"R.C. Sproul was a rare theologian who explained the deepest of subjects in the simplest of terms, and he did so in a way that grabbed people's attention and interest. His gifts shine in the column he regularly wrote, Right Now Counts Forever. On subjects from sports to politics to sexuality, and of course, the life of the church, Sproul's wisdom and wit show us how the truth of God's Word illuminates and transforms all of life."

—Dr. Joel R. Beeke
President and professor of systematic theology and homiletics
Puritan Reformed Theological Seminary
Grand Rapids, Mich.

"R.C. Sproul's legacy is vast, including visual, audio, and print resources stimulating countless believers worldwide. Now, Ligonier has added to it with this thrilling thesaurus, gathered from more than forty years of his monthly contributions to *Tabletalk*. In the early years, he shared his spiritual perception of current affairs, including politics, economics, inflation, the newest A-list books and 'the American dream'; it was as if he had all of these in one hand and his Bible in the other. In the later years, he was more immediately concerned with theological and doctrinal truths. His exposition and application of biblical revelation on subjects such as the doctrine of God, Christology, Jesus' substitutionary death, atonement, the true nature of sin and the new birth, theodicy, the measure and manner of God's forgiveness, conscience, Christian liberty, and scores of other subjects are brilliantly handled.

"I do have a quibble. At one point he wrote, 'There is nothing in my thought that hasn't been said before far more eloquently than I can ever hope to articulate'—commendably modest, but thankfully untrue."

—Dr. John Blanchard
Preacher, teacher, apologist, and author
Banstead, England

"You hold in your hand a veritable gold mine of Christian truth. Flowing from the pen of Dr. R.C. Sproul, here is his work of more than forty

years writing his monthly column Right Now Counts Forever in *Tabletalk* magazine. Dr. Sproul was arguably the greatest teacher of theology in our generation. He was also a lucid and cogent writer, able to take profound truth and make it accessible to everyday readers. This book will take you to the heights of heaven as Dr. Sproul addresses a wide breadth of issues and topics. Though now seated in a cloud of witnesses above, Dr. Sproul continues to instruct us in the vital essentials of Christian living. This book should be required reading for every believer."

—DR. STEVEN J. LAWSON
President, OnePassion Ministries
Dallas

"This collection of columns from four decades offers a treasure trove of timeless reflection on the timely. Dr. Sproul tackles football, commercials, ethical issues, best-selling books, politics, and philosophy—and that's merely the first year of columns alone. You will find wit and humor, always accompanied by deep and faithful theological and biblical reflection. Here you will find wisdom that never goes out of style."

—DR. STEPHEN J. NICHOLS
President, Reformation Bible College
Chief academic officer, Ligonier Ministries

"Spanning more than forty years, Dr. Sproul's prophetic insights on a wide range of ethical and theological issues provide a fascinating historical narrative of cultural change, both in society at large and, sadly, the evangelical church, as well as a breathtakingly clear Christian (biblical) response. Cultural attitudes may have changed as the effects of postmodernity took hold in the late twentieth century, but it is clear from these pages that the Bible is sufficient to address each one. I will be consulting this volume often as issues arise for which I need a clear biblical response."

—DR. DEREK W.H. THOMAS
Senior minister, First Presbyterian Church
Columbia, S.C.

Right Now Counts Forever

R.C. SPROUL

———

RIGHT
NOW
COUNTS
FOREVER

Volume I: 1977–1986

———

 LIGONIER MINISTRIES

Right Now Counts Forever, Volume I: 1977–1986
© 2021 by the R.C. Sproul Trust

Published by Ligonier Ministries
421 Ligonier Court, Sanford, FL 32771
Ligonier.org

Printed in China
RR Donnelley
0000321
First printing

ISBN 978-1-64289-305-2 (Hardcover)
ISBN 978-1-64289-306-9 (ePub)
ISBN 978-1-64289-307-6 (Kindle)

Cover design: Metaleap Creative
Interior typeset: Katherine Lloyd, The DESK

Ligonier Ministries edited and adapted Dr. R.C. Sproul's original text to create this volume. We are thankful to Mrs. Vesta Sproul for her invaluable help on this project.

Bible quotations are the author's translation or are taken from one of the following versions:

Cataloging-in-Publication Data is available from the Library of Congress
LCCN 2020038106 (print) | LCCN 2020038107 (ebook)
LC record available at https://lccn.loc.gov/2020038106
LC ebook record available at https://lccn.loc.gov/2020038107

CONTENTS

FOREWORD

D<small>R.</small> R.C. S<small>PROUL WAS MY FRIEND.</small> When I first came under
his teaching, I immediately appreciated him—not only because
he was such an articulate teacher but because he taught with
passion—passion for truth and passion for God. That passion arose out
of a genuine concern to communicate the unvarnished truth of sacred
Scripture. His fundamental aim was not to please man but to please
God, and the ultimate goal in his teaching was to honor God. I trusted
R.C. because he never attempted to tell me what I wanted to hear but
always told me what I needed to hear. And he did so first as my teacher,
then as my mentor, then as a colleague and friend, and, in many ways,
as a father.

One of the things R.C. and I shared was the death of our fathers when
we were teenagers. I believe it was in part the death of R.C.'s father that
instilled in him an intense passion to help people realize that we don't
know how many days the Lord will give us, and so we must recognize
that every day counts and that right now counts forever. His desire for
people to grasp this truth was out of his deep concern for their souls.
That is one of the reasons there was such urgency in R.C.'s teaching and
writing. He understood the stewardship the Lord had entrusted to him.
He would not squander any opportunity to help people grasp God's truth,
because it was that truth alone that could set them free.

For that reason, R.C. desperately sought to make the truth of God
accessible to everyone. He sincerely believed that theology isn't just for
theologians but is for everyone. Though he was a theologian who could
have pursued a purely academic track in his career, R.C. realized that
what the church most desperately needs is to have the theological truth
of Scripture explained in a simple and accessible way. Thus, R.C. gave

himself to the lifelong task of helping God's people know the truth of who God is. Yet, he wasn't satisfied with simply helping people know who God is—he also wanted people to know the depths of how that knowledge affects every aspect of their lives. That desire came through in every aspect of R.C.'s ministry: in the classroom, behind the lectern, and in the pulpit.

Most who sat under R.C.'s teaching and preaching knew that R.C. didn't use a manuscript, an outline, or notes. What most people don't realize, however, is that it wasn't always easy for him. R.C. had a brilliant mind and memory, but as he aged, he sometimes—though rarely—found comfort in scribbling a few notes or a brief outline on a napkin or scrap of paper, some of which I still have in my possession. The reason he labored so hard not to rely on a manuscript or an outline wasn't because he wanted to demonstrate his amazing memory or his vast knowledge but because he wanted to communicate with people in such a way that they would be fully engaged from the beginning to the very end of his message. Sometimes with humor and often with great intensity, he worked to keep eye contact with his audience in order to help them remain completely focused. He was never just delivering a lecture, only providing information, or merely delivering a sermon. Rather, he was striving by the power of the Holy Spirit to get people on their knees to repent and to rise up to worship and serve our Lord. In every sermon, he gave his all to reach people's hearts and minds with the truth they so desperately needed to know.

When I first began preaching at Saint Andrew's Chapel, I was only twenty-eight years old, and it was terrifying—particularly when R.C. was present. What's more, R.C. didn't want me to use a manuscript, an outline, or a single note when I preached, and I obliged. A couple of years later, I admitted to R.C. how nervous I was to preach in his pulpit, and I will never forget his response. He said: "Burk, that's not my pulpit, and it's not your pulpit. It's God's pulpit, and God is present every time we step into the pulpit. He alone is the One we are to fear, and we preach for His honor and glory alone—not for any man." That reality dominated

R.C.'s preaching and teaching. He had a great sense of the presence of God and a great desire for the glory of God. Ultimately, that is what made R.C. the preacher he was. That, in essence, is what compelled him to try to help others realize that right now counts forever.

—Dr. Burk Parsons
Senior pastor
Saint Andrew's Chapel, Sanford, Fla.

ROOTS IN THE PEPSI GENERATION

MAY 1977

———

W E ARE MOVING TO A new format for our monthly newsletter. Our desire is that the newsletter be not only an update on news and current events of the Study Center, but a modest educational tool as well. Consequently, I've been asked to write a monthly column commenting on current events and issues from a theological perspective.

The column's title, "Right Now Counts Forever," is designed to focus attention on the relevancy of our present lives to the eternal destinies we all face. We live in a culture that places the stress on "Right Now." It's called the "Pepsi Generation"—we are told to live life with "gusto" because we "only go around once." Short range goals, pragmatic methods of problem solving, a quiet hysteria to make it happen "now," all point to modern man's despair regarding the future. The unspoken assumption is that it's "now or never" because there is no ultimate future for mankind.

Our Christian assertion is that there is more to our lives than "now." If there is not then even the now is meaningless. But we say now counts. Why? Now counts because we are creatures who have an origin and a destiny which is rooted and grounded in God.

Did I say "rooted"? Why is that word so important? Recently we've experienced a cultural phenomenon of epic proportions. The televised drama *Roots* has already had a shaking effect on our people. Can we explain the national reaction to Kunta Kinte and "Chicken George" merely in terms of our raw feeling of years of racial strife? I don't think so. Neither does Alex Haley. *Roots* typifies a problem that transcends race. It is the problem of identity for all of modern man. Who am I?

The question of identity can never be answered merely in terms of the

1

present. To know who I am involves a discovery of my past (my origin) and at least a glimpse of my future (my destiny). If I am a cosmic accident springing from the dust and destined for more dust then I am nothing. I am a joke . . . a tale told by an idiot. But if my ultimate roots are grounded in eternity and my destiny is anchored in that same eternity, then I know something of who I am. I know I am a creature of eternal significance. If that's so then my life counts. What I do today counts forever. Now, the now means something.

Roots stirred us deeply because it provoked the hope that if we go back far enough we might find continuity and stability. *Roots* had its messiah figure in Chicken George. The program went through an entire episode with Chicken George never visibly present. Yet his "invisible presence" permeated every scene. I have never seen a television production where a character was so obviously present while not appearing on the screen. When George did appear he led his family in a new exodus to a new land of promise. *Roots* looked backward and forward in such a way as to give the present meaning.

As TV treated us to *Roots* so Hollywood has treated us to *Rocky*—this film has captured the public imagination in a fresh way. Perhaps it represents merely an exercise in nostalgia, a throwback to Frank Merriwell and the original happy ending. Or perhaps it represents a protest to the age of the anti-hero and the story line of chaos that characterizes modern filmdom. Whatever the motive the movie reflects not in the Cinderella motif but the portrayal of human sensitivity displayed in Rocky's mercy as a bill collector for the loan shark and his tenderness on the ice rink.

Applaudable warmth is seen in Rocky's "Lennie-like" love for animals and wayward teenagers and his sentiment for his manager. The fruit of discipline, endurance, and devotion to dignity are actually cast in roles of virtue. Rocky worked and fought not for a momentary prize but for a stand of valor that lasts.

Maybe *Rocky* is a milestone. Maybe we are beginning to see there is more to life than Pepsi-Cola. It's not now or never, but now and forever. Right now counts. It counts . . . for eternity.

THE SEX REVOLUTION AND THE CHRISTIAN

JULY 1977

————

C ULTURAL CHANGE IS ONE THING; revolution is another. As the word suggests, a revolution does not bring mild protest or dissent to existing forms and structures—it brings revolt. When we examine the changes in our own nation's mood and atmosphere regarding sex we see dramatic upheaval with the overthrow of classic ethics and attitudes of sex.

Sometimes we imagine that times are changing when in fact they are not. Sometimes we become alarmists and reactionaries in the midst of small and insignificant cultural changes. Some say about the sexual revolution, "What's the big deal? Sexual problems are as old as the hills. Prostitution is the world's oldest profession." To be sure we have always had sexual problems to deal with but what is happening now is a change, a big change. The sexual revolution is for real.

Think back twenty years (a short span of cultural history). . . . Less than 20 years ago a film was censored in this country for using the word "virgin" on the screen. Outrageous complaints were lodged when *From Here to Eternity* won an Oscar. Why? Because Burt Lancaster appeared in a love-scene embracing his girl in the surf while in a prone position, clad only in bathing suits. Such a scene today would warrant not a whimper and would not even earn a PG rating. Do you remember in the '50s when Frank Lovejoy shocked us with the line "Retreat Hell! We're just attacking in a different direction!"? Gable didn't talk like that on the screen. Profanity was absent from the lips of Bogart, Cagney, Ladd, and Power.

TV situation-comedies in the '50s saw Lucy and Desi having a crisis over sticky wallpaper. *Father Knows Best* had to deal with teenage jealousy over school awards. Today's "situations" concern abortion, homosexuality, and adultery. The new explicitness is heralded as sophisticated realism that prepares children for mature adulthood.

We have our new realism and our new freedom. But how much does it cost? The revolution has not been unbloody. It has brought with it child pornography, a vast increase in sadomasochism for those needing still more intense sexual thrills, a breakdown in the institution of marriage, the abortion business, and black-market babies for sale. These are but a few of the "benefits" of our new enlightenment.

How does the Christian deal with all this? The New Testament makes it clear that chastity is a prime ethical mandate for the Christian. The early apologists of the second century pointed to the exemplary chaste conduct of the Christian community as an "evidence" of its truth-claims. We may not lower our standards to accommodate the drifts of the secular culture.

Several factors need to operate for the Christian to maintain integrity:

1. We must maintain a clear understanding of the New Testament sex-ethic.
2. We must pray for the grace to have moral courage.
3. We must be understanding and patient with those who fall. This point requires elaboration. It is one thing for a person to fall in a perfectly chaste environment. It is quite another to fall when people all around us are falling. The contemporary teen ager is literally bombarded with erotic stimuli and lives in a culture where the peer-pressure to participate in the sexual revolution is overwhelming. Parents, especially, must be aware of these dynamics.

Only a generation ago parental sex-counseling went something like this: "Don't get involved with sex or (1) you'll get pregnant (2) you'll get an STD (3) you'll get a bad reputation." These were the standard "deterrents" used for an ethic of chastity. Today's teenagers have quick answers to these "deterrents." The fear of pregnancy has been neutralized by the pill and abortion-on-demand. The threat of STDs has been minimized by an optimistic view of the power of modern antibiotics. The problem of reputation has been totally reversed to the point that young people who are not involved acquire reputations for being out of it or square.

So what deterrent is left? In the final analysis we are left with the deterrent we started with—the holiness of God and His authority to command obedience from us. We need a new and clear vision of who God is. We need encouragement from the Christian community as a model. We need to see the "more excellent way."

On a community level the Supreme Court has left a crack open in the door for establishing standards of public displays and sale of erotic material. The city of Chicago is taking legal action against child pornography. Cincinnati, Ohio, has been a pioneer city in passing local ordinances prohibiting the sale of pornographic material. This city has avoided the chaos of Boston's "combat zone" and San Francisco's strip district. The same procedures so effective in Cincinnati can be used all over America.

Civil legislation may make a dent in the *atmosphere* of the culture but in the final analysis the Christian must depend on grace and a personal commitment of obedience if he is to maintain chastity in the midst of revolution. How we as Christians deal with the revolution now will count forever.

We have our new realism and our new freedom. But how much does it cost? The revolution has not been unbloody.

"Blessedness is
the ultimate form
of happiness.
There is no
happiness in sin."

—

THE AMERICAN DREAM

AUGUST 1977

———

2 01 AND COUNTING . . . SKYROCKETS, sparklers, and other hooplah
return to the closet for another year. Only 99 more years until we
celebrate the tricentennial of our nation. The annual summer event
of Independence Day passed with differing reactions. For the older generation it was a time of nostalgia, a fond rehearsal of the American dream.
Gone were the days of elm-lined streets in our town with a motor-car
outing on Sabbath afternoon. Gone were the parades of World War I
Dough Boys with their little tin hats. The 48-star flag they proudly waved
is now a relic.

For the middle-aged the 4th was a time of sober reflection and confusion. With one leg standing in the residue of the optimism of the fifties
and the other straddling the struggles of the seventies this generation
didn't quite know whether to salute or sleep in.

For the young it was a time of cynicism with memories of the tragedy
of Camelot, the slaying of Martin Luther King, Kent State, and a vision of
a former Attorney General of the United States being escorted to a new
sanctuary of walls in Alabama.

But the dream goes on . . . Life, liberty, and the pursuit of happiness,
inalienable rights endowed by God. In our dream we find visions of these
rights. Some sparkle with scintillating radiance that gives a euphoric quality to our dream. Others take on a purple hue of nightmarish torment.

Life—Indeed an inalienable right—But not to unborn infants. The
abortion battle casts a shadow of gloom on this right as "life" is abstracted
out of its context of sanctity. The right of life is rooted in the holiness
of God. Its sacred character rests not in the complexity of human biology, but in its foundation in creation. The human life bears the image of
God Himself. The image-bearer derives his dignity from his God. If life

is isolated from sanctity the dream becomes a nightmare and the value of human life is cheapened.

Liberty—When men are enslaved their exodus of liberation is always a cause of celebration. Relief from tyranny and oppression brings with it the highest expressions of human jubilation. But what happens when freedom is confused with autonomy? What happens when the liberated person demands the "right" to do whatever he pleases with no moral restraint? The individual who lives without restraint becomes himself, one who tyrannizes those around him. With the inalienable right of liberty comes the divine obligation of law. Just law does not destroy liberty but is the prerequisite of it. Liberty cannot exist without law. Without law liberty is anarchy. Without liberty law is tyranny.

The pursuit of happiness—If anything will destroy the American dream it will be the confusion of happiness with pleasure. If God is God there can be no happiness in disobedience. The law of God is designed for the welfare and happiness of the entire creation. The obedient person is blessed. Blessedness is the ultimate form of happiness. There is no happiness in sin. But there is pleasure. Disobedience to God would hardly be a temptation if it offered no pleasure. The diabolical lie that torments us is the false promise that unless we sin we cannot be happy. Our lust for pleasure enslaves us and again turns the dream into a nightmare. The lust of pleasure is not our inalienable right. To do our own thing is not our inalienable right. The pursuit of happiness is our right and our duty.

Life . . . Sanctity
Liberty . . . Law
Happiness . . . Obedience

Divorce them now and it destroys forever.

GOD, VIOLENCE, PRO FOOTBALL

SEPTEMBER 1977

———

I N THE NEW TESTAMENT WE FIND AN AWESOME description of the radical corruption of natural man. By "radical" is meant the corruption penetrates the *radix* or root of man's nature. Our fallenness is not a matter of slight external blemishes which touch only the periphery of our lives. Our sin comes from the core or the heart of our being. To illustrate the depths of this corruption the New Testament points to our natural love of violence as a manifestation of our root corruption.

The enjoyment of violence is not a recently acquired taste of modern culture. It cannot be explained as a simple form of escape from ennui or boredom. Rather it is a manifestation of a disposition that perpetually fights against the restraints civilized nations have attempted to provide for it.

Consider the moral situation that characterized the world at the time of Noah. What was so distinctive of that culture that provoked God to an expression of wrath that was unparalleled? Here is how the Old Testament describes the situation:

> The earth also was corrupt before God, and the earth was filled with violence.... And God said unto Noah, The end of flesh is come before me; for the earth is filled with violence through them; and behold, I will destroy them with the earth. (Gen. 6:11–13)

What about now? We are living in a civilized world marked by sophisticated levels of education. This isn't the rip-snorting era of the wild west when everyone packed a shooting iron on his hip. This isn't the blood-soaked age of Roman debauchery where people got their thrills at the Circus Maximus watching lions feeding on the flesh of Christians. Our appreciation for violence is much more subtle but still reveals a thirst for blood.

The carnage of Indianapolis, the penchant for vicarious pleasures of violence in Hollywood films, the increased "realism" of television programming all attest to our corporate appetite for violence.

As we approach the start of a new season of professional football we come with a sense of gloom and concern for the fun of the sport. The preseason focus has not been on the promising talents of the current crop of rookies making their bid for stardom. Rather the spotlight has been on the Atkinson-Noll trial which has been a sensational legal battle over the limits of sportsmanship and brutality in the National Football League. Stemming from an incident in a Steeler-Raider game in which Lynn Swann received a staggering blow to the head from defensive back George Atkinson, the trial has received national coverage. Steeler coach Chuck Noll complained of unnecessary violence in the game citing the intrusion of a "criminal element" into the league. With the criminal element charge obviously aimed at him, Atkinson responded by filing a slander suit against Noll. Though Noll was acquitted of the charge of slander, the trial became an embarrassment to him and his own players. During intense cross-examination Noll admitted that such an "element" existed on his own team. Among those listed in Noll's admission was all-pro defensive back Mel Blount, who was elected as the Steelers' most valuable player in 1975. Blount has responded by refusing to report to the Steelers and threatens another slander suit of $5,000,000 against his own coach.

To restrict violence in the NFL the rules committee outlawed the "head slap," a play enjoyed by defensive linemen as they start their charge against the offense. Such rule amendations are helpful but much more is needed to curb the violence that professional sport is assuming. In the final analysis, it is the public who must make their protest felt. As long as the fans cheer lustily when violence is occurring the league and players will do little to curb it. Football is still a spectator sport.

One of the ironies emerging from the Atkinson-Noll trial is the way the league responded to some of Atkinson's charges. At the heart of Atkinson's damage suit was the assertion that the label of "criminal" and "vicious" would jeopardize his playing career and consequently his ability to make money from his career. Oddly enough the league testified that in their judgment Atkinson's career was under no threat.

If Atkinson's career has not been threatened by public charges that he is unnecessarily violent and vicious, why hasn't it? Is it because Atkinson has so proven his sportsmanlike character that a few angry remarks from an opposing coach won't affect his image? If that's the case then why was Noll acquitted? Maybe there is another reason why Atkinson won't suffer. Because the fans don't really care about excessive violence. I hope that is not the rationale the league officials had in mind.

In sports there is a time to cheer and a time to boo. The time for appropriate booing is not when someone makes a mistake in play execution. The time for booing is when violence is committed for violence's sake.

Christ warned that in the last days the culture would again manifest the characteristics of the days of Noah. Lovers of violence would be heroes. Who are your heroes today? Their virtues or lack of them may influence you and others to acts which count forever.

GOD AND THE JOHNSTOWN FLOOD

OCTOBER 1977

———

T HREE DAYS AGO WORKMEN UNCOVERED the body of a 10-year-old girl amidst the rubble of flood-ravaged Johnstown. The discovery moved the grim list of the known dead in this disaster to 75. National press coverage has given this town in Western Pennsylvania a certain notoriety for its history of devastating natural calamities. How do we respond to the violence of nature? How does our theology deal with such wanton destruction that knows no respecting of persons? The elderly, infants, and helplessly infirm experienced no mercy in the face of the torrents of water that swept away everything in its path. The question on many people's lips was, "How could a good God allow such a thing to happen?"

Nature's angry tirades have produced endless speculation from philosophers and theologians. It was Voltaire's satirical response to the Lisbon Earthquake that produced *Candide* with its biting critique of Dr. Pangloss and his "best of all possible worlds." Behind the mythical character of Pangloss perhaps lurked the work of the philosopher Leibniz. Leibniz worked out an elaborate "theodicy" to explain the problem of evil and suffering in this world. A "theodicy" is an attempt to justify and vindicate God for the presence of evil in the world. Theologically, Leibniz's answers do not satisfy. How do we, as Christians, respond to the problem of evil and suffering in the world?

Scripture provides no final answer to the problem of evil and suffering. Some helpful guidelines, however, are provided.

1. Evil is real

The Bible never seeks to minimize the full reality of suffering and misery. No attempt is made to pawn these realities off as mere illusions. Nor is there any call to a Stoic attitude of imperturbability or detachment from such reality. The Biblical characters speak openly of calamity; they weep real tears; they rend their garments and pen their lamentations. The Christ of Scripture is a man of sorrows who is acquainted with grief. His road is the *Via Dolorosa*.

2. Evil is not ultimate

Though Christianity recognizes the total force of evil it is never regarded in ultimate categories of dualism. Evil is dependent and derived. It has no independent power above and over God. It is redeemable. Though the Scriptures take evil seriously, its message is one of triumph. Though the whole creation groans in travail waiting for its redemption, that groan is not futile. Over all creation stands the Cosmic Christ who at the same time is *Christus Victor*.

3. God is not capricious

The God of Christianity is not a frivolous God. He is not given to caprice or arbitrary acts of violence. His actions are not irrational expressions or whims. We do not know why at a given place or a given time natural catastrophes take place. Easy equations of guilt and disaster are ruled out by such statements as the Book of Job and the ninth chapter of John's Gospel. When inexplicable disasters do occur we must say with Luther, "Let God be God." When Job cried out, "The Lord gave and the Lord takes away, blessed be the name of the Lord," he was not trying to sound pious or give superficial praise to God. He was biting his lip and gripping his stomach as he sought to remain faithful to God in the midst of unmitigated anguish. But Job knew who God was and cursed Him not.

4. This is not the best of all possible worlds

Whatever else this world is, it is fallen. Suffering is inseparably related to sin. That is not to say that all suffering is a direct result of sin or that there is a measurable ratio of an individual's suffering with his sin. (Again Job and John 9 militate against such thinking.) However, suffering belongs to the complex of sin. As long as this world suffers from the violence of men it returns such violence in kind. The Scripture often personifies nature as being angry with its human master and exploiter. Instead of dressing, keeping, and replenishing the earth we exploit it and pollute it. The world is not yet redeemed. We look for a new heaven and a new earth. We yearn for a land without tempest, flood, or earthquake. Such yearning may be regarded as an exercise or fantasy or a hope that is an anchor for the soul. How we regard it now will count forever.

"Over all creation stands the Cosmic Christ who at the same time is *Christus Victor.*"

THE PRESS: PROPHETS OR CYNICS

NOVEMBER 1977

———

WITH THE RESIGNATION OF BERT LANCE from the Carter administration, the Democrats' "mini-gate" is beginning to blow over. In the wake of the controversy comes renewed interest on the question of the role of the press in American Society.

In the Lance episode public opinion was sharply divided between those convinced that Lance was both incompetent and unethical and was justly pressured from office, and those who believe Lance was an innocent victim of "trial by press." Perhaps the truth will never be known. But the deeper question of the role of the press in our culture continues to plague us.

The Press as Prophets

The prophets of ancient Israel are frequently thought of as a group of mystical soothsayers whose chief distinction was their ability to predict future events with uncanny accuracy. Yet future prediction was not the only function of the Biblical prophet. Indeed prediction was not even the chief task assigned to the prophet. A popular distinction between "fore-telling" and "forthtelling" focuses on the primary task of the prophet to "speak forth" God's Word to the nation. The primary message areas are described as social criticism. Government policy, economic oppression, public morality, and social justice were frequent themes of these divine spokesmen. Bruce Vawter, a leading Roman Catholic Biblical theologian, wrote a study of the prophets of Israel under the title *The Conscience of Israel*. As the title suggests Vawter focuses on the role of the prophet to speak to and in a sense "be" the conscience of the nation.

Biblically the role of prophetic criticism of society falls to the church. Though we no longer have divinely inspired Prophets with a capital

P the function of prophetic criticism remains vitally necessary for the health of a nation. But the church has largely abdicated its responsibility of social and political criticism. At times the church speaks merely as an echo of secular critics after the criticism has achieved the level of a popular cause. At other times the church refuses to speak on the grounds that involvement on such matters is none of the church's business. Such a view reflects a serious misunderstanding of the principle of the separation of church and state. To be sure the power of the sword is given by God to the state, not the church. But the power of the Word is given to the church.

With abdication of prophetic criticism by the church the responsibility (largely by default) has fallen to the secular press. It was the press who blew the whistle on Watergate and brought about the fall of a President and the incarceration of an Attorney General. It is the press who plays the role of Elijah challenging Ahab's oppressive policies and John the Baptist criticizing the morality of Herod. The press has stepped into the vacuous breach left by the church's timidity. At this point the press offers a vital service to the people of America.

The Press as Cynics

Though Biblical prophets were critics they never became cynics. Cynicism was utterly foreign to their make-up as men committed to reformation and redemption. Unfortunately the same cannot be said for the secular press. The cynic is infected by a chronic spirit of negativism which offers no hope of redemption. His attitude can easily lead him into the role of the "muckraker." Unhappily, cynicism, as a form of pseudo-intellectualism, offers the cynic a cheap form of intellectual recognition for he stands "above it all" and never indulges in the romantic sentiment of hope. A member of the press faces a difficult temptation to fall into cynicism. His job causes him to focus his attention on an inordinate amount of what is evil and depressing in this world. His close scrutiny of public figures who appear bigger than life to the general populace provides easy disillusionment. The journalist gains a birds-eye view of the clay feet of popular heroes. This disillusionment can easily give way to anger and despair culminating in cynicism. When cynicism comes, the correspondent or commentator can no longer be a healthy critic.

Prophetic criticism . . . yes. Cynical destructive criticism . . . no. Perhaps it is time for the church to be the church and to be a healthy conscience to the secular culture including the press. For without a conscience the press cannot be the press.

"The press has stepped into the vacuous breach left by the church's timidity."

———

THE "ELVIS" PHENOMENON

DECEMBER 1977

S HOCKWAVES OF GRIEF WENT AROUND the world when Rudolph Valentino succumbed to appendicitis at the pinnacle of his career. Morbid fascination and a cultic spirit followed the death of James Dean in a flaming crash of his sports car on an isolated country road. Roses and a shroud of mystery followed Marilyn Monroe to her crypt in Forest Lawn Cemetery. Already the casual moves of the crooner Bing Crosby are missed. But the reactions to the death of these notables is but a whimper compared to the bizarre and ghoulish atmosphere that has followed the demise of Elvis Presley.

Never in the history of our nation has so much emotion been released following the death of an entertainer. Will Rogers, Judy Garland, John Garfield, Jayne Mansfield, Jack Benny, and Louis Armstrong will be remembered as legends. But Elvis is in a class by himself. His legend is already titanic. TV specials, portraits in watercolor and oil, special-release record albums, tee shirts, drinking mugs, and other marketing gimmicks are reaping an exploiter's dream. Why? Why Elvis rather than Crosby or Garland?

If ever a star's rise to fame was meteoric it was Elvis'. His appearance on the *Ed Sullivan* show in the fifties made him an overnight sensation. The initial response to the uninhibited gyrations of the droopy-eyed singer from Memphis was one of frenzy. Parents were furious and kids were ecstatic over the new barbarian of rock and roll. On his second appearance with Sullivan the cameras were restricted to shooting Elvis from the waist up. Still his magic was not eclipsed. With instant fame and fortune Elvis traded in his panel-truck for two or three Cadillacs, one gold and one pink. He spent money like a peasant who just won the state lottery. *Variety* magazine described the new "Elvis" rage as a teenage fad and predicted a very short tenure to this "flash in the pan." But twenty-five years later, the pan was still flashing. Why?

Before his last concert, newsmen interviewed Elvis' fans asking them why they were so devoted to their hero. The responses were strange but revealing. "He is so kind to his mother." "I love his eyes." "He is so honest." Can we really explain the phenomenon of Elvis in terms of his love for his mother? If we can, then what in the world will happen when Liberace dies? Other performers have had exciting eyes. But the last quote is significant. "He is so honest."

When people responded to Elvis' honesty, what were they talking about? Elvis Presley was not George Washington. His reputation for honesty was not built upon what he said. His "honesty" was not a matter of words but of personal openness. Elvis' stage presence was unique. Even Sinatra, the master of timing, could learn something from Elvis. Elvis was always in deep, open communication with his audience. All of the barriers that isolate a performer from his audience were shattered by his personal magnetism. Elvis let people in. He gave himself with intensity to every person in the theater. That is the most costly thing a performer can do.

Elvis Presley had what people call "warmth." With his fame and fortune he never quit being a truck driver. He never became sophisticated. His music was simple and earthy. Though his early pelvic gyrations were considered shocking, his music never became vulgar. He sang of intense emotions but not illicit ones. His music spoke of "tenderness," "cruelty," puppy dogs, and blue suede shoes. His "warmth" made him appear open. His openness made him appear honest.

Elvis Presley was not a saint to be imitated by every Christian. But his personal warmth was a quality we can learn from. Sociologists tell us that we are living in such a highly mobilized society that our lives have become anonymous. We suffer from cultural frigidity. We deal with the grocer and the gas station attendant in impersonal ways. The loss of close community relationships has created a crisis of coldness. Elvis broke through that coldness with a costly gift of warmth. At the end he was drained and confused. His public had come close to emptying him. His reservoir of warmth was running dry. But his followers will not let him die. They want more warmth. I wonder where they will find it.

"Unless the Christian Church takes the marketplace seriously, revolution is inevitable."

—

MARX OR JESUS?

FEBRUARY 1978

———

I N THE DECADE OF THE FIFTIES the "peril" of communism was a grave national concern. Following the Berlin Blockade we went through the hysteria of the McCarthy Era, Hoover's "Enemy Within," the "Three Lives of Herbert Philbrick," the Korean Conflict, the Hungarian Revolution, and ultimately the Berlin Wall and Checkpoint Charlie. During the fifties the estimated population of the world was two billion persons.

Today the communist hysteria is over as we worry about energy crisis, economic inflation, and the conflict in the Middle East. In the meantime two billion persons are now living under the tyranny of communism. That's right. The same number of people that made up the world's population twenty years ago is the number that now live behind the Iron Curtain. Though the hysteria is gone the success of communist expansion has been staggering.

Why has the communist movement been so "successful"? Its goals are clear—revolution led by an awakened proletariat. Its strategy is simple. Recruit the working man. Reach the worker with the promise of a new and better life. Show the worker how he has been a victim of the tyranny of the owners.

Karl Marx was no dummy. He understood clearly one fundamental point of human existence. He understood that man's life is very closely bound up with his work. Marx called man *Homo faber* (man the maker or fabricator). Work, means of production, ownership are all vital to man's human aspirations for dignity. When man's work is an exercise of frustration, when he feels a loss of dignity at his job, when he is treated as anything less than a valued person, he is vulnerable to the empty promises of a glorious proletariat revolution.

The guardians of American capitalism put their trust in huge defense budgets, the C.I.A., and things like Radio Free Europe to withstand the tide of a world-conquering movement. In the meantime the most frustrated group of people in this country is the labor force. High unemployment and a sense of deep alienation exist between the worker and the manager. The worker gives about 10% of his ability toward production goals because he is so alienated from management. The manager sees the lack of production of the worker and responds with anger and hostility. Strikes increase and the bargaining table becomes a battle ground.

What does the laborer do with his frustration and anger? He brings it home and takes it out on his wife and children. The kids flee to drugs to escape the atmosphere of home and the divorce rate soars near the 50% mark. Meanwhile, the frustrated managers watch their production goals fall short and see an inflationary spiral that opens the door for foreign competitors to take away their business. The manager also goes home frustrated and turns the guns on his wife and children. More drugs, more divorce, more alienation as the downward spiral strikes at the heart of American culture.

Marx went straight to the labor world with his gospel. Christians are careful to stay clear of this arena. Unless the Christian Church takes the marketplace seriously, revolution is inevitable. Christ came to reconcile all things to Himself. Where there is alienation, Christ is desperately needed.

The story I wish every American could know and ponder is that of the radical changes wrought in a steel foundry in Pittsburgh by the efforts of one man who thought Christ had more to say about man and his work than Marx. Standing alone, with no precedent or institution to back him, Wayne Alderson proved that labor-management alienation can be overcome by the solid application of Christian principles.

This year at the annual Presidential Prayer Breakfast in Washington, D.C., a new dimension of concern will be expressed. A special seminar on labor-management relations will be held featuring such persons as Mr. Alderson. That seminar is crucial to the awakening of this nation to the profound needs of the work world. Pray for the special seminar in Washington. Look for ways where you can apply Christ to your work; not with bumper stickers or signs on your desk, but with people. It may well be reformation or revolution; Marx or Jesus.

SPIRITUAL GIANTS

MARCH 1978

———

"**N**EVER PREACH ABOVE AN EIGHTH-GRADE** level to a college educated congregation. . . ." These words are still echoing in my ears and stabbing me in the soul. They were uttered by my professor of homiletics in seminary. He was trying to teach us how to be "successful" preachers. He went on to explain that people may have college degrees in their fields of specialty but in matters of religion and theology the majority of them have no better than a Sunday School understanding. The way to success is to "keep it simple."

The way to success is to "keep it simple." Something deep within me reacted to this advice. I refused to accept it then. I refuse to accept it now. The advice carries within it a double insult. The first insult is to God's people. To assume that adults cannot grasp the things of God beyond an eighth-grade level is to slander both their intelligence and maturity.

The second insult is far greater. It is an insult to the majesty of God and to the work of God the Holy Spirit in revealing the deep things of God for us. We will spend thousands of dollars to educate ourselves and acquire knowledge to enhance our careers. We understand the importance of knowledge in many areas of life. Our public education system does not terminate at eighth grade. We would be ill-equipped for the conversations we have in our businesses if our knowledge of the English language reached only the eighth-grade level.

What are the standard clichés that abound in the Christian community? Have you heard them? "We must have a childlike faith." "I don't need to know any theology, I just need to know Jesus." "Christianity is simple: 'Jesus loves me this I know, for the Bible tells me so.' "

It is easy for us to confuse a childlike faith with a childish faith. We are to have the kind of implicit trust in God that a child has in its parents. But we are called to fullness of maturity in terms of our understanding God.

The Apostle Paul put it this way: "Brethren, do not be children in your thinking; yet in evil be babes, but in your thinking be mature" (1 Cor. 14:20).

To say we don't need to know theology, only Jesus, raises the immediate question, "Who is Jesus?" As soon as we begin to answer that question we are instantly involved in theology. As Christians we simply cannot avoid theology. We aren't all expected to be theologians in a technical or academic sense but we are all theologians with a small "t." The question is not will we be theologians or not be theologians but will we be good theologians or poor theologians?

"Jesus loves me, this I know . . ." There is no more basic truth to Christianity than that. As an adult I still love to sing the song. But I also like to sing "Holy, Holy, Holy," "A Mighty Fortress Is Our God," and "Immortal, Invisible, God Only Wise."

Christianity has simplicity but it is not simplistic. The depths and riches of God are profound enough to keep us busily engaged in earnest pursuit of the knowledge of God for the rest of our lives. Its basic truths are easy enough for a child to grasp but its deeper truths require disciplined study.

There is the famous story of the meeting of the theologian and the astronomer. The astronomer said to the theologian: "I don't understand why you theologians fuss so much about predestination and supralapsarianism, about communicable and incommunicable attributes of God; of imputed or infused grace and the like; to me Christianity is simple; it's the Golden Rule, 'Do unto others as you would have others do unto you.'" The theologian replied, "I think I see what you mean. I get lost in all your talk about exploding novae, expanding universes, theories of entropy and astronomical perturbations. For me astronomy is simple: It's 'Twinkle, twinkle little star.' "

Last week a woman said to me, "I was a Christian for eleven years before I found out who God was. It was after viewing your video series on the 'Holiness of God' that I first understood the majesty of God." She went on to say, "I suddenly felt cheap about having a bumper sticker on my car saying 'Honk if you love Jesus.' It seemed to make God seem so small." As delighted that I was that the woman had moved to a deeper understanding of God I tried to reassure her about her bumper sticker. She was trying to do something "visible" to indicate her commitment to Christ. We all start our Christian walk as babes and don't always know the best way to articulate our faith. This woman wanted to go deeper.

To be satisfied with a simple faith that is maintained on a milk diet stunts your growth as a Christian. The problem is as old as the church itself. On occasion the Apostles had to admonish their spiritual children on this point. We read: "Therefore, leaving the elementary teaching about the Christ, let us press on to maturity" (Heb. 6:1). Again: "... Until we all attain to the unity of the faith, and of the knowledge of the Son of God, to a mature man, to the measure of the stature which belongs to the fullness of Christ. As a result, we are no longer to be children, tossed here and there by waves and carried about by every wind of doctrine ..." (Eph. 4:13–14, NASB).

God wants you to be a spiritual giant. There are different ways to define the word "giant." We would describe a giant as a grotesque creature who is a freak of nature. We could define a giant as a mythical character who is featured in fairy tales like "Jack and the Beanstalk." But God does not want you to be a grotesque freak or a mythical person who says Fee Fi Fo Fum ... A spiritual giant is a different kind of giant. In this sense a giant is simply a normal person who never quits growing.

Christian education is an educational process that has no graduation date until we die. We may complete special or particular courses of study but we pursue our knowledge of God as long as we live. Christian education involves a life-long pursuit of God Himself.

The Bible speaks of seeking God. Again and again we hear the words, "Seek and ye shall find." But in almost every case where the Bible speaks of seeking after God it is speaking to and about believers. Jonathan Edwards said, "The seeking of God is the main business of my life."

It was to believers Jesus said, "Seek ye first the Kingdom of God and His righteousness and all these things will be added unto you." To seek after God is to have an unquenchable thirst to know Him deeply.

Life-long Christian education is what Ligonier is all about. We want to help you grow into giants. We want to help you learn as much as you can about the things of God. We want to make seminary available to the layman. We want to provide you with tools of knowledge of the Bible, of theology, of church history, practical aids to personal growth, to the whole gamut of Christian education.

We want you to be knowledgeable and articulate Christians, not so that you can win arguments or boast of your brilliance but so that you can have the food you need to be a giant for God.

"Christianity's basic truths are easy enough for a child to grasp but its deeper truths require disciplined study."

HEROES

APRIL 1978

———

WHAT ARE THE MAGIC QUALITIES THAT add up to the portrait of a hero? Are heroes merely legends invented by the creative imagination of the bored or disenfranchised? Are they plastic images created by the magicians of Madison Avenue? Or are there still bona fide, genuine, flesh and blood heroes who walk the face of the earth?

Nietzsche yearned for the advent of the superman. He had visions of the master leader who would lift Europe to new heights of aspirations and carry her to new and glorious conquests. Kierkegaard had the same kind of longing. He said, "My complaint is not that this age is wicked but that it is paltry . . ." Where have all the heroes gone?

Last week I had the double experience of visiting the tomb of Marilyn Monroe in Los Angeles and later driving across the bridge over San Francisco Bay where Dustin Hoffman rode off in the sunset in *The Graduate*. Strains of "Here's to you, Mrs. Robinson" echoed in my ears. The song brought memories of Mrs. Robinson, Jesus, and Joe DiMaggio. The aura of Joe DiMaggio linked my tale of two cities as my thoughts moved from the bridge to the tomb of Marilyn Monroe. At Marilyn's crypt was the single fresh rose supplied daily by the order of Joe DiMaggio. I remember Joe. The painful heel spur that ended his career; the excitement he generated during the years of world war: I remember reading his autobiography as a boy, *Lucky to Be a Yankee*. Jolting Joe, "The Yankee Clipper," an authentic hero whose impact is still felt in Los Angeles, San Francisco, Yankee Stadium, and wherever people use Mr. Coffee coffee-makers.

The world of sports gives us heroes. The film industry creates people bigger than life. But what of the Church? Where are the people whose lifestyle is that of the heroic? Where are the Ridleys and the Latimers, the Polycarps and the Luthers?

We've seen a few authentic heroes in recent years rising out of the Christian community. We can point to people like Corrie ten Boom, Chuck Colson, and Anita Bryant. None of these have the glamour of Joe DiMaggio but they each have a quality which is a primary quality of the heroic—courage. In the primary definitions given by the dictionary of the meaning of the term *hero*, the adjective *courageous* is used liberally. It is this quality of courage that is the essence of the heroic.

Fear is a necessary requisite for courage. It requires no courage to do what you are not afraid to do. But to do what you face with cold, stark terror requires courage. Corrie ten Boom standing for Christ in the midst of a hostile prison camp, Chuck Colson boldly telling a cynical press corps that he is "born again," and Anita Bryant risking her entire career on a moral stance is the stuff that courage is made of.

The courageous person is one who is inevitably a non-conformist. He is not one who refuses to conform for the sake of nonconformity but one who chooses nonconformity because conformity means compromise of personal integrity. To choose scorn over accolades requires either courage or masochistic tendencies. Anyone can be a non-conformist, and for many reasons. Non-conformity can be a quick and cheap way for recognition. Being different may bring a measure of public scrutiny. But non-conformity for moral reasons is another matter. The normal non-conformist is not a martyr for issues of moral trivia like dancing or the wearing of lipstick; the heroic non-conformist takes his stand on issues that touch the soul of life. For Colson it is prison reform; for Bryant it is sexual integrity.

The Christian life carries with it a call to the heroic. The conquest of fear is the secret of the saints. We need some Joe DiMaggios in the Kingdom. We need a Luther, Joan of Arc, who will provide us with models of courage. Without such models we succumb to the pressure of fear and join the unthinking herd and make Nietzsche a prophet instead of a mad man.

THE FRUITFUL MOMENT

I N BIBLICAL CATEGORIES OF TIME AN IMPORTANT distinction is made between *chronos* and *kairos*. This distinction carries within it the assumption that individual moments can have a dynamic impact on a whole life. The New Testament distinctive is like this: *chronos* refers to the normal linear passing of time; moment by moment, day by day, year by year. *Kairos* refers to a specific moment within time which is of crucial significance. It is the moment that gives lasting significance to history. Examples of kairotic moments in the Bible would be the Exodus, the anointing of Saul, the Exile, the birth of Jesus, and the cross.

Perhaps the closest thing we have to this distinction is the difference between the words *historical* and *historic*. Every event that takes place in June is historical, but not every event is historic. Historic events change the course of history and become the cause of future celebration, mourning, or memorial. The signing of the Declaration of Independence was historic, as was the first human steps on the moon.

Within our private individual lives there are also historic moments, special events which shape and mold our personalities and the direction of our energies. The world of art is often engaged in the quest for those moments as the artist seeks to capture in stone, oil, or film the essence of a life in one frozen moment. The artist calls such a moment the *fruchtbare Augenblick* (the fruitful moment). Part of the genius of Michelangelo was his uncanny ability to capture in one frozen pose, the essence of the subject of his art. David, as he readies his sling for battle, illustrates the principle of the fruitful moment. Perhaps the greatest master of the fruitful moment was Rembrandt. Rembrandt often sketched hundreds of poses of his characters before he selected the one that captured the whole personality in one scene. His *Jeremiah Lamenting the Destruction of Jerusalem* and *The Descent from the Cross* show the mastery of the Dutch painter.

Each of us has fruitful moments in our lives. As I think about my past, I remember, with some degree of maudlin sentiment, the song "Moments to Remember." What we want the most from life will often be "meshed" or "disguised" beneath the veneer of our nostalgic memories. With our aspirations to significance we manifest part of what it means to be human and in the image of God. If we want to be important we would tend to relive in our minds those moments which seemed to indicate we might be important. If we delve more deeply in these memories we can discover a great deal about who we are. Reflections on things of the past you might prefer to forget may provoke feelings of guilt and/or fear. Yet we must live with our past. The historic in our lives defines our history. There is a real sense in which we are our history. I cannot disassociate my identity from the past. Even if I become a "new person" in Christ I still carry the "old man" around with me until I die.

For a little fun as well as an important look into the pages of your history take a few minutes for a simple exercise. Take a pencil and paper and jot down the five most meaningful compliments you've ever received. They may have been verbal or non-verbal, direct or indirect. On your paper note: (1) the nature of the compliment, (2) when it was given, (3) who gave you the compliment and what role did that person represent to you?

After completing this exercise try another. Write down the five most important events of your life. Then write briefly why these "historic" moments are so important to you.

These two exercises represent a simple means by which you can come to grips with who you are. To finish the exercise ask yourself if Rembrandt could only paint one portrait of you what would he have you doing in the portrait? What is your fruitful moment? Maybe tomorrow will bring a moment that will redirect your personal history.

Our history is not the result of blind fate or the impersonal forces of chance. My personal history and yours is bound up with the author and Lord of history who makes my personal history count . . . forever.

TERRORISM

JULY 1978

——

A LDO MORO IS DEAD.* THE SAVAGERY OF HIS murder produced shock waves of international revulsion. Newsmen, heads of state, and the general public have expressed outrage and concern for proliferation of terrorism. William Buckley expressed disappointment that Moro, a professed Christian, failed to die like a Christian.

Moro's kidnapping and subsequent slaying has brought the issue of terrorism to international center stage. Though terrorists have always been with us there has been a marked increase in terrorist activity in the past decade. In a special report *U.S. News & World Report* catalogued the following chronicle of terrorism in the 70's:

Palestinian skyjacking: 1970 (3 airlines blown up)
Lod Airport Massacre: 1972 (Japanese Red Army kills 28)
Munich Massacre: 1972 (11 members of Israeli Olympic team killed)
Mass OPEC kidnapping: 1975 (sixty officials kidnapped)
Israeli Bus Massacre: 1978 (37 Israelis killed by Palestinians)

In the U.S. we have lived through the Weathermen, the Black Liberation Army, and the saga of Patty Hearst and the Symbionese Liberation Army. We've seen the Hanafi Muslim affair involving 134 hostages in Washington D.C. in 1977 and the death of 11 people at La Guardia Airport via a terrorist bomb.

Almost weekly we read of diplomats and international businessmen who are captured and held hostage for political or economic ransoms. The growth of multinational businesses such as Coca-Cola, Sony, DuPont, Volkswagen, and other such companies makes the terrorist pie all the sweeter.

——

* Aldo Moro (1916–78) was prime minister of Italy from 1963 to 1968 and 1974 to 1976. He was kidnapped by a militant group called the Red Brigades, which hoped to exchange him for a group of prisoners. The Italian government refused to negotiate, and Moro was killed.

In a monograph prepared for the International Association of Chiefs of Police (IACP) Dr. Vernon Grose of California says:

> The problem of maintaining security in a large corporation—particularly a multinational corporation—is becoming increasingly severe. Industrial espionage, vandalism, internal pilferage, and, of course, international terrorism all seem to defy traditional methods of control.

Grose points to a large spectrum of threats to the security of governments, public institutions, and corporations. Among the threat-factors Grose lists:

1. The technological capability of criminals to override or thwart the most sophisticated safeguards for security.
2. The combined immobility and vulnerability of physical plants and other stationary facilities which cannot be relocated or adequately modified for either economic or political reasons.
3. The wide range of data and information regarding the management, operations, and assets of a corporation available to the public.
4. The increased utilization of violent or criminal means to achieve goals—whether they be nationalistic, anarchistic, political, or personal.

Obviously the problem of terrorism is a complex problem which will require complex solutions and preventions. However, whatever else is done it is imperative that public opinion stand strongly opposed to such acts. To glamorize the terrorist is to help him detonate his next bomb.

The press must help in exposing the hypocrisy of the ideological terrorists. It is almost axiomatic for such terrorists groups as the Red Brigades to glorify their acts as heroic deeds done in behalf of the liberation of the exploited and oppressed. But nothing is as exploitive as terrorism. People must not be conned into thinking that a government established by terrorism would be any less oppressive than the one it supplants. I for one would dread to live under the rule of men or women who value life so cheaply as to murder and destroy indiscriminately.

U.S. News & World Report quotes Alberto Franceschini as saying, "Violence is the only road to social change."* In a recent court-man conflict Franceschini told the court:

> "None of us has any acrimony against you judges.... As I was saying to the prosecutor, 'I've got nothing against you. It's your toga I hate.' So if I shoot at your toga, and there happens to be a man inside, I'm sorry, but there's not much I can do about it. There might even be a mannequin under those robes—how do I know? It's your function I want to eliminate. You're not a man, you're a judge. No one here is innocent."

Franceschini and the rest of the Red Brigades have a neat way of finding if men or mannequins are under the outer apparel. Mannequins don't bleed when they're shot in cold blood.

Nothing can make a murderer a hero except the distorted applause of a duped public.

---

* Alberto Franceschini was one of the leaders of the Red Brigades.

"Though repudiating socialism as an alternative, Solzhenitsyn concludes that he could not offer America as a model for reshaping the Soviet Union."

—

SOLZHENITSYN SPEAKS OUT

AUGUST 1978

———

"**S**OUR GRAPES!**" **"HE IS BITING THE HAND** that feeds him!" These were some of the milder epithets hurled at Aleksandr Solzhenitsyn on the occasion of his commencement address at Harvard.* For some it was difficult to listen to a critique of their homeland by one who is an alien.

The written text of Solzhenitsyn's speech carries a clear stress on the author's intent not to be heard as an adversary but as a friend. Though the critique of our culture is penetrating and comprehensive the tone is one of pleading concern rather than bitter denunciation. Perhaps we need to hear the Poet Laureate of the Gulag.

In probing America's weaknesses Solzhenitsyn first cites a decline in civic courage as the most striking feature of our culture. He said, "Such a decline in courage is particularly noticeable among the ruling groups and the intellectual elite; of course there are many courageous individuals, but they have no determining influence on public life."

Coupled with a deterioration of courage is a growing legalistic base for society. What he means by "legalism" is not a zeal for righteousness but an attempt to identify and equate the righteous with the legal. That is, if it is legal it is moral and upright seems to be the ethical order of the day. Says the Russian, "A society with no other scale but the legal one is not quite worthy of man.... Whenever the tissue of life is woven of legalistic relations, there is an atmosphere of moral mediocrity, paralyzing man's noblest impulses."

———

* Aleksandr Solzhenitsyn (1918–2008) was a Russian writer and activist who helped raise awareness of the Soviet Union's Gulag prison system. He was expelled from the Soviet Union in 1974 and later moved to the United States. He was sharply critical of Western culture, including at his famous Harvard commencement address in 1978.

Legal restraints have so protected individual rights that society as a whole is vulnerable to the ruthless individual. Freedom, says Solzhenitsyn, is tilted in the direction of evil. That is, what is understood by "freedom" is not the right to pursue noble aims without government interference but the right to be morally corrupt with impunity. He concludes, "It is time, in the West, to defend not so much human rights as human obligations."

Examining the freedom of the press we enjoy in the U.S., Solzhenitsyn asks more disturbing questions. Asserting that the press has become the most powerful estate in the Western world, he inquires, "By what law has it been elected and to whom is it responsible?" The press produces a public opinion trend or power-bloc which tends to a hard mentality which squelches creative and imaginative thought.

Perhaps the strongest element of criticism is leveled at the style of Western living. Though repudiating socialism as an alternative, he sadly concludes that he could not offer America as a model for the reshaping of his own nation. That conclusion wounds the pride of the patriot. Hear the man out however, as he cries, "After suffering decades of violence and oppression, the human soul longs for things higher, warmer, and purer than those offered by today's mass living habits, exemplified by the revolting invasion of publicity, by TV stupor, and by intolerable music."

The West has lost its will-power. The roots of its decay are found in the Enlightenment with its view of rationalistic humanism. This period of Western development spawned the human cry of the autonomy of man, an exercise at once arrogant as well as deluded. Solzhenitsyn defines this in terms of anthropocentricity. In this schema man is seen as the center of everything that exists. Communism reflects merely a naturalized version of humanism.

Solzhenitsyn calls for a kind of reformation with the re-emergence of vital values which were characteristic of democracies in their infancy. He said:

At that, in early democracies, as in American democracy at the time of its birth, all individual human rights were granted because man is

God's creature. That is, freedom was given to the individual condition-ally, on the assumption of his constant religious responsibility. Such was the heritage of the preceding thousand years. Two hundred years ago—even fifty years ago—it would have seemed quite impossible, in America, that an individual could be granted boundless freedom simply for the satisfaction of his instincts or whims.

Aleksandr Solzhenitsyn is a disappointed man. He looks to the West and weeps. His adopted land is treating him as a bastard son. A man without a birthright. Yet he who has ears to hear may hear this man.

CLASSICAL CHRISTIANITY

SEPTEMBER 1978

———

I T IS BEING SAID REPEATEDLY, "We are living in the age of secularism; the post-Christian era." Such is the evaluation of historians and other cultural analysts. The appraisal is not offered because of a radical decline in Church membership or benevolent giving. It is offered because of the obvious lack of impact on culture by Christianity. Charles Colson recently mentioned that one third of the population of the United States claims to be "born again" yet there is precious little viable impact on cultural values, morals, or institutional standards by this large segment of our society.

What Is Secularism?

What is secularism? Secularism as an -ism finds its essence in limiting the significance of mankind and human activity to this time (*saeculum*). The existence and relevance of a transcendent personal God is flatly denied. The public sphere of value and morality is not regulated or governed by theological considerations. Secularism does not prohibit or outlaw "religion." Religion is regarded as a viable human option to be exercised freely (as the Constitution allows). However, the unwritten but nevertheless dominant law of secularism is that religion is a private matter and is never to be brought into the public sphere of life. Religion is to be practiced within the sphere of the Church alone. It is not permitted to penetrate public education, government, industry, or law courts. Religion is confined to a reservation. If the Christian behaves and keeps his religion to the perimeters of the reservation he will find no quarrel from the secularist. But if the believer dares to step off the reservation the secularist community rises up like so many General Custers to put the Christian back "in his place." The Church continues to exist but is confined to an ecclesiastical ghetto with the hope that she will soon die a death of cultural irrelevance.

Separation of State and God

With the cherished American principle of separation of Church and state came the freedom for all churches to exist apart from state controls and establishmentarianism. With a clearly defined "division of labor" the Church agreed that it was not its business to wield the sword, levy taxes, or build highways. Likewise the state acknowledged that it was not its business to preach the Gospel or administer sacraments. But from a division of labor "under God" whereby both state and Church were seen to have different tasks under the authority of God, has come a not-so-subtle shift to the concept of separation of state and God. For the secularist the state exists apart from any consideration of God. God does not belong in the marketplace. The state has claimed "sphere sovereignty" whereby it views itself as being in no wise answerable or accountable to God.

The Death of Monotheism

With the advent of secularism we have witnessed the death of one kind of God, a monotheistic God. In its place has come a revival of ancient henotheism. Henotheism is a variety of polytheism which views individual gods or goddesses ruling over certain geographical or ethnic "territories." Outside his private territorial domain the deity has no power or influence. Within the territory the god is sovereign and carries weighty authority. Henotheism has no provision for a "high" god who exercises authority over all lesser territorial deities. Each territorial god is as great and powerful as the size or strength of his particular territory.

Secularism has revived a modified version of ancient henotheism. There is no single God who rules over everything, no high God before whom both Church and state must bow. Gods are tolerated only within sharply defined territories. The Christian God is viewed as such a henotheistic deity having authority over the Church and the Christian reservation.

Astonishingly the Christian community seems willing, indeed eager, to accept such a view of God. Christian men and women in government and industry often speak the loudest in favor of perpetuating this henotheistic system. Even more astonishing is the frequency with which clergy promote the same order.

Henotheism is essentially and fundamentally opposed to monotheistic Christianity. If God is not sovereign over all spheres of human activity He is not God. If Christ is not sovereign over the state He is not the King of Kings but a mere ghetto prince. We must be very careful to notice the gigantic difference between separation of Church and state and separation of God and state. One is compatible with Christianity while the other is the denial of it.

"According to secularism, religion is a private matter and is never to be brought into the public sphere of life."

———

THE ANTINOMIAN SPIRIT

OCTOBER 1978

———

"**E**VERYBODY DO YOUR OWN THING.**"** This worn cliché from the sixties characterizes the spirit of our age. Increasingly freedom is being equated with the inalienable right to do whatever you please. It carries with it a built-in allergy to laws which restrain, whether they be the laws of God or the laws of men.

So pervasive is this anti-law or antinomian attitude that is so reminiscent of the Biblical epoch which provoked God's judgment because "everyone did what was right in his own eyes" (Judg. 17). In the secular world this is reflected in the notion that it is not the function of the state to legislate morality. Morality is a private matter, outside of the domain of the state and even of the Church. A subtle shift in word meaning has occurred which many have missed. The original intent of the concept "you cannot legislate morality" was to convey the idea that passing a law prohibiting a particular kind of activity would not necessarily eliminate such activity. The point of the phrase was that laws do not *ipso facto* produce obedience to those laws. In fact, on some occasions the legal prohibition of certain practices has only incited greater enticement to practice that which is outlawed.

The present interpretation of legislating morality differs from the original intent. Now, in the minds of many, it means the legislative bodies of government ought not be involved with moral issues. Instead of saying the government *cannot* legislate morality it says the government *may not* legislate morality. Government should stay out of matters such as the regulation of abortion, deviant sexual practices, marriage and divorce, and other issues which are of a moral nature since morality is a matter of conscience and the private sector. For the government to legislate in these areas is often viewed as an invasion of privacy by the state and represents a denial of basic freedoms for the individual.

If we take this kind of thinking to its logical conclusion we leave the government with little to do. If the government may not legislate morality its activity will be restricted to determining the colors of the state flag, the state flower, and perhaps the state bird. (But even questions of flowers and birds may be deemed "moral" as they touch on ecological issues which are ultimately moral in character.) The vast majority of matters which concern legislation are of a moral character. Regulation of murder, theft, and civil rights are moral matters. How a person operates his automobile on the highway is a moral issue as it touches on the well-being of fellow travelers.

Questions of the legalization of marijuana often focus on the fact that a majority of certain age groups are violating the law. Since disobedience is so widespread doesn't this indicate that the law is bad? Such a conclusion is a blatant *non sequitur*. Whether or not marijuana should be decriminalized should not be determined by levels of civil disobedience. The point is, however, a vast number of Americans reflect an antinomian spirit regarding marijuana. Such disobedience is hardly motivated by noble aspirations to a higher ethic suppressed by tyrannical government. Here the law is broken as a matter of convenience and physical appetite.

Within the Church the same spirit of antinomianism prevails. Pope John Paul I faces the embarrassing legacy of his predecessor as he tries to explain to the world why a majority of his American adherents tell the pollsters they practice artificial means of birth control in spite of its being explicitly forbidden by papal encyclical. One must ask how people can confess their belief in an infallible magisterium of their church and at the same time take a position of obstinate refusal to submit to that magisterium.

Within the Protestant churches individuals frequently become irate when church disciplinary boards call them to moral accountability. They often declare that the church has no right to intrude into their private lives. This, in spite of the fact that in their membership vows they publicly vowed to submit themselves to the moral oversight of the church.

There is no sphere of life where antinomianism should be more rare than in the evangelical Christian community. Sadly the facts do not fit the theory. So blasé is the typical "evangelical" toward the law of God that the prophecies of doom Rome thundered at Luther are beginning to come true. Some "evangelicals" are indeed using justification by faith alone as a license to sin. I put "evangelical" in quotes for such can only be deemed properly as pseudoevangelicals. Anyone who has the most rudimentary understanding of justification by faith knows that authentic faith always manifests itself in a zeal for obedience. No earnest Christian can ever have a cavalier attitude toward the law of God. Though obedience to such laws does not justify, the justified person will surely endeavor to obey them.

To be sure there are times when the commandments of men are on a collision course with the laws of God. In such instances Christians not only may disobey men but they must disobey men. But we are talking here not of isolated moral issues but of attitudes. The Christian must be particularly scrupulous in this age of antinomianism. We must be careful not to get caught up in the spirit of the age. We are not free to do what is right in our own eyes. We are called to do what is right in His eyes. Freedom ought not be confused with autonomy. As long as evil exists in the world the moral restraint of law is necessary. It is an act of grace by which God institutes government. Government exists to restrain the evildoer. It exists to protect the innocent and the righteous. The righteous man is called to support it as much as he possibly can without compromising his obedience to God.

BORN AGAIN

NOVEMBER 1978

——

I T'S MOVIE TIME AGAIN. I CAN'T RESIST IT. A film has been released that is rare in its import as Hollywood goes, and consequently warrants some comment. The film is *Born Again* and represents Hollywood's attempt to dramatize and document Charles Colson's conversion to Christianity. It is not often that a religious theme like this is handled in the secular screen world. The initial reaction of the public has been mixed. The world premiere in Washington was successful as have the other regional premieres. The advanced theater bookings have been unusually high. However, in the short time the film has been playing it has been a disappointment at the box office. People are staying away in droves. Why?

The secular press has been unusually critical of this film. There has been an acid tone of overt hostility in many of the reviews. It seems the press can never forgive Colson for being Nixon's hatchet man. The deep-rooted hostility the press has for Nixon continues to spill over onto Colson. Add to that the perennial tone of cynicism the press exhibits to all things religious, and it is no surprise the reviews have been as vitriolic as they have been.

This is not to suggest the film is without weaknesses. It does have a slow beginning and some problems with casting. The movie can logically be divided into three segments. The first deals with Colson's Nixon years and the Watergate fiasco. Here casting is a problem. Dean Jones does not capture the pre-Christian Colson. Jones suffers from his image as a Walt Disney character.* The viewer has difficulty seeing Jones in the role of the tough sophisticate that Colson was and continues to be. The political alley cat emerged as a pussycat and was simply not believable. It was not Colson. (The irony of this, however, is that much of Colson's "tough guy

———
* Dean Jones (1931–2015) was known for his appearances in Disney films, including *That Darn Cat!* and *The Love Bug*.

image" was the creation of the press. Now the press whines when their own created image is not played back for them in living color.) Though Colson is not what the press caricatured him to be, he is still a long way from Walt Disney.

The White House scenes also failed. Attempts to re-create Nixon and his cabinet detracted from the film. Efforts at realism resulted in parody with all of the idiosyncrasies of Nixon and Kissinger that night club comedians mimic, overdone.

The second segment, documenting Colson's religious crisis, was more effective. Jones warmed to his role and the conversion scene was moving. The segment was hampered a bit by a few moments of saccharine dialogue and the standard caricatures of Christians as seeming plastic. Of course it is no easy task to capture on film the intense drama of conversion. It was achieved to a degree but not to the magnificent level captured in Colson's book version of *Born Again*.

The third segment of the film, which the reviewing press has virtually ignored, is so excellent that it redeems the entire production and makes *Born Again* a must-see film for every Christian. This segment empathetically escorts the audience into prison with Charles Colson. At this point Jones sparkles and his work is greatly enhanced by giant performances turned in by Jay Robinson and Raymond St. Jacques. The humiliation and deprivation characteristic of prison life is crippling. Colson's personal struggle to be a Christian behind bars is powerful. Jay Robinson, as Shapiro, Colson's law partner and defense attorney, re-establishes himself as a superb actor. His story would be worthy of a film documentary in itself. He was catapulted to instant fame as a young actor for his performance in the role of Caligula, the mad emperor of Rome who was tormented by the thought of Christians and their leader's garment in the classic movie *The Robe*. His performance in that film was hailed as one of the ten best acting performances in Hollywood history. After *The Robe*, however, Robinson's life went into a tailspin marked by alcoholism, drug addiction, and crime which culminated in a prison term in a federal penitentiary in California. Robinson lived out the classic tragedy of the "poor player who struts and frets his hour on the stage and then is heard no more." But in *Born Again*, Robinson is heard once more. During the filming Robinson had his own religious crisis. He was converted to Christ on the set. The mad emperor finally embraced the robe of Christ and is a new person. The tragic years of obscurity and humiliation have not eroded his skills, but deepened them. The world premiere in Washington was a special time for Robinson as it marked, to the day, the twenty-fifth anniversary of the world premiere of *The Robe*.

Raymond St. Jacques brought realism and intensity to the role of Jimmy Newsom, the tough black inmate who befriended Colson in prison. This segment of the film gives ringing testimony to the urgency of Colson's new ministry of Prison Fellowship. The work Colson is presently engaged with in federal prisons is a more vital vocation than his role of special counsel to the President was. Prison Fellowship is authentic Christianity in action. It deserves the total backing of the entire American Christian Community. Prison Fellowship is an agency of God for changing lives in the midst of prisons. The impetus of Christ's own ministry is carried on there. The film captures the urgency of that mission. In Washington we were given the extra treat of hearing from twelve inmates who have gone through the Prison Fellowship program. These men are living evidence of the power of Christ to change lives. They represent what the film is about ultimately.

America needs to view this film. They will discuss it. They will surely critique it. Don't let America miss the point. It counts forever.

CHICAGO SUMMIT

DECEMBER 1978

———

T HE END OF OCTOBER BROUGHT A NEW dimension to interdenominational cooperation among evangelicals. Hosted by the International Council on Biblical Inerrancy (ICBI), approximately three hundred scholars, pastors, and Christian leaders met to discuss matters relating to Biblical authority. The Summit meeting was held at the Regency Hyatt on the grounds of Chicago O'Hare International Airport.

Representatives from Germany, Switzerland, France, Africa, South America, and other nations joined with American Christian leaders for three days of intense study and dialogue concerning Holy Scripture. Fourteen scholarly papers on issues relating to the integrity of Scripture were presented at seminar sessions. Five plenary sessions were held with major addresses given by men such as J.I. Packer, W.A. Criswell, Edmund Clowney, and Robert Preus.

The conference hosted such Christian leaders as William Bright of Campus Crusade, Kenneth Kantzner, editor of *Christianity Today*, Josh McDowell, A. Wetherell Johnson, James Kennedy, James Montgomery Boice, Harold Ockenga, and a host of other well-known scholars, pastors, and leaders.

The Doctrine of Scripture

The meeting represented an attempt by evangelicals to produce a united statement on the doctrine of Holy Scripture. The proceedings were marked by a high sense of dignity and cordiality. Noticeably absent were demonstrative harangues or bitter denunciations of those not in sympathy or agreement with those present. Though the delegates represented a wide diversity of ecclesiastical and theological backgrounds, the group was able to reach unity on their view of Scripture.

Delegates ended the conference by signing a unified statement of Scripture which included a lengthy introductory essay by J.I. Packer (which was not included in the content being affirmed by signatures but served as a preliminary exposition to the short statement of faith and nineteen articles of affirmation and denial which were affirmed by the signatures of the delegates).

The Chicago Statement represents one of the fullest statements on Scripture ever endorsed by such a wide diversity of evangelical thinkers. The essence of the document upholds the authority, inspiration, infalli-bility, and inerrancy of Scripture.

The Authority of Scripture

The primary concern of the meeting was to reaffirm the full authority of Scripture over the lives of Christians. The erosion of biblical authority in the world and in the Church has been a critical problem for Christians living in the Twentieth Century. Perhaps the Summit will be a watershed that will help turn the drift of skepticism around.

The meeting was a sober one with open recognition given to the difficul-ties raised by forms of higher criticism. Yet the conference also manifested a strong sense of unity and clarity about what is meant by Biblical author-ity. Men and women came away from Chicago at once encouraged and strengthened by this meeting of minds on Scripture.

Nine Years of Research

ICBI outlined plans for nine more years of research, publications, and conferences to help pastors, teachers, and the laity to work through mod-ern problems and issues concerning the Bible. The seminar papers and plenary addresses will soon be published and available for wide distri-bution. The conference marked the future release of ICBI's first effort in publication: a volume of essays entitled *The Foundation of Biblical Author-ity*, edited by Dr. Boice.

It is the hope of ICBI council that more and more Christian leaders will sign the Chicago Document and present a unified front to a world des-perately in need of a clean and certain voice from the Church.

A TIME FOR TRUTH

MARCH 1979

———

ECHOING THE SENTIMENTS OF THE PROPHET Amos in another sphere, I must preface this article by saying, "I am not an economist, nor the son of an economist." So far removed from expertise in the field of economics am I that it may appear presumptuous to even offer comment on the current crisis of American economics. What follows is a layman's response to a bestselling book that has captured the attention of hundreds of thousands of people.

William Simon, former Secretary of the Treasury and former Energy Czar, has written a book entitled *A Time for Truth*, in which he gives a severe critique of current government policies of economic controls, regulations of business and industry, and general interference in the private sphere of life.

Such a book dealing with questions of fiscal responsibility, balancing budgets, gross national debts, and inflationary practices is rarely the fodder of best-sellers. In an interview granted to *Book Digest Magazine*, Simon was asked whether or not he thought his book would do as well as it has. His response was, "I most certainly did not." (The book has already gone through eleven printings and is expected to sell over a million copies.) Simon went on to say, "It seems to have captured a mood in the country.... The whole issue of what our economic policies are doing to our society is still unclear. But we are living with double-digit inflation, and in a public climate which supports Proposition 13. People are becoming dissatisfied. I think I was lucky to come out with my book now."

The central theme is the premise that there is a direct correlation between economic freedom and political freedom. Simon speaks somewhat as a prophet of doom arguing, at times very convincingly, that America is moving at an alarming rate towards a coercive centralized bureaucratic government that has a strangle hold on the nation's economic freedom.

He argues that with the increasing loss of economic freedom for business and industry in the private sector there is at the same time a corresponding loss of real political freedom. Using models of the economic growth and development of two different nations, Simon traces the history of movements and trends in plotting the destiny of nations with respect to their economic growth and freedom. His two chief paradigms are post-war England and West Germany. Where England has moved in the direction of a socialized democracy, West Germany has established its economic and political system on much more of a free market approach. In addition, Simon gives a critique of the events that led up to and culminated with the bankruptcy that has plagued the city of New York. His evaluation of the long-range implications of continued deficit spending and government regulation is scary, to say the least.

From a theological perspective, I was most interested to read his critique of the philosophical foundation for socialized democracy and "Liberal America." He points out that the primary philosophical concern and motive for liberal tendencies in American government is born out of a genuine desire to help the poor, the oppressed, the underprivileged, and the disenfranchised peoples of our nation through proliferating government programs. His studies show that, noble as the motives for such socialized legislation are, they have in fact been a miserable failure. Most disconcerting is that the very philosophy that has been designed to help the poor and oppressed has in the final analysis only served to cripple and hamper the poor and underprivileged all the more. Runaway inflation's worst victims are those on meager and limited incomes. The liberal policies of government programming and spending, generally speaking, have had an adverse effect on the very constituents they are trying to assist.

I am not in the position to know for sure how correct the evaluation of Simon's analysis is, but Mr. Simon gives statistics that are cause for sober reflection. For example, he points out that our national budget has grown from about one hundred billion dollars fourteen years ago to five hundred billion dollars today. Such an enormous growth of government spending has resulted in the fact that forty cents of every dollar that is spent in this country is now spent for government programs. In order to fund the huge deficit programs, the government has resorted to printing money at a rate that far exceeds our backup reserves and resources. This excessive printing of money has an almost immediate adverse effect on the world evaluation of the American dollar. Fundamental principles of economics are upset when the government proliferates such practices. The increase in taxation that comes in the wake of such deficit spending affects radically the lower income wage earners in this country. We are told, at the present time, that the average wage earner must work for four months out of the year just to pay his taxes.

The initial effect of Proposition 13 in California has not proven the doomsday opponents of it predicted. Needed human services have not been destroyed as a result of this mandated restriction on government spending. On the contrary, the people of California are voicing loudly an enormous sense of relief from taxation. For example, I spoke with a widow recently, who owns property outside San Francisco, and who makes less than twenty thousand dollars a year. She was elated because the immediate effect of Proposition 13 was to reduce her property taxes by three thousand dollars a year. She indicated that this meant to her the same as a three thousand dollar a year raise. That sense of relief from taxation has been multiplied throughout the state of California. Simon raises the question that perhaps it is time for a national Proposition 13 to force the government to trim their ship of excess cargo and get rid of duplicating programs that waste and squander the taxpayers' money.

One of the strongest cases that Simon presents in the book is the case that private businesses and industry have more competence to meet the needs of minority groups and underprivileged people through privately funded, non-profit institutions. However, government regulations and high levels of taxation make it difficult for such privately funded charitable organizations to function at peak capacity. The solving of problems that occur in the private sector through government intervention will frequently cost two to five times as much money and energy as it would take private institutions to do the same job.

I do not know if Simon is right in his central thesis. His book has raised profound questions in my mind and in the minds of others. I suggest this book as serious reading for Christians who are interested in the current economic crisis facing our nation. This crisis will touch the life and the effectiveness of the Christian church. As our nation's resources are jeopardized there is an immediate effect on the ability of the church to finance the work of the kingdom of God. All our passionate concerns for missions, for the poor, for the underprivileged, are affected deeply by the economic stability of our government. I, for one, would welcome an opportunity to read a critique of Simon's book so that there can be a balance in any dialogue over these matters. Here is a book that has become a pivotal focal point for evaluation of the fiscal crisis plaguing our government. Simon has thrown down the gauntlet and it's up to others to respond. Maybe it's time to resurrect our win buttons that had a short and painless death during the Ford Administration. We have neither won the war on inflation nor have we whipped inflation, and we are in danger of being whipped by inflation.

THE JUST SHALL LIVE BY FAITH

APRIL 1979

H ABAKKUK'S FAMOUS STATEMENT "The just shall live by faith" is picked up and employed three times in the New Testament. It has become a slogan of Protestantism whose emphasis has been upon the evangelical doctrine of justification by faith alone. In this slogan is contained a hint of the essence of the Christian life. The focal point of it is in the Biblical concept of righteousness.

One of Jesus' most disturbing comments was the statement made, "Unless your righteousness exceeds that of the Scribes and the Pharisees you will in no wise enter the kingdom of God." It is easy for us to assume that what Jesus meant was that our righteousness must be of a higher sort than that characterized by men who were hypocrites. The image that we have of Scribes and Pharisees from the New Testament period is that of unscrupulous, ruthless practitioners of religious fraud and deceit. We must bear in mind, however, that the Pharisees as a group were men who historically were committed to a very lofty level of righteous living. Yet Jesus tells us that our righteousness must exceed theirs. What did he mean?

When we consider the Biblical notion of righteousness we are dealing with a matter that touches virtually every plane of theology. In the first instance, there is the righteousness of God by which all standards of rightness and wrongness are to be measured. God's character is the ultimate foundation and model of righteousness. In the Old Testament righteousness becomes defined in terms of obedience to the commandments delivered by the God who Himself is altogether righteous. Those commands included not only precepts of human behavior with respect to our fellow man but also matters of a liturgical and ceremonial nature.

What happened in Old Testament Israel and with the New Testament Pharisees was that many people substituted liturgical righteousness for authentic righteousness. That is to say, men became satisfied in obeying the rituals of the religious community, rather than the broader implications of the law. The Pharisees, for example, were rebuked by Jesus for tithing their mint and their cumin while omitting the weightier matters of the law, justice and mercy. Jesus indicated that the Pharisees were correct in giving their tithes but were incorrect in assuming that their liturgical exercises had completed the requirements of the law. Here liturgical righteousness became a substitute for true and full obedience.

Within the evangelical world, "righteousness" is a rare word indeed. We speak of morality, spirituality, and piety. Rarely, however, do we speak of righteousness. Yet the goal of our redemption is not piety or spirituality but righteousness. Spirituality in the New Testament sense is a means to the end of righteousness. Being spiritual means that we are exercising the spiritual graces that God has given to us to mold us after the image of His Son. That is, the discipline of prayer, Bible study, church fellowship, witnessing, and the like are not ends in themselves but are designed to assist us in living righteously. We are stunted in our growth if we assume that the end of the Christian life is spirituality. Rather, spiritual concerns are but the beginning of our walk with God. It is a constant danger and subtle trap that is set before us to think that spirituality completes the requirements of Christ. To allow this to happen is to fall into the trap of the Pharisees, to substitute liturgical or ritualistic practices for authentic righteousness. We are to pray; we are to study the Bible; we are to bear witness in Evangelism. By all means. But we must never rest at any point in our lives in our own pursuit of righteousness.

The righteousness of God is imputed to us in our justification. But in our justification we become righteous in the sight of God by means of the cloak of Christ's righteousness. However, as soon as we are justified we are to have evidence in our lives of personal righteousness that flows out of our justification. It is interesting to me that the whole Biblical concept of righteousness is contained in one Greek word. That same

Greek word is used to refer in the first instance to the righteousness of God; in the second instance to what we call justification; and in the third instance to righteousness of life. Thus, from beginning to end from the nature of God to the destiny of man, our human duty remains the same, that of righteousness.

True righteousness must never be confused with self-righteousness. Since our righteousness proceeds from our justification which is by the righteousness of Christ alone we must never be deluded into thinking that the works of righteousness we endeavor to perform have any merit of their own. Yet as Protestants, zealously maintaining our doctrine of justification by faith alone, we must be ever mindful that the justification which is by faith alone is never by a faith that is alone. True faith is a faith that manifests itself in righteousness, a righteousness which exceeds that of the Pharisees and the Scribes; a righteousness which is concerned with the weightier matters of the law, justice and mercy.

To be "spiritual" and unconcerned with justice is to miss the point of righteousness. To be pious and lacking mercy is to turn our piety into hypocrisy. God requires a kind of piety and spirituality which issues in justice and mercy; with a passionate concern with the weightier matters of the law. We are called to bear witness to the righteousness of God in every area of our life—from our prayer closets to our courtrooms, from our pews to our marketplace. The top priority of Jesus is to seek first the Kingdom of God and His righteousness and all other things will be added unto that.

"To reconcile the basic teachings of Jesus with those of Mohammed would take the skill of one greater than a theologian. It would take a magician."

—

KHOMEINI—ARE ALL RELIGIONS THE SAME?

MAY 1979

—————

T HE SHAH IS ON THE ROAD—forced into exile, banished in disgrace, the Shah is no longer a factor in Iran. Noted for a ruthless tyranny, many in the West welcomed the ouster of Shah Mohammad Reza Pahlavi.* Though pro-Western and seemingly a friend of the U.S., the Shah's tactics were repugnant to peace-loving and equity-minded Americans.

Visions of an aged holy man directing the coup from afar gave the impression of a contest between the benign and the malignant, the righteous and the wicked.

Ayatollah Ruhollah Khomeini entered Iran in triumph.† The popular acclamation of the masses resembled a new Palm Sunday. Only the donkey was missing.

Khomeini promised a spiritual revolution. He got his revolution, but it has hardly been spiritual. In his zeal to create a new Islamic Republic, a theocratic state under the rule of Allah, Khomeini brandished the scimitar. This renaissance of orthodox and fundamentalist Islam brought in its wake an ugly blood-bath of terrorism. Khomeini promptly introduced a purge. The purge featured sudden arrests, kangaroo court proceedings and summary executions of those considered disloyal to the new regime. Over sixty people were thus liquidated.

—————————————

* Mohammad Reza Pahlavi (1919–80) was the last shah (king) of Iran, whose overthrow during the Iranian Revolution in 1979 ended 2,500 years of continuous Persian monarchy.
† Ayatollah Ruhollah Khomeini (1902–89) was an Iranian Shiite cleric and politician. He was leader of the 1979 Iranian Revolution that overthrew Shah Mohammad Reza Pahlavi and founder and supreme leader of the Islamic Republic of Iran.

People in the West were shocked and horrified. How could this plain looking "holy man," who resembled an Indian guru, be so ruthless?

Easy. Khomeini is not a Muslim heretic. The ancient virtue of "death to the infidel" is perfectly consistent with orthodox Islamic religion. It was born with a sword and expanded via military conflict. Mohammed himself, the self-styled prophet of Allah, is pictured most often with a sword. He was hardly the Prince of Peace.

In the nineteenth century it was fashionable for historians, philosophers, and anthropologists to search out the "essence" of religion. Thus the unique characteristics of world religions were ignored or discarded in favor of a common core or least common denominator. The naive conclusions of the experts on world religions featured the simplistic idea that at the core, all religions were basically the same.

From this effort came the oft-quoted "mountain analogy." In this image God is pictured as sitting atop a high mountain. Many roads or paths trace their way from the bottom to the pinnacle. The many roads, of course, represent the various religions of the world. Some proceed along a direct route up the mountain. Other paths are more circuitous. Some of the roads are smooth; others are bumpy. But, as the analogy goes, they all arrive at the same place sooner or later.

Jesus didn't believe that. He taught that the road to God was narrow and straight. The broad road and the wide gate, He said, lead to destruction. The mountain analogy is on a collision course with the New Testament.

To reconcile the basic teachings of Jesus with those of Mohammed would take the skill of one greater than a theologian. It would take a magician.

Some might say, "Has not the Christian Church been guilty of sanctioning and initiating more bloody actions in history than Khomeini's little coup?" The answer is obvious. Indeed the Christian Church has been guilty all too often of perpetrating shameful and heinous crimes. The Church's historical "black eyes" are well documented.

So what's the difference? Why pick on Khomeini or Islam? For one fundamental reason. When the Muslim kills the infidel, he is honoring

Allah and bringing glory to Mohammed. When a Christian kills an infidel, he disgraces God and disobeys Christ. Jesus may sanction the civil magistrate's use of the sword, but not the Church's.

Biblical principles of justice could never condone a kangaroo court system which summarily executes political dissidents.

Perhaps one good thing will come out of Iran's upheaval. Perhaps it will awaken people to the folly of the mountain analogy. Perhaps people won't be so quick to embrace the idea that all religions are the same.

Maybe the hysteria that followed Jonestown will be sobered by a new awareness that you cannot lump all religions together.

Perhaps we will be more inclined to examine the differences between religions as well as their similarities. We may be grateful that medical science is so discriminating. We know that the differences between diseases, not their similarities, are what counts—often a difference between life and death, between indigestion and cancer.

That Jesus claimed to be God and Mohammed claimed to be a prophet is an essential difference. That Buddha was an atheist and Christ a theist is an essential difference. That Confucius died and Christ was resurrected is an essential difference. That Jim Jones advocated suicide while Jesus preached patient endurance is a radical difference. That most religions teach salvation by good works while Christianity teaches salvation by grace is an essential difference. That Christianity features an atonement and a mediator who reconciles and redeems is an essential difference. That some men worship idols while others worship a transcendent God is an essential difference. The worship of Yahweh is a far cry from the worship of a cow.

Only the unreligious say all religions are the same.

SEPARATION OF CHURCH AND STATE

JUNE 1979

———

J UST AS VIOLENCE TENDS TO BREED violence so hysteria breeds hysteria. The national reaction to Jonestown is a case in point.* The Jonestown massacre has prompted many in the fields of legislation to take a second glance at the traditional protections and exemptions that are afforded religious institutions and organizations.

Jonestown as an event in history is one that is characterized by hysteria. We must be careful, however, that our reaction to Jonestown not be one that manifests the same kind of hysteria. If we look at Jonestown in the light of the history of religious tradition with any kind of objectivity, we will be quick to admit that Jonestown ranks as one of the most unusual and bizarre episodes of organized religion in the history of mankind. It would hardly be rational to assume that Jonestowns are commonplace in the religious world. Now is not the time to push the panic button.

One of the most important amendments to the United States Constitution is the first one, which guarantees freedom of religion. That the founders of this country considered freedom of religion important is indicated by the fact that they guaranteed it by the first amendment to the Constitution. To obscure it in this day and age would have far reaching implications for our culture.

One congressman recently stated in a news conference that separation of Church and State must be maintained at all costs, however, when the Church is involved in any way with the public domain then all requirements that would be true for a secular institution must also be imposed

———

* Jonestown is the name given to a settlement in Guyana of the Peoples Temple, a cult under the leadership of Jim Jones. It gained notoriety when on November 18, 1978, Jones directed the members to commit suicide by drinking cyanide-laced Flavor Aid; 909 people were killed.

upon the Church. Think about that statement for a minute. What is affirmed in the first half of the statement is denied by the second half. If we have separation of Church and State but that separation is disallowed when the Church is involved in public matters what does that mean? Does this not mean that the government will only sanction the Church when it is utterly irrelevant to public life?

Let us look at the question of Christian colleges which operate in the arena of public education. One issue that has been discussed heavily is the issue of coeducational dormitories and housing. Many Christian institutions believe as part of their value system that it is improper to practice open housing for men and women. If Christian colleges are to be governed by the same standards that apply to secular universities then it would require Christian colleges to abandon their value system in order to meet those standards. In other words, the Christian institution must be secularized if it is allowed to continue in operation.

Historically the First Amendment guaranteed not only the right of private religious beliefs and the free expression of those beliefs, but it also has guaranteed the right of the Church to be involved in the educational enterprise. Christian institutions of learning exist to communicate a Christian life and world view, by incorporating in the curriculum Christian values and behavioral standards. If the secular State imposes restrictions that deny Christian distinctives from full expression then we have seen the end of separation of Church and State and a radical violation of the First Amendment. It must be added that any Church institution that would be discriminatory with respect to race or ethnic origin would in fact be violating their own religion. Thus, it is important that what I am writing is not understood to be a defense in any way for racial or ethnic discrimination in Christian institutions. The issue is the degree to which secular values may be imposed by law upon Christian institutions. We must not think that separation of Church and State can ever mean that the Church has no role to play in the public domain.

There is a deep resistance against religious groups lobbying for public legislation on moral issues such as abortion, and homosexual practices, and the like. The Church is beginning to face a backlash of reaction to its involvement in promoting certain levels of moral legislation. Many say that the Church has no right to speak out on legislative issues. If that were so, then of course we would have to exclude the right of any organization to speak out on moral issues. Why would the Church have any more or any less right to speak out on moral questions than the Daughters of the American Revolution or members of NOW and other such groups? In classical democracy, any group or any individual has the freedom of expression to encourage people to vote for laws. Whether or not the Church has the right to do it in a democratic society has already been decided.

Perhaps the most volatile issue of Church and State that we will face in the eighties is the whole question of tax exemption for the Church. Not only would the Church suffer economic disaster by losing tax exempt status, but all charitable organizations, religious or otherwise, would face the same dilemma. What would happen to the work that is being done by churches and charitable organizations which has been specifically designed to meet social problems in our culture? The only solution would be for the government to take over, adding to the tax burden of the whole nation. And, the government has demonstrated again and again that their involvement in programs of social concern has produced bureaucratic inefficiencies that become increasingly less personal and alarmingly more expensive. Thus, there is more at stake here than controlling the likes of Jim Jones. The whole question of ministry to the disenfranchised is ultimately at stake.

As we come to the eighties we need to be prepared to face the growing militancy of a secular spirit that is becoming less and less tolerant to religious convictions and values. Christians should be the first people to work to curb any abuses of the privileges they enjoy in the present structure of Church and State. The Tax Reform Act, for example, has gone a long way to curb abuse of non-profit organizations. Christian institutions should happily volunteer to make available to the public their financial records and statements. Full financial disclosure should be a normal policy on a

volunteer basis of all charitable organizations. If Christians would cooperate at this level perhaps some of the hostility that is growing within
the secular world would be quieted.

Finally, it is the Christian's job to prove in every generation that in
addition to the Church's unique values of religious conviction, belief,
worship, and the like, the Church in fact is an institution and an agency
of mercy that brings healing of a general nature promoting the general
welfare of all people. When the Church is first a priest, then and only
then can she be a prophet.

THE JOY OF RUNNING—
OR THE MARQUIS DE SADE
REVISITED

JULY 1979

———

AMERICA IS RUNNING. CARS AREN'T doing so well but people are moving with loping strides everywhere. Joggers clog the park trails, suburban streets, even hotel lobbies, as millions of people are taking up our newest national pastime. Some even dare to call it "sport."

The testimonies of the legions of running converts drip with saccharine beads of extravagant praise. Reams of articles and volumes of books are appearing, extolling the wondrous bliss of running. The apostles of jogging tell us how marvelous it is to move with the grace of a deer, gliding along trails beholding the treasures of nature: wildflowers in bloom, rabbits scurrying for shelter, birds singing lilting choruses, and trees sparkling with the reflected hues of their springtime blossoms. They speak of experiencing mystical highs without resorting to hallucinogenic drugs, and of the euphoria that attends long distance runs. The over forty crowd acclaim the rejuvenating powers of running for bodily health. They are giving up their Serutan* as "natures" spelled backwards now comes out "running."

How could I resist such enticement? It sounded just like what I needed to recapture my faded youth, a pleasant way to get in shape. Not that I'm ever worried about heart trouble, as my parents lived 105 years before their hearts gave out. (That is, 105 combined years.) Or that it bothers me that my middle-aged paunch is the topic of friendly barbs like, "I see you buy your shirts with a bump in them," or "You must be on the level, R.C., because you have a bubble in the middle." There are, after all,

———

* Serutan was a laxative whose advertisements encouraged consumers to read the name backward, which spelled "natures."

certain advantages to a little extra weight. Some ladies like to pat me in the tummy and make me feel so mothered.

So, I joined the team of runners coached by Dr. William Harry White, Ligonier's answer to Simon Legree.* I started out for the two-mile run inspired by visions of Roger Bannister breaking the four-minute mile, of multitudes of wiry athletes running through the streets of Boston in the annual Marathon, of "Rocky" jumping with jubilance, fists stretched out to heaven in triumph, as he reached the top step of the plaza in Philadelphia. These visions inspired me to greatness, for the first hundred yards.

I discovered the joys everybody talks about. I love it. Who can describe the thrill of coming in last in a group of fifteen runners? Isn't it great to be able to brag to your friends that you were able to run the first mile in slightly under twelve minutes? I can see the headlines: "Sproul breaks 12-minute mile in Stahlstown Marathon."

I love the getting-in-touch-with-nature part. I see the rabbits scurrying, and think about how great it would be to have four legs to run with. I find myself coveting the equipment God gave the bunnies. I hear the birds sing—the only problem is they all seem to be mocking birds, laughing at me from their tree top perches. I watch the beauty of the raindrops as they drip off the end of my nose and bring such exhilarating shivers through my body.

My body—that's the really fun part. I'm gaining a whole new education in anatomy. I used to think calves were baby cows until I discovered the warm feeling of my own calves throbbing with pain. I used to think shin-splints were something you put on broken bones. It's so nice to be able to limp around the house all day basking in the rewards of my new physical fitness "sport"—a sport designed by sadists for us masochists.

Who has time for mystical highs when your lungs are screaming for breath and your heart is pounding at your chest like a jack hammer? I feel like a deer, alright, a deer that has been savagely shot by a hunter and is using every ounce of will power to run one more step. I see the trees

---

* Simon Legree is a character in Harriet Beecher Stowe's novel *Uncle Tom's Cabin.* He is a cruel slave master.

along the road, but I'm not looking at the blossoms, I'm just praying that the big fat tree that marks the half mile spot will come into view before I drop. As I run up a mere five percent grade I feel like the star in *The Eiger Sanction** or like Hillary on the slopes of Everest.†

The truth is folks, I hate it. I hate every minute, every pace of it. It's no fun at all for me. It's cruel and unusual punishment. It's barbarous torture that should be outlawed.

Why in the world then, do I look forward to it? Why, when I miss a day do I feel bad not because of guilt but because I feel cheated? Why would I feel terribly disappointed if I had to stop?

I don't know for sure. Maybe it's because I like the problems it produces. Maybe I'm glad when I have to go out and buy new socks because my old ones won't fit over my calves anymore. Maybe I like saving my money to go to a tailor to have my clothes altered. Maybe I enjoy seeing my pulse rate after two miles coming down from 188 to 140. Maybe I enjoy feeling the emotional stress of the day flowing right out of my body through my feet as I run. I must like the clear-headed feeling that comes from vastly improved circulation. I like being able to sleep at night and being able to walk around a golf course instead of riding in a cart. I like starting the course with my teenage son and seeing him standing at the finish line, greeting me with a grin as I come in over seven minutes later than he. I like looking forward to summer softball games instead of dreaming up excuses for a gracious retirement. I like the camaraderie of runners, people who abandon ruthless competition for a spirit of mutual encouragement. I like the feeling that comes when I cross the finish line, knowing that I completed the task. I like standing in the shower with warm jets of water soothing my aching muscles. I like stepping on the scale at the end of the day.

I think of Francine, my friend in Amarillo, Texas, who was brutally shot,

---

* *The Eiger Sanction* is a 1975 film starring Clint Eastwood whose plot involves an assassination scheme in the Swiss Alps.
† Sir Edmund Hillary (1919–2008) was a New Zealand mountaineer and explorer. On May 29, 1953, he and the Sherpa mountaineer Tenzing Norgay (1914–1986) became the first climbers to reach the summit of Mount Everest.

six times, by her estranged husband, two months ago. I think of talking to this woman on the phone as she speaks to me from her hospital bed, crying tears of jubilation because that day she reached a new milestone in her process of recovery—she was able to walk four hundred feet. Sixty days ago her joy was boundless when she was able to move her thumb an eighth of an inch. I think of Francine when I run, knowing that very soon she will be running too.

I'm starting to discover why the multitudes are running. They have discovered something—something good, something worthwhile, something very human. I don't want to stop running ... ever.

"MY PEOPLE PERISH ..."

AUGUST 1979

T HIS MOURNFUL LAMENT CAME FROM God Himself as He gazed from heaven on His people Israel. He spoke these awful words through the lips of the Prophet Hosea.

Why were God's people perishing? What was it that moved God so deeply? What was behind the urgency of these words? Let Hosea answer: "My people perish for lack of knowledge."

God's people were not destroyed for lack of military troops; nor for lack of wealth; nor for lack of gasoline or other natural resources. The people did not perish because of disease or economic inflation. They were perishing because they were lacking in the knowledge of God.

Hosea gives us a grim portrait of the state of Israel's national health as a result of the lack of the knowledge of God. The consequences were radical, touching the heart of the land: "There is no truth, no mercy, no knowledge of God in the land. There is swearing, deception, murder, stealing and adultery. They employ violence, so that bloodshed follows bloodshed. Therefore, the land mourns, and everyone in it languishes."

Is our modern world any different? Education has become a major industry where certain levels of literacy are simply assumed throughout the Western world. Yet when it comes to knowledge of God, we wonder still if Johnny can read?

We are living in an age which some historians have described as the era of the eclipse of God, the "Post-Christian" era. Some tell us that knowledge of God is neither possible nor desirable. We need to learn more practical things, things that are more relevant to our daily lives. It is precisely the "practice" of the people that is most deeply affected by a lack of the knowledge of God. Our land mourns and our people are languishing. We look to our own culture to examine our values. Is there truth in our land? Is truth a highly valued commodity to the American people? When we consider the events of the past few years emanating from national government, events which produced a new expression in our vocabulary, "the credibility gap," we see that we have reached a point in our national development where truth is played with very loosely. The self-appointed watchdog of truthfulness has become the press. Yet the press has manifested again and again a tendency for distortion and the publishing of half-truths. Where are the writers who have a scrupulous passion for accuracy? The press has become a creative enterprise creating images used to manipulate the masses and truth is slain in the streets. In the world of theology truth has been reduced to relativism where what classically were understood to be eternal verities have now become simply expressions that change with each culture and each congregation. We are told that there are no absolutes, there are "truths" but no truth.

But in biblical categories truth is not merely an abstract conception. Truth has to do with action as well as with thinking and reporting. When God mourned the loss of truth in Israel He was concerned as well with the loss of justice. One of the critical areas of our culture today is in the area of criminal justice. We see deficiencies at both sides of the debate over crime and punishment. On the one hand we see a growing sense of indulgence towards criminal activities where the victims of crime are left without retribution. We are so concerned for the rights of criminals that often the victims of crime are overlooked and neglected. Yet on the other hand, within the context of the punitive system of criminal justice, namely within the walls of penitentiaries and county jails, we see not justice but dehumanization of prisoners. It is one thing to punish a person guilty of a crime, it is another one to strip that person of his dignity in the midst of that punishment. Radical reform is needed on both sides of the question of crime and punishment. In Israel justice was no longer valued and the people were perishing.

What about mercy? When the Bible speaks of mercy it is not speaking simply of a weak kind of love that indulges every sin but rather it has reference to a commitment of steadfast love and loyalty in relationships. A few months ago Charles Colson was addressing the student body of a university.

The normal questions of Watergate were being asked by the audience which was obviously very hostile. At one point in the meeting an angry student challenged Colson about his relationship to Richard Nixon. Colson hesitated before responding, then looked up and said quietly but firmly into the microphone, "Richard Nixon is my friend." With that statement, which Colson expected would bring down the wrath of the multitude upon him, the student body erupted into spontaneous applause. Somehow Colson had touched a vital nerve by making a public expression of the value of loyalty. Of course, the Bible is not speaking of blind loyalty that condones every conceivable wicked action. On the contrary, it is speaking of a loyalty in human relationships that transcends pettiness, that overcomes minor grievances, and develops relationships where people are willing to pay the price to sustain a rich and constant friendship. If there is any place that such loyalty is needed it is within the fellowship of the Christian Church. The Communion of Saints means that as Christian people, in spite of the differences that may separate us on Sunday morning or may tug us in different directions in terms of our major concerns, nevertheless there must be an abiding commitment of loyalty to every man and woman within the body of Christ because God is committed to every one of His people. That means simply that I must be just as committed to every one of His people.

God's people were destroyed not only because truth, mercy, and justice were lacking, but because there was no knowledge of God in the land. When there is no knowledge of God in the land it is inevitable that swearing, deception, murder, stealing, and adultery will flourish. Violence becomes the order of the day as bloodshed stains the national scene. That happens when the knowledge of God is eclipsed. The conclusion of Hosea's words is that because of these things the land mourns and people languish. It would seem that in light of this dreadful picture painted by the prophet that knowledge of God must become a priority to any healthy nation. Without the knowledge of God the people perish and the nation is weakened at its core.

Is it any wonder that in the New Testament when Jesus gives His great commission to His disciples and lays out the plan for the building of the

Kingdom of God that He puts a strong accent on teaching? He tells us to go into all the world teaching all nations the things that He has revealed to us about God. This mandate to teach is not fulfilled with the simple act of evangelism or proclamation. Talk to Archie Parrish, Executive Director of Evangelism Explosion, who travels the globe to Africa, China, behind the Iron Curtain, and Western Europe spreading the techniques and methods of evangelism to the nations. Listen to the burdens of his heart as he talks of the eagerness and enthusiasm with which people are responding to the gospel around the world and how that initial thrust of enthusiastic response is often dissipated and the movement of the people aborted because there are no materials available to these people for Christian growth and nurture. There is no teaching ministry to follow-up the work of evangelists. Sit in my office and listen to Archie Parrish plead with me and with our staff to produce more and more educational materials so that people may have their faith grounded not in superstition but in the solid content of the Word of God. Our task of Christian education is of supreme importance to the building of the Kingdom of God in our day. Christian education must be available to the masses.

I have often pondered what elements God used to bring about the reformation of His Church in the sixteenth century. I see that He raised up great men of God, great thinkers, fully equipped scholars, who were capable of probing the most delicate intricacies of Scripture and the technical dimensions of theology. We see men like Calvin, Luther, and Knox emerging as the leaders of the movement of the Sixteenth Century. But as able and as fully equipped as scholars as these men were, we see that in each case these leaders were able to take their teaching gifts and their skills of communication outside of the restricted halls of academia and get their message to the people. We think of Luther, after the Diet of Worms, undertaking his first great theological task, translating the Bible into German so that every literate German person, peasant or prince, would have an opportunity for understanding the Bible for himself. This was an effort of mass communication, of getting the Gospel to the people. We see that Luther and Calvin were very much involved with making theology simple, of making it clear so that the people in the streets and in the marketplace could understand the things of God. They were not interested merely in publishing technical works for the applause of the scholarly world, but were willing to risk their academic reputations in order to minister to the people. We need scholars today who have a burden for the educating of Christians everywhere.

So often adult education is left to educational sources that are at best frivolous. There are a multitude of books in the Christian bookstores that have no depth of content, no serious level of research behind them. We have become a generation where the blind lead the blind. The real effort of reformation in our day must be met head-on by the finest scholars that the Church has produced. They should spend at least a portion of their time communicating, writing, and preparing materials for the laity. That is a task to which the Ligonier Valley Study Center is committed, knowing full well that our effort is a very tiny element and dimension of what needs to be done. Certainly the materials that we present can be improved and we call upon those who are far better equipped than we to join in the task of reaching the multitudes with a clear understanding of the truth of God. This is our vision and it is our burden. Two years ago we mentioned that our goal was to have a hundred thousand students using our materials by 1982. Frankly, we are way behind that goal at the present time. But we have not abandoned the task. We intend to press on. With the help of God and with your help we want to raise the consciousness of Christian people to the need to understand who God is and what it is that pleases Him.

AMERICAN CAESAR

NOVEMBER 1979

———

"HE WAS A GREAT THUNDERING PARADOX of a man, noble and ignoble, inspiring and outrageous, arrogant and shy, the best of men and the worst of men, the most protean, most ridiculous, and most sublime."

These words sound like they were penned by Charles Dickens. They introduce, however, not a tale of two cities, but a tale of two men, one an imperious, ruthless, ambitious military leader, the other a duty-driven, family-loving man trying to live up to his father's achievements of heroism. Both men lived in the same body under the same name, Douglas MacArthur.

In completing the lengthy (712 pages) biography of MacArthur one feels as though he has just walked on Mt. Olympus, being at once overwhelmed by the force of the General's personality and exploits, as well as being humbled by his scribe, equally awesome in his literary might. William Manchester writes as one giant probing the strengths and weaknesses of another.

It is rare that I have the opportunity to enjoy such a well written, well documented volume. *American Caesar* offers not only an exquisite portrait of a man but a fascinating history of the United States from the Civil War to the present. The book opens with the narrative of the "boy Colonel," Arthur MacArthur Jr. (Douglas' father), winning the Congressional Medal of Honor at age nineteen in the Civil War battle of Missionary Ridge near Chattanooga. From their frontier life at Fort Leavenworth featuring skirmishes with the Indians to the events culminating in Vietnam, the history of the MacArthur family is chronicled. Detailed insights of the military and political machinations of World War I, portraits of John J. Pershing, and the rise of Franklin Roosevelt set the stage for the conflagration of World War II. The book is so vivid that one feels like he is eavesdropping at the White House and in the Pentagon during these years.

The fall of Corregidor and the death march at Bataan reveal the harsh realities of war. The mystery of the east—the Pacific Theater of World War II is unraveled for us—the rivalries of ego-filled generals are exposed. MacArthur's growing paranoia with Washington is probed as the stage is set for his ultimate confrontation with President Truman.

Manchester provides an extra bonus by explaining to the occidental mind the culture of pre- and post-war Japan, highlighting MacArthur's work of framing the new Japanese democratic constitution. Perhaps most surprising and at the same time most poignant is Manchester's ability to capture with words MacArthur's deep visceral hatred of war.

When the forces of Japan surrendered to the Allies aboard the Battleship *Missouri* in Tokyo Bay, Douglas MacArthur spoke these words which were beamed to the American homeland. They are not as famous as "I shall return," the "Old soldiers never speak to Congress," or the "Duty, honor, country" motif of his final address at West Point—but they are relevant to us today:

> Men since the beginning of time have sought peace, but military alliances, balances of power, leagues of nations, all in turn failed, leaving the only path to be by way of the crucible of war. . . . We have had our last chance. If we do not now devise some greater and more equitable system, Armageddon will be at our door. The problem basically is theological and invokes a spiritual recrudescence. . . . It must be of the spirit if we are to save the flesh.

THE CHURCH FACES THE EIGHTIES

JANUARY 1980

———

A S A SEMINARY STUDENT IN THE EARLY YEARS of the decade of the sixties, I was surprised by an oft-repeated question posed in the classroom. The question simply was, "How can we make the Church relevant for our times?" The question perplexed and at times annoyed me. It distressed me to hear talk about making the Church relevant. My unspoken thought was, "Why try to make the Church what she already is?" It never occurred to me that the Church might be irrelevant. In its weakest hour the Church is ever the most relevant institution on earth. Yet here I was, almost daily listening to suggestions, programs, and strategies all designed to make the Church relevant.

The sixties have passed with their days of violent upheaval. The seventies, a decade of sober iconoclasm of the American dream, are behind us. Cultural fads, musical trends, pop religious movements have come and gone—yet still Churchmen gather to ponder the question, "How can we make the Church relevant for our times?"

My youthful assertion abides . . . unshaken by the changes of our times. The Church is relevant; no one has to make it relevant. I maintain, yea insist, that the Church objectively, as it is right now, is relevant. But such an assertion may not simply be made, uttered dogmatically, and then left to function as an uncritically accepted assumption. Our assertion is challenged on every side and requires a defense—a careful apology.

How then do we defend the assertion of the Church's objective in an age where the Church is viewed by many as a museum of a former era, a monument to the death of God, a vestigial appendage of a pre-enlightened, pre-scientific period? Such a defense may begin by appealing to the historian to offer data from the past to indicate the role the Church has played down through the ages in ministering to the needs of mankind. We could rehearse the Church's role in paving the way for the abolition of slavery, for the university movement, the international establishment of public hospital care, orphanages, and the like. But modern man seems not so interested in the testimony of the past. The question of relevancy always seems to have the ring of present concern to it. The question is not so much about what the Church did yesterday, but what is it doing today? Here the arguments from history and philosophy fail us. The world does not want to hear that the Church is relevant—it wants to see it.

Let's stop a minute to consider a rather bizarre analogy. Suppose a secularist wished to issue a telling criticism against Mormonism. The critical attack follows this pattern: "Mormonism is not credible because its young missionaries are so uncouth. They march through our communities dressed as wild men, ringing doorbells while dressed in unslovenly clothes. Their manners are crude and abhorrent, violating the sensibilities of our cultured citizens. Add to that the fact that all Mormons live so riotously—given to drunkenness and other forms of sensuous debauchery."

Bizarre? Indeed. Who would ever listen to such an obviously false portrait of Mormon behavior? If one would offer a penetrating critique of Mormonism he would do better to question the Mormon's defective view of God, Christ, and redemption. It would be apologetic suicide to attack them at the point of the manners of their missionaries, which are, by contemporary standards, exemplary.

Critics of Mormonism do not feel safe in leveling their guns at Mormon courtesy—yet critics of Christianity feel comfortable and secure telling the world the Church is no longer relevant. I wonder why that is? Why does the lie have such a secure resting place in our world? Perhaps it is because we are failing to show—by concrete demonstration—that Christ and His Church are relevant to the needs of our time.

The prophets of doom look to the eighties with foreboding—fearing the imminent collapse of Western civilization. Yet the Church of Christ looks to the future and sees countless opportunities for ministry. There is indeed a crisis of faith in our day. Man's faith in the empty promises of humanism is cracking into pieces. The utopian dreams are becoming nightmares. Liberalized Christianity has declared bankruptcy for their program of building the kingdom of God on a base of naturalism. Now the Church, empowered by the Holy Ghost, has an opportunity to step into the vacuum with the ministry of Christ to meet the needs of people that are not being met. The Church does not have to become relevant—but it must show in this hour that it is relevant by ministering to the needs of a broken world.

> "The Church is relevant; no one has to make it relevant. I maintain, yea insist, that the Church objectively, as it is right now, is relevant."

RELIGION IN AMERICA

FEBRUARY 1980

———

RECENTLY I WAS ASKED TO COMMENT ON the significance of the latest Gallup Poll on religious life, beliefs and practices in America—the most comprehensive poll, I believe, ever taken on this subject in the United States. *Christianity Today* is running several articles of analysis of this poll.

Here are a few basic statistics from the poll:

42% of the people believe the Bible is the Word of God and is not mistaken in its teachings and statements.

Of this category who have a high view of Scripture, the following applies:

60% claim to have had a conversion
76% claim to be frequent Bible readers
58% claim to be frequent churchgoers
70% claim to give 10% or more of their income to God's work
54% claim to do volunteer work

This breakdown indicates the highest ratio in each category. The obvious conclusion is that there is a clear correlation between a person's view of Scripture and their involvement in the life of the Church and Christian activities. This point underscores a matter I alluded to last month. Many people are wearied by the contemporary issue of the trustworthiness, inspiration, infallibility, and inerrancy of the Bible. I've heard it said, "Why argue about doctrine? It's a waste of time. Let's get on with the business of the ministry of the Church."

Zeal for ministry is indeed noble—but misguided when it assumes that the doctrinal base for ministry is unimportant.

Why do we do what we do? For every practice there is a corresponding theory. We may not have a pointed analysis of our theory or a reasoned apologetic. We may not be able to articulate it at all. But we have theories—points of understanding, ways of thinking about things which have a direct bearing on our behavior.

Let's compare briefly the relationship of tithing to one's view of Scripture. The poll offered three views of Scripture from which to choose "the one closest to your own."

1. The Bible is a collection of writings representing some of the religious philosophies of ancient man.

   PUBLIC RESPONSE (23%)

2. The Bible is the word of God but is sometimes mistaken in its statements and teachings.

   PUBLIC RESPONSE (30%)

3. The Bible is the word of God and is not mistaken in its statements and teachings.

   PUBLIC RESPONSE (42%)

Now let's examine the breakdown of these three groups in terms of tithing.

Group 1: 8% give 10% or more of their income
Group 2: 22% give 10% or more of their income
Group 3: 70% give 10% or more of their income

The same kind of ascending percentage is reflected in volunteer work.

Why is this so important? It is one thing for someone to persuade me to give away 10% of what I earn; it's quite another for God to command me to do it. If the tithe represents merely a part of ancient man's religious philosophy, I can escape obligation and religious duty. If it reflects the divinely authoritative command of God, there is no moral escape hatch.

The issue of the nature of Scripture is inseparably related to the *authority* of Scripture. In turn, the authority of Scripture is inseparably related to the faith, practice, behavior, and obedience of the Christian. To be sure, sacrificial behavior and obedience do not, in themselves, prove that the "high" view of Scripture is correct. What it does show is that the practical ramifications of one's view of Scripture are crucial. Therefore, we ought not flee from the issue of the nature of Scripture on the grounds that it is irrelevant.

"If the tithe reflects the divinely authoritative command of God, there is no moral escape hatch."

WHAT HAPPENED TO THE HUMAN RACE

MARCH 1980

I AM A GRANDFATHER! I'VE BEEN CALLED MANY THINGS in my lifetime but not many of them provoke the "warm fuzzies" that the title "grandpa" does. I remember the day our firstborn child was born. I was filled with intense emotion as I looked at her through the nursery window for the first time. She was our daughter and as far as I could see, she appeared healthy and normal. My mind snapped immediately to the words of the compassionate nurse who sought to console me months earlier. My wife was in the hospital room in the midst of serious hemorrhaging—for the third time—and the verdict was to be that she would probably lose the baby through miscarriage. Comforting me, the nurse said: "It's better this way—if she keeps the baby now it will probably be deformed."

Of course, I didn't relay that grim proposal to Vesta during the rest of her pregnancy, which she was able to sustain without miscarriage. The joy and relief I felt at seeing our baby daughter Sherrie was indescribable. But now Sherrie is a mother herself. Our baby has had a baby. Her name is Kelly Ann, and Vesta and I are beside ourselves with pride and joy. We are reliving those magic moments—moments of emotion and sentiment—of watching the baby focus her eyes, begin holding things, and daily manifesting more of those things that we add up to spell personality.

I thank God that Kelly Ann is not a statistic. I'm personally thrilled that she was not one of the seven million unborn children whose gestation was terminated by legal abortion since the Supreme Court decision. Kelly Ann does not represent a "blob of protoplasm" to us—she is the result of the natural process that God created and sustained in nature. That process was not arbitrarily aborted because someone thought she should not be allowed to be born.

Abortion is an issue. It's a controversial and emotional issue—one that produces anger, rancor, fighting, and all sorts of ugly protests. My concern is that the issue is not emotional enough. From a Christian perspective, abortion for convenience is a heinous sin, an evil that should provoke serious protest, not just calm debate, from any person who values life. This is not an issue of women's rights but one of human dignity and the sanctity of life.

The camps of controversy are divided basically three ways:

1. Pro-Life
2. Pro-Abortion
3. Pro-Choice

The third group (Pro-Choice) does not necessarily endorse abortion on demand but defends the legal rights of individual choice in the matter, usually arguing that it is not the prerogative of government to interfere in this private matter. In reality, the advocates of pro-choice are aiding and abetting the militant pro-abortionists. Theirs is a stance which is ultimately against the Pro-Life Movement. The folly of their position is as shocking to me as the wickedness of the pro-abortionist position. To argue that the government has no right to interfere in matters like this is to take away from government its most fundamental duty and responsibility—namely the protection, maintenance, and sustenance of human life. This is the government's very reason for being. The issue is life—its sanctity, its protection, and its maintenance.

Francis Schaeffer and Dr. C. Everett Koop have produced a remarkable book and film series entitled *Whatever Happened to the Human Race?* I hope that every church will show it and every Christian will see it. This is not a Roman Catholic issue—it's not even simply a Christian issue—it's a human issue. I urge you to join the protest—passionately. We've tried to be calm. Now it's time to step up the campaign to reverse the courts on this. Christians need to let their voices be heard. It matters.

This outstanding film series is available for viewing in churches, schools, and civic groups through:

Gospel Films
Box 455
Muskegon, MI 49443
Phone: 616-733-3361

The series consists of five, one-hour episodes. A Complimentary Teaching Package comes with each rental of the series and includes a book, a record, and a study guide. Also available for purchase are additional study guides, posters, and bulletin inserts. Plan to use this excellent tool to inform Christians on this important issue in your church today.

"Abortion is not an issue of women's rights but one of human dignity and the sanctity of life."

THE NEW KING

APRIL 1980

Q UESTION: **WHAT DO YALE, HARVARD,** Princeton, and Temple Universities have in common?

Answer: These institutions all began with a deep commitment to higher education based on a Christian philosophical framework and commitment. Yet all of these institutions have become basically secularized since their foundation. The pattern that may be seen in these institutions has been repeated literally hundreds of times in American church history. A vast number of church related colleges which began with a clear commitment to a unique Christian education have followed the route of the larger universities to become at best only loosely related to their parent denominations and have followed the course of secularized education. Once the trend towards secularization of an institution of higher education moves into high gear, it is almost unheard of that such an institution would have an about-face and return to its original purpose and goal of providing education within the framework of a deep commitment to classical Christianity. On rare occasions such turnabouts have come forth. One of the most interesting, of course, is the story of Grove City College in Western Pennsylvania, which had embarked on a process of secularization but has since turned around and become once again an educational institution that has increased its academic level of performance and renewed its commitment to Christian principles of education.

But perhaps the most dramatic story of turnaround is one that has taken place south of the Mason-Dixon line, in Bristol, Tennessee, at a college known simply as King College. In 1979, King College, after a history of 112 years of service to the Southern Presbyterian Church, was on the brink of financial collapse with a deficit of 1.5 million dollars. It was a college about to close. As a last-ditch effort to save the school, the trustees intended to sell the school property to the state, merging the college with East Tennessee State. Had that solution been consolidated, King College would have been thoroughly and completely secularized.

At that point in history, a group of concerned evangelical Southern Presbyterians offered a creative alternative to the school's financial problems. A group of pastors and laymen including Dr. Clayton Bell, Pastor of the Highland Park Presbyterian Church of Dallas, Texas, Dr. Cortez Cooper, Pastor of the First Presbyterian Church of Nashville, Tennessee, and Dr. George Long, Pastor of the Lookout Mountain Presbyterian Church of Lookout Mountain, Tennessee, conceived of a bold, creative, and innovative plan to save the college. With the help of key laymen including Mr. Hugh O. MacLellan Jr., Chairman of the Providence Life Insurance Company of Chattanooga, Tennessee, the group of evangelical pastors offered the college a plan of financial rescue. Their condition, however, was "to make the school unapologetically and enthusiastically an evangelical institution of higher Christian education."

At a meeting in Nashville airport, the evangelical group made an offer to pledge $300–$400,000 to the school over the next three years. This offer was unanimously accepted by the old Board of Trustees. The stipulation of the evangelical group's pledge was that the funds would be provided only if the group could: (1) secure faculty and staff who were committed Christians, and (2) make the Christian climate the most distinctive feature of campus life, and require a Christian perspective throughout the curriculum of the school. Their offer was accepted and the old Board of Trustees engineered transfer of school control to a new Board of Trustees that had as its nucleus the committee of pastors mentioned above. The transition took place on May 31, 1979.

The new Board selected Dr. Donald Mitchell, formerly the Vice President for Academic Affairs at Wheaton College, as the new President of King. His first task was to replace the school's two Bible professors and one philosophy professor who resigned after a change toward a more conservative evangelical stance was announced. Before the transition took place, the evangelical group had already raised $900,000 in pledges, believing that the college would succeed because of its renewed evangelical commitment.

In the fall of 1979, the new King College opened its doors for the school year's first term.

What has happened at King College is exciting and encouraging to all Christians who are alert to the crisis in higher education that we face in this day. Because of the boldness of a few Christian men and of their commitment, the school has been redeemed from secularism, and promises a very bright future of supplying the church with young men and women educated from a solid Christian base. The Presbyteries of Knoxville and Holston have voted to endorse the change of leadership of the college and will have representation on the new Board of Trustees.

King College remains a Presbyterian Liberal Arts Institution with a strong commitment to the integration of faith, learning, and living for students. Members of the Bible department and the Philosophy department are required to affirm without reservation the inspiration and authority of Scripture. This commitment to a Biblically oriented education is a critical dimension of the new reorganization. The campus boasts of an approximately $10 million facility that graces a beautiful 135-acre hilltop campus. Academically, King has a prominent record among small colleges. Its past performance has been one of excellence in academic programs, where approximately 80% of its faculty holds earned Doctors degrees. Since 1974, 80% of the graduates applying to law schools and 85% of those applying to medical schools have been accepted. Their quality teaching program is partly the result of a student/teacher ratio of 1/10, which is, of course, unusually low. Some of the more popular academic programs at King are prelaw, business, pre-health, psychology, and education. A dual degree program provides special opportunities in cooperation with the engineering schools of the Universities of Tennessee, Maryland, and Georgia Tech.

Student enrollment at King is up, but it is very important that a high level of enrollment be sustained if the college is going to stabilize financially for the long haul.

One of the questions that I am asked most frequently is that asked by deeply concerned parents, "Where should I send my son/daughter to college?" For those parents who are looking for an institution that offers a combination of high quality academic preparation with a profound commitment to Biblical principles and lifestyle, the new King College is a place that should have top priority in consideration.

I am excited about the new spirit that is present on that campus, about the quality of the new additions to faculty and administrative staff, and especially by the commitment of the new Board of Trustees to make King College a model college for Christian education. King represents a bright spot of hope on an otherwise often dismal horizon of declining emphasis of Christian perspective in higher education. I hope that the Christian world will respond by getting behind this venture in Bristol, Tennessee, as it can have a tremendous impact on the building of the Kingdom of God in this country in the years to come.

"What happens when the aspiration for significance becomes distorted? How easily it becomes a lust for power."

—

WORK WORLD: JUNGLE OR PARADISE

MAY 1980

———

PERHAPS THE METAPHOR OR IMAGE THAT IS used more frequently than any other to describe the work world is the image of the jungle. "Dog eat dog" or being involved in a "rat race" are typical of people's expressions of the work place. When anger is unresolved and violence and hostility permeate an environment, it is hardly a manifestation of paradise.

The symbol of the jungle represents an environment where power becomes the key to survival, where "might makes right." The jungle is where the fittest, the strongest, the most ruthless are able to survive at the expense of the weak and the crippled. The image of the jungle symbolizes chaos. It symbolizes dense vegetation that has gone wild, where predators are hidden in the darkness of the underbrush.

Paradise in biblical terms is described in the imagery of a beautiful garden. It is kept with precision and meticulous care; it is a place of beauty; a place of fulfillment; a place of peace. How different is the image of the garden of paradise from the jungle of our work world. The work world is indeed east of Eden. The ultimate difference, however, between the garden and a jungle is found in the opposing principles of order and chaos. This is the battleground of the modern labor-management scene, the tension between order and a tendency toward chaos.

In the biblical model of creation man is seen as created with aspirations for personal significance. To have aspirations for significance is not a matter of ungodly pride or wickedness. To want and desire that one's life should be meaningful is a mark of man's dignity, not his corruption. But what happens when that aspiration for significance becomes distorted? How easily it becomes a lust for power. That is the choice we face in the work world, a choice between a jungle of opposing power struggles, or a paradise marked by the order and beauty of divine grace where people's aspirations for significance are not frustrated, but mutually enhanced.

In the opening pages of the Old Testament the issues of order versus chaos are set before us in high drama. The very first verse of Genesis provides a model of God's preference for order. We read, "In the beginning God created the heavens and the earth." Every adult American knows that this verse is in the Bible. It was this verse that was read on Christmas Eve from outer space during our space exploration program. Reading on, "The earth was without form and void and darkness was upon the face of the deep." The Old Testament Jew understood the foreboding character of that picture. When God began creating, the illustrative backdrop of His creation was a situation of the void of darkness, of disorder, and of the deep. It was not God's design to leave creation in a state of darkness, in the depths of the abyss, or in a state of chaos. We read that the Spirit of God broods over the waters, and out of the darkness He brings light and order. That is the goal of all creation and it is equally the goal of redemption.

The theme of the opening chapters of the Old Testament is creation; the theme of the rest of all of Scripture is the theme of reconciliation. God created men for harmonious relationships with Himself and with each other. But those relationships have been disturbed, violently disturbed, and the human spirit has suffered enormous wounds. For that fallenness to be redeemed we must be reconciled.

The New Testament cites three areas where men need reconciliation in order to find their fullest expression as human beings. They are between God and man, between man and man, and man with himself. In simple terms, the Bible teaches that man is estranged from God, he is angry with God, he is out of fellowship with God because of his fallenness. The Bible also teaches that as a direct consequence of man's disharmony with God comes man's disharmony with fellow men. Blacks are angry with whites; husbands are angry with wives; labor and management are angry with each other; nations involve themselves in war as anger spills over on to anger; and man becomes estranged from his fellow humanity. Thirdly, we read that man is estranged from himself. How is it possible that it would be otherwise? If there is a God from whom we are estranged and a co-humanity from whom we are estranged, how can we possibly be at peace with ourselves? People who are estranged are not comfortable. There is a nagging, gnawing, inner restlessness that eats away at us until that estrangement can be reconciled, then our anger is resolved. Then we get free to be creative, to enjoy our work, even to be exhilarated by our productivity.

The whole man, in his personal and social relationships, needs to be reconciled. This is the ministry of Christ.

THE REAL WAR

JULY 1980

———

ING RICHARD IS IN EXILE, banished to an island fortress, abandoned in ignominy to write his memoirs. The year is 1980, calling
into remembrance the fateful years following 1815 when Napoleon sought solace from the disgrace of Waterloo on the desolate rock of
St. Helena. Richard's downfall was Watergate, not Waterloo—the result
of what the missing and presumably "late" Jimmy Hoffa described as a
"third rate burglary."

We trust with Gordon Liddy's recent effort, the post-mortems of Watergate are over.* Perhaps now we are ready to hear the voice of an ex-president
crying in the wilderness. The cry is eloquent and penetrating—it is a *cri
de coeur* addressed to the American people—a somber warning from a
man who must rank as our nation's most knowledgeable expert in foreign affairs, Richard Milhous Nixon.

Forget Watergate if you can, and rush to the bookstore and get Richard
Nixon's new book, *The Real War.* Its first few pages made me drop whatever else I was reading to devour its contents. It is Nixon at his analytical
best, revealing the scintillating mind that grasps the nuances of global
politics like few are able.

Nixon's thesis is this: World War III has already begun, breaking out in
earnest with the Allies jockeying for world leadership position during
the closing stages of World War II. This war is not potential, but actual;
it is not imaginary or hypothetical—it is real and it is *now.*

Nixon traces the history of Soviet expansionism from Tsarist days to
the present, setting out for us the broad scenario of Soviet ambitions
and tactics. He reminds us that since 1973 no less than eight nations

———

* G. Gordon Liddy (b. 1930) was one of the key figures in the Watergate scandal during
the Nixon administration, having planned and directed the burglary of the Democratic National Headquarters in 1972. His autobiography, *Will,* was published in 1980.

numbering one hundred million people have come under Soviet domination. He warns that the dreadful specter of a nuclear holocaust ushering in Armageddon with a bang is less likely than a gradual capitulation to Soviet aims that ends Western Civilization with a whimper.

Nixon comes to the geopolitical poker table and explains the stakes. He informs us of the strategic importance of South African nations which are rich in vital mineral resources such as chromium. (One single jet aircraft requires more than 3,600 pounds of chrome. Ninety-six percent of the world's known reserves of chromium are in the Union of South Africa and Zimbabwe Rhodesia.)

Next the ex-president describes the strategic role of OPEC and the Persian Gulf nations—this region he calls "the oil jugular." And so around the world he goes from the Gulf sheikhdoms to Cambodia to Latin America's Grenada, the latest casualty of the Monroe Doctrine sphere.* Nixon's story gives credence to the oft maligned and ridiculed "domino theory" which was once fashionably laughed off as an exercise in "Afghanistanism." Now Afghanistan is real and foreboding—a pitiable cry for help to wake the American slumbering giant.

Nixon is crying that the Bear is at the door—pushing with military, political, and economic muscle. The Bear probes the underbelly of his prey and finds it soft. Lenin established the basic rule of Soviet behavior years ago: "Probe with bayonets. If you encounter steel, withdraw. If you encounter mush, continue."

Nixon is not a defeatist in this matter. He is convinced that there is time to win the war—but not much. The ability of economic productivity favors the West. The big question mark, however, is not weaponry or resources—it is a question of will. Nixon cites repeatedly the formula devised by Sir Robert Thompson, the British expert on guerrilla warfare: "National power equals manpower plus applied resources, times will." Without the will, the equation collapses.

* The Monroe Doctrine is a U.S. policy meant to discourage European colonialism in the Western hemisphere. Grenada, an island nation off the coast of Venezuela, was taken over by a Marxist-Leninist group called the New Jewel Movement in 1979. The United States invaded the island in 1983, leading to democratic elections the next year.

The game is not simply a matter of power politics from which Christians can remain sanctimoniously aloof. The international issues are intensely moral and, in the final analysis, theological. This time we need to hear Richard Nixon.

Nixon dedicates the book to his grandchildren . . .

HIDDEN GOLD: THE REDISCOVERY OF SAMUEL SHELLABARGER

SEPTEMBER 1980

PERHAPS WE SHOULD CALL IT THE "49'ers' disease." It is a malady which strikes those who develop a taste for novel reading, inciting a high fever for discovering gold. We sift through the racks of every bookstore we encounter panning the streams for the 24 karat good stuff. Usually our efforts produce little more than fool's gold—bright and glittering, promising everything and not even producing Arpège. Our new discoveries disappoint and frustrate as they bombard our minds with cynicism and our senses with superficial eroticism.

But every now and then the persevering prospector strikes gold—the real thing—a bonanza. Like Archimedes before him, the lucky discoverer shouts Eureka! That's how I feel with the rediscovery of Samuel Shellabarger.

People over forty may have difficulty remembering the name, but the titles are easily recalled—*Captain from Castile, Prince of Foxes, Lord Vanity, The King's Cavalier*—are some of his better known works. Samuel Shellabarger dominated the Literary Guild Selections of the forties and early fifties. His works were brought to the screen as Hollywood swashbuckling epics—perhaps dooming them for future generations as the saccharine treatment of film cheapened the literary merits of the written mode.

Shellabarger was an authentic artist. He combined skills and expertise in a way that dwarfs all but a few contemporary masters. A student of the renaissance, he became a bona fide "renaissance man" himself. The jack-of-all-trades, multi-gifted personality is often acclaimed as a renaissance man all too glibly. The real title belongs to someone who

achieves a high level of mastery in multiple skills. The description fits
Shellabarger. A Harvard Ph.D., Shellabarger distinguishes himself as a
professor at Princeton University, lecturing both in English and in History. A genuine scholar and master linguist, Shellabarger brings to his
novels a depth of historical research that one might find in Michener or
Manchester but never in an Irving Wallace. Commenting on his work
in *The King's Cavalier*, Shellabarger wrote:

> The research required by such a book is of three kinds: first, and most
> important of all, the author must become psychologically at home in
> his period. The second deals with the externals of an epoch: its clothes,
> food, architecture, means of travel, roads, forms of address, customs, and
> the like. Last, but not least, there is, of course, the historical research.
> fiction must at times take small liberties with history, but it should
> never distort it.

Shellabarger practices his preaching. Never—and I mean *never*—have
I encountered historical novels where such transposition is achieved.
The reader is brought into the immediate presence of a former age. In
Castile, you are transported to sixteenth century Spain—across the ocean
to the new world, marching with Cortés and the conquistadors against
the savage but sophisticated Aztec chieftains under Montezuma. The
theological subtleties of the Spanish Inquisition are handled with careful
appreciation for the most technical nuances. In *Prince of Foxes* you journey to Renaissance Italy to encounter the Medici power and the Borgia
papacy. In *Lord Vanity*, Shellabarger demonstrates his scholarly acumen
in history by moving to the eighteenth century with ease—capturing
the new winds of the Enlightenment in Europe and the emerging order
in America. From Lucretia Borgia to John Wesley, Shellabarger wields
his power of insightful characterization. Shellabarger's romantic novels are lyrical, but never maudlin; provocative, but never crassly erotic;
violent, but never insensitive. Archaic virtues are salvaged, dusted off,
and presented as classical values. Honor emerges as the key virtue for
Shellabarger's heroes and heroines. Sinful flaws abound in his real-life

characters but honor and integrity are celebrated as worthy human aspirations.

The ring of reality that sounds in these books is inspiring. Shellabarger was a neoclassicist—perhaps a living anachronism, or better yet a prophet to our plastic age. Alas, his works are to be found only in libraries as they are out of print—his style no longer in vogue. But I pray that somebody out there will have the good sense to move heaven and earth to get these books reprinted. We need a renaissance of art. We need a literary wind like Samuel Shellabarger to blow through our best seller list today. The gold is there—buried beneath the garbage dump of modern taste. It's time to mine the gold.

THE SECRET SIN

OCTOBER 1980

———

I MAGINE A SOCIETY WITH NO GOVERNMENT, no laws, and no tradition. The scenario calls for a fresh start and you are assigned the task of creating an ideal constitution. You are free to structure the society any way you please, but with one restriction; you must build your society on the substructure of merely ten basic laws. You're the builder—it's your choice—what would your ten foundational laws be?

Surely your list would include a prohibition against murder and one against theft as you would seek to protect the sanctity of life and the right of private property. But do you suppose you would include such things in your top ten as a rule against blasphemy, one to prohibit the dishonoring of parents or the protection of the sacredness of one day in seven?

Maybe you would speak against adultery, seeking to build a society on the inviolate permanence of the family. But would you include perjury in your top priority list?

How odd of God to promote such strange priorities in His Decalogue, the Constitution of Israel. It's strange indeed that God included some of the things He did when He provided the blueprint for the ideal society.

But strangest of all was the inclusion of a prohibition against coveting. Why "waste" a spot with such a harmless matter? It's one thing to prohibit stealing but why put such emphasis on the mere desire to possess another person's property or position? Wouldn't your list substitute something on war, racial discrimination, abortion, or some other major ethical issue?

The Old Testament placed covetousness under a ban and Achan was stoned to death because of it. The New Testament writers talk about it—frequently exhorting the believer to avoid it and other closely related sins such as envy.

Jealousy, envy, lust, greed are all rooted in a spirit of covetousness.

In August's *Remnant Review*,* Gary North writes about the economics of envy. In his essay, North scans the wider issue related to problems spawned in the troubled waters of envy. Distinguishing between jealousy and envy, or perhaps more accurately different levels of envy, North writes:

> Envy runs along these lines: "He's got that. I don't have it. I'd like it, but I know I can never get it. Nobody ought to be allowed to have it if everyone can't have one just like it. I'll destroy it. I'll have the government make it illegal to own one. I'll make sure nobody ever has one like it again."

This attitude—one which can't stomach acts of hatred: An attractive girl in North Carolina throws acid in the face of a beautiful girl—another hacks her roommate's face with a hatchet claiming "envy drove me to do it."

The arsonist burns not merely because he enjoys a maniacal thrill of dancing flames but because he delights in seeing other people's property, hopes, and tangible signs of success go up in smoke.

Terrorism is more often an act of vicious envy than a true effort of ideological revolution. Again, North says: "The act of terrorism is useful only if your political philosophy makes the destruction of society a blessing in itself. If you resent signs of others' success, then terrorism is one way of striking out at what you resent." It is a corporate effort of what Stephen Nash expressed in 1959 after murdering eleven people: "I never got more than the leavings of life, and when I couldn't even get those any more, I started taking something out of other people's lives."

It is difficult to placate the envious person. When envy is rampant, every prosperous or successful person becomes a target. The justification is usually this: "No one who is prosperous or successful could ever get that way honestly. My acts of retaliation are only motivated by my righteous quest for justice." Like the football player who blames every loss on the referee, so the envious seeks to justify his destructive behavior.

---

* *Remnant Review* was a newsletter founded by economist Gary North that was published between 1974 and 2017.

He secretly is gleeful in the news of the setbacks even of his own more prosperous friends. He never applauds the New York Yankees.

Consider the New Testament concern for gossip and slander—the twins of personal character assassination. The gossiper is the arsonist without a physical match, a terrorist minus his Molotov cocktail.

These are but a few of the bitter fruits of envy, the yield of covetousness. Maybe God knew what He was doing when He ordered the structure of a nation.

"It is difficult to placate the envious person. When envy is rampant, every prosperous or successful person becomes a target."

CHRISTMAS 1980

DECEMBER 1980

———

"A DECREE WENT OUT FROM CAESAR AUGUSTUS that all the world should be enrolled ... when Quirinius was governor of Syria ..." These words by Luke, the Gospel-writer, are loaded with significance for our understanding of the Christmas story. Luke has been acclaimed, even by many non-Christian scholars, as the finest historian of antiquity. It is not by accident that he indicates a real historical setting for the Christmas narrative. His book was written in Greek and was probably addressed to people of a Greek background. To proceed to announce the birth of a child, born of a virgin, and to proclaim this child to be God incarnate, was to drop a biological and philosophical bombshell on the playground of Greek thinkers.

The idea of a virgin-born deity was nothing new, as the Greek myths were sprinkled with such stories. As modern critics are quick to point out, virgin born, dying and rising gods, were not unusual to the myths coupled with ancient religions. Ovid's *Metamorphoses* is a classic example of a literary collection of such tales. Rudolf Bultmann, for example, pointed out repeatedly the parallels that are evident between the Biblical account of the life of Jesus and Greek myths, and called Biblical scholarship to the task of demythologizing the New Testament in order to make the vital core of Christianity credible to the modern scientific mindset. Since New Testament literature is "prescientific" it was thought necessary to recast its thought in more modern categories.

But in so doing, Professor Bultmann violated a cardinal principle of modern science. The scientific method of analysis requires that we pay close attention not only to the similarities between objects, events, or other phenomena, but to the differences as well. Indigestion and cancer can both cause stomach aches—it is the difference between them that counts.

When we approach New Testament literature there is a crucial difference evident between it and the mythological literature of the ancient world. That difference rests precisely at the point of the way the Jew (and subsequently the Christian) viewed history. The Greek viewed history in cyclical fashion seeing the world moving in a cycle with no beginning point in time and no ultimate point of consummation. (It is interesting to note that Bultmann's own concept of redemptive history which he calls a "theology of timelessness," has more in common with the Greek view than the Biblical one.) For the Greek, history is the realm of the imperfect Platonic receptacle, where physical things are but shadowy replicas of the eternal ideals. There history, the realm of space and time, is considered intrinsically imperfect. So the Greek never considered that his mythical deities were real historical figures. Indeed, such a notion was repugnant to them. For God to become incarnate—to take upon Himself real human flesh—would be scandalous.

This is precisely the scandal Luke is bold to announce. He is saying that in real history, in a real town, God was incarnate. He is celebrating not simply the birth of a baby, but the incarnation of God. To the Jew, God is the Lord of history. He created time and space—history is under His dominion—it is the theater of His operations.

Caesar Augustus was a real person. There really was an imperial Roman census. There really was a Quirinius who was governor of Syria at that time. There really was a Bethlehem. There really was a King Herod.

This is the message Luke proclaims: God Himself has visited His people. He came to us in "the fullness of time." This message has no need to be demythologized. It already is demythologized. It is dated.

Christmas is not simply a "religious event" that is designed to inspire our souls to some kind of higher moral value system. It means the manifestation of reality in its ultimate sense to the world. The Biblical image that is used more frequently than any other to underline this point is the image of light breaking into darkness. The light dismisses the shadows and by its illuminative brilliance exposes the difference between truth and falsehood, between good and evil. This light is so penetrating that even if men try to obscure it or extinguish it, their efforts are exercises in futility. Put a basket over this light and the light burns through it. Attack it with ominous darkness and the darkness is expelled. Consider the analogy of a room plunged into pitch darkness. There is no moon shining through the cracks of the curtains. It is total darkness. Turn on the light switch and what happens? How long does it take for the light to vanquish the darkness? How impotent the darkness is when exposed to light.

We live in an age of fantasy, a time when people seek all manner and means of escape from the real world. Some describe their lives in terms of the metaphor of the nightmare. Christmas breaks through all that. Christmas puts us in touch with the fullness of ultimate reality. Emmanuel has come. God is really with us—even now. Merry Christmas.

"To deny the reality of hell one must stand firmly opposed to the unambiguous teaching of Jesus."

—

A LOOK TO THE FUTURE

JANUARY 1981

———

HERE IS AN ORWELLIAN BREEZE IN THE AIR, the kind that stings a bit with the mixed attack of invigorating stimulus and icy foreboding. 1984 is approaching. What was once a clever science fiction prediction blended with a prophetic caveat is now almost humorously taken for granted.

It is a question of time—a question of the future. What will the future be like? What will my income be in five years? What will my health be like in three years? Will civilization be safe for my children and my grandchildren? Don't we all ask questions like these even if only to ourselves? Businessmen and missions are given to future planning—to five year plans and ten year plans.

Do you have a 200 year plan? Have you thought of where you will be and what you will be doing two centuries from now? How would you answer the question? Obviously you do not expect to be doing what you are doing presently. You expect that you will have died.

What will your death have brought you? Annihilation? That is, do you expect to pass into total biological disorganization? Do you expect to pass into nothingness? Or do you expect somehow to maintain some continuity of personal existence? Job asked it this way: "If a man die, shall he live again?"

Orthodox Christianity (sadly, we must use the adjectival qualifier "orthodox," as some claiming the name Christian have negotiated virtually all of its content yet retain the name) is unambiguous in its answer to Job's question. The answer is clearly "yes."

If we can trust the teaching of the New Testament in general and of Jesus in particular then we know that in 200 years we will still be existing. The big question is, then—"Where will we be and what will we be doing?" Jesus limited the options to that question to two: heaven and hell.

Modern Christianity in many cases has further reduced the options to one, namely, heaven. The Gallup Poll on Religion in America indicated that the majority of professing Christians believe in life after death. Most of those, however, reject any real idea of hell.

The arguments for a heaven without a hell are based primarily not on sound Biblical exegesis but on human sentiment. People would simply prefer not to believe in hell. It is a subject very few can discuss dispassionately. Yet to deny the reality of hell one must stand firmly opposed to the unambiguous teaching of Jesus. Consider the parable of the Rich Man and Lazarus:

> "Now it came about that the poor man died and he was carried away by the angels to Abraham's bosom; and the rich man also died and was buried. And in Hades he lifted up his eyes, being in torment, and saw Abraham far away, and Lazarus in his bosom. And he cried out and said, 'Father Abraham, have mercy on me, and send Lazarus, that he may dip the tip of his finger in water and cool off my tongue; for I am in agony in this flame.' But Abraham said, 'Child, remember that during your life you received your good things, and likewise Lazarus bad things; but now he is being comforted here, and you are in agony. And besides all this, between us and you there is a great chasm fixed, in order that those who wish to come over from here to you may not be able, and that none may cross over from there to us.' " (Luke 16:22–26)

Note the concept of the great chasm that exists between heaven and hell. It is unbridgeable. Where we are in 200 years is where we will be in 2,000 years and in 2,000,000 years.

But that is just a parable isn't it? Is it not really meant only to instruct us in a moral teaching? Perhaps—but in the didactic portions of Jesus' teachings on the future the issue is even more clear. The New Testament records more teaching on hell from Jesus than it does about heaven.

The very point of this parable is that people are reluctant to heed the Biblical warnings of a judgment that truly is final—with all further appeals exhausted.

"And he said, 'Then I beg you, Father, that you send him to my father's house—for I have five brothers—that he may warn them, lest they also come to this place of torment.' But Abraham said, 'They have Moses and the Prophets; let them hear them.' But he said, 'No, Father Abraham, but if someone goes to them from the dead, they will repent!' But he said to him, 'If they do not listen to Moses and the Prophets, neither will they be persuaded if someone rises from the dead.' " (Luke 16:27–31)

ROBBING HOOD

FEBRUARY 1981

——

A S A BOY MY ALL-TIME FAVORITE MOVIE WAS *The Bandit of Sherwood Forest* featuring Robin Hood and his men—Will Scarlet, Alan-a-Dale, Friar Tuck, Little John, and all the rest—swashbuckling their way across the screen in their idealistic resistance to the malevolent oppression of wicked Prince John and the Sheriff of Nottingham. Ah, those were the days.

Imagine my chagrin and unspeakable horror when my fifteen-year-old son came home from school recently and remarked glibly, "You know, Dad, Robin Hood was a communist." Shades of the Salem witches when even Robin is not safe from such calumny. What possible link did my son see between Sherwood's finest and Karl Marx? He replied, "Robin stole from the rich and gave to the poor, didn't he? Wasn't his work a coercive effort of redistribution of wealth by organized force?" Of course I was quick to defend Mr. Hood, not in terms of his thievery, but in terms of his motives. Were not Robin's actions sparked by a deep compassion for the poor and the oppressed? He was not seeking his own wealth but resisting the greedy merchants of his day. "No matter," says my son, "he still operated on the principle of forceful redistribution of wealth." Vainly I sought to redeem Robin's noble image by arguing that he was merely returning to the poor their own money which was forcibly taken from them by government taxes. "Still," protested my son, "this was returning evil for evil." I quit the debate.

The principle of redistribution of wealth to benefit the greatest number is an idea whose time should be over. The principle recalls another fictional hero—Don Quixote. In every experiment in world history of forceful redistribution of a people's wealth, the bottom line was a lowering of the people's standard of living. As a weapon against poverty it is proven folly. Yet we continue to dream of a great society where everyone will be equally prosperous. Government grows bigger and bigger, taxation becomes heavier and heavier and the nation's wealth shrinks smaller and smaller. The windmills keep winning but the fool grows more determined to finish his errand.

Should not Christians be deeply concerned with poverty? Does not the heart of God beat with compassion toward the under privileged? To ask such questions is to answer them. Of course the Christian must be concerned—indeed the most concerned of all for the poor. But the Christian should be the last to embrace statism as a societal goal—he should be the last to sanction political force as a means of economic redistribution.

Another childhood memory comes to mind. My first visit to a major league baseball game. As I entered the turnstile to the fabulous arena my uncle said to me urgently, "Hang on to your wallet." Dutifully I put my hand in my back pocket and gripped my wallet tightly, not knowing the reason for my uncle's terse warning. He pointed a few rows away to a group of nuns present for the ball game. "Watch out for them, boy. They're always out to get your money." Even at age 10 I regarded my uncle's cynicism with a measure of distaste.

Since my childhood I've learned that the government needs money and the church needs money. The church resorts to every member canvasses, collection plate passing, building fund drives, and so on. The State resorts to force to collect taxes with the threat of prison for the dissenter and evader. During the Christmas holidays I noticed the bonneted women ringing their bells by their Salvation Army pots in the shopping malls. It was nice to be able to give freely, willingly, and cheerfully. We may become annoyed at times with fund appeals, pledge cards, and collection plates. Yet no one will arrest us if we choose to ignore them. Indeed the command of God is there for us to face squarely but even God chose not to use the sword on this world to build the Kingdom.

Imagine this scenario: I would like to have a zoo in my home town. It will cost a lot of money for a nice zoo so I decide to raise it by going house to house with a rifle in my hand collecting "donations" for the zoo by force. The town would be in an uproar and my Robin Hood activity would soon be curtailed by the local constable. Why? Because I would be forcing people to donate against their will.

But that's just an imaginary scene—or is it? We do it every day by imposing our wills on the public budget—by seeking government subsidies which are paid for by other people's tax money. Every time we seek government aid for our private projects we make the burden greater for others.

Who is the heavy? The socialistic liberals? The labor unions? The minority groups? Nonsense. Is the Chrysler Corporation a socialist organization? Is Lee Iacocca a labor leader?* None of us can point the finger to other groups unless or until we stop asking the government to give to us at the expense of others. It is not the job of government to play Robin Hood. We say "No" to Ron Sider when he goes on record to support the use of force to insure Christian charity.† The motives may be noble but the practice is armed robbery.

---

* Lee Iacocca (1924–2019) was an American auto executive. After working at Ford in the 1960s, he famously turned around the troubled Chrysler Corporation in the 1980s, becoming a popular cultural figure and leadership guru.
† Ron Sider (1939–) is an American theologian and activist, founder of Evangelicals for Social Action.

THE PARABLE OF PETER: THE PROFIT-MAKING PORK PRODUCER, OR THE BALLOT IS A BULLET

MARCH 1981

O NCE UPON A TIME IN A MAGIC LAND of freedom and opportunity, there lived an ambitious young man named Peter Profit Maker. Peter set out to make his fortune by becoming a productive pig farmer. He took what money he had and invested in some piglets while learning all he could about his brand-new business. When the day came and his pigs were fully raised, Peter had them butchered, packaged, and made ready for market.

Peter joyfully went to the marketplace to sell his wares and make his fortune. There he met Charlie Customer and Peter said to him, "Hi, Charlie, would you like to buy some of my pork?" Peter was sadly disappointed when Charlie Customer replied, "No thank you, I prefer beef." Peter was even sadder when all of the rest of the customers told him the same thing. Poor Peter . . . It seemed that no one wanted to buy his pork. So he went home to think about his woeful problem.

Peter thought and he thought. "How can I get people to buy my pork?" Suddenly it dawned on him—"It pays to advertise, I hear, so I will try to persuade people to buy my pork by teaching them how good it is and what a bargain they will be getting for their money. I will start a huge campaign to sell my product."

Peter then went to work excited about his new idea. How sad he became when his pocket calculator told him it would cost $100,000 to pay for his advertising scheme. He thought glumly, "I haven't the money to pay to advertise my pork, where will I ever get it?" Peter grew more and more desperate until finally he found a solution. He got a gun and went directly to Charlie Customer's house. When he saw Charlie he pointed his gun at him and said, "Give me $100 or I'll shoot you. I need your money so I can pay to persuade you to buy my pork voluntarily." Reluctantly, Charlie gave him the money. "This is easy," thought Peter, so he went all over town doing the same thing to all the other customers. The customers became very angry and called the police. The police came and arrested Peter and took him to jail. Peter was lucky, though, for the judge was merciful and gave him probation after he returned all the money he stole.

The next day, as Peter walked through the market he noticed another group of profit makers laughing at him. There was Albert Auto Maker, Franky Farmer, Sammy Steel Maker, Eddie Education, and Willie Welfare. "You're so dumb, Peter," they jeered. Peter's feelings were hurt and he said, "Where do you fellows get your money to pay for advertisement to get people to buy your stuff?" Albert replied, "From Gary Government, silly. He sends Tommy Tax Collector to the customers' houses to get their money, then Gary gives it to us so we can get the customers to buy our products cheerfully."

"Wow," thought Peter, "this is great." So he went and stood in a long line until he finally got to Gary Government. Gary was happy to give Peter all the money he needed and gently reminded him to vote for him in the next election.

So Peter had his advertising campaign. It was a great success and suddenly all the customers in town were "thinking pork" and best of all buying pork. Peter was getting richer and richer every day. Then one day Tommy Tax Collector came to Peter's house and demanded money from his profits. "Why are you taking my money?" Peter asked. Tommy replied, "Gary Government sent me because he needs money to give to Albert Auto Maker, Franky Farmer, and the rest, because they all voted for Gary."

Peter was very angry. "I'll not vote for Gary—you can bet on that." From a far part of the country Peter heard of Regal Ronnie. Ronnie promised that if he were elected he'd put a stop to Tommy Tax Collector and Gary

Government. So Peter swore allegiance to Regal Ronnie and worked day and night for his election. Peter rejoiced on Inauguration Day when Regal Ronnie became the new President. Right away Ronnie fired Tommy Tax Collector and Gary Government. All was well with Peter until suddenly he discovered he needed more money to persuade people to buy his pork— so Peter went straight to Ronnie's nice white house and said, "Hi buddy, remember me? It's Peter Profit Maker, you know, the one who worked so hard for your election. I need a little favor. Please give me some money for my pork business." "I'm terribly sorry," Ronnie replied, "I can't do that. I'm not doing that for anybody."

Oh, was Peter mad. He was so mad he pulled out his ballot and bopped Regal Ronnie all the way out of his nice white house. And nobody lived happily ever after.

FRUSTRATIONS OF A CHRISTIAN EDUCATOR

APRIL 1981

———

T**HEY SAY WRITING IS A CATHARSIS,** an opportunity to allow pent up frustrations to be released through the fingers, into the pen, and on to the paper. Let's see if it works. I'm going to indulge myself a bit and see if I feel good or lousy after this essay.

A month or so ago Vesta and I were driving across the desert from Southern California to the airport in Phoenix. Riding with us was Karen Hoyt, who directs the home office of the International Council on Biblical Inerrancy. During our journey Karen related to us an experience she had in tape listening. She said, "I was home alone spending the day in housecleaning. To combat the monotony of my work, I switched on a Ligonier cassette tape on the Transfiguration of Jesus. About halfway through the tape I stopped my cleaning and sat down to give full concentration to listening. When the tape was finished I was so moved that I went over and put Handel's *Messiah* on the record player and just sat there and worshiped God."

Now, when someone relates to me an experience like that I am never frustrated—but overjoyed. The frustrating part came moments later . . . Karen said, "Why don't you feature tapes like these and the *Holiness of God* series more often in your LVSC promotions?" She went on to say that the *Holiness* series had a dramatic impact on her life. Charles Colson had asked the same question when he said the *Holiness* series had him on the floor with his face in the rug in a posture of adoration before God.

In fact this question raised by Karen and Chuck has been asked of me many times—the answer is simple, so here goes:

When we spend money to advertise or promote series like *The Holiness of God* or other "non-practical" teaching tapes, we lose our collective shirts. They are a disaster at the "box office." I know, for example, that if we advertise a lecture series that speaks directly to a felt need, such as improving marriages, dealing with teenage sexual problems, and the like, we will almost certainly break even in our expenses and perhaps even do a little better. But if we attempt to promote something like *The Holiness of God*, I know going in, we are going to incur a serious deficit.

Of course, I regard ministry to practical, felt-need areas of spiritual growth to be very important. But my frustration is this: I am convinced that the deepest need of people there is, is to know God. The more deeply we know God, the more resources we have to deal with the painful practical problems that crop up in our lives. But the effort to focus people's attention on the deeper human needs is a difficult one indeed. Book sellers know that "practical" material sells better than "heavy" content, and as a result the bookstores are overloaded with milk at the expense of meat. There's nothing wrong with milk unless we choose a diet of milk alone.

Content changes lives. This was again impressed upon me recently by an educator from Seattle. After telling me of his experience in California that indicated teachers were not as crucial to the learning process as we are inclined to think, he asked me, "What teachers have really affected your life?"

I responded by saying that I suspect every teacher I've ever had has had some impact on my life—but there are a few who stand out. There was my third-grade teacher, Mrs. MacGraw; my eighth-grade English teacher, Mrs. Gregg; my advisor and college philosophy professor, Dr. Tom Gregory; and my seminary professor Dr. John Gerstner. My friend from Seattle homed in on the latter. "What did Dr. Gerstner do that had such an impact on you?"

After thinking about it awhile I said, "He opened up the book of Romans for me." As I thought more about it I realized that the weight of the impact came not from the rare personality of Dr. Gerstner, but from the force of the themes of the Word of God in Romans.

As a teacher, that is what I long to do for others—to help introduce them to the life-changing content of the Bible; to introduce them to the themes that leave us different because we have really grappled with them. I believe that ultimately this is the most practical course of all.

When one's understanding of things changes—really changes—it is natural that behavioral patterns will also change. It appears that God's method of bringing about real changes in the growth and development of His people is by means of the renewal of the mind through His Word. The Word of God reflects the thoughts and values of God. We want our thoughts and our values to be brought into conformity with His.

INTOLERABLE TOLERANCE

JUNE–JULY 1981

———

T OLERATION IS A VIRTUE APPLAUDED not only in the church, but in the secular society as well. It is by toleration that society itself is made possible. When but two people enter into a relationship it is inevitable that different values, priorities, opinions, tastes, and viewpoints will come into conflict at some point. Each person brings not only his personality and views into the relationship but his sin as well. Imagine a society where every single manifestation of sinfulness were called into sharp focus, coupled with a denunciation or rebuke. Such an atmosphere of intolerance would be intolerable for fallen man.

No wonder then that Scripture uniformly warns against the contentious spirit and the intolerant mind-set. The spirit of contention is viewed biblically as a product of pride and selfishness. It is linked to the behavioral pattern of the fool and is the stimulus for much destruction. The Apostle admonishes to "avoid foolish contentions" for they are deemed unprofitable and futile (Titus 3:9).

By the same token the Bible exacts patience, long-suffering, forbearance, and other ingredients of tolerance as virtues which reflect the very character of God. Far from being contentious about minor things Christians are called to have a spirit of charity which "covers a multitude of sins."

Suffice it to say that God clearly calls us to the virtue of tolerance. But is that virtue to be exercised always and everywhere? Is tolerance a virtue that can, in certain circumstances, become a sin? These questions are indeed rhetorical inasmuch as the Bible balances its call to tolerance with weighty warnings against ill-advised toleration. Though God is long-suffering there is a limit to His tolerance. Though we are to cover a multitude of sins with charity, there are some sins so destructive and so heinous that they call forth discipline. That such lines do exist in the New Testament between things that are to be tolerated and things that are not is clear to almost every Christian. The trouble starts when we differ over where the lines are to be established.

We think of the confusion over tolerance that existed in the Corinthian Church. Paul severely rebuked the Church for "tolerating" the incestuous man in their midst and insisted that the man be disciplined. The Church had tolerated an intolerable sin. Then when the man repented Paul had to rebuke the Church a second time for now the Church refused to tolerate the repentant sinner. How like them we are, tolerating the sin when we shouldn't and refusing to tolerate the repentant sinner when we should.

So Paul rebuked the Corinthians for their misguided tolerance. Jesus rebuked the Church in Pergamos for tolerating the doctrine of the Nicolaitanes of which Christ said "of which thing I hate." Jesus hated the doctrine of the Nicolaitanes and rebuked the Church for tolerating it. The same anger of Christ was directed at the Church of Thyatira for tolerating the Jezebel within their midst (Rev. 2:7–20).

These same incidents manifest that at times tolerance can be a sin, indeed a serious sin involving the betrayal of Christ. In fact the issue of tolerance is frequently measured by its relationship to the matter of loyalty to Christ Jesus spoken in terms of degrees of toleration with regard to God's final tribunal—"It shall be more tolerable for the land of Sodom and Gomorrah . . ."

Toleration has limits. The Proverbs, virtually in the same breath, warn against the contentious spirit and then declare, "He that justifies the wicked, and he that condemns the just, even they both are abomination to the LORD" (Proverbs 17:14–15). Thus toleration does not mean the vindication of evil, nor the oppression of righteousness. If Christians are to contend (indeed there are times when we must or we betray Christ) let it not be over trifles, lest pride and foolishness prevail. Thus wisdom and a great deal of grace are needed to know when toleration should yield to contention and contention give way to toleration. To condemn the tolerable is sin. To tolerate the intolerable is likewise sin. When Christ is betrayed or denied in His Church the Christian must contend with all his might. Compromise at that point would be treason to our King.

Peace, unity, and cooperation are vital ingredients to any happy society. They are precious and greatly to be sought. But no amount of peace, unity, or cooperation is ever worth the loss of Christ. We must never tolerate the intolerable.

"Wisdom and a great deal of grace are needed to know when toleration should yield to contention and contention give way to toleration."

PRACTICAL ATHEISM

AUGUST–SEPTEMBER 1981

"WE MUST LIVE AS IF THERE WERE A GOD . . ." So Immanuel Kant exhorted us to "faith" after he had finished a comprehensive critique of all of mankind's traditional arguments for the existence of God. We could take Kant's advice as a recipe for "practical" theism. Arriving at a point of agnosticism regarding the theoretical possibility of knowing God by reason or by scientific inquiry, Kant was still faced with the burning question of dealing with the practical issues of daily life. The focal point for him was ethics. If there is no God, thought Kant, then there is no ultimate basis for values in general and ethics in particular. In one sense Kant anticipated Dostoevsky's verdict: "If there is no God, then all things are permissible."

What was Kant saying? Simply this: if God does not exist then all ethical values are ultimately arbitrary. Such arbitrariness in ethics is ultimately chaotic making society impossible at worst and a jungle at best. Therefore, to make society possible, we must assume there is a God.

The following generation of thinkers was not satisfied with Kant's approach. Some turned to a rigorous atheism welcoming the vacuum in ethics as a new form of human liberation. Others turned to a truncated form of Christianity, one "safe" from the theoretical attacks of post-Kantian intellectuals. This hybrid form of Christianity which made its impact in the 19th Century was called "Liberalism." 19th Century liberalism reduced Christianity to an ethical core, a practical essence stripped of its supernatural form. Gone were the miracles of Jesus, the Virgin birth, resurrection, atonement, and anything else that intruded into the reduced core of ethical maxims. The "practice" of religion remained with due appreciation for sacrament, liturgy, and other externals of the church. The institution of the Church continued but with a redefined mission and theology.

The "ethical Christianity" of the 19th Century brought a crisis to the church. The "Crisis" theologians of the early part of this century, including Barth, Brunner, and Althaus, protested against the basic dishonesty of 19th Century liberals. Brunner called it a crisis of faith dubbing liberalism as a monument to unbelief. Casserley spoke in more strident tones complaining of what he called "The treason of the intellectual."

Now the organized church is torn with strife and distrust. Ultimately the battle is not so much between conservatives and liberals, evangelicals and activists, fundamentalists and modernists—the issue now is between belief and unbelief; is Christianity true or false, real or unreal?

What is deadly to the church is when the external forms of religion are maintained while their substance is discarded. This we call practical atheism. Practical atheism appears when we live as if there were no god. The externals continue but man becomes the central thrust of devotion as religious concern shifts its attention away from man's devotion to God, to man's devotion to man, bypassing God. The "ethic" of Christ continues in a superficial way having been ripped from its supernatural, transcendent, divine foundation.

Biblical Christianity knows nothing of a false dichotomy between devotion to God and concern for man. The Great Commandment incorporates both. It is because God is, that human life matters so much. It's because of the reality of Christ that ethics are vital. It's because the cross was a real event that the sacraments can minister to us. It's because Christ really defeated death that the Church offers hope. It is because of Jesus' real act of atonement that our forgiveness is more than a feeling.

The Church's life and her creed may be distinguished but never separated. It is possible for the church to believe all the right things and do the wrong things. It is possible also to believe the wrong things and do the right things. (But not for very long.) We need right faith initiating right action. We need a theoretical theism and a practical theism. Both practical theism and practical atheism leave us in a quagmire of dishonesty. Honest faith—joined with honest action—bears witness to a real God and a real Christ.

ESCHATOLOGY: WHAT DIFFERENCE DOES IT MAKE?

OCTOBER 1981

———

RECENTLY AN ANALYSIS OF SOCIO-ECONOMIC classes in America was made public. The report focused on the observable differences evident in value systems, behavioral patterns, and customs that exist between the classes. One of the most interesting dimensions of the findings was with respect to the question of how people regard the present in light of the future. People in the upper levels of the class register tend to be much more future oriented than those in the lower range. The trend in the lower classes is in the direction of immediacy. Consumption of goods, spending money, and other decisions are made with a view of short-range gratification. Planning for the future, sacrificing present impulses for future reserve, capital investment for long-range benefits, and the setting of forward looking goals are endeavors not often found in this segment of society.

On the other hand, capital investment, protracted periods of education, and long-term planning are considered virtues in the upper classes. "Play now, pay later" is the credo of one segment, while the other sings another song, namely, "Save now, play later."

The societal phenomenon illustrates an important lesson for the Christian: "One's future orientation often has a significant impact on one's present patterns of behavior." This impact is not only felt by individuals but by institutions as well.

The church's theology of the future is subsumed under the category of "Eschatology" or the study of the "last things." Not all churches agree on doctrines of the future and these disagreements tend to work themselves out at the very practical level of the churches' agenda.

For example, different churches have differing views about the Millennium and about the Rapture. On the surface the nuances of such differing views would seem to be of little significance. But suppose a person or a church body were convinced that Christ will return before the Millennium but after culture has disintegrated into a radical state of apostasy. What would the tendency of that church's program be? I think history would verify that such a view of the future would tend toward a strong emphasis in personal evangelism as the church would see its top priority as "snatching a few brands from the fire." Issues of social righteousness, cultural reform, and plans to maximize the Christianization of the world tend to be relegated to second-level priorities.

On the other hand, if one expected a final triumph of the Gospel culminating in the inauguration of a Millennial Kingdom before Christ arrives, then the agenda would tend more to penetrating cultural structures with Christian values. Cultural change as well as personal evangelism would be deemed as top-urgent priorities. Reformation beyond revival would be the goal of the church. Bearing witness to Christ in areas of law, politics, economics, education, medicine, and all aspects of cultural life would be crucial to the Church's mission.

What if we assumed a "realized eschatology" as many denominations have, assured that there is no future eschatological chapter to be written? When one opts into this position it leads almost invariably toward an embracing of or capitulation to secularism. Since there is nothing to expect "over there" the accent falls on a purely this-worldly perspective of religious faith. The sacred is swallowed by the secular; the eternal is annihilated by the temporal; and the church becomes "low class" in its behavioral patterns. Theology becomes fixed in the "here and now" divorced both from its past roots in history and its future hope in eternity.

What of the Rapture? Does it matter whether or not Christ comes before the Tribulation or afterwards? It will certainly matter to those alive at the time of the Tribulation. If the church does go through the Tribulation it will require discipline, perseverance, and endurance for the saints. If the

Pre-Tribulation position is wrong, a lot of folks will be caught woefully unprepared to face the crucible of that hour.

Thus the issues of eschatology are not merely exercises in speculation designed for the idle or the curious—they bear on our lives and how we approach them. These issues may have enormous impact on our growth as Christians.

Everybody has some kind of eschatological viewpoint or expectation. The viewpoint may not be consciously developed or carefully worked out but some assumption about the future is made by everyone. It is unavoidable.

The most elementary point relentlessly pursued in this column is that as creatures of time and space we are tethered not only to the past but to the future. Hence we say, "Right now counts forever . . ."

PIE-IN-THE-SKY THEOLOGY

NOVEMBER 1981

———

I T WAS INGMAR BERGMAN WHO CREATED THE forceful dialogue between a knight and Death personified in *The Seventh Seal.*

Knight: "I want knowledge, not faith, not supposition, but knowledge. I want God to stretch out His hand towards me, to reveal Himself and speak to me."

Death: "But He remains silent."

Knight: "I call out to Him in the dark, but no one seems to be there."

Death: "Perhaps—no one is there."

Knight: "Then life is an outrageous horror. No one can live in the face of death knowing that all is nothing."

The mood of despair captured in the words, "life is an outrageous horror" is echoed widely in the culture. From Sartre's assessment that man is a "useless passion" to Camus' conclusion that suicide is the only serious question left for philosophy to explore, the mood is the same. The pessimism of these men is clearly a matter of eschatology. It is the verdict that man's future is the *nihil*, the "nothingness" that evokes these negative sentiments. Look again at Bergman's words: "No one can live in the face of death knowing that all is nothing . . ."

Is death ultimate? Is there hope for the people of God, a hope grounded not in the fantasy of wish-projection but in the reality of truth?

The science of eschatology is concerned with the future events of world history which touch on the Kingdom of God. Questions of the nature and identity of the Anti-Christ, of the appearance of a millennium period of the reign of Christ, and issues about the rapture of the church vis-a-vis the Great Tribulation are questions that involve corporate concerns.

But what about the individual? Do "I" as a living, breathing, conscious person have a concrete hope for my own personal future? What do I have to look forward to? I know that at times when I discover that my own spirit is sagging and a sense of heaviness intrudes on me, I sometimes wonder why the gloomy cloud is perched above my head. When I think about it, I normally discover that I've scheduled myself into a bind with the vacation periods so far off that all seems like labor and weariness. (That, by the way, is a foolish thing to do.) The point is—I tend to be "up" in direct proportion to what I have to look forward to.

I just finished reading a secular treatment of the so-called middle-age male crisis. The analysis of the male crisis syndrome pinpoints several contributing factors, many of which center on the loss of a positive future orientation.

Biblical eschatology gives us solid reasons for expecting a personal continuity of life. Eternal life for the individual is not an empty human aspiration built on myth, but an assurance promised us by Christ Himself. His own triumph over the grave is the Church's hope for our participation in His life.

In a recent series of lectures I gave on eschatology, we examined the common issues of the millennium, etc. But my favorite lecture—the one I enjoyed the most preparing and delivering—was the lecture on Heaven.

We have heard so much ridicule and mocking about "pie-in-the-sky" theology that I'm afraid we've lost our appetite for it. What the Scriptures promise for our future involves a lot more than a perpetual visit to Mother Butler's. Jesus Christ and Simple Simon have very little in common.

The promise of heaven is indeed glorious—a promise which not only anchors the soul but fires the soul with hope. Life is not an outrageous horror, though we witness outrages daily. The outrage is not the bottom line. The sting of death has been overcome.

The victory of Christ is not established by platitudes or conjured up positive mental attitudes. Jesus is not the Good Humor Man. His call to joy is rooted in reality. "Be of good cheer for I have overcome the world." Therein resides our future hope—that Christ has overcome the world. He stared directly into the face of death and death blinked.

THEOLOGY AND "REAGANOMICS"

FEBRUARY 1982

——

N OT SINCE THE BLEAK ERA OF THE Great Depression has economics been so much in the forefront of public attention as it is today. A presidential election focused not on geopolitical issues or law and order debates but on the fiscal condition of the nation. Ronald Reagan swept into office on a platform of returning the nation to a sound economic position. Now the honeymoon is over as the forecast speaks of a 100 billion dollar deficit and the hue and cry is heard over the RIF (Reduction in Force) policy hitting hard at civil service employees. The problems we face are not simple but exceedingly complex, bringing consternation to the professional economists and fierce debate among Christians. Every Christian knows that economic issues are never abstractions but necessarily involve basic issues of values. Though the Bible offers no detailed policy of economics, it majors in values which touch heavily on economic issues.

Even a cursory reading of Scripture makes it evident that God cares about poor people. He speaks in judgment on economic injustice, oppression, and the wasteful consumption of resources triggered by avarice and unprincipled materialism. Yet the same Bible speaks clearly about the dignity of labor, the duty of productivity, and the evil of theft. Private property is protected and regulated by God's law. The Biblical principles are many even as the contemporary problems are many and we must be careful not to put principle and problem together in a simplistic fashion.

What are the practical problems we face today? The most frequently mentioned are:

1. inflation
2. unemployment
3. productivity decline
4. high rates of taxation
5. declining stability of U.S. currency on international markets

Of course there are more problems to deal with but these five are the most visible and most discussed today. To analyze these problems, some basic questions of causal thinking must be faced if a holistic solution may be achieved. Space limits a thoroughgoing answer to each question but let me at least raise the questions that must be faced.

1. What is inflation?
2. What causes inflation?
3. Why is unemployment so high (particularly in the steel and auto industries)?
4. Why do we have a decline in productivity?
5. Why have taxes been elevated to unprecedented levels?
6. Why has the international value of the dollar declined?

If you can give solid causal answers to these questions you will have gone a long way to identify the central issue of economics that plagues our nation.

There is a simple answer that relates to each of the above questions but by no means explains the intricacies involved in the whole picture. The simple answer is An Unbalanced Federal Budget.

No government has an infinite amount of wealth at its disposal. If it fails to take in as much money as it spends it incurs a deficit. Too much deficit over too long a time spells financial collapse—that's axiomatic. Yet we are now talking about a 100 billion dollar deficit. That deficit must be made up. There are basically only three ways to do it:

A. increase government revenue (impose new or increase present tax structure, or issue new fiat currency)

B. decrease government spending

C. seek some sort of combination of A and B

Now go back to questions 1–6 and apply method A to the problems and see what happens. Apply method B and see what happens. If you do these simple exercises you have started to grapple with the issues seriously.

The budget must always be evaluated. But evaluation can only be done in light of values. The conflict in economic policy is a conflict of ethics. A conflict of ethics is rooted in a conflict of philosophy. A conflict of philosophy is rooted in a conflict of theology. We can distinguish between economics and ethics and between ethics and theology but we can never separate them. Bottom line, then, is that our economic issues are ultimately theological in character.

PINOCHLE— A MEANS OF GRACE?

APRIL 1982

G OD DID NOT DESIGN THE GAME OF PINOCHLE as a means of grace, a setting to inspire the exultation of the soul to worship, an occasion for the flight of the spirit to raptured ecstasy. Worship is commonly thought to take place in the church, surrounded by the accoutrements of ecclesiastical architecture and supported by the inducements of a carefully planned liturgy. But God snuck up on me in the midst of erratic bidding and the dexterous shufflings of the cards. The night was oppressive with the heat of the day lingering, clinging to the walls of the hotel room. It was nice to snatch a few moments of frivolous rest after riding the bus all day listening attentively to the fractured English of the tour guide as he fulfilled his debts to the local merchants by directing us to their wares. This was Israel and we were on a pilgrimage to the sacred sites and shrines of the Holy Land.

Weary of travel, intimidated by my stomach's rebellion to all foods foreign, and fearful of being a victim of Ishmael's revenge, I was content to seek respite on a quiet evening in the hotel room. My wife sat with me, keeping score as our perennial struggle for pinochle supremacy was hanging in the balance. She remarked, with a spark of mischief in her eyes, "What would the people think if they knew you turned down an invitation to the Jerusalem Passion Play to sit in our room and play cards?"

"Card playing is considered the device of the devil by some, comparable to visiting the flesh pots of Egypt, but let it be. We shall enjoy this time, hiding from men if necessary, but playing our trump in full view of God as life is to be lived in its fullness *coram Deo*—and that includes moments of mirth as well as moments of mourning," I mused.

It was the Old Testament sage who refused to reduce the thesaurus of living to the boring, the monotonous, the routine, and the humdrum. The spice that is variety is sprinkled by the Creator's own hand to lift the veil a bit that hides the richness of His face. God is never dull as His majesty scintillates with the symmetry of a plethora of attributes all converging in the unity of His being. Should not His creation also sparkle with a myriad of facets, reflecting, as a mirror bounces back the images of lighted candles, His boundless glory? Is there not a time to weep, and a time to laugh; a time to mourn, and a time to dance? Has not God made everything beautiful in its time?

Ah, timing, there's the rub. The fool dances at the funeral and attends the wedding in sackcloth. It is the statue chiseled out of cold stone whose countenance never changes. Flesh and blood knows nothing of the fixed mood; the passions change from anger to joy, from expectancy to apathy, from rancor to felicity. It's the timing that counts. "Time"—the word impels the entrepreneur, torments the prisoner, and haunts the feeble mind of the philosopher. The word defines the boundary of our life span, the arena of our activity. It is the great equalizer of the race. The German has no more hours in his day than the Spaniard; the prince no more minutes in an hour than a beggar. The minute of the manager contains exactly the sum of seconds allotted to the laborer. Time makes creatures of us all, caught in the vortex of the unstoppable movement of the clock. Fill the time—waste the time—redeem the time. No matter, it waits for none of us. God does make everything beautiful in its time but He also, as the Preacher has said, "put eternity into man's mind, yet so that he cannot find out what God has done from the beginning to the end."

Why yield to turgid prose or become rhapsodic about such a time as that expended in a pinochle game? There is little in the game to command more than desultory comment. The game was merely the setting for the rude intrusion into my thoughts of the beauty of holiness. We sat with the sliding glass door open to the terrace. From our vantage point atop the Mt. of Olives we could gaze into the night at the panorama of Jerusalem, its ancient wall illumined by floodlights. The glow of the walls cast a surreal impression on the venerable city below us. It was a living anachronism with taxis competing with donkeys and buses with camels for transportation right of way.

Then we heard it. It was faint at first, giving rise to incredulous feelings of wonder. Was the desert air affecting our senses? Had we imbibed too heavily in letting our imaginations roam freely in this Holy Place? The sound grew louder as the voices drifted over the city, ascending our mountain with growing crescendos. Like a chorus of angels singing on ethereal plains the music pierced our ears and we hastened to the terrace for more acute hearing. Ringing now above the city were the triumphal choruses of Handel. The Victory song of the Lamb was echoing in the Hallelujahs reverberating from the city. "It's the Passion Play," I remarked, for want of more profound comment. My wife said nothing as she stood transfixed by the sound. One tear had gained both volume and momentum as it cascaded from her high cheek bone to plow a furrow in her make-up. Another tear followed in its path making her face take on the look of an eroded hillside.

Now was not the time for cards. Suddenly they were profane as we locked our hands to stand with the angels in the offering of worship to our King. When the spirit of God descends, some men dance, while others weep: on such occasions I am moved to silence, abhorring the slightest interruption to my trance-like posture.

I concentrate on the moment—willing it with fierce determination to freeze in its place—to abide with me beyond those moments of change—to capture forever the touch of eternity when it comes.

As I listened to the strains of the Hallelujah Chorus it was as if I suddenly passed through a warp of time. My eyes focused to the southeastern corner of the Old City. Outside the Dung Gate my vision conjured up shadowy images of a band of people moving stealthily in the darkness. I could see the anguished look on the face of the ghost of King David. It was David leading an entourage of loyal friends into the Valley of Kidron. I could see him beginning the difficult climb up the Mt. of Olives as his friends followed wailing as they moved. The King in exile, fleeing the marshaled forces of his usurping son Absalom. I envisioned Ezekiel observing the

Holy Spirit—the Glory of God departing from the city through the East Gate. Then Jesus, being led by soldiers up the flat stone steps to the house of Caiaphas. Here was the center spot of the earth where the Infinite burst into the finite; the eternal pierced the temporal; the unconditioned intersected the conditioned. It was all in front of me as the stones were crying out.

This is why we are evangelists. Evangelism is a response to God's command to declare to all men what Christ has wrought for us.

A NEW OPPORTUNITY—
A SOLEMN RESPONSIBILITY

JULY 1982

———

O N JANUARY 1, 1982, A NEW DIMENSION emerged in international communications. The first commercial short-wave radio broadcasting station was licensed to operate. Its programs are beamed around the world, being heard in China, Russia, Western and Eastern Europe, South America, Africa, and Australia. The listening audience for this station is approximately twenty million persons. It is a secular station featuring rock music.

In the early part of May, the Ligonier Valley Study Center was granted a prime-time slot for broadcasting the "R.C. Sproul Study Hour" around the world via this new station. Each week, the program will be aired at prime time on Saturday evening and rebroadcast Sunday mornings. The outreach opportunity for teaching the Gospel of Luke by this means is staggering and the sense of awe for the responsibility is equally so.

The import of this opportunity for ministry has affected my awareness as the programs are being taped. It is a weird experience to teach a course while seated at a table in my study or in a control booth at our new media studio. There is no congregation present to interact with and I must conjure up visions of people in my mind driving to church or making breakfast preparations as they listen to the broadcast. I have tried to imagine "Mr. and Mrs. America and all the ships at sea" as I've taped the lectures this year for domestic use. Now the images in my mind have changed. I cannot conceive of twenty million people listening to a program. If such a throng were amassed at one time in one place and I were called upon to address them, I am sure I would be paralyzed with fear and rendered unable to speak.

I don't conjure up visions of huge crowds listening to the programs;

I think of individuals. I think of missionaries seated in tents in remote jungle outposts listening for words of encouragement from home. I think of Christian workers giving themselves to the work of Christ in hamlets scattered throughout India, Australia, and South America. I think of Christians in the underground church behind the Iron Curtain. I think of Josef Tson who electrified the audience at the Congress on the Bible in San Diego with his testimony of suffering persecution in his homeland of Romania. I see his friends listening by the short-wave radio while posting a guard to alert them to the sudden appearance of the Secret Police.

These visions change my perspective and quicken my heartbeat as I am moved by the miserable plight experienced by multitudes of Christ's people who are engaged in the oft perilous task of building the Kingdom of God around the world. I ask you, nay beg you, to pray for this new tool of outreach. Pray that we may be responsible stewards of this gift; that the teaching of Luke's Gospel will bring comfort to the oppressed, redemption to the lost, and hope to those who step close to the border of despair.

Nothing fulfills me more than teaching the Biblical text. Systematic theology is important and I find philosophy stimulating, but it is the exposition of Scripture that is my first love. That love is now married to a new mission to the world. Pray that the communication goes both ways—that we at Ligonier may gain a fresh understanding and heightened sensitivity to the needs of Christians who live and serve beyond the borders of America.

"The birth of Jesus violates the inviolable; it mutates the immutable; it breaks the unbreakable."

—

THE BIRTH OF JESUS

DECEMBER 1982

———

W E MEET WITH CONTROVERSY IN THE PERSON of Jesus before He is even born. The extraordinary narrative of the circumstances surrounding His conception and birth provoke howls of protest from the critics of supernaturalism. The work of de-mythologizing begins early with the scissors wielded on the first page of the New Testament. Following Matthew's table of genealogy the first paragraph of the first Gospel reads as follows: "Now the birth of Jesus Christ was in this way: when as his mother Mary was espoused to Joseph, before they came together, she was found with child of the Holy Ghost."

Though the New Testament is replete with miracles surrounding the person of Jesus, none seems more offensive to modern man than the Virgin Birth. If any law of science is established as immutable and unbreakable it is that human reproduction is not possible without the conjoining of the male seed and the female egg. We may have developed sophisticated methods of artificial insemination and "test tube" intrauterine implantations but in some manner the reproduction process requires the contribution of both genders of the race to succeed.

The birth of Jesus violates the inviolable; it mutates the immutable; it breaks the unbreakable. It is alleged as an act which is pure and simple *contra naturam*. Before we even read of the activity of Jesus' life we are thrust head-first against this claim. Many skeptics close the door on further investigation after reading the first page of the record. The story sounds too much like magic, too much like the sort of myth and legend which tend to grow up around the portrait of famous persons.

Matthew focuses sharply on the extraordinary character of Jesus' birth, capturing the agony of Joseph's consternation. Joseph was a simple man, not privy to the sophisticated technology of our day. He knew nothing of in vitro fertilization and was unfamiliar with debates of parthenogenesis.

He did not understand the simple rules of biology which are common knowledge to today's 10th grade high school student. He lived in a pre-scientific age in a pre-scientific community. However, we must remember that virgin births were as rare in the first century as they are in the twentieth. Joseph did not have to be a skilled biologist to know that babies don't come from the stork.

Joseph was vulnerable in extremis. He had committed his life to Mary, trusting her purity in a society where adultery was scandalous. His betrothed came to him with a crushing revelation. "Joseph, I am pregnant." Mary then proceeds to explain her condition by telling Joseph that she had been visited by an angel who declared that she would be with child by the Holy Ghost. Joseph responded by tenderly considering "putting her away privately." There is no evidence of acrimony or furious rage by Joseph. He chose not to have her stoned, but began thinking of ways to protect Mary from the consequences of her delusions.

It is clear from the Biblical text that Joseph was the first hard-core skeptic of the Virgin Birth until the angel visited him and made him a convert to the "delusion." Nothing else would do. What man would believe such a story with less than miraculous evidence to attest it?

The road from conception to birth, from Zacharias, Elisabeth, Mary, and Joseph to the shepherds outside of Bethlehem was a road trafficked by angels. They appear at every turn, saturating the event in the supernatural.

With the scenario of angels in full play the critic works overtime with his scissors. He needs an electric knife to do the job as angels appear at the birth, the temptation, the resurrection, and the ascension of Jesus. They are promised as part of the retinue of His return. The word "angel" appears more frequently in the New Testament than the word "sin." It appears more often than the word "love." Put the scissors to angels and you are engaged not in Biblical criticism, but you are wreaking Biblical vandalism.

Pilgrims flock daily to the sacred sites of the life of Jesus. They follow the route of the *Via Dolorosa*; they argue about the authentic site of Golgotha and the garden tomb. Modern mountains compete for recognition as the locus of the Sermon on the Mount. But the field outside of Bethlehem is not under dispute as the place where the Glory of God was made visible to peasant shepherds, where the feet of angels stood in the dust of earth. The panorama of blazing effulgence sent these men to Bethlehem, obeying the mandate, "Go and see."

RATIONALISM AND FIDEISM: THE BATTLE OF TWO EXTREMES

FEBRUARY 1983

———

T HE CHRISTIAN LIFE IS LIVED ON THE twin virtues of reason and faith. The two are not identical, neither are they mutually exclusive. To distinguish them is vital; to separate them is deadly. Faith without reason is fideism; reason without faith is rationalism. The Christian must navigate his ship through the shoals of Scylla and Charybdis, maintaining a delicate balance between reason and faith.

The Roman Catholic Church of the nineteenth century understood the importance of the balance of reason and faith. Vatican Council I (which declared the infallibility of the pope in 1870) advocated a middle road between rationalism and fideism. Hans Küng, in his *Does God Exist?*, cites the council's approach to a twofold order of knowledge:

> Above the natural sphere of natural truths (including the knowledge of the existence of God) which are known by natural reason, there is a supernatural sphere of revealed divine truths, which are mysteries of faith and are known only by divine faith. Reason and faith do not contradict one another . . . but can provide mutual aid. Reason establishes the foundations of faith and enlightened by faith works out the science of theology. Man can know the one true God and Creator with certainty by the natural light of human reason. On the other hand, faith frees reason from errors, protects it, and equips it with manifold knowledge.

Vatican Council I marked out two fronts and placed itself in the center between rationalism and fideism. The lines of demarcation were set and a strong warning was issued to avoid the errors of the extreme: There must be no reduction of faith to reason. This is what radical rationalism did, upholding a reason without faith and rejecting everything supernatural. The strong tendency of rationalism is to move in the direction of pure naturalism with God, if there is one, becoming a more impersonal abstraction.

There must be no reduction of reason to faith. This is in fact, what radical fideism did, upholding in practice an irrational faith—a faith without reason—and rejecting any natural knowledge of God.

These twin enemies of Christianity threaten the church in every generation. Their threat, however, is not always at equal strengths. At some periods rationalism looms more powerful while at other times fideism is the more powerful. In our day it is the wolf of fideism that is at the doorstep, and in too many cases has already invaded the house bringing irrationality and pure subjectivism with it.

The appeal of fideism is that it sounds so pious. It promises a pure version of faith unblemished by the intrusions of pagan thought forms. It promises the ultimate safeguard against ungodly rationalism. It provides a sanctuary from the slings and arrows of outrageous reason. James Collins writes about fideism:

> Skepticism about philosophical matters appeared to be the safest way of safeguarding the orthodox faith. This was the motivation behind the fideistic skeptics, who sought to join doubt about the mind's natural powers with faith in supernatural revelation.

Collins' point is perceptive and can be applied to a multitude of varieties of fideists. The desire is for safety to free religion from philosophical attack by removing it from the range of the critics' guns. If religion is relegated exclusively to the realm of "faith" then it can live safely in its protected environment of isolation. But there is safety of this sort in an insane asylum for all who wish to flee the rigors of intellectual debate.

"Take it on faith." "Make a leap of faith."—These are the slogans of the fideist. Biblical faith is reduced to arbitrary decision, a blind choice. The mission of the church becomes proclamation only, discarding the Biblical mandate to give a reason for the hope that is in us. Fideism crucifies the intellect basing faith on the pure arrogance of subjective preference. It brings no glory to God and no honor to Christ. It is reactionary moving so far from rationalism that it embraces irrationalism. Watch for its intrusion into your thinking as it has a subtle power of seduction.

DUTY IS A FOUR-LETTER WORD THAT HAS BECOME A MODERN-DAY OBSCENITY

APRIL 1983

———

T HE HUMAN EAR IS A STRANGE APPENDAGE. Ears come in all sizes and shapes; they are the delight of the cartoonist who can capture a caricature easily by exaggerating their angles. The appendix and the coccyx have been dubbed "vestigial appendices" by those convinced of their relatively useless functional value. No one has ever called the ear "vestigial," as its value is not so much cosmetic but functional. Jesus put it succinctly: "He who has ears to hear, let him hear."

We are endowed by our Creator with certain inalienable responsibilities, among which are love, obedience, and the pursuit of vocation. These may be summed up with one four-letter word which has become a modern-day obscenity: DUTY. Duty involves answering a summons, responding to an obligation, heeding a call.

Our ears are assaulted daily by a cacophony of sounds making it difficult at times to distinguish between a bona fide call and senseless noise. We get phone calls, fire calls, wake-up calls, catcalls, crank calls, house calls, bad calls (by referees), and late calls for dinner. We get calls from our bosses, called on by our teachers, calls to service by Uncle Sam, calls to departure gates, sales calls, nature calls, and are treated to Indian love calls by Nelson Eddy and Jeanette MacDonald and cattle calls by Eddy Arnold.*

———

* Nelson Eddy (1901–67) and Jeanette MacDonald (1903–65) were singers and actors who starred in eight musicals together, including *Rose Marie* (1965), which featured the song "Indian Love Call." Eddy Arnold (1918–2008) was an American country singer who recorded the Tex Owens song "The Cattle Call" in 1944.

Only one call carries the force of absolute and ultimate obligation. I may ignore my phone calls and defy even the call of Uncle Sam, fleeing to Canada nursing a hope for future amnesty. The call of God may also be ignored or disobeyed, but never with impunity. I may marry Betty or Sally, live in Chicago or Tuscaloosa. I may build a small house or a big house or even live in an apartment. I can drive a Cadillac or a Honda—it's a free country. With respect to vocation, however, it is not a free universe. One absolute, non-negotiable requirement of my life is that I be true to my vocation. This is my duty.

We live in daily submission to a host of authorities who circumscribe our freedom: from parents to traffic policemen to dog catchers. All authorities are to be respected and, as the Bible declares, honored. But only one authority has the intrinsic right to bind the conscience. God alone imposes absolute obligation and He does it by the power of His holy voice. He calls the world into existence by divine imperative, by holy fiat. He calls the dead and rotting Lazarus to life again. He calls people who were no people, "My people." He calls us out of darkness and into light. He effectually calls us to redemption. He calls us to service.

Our vocation is so named because of its Latin root *vocatio*, "a calling." The term vocational "choice" is a contradiction in terms to the Christian. To be sure we do choose it and can, in fact, choose to disobey it. But prior to the choice and hovering with absolute power over it is the Divine summons, the imposition to duty from which we dare not flee. It was vocation that drove Jonah on his flight to Tarshish and caused his terrified shipmates to dump him in the sea to still the vengeful tempest. It was vocation that elicited the anguished cry from Paul, "Woe is me if I preach not the Gospel." It was vocation that put a heinous cup of bitterness in the hands of Jesus.

The call of God is not always to a glamorous vocation and its fruit in this world is often bittersweet. Yet God calls us according to our gifts and talents and directs us to paths of the most useful service to His kingdom. How impoverished we would be if Jonah had made it to Tarshish, if Paul refused to preach, if Jeremiah really would have turned in his prophet's card, or if Jesus would have politely declined the cup.

Vocation has its own reward in the Kingdom of God. God is no Pharaoh who withholds straw for the building of bricks or unscrupulous Ahab who rewards fidelity with exile. Our Father stores up treasures for those obedient to their calling and is pleased to give them the Kingdom.

Our duty is our honor. To fulfill it is to grasp the crown of life, to possess the pearl of great price. Our duty is our privilege as God grants with His command the dignity of His own person upon it. Whom we serve, whom we work for has the catalytic power to transform drudgery into exaltation and noise into the words of life.

"One absolute, non-negotiable requirement of my life is that I be true to my vocation. This is my duty."

THE PHILISTINE CROSS

JUNE 1983

———

I T WAS BONAVENTURA WHO OFFERED the thought: "In order that we may be able to extol and glorify God, and in order that we may advance to the knowledge of God, we must transfer to the divine that which pertains to the creature... nearly all creatures possess certain noble characteristics which furnish a source for our understanding of God, e.g., the lion possesses fortitude; the lamb, meekness; the rock, solidity; the serpent, prudence;—hence it is necessary that many names be transferred to God."

Calvin agreed with these sentiments. "There is not an atom of the universe in which you cannot see some brilliant sparks at least of his glory."

The earth; nature that surrounds us; the world—everything is full of God. Nature is a glorious theater, a spectacular sound and light show of the beauty of God. But nature is not God. To worship the whole or any part of nature is idolatry. To confuse God and nature is to fall into pantheism, an intolerable monism that obscures the distinction between creatures and Creator.

But ... the universe is God's handiwork—it sparkles with the revelation of its Maker. It is not an independent entity existing alongside of and apart from God. There is no dualism divorcing God from the world. The earth is the Lord's.

So what? The biblical view of the relationship between God and the world has weighty implications for our understanding of culture—of natural human science, art, recreation—all that is. If we abhor nature; despise culture; eschew natural science—we put a veil on the general revelation of God. We make of nature a means of concealing God, a silent, mute shroud of darkness. Let me diagram:

Monism	Biblical View	Dualism
nature is God—idolatry	culture—nature revealing God	silent universe agnosticism (theoretical atheism)

We move easily across the lines in either direction, to monism or to dualism. Liberalism tends to cross the border to monism confusing nature with God. Fundamentalism tends to cross the border to the right, embracing unawares a world-denying agnosticism.

A spiritual life that denies the revelatory character of the world is not spiritual in the biblical sense, but demonic. It is a pious rejection of God's creation. Ask the Christian artist. Ask him where the weight of his most burdensome criticism comes from the Evangelical community. Art, we say, is worldly.

I remember my first visit to Amsterdam's famous Rijksmuseum. It was a religious experience. I felt as if I were treading on holy ground. The majestic Goyas seemed to leap from their frames with brilliant blacks and reds. Degas, Matisse, Rubens, Vermeer, Hals—they were all there. But nothing compared with the vast hall, the inner sanctum of hushed mystery devoted exclusively to the master of the Muiden Circle, Rembrandt van Rijn. The tourists flocked to the huge, wall-size *Night Watch* or to the *Burgomasters*, with Americans making jokes about Dutch Masters cigars.

I was drawn to the smaller works. I gazed at the intricate lines etched on the face of the Apostle Paul and at the figure of Christ in the *Descent from the Cross*. My favorite, which hung alone in a dimly lit corner of the hall, was a portrait of the prophet Jeremiah lamenting the destruction of Jerusalem. There, the aged prophet, attired in Rembrandt fashion in the clothes of seventeenth century Dutch nobility, was hunched over an ancient text of Scripture, his head hanging in pitiful despair. Hidden in a blaze of light bursting out of darkness (a Rembrandt signature) was the faint outline of the city of Jerusalem in flames, with delicately etched figures of its inhabitants groping wildly in the agony of the inferno.

It was a work to study, to stare at for hours. So, too, the exhibit of early Van Gogh sketches displayed at the Stedelijk Museum. These were not the famous and easily detected later impressionistic paintings of the one-eared madman who whiled away his time in a sanatorium painting choppy broad strokes of sunflowers illumined by a blazing sun, or wild-eyed self-portraits of dementia. These were sketches made in Van Gogh's early twenties when, as a seminary student, he spent his summers in Belgium, working in a mission to Flemish coal miners. I stood mesmerized before an easel that displayed a Van Gogh sketch of a single shoe of a coal miner. The shoe captured life. Its creases, laces, and bent eyelets offered mute but powerful testimony to the misery of these workers. The groans of the people could be heard in the hall. God was in that place.

Biblical theology must draw a circle around the triad of virtues that include the good, the true, and the beautiful. Any religion that despises art is not merely truncated; it is sinister. To exclude the beautiful, to banish the aesthetic from the realm of God, is to crucify theology on a Philistine cross.

THERE'S MORE TO LIFE THAN MEETS THE EYE

SEPTEMBER 1983

———

THERE IS MORE TO LIFE THAN MEETS THE EYE. Reality transcends what we see with our eyes and hear with our ears. Reality goes beyond sense perceptions. It is not less than what we perceive, but it is certainly more.

Classically the Church has made an important distinction between the realm of the supernatural and the realm of the natural. Nature and supernature—two dimensions of the fullness of reality. Even within the realm of nature there is more there than meets the eye. We live in a world inhabited by micro-organisms that are invisible to the naked eye. The microscope may reveal swarms of real entities that can invade our bodies and destroy us. They exist. They are real. They are out there. But until they make us sneeze or provoke more severe discomfort we are largely oblivious to them.

There are other forces of nature that affect our daily lives that we see not. We do not see electricity; we do not observe gravity; we fail to observe energy. But we see the results of these things and know that they are there. In a sense we take them by faith.

We need a Christian epistemology, a Christian theory of knowledge. We must gain an understanding of the role of reason, the role of sense perception, the role of revelation, and the role of faith. Too often faith is understood to be the antonym of reason. A recent novel contained the comment about a dialogue between a priest and a scientist that "the priest expressed his faith, and the scientist stated his reasons."

This is the way many think. Faith is opposed to reason and/or to science. This is not the way the Bible defines it. In biblical terms faith functions with reason and sense perception, not apart from or against these aspects of knowledge. The author of Hebrews says it this way: "Now faith is the substance of things hoped for, the evidence of things not seen."

Faith, in this definition, is related to the evidence of things not seen. It is not a blind belief, an irrational gratuitous leap into irrationality. Faith is elsewhere depicted as being eminently rational and established on the foundation of things seen. The Apostles proclaimed what they saw with their eyes and heard with their ears. The content of faith is based upon both reason and sense perception. Paul tells us that the invisible things of God are perceived through the things that are made. The key concept is revelation. Christianity is a revealed religion. Revelation is at the heart of Christian epistemology. There can be no Christian education without it. Revelation takes us beyond what reason can deduce and the senses perceive.

Revelation rests on a foundation of rationality and sense perception but takes us above and beyond the foundation. The God who made all things visible and invisible communicates to us what otherwise would be inaccessible. The study of biblical faith is the study of transcendent revelation. We call the Bible the Word of God not because it dropped from heaven by parachute or because God Himself wrote it with His own hand. Rather we call it the Word of God because He is the source of its content. The Bible does not merely point us to revelation—it is itself revelation. Its content has its source in God. Any epistemology that discounts this dimension of faith, this content of revelation, is not fit to be called Christian. Take away word-revelation and you take away Christianity.

We need a Christian cosmology. A Christian view of knowledge, a Christian epistemology yields information about the world in which we live. Educational systems vary and compete with each other about such issues as how we should view our world. Our understanding of the world, of the cosmos (cosmology) is tied to our epistemology in one direction and to our behavior in another direction. How I view life has a strong impact on how I live life. If I want to live a Christian life I must first have a Christian cosmology.

We need a Christian theology. It is not merely the world we must understand to live Christian lives. We must also understand the character of the God we are seeking to serve and to please. There are many theologies that seek to establish themselves upon some other basis than revelation. Just as a Christian cosmology depends upon a Christian epistemology, so does a Christian theology rest on the foundation of a Christian epistemology. The method of knowing strongly influences the content of what is learned.

Christian education seeks a view of God, the world, and ourselves from the perspective of God's understanding of these things. His perspective is made known to us via revelation. That revelation comes partly via nonverbal communication in nature and in the activities of historical events. But the meaning of nature, the interpretation of events comes to us in words, in the verbal content of the Sacred Scriptures.

The verbal content of Scripture is the prime subject matter of Christian education. Here the believer is instructed in the school of revelation. Here is where the mind of Christ is communicated. Here we learn the values of God—reality as He sees it. It opens the windows of the soul to a broad vista, penetrating the realm of the invisible.

GOING FOR THE BRASS RING

DECEMBER 1983

SOMETIMES I FEEL LIKE A FIVE-YEAR-OLD child stretching my arms to the limit, wrapping my legs tightly around a plastic horse, reaching my fingers toward the prized brass ring. I know the strategy: I must not cling to the horse if the prize is to be won. The ring cannot be grasped from a safe position. But it's hard to let go, to reach into space, to take the risks. Then someone shouts "Go for it!" The adrenaline begins to pump and somehow my arm grows longer and the ring is won.

The exhortation "go for it" is at once exciting and scary. It's exciting because it promises new vision, new opportunity, new frontiers to be explored. It's scary because it means venturing into unknown territory, taking new risks.

But sometimes new risks are only risks. Sometimes it's much wiser to simply do more of what you are already doing, and do it even better, always reaching further.

For the past nine months the staff of the Ligonier Valley Study Center has been involved in a rigorous process of analysis and future planning. At the behest of the Board of Directors we have analyzed in detail the effectiveness of our ministry in the past and have very carefully reached several decisions for the future. We have been aided by the input and assistance of several top-flight Christian ministry consultants including experts in radio and television ministry, administrative management, ministry growth and expansion, and the like.

After careful study and strategy planning we have made these decisions:

1. Not to bring a program of our own into the arena of broadcast television.

2. To focus on the production of video teaching tapes for churches and Christian leadership groups.

3. To continue on-site seminars for Christian leaders, both clergy and lay persons, emphasizing one-week long and weekend conferences.

4. To expand our outreach of teaching by audio cassette tapes.

5. To continue speaking at strategic functions off-site.

6. To continue teaching the winter semester at Reformed Theological Seminary, and writing for publications.

7. To develop more curriculum materials to aid people using our materials toward a more effective total learning experience.

Each of these decisions has an important rationale, which I will outline briefly.

1. Broadcast: Though our desire is to teach as many people as possible, the experts tell us that my gifts are not used most effectively in normal broadcast media. Though our content on radio has received high ratings, we have been advised to change the format radically in order to appeal to a broader base. The changes necessary to pull this off would involve an annual expenditure of over $250,000.

   Since our ministry focuses on in-depth teaching, our audience is restricted to people motivated to go beyond the basics. We thought it better to put our resources into a more specifically targeted audience such as those who gather in churches and homes for video study because they are already motivated to seek a deeper understanding of their faith. Broadcast television was nixed primarily by me. Broadcast TV is enormously expensive and virtually requires repeated fund appeals and a highly simplified message to succeed. I recognize the importance of Christian broadcast television but its requirements do not fit my gifts, my passions, and my personality. Candidly, it simply is not who I am and what I believe I am called to do.

2. Video Teaching Tapes: This aspect of our ministry thrills my soul. The impact of it is zooming. For example, in October of 1982 we shipped 172 programs to churches. This October we sent out over 300 programs. That means that in the month of October I was able to teach 300 classes of adults averaging 30 persons per class. In addition, some local churches sponsored the showing of these teaching series on cable television. They were viewed, for example, in Manhattan on New York's largest cable station and in Los Angeles. The above figures do not include the video tapes distributed through over 90 bookstores nationally via Tyndale Christian Video. We did almost no advertising this year for video apart from what Tyndale did. Our goal is to ship 1,000 tapes a month by the end of 1984. We are also planning a major production of *The Holiness of God* series under the guidance of a professional producer.

3. Seminars: This past year we discontinued the 10-week terms for resident students. Instead, we have begun offering several one-week seminars for Christian leaders and special weekend seminars in addition to our regularly scheduled seminars for inmates of federal penitentiaries in cooperation with Prison Fellowship. This year's attendance of seminars at LVSC reached an all-time high.

4. Audio Tapes: This past year we shipped approximately 32,000 audio tapes. Of course, many individuals use multiple tape series. Our goal for 1984 is to have 20,000 individuals become LVSC audio tape "students."

5. Outside Speaking: This fall took me to Memphis, Atlanta, Chattanooga, Lafayette (Purdue), and Chicago for teaching missions. Next year's schedule is already booked giving me the heaviest speaking schedule I've ever attempted.

6. Seminary Teaching and Writing: For the past several years the Board has granted me a three-month block of time to go away to concentrate on writing. This past year we tried an experiment. During the three months of writing I lectured two days a week

at Reformed Theological Seminary in Jackson, Mississippi. With the added advantages of the library there and the academic atmosphere, I was able to increase my writing production plus get my batteries charged by being back in a formal classroom situation. We have decided to continue this program with the seminary, teaching Systematic Theology in the winter semester. This year I completed a book in Christian apologetics done jointly with Dr. John Gerstner and Dr. Art Lindsley. The book is scheduled for release July 1, 1984, by Zondervan. I also finished two 100-page booklets for Tyndale on *Prayer* and *Knowing the Will of God.*

For the first time I have attempted to write fiction. Through the urging of an editor, a consultant, and Dr. Gerstner I attempted to write a novel, using theological symbolism in a contemporary setting. The writing of the novel was the most exhilarating and excruciating literary attempt I've ever made. The novel, *Johnny Come Home*, is scheduled for release in July 1984 by Regal Books.

7. Curriculum: We are seeking funds and educational experts to help us produce an organic curriculum to aid laymen in the mastery of biblical truth.

This is where we have been and where we, by the grace of God, are headed, in a nutshell. Since you are the people closest to our ministry, I wanted you to have this capsule summation straight from the horse's (or is it the mule's?) mouth.

"When our souls
are stirred to
delight in the
things God delights
in, we are in touch
with Beauty."

—

THE SOUL'S HUNGER FOR BEAUTY

FEBRUARY 1984

———

An immortal instinct, deep within the spirit of man, is thus, plainly, a sense of the Beautiful ... just as the lily is repeated in the lake, or the eyes of Amaryllis in the mirror, so is the mere oral or written repetition of these forms, and sounds, and colors, and sentiments, a duplicate source of delight ... We still have a thirst unquenchable ... This thirst belongs to the immortality of man ... It is the desire of the moth for the star ... a wild effort to reach the Beauty above.

"**A** WILD EFFORT TO REACH THE **BEAUTY** ABOVE." These are the sentiments of Edgar Allan Poe. For Poe the function of the beautiful is to elevate, or excite the soul.

But what is the beautiful? Can we find a formula for it or does it remain impenetrably concealed in the private, subjective recesses of the retina of the beholder? Is beauty merely a matter of taste, like ice cream cones and cooked vegetables? Or is there some objective measuring rod by which a thing may be said to be ultimately beautiful or ugly?

The science of Philosophy proper concerns itself with discovering norms for Truth. The science of Ethics searches for norms of the Good. The science of Aesthetics seeks for norms of the Beautiful.

In the madness, the insanity of modern thought, the robber barons of the mind have sought to reduce all three, the True, the Good, and the Beautiful, to the nadir of sheer subjectivism. Truth is deemed relative, the Good knows of no absolutes, and the Beautiful is an arbitrary preference. If so, then the triad of foundational principles crumbles into chaos and the words *true, good, beautiful* become ultimately meaningless. If they are ultimately meaningless they cannot be penultimately meaningful. If the skeptics are correct, we must resign ourselves to living in a world that is vacant of any truth, any goodness, any beauty. Without objective standards we must also banish our concepts of falsehood, evil, and ugliness. But such a consistent skepticism cannot be carried out. The skeptics continue to write, arguing for the truth of their skepticism, objecting all the while to evils committed, and recoiling in horror from what they deem ugly. No man, sane or insane, sober or drunk, objectivist or subjectivist, can live without this foundational triad.

The classical thinkers understood that somehow Beauty, the most elusive of the three, has some inner relationship to the True and the Good. St. Thomas, for example, saw a fundamental, though not absolute, identity between beauty and goodness. He listed three conditions for beauty: integrity or perfection, proportion or harmony, and brightness or clarity. If these things are present in a work of art then the image is beautiful even if all it does is perfectly, proportionately, and clearly represent an ugly thing. Here is implied an imitation or correspondence theory of beauty.

Correspondence is crucial to truth and goodness if we are to escape the abyss of subjectivism. John Locke defined truth as that which corresponds to reality. But we must ask, "Reality as perceived by whom?" Who among us has an absolute, infallible perception of reality? Clearly none of us. Hence the temptation toward skeptical relativism. The Christian must modify the correspondence view by defining truth as "that which corresponds to reality as it is perceived by God." Likewise Goodness "corresponds to the judgment of God." God is clearly the ultimate Standard of Truth and Goodness.

What about Beauty? Ultimately the supreme norm of Beauty is likewise located in the character of God. It is what stirs delight in the mind of God. When our souls are stirred to delight in the things God delights in, we are in touch with Beauty.

For us, an appreciation of Beauty involves the mind and the senses (particularly the senses of sight and sound). Jacques Maritain, following Augustine, Albertus Magnus, and St. Thomas, declares:

Every sensible beauty, no doubt, implies a certain delight of the eye or the ear or the imagination: but there can be no beauty unless the mind also is in some way rejoiced ... the beautiful is essentially delightful; it stirs desire and produces love ...

The mind, the senses, and delight are the ingredients. Imitation is not mere external reproduction. It is the capturing of the brilliance or excellence of a form, a thought, a vignette of reality that elevates our souls. It is not mere copying but, as Maritain suggests, "is the faculty of producing, not of course *ex nihilo*, but out of a pre-existing matter, a new creature, an original being capable in its turn of moving a human soul."

A personal footnote: Recently I browsed in a Christian bookstore, scrutinizing in particular the cover designs of Christian works of fiction. (I have a vested interest here. I have written my first novel and was fearful that it would be destroyed by a tacky cover.) I left the store in panic and went home and called my publisher. "Please," I said, "let me see the cover design for my novel before you print it." I had never made such a request before and the publisher assuaged my fears. But the impact of my visit to the bookstore filled me with alarm about where the Evangelical Christian world is with respect to art. My soul was not elevated to worship. It hungers to be fed. I need Truth. I need Goodness. I need Beauty. With the third, the contemporary Christian world is starving me to death.

A FUNNY THING HAPPENED ON THE WAY TO CARNEGIE HALL

APRIL 1984

———

MILLIONS OF CHILDREN IN THE UNITED STATES begin piano lessons. I was one of them. At age eight, I embarked on a musical career that featured a blazing start and a whimpering finish. My teacher introduced me to the magic of the keyboard with the first lesson of the first volume of the ancient and venerable John Thompson instruction series. I will always remember the first lesson. The text of the booklet read: "I am playing middle C. I can play it well you see." It was a snap. I placed my right index finger on middle C and played it repeatedly to the end of the text.

The first lesson was simple. So was the entire first book. I raced through it in what I was sure was record time. In a matter of weeks I finished Volume I and began Volume II. Five years later, I quit taking piano lessons. I was still in Volume II. I had reached a plateau of difficulty and could not progress further without serious practice and discipline. I became a piano dropout like millions of other children. Some, like Van Cliburn, didn't quit.* A few became world class pianists. Others reached high performance plateaus before they leveled off. Most, however, dropped out when the going got tough.

As a seminary student, I resolved to start again. I wanted to be able to play the classics. I enrolled with a piano teacher and explained to her that I wanted to learn to play Mozart, Chopin, and Debussy. She smiled and explained that I was not quite ready to tackle their original compositions.

———

* Van Cliburn (1934–2013) was an American pianist. He started playing piano at age three.

She wanted me to go back to Volume II of John Thompson. I insisted that I wanted to play Chopin "right now." We made a deal. She promised to teach me Chopin if at the same time I would work on rudimentary scales and other simple exercises. She let me work on Chopin by practicing one measure a week. After a year, voila! I could play Chopin. (At least one piece.)

I moved away after seminary and ceased taking piano lessons. I was confident that I could progress on my own without the aid of a teacher. It didn't work. I wound up playing the songs I already knew and could not bring myself to practice the difficult sections of new ones. I had reached a new plateau, but I was as stuck on that one as I had been in Volume II of John Thompson.

So what? The story of my music woes is an illustration of what is typical of us in a multitude of endeavors. It is particularly tragic when we see the same pattern emerging in Christian growth. Multitudes start the Christian life with a flair. They learn a few Bible verses, make a cursory reading of the New Testament, take a crash course in evangelism, learn a few perfunctory prayers, and then level off on a plateau of stagnated growth. We are satisfied with echoing Christian jargon and subsisting on a spiritual diet of milk. Strong growth requires a healthy diet. It requires what the Apostle Paul called meat. We need the discipline of study, the discipline of prayer, the discipline of service. Most of us require being disciplined under the authority or tutelage of another. Self-discipline is merely the extension of discipline learned under another. It does not come by magic. If you desire to break out of the plateau on which you are paralyzed, then it is imperative that you get under the discipline of someone qualified to take you further and deeper into the Christian life. Your pastor is the most obvious person to help. Refuse to be satisfied with milk. It is possible to break out of stagnation and move ahead into a growing, enriching development. We are called to be disciples; not for one year, but for our lives.

The breakdown point of the piano lesson analogy is that it is ultimately impossible for the Christian to quit his growth lessons. Our master teacher is God the Holy Spirit. If the Spirit dwells in us, He will not allow us to remain stagnant in our growth. He is the sanctifier. We must remember, however, that sanctification is a cooperative process. The Spirit is at work within us, yet we are called to work and to work diligently under His divine supervision. The degree of our growth is dependent in large measure on our practice in godly discipline. We still may experience the frustration of getting stuck at various plateaus of spiritual growth. In order to progress beyond them, we need meat and practice, practice, practice.

A potent device of the enemy to effect our paralysis is to convince us that we have "arrived." If Satan can delude us into being satisfied at a level of stunted growth, he need only to worry about a Christian army made up of pygmies rather than giants. Christ calls us to be giants; fully grown, fully mature, edified Christian men and women.

THE PROTESTANT OVER-REACTION

JUNE 1984

———

"**C**HURCH IS BORING.**"** This is the most oft-stated reason why people stay away from church. It raises some important questions. How is it possible that an encounter with a majestic, awesome, living God could ever be considered boring by anyone? God is not dull. If worship is boring to us it is not because God is boring. Sermons can be boring and liturgies can be boring but God simply cannot be boring. The problem, I think, is with the setting, the style, and the content of our worship.

The New Testament gives us little information about proper Christian worship. Some guidelines are established but not much content is offered. In contrast the Old Testament provides a panorama of worship information. This poses some dangers as well as some vital clues for worship. We cannot simply reinstitute the elements of Old Testament worship because many of them are clearly fulfilled once and for all with the finished work of Christ in His offering of the perfect sacrifice.

The Old Testament does provide a key to elements involved in worship. We see, for example, that the mind must be engaged in worship. The centrality of preaching underscores the crucial role of the Word. That the pulpit is featured in Protestant worship is a protest to the central place of other elements of liturgy in Roman Catholic worship.

Full worship, however, is both verbal and non-verbal. The whole person is addressed and involved in a worship experience. We note that in the Old Testament all five senses were intimately involved. Old Testament worship involved sight, sound, touch, smell, and taste.

The visual impact of the furnishings and the building itself, of both tabernacle and temple, was awesome. The eyes were dazzled with a sense of the splendor of God. The Gothic cathedral in Christian history has had the same impact. The vaulted ceilings and high arches sweep the soul into a sense of the majestic loftiness of God. Does your church building have that effect? Sadly, many Protestant centers of worship imitate a town meeting hall where the accent is on human fellowship rather than passing over a threshold to a sacred place of adoration.

Sound was vital to Old Testament worship. The choral compositions of the Psalms were moving to the spirit. They were accompanied by the full harmony and rhythm supplied by the harp, the lyre, the flute, and trumpets. The piano and the organ are marvelous instruments but they cannot produce the sounds that the other instruments provide. Hymns and choral anthems are greatly enhanced when they are supported with greater orchestration. The Philadelphia Conference on Reformed Theology has seen the vital impact made on the congregation by the use of a brass ensemble.

The element of touch is missing in most Protestant worship. Charismatic groups emphasize the laying on of hands, which meets a strong human need for a holy touch. Early Christian worship involved the placing of the pastor's hands on each person with the pronouncement of the benediction. When congregations got too large for such personal attention the act gave way to the symbolic gesture of the benediction spoken by the pastor with outstretched arms. This was a simulation of the laying on of hands, but the actual touch was lost. Old Testament worship included taste and smell. The fragrance of incense burned gave a peculiar sense of a special aroma associated with the sweetness of God. One of the first gifts laid at the foot of the manger of Jesus was that of frankincense. Most Protestants reject incense as being popish without giving any substantive reason for its rejection.

Taste was central to the Old Testament feasts as well as the New Testament celebration of the Lord's Supper. The injunction to "Taste and see that the LORD is good" is rooted in the worship experience. The people of God "tasted the heavenly gift."

Space does not permit a full elaboration of these aspects. This brief article is written to suggest that perhaps we have over-reacted. We have stunted worship by excluding elements that God once commanded be included. The mind and the senses—all of the senses—must be involved if we are going to be totally involved in the worship of God.

"Full worship is both verbal and non-verbal. The whole person is addressed and involved in a worship experience."

THE ULTIMATE VISION

SEPTEMBER 1984

"**WITHOUT A VISION THE PEOPLE PERISH . . .**" We hear this verse quoted frequently in order that we may be inspired and challenged to move with intensity toward a future goal. We applaud the leader who is a visionary, one who can paint a picture of a better future and show us the way to attain it. We are a goal-oriented society. We need a dream, a target to be aimed for, if we are to get our adrenaline moving and our passions stirred.

Every goal, every short-range vision must be measured against the supreme and final norm of all future Christian visions. We must keep before us the Ultimate vision of the people of God. That vision is variously called the *visio Dei* or the "Beatific Vision." It is the vision of God Himself.

I have never seen God. I have felt His presence and reasoned through His existence. I have read His Word and heard of dazzling displays of His glory. But I have never seen Him. He is invisible. Not only have I never seen Him face to face, but no one else has seen Him either. The Creation heralds His majesty; the stars declare His handiwork. We can view the work of the artist but the artist Himself remains unseen.

Why can't we see God? It is not because He is a spirit; nor is it because He is not present. He is here; there is no question about that. We live in a world of real entities that we cannot see with the naked eye. What is invisible to our eyes can have dramatic effects upon us. The forces of electricity and nuclear power inform our daily lives though we see them not. Our bodies may be invaded at any moment by life-threatening microorganisms. We live in a world where there is much more than meets the eye. The sophisticated instruments of telescopes and microscopes reveal a dimension of reality that escapes our naked glance.

There is no microscope powerful enough, however, to penetrate the veil that covers the face of God. There is no lens capable of magnifying our weak eyesight to the level of seeing God. Our problem is not a weakness of visual strength. It is not the optic nerve that is deficient. The deficiency is in our heart, not our eyes. We cannot see God because He is holy and we are not. It is because of sin that we are told: "No man can see God and live."

In a sense we are fortunate that we cannot see God. If for one second the veil were removed and we caught a brief glimpse of the face of God, we would perish instantly. His effulgence is so brilliant, His glory so dazzling that in our present corrupted state we could not bear the sight of Him. He remains invisible both as a curse and as an act of protecting grace. As long as we remain infected by sin we are doomed to wander in His world sightless with respect to Him. We may be comforted by His Word and healed by the secret ministration of His Spirit, but we cannot see the supreme beauty of His face.

But we have a dream; nay, more than a dream. We have the sure and certain promise that sometime we will see Him face to face. The heart of every Christian longs for the face of Christ. We yearn to look directly at God Himself without fear of being consumed. That deep yearning will one day be fulfilled.

The future vision of God is called the "Beatific Vision" because it will bring in its wake the consummate blessedness for which we were created and redeemed. One of the "Beatitudes" promised by Jesus was: "Blessed are the pure in heart, for they shall see God." In heaven we will be pure in heart. In heaven we shall see God. John tells us:

> Behold, what manner of love the Father has bestowed upon us, that we should be called children of God; and such we are ... Beloved, now are we children of God, and it is not yet made manifest what we shall be. We know that, when he shall appear, we shall be like him; for we shall see him as he is. (1 John 3:1–2)

"We shall see him as he is." We will see more than a burning bush; more than a pillar of fire; more than a *shekinah* cloud. What we shall see will make the glory that shone around the shepherds of Bethlehem seem dim by comparison. What we shall see will eclipse the brightness of the sun and obscure the lightning that blazed at Mt. Sinai. We shall see Him as He is. The invisible shall become visible. The impossible dream will become possible. In that moment we shall be flooded with truth, goodness, and beauty. Blessed are those who long for the beatific vision.

BE YE HOLY

NOVEMBER 1984

CHARLES TURNER REVIEWED *Johnny Come Home* and commented, "The only character in the novel who is holy is . . . God." Turner's comment is correct in the sense that no human character can be portrayed with any accuracy unless he is painted warts and all. A human being without sin is as rare as an incarnate deity. That the greatest of saints continue to struggle with sin long after their conversions is so axiomatic that it is disputed only by the most militant perfectionists.

The obvious fact that we all sin can create an atmosphere of false security among us, leading us to accept with ease the idea that sin is so commonplace that we ought not to be too bothered by it lest we surrender our mental health to a self-deprecating neurosis. Yet in our desire to console ourselves and maintain a good self-image we may push to the backburner the mandate of God, "Be ye holy, even as I am holy."

Evangelical Christians are most vulnerable to succumbing to this distortion. We stress the fact that our justification is by faith alone and insist that our righteousness is found in Christ and in Christ alone. Though these assertions are true it is equally true that the faith by which we are justified is a faith that brings forth fruit in our lives. The slogan of the Reformation was that we are justified by faith alone, but not by a faith that is alone. The instant true faith is present in the heart of the believer the process of sanctification begins. Change begins at once. The Christian begins to be conformed to the image of Christ. We are becoming holy. If we are not becoming holy, then Christ is not in us and our profession of faith is empty.

Martin Luther gave the following analogy: He said that when we are justified it is as though a doctor had just administered a sure and certain remedy for a fatal disease. Though the patient would still endure a temporary struggle with the residual effects of his illness, the outcome was no longer in doubt. The physician pronounces the patient cured even though a rehabilitation process must still be carried out. So it is with our justification. In Christ, God pronounces us just by the imputation of the merits of Christ. Along with that declaration, God administers something to us; He gives us the Holy Spirit. The Holy Spirit begins immediately to work within us to bring us to holy living.

The New Testament contains a ringing paradox with respect to sanctification. The Bible says, "Work out your salvation with fear and trembling, for God is at work within you both to will and to do." Notice that there are two agents working here. We are called to work and God promises to work as well. We call this activity *synergism*. It is a coworking, a cooperative effort between God and man. To be sure our initial regeneration is accomplished by God alone, but our sanctification involves mutual activity.

The two great heresies that have plagued the Church on this matter for centuries are the heresies of activism and quietism. The twin distortions are guilty of eliminating one or the other poles of the paradox. In activism God's working is swallowed up by human self-righteousness. In quietism the human struggle is swallowed up by an automatic divine process.

Activism is the creed of the self-righteous person. He has no need of divine assistance to achieve perfection. Grace is held in contempt, a remedy needed only by weak people. The activist can lift himself up by his own bootstraps. His confidence is in himself and his own moral ability. Perhaps the most arrogant statement a person can make is this: "I don't need Christ."

The quietist insults the Holy Spirit by insisting that God is totally responsible for his progress or lack of it. If the quietist still sins the unspoken assumption is that God has been lacking in His work. The creed of the quietist is, "Let go and let God." No struggle is necessary; no resistance to temptation is required. It is God's job, from beginning to end.

God calls us to the pursuit of holiness. The pursuit is to be undertaken with strength and resolution. We are to resist unto blood; to wrestle with powers; to pummel our bodies, rejoicing in the certainty that the Holy Spirit is within us helping, disposing, convicting, and encouraging. His goal in us is His own name—that we may be Holy.

THE CHRISTIAN IN THE MARKETPLACE

FEBRUARY 1985

———

O N THE MOUNTAIN OF TRANSFIGURATION the disciples were stunned by the breakthrough of the dazzling glory of Christ. What previously was veiled by His humanity, hidden from the sight of mortals, suddenly burst through the veil in translucent radiance. With but one glimpse the disciples were paralyzed. They had but one consuming desire—to abide in that place, basking forever in the light of His countenance. Jesus would have none of it. As Lord of the Church He commanded His disciples to forget about pitching tents and sent them down the mountain and into the world.

The day Christ died those same disciples went into hiding. They retreated to the shelter of the upper room in which they huddled together in fear. When Jesus broke the bonds of death, He went to the upper room. In a sense He broke down the door—not so much to get in, but to get His disciples out. His mandate to them was to await the Spirit and then to go—to get out of the temple and into the world.

The cradle of the Church was the marketplace. From the preaching and public ministry of Jesus to the daily acts of the Apostles, the central scene was the marketplace.

When Paul went to Athens, the cultural center of the ancient world, he "reasoned in the Synagogue with the Jews and with the Gentile worshipers, and *in the marketplace daily* with those who happened to be there" (Acts 17:17). The New Testament word for the "marketplace" is the word *agora*. The *agora* was not only the shopping district but was the center of civic life. The *agora* was surrounded by public buildings, shops, and colonnades. Here children played, the idle loafed, lawsuits were heard, and public events were produced. It was public, not private; open, not secret; dangerous, not safe.

Martin Luther, as a herald of reformation, exclaimed that the Church must be profane. It must move out of the temple and into the world. Luther looked to the Latin roots of the word "profane." The word "profane" comes from *profanus* (outside the temple). If Christ is not relevant outside the Church He is insignificant inside the Church. If our faith is bound to the inner chambers of the Christian community, it is at best a disobedient faith and at worst, no faith at all.

It was the Pharisees who developed the doctrine of "salvation by separation." They were practicing segregationists, believing that holiness was achieved by avoiding contact with unclean sinners. No wonder they were scandalized by the behavior of Jesus who dealt with Samaritans, ate dinner with tax collectors, placed His hand upon lepers, and ministered to harlots. Our Lord was accused of being a drunkard and a glutton, not because He was overweight or given to intemperance, but because He frequented places where these things were commonplace. If guilt by association were a legitimate offense, Jesus would have lost His sinlessness early in His ministry. But He came to seek and to save the lost. He found them gathered in the world . . . in His Father's world.

It was again Luther who declared that a new Christian must withdraw from the world *for a season*, but upon reaching spiritual maturity must embrace the world as the theater of redemptive activity. His message was, "Away with the cowards who flee from the real world and cloak their cowardice with piety."

Perhaps the greatest need for our day is the need to market Jesus Christ. The Church must become expert in marketing; not in the slick, Madison Avenue style, but in an aggressive, yet dignified, way. The marketplace is where we belong. It is where needy people are found. It is not enough for the Church to hang a welcome sign on her door. We dare not wait for the world to come to us.

God never intended the Christian community to be a ghetto. The Church is not a reservation. Yet the pervasive style of modern evangelicalism is that of a reservation or a ghetto. We can argue that it is the secularist agenda to put us there and keep us there. But such arguments won't do.

We are there because it is safe and comfortable to be there. The secularist hates the light and is quite willing to offer us a bushel for it. Shame on us when we buy our own custom-made bushels and willingly place them on our own candles. To hide the light or to restrict it to a reservation is to do violence to the Gospel and to grieve the Holy Ghost.

"It is not enough for the Church to hang a welcome sign on her door. We dare not wait for the world to come to us."

HEROES

APRIL 1985

———

W HEN I WAS A BOY I THOUGHT LIKE A BOY. I behaved like a
boy. I understood like a boy. I was deeply impressed by heroes.
Mostly, they were figures from the sports world. There was
Doak Walker, Charlie "Choo Choo" Justice, . . . Sammy Baugh, . . . Bob
Waterfield, . . . Felix "Doc" Blanchard, . . . Johnny Lujack.

I hoarded, traded, and "flipped" baseball cards. My room was adorned by
glossy photos of Stan Musial, Ralph Kiner, Ted Williams, and my favorite—an autographed picture of Joe Garagiola. I kept scrapbooks for both
boxing and wrestling. I subscribed to *Ring Magazine* and cut out pictures
of Marcel Cerdan, Joe Louis, Sugar Ray Robinson, Willie Pep, Kid Gavilán,
and a host of others.

The basketball hoop in my backyard was a focal point for my secret
Walter Mitty life. It was fantasyland. I practiced shooting between my
own running commentary. "Here we are, folks, at Madison Square Garden.
The finals of the NIT. It's Holy Cross versus Duquesne. Si Green drives
into the lane—he shoots! He scores!"

Daydreams and nightdreams were a thrilling reverie visited by my idols
of the sports world. I even had a vivid dream of playing golf with Arnold
Palmer. In my wallet I carried a picture of my favorite movie star, Alan Ladd.
Every Saturday afternoon I went to the double-feature matinee to watch the
latest offerings of Humphrey Bogart, Boris Karloff, Richard Widmark, Errol
Flynn, Tyrone Power, and Douglas Fairbanks Jr. But none matched the glorious
roles of Alan Ladd in *Shane* and *Whispering Smith*. Not even Van Johnson in
all his wartime romances with June Allyson could compare with Alan Ladd.

My greatest hero was fictional. He was a super sports star created by
Clair Bee. His name was Chip Hilton. Chip Hilton was Bob Cousy, Stan
Musial, and Glenn Davis all rolled into one. He could do more things by
himself than Frank and Joe Hardy could do together.

But I became a man. Somewhere along the way the scrapbooks got lost. The glossy photos ended in the trashcan. Alan Ladd died and Van Johnson was consigned to doing bit parts on TV dramas. In 1956 I moved away from my childhood home and from fantasyland. The house is still there. So is the basketball hoop. I checked. Does anyone still read Chip Hilton? I don't know.

The only difference between men and boys is found in the price of their toys. Not so. The other difference is in the names of their heroes. As we grow older our heroes change, but we don't stop having them. Enter into my home today and it will not take long for you to see who my heroes are now. You can't miss the portraits of Martin Luther, Stonewall Jackson, and Robert E. Lee. You'll see the fading photographs of my father and my grandfather. You'll see the collection of Augustine, Aquinas, and Edwards. You'll hear me speak of Gerstner.

Enter my office and these names will be quickly apparent—a bit incongruous, perhaps, next to the framed portrait of Arnold Palmer.

Strange, isn't it? We need models. We need leaders who inspire us, real people of flesh and blood who embody character traits we admire. For in that admiration and inspiration comes emulation. I know that I shall never be Martin Luther. God and all my golf teachers know I'll never be Arnold Palmer. I cannot be these men. But I can try to be like them. I can imitate their courage. I can be strengthened by their example.

A naive sort of piety suggests that having heroes of fallen men is a kind of idolatry. We call it "hero-worship" and speak of it with spiritual disdain. Baloney! None is more spiritual than the Holy Spirit Himself. Yet it pleased the Holy Spirit to commend people to us as models of the heroic.

Though the "cloud of witnesses" cited in Hebrews 11 is a list of heroes and heroines, they are, nevertheless, people of real flesh and blood whose lives are set forth for us in sacred Scripture. Their portraits are painted there for us, warts and all. We even find something praiseworthy, something worth emulating in the life of the harlot Rahab.

Let us never grow up so far that we can no longer look up.

AN AFFAIR OF THE HEART

JUNE 1985

———

T HE BIBLE HAS MUCH TO say about the heart. In Scripture, the heart refers not so much to an organ that pumps blood throughout the body as it does to the core of the soul, the deepest seat of human affections. It is out of the heart that flow the issues of life.

Jesus saw a close connection between the location of our treasures and the drive of our hearts. Find a man's treasure map and you have found the highway of his heart.

In our fallen condition, the heart is seen as the root of our problem. We are said to have "a heart of stone." I remember two songs from my teenage years that lamented this fact of human nature. One was called "Hearts of Stone" and the other, a Dixieland jazz piece, entitled "Hard-Hearted Hannah, the Vamp of Savannah."

Hardened hearts, of course, are not limited to vamps, nor are they only found in Georgia. They are found in the breasts of fallen creatures everywhere who have no affection for God. The stony heart is calcified. It is like an inert rock. It has no passion for God, no affection for Christ, no love for His Word. The hardened heart knows nothing of a longing for the things of God.

When Jesus told Nicodemus that it was necessary for him to be reborn in order to enter the Kingdom of God, He was telling him that he had heart trouble. Nicodemus had a congenital heart defect—a condition of sclerosis of the heart with which he was born.

We are all born with the same malady. Love for God and affection for Christ are not natural to us.

Before we can love God, something must happen to us. Our hearts of stone must be changed into hearts of flesh, hearts that pulsate with new life and new affection for God. When one speaks of being "born again," he is speaking of this change of heart.

When God quickens us from spiritual death, when He regenerates us by His Holy Spirit, He does radical surgery on our hearts. He turns the stone into living tissue. To be converted is to gain a *new disposition*, a *new inclination*, a *new bent* to our hearts. Where formerly we were hostile, cold, or indifferent to God, now we are warmly attracted to Him.

To be a Christian is to be a new person. We have undergone a transformation that is rooted in the heart. Our new affection, however, must be made to grow. We are called to love God with our whole heart. The new heart of flesh must be nurtured. It must be fed by the Word of God. If we neglect our new heart, it too can undergo a kind of hardening. It will not revert once more to a total heart of stone, but it can get a bit leathery.

The new heart is the creation of the Holy Spirit. That same Holy Spirit is working within us to yield His fruit. As our hearts are more inclined to God, so the fruit of His Spirit is multiplied in our lives. Unregenerate people can perform external acts of righteousness, but no man with a heart of stone can yield the authentic fruit of the Spirit. When we examine the biblical fruit of the Spirit, we see that the accent of true Christian virtue is on those things that flow from the central disposition of our hearts. From whence cometh peace, or patience, or kindness, or gentleness, or longsuffering? These flow from the posture of the heart.

Our sanctification is a matter of the heart. It is an affair of the heart. It is a process that flows from intimate fellowship with God. The more we know of God, the greater is our capacity to love Him. The more we love Him, the greater is our capacity to obey Him. Jesus summarized the matter by showing the link between love and law: "If you love Me, keep My commandments."

"YOU *OUGHT.*"
"YOU *SHOULD.*"
"SEZ WHO?"

AUGUST 1985

———

I S THIS BRIEF BIT OF DIALOGUE FAMILIAR? Words like "ought" and "should" play a major role in our daily vocabulary. They are used so often that they don't seem very scary. But they are loaded terms.

The word "ought" conveys some sort of obligation. "Ought" communicates duty. It suggests a requirement.

Ethics is concerned with "oughtness." It seeks to provide a rationale for why we are required to do certain things and refrain from doing other things. It seeks a reason for behavior. It answers the question, "Why should I?"

All of us feel the pressures of obligation. We all struggle with requirements we don't enjoy and many we don't agree with. Life can be enriched or impoverished by requirements. Duty can be liberating or it can be oppressive. We feel the crunch of the collision between "I want to" and "I ought to."

Requirements that impose obligations upon us are an important element of our daily lives. The government passes laws, parents impose rules, schools have requirements, and business has its regulations. Some of these requirements are just; many are unjust.

We live in a society with a mixed bag of rules. They are created by social forces, cultural customs, lobby group legislation, the biases of authorities, and by a host of other sources. We are bombarded with "oughts," and confronted with the deadly danger of guilt without relief if we disobey.

As children we frequently challenge our parents with the key questions of ethics, "Why should I?" As parents our frustration with the endless "Why?" questions of our children lead us to the final answer

"Because I said so." Children learn quickly that it isn't very wise to keep asking "Why?"

Maybe that has something to do with our penchant as adults to accept laws and regulations, customs and taboos, uncritically.

Try an experiment on any contemporary issue. Keep asking "why" until the very question forces you to think more deeply. Let's do the exercise with the abortion issue.

Q: "Why should abortion-on-demand be legal?"

A: "Because a woman has a right to her own body?"

Q: "Why does she have the right to her own body?"

A: "Because it is hers?"

Q: "Why does that give her the right to destroy a part of it or a growing fetus?"

A: "Because she doesn't want to have a baby."

Q: "Why does that give her the right to abort?"

A: "Because she is entitled to happiness."

Q: "Why?"

A: "Because she wants to be happy?"

Q: "Why is it right to be able to do what she wants if what she wants is not right?"

A: "You're confusing me."

Q: "We were speaking about 'rights' and you changed the discussion to 'wants.' Why?"

A: "Why not?"

Q: "Because we are talking about ethics. We are talking about what we ought to do, not about what we want to do. Why is there a difference?"

A: "I suppose because we don't always want to do what is right."

Q: "Why should we do what is right?"

A: "Because it's right."

Q: "Sez who?"

A: "Sez God."

Q: "Why should we do what God says?"

A: "Because God has authority over us. He has the right to bind our conscience."

Q: "Why?"

A: "Because He created us and because He is the absolute standard of righteousness. He is holy."

Q: "Why are we talking about theology now?"

A: "Because all ethical issues drive us there if we are thinking."

Try the same experiment with any ethical issue. What about tax reform? Prayer in public schools? Nuclear war? Capital punishment?

Do we decide these issues on the basis of preference or principle? Do we have a solid reason for ever saying "ought" or "should"? Who has the right to impose obligations upon anyone? Who has the right to limit or restrict human freedom?

These are the root issues of ethics. Apart from theology they become exercises in personal preferences. Dostoevsky was correct; "If there is no God, all things are permissible."

REGENERATION PRECEDES FAITH

OCTOBER 1985

———

T HERE ARE POIGNANT MOMENTS IN EVERYONE'S spiritual pilgrimage, moments of encounter with the closeness of God, moments of painful conviction of sin with salty remorse added to them, Many of my most pregnant moments have come while fixing my mind upon a passage of scripture. There have been times when the text has made a vigorous attack upon me, sinking its teeth into my soul. Such moments when the Author of sacred writ grips me so tenaciously are difficult to forget.

I remember my virgin reading of the Bible. I was intoxicated with the newness of discovery, infatuated with my first spiritual love. I fell upon the text like a ravenous beast upon its wounded prey. For two weeks, a fortnight of hermitage, I did little else than race through the pages from Genesis to Revelation.

I loved it all. Even the obscurities of Numbers and Leviticus, and the bizarre symbols of Daniel and Ezekiel. There was much I did not understand, but I raced to the finish line anyway. It was in the Gospel of John that my first poignant moment hit. It landed like a blue bolt of lightning, silent for a split second before the thunderclap boomed. I had never read this particular text before. I had never heard of Jimmy Carter or Charles Colson. No one in my life had ever mentioned being born again. But there it was, in John's gospel, chapter three: "Unless a man is born anew he cannot enter the kingdom of God."

When I read these words I wanted to jump up and shout with Archimedes, "Eureka, I have found it." I was annoyed with the muddle-headedness of Nicodemus who failed to grasp these words of Jesus. I wanted to shout through the ages, back into time, into the ears of Nicodemus: "I know what He means; it happened to me."

One year later, as a college sophomore, I signed up for a course in the Gospel of John. Shortly after the course began the professor underwent emergency surgery and was out of the classroom for six weeks. A long-retired professor, Dr. John Orr, was pressed into service for the interim. He was in his eighties but was still keen of mind. His first exam was on the third chapter of John. Never before or since did I enter an exam with more confidence than that one. If I knew anything about anything, I was sure I knew John 3.

My stomach sank in dismal shame when I received my exam paper back. The grade was C-. The venerable professor wrote a kindly note on my test paper and gently suggested that I did not understand the doctrine of regeneration. Then he added the words, "Regeneration precedes faith."

I did not grasp the full import of that statement until I sat in a seminary classroom taught by John Gerstner. He wrote on the board in bold letters: REGENERATION PRECEDES FAITH. Suddenly I remembered having seen that phrase before. This time I listened carefully and was guided through the content of the book of Romans in a way that changed my thinking and my life.

I did not know until I read the interview with Dr. Gerstner that appears in this issue of *Tabletalk*, that decades before Dr. Orr scribbled those words on my test, he had written them on the board for a class that included Dr. Gerstner. What Dr. Gerstner grasped immediately took me years to understand. Without Dr. Gerstner's prodding me with Romans I probably would still be deluding myself with an improper understanding of my own conversion. My goal for this essay is to entice you to read the enclosed interview with Dr. Gerstner. It is vintage Gerstner, candid Gerstner, rhapsodic Gerstner as he rehearses his own pilgrimage with Paul's magnum opus, the book of Romans. Read that interview with rapt attention. Listen with straining ears. Then devour the book behind the rhapsody.

WHO WILL SPEAK TO MY HUSBAND?

FEBRUARY 1986

———

"**W**IVES, SUBMIT YOURSELVES TO YOUR HUSBANDS"—this Biblical admonition is one of the most abused exhortations of Scripture. It is abused on two sides, twisted and distorted beyond recognition by both parties in the dispute.

On the one hand, feminists frantically seek to escape the clear teaching of the Apostle on the matter of headship in the home. They enlist the aid of theologians and New Testament teachers who commit exegetical acts of despair to neutralize a Biblical mandate—all in a good cause. To stop the apparently incessant acts of domestic tyranny committed by arrogant husbands, these exegetes turn the Bible into a nose of wax to be shaped to conform to the latest wind of public opinion.

Wifely subordination to her husband is not a popular viewpoint to espouse these days. The fierce militantism of liberated women gives pause to the man who dares to interpret these injunctions in traditional fashion. What kind of ministry can one have if he alienates 50% of the population on an issue like this?

But enough of this feminist distortion. It will pass. It is the other side that frightens me. Those with a zeal for Biblical orthodoxy can also twist these admonitions to wives into destructive orders. Consider the popularity of the view that is epidemic in the evangelical world today that declares women should *always* obey their husbands in *everything*. This simplistic application of the exhortation ignores other Biblical principles by which we are called to obey God rather than men.

When controversy rages over the issue of wives' submission, men who speak to the issue are a bit suspect. We have a vested interest in this debate. I'd rather hear what Elisabeth Elliot has to say about it.*

Recently a woman said to me, "I know what the Bible says about wives being submissive. But who will talk to my husband about his responsibility?"

Hear this woman's plea. She speaks for thousands and tens of thousands of Christian wives. It is almost impossible these days for a Christian wife to be unaware of what the Bible says about submission. The wives all know it and, to make matters worse, their husbands know it too. The problem is that men don't know and/or don't care to know what God commands of them.

Here is the bad news, men. "Husbands, love your wives."

Why is this mandate not the center of controversy? Why don't we find endless articles about what loving our wives means? Why don't we see essays that speak of "mutual love"? This mandate has not become a hotly contested issue because husbands systematically ignore it. Who will speak to the husbands?

I don't know who *will* speak to the husbands. I do know who *has* spoken to the husbands.

God has spoken. God has laid down a law. That law is clear and inescapable. The law states: "Husbands, love your wives" (Eph. 5:25). How are we to love our wives? Let me count the ways, Elizabeth Barrett Browning to the contrary. Scripture lists basically one way we are to love our wives: AS CHRIST LOVED THE CHURCH AND GAVE HIMSELF UP FOR HER.

No wonder men want to focus on the wives' responsibility in marriage. Our responsibility is to love our wives in a sacrificial way, in a way that demonstrates we are ready to lay down our lives for them.

Christ is the head of the church. The church is not the head of Christ. The church is to submit to Christ; Christ is not subordinate to His bride. Yet Jesus has never tyrannized the church. The bride of Christ has never received a black eye from the brutal fists of her husband.

If husbands loved their wives as Christ loves His church, the question of wifely submission would never be an issue. There would be no need

---

* Elisabeth Elliot (1926–2015) was an American Christian missionary, author, and speaker. Her husband, Jim Elliot, was killed in 1956 by members of the Huaorani tribe of Ecuador; Elisabeth later spent two years as a missionary among the tribe.

for women's liberation. What Godly woman would ever feel demeaned if she were called to be submissive to Christ? If Christ were her husband, would she ever need to hoist a picket sign to denounce Him?

If I am called to love my wife as Christ loves the church, that is my responsibility before God. It would be easier for me to concentrate on my wife's responsibility. Everybody else seems to be more interested in the woman's responsibility. Why can't I be also? But then, who would speak to the husbands?

"Our responsibility is to love our wives in a sacrificial way, in a way that demonstrates we are ready to lay down our lives for them."

NO SECRET CODE

JUNE 1986

——

HERE IS A RIDDLE: WHAT IS YELLOW and sleeps seven? The answer? A Penndot truck. If you got this riddle or were able to chuckle with it, chances are you live in Pennsylvania. People from Colorado are probably saying, "A Penndot truck? What in the world is a Penndot truck?" A Penndot truck is a truck that belongs to the Pennsylvania Department of Transportation. These trucks may be seen along the highway in convenient spots for roadcrews to lean on them while they are resting from their labor. The trucks are yellow.

To get the point of the riddle a person has to have inside information. They had to know the meaning of the word "Penndot." The term Penndot is a word that combines an abbreviation with an acrostic. For strangers to Pennsylvania it seems as if the riddle was in some kind of secret code. Unless you know the code you can't decipher the riddle.

This is how some people approach the Bible. People say to me frequently, "I don't read the Bible as I should because I just can't understand it." There may be some truth in these words. There are parts of the Bible that are indeed difficult to understand. Some sections appear so cryptic that they frighten us. However, I suspect that the words I quoted above are more of a smokescreen than a true statement of the fact. They are a kind of code of their own. To say, "I don't read the Bible as I should because I just can't understand it," may be an encoded form of a slightly different statement. What is really being said is, "I don't understand the Bible as I should because I just don't read it."

The more we read the Bible the easier it becomes to understand. As we become familiar with its language, its style, its geography, its historical setting, and its characters, the easier it is to understand it. There are riddles in the Bible but they are exceedingly few and far between. The Bible is not written in some esoteric code. It is a written document that is set before us just like any other written document. There is only one chief difference between the Bible and other written documents. The ultimate author of the Bible is God. It is His book. He is its source. The information found in it reflects His wisdom, His understanding.

One does not have to live in Pennsylvania to be able to understand the Bible. If we can understand a daily newspaper we can understand the Bible. Of course there are rules for understanding the Bible. There is a science called hermeneutics that focuses on the rules for interpreting the Bible. Such a big word as hermeneutics is scary enough to make anyone think they had better not try to understand the Bible for themselves.

The basic rules of hermeneutics, however, are not so frightening. The first and most essential rule of interpreting the Bible is this: The Bible should be read like any other book. Some who read this rule may choke in apoplexy. Am I ripping the Bible down from the sky and throwing it on the low level of every other book? In one sense, yes. There are no special heavenly rules by which we interpret Scripture. When God speaks He doesn't turn a noun into a verb or an indicative into an imperative. The Word of God uses the same forms of language, the same grammar, the same vocabulary words, the same syntax as the daily paper. There is no magic. God speaks to us in words, in sentences, and in paragraphs. The message of those words is of eternal significance. The message is worth hearing. It is worth studying. It is far more vital than anything you will ever read in a newspaper. What is in the text of Scripture is more important to you than your own birth announcement or your own obituary.

If you *will* read the Bible, you *can*. We need not be frightened by the Scriptures. If we keep at it ... if we refuse to give up our effort to lay hold of the Word of God ... we can achieve a breakthrough into a new delight to His truth.

SIGHT FOR THE BLIND

OCTOBER 1986

A T A RECENT CONFERENCE, A WOMAN related a story to me that she insisted was true. She told of a little girl whose mother was punctilious about two matters, religion and cleanliness. The mother drilled the little girl about the Bible and constantly made her wash her hands and face.

One day the little girl came in the house after playing outside. Immediately her mother said, "Hurry and wash your hands!" The girl responded with a child-like defiance. Putting her hands on her hips she stared at her mother and said, "Jesus and germs, Jesus and germs. That's all you ever talk about and I've never seen either one!" The Jesus we believe in was once visible. He walked the earth clothed in skin. His life was a blaze of visible glory. The record of His life is one of the most documented of history. But we see Him no more. He is no longer visible. Yet we believe in Him.

Belief in Jesus is called *faith* in the New Testament. But the New Testament also defines faith as the "substance of things hoped for, the evidence of things not seen" (Heb. 11:1).

If faith involves the evidence of things *not seen*, does it not follow that true faith is blind faith? We are told by countless preachers that faith is blind, that true faith is something we have that rests upon no visible evidence. In fact visible evidence is seen as the opposite of faith.

This is a serious distortion of Biblical faith. Biblical faith is not blind. It involves both a visible and an invisible element. The *foundation* of faith is based on the visible. The invisible God is revealed in His visible creation (Rom. 1). We receive the witness of Scripture to the visible acts of Christ. But there is also an invisible element. We cannot see the future. We can see where we are right now, but none of us has foresight. We cannot see tomorrow. We trust tomorrow because we trust the God who is Lord of tomorrow.

When Hebrews says faith is the *substance* of things hoped for, it means that by trusting God for tomorrow we have a hope that is based on substance. Our hope is not based on fantasy. We are not like the child who closes her eyes, takes a deep breath, and wishes for future magic. Christianity goes far beyond *Alice in Wonderland.* The invisible is guaranteed by the visible. The history of God's past actions is the solid evidence for our confidence in His promises for the future.

Faith is the evidence of things not seen. I have not seen heaven, but the visible Jesus who appeared visibly in resurrection, promises that heaven is real. By trusting what the disciples saw, we have confidence in what we do not see.

A blind man believes in sunsets not because he has seen one but because he trusts the testimony of people who have seen one. If no one had ever seen a sunset there would be no reason to believe in them.

Jesus, in the visible incarnation and resurrection, gives substance to our faith. He is the supreme evidence of things not seen. The Bible calls us not to blind faith but to a faith that responds to Jesus with eyes wide open.

"Virtually every Christian denomination has some doctrine of predestination. The reason for that is clear: Predestination is a Biblical concept."

—

PREDESTINATION: A SOLEMN WARNING

DECEMBER 1986

———

" **T**HE SUBJECT OF PREDESTINATION, WHICH IN** itself is attended with considerable difficulty, is rendered very perplexing, and hence perilous by human curiosity."

This sober caveat was penned centuries ago by John Calvin, whose name is constantly linked with the doctrine of predestination. Calvin was alarmed by any treatment of this doctrine that was cavalier. Calvin himself gave relatively little space to the doctrine in his famous *Institutes of the Christian Religion*. He said little or nothing of the matter that was not already forcibly set forth by Augustine and Luther.

Calvin insisted that the doctrine of predestination allowed no room for extra-Biblical speculation. He insisted that a study of it be focused on what the Bible says. He wrote further this admonition:

> For it will show us that the moment we go beyond the bounds of the Word we are out of the course, in darkness, and must every now and then stumble, go astray, and fall. Let it, therefore, be our first principle that to desire any other knowledge of predestination than that which is expounded by the word of God, is no less infatuated than to walk where there is no path, or to seek light in darkness.

To treat predestination rashly is as foolish as it is perilous. On the other hand our desire for circumspect study may lead us to the other extreme of neglecting the whole counsel of God. We can err by avoiding the matter altogether, which God has set forth for our instruction.

Virtually every Christian denomination has some doctrine of predestination. The reason for that is clear: Predestination is a Biblical concept. It is a Biblical word. It was not invented by Calvin or Luther. It comes from the pen of the Apostle Paul. It pleased God to include the doctrine in sacred Scripture. To avoid it altogether is to do violence to the Holy Spirit.

The issue for us is not will we have a doctrine of predestination, but what will our doctrine of predestination look like? We must be careful that in our attempts to explain this difficult doctrine we not end up, as so many do, explaining it away. I have seen many doctrines of predestination that have no predestination in it. Attempts to reduce predestination to mere foreknowledge or prescience are cases in point.

We study this doctrine not to boast of profound knowledge or to flaunt theological expertise. We study it to discover the answer to the question, "What has God wrought?"

Let us hear Calvin once more:

> We shall never feel persuaded as we ought that our salvation flows from the free mercy of God as its fountain, until we are made acquainted with his eternal election . . . It is plain how greatly ignorance of this principle detracts from the glory of God, and impairs true humility.

True humility is what is required if we are to discover the depths and riches of God's grace. A fresh and deeper understanding of grace is the reward offered to those who humbly and diligently seek to understand what the Bible teaches about predestination.

Recently a mature Christian leader told me that in this past year he has made a serious study of predestination. He said two things that are noteworthy. "I never really understood grace before. Now I see predestination in almost every page of Scripture." I am convinced the man is merely seeing what has been there all along.

Humility should drive us to a deeper study of grace. Grace is not properly grasped until we understand that salvation is of the Lord.

"R.C. Sproul was a rare theologian who explained the deepest of subjects in the simplest of terms, and he did so in a way that grabbed people's attention and interest. His gifts shine in the column he regularly wrote, Right Now Counts Forever. On subjects from sports to politics to sexuality, and of course, the life of the church, Sproul's wisdom and wit show us how the truth of God's Word illuminates and transforms all of life."

—Dr. Joel R. Beeke
President and professor of systematic theology and homiletics
Puritan Reformed Theological Seminary
Grand Rapids, Mich.

"R.C. Sproul's legacy is vast, including visual, audio, and print resources stimulating countless believers worldwide. Now, Ligonier has added to it with this thrilling thesaurus, gathered from more than forty years of his monthly contributions to *Tabletalk*. In the early years, he shared his spiritual perception of current affairs, including politics, economics, inflation, the newest A-list books and 'the American dream'; it was as if he had all of these in one hand and his Bible in the other. In the later years, he was more immediately concerned with theological and doctrinal truths. His exposition and application of biblical revelation on subjects such as the doctrine of God, Christology, Jesus' substitutionary death, atonement, the true nature of sin and the new birth, theodicy, the measure and manner of God's forgiveness, conscience, Christian liberty, and scores of other subjects are brilliantly handled.

"I do have a quibble. At one point he wrote, 'There is nothing in my thought that hasn't been said before far more eloquently than I can ever hope to articulate'—commendably modest, but thankfully untrue."

—Dr. John Blanchard
Preacher, teacher, apologist, and author
Banstead, England

"You hold in your hand a veritable gold mine of Christian truth. Flowing from the pen of Dr. R.C. Sproul, here is his work of more than forty

years writing his monthly column Right Now Counts Forever in *Tabletalk* magazine. Dr. Sproul was arguably the greatest teacher of theology in our generation. He was also a lucid and cogent writer, able to take profound truth and make it accessible to everyday readers. This book will take you to the heights of heaven as Dr. Sproul addresses a wide breadth of issues and topics. Though now seated in a cloud of witnesses above, Dr. Sproul continues to instruct us in the vital essentials of Christian living. This book should be required reading for every believer."

—Dr. Steven J. Lawson
President, OnePassion Ministries
Dallas

"This collection of columns from four decades offers a treasure trove of timeless reflection on the timely. Dr. Sproul tackles football, commercials, ethical issues, best-selling books, politics, and philosophy—and that's merely the first year of columns alone. You will find wit and humor, always accompanied by deep and faithful theological and biblical reflection. Here you will find wisdom that never goes out of style."

—Dr. Stephen J. Nichols
President, Reformation Bible College
Chief academic officer, Ligonier Ministries

"Spanning more than forty years, Dr. Sproul's prophetic insights on a wide range of ethical and theological issues provide a fascinating historical narrative of cultural change, both in society at large and, sadly, the evangelical church, as well as a breathtakingly clear Christian (biblical) response. Cultural attitudes may have changed as the effects of postmodernity took hold in the late twentieth century, but it is clear from these pages that the Bible is sufficient to address each one. I will be consulting this volume often as issues arise for which I need a clear biblical response."

—Dr. Derek W.H. Thomas
Senior minister, First Presbyterian Church
Columbia, S.C.

Right Now Counts Forever

R.C. SPROUL

RIGHT
NOW
COUNTS
FOREVER

Volume II: 1987–1996

 LIGONIER MINISTRIES

Right Now Counts Forever, Volume II: 1987–1996
© 2021 by the R.C. Sproul Trust

Published by Ligonier Ministries
421 Ligonier Court, Sanford, FL 32771
Ligonier.org

Printed in China
RR Donnelley
0000321
First printing

ISBN 978-1-64289-308-3 (Hardcover)
ISBN 978-1-64289-309-0 (ePub)
ISBN 978-1-64289-310-6 (Kindle)

Cover design: Metaleap Creative
Interior typeset: Katherine Lloyd, The DESK

Ligonier Ministries edited and adapted Dr. R.C. Sproul's original text to create this volume. We are thankful to Mrs. Vesta Sproul for her invaluable help on this project.

Bible quotations are the author's translation or are taken from one of the following versions:

The ESV® Bible (The Holy Bible, English Standard Version®), copyright © 2001 by Crossway, a publishing ministry of Good News Publishers. Used by permission. All rights reserved.

The New American Standard Bible® (NASB), Copyright © 1960, 1962, 1963, 1968, 1971, 1972, 1973, 1975, 1977, 1995 by The Lockman Foundation. Used by permission. www.Lockman.org

The New King James Version®. Copyright © 1982 by Thomas Nelson. Used by permission. All rights reserved.

The Holy Bible, New International Version®, NIV®. Copyright © 1973, 1978, 1984, 2011 by Biblica, Inc.™ Used by permission of Zondervan. All rights reserved worldwide. www.zondervan.com The "NIV" and "New International Version" are trademarks registered in the United States Patent and Trademark Office by Biblica, Inc.™

The King James Version. Public domain.

Cataloging-in-Publication Data is available from the Library of Congress
LCCN 2020038106 (print) | LCCN 2020038107 (ebook)
LC record available at https://lccn.loc.gov/2020038106
LC ebook record available at https://lccn.loc.gov/2020038107

CONTENTS

THE PRESENCE OF
THE INVISIBLE GOD

FEBRUARY 1987

———

W E SPEAK OF GOD AS THE IMMORTAL, Invisible, Only-Wise God. This string of attributes gives some comfort and no small amount of dismay. That God is immortal makes me glad. It means simply that He cannot and therefore will never die. I need not worry that He will ever wear out or be replaced. His throne is established forever. He reigns eternally in His omnipotence. That is good news for a perishing humanity. I rejoice also that He is All-Wise. This sets Him apart from every man. It was Aristotle who taught that in the brain of every wise man could be found the corner of the fool. There is no foolish corner in the mind of God. I find solace in the certain truth that the One who rules the affairs of the universe is not given to blunders or lapses into incompetency.

I rejoice in God's wisdom and in His everlasting power. It is His persistent invisibility that saddens me.

It is difficult for sensual creatures to enjoy fellowship with One who cannot be seen, heard, tasted, touched, or smelled. God remains beyond my senses. How then, can I ever relate to Him with intimacy? My heart longs for fellowship with Him. I long to hear His voice as the sound of many waters and to catch one glimpse of His refulgent glory.

As a college student I took a course in classical hymnology. Our professor was a sophisticated sort who ridiculed the maudlin hymns that have crept into popular usage. We shared his cynicism toward such songs as "In the Garden" with lyrics like "He walks with me and He talks with me, and He tells me I am His own."

Such verse seems tawdry. But I cannot deny that in the simplest of terms they express the longing of my heart. Oh, to walk with Him, and to talk

1

with Him. I would crawl over glass to hear audible words from heaven saying to me, "R.C., you are my own."

Is there any one of us who claims Jesus as Lord whose heart does not beat with a passion to hear the voice of God? Who wouldn't sell every possession to be able to walk in a garden alone with Jesus?

The disciples walking the road to Emmaus twenty centuries ago had this experience. He concealed His identity so that they didn't recognize the "stranger" at their side. These men were not in a garden. There were no roses covered with dew. But they walked and talked with the risen Christ. What was their experience like? When their eyes were finally opened and they recognized Jesus. He suddenly vanished. Here is their "on the scene" reaction: "And they said to one another, 'Were not our hearts burning within us while He was speaking to us on the road, while He was explaining the Scriptures to us?' " (Luke 24:32).

That is the normal human reaction to the immediate presence of Christ— "Hearts burning within us." My heart would be scorched to a cinder if I could hear His voice. My soul would explode in joy if I could walk with Him and talk with Him. I would travel the world to find a garden where He was visibly present.

But the truth is that I can't see God. I can't even see His shadow. He leaves no footprints in the sand, no fingerprints on the doorknob, no lingering aroma of aftershave in the breeze. He is invisible because He is immaterial.

That God is invisible confounds me. We human beings are sensual creatures. We respond to what we can see, hear, and touch. Like Thomas, the Doubting One, we long to place our fingers into Jesus' wounds and verify with our senses that it is really He.

I have often wondered how different my life would be if I could see the invisible God. It is hard to love and to serve someone my eyes have never seen. Unfortunately, the axiom "Out of sight, out of mind" seems to be painfully true with our faith.

What I crave is a relationship with God that is both intimate and personal. The great barrier to intimacy is God's invisibility. Because I cannot see Him, I tend to doubt His presence. But He is there and promises communion and fellowship with Him. The tool He provides to overcome the barrier is the tool of prayer.

Prayer offers us a link to intimate fellowship with God. Here is where we find what the saints call "mystic sweet communion." One need not be a mystic to enjoy this sweet communion. Prayer is access to God. He hears what I say to Him in prayer. He responds. Not audibly or with a vision of Himself. But His response is real and encourages more prayer. The sweetness of prayer is found in adoration. When we move beyond speaking our requests or placing our petitions before Him, we enter into the vale of sweet communion. Here we penetrate the invisible and delight in the glory of His presence.

"To divide event revelation from propositional revelation is to leave us with a story without an interpretation."

—

THE CROSS:
A NAKED EVENT OR
A SUPERNATURAL ACT

APRIL 1987

———

WHAT REALLY HAPPENED ON THE CROSS? Was the death of Jesus a human tragedy whereby a good man was brutally and unfairly slain? Was His death an example of faith, obedience, and self-sacrifice? Was it a ransom paid to the devil? A victory over the devil? A manifestation of moral influence?

Was the cross an atonement? Did it involve expiation and propitiation for sin? Was it a supernatural act done to satisfy the wrath and justice of God? Each of these individually and several in combination have been set forth as the real meaning of Christ's death. How we understand the cross of Jesus in large part is determined by our view of the Bible. If we view the Bible as a primitive, pre-scientific expression of human religion, we will be inclined toward a purely natural view of the death of Jesus. It will represent at best an example of an heroic human act of self-sacrifice. Jesus is the existential hero of self-giving.

If we take the popular so-called neoorthodox view of Scripture, we will take a different approach to the cross. The neoorthodox view of the Bible denies that the Bible gives us *propositional revelation*. Rather, the Bible is seen as a witness to revelation that takes place in *events*.

To divide event revelation from propositional revelation is to leave us with a story without an interpretation. The Bible teaches that there was a *crucial* event, an event of the cross. Jesus of Nazareth was crucified. The significance of that death was not agreed upon by those who were a party to it or spectators of it. For the Sanhedrin it was an act of expediency. It was necessary for Jesus to die, lest the Jews experience the wrath of the Romans. Likewise from Pilate's vantage point, it was a matter of expediency for him to satisfy the demand of a raging mob. The thief on the cross saw it as an expression of injustice.

The Apostle Paul wasn't even there. Yet he declared that this act was an act of cosmic and supernatural proportion.

This was a real drama of theological redemption. Here the curse of God's law was visited on a man who bore the sins of His people. For Paul the crucifixion was the pivot point of all history. Paul was not satisfied to give an account of the event. While affirming the historicity of the crucifixion Paul added the Apostolic *interpretation* of the meaning of the event. He set forth *propositions* about the death of Christ. The issue before the Church is this: Is the Apostolic propositional interpretation of the cross correct or not? Is Paul's view merely a first century Jewish scholar's speculation on the matter or is it a view inspired by God Himself?

What difference does it make? This is not a trifling matter of a pedantic point of Christian doctrine. Here nothing less than salvation is at stake. *To reject the biblical view of atonement is to reject the Atonement itself. To reject the Atonement is to reject Christ. To reject Christ is to perish in your sin.*

Please let us not soften this with an appeasing dance. Let us be clear. Those teachers in the Church who deny that the death of Christ was a supernatural act of atonement are simply not Christians. They are enemies of Christ who trample Jesus underfoot and crucify Him afresh.

The only sound view of the death of Christ is the Apostolic view. The Bible gives us not only events, but a divine interpretation of those events.

Divine events. Divine interpretation. That is the revelation we trust for our salvation.

ONE HOLY PASSION

JUNE 1987

——

AN ANECDOTE SURVIVES ABOUT ALBERT EINSTEIN. He was once asked by a student, "Dr. Einstein, how many feet are there in a mile?" To the utter astonishment of the student, Einstein replied, "I don't know."

The student was sure the great professor was joking. Surely Einstein would know a simple fact that every schoolchild is required to memorize. But Einstein wasn't joking. When the student pressed for an explanation of this hiatus in Einstein's knowledge he declared, "I make it a rule not to clutter my mind with simple information that I can find in a book in five minutes."

Albert Einstein was not interested in trivial data. His passion was to explore the deep things of the universe. His passion for mathematical and physical truth made him a pivotal figure in modern world history.

We are called to a similar passion, a passion to know God. A thirst for the knowledge of God should drive us to drink deeply at the fountain of Scripture. We are equipped with more than enough unholy passions. Our appetites for lesser things at times threaten to consume us. Yet few of us are in danger of being consumed by a passion to know God. The Scripture says of Jesus that zeal for His Father's house consumed Him.

In His humanity Jesus was a man of passion. He was neither hostile nor indifferent toward the knowledge of His Father. He was a man driven in His pursuit of God.

I remember a stained glass window that adorned the library of my Alma Mater. It was situated above the stairwell at the second floor landing. In leaded letters the words in the window declared: *Knowledge Is Power*.

Every time I ascended or descended that staircase I cringed at those words. I did not like them. There was something arrogant about them. I could not deny that the words were true. Knowledge is power. But the lust for power is not a sound motivation to gain knowledge. The Bible is right: knowledge puffs up; love builds up.

Even the pursuit of the knowledge of God can become a snare of arrogance. Theology can become a game, a power game to see who can display the most erudition. When it is such a game it proceeds from an unholy passion.

A holy passion is a passion inflamed by a godly motive. To pursue the knowledge of God to further our understanding of Him and deepen our love for Him is to embark upon a quest that delights Him. Jesus encouraged such a pursuit: "If you abide in My word, you are My disciples indeed. And you shall know the truth, and the truth shall make you free" (John 8:31–32).

Jesus linked knowledge not with power, but with freedom. Knowing the truth is the most liberating power in the world. It is a liberating power. Not the power to dominate; not the power to impress: These are not the powers we seek. But the power to set free—to give true liberty—is tied to a knowledge of the truth.

We all want liberty. We want to be free of the chains that bind us. That liberty comes from knowing God. But the pursuit of that knowledge may not be casual. Jesus spoke of "abiding" in His Word. The pursuit of God is not a part-time, weekend exercise. If it is, chances are you will experience a part-time, weekend freedom. Abiding requires a kind of staying power. The pursuit is relentless. It hungers and thirsts. It pants as the deer after the mountain brook. It takes the Kingdom by storm, pressing with violence to get in.

It is a pursuit of passion. Indifference will not do. To abide in the Word is to hang on tenaciously. A weak grip will soon slip away. Discipleship with Jesus requires staying power. We sign up for the duration. We do not graduate until heaven. We gain earthly benefits of freedom. The eternal benefits are even greater. To know God is to have life, and to have it more abundantly.

LIFE UNDER THE SUN

AUGUST 1987

———

I N 1884 FRIEDRICH WILHELM NIETZSCHE published the third part of his most famous work, *Thus Spake Zarathustra* (*Also Sprach Zarathustra*). The third section embodies what Nietzsche considered the most important and fundamental thought of the book, the theme of "eternal recurrence."

The idea of eternal recurrence maintains that in infinite time there are periodic cycles in which all that has been is repeated over again. The drama of human life is a play with one encore after another.

At first glance eternal recurrence suggests a total pessimistic view of life. It is the pessimism of Schopenhauer that depicts life as tragic—it is terrible, mysterious, and fraught with peril. It is this worldview the book of Ecclesiastes struggles with where it seems that all is vanity and that there is nothing new under the sun.

Nietzsche looked to ancient Greece to see how people coped with a cyclical view of history. He saw two conflicting images at work, the images of Apollo and Dionysus. The style of Apollo is to look beyond this world for some kind of higher order that makes sense out of the apparent chaos of this world. It seeks the ideal of order and form. It covers the chaotic with systems of logic and beauty. Dionysus yields to the dark forces of life that rush in a turgid torrent of passion and impulse. Dionysus affirms and embraces life in all its horror without seeking an escape in some ideal world of form and unity.

Here is the role of Superman. He neither succumbs to suicide nor does he retreat into some sort of escapist religion. He sees the cycle as a test of his strength. It is a challenge to his courage to create his own values without a fanciful flight to God. It is what Nietzsche called an "active nihilism," a nihilism that will usher in the overthrow of Christianity.

Ecclesiastes chooses neither the courage of Apollo nor Dionysus. The issue is not how we cope with a cyclical movement of history but whether or not history is indeed merely cyclical. Underlying the book of Ecclesiastes is the Hebrew view of the world.

The primary thesis of the Hebrew view is that the world had a beginning. It was created by God. In this sense history resembles a line more than a circle. A circle has no beginning and no end. It merely turns round and round, going nowhere. A line has a starting point, a middle, and an end.

To be sure, the author of Ecclesiastes sees the appearance of cycles in this world. The sun does rise and set. The seasons do follow an annual cycle. But above all this stands a sovereign God who rules over time and space.

Nietzsche saw clearly that with the destruction of Christianity and its view of the world a spiritual crisis would emerge that would effect radical changes in culture. The first realization would be that there is no absolute truth. Science, ethics, politics, indeed life itself would succumb to a land of utilitarianism. Man's most essential drive is the Will to Power. Science is a result of man's quest to master his environment. Ethics are a result of individuals or groups seeking to justify their own preferences. Even logic is merely a myth man invents to master his environment by imposing order on chaos.

All knowledge functions as an instrument of power. The aim of knowledge depends upon the Will to Power—it involves an impulse to master an area of reality and bring it into one's service as a weapon of power. All truth is a fiction. Truth is merely a mythical interpretation of experience.

The Jesuit philosopher Frederick Copleston replies to Nietzsche by saying:

> The obvious comment on Nietzsche's general view of truth is that it presupposes the possibility of occupying an absolute standpoint from which the relativity of all truth or its fictional character can be asserted, and that this presupposition is at variance with the relativist interpretation of truth.

The author of Ecclesiastes takes us beyond relativism. It lifts us above the circle to the line that reveals an Alpha and Omega. He does this without a philosophy of escape but by grappling with the reality of human pain and frustration that is lived out "Under the Sun."

"Nietzsche saw that with the destruction of Christianity and its view of the world a spiritual crisis would emerge that would effect radical changes in culture."

WHAT'S THE BIG IDEA?

OCTOBER 1987

———

I REMEMBER MAMA. I REMEMBER MAMA standing in front of me, her hands poised on her hips, her eyes glaring with hot coals of fire and saying in stentorian tones, "Just what is the big idea, young man?"

Instinctively I knew my mother was not asking me an abstract question about theory. Her question was not a question at all, but a thinly veiled accusation. Her words were easily translated to mean, "Why are you doing what you are doing?" She was challenging me to justify my behavior with a valid idea. I had none.

Recently a friend asked me in all earnestness the same question. He asked, "What's the big idea of the Christian life?" He was interested in the overarching ultimate goal of the Christian life.

To answer his question I fell back on the theologian's prerogative and gave him a Latin term. I said, "The big idea of the Christian life is *Coram Deo*." *Coram Deo* captures the essence of the Christian life.

The phrase literally refers to something that takes place in the presence of, or before the face of God. To live *Coram Deo* is to live one's entire life in the presence of God, under the authority of God, to the glory of God.

In the Presence of God: To live in the presence of God is to understand that whatever we are doing and wherever we are doing it, we are acting under the gaze of God. That happens—indeed it always happens, whether or not we are *aware* of it. God is omnipresent. There is no place so remote that we can escape His penetrating gaze.

But God's presence is invisible. Because He is invisible we easily fall into the "out of sight, out of mind" trap. Imagine how our lives would change if we could see the face of Christ and feel His eyes upon us every moment of every day. This concept is behind the popular concept of spiritual growth that encourages us to "practice the presence of God." It involves a highly sensitized habit of what has been called "*God consciousness.*"

Under the Sovereignty of God: To be aware of the presence of God is also to be acutely aware of His Sovereignty. The uniform experience of the Saints is to recognize that if God is God, He is indeed Sovereign. When Saul was confronted by the refulgent glory of the risen Christ on the road to Damascus, his immediate question was, "Who is it, Lord?" He wasn't sure who it was who was speaking to him but he knew that whoever it was, was certainly Sovereign over him.

To the Glory of God: Living under divine sovereignty involves more than a reluctant submission to sheer sovereignty, motivated out of a fear of punishment. It involves recognizing that there is no higher goal than offering honor to God. Our lives are to be living sacrifices, oblations offered in a spirit of adoration and gratitude.

To live all of life *Coram Deo* is to live a life of integrity. It is a life of wholeness that finds its unity and coherency in the majesty of God. A fragmented life is a life of disintegration. It is marked by inconsistency, disharmony, confusion, conflict, contradiction, and chaos.

The Christian who compartmentalizes his life into two sections of the religious and the non-religious has failed to grasp the big idea. The big idea is that *All of Life Is Religious or None of It Is Religious*. To divide life between the religious and the nonreligious is itself a sacrilege.

This means that if a person fulfills his or her vocation as a steelmaker, attorney, or homemaker, *Coram Deo*, then that person is acting every bit as religiously as a soul-winning evangelist who fulfills his vocation. It means that David was as religious when he obeyed God's call to be a shepherd as he was when he was anointed with the special grace of kingship. It means that Jesus was every bit as religious when He worked in His father's carpenter shop as He was in the Garden of Gethsemane.

Integrity is found where men and women live their lives in a pattern of consistency. It is a pattern that functions the same basic way in church and out of church. It is a life that is open before God. It is a life in which all that is done is done as unto the Lord. It is a life lived by principle, not expediency; by humility before God, not defiance. It is a life lived under the tutelage of a conscience that is held captive by the Word of God.

Coram Deo: Before the face of God. That's the big idea. Next to this idea our other goals and ambitions become mere trifles.

"To live all of life *Coram Deo* is to live a life of integrity. It is a life of wholeness that finds its unity and coherency in the majesty of God."

THE COSMIC CHRIST

DECEMBER 1987

———

J OHN'S GOSPEL BEGINS WITH THE WORDS: "In the beginning was the Word..." That this opening line mirrors the first words of Genesis, "In the beginning," was no accident. A dramatic link is made here between creation and redemption.

Nothing preoccupied the minds of the theologians of the first three centuries more than John's use of the term *Logos* to refer to the pre-incarnate Christ. The concept of the *Logos* served as an enticing bridge between Christian theology and Greek philosophy.

The concept of the *Logos* was a loaded term in Greek philosophy. The ancient Greeks pursued in speculative fashion, the source of ultimate reality. They debated among themselves whether ultimate reality was singular or plural, physical (corporeal) or spiritual (incorporeal). They were searching for some overarching principle that would unify the vast diversity of experience by some ultimate power of coherency.

The concept of the *Logos* emerged as an abstract force or principle that gave coherency, order, and purpose to the nature of things.

Early Christian apologists jumped on this theme and saw a connection between the Greek concept of the unifying principle of the Logos and John's view of Christ. The New Testament speaks of Christ as the One in whom, by whom, and for whom all things were made. In this respect there is a remarkable parallel between the Greek concept and the Biblical one. But we would be mistaken to assume that John simply borrowed a Greek concept and dressed it in Christian garb. We must note the differences as well as the similarities between John's Logos and that of the Greeks. The differences are tied to the profound differences between Greek and Hebrew thought.

There is a great difference within Greek thought between Greek philosophy and Greek mythology, both of which differ from Hebrew thought.

For example, in Greek mythology God does not create the world; rather the world creates the gods. The order goes like this: The heavens and the earth beget the original Titans who in turn beget the Olympian gods such as Zeus, Hermes, Poseidon, and the rest. The mythological cosmogony would read like this: "In the beginning the heavens and the earth created the gods"—a radical difference from the Biblical view of the eternal primacy of God.

In Greek philosophy the Logos remains an impersonal force, a lifeless abstract philosophical concept that is a necessary postulate for the cause of order and purpose in the universe.

In Hebrew thought the Logos is *personal.* He indeed has the power of unity, coherence, and purpose, but the distinctive point is that the Biblical Logos is a He, not an it.

All attempts to translate the word "Logos" have suffered from some degree of inadequacy. No English word is able to capture the fullness of John's "Logos." Gordon Clark once suggested that we can use the word "logic." "In the beginning was logic, and logic was with God, and logic was God." Of course, Clark was not suggesting that the Logos was simply an abstraction for the rules of immediate inference or an impersonal principle of deduction. Rather he was pointing to the Logos as an integral and co-essential dimension of the rational character of the being of God.

Goethe's *Faust* also played with the concept of Logos by translating it first as "Feeling" and finally as "Act" or "Deed." This reflects in part a drift away from a concept of ultimate rationality in Western philosophy to put the accent either on will or action as seen in nineteenth century voluntarism and twentieth century existentialism. It reflects something of the anti-mind prejudice of modern society.

God's Logos does include action. The Logos is the Eternal-Word-in-Action. But it is no irrational action or sheer expression of feeling. It is the divine Actor, acting in creation and redemption in a coherent way who is announced in John's Gospel.

"The Word became flesh and dwelt among us" is the startling conclusion of John's prologue. The cosmic Christ enters our humanity. The birth of Jesus is the very center or core of human history. It is the supreme moment of visitation of the eternal with the temporal, the infinite with the finite, the unconditioned with the conditioned. It is the center point of the very meaning of human history. It is Christmas, the moment of nativity when the eternal God became flesh for our redemption.

THE IRONY OF
A CLOSED MIND

FEBRUARY 1988

E VERY NOW AND THEN A BOOK SKYROCKETS to the top of the bestselling lists, confounding all the marketing prognostications. For such a phenomenon to take place, the book must strike hard at an undetected raw nerve. This anomaly has occurred again with the recent success of Allan Bloom's *The Closing of the American Mind.*

Bloom has examined the American academic scene and has been bold to declare that the Emperor has no clothes. He dares to blow the whistle on a bankrupt system in which philosophical relativism has torn the guts out of any sober quest for truth.

Bloom, himself, is an educated man. He has spent too much time with Plato, Descartes, and Rousseau to be suckered into the contemporary abyss of intellectual anarchy that characterizes the university scene. He qualifies as a bona fide neo-gadfly to prick and prod at the thin veneer of cultural relativism.

Bloom introduces his study with these words:

> There is one thing a professor can be absolutely certain of: almost every student entering the university believes, or says he believes, that truth is relative . . . They are unified only in their relativism and in their allegiance to equality. And the two are related in a moral intention. The relativity of truth is not a theoretical insight but a moral Postulate, the condition of a free society, or so they see it. (p. 25)

The tragic irony that Bloom reveals is that the starting point assumptions with which the student enters the university are not challenged but reinforced by his "higher education." The student is inculcated with one overarching virtue: to be "open." "The purpose of their education is

not to make them scholars but to provide them with a moral virtue—
openness."

The irony of this openness is that when it is assumed to be based on
the presupposition of relativism, the student's mind is being slammed
shut against any hope of discovering truth.

Openness to truth where truth may be found is a long-standing traditional virtue which worked on the assumption that there is such a thing
as objective truth to which we should be open.

Now the mind is being systematically closed to truth as a possibility.
Truth, as well as morality, is and can only be reduced to sheer personal
preference in a relativistic system. This relativism eschews any form of
fixed objective values or truth. Its simplistic creed is that "there are no
absolutes" (except of course, the axiom that there are absolutely no absolutes). We can't even properly speak of a relativistic system because the
word "system" implies some sort of coherency.

Without objective standards of truth the student is left with feelings,
impressions, and intuitions which can never be judged as either false or
bad. The bottom line of such an approach is not merely ignorance and
skepticism but the ultimate dehumanization of persons. If everybody is
"right," nobody is right. If every viewpoint is equally valuable, no viewpoint is valuable.

The academic world is under siege. The quest for objective truth usually
requires conflict, debate, and controversy. The new *pax academia* disallows
such conflict. We are facing an academic Munich* where appeasement
with the forces of intellectual chaos is the order of the day.

Sadly, the church has a tendency to drift with the current of the secular academic world. Our own leadership "crosses the street" to gain their
academic credentials from prestigious universities. They often return
to the church with their faith intact, but carrying with them uncritical
assumptions gathered in the foreign land. Pretty soon the teaching in

---

* The Munich Agreement was a pact agreed to on September 30, 1938, by Nazi Germany,
the United Kingdom, France, and Italy. It allowed Germany to annex the Sudetenland
region of Czechoslovakia in an attempt to appease Adolf Hitler and prevent war.

Christian colleges, seminaries, and even pulpits begins to sound like an echo of the secular worldview.

We face twin enemies, both of which are deadly.

On the one hand, we are tempted to embrace the thought patterns of the secular world in order to be modern and relevant in our thinking. We are terrified of being perceived as being "out of it." On the other hand, we may be tempted to a new form of monastic isolationism, in which we surrender science, logic, and education to the secular world while we try to live by an empty, contentless faith on an island of religious feeling.

Either option ends at the cemetery with a morbid funeral service for Truth. A burial is a decent thing to do for a body that has been left where it was slain.

WHAT IS A BORN AGAIN CHRISTIAN?

APRIL 1988

————

I N THE CURRENCY OF CONTEMPORARY journalism we frequently see the descriptive phrase, "born again Christian." In strict terms this phrase is a redundancy. If a person is a Christian, he is born again; if he is born again, he is a Christian. There is no such thing as an unregenerate Christian.

To be sure, the term "Christian" has been subjected to a wide diversity of definitions, some of which are flat out contradictory. The word has been identified with "church member" or as I once read, with a "civilized person."

From a biblical perspective, however, we understand that it is possible to be a church member without necessarily being a Christian. The church is always a mixed body that includes both wheat and tares. It is possible to profess faith without having faith. It is possible to confess Christ without loving Christ. Jesus warned His contemporaries, "This people honors me with their lips while their hearts are far from me."

The phrase "born again Christian" arose when people wanted to distinguish themselves as those who had had some sort of conversion experience. Still the phrase "born again Christian" can be translated as a "Christian-Christian." It is a kind of theological stuttering, similar to Francis Schaeffer's famous dictum concerning "true truth."

We agree that the phrase "born again" Christian is a redundancy because Jesus declared that rebirth is a necessary prerequisite for entrance into His Kingdom. It is the *sine qua non* of redemption.

Jesus warned Nicodemus that "unless a man is born again he cannot see the Kingdom of God." He repeated the assertion by stating that rebirth is necessary to enter the Kingdom. In propositional terms, we can render Jesus' words as a conditional clause. Unless A takes place (rebirth) B cannot follow (see or enter the Kingdom). Therefore, we conclude that Jesus set forth regeneration as a *necessary condition*, or *requirement* for inclusion in His Kingdom.

Since regeneration is a necessary condition for redemption, it is imperative that we have some understanding of what it is. Prior to regeneration we are in such a fallen state that we are disinclined or undisposed to the things of God. We are spiritually dead. Our desires are not inclined toward Christ. We are bound in a state of moral inability toward God. We suffer under the bondage of sin, which Augustine described as the *non posse non peccare* (the inability to not sin).

To embrace Christ in faith we must first be "quickened" (Eph. 2) or "made alive" to the things of God. This quickening is accomplished by the work of the Holy Spirit. It is a supernatural, immediate, creative act of God that no man can accomplish in his own power.

Regeneration is the work of the Holy Spirit. It is a *monergistic* work. That is, the only power that is working in regeneration is the power of God. It is not a cooperative activity, not a joint venture between man and God.

To be sure there is much that is cooperative or *synergistic* in the Christian life. Our sanctification for example, is a joint enterprise between God and us. We must work out our salvation with fear and trembling, taking comfort that while we are endeavoring to progress in grace, God is at work within us to assist us in growth.

But there is a difference between birth and life. Growth, with all its cooperation, is a part of the Christian life. Regeneration, however, is related to *birth*. It has to do with the very *beginning* of Christian life. It is the starting point that rests upon the Divine Initiative. It is the Spirit who alone can resurrect our spiritually dead nature. We are as dependent on the Spirit of God to raise us from spiritual death, as Lazarus was dependent upon Christ for his physical resurrection.

Those whom the Spirit regenerates do in fact come alive. Regeneration is not unto potential spiritual life; it is into actual spiritual life. Those whom the Spirit regenerates come to Christ. All who are born again become Christians.

There are no born again non-Christians, just as there are no unregenerate Christians. The work of the Spirit applies the work of Christ to us, and applies us to the work of Christ. It is the divine and supernatural work that moves us from darkness to light, from spiritual death to spiritual life. It accomplishes what it intends. We are born again *into* eternal life. From quickening we move to faith. From faith we are justified. From justification we move to sanctification. From sanctification we move ultimately and inexorably to glorification, the final goal of the Christian life.

"There is no greater benefit to the king-elect's friends than that he ascends to the throne."

—

QUO VADIS?

———

I T WAS 3:00 A.M.—AMSTERDAM, 1965. I couldn't sleep. I was
pacing the floor of our apartment like a caged lion. My body was
more than ready for sleep, but my mind refused to shut down. That
day had been spent studying the doctrine of the ascension of Christ, the
climactic moment of His departure from this world. One statement of
Jesus gripped my mind in a vise. The statement was part of Jesus' farewell discourse to His disciples in the Upper Room. He said: "Nevertheless
I tell you the truth. It is to your advantage that I go away; for if I do not
go away, the Helper will not come to you; but if I depart, I will send Him
to you" (John 16:7).

I paced the floor mulling over this astonishing statement. How could
it possibly be better for the church to experience an absentee Lord? Part-
ing with loved ones is not a "sweet sorrow." One would think that to
part with the incarnate Jesus would be an utterly bitter sorrow, a total
dissolution to the soul.

Yet Jesus spoke of a certain "expediency" of His departure. The word
translated "advantage" or "expedient" in John 16 is the word *sumpherei*, the
same word employed by Caiaphas in his ironic "prophecy" (John 18:14).

The advantage of Jesus' departure from earth is found partially in answer
to Peter's earlier question: "Lord, where are you going?" (*Quo vadis?*). We
might say that the entire farewell discourse of John 14 was given in answer
to that question. But equally important is that Jesus answered Peter by
telling him not only *where* He was going, but *why* He was going.

The "Where" of Christ's Departure

When Jesus left this world He went to the Father. His ascension was to a
certain place for a particular reason. To ascend did not mean merely "to
go up." He was being elevated to the Right Hand of the Father. He was

advancing to what the church calls the *Sessio*, the *session* or seating at the Right Hand of God. The seat He occupies on His departure is the royal throne of cosmic authority. It is the office of the King of the Kings and the Lord of the Lords.

Imagine an earthly situation where the heir-apparent to the throne meets with his closest friends on the eve of his own coronation. The new king's friends would hardly desire that the king skip his own coronation.

There is no greater benefit to the king-elect's friends than that he ascends to the throne.

Jesus was not departing in exile. He was leaving for His coronation. He was passing from humiliation to exaltation. The extraordinary benefit in this for every Christian is that he can live in the full assurance that at this very moment the highest political office in the universe is being held by King Jesus. His term of office is forever. No revolution, no rebellion, no bloody coup can wrest Him from the throne. The Lord Christ omnipotent reigns.

The "where" partially explains the "why." There is more to be added, however. The King serves in a dual capacity. He is not an ordinary monarch. At the same time He reigns as King, He serves His subjects as their Great High Priest. The King kneels before His own throne in supplication for His people. In addition to the *session* there is also *intercession.* Jesus' throne is linked to the heavenly Holy of Holies.

There is still another vital aspect to the "why" of Jesus' departure. He said, "If I do not go away, the Helper [Paraclete] will not come to you; but if I depart, I will send Him to you." Jesus' departure was tied to Pentecost. There is no Pentecost without Ascension. As the invested King of Kings, Jesus had the authority together with the Father to send His Holy Spirit in a new and powerful way upon the church. Jesus spoke of a certain necessity of His leaving in order for the Spirit to come. Herein was another great advantage. He declared, "Ye shall receive power, *after* that the Holy Ghost has come upon you" (Acts 1:8).

Two remarkable things happened to the disciples after Jesus departed. The first is that they "returned to Jerusalem with great joy" (Luke 24:52).

They were not despondent over the departure of Jesus. Obviously they finally understood why He was leaving. They understood what, for the most part, the church since then has failed to understand. We live as if it would not have been better for Jesus to leave.

The second obvious change in the lives of the disciples was in their spiritual strength. After Pentecost they were different people. No longer did they flee like sheep without a shepherd. Instead they turned the world upside down. They turned the world upside down because they fully understood two simple things: the where and the why of Jesus' departure.

A TWO-HANDED KING

———

I T WAS LUNCH TIME IN THE SENATE DINING ROOM. The famous bean soup was on the menu. I sat in shocked incredulity as I listened to a United States senator utter these words: "I don't believe that the government ever has the right to coerce its citizens to do anything." But for the grace of God, I would have choked to death on a single navy bean. "Senator," I replied, "what I hear you saying is that the government has no right to govern."

The key word in the exchange was the word *coerce.* Coercion involves the use of power to force someone to do something they do not want to do. Coercion is rule by force. That is what government does. All government. Everywhere. Government is force. The very essence of government is legal force. Government passes laws and then backs up those laws by various types of law-enforcement. No government rules by *suggestions.*

The use of government force can be oppressive, tyrannical, and arbitrary. It can also be just. But just or unjust, tyrannical or benevolent, capitalistic or communistic, democratic or despotic, government involves force.

St. Augustine taught that government is not a necessary evil; rather, it is necessary because of evil. Earthly government began when God posted a guard at the entrance to Eden. When Adam and Eve were banished from paradise, their return was blocked by an angel brandishing a flaming sword. The sword was not made for rattling but to exert force upon the exiles should they seek re-entry to the garden. So Paul writes in Romans 13 that God gives the sword to the civil magistrate. It is the symbol of the magistrate's force.

The Bible makes it clear that it is God who ordains and institutes civil government. Government is both an expression of the wrath of God and of the mercy of God. It expresses His wrath when it uses force to punish evil-doers. It expresses His mercy when it protects and defends the innocent. Its function is to restrain evil and to protect life and property.

Luther's view of civil government has stirred wide debate. What stands out in Luther, however, is his concept of the two kingdoms. He saw secular government as a part of God's kingdom. But human government is the "kingdom of the left hand of God." The kingdom of the right hand is the spiritual realm of the church.

With this distinction between the kingdom of the right hand and kingdom of the left hand, we note two important ideas. The two kingdoms are distinguished and separated with respect to their peculiar roles and responsibilities. But both are under the sovereignty of God. Both are accountable to God.

No human government, no human authority is autonomous. To separate church and state is not to separate God and state. A state that refuses to acknowledge its subordination to God is on a collision course with the Lord of history.

Calvin also made a sharp distinction between church and state but insisted that one of the tasks of the state is to protect the interests of the church. There is to be mutual respect and honor between church and state. It is the duty of the church to pray for those who manage the affairs of state and to be models of civil obedience wherever and whenever conscience permits. It is also the duty of the church to exercise prophetic criticism against the state if and when the state functions unjustly or departs from its divinely appointed task. For example, one of the chief tasks of any government is to protect, honor, preserve, and defend human life. When the state legitimizes abortion, it arouses protest from the church, not because it is failing to do the church's mission, but because it is failing to do the task for which God instituted government in the first place. When the state sanctions abortion, it uses the sword (or the scalpel) for evil rather than for good.

The state, according to Calvin, is not to perform the functions of the church but to protect the church's liberty to carry out its mission. The state must not retard the work of the church but insure its rights to exercise its duty.

The church is not above the state. God is above the state. The state is not above the church. God is above the church. The two institutions are both ordained by God and are accountable to God. Both are capable of radical disobedience. The state can become an instrument of tyranny, the church, a body of apostasy. Both are ordained of God. The prince or the president is as much an ordained minister of God as a clergyman. Both have a sacred vocation to fulfill. Both will give an accounting to God for how they carried out their duties.

"Government is both an expression of the wrath of God and of the mercy of God."

SUFFERING AND MERIT

FEBRUARY 1989

———

MARTIN LUTHER ONCE DECLARED THAT if anybody could go to heaven by monkery it was he. Luther's tenure in the monastery was a time of spiritual desperation. He was tormented by unrelieved guilt coupled with a gripping fear of the wrath of God. If ever a man pursued spiritual peace with all his might, it was Luther.

Why would an educated man retreat to a barren cell and abuse himself with self-inflicted physical punishment? Why would a believer go out of his way to find personal suffering?

The answer may be found partially, though not totally, in a concept that emerged in church history that equated suffering with merit. Monks fled to the desert to seek rigorous forms of asceticism and self-denial not only as a form of spiritual discipline to maintain a healthy dependence on the grace of God, but also in quest of sanctifying merit.

A Biblical text that was often cited as Scriptural warrant for such activity is found in Colossians 1:24. Paul writes:

> I now rejoice in my sufferings for you, and fill up in my flesh what is lacking in the afflictions of Christ, for the sake of His body, which is the church.

The key words of this verse are "fill up ... what is lacking in the afflictions of Christ."

A theology of suffering and merit emerged that was built on the hypothesis that the meritorious suffering of Jesus, though necessary for the redemption of God's people, is not complete. In addition to the merit Jesus acquired in His perfect obedience as the suffering servant, there is additional merit that can be added to this by the suffering of the saints. Therefore the merit of Christ can be augmented by our merit.

This concept is part of the foundation for the Roman Catholic doctrine of the *treasury of merit.* The treasury of merit is like a heavenly bank account from which the church can draw to help people who have a short fall of merit in their account.

It works something like this: To be justified a person must be just. He needs so much merit to be redeemed. Some people fall short of the necessary merit. Others, whom the church canonizes as "saints," live lives of such great virtue that they accrue more merit than they need to get into heaven. This "excess merit" is then deposited in the treasury of merit. The "power of the keys" is given to the church to distribute to the needy by way of papal indulgences and the like.

How does this relate to suffering? Another concept developed in Roman Catholic theology is called "works of supererogation." A work of supererogation is a work above and beyond the call of duty and earns for the believer extra merit. One example in the lives of saints is martyrdom.

It was these ideas that resulted in the worst fracture of the historic Christian church. The furious debate was and is at two crucial points. The first is the ongoing debate over merit and grace. The second focuses on the question of the sufficiency of the merit of Christ.

Luther's "justification by faith alone" was a battle cry for the sufficiency of the merit of Christ and for the graciousness of redemption. His slogan *sola fide* (by faith alone) was merely an extension of Augustine's earlier credo, *sola gratia* (by grace alone).

What is lacking in the afflictions of Christ is not merit. No one can possibly subtract from or add to the merit of Christ. His merit is capable of neither diminution or augmentation. Our best works are always tainted by our sinfulness. We are debtors who cannot pay our debts, let alone accrue a surplus of excess merit. To interpret Colossians 1:24 in the way I mentioned is to cast a grotesque shadow over the utter perfection and fullness of Christ's meritorious suffering.

What then does Paul mean by filling up what is lacking? If the lack is not merit, what is it? Paul repeatedly stresses the idea that the church, the body of Christ, is called to a willing participation in the humiliation and suffering of Jesus. For Paul, as with any Christian, it was a singular honor to be persecuted for righteousness' sake. But it is one thing to suffer for righteousness' sake; it is quite another to suffer for merit's sake.

The irony of the theology of meritorious suffering is that it tends to produce the very opposite effect from its original intention. What began as a call to humble willingness to suffer became an insidious tool for self-righteousness. Perhaps the most difficult task for us to perform is to rely on God's grace and God's grace alone for our salvation. It is difficult for our pride to rest on grace. Grace is for other people—for beggars. We don't want to live by a heavenly welfare system. We want to earn our own way and atone for our own sins. We like to think that we will go to heaven because we deserve to be there.

All the suffering I could possibly endure could not earn me a place in heaven. Nor can I merit the merit of Christ through suffering. I am altogether an unprofitable servant who must rely on someone else's merit to be saved. With Paul we can rejoice in our sufferings if they enhance the glory of Christ. We can rejoice in our persecutions and look forward to the promised blessing of Christ. But the blessing Christ promised, the blessing of great reward, is a reward of grace. The blessing is promised even though it is not earned. Augustine said it this way: Our rewards in heaven are a result of God's crowning His own gifts. *Sola Gratia.*

WHAT'S GOING ON HERE?

MARCH 1989

———

EVERY SUNDAY MORNING WE OBSERVE a strange phenomenon in our cities, towns, and villages. Millions of people leave their homes, take respite from their jobs and recreation, and gather in a church building for services of worship. People sit quietly and listen while one person stands before them and gives a speech. We call the speech a sermon, homily, or meditation.

What's going on here? Is this sociological happening a vestigial rite from former days? Is it a painful price people pay to get the opportunity to gather with friends and neighbors?

Different denominations have different views of the place of the sermon in Sunday worship. For example, there is a profound difference between the Roman Catholic view of the matter and the view of historic Protestantism. If we note the architecture of most Roman Catholic sanctuaries we see that the altar, not the pulpit, is the central focal point.

Why? We remember that in the sixteenth century Reformation the central issue of debate was the question of justification. Both Rome and Protestants agreed that justification is a vital concern of Christianity. Both agreed that sinful people are in need of justification. The question was—"How is a person justified?" Luther insisted that justification is by faith alone.

Most of us are familiar with the crucial debate about the word "alone" in Luther's formula. Justification by faith alone means justification by the merits of Christ alone. There is no admixture of human merit that adds to or dilutes the sole sufficiency of the merit of Christ.

But the issue went deeper. The little word "by" was also at the core of the debate. Here the question was and is: "What is the instrumental cause of justification? What is the means by which a person is justified?"

The Reformers insisted that the instrumental cause of justification is faith. Rome declared that the instrumental cause of justification is baptism (see the decrees of the Council of Trent). In baptism, justifying grace is infused into the soul resulting in justification. This operation of infusion is accomplished virtually automatically. Rome teaches that the sacraments work *ex opere operato*, by the working of the works.

Baptism effects justification. But the grace of justification can be lost by mortal sin. Mortal sin is called "mortal" because it "kills" justifying grace. However, a Catholic who has sinned mortally is not required to be re-baptized. The original baptism confers an "indelible mark." This uneradicable mark remains, though justifying grace is destroyed.

Rome has another sacrament that effects justification. It is the sacrament of penance (which lay at the eye of the Reformation tornado). Trent called penance the "second plank of justification for those who make shipwreck of their souls." Via penance there is a fresh infusion of justification by which the penitent sinner is restored to a state of grace.

The Roman Catholic system is called *sacerdotalism* because the instrumental cause of justification is found in the sacraments. Of course Rome also teaches that people are to have faith and the sermon has a place in worship. Protestantism holds the sacraments of baptism and the Lord's Supper in high esteem—but the accent mark in worship tends to be placed on the sermon.

The sermon is of crucial importance because of its link with faith. Paul wrote, "So then faith comes by hearing, and hearing by the Word of God" (Romans 10:17). Romans 10 provides the classical biblical study of the crucial role of preaching in the life of the church. The "foolishness" of preaching is the divinely instituted and ordained means by which God calls people to faith, a faith that must be operative not only in justification but in sanctification as well.

Preaching is a supernatural event. By that I do not mean that it is a miracle. All miracles are supernatural events; but not all supernatural events are miracles. Nor do I mean that preachers are supernatural persons or have in themselves supernatural powers. Preaching is also a human event. It is done by humans and heard by humans. But where the Word of God is faithfully preached we can be assured that it will be accompanied by the Holy Spirit. The Holy Spirit works through human preaching to quicken sinners to justifying faith and to move them from faith to faith in the growing process of sanctification.

The power of preaching is found in the Spirit's working with the Word of God, and through the Word of God. God promises that His word will not return to Him void. Its power is located not in the eloquence or erudition of the preacher but in the power of the Spirit. Preaching is a tool in the hands of the Spirit of God. The Holy Spirit is a supernatural being, the Third Person of the Trinity. His presence in preaching is what makes it a supernatural event.

Salvation is a divine achievement. No man can save himself. God sovereignly ordains not only the *end* (salvation) but the *means* to the end (preaching). We conclude then that what is going on Sunday morning when the Word of God is truly preached is a divine drama of redemption.

THE BIBLE AS HISTORY

MAY 1989

———

L UKE'S ACCOUNT OF JESUS' BIRTH is recorded in these words: "And it came to pass in those days that a decree went out from Caesar Augustus that all the world should be registered. This census took place while Quirinius was governing Syria."

These introductory words to the nativity of Jesus are often passed over lightly in our Christmas celebrations in favor of the miraculous Virgin Birth. The supernatural events surrounding Jesus' birth have been an endless topic of critical debate. Were there really angels present? Did a woman really conceive and bear a child without the normal process of biological propagation?

One looks in vain to the science of archaeology to answer the question of angelic visitors. We have no fossil record of ossified feathers from angel wings, and no autopsy report with tissue samples from Mary. What we have in the way of historical data is a book that records purported eyewitness testimony to these things. The question then becomes, Is this testimony credible or does it reflect an intrusion of legend and myth into the biblical record?

Because of such difficulties there has been a powerful trend in New Testament theology to remove the essence of Christian faith from the space-time realm of history. We are urged to consider that the Bible is not history, as such, but is *redemptive* history. Here the accent is on the *redemptive* rather than the *historical*. Rudolf Bultmann, for example, stressed what he called the *punctiliar* view of salvation. Salvation is something that occurs *vertically*, rather than *horizontally*. That is, in the course of my spiritual life I have a "here and now" existential encounter that evokes faith in me. That is what matters. Whether or not Jesus ever lived has little or no redemptive significance. He represents a symbol of existential faith, which is not bound to, nor by, history.

This approach to Christianity is about as far removed from the biblical perspective on salvation as possible. It so redefines Christianity by relativizing and de-historicizing it that it becomes more accurate to describe it not so much as neo-Christian, or liberal-Christian as anti-Christian. The New Testament scholar Herman Ridderbos was correct when he insisted that though the Bible is indeed redemptive history, we must always remember that it is redemptive *history*. If we do away with the history, we do away with the redemption, also.

Luke's account says, "And it came to pass." What he intended to convey was: "It *happened*. It really took place in time and space." It is one thing to say, "Well, I don't believe it really happened. Luke was either deluded or dishonest." It is quite another to try to reshape the biblical text in a way that neutralizes its commitment to real history.

The opening verses of Luke refer specifically to two historical personages, one historical event, and one specific geographical location. We read of Caesar Augustus, Quirinius, a decree of enrollment, and Syria. These are matters of historical detail that fall under the critical scrutiny of historical and archaeological research. Here Luke's accuracy can be critically evaluated by history-science.

Archaeological research has shown that there was a Roman emperor named Augustus. F.F. Bruce writes that it is "practically certain" that a census was held in 10–9 B.C. and repeated every 14 years. The archaeological record also attests that there was in fact a census authorized by Quirinius of Syria.

For the past century there has been a growing rift between speculative higher criticism and the science of archaeology. Again and again the former so-called "assured results" of higher criticism have been shattered by 20th-century archaeological discoveries. It seems that with every thrust of the shovel another pet-theory of the critics is exploded to their scholarly embarrassment. The trend in archaeological research is clearly in the direction of verifying the biblical record rather than falsifying it. But "liberal" theories die hard.

To catch something of the flavor of the current dispute I conclude with a citation from the 20th-century dean of biblical archaeology, Professor William Foxwell Albright. Albright was to archaeology what Einstein was to physics. Though Albright did not press for an inspired or infallible Bible, he did have this comment to make in one of his last published works (found in the preface of the Anchor Bible series *Matthew*):

> For much too long a time the course of New Testament scholarship has been dictated by theological, quasi-theological, and philosophical presuppositions. In far too many cases commentaries on NT books have neglected such basic requirements as up-to-date historical and philological analysis of the text itself. The result has often been steadfast refusal to take seriously the findings of archaeological and linguistic research.
>
> So anti-historical is this approach that it fascinates speculative minds which prefer clichés to factual data, and shifting ideology to empirical research and logical demonstration.

PRAYER

———

PERHAPS NO THEOLOGIAN OF THE CHURCH has been more viciously maligned by critics than John Calvin. Scurrilous distortions of his character have portrayed him as being stern, severe, unfeeling, rigid, and austere. So widespread and deeply entrenched is this caricature that I tread in fear and trembling when I assign readings from the *Institutes of the Christian Religion* to my seminary students.

To cut through the false mask of Calvin, I ask my students to begin reading the *Institutes* not at chapter 1 but at book III, chapter 20. This is Calvin's treatment of prayer—a classic study not only in this godly exercise on faith but of Calvin himself. It reveals a man whose heart soars in adoration, a man who has a passion to be pleasing to God.

For Calvin prayer was like a priceless treasure that God has offered to His people:

> To prayer, then, are we indebted for penetrating to those riches which are treasured up for us with our heavenly Father. For there is a kind of intercourse between God and man, by which, having entered the upper sanctuary, they appear before Him and appeal to His promises, that when necessity requires, they may learn by experience, that what they believed merely on the authority of His word was not in vain. Accordingly, we see that nothing is set before us as an object of expectation from the Lord which we are not enjoined to ask of Him in prayer, so true it is that prayer digs up those treasures which the Gospel of our Lord discovers to the eye of faith.

The first rule of prayer for Calvin was to enter into it with a full awareness of the One to whom we are speaking. The key to prayer is a spirit of reverence and adoration.

Let the first rule of right prayer be, to have our heart and mind framed as becomes those who are entering into converse with God.

Calvin speaks of how easy it is for our minds to wander in prayer. We become inattentive as if we were speaking to someone with whom we are easily bored. This insults the glory of God:

Let us know, then, that none duly prepare themselves for prayer but those who are so impressed with the majesty of God that they engage in it free from all earthly cares and affections.

The second rule of prayer is that we ask only for those things that God permits. Prayer can be an exercise in blasphemy if we approach God entreating His blessing for a cooperation with our sinful desires.

I lately observed, men in prayer give greater license to their unlawful desires than if they were telling jocular tales among their equals.

The third rule is that we must always pray with genuine feeling. Prayer is a matter of passion:

Many repeat prayers in a perfunctory manner from a set form, as if they were performing a task to God. . . . They perform the duty from custom, because their minds are meanwhile cold, and they ponder not what they ask.

A fourth rule of prayer is that it be always accompanied by repentance.

God does not listen to the wicked; that their prayers, as well as their sacrifices, are an abomination to them. For it is right that those who seal up their hearts should find the ears of God closed against them. . . . Of this submission, which casts down all haughtiness, we have numerous examples in the servants of God. The holier they are, the more humbly they prostrate themselves when they come into the presence of the Lord.

If I can summarize Calvin's teaching on prayer succinctly I would say this: The chief rule of prayer is to remember who God is and to remember who you are. If we remember those two things our prayers will always and ever be marked by adoration and confession.

"The chief rule of prayer is to remember who God is and to remember who you are."

THE NEED FOR SYSTEMATIC THEOLOGY

JULY 1989

——

MY FIRST PIANO LESSON WAS EASY. It was a one-note melody. I sat at the keyboard and used my index finger to play middle C. I still remember the ditty: *I am playing middle C, I can play it well, you see.*

That was over 40 years ago. Now I am taking lessons in modern progressive jazz. It's not so easy. Every Tuesday night I leave my piano lesson in a state of panic. I'm confused and feel lost in the maze of intricate harmonic patterns. Playing a one-note melody is simple. It is the *harmony* that gives me problems. In modern jazz the harmonies get more and more intricate, more and more complex. The more complex it gets, the more confused I get. The more confused I get, the more mistakes I make. Yet in the most intricate harmony there is a logic operating, a strict mathematical ratio that is coherent rather than chaotic.

In music we seek symphony, not cacophony. So it is with systematic theology. It is the quest for a coherent understanding of the whole of Scripture. It is an attempt to understand how the individual parts fit together.

Recently I heard of some men who undertook the task of rebuilding the engine of an antique sports car. They worked on the project for six months. When the task was finished and the engine was reassembled, they were distressed to discover they had several bolts left over. They could find nowhere to put them. So they put them in a basket and drove the car merrily away.

The Word of God has no useless parts. Every word that proceeds from the mouth of God is important. The goal of systematic theology is to understand how *all* the parts fit together.

We live in an age that tends to hold systematic theology in disdain.

The word *system* itself has become a dirty word. We are fearful or hostile to logic. The influence of antilogical, antisystem, and antirational existentialism has been pervasive. The common charge is that systematic theology involves an artificial imposition of some foreign philosophical structure on the Word of God. The Bible is seen to suffer the fate of Procrustes, whose legs were cut off to force-fit him to his bed.

Surely it is possible to try and squeeze the Bible into a preconceived philosophical system. That is certainly not the proper task of systematic theology.

However, it is one thing to force a system upon the Scripture; it is another thing to discover the system of truth that is already there. To find the system involves nothing more and nothing less than to discover the coherency and consistency of the Word of God.

Systematic theology does assume that God is coherent and consistent. It assumes that God does not speak with a forked tongue. Classical systematic theology works on the premise that God is the author of the Bible. There is no place for atomistic exegesis of Scripture. Those who tend toward atomism are those who first deny the divine source of Scripture. They work on the assumption that the Bible is merely a human book written by human authors without the aid of divine superintendence. As a result they see as many disparate theologies in Scripture as there are authors. Indeed they find more, distinguishing between "early" Paul and "later" Paul or between "rabbinic" Paul and "Christian" Paul. In this approach the Bible becomes a textbook for pluralism, or as Luther argued, a "waxed nose" that can be shaped and formed to agree with anyone's bias.

The Reformed systematic theologian is committed to the Reformed hermeneutic whose cardinal principle is this: "Sacred Scripture is its own interpreter." That means that we are to interpret Scripture by Scripture, refusing to set one part of Scripture against another part of Scripture. It means seeking the harmony that is already there based on the assumption that God is coherent and consistent.

It has been argued that "consistency is the hobgoblin of small minds."

If that is so then God must have the smallest mind of all. The Deity must suffer from an overload of hobgoblins.

I am convinced that inconsistency is the hobgoblin of small minds. It is the mark of confusion or the lack of clarity of thought. We seek clarity in our understanding of the Word of God, a clarity found by wrestling with all its parts that we may understand its coherent whole.

"Just as when good is commanded, its opposite evil is prohibited, so when evil is prohibited its opposite good is commanded."

—

ELLIPTICAL GUILT

AUGUST 1989

———

T HE WESTMINSTER CATECHISM DEFINES SIN as "any want of conformity to or transgression of the law of God." We notice here that sin is defined both in negative and positive terms. The negative aspect is indicated by the words *want of conformity*. It points to a lack or failure on moral performance. In popular terms it is called a sin of omission. (I once had a theology professor who denoted a sin of omission as the failure of the second baseman to cover the bag in a double play.) A sin of omission occurs when we fail to do what God commands us to do.

The positive aspect of the catechetical definition of sin refers to overt, actual stepping over the boundaries of God's law. It is a sin of commission.

Both sins of omission and sins of commission are real sins. They incur real guilt. When we do what God forbids, we are guilty of a sin of commission; when we fail to do what God commands, we are guilty of a sin of omission. In both cases the law of God is violated.

Sometimes God expresses His laws in negative terms (Do not do...) and sometimes in positive terms (Do...). The Ten Commandments contain both forms (Do not steal; Honor your father and mother).

That God's commands appear in both positive and negative forms hints at the elliptical character of the law. Calvin stated it this way:

> There is always more in the requirements of the Law than is expressed in words.... It is true that, in almost all the commandments, there are elliptical expressions, and that, therefore, any man would make himself ridiculous by attempting to restrict the spirit of the Law to the strict letter of the words (*Institutes* II/VIII/8).

Calvin's distinction between the letter and the spirit of the Law follows Augustine, and more importantly, the teaching of Christ. It is not intended to say we are to keep the letter of the Law and ignore the spirit, or keep the spirit of the Law and ignore the letter. The spirit and the letter of the Law may be distinguished but never divorced. God requires that we keep both the letter and the spirit of the Law.

The spirit of the Law is often elliptical to the letter. That is, it is not overtly stated but is left implied or tacitly understood. This is the crucial point the Pharisees missed and which Jesus carefully expounded in the Sermon on the Mount.

It is usually clearly understood that when God positively commands some good, by implication the evil opposed to it is forbidden. For example when God says, "Honor your father and your mother," we understand that we are not permitted to *dishonor* our parents.

It is not so clear to us when we work in the opposite direction from vice to virtue. When the Pharisees looked at the prohibitions "Thou shalt not kill" and "Thou shalt not commit adultery," they assumed they were guilt-free if they merely abstained from the letter of the prohibition. They missed the ellipse that called attention to the whole *complex* of the commandment. Jesus explained that the prohibition against murder contained implicitly within it the whole complex of inflicting injury against our fellow man. To hate a person or be angry against a person is implicitly forbidden along with the explicit prohibition against murder. Likewise, sexual impurity including lust, is prohibited on the full import of the Law against adultery.

But the Law goes deeper. Just as when good is commanded, its opposite evil is prohibited, so when evil is prohibited its opposite good is commanded. The Law *against* adultery is a law *for* sexual purity. The Law *against* idolatry is a law *for* true worship. The law *against* murder is a commandment *for* the sanctity of life. Again Calvin comments:

> When evil is forbidden, its opposite is enjoined. . . . Censure of vice is commendation of virtue. . . . Hence the commandment. "Thou shalt not kill," the generality of men will merely consider as an injunction to abstain from all injury, and all wish to inflict injury. I hold that it moreover means, that we are to aid our neighbor's life by every means in our power (*Institutes* II/VIII/9).

If we fully grasped the elliptical character of the Law, I trust, for example, that the argument among Christians over abortion on demand would be ended once and for all.

When we consider the elliptical character of the Law we discover that God's law is far deeper and broader than we ever imagined. We also discover that our guilt is far deeper and broader than we ever imagined. It is the elliptical guilt we often overlook when we flatter ourselves for our virtue. When we see it and see it clearly, we fly to the Savior and His fountain of grace.

"The true, the good, and the beautiful may be distinguished, but to separate them or isolate one from the others is to have a distortion of the character of God."

—

BEAUTY & HOLINESS

SEPTEMBER 1989

———

FREQUENTLY I HAVE WRITTEN ABOUT the triad of Christian ideals: the good, the true, and the beautiful. God is the fountainhead of these three, the source from which they flow, and the standard by which they are judged.

Like Ahab in Melville's *Moby Dick*, we all have a tendency toward monomania. Imprisoned by a fetish for reductionism, we tend to make the complex simplistic, and the multifaceted one-dimensional. It is a matter of emphasis, at times even preoccupation.

Church history bears witness to our monomial predilections. We have seen the impact of intellectualism, which so stresses the importance of doctrinal truth that it has little concern for ethics and aesthetics. We have seen moralism that reduces Christianity to right conduct without a view toward theological truth and often coupled with a contempt for art. We have seen aestheticism which has equated beauty with God and rested in liturgy at the expense of truth and conduct.

Indeed the true, the good, and the beautiful may be distinguished, but to separate them or isolate one from the others is to have a distortion of the character of God. Authentic beauty is wed to truth and goodness as authentic goodness is both true and beautiful.

In this issue we are concerned with one aspect of the triad, the beautiful; but not in isolation from or contradiction of the good and the true. We are also concerned with the relationship between the beautiful and the holy.

The Bible speaks of the "beauty of holiness" (1 Chronicles 16:29). We now ask if this phrase is in any way tautological; that is, we ask if it can be reversed and still hold true. We've seen what happens when we take the phrase "God is love" and make it a symmetrical equation, a copula that translates into "love is God." Then romance becomes an idol worshiped in the place of the living God.

All that God is, is beautiful. But not all that is beautiful is God. It may come from God and bear witness to God, but it is not God. Nature is beautiful, but nature is not God.

The Enlightenment of the 18th century saw a rise in aestheticism, whereby the arts were assigned the function of shaping human thought and behavior. The chief epistemology of Enlightenment thought was the analytical method, which involved a search for "the logic of facts"—it was an attempt to apply the scientific method that gave weight both to induction and deduction. Art was seen as a bridge between science and life. The chief span of the bridge was found in mathematics. Art involves a grasp of mathematical balance, proportion, harmony, and symmetry. As music was said to "charm the savage beast" (a la David's music for Saul) the arts could be useful to instruct the human mind and shape the human spirit toward a good, proportional, balanced life.

The aestheticism of the Enlightenment, however, sought to find the relationship between the beautiful and the good without dependence upon biblical truth. It was a naturalistic form of aestheticism. The chief opponent of Enlightenment thought in this area was Johann Sebastian Bach. Bach's view of beauty was specifically Christian. For him, beauty was demonic if it was not subordinated to the Word of God.

Jaroslav Pelikan summarized the key points of Bach's view in his book *Fools for Christ*. The following propositions capture Bach's Christian aesthetic:

Proposition #1. The highest activity of the human spirit is the praise of God. Such praise involves the total activity of the Spirit. Any object of the uplifted heart short of the Lord Himself is unworthy of human aspirations. Bach strove to honor the holiness of God even in his "secular" compositions.

Proposition #2. As the praise of the eternal God, Christian art is an expression of boundless freedom; but as the praise of God who became incarnate, it bends itself to form.

Proposition #3. As the medium of a historical faith. Christian art has to be cast in terms of historical tradition; yet as an expression of faith in the living God, it has to be relevant and contemporary. (Bach's setting of the

Nicene Creed in a contemporary style reflects this blend.) There is a marriage of the classic and the fresh; of the orthodox and the contemporary. Orthodoxy itself does not change, but its expression is contemporary.

Proposition #4. Christian art illumines or even transcends the content of the words with which it is joined. Art is never to be set in competition with the Word of God. Rather it is a *response* to the Word and reinforces the Word. Bach saw art as a kind of quasi-sacramental medium of communication. That is, it is dependent for its validation upon the Word yet aids in the communication of the Word.

Beauty, then, for Bach, was a channel by which the holiness of God was communicated to the human spirit. Pelikan summarizes Bach's view:

> The Holy is not, first of all, a highest Good, a sublimely True, an ultimately Beautiful. Yet that Holy which men have vainly tried to grasp with their systems of thought, their categories of ethics, and their depictions of beauty; that Holy which has eluded every human attempt to take it captive and to tame it; that Holy has been made flesh and has dwelt among us in Jesus Christ.

THE BIBLICAL SEX ETHIC

OCTOBER 1989

The NT is characterized by an unconditional repudiation of all extra-marital and unnatural intercourse. In this respect it follows to a large degree the judgment of OT and Israelite preaching and transcends the legalistic practice of later Judaism, which is shown to be inadequate by the Word of Jesus. Jesus can and does effect this radicalizing because the Gospel as saving forgiveness manifests the divine dynamic in this age. A further result of this is a basically new attitude to woman. She is no longer man's chattel but a partner of equal dignity before man and God (Hauck/Schulz, "porneia," *Theological Dictionary of the New Testament*).

WHAT IS NOTEWORTHY ABOUT THIS paragraph is its source. It comes from higher critical scholars in the most comprehensive lexicographical tool available for contemporary biblical research. The scholars who produced this work are not known for their commitment to biblical orthodoxy.

They are neither conservatives in theology or in ethics. Yet they have distinguished themselves for precision in detail and accuracy in the setting forth of biblical teaching. They may not believe or accept what the Bible teaches on certain matters but they have been scrupulous in giving historical and grammatical definition to those teachings.

The opening sentence of the paragraph jumps out at us: *The NT is characterized by an unconditional repudiation of all extra-marital and unnatural intercourse.* While many church groups consider the propriety of homosexuality and write position papers accepting types of pre- and extramarital intercourse, they do so against a clear biblical mandate that disallows such practices. People may debate the authority of the Bible on these issues, but there is no legitimate debate about the biblical message on these issues.

With respect to premarital, extramarital, and unnatural sexual practices, the Bible says "No," and says it emphatically.

In Acts 15, minimal requirements are set forth for the Christian community, including the prohibition of fornication. The *Theological Dictionary of the New Testament* calls this a "moral catechism," which cites the three chief sins as idolatry, murder, and fornication. In the writings of Paul there is a clear incompatibility between fornication and the kingdom of God. (See, for example, Romans 1:10ff; 1 Corinthians 6:9, 19; 10:1–13; 2 Corinthians 11:2; Ephesians 5:5; 1 Thessalonians 4:1–5.)

Revelation 9:21 lists sexual indulgence as one of the leading pagan sins to which men will cling in the last days despite all the divine judgments against them. In our recent Ligonier survey of guilt, the number one problem male responders mentioned was that of sexual temptation and sin. The moral struggle at this point is severe. Sexual chastity is difficult even when one lives in an setting where the biblical ideal is stressed and to a high degree maintained. But when living in a culture that tolerates and even encourages unrestricted sexual indulgence, the struggle becomes even more acute.

In our society the cultural taboos against pre- and extramarital sex have been removed. It is expected that single people will be sexually active. There is an atmosphere of "everybody is doing it" that has removed the moral stigma from casual sex. In addition, we live in an age where sex is exploited beyond measure to sell products and to stimulate interests in books, plays, films, music, and T.V. Sex sells because sex interests.

A person trying to live out the biblical sex ethic today is bombarded daily with erotic stimuli couched in respectability. In an effort to ease the consciences of those suffering from the pangs of guilt, many churches have moved from a posture of offering forgiveness to repentant sinners to sanctioning the activities themselves.

Yet every Christian knows from even a cursory reading of Scripture that ours is a higher call. We are not to look at the culture but to our Lord for our sexual ethic. God's law on the sanctity of sex has not changed. No church group ever has the right to revise the rule of Christ.

To those who fall and genuinely repent, we still have Jesus who says, "Neither do I condemn you. Go and sin no more." We must hear both parts of this statement: Christ does not condemn the penitent; He forgives them. But with the forgiveness comes the command: "Go and sin no more."

"With respect to premarital, extramarital, and unnatural sexual practices, the Bible says 'No,' and says it emphatically."

———

THE MESSAGE
OF THE SIGN

NOVEMBER 1989

———

O NE OF THE MORE FAMOUS QUOTES FROM moviedom comes from the classic film *Cool Hand Luke*. The corrupt redneck lawman torments Luke by saying in an exaggerated southern drawl, "What we have heya . . . is a failya to communicate."

Failures in communication do not occur simply because the wrong word or an imprecise phrase is used. Communication is enhanced or weakened by the voice inflections and/or gestures that accompany our words. The nonverbal is an integral and crucial accompaniment to the verbal. Cement my face into a frown or tie my hands behind my back and I could not deliver a sermon.

One role of a sacrament is to be a nonverbal message from God. It does not ever stand apart from His Word or against His Word, but with the Word it communicates, and communicates powerfully.

When Jesus glanced at Peter in the midst of His trial after Peter had steadfastly denied Him, Peter went out and wept bitterly. Presumably no words were exchanged at the moment. Peter's eyes met the eyes of Christ. Yet in that brief look, profound communication took place.

God is a God of the Word. The Word of God is so-called because the Bible is filled with words. Words are combined into sentences, sentences into paragraphs, paragraphs into books—all verbal communication. But what is a word? A word is merely a sound or a configuration of letters that are signs for ideas. These signs convey content. A sacrament is also a sign. It does not involve letters but as all signs do, it points beyond itself to some kind of message. A sign is called a sign because it is significant; it conveys meaning.

Sacraments are often called "outward signs" because they are visible. They are empirical. The sensory organs of the human body are all involved. In the Lord's Supper, for example, we can see the sign of bread and wine. We can feel the texture of the bread. We can taste the elements. God's verbal promise of a new covenant wrought in the blood of Christ is empirically impressed upon us by this outward sign.

The sacraments are never *nuda signa*, "naked" or "empty" signs. No gesture of God is meaningless. The sacraments are indeed divine gestures, added to His Word to confirm and seal His promises.

In the Old Testament God instituted the Passover. He commanded the children of Israel to smear blood from a slain lamb upon the doorposts and lintels of their houses. For whose benefit was the blood to be sprinkled? Was this outward sign for God's eyes that He not make a mistake and send the angel of death to the wrong house?

By no means. God did not require an outward sign to be aware of who were His. God said, "The blood shall be a sign for *you* on the houses where you are" (Exodus 12:13). The sign of blood on the doorpost was given as a perpetual memorial: "Obey these instructions as a lasting ordinance for you and your descendants" (Exodus 12:24).

Circumcision was a sign instituted by God. Baptism is a sign instituted by God. The Lord's Supper is a sign instituted by God. The outward signs ordained by God are matters of high drama. God is not only a God who speaks; He is a God who acts. He is the star actor in the drama of redemption. We also are involved in action in the drama. We participate in the signs God has given us. Dramatic participation moves beyond mere recitation or a "going through the motions" of external rites and rituals.

Because the sacraments are rich in content, the mind must be engaged in the partaking of them. They are matters of discernment (though in the case of circumcision of infants in the Old Testament and baptism in the New Testament, the discernment may come after the sign is administered). As the sacrament undergirds the Word, so the Word undergirds the sacrament. The two may be distinguished but never separated.

The sacraments are divine and supernatural but never a matter of magic. Only when the mind is disengaged and discernment fails do we allow the sacraments to degenerate into superstition and magic. The very expression "hocus pocus" derives from a bastardization of the Latin formula for the words of Jesus, "*Hoc est corpus meum*" (this is My body).

The sacraments also must engage the heart. As we understand the message of the sign, our hearts are set aflame by the promises of God signed and sealed by divine institution.

THE LORD OF GLORY

DECEMBER 1989

―――

T HE BOOK OF JAMES HAS an unusual sentence construction that links the word *glory* with the name of Jesus. In Chapter 2, verse 1, we read: "My brethren have not the faith of our Lord Jesus Christ, the Lord of glory, with respect of persons" (KJV). In this verse the words *Lord of glory* have alternate renditions. Some translations read, "Our glorious Lord." Still another possible translation reads, "Jesus Christ, who is the glory."

B.B. Warfield, in his book *The Lord of Glory*, says, "Jesus was, in a word, the glory of God, the Shekinah." According to the Old Testament the Shekinah was the visible manifestation of the invisible God. The Shekinah was a radiant cloud or brilliant light within a cloud and signaled the immediate presence of God. For Jesus to be identified with the Shekinah was to be equated with the presence of God Himself. In Jesus we see the full manifestation of the majesty of God.

That the New Testament writers ascribed glory to Jesus was a clear indication of their confession of His full deity. Glory, in the sense it is used with reference to Jesus, is a divine attribute. It is the glory of God that He refuses to share with any man.

John, in his gospel, makes reference to the glory of Jesus: "And the Word became flesh and dwelt among us, and we beheld His glory, the glory as of the only begotten of the Father, full of grace and truth" (John 1:14).

In Jesus' High Priestly Prayer in John 17, Jesus says: "And now, Father, glorify Me together with Yourself, with the glory which I had with You before the world was" (v. 5). Here Jesus alludes to a position He held before creation. It is a tacit claim to His participation in the eternal glory of God.

In the fourth century, the church faced a serious crisis with respect to the deity of Christ. The Arian heretics denied the deity of Christ, claiming that Jesus was a creature who was adopted into a special relationship with God. In their controversy with orthodox Christians, the Arians used ribald and derogatory songs as a method of propaganda.

In response to the Arian attacks the orthodox Christians composed their own songs to affirm the deity of Christ. Perhaps the most important of these songs was the *Gloria Patri*. Note the words of this well known song: *Glory be to the Father; and to the Son; and to the Holy Ghost. As it was in the beginning, is now and ever shall be, world without end, Amen.*

Here the attribute of glory is ascribed to all three members of the Trinity. This glory is then confirmed as a glory that is eternal. It is not something added to or acquired by Jesus at some point in His earthly life and ministry. He held this glory at the beginning and will possess it for eternity.

In its inception the *Gloria Patri* functioned as a type of fight song, a rallying cry for orthodox Christianity. That original function has been lost through the passing of time so that it is now used as a liturgical response. We no longer sense the extraordinary significance of ascribing glory to Christ.

The life of Jesus was shrouded in the cloak of His humanity. His deity was not exhibited by an ostentatious display of constant refulgent majesty. He voluntarily took upon Himself the form of a servant, subordinating His glory to humility. The *Kenotic* (humility) hymn of Paul in Philippians 2:4–11 called attention to this factor:

> Each of you should look not only to your own interests, but also to the interests of others. Your attitude should be the same as that of Christ Jesus: Who, being in very nature God, did not consider equality with God something to be grasped, but made Himself nothing, taking the very nature of a servant, being made in human likeness. And being found in appearance as a man, He humbled Himself and became obedient to death—even death on a cross! Therefore God exalted Him to the highest place and gave Him the name that is above every name, that at the name of Jesus every knee should bow, in heaven and on earth and under the earth, and every tongue confess that Jesus Christ is Lord, to the glory of God the Father.

Though the form of servanthood covered Jesus and His life was marked by a willing humiliation, nevertheless there were moments in His ministry where the glory of His deity burst through. It was these moments that provoked John to write: "And we beheld His glory."

"That the New Testament writers ascribed glory to Jesus was a clear indication of their confession of His full deity."

———

A NEW DARK AGE?

JANUARY 1990

———

W HEN I OBSERVE A PHOTOGRAPH or a painting that evokes a visceral reaction within me, I like to reflect on it a bit to pinpoint the reason for the stirrings. So it is with the cover of this issue of *Tabletalk*.

I wonder what the artist had in mind with the composition of this piece. I sense a varied contrast of images here. My eyes went first to the image of the knight on horseback. The solitary figure suggests a posture of abject defeat. He rides low in the saddle, his shoulders slumped, and he drags his banner on the ground behind him. Where is the valiant demeanor of the heroic combatant of yore? It is absent.

Obviously the knight's mission has failed. His crusade is over. He is in retreat. He is weary.

Yet the painting is not monolithic in its images. In vivid contrast to the forlorn darkness of the rider is the lush brightness of the field of flowers. The garden is a magnificent display of color. No weeds intrude on the symmetry of the vibrant field. Each blossom is pure. No fading petals, no blotches of disease mar the landscape.

But something is terribly wrong here. Knights can be defeated. Warriors can be conquered. The greatest of heroes can grow tired. But this knight has lost more than a battle. He has lost the very essence of his knighthood; he has surrendered his honor; he has negotiated his own dignity.

We remember the credo of the ancient Spartan warriors: "Come back from the battle with your shield or on it." We remember the medieval knight's code of honor. He was trained in and committed to the etiquette of the court. He spoke of "me lady" and "me lord." It was unthinkable that one dubbed to the order of knighthood would ever engage in a thoughtless act of vandalism. His was an office of grace, honor, and nobility. He was sworn to the maintenance of virtue.

What knight there, in his moment of darkest gloom, would dare to plod his horse through somebody's beautiful garden? As I look at the picture I want to shout, "Hey! Get that horse out of the flowers!"

But the knight has been brought so low that he seems oblivious to his surroundings. Never mind that his banner, once so proud, is now merely an instrument he drags to lop off the blossoms of nature's beauty.

Who is this knight? Is he modern man-in-defeat? Is he Western culture-in-retreat? I don't know, but his image suggests both of these concepts.

In his most recent book Charles Colson speaks of a modern "return to the Dark Ages." When I think of the original Dark Ages I think of a period when culture was in decline and the progress of knowledge was static.

But today we read of the problem of the explosion of knowledge. It is a time when information and communications are big business. We hear the cry from the universities that knowledge in every field of investigation is increasing so rapidly that no one can assimilate it, even in the most narrow of specialties. The age of the "expert" is over. The word *expert* must now be defined in relative terms.

Where, then, is the darkness? If knowledge is light and the light is exploding in magnitude, how can we speak of a new Dark Ages?

The darkness is in the heart. It is a darkness produced by a shroud covering the face of God. Thirty years ago I read a book written by the Jewish philosopher and theologian Martin Buber. Buber's book had an ominous title: *Eclipse of God.*

That is the eclipse of our age. A shadow has passed over the glory of God. We are a people who will not have God in our thinking. We have returned to Plato's cave in which we prefer the dancing shadows on the wall of ungrounded opinion over the light of truth. As Allan Bloom declared, we have closed our minds to truth.

In the event of a solar eclipse the sun is not destroyed; it is obscured. The shadow hides but does not annihilate. The sun itself is no less bright in itself nor less refulgent in its nature when its view is blocked from our sight. The light is still there.

I think of Romans 1 where Paul speaks of the clear and manifest revelation God gives of Himself to all men:

For since the creation of the world His invisible qualities—His eternal power and divine nature—have been clearly seen, being understood from what has been made, even His eternal power and Godhead, so that men are without excuse (Romans 1:20).

Like our knight in the garden we pass through an arena, a theater of blazing glory where the light of God is manifest. Though we cannot see the eyes of the knight in the painting, there is no reason to assume that the defeated rider is blind. He rides aimlessly in the midst of the field of flowers as if they were not plain to see.

This is our course. We ride into the decade of the nineties *as if* we had no light from God. We are proving the thesis of the Apostle: *For although they knew God, they neither glorified Him as God nor gave thanks to Him, but their thinking became futile and their foolish hearts were darkened (Romans 1:21).*

Futile thinking—the thinking of vanity is the consequence of a darkened heart. It is our own minds that cast a shadow over the light of God. There is no shadow of turning in Him. We are the shadow of the eclipse. Our refusal to honor God means the very loss of honor itself. When we trample on the flowers of divine dignity we sacrifice our own.

The cultural struggles of the 90s will surely reflect this crisis. Abortion will continue to divide the nation, as the issue of the sanctity and dignity of human life will be debated. Law will be discussed and enacted not by appeals to the light of nature but by the test of collective preferences.

Church and state issues will multiply. The state will become more jealous for its autonomy. Separation of church and state will progressively (or regressively) be more and more interpreted to mean separation of state and God. Some churches will capitulate. They will drag their banners behind them as they surrender meekly to the state. Other churches will fight for their lives to save the flowers. They will come home with their shields or on them.

I see a deep struggle coming. Indeed it is already here. It is a time that calls for honor—the honor of God is at stake. And with it the dignity of every human being.

TRUTH IN THE MEDIA

FEBRUARY 1990

———

I REMEMBER MY FIRST EXPERIENCE OF disillusionment with the news media. As a graduate student at the Free University of Amsterdam I longed for news from my homeland. I subscribed to the international edition of *Time* magazine. Each week I devoured the magazine, reading each section or department carefully. I always paid close attention to the Religion page. I became more and more disturbed as I noticed glaring inaccuracies in reports of what was going on in the theological world. It was not simply a matter of differing theological positions but rather a question of accuracy in reporting. After a while I began to wonder—"Are the reports in the fields of art and science as inaccurate as in the field of theology?" I did not know the answer. But the reports in theology were so sloppy that I finally lost confidence in the credibility of the magazine and finally canceled my subscription.

I also remember the first time I saw my name in a newspaper. It was heady stuff. It proved the maxim that everybody is famous for at least fifteen minutes in their life. Together with two friends, Bowden Anderson and Eddie MacIlvane, I found a crayfish that we brought home and adopted as our mutual pet. We named the crayfish Sam, an acrostic of Sproul, Anderson, and MacIlvane. Eddie's next door neighbor was a reporter for the local newspaper. She thought our crayfish escapade was cute, so she wrote it up in the paper. There, for the first time, I saw my name in print.

When I grew up and became involved in speaking in various cities, I was often invited to be interviewed by the religion editor of various newspapers. After several such interviews I finally adopted a policy born of despair of declining interviews whenever possible. The reason was a sense of frustration that emerged after countless misrepresentations and misquotations in the press. It wasn't a question of whether or not the reporter agreed or disagreed with me; it was a matter of sheer accuracy in reporting. I remember specifically one such interview in Phoenix. The reporter had a Ph.D. in religion and was well-conversant in the field. He was cordial throughout the two-hour interview. I was comfortable with his manner of questioning and impressed by his ability to grasp crisp and important distinctions. Then I read his article in which he articulated the concepts I had carefully set forth to him. I could hardly recognize the interview. The man quoted me as saying things I wouldn't say with a gun to my head. I don't know if that reporter was malicious or simply grossly muddled or incompetent. In either case I found the results so distorted that I despaired of most interviews.

Newspapers are businesses. Businesses seek to make a profit. Sometimes controversy sells. Sadly it seems that zeal for sales creates controversy by the distortion of views. When that happens, truth is sacrificed upon the altar of profitability.

The current climate of media reporting sometimes reveals a commitment to a form of philosophical relativism that is agnostic with respect to objective truth. We live in an age of neo-sophism. Like the sophists of antiquity who awakened Socrates to action, we are besieged by a kind of skepticism that inevitably follows in the wake of relativism.

The ancient sophists, who with their *sophistry*, were both *sophisticated* and *sophomoric*. They excelled in the science of *rhetoric*. What began as a science of training in debate and forensics with the noble goal of teaching students sound reasoning and skills of clarity in communication degenerated under the sophists to a science dedicated to the goal of learning how to persuade or win arguments whether or not the propositions argued were true. Persuasion became the all-consuming pragmatic expedient at the loss of any concern for truth. This was the practice that Socrates refused to tolerate. Socrates could not, nay, would not live on Madison Avenue.

Freedom of the press is a vital national interest. It is rightly defended by the Constitution of the United States. What we need today is a corresponding commitment to the responsibility of the press. Freedom demands responsibility. A man may be legally free in certain societies to distort the truth. But no man is ever morally free to corrupt the truth. A good press is a press with a conscience, a press that holds truth in the highest regard.

There are few news agencies that say they are opposed to the truth. Even the leading news agency of the Soviet Union is named "Truth" in Russian.* But to claim to tell the truth and to tell the truth are two different things. We need news agencies that are as zealous for the deed as they are for the claim.

---

* *Pravda,* meaning "truth," is a Russian newspaper based in Moscow. During the Soviet era, it was the official newspaper of the Communist Party of the Soviet Union.

SOVEREIGNTY AND FREE WILL

MARCH 1990

I F GOD IS SOVEREIGN, CAN man have free will? If man has free will, can God be sovereign? Classical Christianity answers *yes* to both of these questions. However, the *yes* is often qualified by tortuous explanations that reveal the idea that the two affirmations involve believing on two poles of a contradiction. We hear these dual affirmations being called "antinomies" or contradictories that both must be embraced by faith.

A faith that embraces two poles of a contradiction is not faith but credulity. It necessitates a flight into irrationality that casts a shadow on the fruitfulness of God. If we conceive of divine sovereignty and human freedom in contradictory terms, then we are both intellectually and morally obliged to deny one or the other, if not both of the propositions. If two propositions are equally true then they cannot be contradictory. If two propositions are contradictory they cannot both be true.

Suppose we construct the following syllogism: All men are not men. Socrates is a man. Socrates is not a man.

Is the argument indicated by the syllogism valid or invalid?

Most people answer that question by saying "invalid." However, according to the rules of logic, the argument is valid. "But," you say, "the conclusion is not true." Right. The conclusion is not true but the argument is still valid. Arguments, according to logic, are neither true nor false; they are either valid or invalid. Propositions, on the other hand, are either true or false.

Now ... to complicate matters further we must insist that the *conclusion* of an argument may be true and the argument itself invalid. By a happy inconsistency we can arrive at a true conclusion by an invalid argument just as we can reach a false conclusion by a valid argument.

For the conclusion to be true and the argument valid, two requirements must be met. The propositions that make up the premises must be true and the argument itself must be valid. The problem with the syllogism above is that its first premise is not true. The proposition "all men are not men" is a false proposition because it is contradictory. Arguments are valid when and if their conclusions flow from the premises. An argument's validity then does not depend on the truth of the premises but upon the logical relationship of the premises.

Therefore if we conclude that God is sovereign and that man has free will, then our conclusion itself becomes a new conjunctive proposition. If the proposition is *true*, it cannot be contradictory. For the conjunctive proposition to be true and not contradictory, one side of the proposition at least must be limited. That is, either God's sovereignty is limited by man's free will or man's free will is limited by God's sovereignty.

To limit God's sovereignty by human free will allows the proposition: God is sovereign over everything except man's free will; or the proposition: Man's free will is not limited by God's sovereignty. Both of these are logical possibilities but theological impossibilities. If God's sovereignty is limited by the creature's will, then God is not sovereign over His creatures. If God is not sovereign over His creatures, God is not sovereign. If God is not sovereign, God is not God.

On the other hand, if man's free will is limited by God's sovereignty, we have a proposition that is both logically sound and theologically sound.

To say that man's free will is limited is to agree with Scripture. If man's free will is unlimited, then man is autonomous. In this case man, not God, would be sovereign.

It is divine sovereignty and human autonomy that are mutually exclusive contradictories. If God is sovereign, man could not possibly be autonomous. If man is autonomous, God could not possibly be sovereign.

But the Bible nowhere teaches that man is autonomous. It everywhere teaches that God is sovereign. Man has freedom—but his freedom is always and everywhere limited by God's sovereignty. Both God and man can simultaneously be free moral agents but not to the same degree. If man's limited freedom collides with God's unlimited sovereignty, something has to give. It is not God who yields.

In my house there are several people living together, each of whom is a free moral agent. For example, I have a free will and my son has a free will. I have more freedom than my son in the sphere of our relationship because I have more authority and power than he does. If his free will bumps up against my free will, my son is the one who usually experiences the limitation. Of course neither of us is sovereign; that role is usually held by my wife (*sic*).

We conclude then that divine sovereignty and human freedom are not antinomies as long as we understand that divine sovereignty imposes a limit on the extent of human freedom. Human freedom, though less than autonomous, is real. Its limitation by divine sovereignty does not involve its annihilation.

TIME WARP

———

"PERHAPS WHEN WE PASS THE DIMENSIONAL veil from this world to the next, we will dwell in that place of light inaccessible where time and eternity meet."

In 1905, a sixteen-year-old boy was walking alongside a river in Switzerland. His mood was one of contemplative reverie. He was entranced by the patterns of the meandering river. As children gaze at the clouds and allow their imaginations to roam freely, "seeing" images and shapes of animals and people formed by the clouds, so this young man began to think about sunbeams. He thought about what it would be like to chase a beam of light.

This reverie was not unlike that of the child who is afraid of the dark and walks to the light switch by the door. He assumes a racer's poised stance at the blocks then switches off the light and rushes toward his bed in a frantic effort to get there before the light goes out. Every child who has entered such a race against light or darkness has lost.

But the boy in Switzerland imagined that he could run as fast as the light. He saw himself chasing down a beam of light. His mind became fixed on the idea. By the time he had reached his twenty-sixth birthday, he had formulated a theory based on his imaginative reverie and delivered a lecture on it in Zurich at the Carpenter's Union hall. His first lecture sounded like the ravings of a crank, a kind of "Gyro Gearloose" fantasy.*

This was the introduction of a theory now known to the world as the "special theory of relativity" introduced by the boy-dreamer, Albert Einstein.

In the special theory, Einstein challenged a concept that had been assumed by man as long as there have been men or women to make assumptions. He challenged the idea that time is a fixed, inherent, objective reality. He challenged the axiom of Sir Isaac Newton that "absolute

———

* Gyro Gearloose is a character in Walt Disney cartoons. He is a prolific inventor, the stereotypical eccentric genius.

time and mathematical time, of itself, and from its own nature, flows equally without relation to anything external."

We are accustomed to thinking about time in Newton's way. We measure it by observing the succession of moments by space and motion. How do our "clocks" work? The sundial measures time by the movement of a shadow across the surface of a dial. We watch a second hand sweep around the face of a numbered circle. We count the swings of a pendulum moving from left to right and back again. Gears turn, elements pulsate, water drops. These and other methods help us to count moments. In all these forms of timekeeping there is some kind of motion measured against some kind of reference point in space.

Einstein's theory argued that neither space nor time are absolute objective realities. He came to this by examining the strange phenomenon of light.

Einstein had some interesting things to say about light. The first was that the velocity or speed of light is inherent in light itself. It is the same for all observers whether the observers are at rest or in motion. For example, if I am traveling west at 50 miles per hour and another car is traveling east directly toward me at 50 miles per hour, the rate of approach of the two cars is 100 miles per hour. However, according to the special theory of relativity, if a beam of light approaches me at 186,272 miles per second and I am moving toward it at the rate of 100,000 miles per second the rate of approach stays fixed at 186,272 miles per second. The theory contends that nothing can accelerate to the speed of light and that nothing can exceed the speed of light. The speed of light seems to be the cosmic speed limit over which nature has an inherent governor.

As we approach the speed of light, mass increases and time slows down. Einstein imagined that if he ever caught up to his sunbeam he would enter a condition where time would stand still. Ernst Mack, with whom Einstein agreed, argued that "all masses and all velocities, and consequently all forces, are relative."

In heaven we are told that time shall be no more. Perhaps when we pass the dimensional veil from this world to the next, we will dwell in that place of light inaccessible where time and eternity meet. Perhaps in heaven, we will catch Einstein's sunbeam.

"Though God's grace tempers His just and righteous anger, it by no means annuls it."

—

THE LIMITS OF GOD'S GRACE: JONATHAN EDWARDS ON HELL

JULY 1990

A S A COLLEGE STUDENT I WAS INTRODUCED to Jonathan Edwards' sermon "Sinners in the Hands of an Angry God" in two ways. The first was in an anthology of American literature. The second was in a textbook of psychology. The psychology text made reference to Edwards' sermon as an example of sadism. Edwards' graphic description of the flames of divine wrath was cited as an illustration of a psychological disorder that reflected the aberrations noted in the Marquis de Sade. Edwards was charged with a preoccupation with hell and divine wrath by which he terrorized his congregation with a sadistic "scare theology."

If we know anything about the real Jonathan Edwards, we know that whatever else he may have been, he was not a sadist. I say this for several reasons, not the least of which is that Edwards clearly believed in the reality of hell. He also exhibited a profound concern that his people never experience that reality. A sadist who believed in hell would probably be more likely to give assurances to people that they were in no danger of hell, so he could deliciously relish the contemplation of their falling into it.

Edwards has been widely recognized as a giant among American philosophical geniuses. He was conversant with the latest developments in eighteenth-century British empiricism. The empiricists, especially David Hume, were concerned about epistemology, how we learn, know, experience, and recall ideas. For example, David Hume argued that ideas are remembered by the mind in direct proportion to the *intensity* and *vivacity* by which they were first experienced. Edwards in turn, was not a sensationalist in the journalistic sense but philosophically he was acutely aware of the importance of intense and vivid sensations to make a deep and lasting impression on the mind. Perhaps no preacher in history provides more graphic mental images than did Edwards.

We cite the following images from "Sinners in the Hands of an Angry God": "The wrath of God burns against them, their damnation does not slumber; the pit is prepared, the fire is made ready, the furnace is now hot, ready to receive them; the flames do now rage and glow. The glittering sword is whet, and held over them, and the pit hath opened its mouth under them."

Again we read: "The bow of God's wrath is bent, and the arrow made ready on the string, and justice bends the arrow at your heart, and strains the bow, and it is nothing but the mere pleasure of God, and that of an angry God, without any promise or obligation at all, that keeps the arrow one moment from being made drunk with your blood."

Again: "You hang by a slender thread, with the flames of divine wrath flashing about it, and ready every moment to singe it and burn it asunder...."

When we examine the terrifying images that Edwards used in this sermon, we see that almost all of them are taken directly from Sacred Scripture itself. If we read this sermon armed with a broader knowledge of Edwards' preaching and teaching, we may see something in it that goes beyond the images of fire, bow, and wrath. We know that at the core of Edwards' theology was a profound emphasis on the grace of God. He repeatedly spoke of the "sweetness and excellency" of Christ and of God's grace.

Is there any grace in this sermon? By all means. We see it in the image of the hands of God. It is the hand of God that stops the bow and keeps the sinner from falling into the pit. Yet Edwards observes that these gracious hands belong to a God who is angry. The warning is clear against presuming upon grace. Though God's grace tempers His just and righteous anger, it by no means annuls it. If one fails to avail himself of God's long-suffering patience and extended offer of grace, there comes a moment when the limit of that grace is reached and the hand of God lets go. The straining bow is released. The upholding hand is removed and we fall into the pit.

The sermon is a due warning about the human neglect of divine grace. The dual theme is seen in these words: "God hath had it on His heart to show to angels and men, both how excellent His love is, and also how terrible His wrath is."

PARABLES: A TWO-EDGED SWORD

AUGUST 1990

———

T HERE IS AN OFT-NEGLECTED PRINCIPLE taught in the New Testament. I call it the principle of "graduated responsibility." This principle is taught by Jesus in Luke 12:48: "From everyone who has been given much, much will be demanded. . . ."

This saying is part of the parable of the faithful steward. It underscores the terms of the judgment the lord in the parable renders to his servants. The punishment meted out is given in direct proportion to the prior knowledge each servant had:

> That servant who knows his master's will and does not get ready or does not do what his master wants will be beaten with many blows. But the one who does not know and does things deserving punishment will be beaten with few blows (vv. 47–48).

Here we see that judgment and punishment are rendered according to knowledge as well as action. The greater the knowledge, the greater the accountability.

The principle of graduated responsibility sheds light on the difficult New Testament teaching regarding Jesus' use of parables:

> He told them, "The secret of the kingdom of God has been given to you. But to those on the outside everything is said in parables so that 'they may be ever seeing but never perceiving, and ever hearing but never understanding; otherwise they might turn and be forgiven!'" (Mark 4:11–12).

We tend to view the parables of Jesus as simple illustrations that shed light on great truths. Indeed they do function in that way in part. However, at the same time, the parables double as a kind of riddle whose purpose is to conceal or obscure the meaning from some. To some, the parables reveal the mystery of the kingdom of God, while to others, they hide it from them.

As a two-edged sword the parable is at once a tool of redemption and an instrument of judgment. The use of parables reflects the "crisis" character of Jesus' ministry. The English word *crisis* derives from the Greek word *krisis*. The Greek word, however, is usually translated by the word *judgment.*

Though Jesus came as Redeemer, He also came as Judge. The judgment He brings is the supreme crisis for the world. To those who have ears to hear, His words are life; to those who are deaf to the things of God, His words are death. Jesus' life and ministry are the ultimate division brought before mankind.

That the concealing aspect of parables reflect the judgment of God is foreshadowed by the prophet Isaiah:

> He said, "Go and tell this people: 'Be ever hearing, but never understanding; be ever seeing, but never perceiving.' Make the heart of this people calloused; make their ears dull and close their eyes. Otherwise they might see with their eyes, hear with their ears, understand with their hearts, and turn and be healed" (Isaiah 6:9–10).

Here God's call to Isaiah is to be a vehicle of divine judgment. When the people refuse to see the glory God reveals of Himself, His response is to make them blind. When the people refuse to hear the Word of God, God makes them deaf. This is a kind of poetic justice by which God punishes in kind.

This type of judgment is articulated by Paul in Romans 1: "Since they did not think it worthwhile to retain the knowledge of God, he gave them over to a depraved mind, to do what ought not to be done" (v. 28).

The worst punishment that can befall us is to be given over or abandoned to our sin by God. This anticipates God's verdict at the final judgment: "Let him who does wrong continue to do wrong; let him who is vile continue to be vile" (Revelation 22:11a).

Every time God's Word is proclaimed it changes all of those within its hearing. No one ever remains unaffected by God's Word.

To those who hear it positively, there is growth in grace. To those who reject it or are indifferent to it, calluses are added to their souls, and calcium to their hearts. The eye becomes dimmer and dimmer, the ear heavier and heavier, the mystery of the kingdom more and more obscure.

He who has ears to hear, let him hear.

"I WAS A STRANGER
AND YOU INVITED ME IN"

SEPTEMBER 1990

———

THE BOOK OF ACTS RECORDS a curious phenomenon:

> On that day a great persecution broke out against the church at
> Jerusalem, and all except the apostles were scattered throughout
> Judea and Samaria (8:1).

> Those who had been scattered preached the word wherever they
> went (8:4).

It is clear that the whole church, save their Apostolic leaders, were scattered. Those who were scattered (the whole church) went about preaching the Word.

The New Testament church was a mobilized community. All of the rank-and-file members were involved in ministry. This is the kind of church that "turned the world upside down."

In the sixteenth century Martin Luther formulated the concept of the "Priesthood of All Believers." Contrary to widespread misconceptions of this doctrine, Luther did not mean by it the abolition of any distinction between clergy and laity. Rather, Luther's point was that every Christian must participate in the ministry of the church and that every Christian must endeavor "to be Christ to his neighbor."

To be Christ to your neighbor is not to be your neighbor's Lord and Savior. Rather, it is to be Christ's *representative* to your neighbor. We are to represent the mercy and ministry of Jesus to all who are around us.

Nineteenth-century liberal theology in Germany saw the publication of countless volumes of theology containing the German word *wesen*, which means "being" or "essence." Liberals sought to reduce the supernatural concern of personal redemption to a core or essence of social concern.

In reaction to the modernist-fundamentalist controversy many evangelicals, zealous to retain the biblical concern for personal redemption, began to minimize or even reject the social agenda of the New Testament. Social concern and social relief ministry became identified with Liberalism. Ministry to the poor, the homeless, the hungry, and the imprisoned was often all-too-willingly surrendered to the state or the liberal church.

This reaction was utterly foreign to and in violation of the clear mandate of Scripture, the Scripture that evangelicals were so jealous to defend. James wrote concerning the *wesen* or essence of pure religion:

Religion that God our Father accepts as pure and faultless is this: to look after orphans and widows in their distress and to keep oneself from being polluted by the world (James 1:27).

James was not a liberal. James, the brother of Jesus, was more concerned about evangelism and personal salvation than any evangelical. He saw no tension between concern for the soul and concern for man's material welfare. In this James was merely echoing the teachings of his brother and Lord:

"For I was hungry and you gave me something to eat, I was thirsty and you gave me something to drink, I was a stranger and you invited me in, I needed clothes and you clothed me, ... I was in prison and you came to visit me" (Matthew 25:35–36). "I tell you the truth, whatever you did for one of the least of these brothers of mine, you did for me" (v. 40).

We do not need volunteers driven by guilt manipulation or looking for merits to be redeemed. Christ has taken our guilt and supplied all the merit we need. We need volunteers because in the least of His brothers, Jesus is hungry; Jesus is thirsty; Jesus is homeless; Jesus is sick; Jesus is imprisoned.

We need volunteers who love Jesus in the afflictions of His least brethren.

SAVING THE PHENOMENA

OCTOBER 1990

A TOP THE ENTRANCE TO PLATO'S Academy outside of Athens, the following words were affixed: *Let None But Geometers Enter Here.* Few moderns think of Plato's Academy as a school of geometry. We usually associate Plato with the discipline of philosophy, not mathematics, though it is widely known that Plato was intrigued by the quasi-mystical significance Pythagoras had attached to numbers and math. Pythagoras' blend of math and philosophy had a clear influence upon Plato.

It is the link between math and philosophy that explains the sign over Plato's door and gave rise to a phrase popularized by Plato that has been a crucial legacy to subsequent generations of scientists. The phrase *save the phenomena* crystallizes Plato's conviction that one of the primary tasks of science is to provide a model that would adequately explain the perceivable world of the senses.

For Plato there was an inseparable relationship between science and philosophy. He saw the task of philosophy (science/knowledge) to get beyond the realm of the physical (opinion) to the ultimate or metaphysical realm.

Plato's philosophy has been called a theory of forms, because ideas represent formal or rational reality. To understand the external world, one must grasp the proper *forms* or *ideas* that lie behind the imperfect copies we perceive around us. In this regard, Plato was searching for a formal (rational) explanation for the material (sensory) realm. Hence his vital concern for geometry. Geometry explores various forms such as circles, triangles, and squares and seeks to discern the mathematical relationships that govern them.

Since Plato (and even before him), scientists have sought to discover the mathematical laws that govern reality. They have sought to quantify nature in an effort to provide a coherent, symmetrical pattern of order by which observable things may be explained and *predicted*. To *save the phenomena* is to make sense out of the diversity of natural experience. The phenomena are saved when an adequate mathematical formula can account for them and render them predictable.

At this point, science is concerned with something eminently practical. In the ancient world, literally life-and-death decisions were made based on mathematical calculations of time and seasons. The patterns of the phases of the moon and the movement of the stars were observed and analyzed for purposes of navigation (a life-and-death enterprise) and especially for the tasks of planting and harvesting (again, real life-and-death matters).

The pattern of the movement of the stars posed a vexing problem. Though most of the stars moved in a relatively easy-to-predict pattern, there were a few stars that violated the regular patterns. These stars seemed to "wander" about the sky like so many loose cannons on the deck of a ship. The word *planet* comes from the Greek word that means "wanderer."

In an effort to save the phenomena of the stars, the ancient philosophers/astronomers tried to figure out how the universe was constructed (cosmology). To the naked eye the sky appeared as a canopy or a ceiling over a stationary earth. The sky was conceived as a crystalline sphere to which stars were attached. As the sphere revolved, the stars moved in their observable patterns. Because the canopy-sphere was made of crystal it was invisible to the naked eyes of human observers. However, to explain the movements of the planets in an orderly, predictable pattern, special adjustments had to be made. For the math to work, a series of smaller crystal spheres were postulated with individual patterns of motion called *epicycles*. What emerged was a complex geometrical theory of wheels within wheels that made mathematical sense. The epicycle theory went through numerous modifications, revisions, and adjustments until a cumbersome and complex series of over fifty epicycles emerged. As contrived and cumbersome as this theory became, the astonishing thing is that for all practical purposes, it worked. It worked with amazing precision in terms of the life-and-death issues of predictability.

The crystalline sphere-cum-epicycle theory saved the phenomena. Indeed, the phenomena were considered saved, sanctified, and sanforized. Never mind that the theory was false in the sense that it did not correspond to reality. It assumed geocentricity, namely that the earth was the center of the solar system, and a host of other since-discredited assumptions. The theory persisted as accepted fact for well over a thousand years and is often pinpointed as a monumental obstruction to progressive scientific discovery.

When the old geocentric theory was overcome by the heliocentric (sun-centered) solar system of Copernicus, this victory was described as a "revolution." The Copernican revolution created a crisis of credibility both for the church (the church had "baptized" the geocentric model) and for orthodox scientists. In a word, Copernicus' work smashed the crystalline spheres of the ancient world and opened the door for fresh avenues of exploration for modern science.

A supreme irony emerged, however, out of the Copernican revolution. Though the heliocentric theory clearly had a much closer understanding of actual reality than geocentricity, it didn't work as well in the practical realm of prediction. Copernicus made a serious error in his theory. He assumed that the orbits of the planets around the sun were circular.

It was not until Kepler defined and quantified the orbital path of planets as being elliptical rather than circular that the problem was solved. Kepler's adjustments served to bring the scientific model into closer conformity to reality as well as saving the phenomena with accuracy superior to geocentricity.

There is a gigantic lesson to be learned in all this. It is the lesson that scientific models may work fine for practical purposes and be false with respect to reality. The history of science has witnessed an as yet never-ending series of models that are constantly being revised or jettisoned as new knowledge is uncovered. Some models work fine to a point. The point at which they fail is the point they encounter anomalies that cannot be accounted for adequately by the current model. Anomalies threaten to disrupt the model; like planets were to the ancients, they are those pesky data that defy salvation by a working model. They belong to phenomena that refuse to be saved until a better model or theory is devised.

This observation is not meant to disparage the efforts of modern science. On the contrary, I for one stand in awe at the relentless pursuit of judicious scientists to improve working models to get a more accurate view of truth. The advances in the realm of cosmology over the last five hundred years have been almost superhuman in their brilliance.

It is precisely because of the marvelous discoveries of recent times that a sober caution is in order. We can become so intoxicated by the progress of science that we delude ourselves into thinking the present working models are more trouble-free than they are. We can also fall into the same trap that earlier thinkers did: by assuming that because something works for practical purposes, it therefore must necessarily describe reality. That would be as naive as it is arrogant.

In the novel *The Sand Pebbles*, unskilled and uneducated natives became assistants of the hero, working with him in the engine room. The assistants had no technical knowledge of the machinery they were charged to maintain. They literally "played it by ear." They were in tune to the rhythmic sounds of the engines. When the engines went "thumpity-thump," they were fine. When they heard "thumpity-da-thump," the assistants not only knew something was wrong, they knew exactly what to do without knowing anything about physics or mechanics. They could save the phenomena practically without understanding the deeper truths behind the phenomena.

In like manner, my six-year-old grandson is the person whose expertise I rely upon when I can't get our VCR to work. He knows the right buttons to push in the right sequence to get the desired results, without any understanding of the mysteries of electronics.

To save the phenomena the way Plato wanted to save the phenomena was to discover models that both work and are true. In this enterprise the Christian ought to be an active participant. The scientific goal of achieving truth is a sacred task. The practical concerns of predictability and managing the phenomena are also sacred tasks implied in the divine mandate to have dominion over the earth. At this level the Christian must never be an enemy of science. To oppose science in these pursuits is to be faithless rather than faithful.

"The history of science has witnessed an as yet never-ending series of models that are constantly being revised or jettisoned as new knowledge is uncovered."

THE GREAT
AND THE GOOD

NOVEMBER 1990

———

A S A CHILD, THE FIRST prayer I ever learned was a simple table grace. It went like this: "God is great, God is good. And we thank Him for this food." At the time, I did not realize that a single biblical word captured the twin ideas of God's greatness and His goodness. The single word is *holy*.

The earliest traceable form of the Semitic root of the word *holy*, reaching to a Canaanite source, carried the meaning "to divide." Anything that was holy was divided or separated from all other things. It pointed to the difference between the ordinary and the extraordinary; the common and uncommon; the average and the great.

In religious terms the word *holy* divided God from all other things to put Him in a category that was *sui generis* (in a class by Himself). The Holy One is the One who possesses the supreme perfection of being. He transcends or is divided from all things creaturely. He is the most majestic, most exalted, most awe-provoking Being. Since He is both marvelous and wonderful in His very essence, the creature, when contemplating the Holy God, responds in marvel and wonder because of His greatness.

We see, then, that in the first instance God is called *holy* not because of what He does, but because of who He is. Originally the term was more a noun than a verb, referring to God's being, not His action or behavior. When Amos caused God to swear by His holiness (4:2), God was not swearing by His ethical or moral purity; He was swearing by his august essence, by His very divine Being. This referred to the gravity (*gravitas*) of God's inner nature. Since ontology is the science of being, we can say that in the first instance the word *holy* refers to God's ontological perfection rather than His moral perfection. His Being is clearly divided from all creaturely being. His Being is a higher order of being from all created being. Creatures great and small cannot be at all safe, as in Him they live and move and have their being. All lesser beings are contingent, derived, and dependent upon the greater and prior Being of God.

Yet if our childhood prayer stopped with the first predicate adjective ascribed to God ("God is great"), the prayer would be naked. It would be vulnerable to serious misunderstanding.

It is not enough for the Christian to believe that God is great. In human terms of power, Joseph Stalin was great. His power was overwhelming. But Joseph Stalin was not good.

As the word *holy* developed in biblical usage it took on an added dimension that clothed the naked being of God with garments of purity. The biblical writers came to understand that there was another crucial line of division between God and creaturely humans. This was a line that distinguished the quality of action between mortals and God. God alone possesses moral perfection. What He does is consistent with what He is. An aspect of His innermost being is His absolute purity. Not only is there nothing contingent, derived, or dependent in God's being, so is there nothing in His innermost character that is evil. The God who is great is also the God who is good. He is the *summum bonum* (highest good) not only in the sense that His excellency is the highest good for us to contemplate, but He is the *summum bonum* in the sense that perfection is inherent in His character. He is both the source and the norm of all good. In Him the good itself lives and moves and has its being. He is the norm of norms and without norm.

Before the moral perfection of God no man is holy. As Isaiah realized before the unveiled splendor of divine majesty, we are all unclean. We are *akathartos*. For us to be called *saints* (holy ones), we must have a catharsis. We must be made clean. No unclean thing can stand before the presence of a holy God. That which is unclean is profane in His eyes. For us to be holy unto God we must have our unclean, unholy moral imperfection purged and our sin removed from us. That is why the absolutely necessary condition for redemption is atonement. Without atonement we would remain always and forever unclean and unholy before His penetrating gaze.

No human is holy in himself. Holiness is foreign to us. It is alien. That is why we require the righteousness of Another to cover our moral nakedness. The Holy One has given us the holiness we need in the cloak of Christ's righteousness. Therefore we pray: God is great, God is good. And we thank Him for the food . . . that has come down from heaven for us.

AFTER DARKNESS, LIGHT

JANUARY 1991

———

I T WAS A BAPTISM OF SORTS, an immersion in history. Our trek
through Europe last summer included visits to England, Scotland,
Austria, Germany, Switzerland, and France. There were two foci in
view. The first was the Vienna conference on theology for pastors from
behind what was called the Iron Curtain. The second was a Reformation
study tour with special emphasis on the work of Martin Luther in Germany and John Calvin in Switzerland.

When one is immersed in anything he runs the risk of being inundated to the point of eventual suffocation. The deluge of history was
so powerful that I still have not sorted it all out. I am left with impressions. Vivid impressions from the past that suggest needed action in
the present.

In England I spent as much time reading as I did observing and listening.
We walked through the pages of British history (which is our history),
beginning with the mute remains of Roman settlements dating back to
the first century. We noted the impact of the Saxons, the Normans, and
the violent assaults from the Vikings. I saw the legacy of Edward the
Confessor. What began as a small abbey chapel expanded ultimately
into what is now Westminster Abbey. I tried to chart the maze of British
monarchs from Harold through Henry I and II, the Jameses, the Charleses,
the Georges, and others. What affected me the most, however, was the
brief period of severe struggle in the sixteenth century marked by the
reigns of Mary Tudor and Elizabeth I. I sat in the chapel at the Tower of
London and then stood by the Traitor's Gate where Bloody Mary sent her
half-sister Elizabeth as a captive. I visited Oxford and stood on the spot
where, after the executions of Bishops Latimer and Ridley. Mary ordered

the burning of Archbishop Cranmer—the funeral pyre whose sparks set England aflame for reformation.

North to Yorkshire and on to Scotland. There I preached in a small village church pastored by a man of singular devotion. I listened as he told me that only four percent of Scots attend church on a given Sunday, and the vast majority of them were attending a state church whose theology is chiefly a theology of unbelief.

Then came the standard European fare of C^2. C squared represents castles and cathedrals. St. Giles in Edinburgh afforded me a glimpse of breathtaking stained glass and the raised pulpit where John Knox thundered, at times impolitely, to the severe agitation and vexation of Mary, Queen of Scots. Knox is now buried in an unmarked grave somewhere beneath the asphalt parking lot around the corner from St. Giles.

Refreshing my memory of the spiritual pilgrimage of Luther in Germany fired my soul and shamed my conscience for my own insipid devotion. In Geneva I consorted with the ghosts of Farel, Calvin, and Beza. I stood at the Wall. *The* Wall. Not the Berlin Wall—the Reformation Wall, a long monument of stone that commemorates the Reformation. Towering in relief are the figures of Farel, Calvin, Beza, and Knox. Chiseled in the stone are the Latin words: POST TENEBRAS LUX—"After darkness, light."

But the depth-dimension of my baptism occurred in Vienna. There I met with 82 pastors from Eastern Europe. The largest group was from Romania, followed by contingents from the Soviet Union, Czechoslovakia, Hungary, Poland, Bulgaria, and East Germany. Nearly every individual who came was making the first trip of his life outside the Iron Curtain. They came to study theology. I learned that the average pastor in Eastern Europe owns the paltry total of six books. Their most treasured volume is, of course, the Bible. These men not only love the Bible, they know what's in it. They exhibited an extraordinary grasp of Sacred Scripture. But they yearned for in-depth theological instruction. As a teacher I had no worries of trying to motivate my students. They simply could not get enough. I lectured (via translators) for seventeen 90-minute segments in which I presented 34 units of theology covering the doctrine of God, the person of Christ, and the work of the Holy Spirit.

I did not want to leave. These pastors took my heart captive. Their faith and steadfast loyalty to Christ had been at great personal risk and cost. They had been imprisoned, shunned, dismissed from their jobs, and constantly harassed. But they displayed a joy and serenity that mirrored the martyred saints of the past.

I was left with this gestalt impression. What happened in England, Scotland, Germany, and Switzerland in the sixteenth century was the result of God's providential hand upon an exceedingly small group of people with an exceedingly large capacity for devotion and fidelity. If a new reformation comes to our planet, I would not be surprised to see it emanating from Eastern Europe. The devotion is there. And surely the hand of Providence is there. These are the chief ingredients needed. The central authority of Scripture musters their lives. They are living out what they believe.

I must go back.

WHAT THE *DUCE* HAS HAPPENED TO EDUCATION AND OTHER TRIVIA?

FEBRUARY 1991

———

W**E NEED TO PUT THE** *duce* back into education. The word *educate* is derived from the Latin *educare*, which means "to lead or guide out of" (from ignorance?). Two other crucial words derive from the same root: *induce* and *deduce*.

The modern scientific and technological revolution that has radically altered human life and culture may be traced to the triumph of the scientific method. At root the scientific method is based upon a combination of induction and deduction. The whole "knowing person" is engaged in the task of acquiring knowledge. That is, knowledge or "science" is achieved by using both the mind (rational) and the senses (empirical). Induction places the accent on the sensory, while deduction stresses the mental.

Induction derives from the Latin *inducere*, meaning "to lead in" or "to persuade." Induction moves from the particular to the universal or from the specific to the general. That is, by observation, experimentation, notification, and the like, we learn the particular data bits from which knowledge is constructed. Here we engage in the task of individuation. For example, we examine and observe a particular entity. We note that this entity is alive, is warm-blooded, is a vertebrate; it is a quadruped, has a bushy tail, and likes to store nuts. Since it looks like a squirrel and acts like a squirrel we acknowledge that it is a squirrel. Then we look at 10,000 more squirrels and see that they all have bushy tails. Finally we draw the conclusion that all squirrels have bushy tails. We move from the particular squirrel to the universal premise that all squirrels have bushy tails.

Once we establish our universals or "laws" then we are able to make deductions from them. The word *deduct* comes from the Latin *deducere*, meaning "to lead down" or "to draw out." The process of deduction moves from the universal to the particular, from the general to the specific. For example, we reason in the following manner: *All squirrels have bushy tails. This animal is a squirrel. This animal has a bushy tail.*

According to the laws of deduction the conclusion of this syllogism is valid. (It may or may not be true. It is true only if the premises are true.) Propositions are true or false. Arguments based on propositions are valid or invalid, depending upon their conformity to the laws of deduction. Check this syllogism: *All squirrels have bushy tails. This animal has a bushy tail. This animal is a squirrel.*

The conclusion of this syllogism is invalid because the laws of deduction (excluded middle) have been violated. (This same syllogism may actually be describing a fox rather than a squirrel.)

The glaring failure of modern education appears most blatant at the level of deduction. This is the *duce* that is all but missing. Our educational processes put great stress on the inductive side of learning, but all but ignores the deductive side.

Let me illustrate from standard seminary curricula. To prepare the student to be an effective pastor and biblical expositor, the student is required (sometimes) to learn the ancient languages of Hebrew and Greek. This involves learning vocabulary (word-meanings) and grammar. The tense of a verb is important to know to grasp the full impact of the force of the verb's meaning in its context. The student must also study the historical background and culture in which the biblical literature was written. All of these exercises are designed to insure that the student emerge from his studies as a competent exegete and interpreter of Scripture.

However, one thing is missing. I know of no seminary that requires the study of logic as a necessary tool for biblical interpretation. Yet I venture to guess that the single most frequently committed error in biblical exegesis and interpretation is an error in deduction. Wrong conclusions are reached because *illegitimate inferences* are made. We may master grammar, lexicography, and historical background and yet reach false conclusions because of errors in deduction.

It is possible, indeed customary, to achieve a Ph.D. in almost every academic discipline there is without ever taking a single course in logic. The deductive side of education has been all but eclipsed.

This is a matter of *trivial concern* (pun intended). In the medieval-classical education the lower division of the liberal arts curriculum three primary disciplines were stressed: These three arts were called the *trivium*. They were made up of *grammar, rhetoric,* and *logic.* The stress was on *reading, speaking,* and *thinking.* Now, progressive education gives us a Johnny who can't read, a Johnny who is inarticulate, and a Johnny who can't think. What the *duce* is going on?

We don't want to jettison the inductive. But if we are interested in sound conclusions, in real and valid knowledge (science), we must restore a balance between inductive and deductive skills and recover what Dorothy Sayers called the "lost tools of learning."

PERSONAL TRINITY

MARCH 1991

THE WORD *TRINITY* DOES NOT appear in Scripture. Nor do the terms *homoousios* or *persona* as such appear. That such language has entered the vocabulary of the church, indeed the touchstone expressions of orthodoxy itself, is decried by many as an intrusion into biblical faith of speculative philosophy in general and of Greek modes of thinking in particular.

However, the *concepts* these words convey *are* found in Scripture, and they have been usefully employed in the church. Like it or not, the English language is tied inseparably to concepts of early Greek discrimination. For example, the concepts of *being*, *essence*, and *existence* are so deeply rooted in our language, it is hard to imagine speaking for long without recourse to them. How long can we speak or write without using some form of the verb *to be*? It is also important to remember that it did not offend the Holy Ghost to use the Greek language as a vehicle for revelation.

What, then, do we mean when we express our faith in the Trinity by the formula: God is one in essence, and three in person? In addition to the numerical differences, the key distinctive concepts are *essence* and *person*. Essence, we know, refers to the being, substance, or stuff of any entity. Essence is what something ultimately *is*. In the formula of the Trinity it is the concept of *person* that is most troublesome.

The term *person* comes from the Latin term *persona*. It corresponds to the Greek word for *face*. In the ancient theater one actor could perform more than one role in a play. To assume the role of a different character the actor donned a persona or mask to dramatize the different character.

This human analogy breaks down, however, when applied to God. In the human drama we have one person assuming the roles of multiple persons. The Trinity means more than that God is one person with three faces. In human terms our point of reference to persons is that each singular person is a singular being. Likewise each individual person, even if suffering from a psychotic manifestation of a split personality or multiple personalities, is still a single person.

Key words are used to define what is meant by "person" in the Trinity. Some important terms are *subsistence, individuum,* and *hypostasis.*

The term *subsistence* may be compared with and contrasted with the word *existence.* Originally the word *exist* meant "to stand out of" (from *existere*). From what does existence stand out? It stands out of pure being or essence. It also stands out of nonbeing. The Greek philosophers struggled to define the difference between pure being, which is unified and eternal, and creaturely entities that are marked by change. Being is . . . but creaturely entities are always changing. They are "becoming." As they are becoming something they are not nothing, they are something. But what they are, is changing. These entities "stand out" of pure being, and out of nonbeing. In a word, they exist. In this sense God does not exist. He is . . . He is not becoming.

The term *subsistence* differs from *existence* in that it stands "under" being, not "out" of it. The difference between being and existence is essential. It is a difference in essence. The difference between subsistence and being is not essential. Subsistence refers to a distinction within essence. We can state it another way. The distinction of persons in the Godhead is a matter of a difference that is *real,* but not *essential.* They are distinct *hypostases* or subsistences. Each has a real, but not essential individuality (*individuum*). A divine person is not a species of God nor a part of God. The three persons are equal to each other in deity, dignity, power, and glory. They are distinguished in name, in the order of their being, in the mode of their action, and in their effects.

The psychological model of the Trinity has been attractive to many theologians, especially Jonathan Edwards. In brief it relates to the perfection of God's knowledge of Himself. God's knowing is inseparable from His being. He knows Himself perfectly and eternally. God's self-knowledge has a subject and an object. The object of His knowledge is Himself. God's self-knowledge bends back and returns from eternity upon itself.

Because God knows Himself most perfectly from eternity, He conceives and begets in Himself the perfect image of Himself. It is both a conception and an eternally generated idea of Himself. This is the second person of the Trinity, the Son or the Divine Logos.

Within the Divine Being there is not only knowing, but willing (volition). God wills nothing except as He knows it. What He wills, He wills perfectly. By His perfect will, He desires or wills Himself as the supreme good. As in the case of His self-knowledge, so God's self-willing returns eternally upon Himself. The Father conceives and perfectly wills the image of Himself, the Son. Perfect love proceeds from the Father to the Son and from the Son to the Father. By the conjunction of the knowledge and will of them both a third subsistence is posited in the Godhead, called the Holy Spirit. The Spirit proceeds from the mutual willing or longing of both the Father and the Son.

In an essence in which there is perfect knowledge bending back upon itself, an image is begotten and a Spirit proceeds on the impulse of the will. And yet these things inhere in the one, most single essence of God.

"Jesus is a living lightning rod, attracting to Himself both the fury of man against God and the wrath of God against man."

—

GOD: FRIEND OR FOE?

APRIL 1991

———

A S CHILDREN WE PLAYED GAMES DRAWN from the scenario of war. When a friend approached we pretended that we were sentries. The dialogue was simple: "Halt! Who goes there? Friend or foe?" Our categories left no room for indifferent neutrality. They were restricted to two options, friend or enemy.

Those are the only options we have in our relationship with God. No one is neutral. We are either God's friends or God's enemies. Men protest vociferously against this either/or situation, proclaiming that though they have no zeal for God, nevertheless they are not hostile, either. To suggest that people have a burning hatred for God is to provoke many to a burning hatred for us.

Jonathan Edwards once preached a sermon entitled "Man, Naturally God's Enemies." In this sermon Edwards declared:

> Men in general will own, that they are sinners. There are few, if any, whose consciences are so blinded as not to be sensible they have been guilty of sin.... They will own that they do not love God so much as they should do; that they are not so thankful as they ought to be for mercies; and that in many things they fail. And yet few of them are sensible that they are God's enemies. They do not see how they can be truly so called; for they are not sensible that they wish God any hurt, or endeavor to do Him any.

Yet, despite human protestations to the contrary, Scripture clearly describes natural fallen men as enemies of God. Paul, in speaking of our salvation, wrote: "For if, when we were God's enemies, we were reconciled to Him through the death of His Son" (Romans 5:10). Again, "Once you were alienated from God and were enemies in your minds because of your evil behavior" (Colossians 1:21). Also, "The sinful mind is hostile to God" (Romans 8:7).

Unregenerate man is consistently described as being in a state of alienation and enmity. This is the condition that makes reconciliation necessary. Reconciliation is necessary only when a state of estrangement exists between two or more parties. Estrangement is the natural fallen state of our relationship to God.

How are we enemies of God? Edwards provides an insightful summary of the problem. He lists several points of tension between God and man:

1) By nature we have a *low esteem* of God. We count Him unworthy of our love or fear.
2) We prefer to *keep a distance* from God. We have no natural inclination to seek His presence in prayer.
3) Our *wills are opposed* to the law of God. We are not loyal subjects of His sovereign rule.
4) We are enemies against God in our *affections*. Our souls have a seed of malice against God. We are quick to blaspheme and to rage against Him.
5) We are enemies in *practice*. We walk in a way that is contrary to Him.

The enmity we have by nature is neither mild nor slight. Edwards calls it a "mortal" enmity. It is mortal in the sense that if it were in our power to kill God, His life would not be safe among men for an instant. This charge may be more than we can bear unless we have absolute evidence to support it. History provides the proof. When God became incarnate by taking upon Himself a human nature, He was viciously hated, persecuted, and destroyed. The cry of the crowd, "Crucify Him," exhibited the deep-rooted lust for the blood of God.

Where such deep-rooted estrangement exists reconciliation seems almost impossible. To mediate such a dispute would require mediation beyond the scope of natural power. Herein is seen the depth and the riches of the mediatorial work of Christ. As the perfect mediator between God and man, Jesus effects our reconciliation. He is a living lightning rod, attracting to Himself both the fury of man against God and the wrath of God against man. His work on the cross placated the wrath of God in our behalf. All enmity between us and the Father has been removed for us by our Mediator.

The first fruits of our justification, as the Apostle Paul declared, is that we have "peace with God." For the redeemed all warfare with God is over. An eternal truce has been declared for us in Christ. Now, we are no more enemies but friends of God, indeed more than friends, as we have been adopted into His family.

WORKS OR FAITH? WHAT IS THE ROLE OF WORKS IN EFFECTING OUR JUSTIFICATION BEFORE GOD?

MAY 1991

T EVYE, IN HIS ROLE OF patriarch in *Fiddler on the Roof*, weighed the issues that befuddled him by saying, "On the one hand. . . . On the other hand."

Like Tevye we face a puzzling question regarding the role of works in effecting our justification before God. On the one hand the Bible says unequivocally, "By observing the law no one will be justified" (Galatians 2:16b).

On the other hand the only possible way any person can ever be justified before God is by good works. Good works and their consequent merit is the only way the demands of God's justice can be met.

Did I just write what it seems like I wrote? Indeed I did. Perhaps I can spell it out even more clearly by saying, "Ultimately, justification is by works alone."

Haven't I just repudiated the cardinal point of evangelical Christianity, justification by faith alone? By no means. Ironically justification by faith alone ultimately means justification by works alone.

Has Sproul lost his mind? Or his faith? Is this the man who ceaselessly insists that there is no room for contradiction in Christian truth now entertaining contradiction in the doctrine of justification?

God forbid. The key word is *ultimately*. When I say that ultimately justification is by works alone I mean that at the highest level good works must be performed to satisfy the demands of God's justice. Those good works are indeed performed by Christ, and by Christ alone. Christ alone earns the merit that is necessary to satisfy the requirements of God's justice.

When Luther and others declared that justification is by faith alone, he meant that justification is by Christ alone. The basis of my justification, the meritorious cause, is the righteousness of Christ. I am justified by works. They are not my works *per se*; they are the good works of Christ.

When we say that justification is by faith alone we are speaking not of the ultimate basis of our justification (which is always and ever the meritorious righteousness of Christ), but of the means by which the merit of Christ is appropriated to us.

When I say I am justified by faith alone I am saying that the means (the instrumental cause) by which the merit of Christ is reckoned to my account before God is faith. It is by faith and by faith alone that we receive the imputation of the merits of Christ.

There is nothing I can do to earn the application of Jesus' merits to my account. All of my "righteousness" is but filthy rags (Isaiah 64:6) compared with the cloak of Christ's righteousness. His merit alone is sufficient. I can never "merit the merit." That is, I can never perform works good enough to deserve the transfer of Christ's merits to my account. It is only by faith that I am joined to Christ in such a union that will result in God's utterly gracious act of imputing Jesus' merit to me.

We must remain constantly clear about the issue of justification. It is not so much an issue about faith and works as it is an issue of merit and grace. My justification is by grace alone (*sola gratia*) precisely because it is based upon someone else's merit. My justice or "justness" before God is an alien justice (*justitia alienum*), a righteousness that is foreign to me personally, precisely because it is performed by someone else, namely by Jesus. His righteousness was perfect. He satisfied every demand of God's law. He earned a crown of righteousness. By His good works salvation is earned. The merit is His and His alone.

Yet, by grace, God offers the righteousness of Christ to all who put their trust in Him. For all who believe, all who have faith in Him, the merit of Christ is reckoned to their account.

Does this exclude good works in the life of the believer? By no means. Our justification is always *unto* good works. Though no merit ever proceeds from our works, either those done before our conversion or those done afterwards, nevertheless good works are a necessary fruit of true faith.

"Necessary fruit"? Yes, *necessary*. Good works are not necessary for us to earn our justification. They are never the ground or basis of our justification. They are necessary in another more restricted sense. They are necessary corollaries to true faith. If a person claims to have faith yet brings no fruit of obedience whatsoever, it is proof positive that the claim to faith is a false claim. True faith inevitably and necessarily bears fruit. The absence of fruit indicates the absence of faith. We are not justified by the fruit of our faith. We are justified by the fruit of Christ's merit. We receive His merit only by faith. But it is only by true faith that we receive His merit. And all true faith yields true fruit.

This is what is meant by the Reformation slogan "Justification is by faith alone, but not by a faith that is alone."

The difference between Rome and the Reformation can be seen in these simple formulas:

Roman view
faith + works = justification

Protestant view
faith = justification + works

Neither view eliminates works. The Protestant view eliminates human merit. It recognizes that though works are the evidence or fruit of true faith they add or contribute nothing to the meritorious basis of our redemption.

The current debate over "Lordship salvation" must be careful to protect two borders.* On the one hand it is important to stress that true faith yields true fruit; on the other hand it is vital to stress that the only merit that saves us is the merit of Christ received by faith alone.

---

* The Lordship salvation controversy was a dispute during the 1980s and 1990s that centered on the place of works in the life of a Christian. One side said that a true Christian will always manifest his belief in form of good works after salvation. The other side argued that such a position is tantamount to making works necessary to salvation, which destroys the doctrine of justification by faith alone. Briefly, the question was whether it is possible to have Jesus as one's Savior (and thus to enjoy salvation) without having Him as one's Lord (and thus not to live a life of obedience).

AN APOLOGY FOR APOLOGETICS

JULY 1991

———

THE TERM *APOLOGETICS HAS ITS* origin in the Greek word *apologia* meaning "a reply." It is not to be confused with a hat-in-hand expression of remorse for having done something wrong. The role of the apologist is not to say, "I'm sorry for being a Christian."

Apologetics as a special science was born out of a combination of a divine mandate and the pressing need to respond to false charges leveled against the early church. God requires that we be prepared to give a "reason for the hope that is within us" (1 Peter 3:15). In this regard the apologist echoes the work of the Apostles who did not ask people to respond to Christ in blind faith. For example, Peter said, "We did not follow cleverly invented stories when we told you about the power and coming of our Lord Jesus Christ, but we were eyewitnesses of His majesty" (2 Peter 1:16). The Apostolic testimony to Christ was buttressed both by rational argument and empirical evidence.

The early church apologists, such as Justin Martyr, gave "replies" (usually addressed to the Roman emperor) to clarify and defend the faith against false charges. It was reported, for example, that the emerging sect of Christians was seditious, irrational, and cannibalistic (meeting in secret to eat somebody's body and blood). Justin replied by clarifying the Christian position on civil obedience, philosophy, and the Lord's Supper.

At first the stress on apologetics was defensive. It replied to objections and misrepresentations used against Christian truth claims. Later it developed into a more proactive science in seeking to develop a full-orbed Christian philosophy in which the truth claims of Christianity were set forth in a reasoned intellectual system of thought.

In our day it is becoming increasingly necessary to provide an apology for apologetics. In many quarters the reasoned defense of Christianity is considered at best a waste of time and at worst a degeneration into a sub-Christian or even anti-Christian elevation of reason over faith.

Ours is an age of unprecedented fideism in which it is thought virtuous to believe without reason or even against reason. Karl Barth, for example, insisted that to embrace contradictions is a mark of Christian maturity.

Reformed theology has a firm conviction that only God can convert the sinner. No amount of rational argument, cogent evidence, or forceful persuasion can change the heart of the unbeliever unless that sinner is first regenerated by God the Holy Spirit. Armed with this conviction some in the Reformed camp conclude that rational apologetics is either an exercise in futility or positively harmful.

As one thoroughly convinced of Reformed theology, I am in total agreement with the thesis that apologetics alone cannot convert the sinner. But I do not further conclude that apologetics is therefore unnecessary.

There are several vital tasks left for apologetics to perform. I will provide here a brief list:

(1) *Pre-evangelism.* In defining the essence of saving faith the Reformers distinguished among three elements: (a) content or data of faith (*notitia*); (b) objective truth of the content (*assensus*); (c) personal trust or reliance on the truth (*fiducia*). The third, *fiducia,* can only be wrought by the operation of the Holy Spirit via regeneration. The first two are assisted by apologetics. The heart cannot trust what the mind does not affirm. There can be assent (*assensus*) without trust (*fiducia*) but not trust (*fiducia*) without assent (*assensus*).

(2) *Restrain evil.* Calvin argued that one value of apologetics was to "stop the mouths of the obstreperous." Here apologetics, though not able to convert the infidel, can restrain the unbeliever from unbridled assault against the faith. Apologetics provides an atmosphere in which the unbeliever must guard his tongue against accusing Christianity of being intellectually foolish.

(3) *Support believers.* Converted Christians can become so easily intimidated by intellectual critique that they lose their boldness to proclaim the Gospel. They are also vulnerable to being assailed by doubts. For example, as a college student I listened to learned professors who ridiculed Christianity. At that time I read Cornelius Van Til's remarkable critique of opposing world views to Christianity. Though I did not embrace Van Til's method of proactive support of Christianity, I was greatly aided by his critique of opposing philosophers.

(4) *Commonplace benefits.* Closely related to (2) is the benefit to culture derived when Christianity enjoys a status of intellectual credibility. When the faith is relegated to a reservation of personal religion or piety based solely on sentiment, it has difficulty informing the institutions that shape culture. Where Christian truth is established with credibility, it has a salutary effect on culture.

The apologetic task is difficult, complex, and never-ending. Yet it is the mandate of God to us. The responsibility is ours; its success is God's.

AN OBJECTIVE LESSON IN SUBJECTIVE THEORY

SEPTEMBER 1991

V ALUE IS IN THE EYE OF THE BEHOLDER.
Which is the better flavor of ice cream, vanilla or chocolate? If I
asked you such a question you may be inclined to respond, "Better, in what way? Do you mean more healthy? More flavorful? or what?"
Isn't it simply a matter of taste? When we speak in these terms we are
describing personal preferences. Such preferences vary from individual
to individual. There is no universal preference of ice cream flavors.

Personal preference lies at the heart of the subjective theory of value.
To prefer one thing over another is to value it more highly than the other.
In this sense value is relative; it is relative to one's preference.

Does that sound like relativism or subjectivism? It may sound like relativism; it may seem like relativism; but it is not relativism. Relativism is
a philosophy that denies ultimate norms for truth. It reduces truth itself
from objective correspondence to reality to subjective preference. Likewise subjectivism reduces truth to personal preference or perception.

We are not discussing truth here. We are discussing values; the worth
we attach to certain things. It may be that no two people on this planet
have exactly the same value systems. This is one reason why finances are
often a serious stress point on marriages. A married couple doesn't always
agree on how $100 should be used. The husband may want to spend it
on tools and the wife on the children's clothes.

Because people have different priorities and preferences, value is related
to the subject who makes the financial decision. It is because value is
subjective that commerce is possible and necessary.

From earliest times mankind has been involved with an important
division of labor. Since no human being is utterly self-sufficient, we must

exchange goods and services with other people. The early forms of trade by bartering illustrate this principle. Suppose one man was a shoemaker. He produced one hundred pairs of shoes. His neighbor is a cattle rancher. The shoemaker produces more shoes than he can wear; the cattleman has more beef than he can eat. The shoemaker's feet are warm, but he is hungry. The cattleman's stomach is full, but his feet are cold. They get together and say, "Let's make a deal."

When the two men work out a trade they both profit. Each receives something that he values at the time more than what he gives up. The same thing happens every time we make a purchase that is not coerced. I never freely buy anything unless I value the purchase more than I value the money I give up in payment for it. I may gripe about the price. I might prefer that the price be lower. But the moment the price reaches a level that is higher than I'm willing to pay for it, I don't buy.

This elementary point is misunderstood every day. It is one reason why many businesses fail. The buyer is not interested in how much the product costs to make. The buyer is simply concerned with his own subjective value of the product. Prices, unless imposed coercively by government or extortion, are ultimately set by the customer. It is the customer who ultimately determines whether the product is worth the asking price to him or to her.

A few years ago I went shopping for a car. In the negotiations the salesman offered me so many dollars trade-in on my car. When I demurred he quickly produced a little book, showed me a number written in it, and declared, "This is the *actual* value of your car." I replied, "No, it is the actual value of my car to *you*; it is not the actual value of my car to *me*." I left and went to another dealer whose "actual" value of my car was $2,000 more than the first dealer and made a trade.

The subjective theory was challenged by Karl Marx. Marx argued for the "Labor Theory of Value." As the name suggests, value is to be decided (by government) on the basis of the labor exerted to create the product. The more labor, the higher the value and subsequently the price. The only way this scheme can work is via some sort of coercive tyranny. If prices are fixed and competition is ruled out then the customer is left with little voice in the transaction (except the customer will still exercise his subjective value with whatever funds he has, usually by not buying anything except what he absolutely needs). Imagine applying the Marxist theory to art. If a novice painter works ten times harder to produce a less excellent painting than Rembrandt could produce with ten times less effort, the inferior painting would be priced at a rate ten times higher than the Rembrandt. This illustration is purposely extreme to reveal the absurdity of such a system.

"But," the Christian asks, "don't Christian ethics have anything to say about values?" Indeed they do. The highest value is determined by the Highest Subject. It is a goal of the Christian life to bring our personal values into conformity with the values of Christ. We seek to grow to the point that we love what He loves, and hate what He hates. To be sanctified involves being sanctified in our preferences as well as our duties.

REPENTANCE REQUIRED

" **T**HEN **I** WILL TELL THEM PLAINLY, 'I never knew you.'"
The widespread controversy concerning "lordship salvation" has
spawned other controversies in its wake. One of the ancillary
issues that has been raised focuses on the question of the role of repentance
in salvation. Dr. Charles Ryrie, retired professor of systematic theology at
Dallas Theological Seminary, makes the following observation:

> Is repentance a condition for receiving eternal life? Yes, if it is repen-
> tance or changing one's mind about Jesus Christ. No, if it means to be
> sorry for sin or even to resolve to turn from sin, for these things *will
> not save*. Is repentance a precondition to faith? No, though a sense of
> sin and the desire to turn from it may be used by the Spirit to direct
> someone to the Savior and His salvation. . . .

Rarely have I been more surprised by a statement written by an esteemed
theologian than when I read the words above. I keep hoping that I have
misunderstood them. The troublesome portion is found in the words, "No,
if it means to be sorry for sin or even to resolve to turn from sin." I take
Dr. Ryrie to mean that repentance from sin in this sense is not a necessary
condition for salvation. I take it that he means that an impenitent person
with no contrition and no resolve to turn from sin can change his mind
about Jesus and have saving faith in Him in his impenitence from sin.

There is a strange twist to his argument that raises questions for me
about whether I understand Ryrie. The phrase that follows the troublesome words reads: "For these things *will not save*." I assume the word *for*
here means "because"; that is, it introduces Ryrie's explanation for why
such repentance from sin is not a condition for receiving eternal life.

It is crucial to see that Ryrie does not qualify the "condition" in his assertion. What kind of a condition is he referring to? His opening question (Is

repentance a condition for receiving eternal life?) suggests that the type of condition he has in view is what we call a *necessary condition*, something that must take place for a desired effect to follow. If this is what Ryrie means, then he has made an error in logic as well as an error in theology.

To argue that repentance is not a necessary condition for salvation because it in itself *will not save* is a fallacious deduction. This is to say that a thing (repentance) cannot be a necessary condition because it is not a *sufficient condition.*

Let me explain the difference between a necessary condition and a sufficient condition. A necessary condition is something required for an effect to take place, but by itself will not assure that the effect takes place. A sufficient condition is a condition which if met, assures that the effect will indeed take place. For example, the presence of oxygen is a necessary condition for fire to take place. However, the mere presence of oxygen will not guarantee that fire will break out. Other factors are also necessary.

If Ryrie simply means that repentance from sin by itself (without chang-ing one's mind about Christ) is not a sufficient condition for salvation, then we have no quarrel with him. (Nor would any orthodox theologian.)

If, however, he means that a person can be saved by changing his mind about Christ and believing in Him as Savior without repenting of his sin, then Ryrie is manifestly guilty of crass antinomianism. Though Ryrie wants to connect repentance with faith, the repentance so connected with saving faith is restricted to "changing one's mind about Jesus."

Again Ryrie seems to be saying that because repentance from sin is not a sufficient condition for salvation, it is not a condition at all. It may be a helpful condition or a desirable condition but certainly not a necessary condition. Ryrie is not opposed to repentance. He not only recommends it, he urges it, particularly in the life of a Christian. He insists, however, that it is not necessary for salvation.

To define *repentance* requires the same process involved in the defini-tion of any word. The lexicographer is concerned with various matters. He considers the etymological derivation of the word. In the case of the biblical word for *repentance* the Greek word is *metanoia*. This word comes from the prefix *meta* and the root for the Greek word for "mind." The prefix *meta* can mean "with," "after," or "behind." In ancient Greek the term came to refer to a change of one's mind (as a kind of "afterthought"). It referred to the adopting of a different view of something. Later the idea of "regret" or "remorse" was added. The idea of a conversion from a sinful lifestyle was not in view in the Greek concept.

When the Bible adopted this Greek word, however, there was a clear change in emphasis. The second and most important consideration for the lexicographer is the *customary usage* of a term. Words and their meanings go through developmental changes as their usage changes. By the time the New Testament was compiled, the use of *metanoia* communicated far more than merely changing one's mind about a matter.

In Kittel's analysis of *metanoia* (TDNT), stress is laid on conversion from sin. It refers to the "ancient prophetic summons for conversion, for a break with the ungodly and sinful past, for turning to God. . . ." In the teaching of Jesus it "demands radical conversion, a transformation of nature, a definitive turning from evil, a resolute turning to God in obedience." (See Luke 13:1–5.) Here repentance is a necessary condition in order to avoid perishing. This repentance is linked to faith in Christ and is a necessary element of it. One embraces Christ as his Savior from sin when he is awakened to contrition for his sin. An impenitent person does not flee to Jesus as Savior or Lord.

The call to repentance from sin was an integral, indeed central, part of the Apostolic kerygma. The *kerygma* refers to the "proclamation" or "preaching" of the early church. Here repentance included not only the changing of one's mind about Jesus but a turning away from evil (see Acts 3:26; 8:22; Heb. 6:1; Rev. 9:20; 16:11).

To embrace Jesus without repenting of sin is to be numbered among the workers of lawlessness who cry to Jesus, "Lord, Lord," to whom Jesus will respond: "I never knew you: depart from me, you that work iniquity" (Matthew 7:23).

SMILE, GOD LOVES YOU …
AND HAS A WONDERFUL
PLAN FOR YOUR LIFE

NOVEMBER 1991

———

D OES GOD REALLY LOVE YOU, and does He have a wonderful plan for your life? Not if your name is Esau, in which case He hates you; or if you are a vessel fit for destruction, in which case God's plan for your life is eternal damnation.

How are we to reconcile the seemingly conflicting ideas found in Scripture concerning the love of God and the hatred of God? Are we being naively facile, or even worse, telling them a falsehood when we announce to people that God has a wonderful plan for their lives? The question focuses on the propriety of assuming the universal love of God for every person in the world. A universal affirmation of anything allows for no exceptions. One of the most fundamental rules of logic is the law of immediate inference. In classic truth tables it is clear that one may not properly combine a universal positive with a particular negative. The following premises are utterly incompatible:

Premise A: God loves all persons.
Premise B: God does not love some persons.

It does not require the brains of a rocket scientist to see that these two premises cannot both be true at the same time and in the same relationship. They may be acceptable to the mind of a Hindu but not to the mind accustomed to thinking in logical categories.

Obviously, if there is one person God hates, and if hate is contrary to love, then, by resistless logic, we must conclude that God does not love everybody.

We all know the Bible teaches that God is love and that God so loved the world that He gave. . . . If God so loved the world that He went so far as to give His only begotten Son to die, doesn't this radical degree of sacrificial love strongly imply that in loving the world God loved each and every person in it?

It would seem so, and we may even be driven to that conclusion if that is all the Bible ever said about the love of God. Yet right there in Holy Writ, boldly inscribed on the sacred page are the words "Jacob have I loved; Esau have I hated" (Malachi 1:2–3; Romans 9:13).

This is a tough nut to crack. How can we square this statement with the assumption of the universal love of God for all persons?

Various attempts of handling this difficult passage have been set forth. The first thing we see about it is that it is structured in the literary form of antithetical parallelism. A vivid contrast is intended between what God does for Jacob and what He does not do for Esau. Since there is an antithesis set forth between "love" and "hate," all we have to do is discern what love means in the passage and then understand the use of the word *hate* to refer to its opposite.

This is the tack most interpreters follow. The argument goes like this: When the Bible says that God "hated" Esau it simply means that God gave a special benefit to Jacob that He withheld from Esau. God bestowed the unmerited favor of electing grace on one of the twins; the other (Esau) He passed over. Jacob received God's mercy ("I will have mercy upon whom I will have mercy" [Romans 9:15]). Esau received God's justice. The dispensing of justice to Esau does not require that God act in a spiteful or "hateful" manner. Even those, such as Esau, who are not the objects of divine election, still in this life receive the common grace of God that flows out of His benevolence.

In this view of the passage, the contrast between God's love and hatred has nothing to do with God's affection or lack of it for either party. It merely refers to God's actions with respect to each.

This may, indeed, be the proper meaning of the passage. However, it still does not get us off the hook. We are still left with the nagging problem that *in some sense* God does not love all persons equally in the same manner. God's disposition may be benevolent toward all men in the sense that He pours out His common grace on all. The rain, with its nourishment, falls on the unjust as well as the just.

If we probe more deeply, however, we discover that even the blessings God bestows upon the impenitent sinner are not ultimately a blessing but a curse. Each gift God gives to the reprobate that is not received with gratitude and honor to the Giver becomes the occasion for fresh sin on the part of the recipient. With each fresh sin comes more guilt and an increase in the wrath of God to which the sinner is exposed. The gifts of God toward the reprobate become ultimately part of the treasure of wrath the sinner is heaping up against the Day of Judgment (Romans 2:5). It would be better for the sinner that God were not so loving.

When we examine Esau as a case study of the reprobate, we realize that there is nothing lovable about him. It would be perfectly just and righteous of God to regard Esau as odious in His sight. God has every right to hate the sinner as much as He hates the sin in the fullest sense of the word *hate*. In our sin we are all loathsome to God. Esau was a vessel fit for destruction. It was fitting for God to hate him.

David, in an imprecatory Psalm, declared that he hated his enemies with a "perfect hatred" (101:2–3; 119:104; 139:21–22). Is such a posture legitimate for men? It would seem that David's hatred for his enemies, no matter how "perfect," was incompatible with Jesus' command to us to love our enemies and with the Great Commandment of the Old Testament, which includes the mandate to love our neighbors as ourselves. Perhaps the Spirit's inspiration of David's Psalm goes no further than to ensure that David's sinful attitude toward his enemies is accurately recorded. However, the broader context of the imprecatory psalms seems to indicate that not only the record of David's perfect hatred but the perfect hatred itself is inspired of God. If so, then obviously perfect hatred would be a virtue and not a vice.

If there is such a thing as a perfect hatred it would mirror and reflect the righteousness of God. It would be perfect to the extent that it excluded sinful attitudes of malice, envy, bitterness, and other attitudes we normally associate with human hatred. In this sense a perfect hatred could be deemed compatible with a love for one's enemies. One who hates his enemy with a perfect hatred is still called to act in a loving and righteous manner toward him.

This issue is far too complex and vexing to resolve in a short essay, if I could resolve it at all. Its difficulty, however, should give us pause before we blithely announce to everyone indiscriminately, "Smile, God loves you."

WORSHIP: A TALE OF TWO FRIENDS

DECEMBER 1991

I HAVE TWO CLOSE FRIENDS WHO ARE struggling about worship. One is excited; the other is angry.

My angry friend is a psychologist from California. She understands the dynamics of personal anger. She is adept at counseling people with unresolved anger problems. She knows the symptoms of misdirected anger, situational anger, and the like. She knows what she is angry about and with whom she is angry.

She is angry with the church. She said, "I almost get the feeling that my minister is intentionally concealing the character of God from us on Sunday morning. The God he preaches is innocuous. He is not worthy of worship." The atmosphere of worship in her church resembles more a town meeting called to discuss local political problems than an event where people gather to adore God.

My other friend is a clergyman. He loves worship. He can't wait to get to church on Sunday morning to experience worship. It's not so much that he is eager to preach; his excitement rests on his delight in the elements of worship in the entire "worship service." He says that for him, "worship is a taste of heaven." His "taste of heaven" includes a powerful sense of being in the presence of God with his soul filled with the delight of reverence, adoration, and the sweet communion of prayer.

There is a crisis of worship in our land. People are staying away from church in droves. One survey indicated that the two chief reasons people drop out of church are that it is boring and it is irrelevant.

If people find worship boring and irrelevant, it can only mean they have no sense of the presence of God in it. When we study the action of worship in Scripture and the testimony of church history, we discover a variety of human responses to the sense of the presence of God. Some people tremble in terror falling with their face to the ground; others weep in mourning; some are exuberant in joy; still others are reduced to a pensive silence. Though the responses differ, one reaction we never find is boredom. It is impossible to be bored in the presence of God (if you know that He is there).

Nor is it possible for a sentient creature to find his or her encounter with God a matter of irrelevance. Nothing—no one is more relevant to human existence than the Living God.

I have said these things before in the context of an analysis of preaching. But worship is more than preaching—far more.

Biblical worship invades the human soul. It is the soul that too often has been banished from modern worship. Since Immanuel Kant assigned the "self" to the realm of the *noumena*, along with God and metaphysical essences, it has been deemed unknowable at best and irrelevant at worst. We are a people preoccupied with self-image, self-esteem, and self-gratification. Yet in all this we don't even know what a "self" is.

The human soul is in exile from our thinking. No wonder, then, that it is not considered relevant to worship. Heaven is too distant to contemplate. Our lives are lived within the restricted boundaries of our terrestrial horizon. We have so despised the notion of pie-in-the-sky that we have lost our taste for it altogether.

But when our souls are engaged in worship, our gaze is lifted heavenward, our hearts are set aflame by the divine fire, and we are ready to have done with this world. There is such a thing as mystic sweet communion with Christ in worship. Hear it there in Bunyan, here in Edwards, over there in Luther and Calvin. All the saints testify to the sweetness of the taste of heaven that can and does occur in worship.

I'm speaking about something that goes beyond emotion (but includes it), that transcends passion (but doesn't annul it), that penetrates to the deepest core of our being where we sense; nay, we know that we are in the presence of the living God.

The model of worship found in the Old Testament is a model instituted by God Himself. Though its elements cannot be carried willy-nilly into Christian worship without falling into the Judaizing heresy, its *principles* are instructive.

The worship of Israel was formal and liturgical. Solemn rites were central to the experience. The setting of temple worship was anything but casual. The meeting place had an ambiance of the solemn and the holy. The ritual was designed for drama. The literature and music were high and majestic. The content of songs (the Psalms) was inspired by God Himself. The articles of art were fashioned by the finest craftsmen who were filled by the Holy Spirit. The vestments of the priests were designed by God for "beauty and holiness."

Everything in Israelite worship, from the music to the building to the liturgy, focused attention on the majesty of God. God, in His holiness and in His redemptive work, was the content of the form. It was solemn because to enter the presence of God is a solemn matter.

But even God-ordained patterns of worship can be corrupted. Liturgy can degenerate into liturgicalism, or even worse, sacerdotalism, by which the rites and sacraments themselves are seen as the instruments of salvation. The forms of worship can devolve into formalism and the externals into externalism.

It is important to note, however, that when Israel's prophets denounced the corruption of Israelite worship, they sought reform, not revolution. Though they vehemently criticized liturgicalism, they never attacked the liturgy. Though they railed against externalism and formalism, they never sought to remove the externals and forms God had instituted.

For the forms of worship to communicate the content they are designed to convey, there must be constant instruction so that people understand their meaning. The sacraments are not naked symbols. They must be clothed with the Word. Word and sacrament must go together. Sacrament without Word inevitably yields formalism. Word without sacrament inevitably yields a sterility of worship.

We need a reformation of worship, a new discovery of the meaning of classical forms. I cannot be casual about worshiping God. God stripped of transcendence is no God at all. There is such a thing as the Holy. The Holy is sacred. It is uncommon. It is other. It is transcendent. It is not always user-friendly. But it is relevant. It provokes adoration, which is the essence of godly worship.

"If people find worship boring and irrelevant, it can only mean they have no sense of the presence of God in it."

THE ANATOMY OF DOUBT

JANUARY 1992

———

*S*PIRITUS *SANCTUS NON EST SKEPTICUS*—"The Holy Spirit is not a skeptic." So Luther rebuked Erasmus of Rotterdam for his expressed disdain for making sure assertions. Luther roared, "The making of assertions is the very mark of the Christian. Take away assertions and you take away Christianity. Away now, with the skeptics!"

Doubt is the hallmark of the skeptic. The skeptic dares to doubt the indubitable. Even demonstrable proof fails to persuade him. The skeptic dwells on Mt. Olympus, far aloof from the struggles of mortals who care to pursue truth.

But doubt has other faces. It is the assailant of the faithful striking fear into the hearts of the hopeful. Like Edith Bunker, doubt nags the soul.* It asks "Are you sure?" Then, "Are you sure you're sure?"

Still doubt can appear as a servant of truth. Indeed it is the champion of truth when it wields its sword against what is properly dubious. It is a citadel against credulity. Authentic doubt has the power to sort out and clarify the difference between the certain and the uncertain, the genuine and the spurious.

Consider Descartes. In his search for certainty, for clear and distinct ideas, he employed the application of a rigorous and systematic doubt process. He endeavored to doubt everything he could possibly doubt. He doubted what he saw with his eyes and heard with his ears. He realized that our senses can and do often deceive us. He doubted authorities, both civil and ecclesiastical, knowing that recognized authorities can be wrong. He would submit to no *fides implicitum* claimed by any human being or institution. Biographies usually declare that Descartes was a Frenchman but his works reveal that he was surely born in Missouri.

———

* Edith Bunker was a character on the 1970s American sitcom *All in the Family.*

Descartes doubted everything he could possibly doubt until he reached the point where he realized there was one thing he couldn't doubt. He could not doubt that he was doubting. To doubt that he was doubting was to prove that he was doubting. No doubt about it.

From that premise of indubitable doubt, Descartes appealed to the formal certainty yielded by the laws of immediate inference. Using impeccable deduction he concluded that to be doubting required that he be thinking, since thought is a necessary condition for doubting. From there it was a short step to his famous axiom, *cogito ergo sum*, "I think, therefore I am."

At last Descartes arrived at certainty, the assurance of his own personal existence. This was, of course, before Hume attacked causality and Kant argued that the self belongs to the unknowable noumenal realm that requires a "transcendental apperception" (whatever that is) to affirm at all. One wonders how Descartes would have responded to Hume and Kant had he lived long enough to deal with them. I have no doubt that the man of doubt would have prevailed.

There were clearly unstated assumptions lurking beneath the surface of Descartes' logic. Indeed there was logic itself. To conclude that to doubt doubt is to prove doubt is a conclusion born of logic. It assumes the validity of the law of non-contradiction. If the law of non-contradiction is not a valid and necessary law of thought, then one could argue (irrationally to be sure) that doubt can be doubt and not be doubt at the same time and in the same relationship.

The second assumption was the validity of the law of causality (which, in the final analysis, is merely an extension of the law of non-contradiction). Descartes could not doubt that an effect not merely may, but *must* have an antecedent cause. Doubt, by logical necessity, requires a doubter, even as thought requires a thinker. This is nothing more than arguing that action of any kind cannot proceed from non-being. Hume's skepticism of causality was cogent insofar as he brilliantly displayed the difficulty of assigning a particular cause to a particular effect or event. But not even Hume was able to repeal the law of causality itself. It is one thing to doubt what the cause of a particular effect is; it is quite another to argue that the effect may have no cause at all. This is the fundamental error countless thinkers have made since Hume. I once read a critical review of *Classical Apologetics* in which the able and thoroughly Christian reviewer observed, "The problem with Sproul is that he refuses to acknowledge the possibility of an uncaused effect."

I wrote to my reviewing colleague and pleaded guilty to the charge. *Mea culpa.* I do refuse to acknowledge even the most remote possibility of an uncaused effect. I have the same obstreperous stubbornness for circles that are not round and for married bachelors. I asked my friend to cite but one example, real or theoretical, of an uncaused effect and I would repent in dust and ashes. I'm still waiting for his reply. If he reads this perhaps it will jog his memory and induce him either to deliver the goods or admit his glaring error.

I certainly allow for an uncaused being, namely God, but not for uncaused effects. An uncaused effect is an oxymoron, a veritable contradiction in terms, a statement patently and analytically false, which Descartes could refute in his Dutch oven without the benefit of empirical testing.

So how does this affect the Christian in his struggle with the doubts that assail faith? The content of Christianity, in all its parts, cannot be reduced simplistically to Cartesian syllogisms. The lesson we learn from Descartes is this: when assailed by doubt, it is time to search diligently for first principles that are certain. We build upon the foundation of what is sure. This affects the whole structure of apologetics. It is a matter of order. It seems astonishing to the lay person that anybody would go to the extremes Descartes insisted simply to discover that he existed. What could be more self-evident to a conscious being than one's own self-consciousness? But Descartes was not on a fool's errand. In a world of sophisticated skepticism, Descartes sought certainty for something that could serve as a foundation for much, much more. He moved from the certitude of self-consciousness to the certitude of the existence of God, no small matter for the doubt-ridden believer. Descartes and others like him understood that to prove the existence of God is prior to affirming the trustworthiness of Scripture and the birth and work of the person of

Christ. Once it is certain that God exists and reveals Himself in Scripture, there is ground for a legitimate *fides implicitum.*

But the order of the process to destroy doubt is crucial. For example, the miracles of the Bible cannot and were never designed to prove the existence of God. The very possibility of a miracle requires that there first be a God who can empower it. In other words, it is not the Bible that proves the existence of God, it is God who through miracle attests that the Bible is His Word. Thus proven, to believe the Bible implicitly is a virtue. To believe it gratuitously is not.

The most important certainty we can ever have is the foundational certainty of the existence of God. It is this matter that prompted Edwards to declare: "Nothing is more certain than that there must be an unmade and unlimited being" (Miscellany #1340).

On this bedrock of certainty rests the promises of that unmade, unlimited Being. On these promises we rest our faith. Doubting served Descartes well, but Edwards knew that ultimately, it is dubious to doubt the indubitable.

FEAR NOT

FEBRUARY 1992

———

W E ARE FRAGILE MORTALS, GIVEN TO fears of every sort. We have a built-in insecurity that no amount of whistling in the dark can mollify. We seek assurance concerning the things that frighten us the most.

The prohibition uttered more frequently than any other by our Lord is the command, "Fear not . . ." He said this so often to His disciples and others He encountered that it almost came to sound like a greeting. Where most people greet others by saying "Hi" or "Hello," the first words of Jesus very often were "Fear not."

Why? Perhaps Jesus' predilection for those words grew out of His acute sense of the thinly veiled fear that grips all who approach the living God. We fear His power, we fear His wrath, and most of all we fear His ultimate rejection.

The assurance we need the most is the assurance of salvation. Though we are loath to think much about it or contemplate it deeply, we know if only intuitively that the worst catastrophe that could ever befall us is to be visited by God's final punitive wrath. Our insecurity is worsened by the certainty that we deserve it.

Many believe that assurance of eternal salvation is neither possible nor even to be sought. To claim such assurance is considered a mask of supreme arrogance, the nadir of self-conceit.

Yet, if God declares that it is possible to have full assurance of salvation and even commands that we seek after it, then it would be supremely arrogant for one to deny or neglect it.

In fact, God does command us to make our election and calling sure: "Therefore, my brothers, be all the more eager to make your calling and election sure. For if you do these things, you will never fall" (2 Peter 1:10).

This command admits of no justifiable neglect. It addresses a crucial matter. The question, "Am I saved?" is one of the most important questions I can ever ask myself. I need to know the answer; I must know the answer. This is not a trifle. Without the assurance of salvation the Christian life is unstable. It is vulnerable to the debilitating rigors of mood changes and allows the wolf of heresy to camp on the doorstep. Progress in sanctification requires a firm foundation in faith. Assurance is the cement of that foundation. Without it, the foundation crumbles.

How, then, do we receive assurance? The Scripture declares that the Holy Spirit bears witness with our spirit that we are the children of God. This inner testimony of the Holy Spirit is as vital as it is complex. It can be subjected to severe distortions, being confused with subjectivism and self-delusion. The Spirit gives His testimony with the Word and through the Word, never against the Word or without the Word.

Since it is possible to have false assurance of salvation it is all the more urgent that we seek the Spirit's testimony in and through the Word. False assurance usually proceeds from a faulty understanding of salvation. If one fails to understand the necessary conditions for salvation, assurance would be at best a lucky guess.

Therefore, we insist that right doctrine is a crucial element in acquiring a sound basis for assurance. It may even be a necessary condition, though by no means a sufficient condition. Without sound doctrine we will have an inadequate understanding of salvation. However, having a sound understanding of salvation is no guarantee we have the salvation we so soundly understand.

If we think the Bible teaches universal salvation we may arrive at a false sense of assurance by reasoning as follows: Everybody is saved. I am a body; therefore, I am saved.

Or, if we think salvation is gained by our own good works and we are further deluded into believing that we possess good works, we will have a false assurance of salvation.

To have sound assurance we must understand that our salvation rests upon the merit of Christ alone, which is appropriated to us when we embrace Him by genuine faith. If we understand that, the remaining question is, "Do I have the genuine faith necessary for salvation?"

Again two more things must be understood and analyzed properly. The first is doctrinal. We need a clear understanding of what constitutes genuine saving faith. If we conceive of saving faith as a faith that exists in a vacuum, never yielding the fruit of works of obedience, we have confused saving faith with dead faith, which cannot save anyone.

The second requirement involves a sober analysis of our own lives. We must examine ourselves to see if the fruit of regeneration is apparent in our lives. Do we have a real affection for the biblical Christ? Only the regenerate person possesses real love for the real Jesus. Next we must ask the tough question, "Does my life manifest the fruit of sanctification?" I test my faith by my works.

I call this last question the tough question for various reasons. We can lose assurance if we think perfect obedience is the test. Every sin we commit after conversion can cast doubt upon our assurance. That doubt is exacerbated by the assault of accusation made by Satan against us. Satan delights in shaking the true Christian's assurance.

On the other hand, we can delude ourselves by looking at our own works with an exalted view of our goodness, seeing virtue in ourselves when there is none. Here we quake in terror before our Lord's warning:

"Many will say to Me on that day, 'Lord, Lord, did we not prophesy in Your name, and in Your name drive out demons and perform many miracles?' Then I will tell them plainly, 'I never knew you. Away from Me, you evildoers!' " (Matt. 7:22–23)

Real assurance rests on a sound understanding of salvation, a sound understanding of justification, a sound understanding of sanctification, and a sound understanding of ourselves. In all these matters we have the comfort and assistance of the Holy Spirit who illumines the text of Scripture for us, who works in us to yield the fruit of sanctification, and who bears witness with our spirit that we are the children of God.

THE POLITIZATION OF TRUTH: THE NEW SOPHISM

MARCH 1992

I
N OCTOBER OF 1991, THE AMERICAN PEOPLE were riveted to
the drama of the Supreme Court nomination of Clarence Thomas.
Then, a twist of biting irony took place when Anita Hill emerged with
allegations of sexual harassment. After Professor Hill testified before a
watching world, Clarence Thomas reappeared before the Senate Judi-
ciary Committee.

But something had changed. A marked contrast appeared in the demeanor
of Judge Thomas from what he described as his "real" confirmation hearing. Thomas was angry. Sensing that his appointment to the Court was
lost and that he had nothing else of a political nature to lose, he waded
into the fray with fists flying. Gone was the elusive, evasive, "politically
correct" respondent. Now Thomas spoke with the candor of fury, accusing those who sat in judgment on him of a "high-tech lynching." Thomas
was obviously unconcerned about further alienating his antagonists.

I don't know if Thomas spoke the truth. I know, however, that he spoke
differently, and the nation responded positively to his less-than-cautious
replies. He broke all the rules of political sensitivity and got away with it.
That part, at least, was a breath of fresh air, a political *aggiornamento* (an
Italian term used by Pope John XXIII meaning "to open the windows")
in an atmosphere of choking blue smoke.

Politics in America has degenerated to the nadir of the rhetoric of sophistry. It was not truth that kindled the spark that brought Socrates to the
fore in Athens. It was the sophists of antiquity with their multitude of
empty phrases and vacant words designed for persuasion. The "gadfly of

R . C . S P R O U L

Greece" was convinced that sophism was a clear and present danger to the very survival of civilization, and that made him willing to drink the bitter dregs of hemlock to sound his protest.

Socrates, with his protégé Plato, and in turn, Plato's most gifted student, Aristotle, restored truth over perception and science over political opinion, and delayed the disintegration of Western civilization.

With the advent of Christianity, the quest for ultimate truth and the priority of ethics over vested interests conquered the new pragmatism of Roman morals.

Now, however, it seems that once again civilization is threatened by neo-sophism. To understand this, we need a brief recapitulation of ancient sophism. Sophism emerged in ancient Greece after science and philosophy reached an impasse in the metaphysical tension between Parmenides and Heraclitus.

Parmenides postulated a land of metaphysical monism by declaring the ultimacy of being with his famous maxim, "Whatever is, is." He rejected the physical world of changing entities as being ephemeral and illusory.

Heraclitus responded by asserting the ultimacy of change, arguing that whatever is, is changing. The only thing permanent is change itself. Everything is always and everywhere in a state of flux.

This metaphysical debate left the public with a collective Excedrin headache. The man in the street reasoned, "If these two titans of theoretical thought cannot agree, how can we ever resolve such ultimate issues?" Ultimate truth was then deemed unknowable and equally unnecessary. What was left was the pragmatic concerns of daily living.

The cry of the sophist was, "Give us some news we can use." Ultimate truth is not possible; what matters is the here and now in my political situation. Sophism gave rise to "how to" schools that majored in the art of political expediency. The new science of rhetoric became popular. This "science" was not concerned about discerning truth through argument and debate. Rather, rhetoric stressed the importance of political persuasion. Whatever is persuasive is true. Science was reduced to popularity opinion polls. Does this sound familiar? Sophism became equated with superficiality where truth and ethics were relativized and politicized.

Western civilization experienced a renaissance of culture with the emergence of modern forms of democracy. The supreme model for the new experiment was the republic of the United States. It was formed not as a pure democracy but as a republic. The difference between a pure democracy and a republic is crucial, though this difference is being more and more obscured with each passing day. The republic is defined as "rule by law," whereas a pure democracy is defined in terms of majority rule. The chief safeguard of a republic is embodied in a constitution that guarantees certain rights to every person in the society, individual rights that may not be usurped via a tyranny of the majority.

When the American experiment began, the Frenchman Alexis de Tocqueville warned of two eventualities that could destroy the plan. Both involved the threat of the politicization of economics. He said that when people discover that the vote is worth money, the republic is in trouble (bribes and financial support can corrupt statesmen and turn them into prostituted politicians); and when people discover that they can vote for themselves largess from the government, it's over.

What de Tocqueville apparently did not anticipate was the politicization of education. Once economics is politicized, the public education system follows. We are accustomed to distinguishing in our culture between public schools and private schools. Perhaps a more accurate designation for "public schools" is "government schools," or more precisely, "politicized schools."

The relativization of higher education philosophy was documented by Allan Bloom's book *The Closing of the American Mind*. Now, the politization of American higher education is documented in the recent work of Dinesh D'Souza entitled *Illiberal Education: The Politics of Race and Sex on Campus*. D'Souza traces the pattern of the new sophism as it has moved through institutions such as Stanford, Harvard, Duke, and other universities that had achieved the highest level of credibility in education. Now, hiring policies, entrance policies, and curricula are being reshaped by a left-wing activistic political agenda.

The book jacket asserts: "Student activists march under the banners of pluralism and diversity. They have demanded an admissions policy based not on academic merit but on ethnic representation; a curriculum and faculty assembled not by intellectual standards but by race and gender categories; and sensitivity training which borders on the totalitarian in its invasive insistence on a new social and political orthodoxy."

The structural innovations D'Souza documents are as scary as they are silly. The politics of intimidation are used to enforce a radically leftist political agenda on liberal arts education. D'Souza did well on exposing the illiberal character of this movement. We need a new Socrates who would prefer hemlock to such a distortion of the academic enterprise.

"You gotta love the church. You can't love Christ and despise His body. You can't reject His bride."

—

DEAR BOB

APRIL 1992

———

D r. R.C. Sproul
Ligonier Ministries
Orlando, Florida

Dear Dr. Sproul:

I need your help.

For the past three years I have been a ministerial student at an old and respected seminary. Before coming to school, my goal in life was to obtain the credentials necessary for service in my denomination. I have some grave doubts nearing the completion of that goal. I can't believe what my education in "divinity" has done to my faith.

It all started in my first class. It was in Church History where the professor told us that the history of the institutionalized church is one of continued conflict over ideology, ending in schism, more struggle, and irrelevance. Then in Dogmatics, the instructor openly humiliated a student who attempted to defend the efficacy of Christ's death. Throughout that first year, my faith was undermined more than it was strengthened. Has it always been this way? What is the problem?

Seminary was attractive to me because I loved Christ and His church. I wanted to give my life in service to the body of Christ. Now, however, I despise the institution and feel real shame over her prideful ignorance. My perceptions were sadly confirmed during a two-year internship. I can no longer define the church. What is it? Where do I find it? Is such a thing still alive?

My only comfort is that God is sovereign and that He might one day effect a great revival of true Christianity. But what about now? Have I wasted three years chasing after a dream only to discover it is a nightmare? I know that Paul warned the elders in Ephesus that wolves would come into the fold and not spare the sheep. I understand that—but this is ridiculous. The wolves have become the shepherds. Help me. Please give me some direction.

Sincerely yours,
Bob

Dear Bob,

Your letter struck a raw nerve with me. I felt a sense of déjà vu. My mind snapped back to my own seminary days and subsequent early years of ministry.

The first memory it sparked was of occasions as a young man when I expressed my frustrations to older men who responded to me by saying, "You're too young and idealistic to understand these things. Wait until you get more experience."

That type of answer only fueled my frustration. I wanted cogent answers and sound arguments, not patronage from my elders.

My seminary experience was much like yours. I had professors who openly attacked the doctrine of Christ's substitutionary atonement, the deity of Christ, and ridiculed anyone who believed the Bible was God's Word. I experienced shock, hurt, and anger. When I expressed these concerns to older people in the church, they added to my dismay by insisting that I must be mistaken and that I was being a troublemaker.

Day after day in seminary classes I was exposed to a rigorous skepticism toward everything I held sacred. Fortunately (I should say *providentially*), I had one professor who brilliantly defended the biblical faith and who supported me in my trials. I really don't know what I would have done without Dr. Gerstner.

There were two simple passages from the Bible to which I clung tenaciously. The first was from Psalm 37:1: "Do not fret because of evil men." That hit home with me because I was doing a lot of fretting and it wasn't helping my spiritual life.

The second passage was from Jeremiah. When the prophet complained to God bitterly and threatened to quit because false prophets were undermining his ministry, God rebuked him and said, "Let the prophet who has a dream tell his dream, but let the one who has My word speak it faithfully" (Jeremiah 23:28).

The application of those words to my life was simple. I realized that God was not going to hold me accountable for what other ministers said or did. Rather, He was going to hold my feet to the fire for what I say and do. I had my marching orders, and so do you.

When I hear your anguish, I have two conflicting responses in my heart. On the one hand I want to rush to your side and offer you whatever encouragement I can. I want to weep with you as you weep. On the other hand, as a battle-scarred veteran, I want to kick you in the pants and give you a "Pattonesque" bop on the chin. I want to say, "If you can't stand the heat, get out of the kitchen." The ministry is no place for cowards. You know as well as I do that this all goes with the territory. When was it ever any different? We are called to serve a Master who was despised and rejected of men. We join a company of those whom the world hated and slew.

I know what you're thinking. Yeah, it's easy to put up with the hostility of the world. We expect it. It's getting shot in the back from within the church that is hard to take. Even then we tend to rise to the occasion when the issues are big and important. It's the pettiness that wears us down.

Again, mature faith requires that we be willing and able to absorb petty slights and insults. How does it go for you on Sunday mornings? You stand at the door to greet your flock and fifty people tell you that they appreciated your sermon. Then one person expresses a criticism. What do you remember for the rest of the day? Right . . . me too. You tell yourself that you're supposed to be able to handle criticism, but it still wounds. Chances are, if the person knew how much they wounded you they would be horrified. Most of the petty hurts we endure are unintentional. Understanding that can go a long way to salving the wound.

But there is a bigger issue to be dealt with from your letter. It involves our understanding of the church itself. You need to understand that the church is the most corrupt institution on earth. It's more corrupt than the government. It's more corrupt than the *cosa nostra*.

Surely I exaggerate? By no means. I am rating corruption according to a standard of giftedness. God says that to whom much is given, much is required. No institution has been invested with more divine grace than the church. Here is where both grace and the means of grace are particularly concentrated. Again, no institution on earth has such a holy vocation. If the church is the most corrupt institution in the world, it is because it is the most important institution in the world. All things being equal it is nowhere near the actual corruption of government or of the mafia. But judged by its gifts and its sacred vocation, relatively speaking its corruption grows in proportion.

Because the church is so important, it is the central target of hell. The devil doesn't have to work up a sweat to induce the mafia to evil. Junior-grade demons can plunge a government into decadence. But the church—the bride of Jesus, the family of God, the fellowship of the Holy Spirit—that institution invites the unbridled assault of hell at every point. This isn't a simple problem of wrestling with flesh and blood. It is a struggle with principalities and powers.

We know that there have been periods in history when the church was more or less pure. But it has always been what St. Augustine described as a *corpus per mixtum*, a mixed body. Our Lord described the church as an institution that included both tares and wheat. Sometimes the tares gain the upper hand and lead the church into apostasy. Some churches have degenerated to such a low degree that they cease being churches at all. But no church in any age has been utterly pure. It was the clergy who gnashed their teeth in hatred of Jesus and plotted His death. It was the church that condemned Luther, banished Calvin from France, and dismissed Edwards from Northampton. It was during the century of the Great Awakening in our land that Gilbert Tennent wrote *The Danger of an Unconverted Clergy*. The sheep have always suffered at the hands of wolves cleverly disguised as sheep themselves. But will not God vindicate His elect who cry unto Him day and night?

You gotta love the church. You can't love Christ and despise His body. You can't reject His bride. He has promised to present His bride to the Father without spot or wrinkle. Right now we may be discouraged. Her wedding gown has been torn to shreds as if by a wolf. But the groom will surely take care of all that. He will remove every spot, mend every tear, and smooth every wrinkle. Remember, it is we who are the spots and the wrinkles. If we despise them we despise ourselves.

Now it is time to gird up yourself like a man. Stir up the gift that is within you and look to the Author and finisher of your faith to rekindle a fire in your bones. It's worth it.

Love in Christ,
R.C.

THE ORIGIN OF THE SOUL

JUNE 1992

———

S TUDENTS OF PHILOSOPHY ARE WELL aware of the watershed significance of Immanuel Kant's epochal work *The Critique of Pure Reason*. In this volume Kant gave a comprehensive critique of the traditional arguments for the existence of God, wreaking havoc on natural theology and classical apologetics. Kant ended in agnosticism with respect to God, arguing that God cannot be known either by rational deduction or by empirical investigation. He assigned God to the "noumenal world," a realm impenetrable by reason or by sense perception.

The impact on apologetics and metaphysical speculation of Kant's work has been keenly felt. What is often overlooked, however, even among philosophers, is the profound impact Kant's critique had on our understanding of the soul.

Kant placed three concepts or entities in his noumenal realm, a realm above and beyond the phenomenal realm. The triad includes God, the self, and the thing-in-itself, or essences. If God resides in this extraphenomenal realm, then, the argument goes, we cannot know anything about Him. Our knowledge, indeed all true science, is restricted to the phenomenal realm, the world perceived by the senses. Kant argued that we cannot move to the noumenal realm by reasoning from the phenomenal realm (a point that put Kant on a collision course with the Apostle Paul).

Kant's agnosticism moved beyond theology to metaphysics. Since metaphysics is concerned with that which is above and beyond the physical, it is deemed a fool's errand to seek knowledge of essences. The phenomenal realm is the world of *existence*, not of metaphysical essences or "things-in-themselves." There may be metaphysical essences but they cannot be known by human reason. That Kant did a hatchet job on metaphysics as well as theology is clear.

Again, what is often overlooked is that the hatchet had more work to do. By assigning the self to the noumenal realm, Kant also hacked away at the concept of the human soul. This has had a devastating impact on subsequent views of anthropology. Pre-Kantian thought gave heavy weight to the importance of the human soul. Post-Kantian thought has as all but eliminated the soul from serious consideration.

The nature of the self remains a concern of psychology, but its nature is enmeshed in enigma. Descartes arrived at a knowledge of the self as a clear and distinct idea via a rigorous doubting process. He resolved to doubt everything he could possibly doubt. The one thing he couldn't doubt was that he was doubting. There was no doubt about that. For anyone to doubt that he is doubting, he must doubt to do it. Since doubting is a form of thinking and thought requires a thinker, Descartes arrived at his famous conclusion: *Cogito ergo sum*, "I think, therefore I am." We notice that in this formula there is an "I," a *self*, that is necessarily involved in the process.

Kant, himself, could not rid himself of the awareness of his self. He appealed, however, not to a rational deduction by which he came to a conclusion of his self; rather, he coined the idea of the "transcendental apperception of the ego." This technical language is somewhat cumbersome but nevertheless significant. Kant saw the self not as something *perceived* by the senses. It is an apperception and a *necessary* apperception for all thought. It transcends the normal process of knowing according to Kant.

What is crucial is that some notion of the self beyond the physical is inescapable. We may argue about *how* we know we are selves but we cannot deny *that* we are selves. Descartes was correct: It takes a self to deny the self.

That the human self involves more than the body is clear to all except the most rigorous material determinists who reduce all reality to the purely physical, including thought as mind itself. They reject the Gerstnerian formula: "What is mind? No matter. What is matter? Never mind."

Classical Christian anthropology views man as a *substantial dichotomy*. This concept is likewise under attack in evangelical circles, not only from the side of trichotomists but also from those who see in it an unwarranted intrusion of Greek philosophy into Jewish-Christian thought. It is rejected by Murray Harris, for one, and was attacked by Philip Hughes, to mention another evangelical scholar.

In my judgment, the rejection of substantial dichotomy rests upon a fundamental error of understanding, a fatal false assumption. Harris and others attack substantial dichotomy because they hear in it a recapitulation of Greek dualism. The Greeks viewed man as a creature locked in a conflict between two opposing and irreconcilable substances, the body and the soul. To the Greek the soul is eternal and good; the body is temporal and intrinsically imperfect. For Plato the nonmaterial *ideal* realm is the realm of the good. The physical is at best an imperfect receptacle or copy of the ideal. Hence the view emerged in Greek philosophy that the body is the prison house of the soul. Redemption means the release of the soul from the body.

Pythagoras was the source of Plato's theory of the transmigration of the soul, an early version of reincarnation. The soul is eternal but may become entrapped in a series of incarnations during its eternal migration. Redemption occurs when the chain or series of incarnations end and the soul is free to live a bodiless existence.

Herein is the dualism so repugnant to Christian thought. But the problem with the Greek view is not that it has two distinct substances, body and soul, but that it views them as in total conflict with each other, because the physical is inherently evil (at least in the metaphysical sense of evil).

Jewish-Christian thought, however, sees man as made up of two distinct substances that are not in conflict. Nor does the Bible view matter as being inherently evil. For the Christian, redemption is *of* the body, not *from* the body. The Christian doctrine of substantial dichotomy is not dualistic. Man is not a *dualism* but a *duality*. That is, we have a real body (material substance) and a real soul (immaterial substance). There is an analogy with the person of Christ in that He has two natures or substances, divine and human, united in one person. That He has two substances does not necessitate a dualism in His person. (Of course the human nature of Christ also includes a human body and a human soul.)

That we are made up of body and soul is indicated in the creation account:

And the LORD God formed man from the dust of the ground, and breathed into his nostrils the breath of life, and man became a living soul (Genesis 2:7).

In the creation imagery man's body is formed first. But the body without the soul remains lifeless. When God breathes the breath of life into the body, then man becomes a living soul. In this account there is no hint of an eternal or preexistent human soul. The soul is as much a creation as is the body. That the soul survives the grave is not a testimony to its indestructibility or of its intrinsic immortality. The soul as a created entity is mortal. It survives the grave only because it is sustained and preserved by the power of God. It is preserved for eternal felicity for the redeemed; it is preserved for eternal punishment for the damned.

The soul of man can live without the body; the body cannot live without the soul. Jesus exhorted His hearers: "Do not be afraid of those who kill the body but cannot kill the soul. Rather, be afraid of the one who can destroy both the soul and the body in hell" (Matthew 10:28).

From biblical revelation we know we have souls. The Bible does not banish the soul to some "never-never" noumenal world of agnosticism. Not only do we have souls, but the nurture and care of our souls is a top priority for the Christian life.

CHILDREN OF THE COVENANT

JULY 1992

———

W HAT DOES IT MEAN TO be a "child of the covenant"? In its barest form the expression refers to children born into a family, where at least one parent is a member in good standing of a visible church. The church is viewed as the covenant community, the visible body of Christ. The church possesses the sign of the covenant, baptism, and is called to perform all the sign signifies.

In 1 Corinthians 7:14, Paul declares that the children of at least one believing parent are considered "holy" and not "unclean." To be unclean in this biblical sense is to be outside the covenant community, unconsecrated, or set apart from God. So, we conclude that in some sense, however restricted, children of a believer are within the covenant of grace. We recognize that God's promise of gracious salvation is made to believers and to their seed (Genesis 17:7; Luke 1:55).

With these givens we are still left with several controversial questions. They include the following:

1) Should infant children of believers be given the sign of the new covenant, *baptism?* Those who answer yes to this question do so largely because they see a *continuity* (though not *identity*) with the old covenant. In the old covenant, the covenant sign of circumcision was not only permitted to be administered to infants, it was commanded. Among other things circumcision was a *sign* of faith in God's covenant promises. In the case of adults, such as Abraham, the sign of faith was given *after* faith was present. In the case of the infant Isaac, circumcision was given *before* faith was present. This indicates at the very least that, in principle, a *sign* of faith need not be tied to the antecedent *presence* of faith.

Those who answer no to this question usually argue on two main premises. The first is that in the new covenant, faith is not only a condition to receive the *promises* of the covenant, it is also a necessary condition to receive the *sign* of the covenant. The second is that in Israel, the concept of a divine theocracy was operating which is not in effect in the new covenant. Though not necessarily conveying salvation, circumcision did have biological significance. Ethnic separation was marked by circumcision. Since there is no ethnic separation in the New Testament, there is no reason to continue the inclusion of children in the reception of the covenant sign.

2) Does baptism regenerate infants? Many who practice infant baptism believe in baptismal regeneration. In this case the sign *conveys* what it signifies. For example, the Roman Catholic Church views baptism as the *instrumental cause* of justification, by which saving grace is infused into the infant *ex opere operato* ("by the doing it is done"). However, others who practice infant baptism do not believe in baptismal regeneration.

3) If baptism does not regenerate or place the child in a state of grace, the question then is raised, What happens to infants who die in infancy? This question is dealt with at length by John Gerstner in his recent book *The Rational Biblical Theology of Jonathan Edwards*, vol. II. Gerstner distinguishes among three different views of covenant children affirmed by those who hold to infant baptism.

Infants are "little saints." Calvin, for example, believed that covenant children are elect and regenerate at birth. Here the greatest "Calvinist" of all time, Calvin himself, adopted a position that was utterly contradictory to Calvinism. Calvin assumed that all children of all believers are elect. He apparently missed the implication that this would mean that every human person was elect. According to Calvin, all the elect come to faith and none are ever lost. This would amount to universalism. Every human alive has some ancestor who was a believer. If Adam and Eve were redeemed, all the progeny would be numbered among the elect. But if ever there was a theologian who was not a universalist it was John Calvin.

The "as if" view. Though not assuming that all covenant children are elect, this view assumes that *most* are elect. Since we do not know who are and who aren't, the children are treated "as if" they are elect until they give convincing evidence to the contrary.

Infants are "little sinners." Edwards and most current Reformed groups see covenant children as being born into the *obligations* of the covenant. Here the church has a solemn duty not to take their election for granted or as an assumption. These children do not have the privileges of full communicant membership until they make a credible confession of faith. Their parents, the church, and they themselves are urged to "seek" salvation.

Though baptism does not automatically convey salvation or communion privileges and places the child under covenant obligation, there remains an advantage for these children. They are placed in the context of the covenant community where the means of grace are strongly focused.

When the Apostle Paul repudiated the erroneous idea that ethnic identity or biological inheritance insured salvation among the Jews, he nevertheless reaffirmed that there was a great advantage to being Jewish in the Old Testament. He answers his own question, "What advantage is there in being a Jew?" by declaring, "Much, in every way!" (Romans 3:1–2). The Jews had the oracles of God. Since faith, the condition for salvation, comes by hearing, and hearing by the Word of God, it is an enormous advantage to be where the Word of God is preached.

The child of believers then enjoys the environment where God chiefly works to bring His people to Himself. The sign of baptism is not an empty sign. It is a sign of God's promise to redeem all who believe. God does not promise to save all who are baptized. But He does promise to save all who possess by faith all that baptism signifies. To have the sign is to have the promise, but not the condition of the promise. To have the promise without the condition is both a privilege and an obligation. The obligation is to meet the condition; the privilege is to have the promise that attends the meeting of the obligation.

The obligation does not stop with the child. A heavy obligation rests upon the parents and the whole church for the nurture and admonition of these children. The church together with the parents have the role of spiritual caretakers of the covenant children.

BACK TO THE CAVE

AUGUST 1992

———

I N HIS FAMOUS *REPUBLIC*, PLATO spoke of prisoners in a cave, shut off from the outside world, limited in their vision to gazing at shadows on the wall. For these men the shadows were their window on reality. In time they began to mistake the shadows for the reality. The cave served as a parable for Plato to describe the difference between *opinion* and *knowledge*, between transcendent truth and its imperfect earthly copy.

Modern man has returned to the cave. We have locked ourselves in a dark place where the windows are blackened and the door is barred. We seal the cracks lest light might seep through from above and reveal the ephemeral quality of our eyes. We dance with the shadows as we stumble in the dark.

When people shut themselves off from the transcendent they become blind to ultimate truth. We lose sight of the sublime; we become indifferent to wonder. The sense of awe is extinguished and we are reduced to the contempt of the familiar. We are surface-bound creatures, content to live by the creed "What you see is what you get." The depth-dimension of reality eludes us not so much because it is inaccessible but because we are not interested in it, or even more seriously, hostile to it. It is what Calvin meant when he said that we are like people walking blindfolded through a glorious theater.

When Rudolf Otto published his work on the holiness of God, the original German title of the book was *Das Heilige*. A direct translation of this title into English would read simply, *The Holy*. However, when the book was rendered into English the title that appeared was *The Idea of the Holy*. I wonder if Otto, himself, knew of this title. I can't imagine that he would have approved of it. Otto wasn't concerned about the *idea* of the Holy; he was consumed by the *reality* of the Holy.

For Plato there was no essential difference between idea and reality.

For modern man there is a profound difference. For us, concepts *follow* an awareness of something. An infant does not think with words. The infant knows no words. He must *acquire* verbal skills. He learns a language, which is a system of sounds related to concepts or ideas that are associated with perceived reality. He begins not with words or concepts; he begins with awareness.

We don't speak much about transcendence. Indeed, the word itself is not active in many people's vocabulary. The concept tends to be ignored. That is because we repress our awareness of the transcendent.

Rabbi Abraham Heschel, in his *God in Search of Man: A Philosophy of Judaism*, decries the loss of wonder and awe in modern man. He writes: "The surest way to suppress our ability to understand the meaning of God and the importance of worship is to *take things for granted*. Indifference to the sublime wonder of living is the root of sin."

My only objection to Heschel's observation is to his use of the word *indifference*. Our problem, the problem of sin, is not so much indifference as it is hostility. We are alienated and estranged from the Holy and the transcendent. (The Holy is the transcendent, and the transcendent is the Holy.) We are estranged because the Holy Transcendent is *alien* to us. On the other hand, if indifference is the most egregious form of hostility, a calm expression of contempt, then I have no quarrel with Heschel's use of the word.

The loss of transcendence via the route of indifference describes the loss of the "sacred umbrella." The Holy once was the coverall by which all of human existence was defined. It was the stimulus to high culture, to virtue, and to nobility. First the umbrella sprang a leak and society became water-stained. Now the umbrella is in shreds, tattered beyond repair. Modern man stands in a deluge without an umbrella. We have replaced high culture with low culture, virtue with vice, and nobility with ignominy.

Awareness of God begins with wonder and ends with wonder. Science without wonder is mere arrogance in disguise. The quest for knowledge should heighten awareness, not diminish it. It presses toward light, not the obscurity of the cave. As long as man's pursuit of knowledge resists the transcendence, it is a charade, a masquerade. It is not a quest for light but a flight from the light. It rests in the security of the cave.

The wonder that provokes the initial quest for truth will, in the honest quest, produce more wonder, not less. When the seeker stops wondering, his quest has become an abortion.

This is not the credo of the skeptic who is always learning but never coming to a knowledge of truth. I am not saying that the quest evoked by wonder ends in ignorance. Wonder does lead to knowledge if diligently and honestly pursued. The point is that the more knowledge of truth we gain, the more wonder there is to contemplate. It is not that the less we know the more we wonder. On the contrary, the more we truly know, the more we truly wonder.

Kant understood this when he wrote: "Two things fill the mind with ever new and increasing admiration and awe, the more often and more steadily we reflect on them: the starry heavens above and the moral law within."

It's a shame Kant was content with starry heavens when the very awe they produce points so clearly beyond themselves to the transcendent Creator of the starry heavens and the Author of that moral law.

Hebrew wisdom declares that the "fear of the Lord is the beginning of knowledge" (Proverbs 1:7). Heschel translates it: "The *awe* of God. . . ." Something sacred and awe-evoking is present in every object we perceive and every event we experience. The whole earth, indeed the whole of existence, is full of His glory. All of nature manifests God. This does not mean that all of nature *is* God. It does mean that God is *in* all of nature and reveals Himself *through* all of nature. This is ultimate consubstantiation, by which God is in, under, and through all things. It is in Him that we live and move and have our being (Acts 17:28a).

This means that the transcendent is also immanent. We can have an awareness of the transcendent because though He is above and beyond us, He is also present with us. He is both hidden and revealed, partially concealed in His revelation, and partially manifest in His hiddenness. It is the God who dwells in thick cloud who speaks from Sinai.

Again Heschel observes: "The outwardness of the world communicates something of the indwelling greatness of God, which is radiant and conveys itself without words."

The whole earth, then, is full of the *presence* of God. That presence even invades our cave. It will not permit us to be content with shadows. Indeed it is the reality that makes shadows possible in the first place.

For there even to be shadows, there must be some source or power of light. If the light is totally extinguished and the cave is plunged into absolute darkness, then even the shadows vanish from view.

It is awe and wonder before the transcendent majesty of the glory of God that moves, nay, impels us to turn on the lights and get out of the cave. One glimpse of the screen in the glorious theater, one peek over the cloth, is enough to make us rip the blindfold from our eyes and behold the fullness of His glory.

STATISM:
LAND OF THE FREE

SEPTEMBER 1992

———

A NUMBER OF YEARS AGO I shared a taxi with Francis Schaeffer in St. Louis. During our cab ride I asked Dr. Schaeffer, "What is your greatest concern for the future of America?" Without hesitation or interval given to pondering the question, Schaeffer replied simply, "Statism."

What did Schaeffer mean? What was at the heart of his concern? To answer these questions, we need a clear understanding of statism. Our understanding of the term is often obfuscated by a tendency to think of statism as a phenomenon that only exists in autocratic totalitarian governments. We tend to associate it with dictatorships, not with democracies.

Upon closer scrutiny we realize that statism, as an *ism*, can function within the structure of any form of government, be it a monarchy, an oligarchy, a democracy, or a dictatorship. Statism is chiefly a philosophy, an ideology that attends one's view of government. The philosophy usually yields certain results that culminate in tyranny, but the results must not be confused with the philosophy.

Statism involves a philosophy of government by which the state (or government) is viewed not only as the final ruling authority but the ultimate agency of redemption. In this sense the state does not simply coexist with the church. It supplants the church.

Statism can never function "under God." If the state is deemed to be under God in the sense of being under God's authority and accountable to God for its actions, then the state cannot be the ultimate authority.

In the philosophy of statism, the government is conceived of as *autonomous*. It may take shape in an autonomous king, an autonomous dictator, an autonomous committee, or even in an autonomous democratic populace.

The classical safeguard against autonomous government is the concept of law, which is usually embodied in some form of constitution. The Greek word for *law* is *nomos*. To be autonomous means to be a law unto oneself (autonomy = self-law).

Herein lies the essential difference between a constitutional monarchy and an absolute monarchy, or the difference between a *republic* and a *democracy*. In a pure democracy, the ultimate authority rests with the will of the majority. Here the majority rule of the people gives autonomy to the majority over the minority or the individual. There is no higher authority than the majority vote. In this view the people's autonomy is expressed by their representative government. A government by the people, of the people, and for the people can be statist. It allows for the possibility of a tyranny of the majority over minorities and individuals as the Frenchman Alexis de Tocqueville warned.

In a republic the authority rests with the law. The classic formula for a republic is "Rule by law, not rule by men." The purpose of a constitution is to establish inalienable rights protected by law. Such laws are designed to guarantee certain rights to minorities and individuals. In practical terms this means that an individual's rights cannot be taken away by the simple vote of a majority. This is what the civil rights battle was all about.

If, for example, one hundred Americans in a given community vote to prohibit one person's expression of religion or speech, the individual can appeal to the First Amendment to protect his rights against the will of the majority. In pure statism the rights of individuals are swallowed up by the state. Law does not rule. Rulers rule and rule autonomously.

The second critical idea of statism is that the state supplants the church as the chief instrument of redemption. People look to the state, not to God, for "salvation." That Marx consciously developed such a view is well documented. For him the eschatological agent of redemption was the state.

As I am writing this article, the city of Los Angeles is burning. Sociologists, historians, and psychologists are musing on the causes for this mob violence. Once the Rodney King trial ended in the jury's acquittal of the L.A. police officers, the city exploded in violence, resulting in untold millions of dollars in property damage, hundreds of fires, hundreds wounded, and scores left dead.

The question we ask is why? Certainly the contributing factors are many and complex. One of those factors, however, that will probably be overlooked involves the people's reaction to the state. On the one hand, the riots may be viewed as a reaction *against* statism. The uprising in Tiananmen Square in China, the myriad of uprisings in the Soviet Bloc that led to the disintegration of the Soviet Union may all be viewed as violent protests against statism. In Los Angeles people were enraged against the state because they believed Rodney King's rights were violated. They perceived that the state failed to uphold the law. The irony is that their response was an act of unbridled lawlessness. Angered by the state's disregard for the law, they took to the streets to protest by radically violating their neighbors' rights. They burned, they looted, they beat, and they shot their neighbors with a savagery that far exceeded what King himself endured.

What is astonishing about all this is the attitude some of the looters expressed. One, interviewed on CNN, was asked, "Why did you take that television set from the store?" He replied, "It was free."

The assumption of some of the looters was one of entitlement. It was a thinly veiled protest against the state's promise of redemption via proliferating entitlements. The state had failed to "deliver the goods," so they simply helped themselves to the goods.

In this sense and to this degree, the riots in Los Angeles were not so much a protest against statism, but a result of the myth of statism. It was a demand for *more* statism.

Democratic statism lives by the myth of state redemption. The dream is that the state will provide all my needs. It will provide food for my table, education for my children, money for my bank account, employment for my career, and a host of other benefits that will cover me from the cradle to the grave.

I begin with *appreciation* for such provisions, move quickly to an *expectation* of these provisions, and then finally to a *demand* for these provisions.

When the demand is not met, I take to the streets like a child in a temper tantrum.

I call the dream of statist redemption a myth because it cannot become a reality. The dream quickly becomes a nightmare. The size of government increases geometrically as more and more demands are placed upon it. The power of government increases geometrically as more hope is invested in it. Finally the cost of government increases geometrically as the price tag for the provisions escalates. While all this happens, the ability of government to function diminishes geometrically as it builds bigger and bigger deficits and drains more and more of the nation's resources. Its laws become confused and contradictory, its operation becomes unwieldy and paralyzed, and its excellence diminishes with the diminished quality of its leaders.

As long as the statist philosophy—or more accurately, mythology—persists, the nation languishes. The people become like the proverbial frog which is boiled alive while the water heats so gradually that by the time the frog realizes he's in hot water, it's too late to jump out.

During the recession the nation faced high unemployment. Those unemployed demanded more unemployment benefits, which placed more strain on the budget, more tax burden on the people and on businesses, and resulted in more unemployment . . . and the beat goes on as the myth refuses to die.

Meanwhile, Francis Schaeffer enjoys the final refuge from statism as he beholds the reality of his own redemption.

GOD: BETWEEN A ROCK AND A HARD PLACE

NOVEMBER 1992

———

T EACHERS OFTEN ENCOUNTER THE PROBLEM of the fast-draw gunslinger. As the official expert of a given field, the teacher is expected to have all the answers, to take all comers. Some students view education as a contest, and their purpose is to "stump the wizard." When the arena is theology, students invariably throw down the gauntlet with this brain teaser: "Can God make a rock so big that He Himself can't move it?" The difficulty is apparent. If we respond in the negative, we seem to deny His sovereignty. We conclude that there is at least one thing He cannot do, make such a rock. To answer positively, however, likewise affirms that there is at least one thing He cannot do, move such a rock. Either way we seem to deny that God is omnipotent, all-powerful.

Such a question reveals a bit of ignorance by the questioner. In the first place, the question, properly understood, involves a contradiction. It could read, "Is God so omnipotent that He could stop being omnipotent?" Secondly, when theologians speak of omnipotence, they do not make the claim that God can do anything. There are many "things" that God cannot do. God is not able to lie. God is not able to make a square circle. He cannot create a self-existent being. He cannot sin. Is God then subservient to some set of rules, standards above Himself? Is God *sub lego* (under law)? Some argue that God's power to rule creation is limited by creaturely freedom. It is said, "God's sovereignty is limited by man's freedom." Is human freedom the immovable object that reduces God's power to a resistible force? Happily this is not what Christians usually mean when they say God's sovereignty is limited by human freedom.

Rather, what is meant is that God does not have the *authority* to limit, foreordain, or in any way intrude upon human volitional actions (authority being not the ability but the right to impose obligation). To do so, it is believed, would be to violate some law that governs God's behavior. It would mean that God would act unjustly toward His creatures, which God is forbidden to do. This law imposes restraint upon God, limiting His authority and the use of His power. It would seem that God is governed both by the rules of reasoning (thus the impossibility of the square circle, a shape having simultaneously no angles and four angles) and by laws of morality (thus the prohibition against lying, or interfering with human choices as some claim).

With this question now before us, we are well beyond the rock and into the hard place. It would seem that God has become impaled on the horns of a dilemma. If we say that God operates outside the law (*ex lex*) we are vulnerable to the charge that God is lawless and arbitrary, that His rule is characterized by caprice. He reigns by sheer power and is the paradigm of the axiom "Might makes right." If, on the other hand, we say that God is under law (*sub lego*), meaning that there is some cosmic law or extra-divine *summum bonum* (highest good) to which God is accountable, then we are left with a god who is not sovereign. He is subject to this other higher authority.

Jonathan Edwards and his study of the human will provide some insight for how we can navigate through this dilemma. In his essay "The Freedom of the Will," Edwards discusses how it is that we make choices. The will, he says, is the mind choosing. He reasoned that we are free in the sense that we can choose whatever we most desire in a given moment. We are not free in the sense that we can choose other than what seems best. Edwards pointed out that we always choose according to our strongest inclination at the moment. As unregenerate sinners at enmity with God, our strongest inclination is always to choose sin. It is only after the sovereign intervention of the Spirit giving new life that a person can do the good.

In defining the sovereignty of God, Edwards uses much of the same reasoning, though noting some differences between God and man. His definition of sovereignty as it applies to God is "God's absolute, independent

right of the disposing of all creatures according to His own pleasure."
But this, as John Gerstner points out (in *The Rational Biblical Theology
of Jonathan Edwards*, vol. II), is not a form of raw voluntarism by which
God acts upon some sheer absolute power in a manner that is arbitrary
or capricious. God's "choices" are no more uncaused than ours. He, like
us, chooses according to His own rational judgment. Just as we choose
according to what seems good to us at the moment of choice, so does
God. The great difference is that there is no "seeming" good to God. He
knows the good absolutely and always chooses not what merely seems
good but what actually is good.

We are beginning to see that whether God is *sub lego* (under law) or *ex
lex* (outside law) is a false dilemma. Historically, the church has rejected
both horns of this false dilemma. There is a *tertium quid*, a third option.
God is neither lawless nor subject to law outside of Himself. He is governed, but He is governed by Himself. He is, in the fullest sense, a law
unto Himself. This law is internal, not external. It is the law of His own
holy character. God acts according to His own being. His moral attributes
are a part of His essence. His goodness is not accidental to Him. He acts
according to who He is. He is altogether holy. Something is good or right
not simply because God does it. Rather, God does only what is good and
right because He is good and right. This is no mere distinction without
a difference. It makes all the difference in the world. It is the difference
between righteousness and caprice, between goodness and whim. God
is able (has the power) and has the sovereign authority to do whatever
He pleases with His creation. His will is not and cannot be determined
by anything outside Himself.

We are doomed to confusion when we seek to pit one of God's attributes
against another. We must not conceive of God as a mere conglomera-
tion of attributes, as if His holiness, omnipotence, and omniscience were
various pearls upon a string. God is a unity; He is of one piece. We can
distinguish His various attributes, but we can never separate them. This
is the doctrine of divine simplicity. In explaining this doctrine, Aquinas
argued that God is identical with His nature. In God, essence and nature

are the same. God, therefore, does not *possess* the attributes of goodness and omnipotence. Rather, God *is* goodness and omnipotence. We cannot pit one attribute against another because they are the same.

Our God then remains incomprehensible and retains His simplicity. He tells us in His Word that He is not a God of confusion but of order. He is not at war with Himself. He is neither *sub lego* nor *ex lex*. Rather, He was, is, and evermore will be a law unto Himself. He is altogether good, altogether holy, and altogether sovereign. This we must affirm to maintain a biblical concept of divine sovereignty. Yet we must always balance this understanding with a clear understanding that God *always* exercises both His power and authority according to His holy character. He chooses what He chooses according to His own good pleasure. It is His pleasure He does. He chooses what is pleasing to Himself. But that pleasure is always His *good* pleasure, for God is never pleased to will or to do anything that is evil or contrary to His own goodness.

In this we can rest, knowing that He wishes for, and has the power to bring about, all good things for us His children (Romans 8:28).

TAKE UP AND READ
CHRISTIAN CLASSICS

JANUARY 1993

———

T OMMY LASORDA, THE WALKING SYMBOL of "Dodger Blue," was there. Poised to watch a game between the San Francisco Giants and the Pittsburgh Pirates, I was surprised to see Lasorda take a seat in the stands at Three Rivers Stadium. The Dodgers were in town awaiting the beginning of their three-game series against the Pirates to begin the following day.

From the moment Lasorda took his seat, a line began to form in the aisle. Autograph hounds besieged him during the entire game. After signing at least two hundred autographs over a space of two hours, an usher rescued Lasorda by dispersing the remaining group in line. One man erupted in a paroxysm of obscenities complaining that this was the one time in his life that he had the opportunity to get Lasorda's autograph.

There was irony here. Seated two rows in front of Lasorda was Chuck Tanner. A few rows behind me, flashing his ubiquitous smile, was Manny Sanguillén. Both Tanner and Sanguillén sat in obscurity, unrecognized by the fans. No one asked Tanner, the former manager of the Pirates, for his autograph. No one approached Sanguillén either. The irony was compounded by another obscure historical note. When Sanguillén was an All-Star catcher for the Pirates, he was traded to Oakland, not for a player but for their manager, Chuck Tanner—one of the most bizarre trades in baseball history. I doubt if either man was aware of the other's presence at the game.

Why all the attention to Lasorda and none to Tanner or Sanguillén? The answer is obvious. Lasorda is current. He is "now." Tanner and Sanguillén are pages out of the past. Their hour on the stage is over. Now they walk the idiot's stage.

I couldn't help but wonder.... What if Ted Williams walked in? Surely the crowd would have deserted Lasorda and flocked to Williams. Why? Because though the Splendid Splinter is no longer current, he is a legend. He is not merely past; he is a classic, one of the all-time greats.

It's not much different with books. In 1991 the best-selling book in Christendom was Benny Hinn's *Good Morning, Holy Spirit.* There is little risk that Hinn's book will become a classic. I won't require it as a text book for my students in theology. If you haven't read it, wait a couple years. You'll be able to buy a copy for a dime at somebody's garage sale.

Two years ago I found an antiquary in Geneva, Switzerland, near St. Peter's Church. I found a copy of Calvin's *Commentary on the Psalms*, published two years before the Reformer's death. I could not believe my good fortune. I was able to buy it for $500. When I brought it home it was appraised at $5,000. (No, I won't sell it for $5,000. No way.)

My students are still required to read Calvin's *Institutes.* Since the sixteenth century there have been numerous systematic theologies written. Many of them are excellent. But none equals Calvin's prodigious work on the subject. I assign many contemporary works, but always sprinkled among them are titles from the giants: Luther, Edwards, Augustine, et al.

Books become classics when they stand the test of time. They rise above the novel. They transcend the new and different. They defeat the spirit of the philosophers who gathered at the Areopagus eager to discuss whatever was "new." Those of us who live to write of theology in our impoverished era are at best dwarfs standing on the shoulders of yesterday's titans.

Many years ago I purchased an English translation of St. Athanasius' classic work on the Incarnation (*The Incarnation of the Word of God*), published in London in 1944. I was delighted to discover that the introductory essay for this volume was written by C.S. Lewis. This essay was later included in the collection of Lewis' writings in the volume entitled *God in the Dock* under the title "On the Reading of Old Books."

In this essay Lewis notes the penchant of modern Christians to restrict their reading to contemporary literature. They may read about the classics, while ignoring the classics themselves. He writes:

Now this seems to me topsy-turvy. Naturally, since I myself am a writer, I do not wish the ordinary reader to read no modern books. But if he must read only the new or only the old, I would advise him to read the old (p. 201).

My sentiments exactly. I would gladly have all the books I have written summarily discarded if the reader would exchange them for the classics. Everything I have ever written has been said better and more profoundly by the fathers. My books are designed to pique an interest in the reader to go deeper—to flee my work for the work of the true masters. Lewis continues:

And I would give him this advice precisely because he is an amateur and therefore much less protected than the expert against the dangers of an exclusive contemporary diet. A new book is still on its trial and the amateur is not in a position to judge it. It has to be tested against the great body of Christian thought down the ages, and all its hidden implications (often unsuspected by the author himself) have to be brought to light.... The only safety is to have a standard of plain, central Christianity ("mere Christianity" as Baxter called it) which puts the controversies of the moment in their proper perspective. Such a standard can be acquired only from the old books. It is a good rule, after reading a new book, never to allow yourself another new one till you have read an old one in between (pp. 201–202).

Lewis notes that every age has its own peculiar outlook. Every generation has its unique perspective. We are almost two thousand years removed from the New Testament. Those who seek to "revise" the ancient Gospel or accommodate it for the benefit of modern ears shriek their laments that the Bible is "culturally bound." Indeed, the Bible does reflect a first-century perspective, but that is only half the problem in penetrating its meaning. The problem is not that the Bible is culturally bound: It is that we are. We are tethered to the perspective of our own time. We bring contemporary baggage to the New Testament. We are blinded by the errors of our own age. Lewis exhorts:

The only palliative is to keep the clean sea breeze of the centuries blowing through our minds, and this can be done only by reading old books. Not, of course, that there is any magic about the past. People were no cleverer then than they are now; they made as many mistakes as we. But not the same mistakes.... To be sure, the books of the future would be just as good a corrective as the books of the past, but unfortunately we cannot get at them.

I try to read every book, except the Bible, "with a comb." When I comb my hair, loose, dead hair is removed. This hair is of no value to me. It just adds fluff to my crown. Every book is measured by such excess weight. The breeze of the ages acts as a comb for contemporary dross.

A classic, then, stands the test of time. It is, however, more than that. A true classic must pack a double punch; it must be able to instruct and inspire. Dry, dusty tomes can explain to us technical nuances, dissecting God and His redemptive history as an anatomy text dissects the body. Too many devotional books turn us inward, focusing on our feelings as we monitor ourselves to see if we can muster the proper response. A classic points us outward to our evocative God, and we respond in awe and worship. Lewis, a writer of modern classics, makes that commitment, to look to God, to learn from the greats and respond *coram Deo*:

> For my own part, I tend to find the doctrinal books often more helpful in devotion than the devotional books, and I rather suspect that the same experience may await many others. I believe that many who find that "nothing happens" when they sit down, or kneel down, to a book of devotion, would find that their heart sings unbidden while they are working their way through a tough bit of theology with a pipe in their teeth and a pencil in their hand.

HARMONY OF CREATION

FEBRUARY 1993

———

M Y WIFE VESTA AND I WERE WALKING on the Charles Bridge in Prague, Czechoslovakia. Tourists crowded around us as they made their way either to John Hus Square or to the slope to view the magnificent Gothic architecture of St. Vitus Cathedral. The bridge, built over 600 years ago, is closed to traffic but is the daily workplace of myriad artists. The painters, woodworkers, metalworkers, and sculptors displayed their wares on the sides of the bridge. Musicians of all types played: A blind woman sang hymns—a combo played Dixieland jazz—two unemployed opera singers performed rich arias.

We stopped to listen to the musicians; we listened to opera for over an hour. Then, only a few paces away, we were attracted to a man playing "Edelweiss." His "instrument" was composed of about thirty crystal goblets filled with various levels of water. He "played" the glasses with his moistened finger tips, making the goblets sing as he glided his hands over their rims.

Vesta said to me, "How does that work?" I could only offer a most simplistic reply. It was like asking me how a piano works. I wanted to say, "You strike a key and a tone sounds." Yet I knew it was far more complex than that. I am afraid that if I were the sole survivor of a nuclear holocaust, civilization would retreat to the stone age. I would have trouble reinventing the wheel. My only contribution to future science of the race would be to write fiction about strange creations like electric light bulbs and combustion engines, but I wouldn't be able to tell anyone how to make them.

In answering Vesta's question, I thought back to my days in elementary school. I did a crude science project on the marvels of sound. My project was to take a board and attach wires to it in guitar-like fashion. I learned two things about music doing that. The first was that the thicker the wire, the lower the sound. I also discovered that if I pressed down the wires at various places along the board, I could alter the tones of the sound. If I shortened the wires by depressing them with my fingers, I got a higher pitch. The shorter the wire, the higher the pitch. If I carefully measured the distance of my board and inserted fret lines at the appropriate intervals, I could regulate the lengths of the wires so as to produce the various sounds of a twelve-tone scale.

Relying on that experience, I could now speculate to Vesta, "I don't know how he gets 'Edelweiss' out of those glasses, but I think it has to do with a carefully measured size and volume of each glass in proportion to the others." The two key words in the equation are *measure* and *proportion*. There is a profound difference between noise and music. Music makes noise, but not all noise is music. For noise to become music, it must be measured and put in proportion.

Music has three basic elements: melody, harmony, and rhythm. Each is equally amazing. Melody is the rise and fall of pitch. Go to a piano and find middle C. Strike the key and listen to the tone. Strike the next black key up and you will hear C sharp (or D flat as they are enharmonic). Continue up the keyboard striking every black and white key until you reach C again. How many tones have you heard? That's right, you've heard twelve (C, C♯, D, D♯, E, F, F♯, G, G♯, A, A♯, B).

Twelve distinct tones. That's all. Yet virtually every melody you've ever heard was created by some combination of only twelve distinct tones. It is hard to imagine so many melodies from so few tones. The possible combinations of those twelve tones provide a virtually infinite number. Beethoven worked with the same number of tones as did Elvis Presley or Thelonious Monk.

Next comes harmony. When we strike, play, or sing together more than one tone at a time, we create the possibility of harmony. Simple chords are based on three tones played at the proper intervals. Complex chords have more than three tones. The more tones we incorporate in music, the more we realize how crucial proportionality is. Indiscriminate banging on the piano creates noise. It is only when the tones fit together in proportionate ratio that we achieve *harmony*.

Music is applied mathematics. Most occidental music is based on a proportionate ratio of the "third." Oriental music tends to build upon "fourths." But both employ a mathematical ratio of sounds to one another. Harmony reflects the triumph of creation over chaos, order over disorder, sanity over confusion, beauty over ugliness.

The ancient scientist-philosophers sought the secrets of the cosmos in mathematical proportion. The Pythagoreans were not simply religious mystics. Like Plato, they sought the "harmony of the spheres."

Rhythm. Duke Ellington said, "If it ain't got that swing, it don't mean a thing!" He was referring to the distinct rhythm of jazz. But every type of music has some kind of rhythm. Life is filled with matters of rhythm—the tick of a clock, the beat of the heart, the tempo of the golf swing, the cadence of the marching command.

Rhythm has to do with time. The author of Ecclesiastes notices the rhythm of life itself. There is a proper timing for things, a time to laugh and a time to mourn; a time to sow and a time to reap. In agriculture timing is everything. Calendars were first invented out of the necessity to be able to measure the proper seasons for planting and harvesting.

Good rhythm is measured carefully. I can't stand it when my piano teacher tells me to play a song in strict tempo. I prefer to *ad lib* the rhythm. When he measures me against the metronome (the most diabolical of human inventions), I usually get failing marks. Most of our hearts do not require a metronome to keep us alive. The Creator grants us a natural pacemaker to keep a proportionate supply of blood circulating through our bodies in a proportionate manner.

The Bible is replete with allusions to music as evidence of the grandeur of creation. The dawn of creation is described as the moment when the morning stars sang together with joy (Job 38:7). Every harmony, every melody ever composed since Creation bears witness, even at times hostile or reluctant witness, to the Fountainhead and Author of all harmony.

It was no mistake that when C.S. Lewis wrote of the creation of Narnia, he had Aslan, the Son of God, sing all things into being. Our God is a God of harmony, of order, of beauty.

When the world opts for irrationality, when people claim to be relativists, when the immoral say there are no absolutes, when the culture is assaulted by the din of dissonance, when the beautiful is vandalized, then it is time for the sound of music, the music that reverberates with the echo of the Creator's voice.

RELATIVISM: A PHILOSOPHICAL ABORTION

MARCH 1993

———

WITH RELATIVISM, INTELLECTUAL INQUIRY fails to reach full term in the gestation process and the fetus dies and is ejected. The baby that is lost is Truth.

To continue the metaphor, if the baby is Truth, then revelation is the midwife. Without the assistance of the midwife the baby cannot be born.

Relativism is linked inseparably with subjectivism. Truth is determined by individual preference. It is locked into the subject without recourse to the object. Objective truth is related to a discovery of reality that exists outside of and apart from us.

For knowledge of the external world to get into my mind, there must be a process or source. My body is my transition to the world external to my mind. I apprehend the world via sense perception. I hear things, see things, taste things, touch things, and smell things outside myself.

Each of the senses gives access to the objective world. If one of the senses is lost, we must rely on the others for that access. Recently, I watched an event I had never seen before. At the conclusion of our 1992 San Diego Conference, about thirty deaf participants spontaneously moved to the platform and surrounded the Westminster Brass as they played the postlude, putting their fingers on the instruments. Because they could not hear the music being played, they wanted to feel the vibrations of the horns. It was literally and spiritually a "touching moment." These deaf people wanted to experience a reality that was outside of themselves. They wanted to touch objective truth.

Knowledge is in the mind. The question is, How does it get there?

Christianity asserts that all knowledge is based on and dependent upon revelation. God is the source of truth. His self-disclosure (revelation) is the necessary condition for knowledge. We have natural faculties for knowing, but the content ultimately depends upon God.

The Bible teaches that God reveals Himself in nature. This natural revelation is called general revelation. General revelation is distinguished between two types: *immediate* and *mediate*. Immediate general revelation refers to knowledge God plants directly in the mind. We are born with an innate sense of God and innate sense of right and wrong. God, as the Apostle Paul contends, writes His law on our hearts. This "immediate" knowledge is so-called because it is not mediated to us through the objects present in the external world. It comes directly from God. Innate knowledge does not come from the slime. Slime is ignorant. This innate knowledge can only be imparted by a knowing subject.

Mediate general revelation comes through and by means of the external created order. We learn it through the senses. But the senses require a midwife. Consider sight as an example. Both St. Augustine and then St. Thomas Aquinas saw an analogy between revelation and sunlight. To see objects in the external world, three things are necessary: (1) There must be objects out there to see; (2) there must be the faculty of vision (eyes, optic nerves, and all the equipment we have for sight); and (3) there must be light. If the object is out there and my vision is sound, I still cannot see anything if I am in total darkness. The light is the "extra," the necessary midwife for the visual experience to take place.

God's existence is "objective" in the sense that He is a being different from me who exists apart from me whether I acknowledge His existence or not. God's existence is not dependent upon my subjective whim. The existence of God is not a relative matter. It is truly either/or. Either God exists apart from me or He does not. How I *feel* about God may be a matter of subjective response, but His reality is not. If God exists apart from me, I cannot destroy Him by my relative feelings on the matter. Nor can I create God subjectively if He does not exist.

Integral Aristotelianism, as the name suggests, was an attempt to merge

R . C . S P R O U L

or integrate the religion of Islam with the philosophy of Aristotle. What resulted was a new form of relativism, manifest in the embracing of a "double-truth" theory. The double-truth theory declared that what is true in faith may be false in reason; what is true in theology may be false in science. This intellectual schizophrenia relativized truth. It provoked a fatal rupture of nature and grace.

It was into this morass that St. Thomas Aquinas stepped to provide a Christian apology. One of the great ironies of modern church history is that a commonly assumed "truism" of evangelical assessment of St. Thomas is that he was the chief culprit in causing the modern divorce between nature and grace. Francis Schaeffer relentlessly laid this blame at Aquinas' doorstep. The irony is this: Probably no Christian thinker in history fought against the separation of nature and grace as did Thomas Aquinas.

Whatever Thomas' errors may have been, they did not include a separation of nature and grace. On the contrary, he abhorred such a separation. What Thomas did was this: He *distinguished* between nature and grace in an effort to demonstrate their ultimate unity. He argued that there are certain truths that are learned by nature that are not learned by grace and certain truths that are learned by grace that are not learned by nature. He also maintained that there are "mixed articles" (*articulus mixtus*) whereby certain truths (such as the existence of God) are known through both nature and grace.

The distinctive "nature" and "grace" can be and has been misleading. Aquinas is accused of setting up naked human reason against divine revelation. However, according to Thomas *all* knowledge is based on and dependent on revelation. At this point he was at one with Augustine, of whom he never tired of citing. Aquinas' distinction between nature and grace is basically a distinction between general revelation and special revelation. Both nature and the Bible reveal the existence of God. This "mixed article" was formulated by Aquinas via a lengthy exegesis of Romans 1.

Aquinas was jealous to show that general and special revelation are harmonious. There are no double truths. Though faith and reason are distinct, they are not in conflict. All truth is God's truth and all truth meets at the top. Faith is not irrational. Yet reason depends upon revelation to make knowledge of the world possible. To set faith in opposition to reason is to reduce Christianity to gnosticism.

Though the world has grappled with a multitude of philosophical systems and methods, there is one such view that can't possibly be true. That view is relativism. Relativism cannot be "true" because it denies truth itself. It has to, in order to be entertained at all. Relativism not only makes truth impossible, it makes life impossible. Perhaps that is why people who embrace relativism do it selectively. That is, they become relativists when it suits them (usually to excuse unethical behavior). People who are relativists are only "relative" relativists. No one is an "absolute" relativist because pure relativism is fatal. When people drive their cars to a major intersection, they do not relativize their situation. They know that the presence of an oncoming truck is not a relative matter. They understand that if they proceed into the path of the truck they will not end up relatively dead.

AN UNCHANGING STANDARD

APRIL 1993

———

RECENTLY, THE VATICAN ANNOUNCED THE release of a new catechism, a massive work years in the making. I am eagerly awaiting its translation into English. My interest is not dominated by a new theological dictum but by what the document will say on the field of biomedical ethics.

Roman Catholic moral theology has been one of the church's strong suits. Catholic scholars have placed a premium on the careful exploration of ethical issues. Though I frequently differ with Rome in its moral theology, I have an abiding respect for the care of its work. Rome refuses to be held hostage by societal shifts in customs or mores. They don't decide moral issues by referendum.

In the arena of biomedical ethics, we face a unique kind of problem. In the general field of ethics, we have the advantage of 2,000 years of careful research, debate, and insight into complex and weighty problems. With biomedical ethical issues that presently confront us, however, we do not have the benefit of such long-term investigation. Modern technologies have introduced ethical questions that are new. The use of life-support systems, in vitro fertilization, and other technologies have introduced new dilemmas and pose new ethical questions.

To address these questions, we have the advantage of manifold basic principles. It is the application of such principles to complex new problems that is difficult.

These problems are not restricted to abstract theoretical questions. They are issues that touch heavily on life itself. With increasing regularity pastors are called to assist in decision-making crises that involve the use of life-support systems. The question of when to "pull the plug" touches life issues so poignantly that in order to avoid paralyzing guilt problems, the pastor, along with the attending physician, is asked to "play God."

But no pastor is God. We look to our pastor to give us the voice of God. We want God's guidance in these ethical dilemmas. The Supreme Court is not an adequate substitute for the person who is more concerned to discern and to carry out what is right rather than simply what is legal.

To solve such dilemmas we need clear and normative principles. Principles exist in the abstract. Decisions must be made in concrete life situations. Situations, however, do not dictate the decision. Situations are the real-life arena where principles must be applied. Real-life situations demand a decision. We do not have the luxury of making no decision. To make no decision is to make a decision.

What we are after in biomedical ethics are clear and certain principles that are not arbitrary. We need principles that are absolute and normative. The legal code of society can never provide an absolute norm. In societies where laws are enacted according to popular will, we discover conflicting and contradictory laws. In the United States abortion is legal. In Ireland abortion is illegal. Does this mean that it is ethically "right" to abort American babies but "wrong" to abort Irish babies? Or, to put it another way, was it ethically wrong to have an abortion before *Roe v. Wade*, but ethically proper after *Roe v. Wade*? If legal rights are an absolute norm we would say yes.

The ultimate standard of right and wrong is the character of God as revealed in His law. God's law is always situational in the sense that it must be applied in given situations. It is never situational in the sense that the good is dictated by the situation. The situation is subordinate to the principle, not the principle to the situation.

The "new morality" follows the situation ethics set forth popularly by Joseph Fletcher. Fletcher summarized his view of ethics by saying, "We must always do what love requires in the situation."

This maxim, if it stood alone, would be sound. We are always responsible to do what love demands in a situation. Love is the linchpin of the law of God. The problem remains, however, how do we know what love requires in a given situation? God's law reveals what God's love requires.

When Paul speaks of the ethics of love he says, "And live a life of love, just as Christ loved us . . ." (Ephesians 5:2).

But the Apostle does not stop with an ambiguous appeal to love. In the next breath he says, "But among you there must not be even a hint of sexual immorality, or of any kind of impurity, or of greed, because these are improper for God's holy people" (Ephesians 5:3).

Here the law of God defines what is consistent with love. Appeals to love are frequently used to excuse sin. The oldest ploy in the world for sexual seduction is, "If you love me, you will." Yet Paul declares, "If you love God, you won't. Ever."

Most ethical decisions we face involve the application of more than one principle. It is balancing the myriad principles of the law of God that requires wisdom. To face the new questions posed in the field of biomedical ethics, we must grasp the relevant principles that apply.

Professor John Frame of Westminster Seminary West has contributed greatly to the discussion with his book *Biomedical Ethics*. Likewise, John Jefferson Davis has also helped with his work, *Evangelical Ethics*. We must continue to study the questions in light of biblical principles as we seek to live under the authority of God and for His glory. The principles revealed in God's law are not subject to the shifting sands of cultural or legal relativism.

God's law is law. It requires a response of obedience for which we are held accountable, absolutely. The Last Judgment prophesied by the New Testament refers to a final and absolute tribunal from which there is no court of appeal. This tribunal is a cosmic Supreme Court.

The Final Judgment will be the occasion for final and ultimate law enforcement. Lawlessness and disobedience will be punished according to justice. Obedience will result in the distribution of rewards.

In the scenario of Final Judgment, the folly of relativism will be fully exposed. The wisdom and excellence of divine law will be made manifest.

The absolute law of God reveals the absolute glory and righteousness of God. It reflects God's own character, His own righteousness. It also expresses the *authority* of God by which He rules by divine right. As the *author* of creation, God has the *authority* to command from His creatures what He deems right.

Herein is the great conflict between relativism and absolutism. It is the conflict between the will of the creature and the will of the Creator. In relativism the individual person is the final authority for behavior. It involves the syndrome described by Scripture as each person doing "what is right in his own eyes." This conflict is not modern but is as old as human experience after the Fall.

The law of God transcends individual preferences. It provides an objective norm, a norm that governs everybody's behavior. The norm is not concealed—it is revealed, giving each of us the opportunity and the responsibility to know what righteousness requires. We are left with no excuse.

THE GOSPEL: A TWO-EDGED SWORD

MAY 1993

I N A CRISIS SITUATION WHEN ANXIETY CLUTCHES the heart as we await the outcome, we are prone to exclaim, "No news is good news." In the absence of *any* news we prefer silence (as suspenseful as it is) to *bad* news. We hope for the good news while enduring the silence of no news. Just don't give me bad news.

We enjoy the comedy that plays off the tension between good news and bad news. The jokes are endless. Take, for example, the pope's response to the bishop who is an avid golfer. The bishop inquires if there is golf in heaven. The pope prays and returns with an answer: "I have good news and bad news. The good news is there is golf in heaven. The bad news is that you tee off at 10:00 o'clock tomorrow morning."

In the ancient world, people understood that bad news can bring sorrow and mourning to the hearers. Likewise, good news elicits joy. Because of the consequences of the news, messengers were held responsible for the news they carried. The messenger of good news was rewarded; the herald of bad news was punished.

In 2 Samuel 4:10 we read, "When a man told me, 'Saul is dead,' and thought he was bringing good news, I seized him and put him to death in Ziklag. That was the reward I gave him for his news!"

Later in 2 Samuel, David heard from another messenger who also brought news of the outcome of a battle. In this battle the rebellious son of David, Absalom, was killed. Ahimaaz was eager to bring the news to David. He said, "Let me run and take the news to the king, that the LORD has delivered him from the hand of his enemies" (2 Samuel 18:19). Joab warned Ahimaaz of the severe jeopardy of this task: "You are not the one to take the news today. You may take the news another time, but you must not do so today, because the king's son is dead" (v. 20).

This counsel undoubtedly saved Ahimaaz's life. When he did report to David, he delivered the news carefully. When the watchman reported the sight of two runners approaching David, he recognized the approach of the first runner as Ahimaaz. David said, "He is a good man. He comes with good news" (v. 27).

Notice how Ahimaaz delivered his report: "Then Ahimaaz called out to the king, 'All is well!' He bowed down before the king with his face to the earth, and said, 'Praise be the LORD your God! He has delivered up the men who lifted their hand against my lord the king'" (v. 28).

David inquired immediately about the fortunes of his son: "Is the young man Absalom safe?" And Ahimaaz answered, "Just as Joab was about to send the king's servant and me, your servant, I saw great confusion, but I don't know what it was" (v. 29).

Ahimaaz was creative in his approach. His answer was both deceitful and cloaked in ambiguity. He restricted his report to the good news of victory but left David with an ambiguous answer to his query about Absalom.

The full answer was provided by the second runner, a Cushite who also answered indirectly: "May the enemies of my lord the king and all who rise up to harm you be as that young man" (v. 32).

David got the message . . . and the messengers escaped with their lives.

Just as the bearer of bad news was in mortal danger in ancient times, so the herald of good news is deemed worthy of honor and reward. Homer used the Greek word *euangelion* (*gospel*) to mean a "reward for good news." For Plutarch, *gospel* meant news of victory. Kittel notes: "The messenger appears, raises his right hand in greeting, and calls out with a loud voice: 'We are victorious.' By his appearance it is known already that he brings good news. His face shines, his spear is decked with laurel, his head is crowned, he swings a branch of palms, joy fills the city, 'gospels' are offered, the temples are garlanded, a contest is held, crowns are put on for the sacrifices, and the one to whom the message is owed is honoured with a wreath" (*Theological Dictionary of the New Testament*, Vol. II).

In Greek mythology, Hermes, the messenger of the gods, like his Roman counterpart, Mercury, is often depicted with wings on his feet and a wreath on his head.

This imagery is found in both Testaments. In Romans 10:15, Paul alludes to Isaiah 52:7: "How beautiful on the mountains are the feet of those who bring good news, who proclaim peace, who bring good tidings, who proclaim salvation, who say to Zion, 'Your God reigns!' "

Notice that the content of the announcement concerns the *reign of God*. It is Isaiah's proclamation of the Gospel of the kingdom of God.

The New Testament Gospel

The term *gospel* is used in the New Testament in at least three distinct ways. The first refers to the preaching of Jesus who proclaims the "Gospel of the kingdom of God." The second is in the Apostolic writings where the Gospel is a proclamation about the person and work of Christ. It is the Gospel of (about) Jesus Christ. The third is to refer to a form or genre of literature—the narrative records of Matthew, Mark, Luke, and John, which we call "Gospels."

The New Testament Gospel is a double-edged sword. It is good news that is also at the same time (but in a different relationship) *bad news*. The feet that are beautiful on the mountain to some are ugly to others. The sweet fragrance of life that emanates from the Gospel is malodorous to those who perish. For the redeemed the Gospel is an announcement of peace; for the damned it is a declaration of war.

The announcement of the Gospel is the report of a crisis. It is a major crisis. Indeed, it is a crisis of cosmic proportion.

The theology of Karl Barth has been called alternately neo-orthodox theology or "dialectical theology" and also frequently "crisis-theology." Why the designation "crisis theology"? Barth provided a bit of wordplay with the term *crisis*. The English word *crisis* derives from the Greek *krisis*, which is the New Testament word for "judgment." The coming of Jesus brings a crucial time of judgment. He appears on earth as the Son of Man. The role of the Son of Man is chiefly that of a heavenly Judge.

Jesus declared that He came not to bring peace but a sword. He came not to unite but to divide (Matthew 10:34f). His coming onto the scene is heralded by John the Baptist as a time of supreme crisis: "The ax is already at the root of the trees, and every tree that does not produce good fruit will be cut down and thrown into the fire" (Matthew 3:10).

Again, John warns: "His winnowing fork is in His hand, and He will clear His threshing floor, gathering His wheat into the barn and burning up the chaff with unquenchable fire" (3:12).

The winnowing fork is an instrument of separation. It is a tool used to divide the wheat and the chaff. Before the fork is applied, the wheat and the chaff are mixed together in a pile. That mixture is temporary. It is the farmer's design to establish a different destination for the wheat and the chaff. The destiny of the wheat is the harbor of the barn. There it is "saved" from destruction. The destiny of the chaff is the fire that no water can quench.

The Gospel is like the winnowing fork. For the believer it is the power of God to salvation (Romans 1:16). For the unbeliever it is the kiss of death; it is the power of God unto damnation.

Perhaps the most popular verse in the Bible is John 3:16. There the Gospel is proclaimed in a nutshell. But John 3:16 has a context. It provides the bad news as well as the good news: "Whoever believes in Him is not condemned, but whoever does not believe stands condemned already because he has not believed in the name of God's one and only Son. This is the verdict: Light has come into the world, but men loved darkness instead of light because their deeds were evil" (John 3:18–19).

No one can be neutral toward the Gospel. Those who are not with Christ are against Him. Those who reject His good news will hear His bad news. Those who reject the Gospel of the kingdom of God will not enter the kingdom of God. They will remain enemies to the King of the kingdom. Those who reject Christ as Savior and Lord will have Christ as their Judge. For the redeemed, the day of the Lord will be a time of peace, joy, and light. For those who reject the Gospel, there will be no peace, no joy, and no light. For them, the day of the Lord will be a day of darkness with no light in it. That is bad news, the worst of all possible news.

WHAT IS HEAVEN LIKE?

JUNE 1993

———

WHEN WE ASK QUESTIONS ABOUT matters that elude our full understanding, we tend to look for models or patterns that are *similar* to what we do understand. We seek for clues to a new and different paradigm. The shift from earth-bound thinking to conceiving of heaven is a massive paradigm shift.

To speak of our mysterious future is to search for analogies that will give us a hint about what to expect. We cannot say what heaven *is*, but the Bible does give us hints as to what it is *like*. We try to imagine the unknown in the light of what *is* known. John tells us: "It has not yet been revealed what we shall be, but we know that when He is revealed, we shall be like Him, for we shall see Him as He is" (1 John 1:2).

We do not know for sure to whom the "He" and the "Him" refer. Do they refer to God the Father or to Christ? God the Father is the subject of the preceding verses, but what follows seems to indicate Christ.

The difficulty of the reference is mollified when we realize that to be Christ-like is to be God-like. The firstfruits image of Christ in His resurrection indicates that, ultimately, we shall be like Christ. As Christ rose with a glorified body so we too will enjoy glorified bodies at the final resurrection.

We can say, then, that we will be in some *place*. The place will be similar to places we occupy now. But there will also be differences. The heavenly place will be a place of manifest glory. Our bodies will have continuity with our present bodies. There will also be discontinuity. Our new bodies will be glorified. What that means is shrouded in mystery—we see through the glass darkly. Yet we receive hints about our glorified bodies by comparisons to Jesus as well as by His words that we will be "like the angels."

Paul gives further hints: After discussing various kinds of bodies we experience on this planet, and various levels of glory of created objects, he adds: "The body that is sown is perishable, it is raised imperishable; it is sown in dishonor, it is raised in glory; it is sown in weakness, it is raised in power; it is sown a natural body, it is raised a spiritual body" (1 Corinthians 15:42–44).

We understand corruption, dishonor, weakness, and natural bodies. Only by contrast or eminence do we contemplate an incorruptible, glorified, powerful, spiritual body. The new body will be clothed with immortality. It will receive a garment it does not presently or intrinsically possess.

John's vision in Revelation gives us further clues about heaven.

The first thing John mentions about the new heaven and new earth is that there was no more *sea*. This is an interesting observation, especially since a large percentage of the globe is covered by water. We look toward the poetic significance of the sea. In Hebrew poetry, the sea is a negative image. It is the symbol of primordial chaos, the habitation of the threatening sea monster. In Jewish history, the sea is the place of rocky coasts and the origin of violent storms. Their classic enemy, the Philistines, were a coastal people. The sea "rages"—it stands in contrast to the River Jordan, whose springs make glad the people of God. The New Jerusalem has no sea, but it does have a river—a river of life, clear as crystal, that proceeds from the throne of God and the Lamb. This river is adorned on its banks by the Tree of Life and the leaves that produce the healing of the nations.

The vision of heaven is also charged with the absence of things that are conspicuously present in our earthly environment. What is absent? Some of the missing things include tears, death, sorrow, and pain: "He will wipe every tear from their eyes. There will be no more death or mourning or crying or pain, for the old order of things has passed away" (Revelation 21:4).

Certain types of people will also be absent. There will be no need for locks on doors as the ultimate security gate will guard the city from trespassers. No unbelievers, abominable and sexually immoral people, murderers, sorcerers, idolaters, or liars will live in that place. This indicates that heaven will be a place where sin is totally absent. This may sound like Utopia, but it is not Utopia. *Utopia* means "no place," and heaven will be a real place.

The New Jerusalem will have neither tabernacle nor temple. These were but earthly types, shadows of what is to come. When the reality appears, the shadows depart. "I did not see a temple in the city, because the Lord God Almighty and the Lamb are its temple" (Revelation 21:22).

The new heaven will have no sun nor moon. They are unnecessary luminaries: "The city does not need the sun or the moon to shine on it, for the glory of God gives it light, and the Lamb is its lamp" (Revelation 21:23).

In this world the sun sets each evening as day turns into night. In heaven there is no night. Nothing can eclipse or dim the light of the refulgent glory of God. No darkness can overcome or even intrude into the splendor of the One who is the Light of the World.

Finally, there will be no curse there. The curse on the cosmic order, which produces groans from the whole creation, will be lifted. It will be banished from heaven. No death, no pain, no struggle will curse the human enterprise.

On the positive side, John's vision provides a glorious picture of what *will* be in heaven. There will be a high wall with twelve gates and twelve angels at the gates. The wall will have twelve foundations. The gates will be named for the twelve tribes of Israel and the foundations for the twelve Apostles.

The city will be four-square with walls of jasper. The walls' foundations will be adorned with precious gemstones. The city itself will be constructed not of brick and mortar or steel and glass. It will be made of pure gold—translucent gold, like clear glass. The gates will be pearls and the streets paved not with tarmac but transparent gold.

These images of breathtaking beauty and opulence pale into insignificance, however, when we consider the most important presence in the Holy City: "The throne of God and of the Lamb will be in the city, and His servants will serve Him. They will see His face, and His name will be on their foreheads" (Revelation 22:3–4).

Heaven is the place of the unveiled presence of God. Christ, in all His splendor, will be there. We shall see Him. We shall speak to Him. We shall hear His voice. We shall serve Him in unspeakable joy.

We don't know exactly what heaven will be. The reality will surely exceed all images or symbols of it. This we do know, heaven is where Jesus is, and it is our destiny.

"Heaven is the place of the unveiled presence of God. Christ, in all His splendor, will be there. We shall see Him. We shall speak to Him."

LUCIFER: DARK ANGEL OF LIGHT

JULY 1993

———

"**I**F THE RIGHT HAND DOESN'T GET YOU, then the left one will." This maxim expresses the double jeopardy faced by a prizefighter in the boxing ring. Like the ambidextrous pugilist, our adversary Satan has a two-pronged strategy. To defeat him we must wage war on two fronts.

It is the nature of Satan to be deceptive. He is called a liar from the beginning. His first appearance in Scripture comes under the guise of a serpent. The credentials of this malevolent creature are announced in his initial introduction: "Now the serpent was more cunning than any beast of the field which the LORD God had made" (Genesis 3:1a, NKJV).

These words fall as a sudden intrusion into an otherwise glorious account of God's majestic work of creation. With the words "Now the serpent," the whole atmosphere of the biblical record changes dramatically. A sudden and ominous sense of foreboding enters the narrative. An uninspired author of Genesis 3 may have introduced the record of the Fall by saying, "It was a dark and stormy day." But such hackneyed prose would have failed to yield the foreboding dread contained in the words "Now the serpent was more cunning."

Cunning. Craftiness. Subtlety. Guile. These are the descriptive qualifiers that paint the biblical portrait of Satan. This guile is nowhere more evident than in Satan's two-fisted, double-front strategy by which he cloaks his own nature and identity.

The tactic is simple. He conquers by spreading disinformation about himself. He divides the church by creating two myths, two erroneous views of his own identity.

The Devil as Myth

The first deception from Satan about Satan is that he is a ridiculous myth. As a mythical figure, he can be put in the category of goblins, ghosties, and things that go bump in the night. Nothing pleases Satan more than to persuade people that he doesn't exist at all. If we are convinced that Satan doesn't exist, we will hardly waste time preparing to make war against him or finding ways to resist him. To put on armor to ward off imaginary fiery darts is as much a fool's errand as Don Quixote's tilting at windmills.

On the other hand, a stealth bomber can have its way, unimpeded in its mission, if the enemy is persuaded that there is no such thing as a stealth bomber.

Satan loves the modern image of himself. Who gives credence to an ugly little imp in red flannel underwear with cloven feet, horns on his head, bearing a trident, and flashing a diabolical grin?

I once asked a college philosophy class, "How many of you believe in God?" Out of 30 students, 27 raised their hands in the affirmative—three demurred. Then I asked, "How many of you believe in Satan as a personal reality?" This time the vote was reversed.

I pursued my inquiry. I asked, "Why do you believe in a supernatural personal being who has the capacity to influence us for good (God) and not in a supernatural personal being who has the capacity to influence us for evil (Satan)?" Their answers indicated that the devil they were rejecting was the nonexistent mythical caricature noted above.

Many qualified their positions by saying, "I do believe in the reality of an impersonal force of evil in the world." I found this response fascinating. I asked them, "How can an *impersonal force* be evil?"

What is this mysterious impersonal force? Cosmic dust? Radioactivity? Impersonal objects, forces, or powers can be many things. One thing they cannot be is morally evil. Only volitional agents, *personal beings*, can be morally evil. Here the attempt to be modern and sophisticated becomes an exercise in intellectual regression. Are we reverting back to a primitive form of animism, imputing evil spirits into rocks and whirlwinds?

At least the primitive animist realized that if the forces were evil they had to be animated.

The Devil as God's Equal

The devil-as-myth view is Satan's right-hand punch. If that one doesn't get you, then watch out for his left hook.

The left-hand attack moves the disinformation to the opposite extreme. If Satan can't get you to ignore him by denying his very existence, he will cunningly lead you to attribute power to him far beyond what he actually possesses. He will seek to persuade you that he is virtually equal to God.

Dualism, as a philosophy and a religion, has vied with Christianity from the beginning. Dualism affirms that the universe is the staging area, the combat zone, for two equal and opposite beings who struggle with each other eternally. It has virtually two gods: a good god and an evil god, a yin and a yang, a power of darkness and a power of light.

This struggle is never resolved. It cannot be resolved because the combatants are equal. The struggle between good and evil must stretch on into eternity because neither participant has the ability to gain the upper hand. It is a cosmic standoff.

Most evangelical churches would emphatically deny dualism. They understand that it fundamentally denies the very essence of Christianity. Yet when we examine views of Satan in popular religion, we see indicators of an implicit dualism. Every day I hear Christians talk about Satan as if he had divine attributes. He is described in terms of omniscience, omnipresence, and the power to do actual, not merely counterfeit, miracles. He is given attributes orthodox Christianity labels as the incommunicable attributes of God. And he is assigned power over nature that rivals the Creator's.

In this view Satan is elevated above his actual being as an angel. The Bible teaches that Satan is an angelic being. He is a spiritual being. He is not an eternal spiritual being. He is not an infinite spiritual being. He is temporal, finite, and created. In a word, he is a *creature*. He is a higher order of creature than humans, but he remains a creature. He is more powerful than we, but he is not omnipotent. He is not immutable, as God is. Indeed, Satan's mutability is profound. His most obvious mutation is his fall. He was created a good angel. He fell from his original righteousness and is now totally malevolent.

As a creature Satan is not *ubiquitous*. He is iniquitous, but never ubiquitous. He cannot be at more than one place at a time. The theological maxim *finitum non capax infinitum*—the finite cannot contain the infinite—is true of Satan, a finite creature.

This is not to say that Satan doesn't cover a lot of ground. He goes about as a roaring lion seeking those whom he may devour. Yet when he is resisted, he flees (1 Peter 5:8–9). He removes himself. And once he is absent, he cannot still be present.

As relentless as Satan was in stalking Jesus, he still departed from Him at least for a season. The demons Jesus expelled and sent into the pigs were first in the man and not in the pigs—and then in the pigs and not in the man. They were not able to be in both at the same time. Satan, as with any angel, is always limited to a single location. Thankfully, this archenemy of the soul spends most of his time in the pursuit of bigger game than you or I.

Satan is powerful. He is far more powerful than we are. That is why we desperately need the armor of God. But as powerful as he is, he is far less powerful than God. That is why the Bible declares that greater is He who is in you (the Holy Spirit) than he who is in the world (Satan). Satan's darts are quenchable; God's are not. You can flee the presence of Satan; you cannot flee the presence of God.

Finally, we must be wary not only of his right and left fists. He is a kickboxer as well. Just when we shield ourselves from his hands, he cheats: He uses his feet. Here his guile is most effective.

One characteristic of Satan is his metamorphic power. He has the cunning and uncanny ability to appear *sub species boni*—"under the auspices of the good." He can transform himself into the appearance of an angel of light. You don't find him so much in the Saddam Husseins of this world. He is not so crass. He appears as a saint, a paragon of virtue, waiting to seduce you.

He is, above all, a fraud. His work is anti-Christ not merely in the sense of working against Christ, but in the sense of seeking to act as a substitute for Christ.

The good news about Satan is this, as Luther so clearly understood: his doom is sure, and one little word can fell him.

"Satan is far more powerful than we are. That is why we need the armor of God. But as powerful as he is, he is far less powerful than God."

GOD'S WILL & TESTAMENT

AUGUST 1993

———

"I T IS THE WILL OF GOD."

How easily these words fall from the lips or flow from the pen. How difficult it is to penetrate exactly what they mean. Few concepts in theology generate more confusion than the will of God.

One problem we face is rooted in the multifaceted way in which the term *will* functions in biblical expressions. The Bible uses the expression "will of God" in various ways. We encounter two different Greek words in the New Testament (*boulē* and *thelēma*), both of which are capable of several nuances. They encompass such ideas as the counsel of God, the plan of God, the decrees of God, the disposition or attitude of God, as well as other nuances. Further distinctions in historical theology add to the labyrinth of meanings attached to the simple formula "the will of God."

Augustine once remarked, "In some sense, God wills everything that happens." The immediate question raised by this comment is, In what sense? How does God "will" the presence of evil and suffering? Is He the immediate cause of evil? Does He *do* evil? God forbid. Yet evil is a part of His creation. If He is sovereign over the whole of His creation, we must face the conundrum, How is evil related to the divine will?

Questions like this one make distinctions necessary—sometimes fine distinctions, even technical distinctions—with respect to the will of God. Some of those distinctions made by theologians include the following:

The Decretive Will of God

This is sometimes described as the sovereign efficacious will, by which God brings to pass whatever He pleases by His divine decree. An example of this may be seen in God's work of creation. When God said, "Let there be light," He issued a divine imperative. He exercised His sovereign efficacious will. It was impossible for the light not to appear. It appeared by the sheer necessity of consequence. That is, the decretive will can have no other effect, no other consequence than what God sovereignly commands. He did not request the light to shine. Nor did He coax, cajole, or woo it into existence. It was a matter of the authority and power vainly sought by the king of Siam when he said to Anna (to no avail), "So let it be said; so let it be done." No creature enjoys this power of will. No man's will is that efficacious. Men issue decrees and then hope they will bring about their desired effects. God alone can decree with the necessity of consequence.

The Preceptive Will of God

The preceptive will of God relates to the revealed commandments of God's published law. When God commands us not to steal, this "decree" does not carry with it the immediate necessity of consequence. Where it was not possible for the light to refuse to shine in creation, it is possible for us to refuse to obey this command. In a word, we steal.

We must be careful not to make too much of this distinction. We must not be lulled into thinking that the preceptive will of God is divorced from His decretive will. It is not as though the preceptive will has *no* effect or *no* necessity of consequence. We may have the power to disobey the precept. We do not have the power to disobey it with impunity. Nor can we annul it by our disregard. His law remains intact whether we obey it or disobey it. Even this law cannot ultimately be frustrated. There will come a time when no one will steal. The sinner in hell will be forcibly restrained from stealing. The saint in heaven, in the glorified state of perfected sanctification, will be totally disinclined to theft.

In one sense the preceptive will is part of the decretive will. God sovereignly and efficaciously decrees that His law be established. It is established and nothing can disestablish it. His law exists as surely as the light by which we read it.

Yet we still observe the acute difference between the light's obedience to God's creative decree and our disobedience to God's moral, preceptive decree. How do we account for this?

A common way to resolve this conundrum is by appeal to a distinction between the sovereign will of God and His permissive will.

The Permissive Will of God

The distinction between the sovereign will of God and the permissive will of God is fraught with peril, and it tends to generate untold confusion.

In ordinary language the term *permission* suggests some sort of positive sanction. To say that God "allows" or "permits" evil does not mean that He sanctions it in the sense that He grants approval to it. It is easy to discern that God never permits sin in the sense that He sanctions it in His creatures.

What is usually meant by divine permission is that God simply lets it happen. That is, He does not directly intervene to prevent its happening. Here is where grave danger lurks. Some theologies view this drama as if God were impotent to do anything about human sin. This view makes man sovereign, not God. God is reduced to the role of spectator or cheerleader, by which God's exercise in providence is that of a helpless Father who, having done all He can do, must now sit back and simply hope for the best. He permits what He cannot help but permit because He has no sovereign power over it. This ghastly view is not merely a defective view of theism; it is unvarnished atheism.

Obviously the motive behind this specious theology is virtuous. It is fueled by a desire to exonerate God from any culpability for the presence of evil in the world. I am sure God is pleased by the sentiment but repulsed by a theory that would strip Him of His very deity. Calvin said of this:

> Hence the distinction was devised between doing and permitting because to many this difficulty seemed inexplicable, that Satan and all the impious are so under God's hand and power that He directs their malice to whatever end seems good to Him, and uses their wicked deeds to carry out His judgments. And perhaps the moderation of those whom the appearance of absurdity alarms would be excusable, except that they wrongly try to clear God's justice of every sinister mark by upholding a falsehood (*Institutes* I.xviii.1).

Calvin locates the scurrilous untruth in the faulty distinction between *willing* and *permitting*:

> It seems absurd to them for man, who will soon be punished for his blindness, to be blinded by God's will and command. Therefore they escape by the shift that this is done only with God's permission, not also by His will; but He, openly declaring that He is the doer, repudiates that evasion. However, that men can accomplish nothing . . . except what He has already decreed with Himself and determines by His secret direction, is proved by innumerable and clear testimonies (*Ibid.*).

Calvin goes on to enumerate several passages that support his thesis, looking to Job, Satan and the Sabeans, the role of Pilate and Judas in the execution of Christ, the role of Absalom in Jewish history, etc.

The key phrase is this: "Therefore they escape by the shift that this is done only with God's permission, not also by His will."

Here the operative word is *only*. If we are in any just way to speak of God's permissive will, we must be careful to notice not only the word *permissive* but also the word *will*. Whatever God "permits" He sovereignly and efficaciously *wills* to permit. If I have a choice to sin or not sin, God also has a choice in the matter. He always has the ability and the authority to stop me from exercising my will. He has absolute power to restrain me. He can vaporize me instantly if it is His pleasure. Or He can keep me on a long leash and let me do my worst. He will only permit me to do my worst if my worst coincides with His perfect providential plan.

In the treachery perpetrated by Joseph's brothers, it was said, "You meant it for evil; God meant it for good." God's good will was served through the bad will of Joseph's brothers. This does not mean that since they were only doing the will of God the acts of the brothers were virtues in disguise. Their acts are judged together with their intentions, and they were rightly judged by God to be evil. That God brings good out of evil only underscores the power and the excellence of His sovereign decretive will.

We sometimes get at this same problem by distinguishing between God's *active* will and His *passive* will. Again we face difficulties. When

God is "passive," He is, in a sense, *actively passive*. I do not mean to speak nonsense but merely to show that God is *never* totally passive. When He seems to be passive, He is actively choosing not to intercede directly.

Augustine addressed the problem this way: "Man sometimes with a good will wishes something which God does not will, as when a good son wishes his father to live, while God wishes him to die. Again it may happen that man with a bad will wishes what God wills righteously, as when a bad son wishes his father to die, and God also wills it. . . . For the things which God rightly wills, He accomplishes by the evil wills of bad men."

I BELIEVE

SEPTEMBER 1993

———

*C*REDO . . . THIS LATIN WORD MEANS SIMPLY "I believe." It never can properly stand alone. To believe means to believe something. We can believe in or believe that, but we cannot simply believe. Belief always has a content.

Faith always has an object. That is why the church has creeds. A common cliché we hear is "It doesn't matter what you believe, as long as you are sincere." Such sentiment is on a collision course with Christianity.

A few miles outside of Waco, Texas, there is a smoldering ruins of what once was the headquarters of a religious sect descended from the Branch Davidians. Scores of charred bodies were recovered from that site. These were the bodies of people who believed in David Koresh. I don't know if David Koresh was sincere in his belief that he was Christ, but it seems clear that there were some people who sincerely believed in him.

A day or so after the conflagration that consumed most of Koresh's followers, one woman who was spared affixed a sign to the ashes with words declaring her faith that Koresh was still alive. I don't know if she still believes it or not, but this I do know: What she believes or believed about Koresh matters to her. It matters profoundly to the surviving relatives of those who perished in the inferno.

Recently a famous evangelist was interviewed on national television. In the course of the interview, he made a comment that Protestants, Catholics, and Jews all believe in the same God. I was surprised by that. The creeds of Roman Catholicism and Protestantism differ sharply at crucial points. The faith of Judaism differs significantly from that of Christianity.

For example, historic Judaism is monotheistic. So is historic Christianity (as well as Islam). These religions all claim to believe in the God of the Old Testament. Yet how the Muslim understands the nature and character of God differs seriously from how He is understood by Judaism or Christianity. The Christian faith affirms that God is *triune*; the Jewish faith does not agree. It clearly repudiates the Trinity. We must ask: Are a triune God and a non-triune God the *same* God? Christianity rests on the assertion that God has become incarnate in Christ. Judaism flatly denies that.

These differences in theology are real and they matter. If Judaism is right in its concept of God, then it follows inexorably that Christianity is guilty of an idolatrous view of God. By the same token, if Christianity is right, then Judaism is guilty of denying the true Incarnation of God.

The conflict inherent in these differences cannot be resolved by relativizing the content. It may be politically correct to say we all believe in the same God, but it is not theologically correct. It is theologically naïve in the extreme.

Nor does it help to assume that it doesn't matter what you believe about God. That might be true if God didn't exist. If that is the case, I would insist that it doesn't matter what you believe. I would go even further and say, not only does it not matter what you believe, but it doesn't matter what you do, for ultimately nothing matters at all. I say with Dostoevsky, "If there is no God, all things are permissible."

The Reformation was, in some respects, a tragic necessity in church history. It was tragic in that it resulted in a woeful fragmentation of Christendom into literally thousands of disparate and conflicting faiths. It was a time of theological tempest.

The Reformation was a debate about faith. It was a serious conflict about the content of faith, and of the role of faith in salvation. If we compare the historic Protestant creeds with those of Rome, we will see important points of agreement—but also points of serious difference.

For example, Rome believes justification in the first instance is effected through the instrumental cause of baptism and can be restored by the sacrament of penance. Protestantism, on the other hand, insists that the instrumental cause of justification is faith.

Many today argue that the historic debate over justification between Rome and Protestantism has finally been resolved and no serious issue remains. I am less sanguine about it. Indeed I am baffled by the assertion. For example, how anyone is able to resolve the canons and decrees of the Council of Trent with Protestant creeds such as the Westminster Confession of Faith escapes me. The last time I looked, Rome had not repealed those canons, especially those of the Sixth Session, which unambiguously anathematize the Protestant doctrine of justification by faith alone.

The issue of justification by faith alone was a creedal issue with massive practical ramifications. Luther insisted that justification by faith alone was the article upon which the church stands or falls. But its seriousness does not stop at the institutional level. It is an individual and personal issue, for it addresses the question, *How* is a person saved?

From the prophets of the Old Testament to the Apostles in the New Testament down through the ages of church history, the content of faith has been regarded as a serious matter indeed. From the beginning the church has understood that it matters profoundly what we believe.

We can have a correct understanding of the content of the Christian faith, even affirming its truth, and still not rise above the level of demons. The demons knew the truth of Christ, but they hated the content they knew to be true. Theology does not save. Creeds do not save. Only Christ can save. But what we believe *about* Christ is essential to that salvation. If the New Testament is correct, then it matters eternally what we believe.

To separate doctrine from life or life from doctrine is to sue for a groundless divorce. God has joined them together, and what He has joined together, we must never put asunder.

"Man's dignity is derived and dependent, not intrinsic. It is nevertheless real. It rests upon a divine assignment."

—

VICE-REGENTS OVER
A DIVINE CREATION

OCTOBER 1993

———

I T WAS ALEXANDER POPE WHO DECLARED that "the proper study of mankind is man." If Pope was correct, then the man who bears Pope's name as a title is wrong when he urges the study of God as the highest endeavor of learning.

Ultimately, there are two conflicting views of man and the world. The first is anthropocentric; it centers on and revolves around man himself. The second is theocentric, pivoting around the central concept of God. How we view ourselves and our relationship to the created order will be radically affected by what we view as central.

A man-centered view sees man as the measure of all things, reaching back to the motto of Protagoras: *homo mensura*, or "man, the measure." This is the vital nerve center, the credo of all forms of humanism.

Modern humanism celebrates the importance of man while whistling in the dark. He is on a roller coaster made all the more thrilling because the coaster has no brakes.

He is whistling in his free fall because he dreads the darkness that looms over the question of his origin and of his destiny. He is told that he emerged from the primordial slime by the chance collision of atoms.

Though we spend our days between the slime and the abyss, the anthropocentric humanist extols the dignity of this mass of protoplasm, exhorting us to a noble concern for ecology. We are to be careful to preserve the slime. Life is an idiot's tale, full of sound and fury, signifying nothing—which cannot be twisted to mean a little something.

In sharp contrast to this view of man and his environs is the biblical view of creation and redemption. Here man is celebrated as a creature with enormous dignity because he is rooted and grounded in God's creation. His origin is not slime but a gloriously adorned garden.

Man's dignity is derived and dependent, not intrinsic. It is nevertheless real. It rests upon a divine assignment. God assigns us dignity by making us in His own image:

> Then God said, "Let Us make man in Our image, in Our likeness, and let them rule over the fish of the sea and the birds of the air, over the livestock, over all the earth, and over all the creatures that move along the ground." So God created man in His own image, in the image of God He created him, male and female He created them (Gen. 1:26–27).

In this text God determines to create man in His image and likeness. Two distinct Hebrew words are used: *tselem* and *demuth*. Do *image* and *likeness* refer to two *distinct* aspects of man as Rome suggests? Most Protestant scholars say no, seeing here a literary structure called a *hendiadys*, by which two different words describe one and the same thing.

Image and *likeness* describe some point of similarity between God and man. This similarity does not imply identity. Man is not a god and God is not a man.

Classical theology described this likeness as an "analogy of being" (*analogia entis*). The idea of this analogy of being has come under sharp attack in the 20th century, especially by the noted Swiss theologian Karl Barth. Barth feared that the analogy concept involved a kind of natural theology, by which both God and man were subsumed under some abstract concept of Being.

Barth also reacted strongly against 19th-century theologies of pantheism. In both natural and pantheistic theology, Barth feared that the unique character of God would be lost in some abstract form of "being."

Instead of an analogy of *being*, Barth preferred to speak of an analogy of *relationship* (*analogia relationes*) between man and God. Man is created *male* and *female*. Just as God is an eternal relationship among the persons of the Godhead, so we are created in and for human relationships.

Barth's rejection of an analogy of being was taken to another level with the popularity of the phrase *wholly other* (*totaliter aliter*). This phrase was used to refer to the uniqueness of God to protect against confusing God with creation. This concern is a serious one because confusing God with part or all of creation is the essence of idolatry.

The problem with the phrase *wholly other* is this: Unless it is taken as hyperbole, it asserts too much. Zealous to protect God from being confused with creation, it leaves us back at Mars Hill with a modern altar to an "Unknown God."

I had a discussion with some theologians several years ago. These theologians were critical of my assertion of an analogy of being. They insisted that God was "wholly other." I asked them a simple question: "If God is wholly other how can you know anything about Him?" They answered immediately, "We know Him by His revelation." I pushed the question, "*How* can He reveal Himself?" Again they answered quickly, "He reveals Himself through creation, history, the Bible, and through Christ."

I said, "I don't think I'm making my question clear. If God is wholly other, or utterly dissimilar from us, if there is no common point of reference between us, how can He communicate anything about Himself to us?"

Finally they got the point. One of them replied and the others agreed, "Perhaps we shouldn't say that He is wholly other." Then I finished my point by explaining the obvious. If God is not wholly other (in the sense of dissimilarity), then there must be some analogy or likeness between us and we should stop denying an analogy of being. Let us say instead that God is *other* and that He is *holy* other, but not *wholly* other.

The question of analogy is foundational to our understanding of ourselves, of God, and of the world. Because God has created us in His image it is possible for Him to communicate with us. It makes divine revelation possible. With that revelation we learn our place in the cosmos. Our ecological responsibility rests in our prior responsibility to obey our Creator. We are called to dress, till, and keep the earth because it is our

Father's world. In creation He has given us dominion, but that dominion is not absolute. We remain always under His authority. We are not autonomous czars over slime; we are vice-regents over a divine creation.

The Christian concern over the environment is theocentric. It is a matter of obedience to a Holy Other who has created the world and who has spoken decisively to us.

MOBILIZING THE LAITY

NOVEMBER 1993

S EVERAL IMAGES ARE USED IN THE BIBLE to describe the church: the body of Christ, the elect, the house of God, the saints. One of the most meaningful expressions the Bible uses is "the people of God," the *laos theon*.

When we speak of the laity, we are speaking of people—the people who together with Christ and the Apostles comprise His body, the church.

The church, then, is *people*. Rome once declared, "Where the bishop is, there is the church." The Reformation declared, "Where the people of God are, there is the church—the church under the Lordship of Christ and indwelt by the Holy Spirit."

The church is not a building, it is not the clergy, it is not an abstract institution—it is the people of God. When Martin Luther articulated his vision of the priesthood of all believers, he did not denigrate the legitimate role of the clergy. He understood that Christ has given pastors and teachers to His church, along with other offices, with specified tasks. What Luther was getting at, however, is that the priestly ministry of Christ is passed on in some measure to every believer.

Luther also declared that every believer is called to be "Christ to his neighbor." I cannot be Christ to my neighbor in the sense of offering an atonement or being my neighbor's savior. Rather, I must *represent* Christ to my neighbor in the sense of bringing the ministry of Christ to him or her.

In this sense, then, every believer is called to be a minister. We are not all pastors; we are all ministers. To be included in the laity is to be included in the ministry.

In Acts we read the following account:

At that time a great persecution arose against the church which was at Jerusalem; and they were all scattered throughout the regions of Judea and Samaria, except the apostles (Acts 8:1b, NKJV).

This account records the scattering of the church beyond the confines of Jerusalem. We note that in this dispersion the people (*laos*) were spread out, but the Apostles (clergy) remained in Jerusalem.

In verse 4 we read, "Therefore those who were scattered went everywhere preaching the Word."

This incident is striking in that the outward expansion of the Gospel was done not by the Apostles but by the whole body of believers. This is the supreme model for the mobilization of the church. Christ's people became Christ's ministers wherever they went. They did not leave the business of ministry exclusively in the hands of the Apostles.

More than 20 years ago, I went to Coral Ridge Presbyterian Church to be trained in the Evangelism Explosion program. A Christian company was there filming the story of Coral Ridge. They entitled the film *Like a Mighty Army.* I was stunned to see an army of lay people trained and involved in evangelism. It was a ministry-changing paradigm shift for me. Not only did I learn how to do evangelism myself, but I learned how to train the laity for it as well.

I returned to my job in Ohio and trained about 250 people in the Evangelism Explosion program. The laity involved caught a vision for ministry. Out of their experiences in evangelism, several things happened in a chain reaction. The laypersons themselves started specialized ministries to the unemployed, to prison inmates, to poor communities, to those needing marriage counseling, to name but a few. I also witnessed a quantum leap in the laity's interest in adult education.

A wonderful symbiosis developed. The more the laity became involved in ministry, the more they wanted to deepen their understanding of the Word of God. The more they deepened their understanding of the Word of God, the more they wanted to put that understanding to work in ministry. It was in that arena that the concept of Ligonier Ministries was born—driven by a vision to mobilize the laity via education and training.

Since that time I have seen extraordinary examples of laypersons who have taken their faith to the marketplace in the form of ministry. I think of Charles Colson who went from the White House to prison. When Colson was released from prison, he was not released from ministry. Indeed, from his own experience grew a vision to minister to prison inmates in the name of Christ, a ministry that now reaches tens of thousands of people in virtually every country.

I saw Wayne Alderson, a layman, put his faith to work in the violent arena of labor-management relations. He has taken that ministry around this nation ministering to people in corporate board rooms, coal mines, and labor union halls.

The list could easily include a multitude of ministries that involve the laity. Without the laity the church would not have conquered the ancient world. Without the laity no one would ever have heard of Luther's academic dispute at Wittenberg. The Reformers understood that for real reformation to happen, the laity had to be educated, trained, and mobilized. Luther took a leave of absence from the university in order to translate the Bible into German so that every believer could personally read the Scriptures. Calvin's *Institutes* were originally penned as an instruction manual for the laity. Many of the works of Edwards were originally composed for the benefit of his congregation, many of whom were known to be studying their Greek New Testaments while they were plowing their fields.

Over the years I have kept one foot planted in the academic world via seminary teaching. But my greatest passion has been adult education for the laity. My dream has been to see an army of knowledgeable and articulate lay persons applying their faith to ministry. I dream to see our nation, indeed the world, flooded by such people. Training pastors is important, but chiefly to the degree that they in turn will catch the vision to equip the saints for ministry.

One thing that disturbs me about contemporary Christian jargon is the inexact use of the word *witness*. Too often people use the terms *evangelism* and *witnessing* interchangeably, as if they were synonyms. They are not. All evangelism is witness, but all witness is not evangelism. Evangelism is a specific type of witnessing. Not everyone is called to be a pastor or teacher. Not everyone is called to administration or specialized ministries of mercy. Not everyone is called to be an evangelist (though we are all called to verbalize our faith). We are all called to be witnesses to Christ—to make His invisible kingdom visible. We witness by doing the ministry of Christ. We witness by being the church, the people of God.

Some of us can plant. Some of us can water. When we plant and water, God will bring an increase.

MARLEY'S MESSAGE TO SCROOGE

DECEMBER 1993

———

B AH! HUMBUG! THESE TWO WORDS are instantly associated with Charles Dickens's immortal fictional antihero, Ebenezer Scrooge. Scrooge was the prototype of the Grinch who stole Christmas, the paradigm of all men cynical.

We all recognize that Ebenezer Scrooge was a mean person—stingy, insensitive, selfish, and unkind. What we often miss in our understanding of his character is that he was preeminently profane. "Bah! Humbug!" was his Victorian use of profanity.

Not that any modern editor would feel the need to delete Scrooge's expletives. His language is not the standard currency of cursing. But it was profane in that Scrooge demeaned what was holy. He trampled on the sanctity of Christmas. He despised the sacred. He was cynical toward the sublime.

Christmas is a holiday, indeed the world's most joyous holiday. It is called a "holiday" because the day is holy. It is a day when businesses close, when families gather, when churches are filled, and when soldiers put down their guns for a 24-hour truce. It is a day that differs from every other day.

Every generation has its abundance of Scrooges. The church is full of them. We hear endless complaints of commercialism. We are constantly told to put Christ back into Christmas. We hear that the tradition of Santa Claus is a sacrilege. We listen to those acquainted with history murmur that Christmas isn't biblical. *The Church invented Christmas to compete with the ancient Roman festival honoring the bull-god Mithras*, the nay-sayers complain. Christmas? *A mere capitulation to paganism.*

And so we rain on Jesus' parade and assume an olympian detachment from the joyous holiday. All this carping is but a modern dose of Scroogeism, our own sanctimonious profanation of the holy.

Sure, Christmas is a time of commerce. The department stores are decorated to the hilt, the ad pages of the newspapers swell in size, and we tick off the number of shopping days left until Christmas. But why all the commerce? The high degree of commerce at Christmas is driven by one thing: the buying of gifts for others. To present our friends and families with gifts is not an ugly, ignoble vice. It incarnates the amorphous "spirit of Christmas." The tradition rests ultimately on the supreme gift God has given the world. God so loved the world, the Bible says, that He *gave* His only begotten Son. The giving of gifts is a marvelous response to the receiving of such a gift. For one day a year at least, we taste the sweetness inherent in the truth that it is more blessed to give than to receive.

What about putting Christ back into Christmas? It is simply not necessary. Christ has never left Christmas. "Jingle Bells" will never replace "Silent Night." Our holiday once known as Thanksgiving is rapidly becoming known simply as "Turkey Day." But Christmas is still called Christmas. It is not called "Gift Day." Christ is still in Christmas, and for one brief season the secular world broadcasts the message of Christ over every radio station and television channel in the land. Never does the church get as much free air time as during the Christmas season.

Not only music but the visual arts are present in abundance, bearing testimony to the historic significance of the birth of Jesus. Christmas displays, crèches, Christmas cards, yard displays all remind the world of the sacred Incarnation.

Doesn't Santa Claus paganize or at least trivialize Christmas? He's a myth, and his very mythology casts a shadow over the sober historical reality of Jesus. Not at all. Myths are not necessarily bad or harmful. Every society creates myths. They are a peculiar art form invented usually to convey a message that is deemed important by the people. When a myth is passed off as real history, that is fraud. But when it serves a different purpose it can be healthy and virtuous. Kris Kringle is a mythical hero, not a villain. He is pure fiction—but a fiction used to illustrate a glorious truth.

What about the historical origins of Christmas as a substitute for a pagan festival? I can only say, good for the early Christians who had the wisdom to flee from Mithras and direct their zeal to the celebration of the birth of Christ. Who associates Christmas today with Mithras? No one calls it "Mithrasmas."

We celebrate Christmas because we cannot eradicate from our consciousness our profound awareness of the difference between the sacred and the profane. Man, in the generic sense, has an incurable propensity for marking sacred space and sacred time. When God appeared to Moses in the burning bush, the ground that was previously common suddenly became uncommon. It was now holy ground—sacred space. When Jacob awoke from his midnight vision of the presence of God, he anointed with oil the rock upon which he had rested his head. It was sacred space.

When God touches earth, the place is holy. When God appears in history, the time is holy. There was never a more holy place than the city of Bethlehem, where the Word became flesh. There was never a more holy time than Christmas morning when Emmanuel was born. Christmas is a holiday. It is the holiest of holy days. We must heed the warning of Jacob Marley: "Don't be a Scrooge" at Christmas.

VANITY OF VANITIES, ALL IS VANITY

JANUARY 1994

HAT IS VANITY? I KNOW at least three distinct usages of this word. The first meaning I ever learned was in reference to a piece of furniture that was in my grandmother's bedroom, a kind of desk with a large mirror, before which she sat in order to apply her make-up.

The second usage I learned in junior high school. The school principal entered the men's room and observed me taking great pains to comb my hair properly. He warned me against "vanity"—a synonym for narcissistic pride or egotism, the kind of attitude Jimmy Connors says impels him to be concerned with using the proper deodorant.*

But the vanity of which Ecclesiastes speaks is a matter far deeper. It is the vanity of meaninglessness, the vanity of futility. It captures the essence of a philosophical position called "nihilism." To say "all is vanity" is to say that *nothing* has meaning or significance ultimately. Nihilism means literally "nothing-ism." The *nihil* corresponds to what Nietzsche called *"das Nichtig"* (the nothing).

Nihilism has two traditional enemies—theism and naive humanism. The theist contradicts the nihilist because the existence of God guarantees the ultimate meaning and significance of personal life and history. Naive humanism is considered naive by the nihilist because it rhapsodizes—with no rational foundation—the dignity and significance of human life. The humanist declares that man is a cosmic accident whose origin was fortuitous and whose destiny is annihilation. The two poles of human existence—origin and destiny—are both entrenched in meaningless

---

* Jimmy Connors (1952–) is an American former professional tennis player. He starred in commercials for Power Stick deodorant in which he admitted to being vain.

insignificance. Yet in between the humanist mindlessly crusades for, defends, and celebrates the chimera of human dignity.

Philosophers like Jean-Paul Sartre and Albert Camus saw the glaring pollyannaish naivete of such forms of humanism. Camus saw the only serious question left for the philosopher was the question of suicide. Sartre punctuated his literary career with his little volume titled *Nausea*, in which he concluded that man is a "useless passion."

It is one thing to be useless. It is quite another to have feelings about it. When we discard a piece of junk and throw it in the garbage, we declare it "useless." Now if the object thrown away is a piece of metal scrap, we do not risk hurting its feelings. A metal scrap has no passion. It does not care about its destiny. It is mindless and feelingless.

But if we discard a living human person, if we declare it useless, then we are dealing with real passion. Twentieth-century existential philosophy has been almost preoccupied with the concept of *Besörgen*. This refers to "care." Human beings are caring creatures. They have feelings and passions. They care because what happens in their lives matters to them.

Herein is the dilemma: Nihilism declares that nothing really matters ultimately. It may matter to us, but that does not mean that it matters ultimately. We may care but the blind forces of the universe do not care. They do not care at all.

To be in an environment of ultimate carelessness is the worst fate that can befall a caring creature. It is to be sentenced to a life of ultimate futility. Perhaps the naming of a mirrored table as a "vanity" suggests that efforts to disguise our lack of beauty by external cosmetics is an exercise in futility. It is a cover-up of the real—an illusion designed to camouflage the truth.

There is a common fallacy committed in philosophical reflection. It is labeled the either/or fallacy, or the fallacy of the false dilemma. It occurs when we simplistically reduce all options to two when there are many more. Because of the pervasive abuse of this fallacy, we tread on dangerous ground when we attempt such reductions. But there are times when the peril must be ignored and the stance taken. There are some issues that do resolve to either/or status. For example, either God exists or He does not. There is no *tertium quid.*

When we ask the question of ultimate meaning, we have a similar either/or option. Either human life matters ultimately, or it does not. If it does not, then the conclusion cannot be resisted: "Vanity of vanities, all is vanity."

The author of Ecclesiastes is not wrestling with shadows or dealing with trifles. He is probing the ultimate question of human life, human passion, human aspiration, human care—the question of meaning and significance. He understands an equal ultimacy about the question. He knows that the question of ultimate meaning is a theological question. He understands that the question of ultimate meaning is linked inexorably to the question of ultimate being.

As a student and later a professor of philosophy, I have been long convinced that ultimately there are only two serious philosophical options open to theoretical thought: nihilism or full-orbed theism. I realize that between these polar opposites there resides an almost endless number of variant philosophical schools. But the iron hand of logic forces all the hybrids to resolve to one or the other. All other systems are parasites. They live off the capital borrowed either from theism or nihilism. They suffer the gourmet's paradox: You cannot have your cake and eat it too.

In my judgment, no philosophical treatise has ever surpassed or equaled the penetrating analysis of the ultimate question of meaning versus vanity as that found in the book of Ecclesiastes.

VANITY OVERWHELMED BY PURPOSE

FEBRUARY 1994

———

W HY? THIS SIMPLE QUESTION, which we utter many times a day, is loaded with assumptions of what philosophers call "teleology." Teleology is the study or science of purpose. It comes from the Greek word *telos*, which is sprinkled liberally through the New Testament.

The "why" questions are questions of purpose. We seek to discover the reason for things happening as they do. Why does the rain fall? Why does the earth turn on its axis? Why did you say what you said?

When we raise the question of purpose, we are concerned with ends, aims, and goals. All of these terms suggest intent. They assume meaning rather than meaninglessness.

Last month we considered the question of vanity. That which is vain is ultimately a-teleological; it lacks a definite purpose. It is the opposite of purpose.

The cynic may respond to the question "Why?" by a glib retort: "Why not?" Yet even in this response there is a thinly veiled commitment to purpose. If we give a reason for *not* doing something, we are saying that the negative serves a purpose or fulfills a goal. Human beings are creatures committed to purpose. Intent informs our actions.

Edmund Husserl defined the uniqueness of our humanity in terms of our capacity to act with "intentionality." That simply means that we do things for a reason—with a purpose in mind. The hunter aims his gun. The golfer lines up his putt. The business executive sets goals. The football player cuts toward the end-zone.

In the quest for purpose, we must distinguish between *proximate* and *remote* purposes. The proximate refers to that which is close at hand. The remote refers to the distant, far off, ultimate purpose. The football players' proximate goal is to make a first down. The more remote goal is the touchdown. The even more remote goal is to win the game. The ultimate goal is to win the Super Bowl.

We remember the poignant meeting between Joseph and his brothers in which the brothers feared recriminations from their powerful brother for the treachery they had committed against him. But Joseph saw a remarkable concurrence at work between proximate and remote intentions. He said, "You meant it for evil; God meant it for good."

Here the proximate and the remote seemed to be mutually exclusive. The divine intention was the exact opposite of the human intention. Joseph's brothers had one goal; God had a different one. The amazing truth here is that the remote purpose was served by the proximate one. This does not diminish the culpability of the brothers. Their intent was evil and their actions were evil. Yet it seemed good to God to let it happen that His purpose might be fulfilled.

With us there are accidents, indeed tragic accidents. Last fall our receptionist cut her fingers severely with an electric hedge clipper. She did not mean to cut her fingers. Her goal was to cut the bushes. In a proximate sense she had an accident. She may have asked, "Why did God allow it to happen?"

This question seeks to probe the remote or ultimate purpose. The question assumes something crucial to our understanding of God. It assumes that God *could have* prevented it. If we deny this verity we deny the very character of God. If God could *not* have prevented it, He would no longer really be God. By asking "Why?" we also assume something else that is vital. We assume there is an answer to the question. We assume that God had a *reason*, or a *purpose*, for its happening.

The question remains—"Was God's reason or purpose a good one?" To ask the question is to answer it if we know anything about God. We err in our reason. We establish futile goals. We rush off on fools' errands. We pursue sinful ends. Let us not project the same kind of vicious intentionality to God.

The only purpose or intention God ever has is altogether good. When the Bible speaks of the sovereign exercise of the pleasure of His will, there is no hint of arbitrariness or wicked intent. The pleasure of His will is always the *good* pleasure of His will. His pleasure is always good; His will is always good; His intentions are always good.

When Paul declares the mysterious and breathtaking promise that "all things work together for good to those who love God, to those who are called according to His purpose" (Rom. 8:28), he is musing in teleology. He is dealing with the realm of the remote rather than the proximate. This insists that the proximate must always be judged in the light of the remote.

Our problem is this: We do not yet possess the full light of the remote. We are still looking in a dark mirror. We are not utterly devoid of light. We have enough light to know that God has a good purpose even when we are ignorant of that good purpose.

It is the good purpose of God that gives the final answer to the appearance of vanity and futility in this world. To trust in the good purpose of God is the very essence of godly faith. This is why no Christian can be an ultimate pessimist. The wicked aims of mice and men that surround and beset us daily may incline us toward pessimism—but only at the level of the proximate. I am not optimistic about human government or the innate good will of men. I am utterly optimistic about divine government and the intrinsic good will of God.

The world in which we live is not a world of chance. Its beginning was not an accident . . . its operation is not an accident . . . its *telos*, or goal, is not an accident. This is my Father's world and He rules it without caprice. As long as God exists, vanity is a manifest impossibility.

"The turmoil in America is not ultimately about changes in laws or about the behavior of Congress or the Supreme Court. Government follows culture; it does not lead it."

—

AND NOW
THE NATION MOURNS

MARCH 1994

———

L ONDON. ROME. ATHENS. JERUSALEM. Each of these four great
cities contributed a thread, which when woven together formed
the tapestry that is called America. To change the metaphor, these
cities may be seen as vital roots that together produced the tree.

In his book *The Roots of American Order*, Russell Kirk traces the philosophical and cultural roots of the American Revolution. He analyzes the
philosophical contributions of Locke, Hume, Burke, Blackstone, Mon-
tesquieu, and others. The crux of his study, however, traces the cultural
roots of America.

America did not begin with an abstract ideology that was then implemented into a nation. That experiment was tried in the French Revolution
and the Russian Revolution, both of which ended in disaster. Rather, the
United States as an independent republic grew out of an existing order,
an order that was already long established.

America is a nation that cherishes "law and order." The crux of Kirk's
thesis is that these realities develop from order to law, not from law
to order. That is, cultures develop in such a way that their laws reflect
rather than create the order. Anarchy produces no laws. Order must
come first.

By 1775, order, culture, and way of life in America was already established. Our local law reflected the common law of England. The great city
of London was our most immediate cultural root. The British system of
law carried to our shores was heavily influenced by earlier civilizations
and cultures. Roman law and civilization had an enormous influence on
shaping the culture of the West, including England.

Athens was not without a mighty influence as well. From contributions in art, philosophy, and science, the Greeks also loaned the wisdom of Solon and Pericles to the emerging world civilization.

Though our roots include London, Rome, and Athens, the tap root—the main source of nutrition that fed the emerging American nation was that of Jerusalem, the cradle of Judeo-Christian religion, reflecting the origins of Exodus and Sinai. Kirk remarks:

> The tap-root of American order began to grow some 13 centuries before the birth of Jesus of Nazareth. Through Moses, prophet and law-giver, the moral principles that move the civilization of Europe and America and much more of the world first obtained clear expression (p. 11).

The instigators of the American Revolution defended it not as a revolution but as opposition to a revolution. That is, changes in the customary relationship between the colonies and England signaled a threat to the current American order and culture.

Kirk observes: "Yet the War of Independence really was not fought about cups of tea.... The Americans, in essence, meant to keep their old order and defend it against external interference" (p. 395).

In other words, says Kirk, the American Revolution and the French Revolution were fundamentally different. The American Revolution *prevented* a revolution of the legal order (the English crown and parliament) against the cultural order. The French Revolution *perpetrated* a revolt against both the legal and cultural order of late-18th-century France.

At the time of the American Revolution, Christians were divided as to whether revolution was justified. Those who supported the crown insisted that Romans 13 demanded submission to the crown and parliament, even though the king was changing traditional cultural practice. Christians who supported the Revolution were equally convinced they were supporting the existing structure of law and order by resisting an illegal act of governmental tyranny.

Was the Revolution biblically justified? Though I have enormous respect for Kirk's brilliant historical analysis and enormous sympathy for the cause of the Revolutionaries, I must admit that I am not yet persuaded that warring against the British government was a moral act. Because of Paul's injunction in Romans 13 to submit to the governing authorities, the loyalists of the Revolutionary period, biblically speaking, had the better argument.

Regardless of one's opinion on the justifiability of the American Revolution, this much is certain: When nations cut off their roots, they are in trouble. The revolution in America that began in the 1960s and '70s resembles the French Revolution—a revolt against the cultural order. The tap-root of American culture, remember, was Jerusalem. But since the '60s, the secularist axe slams hard, severing America from its biblical roots. The Law of Moses no longer commands respect. Separation of church and state now means separation of state from God.

The turmoil in contemporary America is not ultimately about changes in laws or about the behavior of Congress or the Supreme Court. As Kirk so masterfully demonstrates, government follows culture; it does not lead it.

The institution for cultural renewal ordained by God is the church. The collapse of the church precipitated the decay of our culture. When Alexis de Tocqueville visited America in the early 1800s, he observed in his tour de force *Democracy in America* that Americans shared a biblically informed conception of the common good. This idea restrained their natural individualism, preventing them from doing what they might. But as the church decayed, a common idea disappeared, paving the way for individualism to run wild.

And now the nation mourns. Taxes on tea pale into insignificance.

The Apostle Paul wrote the epistle to the Romans in the midst of a decadent, immoral, statist empire. Even so, he forbade physical revolt. Paul knew that the small band of Christ's followers had better cultural weapons than swords and shields of iron. They had the sword of the Spirit, the breastplate of righteousness, the helmet of salvation, feet shod with the Gospel of peace.

Those weapons transformed the Western world. They planted a new cultural order—one rooted in truth. There is no reason to suppose they cannot do the same today.

NONE DARE CALL IT HERESY

APRIL 1994

I S THE FLAMBOYANT FAITH HEALER Benny Hinn a heretic? He was so branded by Hank Hanegraaff, the "Bible Answer Man," in his recent book *Christianity in Crisis*. Hanegraaff's charge resulted in a radical outburst of indignant cries directed not at Hinn but at Hanegraaff.

It seems that the only real and intolerable heresy today is the despicable act of calling someone a heretic. If the one accused is guilty of heresy, he or she will probably elicit more sympathy than his accuser. Anyone who cries "Heretic!" today risks being identified as a native of Salem, Massachusetts.

After Hanegraaff made his charge in print, a couple of things happened. One is that Hinn recanted his own teaching that there are nine persons in the Trinity and apologized to his hearers for that teaching. Such recantations are rare in church history, and it is gratifying that at least in this case on that point Hinn repented of his false teaching.

The second interesting footnote to the Hanegraaff-Hinn saga was the appearance of an editorial by the editor of a leading charismatic magazine in which Hanegraaff was castigated for calling Hinn a heretic. At the 1993 Christian Booksellers Association convention, I was present for and witness to a discussion between Hanegraaff and the magazine editor. I asked the editor a few questions. The first was, "Is there such a thing as heresy?" The editor acknowledged that there was. My second question was, "Is heresy a serious matter?" Again he agreed that it was. My next question was obvious. "Then why are you criticizing Hanegraaff for saying that Hinn was teaching heresy when even Hinn admits it now?"

The editor expressed concern about tolerance, charity, the unity of Christians, and matters of that sort. He expressed a concern about witch hunts in the evangelical church. My sentiments about that are clear. We don't need to hunt witches in the evangelical world. There is no need to hunt what is not hiding. The "witches" are in plain view, every day on national television, teaching blatant heresy without fear of censure.

Consider the case of Jimmy Swaggart. For years Swaggart has publicly repudiated the orthodox doctrine of the Trinity. Swaggart was not challenged (to my knowledge) by his church for his heresy. He was censured for sexual immorality but not heresy. I guess this church regards romping with prostitutes in private a more serious offense than denying the Trinity before the watching world.

As I documented in *The Agony of Deceit*, Paul Crouch teaches heresy. So do Kenneth Copeland and Kenneth Hagin. These men seem to teach their heresies with impunity.

But what do we mean by *heresy?* Is every theological error a heresy? In a broad sense, every departure from biblical truth may be regarded as a heresy. But in the currency of Christian thought, the term *heresy* has usually been reserved for gross and heinous distortions of biblical truth, for errors so grave that they threaten either the essence (*esse*) of the Christian faith or the well-being (*bene esse*) of the Christian church.

Luther was excommunicated by Rome and declared a heretic for teaching justification by faith alone. Luther replied that the church had embraced a heretical view of salvation. The issue still burns as to who the heretic is.

In Luther's response to Erasmus' *Diatribe*, he acknowledged that many of the points at issue were trifles. They did not warrant rupturing the unity of the church. They could be "covered" by the love and forbearance that covers a multitude of sins. When it came to justification, however, Luther sang a different tune. He called justification the article upon which the church stands or falls, a doctrine so vital that it touches the very heart of the Gospel. A church that rejects justification by faith alone (and anathematizes it as a deadly heresy) is no longer an orthodox church. Luther wasn't shadow boxing on that issue; nor was the Reformation a mere misunderstanding between warring factions in the church. No teapot was big enough to contain the tempest it provoked.

In graduate school in Holland, it was the custom of my tutor, Professor G.C. Berkouwer, to lecture on one doctrine per year. In 1965 he departed from his normal policy and lectured on "The History of Heresy in the Christian Church."

Berkouwer canvassed the most important struggles the church faced against heresy. It was Marcion's heretical canon that made it necessary for the church to formalize the contents of the true canon of sacred Scripture. It was Arius's adoptionism that necessitated the conciliar decrees of Nicaea. It was the heresies of Eutyches (Monophysitism) and Nestorius that provoked the watershed ecumenical council of Chalcedon in 451. The heresies of Sabellius, Apollinaris, the Socinians, and others have driven the church through the ages to define the limits of orthodoxy.

One of the major points in Berkouwer's study was the historical tendency for heresies to beget other heresies, particularly heresies in the opposite direction. For example, efforts to defend the true humanity of Jesus often led to the denial of His deity. Zeal to defend the deity of Christ often led to a denial of His humanity. Likewise the zeal for the unity of the Godhead and monotheism have led to the denial of the personal distinctions in the being of God, whereas zeal for personal distinctives have led to tritheism and a denial of the essential unity of God. Likewise, efforts to correct the heresy of legalism have produced the antinomian heresy and vice versa.

We live in a climate where heresy is embraced and proclaimed with the greatest of ease. I can't think of any of these major heresies that I haven't heard repeatedly and openly on national TV by so-called "evangelical preachers" such as Hinn, Crouch, and the like. Where our fathers saw these issues as matters of life and death, indeed of eternal life and death, we have so surrendered to relativism and pluralism that we simply don't care about serious doctrinal error. We prefer peace to truth and accuse the orthodox of being divisive when they call a heretic a heretic. It is the heretic who divides the church and disrupts the unity of the body of Christ.

THOMAS AQUINAS: A TRUE GIFT OF GOD

MAY 1994

———

WITHIN PROTESTANT CIRCLES ST. THOMAS AQUINAS has been the victim of a bad rap.

"Aquinas bashing" has become a popular pastime with some Protestant scholars.

Viewing Aquinas as a theological ogre may be linked to a form of "Catholicophobia." Since Rome claims Thomas as the "Doctor Angelicus," his status as "the" theologian of the church makes him the target of much Protestant criticism.

Though the criticisms of Aquinas are legion, the two most often cited complaints are these: (1) Thomas is guilty of "baptizing" the pagan philosophy of Aristotle, allowing an unwarranted intrusion of Greek philosophy into biblical thought; (2) His system of apologetics created a separation of nature and grace that ultimately led to the destruction of Christian culture and the triumph of secularism.

Aquinas & Aristotle

There is little doubt that St. Thomas made much use of Aristotelian philosophy. His thought does indicate a kind of synthesis between Aristotelian philosophy and Christian theology. Many of the categories of Aristotle's philosophy appear in Aquinas's reasoning. This is true not only with respect to Aquinas but more broadly throughout Roman Catholic theology.

In the doctrine of transubstantiation, the miracle of the Mass is formulated in Aristotelian terms when the church declares that the substance of the bread and wine is changed into the substance of the body and blood of Christ, while the *accidens* (the external qualities) remain the same. This formulation is unintelligible apart from Aristotle's metaphysical or ontological distinction between substance and accidens. This involves a double miracle (something foreign to Aristotle) in that you end with the substance of one thing and the accidens of another and vice versa.

A parallel may be seen with St. Augustine. Augustine is claimed both by Rome and by Protestantism as a theological "patron saint." Augustine's influence on Luther (an Augustinian monk) is well documented. His influence on Calvin is even more evident. Augustine is quoted more often in Calvin's *Institutes* than any other extra-biblical writer. Indeed, Calvinism is often designated by the alternate name: Augustinianism. Augustine fought a life-long battle against neo-Platonic philosophy, yet he adopted many of his opponents' premises. It is often said of Augustine that as Aquinas achieved a synthesis between Christian theology and Aristotelian philosophy, so Augustine achieved a synthesis between Christian theology and Platonic (or neo-Platonic) philosophy.

The influence upon Western thought exercised by Plato and Aristotle is so enormous that it is hard to overestimate it. It has been said, perhaps a bit hyperbolically, that the history of western philosophy is but a footnote to Plato and Aristotle.

Every generation of Christians has found it necessary to address its culture in terms of the prevailing philosophies of the times. The danger of accommodation or seduction by alien philosophy is always there, and I suppose never entirely avoided.

Nature & Grace

The second rap against Aquinas is perhaps the most prevalent. The charge that Aquinas separated nature and grace is most common among Protestants, becoming virtually axiomatic, almost a Protestant truism. This charge has caused Norman Geisler to quip that the modern Protestant theme song is: "Should old Aquinas be forgot, and never brought to mind?"

This charge against Aquinas disturbs me because it simply is not true. It is a serious distortion of Aquinas, driven either by a misunderstanding of St. Thomas, or worse, a woeful ignorance of his writings. I fear that this "bad rap" is received uncritically by one generation of Protestants and then passed on to the next.

If there was anything St. Thomas did not do, or certainly did not desire to do, it was to separate nature and grace. He fought his most strenuous battle against those who did separate nature and grace. At a time when Christianity faced its most serious threat with the use of the Islamic religion as a world-conquering force, Aquinas rose as the champion of the Christian church to engage the Islamic philosophers in intellectual warfare.

The Arab philosophers, chiefly Averroes and Avicenna, created a synthesis between Aristotle's philosophy and Islamic theology. It was called "Integral Aristotelianism" precisely because it sought an integration between Islam and Aristotle.

For Aquinas the most repugnant element of this Islamic synthesis was its "Double Truth theory." The double truth theory maintained that something could be true in religion (grace) and at the same time be false in philosophy or science (nature). It would be similar to someone today saying that he believes man emerged from the slime as a cosmic accident and, at the same time, was created by the purposive act of God. This involves a radical separation of nature and grace.

To overcome the separation of nature and grace inherent in the double truth theory, Aquinas sought to maintain their unity. He saw both united under God's rule and dominion. He also saw both as spheres of divine revelation.

What Aquinas *did* do was to make a *distinction* between nature and grace (following his exegesis of Romans 1). We must learn to make a distinction between distinguishing between things and separating them. We distinguish the two natures of Christ, the divine and human. We do not separate them, unless we embrace the Nestorian heresy. We distinguish between a person's body and soul. We do not separate them unless we kill them. It is one thing to distinguish between a husband and a wife. To separate them is to do violence to their marriage.

Aquinas distinguished between those things that are learned exclusively by special revelation (the Bible) and those things that are learned by a study of general revelation (nature). In addition he spoke of "mixed articles" (*articulus mixtus*). The mixed articles refer to those truths that may be learned either by reading the Bible or by "reading" nature. Most prominent of the mixed articles is the existence of God, which is revealed both in Scripture and in nature. Far from divorcing nature and grace, Aquinas sought to show their unity. He was convinced that all truth is God's truth and that all truth "meets at the top." Aquinas refused to put asunder what God had joined together.

The whole Christian world owes an abiding debt to Thomas Aquinas. He is a giant of the faith upon whose shoulders we who are dwarfs are compelled to stand. We dare not simply bash him, or ignore him. He is a true gift of God to His church.

WAR BETWEEN
THE STATES

JUNE 1994

———

D R. JEKYLL AND MR. HYDE. This story could be an allegory for
the Christian life. There is a war in our members, a constant conflict between the old and the new, between vice and virtue, sin
and obedience. We seem to be moral schizoids. It is a struggle between
what the Bible calls the "old man" and the "new man."

Whenever I hear an evangelist declare, "Come to Jesus and all your
problems will be over," I cringe. I cringe because I am hearing false advertising. I cringe because it conflicts with my own experience and my own
spiritual pilgrimage. In one sense my life didn't become complicated until
I became a Christian. Before my conversion I only had one man with
which to contend—the old man. My spiritual life was one dimensional.
I was Mr. Hyde. Dr. Jekyll never showed up to bother me.

Prior to my conversion I was dead in trespasses and sins. As Paul describes
the course of the unregenerate person in Ephesians 2, I "walked according
to the course of this world, according to the prince of the power of the
air, the spirit who now works in the sons of disobedience."

But now I am a Christian. I have been made alive to the things of God,
being quickened to new life by the regenerating grace of God. As Christians
we are new creations. Our hearts of stone have been turned into hearts of
flesh. In this metaphor *flesh* is used as a positive figure, not a pejorative
one. Where once my heart was reified, cold and recalcitrant, dead and
inert to the things of God, now it throbs and pulsates with spiritual life.
Once I was biologically alive but spiritually dead. Now I am biologically
alive and spiritually alive as well. I am a new person.

There is radical discontinuity between my new self and my old self. This radical discontinuity, however, is not *total* discontinuity. A link between the old and the new man remains. The old man has been dealt a mortal blow. His total destruction is certain, but he is not yet dead.

I once described the old man's condition as similar to that of a chicken with its head cut off. I said that the beheaded chicken runs around the barnyard squawking like mad. Later a farmer corrected me. He said that decapitated chickens may run around and create a mess, but they don't squawk. Their "squawkers" had been destroyed.

I still don't know first-hand how such chickens behave; I've never actually seen one. One thing I do know, however, is that once their heads have been chopped off, they die.

The old man has been beheaded. His death is certain. But in his death throes he still can create a mess of things.

Many movements in Christian history have promised a kind of deeper life of perfectionism for the Christian. They all err in seizing prematurely an eschatological promise. We are on our way to perfection, but we will not reach it until we are glorified in heaven. Every variety of perfectionism I've encountered falls into one of two theological traps. The first is the trap of lowering the standards of perfection so that we may think we have reached them (a theological Procrustean Bed). The second is the trap of deluding ourselves into thinking we have reached a higher level of virtue or sanctification than we have actually achieved.

The conflict of the Christian life is a struggle with sin. Sin no longer has dominion over us if we are in Christ, yet sin is still in us. Regeneration liberates us from the bondage of original sin, but our corrupt nature is not totally annihilated this side of heaven. Paul speaks of the warfare that goes on between the flesh and the spirit:

> For the flesh lusts against the Spirit, and the Spirit against the flesh; and these are contrary to one another, so that you do not do the things that you wish (Gal. 5:17).

As Christians we are called to mortify the flesh. This is not a call to the flagellation of the body but to the destroying of the old nature. We are to feed the new man with the means of grace and starve the old man by denying him the occasions for sin.

The old man is dying daily. As we grow in the grace of sanctification, the new man is strengthened and the old man is weakened. The Spirit works to renew us from within as we struggle in this spiritual warfare.

The modern distinction between the "carnal Christian" and the "Spirit-filled Christian" is a dangerous one. If a carnal Christian is described as one whose fallen nature has not yet been changed by grace, it is a contradiction in terms. If a person is carnal in the sense that the Holy Spirit resides in him without affecting his constituent nature in any way, then he is simply not a Christian. To view regeneration as not effecting any real change in the person is a serious distortion of regeneration. Here the Holy Spirit indwells but does nothing to effect change in the person. This is simply no regeneration at all.

If a Spirit-filled Christian is defined as one in whom the flesh is absent entirely, then the only Spirit-filled Christians are those now in heaven. Every Christian is to some degree carnal in this world, insofar as the remnants of the flesh are still there provoking warfare. In this sense the Apostle Paul, after his conversion, was a carnal Christian. Every Christian is also spiritual in that the Holy Spirit indwells him and works in him, through him, and upon him.

To have the Holy Spirit indwelling but not changing is to have real schizophrenia by which two persons simply coexist, a human person who is still entirely flesh, and a divine person who is totally perfect. The biblical view involves the indwelling of a divine person within a human person who has been truly regenerated by the power of the divine person. The human person has changed. His old nature is dying, and by cooperation with the grace of the Holy Spirit, the new man is growing into conformity to Christ.

"Sexual union is not merely for recreation or for procreation. It includes the mystery of the two becoming one flesh."

—

THE MYSTERY OF MARRIAGE

JULY 1994

———

P AUL'S LETTER TO THE EPHESIANS CONTAINS one of the most
neglected texts found in the New Testament (5:31–32): " 'For this
reason a man shall leave his father and mother and be joined to
his wife, and the two shall become one flesh.' This is a great mystery, but
I speak concerning Christ and the church."

In this passage Paul refers back to the original institution of marriage
in creation. He cites Genesis 2:24 including the reference to the result of
marriage by which the two become "one flesh."

In what sense does marriage effect a union of one flesh? This question
catapults us squarely into the face of mystery. Surely the marriage union
does not annihilate the personal identities of the individuals who are
united. Before the wedding there are two distinct persons with two distinct personalities. After the wedding there are still two distinct persons
with two distinct personalities. Yet now the two have become "one flesh."

This change, traditionally has been indicated by the couple's now sharing a single last name. My wife's name was Vesta Voorhis. Now her name
is Vesta Sproul. Together we are called Mr. and Mrs. Sproul. (I am aware
that in our time the custom of sharing a common last name—that of
the husband—has been repudiated in certain circles. I wonder at times
if this assault on tradition is in any way tied to the neglect of the biblical
concept of union into one flesh. Perhaps it may simply be resistance to a
convention that is viewed as one rooted in male chauvinism. I hope that
is all that is involved.)

I have a friend whose young son calls me "R.C. and Vesta." He thinks
that is my name. He calls my wife "Mrs. R.C. and Vesta." He hears his
parents talking about "R.C. and Vesta" as a tandem so often that he has

come to believe that *I am* "R.C. and Vesta." Perhaps this child is closer to the biblical concept of marriage than any of us realize.

It is facile to assume that the phrase "the two shall become one flesh" refers exclusively to a spiritual union that is to occur in the bond of marriage. Certainly marriage is designed to effect a spiritual union. There is to be a oneness of mind and spirit. But the Bible speaks of one "flesh." The union is holistic. Two persons come together to effect a physical as well as spiritual union.

The physical union of marriage may involve something more than a sexual union but by no means less. The sexual union is a vital part of the marriage relationship. The Apostle elsewhere declares that the sexual union is not an optional element of marriage. It is mandatory. He says, "Let the husband render to his wife the affection due her, and likewise also the wife to her husband. The wife does not have authority over her own body, but the husband does. And likewise the husband does not have authority over his own body, but the wife does" (1 Cor. 7:3–4).

This mandate speaks directly to the role of sexual union in marriage. If ever the great titan of theology St. Augustine erred, it was regarding the role of sexual union in marriage. His view that sex was a necessary evil only to be indulged in with a view specifically to propagation has had enormous influence in church history. His view seems to derive more from his earlier instruction in Manichaeism, which denigrated all things physical, than from the New Testament.

Sexual union is not merely for recreation or for procreation. It includes the mystery of the two becoming one flesh. So crucial to the sexual union is the becoming of one flesh that Paul appeals to this mystery as grounds for avoiding illicit sexual relationships. He forbids fornication, indeed calls us to "flee" from it in the context of saying: "Or do you not know that he who is joined to a harlot is one body with her? for 'the two,' He says, 'shall become one flesh'" (1 Cor. 6:16).

Here it seems that the sexual union itself, even with a harlot, by virtue of the act itself effects a union of flesh. If an unmarried man enters a harlot, in a real sense he marries her. Likewise, when a married person commits adultery, he or she, in effect, commits bigamy. The sacred union of husband and wife is radically violated by adultery and becomes a real ground for divorce. The act itself is tantamount to divorce because the previous union has been broken and a new union effected with another person.

The context of this discussion in Corinthians includes a link between our union with Christ and our union with our mates. Paul says, "Do you not know that your bodies are members of Christ? Shall I then take the members of Christ and make them members of a harlot? Certainly not!" (1 Cor. 6:15).

Here Paul links our union with Christ and His body with the mystery of sexual and marital union. We recall that in Ephesians Paul said, "This is a great mystery, but I speak concerning Christ and the church."

At the heart of Christianity is the doctrine of the mystical union of the believer with Christ. The New Testament does not only call us to believe *in* Christ (*en Christo*) but to believe *into* Christ (*eis Christon*). Faith links us directly into Christ. We become *in* Him and He *in* us. This mysterious union is carried over into the relationship between Christ and the church. The church is His bride with whom He has effected a real, profound, and powerful union.

We normally assume that the image of the church as the bride of Christ is a metaphor borrowed from the institution of human marriage. In this case the earthly serves as the model for the heavenly. Perhaps that is the intent of Scripture. I am not sure. It may well be the other way around. It may be that the earthly estate of marriage is based upon the heavenly model of the mystical union of Christ and His bride. Marriage is the reflection of the heavenly reality, not the basis for a heavenly image.

The perfect unity of persons existed in eternity in the nature of the Trinity itself. Though the Father, Son, and Holy Spirit are not "one flesh," they are one Being in perfect eternal harmony. In the Godhead there is no possibility of divorce. It is a union that cannot and will not ever be broken. It is the eternal pattern of relationship that defines our human relationship. We share with God not only an analogy of being (*analogia entis*) but also an analogy of relationship (*analogia relationis*). It is found in the mystery of marriage.

FAREWELL TO THE AMERICAN FAMILY

AUGUST 1994

O UR LAND MOURNS. IT GROANS FROM economic depression, from social disintegration, from government corruption, from violent crime, and decline in health. Not one of these areas, featured in daily news report and daily debates in state houses and Congress, can be isolated from the stark reality of the breakdown of the American family.

The family is the root social unit. It is the cohesive force of any organized society. When this glue melts, the society comes apart at the seams. All the rhetoric about "traditional values" finds its primary *focus on the family*. I used the last phrase intentionally. The organization Focus on the Family is so called for a reason. A good reason. A compelling reason. It recognizes that if we are concerned with the well-being of our nation, we must fix our focus on the family.

In 1948 the Harvard historian-sociologist Pitirim A. Sorokin sounded an alarm about the impending disintegration of American society. Twelve years before the "revolution" of the '60s began, Sorokin wrote:

> An illiterate society can survive, but a thoroughly anti-social society cannot. Until recently the family was the principal school of socialization for the new-born human animals, rendering them fit for social life. At present this vital mission is performed less and less by the family.

What provoked Sorokin's alarm was a phenomenon that could be objectively measured in social behavior. He expressed shock that in 1948 the divorce rate in America had soared to 25 percent. In 1910 the divorce rate was 10 percent. In a period of 38 years the rate increased by 150 percent. Once the rate of failed marriages rose from one in ten to one in four Sorokin predicted social catastrophe.

I wonder what Sorokin would say now. By 1970 the rate had risen to 33 percent. Today it is over 50 percent. From the time Sorokin sounded the alarm until the present, there has been a 100 percent increase in the divorce rate, not to mention the multitudes of couples who have opted out of marriage by living together or the multitudes of women who choose to be single-parent mothers.

How does this affect society? It dramatically impacts the national economy. Sexual disease takes a grim toll. The moral climate deteriorates. Perhaps most ominous is the rise of statism by which the government supplants the family. It is a human horror story.

To stem the rising tide of divorce, the government has taken crucial steps. Because of acrimony, bitterness, and costly legal disputes over divorce, the government has implemented the "wisdom" of no-fault divorce. Here the raging fire is being doused by a heavy dose of gasoline.

Over against this cultural madness stands the commands of God and the ethic of Jesus. Matthew records Jesus' teaching on divorce:

> The Pharisees also came to Him, testing Him, and saying to Him, "Is it lawful for a man to divorce his wife for just any reason?" (19:3).

In response Jesus referred back to the creation ordinance of marriage and said, "Therefore what God has joined together, let not man separate" (19:6).

This strong statement provoked immediate reaction from the Pharisees. They quickly pointed to Moses' provision for divorce in the Old Testament. Jesus did not deny the provision of Deuteronomy 24 but reminded them of the original intent of marriage, explaining that the Old Testament provision was given against the backdrop of the hardness of the human heart due to sin. Then Jesus gave His famous dictum that included the often-debated "exceptive clause":

> And I say to you, whoever divorces his wife, except for sexual immorality, and marries another, commits adultery (19:9).

This is the ruling of the Lord of the church and the Lord of the world. It is a perilous thing for individuals or governments or churches to defy this edict from the King of Kings, who is Lord of the entire institution of marriage.

To be sure, Paul extended the teaching of Christ in this matter with respect to the desertion of the unbeliever. Some want to argue for no grounds of divorce on the basis of Jesus' appeal to creation and the original intent. But the reason for the Mosaic provision is still intact. Marriages are still violated by the sin of immorality.

More importantly, Jesus did explicitly give an exception, which must not be ignored. He did except immorality as a legitimate ground for divorce. It is, however, an exception to a rule, not a license for divorce on a multitude of grounds. Nor does He make any provision whatever for "no-fault" divorce.

For God and for Christ, there is nothing cavalier about marriage and divorce. These are matters of the utmost seriousness. To trifle with them is to defy God Himself. No wonder the land mourns.

What God has put together, men everywhere for every conceivable reason are tearing asunder. They are thereby tearing families and nations asunder at a woeful economic, moral, societal, and spiritual cost. It is cultural insanity.

Every day lawyers, counselors, and clergymen recommend divorce where Christ does not permit it. The epidemic has reached the highest levels of Christian leadership. It reflects a loss of a sense of obedience to Christ. It is corporate treason. If the specter of antinomianism is anywhere evident in the life of the church, it is here—at the altar of marriage and the garbage dump of divorce.

YOU SHALL NOT BE GODS

SEPTEMBER 1994

———

"**Y**OU SHALL BE LIKE GODS.**" This was the original temptation, the archetypal seduction aimed at our first parents by the serpent. Created as vice-regents with dominion over the earth, Adam and Eve wanted more. They reached for autonomy, stretching greedy arms toward the throne of God, only to fall headlong into the abyss of evil.

Expulsion from Eden was their fate. They could not go back. Paradise was lost. An angel with a flaming sword stood guard at the gateway to the Garden. This is the first reference in Scripture to a weapon of any sort. Before God gave the "power of the sword" to men, He gave it to the angel to patrol and guard the border west of Nod.

With the Fall came a rapid expansion of sin. One son of Adam and Eve murdered his brother, introducing fratricide to human history. This violence was followed by Lamech, who celebrated warfare in his famous "sword-song" (Gen. 4:23–24). Man, originally given dominion and called to dress, till, and replenish the earth, used his nascent technology to turn the tools of farming into implements of war. The plowshare became a sword, and the call to subdue the earth was distorted into a conspiracy to conquer one's brother. The means of production became the means of destruction, and human technology and scientific discovery were used not to honor God but to assault Him, by attacking His creation and His image-bearers.

Then God said NO! to the expansion of corruption and brought the Flood, a storm of judgment upon the earth, a deluge to clean the planet.

After the Flood, Noah and his family began to repopulate the earth. Noah's descendants became hunters (Nimrod) and builders. A new technology emerged to provide more stable and suitable shelter. Brick and mortar became the means by which whole cities could be built:

"Come let us make bricks and bake them thoroughly." They had brick for stone, and they had asphalt for mortar. And they said, "Come, let us build ourselves a city, and a tower whose top is in the heavens; let us make a name for ourselves..." (Gen. 11:3–4).

Immediately after the Flood, Noah erected an altar, a structure upon which to offer the sacrifice of praise and worship. The building project at Babel was something else. Again it was a reach of pretended autonomy, a stretch for heaven, an attempt to rip God down from His throne that man might make for *himself* a name. The result of this effort, this primitive scientific undertaking, was chaos. The language of man was confused and communication gave way to babbling.

This pattern has not changed. The greater the technology, the greater the chaos. The more sophisticated the tools, the more sophisticated the violence. The 20th century is the age of high technology. The technological advances of our age have eclipsed all previous generations. The most peaceful century in human history was the 1st century. The second most peaceful century was the 19th. It was the 19th century that evoked an unprecedented spirit of human optimism. The Enlightenment concluded that man no longer needs the God-hypothesis to explain his origins and purpose. An optimistic humanism was born that promised a coming utopia. Education, science, and technology would produce the acme of evolutionary development. Peace would prevail and poverty, disease, crime, and war would be banished by the modern techniques of government, economics, and education.

World War I temporarily burst the bubble until it was decreed to be the war to end all wars. Somebody forgot to tell that to the sons of Lamech: Mussolini, Tojo, Stalin, Mao, and the corporal from Bavaria. The 20th century brought a new horror to world history, the phenomenon of global war. The new warfare engaged alliances from east and west in wars numbered by Roman numerals and punctuated by a mushroom cloud.

We cannot blame this on technology. It is not the instruments that are culpable; it is the users of the instruments. The same scalpel that is used to save a life in surgery is now used to hack into pieces millions of unborn babies. The same atomic energy that supplies power for living is harnessed for weapons of incalculable destruction.

The technological explosion proliferates in geometric proportion. Yet the human spirit of corruption remains. We are still trying to be as God. We still grasp for autonomy, refusing to have God rule over us. We now reach beyond the heights of an ancient ziggurat. We walk on the moon and call it a real step forward for mankind.

We are indeed "enlightened." No longer do students carry switchblades to school. They carry guns. Gangsters don't use Tommy guns. Machine Gun Kelly* has become obsolete in the face of assault weapons and rocket launches. The battering ram has yielded to the ICBM. Our cities are armed fortresses, and we need more brick and mortar for prisons. We are still confused. Our politicians babble to us daily on the magic technology of television. And still everyone does what is right in his own eyes.

Marx believed that whoever controls the means of production (tools) controls the world. The race for technological supremacy is the race for dominion. Autonomy is the objective. But there is no technology sophisticated enough to fulfill the serpent's seductive promise. We are not gods. We shall not be gods. We cannot be gods. Only God can be God. Only God can be supreme. The issue in Eden is the issue today: Who will have dominion over man and man's technology? Our margin of error shrinks each day. Now we have the technology and techniques not to destroy God but to destroy ourselves. It is technological madness.

---

* George Kelly Barnes (1895–1954), better known as Machine Gun Kelly, was a American gangster active during the prohibition era. His nickname was derived from his preferred weapon, a Thompson submachine gun or "Tommy gun."

"Christianity is not about techniques. It offers its initiates no mystic secrets to take them to a higher consciousness. It is first about utter dependence."

—

SEARCHING FOR SHORTCUTS

H AVE YOU SEEN THE BUMPER STICKER "Visualize world peace"? Did you try it? Did it work? Presumably we are asked to create this mental picture in the hope that it will make the picture a reality. I don't know what world peace would look like, but if I did, the picture would not bring it to pass. What boggles my mind is that people would actually believe such a silly technique could effect such a desirable end.

The idea is that with the right mental technique, one could control the external world. This form of mental magic is not significantly different from the pagan lore wherein saying the magic words brings about the desired effect. Such magic brings forth wrath from God, and ridicule from other humans. Hence the cynical alternative: "Visualize whirled peas."

Perhaps the cynicism results from the necessary brevity of bumper sticker theology. Given enough time for explanation, one could wrap a nice veneer around the nonsense and people might buy it. Try a little business veneer and suddenly it's what Tony Robbins and his clones shout at us.* "If we only believe we can accomplish it, we can!!!" Too crass for you? Try the Eastern mystic veneer. Center your chakra, repeat your mantra, and only then visualize, and your dreams will all come true. Wrong spirituality for you? Try the Christian version, neatly wrapped in the Bible, first name your wish, next mutter Jesus' mighty name, then believe it will happen—visualize and it shall be given unto you.

We are a people in search of the right technique. We are on the long and winding road to discover the shortcut, the secret, the magic wand that will turn our wishes into reality. As Christians we search the Scriptures

---

* Tony Robbins (1960–) is an American motivational speaker known for encouraging his students to make use of self-help and positive-thinking techniques.

seeking the key to spiritual growth, all the while missing the thick and cumbersome answer. It's not hidden in the Book; it is the Book. We snicker and sneer at the world's spiritual alchemy, only to practice a baptized alchemy.

This is the modern age. Shortcuts abound. It should not surprise us, then, when we mistakenly believe that we can find spiritual conveniences to match. Technology has eased our bodies; can it not also give rest to our souls? A thousand theories say yes, and each one fails. Go to your local bookstore, look at the self-help section. Book after book purports to hold the secret technique for your happiness. The only place you'll find a broader selection is at your local Christian bookstore. Shelf after shelf holds books promising happiness, higher self-esteem—oh, and spirituality in twelve, seven, or three easy steps if you're in a real hurry.

The search for a shortcut, however, is not strictly a modern phenomenon. It goes back to our beginnings. While our technological prowess tempts us to seek spiritual techniques, the temptation began long before the industrial revolution. The Apostle Paul (Saul) had the technique down; he had been the ultimate Pharisee. His technique, and his pride in all it accomplished in his soul, led him to murder the early Christians. Soul exertion nearly drove Martin Luther out of his mind. His monkery, the preferred technique of his day, led not to some exalted spiritual plane but to a deep and foreboding abyss.

Soul-building techniques are evidence of our drive for autonomy. Too many of us are like Saul, seeing our religion not as an end but as a means to fulfillment. Our evangelists tell us to come to Christ not because He is the end of our existence but because He will make us happy, restore our self-esteem, and make us more "spiritual." Jesus is now a means to get our finances together, improve our marriages, and free us from every compulsive behavior from overwork to laziness. Christ, of course, can do all those things. He does them, however, finally for His glory.

Christianity is not about techniques. It offers its initiates no mystic secrets to take them to a higher consciousness. It is first about utter dependence.

Our souls cannot climb out of the mire because they are dead. Salvation comes not to those who cry out, "Show me the way to heaven," but to those who cry, "Take me there for I cannot."

Lest we see the sinner's prayer as mere technique, we must remember that Christ raises the dead that they might walk. We do not mumble the magic words and then wait to die. Christianity is about spiritual growth as well. It is about work, the hard work of sanctification. Regeneration is monergistic, God's work alone. Sanctification, the process by which we are made holy, is synergistic, God's work with us.

God's part is easy for Him. He needs no shortcuts because He never tires. We, however, must ever fight the temptation to seek the shortcut. No technique will make us holy. No technique of the devil's, however, can stop the process of Christ making us into His image. Those whom He calls He sanctifies. He has given us no techniques, but He has given us gifts. Our responsibility is to devote ourselves to those gifts.

Our sanctification requires the Spirit of God and, because He has so ordered His world, sanctification requires the disciplined and repeated use of the means of grace. Five minutes a day of Bible study smells like technique. And it is sure to fail. We must immerse ourselves in the Word of God. We must continue in the Word. Then, as Jesus promised, we will know the truth and the truth will set us free. Then we will be His disciples (John 8:31–32).

A casual attention to the things of God will do little to nurture our growth in grace. This learning process is lifelong. It has no graduation ceremony this side of heaven. Visualizing our sanctification will accomplish nothing. We must work, with fear and trembling, to begin to see the fruit of the Spirit of God in our lives.

AFTER LIGHT, DARKNESS

NOVEMBER 1994

———

T HE REFORMATION WALL IN THE old city of Geneva, Switzerland, is adorned with the motto of the Protestant Reformation chiseled into stone: Post Tenebras Lux, "After Darkness, Light." The darkness was the eclipse of the Gospel that gradually emerged in the Dark Ages and reached its nadir at the Council of Trent, when Rome put the doctrine of justification by faith alone under anathema. With this action Rome condemned what the Reformers believed was the biblical Gospel. This resulted in the most widespread fragmentation of the visible church in history.

It was a heavy price to pay. Luther had been warned that his stance would cause "a floodgate of iniquity to be opened." Luther replied, "If a floodgate of iniquity be opened, so be it." Luther was not being glib. He had no desire to open a floodgate of iniquity. But he was willing that it should happen if that is what it would take to rescue the truth of God from eclipse. Luther was addressing matters that he regarded to touch the *cor ecclesia*, the very heart of the church. He considered justification by faith alone to be "the article upon which the church stands or falls."

The Reformation was not a pedantic controversy over trifles nor a simple misunderstanding. It was a dispute about the essence of the Gospel of Jesus Christ.

The doctrine of justification by faith alone is the "cement" that has brought unity to a multifaceted and diverse group of Christian communions that differ on many other points of doctrine. That unity in the Gospel has held firm for centuries.

Today the cement of evangelical unity is crumbling. Two major issues have cast a shadow over that unity. The first was the "lordship salvation" controversy.

The second issue was provoked by the public announcement of a document issued by a joint group of 15 evangelical and Roman Catholic leaders drafted chiefly by Charles Colson and Richard John Neuhaus entitled *Evangelicals and Catholics Together: The Christian Mission in the Third Millennium.* The document, released on March 29, 1994, was endorsed by another 25 notable leaders from both groups.

One of the concerns I had initially was that the document would *create* a serious rift among evangelicals and disturb the unity that had existed for so long. As I reflected on this I came to the conclusion that the document did not and could not destroy such unity.

The Colson-Neuhaus document did not cause disunity but *exposed* a serious rift within evangelicalism. The rift concerns the place *sola fide* (justification by faith alone) has in Christian doctrine. *Sola fide* was not denied in the document. Neither was it affirmed. The evangelical understanding of *sola fide* was simply not mentioned. It was utterly ignored. A unity of justification was declared with no mention of *sola fide* or its exposition of justification solely by the *imputation* of the righteousness of Christ. That is, the *forensic* character of justification, which was central and normative to historic evangelicalism, was passed over in silence.

The question that is left in the wake of the Colson-Neuhaus document is the question, Is *sola fide* an *essential* and *necessary* element of the one true Gospel?

Alister McGrath summarized the four characteristics of the Protestant doctrine of justification that were established by 1540:

1. Justification is the forensic declaration that the Christian is righteous, rather than the process by which he or she is made righteous. It involves a change in status rather than in nature.

2. A deliberate and systematic distinction is made between justification (the external act by which God declares the believer to be righteous), and sanctification or regeneration (the internal process of renewal by the Holy Spirit).

3. Justifying righteousness is the alien righteousness of Christ, imputed to the believer and external to him, not a righteousness that is inherent within him, located within him, or in any way belonging to him.

4. Justification takes place *per fidem propter Christum* (by faith because of Christ), with faith being understood as the God-given means of justification and the merits of Christ the God-given foundation of justification.

Here McGrath gives an exposition of *forensic justification*. The central issue here is the question of the *grounds* of justification. Are we justified by a righteousness that is *apart* from us (*extra nos*) or by a righteousness that is *inherent in* us? Rome made it clear at Trent that we are not justified apart from faith, apart from grace, or apart from Christ. They taught that the sinner is justified when, after receiving the grace of the *infused* righteousness of Christ, they cooperate and assent to this infused grace to the end that they become inherently just. Justification then rests not on the *imputation* of Christ's righteousness but on the infusion of grace within us by which we are *made* righteous. God only declares to be just people who are actually just.

The Protestant Reformation insisted that justification is God's gracious declaration by which we are reckoned or counted just by the imputation of the righteousness of Christ when we are still sinners. Our justification comes to us through the instrumental cause of faith alone. The believing person is a changed person. He is regenerate and indwelt by the Holy Spirit. But he is still a sinner whose righteousness before God rests solely on the imputed righteousness of Christ alone. This, the Reformers believed, is the biblical Gospel, the Gospel Paul declared was the only Gospel, the denial of which was worthy of anathema. This is the very Gospel Rome anathematized at Trent, thereby condemning the biblical Gospel. Luther, as well as the other Reformers, believed that when Trent anathematized *sola fide* she fell into apostasy.

Many evangelicals today believe either that Rome has so modified her views of justification that she no longer condemns *sola fide* or that the historic differences are not as serious as once supposed. In light of the present threat of post-Enlightenment modernity and the hostility of secularism to Christianity, many think it is time for Catholics and evangelicals to close ranks to face a common foe. The threat of modernity is deemed so great that whatever doctrines have divided us historically pale into relative insignificance. McGrath observes:

> There exist real differences between Protestants and Roman Catholics over the matter of justification. The question remains, however, as to the significance of these differences. How important, for example, is the distinction between an alien and an intrinsic justifying righteousness? In recent years there appears to be increasing sympathy for the view that these differences, although of importance in the Reformation period, no longer possess the significance that they once had....

McGrath attributes this shift in concentration to the "real threat" that comes from the rationalism of the Enlightenment.

McGrath's observation begs a question. Why would a difference in the doctrine of justification be significant in one century but not in another? Though cultures change from age to age, the Gospel itself is bound neither by time nor by culture. I can't imagine any threat from rationalism or secularism that is more dangerous than a threat to the essence of the Gospel itself. If *sola fide* is essential to the Gospel and to Christianity, it must never be compromised or negotiated for the sake of peace.

The Colson-Neuhaus document declares agreement that we are justified by grace, through faith, because of Christ. The issue was and is, Are we justified by grace *alone*, by faith *alone*, and because of Christ *alone*? This *solecism* was and is the central issue that divided Protestantism and Roman Catholicism. It is *sola fide* that is now in danger of being shrouded once again in darkness.

We are living in a time when some evangelicals are willing to affirm *sola fide* but apparently unwilling to deny falsehoods that negate or deny it. We are willing to say what we are *for*, but unwilling to say what we are *against*. This may be because we are convinced that though *sola fide* is true it is not an essential truth. The question raised in my mind by the Colson-Neuhaus document is, Do the evangelicals who signed it believe that *sola fide* is essential to the Gospel? If they do, I pray that they will say so without horns and in no uncertain terms. In the meantime the question is clouded by the uncertain message conveyed by the document. Let the light of the biblical Gospel shine without confusion and without any shadow of darkness. This matters, now and forever.

"The Reformation was not a pedantic controversy over trifles nor a simple misunderstanding. It was a dispute about the essence of the Gospel of Jesus Christ."

—

FROM ETERNITY
TO HERE

DECEMBER 1994

———

W HAT DOES IT MEAN TO believe in something? Children are asked if they believe in Santa Claus. We are asked if we believe in God or believe in miracles. In each of these instances, the preposition *in* is used. The word *in* can be substituted by the word *that*. When we say we believe *in* something we usually mean that we believe *that* something is true. It is a matter of intellectual assent to a certain proposition. We are saying yes to a certain thesis, making an affirmation about the truth of something.

At other times when we say "we believe in," we are referring to more than a mere intellectual proposition. We are indicating something that we trust or upon which we rely. James says, "You believe that there is one God, you do well. Even the demons believe—and tremble!" (James 2:19).

Here sarcasm drips from James's pen. There is a kind of belief that is shared even by devils. It is a mere belief "that." The demons believe *that* Christ is Lord. They do not believe *in* Christ. They do not rely on Christ, neither do they trust in Christ.

When the Reformers spoke of the faith that alone justifies, they spoke of a faith that included not only intellectual assent about certain propositions or data but a *fiduciary* trust or reliance upon Christ.

However, the idea of believing *in* Christ means even more than possessing a living, authentic saving trust or reliance. True faith *in* Christ is a result of our mystical union *with* Christ, which is effected in our regeneration. In the May 1994 issue of *Tabletalk* Dr. John Gerstner wrote,

When Jesus Christ unites Himself with an elect soul, that person is so united with Him that his regenerated soul trusts Christ for eternal salvation, his sin's guilt is remitted, and divine righteousness received. In this act, instantly and forever after, the soul believes and obeys Jesus Christ.

Later in the same article, regarding Thomas's view of infused grace, he said,

We do insist that the Holy Spirit unites the regenerate soul with Christ and produces faith and all virtues along with it forever, which is the very substance of infused grace. . . . I diagram *evangelical justification* in a way, I believe, Aquinas would not have objected:

(Union with Christ produces)

Faith → Justification + Works.

The point that Gerstner makes is that our entire salvation is tied to our mystical union with Christ, a union that in one respect moves from eternity past to eternity future.

In the Roman Catholic view of justification, we are made just through the grace of the infusion of the righteousness of Christ, with which grace we must cooperate in order to become *inherently* righteous.

The Reformation protest against the Roman view stressed that the ground of our justification is the righteousness of Christ alone, which righteousness is imputed to the believer by faith. This crucial issue, whether the righteousness by which we are justified is *our* righteousness inherent in us, or *Christ's* righteousness imputed to us remains the chief point of dispute between Rome and evangelicalism.

What is easily missed or obscured by the evangelical stress on imputation vs. infusion is that evangelical theology *also affirms* the reality of the *infusion of grace.* In indwelling us the Holy Spirit unites us mystically with Christ so that we become *in* Christ, and Christ is in us. Gerstner argues that infused grace indeed *is* the cause of the *virtues* of the Christian but not the cause of justification.

The Christian life is lived in the context of mystical union with Christ.

This union finds its initial origin in eternity. Our salvation is from the foundation of the world, resting in the grace of God's sovereign election. Paul indicates this in Ephesians 1:3–6:

> Blessed be the God and Father of our Lord Jesus Christ, who has blessed us with every spiritual blessing in the heavenly places in Christ, just as He chose us in Him before the foundation of the world, that we should be holy and without blame before Him in love, having predestined us to adoption as sons by Jesus Christ to Himself, according to the good pleasure of His will, to the praise of the glory of His grace, by which He made us accepted in the Beloved.

It is *in the Beloved* that our redemption is found. From eternity God considers the elect to be *in Christ*. Before our mystical union is effected with us in time, it is already a present reality in the mind of God.

Just as Christ invaded time from eternity 2,000 years ago, so our eternal union intrudes in time through the work of the Spirit. What has always existed in the mind of God in eternity becomes a time-bound reality in the heart of the regenerate. The result is that in Christ, through the Spirit, we will behold the Father at our death and from there to eternity. We are sons and daughters of the Father, as it was in the beginning.

Our salvation is *by* Christ and *in* Christ. By His righteousness we are made just. By His atonement our sins are forgiven. Calvin comments on our election in Christ as Paul asserted in Ephesians:

> When he adds *in Christ*, it is the second confirmation of the freedom of election. For if we are chosen in Christ, it is outside ourselves. It is not from the sight of our deserving, but because our heavenly Father has ingrafted us, through the blessing of adoption, into the Body of Christ. In short, the name of Christ excludes all merit, and everything which men have of themselves, for when he says that we are chosen in Christ, it follows that in ourselves we are unworthy.

LIVING EAST OF EDEN

JANUARY 1995

——

ST. AUGUSTINE STOOD BY THE shores of the Mediterranean. He had heard of the hordes of barbarians that were moving as a juggernaut against Rome and the empire. The reports were ominous, foreboding, lending little reason for hope of the survival of the Roman culture. Augustine said a prayer in three parts. In the first part he implored God to save the empire. In the second part he asked for grace to accept the destruction of civilization as he knew it, if that should be the will of Providence. In the third part he asked that in either case he might be permitted soon to die and enter his eternal rest.

Like Abraham before him, the venerable Bishop of Hippo sought a better country—a heavenly city with foundations, whose builder and maker is God. The author of the Christian classic *The City of God* held no illusions about the city of man.

Human kingdoms come and go according to the persevering grace of God. The human city is always a monument to human corruption. The endurance of such monuments is subject to the patience of the One who will not always strive with men.

The first residence of mankind was a garden. There was no metropolis. After the Fall our primordial parents were sent into exile. It was history's first deportation. The first sin of mankind led quickly to the second and the third in rapid expansion, escalation, and proliferation of evil. The trespass of Adam and Eve was followed by the crime of Cain—fratricide, the cold-blooded murder of his own brother, whose blood screamed from the earth and was heard by the ears of God. So Cain was cursed. He was sentenced to be a fugitive, a vagabond upon the earth.

But Cain was not content to roam. He acquired a wife, and she gave him a son named Enoch. Then Cain did something that was a first in biblical history. Cain built a city. The name of the city was "Enoch."

It was a city of man. It was designed by man, built by man, inhabited by man, and named to the glory of man.

As Cain's family grew so grew the city. It became the home of the first polygamist. It had a fine artist's colony. Its most prominent citizen became Lamech, whose famous sword-song celebrated his own propensity for violence.

From this degenerate group came the descendants who gathered on a plain in Shinar with a blueprint for human progress. Their dream was to erect the ultimate city of man. They said to one another:

> "Come, let us build ourselves a city, and a tower whose top is in the heavens; let us make a name for ourselves, lest we be scattered abroad over the face of the whole earth" (Gen. 11:4).

Like the third and most astute of the three little pigs, the city planners of Babel decided to build their city of brick and mortar. They were looking for permanence. They wanted a city that was safe, secure from invasion.

They also sought a monument. Their monumental quest was not to glorify God but to rival Him. They sought their own glory, the control of their own destiny. Their only altar was to the divine Pelagius, the patron saint of human arrogance.

It was a marvelous tower. But it didn't quite make it to heaven. They made a name for themselves that is now a synonym for chaos and confusion. God peered down at their city building project and said "No!"

The Tower of Babel is no more. The hanging gardens of Babylon have gone to weeds. The Sphinx has had his nose fall off. Other monuments remain. But these too will perish. Human monuments all do. No earthly city is eternal, not even Rome.

Permanence and security cannot be found in concrete. Concrete crumbles. Glass shatters. Steel melts. When God says "No!" the cities and kingdoms of men come to ruin. God simply will not tolerate man's quest for autonomy—his lust for idols of his own making. No city, no nation, no culture can survive the judgment of God.

Christians love America. Some see in her the last hope of creating a

Christian nation. But it is not a Christian nation. It is pagan to the core. It is in danger of becoming, if it is not already, the new "Evil Empire." The Mayflower Compact is a museum piece, a relic of a forgotten era. "In God We Trust" is now a lie.

Yes, we must always work for social reform. Yes, we must be "profane" in Luther's sense that we go out of the temple and into the world. We do not despise the country of our birth. But in what do we invest our hope? The state is not God. The nation is not the Promised Land. The president is not our King. The Congress is not our Savior. Our welfare can never be found in the city of man. The federal government is not sovereign. We live—in every age and in every generation—by the rivers of Babylon. We need to understand that clearly. We must learn how to sing the Lord's song in a strange and foreign land.

America will fall. The United States will inevitably disintegrate. The Stars and Stripes will bleed. The White House will turn to rubble. That is certain. We stand like Augustine before the sea. We pray that God will spare our nation. If He chooses not to we ask for the grace to accept its demise. In either case we look to Him who is our King and to heaven, which is our home. We await the city of God, the heavenly Jerusalem, whose builder and maker is God.

THE COMMUNITY
OF FAITH

FEBRUARY 1995

E LLIS ISLAND. RESTING WITHIN THE shadow of the Statue of Liberty, this small piece of real estate has become a symbol of American history. There emigrants assembled upon arrival to our nation. They came from many places for many different reasons. They all looked to Miss Liberty for hope—this despite her somewhat hypocritical smile inasmuch as she was erected two years after Congress passed a law limiting immigration.

Two of my ancestors arrived at Ellis Island. One came from Ireland to escape the potato famine. He left a thatched-roof home with a mud floor. The other one came from Yugoslavia, where he was a member of the aristocracy of Croatia.

The two shared a common goal. They both left their homeland seeking a better country. They were pilgrims, sojourners in a foreign land. They, like Abraham, went out seeking a city. Yet unlike Abraham my ancestors sought the city of man.

Every Christian is called to be a pilgrim. We are pilgrims and sojourners upon the earth. Our home is in the city of God. Our community is the church, the visible testimony to the invisible kingdom of God. It is our community—a community of faith.

In the community of faith, Abraham is considered the father of the faithful. He stars in the roll call of faith:

> By faith Abraham obeyed when he was called to go out to the place which he would receive as an inheritance. And he went out, not knowing where he was going. By faith he dwelt in the land of promise as in a foreign country, dwelling in tents with Isaac and Jacob, the heirs with

him of the same promise; for he waited for the city which has foundations, whose builder and maker is God (Heb. 11:8–10).

Centuries later a new tent appeared in the land of promise. It was Immanuel who "dwelt" or "tabernacled" among us. Christ was the living tabernacle who pitched His tent among His people. His appearance signaled the intrusion of the city of God. He said of the Old Testament patriarch, "Abraham rejoiced to see My day," and "Before Abraham was, I AM" (John 8:56, 58).

Christ came as the anointed King of the kingdom of God. He is the King of the heavenly city. But His kingdom differs radically from the kingdoms of this world. During His trial before Pilate, Jesus made this point:

"My kingdom is not of this world. If My kingdom were of this world, My servants would fight, so that I should not be delivered to the Jews: but now My kingdom is not from here" (John 18:36).

Pilate asked directly, "Are You a king then?" (v. 37). Obviously Pilate could not see how a person could be a king if his kingdom had no earthly locus.

If Pilate was bewildered by Jesus' first reply he was more confused by the second:

"You say rightly that I am a king. For this cause I was born, and for this cause I have come into the world, that I should bear witness to the truth. Everyone who is of the truth hears My voice" (v. 37).

This is an enigmatic saying. Jesus confirms that He is indeed a King. But He goes on to affirm that He came into the world to bear witness to the truth. Whatever else the kingdom of God may be, it is at its core a kingdom of truth. In the city of God there is no falsehood, no delusion, no lie.

When Jesus ascended to His coronation, the last question His disciples asked Him was, "Will you at this time restore the kingdom to Israel?" They were still looking for a kingdom in this world. Jesus replied:

"It is not for you to know times or seasons which the Father has put in His own authority. But you shall receive power when the Holy Spirit has come upon you: and you shall be witnesses to Me in Jerusalem, and in all Judea and Samaria, and to the end of the earth" (Acts 1:6–8).

Jesus spoke of Pentecost, of the receiving of power. That power was given to fulfill the mandate to *bear witness* to Him. The task of the church, the mission of the community of faith, is to make the invisible kingdom of Christ visible. We bear witness to the truth. The timetable of the earthly manifestation of the kingdom belongs to God. Our task is to participate in the very vocation of Christ to "bear witness to the truth."

A church that cares not for truth is a community that rejects its very mission. The person who says, "I'm not interested in doctrine or theology" is not "of the truth." They have missed the voice of Jesus.

For the church to be the church, she must bow before her King and embrace the mission He has given to her. Yes, we desire a cultural reformation and a restoration of public morality. But that is secondary to and dependent upon our mission to bear witness to the truth. Doctrine is important because its central concern is for an understanding of truth, without which there can be no godliness. It is the truth that sets us free, reforms our behavior, and defines us as disciples of Christ.

The world does not see or understand the city of God. It is a hidden city, a concealed kingdom. It is veiled by falsehood, by the lie that seeks to obscure the truth. The truth is that at this moment Jesus is the King of kings. This world is under His dominion. We are citizens in His realm. We must not negotiate or retreat from that affirmation. The kingdom of God is comprised of those people who believe what God says and obey what God commands.

WISDOM AND THE MIND

MARCH 1995

———

THE BIBLICAL CONCEPT OF WISDOM demands disciplined study of Scripture. The Christian is called to be enrolled in the school of Christ; careful study is necessary for true discipleship.

The word *philosophy* derives from a combination of two Greek words: *phileō* ("to love") and *sophia* ("wisdom"). Literally *philosophy* means "love of wisdom." The current discipline of philosophy usually has little to do with a pursuit of wisdom, concentrating instead on questions of metaphysics, epistemology, or linguistic analysis. The science of ethics is still subsumed under the generic heading of "philosophy" but is often speculative rather than practical in its orientation.

The ancient Greeks, who are usually credited with developing the science of philosophy, were also concerned with abstract metaphysics and epistemology. However, the question of ethics was of paramount importance to Socrates, Plato, and Aristotle. Socrates sought to reduce virtue or ethics to "right knowledge." Plato sought the ultimate standard of the good. Aristotle wrote the *Nicomachean Ethics*.

The Jewish thinkers of the Old Testament did little in the area of metaphysical speculation. The Scriptures begin with the affirmation of God, known not via intellectual speculation but by His own revelatory self-disclosure. The overarching concern of Jewish philosophy was indeed a love of wisdom. The wisdom in view, however, was not speculative but practical. Hebrew wisdom was concerned with life, with living a life pleasing to God. The Jewish thinker asked, "What does obedience involve? How is God glorified in my behavior?" Because of this focus, the Old Testament declared that "the fear of the LORD is the beginning of wisdom" (Prov. 9:10a).

The starting point for wisdom is reverence for God. The fear of the Lord is not a servile fear but a filial fear born of adoration. Here wisdom is a religious matter. Because it was religious, modern Christians tend to think it was not an intellectual matter. Our generation may rank as the most anti-intellectual generation of all Christian history.

We may describe our age as an era of neo-gnosticism. The Gnostic distortion is found not only in New Age thinking, in elements of existential theology, and in Eastern forms of mysticism, it is found pervasively in evangelical circles.

Gnosticism took its definition from the Greek word for knowledge (*gnōsis*). The Gnostics of early church history eschewed knowledge of God either through normal rational channels or through sense perception. Knowledge was achieved through a kind of direct, immediate, mystical intuition. This knowledge was a kind of super knowledge available only to an elite group of spiritually oriented persons called "the *Gnostikoi*" or "those in the know." The heretics of the second and third centuries claimed knowledge superior to that sought by the Apostles. The Apostolic revelation was meant to be intelligible to the mind. Christianity, though based upon revelation and intensely religious in scope, is nevertheless fundamentally an intellectual faith. That is, God's Word is directed to the mind and is meant to be understood by the mind. It is not intellectualism, but it does address the intellect. We are called to love God with our whole mind as well as with our whole heart. Indeed we cannot not love God or anything else with our hearts unless there is some understanding of the object of our affection in our minds.

Today's neo-gnosticism replaces biblical understanding with private "leadings of the Spirit." In contrast, the biblical concept of wisdom demands rigorous disciplined study of Scripture. Indeed the very word *disciple* is closely linked to the idea of discipline. The New Testament word for disciple means literally "a learner." The Christian is called to be enrolled in the school of Christ. Careful study of the Bible is necessary for true discipleship.

Jesus said to His own students, "If you abide in My word, you are My disciples indeed. And you shall know the truth and the truth shall make you free" (John 8:31–32). Our Lord calls for a continued application of the mind to His Word. A disciple does not dabble in learning. He makes the seeking after an understanding of God's Word a chief business of his life.

The wisdom literature of the Old Testament distinguishes between knowledge and wisdom just as the New Testament distinguishes between knowledge and love. Knowledge without love merely puffs up with pride. Yet the love that edifies is not a contentless love. Likewise the Old Testament makes it clear that one can have knowledge without wisdom. The biblical "fool" might be highly intelligent and highly knowledgeable.

It is because we understand that knowledge must never be an end in itself that we step into the error of denigrating its importance. Since we can have knowledge without love and/or knowledge without wisdom, we tend to downplay the importance of knowledge.

The wisdom literature of the Old Testament never views the difference between knowledge and wisdom as a difference between the bad and the good. Rather, the distinction is one between the good and the better. It is good to attain knowledge; it is better to achieve wisdom.

It is possible to have knowledge without having wisdom. It is not possible, however, to have wisdom without having knowledge. Knowledge is a necessary precondition for wisdom. The practice of godliness demands that we know and understand what godliness requires.

The Christian life is a transformed life. The transformation of life comes about, as the Apostle Paul declares, through the renewal of the mind. The mind is renewed by an understanding of the Word of God. The Word of God expresses the mind of God to us.

Our minds are to be conformed to the mind of Christ. That conformity does not automatically or instantly occur with conversion. Our conversion by the power of the Holy Spirit is not the end of our learning process but the beginning. At conversion we enroll in the school of Christ. There is no graduation this side of heaven. It is a pilgrimage of lifelong education.

The pursuit of wisdom is the pursuit of the knowledge of God. In one sense Socrates was right in his insistence that right conduct is right knowledge. This is not in the sense that correct knowledge guarantees right behavior but in the sense that knowledge, when it grows to wisdom, leads into right behavior. Thus philosophers can become *philo-theos*, lovers of God.

THE HISTORY OF THE REFORMATION

APRIL 1995

"A CESSPOOL OF HERESIES." THIS WAS the judgment rendered by Holy Roman Emperor Charles V on May 26, 1521, shortly after Luther took a stand at the Diet of Worms.

Earlier, in the bull *Exsurge Domine*, Pope Leo X described Luther as a wild boar loose in the vineyard of Christ and as a stiff-necked, notorious, damned heretic. On May 4, 1521, Luther was "kidnapped" by friends and whisked off to Wartburg castle, where he was kept secretly hidden, disguised as a knight. There Luther immediately undertook the task of translating the Bible into the vernacular.

Frequently the Reformation is described as a movement that revolved around two pivotal issues. The so-called "material" cause was the debate over *sola fide* ("justification by faith alone"). The "formal" cause was the issue of *sola Scriptura*, that the Bible and the Bible alone has the authority to bind the conscience of the believer. Church tradition was regarded with respect by the Reformers but not as a normative source of revelation. The "protest" of Protestantism went far beyond the issue of justification by faith alone, challenging many dogmas that emerged in Rome, especially during the Middle Ages.

In a short time, the Reformation swept through Germany but did not stop there. Aided by the translation of the Bible in other nations, the reform spread to the Huguenots in France, to Scotland, England, Switzerland, Hungary, and Holland. Ulrich Zwingli led the Reformation movement in Switzerland, John Knox in Scotland, and John Calvin among the French Protestants.

In 1534 Calvin delivered a speech calling the church to return to the pure Gospel of the New Testament. His speech was burned, and Calvin fled Paris to Geneva. Disguised as a vinedresser, he escaped the city in a basket. During the next year, some two dozen Protestants were burned alive in France. This provoked Calvin to write his famous *Institutes of the Christian Religion*, which was addressed to the King of France. His thought contained in the *Institutes* developed into the dominant theology for the international expansion of the Reformation.

The first edition of the *Institutes* was completed in 1536, the same year Calvin was persuaded by Farel to come to Switzerland to build Geneva into a model city of reformation. In 1538 Farel and Calvin were forced to leave Geneva. Calvin lived and ministered in Strasbourg for three years until he was recalled to Geneva in 1541.

Calvin's theology stressed the sovereignty of God in all of life. His chief passion was the reform of worship to a level of purity that would give no hint to or support of the human penchant for idolatry. Geneva attracted leaders from all over Europe who came there to observe the model and be instructed by Calvin himself.

During this period turbulence spread to England when King Henry VIII resisted the authority of Rome. In 1534 Henry became the Supreme Head of the Anglican Church. He undertook the persecution of evangelicals, which escalated under "Bloody Mary," causing many to flee to Geneva for refuge.

The persecutions were suspended under "Good Queen Bess," Elizabeth I, whose stance provoked a papal bull against her in 1570. The Reformation spread rapidly to Scotland, largely under the leadership of John Knox, who served 19 months as a galley slave before he went to England and then to Geneva. In 1560 the Scottish Parliament rejected papal authority. In 1561 the Scottish Reformed "Kirk" was reorganized.

One interesting footnote to this is that the first man John Knox ordained into the ministry of the church was an obscure clergyman by the name of Robert Campbell Sproul, of whom I am a direct descendant.

In the early 17th century, the Reformation spread to the new world with the arrival of the Pilgrims and colonies of Puritans who brought Reformed theology and the Geneva Bible with them.

Reformation theology dominated Protestant evangelicalism for decades but became diluted later under influences of Pietism and Finneyism.

By the end of the 20th century, Reformation theology declined dramatically in the Western world, being assaulted by 19th-century liberal theology on the one hand, and the influence of Arminian theology on the other. This was especially true in America.

In the present scene of American evangelicalism, Reformation theology is a minority report. The dominant strands of theology that reign in current evangelical circles are dispensationalism and neo-Pentecostal charismatic thought. The phenomenal spread and growth of dispensational theology in America is a fascinating chapter in church history. Having its roots in British Plymouth Brethren suppositions, dispensationalism spread rapidly in the late 19th and early 20th centuries. Fueled by the Bible School movement, prophecy conferences, and the preaching of men like D.L. Moody, dispensationalism gathered enormous popular support.

The American version of dispensationalism got a great boost by the publication of the *Scofield Reference Bible*. The *Scofield Bible*, with its study notes, served as a popular tool for the spread of dispensational theology. This theology was forged by men who had their roots predominately in Reformation thought. The themes of classical Reformed theology were modified significantly by this movement.

The *New Geneva Study Bible* is the first distinctively Reformed study Bible in English to appear since the Geneva Bible in the 16th century. It seeks to recover the theology of the Reformation and provide a guide for the laity to understand its historically, doctrinally, and biblically rich system. Its importance to American Christianity is enormous. It is my hope that it will help guide English-speaking evangelicals back to their Reformation roots. More importantly, it is designed to call evangelicals back to the Bible itself and to their historic confessions of biblical theology.

Beyond the borders of America, the *New Geneva Study Bible* may be used to expand the light of the Reformation to lands where the original Reformation never reached, especially to Russia and Eastern Europe.

In our day we have seen a revival of interest in the Bible and a renewed commitment to the authority and trustworthiness of Scripture. But the Reformation was more than a doctrine about the Bible. It was sparked by a deep and serious study of the Bible. It is not enough to extol the virtue of Scripture—we must hear the teaching of Scripture afresh. It is only by a serious and earnest recovery of biblical truth that we will be able to avoid falling into a new cesspool of heresy.

"In our day we have seen a revival of interest in the Bible and a renewed commitment to the authority and trustworthiness of Scripture."

DEUTERONOMY: JOSIAH AND THE DISCOVERY OF THE LAW

MAY 1995

When they brought out the money that was brought into the house of the LORD, Hilkiah the priest found the Book of the Law of the LORD given by Moses. Then Hilkiah answered and said to Shaphan the scribe, "I have found the Book of the Law in the house of the LORD." And Hilkiah gave the book to Shaphan. So Shaphan carried the book to the king.
—2 Chronicles 34:14–16a

IN THE MIDDLE OF THE 20TH CENTURY, a small monograph was published by George Mendenhall of the University of Michigan. The title of the work was *The Law and the Covenant in the Ancient Near East*. The book was provoked by archaeological discoveries that revealed the structure of treaties from the Hittite civilization. These suzerain treaties followed a format that was similar to the form and structure of biblical covenants.

Further elucidation of the covenant structure was given by Dr. Meredith Kline, particularly in his two books *Treaty of the Great King* and *By Oath Consigned*. Kline shows how the basic structure of ancient Near Eastern treaties is incorporated in the Old Testament, especially in the so-called "second book of the Law," or Deuteronomy.

One feature that stands out in this structure is the feature of *stipulations* that define the terms and obligations of the covenant. In a word, the stipulations are the law of God. It is important to remember that God's law is not given in a vacuum. The context of the Old Testament Law is the covenant. Covenantal duty and obligation is expressed in the Law.

God's law is God's Word; God's Word is law. Even the Gospel, which is distinguished normally from God's Law, has stipulations. That is, Law and Gospel may never be absolutely separated. The Gospel as God's Word imposes obligations on the believer.

We live in an age in which both Law and Gospel have been obscured. As a result evangelism often is expressed simply as an announcement of redemption without obligation. We hear preachers declare, "God loves you unconditionally." What does this mean? The danger with such declarations is that they are heard or understood to mean that God's love imposes no conditions or obligations upon people. It suggests that I can have a loving relationship with God even if I do not repent or if I do not embrace the Gospel. It suggests that I am acceptable to God just as I am. This sounds more like Mr. Rogers' neighborhood than the kingdom of God.

In the Old Testament, God's Law was forgotten and the spiritual vitality of Israel fell into ruins. The "reformation" in Israel (as brief as it was) took place with the rediscovery of the Law under King Josiah. The biographical sketch of Josiah presented in 2 Chronicles 34 observes: "And he did what was right in the sight of the LORD, and walked in the ways of his father David; he did not turn aside to the right hand or to the left" (34:2).

Doing what was right in the sight of the Lord stands in contrast to the biblical judgment pronounced against doing "what was right in their own eyes."

Doing what is right in God's sight is to live in *theonomy*, under the Law of God. Doing what is right in our own eyes is to live in a delusion of *autonomy*, which is nothing less than antinomianism.

In the 19th century, Friedrich Nietzsche, who carried no brief for Christianity, lamented the state of European culture, claiming that the manners and customs of the people reflected a "herd morality." A herd morality is a thoughtless morality. It is a morality greased by conformity to current customs and behavioral patterns.

Our culture is marked by a herd morality. We live according to what is in vogue. Think of the national climate of abortion. Thirty years ago abortion on demand was widely considered to be a monstrous evil practiced only by the most decadent people. Today it is favored by the majority and lauded by many as a virtuous act. Did the foundation for this ethical issue change, or did cultural custom and mores change?

Living like everybody else in slavish imitation of prevailing custom is what destroyed the soul of Israel. She began to imitate her pagan neighbors and lapsed into a crass religion of idolatry. Life became directed by custom rather than divine law.

Israel's reformation came via a rediscovery of the Law, which created a brief awakening to the bankruptcy of a corrupt nation. As a young man, King Josiah began the process of reformation with a spiritual purge, a cleansing of pagan elements from the religious life of the nation. The Bible says: "And in the twelfth year he began to purge Judah and Jerusalem of the high places, the wooden images, the carved images, and the molded images" (2 Chron. 34:3b).

A few years later, Hilkiah found the Book of the Law of the Lord given by Moses. A scribe brought the book to King Josiah and read it to him. The result was dramatic: "Thus it happened, when the king heard the words of the Law, that he tore his clothes" (v. 19).

Josiah was awakened to the greatness of the wrath of God. He realized that God had been pouring out that wrath upon the nation of Israel. He further understood that this divine judgment on the nation was a direct result of sin: "Great is the wrath of the LORD that is poured out on us, because our fathers have not kept the word of the LORD, to do according to all that is written in this book" (v. 21).

The most apparent immediate change in the national reform of Israel was seen in the restoration of true worship, a worship purged of idolatry and rooted in a sound understanding of the character of God and of His Law.

The Reformation of the 16th century also saw an accent upon the restoration of sound theology and proper worship. The Reformers were not legalists, nor were they Judaizers. But they did herald a recovery of the Old Testament particularly as the Old Testament reveals the character of God. As such the Reformation was not only a rediscovery of the Gospel, it was also a rediscovery of the Law.

The work of Christ in our salvation was understood by the New Testament writers in terms of Jesus' fulfillment of the stipulations of the old covenant, particularly as they are summarized in Deuteronomy. Deuteronomy gives us the Law in summation and points toward the Gospel.

We need a new discovery of the Law of God and the Word of God in our land. Yes, it needs to be rediscovered in the public square—but even more importantly it must be rediscovered in the house of God. Josiah's mandate to the priests of Israel must be recovered as God's mandate to us:

"Now serve the Lord your God" (2 Chron. 35:3).

THE WRATH OF GOD

JUNE 1995

> God is angry. He is angry with the wicked every day. His wrath is revealed from heaven against all that work iniquity. If it were not so, He would not be a moral being: For every moral being must burn with hot indignation against all wrong perceived as such.... If we do not react against the wrong when we see it, in indignation and avenging wrath, we are either unmoral or immoral. —B.B. Warfield

"MY GOD IS NOT A GOD OF WRATH; my God is a God of love." I cannot provide a footnote to this quote to indicate the source of it. To do so it seems I would have to footnote the world. Perhaps I should simply ascribe it to the most prolific of all authors, Anonymous.

Much is revealed in this quote. The first is that it is an expression of idolatry. To embrace a god who is wrathless is to worship a god who is not God. It is to be infatuated with an idol. The qualifier "my" before "God" indicates that the god who is confessed is a personal deity of one's own subjective creation.

The second revelation found in this quote is that it indicates a view that wrath is incompatible with love in the character of God. It assumes that if God is loving He cannot be wrathful, or that if He is wrathful He cannot be loving.

What are we to make of this? It is not enough merely to dismiss it as a false dilemma, which indeed it is. We must show why it is a false dilemma. If God is good as well as loving, He must punish evil. If He refuses to punish evil, then He would be neither good nor loving. A parent who refuses to correct his own children does not love his children. He cares not for the child's well-being.

God is wrathful because He is loving. His anger rages against sin because sin is destructive to those whom He loves. He loves people. He also loves righteousness and justice. His wrath is never directed against righteousness; indeed His indignation is always righteous indignation.

The Scripture repeatedly warns us of the wrath of God. It is the visitation of His righteous punishment on the ungodly. Though He is indeed slow to anger He is also sure to anger.

The wrath of God was perfectly displayed in the life of His incarnate Son. Jesus, in His perfect and sinless humanity, expressed anger. His fury with the money-changers in the temple is part of the Gospel record. Here, the Prince of Love demonstrated the compatibility of love and wrath.

But how do we reconcile the doctrine of the impassibility of God with the multitude of biblical references to His wrath?

While a seminary student I listened to a chapel speaker who mutilated Reformed theology. When chapel was over I walked outside with Dr. John Gerstner. I said, "If John Calvin would have heard that, he would have turned over in his grave." Gerstner stopped in mid-stride, turned to me and said, "Roberto [a term of affection borrowed from Pittsburgh's great one, Roberto Clemente], don't you know that nothing could possibly disturb the felicity John Calvin is enjoying at this very moment?"

Gerstner's point was clear. When the saints enter into their eternal rest they enjoy a state of blessedness that goes forever uninterrupted. It is not that they become devoid of feelings. On the contrary, the beatific vision they behold stirs the very depths of their sanctified souls. They know constant joy and bliss. Such bliss cannot be diminished by anything that occurs on earth or in heaven.

In heaven there is no sadness, no grief, no pain, no mourning. Neither is there anger among those who inhabit eternity.

When we consider the nature of God we realize that nothing can possibly destroy or impair His internal and eternal blessedness. God is not given to mood swings. His wrath must never be conceived as an eruption into paroxysms of anger in which He loses His temper. His anger reflects His manifest disapproval of wickedness. But even this Divine displeasure, which the Bible expresses in anthropomorphic language, cannot create an emotional crisis in the Divine being. We are not to view God as a disinterested spectator of human affairs. Yet neither may we view Him as an anxious Olympian who wrings His hands in nervous frustration at the vicissitudes that befall His creation. All things are under His sovereign control. Anxiety is an intrinsic impossibility for Him. So is disappointment. All that occurs occurs by His sovereign will. Even His anger is part of his eternal will. He wills to display His indignation against the wicked activities of His creatures.

When we consider the relationship between the wrath of God and the wrath of human beings we must be careful to remember the difference between God and us. Though we are created in God's image and that carries the result that there is some similarity between God and humanity, an analogy of being, that similarity must not be seen as an equation of exactitude. Along with similarity there is also dissimilarity. Though there is an analogy of being there is not an identity of being. St. Augustine maintained that what is attributed to God in an analogical sense must be denied in its universal sense. This means simply that when we speak of the wrath of God we must remember that His wrath is not exactly like our wrath.

We, as God's creatures made in His image, are called to mirror and reflect His character. That reflection extends to anger. As God's image bearers we are called to be angry. Our anger is to be a reflection of God's anger. We are to mirror God's indignation at injustice and unrighteousness.

This is part of our quest to have the mind of Christ in us. We are called to love what Christ loves and hate what Christ hates. We are to approve what God approves and disapprove what He disapproves.

Though there is no sin in God's anger, there can be sin in ours. Even righteous indignation for us may be an occasion for sin. Our wrath, like that of God's, must be grounded on, not opposed to, love. We must love the truth enough to be angry about its distortion. We must love justice enough to be angry with its violation. We must love righteousness enough to be angry with its corruption.

WILLFUL JOY

JULY 1995

———

"**D**on't Worry. Be Happy!**"** * From popular music to a cultural slogan this adage is stated in the form of an imperative. It reflects the idea that happiness can be evoked by an act of the will. Yet the prevailing assumption among us is that happiness is something that happens to us or in us. It is a passive experience. We may be active in seeking it as its pursuit is considered one of our inalienable rights. But the thing itself, as elusive as it may be, is often regarded as something involuntary despite the imperative form of the maxim, "Be Happy."

There is a difference between happiness and the joy of which the Scripture speaks. The term *happiness* tends to be broader than the term *joy*. Happiness tends to include a notion of contentment and satisfaction along, perhaps, with feelings of joy. Joy suggests something more intense—a strong feeling of gladness.

Since joy is so often associated with feelings, indeed even intense feelings, it seems all the more incapable of being achieved by an act of the will. We cannot turn a switch or press a button and create *de novo* a feeling of joy. Yet in biblical terms joy is often set forth as a mandate, a command to be obeyed, suggesting that it is a matter of the will to some degree.

When God spoke judgment upon His people Israel, He said: "Because you did not serve the Lord your God with joy and gladness of heart . . ." (Deut. 28:47). Here God punishes Israel not merely because they failed to serve God, but because they failed to serve Him with joy and gladness. Serving God with joy is not an option or added luxury—it is a duty and obligation. This does not imply the joy is totally a matter of will. There may be a passive or involuntary element to it. But joy surely comes with

———

* "Don't Worry, Be Happy" is a song by the American musician Bobby McFerrin released in September 1988.

behavioral practices that are a matter of the will. If we are serving God without joy there is something wrong with that service.

Still the command to rejoice is clearly present in Scripture. In Philippians Paul commanded Christians to rejoice: "Rejoice in the Lord always. Again I will say, rejoice!" (4:4). The note on this text in the *New Geneva Study Bible* reads: "The command to rejoice can always be obeyed, even in the midst of conflict, adversity, and deprivation, because joy rests not on favorable circumstances, but 'in the Lord.' Paul uses repetition to emphasize this truth."

This does not mean that adversity is enjoyable. I do not take pleasure in the sensation of the dentist's drill. But the ground of our rejoicing is "in the Lord." All of our life is lived *coram Deo*, before the face of God. The Christian is a person who is in Christ and Christ is in the person. This, in itself, is enough to occasion joy in us no matter what the circumstances are. Joy can be present in the midst of pain and sorrow.

Paul in Romans reminds us of a critical point regarding joy and sorrow. He gives us the simple promise: "And we know that all things work together for good to those who love God, to those called according to His purpose" (Rom. 8:28). This passage has become something of a cliché, particularly when it is used to try to comfort the grieving. Like most clichés, however, this passage attained that status for the simple reason that it is true, and it should comfort. Unlike most clichés, this one is God's Word and hence cannot become over-used. The degree to which we believe this promise is the degree to which we can experience joy while enmeshed in sorrow.

In this regard joy is both a possibility and a requirement. Our wills do operate in the focus of our thoughts and in our quest for the knowledge of God. If joy is not characteristic in our lives, it may be a sign that we are not Christians at all. Indeed, if there is no joy in our lives, it would be proof positive that we are unregenerate; we would not be in Christ or He in us. It is simply impossible to be in Christ and not partake of His joy.

Too often we Christians seek to heed this command not by possessing joy but by professing it. We pretend joy, adding to our failure to achieve joy the sin of hypocrisy. We move through our days like clowns, with painted smiles. We seek to fulfill an image of joyful Christian living, masking reality.

Our options, however, are not merely either a false joy or an honest misery. We cannot excuse a sour disposition with an atonement of honesty. The third option is what Paul commands, real joy.

In John's Gospel Jesus expounded His declaration that He is the vine and we are the branches: "These things I have spoken to you, that My joy may remain in you, and that your joy may be full" (15:11).

This text indicates that the joy of the Christian is not the natural joy of human life. It is a supernatural joy insofar as it has a supernatural source. It is the work of Christ within us. Though Jesus spoke of His joy being in us, it is still *our* joy once it is in us. He is its source and its power, but it is still our joy. Jesus also spoke of the end or purpose of His joy remaining in us, namely that our joy may be full. The term "full" speaks of a degree, in this case an ultimate degree. There is no more joy than full joy. Yet we can experience partial joy or less than full joy, not because there are fluctuations in Jesus' joy but because there are fluctuations in the degree of our abiding in Christ. We cannot fall out of Christ, but in the process of sanctification we experience greater and/or lesser degrees of clinging closely to Him. Here our wills are important in that we are called to abide in Christ. There are things we are to do such as making diligent use of the means of grace. We are to abide in His Word, be constant in prayer, remain faithful in worship, all of which yield a greater intensity of the joy of Christ.

In Galatians Paul admonished us to walk in the Spirit. Failure to walk in the Spirit has consequences. Walking in the Spirit also has consequences. These consequences the Apostle called fruit. Fruit is something that is produced, a by-product of labor, planting, cultivating, and the rest. To be sure, it is the necessary consequence of being in Christ. One cannot be a Christian and have no fruit. Indeed all Christians yield some measure of all the fruit of the Spirit. It is not that one receives the fruit of love and another the fruit of joy. All the fruits are to be manifest in all Christians.

The degree of the manifestation of the fruit of the Spirit may vary from

Christian to Christian and even episodically in the individual Christian's life. The fruit is produced by the Holy Spirit. But the fruit of the Spirit is part of the Spirit's work of sanctification. Sanctification is not a monergistic work, it is synergistic: It involves and requires the cooperation of the believer. We are working out our salvation while at the same time God is working within us.

All of our labor in sanctification would yield no fruit if God were not working in us. Ultimately it is His fruit in that He is the source of it and power for it. But the full measure of the fruit of the Spirit does require that we work. We are to work not casually or occasionally. Our labor is to be done in fear and trembling. This indicates a most sober and serious work. It is intensive and diligent. This cooperative work yields fruit, the second of which mentioned by Paul is joy.

The joy we receive is a joy that rejoices in truth, rejoices in adversity, and discovers its impetus in our delight in God Himself and in our names being found written in the Lamb's Book of Life.

THE END OF
ALL DISPUTE

AUGUST 1995

———

T THE END OF HIS life Joshua called the people of Israel together for a solemn assembly. It was the occasion of his departure from this world and the occasion for the people to renew their covenant with God. It was here that Joshua uttered his famous words, "And if it seems evil to you to serve the LORD, choose for yourselves this day whom you will serve . . . but as for me and my house, we will serve the LORD" (Josh. 24:15).

Before he made this famous utterance Joshua brought the history of God's covenant relationship to His people up to date. He said: "Behold this day I am going the way of all the earth. And you know in all your hearts and in all your souls that not one thing has failed of all the good things which the LORD your God spoke concerning you. All have come to pass for you; not one word of them has failed" (Josh. 23:14).

Joshua reminded the people of the promise God made centuries earlier to Abraham. It had taken three centuries for the people of God to realize the occupation of the promised land. Though God's promises tarried long on their fulfillment they came to pass. Not a single word of God's promises failed.

I have said many times that if I were ever incarcerated and shut up in solitary confinement the one book I would want in my possession would be the Bible. If my options were reduced to one book of the Bible it would be Hebrews. If I were further limited to one chapter it would be Genesis 15. If I had but one verse to read day after day it would be Genesis 15:17: "And it came to pass, when the sun went down and it was dark, that behold, there appeared a smoking oven and a burning torch that passed between those pieces."

When I tell people that this is the verse I would want to comfort me in times of trouble they look at me as if I had taken leave of my senses. "Why," they ask, "would you take comfort in a smoking oven and a burning torch?"

The answer lies in the significance of what is going on here. It is not so much on the *what* of the oven and torch but in the *Who* of them and the *why* of what they are doing.

The smoking oven and burning torch are symbols. More specifically they are theophanies. A theophany is a visible manifestation of the invisible God. Perhaps the most well-known theophany in the Old Testament is God's appearance in the burning bush in the Midianite wilderness. God appeared variously as a pillar of cloud or pillar of smoke. He is referred to as an "all-consuming fire" (Heb. 12:29).

The oven and torch represent the presence of God. The chief importance of Genesis 15:17 is found in what God is doing. He is passing between the pieces of animals that have been hewn in two. It is a solemn ceremony, perhaps the solemnest of all ceremonies, the ceremony of covenant with Abraham and his seed. In covenants of the ancient Near East the sovereign in the treaty had the power and authority vested in him. The lion's share of obligation rested in the vassals. But in the covenant in Genesis 15 God takes upon Himself a solemn obligation to keep His promise to Abraham.

Abraham had asked God the question every Christian asks at one time or another, "How can I know for sure?" Abraham had faith, indeed he is called the father of the faithful, yet even his faith was mixed with an element of doubt. He was trusting God but he yearned to be sure God would do what He said He would do.

Then came the strange ceremony in which the oven and torch passed between the pieces. The *New Geneva Study Bible* offers this note: "As other Near Eastern texts and Jeremiah 34:10 indicate, by passing between the torn animals (signifying the punishment due others who break the covenant), God invokes a self-maledictory oath or curse upon Himself should He fail to keep His covenant. Because He can swear by no higher authority, God swears by Himself to keep the covenantal terms."

Here God says to Abraham in graphic terms, "Here's how you can know for sure—I will swear a solemn oath to you. If I do not keep My promise to you may I be torn in two even as these animals have been torn asunder." God swears by Himself, by His solemn divine nature. He is saying that if He doesn't keep His word that curse will come upon Himself. His immutable nature will suffer mutation. His indivisible being will be divided. The light of His own countenance will be shrouded in darkness. God puts His own deity on the line to give Abraham assurance.

This event is in view when the author of Hebrews declares: "For men indeed swear by the greater, and an oath for confirmation is for them an end of all dispute. Thus God, determining to show more abundantly to the heirs of promise the immutability of His counsel, confirmed it by an oath. That by two immutable things, in which it is impossible for God to lie, we might have strong consolation, who have fled for refuge to lay hold of the hope set before us. This hope we have as an anchor of the soul, both sure and steadfast, and which enters the Presence behind the veil, where the forerunner has entered for us, even Jesus, having become High Priest forever according to the order of Melchizedek" (Heb. 6:16–20).

The strong consolation given to Abraham is given also to us. This consolation rests upon the immutability of God, which immutability makes it impossible for God's word of promise to fail. If something is impossible then manifestly it cannot happen. For God to break His promise, which He sealed with a vow, He would have to lie. But He cannot lie. He is incapable of lying. It is impossible for Him to lie. With all His power, His very omnipotence, there is a limit. There is something He cannot do. He cannot lie. He cannot break His covenant promise. Herein is the anchor of our soul.

EXPERIENCE ET AL.

SEPTEMBER 1995

———

T HE AXIOM GOES: "A PERSON with an experience is never at the mercy of a person with an argument." While we're at the business of citing cultural folklore we might as well quote another one: "If you repeat a lie often enough people will begin to believe it."

These popular adages all speak to the question of the relationship between passion and reason. Let us examine them *seriatim*.

1. A Person with an Experience Is Never at the Mercy of a Person with an Argument

This adage assumes yet another, namely that experience is the best teacher. Indeed experience is a valuable tutor. It serves as the threshold from the theoretical to the practical, from the abstract to the concrete. Experience provides the nuances drawn from the complexities of real life. But there are different kinds of experiences. Experience may refer to empirical or sensory validation or verification of a theory, or its falsification. In criminal investigations circumstantial evidence may suggest a certain theory, which theory may be verified or falsified by eye witness testimony or hard evidence. Or consider the case of Roger Bannister. The theory was that it was impossible for a human being to run a mile in less than four minutes. Bannister had an experience that refuted the theory. Later his experience was confirmed by many others.

These illustrations seem to verify the adage that a man with an experience is never at the mercy of a man with the argument. Such a conclusion would be premature. Indeed, there are circumstances in which experience outweighs argument, particularly when the argument rests on speculation. The operative word in the adage however, is the word "never." There are times when experience is trumped by a sound argument. This is particularly true when the debate concerns personal experience versus a sound understanding of the Word of God.

I once was approached by a sweet lady who said to me, "Dr. Sproul, I have a problem. I am married to a man who is a nice person, a good provider, and a kind companion. But he is not a Christian. He doesn't share the most important thing in my life with me. So after thirty years of marriage I couldn't take it anymore and I left him. Now he calls me every day and begs me to come back. What is God's will for me?"

I told the woman that she had no biblical grounds for leaving her husband and that it was her duty to return to him, citing Paul's exhortations in 1 Corinthians. Suddenly this sweet woman became enraged with me and said bitterly, "What do you know about it? You don't have to live with him!"

I replied, "Ma'am, you didn't ask me what I would do if I were in your shoes. Perhaps I would have backed out long before you did. You asked me about the will of God, and that is clear in this matter. Your experience is not a license to disobey God."

The woman calmed down and finally acknowledged that she was asking God to make an exception in her case. She repented and went back to her husband.

This was an isolated case but one that is duplicated every day among many Christians who would elevate experience over the Word of God. When God's law doesn't fit our experience, something has to give. Too often it is the law of God that is negotiated. When this occurs we take refuge in the court of public opinion or in the latest dicta of psychological research or sociological surveys. What is customary in the culture becomes normative for us. The collective experience of fallen humanity begins to outweigh the wisdom and authority of God.

Experience is a *good* teacher. But experience is not the best teacher. The best teacher, obviously, is God. God alone instructs *sub species aeternitatis* from the vantage point of eternity and out of the fount of His omniscience.

I am amazed at the number of times I have heard Christians declare that the Spirit had led them to do things Scripture clearly forbids, or that they had prayed about a matter and God gave them peace about their decision to act, which action was contrary to the law of God. This involves nothing less than slander against the Holy Ghost, to appeal to Him and His guidance as an excuse for sin. It's one thing to say, "The devil made me do it," quite another to appeal to the Spirit of Holiness Himself as the One who incites us to evil.

Christians quickly learn that one of the most powerful manipulation devices designed to squelch any question about one's behavior is to exclaim, "The Spirit led me to this . . ." Who wants to challenge the authority of the Holy Ghost? Yet the Scriptures indicate that it is the work of the Holy Ghost to lead us to holiness, not to sin, ever. "Rhapsody without realism is not Christ-like, and it is a failure in holiness rather than a form of it" (J.I. Packer, *Rediscovering Holiness*, p. 164).

2. If You Tell a Lie Often Enough People Will Begin to Believe It

One of the most common informal fallacies of logic is the *argumentum ad populum*. This is an argument based on an appeal to public opinion, the assumption that fifty thousand Frenchmen can't be wrong. In reality, fifty thousand Frenchmen, Americans, or Italians can be wrong and often are wrong. Truth cannot be determined by counting noses.

I once conducted an experiment in one of my college philosophy courses. We were discussing epistemology, or the science of knowing. I asked the class, "How many of you believe that all life on this planet has evolved from a single cell?" Out of about forty students in the class all but three raised their hands in the affirmative. I asked the students to give me the arguments that persuaded them of their conviction. The only "argument" I was able to elicit from them was, "This is what my teacher told me."

This is not to say that no arguments can be offered in favor of macro-evolution. My experiment was not about evolution; it was about critical evaluation of arguments. I wondered how many of their teachers were merely repeating what their teachers had proclaimed to them. Proclamation by itself is not an argument for anything.

We are all susceptible to this sort of thing. We must frequently turn the critical guns inward and aim them at ourselves as we ask ourselves why we believe what we believe.

Experience must always be interpreted. The meaning or significance of an experience must be understood in light of objective reality and rational analysis. Experiential religion is a slave to the emotions and must always be subjected to the interpretation and evaluation of the teaching of biblical principles. The Christian who lives by experience alone is doomed to being tossed to and fro with every wind of doctrine and tends to be only as strong as the intensity of feelings drawn from his most recent experience. Christians are free to enjoy the pleasure of spiritual experience but we are called to live not by feeling but by every word that proceeds from the mouth of God.

A MAN FOR ALL SEASONS

OCTOBER 1995

———

O F ALL THE FAMOUS THEOLOGIANS of church history, the titans of knowledge upon whose shoulders we stand, none has been more maligned or vilified than John Calvin. The public caricature of Calvin portrays him as nothing less than a monster, a mean-spirited ogre who ruled Geneva with an iron hand, sent poor Michael Servetus to his death, and introduced a diabolical view of predestination to the church. If Christ's beatific promise applies, "Blessed are you when they revile and persecute you, and say all kinds of evil against you falsely for My sake. Rejoice and be exceedingly glad, for great is your reward in heaven," then John Calvin needs a tractor trailer to cart around his heavenly reward.

When I consider the great theologians of the church, I think immediately of my list of the top five: St. Augustine, St. Thomas Aquinas, Martin Luther, John Calvin, and Jonathan Edwards. These are the giants with which God has gifted His church. They comprise the all time all-star team in the roll call of theologians.

Each of these men had a distinctive personality. Each brought to the theological arena different strengths and weaknesses. They were not cookie cutter copies of each other. Three of the five were gifted with keen philosophical minds: Augustine, Aquinas, and Edwards. Their intellectual power in probing abstract metaphysical concerns rank them among the top philosophers of western civilization.

Augustine was the dominant Christian thinker of the first millennium of church history. He worked under the disadvantage of not having someone like himself to go before him. He blazed trails where no pioneers had previously trod.

Aquinas was the dominant theologian of the Middle Ages. His monumental works, the *Summae*, are of lasting value to the church. Aquinas seemed almost superhuman. His penetrating thought and combined grasp of philosophy and theology rightly earned him the title conferred upon him by the Roman Catholic Church, *Doctor Angelicus.*

Luther was a man of great passion. Erudite and highly skilled in biblical thought and philology, he was a master of vignettes of insight. His perceptions, though not always systematic, were brilliant in their clarity and lucid in their penetration. He was a great leader of men who mixed the ability of dealing at the academic level and communicating to the popular masses as well as to children.

Edwards, the least feted among my top five, was perhaps most brilliant of them all. He is second only to Calvin in terms of being vilified, portrayed as a sadistic, narrow-minded Puritan, preoccupied with hell and the wrath of God. This is the image garnered from English anthologies that expose students to one sermon, "Sinners in the Hands of an Angry God," perhaps the most misunderstood sermon in history.

Calvin was perhaps the most gifted systematician of the "big five." His knowledge of Scripture and theology was encyclopedic. He was known to quote lengthy passages from the church Fathers, especially from Augustine, from memory at the drop of a hat. His ability in debate was unmatched. His literary output was phenomenal. His literary skill matched his theological genius. Reading Calvin at times is like reading lyric poetry. The majesty of his language was appropriate to the loftiness of the subjects he treated. He was a man intoxicated by the majesty of God. No theologian, before or since, had such a grasp of His beauty and loveliness. This marks everything that Calvin wrote and did.

If anything drove Calvin's theology and ministry it was his love for the excellence of God and conversely his abhorrence of all forms of idolatry. His legacy includes a revolution of Christian worship marked by a theocentric focus on the praise and reverence for the nature and character of God. His love for the law of God reflects his love for the Being whose character is expressed in that law. Calvin's work of reform was designed to bring Christian truth and Christian living together, molded by a deep spiritual affection. He was no mere moralist but a profound thinker whose concern for true spirituality earned him the sobriquet, "The theologian of the Holy Spirit."

The caricatures of Calvin as a dour, stiff, cold tyrant are drawn by those who have never plumbed the depths of his thought. To counteract these distorted images I often have my students read his chapter on prayer in the *Institutes* before they read anything else of Calvin. Here they get a glimpse of a man as they eavesdrop on a soul naked before God.

The fame or infamy of Calvin with respect to the doctrine of predestination is a strange thing. There is certainly nothing in Calvin's doctrine of predestination that was not first in Luther. Luther wrote more, and more polemically, about this doctrine than did Calvin, and referred to the doctrine of election as the *cor ecclesiae*, the very "heart of the church." But Luther's trusted comrade, Melanchthon, later modified Luther's view, leaving Calvin to expound the doctrine more consistently. Calvin echoed not only Luther but Augustine in his exposition of the biblical and especially Pauline doctrine of predestination.

Calvin's theology was formative to a broad spectrum of church confessions. His teaching is clearly seen in the Thirty-Nine Articles of the Church of England, which formed the historic theological foundation of Anglican and Episcopal thought. His theology was virtually codified in the Scots Confession and the Westminster Confession, forming the bedrock of historic Presbyterianism and Reformed and Congregational Christianity. The influence is likewise apparent in historic Baptist confessions and creeds.

Modern Evangelicalism owes an enormous debt to John Calvin. Dispensationalism, which is a serious distortion of historical Calvinism, nevertheless grew out of the thought of men deeply influenced by the Reformer. Even James Arminius was a child of Calvin. Modern neo-orthodox thought, chiefly through the work of Karl Barth, appeared on the theological scene as a kind of neo-Calvinism (though some have argued that the *neo* would be better spelled without the *e*).

Calvin's disciples include John Knox, Francis Turretin, the Puritans such as John Owen, Richard Baxter, Jonathan Edwards, as well as such modern theologians as B.B. Warfield, Charles Hodge, James H. Thornwell, Robert Dabney, J. Gresham Machen, G.C. Berkouwer, Cornelius Van Til,

Gordon Clark, Francis Schaeffer, J.I. Packer, John Gerstner, Roger Nicole, James Boice, et al.

Beyond Calvin's legacy in the world of theology he also exercised an uncommon influence on the shaping of modern culture, government, and civilization. Max Weber in *The Spirit of Capitalism* documents Calvin's influence not only in the shaping of modern democratic forms of government modeled after Calvin's Geneva, but also in the emergence of free market capitalism as the basic structure of economics in the free world.

Calvin is also seen as the inspiration for the formative influence of the so-called Puritan work ethic. Calvin's sweeping doctrine of Providence influenced generations of Christians who saw their labor as a vocation from God and their diligence as an offering to God. The fruits of their labor were received as from His gracious hand, giving impetus to thanksgiving and due diligence in the stewardship of worldly goods.

American society, particularly with respect to its strengths, is unthinkable apart from this extraordinary individual. Scholar, teacher, pastor, reformer, administrator, author, civic leader—John Calvin, in exercising these multitude of gifts, has been to the church of Christ a man for all seasons.

WILLY NILLY

NOVEMBER 1995

TWO MEN MET EACH OTHER in the church parking lot after morning worship. Their names were Roger Rational and Sammy Sensual. The following conversation ensued:

Sammy: "Good morning, Roger. How do you feel?"

Roger: "I feel fine, Sammy. What do you think?"

Sammy: "I don't. I don't really believe in thinking. I believe that thinking is dangerous to the soul."

Roger: "How can you believe that without first thinking about it? Indeed, how can you believe anything without thinking about it?"

Sammy: "I believe it because that's what I feel. It has nothing to do with thinking."

Roger: "What has nothing to do with thinking?"

Sammy: "What I believe."

Roger: "Then how do you know what it is you believe?"

Sammy: "I told you, I *feel* it."

Roger: "Where do you feel it, in your elbow?"

Sammy: "Of course not; I feel it in my heart."

Roger: "I see. In which part of your heart? The left ventricle? The aorta?"

Sammy: "I don't know."

Roger: "Don't you mean that you don't *feel*? If you don't think then you cannot know."

Sammy: "That's right, that's what I said, I don't *know*."

Roger: "But you just said, 'That's *right*.' How do you know what's *right*?"

Sammy: "I don't know what's right. I feel that it is right. That's good enough for me."

Roger: "There you go again. You are talking about the *good*. How do you know what is good without thinking about it?"

Sammy: "That's easy. If it feels good it is good. I don't have to think about it."

Roger: "Let me see if I understand what you are saying. You are saying that what you believe, what is right, and what is good are all matters of feeling?"

Sammy: "Bingo! You understand exactly what I am saying."

Roger: "Good. I'm glad that I am understanding what you are saying. That makes me feel good."

Sammy: "See, now you are getting with it. You are starting to feel."

Roger: "Yes, but my feeling good is a result of my understanding. But I wonder if you can understand what I am saying."

Sammy: "Of course I understand what you are saying. You are saying that what you believe, what is right, and what is good is a matter of thinking, not just feeling."

Roger: "Bingo! Now you're thinking, not just feeling; else how could you understand what I am saying?"

Sammy: "Oh no you don't. You're trying to trap me. I *understand* what you are saying because I am in touch with your feelings. That's how I see what you mean."

Roger: "Do you mean when you say that you see what I mean that it is something you do with your eyes?"

Sammy: "Don't be silly. When I say 'I see,' I mean 'I feel.' "

Roger: "You sound like the man who went to the symphony to see what the orchestra would sound like."

Sammy: "What's wrong with that?"

Roger: "Well, going to the symphony to see what the orchestra sounds like is like listening to a sunset to hear what it looks like."

Sammy: "That's absurd. You can't 'hear' what something looks like."

Roger: "Now we're getting somewhere. You recognized an absurdity when I uttered it. To recognize absurdities requires logical thought, doesn't it?"

Sammy: "Of course not. I said it was absurd because it feels absurd to me."

Roger: "Why does it feel absurd? You said you can't hear what something looks like. Isn't that a conclusion drawn from thinking about the meaning of words?"

Sammy: "Words can mean whatever you want them to mean. And to want something is a matter of desire, and desire is a feeling."

Roger: "Sounds like you've given some thought to what a desire is and what the word 'want' means."

Sammy: "You keep trying to twist my words. You're really reacting with feelings but you just won't admit it. You are trying to cloak your feelings with some kind of abstract 'thought.' "

Roger: "Do you think so?"

Sammy: "No, I *feel* so. That's what I perceive. It's a matter of perception."

Roger: "Is there no such thing as objective reality?"

Sammy: "No, only perceptions and feelings."

Roger: "Do you believe that Jesus is the Son of God and your Savior?"

Sammy: "Yes, I surely believe that."

Roger: "Is that just a feeling or perception, or is He *really* the Son of God?"

Sammy: "It doesn't matter. What matters to me is that is what I perceive Him to be. Since I perceive that Jesus is the Son of God, then for me He is the Son of God."

Roger: "But what if someone else perceives that Hulk Hogan* is the Son of God and the Savior of the world?"

Sammy: "Then, for that person Hulk Hogan is the Savior. It's all a matter of perception."

Roger: "So, there is no such thing as objective truth?"

Sammy: "No, only feelings and perceptions."

Roger: "Is it true then that there is no such thing as objective truth?"

Sammy: "That's how I perceive it and how I feel about it."

Roger: "Do you perceive that it is objectively true that there is no objective truth?"

---

* Hulk Hogan (1953–; real name Terry Bollea) is an American retired professional wrestler who is widely considered the most popular wrestler of the 1980s.

Sammy: "Who cares? Objective truth doesn't matter. It's relationships that matter."

Roger: "What do you mean?"

Sammy: "I mean that what really counts is how people feel about each other and how they treat each other."

Roger: "Does the Bible give us truth about how we *ought* to treat each other?"

Sammy: "I feel that it does."

Roger: "Is that truth objective? Must we not first understand how we ought to treat each other before we can move to acting properly?"

Sammy: "No. Don't you see what you are doing? You are arguing with me about truth and that doesn't make me feel very good. I'll grant you that you have done so cleverly, with wit, but I am not amused."

Roger: "Ah, but you are 'a-mused.' 'Amuse' comes from the Latin *a* meaning 'not' and *muse* meaning 'think.' It's not me that's amusing; you're amusing yourself."

Sammy: "So what's wrong with 'amusement,' with not thinking? Remember Paul extolled love while condemning knowledge. You need to give your mind a rest and let your feelings go."

Roger: "Go where? When our minds don't direct our feelings someone else's mind will, or someone's will will. If I am to love love I must do so because my mind tells me that Scripture calls me to love love. Without my mind to guide me I won't love what God commands me to love, but will love willy-nilly."

Sammy: "You know Willy? He's one of my best friends. . . ."

MOTHER OF GOD

DECEMBER 1995

———

Hail Mary, full of grace, blessed art thou among women, and blessed is the fruit of thy womb, Jesus. Holy Mary, mother of God, pray for us sinners, now and in the hour of our death. Amen.

THESE EXCERPTS FROM THE ROSARY ARE an important dimension of the devotional life of millions of adherents of Roman Catholicism. The first section is taken virtually from Scripture itself, reflecting Elizabeth's words to Mary on the occasion of Mary's visit to her during their pregnancies (see article on pp. 8ff.). The second is an appeal to Mary's intercession for sinners both in the present and at the time of death.

In the Rosary, Mary is addressed as the "Mother of God." This title has its roots in the creedal formulations of the ancient church wherein Mary is called *Theotokos* or "mother of God" (more technically the "bearer of God"). The intent of this formulation was not so much designed to tell us something about Mary, but to make a bold affirmation concerning the child that she bore. Mary is the mother of God not in the sense that Jesus derived His divine nature from her but in the sense that Mary was the mother of a child who indeed is God incarnate. Given the church's full confession of the deity of Christ it is a perfectly appropriate title for the woman who was His earthly mother.

To esteem Mary as the mother of God is the common heritage of all Christendom and should not be a point of dispute among us. That Mary performs a role of intercessor *is* a point of dispute between Roman Catholicism and historic Protestantism.

The issue of the veneration of Mary has engendered a doctrinal conflict of long standing. It reached severe proportions during the 16th-century Reformation. However, the dispute was not limited to or contained within that era. Many events have transpired since that period to aggravate the problem. Most of the Mariological decrees that separate Protestants and Catholics have been issued in the past 200 years, long after the Reformation. De fide declarations and papal encyclicals regarding Mary have decreed such doctrines as (1) the Immaculate Conception of Mary, (2) the Sinlessness of Mary, (3) the Perpetual Virginity of Mary, (4) the Bodily Assumption of Mary into Heaven, and (5) the Coronation of Mary as Queen of Heaven.

It should be noted that when Rome officially decrees a particular doctrine they do not intend to declare something to be presently true that was not always the truth. That is, though the Encyclicals that define these doctrines are of recent origin, they are considered to make clear what has always been the faith and teaching of the church.

In the 16th century Calvin and the magisterial Reformers objected to the veneration of Mary by Rome. The Reformers accused Rome of promoting an idolatrous veneration of Mary. Rome defended the veneration of Mary against the charge of *Mariolatry* by distinguishing between *Mariology* and *Mariolatry*. The suffix *ology* refers to a word or teaching about Mary whereas the suffix *olatry* indicates a worship of Mary. Rome denied the practice of the worship of Mary. Rome distinguishes between the Greek words *latria* and *dulia*. *Latria* refers to worship while *dulia* refers to service. *Latria* (or worship) is not to be given to the saints, to Mary, or to idols. The word idolatry comes from *idol-latria* or the worship of idols.

Rome insists that *latria* (or worship) is not to be given to saints or to Mary. *Dulia* (or service) is offered to the saints in their veneration. What is to be accorded Mary is *hyper-dulia* or "hyper-service." She is to receive supreme veneration, higher than that accorded to the saints, but lower than the worship given to God.

Calvin objected to this calling it a distinction without a difference. The shrines that appear throughout the world to Mary, the private backyard grottoes of the people, and the customary devotion to Mary that is central to Roman Catholic worship obscures the distinction between *hyper-dulia* and *latria*. To be sure Mary is worthy of honor in the church, but the line between honor and worship must be kept so clean and clear that we cannot miss it.

This subject was a major concern at the Second Vatican Council. Vatican II saw a sharp debate between two wings of the Roman Catholic Church. The two parties were distinguished as the *Maximalists* and the *Minimalists* and tended to follow the lines of struggle in the church between the Western wing and the Latin wing. The Western wing, being influenced by the so-called *theologie nouvelle* (the new or progressive theology), was more inclined to the minimalist view, while the Latin wing (Italy, part of France, Portugal, Spain, Latin America, etc.) was more conservative and favored the maximalist view.

One issue that divided the camps focused on the question of Mary's role as co-redemptrix. Does Mary occupy a place beside her Son in the work of redeeming fallen sinners? Thomas Aquinas, the Doctor Angelicus of the church, had centuries before answered in the negative calling attention to Mary's words in the *Magnificat*, "My soul doth magnify the Lord and my spirit doth rejoice in God my *Savior*." Thomas saw that Mary's Son was also Mary's Savior because Mary, like other human beings, was a sinner. This view was given, however, before the Roman Church declared the sinlessness of Mary. The doctrine of the Immaculate Conception of Mary does not refer to the virgin birth of Jesus or His conception in the womb of Mary. Rather, the Immaculate Conception refers to Mary's conception in the womb of her mother, St. Anne, in order to insure Mary's freedom from original sin.

The issue of the so-called Eve-Mary Parallel was also discussed. John XXIII insisted that Mariological matters be treated under the heading of *Ecclesiology* rather than *theology*, a subtle but important distinction. The Eve-Mary Parallel stands in analogy to the Adam-Christ parallel. As in Adam ruination came into the world and in Christ came redemption, so as in Eve destruction came into the world so in Mary salvation came into the world.

Crucial to the Eve-Mary Parallel is the Roman Catholic concept of "Mary's Fiat." This refers to Mary's response to Gabriel's annunciation to her of the impending Virgin Birth of Jesus. When Gabriel made his announcement Mary responded with the words, "Let it be to me according to your word." In the Latin Vulgate the "Let it be" is rendered as *fiat*, the imperative form of the verb "to be." An imperative indicates a command. Rome historically interprets this to mean that Gabriel was subject to the authoritative command of Mary. The whole plan of redemption rested upon Mary's agreement to the announcement. By her command the plan was set in motion.

Protestant interpretation is radically different. The Greek text (which preceded and was the basis for the Latin) contains not an imperative verb but an optative which expresses a desire rather than a command. It indicates Mary's humble submission to the will of God. The whole demeanor of Mary in the narrative is one of acquiescence to the will of her God.

Mary, as the mother of God, the bearer and nurturer of our Lord, serves as a marvelous model of godliness. She is to be emulated but not venerated, honored but not worshiped. She bore for us our Redeemer, and her life points us to Him as our one and only redeemer and intercessor.

OUR STRONG FATHER

JANUARY 1996

———

MY SON IS THE EDITOR OF *Tabletalk*. Each month he gives me a sheet of written instructions for my articles. He is a tough taskmaster, not unlike Pharaoh, who is loath to give me straw for my quota of bricks. This month's instructions included the comment: "I'd hate to have to write on the frustrations of having your father work for you reluctantly. You need to be more zealous for these articles than I ever was about tending your yard."

The yard reference was provoked by a comment I made to him recently. My son now owns his own home. I noticed that he is inordinately fussy, indeed punctilious, about the care he gives in manicuring his yard. I said to him, "Why didn't you give this kind of tender-loving-care to my yard when you used to cut the grass as a boy? I guess things change when you are tending your own yard rather than someone else's. It must be pride of ownership." So now it's turnabout and fair play.

I write my articles and books in the men's locker room where I play golf. I have four lockers, one for my golf gear and three for my books. It is nice to have a not-so-quiet place where I have a constant supply of iced tea and a huge table to spread out my stuff and work. I am deaf to the rowdy by-play that goes on around me, even though it is often directed at me.

I live in two different worlds, the world of church and kingdom, and the secular world that finds its microcosm in the men's locker room. It is an exercise in contrast, yet one in which I find heartening intrusions of grace wherein the distinctions between sacred and profane are sometimes blurred.

I love the guys who are the denizens of the locker room. They are men in every sense of the word, and for them this place is their sanctuary. There is "Big Al" with his ponytail, gruff voice, and perpetual twinkle in his eye; "Rifle" the Polish golfer who endures endless ethnic jokes; "Fultie" the South African "bull" who is a regular on the PGA Tour; "The Buck" (a.k.a. "Wild Bill," the former NFL player); and a host of others including "Tommy," "Fearless," "Pudge," "Chuckles," "X" (whose name is really Malcombe), "John," "Pat," "Doc," and "Guy." Guy is incorrigible. His favorite pastime is teasing R.C. Then there is "Lee" who erupts every time I walk in the room. He raises his hands over his head and shouts, "Praise the Lord," and likens me to Benny Hinn. Lee's nickname is "Home Doggy" (figure that one out).

The locker room is the quintessential arena for male bonding. It is the place where "Skippers" and the boys all call each other "pards." Every day golf games are made, bets are arranged by strokes, first tee arguments are settled, and Ron is heard to shout, "Call Rangoon," when he lays his cards on the table for gin. The locker room/grill room is off limits to women. It is a feminist's worst nightmare. It is a place of refuge where men are men, with all that that means, good and bad. It is a place for hard drinking, hard cursing, where men act like kids and are as rowdy as sailors on shore leave. It is also the place the guys refer to as "R.C.'s office," a term they use when they answer the corner phone.

Recently I walked into this place after being on the road for three weeks. Things were strangely quiet as the guys were absorbed in card games. Doc Albert looked up and saw me enter. In a sing-song voice he loudly declared, "He's back!" After a perfectly timed Jack Bennyesque pause, he added in the same cadence, "Who cares?"

This is how I am treated in this place. I love every minute of it. These men tease me to death. They call me "Preacher" and make me the butt of a thousand jokes. They squirt me with water pistols while I'm writing and dump ice down my shirt if I turn my back to them. Yet I know they do care. And several of them come regularly to a weekly Bible study I teach, which was started at their request.

Men long for the love of a woman. But what they are sheepish to admit is that they also long for the love and concern of their comrades. Most of them are fathers. All of them are sons. All of them want the caring love of their fathers. Not all of them received it. They all wanted it; they all needed it. But they all didn't get it.

I was one of the fortunate ones. No man ever displayed more care and affection for me as my father did. Like most boys, my father was my first and greatest hero. Though he left this world almost forty years ago (Oops, I was just interrupted. "Pudge" walked by and hollered, "What's happening, 'Rev'?"), I have vivid memories of him and evoke them frequently. These memories are a rich legacy that endures. One such memory jumps to my mind at this moment:

I had just returned from playing baseball. As I approached our driveway, still in uniform, lugging my bat over my shoulder with my spikes and glove dangling from the end of the bat, my next door neighbor, Mr. Davies, called, "Did you win, Kiner?" I lit up inside, smiled, and said, "Yes, we won." I loved it that he always called me "Kiner," a reference to Pittsburgh's legendary homerun king, Ralph Kiner.

I proceeded down my driveway where my father was standing by our back-yard barbecue pit while thick, juicy steaks were sizzling on the grill. My dad said, "How'd you do?" I said, "Great, Dad, I went three for four, two singles and a double." He replied, "What did you do the other time?" "I struck out." With a mock frown he said, "Struck out!—Then no steak for you for dinner."

I knew he was kidding. I knew he was really pleased, but it was his way to remind me that I still had lots of room for improvement. I knew that he cared. When he died a couple of years later my world fell apart. My anger raged against God for taking my father from me. It was not until I became a Christian that this rage was supplanted by love and delight in my heavenly Father. There are many people who have trouble relating to God as Father. Their earthly fathers were so abusive and uncaring that they flinch when they hear God referred to as "Father." That is not my problem. Though even God cannot completely fill the hollow place left in my soul by the absence of my earthly father, He fills a greater void for me than the world's greatest earthly father could never fill.

God is the supreme Father of care. He loves, chastens, rebukes, corrects, disciplines, and instructs. But above all, He cares. I take umbrage at those who, in their zeal for "political correctness," seek to strip the Bible of its masculine imagery and produce a version of gender-neutral language. This does grave insult to the Holy Spirit, who, without a view toward P.C. language, was pleased to inspire language drawn from fallen humanity, both male and female, that is an adequate vessel to communicate the character of God. Whatever else I may be, I am a man. I was born male and maleness is part of my identity just as femaleness is part of my wife's personal identity. That God is my Father means that He cares for me, that when I ask for bread I will not receive a stone or a scorpion. His arms are strong. He is mighty in battle, a strong fortress for my soul. These terms may be masculine, but they are images of a strength that is tempered by tenderness, virtues every child, boy or girl, long for in their earthly father.

HOLY MOTHER CHURCH

FEBRUARY 1996

———

HISTORIANS ARE NOT CERTAIN WHO said it. The statement has been attributed by some to Cyprian, by others to Augustine. The assertion has survived since the early centuries of Christian history: "Who does not have the church as his mother does not have God as his Father." From its earliest days the church was given the appellation "Mother."

The use of paternal and maternal language is an intriguing phenomenon in religion. The pattern of comparative religion indicates a strong tendency among people to seek transcendent models in both male and female figures. The Greeks had both gods and goddesses in their pantheon. The Egyptians revered Isis, the wife of their ruling god. So the Roman goddess Juno corresponded to the Greek Hera. Mythological deities commonly include a queen as well as a king.

The role of Mary in Roman Catholic religion is significant. She reigns as the "Queen of Heaven," and is the Holy Mother to whom the faithful can go for solace. The recent gnostic apotheosis of "Sophia" provides a rallying point for the feminization of Christianity.

However we respond to these developments, we cannot deny the virtual universal tendency to seek ultimate consolation in some sort of divine maternity. We have all experienced the piercing poignancy that attends the plaintive cry of a child who, in the midst of sobs, says, "I want my mommy." Who of us when we were children did not ever utter these words? Who of us, who are parents, has not heard these words? As a father I recall my own children sobbing them. Nor did I experience jealousy or a sense of rejection when they cried for their mother. I can identify with them and still remember those words as they crossed my own lips. Nor is this a cry restricted to children. It is a matter of record that soldiers mortally wounded in battle often cry out for their mothers in their dying words. Football players when caught in the eye of the TV camera rarely say, "Hi, Dad."

The Bible itself describes God not only in the masculine image of Father but also borrows from feminine imagery at times. Some scholars argue that the Semitic, linguistic roots of the title *El Shaddai* referred to the "multi-breasted one," the One who was capable of providing succor and nourishment to the nation. Jesus Himself, in His lament over Jerusalem, cried, "Oh, Jerusalem, Jerusalem, the one who kills the prophets.... How often I wanted to gather your children together, as a hen gathers her chicks under her wings, but you were not willing!" (Matt. 23:37). The brooding of the Spirit over the primordial waters conjures up a similar maternal image.

In the Bible the supreme feminine image is ascribed not to a goddess or to a female consort of God; it is the image ascribed to the church. Before the church is ever seen as mother, she is first revealed as a bride. In the Old Testament the commonwealth of Israel is the bride of Yahweh. In the New Testament the church is the bride of Christ.

The resulting familial imagery is somewhat strange. God is Father; Christ is the Son. As the Son of God, Christ is then referred to as our Elder Brother. The church is His bride. In the language of family this would then mean that the church is our sister-in-law. But whoever speaks of Holy Sister-in-Law Church? It is rare in family life that younger siblings look to their older brother's wife as an ersatz mother, though at times such a wife may exercise that role.

But we, both men and women, are given the title "Bride of Christ." I am male, yet I am part of a body that is described in feminine terms. What is more strange is that the same entity that is called bride, of which I am a part, is regarded as my mother. I cannot be my own mother.

These images are not the result of a jumbled mass of nonsense or confusion. It is not a matter of nonsense to refer to the church as mother. Though we are born of the Spirit it is chiefly within the cradle of the church where we are birthed into spiritual life. If the church is not our birthplace, it is surely our nursery. It is in her bosom that the means of grace are concentrated. The church nurtures us unto mature faith.

This nurturing function of the church most clearly links it to the maternal image. It is in the church that we are given our spiritual food. We gain strength from the sacraments ministered to us. Through the Word we receive our consolation and the tears of broken hearts are wiped clean. When we are wounded we go to the church for healing.

When someone asks, "Is the church an army or a hospital?" their question posits a false dilemma. It is both. It is an army, called to be the church militant. But no army worthy of the name shoots its own wounded. It is also a hospital, erected by Christ Himself and entrusted with the care of wounded souls.

The church is our *mother*, but it is Christ's *bride*. In this role we are the objects of Christ's affection. We, corporately, are His beloved. Stained and wrinkled, in ourselves we are anything but holy. When we say that the church is holy or refer to her as "holy" mother church, we do so with the knowledge that her holiness is not intrinsic but derived and dependent upon the One who sanctifies her and covers her with the cloak of His righteousness. As the sensitive husband shelters his wife and in chivalrous manner lends his coat to her when she is chilled, so we are clad from on high by a Husband who stops at nothing to defend, protect, and care for His betrothed. His is the ultimate chivalry, a chivalry that no upheaval of earthly custom can eradicate or make passé. This chivalry is not dead because it cannot die.

The bride of Christ is soiled but will one day be presented spotless to the Father by the Son who bought her, who loves her, and who intercedes for her every day. If we love Christ we must also love His bride. If we love Christ we must love His church. For he who does not have the church as his mother does not have God as his Father.

"In biblical terms there is a close connection between values and ethics. It is an ethical concern to adjust our values according to the value standards of God."

—

COUNT THE STARS

MARCH 1996

A N EVENT OCCURRED RECENTLY THAT changed my life forever. Indeed it was not only my life that was changed but the lives of many people who are close to me. This life-changing event was the birth of a baby. Recently my son and daughter-in-law became the parents of a baby boy whose name is Robert Campbell Sproul. Campbell, as he is called, represents the fifth generation of R.C. Sprouls. When he was born I said to my son, "Now I have an heir." He replied, "Perhaps there is something you have forgotten, Dad; you already have an heir." My daughter would be quick to change that from the singular to the plural "heirs."

My son was correct. Now I have another heir, another grandchild. The arrival of this new grandchild will change more than my last will and testament. It will change the entire dynamic of our family relationships. When Campbell was being born his two-year-old sister, Darby, stayed with my wife and me at our home. When we received word of Campbell's arrival we told Darby that she had a new brother. She had little understanding of what that meant. As we traveled to the hospital with Darby we tried to generate excitement about her new brother. When we arrived, Darby was more interested in the elevator than she was in Campbell. Darby didn't realize it but her life would never be the same. Her family had suddenly changed. She was no longer an only child. My son and his wife would also experience a radical change in their lives. There is now another mouth to feed, a child to tutor, a son to love and embrace.

As our modern culture ceases to value families we often hear talk of the crisis of "family values." I notice in the rhetoric a subtle equivocation in the meaning of the word "values." The tendency is to use the term "values" as a synonym for "ethics." But values and ethics are not the same thing. Ethics is concerned with norms, with objective standards of right and wrong. To be sure we live in an age wherein ethics are relativized and reduced from the status of norms to the level of mere preferences. Perhaps this is why it has become easy to slide between values and ethics as if they were identical.

Values have to do with preferences. They are subjective. The subjective theory of value declares that the value of goods and services is determined not by the cost of their production but the worth attributed to them by those who desire them or have a lack of desire for them.

Because values are subjective and ethics are objective we may leap to the conclusion that they are not related. But in biblical terms there is a close connection between values and ethics. It is an ethical concern to adjust our values according to the value standards of God. We ought to value our souls more than the goods of the whole world, our faith more than our reputation.

The crisis of family values begins with how we value people. In biblical categories children were viewed as gifts from God that are of inestimable value. In the Old Testament a large family with a "full quiver" of children was seen as a great blessing. Conversely the barren womb was seen as a great calamity. We see this vividly in the case of Abraham (Gen. 15:1–5):

> After these things the word of the LORD came to Abram in a vision, saying, "Do not be afraid, Abram. I am your shield, your exceedingly great reward."
>
> But Abram said, "Lord GOD, what will You give me, seeing I go childless, and the heir of my house is Eliezer of Damascus?" Then Abram said, "Look, You have given me no offspring; indeed one born in my house is my heir!"
>
> And behold, the word of the LORD came to him, saying, "This one shall not be your heir, but one who will come from your own body shall be your heir." Then He brought him outside and said, "Look now toward heaven, and count the stars if you are able to number them." And He said to him, "So shall your descendants be."

Abraham was one of the wealthiest men of the ancient world. His herds and flocks were huge. When God appeared to him He declared that He would be Abraham's great reward. Abraham's response borders upon cynicism: "What will you give me, seeing I go childless?" This question reveals volumes about Abraham's value system. Despite his riches he felt impoverished because he had no children. His wife was barren. He had goats and sheep, but no descendants. He complained to God that his only heir was a servant who worked for him.

For Abraham the chief component of the patriarchal blessing he was promised (apart from redemption) was the blessing of children and grandchildren. He was to receive a gift from his own loins that would be flesh of his flesh and bone of his bone. Throughout the Old Testament the abundance of children was seen as a manifold blessing from God, while the lack of children a great disaster. Somebody forgot to tell the people of God that the ideal family consisted of a husband, wife, and two children. They were not informed of the niceties of family values by Planned Parenthood.

Recently I was doing a taping for our radio broadcast. Six people in the studio audience indicated that they were from Pittsburgh, the city of my birth and childhood. I asked these people where they were born. They mentioned various different hospitals in the Pittsburgh area. Among the hospitals named was a hospital that enjoyed the reputation years ago of being Pittsburgh's "baby hospital." Of course all of the hospitals had maternity wards but this one hospital specialized in maternity care. Today that has changed. Now that same hospital is known as Pittsburgh's largest abortion mill.

Each year in America one and a half million unborn babies are legally slaughtered. This reflects a major crisis in family values. The chief justification for this modern slaughter of the innocents is that they are "unwanted children." For a child to be unwanted means that a low value is assigned to it. Indeed the value is so low that in the case of one and a half million pregnancies the child conceived in the womb is considered a liability rather than an asset.

Sociologists have explained the radical shift in the value of children from ancient cultures to our own day by virtue of the societal shift from being based in an agrarian economy to an industrial or technological economy. In antiquity a large family, particularly of sons, meant cheap labor in the fields. Now an additional child means an additional economic burden. It means the cost of food and clothes, of braces and college tuition. We have been told that we simply cannot "afford" to have more than two children.

This economic calculus of the relative value of children is an exercise in insanity. Imagine speaking in these terms while living in the wealthiest nation in the history of the world. Imagine this value judgment in a land where poor people enjoy more amenities and luxuries than most of the kings who ever lived enjoyed. What would Henry VIII have given for an electric light or a flush toilet? Beyond this economic madness is the consideration of the relative degree of joy and meaning we gain from our children over against our disposable goods. For most of us our children are not considered disposable goods. Most of us would not hesitate to divest ourselves of our cars or stereo sets in order to save the life of one of our children. Cars and the like may give us some measure of comfort and pleasure, but can they ever take the place of the joy we receive from the hugs of our kids?

I like people. I've met thousands of them in my lifetime. I enjoy my friends. But there is nothing like family. The closest people to me in all the world are my family. My greatest griefs have been the loss of family members to death. My greatest joys have been found in my relationships with my family.

The arrival of Robert Campbell changes my life. I believe it is a change for the good. The bundle in which he was wrapped when he came home from the hospital is indeed a bundle of joy. It came not from the stork but from the Creator of storks. Campbell already occupies a place of inestimable value in my life.

CAPTIVE HEARTS, CAPTIVE CHURCH

APRIL 1996

D URING THE PROTESTANT REFORMATION Martin Luther wrote a little book that was highly controversial. It was a massive critique of the Roman Catholic sacramental system, entitled *The Babylonian Captivity of the Church*. Luther likened the oppressive regime of Rome in the sixteenth century with that of Israel's plight while held captive by the rivers of Babylon.

I have often wondered how Luther would assess our own age and the state of the church today. I suspect if he wrote for our time his book would be entitled *The Pelagian Captivity of the Church*. I suspect this would be the case because Luther considered the most important book he ever wrote to be his classic *magnum opus*, *The Bondage of the Will* (*De Servo Arbitrio*). This work focused on the issue of the enslaved will of man as a result of original sin. It was a response to the *Diatribe* of Desiderius Erasmus of Rotterdam. In the translator's introduction to this work it is said that Luther "saw Erasmus as an enemy of God and the Christian religion, an Epicurean and a serpent, and he was not afraid to say so."

I think Luther would see the great threat to the church today in terms of Pelagianism because of what transpired after the Reformation. Historians have said that though Luther won the battle with Erasmus in the sixteenth century he lost it in the seventeenth century and was demolished in the eighteenth century by the conquest achieved by the Pelagianism of the Enlightenment. He would see the church today as being in the grasp of Pelagianism with this adversary of the faith having a stranglehold on us.

Pelagianism in its pure form was first articulated by the man for whom it is named, a fourth century British monk. Pelagius engaged in a fierce debate with St. Augustine, a debate provoked by Pelagius' reaction to

307

Augustine's prayer: "Command what Thou will, and grant what Thou dost command." Pelagius insisted that moral obligation necessarily implies moral ability. If God requires men to live perfect lives then men must have the ability to live perfect lives. This led Pelagius to his wholesale denial of original sin. He insisted that Adam's fall affected Adam alone; there is no such thing as an inherited fallen nature that afflicts humanity. He further claimed grace is not necessary for salvation, that man is able to be saved by his works apart from the assistance of grace. Grace may *facilitate* obedience, but it is not a necessary condition for it.

Augustine triumphed in his struggle with Pelagius, whose views were consequently condemned by the church. In condemning Pelagianism as heresy the church strongly affirmed the doctrine of original sin. In Augustine's view this entailed the notion that though fallen man still has a free will in the sense that he retains the faculty of choosing, the will is fallen and enslaved by sin to such an extent that man does not have moral liberty. He cannot not sin.

After this struggle passed, modified views of Pelagianism returned to haunt the church. These views were called *semi-Pelagianism.* Semi-Pelagianism admitted to a real Fall and a real transfer of Original Sin to the progeny of Adam. Man is fallen and requires grace in order to be saved. However, this view says we are not so fallen that we are left totally enslaved to sin or totally depraved in our nature. An island of righteousness remains in fallen man by which the fallen person still has the moral power to incline himself, without operative grace, to the things of God.

Though the ancient church condemned semi-Pelagianism as vigorously as it had condemned Pelagianism, it never died out. In the sixteenth century the magisterial reformers were convinced that Rome had degenerated from pure Augustinianism and fallen into semi-Pelagianism. It was not an insignificant detail of history that Luther himself was a monk in the Augustinian Order. Luther saw his debate with Erasmus and Rome as a renewal of the titanic struggle Augustine had with Pelagius.

In the eighteenth century, Reformation thought was challenged by the rise of Arminianism, a new form of semi-Pelagianism. This captured the thinking of such prominent men as John Wesley. The split over doctrine between Wesley and George Whitefield focused on this point. Whitefield sided with Jonathan Edwards's defense of classic Augustinianism during the American "Great Awakening."

The nineteenth century witnessed a revival of pure Pelagianism in the teaching and preaching of Charles Finney. Finney made no bones about his unvarnished Pelagianism. He rejected the doctrine of original sin (along with the orthodox view of the atonement and the doctrine of justification by faith alone). But Finney's evangelistic methodology was so successful that he became a revered model for later evangelists and is usually regarded as a titan of Evangelicalism, this despite his wholesale rejection of Evangelical doctrine.

Though American Evangelicalism did not embrace Finney's pristine Pelagianism (that was left for the Liberals to do), it was deeply infected by forms of semi-Pelagianism to the extent that today semi-Pelagianism is far and away the majority report within Evangelicalism. Though most Evangelicals will not hesitate to affirm that man is fallen, few embrace the Reformation doctrine of total depravity.

Thirty years ago I was teaching theology in an Evangelical college that was heavily influenced by semi-Pelagianism. I was working through the five points of Calvinism using the acrostic TULIP with a class of about thirty students. After giving a lengthy exposition of the doctrine of total depravity, I asked the class how many of them were convinced of the doctrine. All thirty students raised their hands in the affirmative. I laughed and said, "We'll see." I wrote the number 30 in the upper left hand corner of the blackboard. As we proceeded to the doctrine of unconditional election several of the students balked. I counted their number then went to the board and subtracted that number from the original thirty. By the time we got to Limited Atonement the number was reduced from thirty to about three.

I then tried to get the students to see that if they really embraced the doctrine of total depravity that the other doctrines in the Five Points were but footnotes. The students soon discovered that they didn't really believe in total depravity after all. They believed in depravity, but not in the sense of total. They still wished to retain an island of righteousness unaffected by the Fall whereby fallen sinners still retained the moral ability to incline themselves to God. They believed that in order to be regenerated they must first exercise faith by the exertion of their wills. They did not believe that the divine and supernatural work of regeneration by the Holy Spirit was a necessary precondition for faith.

Erasmus had won. Again the authors of the introductory essay of *The Bondage of the Will* assert:

Whoever puts this book down without having realized that evangelical theology stands or falls with the doctrine of the bondage of the will has read it in vain. The doctrine of free justification by faith only, which became the storm-centre of so much controversy during the Reformation period, is often regarded as the heart of the Reformers' theology, but this is hardly accurate. The truth is that their thinking was really centred upon the contention . . . that the sinner's entire salvation is by free and sovereign grace only. . . . Is our salvation wholly of God, or does it ultimately depend on something that we do for ourselves? Those who say the latter (as the Arminians later did) thereby deny man's utter helplessness in sin, and affirm that a form of semi-Pelagianism is true after all. It is no wonder, then, that later Reformed theology condemned Arminianism as being in principle a return to Rome . . . and a betrayal of the Reformation. . . . Arminianism was, indeed, in Reformed eyes a renunciation of New Testament Christianity in favour of New Testament Judaism; for to rely on oneself for faith is no different in principle from relying on oneself for works, and the one is as un-Christian and anti-Christian as the other.

These are strong words. Indeed for some they are fighting words. But of one thing I am sure: They mirror and reflect accurately the sentiments of Augustine and the Reformers. The issue of the extent of Original Sin is tied inseparably to our understanding of the doctrine of Sola Fide. The

Reformers understood clearly that there is a necessary link between Sola Fide and Sola Gratia. Justification by faith alone means justification by grace alone. Semi-Pelagianism in its Erasmian form breaks this link and erases the Sola from Sola Gratia.

"Though most Evangelicals will not hesitate to affirm that man is fallen, few embrace the Reformation doctrine of total depravity."

FROM HERE
TO ETERNITY

MAY 1996

———

I N JUNE OF 1960 MY WIFE AND I WERE MARRIED in a "double ring"
ceremony. The congregation witnessed the exchange of rings between
us, but what they could not see was the inscriptions engraved on the
inner surface of our rings. On the inside of my ring is written: "Your people, my people." On the inside of her ring is written: "Your God, my God."

These words recall and are taken from the famous plea of Ruth to her
mother-in-law, Naomi, when she said: "Entreat me not to leave you, or
to turn back from following after you; for wherever you go, I will go; and
wherever you lodge, I will lodge; your people shall be my people, and
your God my God. Where you die, I will die. And there will I be buried.
The LORD do so to me, and more also, if anything but death parts you and
me" (Ruth 1:16–17).

This plea is not merely an entreaty; it is a sacred oath and vow that
sealed a covenant meant for life. It provides a window to the soul of a
woman who understood the character of God and mirrored that character in her own life.

What is extraordinary about this promise is that it is taken in the name
of *Yahweh* by a woman who was not a Jewess by birth. Ruth was a Moabitess, a person who, according to her ethnic background, was a stranger
to the covenant of Israel. Martin Luther made much of this, pointing to
the universal relevance of Ruth's greater Son who would die not only for
Jews but for Gentiles as well. From the womb of Ruth would come David
and from David's loins, Christ. Within the bloodstream of Jesus' human
nature was the blood of His ancestor, Ruth.

Ruth is a character study in loyalty. When the prophet Micah wrote
the summary of God's commands answering the question, "What does

the LORD require of you?" the reply was "To do justly, to love mercy, and to walk humbly with your God" (Micah 6:8). The accent on loving mercy is rooted in a term that occurs frequently in the Hebrew Scriptures. It is the word *hesed*. The word is sometimes translated by "mercy" or "loving-kindness." Some translators prefer the words "loyal love." It is used chiefly to describe the character of God Himself. The God of Israel is a God who is supremely loyal in His love.

It is this trait of God that is mirrored in the life of Ruth. She was a woman of consummate loyalty. We see it in her loyal love of Naomi. We see it in her loyal love for Boaz. We see it supremely in her loyal love for God.

Ruth's portrait is not a cameo sketch of loyalty in the abstract. Hers was a loyalty in the trenches, in the anxiety of struggling for an identity in a foreign land. It was a loyalty in the midst of poverty where her fingernails were broken and caked with mud. It was a loyalty purified of its dross by the beating Palestinian sun.

Loyalty is a virtue that is linked to the biblical concept of faith. We tend to restrict or limit our understanding of faith to an act of believing, a kind of intellectual assent to the truth of a proposition. We know, however, that saving faith includes more than assent; it includes personal trust.

When we probe the depths of this trust we discover that it is multi-faceted. It is within the nature of trust that we see the link between faith and loyalty. Together, faith and loyalty yield *fidelity*. In our language loyalty and fidelity serve as virtual synonyms. Fidelity means faithfulness. A loyal friend is a faithful friend. A loyal believer is a faithful believer. So to live by faith is not only to exercise faith and trust; it is to be faithful.

The motto of the United States Marine Corps is *Semper Fidelis*, or "always faithful," sometimes shortened to the abbreviated cry "Semper Fi!" The prototypical "Marine" was not John Wayne, but the Moabitess Ruth. She was *semper fidelis*, always faithful. She embodied "Ruthfulness" rather than "ruthlessness."

I once rode on an airplane with Edward DeBartolo, the entrepreneur owner of the San Francisco 49ers. I asked him what he valued the most in his employees and players. He answered without hesitation, "Loyalty!"

On the surface this may have been interpreted as the desire of a leader to be surrounded by yes men or a band of sycophants. But "yes men" are not really loyal. They are driven more by self-preservation rather than fidelity.

A faithful friend does not exhibit a blind loyalty that refuses to recognize the errors or faults in their friends or bosses. Rather they exhibit the biblical love that covers a multitude of sins. They remain faithful in the midst of failure and shortcomings.

The loyalty of Ruth was not naive. Naomi was not perfect; neither was Boaz. Perfection belongs to God alone. We have no reason not to be loyal to Him. But our earthly friends are not perfect. Here loyalty is often part of a fierce test. Loyalty can be misguided, resulting in aiding and abetting sin. This type of "loyalty" is not authentic, but specious. True loyalty rebukes, admonishes, and corrects, while remaining steadfast in love. Loyalty is what binds families together. It is especially rich when it transcends family boundaries. It is usually expected in relationships of consanguinity, the relationship of blood relatives. Ruth's relationship to Naomi was one of affinity. Naomi was not her mother but her mother-in-law. But this loyalty was thicker than water, it was as thick as blood.

We all have thousands of acquaintances but far fewer friends. It is a bonus to have loyal friends. If we need more than one hand to count them we are blessed indeed.

THE RIGHTS OF PEOPLE

JULY 1996

———

"RHETORICAL NONSENSE—NONSENSE ON STILTS." THIS was the cynical assessment of Jeremy Bentham of his tutor's (Sir William Blackstone) theory of natural rights, and by extension the grounds for his judgment that the American Declaration of Independence was a confused and absurd jumble of words.

The utilitarian Bentham would surely have joined Joe Biden in his scorn of Clarence Thomas' appeal to natural law during his Supreme Court confirmation hearings.

The Declaration appealed to "inalienable rights" that are given to us or endowed by the Creator. An "alien" is a stranger or a foreigner. Something that is deemed "inalienable" is that from which we are not to be "estranged," that which should not be made foreign to us. These rights of which the Declaration spoke are said to be an endowment. That which is endowed is possessed. An endowment passes ownership from one party to another. Since it involves a transfer it cannot be perceived as inherent to the one who receives it or benefits from the reception of it. If rights come from an endowment (from God or the state) they are not intrinsic but extrinsic.

If rights are not inherent or intrinsic how can they be said to be inalienable? If the endowment is made by the Creator then the force of His authority or His Law is what serves as the ground of their "inalienableness."

They are not inalienable because they are inherent or essential to humanity. Rights are "accidental" to humanity in that they are something "added to" us. But if they are a kind of *donum superadditum* (a super-added gift) and the donor is God Himself, then to alienate a person from his or her rights is not only to do violence to the donee but to violate the will and the Law of the Donor.

We may read separation of the church and state between the lines of the foundational documents of the American nation but we cannot legitimately read into them a separation of the state from God. The very foundation of the Bill of Rights rests upon a theistic basis. If this foundation is removed or ignored, the inalienableness of our rights is vitiated and the rights themselves may be seen as slanting precariously upon rhetorical nonsense or the tottering stilts of nonsense.

The framers of the American Declaration looked beyond the state to find a secure foundation for human rights. They looked to a transcendent authority beyond the will of the majority or the preferences of a ruling class. This was not naked law positivism. It was an appeal to natural law (*lex naturalis*) with a vengeance.

The effort to ground human rights in something beyond contemporary community standards, customs, tradition, or personal preference was not a recent concern growing out of the Enlightenment or the theories of Locke or Blackstone. It is an ancient quest sought after by Plato, Aristotle, and the architects of Roman jurisprudence. Perhaps the most significant contribution to the stoic philosophies made to the development of Western civilization was their doctrine of a universal natural law. Cicero argued:

> Since reason exists both in man and God, the first common possession of man and God is reason. But those who have reason in common must also have right reason in common. And since right reason is Law, we must believe that men have Law also in common with the gods.

Cicero's sentiments reveal that the ancient view of natural law was rooted in something higher than nature itself. The Stoics anticipated the views of Augustine and Aquinas that the law of nature is rooted in and is a reflection of the law of God. Above the *lex naturalis* stands the *lex aeternitatis*, the eternal law of God. Law that is eternal is universal. It is not to be confused with conventional law or law established on the basis of human conventions.

Human law is to be judged against the norm of natural law, which in turn is based upon the eternal law of God. This is the sentiment that clearly underlines the American Bill of Rights. Take away the philosophical premises of the Declaration and we reduce the Bill of Rights to mere convention.

The French philosopher Frédéric Bastiat understood this. He noted the crucial difference between a democracy and a republic. A democracy is a structure by which the *rule by men* is manifested. By contrast a republic is defined as a structure by which the rule is *by law*. At first glance this may be seen as a distinction without a difference, since all republics are governed by men. What is meant, however, is that the authority resides not in the will of the majority in a republic. The majority does not have the "right" to impose their will on the minority or the individual in such a way as to deprive them of their universal inalienable rights. This is what the Bill of Rights is all about. It is designed to protect certain rights that are endowed to all persons regardless of the will of the majority in an election or the decisions of the majority of legislators. This is also what the civil rights movement was all about wherein statutes that discriminated against the rights of minorities were challenged and stricken as being in violation of constitutional rights.

The idea of rights being based upon something higher than the preferences of the ruling class or the will of the majority argued by the ancient Greeks and Romans was anticipated much earlier in Hebrew law. The Old Testament saw justice and rights as inseparably related. Justice and righteousness are married. A law is only as just as it is righteous. A right is bestowed upon the creature not because it is preferred but because it is just. That which is "right" or "just" indeed ought to be preferred, but mere preference does not make it so. Unrighteous mortals often prefer what is not right and inflict injustice upon their neighbors. We never have the "right" to do what is wrong. We never have the right to inflict injustice upon human beings.

The biblical concept of sin includes the notion of everyone's doing what is right in their own eyes. This reflects the judgment of the Creator on the idea of rights being grounded simply upon personal preference. It is a judgment lodged against a relativistic ethic whose credo is "Everybody has a right to do their own thing." Here the will of the individual becomes supreme and every person their own god. It is the grasping after moral autonomy by which society itself becomes impossible and civilization becomes barbarian.

Plato depicted the thought of ancient Sophism in the character of the skeptic Thrasymachus. Thrasymachus argued that justice is something pursued by simpletons and results in weakness. He insisted that each person should aggressively pursue his or her own interests in unlimited self-assertion. "Justice" is merely the vested interests of the strong (anticipating both Marx and Nietzsche). This is the philosophy of "might makes right," the law of the jungle and the ethic of barbarianism.

Rome fell to barbarians. We tend to think of barbarians as sub-human monsters. But the Huns, the Goths, and the Visigoths were human beings. They were real people. Indeed they were people of violence who lived out the creed of might makes right. Their creed was a mere extension of ethical relativism and the notion that right is grounded in personal preference.

When people separate the just and the right they tear asunder what God has joined together. We are rapidly moving toward, if we have not already reached it, a neo-barbarian culture.

WHY LIGONIER?

AUGUST 1996

———

C ENTURIES AGO THE PHILOSOPHER ARISTOTLE examined the notion of causality. In his analysis he distinguished among four kinds of causes: (1) the formal cause of a thing, (2) the material cause, (3) the efficient cause, and (4) the final cause. Aristotle was moved to this analysis by reflecting upon the world around him. He noticed that things change. They move, grow, generate, and decay. He wanted to know *why things change*. He said that of anything that exists we may ask, What is it? What is it made of? By what is it made? and For what end is it made?

It is the last of these four questions that Aristotle defined in terms of the *final cause* of a thing. The question of final causality is a teleological question. That is, it is a question of *purpose*. The Greek word *telos* means end, purpose, or goal.

When we ask the question, "Why Ligonier Ministries?" we are inquiring into its final cause, its *raison d'être*. Most organizations seek to answer the question of its reason for being by drafting some sort of purpose statement. The reason or the purpose for a purpose statement is to provide a *focus* for the direction of the organization. All organizations change. They move as they grow and develop. If the focus is fuzzy and the purpose is unclear, they tend to stray and wander about responding and reacting to all sorts of influences.

At Ligonier we have re-written our purpose statement many times. In my mind the overarching purpose of the ministry has never really changed. Yet the purpose statements have changed as we seek a better way to articulate our purpose so that it will be sharp in our focus. Organizational goals and objectives, tactics and strategies, must not be seen as ends in themselves. They are to be designed in light of and directed to serve the *purpose* of the organization. That is why we seek to sharpen our own understanding of our purpose as the purpose is the norm by which these other things are to be judged.

In my thinking the original vision for Ligonier took place as a result of various factors. One was my own reflection on the Protestant Reformation of the 16th century. I saw that two crucial factors were important to the sweeping changes that were wrought in the world and the church. One was that Christian scholarship was returned to the base of the authority of Scripture and the church was enriched by the teaching of its pastors by such giants as Luther and Calvin. But a second factor was also crucial for the renewing of the church and the culture. That was that the teaching of the content of Scripture was extended far beyond the walls of the university and reached the people. The message of Calvin and Luther got to the people and the church became filled with knowledgeable and articulate lay persons who carried their faith into the world, becoming change agents to re-form or restructure society.

The second formative factor for my thinking grew out of personal experience. I was teaching Systematic and Philosophical Theology at the Conwell School of Theology on the campus of Temple University in Philadelphia. My chief vocation was that of being a seminary professor. However, I also preached in various neighboring churches on Sundays. The church where I and my family attended requested that I give a series of lectures in their adult education classes. That series would be pivotal for my personal future. I discovered that adults from all walks of life had a deep hunger for learning the things of God, wanting to go beyond the learning they had gained in Sunday school as children. I grew excited about working with the laity as I watched them "turn on" to learning.

When Conwell merged with Gordon Seminary and the two schools were amalgamated into a single campus in Massachusetts I elected to respond to a call to be the Associate Minister of Theology at the College Hill Presbyterian Church in Cincinnati. Suddenly my vocation changed. Instead of dabbling in adult education I was majoring in it, doing it full time. It was a delightful experience as I watched a small army of lay people become mobilized for ministry as they were being deepened in their understanding of the things of God.

It was during this period that I was approached by a group of people in the Pittsburgh area who were involved both in adult education in area churches and in outreach ministry to college and university campuses. They expressed a desire to have a study center that would be a kind of battlefield seminary for laypersons who were actively engaged in ministry. They asked me to come and start such a center for lay education. I agreed on the condition that the work be sanctioned by the church.

In the early days of Ligonier we forged purpose statements that said things like, "To help Christians know what they believe and why they believe it.…" The expressions changed but the underlying purpose never did. As Ligonier grew we discovered that there was a deep interest in the church beyond the confines of Ligonier for educational materials. The lectures given on site were tape recorded and then video taped for broader distribution. They began to be carried far and wide.

When the chief benefactress of Ligonier died, the ministry faced a financial hardship as the cost of maintaining a campus facility escalated. The board decided to carry on the ministry chiefly outside the grounds of the campus by hosting conferences and seminars around the country and by continuing to produce educational materials for the laity. Still the chief purpose was to help strengthen the church by providing resources for its people. This grew out of the conviction that as the church goes, so goes the world. We see the church as the most important institution on this planet being founded and commissioned by God and being ruled by its Head and Savior, Christ.

Ligonier was incorporated as a non-profit educational institution, much like a seminary or college. It was designed to be a seminary for the laity. One of the chief delights of our experience has been to see that not only the laity has availed itself of Ligonier resources, but that multitudes of pastors have also made use of the educational materials to augment their own study and training.

I always cringe when Ligonier is described as a "para-church ministry."

A para-church ministry exists and functions "along side of" the church. It is not the church or a particular church. Because para-ministries are not integral to an institutional church they sometimes function as a substitute for the church, competing with the church, and at times working against the church. Hence the term "para-ministry" has become a pejorative term in many circles. I cringe at the pejorative because it has never been the purpose of Ligonier to supplant the church.

Yet Ligonier is a para-ministry in the technical sense. But it exists to help the church and serve the church. Its job is to help equip the saints for ministry. Our current purpose statement reads: "To help awaken as many people as possible to the holiness of God in all its fullness." One cannot be so awakened without seeing the church as the people of God who are summoned to worship Him, serve Him, and obey Him. To worship God means chiefly to join with the corporate body. To serve and obey Him is to serve and obey Him by serving His church.

THE DISCIPLINE
OF DISCIPLESHIP

SEPTEMBER 1996

———

T HERE IS A STRANGE DICHOTOMY IN the language of the contemporary church. Much is said and written about the important function of "discipling" new Christians, while at the same time the function of church discipline has vanished almost to the horizon point. Today "discipline" is a word used to refer to the instruction and nurture of the believer. It does not usually carry the connotation of ecclesiastic censure or punishment.

In one sense this modern version of "discipling" is linked to the New Testament model. The term "disciple" in the New Testament means "learner." The disciples of Jesus were students who enrolled in Jesus' peripatetic Rabbinic school. They addressed Him as "Rabbi" or "Teacher." To "follow Jesus" involved a literal walking around behind Him as He instructed them (peripatetic being from the Greek word *peripateō*, to walk).

In modern language the idea of providing "discipline" usually suggests some form of punishment. Spanking children is a form of discipline that involves corporal punishment. Yet the link to teaching and nurture is evident. This form of "discipline" is viewed as a form of teaching and nurture by which the student is "taught a lesson" that certain patterns of behavior are unacceptable.

In the New Testament church discipleship involved discipline. Part of Apostolic nurture was seen in the rebuke and admonition. The church had various levels or degrees of such discipline ranging from the mild rebuke to the ultimate step of excommunication. On the one hand the New Testament community was forbearing and patient with its members, embracing a love that covered a multitude of sins. Formal discipline was reserved for gross and heinous sins. There was only one sin that could result in excommunication, namely the sin of impenitence. There were many sins that could be grounds for the beginning of the *process* of discipline. But the process included several steps, each designed to turn the wayward person from his sin. Only if the sinner persisted in impenitence throughout the process would the final step of excommunication be taken. Even that step was viewed as remedial in that there remained the hope that by removing the impenitent person from the fellowship of the church the person might then repent and be fully restored to church fellowship.

It is rare in church history that the church has gotten it right. The incident recorded in 1 Corinthians of the impenitent incestuous man provoked Paul's rebuke of the church for tolerating this scandalous behavior and his Apostolic command that the man be properly disciplined. When the man was so disciplined he did repent and Paul had to admonish the church later to restore him to fellowship. This episode represents a microcosm of church history. First the church was too lenient; later they were too harsh.

The history of church discipline follows the pattern of a pendulum that swings from the extreme of harsh and cruel punishment to the other extreme of latitudinarian indulgence of sin wherein almost any sinful behavior and/or heresy is tolerated.

I have been in museums in Europe that exhibit ingenuous and ghastly inventions of torture used by the church to discipline its lapsed members. I have stood in the spot in Oxford where Ridley and Latimer were burned at the stake under the regime of "Bloody Mary."

Such ecclesiastical practices of the Inquisition, etc., seem barbaric to the modern church. Today the pendulum has swung to the opposite extreme. Rare is the heresy trial by which a false teacher is even admonished, let alone excommunicated. The defrocking of clergy is virtually limited to scandalous public sins of criminal activity or gross sexual immorality.

Several years ago a mainline Protestant denomination had a celebrated heresy case in which one of its ordained ministers refused to affirm the deity of Christ and flatly denied the vicarious atonement of Christ. The church handled this in a bizarre manner. First they reaffirmed their historic creeds and confessed anew their belief in the deity of Christ and His vicarious atonement. Then they ruled that the man's views were "within the acceptable limits of interpretation of the creeds." I call this bizarre because the church, though reaffirming its historic faith, decreed that a person who taught the exact opposite of the creeds was within the acceptable limits of interpretation of the creeds.

A few years later this same denomination faced another controversial crisis. A team of clergy and seminary professors composed a report on sexual ethics that sanctioned certain sexual behavior that is clearly condemned in the New Testament. Conservatives in the denomination were greatly distressed by this report and worked hard to get the church to refuse its adoption. The church subsequently refused to adopt the report. At this time the conservatives breathed a collective sigh of relief and rejoiced in their victory. But it was an empty victory. Those who prepared the report were not disciplined. The *de facto* result was though the church would not endorse the views expressed in the report, the church did not discipline those who taught them. This sent a message that though the report did not represent the official policy of the church, those who espoused the views within it could teach them with impunity. The conservatives won the *de jure* battle but lost the *de facto* war.

After the Protestant Reformation Christendom experienced a broad proliferation of churches and sects. This prompted the question: What are the marks of a true church? Stated negatively the issue was, How much error can there be in a church and the church still be a valid or legitimate church?

Historically the marks of a true church were reduced to three or four essentials, depending upon whether the third and fourth were combined. These marks include (1) a preaching of the true Gospel, (2) a valid administering of the sacraments, (3) a valid form of church government, and (4) the proper practice of church discipline.

Negatively this meant that a church was apostate if it denied any essential truth of the Gospel, if it desecrated the sacraments, if it had no sound government, if it was deficient in the basics of church discipline. For example, Mormonism was not accepted as a true church because of its emphatic denial of the deity of Christ. It would also mean that if a church refused to discipline a person who denied an essential truth of the Gospel, who desecrated the sacraments, or who openly lived in impenitent gross sin, that church would be not valid but rather apostate.

If the historic criteria of the marks of a true church are accurate then we obviously face a serious crisis in the church today, not only in liberal communions but in professing evangelical churches as well. We live in a time wherein churches and individuals are willing to affirm the truths of the Christian faith but are loath to repudiate or deny the antitheses of these truths. Church discipline has become politically incorrect, setting the church adrift from its biblical and confessional base. The corrective for this is not to swing the pendulum back to cruel punishment but back to the biblical norms of true discipline.

THOU SHALT FEAR

OCTOBER 1996

———

I RECENTLY HEARD A YOUNG CHRISTIAN REMARK, "I have no fear of dying." When I heard this comment I thought to myself, "I wish I could say that." I am not afraid of death. I believe that death for the Christian is a glorious transition to heaven. I am not afraid of going to heaven. It's the process that frightens me. I don't know by what means I will die. It may be via a process of suffering and that frightens me. I know that even this shouldn't frighten me. There are lots of things that frighten me that I shouldn't let frighten me. The Scripture declares that perfect love casts out fear. But my love is still imperfect and fear hangs around.

There is one fear however that many of us do not have that we should have. It is the fear of God. Not only are we allowed to fear God, we are *commanded* to fear Him. A mark of reprobation is to have no fear of God before our eyes.

Luther made an important distinction concerning the fear of God. He distinguished between *servile fear* and *filial fear*. He described servile fear as that kind of fear a prisoner has for his torturer. Filial fear is the fear a son has who loves his father and does not want to offend him or let him down. It is a fear born of respect.

When the Bible calls us to fear God it is a call to a fear born of reverence, awe, and adoration. It is a respect of the highest magnitude.

Luther's distinction is comforting to me. It is important to know the difference between servile and filial fear. These are different *kinds* of fear. But there are also both different kinds of *fear*.

The unbeliever may experience the way of the wicked who flees when no one pursues him, or the pagan who trembles at the rustling of a leaf. These are types of servile fear. The unbeliever has far more to fear than he is usually ready to acknowledge. It is a fearful thing indeed to fall into the hands of the living God who reigns as a consuming fire. The paradox here is that the unbeliever has "no fear before God" he is still said to flee at his shadow. Perhaps this means the unbeliever's fear is subliminal. He wills not to have God in his knowledge; he suppresses the truth of God that is plainly manifest to him. But suppression does not destroy knowledge. It buries it but it gnaws away at the uneasy conscience.

The filial fear the believer has differs from the fear of the unbeliever but it is fear nevertheless. We are called to fear Him and keep His commandments. We are called to work out our salvation in fear and trembling.

It is because God is a loving Father to us that Luther spoke of filial fear. It is an analogy drawn from family life. Some people have a hard time even thinking of God as "Father" because of the horrible abuse they suffered from their earthly father's hands. But God is a Father who never abuses His children. But He does punish them. He chastens those He loves. It is wise for the child of God to fear the corrective wrath of the Father.

I loved my earthly father deeply. In fact, I idolized him. I was secure in his love as he was constant in showing affection for me. I feared him in the sense that I didn't want to disappoint him or let him down. I had the "fear" of respect for him. But I also feared his wrath and discipline. Even though, in general, I didn't want to disappoint him or grieve him, nevertheless I often disobeyed him. That meant facing his discipline.

I was spanked as a child. The instrument used for this purpose was a wooden spoon (I remember hiding it on one occasion when I knew I was in trouble). It was always my mother who wielded the wooden spoon. Never my father. My father never spanked me. Yet I feared his discipline far more than my mother and her spoon. When my father disciplined me he always announced it to me by saying, "Son, we have to have a session." That meant I had to follow him into his office, close the door behind me and set in a chair in front of him. He wouldn't raise his voice. He would calmly tell me what I did wrong and why it was wrong. He instructed me in such a way that I was devastated. He always ended the session with a warm embrace. But talk about the conviction of sin . . . whew!

I had a football coach who had hands the size of catchers' mitts. When we got out of line he would stand in front of us and place his hand on our shoulders. As he rebuked us he would begin to squeeze our shoulders. When he did that to me I could hardly keep standing. During my days in seminary I went through a difficult period. I went to Dr. Gerstner for counsel. When I told him what I was experiencing he made the simple comment, "The Lord's hand is heavy on you right now." I immediately thought of my football coach. I had vivid memories of a heavy hand on me.

When God puts His heavy hand on me it hurts far worse than any punishment wrought by my football coach. This is not to suggest that God is "heavy handed" in the pejorative sense. But His hand of discipline can be heavy indeed. It would be far worse, of course, if I screamed at Him, "Take Your hands off me!" . . . and He did. If God ever took His hands off us we would perish in an instant.

One of the most poignant episodes of the judgment of God occurred in the Old Testament case of Eli. Eli was a judge and priest over Israel. He was, for the most part, a godly man. But his sons were wicked and profaned the house of God. Eli rebuked them but did not fully restrain them. God revealed to Samuel that He would judge the house of Eli:

> Behold, I will do something in Israel at which both ears of everyone who hears it will tingle. In that day I will perform against Eli all that I have spoken concerning his house, from beginning to end. For I have told him that I will judge his house forever for the iniquity which he knows, because his sons made themselves vile, and he did not restrain them . . . (1 Sam. 3:11ff).

When Eli persisted in asking Samuel what God had said, Samuel finally told him. When Eli heard the words, he said: "It is the LORD. Let Him do what seems good to Him" (v. 18).

What seemed good to God was to punish the house of Eli. Eli recognized the word of God when he heard it because he understood the character of Him whose word it was. A God before whom we need to have no fear is not God but an idol made by our own hands.

THE PILGRIM

———

"This world is not my home . . . I'm just a passin' through . . ."

S O GO THE LYRICS OF the old-time spiritual that captures the essence of the Christian pilgrimage. And a pilgrimage it is. We are men and women without a country, finding ourselves sojourners in a strange and foreign land.

My wife and I were traveling in Eastern Europe with Bob and Marjean Ingram. When we crossed the border from Hungary to Romania three burly, rough looking soldiers boarded the train to check our passports and examine our luggage. Their leader indicated that he wanted to see our passports. As we handed them to him he pointed to our luggage. As I rose to reach for a large suitcase he suddenly stopped me. In broken English he said, "Wait! You not American!" Then he looked at Marjean and said, "You not American."

I must confess I was gripped by a vice of fear. The man pointed to a paper bag Marjean had on the seat beside her. "What is that?" he asked, pointing to the edges of a book that protruded out of the top of the bag. Marjean pulled out her Bible. I gulped, thinking to myself, "Now we are in real trouble."

The policeman took the Bible and began to leaf through its pages. He opened to the Book of Ephesians and pointed to chapter 2:19. He ordered: "Read." We read it aloud: "Now, therefore, you are no longer strangers and foreigners, but fellow citizens with the saints and members of the household of God . . ."

Instantly the policeman's face radiated with a benevolent smile as he said, "You not American. I not Romanian. We are citizens of heaven." Then he turned to his fellow officers and said, "These people okay." He returned our passports and bid us God-speed.

We were left stunned and amazed by this serendipitous touch of the sweetness of divine providence. As we continued through the countryside we passed through Transylvania, the mythical home of Count Dracula. We noticed the gypsy camps and the chief mode of transportation in the rural areas, wooden carts with large rubber tires, pulled either by horse or donkeys. We noted the uneven rows of corn, parched and stunted in their growth. What was most moving was the sight of elderly women dressed in black blouses and black skirts, all adorned with black babushkas, stooped over, working the fields with crude wooden rakes. I saw these peasant women the following Sunday morning. As I stood in the pulpit to preach (with a translator) in a church crammed to the walls with people, many standing throughout the two-and-one-half-hour service, I noticed that seated beneath the pulpit was a bloc of peasant women all dressed in the same drab black, with black high-top shoes. Their faces were wrinkled—years of toil etched in their countenance. They had the look of serenity, a seraphic appearance by which their eyes indeed served as windows for their souls.

As I spoke, my gaze kept returning to this group of women who were listening in rapt attention. Occasionally I noticed a tear escape from the side of one or another's eye. It was obvious that they found supreme solace and delight from the hearing of the Word. I felt like they should be preaching and I should have been seated in the pew. I felt an immediate bonding of the soul with these people. Our customs were radically different—our cultures and life-styles had little in common—but there was the blessed tie that binds all citizens of heaven into a common "nationality." It is the heritage of all who are pilgrims and sojourners in this world. We experienced these in Romania, again at a communion rail in Budapest, and in the sanctuary of a Baptist church in Prague in the Czech Republic.

More recently we experienced this bond in our travels following the footsteps of Martin Luther in the region that was known until recently as East Germany. We felt it at "Checkpoint Charlie" in Berlin, which is now marked by a small museum that houses photos and artifacts of people's desperate and heroic attempts to escape the confines of "The Wall."* Some of the devices they used were ingenious. There was a display of two ordinary suitcases that were set side by side. What was not evident to the naked eye was that these suitcases were cleverly connected to each other with their adjacent ends hollowed out so that a woman was concealed within them. By this device she was able to effect her "exodus."

It was the Exodus of the Old Testament that earned the name of pilgrims and sojourners for the ancient Israelites. They were a semi-nomadic people who lived the life of what Harvey Cox once likened to a floating craps game. They moved from place to place. Even their church was a tent that had to be pitched and torn down repeatedly as they followed the lead of God in the wilderness. This very image figures prominently in the New Testament portrayal of the Incarnation. In John's Gospel it is written that the Logos, the Divine Word, was "with God" and "was God" from the beginning, "became flesh and dwelt among us . . ." (John 1:1, 14). The word that is translated here *dwelt* literally means "tabernacled" or "pitched His tent" among us.

In this sense it is Christ who is the ultimate Pilgrim. The Incarnation is the supreme sojourn. Christ left His heavenly home to enter into our pilgrimage in our behalf. His was a solidarity with the descendants of Abraham, Isaac, and Jacob.

In the roll call of the heroes of the faith recorded in Hebrews 11 we read: "These all died in faith, not having received the promises, but having seen them afar off were assured of them, embraced them and confessed that they were strangers and pilgrims on the earth. For those who say such things declare plainly that they seek a homeland. . . . Now they desire a better, that is, a heavenly country. Therefore God is not ashamed to be called their God, for He has prepared a city for them" (Heb. 11:13ff.).

---

* Checkpoint Charlie was a well-known crossing point in the Berlin Wall between East Berlin and West Berlin during the Cold War. The Berlin Wall surrounded West Berlin, which was an exclave of West Germany that was enclaved within East Germany. Many people tried to cross over the wall into West Berlin in dangerous attempts to escape conditions in East Germany.

That the pilgrimage did not end with the conquest of Canaan or with the possession of Jerusalem is clear. Even the earthly Jerusalem is not the final city prepared for the people of God. We still await the heavenly city, the new Jerusalem adorned as a bride for her husband. The book of Revelation declares: "Behold, the tabernacle of God is with men, and He will dwell with them, and they shall be His people" (Rev. 21:3).

Not only Old Testament Israel was defined by the metaphor of the pilgrim. Peter, describing New Testament believers said "Beloved, I beg you as sojourners and pilgrims, abstain from fleshy lusts which war against the soul" (1 Pet. 2:11).

I love my homeland. Every time I travel abroad I am always happy to return to America. But the United States is an inn, a resting place in the midst of a higher journey, a roadstop on the way to my true home.

THE PROTO-GOSPEL

I F WE CONSULT KITTEL'S *Theological Dictionary of the New Testament*, we will discover a fascinating study of the word *evangelion*. This is the Greek term that is translated "Gospel." In rudimentary form the word means simply "good news, message, or announcement." The word was employed in antiquity for almost any kind of good tidings such as the good report of the outcome of a battle delivered by a marathon runner who delivered the message. Hence the allusion of Paul in Romans 10 to Isaiah's words:

> How beautiful upon the mountains are the feet of him who brings good news, who proclaims peace, who brings glad tidings of good things, who proclaims salvation, who says to Zion, "Your God reigns!" (Isa. 52:7).

The reference to beautiful feet reflects the joyous anticipation of the watchman who is posted as a look-out for an approaching messenger. Without the benefit of CNN ancient people relied on the reception of reports by runners. The experienced watchman could discern the outcome of the message by the distant sight of the movement of the messenger's feet. If the runner appeared to be sluggard or plodding it indicated the footsteps of despair—bad news. If the messenger's feet were flying, an obvious excitement and eagerness to complete the run, it signaled good news. Hence, the sight of the feet of the runner who brought good news was deemed "beautiful."

In the New Testament there is a progressive movement of the meaning of the term "Gospel." The Gospel is first proclaimed in the New Testament by angels. The term "angel" itself means "messenger." It comes from the same root as the word *evangelism*. Luke records:

> Then the angel said to them, "Do not be afraid, for behold, I bring you good tidings of great joy which will be to all people. For there is born

to you this day in the city of David a Savior, who is Christ the Lord"
(Luke 2:10–11).

Later with the beginning of the public ministry of Jesus the accent was
on the proclamation of the "Gospel of the Kingdom." John the Baptist was
the herald of this announcement. Much of Jesus' teaching, especially in
His parables, focused on the announcement of the advent of the Kingdom of God.

In the writings of Paul the focus changes from the kingdom (which he
does not repudiate) to the person and work of Christ. Paul speaks of the
Gospel of Jesus Christ. This does not mean simply the Gospel that Jesus
Himself announced but rather the good news *about* Jesus Christ.

This progressive change in emphasis does not indicate a disparity
between the Gospel Jesus proclaimed and that proclaimed by Paul and
the other Apostles. The Gospel was and is always about Christ. It finds its
core significance in Him and in what He has accomplished in our behalf.

The Gospel is not an innovation of the New Testament. That it is called
"good *news*" may be a bit misleading. We see the link between the words
"news" and "new." We read the newspaper to find out what's new. But
though there are new aspects revealed about the specific details for the
Gospel found in the New Testament there is a sense in which the good
news of the Gospel is in fact "old news." It is found in a multitude of
places in the Old Testament as the New Testament writers are fond of
pointing out.

Indeed the *news* of the Gospel is as old as the Garden of Eden. The
Gospel was first preached to Adam and Eve. The Preacher who delivered
the message was God Himself. This message is known in the church
as the Proto-Evangelion or the "First Gospel." Technically, the Gospel
was not preached to Adam and Eve directly. Presumably they were
eavesdroppers or bystanders who overheard it. Indeed to the original
audience it was not even a Gospel; it was bad news delivered in the
form of a curse. The original recipient was an audience of one, the serpent who beguiled Adam and Eve. This malediction-turned-Gospel is
found in these words:

> Because you have done this, you are cursed more than all cattle, and more than every beast of the field; on your belly you shall go, and you shall eat dust all the days of your life. And I will put enmity between you and the woman, and between your seed and her Seed; He shall bruise your head, and you shall bruise His heel (Gen. 3:14–15).

There is irony here. We usually understand the Gospel in terms of reconciliation. Yet the first Gospel is couched in terms of enmity and alienation. Christ proclaimed a Gospel of peace, but in Genesis the message is about conflict. As part of the curse God placed upon the serpent, He decreed that He would put enmity between the serpent and the woman, between the serpent's seed and the woman's Seed.

The thinly veiled good news in this decree is found in the divine promise that the mortal enemy of the human race will ultimately be vanquished. It is good news to Adam and Eve and to us that the evil one who led in temptation and fall will not be the friend of fallen people in need of redemption. The enemy of the serpent will emerge as our ally, indeed as our champion in cosmic conflict.

The promise of the proto-Gospel is the promise of victory—it is the promise of One who will come from the Seed of the woman who will be *Christus Victor*.

There is an ominous note contained in the proto-Gospel. The good news is that the head of the serpent will be crushed, fatally bruised by the heel of the Seed of the woman. The image is of a strong man grinding his heel into the head of a snake. It is not merely that the snake will be kicked or merely injured by the confrontation. Nor will the Seed of the woman merely step on the snake's tail, leaving him to wriggle away to safety. No, the good news is that the conflict will not end in a draw or in mild chastisement. The conflict will end by a mortal blow delivered to the serpent.

But the victory will have a price tag. It will not be accomplished without pain to the Seed of the woman. In crushing the head of the serpent, His own heel will be bruised. He must feel the fury of His enemy, the pain of bared fangs that inject venom. But His is not an Achilles' Heel by which He will Himself be destroyed by being bruised in a vulnerable point.

Yes, He will die in the battle, but death will lack the power or authority to hold Him. The wound will be fatal, but not final. His triumph will be complete. The Suffering Servant of Israel will emerge as her risen, glorious King. This is the Gospel in a nutshell.

"The thinly veiled good news in this decree is found in the divine promise that the mortal enemy of the human race will ultimately be vanquished."

"R.C. Sproul was a rare theologian who explained the deepest of subjects in the simplest of terms, and he did so in a way that grabbed people's attention and interest. His gifts shine in the column he regularly wrote, Right Now Counts Forever. On subjects from sports to politics to sexuality, and of course, the life of the church, Sproul's wisdom and wit show us how the truth of God's Word illuminates and transforms all of life."

—Dr. Joel R. Beeke
President and professor of systematic theology and homiletics
Puritan Reformed Theological Seminary
Grand Rapids, Mich.

"R.C. Sproul's legacy is vast, including visual, audio, and print resources stimulating countless believers worldwide. Now, Ligonier has added to it with this thrilling thesaurus, gathered from more than forty years of his monthly contributions to *Tabletalk.* In the early years, he shared his spiritual perception of current affairs, including politics, economics, inflation, the newest A-list books and 'the American dream'; it was as if he had all of these in one hand and his Bible in the other. In the later years, he was more immediately concerned with theological and doctrinal truths. His exposition and application of biblical revelation on subjects such as the doctrine of God, Christology, Jesus' substitutionary death, atonement, the true nature of sin and the new birth, theodicy, the measure and manner of God's forgiveness, conscience, Christian liberty, and scores of other subjects are brilliantly handled.

"I do have a quibble. At one point he wrote, 'There is nothing in my thought that hasn't been said before far more eloquently than I can ever hope to articulate'—commendably modest, but thankfully untrue."

—Dr. John Blanchard
Preacher, teacher, apologist, and author
Banstead, England

"You hold in your hand a veritable gold mine of Christian truth. Flowing from the pen of Dr. R.C. Sproul, here is his work of more than forty

years writing his monthly column Right Now Counts Forever in *Tabletalk* magazine. Dr. Sproul was arguably the greatest teacher of theology in our generation. He was also a lucid and cogent writer, able to take profound truth and make it accessible to everyday readers. This book will take you to the heights of heaven as Dr. Sproul addresses a wide breadth of issues and topics. Though now seated in a cloud of witnesses above, Dr. Sproul continues to instruct us in the vital essentials of Christian living. This book should be required reading for every believer."

—Dr. Steven J. Lawson
President, OnePassion Ministries
Dallas

"This collection of columns from four decades offers a treasure trove of timeless reflection on the timely. Dr. Sproul tackles football, commercials, ethical issues, best-selling books, politics, and philosophy—and that's merely the first year of columns alone. You will find wit and humor, always accompanied by deep and faithful theological and biblical reflection. Here you will find wisdom that never goes out of style."

—Dr. Stephen J. Nichols
President, Reformation Bible College
Chief academic officer, Ligonier Ministries

"Spanning more than forty years, Dr. Sproul's prophetic insights on a wide range of ethical and theological issues provide a fascinating historical narrative of cultural change, both in society at large and, sadly, the evangelical church, as well as a breathtakingly clear Christian (biblical) response. Cultural attitudes may have changed as the effects of postmodernity took hold in the late twentieth century, but it is clear from these pages that the Bible is sufficient to address each one. I will be consulting this volume often as issues arise for which I need a clear biblical response."

—Dr. Derek W.H. Thomas
Senior minister, First Presbyterian Church
Columbia, S.C.

Right Now Counts Forever

R.C. SPROUL

RIGHT NOW COUNTS FOREVER

Volume III: 1997–2006

 LIGONIER MINISTRIES

Right Now Counts Forever, Volume III: 1997–2006
© 2021 by the R.C. Sproul Trust

Published by Ligonier Ministries
421 Ligonier Court, Sanford, FL 32771
Ligonier.org

Printed in China
RR Donnelley
0000321
First printing

ISBN 978-1-64289-311-3 (Hardcover)
ISBN 978-1-64289-312-0 (ePub)
ISBN 978-1-64289-313-7 (Kindle)

Cover design: Metaleap Creative
Interior typeset: Katherine Lloyd, The DESK

Ligonier Ministries edited and adapted Dr. R.C. Sproul's original text to create this volume. We are thankful to Mrs. Vesta Sproul for her invaluable help on this project.

Bible quotations are the author's translation or are taken from one of the following versions:

The ESV® Bible (The Holy Bible, English Standard Version®), copyright © 2001 by Crossway, a publishing ministry of Good News Publishers. Used by permission. All rights reserved.

The New American Standard Bible® (NASB), Copyright © 1960, 1962, 1963, 1968, 1971, 1972, 1973, 1975, 1977, 1995 by The Lockman Foundation. Used by permission. www.Lockman.org

The New King James Version®. Copyright © 1982 by Thomas Nelson. Used by permission. All rights reserved.

The Holy Bible, New International Version®, NIV®. Copyright © 1973, 1978, 1984, 2011 by Biblica, Inc.™ Used by permission of Zondervan. All rights reserved worldwide. www.zondervan.com The "NIV" and "New International Version" are trademarks registered in the United States Patent and Trademark Office by Biblica, Inc.™

The King James Version. Public domain.

Cataloging-in-Publication Data is available from the Library of Congress
LCCN 2020038106 (print) | LCCN 2020038107 (ebook)
LC record available at https://lccn.loc.gov/2020038106
LC ebook record available at https://lccn.loc.gov/2020038107

CONTENTS

HERO WORSHIP
IN THE CHURCH

JANUARY 1997

——

I F I MUSE ON THE PAST WEEK OF MY LIFE I recognize that I have had much interaction with some of my greatest heroes. This morning I taped four programs for our radio show, *Renewing Your Mind*. As I stood at the podium in our studio, I could look through the glass partition into the control room where there hangs a large color portrait of Jonathan Edwards. On the podium itself was a book written by Edwards. This dual presence of Edwards at the tapings may be easily explained: I am an Edwardsian, one who embraces the thought of this theological giant.

The day before I spent much time poring over volumes written by St. Augustine as I was working on a new book. The reason I spent so much time with Augustine is because, in a significant way, I am Augustinian in my thinking.

Two days ago, I had a dual encounter with Martin Luther. First, I gazed at an oil painting I did of Luther, copying Cranach's famous portrait in my own amateurish style. Then, when I arrived at my office I discovered, to my delight, a package that arrived in the mail. It was a beautiful calligraphic work of Luther's speech at the Diet of Worms. This was a gift from friends who participated in our recent tour of the sites in Germany where Luther made history. This wonderful gift came from people who know my love for Luther.

How does all this relate to Paul's rebuke of the Corinthians who were guilty of provoking a factious spirit in the early church? Paul wrote to the Corinthians:

> Now I plead with you, brethren, by the name of our Lord Jesus Christ, that you all speak the same things, and that there be no divisions

among you, but that you be perfectly joined together in the same mind and in the same judgment. For it has been disclosed to me concerning you, my brethren, by those of Chloe's household that there are contentions among you. Now I say this, that each of you says, "I am of Paul," or "I am of Apollos," or "I am of Cephas," or "I am of Christ." Is Christ divided? Was Paul crucified for you? Or were you baptized in the name of Paul? I thank God that I baptized none of you except Crispus and Gaius, lest anyone should say that I had baptized in my own name (1 Cor. 1:10–15).

My activities of the past few days concerning Edwards and the others pale almost into insignificance compared to my experience this past Sabbath evening. This past Sunday marked the fifth anniversary of our church, St. Paul's Presbyterian. We celebrated the feast of St. Paul's, which culminated in a dramatic production of the *Life of St. Paul.* I was credited with being the playwright for this first annual production. But all I did was provide the basic story-line of the play, which was then vastly enriched with musical compositions. As I watched the play I thought of the theme of this article. I wondered—Were we doing the same thing the Corinthians were guilty of, or were we merely highlighting the very word the New Testament provides about the life of the Apostle Paul? Luke's record in the Book of Acts was hardly a manifestation of a contentious or factious spirit, inasmuch as the record was inspired by the Holy Ghost Himself.

What do we mean when we identify ourselves as Augustinian or Calvinistic or Arminian? Are we engaged in a cultic exaltation of mere mortals, ascribing to them a role or rank supplanting that which properly belongs solely to Christ? I certainly hope not.

The two terms I generally use to describe my faith are the words "theist" and "Christian." These words contain suffixes that are commonly used to indicate adherence to a certain belief system. An "ist" is one who embraces a particular "ism." A theist is one who believes in God. The suffix "ian" involves identification with a particular system of thought. A Christian embraces the teaching of Christ, a Barthian, the teaching of

Karl Barth, and an Arminian, the teachings of Arminius. The use of such suffixes are useful shorthand to identify distinctive theological systems.

Frequently, I hear people say, "I'm not a Presbyterian or a Methodist, a Calvinist or a Dispensationalist—I am simply a Christian." This is often coated with a saccharin dose of spiritual superiority, an Olympic aloofness from all divisive parties or competing theologies. The problem is, however, that the term *Christian* come to resemble a chameleon with its variant hues and shades. I once checked the definition of the word *Christian* in a dictionary. One of the entries read "civilized." This indicates that in current usage the word "Christian" has been so abused that it can be and often is used to mean not only different but mutually exclusive things. It has suffered what Antony Flew once called "the death of a thousand qualifications."

It is important to note that in Paul's rebuke of the Corinthians, he was criticizing a party spirit—a contentious attitude that created false dichotomies and destructive rivalries in the church. In reality the theological "systems" of Apollos, Paul, Cephas, and Christ were virtually identical. The teaching of Paul and Peter, for example, revealed a unity in their Apostolic exposition of the teaching of their Lord. It is significant that one of the Corinthian parties identified itself as being "of Christ." That suggested that if they were of Christ they could not at the same time be of Peter or of Paul. But Apollos, Cephas, and Paul were all "of Christ." They did not represent mutually exclusive theological traditions or systems as some modern theological pluralists would have us believe.

Since Apollos, Cephas, Paul, and Christ taught a unified doctrine, how could parties arise focusing on these individuals? This could have happened by different means. The first way is by people misunderstanding the teaching of one or more of the passages, thus failing to see the unity that existed among them. It would be like one person claiming to be Edwardsian and another a Calvinist as if Edwards and Calvin represented mutually exclusive traditions.

Another possibility is that parties arose based on the exaltation of personalities. Rivalries could emerge as some were fans of Apollos and his style, while others preferred the personality of Peter. Such rivalries would surely have grieved both Apollos and Peter, as they were not engaged in a popularity contest with each other. They worked together in a common mission.

Paul asks the Corinthians a rhetorical question: "Is Christ divided?" The obvious answer is "No!" Nor is it true today. Christ cannot be divided. But His earthly body, the church, is divided. The divisions are as serious as they are grievous to behold. Surely some of the division that exists today has to do with personality rivalries. Most of it, however, involves competing and often mutually exclusive doctrinal systems. These systems often claim to be consistent with and recapitulate the unified system of thought contained in Scripture—even those "systems" that claim to be anti-system and those that agree that there is no system of thought found in Scripture.

God has given great men and women to the church. They serve as valuable models, even as the biblical giants function as models despite their imperfections. Were we to elevate Paul, Abraham, or David above Christ, we would be guilty of idolatry. The same would be true if we exalted Luther, Calvin, Aquinas, and others above Christ. But we respect these saints only in so far as they are faithful to Christ and point beyond themselves to Christ. This was certainly the style of the Apostle Paul, who labored tirelessly for the cause of Christ. We love and honor him for that labor. Likewise, we honor the giants of church history. But even the theological "giants" were sub-Apostolic, never speaking or writing with an authority equal to an Apostle.

At the same time we recognize that a vast gulf separates St. Augustine from Jim Jones.* People like Augustine and Luther have contributed theological insight of such magnitude that their names are representative of key thoughts. Few in church history are worthy of such recognition. Candidly, I have had people tell me that they are "Sproulians" or "Sproulites." Thankfully they are extremely few in number. Sproul has never made such a contribution to biblical understanding to warrant a personal following. There is nothing in my thought that hasn't been said before far

---

* Jim Jones (1931–78) was an American cult leader, founder of the Peoples Temple. The group created a settlement named Jonestown in Guyana and gained notoriety when on November 18, 1978, Jones directed the members to commit suicide by drinking cyanide-laced Flavor Aid; 909 people were killed.

more eloquently than I can ever hope to articulate. The suffixes "ian," "ist," or "ite" are valuable to identify truth but have little positive and much negative value when applied to personalities. We know that Augustine, Luther, Calvin, and Edwards were not crucified for us.

"God has given great men and women to the church. They serve as valuable models, even as the biblical giants function as models despite their imperfections."

LOVE

FEBRUARY 1997

———

WITH FLASHING WHITE TEETH Burt Lancaster played the role of the evangelist in the film version of *Elmer Gantry*. One of his ploys was to appear on stage and ask, "What is love?" Then Gantry supplied a flowery answer to his own question— the response of the demagogue: "Love is the morning and the evening star; the inspiration of poets; the substance of philosophers." This "love speak" was designed to mesmerize the crowd with a semblance of truth that substituted for the genuine article.

Love is a popular topic, one that evokes warm feelings and a rush of spiritual adrenaline. Every year the polls indicate that the chapter of the Bible voted "most popular" is 1 Corinthians 13. This is the famous "love chapter" of the Bible. That this chapter holds such perennial appeal for Christians indicates something of the profound concern we have for the entire matter of love. As the adage suggests, "Love makes the world go round." It surely makes our world go around. Our lives are lived out in an arena wherein love, in all its dimensions, is vital. Romantic love is still the dominant motif of the novel, the poem, the movie, and music. It is the holy grail, pursued with reckless abandon.

But beyond the sphere of romantic love is our crying concern for the love that defines our relationships. Indeed the very word *relationship* has become a buzz word in the culture. When people speak of yearning for "meaningful relationships," they are not speaking of relationships marked by hate but those steeped and grounded in love.

This deeply felt human need drives us to 1 Corinthians 13. However, 1 Corinthians 13 is a double-edged sword. It not only comforts us with an inspiring and exalted rhapsody of love, it holds a mirror of the nature of love so clearly manifest that it reveals the flaws and warts of our feeble exercise of love. It shows us how unloving we are. It sets the bar, presenting a norm of love that condemns us for falling so miserably short of it. This makes me wonder why it's so popular. Having one's weaknesses exposed so rudely is not commonly viewed as a thing of pleasure. And pain never reaches a high zone in popularity polls.

Perhaps our delight in the love chapter rests upon a superficial nod towards this biblical paean of love. Maybe we read its eloquent words as if they were merely the lyrics of a romantic ballad. But once we probe the content of the chapter discomfort inevitably sets in.

The ultimate norm of love is God Himself. He is the *ens perfectissimus*, the "most perfect being," whose personal attributes are perfect in every respect. His omniscience is not flawed by any feint of ignorance. His omnipotence is not marred by any hint of weakness. Likewise, His love is utterly perfect, containing no shadow that would obscure its brilliant purity.

If we are to search out the depths and riches of the meaning of God's love, we can approach our quest in two different ways. We can work from the top down or from the bottom up. By working from the top down we can focus on everything the Bible says about the character of God's love, seeing the full expression of the declaration that "God is love," and then seeing how that dimension of God's character is to be reflected by His image-bearers. Or we can proceed from the bottom up, reflecting upon God's commandments to us regarding love and discern from this light of His law something of His own character that stands behind His law and out of which His perfect law proceeds. In this brief essay I have elected to do the latter rather than the former.

Paul writes to the Ephesians: "Therefore be imitators of God as dear children. And walk in love, as Christ also has loved us and given Himself for us, an offering and a sacrifice to God for a sweet-smelling aroma" (Eph. 5:1–2).

The Apostle calls us to imitate God, which imitation is carried out by walking in love. Next, this imitation is viewed as an *imitatio Christo*—an "imitation of Christ"—in that Christ, as the New Adam, perfectly demonstrates the character of the Father's love. He is the beloved of the Father.

He is the supreme lover of God and lover of our souls as well. He shows love both in its vertical and horizontal relationships. He lived out all that Paul enjoins in 1 Corinthians 13.

Let us look then at the love chapter. First Corinthians 13 begins with a comparative analysis designed to show the preeminent value and importance of love. In context love is first mentioned with respect to the extraordinary spiritual gifts enjoyed by the Corinthians. The gifts of tongues, prophecy, knowledge, and faith are shown to have zero value without the presence of love. Eloquence is reduced to noise without it. External power, talent, gift, or ability are all worthless if love is absent. Likewise, extraordinary performance in terms of sacrificial giving of one's goods or even one's life has no profit without love.

The introductory words of this chapter stress the extreme importance and priority of love without yet giving us any information of what love really is, what it looks like. Paul follows this with a definition of love that is described in both positive and negative terms, by explaining what love does and what it does not do.

The love so defined is the love that has been shed abroad in our hearts by God the Holy Spirit. It defines the quality of love divine. This love is defined:

> Love suffers long and is kind; love does not envy; love does not parade itself, is not puffed up; does not behave rudely, does not seek its own, is not provoked, thinks no evil; does not rejoice in iniquity, but rejoices in the truth; bears all things, believes all things, hopes all things, endures all things. Love never fails (1 Cor. 13:4–8).

We could amend this text of Scripture by substituting the word "God" every time the term "love" appears, with the possible exception of "hopes all things." This does not mean that we can view the expression "God is love" as a tautology by which the subject and predicate can be reversed without changing the meaning. Though God is love, love is not God.

God's love is a long-suffering and patient love. It is kind and never mean-spirited. The love of God is incapable of being mixed with envy.

There is nothing above God or equal with God that could provoke envy within Him. He is the all-sufficient One. He is completely satisfied in and by Himself. We are to be satisfied people, but as creatures we are to find our satisfaction in Him. We do have people over us and equal to us. We are given to envy and meanness—because our love is flawed. We tend to be short-suffering and less than kind. We fail at imitating the love of God, and the sweet aroma of the love of Christ is rendered malodorous. At times our futile efforts at love just plain stink with the rotting stench of a decaying Lazarus.

God is glorious but He does not vaunt His majesty in arrogant strutting. There is no conceit or vulgar pride in His character. Love excludes these things so common among us. Imagine attributing rudeness to God. The love of God is a love of a Being who doesn't know how to be rude, discourteous, or impolite.

God does seek His own glory and His own will—but only because it is good for Him to do so. This does not make Him vainglorious or selfish. He does not seek His own in a wicked or selfish manner as we are prone to do.

God is a God of wrath, but He is not ill-tempered or a "hothead." His fuse is not short, as He is slow to anger. His anger is always holy anger and loving anger, not the fury of men who lack self-control.

God thinks no evil. There is never a devious thought in His mind. He takes no delight in wickedness. We find pleasure in sin, which pleasure would vanish if our love were pure.

God is truth. Christ came to bear witness to the truth. He was truth incarnate. God takes great joy in truth. For God, love does not mean that we negotiate or compromise truth for the applause of men or for worldly gain. God's love includes a love of truth. By loving truth God loves Himself, for He is the fountainhead of all truth.

God bears, trusts, hopes, and endures all things. His love transcends all the exigencies that cause mortals to fail in their love. The love of God is never a failure. It is infallible and indefectible. It is preserving love and is the power by which we ourselves are preserved.

I recently completed a 15 lecture series on 1 Corinthians 13 for our radio

RIGHT NOW COUNTS FOREVER

program, *Renewing Your Mind.* I don't know how the audience received it, but the study I enjoyed while preparing the material bordered on a mystical experience for me. I came away shaking my head about two things: the awesome character of God's love and the lack of depth of my own understanding of this mighty power and preeminent virtue.

The greatest of these is still love.

THE WAR OF LIBERATION

MARCH 1997

———

T HE DECADE OF THE SIXTIES evoked what was perhaps the most
far reaching, epochal revolution in American history. The revolution was unbloody in some respects—if bloodiness is perceived
strictly in terms of violent revolution carried out in military fashion. Yet
this revolution wrought far more changes to the cultural behavior of
America than the bloody War of Independence fought against England
in the 18th Century. This war of independence was a war fought not
against King George but against the King of the Cosmos, God Himself. It
reflected the passions of the earthly kings in Psalm 2 who declared, "Let
us cast His bonds from off us."

The Sixties witnessed the beginning of a cultural war that was framed
in the rhetoric of a war of liberation. The cause of freedom that fueled the
Revolutionary War was now draped in the flag of free speech, free sex,
and freedom from oppression. Not only from civil law did these enemies
of democracy demand freedom, but from the oppression of natural law
and the eternal law of God as well. It was a culture war drawn by the primordial grasp for moral autonomy, championed first by the archenemy
of humanity who promised seductively, "You shall be as gods."

In the 19th Century, Friedrich Nietzsche wrote his doctoral disserta-
tion comparing two conflicting models present in ancient Greek culture:
the model of Apollo and the model of Dionysus. Apollo was the god of
Greek high culture that stressed a teleological motif—a commitment to
purpose, harmony, and proportionality. Dionysus symbolized the chaotic and the sensual which was expressed in the orgiastic freedom of the
uninhibited eroticism which undergirded a religion of sex dramatized
later in the Roman Bacchanalia. After consideration, Nietzsche threw his

11

lot with Dionysus, arguing for a new social conscience that would supplant the herd morality of the masses who were repressed by the decadent weakness of the influence of Judeo-Christianity. In Nietzsche's eyes, the morality rooted in the Scriptures kept the authentic individual in chains, doomed to sacrifice his most basic human drive, the "will to power." He awaited the arrival of a "Superman" (*der Übermensch*) who would assume the role of the conqueror to set people free from the chains of belief in the existence of God. Nietzsche's Superman would then fill the vacuum left by the so-called death of God.

Adolf Hitler, before his meteoric rise to power in Germany, once sent Christmas presents to his brown-shirted henchmen. The presents were copies of Nietzsche's most famous work *Also Sprach Zarathustra*. The Bavarian Corporal sought, in his own distorted way, to implement Nietzsche's biological heroism by creating a master race. He failed as the nations of the world rose up in opposition to his dementia.

Sadly, what Hitler failed to accomplish with his Blitzkrieg, the unbloody sons of Nietzsche have accomplished in large measure in the West—a liberation from God that rests in the root impetus of "sexual liberation."

The gay rights movement is only one small aspect of the broader liberation war. This war is fought on several fronts. It includes the abuses of "free-speech," abortion-on-demand, no-fault divorce, and "open-sex." And what do gay liberation, abortion, pornography, no-fault divorce, and "open-sex" all have in common? The answer is as easy as it is obvious: sex. This human drive is now liberated from all forms of oppression that would deny us our inalienable right to pleasure—and pleasure is seen as necessary to human happiness. The war of liberation has freed us from the tyranny of Queen Victoria, the Puritan Ethic, and above all, from the dehumanizing control of Yahweh, the narrow and primitive God of the Old Testament Hebrews.

I have called this liberation movement "unbloody" in quotes, as though it has been accomplished without military weapons, but it has not been without its casualties. The blood of millions of unborn babies, the blood of AIDS victims, the blood of victims of pornographic violence, and the carnage of the destruction of the American family, together have not scorched the earth, but saturated it. The blood of the victims of this war screams from the ground as millions of modern Abels plead for vindication from the hands of their brother, Cain.

Perhaps the greatest casualty in this war is the casualty of sin itself. Sin has been defeated not by virtue but by the wholesale rejection of the very categories of virtue and vice. In the context of moral relativism, these categories no longer carry any meaning. The only sin that remains is the evil of being politically incorrect—a traitor to the cause of the New Independence; a collaborator with the so-called wicked forces of Paul, Moses, and God.

Even the church rushes to accept the laurels of the victors—falling all over herself to accommodate the changes wrought by the Revolution. The church craves relevance and acceptance. Like the Bishops who endorsed Stalin and the ministers who sanctioned Hitler, the church rushes to play catch-up with the culture. It pronounces that the Revolution is merely God's way of declaring to us His favor. He loves us "unconditionally" we are told by the so-called evangelists. We can have reconciliation without repentance, the Kingdom without the Cross, and the Gospel without the Law.

The article on *porneia*, which is Greek for sexual immorality, in Kittel's *Theological Dictionary of the New Testament*, though it carries no brief for orthodox Christianity, is at least clear in its exposition of what biblical Christianity avows, though it makes this judgment in a left-handed sort of way. Consider this proposition: ". . . the hard-headed and exclusive separation of the Pharisees Jesus opposes (with) His message of unconditional forgiveness which is for all who turn from their previous way" (Vol. VI, p. 591).

It would seem to me that if a turning from their previous way is requisite for Jesus' forgiveness then the forgiveness is by no means "unconditional." The essay is less confusing with respect to the teaching of Paul: "As compared with the different judgment of the Greek world and ancient syncretism, the concrete directions of Paul bring to the attention of Gentile Christians the incompatibility of *porneia* and the kingdom of God. No *pornos* (sexually immoral person) has any part in this kingdom" (Vol. VI, p. 593).

The New Testament Gospel is about forgiveness—forgiveness for all types of sin. Forgiveness is not needed if sin does not exist (1 John 1:8–10). To the modern liberationist the Gospel is not good news; it is bad news because it still regards sin as sin. Jesus forgave the woman caught in adultery. He said to her, "Neither do I condemn you . . . Go and sin no more." He clearly recognized adultery as sin, as Paul and Moses also called homosexual practices sin. All kinds of sexual sins are forgivable. But it is one thing to forgive sin; it is quite another to sanction it. To give license to sin is not to free people but to enslave them.

SONG FROM EXILE

APRIL 1997

———

I N EXILE THE PEOPLE OF ISRAEL faced the question: "How do you sing the Lord's song in a strange and foreign land?" The question is similar to that faced by contemporary American Christians. Ours is a spiritual exile as we confront a culture and government increasingly hostile to Christianity.

We look to Nehemiah for clues to guide our own pilgrimage in difficult times. Nehemiah was grief-stricken by the news of the condition of Jerusalem. The walls were broken down and its gates burned with fire. His first emotion over the sad loss of his heritage was grief. It was not bitterness or anger. Nehemiah wept and mourned as Jesus would later weep over the same city.

In his grief, Nehemiah moved to the next step, prayer and fasting. His prayer was first of all a prayer of adoration for the majestic awe of God and for His faithfulness to His people: "O great and awesome God, You who keep Your covenant and mercy with those who love You and observe Your commandments."

Even in exile, Nehemiah praised God for His covenant faithfulness. Then the focus of his prayer turned to repentance, pleading with God to forgive the sins of his own people, acknowledging that they had brought exile upon themselves.

Nehemiah was a cup-bearer to the king. He served in a pagan government as a believer in God. His vocation was that of a servant. He was humble and respectful to the king, but proper fear of his king did not stop him from acting to save his people. He prayed to God and made a request of the king, asking for permission to go to Jerusalem to rebuild it. He also asked for letters that he might present to lesser governors for safe conduct and even a grant for building materials.

Not all the pagan governors were sanguine toward Nehemiah and his plans. Indeed, some were fiercely resistant to them. "When Sanballat the Horonite and Tobiah the Ammonite official heard of it, they were deeply disturbed that a man had come to seek the well-being of the children of Israel" (2:10). But there is nothing unusual about this as it is a common pagan reaction to the mission of the church in any age.

When Nehemiah set about the task of rebuilding, his enemies laughed at him and despised him. Nehemiah, though, did not let his critics determine his agenda. He was polite but firm in his response to them.

When Nehemiah's pagan enemies received word that he had rebuilt the walls (but the doors were not yet hung on the gates), they invited him to meet with them in a special "audience." Nehemiah had no time for this sort of thing, knowing the plans of the enemy were evil. He replied to Sanballat and his cronies, "Why should the work cease while I leave it and go down to you?" Sanballat then sent an open letter accusing Nehemiah of a seditious attempt to become a king and other false charges. Nehemiah sent back a message denying the allegations, noting that the charges were but a thinly veiled form of intimidation.

Nehemiah's temptation would have been to allow Sanballat and his pagan cohorts to alter the plans and engage in a joint-venture of compromise in the mission. That would have eased the burden on his own people, won him both the applause of the Jews and of the pagans. But Nehemiah cared nothing for the applause of men and was totally unwilling to compromise the mission he had undertaken for God.

Instead of worrying about accommodating the pagans, Nehemiah focused on the reforms needed among his own people. It was one thing to rebuild the city; it was quite another to rebuild the people. The paganism Nehemiah feared was not the paganism of the pagans; it was the paganism of his own people. It was not paganism outside the camp that threatened Israel so much as the paganism within the camp.

The key strategy of Nehemiah may be seen in the closing verses of his book: "And one of the sons of Joiada, the son of Eliashib the high priest, was a son-in-law of Sanballat the Horonite; therefore I drove him from me.... Thus I cleansed them of everything pagan" (13:28–30).

Nehemiah is not unique in redemptive history. The people of God in every era are called upon to relate to pagans around them. As the New Testament commands, Nehemiah honored the king and prayed for him. He was diligent to give civil obedience where possible without compromising the commands of God. He sought, as the Apostle Paul did, to live at peace with all men.

But neither Nehemiah nor Paul was able to live at peace with all men. There are always pagans like Sanballat or Demetrius of Ephesus who seek the destruction of the work of God. Neither Paul nor Nehemiah responded to such pagans with hatred. But neither did they enter into unholy alliances with them.

Nor did Nehemiah lead a monastic retreat into the wilderness. Jerusalem was not a monastery, but a city designed to be set on a hill. The task of rebuilding the Holy City was not one of world-withdrawal. Nehemiah understood that the home base of our mission is still the church. The staging zone for the divine operation must be sound if the mission to the world is to be effective.

Our readiness to perform our task becomes critical when we realize the world also has a mission to capture and assimilate the church. And if the church becomes an echo of the world, the mission of the world is accomplished.

When the church is paganized there is no need for walls or gates in the city of God. Then the church doesn't need to worry about singing the Lord's song—it can sing the songs of the pagan culture because there is no longer a strange and foreign land.

But the people of God are always pilgrims. We are always living in exile if we are living in the kingdom of God. We may respectfully serve the magistrates of this world. We may seek their sanction for the building of our cities and churches—but we cannot expect them to build them for us. It is our task to build the city of God. It is supremely costly and extraordinarily dangerous. He who will work to build the kingdom of God must be on guard against arrows that are directed at his face—but perhaps even more on guard for the arrows directed at his back.

Nehemiah's work provoked hostile reactions from some of the pagans. But the real threat was grounded in the fears of God's people. When a leader like Nehemiah, Paul, or Jesus Himself provokes a hostile reaction from enemies, the people are prone to turn on them as they bear the fallout from such attacks. Remember, it was the people who feared the wrath of Rome who turned their wrath on Jesus.

True leaders of the Christian faith, however, love believers and pagans alike and risk the hostility of both to build the kingdom of God.

"If the church becomes an echo of the world, the mission of the world is accomplished."

———

CALVINISM: THE ONCE AND FUTURE QUEEN

MAY 1997

———

T HE ROOTS OF AMERICA'S CULTURE may be traced in large measure to the Protestant Reformation of the sixteenth century. The current tree that has grown from those roots may not resemble the seedling as the light of the Reformation has grown dim in our time. The Reformation motto, *post tenebras lux*, might now be reversed to read *post lux tenebras* (after light, darkness), for the axe of secularism has been laid to the root of the tree. The truths recaptured in the Reformation may now appear as a root out of dry and parched ground. The tree has been pruned and infected by a blight not unlike the Dutch Elm disease, The tree is withered and its fruit sparse and spotty, but the tree is by no means dead.

The third edition of the Westminster Confession of Faith contains a historical sketch entitled "The original and formation of the Westminster Confession of Faith" penned in 1906. It provides a brief overview of the historical development of Reformed thought in the English speaking world.

The reform of the sixteenth century spread through Europe largely through the impetus of the influence of Luther and Calvin. According to the essay mentioned above, by 1540 two distinct types of reform can be noted—one molded by Luther and the other by Calvin. According to the essayist, Luther retained more of medieval doctrine, government, and liturgy than did Calvin. Luther's reform is called "moderate," while Calvin's is called "thoroughgoing." The moderate reform prevailed in northern Europe while the thoroughgoing reform prevailed in France, Holland, Switzerland, Scotland, and southern Germany.

The struggle between moderate and thoroughgoing reform was played out in England where the audience was largely determined by the crown. Though he revolted from Papal rule, Henry VIII was at best ambivalent about reformation. His son, Edward, was a moderate. When Edward was succeeded by "Bloody Mary" the Reformation was bitterly opposed with nearly three hundred Protestants burned at the stake and several hundred others sent into exile. When her half sister Elizabeth ("Good Queen Bess") succeeded her she sought a moderate type of reform.

During the persecution of Mary a party tending to thoroughgoing reform arose in England in opposition to the crown. This party was spurred by Nicholas Ridley and Hugh Latimer, among others. Ridley and Latimer were burned in Oxford. Exiles in this period sought refuge in Calvin's Geneva. Some of these refugees undertook the task of producing the original Geneva Bible. The Geneva Bible became the dominant Bible used by English speaking Christians for 10 years.

The Pilgrims carried the Geneva Bible with them to the shores of America in 1620. The early settlers, bound together by the Mayflower Compact, brought the thoroughgoing form of Reformation to the New World. Puritans, who fled persecution in England, were a dominant force in the early settlement in New England and Virginia. They brought the religion and worldview of Calvinism to America. The founding of educational, political, and ecclesiastical institutions in the seventeenth century was stimulated by this dominant influence. Presbyterians, Episcopalians, and Congregationalists were all part of the movement.

By the middle of the eighteenth century the thoroughgoing reform was in decline. New England was facing the influence of Arminianism, Deism, and the roots of Unitarianism. At this time Jonathan Edwards lamented the shift of American culture away from its roots. The Great Awakening soon followed, flaming the dying embers of reform into a new fire that swept through the colonies and the frontier. The Awakening was led chiefly by three preachers: Jonathan Edwards, John Wesley, and George Whitefield. Of these three Edwards and Whitefield were thoroughgoing Calvinists. Wesley was not. The Wesleyan revival made great inroads on the frontier. Calvinism became entrenched in Pittsburgh, which served as the gateway to the West. The Scottish Presbyterians made Pittsburgh the "Heartland of Presbyterianism" while the Dutch Calvinists settled New York and Michigan. The eighteenth century saw an amalgamation of a plurality of religious influences as America became more of a melting pot of immigrants. Unitarianism and Arminianism captured much of New England. The influence of thoroughgoing reformation was on serious decline. The nineteenth century witnessed the massive influence of liberal theology on the one hand and fundamentalism on the other hand. Though these two parties were bitter rivals and neither one was Reformed in its orientation. Reformation theology was forced to take a back seat to both.

The "revivals" of the nineteenth century saw Charles Finney rise to prominence. Finney was outspoken in his rejection of Reformation thought including his rejection of the substitutionary atonement and the cardinal doctrine of the Reformation, justification by faith alone. In Finney the ancient heresy of Pelagianism saw its most prominent and articulate advocate. Finney's influence on twentieth century methods of mass evangelism is now a matter of record.

When in the nineteenth and early twentieth century theology was deposed as the "Queen of the Sciences," Calvinism fell with her. When Princeton, once under the leadership of stalwarts such as Edwards, the Hodges, and B.B. Warfield, fell, the task of preserving Reformation thought landed largely on the newly organized Westminster Seminary in Philadelphia. Much of current Reformed thought can trace its immediate roots to that institution.

In today's evangelical landscape Reformed thought is a decided minority, being largely overshadowed by Arminianism, Dispensationalism, and Neo-Pentecostalism. Though several Reformed denominations and educational institutions dot the American landscape their influence remains small compared with these other movements.

Contemporary Reformed thought manifests a similar oscillation between moderate and thoroughgoing reform to what was witnessed earlier, particularly in England. We have spawned a generation of Reformed leaders who, perhaps caused by the forces of political correctness, are satisfied to affirm the positive elements of their Reformed faith, but are loath to deny the antitheses of it. They embrace the moderate position for "strategic reasons," eschewing the conflict inherent in the thoroughgoing standpoint.

When asked about the current struggle between the moderate and thoroughgoing wings, Dr. Robert Godfrey pointed to the danger of cowardice by which minority groups are threatened. Reformed theology has been the subject of so much hostility that one is easily intimidated and persuaded to seek cover.

Yet there is a cause for optimism. The growth of Ligonier reveals a growing interest in Reformed theology. The reprinting of Puritan works by Soli Deo Gloria Publishing, Banner of Truth, and Still Waters Revival shows a deep and widespread hunger for Reformed doctrine. The growth of Reformed seminaries and denominations is encouraging. The Cambridge Declaration of 1996 by the Alliance of Confessing Evangelicals is another bright light on the horizon.*

Also the distribution of the *New Geneva Study Bible* in America is a sign of renewed interest in the faith recovered by the Reformers. The roots of Reformed theology are springing new branches—branches that go beyond the boundaries of traditional Presbyterian and Reformed bodies. Thousands of Baptist Christians are recovering their roots in the Reformation and untold numbers of "broad Evangelicals" are looking for more substance and finding it in the historic writings of the thoroughgoing Reformed tradition.

Whether rising or falling, however, Calvinism is a theology at peace, for God is always sovereign.

---

* The Cambridge Declaration is a statement of faith drafted by the Alliance of Confessing Evangelicals at a conference in Cambridge, Mass., in April 1996. It was meant to repudiate contemporary trends in evangelicalism.

TO TELL THE TRUTH

JUNE 1997

———

WHAT IS THE MOST IMPORTANT virtue of the Christian life? To ask such a question is to plunge into an abyss of almost impossible confusion. All virtue is important, and to attempt to single out the most important of all seems like a fool's errand. We immediately think of Paul's words regarding faith, hope, and love—which the apostle does not shrink from rating in importance when he says, "The greatest of these is love."

When James speaks of the priority of virtue he says, "Above all—swear not by . . . but let your yea be yea and your nay be nay." Surely for James it was a matter of top priority that the Christian's word be reliable and trustworthy. Behind this concern lies the whole scope of biblical concern for the sanctity of truth. God Himself is the fountain of all truth and His Word is truth. His incarnate Son is the very incarnation of truth.

The unusual indictment of Scripture against fallen humanity may be seen in the sad conclusion that "All men are liars" (Ps. 116:11). This is a sin endemic to fallen human nature and one that is not instantly cured by regeneration. It is the character trait that clearly distinguishes us from God. God is a covenant-keeper; He speaks no falsehood. We are covenant breakers, spreading lies even in our promises.

It is Satan who is called the "father of lies." Sadly he has sired many children. We are all by nature his offspring in this regard. It was the serpent in Eden who uttered the first lie: "You shall not die . . . you shall be like God" (Gen. 3:4–5). By that lie the human race was seduced and plunged into corruption. It is no small thing that the ruination of original righteousness was provoked by a lie. It was the lie that was the catalyst for the change from original righteousness to original sin.

The judgment of God upon the liar is given. Revelation 21:8 declares that all liars shall have their part in the lake of fire. It avows that the destiny

RIGHT NOW COUNTS FOREVER

of the liar is hell. If this means that everyone who has ever told a lie will end up in hell, then all of us are bound for perdition.

To tell a lie even once makes a person a liar. Since Scripture affirms that all men are liars it would seem to suggest that all will perish. But this is not the conclusion Scripture reaches. Our lies are covered by the Atonement. But this grace is not a license to lie with impunity. The lie means a serious offense against God and our neighbor. To persist in lying is inconsistent with sanctification and the person who is characterized by the habit of lying is not Christian.

Yet Christians lie and often with great facility. We lie because we fear the consequences of the truth. We lie to cover up our sins. The lie tends to take on a life of its own, breeding further lies to cover up the first one.

There are other ways that we lie besides direct distortions. We lie when we fail to keep our word. When we say we will do something and then do not do it we lie. When we say we will not do something and then do the very thing we said we would not do, we lie.

This past summer I had to take two trips to the north that were scheduled about ten days apart. I considered simply staying up north for the entire duration rather than coming home in the interim. But to do so would have required my being absent from home on my daughter's thirty-fifth birthday. Now, for a father to miss his daughter's thirty-fifth birthday may not seem as calamitous as missing her eighth or ninth, but my decision to return home was a "no brainer" for reasons of history. When my daughter was younger I missed several of her birthdays. Each one I missed because I was away for "important" reasons. Each time she said to me, "Daddy, you promised." Daddy did promise and Daddy broke those promises. And Daddy is still haunted by the pain he caused his daughter then.

In the courtroom the witness is "sworn in." He is required to take the oath "to tell the truth, the whole truth, and nothing but the truth" under the penalty of perjury if the oath be broken. This is a strange phenomenon made necessary because we can lie by means of the half-truth. The half-truth is a ploy designed to deceive while technically telling the truth. It is the truth told while the fingers are crossed. It is not the whole truth and thus misleads the hearer. So is the mixed truth that adds the cross of deception to the nugget of truth that is distorted by it.

I can remember running out the door when our phone rang so that my wife could tell the person calling me that I wasn't "in." It was a contrivance designed to bend the truth and seek refuge in a half-truth that was really a lie.

Relationships are harmed and often destroyed by the lie. We have far more acquaintances than we have close friends. We choose our close friends carefully. We seek friends who share our concerns, our likes, and dislikes, etc. . . . but above all we want close friends we can trust with our very lives. The chronic liar has few friends. Nobody wants to trust his or her life to someone whose word is no good.

Dr. John Gerstner, who once remarked, "I'd rather die than lie," told the story of having a contractor do a small repair job for him. The man said he would arrive at a certain time to do the work. Dr. Gerstner arranged his schedule to be home at the appointed time. The workman failed to show up. That evening Dr. Gerstner called him. The man explained that another job opportunity that was far more lucrative opened up for him. He promised that he would do the job the next day. Dr. Gerstner declined the offer and hired another contractor whose yea meant yea.

This sort of thing occurs regularly. The missed appointment. The pledge that isn't paid. The bill that is not paid on its due date.

Perhaps the worst and most damaging lie we speak is not the lie we say *to* someone but the lie we speak *about* someone. This is the slander and false witness that is forbidden explicitly by the ninth commandment. This is the lie that steals a person's reputation and sullies his or her good name. Slander is the stock and trade of Satan, whose very name means "slanderer." His favorite pastime is to bring false accusations against the people of God.

For the Christian we must understand that it is far better to be lied to than to lie, to suffer broken promises to us than to break them, and to be slandered than to slander. We are to pursue the truth and not give place to falsehood.

THE CONSCIENCE

JULY 1997

———

"**M**Y CONSCIENCE IS HELD CAPTIVE by the Word of God. And to act against conscience is neither right nor safe."

These words formed a crucial part of Martin Luther's fateful response to authorities of church and state when he was ordered to recant of his teachings at the Diet of Worms. He was pleading that his intention was to be neither rebellious nor obstreperous but to be faithful to Scripture. What Luther was declaring was not so much that he *would not* recant but that he *could not* recant.

Luther used the metaphor of the prisoner. He was as a man in chains, incarcerated, with no option of liberty by which he was able to do what the authorities commanded. He was not physically restrained. The irons that gripped him were of a moral sort. It was his conscience that had been captured by the Holy Ghost.

The only option by which he could please men was the option to act against his conscience. To act *for* men was to act *against* God. Though the stakes were high the decision was actually a "no brainer." His twin restraints were clear: to act against conscience was neither *right* nor *safe*.

The Scripture declares that whatever is not of faith is sin (Rom. 14:23). This principle is one that complicates ethical decisions that themselves may already be complex. It speaks to those occasions wherein a person is convinced that a particular course of action is wrong. He has conscientious scruples about it. It is possible that the action, considered in itself, is not actually wrong. It may fall into the category of those issues that are *adiaphorous*. The *adiaphora* refers to those areas of human behavior that are neutral. They include those options we face wherein they deal with matters about which God has neither commanded nor forbidden any particular actions. This defines the borders of Christian liberty. Jesus rebuked the Pharisees for creating a tradition of rules that bound people where God had left them free. This garden variety of legalism did not end with the Pharisees; Christians in every generation struggle with humanly devised restrictions that encroach on the arena of freedom.

Frequently we acquire scruples and a conscience bound by rules never legislated by God. We may become convinced that a particular option is forbidden, which in fact is not (such as the case regarding the eating of meat offered to idols). In such a case, even though the conscience has been misinformed, if the person does what he *deems* to be sin (though in itself it is not) the doing of it is actually sin. It is sin because it violates the principle that what is not of faith is sin.

The matter becomes more complex when we consider it from another angle. If God forbids something but I have failed to grasp His law correctly and actually am convinced that He has not forbidden it and therefore go ahead and do it "in good conscience," I am still guilty of sin. My sin is not in following my conscience as such but in doing what God forbids and allowing my conscience to be distorted about it.

To work through these difficulties we must first gain a clear understanding of sin and of the role of conscience. Sin has been defined as a want of conformity to, or transgression of, the Law of God. In this definition sin and guilt are *objective* matters. In this sense sin is not defined by conscience. It is defined by law. If we break the Law of God we sin and we are guilty. A distorted conscience is not an excuse for sin.

Here conscience is a double-edged sword. To act *against* conscience is always sin. But to act *according to* conscience is not always virtue. This apparent conflict regarding acting via conscience is resolved when we look more deeply at the role of conscience. Aquinas defined conscience as the inner voice we have that either accuses us or excuses us for our actions. This "inner voice," however, may reflect the internal conviction of the Holy Spirit or the subtle delusions of Satan or of our own flesh.

It is Jiminy Cricket, not the New Testament, that is the author of the axiom "let your conscience be your guide." The Cricket apparently failed to grasp that the human conscience can become seared and distorted. God, speaking through the prophet Jeremiah, rebuked Israel for having the forehead of a harlot. By repeated acts of disobedience Israel had so dulled her conscience that she lost her capacity to blush.

Like Israel, we have the power to so engage in denial and rationalization. We stultify our consciences and thus experience objective guilt without the appropriate corresponding subjective response of guilt feelings. We become theological psychopaths, being guilty without feeling guilty. But guilt is not determined by feelings but by the objective standard of the Law of God. If I break the law, I am guilty regardless of my feelings about it.

The key for the Christian is to bring one's conscience into conformity with the Law of God. It is only when our consciences are sensitized by the Word that it is safe to let our consciences be our guide. We need to know what God commands and what He forbids, that the realm of freedom be clearly discerned.

For Luther to act against conscience involved doing something he considered to be neither right nor safe. That it was not right is understood in light of the principle that to act without faith is sin. That is, even if Luther's views were wrong (which, of course, we do not think was the case), he would have sinned to recant of them. At the same time, if his views were unsound biblically he would have been duty bound to change them. One is not free to use conscience as a shield to hide behind in the clear light of Scripture.

This is why Luther's opening remarks to his full reply to the Diet are of crucial importance. He repeatedly indicated a willingness to alter his views if it could be shown that his views were contrary to Scripture. He began his answer to the Diet by saying: "Unless I am convinced by Sacred Scripture, or by evident reason, I cannot recant." This was the public birth of the Reformation axiom *Sola Scriptura*, namely that only the Word of God has the authority to bind the conscience absolutely. Luther insisted that he was open to being corrected by Scripture but was unwilling to act against what he was convinced was taught by Scripture simply for political or other reasons of personal expediency. He declared that such an action that involved violating his conscience would be not only not right but not *safe*. Indeed, to comply would have been far and away the "safe" thing to do given the power of the men he was resisting. But he had his eyes on God. It is never safe to act against God, no matter how safe it may be with respect to men.

"If we break the Law of God we sin and we are guilty. A distorted conscience is not an excuse for sin."

BY FAITH ABRAHAM ...

AUGUST 1997

———

I T WAS APRIL, 1964. I was meeting with my mentor, Dr. John Gerstner, in his office at Pittsburgh Theological Seminary. Graduation was only a few weeks away and I was struggling with a major decision regarding my future. The day before I had met with the General Presbyter from a Presbytery north of Pittsburgh. In that meeting I had expressed a desire to find a small rural church where I could begin my pastoral ministry. The gentleman was avuncular in his demeanor and gently counseled me to delay my ministry by extending my studies in graduate school.

His counsel resulted in my meeting with Dr. Gerstner the following day. Gerstner was adamant that I journey to the Netherlands to study under G.C. Berkouwer at the Free University of Amsterdam. I protested, claiming my aversion to foreign languages as a just impediment to studying abroad, and expressed my desire to get a job. I was tired of school and tired of struggling to feed my wife and daughter on our meager resources.

My protests were in vain. Gerstner shot off a letter to his friend Berkouwer and told me to start immediately making arrangements to travel abroad. On the way home, in fear and trembling, I stopped at the office of my mother's next door neighbor, who was a travel agent. She booked passage for me and my family (one way) on the S.S. *Statendam* that was sailing in early May for Rotterdam out of New York City.

While this was happening my wife and daughter were in Ohio visiting relatives. When I got home I called them long distance. I said to Vesta, "Guess where we're going?" She replied, "Where?" My simple answer was, "Amsterdam."

This announcement was followed by a pregnant pause. . . . Finally she said, "O.K.—You know what it says in our rings." She was alluding to the inscriptions etched on the inner bands of our wedding rings. Hers read:

"Your God, My God." Mine read: "Your people, My people"—borrowed from the immortal words of Ruth to Naomi following the declaration, "Entreat me not to leave thee, or to turn back from following after thee; For wherever you go, I will go; And wherever you lodge, I will lodge" (Ruth 1:16ff).

The die was cast. In the following days we sold what little furniture we had, sold our car, and got a loan from the bank to pay our passage and our costs for Holland. The last week of seminary I hitch-hiked 40 miles each way back and forth to school. Then we went to New York, said goodbye to family and friends and sailed for Europe.

We had no permanent residence arranged in Holland and no definite acceptance yet from Berkouwer or The University. It was scary. But we were young and it was an adventure to savor.

Not so Abraham. He too went to a far country at the bidding of God. He was not young and foolish. He was advanced in years, being seventy-five years old when God said to him: "Get out of your country, from your family and from your Father's house, to a land that I will show you" (Gen. 12:1).

Abraham's move was not a temporary trip for purposes of study. It was to be a permanent uprooting for himself and his immediate family. It meant leaving both his father's house and his fatherland. It meant leaving everything that was a part of his security. He left his home, his property, his business contacts, his doctor, and everyone else that was integral to his community. He took his wife, his nephew, and some servants. The only other person who went with him was God.

What made Abraham's departure all the more startling was that he had no idea where he was going. He was a pilgrim with no place to call his home. But he went with a promise, a sacred pledge from God Himself that the Lord would show him a land wherein Abraham would become the father of a great nation.

It is this moment in his life that was memorialized by the author of Hebrews: "By faith Abraham obeyed when he was called to go out to the place which he would receive as an inheritance. And he went out, not knowing where he was going. By faith he dwelt in the land of promise as in a foreign country, dwelling in tents with Isaac and Jacob, the heirs with him of the same promise; for he waited for the city which has foundations, whose builder and maker is God" (Heb. 11:8–10).

We notice in this text that Abraham did four specific things in response to the divine summons. 1. He obeyed. 2. He went out. 3. He dwelt. 4. He waited. The author of Hebrews defines faith as "the substance of things hoped for, the evidence of things not seen." Faith fills the vacuum of hope. Hope, when coupled with faith, has substance and substance is something rather than nothing. Faith also provides evidence for that which is not visible. Faith is not blind. Indeed far from being blind, it is both far-sighted and sharp-sighted. Its evidence rests not upon speculation but upon confidence in a God who does see what we cannot see. It rests on trust in the reliability of every promise that is uttered by God.

It is one thing to believe in God. It is quite another to believe God. Abraham believed God when He said He would show him a better country. He believed God again later when God dramatized His covenant promise in Genesis 15, and by this faith Abraham was counted righteous. He was justified by his faith.

That Abraham's faith was genuine is seen in that by faith he obeyed God. True faith is always obedient faith. Abraham obeyed the call of God on his life. He demonstrated this obedience when he "went out." His faith issued in action.

When Abraham arrived in Canaan it was by no means a great nation. But he dwelt there in the foreign land, living in tents. God may have prepared a mansion for him in heaven but in Canaan all he had was a tent. The only parcel of ground he actually owned was his burial plot.

Most importantly Abraham waited. This is perhaps the hardest test of faith. Unrealized expectations make for bitterness and despair in many people's lives. But Abraham waited in faith, just as God later required of the prophet Habakkuk when He said: "Write the vision and make it plain on tablets, that he may run who reads it. For the vision is yet for an appointed time; but at the end it will speak, and it will not lie. Though it tarries, wait for it; because it will surely come. It will not tarry" (Hab. 2:2–3).

Abraham waited in faith and he died in faith. With the rest of the Old Testament saints it was said: "And all these, having obtained a good testimony through faith, did not receive the promise, God having provided something better for us, that they should not be made perfect apart from us" (Heb. 11:39–40).

"It is one thing to believe in God. It is quite another to believe God."

TIME WELL SPENT

SEPTEMBER 1997

———

W HEN I WAS A CHILD in elementary school people often asked me, "What is your favorite subject?" Invariably my response was one of two things. I either said, "Recess," or "Gym." My answer revealed my deepest predilections. I preferred play to work. Indeed my nascent philosophical musings regarding the cosmic "why?" questions took place as I made a game of walking to school via tiptoeing along a log path, pretending I was a tight-rope walker in a circus. I asked myself the meaning of life wherein I had to spend five days a week doing what I didn't want to do just so I could play on the weekends. I was always at the schoolyard a full hour before school began not out of a zeal for getting a head start on my studies but so I could "redeem" the daily grind by having an hour's worth of fun on the playground before the school bell rang. For me time redemption meant rescuing precious minutes of play from the required hours of work.

I've come to realize that when the Apostle Paul exhorted his readers to "redeem the time, for the days are evil" (Eph. 5:16), my practices are not exactly what he had in mind. His was a solemn call to the productive use of one's time in the labor of Christ's kingdom.

The things we purchase to distract us from labor make up a high component of the Gross National Product. Perhaps this is the origin of the meaning of "gross." The forty-hour week has been made sacrosanct to the American way of life. The Decalogue has been modified to read "Forty hours shalt thou labor and do all thy work." No longer is six days of labor considered a divine mandate.

Forty hours a week? Let's do the math. There are 168 hours in every week. If we allow 56 hours for sleep and 40 hours for work, that comes to 96 hours a week. If we allot another 10 hours a week for drive-time, etc., that gets us to 106 hours. What happens to the other 62 hours? Indeed,

34

only 25 percent of our time is given to work (if we work a full eight hours a day for five days).

Time is the great leveler. It is one resource that is allocated in absolute egalitarian terms. Every living person has the same number of hours to use in every day. Busy people are not given a special bonus added on to the hours of the day. The clock plays no favorites.

We all have an equal measure of time in every day. Where we differ from one another is in how we redeem the time allotted. When something is redeemed it is rescued or purchased from some negative condition. The basic negative condition we are concerned with is the condition of waste. To waste time is to spend it on that which has little or no value.

I am a time waster. When I think of the time I have wasted over the course of my life, I am hounded by remorse. This guilt is not a false one fostered by an over-active work ethic. The guilt is real because the time I have wasted is real time.

The late Vince Lombardi introduced the adage, "I never lost a game; I just ran out of time." This explanation points to one of the most dramatic elements of sports—the race against the clock. The team that is most productive in the allotted time is the team that wins the game. Of course, in sports, unlike life, there are provisions for calling time-out. The clock in a sports contest can be temporarily halted. But in real life there are no time-outs, proving another adage, *tempus fugit.*

Given my propensity to waste time, I have learned a few tricks to help me beat the clock. They may be helpful to some of you.

First, *I realize that all of my time is God's time and all of my time is my time by His delegation.* God owns me and my time. Yet, He has given me a measure of time over which I am a steward. I can commit that time to work for other people, visit other people, etc. But it is time for which I must give an account.

Second, *time can be redeemed by concentration and focus.* One of the greatest wastes of time occurs in the human mind. Our hands may be busy but our minds idle. Likewise, our hands may be idle while our minds are busy. Wool-gathering, day-dreaming, and indulging in frivolous fantasy are ways in which thoughts may be wasted in real time. To focus our minds on the task at hand—with fierce concentration—makes for productive use of time.

Third, *the mind can redeem valuable time taken up by ordinary or mechanical functions.* For example, the mechanics of taking a shower are not difficult. In this setting the mind is free for problem solving, creative thinking, or the composition of themes. Many of my messages and lectures are germinated in the shower. When I used to play a lot of golf, I found that the time I had between shots was a great time for composing messages in my mind.

Fourth, *use your leisure time for pursuits that are life enriching.* Leisure time is often spent on avocations. Reading is a valuable use of time. It enriches life to read outside of your major field or area of expertise. Augustine once advised believers to learn as much as possible about as many things as possible, since all truth is God's truth. Other avocations that are enriching include the arts. I like to study the piano and I dabble in painting. No one will ever mistake me for a serious musician or an accomplished artist. But these avocations open up the world of beauty to me that enhances my view of God and His manifold perfections. I also enjoy working crossword puzzles to warm up the little gray cells and to expand my vista of verbal expression.

Fifth, *find ways to cheat the "Sand Man."* Several years ago I had an epiphany about time management. Though my life-long pattern had been to stay up late at night I realized that for me, the hours between 9 p.m. and midnight were not very productive. I reasoned that if I used those hours to sleep I might secure more time for more productive things. Since then my habit has been to retire between 8–9 p.m. when possible and rise at 4 a.m. This has effected a wonderful revolution for my schedule. The early hours of the day are a time free from distractions and interruptions, a marvelous time for study, writing, and prayer. This pattern has enlarged my appreciation for the sagacity of Ben Franklin. However, it has its down side as my friends have found me less than socially energetic after 7 p.m.

Sixth, *use drive-time for learning.* Driving a car is another mechanical function that allows the mind to be alert to more than what is happening on the roadway. The benefits of audio tape can be put to great use during these times. I can listen to lectures and instructional tapes while driving, thereby redeeming the time.

Finally, *in most cases a schedule is more liberating than restricting.* Working with a schedule helps enormously to organize our use of time. The schedule should be a friend, not an enemy. I find it freeing in that the schedule can include time for leisure, recreation, and avocation. It helps us find the rhythm for a God-glorifying productive life.

THE GERSTNER
I REMEMBER

OCTOBER 1997

———

I WAS PLAYING SHORTSTOP IN A SOFTBALL GAME at a senior class picnic in seminary. Dr. John Gerstner was playing for the opposing team. Four times Dr. Gerstner came to the plate. Four times he hit routine ground balls to me. Four times I gunned him out at first base. I say "gunned" him out because I was not satisfied by merely tossing the ball to the first baseman. I threw as quickly and as hard as I could, not merely to get Dr. Gerstner out, but to insure that he was out by several steps. I didn't want merely to beat him, but to "dust off the spot where he stood."

Pay backs are sweet, especially to a person who is but partially satisfied. I still savor that day because it was the only time in my life I found an arena in which I could beat Dr. Gerstner. In every other arena, he dusted off the spot where *I* stood.

It began in our first encounter. My initial meeting with Gerstner (or my baptism of fire) occurred when he gave a lecture on predestination at Westminster College where I was an undergraduate student. Being Pelagian by nature, I took umbrage at this doctrine. When Dr. Gerstner finished, I went up to him and posed an objection that I was sure would annihilate his position. He calmly fielded my objection and painstakingly answered it in detail. When he was finished, I told him he missed the point of my objection and restated it in a different way. He responded by quoting back to me verbatim the words I used in my original statement and asked, "Is not that what you said?" I said, "Yes, but that's not what I meant." Then I proceeded to tell him what I really meant. Whereupon, he undertook to give another comprehensive reply to my newly stated objection that was even more devastating than the first one. I knew I was licked. Then, in avuncular fashion he put his arm around me and gently said, "Young man, you need to learn how to say what you mean and mean what you say."

I've never fully accomplished the aim of that counsel but, as this recollection attests, I've not forgotten it. I had plenty of opportunities to have the notion reinforced in countless subsequent discussions with Gerstner.

The next time I encountered this professor was in his classroom. I was now enrolled in the seminary where he taught. This time it was not predestination but another issue. He was lecturing on a point that dealt explicitly with an issue I had written my senior research paper on in college, where I was a Philosophy major. He was espousing the very position I had gained an "A" for so lucidly refuting. That research paper was the culmination of four years of study and preparation. I was utterly convinced of my position. So, once again, I challenged Dr. Gerstner. This time I said what I meant and meant what I said. Five minutes. That's all. In five minutes he took my position apart, fully and finally. He didn't browbeat me, bully me, or simply pull professional rank. With razor-like precision he refuted me by clear and compelling reason. What's more, I knew immediately that he had done it. My visceral response was one of panic but intellectually I knew the jig was up.

So far I was 0 for 2 in my debates with Dr. Gerstner. But I was a slow learner. For three years (and beyond) I argued with him incessantly about a myriad of issues. I fought tooth and nail, hammer and claw, toe to toe, head to head, in an arena where no quarter was asked and none was given. I debated him literally hundreds of times. I won once. It was a tiny pedantic point but once, just once, I proved him wrong and he waved the white flag and changed his position. All the rest I lost. If practice makes perfect I became almost the perfect loser in the history of theological debates.

Dr. Gerstner himself acknowledged that no student had ever argued with him as much as I did. I was a thorn in his professional side. We argued frequently; we never quarreled. In Gerstner I learned the difference. He was argumentative but not in the pejorative sense. He was not quarrelsome nor mean-spirited as some of his critics have alleged. Nor did I ever detect in him a desire to win an argument to bolster his own ego or to display his own uncanny erudition. This was a man with a singular passion for truth, particularly the truth of God.

In this regard, Dr. Gerstner mirrored the passion of his own mentors, John Calvin and Jonathan Edwards. He considered himself a dwarf next to these giants but their peculiar devotion to God's truth obviously rubbed off on him. Gerstner never displayed to me that he was a person who "had to be right" in the eyes of men. He was obsessed with defending the rightness of the Word of God. To this end he was uncompromising and controversial. Perhaps John Gerstner was the most vilified theologian of his generation. Yet, I never met a more humble or self-effacing human being. To honor him was to offend him. Like Paul he viewed himself as the chief of sinners. His theology was centered on grace as he had a profound existential sense of the need of it to cover his own unworthiness.

In later years when we worked together he frequently sought to defer to me in debating opponents. He would say to me, "You do the talking. You are winsome and charming and they will listen to you." Now, to be sure, there are many who will dispute Gerstner's assessment of me but there is no doubt that he believed it. Notice that he did not say, "You do the talking because you are more astute, acute, or knowledgeable." That would not have been gracious; it would have been a lie, and we both knew it. Gerstner once said to me off the record, "I would rather die than lie."

John Gerstner was not only my mentor. He was my Barnabas. If he was steady, I am volatile. If he was stoic in his ability to live with criticism and hostility, I am a sissy. If I ever was more "winsome" it was because I was much more concerned about whether people liked me than he was. He didn't have a political bone in his body, and more than any person I've known, sought the approval of God rather than men.

Like Barnabas, Dr. Gerstner never tired of encouraging me. God knows I needed it. To encourage is to incite to courage. Courage itself is contagious, as is cowardliness. I don't think that it was fortuitous that the writer of the Apocalypse indicates that the first group who will be cast into the lake of fire will be cowards. John Gerstner was no coward. His encouragement to me was often tender. He served me also as a Father-Confessor. When

I would go to him to confess some sin I was struggling with, I was often frustrated because he was so lenient with me. However, in some ways he was demanding. But he was always more demanding on himself than he was on others. He always called me "Roberto." Never "R.C." It was a term of endearment and for any kid who ever played baseball in Pittsburgh, a sobriquet of the highest magnitude.

I know there are many who are convinced that I view Dr. Gerstner through rose-colored glasses, but I take comfort in the sure knowledge that I knew him in ways they never did. They saw the polemics. They missed the motive. They were exposed to the mind. I was a beneficiary of the heart. To be sure had Karl Barth ever dueled with Gerstner he would have saved the epitaph of *menschenesser* (man-eater) for him rather than hurling it at Cornelius Van Til, who was himself an extraordinary prince of grace.

If I were asked to carve words on John Gerstner's tombstone I would etch in granite—"Here lies a politically incorrect man." Then I would add the obvious redundancy, "a man of character."

WHEN YOU WALK BY THE WAY

NOVEMBER 1997

———

T HE HYPE FOR THE DR. LAURA SHOW on my local radio station borrows a page from Howard Cosell and promises that she "tells it like it is."* Recently Dr. Laura leveled a broadside against the clergy, chastening us for being little more than camp counselors. I mused on this criticism and considered the degree to which the shoe fits. Camp counselors tend to do little counseling. Their time is taken up organizing and monitoring sports activities, crafts, hiking, and the like (At least that is what I did when I worked as a camp counselor). I guess Dr. Laura had in view the idea that the church often functions in the role of baby-sitting and childcare. We are expected to provide a form of entertainment or amusement in our youth programs and keep the kids occupied for a brief time each week in Sunday school. That our children are enrolled in Sunday school and make an annual summer trek to vacation Bible school salves our consciences regarding our parental responsibilities and our vows to bring up our children in the nurture and admonition in the Lord.

Sunday school is a relatively recent phenomenon. Surely it grew up out of the church's desire to catechize underprivileged children who were not receiving teaching at home. But as time passed and Sunday school became institutionalized it developed more and more into a *substitute* for home training for all classes of children. It became the institutional default position for rigorous nurture in the home. We have been defeated all too often precisely because we have neglected our responsibilities as parents to insure that our children are trained in the things of God. We

---

* Laura Schlessinger (1947–), known popularly as Dr. Laura, is an American talk show host and author. Her radio program was particularly popular during the 1990s.

look both to the church and to the Christian schools to cover for us as they serve on our behalf *in loco parentis*.

When God established Israel as His chosen covenant community He gave rigorous prescriptions for the duty of parents. The expansion of the *Shema* indicates this:

> "Now this is the commandment, and these are the statutes and judgments which the Lord your God has commanded to teach you, that you may observe them in the land which you are crossing over to possess, that you may fear the Lord your God, to keep all His statutes and His commandments which I command you, you and your son and your grandson, all the days of your life, and that your days may be prolonged. Therefore hear, O Israel, and be careful to observe it, that it may be well with you, and that you may multiply greatly as the Lord God of your fathers has promised you—'a land flowing with milk and honey.' Hear, O Israel: The Lord our God, the Lord is one! You shall love the Lord your God with all your heart, with all your soul, and with all your strength. And these words which I command you today shall be in your heart. You shall teach them diligently to your children, and shall talk of them when you sit in your house, when you walk by the way, when you lie down, and when you rise up. You shall bind them as a sign on your hand, and they shall be as frontlets between your eyes. You shall write them on the doorposts of your house and on your gates. So it shall be, when the Lord your God brings you into the land of which He swore to your fathers, to Abraham, Isaac, and Jacob, to give you large and beautiful cities which you did not build" (Deut. 6:1–10).

The term *tradition* has been given a pejorative connotation. We are acutely aware that Jesus rebuked the Pharisees for their substituting the traditions of men for the law of God. What we tend to overlook is that Jesus was not thereby casting aspersions on traditions as such but upon those traditions that were of human origin, that were used to supplant the Word of God. The Scriptures frequently challenge us to be faithful to another kind of tradition, the *parodosis*, or "handing over," of which the New Testament speaks. There is an Apostolic tradition which the Apostles received as it was passed on to them by Christ. Christ, in turn, proclaimed what was given over to Him from the Father. In a word, there is a divine tradition whose passing on to each new generation is a sacred mission of the church and of the people of God.

It is the divine tradition that is in view in Deuteronomy 6. The commandments, statutes, and judgments of the Lord are to be taught to the son and to the grandson. Here the daughters are included by extension. All of the children are to receive this instruction and the designated place for this instruction is chiefly that of the home. The command is clear: "You shall teach them diligently to your children, and shall talk of them when you sit in your house, when you walk by the way, when you lie down, and when you rise up." The accent on this command is found in the word *diligently*.

I have been guilty in my own role as a parent in not fulfilling the biblical mandate to give vigorous instruction to my children and to serve in the capacity of family priest. When our children were little I depended for the most part on the programs of the church to fill these needs. Yes, I read them children's Bible stories at bedtime and said their prayers with them. Since our home was used daily to feed students at the Ligonier Valley Study Center, the topic of conversations in our "Tabletalk" was theology. I assumed that my children would get it by osmosis. They lived daily in a Christian educational environment. But I am grateful to God that my children came to a robust faith despite my negligence in the full duties of parenthood. I am most thankful for their pastor who poured himself diligently into their catechetical instruction.

In some ways I was a child of my own times, blinded to the vital necessity of the family hearth as the modern synagogue. It took my own children to show me my error as both of them have been much more diligent in instructing their children than I was in instructing them. I was both shocked and delighted to watch my granddaughter learn the Children's Catechism when she was two years old. It never occurred to me that infants could learn so much. By age three she had memorized scores of

Bible passages, the Apostles' Creed, and the words to sound hymns. When she was two I asked her, "Darby, why did God make all things?" Without hesitation she replied, "For His gwory..." She couldn't yet pronounce the word "glory" and I doubt if she had much of a grasp of the weightiness of the concept. But this was not merely an exercise in rote memory with no enduring value. On the contrary, she was learning the grammar of the things of God, a grammar that is more valuable than the grammar of any language. She was learning the building blocks for life.

"There is a divine tradition whose passing on to each new generation is a sacred mission of the church and of the people of God."

YOUR JESUS
IS TOO SMALL

DECEMBER 1997

———

I REMEMBER THE REMARKABLE SUCCESS OF the little book published in the middle of this century by J.B. Phillips entitled *Your God Is Too Small.* The book was a ringing challenge to seek a deeper understanding of the nature and character of God. It obviously struck a nerve as multitudes of people devoured the book in a quest to expand their knowledge of the majesty of God.

I wish that someone could provoke the same response with regard to Christ. In my years of publishing and producing educational materials for Christians I have been puzzled by something strange. I have noticed that books about Jesus do not do well in Christian bookstores. I've noticed the same thing about tapes. I am not sure why this is so. Perhaps it has something to do with a widespread assumption that we already know a lot about Jesus or that there may be something irreligious about studying the person and work of Christ too deeply. Perhaps such study might disturb the simple faith we cling to

My teaching career has spanned over thirty years. And though I have taught in the formal setting of colleges and seminaries, the bulk of my time has been devoted to adult lay education. This emphasis began in Philadelphia in the sixties when, while I was working as a seminary professor, I was approached by the pastor of the church my family attended to teach an adult course on the person and work of Christ. My class was composed of housewives, professional people, business people, etc. As we got into the material I discovered a more passionate response to the content of my teaching than I had ever witnessed in the academic classroom. These people had never been exposed to any serious teaching of theology beyond what they had experienced in Sunday school. It was this class that pushed a button in my soul that catapulted me into the full-time endeavor of adult education.

There seems to be something wrong with our understanding of Jesus. We speak in saccharine terms of "gentle Jesus, meek and mild," and of His "sweetness," but the depth and riches of His nature remain elusive to us. Now, I love to speak of the sweetness of Christ. There is nothing wrong with this language. But we need to understand what it is about Him that makes Him so sweet to believers.

When we consider Jesus as the second person of the Trinity, the eternal Logos who became incarnate, we note instantly that in any attempt to plumb the depths of His person we are stepping into the deep waters of searching for the nature of God Himself. The Scripture says of Jesus in Hebrews 1:1–4: "God, who at various times and in various ways spoke in time past to the fathers by the prophets, has in these last days spoken to us by His Son, whom He has appointed heir of all things, through whom also He made the worlds; who being the brightness of His glory and the express image of His person, and upholding all things by the word of His power, when He had by Himself purged our sins, sat down at the right hand of the Majesty on high, having become so much better than the angels, as He has by inheritance obtained a more excellent name than they."

Here the author of Hebrews describes Christ as "the brightness of His glory and the express image of His person." Imagine someone who not only reflects the glory of God as Moses did after his encounter with God on Mount Sinai, but who actually is the very brightness of the divine glory. The biblical concept of divine glory is reiterated again and again in the Old Testament. Nothing can be likened to that glory that belongs to the divine essence and which He has placed above the heavens. This is the glory manifest in the theophany of the *shekinah*, the radiant cloud that displays the pure effulgence of His being. This is the glory of the One who dwells in light inaccessible, who is a consuming fire. This is the glory that blinded Paul on the Road to Damascus. The glory of Christ belongs to His deity as confessed in the ancient hymn, the *Gloria Patria*, composed by Trinitarians as they resisted the heresy of Arianism: "Glory be to the Father, and to the Son, and to the Holy Ghost. As it was in the beginning, is now and ever shall be, world without end, Amen."

St. Athanasius in commenting on Hebrews 1 declared: "Who does not see that the brightness cannot be separated from the light, but that it is by nature proper to it and co-existent with it, and is not produced after it?" Or as Ambrose proclaimed, "Think not that there was ever a moment of time when God was without wisdom, any more than there was ever a time when light was without radiance. For where there is light there is radiance, and where there is radiance there is also light. For the Son is the Radiance of his Father's light, co-eternal because of eternity of power, inseparable by unity of brightness."

But what can be said of Christ's being the "express image of His person"? Are not we all created in the image of God and does not this reference merely speak of Jesus' being the perfect man, the one in whom the *imago Dei* has not been besmirched or corrupted? I think the text means more than that. Phillip Hughes says of this: "The Greek word translated 'the very stamp' here means an engraved character or the impress made by a die or a seal, as for example, on a coin; and the Greek word translated 'nature' denotes the very essence of God. The principal idea intended is that of exact correspondence. This correspondence involves not only an identity of the essence of the Son with that of the Father, but more particularly a true and trustworthy revelation or representation of the Father by the Son."

We remember the request made to Jesus by Philip when he said, "Lord, show us the Father, and it is sufficient for us" (John 14:8). We need to meditate upon the response of Jesus in John 14:9–11: "Have I been with you so long, and yet you have not known Me, Philip? He who has seen Me has seen the Father; so how can you say, 'Show us the Father'? Do you not believe that I am in the Father, and the Father in Me? The words that I speak to you I do not speak on My own authority; but the Father who dwells in Me does the works. Believe Me that I am in the Father and the Father in Me, or else believe Me for the sake of the works themselves."

He who would taste the fullness of the sweetness of Christ and perceive the total measure of His excellence must be willing to make the pursuit of the knowledge of Him the main and chief business of life. Such pursuits must not be hindered by sentimentality or season.

"Nothing can be likened to that glory that belongs to the divine essence and which He has placed above the heavens."

PINPOINTING
EVANGELICALISM

JANUARY 1998

———

W E ARE ACCUSTOMED TO USING LABELS to define ideologies, groups, and positions. At times we react with disdain for the use of labels at all, but they serve a needed function in communication. In a sense all words are labels. Words are signs that point to things, actions, or ideas. The making of language is a large part of what we call taxonomy. Taxonomy is the science of classification by which we distinguish such things in biology as kingdoms, classes, orders, families, and species. For such classification to work we must note both the similarities and differences between things.

In his preface to *Freedom of the Will*, Jonathan Edwards discusses the use of labels in theology. He acknowledges that sometimes labels are born of an uncharitable spirit that is censorious and bitter. Hence the origin of racial slurs and epithets. But he also notes a legitimate and important function for theological labels:

> But yet there is no necessity to suppose, that the thus distinguishing persons of different opinions by different names, arises mainly from an uncharitable spirit. It may arise from the disposition there is in mankind (whom God has distinguished with an ability and inclination for speech) to improve the benefit of language, in the proper use and design of names, given to things which they often occasion to speak of, or signify their minds about; which is to enable them to express their ideas with ease and expedition, without being encumbered with an obscure and difficult circumlocution.

In this regard Edwards noted that the term *Calvinist* had become a term of reproach in his day and though he denied a slavish dependence upon

Calvin for his own theology, Edwards said he would not take it amiss to be called a Calvinist.

So it is with the label *evangelical*. It is a term used as a kind of theological shorthand, designed to speak broadly of a certain group that share a common set of core beliefs. The term came into vogue during the Reformation of the sixteenth century. At this time the term served as a virtual synonym for the word *Protestant*. Historians have often suggested that the two chief causes of the Reformation were the core issues of biblical authority and the doctrine of justification by faith alone. Frequently the issue of biblical authority is called the formal cause of the Reformation, while the issue of justification was the material cause. This distinction between the formal and the material has its roots in Aristotelian philosophy, which influenced the language of the church for many centuries. These two "causes," the formal and the material, led to the twin battle cries expressed by the Latin slogans *sola Scriptura* and *sola fide*. The term *evangelical* was the broad term applied to many groups that, despite their separation into different denominations, agreed on these two basic issues over against the Roman Catholic Church.

The Reformers called themselves "evangelicals" because they believed that the doctrine of justification by faith alone is central and essential to the Gospel. Since the biblical word for "gospel" is *evangel*, they used the term *evangelical* to assert their conviction that *sola fide* is of the essence of the Gospel itself. Thus to be an evangelical in this historic sense was to be a "gospeller," or an advocate of justification by faith alone.

Over time the term evangelical has undergone certain changes of nuance. At the turn of the century the church was embroiled in a fierce theological controversy sparked by the rise of nineteenth-century liberalism, which was often given the label of "modernism." This led to the so-called modernist-fundamentalist controversy. Part of that controversy focused on the question of the mission of the church. Was the church called simply to the building of an ethical humanitarian society by which the ethical values of Christ were to be applied to culture and social relationships? Or was the primary mission of the church to proclaim a supernatural Gospel of personal redemption? What was at stake in large measure was the meaning and significance of evangelism. Fundamentalists insisted that not only was the supernatural portrait of Christ a non-negotiable of biblical Christianity, but that personal conversion by the Holy Spirit's work was "fundamental" to Christianity. Though the original fundamentalists considered the church's role in social care a vital part of the church it was not deemed as the chief function of the church.

As a result of this controversy the term *evangelical* began to take on the nuance of a label to describe people who believed in the importance and necessity of evangelism and personal conversion. In this respect the term *evangelical* was used to distinguish a person from a liberal or a modernist. J. Gresham Machen's book *Christianity and Liberalism* argued strenuously that Christianity and liberalism are two distinct religions and that liberalism is not Christian at all.

In this schema the term *evangelical Christian* would be a redundancy. According to Machen one cannot be a Christian without being evangelical. All who embrace the tenets of evangelicalism are embracing the tenets of Christianity. This is consistent with the original usage of the label during the Reformation. Though the antagonist in the nineteenth century was liberalism, the antagonist in the sixteenth century was Rome. Though liberalism is vastly different from Roman Catholicism and though Rome clearly affirms many vital doctrines of historic Christianity that liberalism and modernism denied, nevertheless Rome and liberalism had this much in common: They both denied *sola Scriptura* and *sola fide*.

In our day we can no longer assume that the label *evangelical* describes one who affirms either *sola Scriptura* or *sola fide*. The inerrancy controversy indicated that many who are within the denominations or groups commonly called evangelical no longer hold to the classic view of *sola Scriptura*. In like manner the "Lordship Salvation" controversy revealed a serious disagreement among professing evangelicals regarding the essential meaning of *sola fide*. The differences between these factions indicate clearly that they cannot both be evangelical in the classic sense, though both claim the label. The controversy over ECT, Evangelicals and Catholics

Together (see Nov. '94 *Tabletalk*), did not indicate that the Protestant sign-ers of the document denied *sola fide* but it raised the issue of whether the Reformation understanding of *sola fide* is essential for Christianity.

In our day the broad meaning of the term *evangelical* tends to indicate that a person is part of a branch or denomination of Christianity that is evangelical in its roots. That it is may refer simply to an organizational sub-culture. Or it may refer simply to those who still affirm the impor-tance of personal evangelism and/or personal conversion. As a result the understanding of the term has lost much of its theological content and tends now to be used to define a certain methodology or broad ecclesi-astical tradition. The term has been virtually stripped of its historical doctrinal content and does little now to define a person's belief system. The term has been used to refer to many different and often opposing things that it is in danger of dying the death of a thousand qualifications. It means so much that it ends up meaning little or nothing.

"We live in a culture where many, if not most, people believe that forgiveness is a necessary requirement of love."

—

REPENT OR PERISH

FEBRUARY 1998

T HE APOSTLES' CREED PROVIDES ONE of the most ancient summaries of the content of the Christian faith. It is short and concise, focusing on the main topics of the believer's confession. Because it is so succinct it is important to note that the original writer or writers of the Creed deemed the forgiveness of sins to be so central to Christianity that it forms an integral part of the Creed. "I believe in the forgiveness of sin. . . ."

There is no other way to gain entrance into the kingdom of God save through the forgiveness of our sins. This is what the Cross is all about. The historic controversy over justification by faith alone was not a tempest in a theological teacup. It was about the ultimate issue of our faith, how a person is reconciled to God and granted eternal life. In a word, it was about the conditions that must be met for a person to be forgiven by God for his or her sins.

In our day there are few who get exercised about the doctrine of justification by faith alone. It has become a negotiable article of faith for many. There are many reasons for the eclipse of this doctrine, which Luther once declared was the article upon which the church stands or falls. One of those reasons has to do with a radical shift in our understanding of what God requires in order to receive His divine pardon.

I frequently hear from the lips of preachers and evangelists the declaration that "God loves you unconditionally." I've often wondered what people mean by this expression. Certainly the Bible teaches that nothing can separate those who are in Christ from the love of God. But this presupposes that a condition has been met, namely the person being *in Christ*. Maybe this is what is meant by the preachers, that God loves all of the redeemed in Christ unconditionally.

Or perhaps what is meant is that God demonstrates His love of benevolence to all men indiscriminately and provides the benefits of His common grace without people meeting prior conditions. Both of these nuances for the pronouncement would make sense. However, what many people hear in the declaration that God loves them unconditionally is that they have absolutely no conditions to meet in order to secure the forgiveness of God for their sins. That is, the requirement of repentance has been dropped from the lexicon of God. God's love is *so* unconditional that a person need not embrace Christ in order to receive the forgiveness of God. I put the word *so* in italics because it really is a redundancy. Unconditionally really admits to no degrees.

Perhaps all these preachers want to convey is not that God's forgiveness is unconditional but that His love is unconditional. What is hidden in the evangelist's fine print is the clause that reads: *God, in His unconditional love for you, may still send you to hell forever.* What is so dangerous about proclaiming the unconditional love of God without careful qualification is that we live in a culture where many, if not most, people believe that forgiveness is a necessary requirement of love. That is, if you or God loves somebody unconditionally, and if someone sins against you or against God, both you and God are required to forgive them unilaterally and unconditionally. The assumption is this: To love is to forgive. You cannot have the one without the other.

Surely to forgive is a loving thing to do and love certainly inclines to that end. But the question we raise is this: Must God forgive us simply because He loves us—without our being repentant? The corollary question is also important: Must we forgive people who have sinned against us if they do not repent? It is clear that we must love them. God commands us to love even our enemies and that love does not rest on the prior condition that our enemies have repented.

Jesus Himself prayed that the Father would forgive even those who executed Him. Was Jesus asking the Father to forgive His enemies even if they didn't repent? That is certainly possible. His prayer could also have been elliptical in that though a condition of repentance was not explicitly stated it was tacitly assumed. But this involves conjecture. Let us assume that what He was asking was that the Father forgive them even if they didn't repent. If this is so then we have an example of Jesus (and by no means the only example) speaking about forgiveness that is unilateral and unconditional. Does this example carry with it the normative principle that we must always and everywhere grant forgiveness to impenitent people?

My answer to the above question may jar or shock many who read it as I answer my own question by saying, "No." I do not believe that the New Testament anywhere imposes upon the Christian the obligation of granting forgiveness unilaterally to the impenitent person. Surely we may grant such forgiveness if we are so inclined, but the question is not "May we forgive the impenitent?" but rather "Must we so forgive?"

This is a complex matter that involves many aspects. On the one hand, it is clear that there are times when we must forgive. If a person sins against us and confesses that sin and repents of it we are obligated to forgive that person. If we refuse to grant our forgiveness then we heap piles of coal upon our own heads. Secondly, the Bible speaks of a love that covers a multitude of sins. I take that to mean that the Christian should be willing to absorb and suffer many slights and injuries without demanding apologies or formal discipline for the actions. We are not to be quick to litigate in church courts against our brethren. There is no room in the kingdom for nit-picking or for harsh judgment for minor offenses.

However, the main reason that I say we are not absolutely required to forgive unilaterally when there is no repentance is precisely because the New Testament establishes formal procedures for discipline. Discipline would be precluded if unilateral forgiveness were mandated. Christians who have suffered serious injury at the hands of believers may seek the help of the church for redress. This is fundamental to historic Christianity. It must be added, however, that no matter how grievous the offense against us has been, we must stand ready at any moment to grant full and complete forgiveness to the one who repents. The example of the controversy concerning the incestuous man Paul had to deal with in the

Corinthian correspondence is a good guideline for us to have as instruction.

Finally, I mention that God does lay down requirements for His forgiveness as we see clearly in the book of Acts. At Mars Hill in Athens, Paul made this declaration: "Truly, these times of ignorance God overlooked, but now commands all men everywhere to repent, because He has appointed a day on which He will judge the world in righteousness by the Man whom He has ordained ..." (17:30–31).

WHO ARE THE POOR?

MARCH 1998

—

I N THE MAKING OF SOCIO-ECONOMIC DISTINCTIONS, the use of the word *poor* can function as an emotive lever for guilt manipulation. We can use the technique of "poor-mouthing" by which we seek to garner sympathy from those who enjoy more financial prosperity than we do. Or we can refer indiscriminately to "the poor" as victims of social injustice or as examples of people who are all guilty of indolence.

There is a popular perception that liberal hearts bleed for the poor and conservatives shut up their hearts from compassion, looking with contempt upon those who are poor. In a word, the term "poor" can serve as an inflammatory piece of rhetoric to incite a wide variety of emotional responses. It becomes a political buzz-word to galvanize a visceral response, either positively or negatively.

Or we can construct a theology of poorness as witnessed by the poverty mysticism that emerged during the Middle Ages by which poverty itself was viewed as a meritorious virtue.

It is easy to simplify the situation by dividing the world into two classes, the rich and the poor, with the implication that all rich folks are evil and all poor people are innocent victims of the exploitation of the powerful. Or we can buy the myth that the only way a person can become wealthy is at someone else's expense. This myth is born out in poker games, but in few other areas.

If we seek a biblical understanding of poverty and the poor, we see that things are simply not so simple. The Bible differentiates among at least four distinct types of the poor and calls for a different response to each. In saying that there are four types, this does not infer that God values one over the other. Though the Bible is not a textbook for Marxism, it clearly declares that God is not a respecter of persons; He shows no partiality on the execution of justice to either the rich or the poor. It is just as evil to steal from the rich as it is to steal from the poor. Yehezhel Kaufmann in *The Religion of Israel* argues that Israelite law, as distinct from other Near Eastern law, recognizes no class privileges. Special favors were prohibited at the bar of justice both for the rich and for the poor. Exodus 23:3 declares: "You shall not show partiality to a poor man in his dispute." Leviticus 19:15 says "You shall not be partial to the poor, nor honor the person of the mighty." The standard of justice is not to be determined by economics or political clout but by righteousness. Class warfare is anathema to God.

Slothfulness

The four distinct groups of the poor set forth in Scripture are directly related to different causes of poverty. The first is slothfulness, which Karl Barth once declared to be one of the three basic sins of humanity, the other two being pride and dishonesty. To be slothful is to be indolent or lazy. This is a moral problem involving the refusal to obey the divine mandate to work. Those who are poor because they are lazy and refuse to work heap the wrath of God upon themselves. The wisdom literature of the Old Testament is replete with negative sanctions rewarding sloth. The lazy person's tossing and turning in his bed is likened to a door that swings on its hinges in the wind. In contrast, the sleep of the working man is sweet (Eccl. 5:12). The lazy are to look to the ant as a model of industry. Though the New Testament effuses with a spirit of compassion for the poor, this compassion is not without appropriate limits. Paul declares, "If anyone will not work, neither shall he eat" (2 Thess. 3:10). For the Apostle, welfare is not for the lazy. Neither the state nor the church is called to indulge the indolent.

In our society there is a growing resentment among those who work diligently but are burdened by taxes to subsidize those who will not work. But, alas, the rhetoric that is heard in some circles sounds as if the sole cause of poverty is laziness. The gratuitous leap of logic is that if a person is poor it simply must be because of a moral defect. But not all poor people are lazy. There are also lazy rich people who accrue wealth by means other than diligent work.

Calamity

The second cause the Bible recognizes for poverty is calamity. Calamity may involve accidents or diseases that leave a person incapacitated and unable to work without crippling restrictions. It may be the result of natural disasters such as flood, storm, fire, or famine.

With respect to those who are rendered poor by such occurrences, the Word of God commands compassion and charity. We are not permitted to close our hearts to those who are victims of such catastrophes. This is the very heart of authentic welfare. We see the New Testament church mobilized to take collections for the aid of people in such circumstances (Acts 11:28–29). The care of the hungry and needy is a priority of Christ's church.

Exploitation

The third type of circumstance that can create poverty occurs when people are made poor because they have been exploited by the powerful. They live in societies where the political, social, and judicial institutions favor the rich and powerful and leave the poor without advocacy. In biblical terms, the most frequent abuser of such victims is government. Government leaders and rulers have tended to exploit the very people they are called to serve. They enslave their own people, as did Solomon (1 Kings 12:4), or other peoples, as did the pharaoh of Egypt. The Exodus was God's response to such wicked exploitation. It happens in modern forms of dictatorial tyrannies, as well as in democratic bureaucracies.

Personal Sacrifice

Some people are poor "for righteousness' sake." They willingly give themselves to vocations of service that are not deemed valuable in the secular marketplace. In America, the two lowest paid professions relative to the education required remain the clergy and teachers. Here the marketplace determines the values of goods and services as it does for everything else. This reveals that the market puts relatively little value on spiritual nurture or education. I suspect this is why these were the two vocations God commanded to be subsidized by the tithe. He obviously places a higher value upon them than does our society.

Few, if any, who enter the vocations of ministry or education do so with the expectation of becoming wealthy. They have chosen to eschew riches for the sake of their service. It is a wicked thing, however, for the society in which they serve to impose poverty upon them or to exploit their willingness to serve by withholding the tithe or financial support from them. This was viewed in the Old Testament as nothing less than robbery of God Himself (Mal. 3:8).

The Bible will not allow us to lump all the poor together as being lazy or being virtuously sacrificial. We must discern the difference.

A ROSE IS A ROSE

A **ROSE IS A ROSE IS A ROSE.** This dictum reinforces the adage that a rose by any other name is still a rose. The idea is that the essence of the rose is not conditioned by what name is attached to it. It is its *res*, not its *nomina*, that determines what it is. In different languages, the same flower is known by different names, but it is still the same flower.

When we apply this idea to theology things get a bit more complicated. Indeed the rose adage has been transferred indiscriminately to religion in order to create a theological concept. The concept is: "God by any other name is still God." Now certainly, it is true that the immutable essence of God is not changed by the alteration of His name. In English, we may say "God," in German "*Gott*," in Greek "*Theos*," yet all these names or words are used to point to the same Deity.

Beyond this, however, things get murky. It is a quantum leap to go from saying that God by any other name is still God, to saying that all the great religions in the world believe in the same Being though they call Him different names.

This irrational leap is prodded by the popular analogy of the mountain. This analogy notes that there are many roads up the mountain. Some progress on a more direct route, while others wind about on more circuitous roads, but sooner or later they all arrive at the same place, at the top of the mountain.

So, it is argued, there are many roads that lead to God. They may be different routes but they all end up in the same place—with God Himself. That is, the differing roads indicate no difference in the God who is found. God's being, then, becomes the lowest (or highest) common denominator of all religions.

The road analogy is buttressed by the democratic truism that all religions are equal under the law. The fallacy in this axiom is thinking that just because all religions enjoy equal tolerance under the civil law, they therefore are all equally valid. That might be true if there were no God, but then it would be better to say that with respect to their ultimate affirmation they are all equally invalid.

To argue that all religions ultimately believe in the same God is the quintessential nonsense statement. Even a cursory examination of the content of different religions reveals this. The nature of the Canaanite deity Baal differs sharply from the nature of the biblical God. They are not remotely the same. This sharp distinction is also seen when comparing the God of Israel with the gods and goddesses of Roman, Greek, or Norse mythology.

The problem becomes even more complex when we consider that sometimes different religions use the same name for God while their views of the nature of God differ radically. Consider, for example, the religion of Mormonism. It claims to embrace the Bible (as well as the Book of Mormon, Pearl of Great Price, and Doctrine of Covenants) and professes belief in the God of the Bible as well as the biblical Christ. Mormons call themselves the Church of Jesus Christ of Latter-day Saints. Yet historic Christianity does not accept the Mormon religion as a branch or denomination of Christianity. Why? Because the Mormon view of the nature of God and of Christ differs sharply at essential points of faith. For example, Mormonism categorically rejects the full deity of Christ. Christ is said to be pre-existent, but not eternal. He is highly exalted—indeed revered—but He remains a creature, not Creator, in Mormon theology.

What about Islam? Islam is one of the largest religions in the world. In the city of Jerusalem, the Dome of the Rock is displayed as one of the most beautiful sacred shrines on the planet. Islam claims to embrace the God of the Old Testament. It holds the biblical patriarchs in high esteem and even accords a certain respect to Jesus as a great prophet, but He pales in significance to Mohammed, who is the supreme prophet in the credo: "Allah is God and Mohammed is His Prophet."

This forces the question, "Is Allah the same God as Yahweh, only under a different name?" Or we could pose the question in a different way: "Is Allah the God of the Bible?"

The answer to these questions depends first of all on the answer to the question: "Is the God of Christianity the God in the Old Testament, that is, Yahweh?" If the Being who is called "God" in the New Testament is the God called "Yahweh" in the Old Testament, then, manifestly, the God of Islam is not the God of the Bible. As Yahweh continues to reveal Himself through the ministry of Christ and the Apostles, it is clear Yahweh is very different from Allah. We cannot legitimately harmonize the theology of Christianity with the theology of Islam. They differ sharply at essential points.

The most obvious difference is with respect to the Trinity. Christians confess the triune nature of God. The language "nature" here may be confusing inasmuch as the Christian doctrine of God affirms that God is one in essence (or nature) and three in person. This means that the distinction of persons in the Godhead is not a distinction of essence, which would leave us with three gods. For precision, we must walk the razor's edge and say that the distinctions of persons in the Godhead is an *essential* distinction, yet not a distinction of *essence*. God is one in being (or essence), but it is important to note the personal distinctions of God, because the Bible goes to great lengths to do so.

Here is a crucial difference between the Muslim understanding of God and the Christian concept: The term *god* does not refer to the same being in each religion because Allah is clearly not triune. For Islam, there is no second person of the Trinity who becomes incarnate and effects our salvation and no third person of the Trinity who applies that redemption to us. So we are left with radically different views of God via the person and work of Christ and the person and work of the Holy Spirit.

There are two other vital differences between Christianity and Islam. Islam has no Cross and no resurrection, articles of the faith that are of the essence of Christianity and of ultimate importance to the plan of the God of the Bible. Mohammed made no atonement for our sins when he died. And when he died, he stayed dead.

There are other crucial differences we could explore of how God is understood in orthodox Christianity and how He is understood in orthodox Islam. It is enough for now to say that Allah and Yahweh are not the same. One is the living God; the other is an idol.

"To argue that all religions ultimately believe in the same God is the quintessential nonsense statement."

———

INDEPENDENCE DAY

MAY 1998

———

I T HAS BEEN AN ENIGMA to me why the ascension of Christ receives so little attention among most evangelical churches. Other momentous events in the life of Christ are feted during the church year, such as Christmas, Good Friday and Easter. Some attention is given to Pentecost, but very little to Ascension day.

It is understandable that the church would desire to celebrate the birth of Christ, His atoning death and the Resurrection. But why does the Ascension suffer neglect by comparison? To be sure, without the Nativity there can be no Cross, and without the Cross there is no Atonement. Also, without the Resurrection, the Cross would be seen as a futile act of self-sacrifice.

The Ascension is vital to the biblical understanding of the ministry of Christ. In one sense it represents the acme or zenith of Christ's incarnate progression from humiliation to exaltation. His entire life was a relentless progression to the point of His coronation as King of Kings. This was a critical aspect of His messianic destiny. He fulfilled the Old Testament prophecies and the psalms of enthronement when He ascended to the seat of cosmic authority.

In America we celebrate July 4th as "Independence Day," on which the colonies broke free from the oppression of King George. But we virtually ignore the day when our King was invested on high and gained independence for us from the Prince of Darkness. The Ascension of Jesus was the most important political event in history because in it He was installed in the highest seat of authority in the cosmos.

The ascension of Jesus was a unique event. Jesus Himself indicated that no one ascends into heaven except He who has descended from heaven (John 3:13). This reality points to two important concepts.

The first relates to the very meaning of *ascension*. The term, in its general usage, simply means "a going up." Pilgrims who visited Jerusalem were said to "ascend" or "go up" to Jerusalem. In this case ascension was merely a matter of geographical or topographical elevation. It was a matter of earthly altitude.

In like manner we speak of people going "up to heaven." We tend to speak of heaven in spatial terms as a place "up there" to which people rise upon their deaths. But going up to heaven is simply a dimensional change that is articulated via spatial language. It may be an "ascension" in the broad sense, but not in the narrow sense in which Jesus speaks of it. In the narrow sense the Ascension refers to "going up" to a specific place for a specific purpose. The place to which Christ ascends is the right hand of the Father. The specific purpose is to be enthroned as the King of the universe. In this narrow sense, Christ, and Christ alone, "ascends." No one else is granted the honor, privilege, and authority that goes with being seated at the right hand of the Father.

The second aspect of the Ascension refers to Jesus' statement that no one ascends save He who has first descended. Indirectly, the Ascension of Jesus bears witness to His pre-existent glory as the second person of the Trinity. When Jesus ascends to heaven, enshrouded by the glory of the *shekinah* cloud, He demonstrates His own origin. He is the One who has first come down from heaven. He is the One who counted His equality with God not a thing to be grasped or tenaciously held on to—He was willing to empty or divest Himself of His eternal glory in order to make Himself of no reputation on our behalf (Phil. 2:5). It was this glory that He had set aside for us and for our salvation that He prayed the Father would restore to Him in His High Priestly Prayer of John 17.

For Jesus the Ascension was a return to glory where He would exercise the authority over all things that had been granted Him by the Father. For His disciples it was an occasion for great joy and celebration. When Jesus first spoke to them about His impending departure from their midst, they received this news in a spirit of despair. The news cast a pall of gloom over them as the thought of separation from their master was an unbearable idea for them. When Jesus declared that He was "going away," Peter responded with his famous question, "*Quo Vadis?*"—"Where are You going?" Once Jesus explained to them the purpose and necessity of His departure, their mood began to change. He told them that it was needful for Him to depart. Indeed, the force of His words is that His absence would be better for them than His presence because of *where* He was going and *why* He was going there.

When the disciples witnessed the actual departure of Jesus from the Mount of Olives, they stood gazing at the rising *shekinah* cloud that bore Him up. When the angel spoke assuringly to them of Christ's return, they returned to Jerusalem rejoicing. Their joy was not at their separation from Him, but obviously from their understanding that His departure did not mark the end of His redemptive work on their behalf. It marked the beginning of a whole new dimension of that work.

Three crucial aspects of Christ's work are linked to the Ascension. The first is that He assumed the seat of cosmic authority upon His investiture as King of kings. His coronation laid waste the mockery of the inscription placed by Pilate over His cross that He was "King of the Jews." The Crucified One was now, not only King of the Jews, but King over the Romans and over all nations. This is the point the church has failed to grasp in its fullness. The kingdom of Christ is not simply a future hope that is as yet unrealized. His reign has already begun. He is King of kings right now.

The last instructions Jesus gave to His disciples and thus to His church were that they should bear witness to His kingship. Presently His kingship is invisible to us but nonetheless real. Calvin argued that the task of the church is to make the invisible kingdom of Christ visible.

The second aspect of the Ascension is its link to Pentecost. It was necessary for Jesus to ascend *before* He could, along with the Father, send the Holy Spirit to empower the church for its expanded ministry. Jesus told the disciples to wait in Jerusalem until they received power to carry out the mandate to bear witness to His kingdom. The reception of that power took place at Pentecost. Without the Ascension there could be no Pentecost.

The third crucial aspect that was linked to the Ascension was Jesus' entering the heavenly Holy of Holies to continue His ministry as our great High Priest. On the cross He made the perfect, once-for-all sacrifice of atonement for His people. But that was not the end of His priestly vocation. Once He entered into heaven, He continued and continues His priestly role in the ministry of intercession. At this very moment Jesus serves as our King and our High Priest, daily ruling over the world and praying for His church as our Priest-King. That is cause for jubilant celebration.

SIGNS AND SEALS

JUNE 1998

———

T HAT BAPTISM IS A SACRAMENT instituted by Christ as an outward sign of the new covenant is a reality embraced by almost all
who profess the name of Christ. This consensus, however, begins
to unravel when we consider the widespread disagreement that erupts
among Christians when we consider the related questions of the full significance of baptism, its mode of execution, its efficacy, and those who
are to receive it.

Though baptism was given as an integral dimension of the unity of the
body of Christ (Eph. 4:5), it has become a focal point of historical controversy among confessing Christian bodies. With respect to the practice of
infant baptism, the church is seriously divided. Although the practice of
infant baptism has been the majority report among Christian bodies in
church history, it has not been monolithic—it has been challenged for
centuries by those groups who restrict baptism to professing believers only.

Part of the debate over paedobaptism is related to other issues such as
the mode, efficacy and significance. In the early centuries of Christian
history, a fierce debate over infant baptism arose in the Pelagian controversy. Pelagius and his followers raised questions about infant baptism,
not for the same reasons modern Baptists object to it, but for a totally
different reason. At issue with the Pelagians was the link of baptism to
the doctrine of original sin. Since baptism was regarded, among other
things, a rite of cleansing from original sin, Pelagius took umbrage at
it. Pelagius denied original sin, arguing that Adam's sin affected Adam
alone, and that no sin nature or moral corruption passed to the progeny
of Adam. He considered that infants were innocent and without moral
corruption at birth, and therefore required no cleansing from sin or its
effects. Against the Pelagian view, the church regarded all infants as being
born corrupted with original sin.

In Roman Catholic sacramentology, baptism is called the "sacrament of faith, without which no man was ever justified," and the "instrumental cause" of justification. In this view baptism is necessary for salvation. This baptism must be either actual or "by desire." The baptism of desire makes allowance for those who intend to be baptized but are so hindered (for example, by sudden death) that they are unable to have it accomplished. Trent decreed, "If anyone says that baptism is optional, that is, not necessary for salvation, let him be anathema" (Canon 5, Session 7).

For Rome baptism effects regeneration, the infusion of grace, the cleansing of original sin, and remission of sin. This is accomplished *ex opere operato*, i.e., by the working of the work. Again, Trent declared, "If anyone says that by the sacraments of the New Law grace is not conferred *ex opere operato*, but that faith alone in the divine promise is sufficient to obtain grace, let him be anathema" (Canon 8 of Sacraments).

Rome does not insist on immersion as the only valid mode of baptism. It allows for sprinkling as well. The remission of sin invokes not only the pardon of sin but the *removal* of sin. The soul is cleansed of original and actual sin. The soul of the infant receives inward sanctification.

Protestants differ among themselves regarding the efficacy of infant baptism, particularly with respect to the question of baptismal regeneration. The issue of baptismal regeneration is a complex one chiefly because of the various ways in which the term *regeneration* has been understood in church history. Sometimes regeneration is used to indicate an *external change*—that is, a translation from the world into the church. In this sense it requires no necessary inward change. Sometimes it refers to a lifelong process by which the soul is gradually transformed into conformity with Christ. Sometimes it is used simply as a synonym for conversion. In contemporary theological usage it usually refers to the supernatural work of the Holy Spirit by which the soul is quickened from spiritual death and is made spiritually alive.

The Church of England teaches that by baptism infants are made members of Christ and children of God. This "regeneration" includes a cleansing from guilt and an inward renewing by the Holy Spirit.

Likewise, historic Lutheranism affirms a doctrine of baptismal regeneration. Baptism conveys to infants all the benefits of redemption. The soul is renovated and the infant receives the gift of the Holy Spirit. However, Lutherans add that there is a necessary condition for the reception of those benefits of baptism. That condition is faith. Without faith baptism is useless or invalid. In the case of adults, both regeneration and faith must precede baptism. In the case of infants, Lutherans teach that they have true faith. This faith is produced by baptism. Lutherans acknowledge that the "faith" of infants is not the fully developed voluntary function of adults, but is worked by grace, because the infants do not voluntarily reject it.

Classic Reformed theology rejects the idea of baptismal regeneration. The Westminster Confession declares, "Although it be a great sin to condemn or neglect this ordinance, yet grace and salvation are not so inseparably annexed unto it, as that no person can be regenerated or saved without it, or that all that are baptized, are undoubtedly regenerated." A crucial point of the Reformed view of baptism is that its efficacy is *not tied to that moment of time* in which it is administered. Baptism signifies many things, including the regeneration of the soul, but that which it signifies is not automatically conferred by the sacramental act itself. The redemptive benefits signified by baptism are contingent upon faith. That faith may be present either before or after the sacrament is received. In the case of adult baptism, a profession of faith must be made before the sign is given. In the case of infants, faith must come after the sign.

What the infant does receive in baptism prior to the exercise of faith is the sign of God's promise to grant all the benefits signified by baptism to all who exercise faith. This sign is not regarded as an empty or naked sign. It marks a real promise of God to all who believe.

Reformed churches restrict infant baptism to children of members of the visible church. In this sense children of the covenant community are given the sign of the new covenant and are marked by that sign as children of the covenant. At this point Reformed churches see a link between new covenant baptism and Old Testament circumcision. This is not to say that Reformed theology sees an identity between circumcision and baptism. The two are different ordinances. There are areas of discontinuity between them, yet they are not so dissimilar as to have no connection. Despite the discontinuity between circumcision and baptism, there remains a continuity between them. Both are outward signs of God's promise of redemptive blessing. Both are signs of faith. Both are covenant signs. In the Old Testament circumcision did not automatically convey salvation. In the New Testament baptism does not automatically convey salvation. What is conveyed is God's faithful promise of salvation unto all who believe.

TWIN PILLARS

JULY 1998

———

E VANGELISM AND APOLOGETICS ARE TWIN pillars upon which the outreach of the church is built. The two may be and must be distinguished, but they ought never be separated. They form a two-pronged attack against the fortress of hell and a double-front of defense against the onslaught of paganism.

What is evangelism? If we answer this question by appealing to the definition of contemporary usage, the answer becomes fuzzy and confused. A "liberal" may define evangelism as an effort to bear witness to the kingdom of God by working to promote social and political change. This is a "social gospel" that seeks the betterment of the human condition without a view to the personal reconciliation of the sinner to God. It involves the redemption of society, the relief of suffering from economic deprivation, and the salvation of whales and turtle eggs.

An "evangelical" answer to the question may focus on the process of mass or personal evangelism designed to get people "saved" from their sin and into personal relationships with Jesus. Here the accent is often on methodology or technique by which the saved person responds to an appeal by "making a decision for Christ," raising a hand, walking an aisle in response to an altar call, or by reciting the sinner's prayer. These techniques may or may not be related to or consistent with biblical evangelism. That is, they may grow out of biblical evangelism or, in some cases, may actually work against biblical evangelism.

If we seek a biblical definition of evangelism, we see immediately that such evangelism contains two essential elements: (1) proclamation; and (2) the Gospel itself. Since the word *evangelism* comes from the Greek word that is translated by the English word *gospel* and transliterated by the term *evangel*, we clearly see that the biblical concept of evangelism is first and foremost about the Gospel. If our evangelism is to be biblical, then it must contain the Gospel.

Herein lies the rub. If biblical evangelism is about the Gospel, then we must have a clear understanding of the meaning and the content of the Gospel. If we search the ancient meaning of *gospel* as it relates to the New Testament, we see that it is used in at least three distinct ways (although in a lesser sense the term may be used for any form of "good news"). The first reference we find is to a specific literary form. The first four books of the New Testament, which to a greater or lesser degree provide biographical sketches of the life of Christ, are called "Gospels." Since John's Gospel focuses much of its attention on the last week of Jesus' life, it is differentiated from the other three Gospels, called the "Synoptic Gospels" because they provide a more comprehensive "synopsis" of the life of Jesus.

The second main reference to the Gospel has to do with Jesus' chief use of the term. Here the term *gospel* refers to Jesus' frequent announcements of the breakthrough of the coming kingdom of God. For Jesus the heart of the Good News is the Gospel of the kingdom. He frequently expanded this message via His parables in which He said, "The kingdom of God is like unto this..." Perhaps it is because the announcement of the kingdom was so central to the teaching of Jesus that some have restricted the meaning of Gospel to a kingdom orientation.

In the New Testament epistles, especially the epistles of the Apostle Paul, the term "gospel" has a different, though by no means antithetical, focus from that of the Gospels. Here the emphasis is on the person and work of Jesus Himself. Jesus is seen as the King of the kingdom through whose work salvation is accomplished. Paul announces the Gospel of God, not in the sense that it is a Gospel *about* God, but that it is God's Gospel. It is news that originates with God Himself.

In this use of *gospel*, the Good News focuses on the objective accomplishments of Jesus on our behalf, and the subjective appropriation of these benefits by the believer. Objectively, the Gospel is about Christ's work of redemption in the Cross, Resurrection, and Ascension. But it also includes the oft overlooked or neglected element of His perfect active obedience. That Christ was sinless and achieved perfect obedience to the Law is essential to the Gospel. That is, His *life*, as well as His death, is vital to the Good News. Without His perfect active obedience, Jesus could qualify neither to die for us nor to live for us. His perfection is necessary for the "blessed exchange" by which our sins were imputed to Him on the cross, and His righteousness imputed to us as the grounds of our justification before God.

The notion of imputation is an essential element of the Gospel in that, without it, either negatively by which our sins are imputed to Him, or positively by which His righteousness is imputed to us, there is no good news. Any gospel without imputation in both directions is "another gospel," which is what Paul called no gospel at all. This issue of double imputation was the center of the controversy that provoked the 16th century Reformation and remains to this day the central issue of the controversy or battle for the Gospel.

For Paul, especially as he contended with heretical Judaizers of the 1st century, whom he placed under the anathema of God and about whom he said with tears that they were "enemies of the cross," the question of the subjective appropriation of the benefits of the work of Christ was both integral and essential to the Gospel itself. Without this aspect the Gospel would be left hanging. The question is, "How do the benefits of Christ's life and death become mine?" The apostolic answer is, "Through faith apart from the works of the Law." This is the core of the Reformation concept of *sola fide*, that the benefits of Christ's work of redemption are received through faith and through faith alone. This defines the classic meaning of the term *evangelical* and must be incorporated in evangelism if indeed it is the Gospel we are preaching.

Secondly, evangelism involves proclamation. We can witness to Christ in many ways by the example of our lives, but such witnessing is not evangelism. For evangelism to take place, there must be proclamation. The Good News is news and it must be communicated or proclaimed with words.

The term *apologetics* comes from the Greek *apologia*, which means "a reply." In the early church the work of the apologist was two-fold. Firstly, the apologists had the task of clarifying the content of the Gospel against distortions of it made by enemies. For example the early Christians were charged with sedition, atheism, and cannibalism. Because Christians spoke of Christ as their King, they were accused of being disloyal to the Roman Empire. Since they would not worship the Roman gods and goddesses, and especially because they would not worship the emperor, they were charged with atheism. Also, rumors abounded that Christians were cannibals in that they met in secret and engaged in the eating of somebody's body and the drinking of somebody's blood. To these charges and others, the apologists gave a "reply," clarifying the church's position on such matters.

Secondly, the task of the apologist was to defend the truth claims of the Gospel. They argued for the truth of the Gospel. In this regard the work of the apologists was basically that of pre-evangelism. They were the "Seabees" of the army of God, providing the basis for intellectual assent to the truth of the Gospel.*

In history the task of apologetics has progressed to include both the defense of the Gospel against the attacks of alien philosophies and religions, and the positive construction of full-fledged Christian philosophy. In this regard apologetics serves the church not only in pre-evangelism, but in post-evangelism as well. It helps the believer counter the objections that are faced in a myriad of settings. It arms and equips the saints for the task of ministry. God has ordained both evangelism and apologetics, and the obedient church is faithful to both tasks.

---

* The U.S. Naval Construction Battalions, known as the Seabees, are particularly famous for their efforts in the Pacific Theater of World War II, which involved hastily clearing fields and building airfields to support subsequent operations.

GLORY

AUGUST 1998

"Oh, let the nations be glad and sing for joy!" —Psalm 67:4

I N THE OLD TESTAMENT ABRAHAM was called of God to be blessed and to be a blessing. The marvelous promises of God that were given to him and to his seed were also, by extension, to be the occasion for the blessing of all the nations of the world. In the New Testament the "mystery" that once had been hidden but was then being revealed was that the Gospel was not for the Jews only, but was "Christ in you, the hope of the Gentiles." Paul's selection as the apostle to the nations was consistent with the Great Commission—that the Gospel would be taken to the ends of the earth, to every tribe, tongue and nation.

The word mission comes from the Latin verb that means "to send." We have *missal*, *missives*, and *missionaries*, all of which are sent by someone or something. When we remit payment for a bill, we send it in. When we gain *remission* of our sins, our sins are sent away from us. Thus, mission is about a kind of sending.

The origin of missions is in eternity. The missionary enterprise of the church began in what is called the covenant of redemption. This covenant is not that made by God with Adam, Abraham, or Moses. It is a covenant made by God with Himself. The impetus for missions began with an agreement within the Godhead among the three Persons of the Trinity. This is important to note, lest we ever fall into the trap of thinking that the Son is engaged in resolving a conflict that He has with the Father, as if the Father and the Son were ever at cross purposes. The only cross purpose they had was the purpose of the Cross, which purpose they agreed on from the foundation of the world.

The New Testament agenda for missions begins with the mission of Christ Himself. Christ is not only the sender or the One who sends the church into the world, but He Himself is the One who is sent. The Father sends the Son into the world. Then the Son sends His church into the same arena in His name and for His sake. In this entire enterprise it is the mission of God that is being carried out. As the Father sends Jesus, so Jesus sends us.

If the enterprise of missions begins in eternity and within God Himself, we are left with the question, "Why?" What is the ultimate purpose of missions? The standard reply to such a question is that the purpose of missions is the salvation of God's people. We are directed to John 3:16: "God so loved the world that He gave His only begotten Son..." Here the reason or purpose for God's giving or sending Christ is His love for the world. That is, the motive of the divine mission is found in the love of God for His creation. The question then is asked, "Is this the only motive or purpose for missions?" Is God's purpose in the work of redemption solely or exclusively based on His concern or benevolence for people?

The latter question has been the subject of much theological debate through the ages of church history. The arguments have been waged that contend that another purpose is for God's own glory. Indeed, at times these two purposes have been placed in opposition to each other as if they were mutually exclusive options. It is argued that, if the ultimate motive of missions is God's own glory, then it cannot be a concern for human redemption.

It may be true that we cannot have two equal and opposite ultimates. Equal ultimacy tends to fall of its own weight on such a construction.

But the question may be resolved by first recognizing that it is often posed in the form of the fallacy of the false dilemma, or what is more commonly called the either/or fallacy.

The question of ultimacy may be postponed for the moment. Before we seek to answer that question, we must first acknowledge that the Bible clearly reveals that God's work of redemption involves both a love and concern for His creatures *and* a concern and "jealousy" for God's own glory.

The psalmist sees no conflict between these two ends when he says "The LORD reigns; let the earth rejoice; let the islands be glad!" (Ps. 97:1).

The joy and gladness of the earth can never be fully realized unless or until we rejoice in the reigning of God.

The Westminster Shorter Catechism begins with the initial question: "What is man's chief end?" The question is not about the "end" of man with respect to a spatial or temporal terminal point. The word "end" here is used to mean "purpose or goal." It is a teleological question that is in view. In modern English we would ask, "What is man's chief purpose?"

The answer given by the Catechism is revealing. It reads: "Man's chief end is to glorify God and to enjoy Him forever." The answer is quite easy to memorize. To understand it fully and to embrace it whole-heartedly is not so easy. The reality and power of sin is found in its insistence that human happiness is incompatible with divine glory. Sin declares that the glory of God is the supreme barrier to my own joy. God cannot be glorified by disobedience. Yet obedience it seems, can only be achieved at the sacrifice of joy. This is the great lie of sin.

Yet the lie works against the very purpose and goal of our humanity. We were made in the image of God. The very purpose of our lives is to be holy as He is holy, to glorify Him by our obedience to Him. It is only when we are in harmony with the purpose for which we were made that the fullness of joy can be experienced. To seek our "fulfillment" in our own glory is not only to work against God but to work against ourselves. To do this is to rob God of His glory and to rob ourselves of our highest possible joy. A thief who robs from others is evil; a thief who robs from himself is stupid. As sinners, we are both evil and stupid.

The goal of missions is the goal of redemption. It involves both the joy and gladness of the nations, and the glory of God. The joy and gladness of the nations are not opposed to the glory of God, but redound to the glory of God. God is glorified in the redemption of His creation and His creation is gladdened by that redemption. We are told that the whole creation groans together in travail as it awaits its final redemption. Travail is likened to the birth pangs of a woman in labor. The pain is bitter-sweet. It is painful in the moment, but made sweet by the hope that it will yield the fruit of a baby and newness of life.

If we are forced to return to the question of ultimacy, we must remember that what is ultimate need not be opposed to what is penultimate. In terms of ultimacy we must regard the glory of God as the ultimate purpose for what God does. This does not cast a shadow of selfishness over the divine purpose because, when God wills to glorify Himself, this will is both holy and just. If God willed to set the glory of man above His own glory, He would be neither holy nor just. For God to exalt the creature above Himself would be for God to commit the heinous evil of idolatry. He would be acting against the very holiness of His own nature. Not only would such a goal violate His own holiness, but it would not be just.

If justice is defined as "giving a person what is his due," then it follows that justice demands that ultimately glory must be given to God above His creatures because it is His due. It would be a gross injustice to assign the creature a greater glory than God Himself. When God wills His own glory, He is acting according to the good pleasure of His will. It is a pleasure that is neither arbitrary nor selfish. It is a *good* pleasure. God is and should be pleased when He is glorified. Here the one who is most glorious is glorified and, in the process, His creatures are able to reach the zenith of their own joy and gladness.

The glory and majesty of God are not the only motives and goals of missions, but they are the highest and supreme goals. The ultimate does not cancel the penultimate, but is reached through it.

THREE SCHOOLS

SEPTEMBER 1998

———

T HE FRENCH PHILOSOPHER BLAISE PASCAL described man as a
creature of profound paradox. Humans are creatures of the highest grandeur and the lowest misery, often at the same time (but
not in the same relationship, of course). Part of our grandeur is located
in our ability to contemplate ourselves. Whether animals are "self-
conscious" in the sense that they can reflect upon their origins and destinies or cogitate about their place in the grand scheme of things is a
debated point, but that man has a complex and superior ability to do
these things allows for little debate.

This gift of contemplation is not without its downside: pain. Our misery is often enhanced by our ability to contemplate a better life than we
presently enjoy, often coupled with the awareness that we are incapable
of gaining or achieving the ideal life. This is the stuff of which dreams
and nightmares are made.

We may enjoy good health, but not perfect health. We can imagine
life free of aches and pains, tooth decay, and crippling diseases, but no
one has yet found a way to insure such physical freedom. We all face the
certainty of agony and of death.

The poor man can dream of riches untold, but be frustrated when the
lottery passes him by. Even the rich man can contemplate an even greater
abundance of wealth, and while abundance has a finite limit, desire does not.

Sick or healthy, poor or rich, successful or unsuccessful, we can be
plagued by the vexing problem that life could provide a better state than
we presently enjoy.

The biblical escape hatch from perpetual frustration for dreams unrealized, aspirations not met, and hopes dashed to pieces is the spiritual
virtue of contentment.

We find a model for this virtue in the Apostle Paul's declaration in

Philippians 4:11, "Not that I speak in regard to need, for I have learned in whatever state I am, to be content."

When Paul uses the word "content," he uses the Greek word *autarkēs*, which means "self-sufficing," i.e., "co-independent of circumstances" (see also 2 Cor. 9:8). The word Paul uses is from the same root as the Greek word *ataraxia*, which has been borrowed as the brand name for a modern tranquilizer.

Socrates spoke of the concept when he was asked the question, "Who is the wealthiest?" He replied, "He that is content with least, for *ataraxia* is nature's wealth."

The New Testament mentions two schools of philosophical thought that were in vogue during Apostolic times. These were the schools of Stoicism and Epicureanism, whose representatives Paul encountered at Mars Hill in Athens. Though their two schools differed sharply with respect to cosmology and metaphysics, they shared a common practical goal for living: the quest for *ataraxia*. The Stoics understood this in terms of what they called "imperturbability." The Stoics constructed a type of material determinism by which humans have no power over their circumstances. Life "happens" via fixed external causes. Our circumstances are a result of what happens *to* us. The only arena over which the self has any significant control is the inner arena of personal attitude. What we can control is how we feel about what happens to us. The goal of Stoic training was to gain the inward state of imperturbability so that, whatever transpired outwardly, the person maintained an inner peace that left him unbothered. This is the classical Stoic attitude of the so-called "stiff upper lip."

The Epicureans were more proactive in their search for *ataraxia*. They sought to maximize pleasure and minimize pain. They were refined hedonists who sought a proper balance between pleasure and pain. Yet, they never solved the "Hedonistic Paradox," which decreed that if you fail to gain the pleasure you seek you are frustrated, but if you gain the pleasure you seek you are bored. So, in terms that anticipate Pascal's paradox, one was left in a state of either frustration or boredom, neither of which captured the contentment of *ataraxia*.

Paul's view of contentment differed radically from that of the Stoic or the Epicurean. Paul, in 1 Corinthians 15, eschewed the credo of "eat, drink and be merry, for tomorrow we die." This hedonistic view which was discussed in Ecclesiastes is a view of ultimate pessimism that held no place in Paul's theology, especially in light of the resurrection.

In like manner, Paul categorically rejected the passive resignation stance of Stoicism. Paul did not believe that our circumstances are ordered by blind, impersonal forces. He had no room for fatalism or mechanistic determination. He was an activist who pressed toward his goals, and who called us to work out our salvation with fear and trembling. He did not advocate a quietism which declared, "Let go and let God."

The contentment of which Paul spoke is not a being "at ease in Zion," by which a godless complacency leaves the soul moribund and the spirit inert. He was never "content" to rest on his laurels or to relax his zeal for ministry.

At countless points Paul expressed his discontent and dissatisfaction concerning the errors, vices and failings of the church, and concerning his own shortcomings. There were many tasks to be finished and problems to be solved in his own life and ministry that required zealous effort on his part.

His contentment was directed to his personal circumstances or the state of his human condition. He expanded his statement of contentment by writing, "I know how to be abased, and I know how to abound. Everywhere and in all things I have learned both to be full and to be hungry, both to abound and to suffer need" (Phil. 4:12).

Here we notice that Paul speaks of learning and knowing. The contentment he enjoyed was a *learned* condition. He *learned* the secret or the mystery of contentment. That secret is partially revealed to us in his following declaration, "I can do all things in Him that strengthens me."

Paul's contentment rested in his mystical union with Christ and in his theology. For the apostle, theology was not an abstract discipline removed from the pressing issues of daily life. In one sense it was life itself, or the key to understanding life itself. Paul's contentment or satisfaction with his state or condition of life rested upon his knowledge of the character of God and his knowledge of how God works. His was not an *ataraxia* based upon passive resignation to the impersonal forces of nature. His was a contentment based on the knowledge that his steps and human condition were ordered by the Lord. Perhaps it was Paul's understanding of the providence of God, more than anything else, that was his secret to biblical contentment. He understood that every good and perfect gift comes from God, and that all things work together for good for those who love God and are called according to His purpose. Paul understood that if he was abased he was fulfilling the purpose of God, and if he abounded he was also fulfilling the purpose of God. For Paul it was a matter of submission to the divine vocation that was the key to his relentless joy.

In our partly sanctified lives, there lurks the godless temptation to assume that God owes us a better condition than we presently enjoy. Such is the misery of sin, which misery is defeated by the triumph of God's saving and providential grace. It is in this grace that Christian contentment may be found.

THE TRUTH OF BEAUTY

OCTOBER 1998

———

IT WAS MIDNIGHT IN AMSTERDAM. The *Concertgebouw* was packed with jazz fans eagerly awaiting the performance scheduled by Thelonious Monk. The audience was teased by the warm up provided by a combo. Finally, the houselights were dimmed and a single spotlight was fixed on the piano. Monk made his entrance. He was wearing a sweatshirt and jeans. On his head was a Russian Cossack hat. His eyes were hidden by sunglasses, and a cigarette dangled from the side of his mouth. Monk didn't walk to the piano; he ambled. The piano bench was situated at a cock-eyed angle to the piano. While the combo played, Monk straddled the end of the bench looking toward the audience. He reached out his left hand and with one finger tinkled an improvised melody. People laughed at what was apparently a "put on." At length, Monk swung around and faced the keyboard. Then, with both hands moving in animated rapidity, he began a concert that dazzled the critics and elated the fans. His harmonic improvisation produced sounds that some likened to Venusian music, sounds from another planet. It was far out with an abundance of dissonance, yet somehow Monk was always able to resolve the tension with a pure harmony.

Monk's music was strange, provoking strong reaction from his listeners, both positive and negative. Yet even Monk's strongest critics never considered his music simply "noise." Some respond by declaring that music, as well as other art forms, is merely a matter of taste or personal preference. The cliché is that "beauty is in the eye of the beholder," or, in this case, "in the ear of the listener."

Part of the pervasive relativism of our age is a growing trend toward reducing aesthetics to pure subjectivism. Yet the question persists: are there objective norms and standards by which beauty may be measured in the arts? Obviously there is always a subjective element in art, at least in art appreciation, because the appreciation is given by people, who are subjects. Animals may give measured responses to art forms, but so far we have not hired dogs or cats to be art critics, though some artists believe monkeys and mules have been variously employed.

From Aristotle, to Thomas Aquinas, to Jonathan Edwards, some of the greatest minds in the history of western civilization have attempted to find objective standards for true beauty. For Aquinas and Edwards, the quest was driven in part by the conviction that the character of God is the fount of all beauty, just as He is the source and foundation of all truth and goodness. The triad of virtues—the good, the true, and the beautiful—all find their root and norm in God Himself.

That God is concerned with beauty may be seen in many ways. It is significant that the first persons recorded in Scripture as being filled with the Holy Spirit were the artisans and craftsmen God ordained to fashion the holy vessels and furniture for the tabernacle. Likewise, the design of the priestly garments of Aaron was given by divine decree, the goal of which was that they be for "beauty and holiness." Though these two categories can be distinguished, they are not unrelated. We are to worship God in the "beauty of holiness." It is easy to see that holiness is a thing of beauty. It is not so easy to see that beauty is a thing of holiness. But insofar as the beautiful bears witness to the character of God, it carries with it an element of the sacred. In this sense all art is sacred even if the artist is profane.

Some of the objective standards philosophers have claimed for beauty include complexity, proportionality, harmony, and excellence.

Complexity

Works of art have variant degrees of complexity. We recognize the difference between a stick-figure drawing and a fresco by Michelangelo. Anyone can draw stick-figures; they are simple. But few can master the complexity displayed by Michelangelo. My first piano lesson was easy. It involved playing one note with one finger, middle C. Once middle C was located, the rest was simple. No one who heard me play the one-note tune mistook me for Thelonious Monk.

We grant that the simple can at times be beautiful, as witnessed by the Gregorian chant or the primitive art of Grandma Moses.

Proportionality

Complexity in itself does not make for beauty. Noise can be complex and ugly. Complexity screams for proportionality and harmony. Proportion is often described mathematically in order to distinguish it from chaos. Chaos, like noise, is complex, but is asymmetrical to the point of confusion. It is disorder rather than order. Creation is complex. Yet it is breathtakingly beautiful. It confirms what Scripture declares: that God is not the author of confusion. Even Carl Sagan chose to call his book *Cosmos*, rather than *Chaos*, because of the display of order that makes science possible. If all were chaos, individualism would be impossible, and without individualism the pursuit of knowledge would be a fool's errand because language itself would be unintelligible gibberish.

Harmony

The ancient philosopher Pythagoras (author of the Pythagorean theorem and tutor of Plato) had a mystical view of numbers that drove his interest in math. Some consider Pythagoras to be the original author of the 12-note scale. He spoke of the movement of the stars in terms of the "harmony of the spheres."

That music is related to mathematics is seen by the proportionality that is involved with harmony. Harmony can be achieved in a multitude of ways, using thirds, fourths, fifths, etc. But the intervals and scales employed all follow a definite mathematical pattern.

One story about J.S. Bach alleges that the day he first heard of the Fibonacci sequence in math, he immediately sat down and composed an extraordinary fugue based on the sequence. It is not disputed that Mozart frequently experimented with mathematical formulas as he composed his music.

In modern art forms such as cubism, distortion seems to be the rule rather than proportionality. Yet, the distortion, like dissonance in jazz, is calculated and given to resolution. Some might argue that painting via hurling paint cans at a canvas may also be beautiful. The technique may leave something to be desired as it "intends" to demonstrate chance or chaos. Yet by its very intention, it excludes pure chance. And if nothing else, the splatter pattern of the paint is still bound by the laws of physics.

Excellence

The element of excellence may refer to technique, expression, mastery of the medium, or the medium itself. Excellence encompasses the skill factor of the artist. In various forms of competition, such as dance, music, diving, gymnastics, etc., points are awarded with reference to the degree of difficulty demanded in the performance. The degrees are related to complexity and the like, but the mastery of the skills involved underlines the quality of excellence.

The media employed by artists also contribute to excellence and beauty. The kind of stone used by the sculptor, the piano or violin employed by the musician, the pigment and brushes used by the painter, tend to augment or diminish the work of the artist.

We've included expression in the category of excellence because the emotive is an integral aspect of beauty. This is the "soul" or "heart" that is expressed in art. Though it is subjective in nature, it may still be measured to some degree in the overall work of the artist. A soul-less performance in music, though correct in notation, does not attain a high degree of excellence.

There are a few elements of art that bear witness to God who is perfect in His complexity, proportionality, harmony, and excellence. To measure each of these elements in art may be an art itself. Though we may fail to achieve total objectivity in our art appreciation, we can at least take solace in the fact that we can distinguish between drawing and scribbling, or symphony and cacophony.

TRUTH
OR CONSEQUENCES

NOVEMBER 1998

———

H ow do you know? This simple question is asked every day by
a multitude of people in a multitude of real-life situations. On the
surface the question seems simple and innocuous enough, yet it
gets at one of the most difficult and complex matters we can ever investigate. It touches the deepest questions there are about truth—namely,
what is truth and how do we learn it?

What Is Truth?

Francis Schaeffer wasn't stuttering when he spoke of "true truth." Nor
was he indulging himself in an exercise in redundancy. With this jarring
and ironic combination of words, "true truth," Schaeffer was addressing a major crisis in our culture, the loss of commitment to the idea
of objective truth, as chronicled and analyzed by Allan Bloom in his
best-selling work *The Closing of the American Mind.* Bloom argued that the
American mind was being systematically slammed shut on the pursuit
of objective truth. He estimated that over 95% of entering freshmen in
our universities come to college embracing a relativistic view of truth.
That commitment to relativism is then set in concrete by four years
of "higher" education that serves to reinforce the notion that truth is
purely subjective, a mere matter of personal taste or preference. In this
scenario "higher" education becomes "lower" education as the human
pursuit of knowledge degenerates into the base grunts and appetites of
brutes. Of course, the argument that truth is subjective would also be
subjective, rendering it meaningless. The confusing axiom most of our
society lives by is that there are no absolutes, except for the absolute that
there are absolutely no absolutes. This is the unofficial creed of the new

barbarianism that seeks liberation not only from God but from truth itself, lest any norm or standard impinge upon the personal desires of the individual. Truth becomes egocentric, based strictly upon whatever I want it to be. This would be as fatal to chimpanzees and grasshoppers as it is to human beings. The chimpanzee knows well enough that he can't turn a bamboo shoot into a banana merely by wanting it to be so. Perhaps I'm giving barbarians and animals a bad name by associating relativists with them.

The bad news is that over 95% of the "me generation" asserts that truth is relative. The good news is that none of them really believe it. If they did believe it, they could hardly exist for 24 hours. The professing relativist quickly abandons his epistemology when he approaches an intersection in the highway. He may prefer that there be no oncoming traffic that thwarts his entrance to the highway, but he knows that there can't be a Mack truck bearing down on him and not be a Mack truck bearing down on him at the same time and in the same relationship. Suddenly his commitment to relativism yields to his deeper commitment to the law of non-contradiction as he puts his foot on the brake. Now he is facing the objective reality of true truth.

Though various definitions of truth compete with each other for acceptance, such as relativism, subjectivism, pluralism, and a purely emotive view; nevertheless the common sense approach by which people actually live is some form of the classic correspondence theory of truth. John Locke, for example, defined truth as "that which corresponds to reality." This was challenged in part by Bishop Berkeley's famous maxim *esse est percepi*, "to be is to be perceived." This philosophical concept has been popularized by the poser, "If a tree falls in the forest and no one is there to hear it, does it make noise?" Berkeley was not trying to reduce truth to mere human perception, but merely trying to make room for God. His idea was that everything that is, and everything that happens, is always known and "perceived" perfectly by God at every moment. He then qualified Locke's definition by defining truth as "that which corresponds to reality as it is perceived by God." Only God knows truth comprehensibly and with perfect accuracy. His view of reality is never subject to distortion. He knows it like it is, perfectly and ultimately.

How Do We Know?

The "how" of knowledge is the big question of the science of science. The term "science," in its most rudimentary form, means "knowledge." So the science of science could also be called the knowledge of knowing. It asks the question, "How do we know what we know?" This is the ancient discipline of epistemology. Epistemology is a subdivision of philosophy which explores the process by which knowledge is attained. Various schools of thought have competed over this issue for centuries. Types of rationalism stress the primacy of the mind or intellect in gaining knowledge, while types of empiricism stress the primacy of sense perception in the process. Some have argued that truth is innate (*a priori*) and that, as Plato supposed, learning is simply a matter of recollection or recalling from the mind what has been there since before birth. Plato sought to demonstrate this in the *Meno* dialogue. In this work, through a series of leading questions, Socrates was able to elicit the Pythagorean theorem from an illiterate slave-boy named Meno. Or we may think of René Descartes, who after searching for clear and distinct ideas (such as the *cogito ergo sum*), thought that he could crawl into his Dutch oven and deduce the nature of reality without the benefit of sense perception, using only innate knowledge.

John Locke, on the other hand, argued that though the mind has an innate ability to organize sensory data into knowledge, it has no innate knowledge. The mind, at birth, is a "blank tablet" (*tabula rasa*), and all knowledge is then gained by experience (*a posteriori*).

Others such as Immanuel Kant and the Enlightenment thinkers who forged the analytical method by which one seeks the logic of the facts posed a kind of synthesis by which both the mind and the senses play key roles in the knowing process.

As human beings it is a given that we are equipped both with a mind and the five senses. Both the mind and the senses play a critical role in the learning process. Both are necessary to gain knowledge of the external world. Without the mind, all of our sense perceptions would be unintelligible hash. We would merely experience a bombardment of indiscriminate sensations, a blob of stimuli, with no ability to individuate or discriminate between sights and sounds, colors or shapes, unity or diversity. The mind is the organ necessary for orderly perception.

Likewise, without the senses our knowledge would be limited to what goes on within our own consciousness. Since we have physical bodies, our transition from the interior chamber of our mind to the exterior world around us is found in the five senses. Our senses of sight, hearing, touching, etc., are the threshold we have to the world. There may be a sunset apart from me, but I can't know about it unless I see it, read about it, hear someone describe it, or feel a record of it recorded in Braille.

If we are going to discover truth at all, we must realize that we are dependent upon both the mind and the senses. Rational thought and sense perception are both necessary conditions of knowledge.

Some might argue that as Christians we need neither reason nor sense perception since we have an infallible source of truth in the revelation of sacred Scripture. While it is true that revelation is a crucial source of truth for us, that very source of truth would be inaccessible to us apart from reason or sense perception. Without sense perception we have no access to the Bible. To gain any knowledge from the Bible we must perceive it. Our eyes, ears, or fingers must be engaged in order to get at the Bible. If we had no rational faculty of mind, the content of Scripture would be unintelligible gibberish to us. But the mind and the senses are part of our creative nature—they are gifts of God granted to us that we may be able to enter into a knowing relationship with Him. In Him we meet the fountainhead of all truth—a truth that corresponds to the reality He creates and governs—a reality that is not vitiated by the personal preferences of His creatures.

WHAT WENT WRONG?

DECEMBER 1998

—

> "The stone which the builders rejected has become
> the chief cornerstone. This was the Lord's doing,
> and it is marvelous in our eyes."
> —Matthew 21:42

T HE SCRIPTURE TELLS US THAT salvation is of the Jews. Historic Judaism was the cradle in which Christianity was born. Yet today Judaism and Christianity comprise two of the world's "great religions," which, while claiming a common source, are not only different religions, but at many crucial points are antithetical to each other.

The primary bone of contention between Judaism and Christianity is the understanding of the person and work of Jesus of Nazareth. Though many adherents of Judaism have complimentary views of Jesus, regarding Him as great moral teacher and virtuous man, they nevertheless demur at any attribution of deity to Jesus, or, perhaps even more basic, to any declaration that Jesus was the promised Messiah of the Old Testament.

Was Jesus the long-awaited Messiah? Christianity says "yes," while Judaism says "no." This difference is truly an irreconcilable difference. Jesus, manifestly, cannot both be the biblical Messiah and not be the biblical Messiah at the same time and in the same way. On this point somebody is wrong. Both views cannot be correct as they are mutually exclusive.

Christianity is so-named because of the central affirmation that Jesus is the "Christ." It is not called "Jesusanity" or "Godianity," but "Christianity." When the New Testament speaks of Jesus Christ, the appellation includes both a proper name and a title. "Jesus" is His name; "Christ" is His title. "Christ" is the English translation of the Greek word *Christos*, which in turn is the Greek translation for the Hebrew word for "Messiah."

Many of Jesus' contemporaries, including the writers of the New Testament, came to the conclusion that Jesus was, indeed, the Messiah of Israel. In the early days of the church, Christians were considered by many to be a sect or subdivision of the Jewish community. The church was born in Jerusalem, the Holy City of the Jews, and its first members were predominantly Jewish. Zacharias, Elizabeth, Simeon, Anna, Joseph, Mary, Paul, Peter, John, et al., as well as Jesus Himself, were all Jewish.

But not everyone in Israel came to the same conclusion. The majority of those who made up other parties of the Pharisees, the Sadducees, and the scribes, rejected the Messianic identity of Jesus. The Gospel writer says of Jesus, "He came to His own, and His own did not receive Him" (John 1:11).

The issue of Jesus' identity was a volatile issue, and the peaceful co-existence of Judaism and Christianity was short-lived. Some place the point of no return that marked the separation of Judaism and Christianity as two separate religions at the martyrdom of Stephen. Others point to the destruction of Jerusalem and the temple in A.D. 70 as the final point of historical division.

It is often surmised that the Old Testament is the sacred book of the Jews and the New Testament is the sacred book of the Christians. Yet historic Christianity does not accept this disjunction. Christianity claims both the Old and New Testaments for its sacred literature. The church argued that the New Testament provides not only the fulfillment of the Old Testament, but is also the normative interpreter of the Old Testament. This claim has its roots in the teaching of Jesus Himself. In His conflicts with the scribes and the Pharisees, Jesus appealed to the Old Testament to vindicate His claims. He claimed that Abraham rejoiced to see His day and that Moses wrote of Him. Obviously the scribes and Pharisees interpreted the Old Testament in a manner different from and contrary to the interpretation of Jesus. While the New Testament writers interpreted many of the "suffering servant" passages of Isaiah and the Messianic Psalms as relating to Jesus, the Jewish authorities did not. In a word, the New Testament writers had a Christological or Christocentric view of the Old Testament, while others of the first century did not.

In the apologetic work of Paul, the Apostle sought to demonstrate that the person and work of Jesus were "according to the Scriptures," referring to the Old Testament. The early Church did not view itself as creating a new religion, but rather as the culmination of an old one.

On the surface the question "What went wrong?" can be answered in terms of misinterpretation or misunderstanding of the Old Testament. It is clear that either Judaism or Christianity has an incorrect understanding of the Old Testament. There remains the logical possibility that both are wrong. Islam, for example, would put a pox on both the houses of Judaism and Christianity. But what is not possible is that both can be right.

It is not enough to say that the conflict between Judaism and Christianity is simply a matter of a difference of interpretation of the Old Testament. We must also ask the provocative question, "Why did someone have it wrong?" This gets into the controversial and explosive issue of the morality of the parties involved. If the Christians were wrong in these views, it would mean that the church is guilty of twisting the pure monotheism of Old Testament Judaism into a pagan system of polytheism that is erected upon the twin foundations of idolatry (the worship of a creature, Jesus Himself) and of blasphemy.

By contrast, if Christianity is correct, then Judaism is guilty of rejecting the Son of God, and thereby of rejecting God Himself. The claim of the New Testament and of Jesus that the Jews who rejected Christ were guilty of heinous sin is particularly offensive to Jews, both ancient and modern. Jews see in these New Testament claims the sowing of the seeds of a virulent anti-Semitism that has wreaked untold suffering upon Jews for centuries—this despite the clear teaching of Jesus regarding love of neighbor and love of one's enemy, and the teaching of Paul wherein he laments the case of Israel and swears an oath regarding his earnest desire for his own people "according to the flesh." It is the well-being of his own ethnic group that drives Paul in his quest to reach them with the Gospel. When a professed Christian advocates hatred for Jewish people, he not only rejects Judaism, he rejects the Christianity he claims to espouse. It is one thing to reject the theology of Judaism; it is quite another to reject the people of Judaism.

It is clear that the New Testament pulls no punches with respect to its judgment upon those among the Jews who rejected Jesus. The chief cause that is assigned to this rejection is the sinful hardness of the heart to the Word of God. To be sure ignorance is mentioned as a mitigating circumstance. That ameliorated God's judgment, at least for a season. Jesus prayed for His executioners, saying, "They do not know what they do." Likewise the Apostles made allowances for ignorance by declaring, "Had they known, they would not have crucified the Lord of glory" (1 Cor. 2:8). But this ignorance did not carry the exculpatory weight of invincible ignorance. It was vincible ignorance, ignorance that could have and should have been conquered or overcome. Jesus Himself sorely rebuked those who walked with Him on the road to Emmaus following His resurrection from the dead. He spoke of them as being stiff-necked and slow of heart to believe all that the Scriptures had declared.

Though it may be argued that the negative judgment of the New Testament regarding Jesus' Jewish contemporaries was biased and self-serving, it is ironic that this judgment on the Jewish nation was not unlike the assessment of the Jewish people found repeatedly in the Old Testament, especially in the prophets. What is important to note, however, is that this proclivity toward hardness of heart and stiffness of neck is not unique to Jewish people. It is not so much a Jewish problem as it is a human problem, a problem that is by no means solved the minute a person joins a Christian church. If Jews are singled out for judgment, it is not because they are any worse than we are, but only because of the singular privilege they enjoyed as the chosen of God. This confirms the biblical principle that the greater the privilege, the greater the responsibility. This should weigh heavily on the minds of every Christian.

A JOURNEY
BACK IN TIME

JANUARY 1999

—

I T HAS BEEN ARGUED THAT NO LESS THAN two thirds of the content of the New Testament is concerned directly or indirectly with eschatology. Eschatology is that subdivision of theology that deals with the "last things," or future prophecy.

Of all the branches of theology, the study of eschatology is the most difficult. There are several reasons for this, among which are the following: (1) Since eschatology concerns the future, we lack the advantage of the "20/20" vision of hindsight. With respect to Old Testament prophecies that were fulfilled by events recorded in the New Testament, we have the authoritative inspired understanding of such fulfillment. For fulfillment of New Testament prophecy, we are left with our own fallible interpretations of post-biblical fulfillment. We are left to interpret the events of history without the benefit of inspired interpreters. (2) The literary form of future prophecy is often difficult to handle because of the tendency of biblical writers to use imaginative and symbolic language. The apocalyptic genre of literature requires skill and soberness in its handling; unfortunately, it is vulnerable to irresponsible, unbridled speculation wherein the literary form is viewed as a license for all sorts of wild interpretations that tell us more about the imagination of the interpreter than the meaning of the text of Scripture. (3) Eschatology is the demagogue's dream. Nothing sells like future prophecy. Human beings all face the fears and hopes of what the future may bring. People want to know what will happen before it does. Preoccupation with the future is what sells tarot cards, horoscopes, palm readings, and the like. The Ouija board remains a hot item for children. The desire to know the future is what made it possible for diviners, necromancers, magicians, soothsayers, and other occultists of antiquity to ply their trade despite the clear divine prohibition of these practices as an abomination to God. The false prophet in Israel exploited this human curiosity. It was the backdrop for the success of pagan prophets such as the Oracle of Delphi. Every age has its own Jeane Dixons as fascination about the future abounds.*

Because of the madness that surrounds such chicanery, it is tempting to dismiss all prophets and all forms of prophecy. To do so, however, would be to throw the baby out with the bath water. The Bible makes a distinction between the false prophet and the true prophet. The true prophets, along with the Apostles, comprise the foundation of the church. The biblical prophets were agents of divine revelation. Unlike the false prophets, who spun out their own dreams, the true prophets were spokesmen for God Himself, who, as the sovereign Lord of History, alone knows what the future will bring. The future is His future and nobody else's. What God says will come to pass must come to pass. His Word is sure and reliable. We can and must trust the future as He has declared it. When God speaks of future matters, it is for our instruction, our warning, and our comfort. What God says about the future has massive import to the church's mission in the present. For these and other reasons, we dare not neglect the biblical prophecies regarding the future, because there is a future for the people of God.

Because of our confession of the deity and humanity of Jesus, and His roles as Redeemer, Lord, and Savior, we must insist that He was more than a prophet. But in this high confession of faith we must not forget that Jesus was not less than a prophet. He was the supreme Prophet, the Prophet par excellence, and His prophecies regarding the future have binding authority upon our consciences.

My own eschatological pilgrimage has been one of vacillation. I have been torn between various systems of eschatology, being drawn at times to the amillennial and historic premillennial positions. I have never been

---

* Jeane Dixon (1904–97) was an American astrologer and self-proclaimed psychic. She was noted for her many well-publicized predictions and for advising Richard Nixon and Nancy Reagan.

enticed by dispensational eschatology, despite its being the contemporary majority report among evangelicals. I rarely gave much credence to the post-mil position, as I usually associated it with a liberal approach to the question in that it was too optimistic regarding the impact of Christianity in a pagan world.

Yet, to my own surprise, I have found myself more and more attracted to an orthodox post-mil position with its moderate preterist perspective. The two most critical considerations that have led me here are my commitments to the absolute authority of Jesus in His prophetic utterances and to the full inspiration and inerrancy of the Bible.

More specifically, it has been my work in the theological defense of biblical inerrancy that has directed my course. How so? In brief, my experience as a student in a liberal seminary brought me in daily contact with professors who not only denied but ridiculed biblical inerrancy. What was clear to me in this academic arena was that the focus of much of the higher criticism of the New Testament was leveled against the prophecies uttered by Jesus and the Apostles, prophecies the critics allege failed to take place within the time frame of the original predictions. The critical assumptions of 19th century liberalism, of Schweitzer's "Parousia Delay," tore away at the prophecies of the New Testament.*

Of all these criticisms, the one that disturbed me most was that regarding Jesus' prophecies in the Olivet Discourse, which is treated in detail by all three synoptic gospel writers, Matthew, Mark, and Luke. In the Olivet Discourse, Jesus speaks of three distinct future events. These events include (1) the destruction of the temple (2) the destruction of Jerusalem, and (3) His own "coming" in glory.

The irony is that if any passage should serve to prove the supernatural origin of the New Testament and attest to Jesus' credentials as a true prophet, it should be the Olivet Discourse. Here Jesus clearly and accurately predicts two future events, events that were unthinkable to His

---

* Albert Schweitzer (1875–1965) was a German theologian who proposed a theory to account for the supposed delay of the second coming of Christ (or *parousia*) after His ascension.

contemporaries, with astonishing accuracy. There is no doubt that the temple and Jerusalem were destroyed in one of the most well-attested events of history, the 70 A.D. destruction of Jerusalem by the Roman general Titus. However, the prophetic passage is seen by critics and believers of biblical inspiration alike as being only two thirds fulfilled. Two out of three accurate predictions would qualify Jesus, in biblical terms, as a false prophet.

It was the third element that turned the Olivet Discourse from an irrefutable proof of biblical and Christological authority into a "proof" of the "errancy" of both the Bible and Jesus, namely, the element relating to Jesus' prediction of His own coming. The critics jump on this precisely because of the time frame in which Jesus said these things would come to pass. The glaring problem is found in Jesus' words, "This generation shall not pass away until all these things come to pass." Evangelical defenders of Scripture have engaged in all sorts of exegetical gymnastics to escape this problem. None of these attempts has ever satisfied me. I am convinced that only within the framework of a moderate preterist position can we escape the devastating assault of the critics. This is why I have written *The Last Days according to Jesus*, to deal with this issue. Other authors in this issue of *Tabletalk* will expand upon this problem and indicate biblical solutions to the Olivet Discourse without abandoning hope, indeed the Blessed Hope, of the still-future final coming of Christ and the consummation of His kingdom.

THE MESSENGER

FEBRUARY 1999

T HE UBIQUITOUS LOGO THAT APPEARS on a window decal at almost every flower store in America, indicating the service of F.T.D. (Floral Telegraph Delivery), displays the image of the mythological deity called Mercury by the Romans and Hermes by the Greeks. Mercury (or Hermes) is depicted as having wings on his helmet and wings on his feet. These wings were used for superhuman speed, an attribute necessary for the deity described as the "messenger of the gods."

The term "hermeneutics" contains the same root that serves as the name of the Greek counterpart to Mercury, Hermes. The root concerns the delivery of a "message." When we read the Bible, we do not believe we encounter the Olympian wisdom of Zeus or Jupiter but the very Word of the Most High God. The Bible is the divine word or "message" of God. It is the message of God because it belongs to God and it comes from God.

Orthodox Christianity affirms the infallibility of the divine message and the inspiration of the human authors God used to deliver that message. The prophets and Apostles did not originate the message; they were merely the deliverers of the message, or God's appointed messengers. (It is ironic that the Apostle Paul once was mistaken for Hermes himself.)

The problem we face with biblical interpretation is that though the message is infallible and the messengers are inspired, the recipients of the message are neither infallible nor inspired (unless you believe in the infallibility of the church—which only removes the problem one more step). Sooner or later the message gets to us, and we are capable of misunderstanding the message and the messengers.

That is why we have a science called hermeneutics—to assist us in gaining the correct interpretation of the biblical message. Notice that I said *the* correct interpretation, not *a* correct interpretation. I used the definite article rather than the indefinite article. My assumption here is that though there may be 1,000 applications of a given text, there is only one correct meaning. We say this because we do not believe that the Bible is a waxed nose capable of being formed or shaped into any figure according to the subjective whim of the reader.

Classical hermeneutics seeks the objective meaning of Scripture before it may properly be applied to the reading subject. In recent decades, this matter of objective meaning has become a huge issue among biblical scholars. At present, a hermeneutical war is being waged on this very point. Rudolf Bultmann, for example, argued that the discovery of the objective meaning of the Bible is not only not possible, it is not desirable. Here the influences of existential and subjective philosophy have taken away the body of Scripture, and we know not where they have laid it.

The Reformation brought an emphasis on seeking the literal sense of the Bible. This principle is often seriously misunderstood. What Luther meant by the *sensus literalis* (literal sense) of Scripture is that the Bible is to be understood and interpreted as literature. It is a written message that employs a wide variety of literary forms and devices. It contains historical narrative, letters (epistles), poetry, etc. It makes use of personification, similes, aphorisms, proverbs, sermons, hyperbole, and the like. To interpret the Bible "literally" is to treat narrative as narrative, poetry as poetry, didactive as didactive, proverb as proverb, etc. To impose the literary rules of poetry on historical narrative or the rules of narrative on poetry is to distort the meaning of the text. In this regard, the Bible, though it is not like any other book in light of its inspiration and divine origin, has to be read like any other book. The inspiration of the Holy Spirit does not turn a noun into a verb or the active voice into the passive voice or a subjunctive into an indicative. To be responsible in interpreting Scripture requires that we learn the rudiments of grammar and of literary interpretation.

Because the Bible has been translated into a multitude of languages, it is important to remember that no translation conforms exactly word for word with the original Hebrew and Greek texts of the Bible. This is why many, if not most, seminaries require a study of the original languages of the Bible.

The Bible also was written in a historical context. It is helpful to the serious student of Scripture to know something of the historical context in which the Bible was written. This helps safeguard us from the tendency to read our own cultural and historical context into the text of the Bible. We are separated culturally, historically, and linguistically by thousands of years from the original texts of the Bible.

Another problem we encounter in interpreting the Bible is a logical problem. Even if we master the ancient languages in terms of vocabulary and grammar, and become expert students of ancient history and culture, that is no guarantee that we will interpret the Bible accurately. One of the most frequent causes of misinterpretation of Scripture is the making of illegitimate inferences from the texts. That is, we make mistakes in logic, drawing gratuitous conclusions from what we read. The rudimentary rules of logic and logical inference from the text are of vital importance to sound interpretation. For example, we need to know the difference between a possible inference and a necessary inference. Let me illustrate. Did Jesus in His resurrected body have the ability to pass through solid objects such as doors? How you answer that question may depend on how you understand the significance of the biblical record that Jesus appeared to His disciples in the Upper Room where they were assembled. The account tells us that the door was shut "for fear of the Jews." Was the purpose of the inclusion of this detail about the door intended by the author to tell us something about the state of Jesus' resurrected body or was it to call attention merely to the state of the disciples (fear) at the time of Jesus' appearance? The Bible does not explicitly state that Jesus walked through the shut door. It merely says that He appeared in their midst. The text may imply that Jesus passed through a solid object but it does not explicitly declare it. That He did pass through solid objects is a possible inference drawn from the text, but not a necessary inference.

This is but one example of a host of texts that are used to build theologies or inferences that are either merely possible or actually illegitimate.

These are some of the reasons the prudent student of the Bible will be diligent in the use of good commentaries, as they often help us prevent our own subjective inclinations from distorting the text.

The final interpreter of the Bible is the Bible itself. The primary rule of biblical hermeneutics is the "rule of faith," that the Scripture is its own interpreter. We must never insult the Spirit of God by interpreting Scripture in such a way as to do violence to what the Scripture says in other places.

SPINNING OUT OF CONTROL

MARCH 1999

―――

"SHAPES." THIS TERM IS STREET SLANG heard in pool halls for the practice of creating cue ball positions for subsequent shots. The expert player is concerned not only with pocketing the shot that faces him but with leaving the cue ball in such a position that he is in good "shape" for the next one. To succeed in this endeavor he must master the subtleties of overspin, backspin, and side spin, all of which influence the movement of the cue ball after it contacts the object ball. In pool, it is axiomatic that one of the most frequent causes of missed shots is the impartation of unintentional spin. Accuracy is lost when spin is imparted to the shot by an incorrect stroke on the cue.

Golfers are also subject to the vagaries of spin. A slice spins the ball erratically to the right (for a right-handed golfer) and a hook spins the ball to the left. As Lee Trevino once mused, "You can talk to a fade [slice], but a hook won't listen." Amateurs tend to drool at the shots hit by touring pros, which land on the green and spin backward. When asked by an amateur how to put backspin on a 5-iron, Sam Snead asked, "How far do you hit your 5-iron?" The amateur replied, "About 150 yards." To which Snead commented, "If that is all the distance you hit it, why would you want to spin it back?"

In sports such as pool or golf, the application of spin can be a benefit or a disaster. In either case, spin affects the net result. In the language of politics, the term "spin" attains a metaphorical meaning for interpreting statements and actions in a politically favorable light. One "spins" the truth to gain a political advantage. In such cases, the use of spin imparts distortion to the truth at the expense of accuracy. The experts at such interpretive legerdemain are called "spin doctors" or "spin meisters." They are proficient in the art of rhetorical illusion.

One noted wag spoke of the literary science of the "declension of personal adjectives." Such declensions may go something like this: "I am frugal, you are tight, he is cheap." Or, "I am dynamic, you are pushy, he is frantic." In such declensions, the same traits are colored or spun in either a positive or negative way.

Traits such as arrogance and confidence are often confused. Yet they are two different attitudes, one a vice and the other a virtue. To call an arrogant person simply confident or a confident person simply arrogant is to distort the character of the individual.

There is no arena in which spinning the truth is more dangerous than in the arena of biblical interpretation. It is one thing to spin the remarks of a politician; it is another thing to spin the Word of God. As obvious as it would seem that to spin the Word of God is to do violence against the Holy Spirit who is the Spirit of Truth, it not only is done by Christians with reckless abandon, but is done as if it were a legitimate method of biblical interpretation.

Many times after I have given an exposition of a biblical text I have been met with this response: "Well, that's your interpretation." The response is not a preface to the offering of a different interpretation, given with an argument to back it up. Rather, the response stands alone, hanging in the air like a dangling participle, as if this response in itself is all that is needed to neutralize my explanation of the text.

What is meant by this ubiquitous response "That's your interpretation"? Is the implied criticism a thinly veiled categorical refutation of the interpretation based simply on the fact that it is mine? Is the unspoken syllogism something like this:

All of Sproul's interpretations are wrong.
This is Sproul's interpretation.
Therefore, this interpretation is wrong.

Surely the syllogism is valid *if* the premises are true.

However, when someone says to me, "Well, that's your interpretation," I don't assume that he means that the interpretation must be wrong simply because it's mine. I guess that my harshest critics would admit that even a blind pig finds an ear of corn once in a while. No, the response is far more insidious than the uttering of a simple slander against me.

I am afraid that what is often meant by the response is something like this: "Well, that's your interpretation, but my interpretation is different and both of our views, though different, are equally valid." Here the unspoken assumption is that of *relativism*, namely that the truth is relative to the individual, even the truth of God.

Where does such a view of relativistic interpretation come from? There may be many sources, but at least three come immediately to mind:

1. *Private interpretation.* Among the principles of biblical hermeneutics established by the Reformers was the right of private interpretation of the Bible. This was designed to offset the Roman claim to magisterial authority in biblical interpretation, by which any interpretations that differed from the church's interpretation were forbidden. Martin Luther challenged this position, arguing for the right of the believer to follow his own conscience in interpreting the Bible. Yet this was not viewed as a license to distort the Bible. With the *right* of private interpretation comes always the *responsibility* of correct interpretation. Private interpretation is never the right to private *mis*interpretation.

2. *Existential subjectivism.* From Søren Kierkegaard's "truth as subjectivity" to Emil Brunner's "truth as encounter" to Rudolf Bultmann's "prior understanding hermeneutic" (*Vorverstandnis*), the desire to be open to the personal application of Scripture to one's subjective situation opened the door to the subjectivization of the biblical truth itself. That meant that Bultmann, for example, could argue that not only is it not possible to ascertain the objective meaning of Scripture, it is not even desirable. For Bultmann, the Bible must be read through the lens of a certain prior understanding, which understanding Bultmann sought to gain from Martin Heidegger's philosophy.

3. *Secular relativism.* As Allan Bloom indicated in his best-selling book *The Closing of the American Mind*, the philosophy of relativism has captured American thinking. Relativism is joined at the hip with its twin,

pluralism. Pluralism argues that there are truths but no truth. Objective truth is ruled out by an epistemic theory of relativity. In this view, it is not so much that the very idea of truth is redefined; it is completely annihilated. Relative truth is no truth.

Any biblical passage may be subject to multiple applications, but only one correct meaning. We must be ever vigilant to maintain the distinction between the objective meaning of the text and its subjective application to our lives. To confuse the two is to turn the Bible into a waxed nose, capable of being twisted and shaped to suit the bias or whim of the interpreter. It is one thing to spin a pool ball or a golf ball. It is quite another to spin the Word of God.

THE ORDER OF CREATION

MAY 1999

———

I N THE CREATION OF THE WORLD, God made man in His own image. The term *man* is used generically, as we see that man was created male and female. In the order of Creation, mankind was given dominion over the earth. In this regard, Adam and Eve served as viceregents for God. Eve shared in this dominion; if we regard Adam's dominion as a kind of kingship over creation, we would see Eve as his queen. Nevertheless, it is clear from the order of Creation that Eve was placed in a position of subordination to Adam. She was assigned the role of "help meet."

Several issues that relate to this Creation order have been brought into bold relief by the feminist movement. For instance, the New Testament passages that call wives to submit to their husbands and men only to lead in the church have been greeted with vociferous protests. Calumnies have been launched against the Apostle Paul for being a first century chauvinist, while others have sought to historicize and relativize these rules by arguing that they were merely culturally conditioned customs relevant to the first century but not to the modern world. It also has been argued that the principle of submission denigrates women, robbing them of their dignity and relegating them to the level of inferior humanity.

With respect to the last point, the erroneous assumption made is that subordination means inferiority or that subordination destroys equality of dignity, worth, and value. Sadly, male chauvinism has often been driven by this very misconception, with men assuming that the reason God commands their wives to be submissive to them is that women must be inferior.

That this inference is patently false is seen in our understanding of the persons of the Godhead. In the economy of redemption, the Son is subordinate to the Father, and the Holy Spirit is subordinate to the Father and the Son. This does not mean that the Son is inferior to the Father, and the Holy Spirit inferior to both Father and Son. Our understanding of the Trinity is that the three persons of the Godhead are equal in being, worth, and glory. They are co-eternal and co-substantial.

Likewise, in an organizational hierarchy, we do not assume that because a vice president is subordinate to the president that the vice president is inferior to the president as a person. It is obvious that subordination does not translate into inferiority.

The question of whether the subordination of wives to husbands in marriage and of women to men in the church is merely a cultural custom of the ancient world is a burning one. If indeed these matters were articulated as cultural customs and not binding principles, it would be a serious miscarriage of justice to apply them transculturally to societies where they don't belong. On the other hand, if they were given as transcultural principles by divine mandate, to treat them as mere cultural conventions would be to do violence to the Holy Spirit and to rebel against God Himself.

In other words, if the biblical passages merely reflect the chauvinism of a first century rabbinic Jew, they are unworthy of our acceptance. If, however, Paul wrote under the inspiration of the Holy Spirit, and if the New Testament is the Word of God, then the charge of chauvinism must be leveled not only at Paul but at the Holy Spirit Himself—a charge that cannot be leveled with impunity.

If we are convinced that the Bible is God's Word and its commands are God's commands, how can we discern between customs and principles? I've written about the matter of culture and the Bible in my book *Knowing Scripture*. In it, I mention that unless we conclude that all of Scripture is principle and thus binding on all people of all times and places, or that all Scripture is simply a matter of culturally conditioned local custom with no relevance or necessary application beyond its immediate historical context, we are forced to discover some guidelines for discerning the differences between principle and custom.

To illustrate the problem, let us see what happens when we hold that everything in Scripture is principle. If that were the case, then radical changes would have to be made in evangelism. Jesus commanded His disciples to "Carry neither money bag, knapsack, nor sandals . . ." (Luke 10:4a). If we make this text a transcultural principle, then we must engage in barefoot evangelism.

Obviously there are biblical matters that reflect a historical custom. We are not required to wear the same clothing that biblical people wore, or pay our tithes with shekels or denarii. Things such as clothing and monetary units are subject to change.

One of the chief considerations in determining the question of principle or custom is whether the matter involves a Creation ordinance. Creation ordinances may be distinguished both from old covenant laws and new covenant commands. The first consideration concerns the parties to the various covenants. In the New Testament, the covenant is made with Christian believers. For example, Christian believers are called to celebrate the Lord's Supper. But that mandate does not extend to non-believers, who indeed are warned not to participate in the sacrament. Likewise, there were laws in the Old Testament that applied only to the Jews.

But we ask, who are the parties to the covenant of Creation? In Creation, God makes a covenant not simply with Jews or with Christians, but with man *qua* man. As long as humans exist in a covenant relationship with the Creator, the laws of Creation remain intact. They are reaffirmed in both the old covenant and the new covenant.

If anything transcends a cultural custom, it is a Creation ordinance. Thus, it is a dangerous business indeed to treat the matter of subordination in marriage and in the church as a mere local custom when it is clear that the New Testament mandates for these matters rest upon apostolic appeals to Creation. Such appeals make it crystal clear that these mandates were not intended to be regarded as local customs. That the church today often treats divine rules as mere customs reflects not so much the cultural conditioning of the Bible but the cultural conditioning of the modern church. Here is a case where the church capitulates to the local culture rather than being obedient to the transcendent law of God.

If one studies an issue such as this with care and is not able to discern whether a matter is principial or customary, what should he or she do? Here a principle of humility comes into play, a principle set forth in the New Testament axiom that whatever is not of faith is sin. Remember the old adage, "When in doubt, don't"? If we are over-scrupulous and regard a custom as a principle, then we are guilty of no sin—no harm, no foul. On the other hand, if we treat a principle as a custom that can be set aside, we are guilty of disobeying God.

Creation ordinances may be modified, as the Mosaic Law did with regard to divorce, but the principle here is that Creation ordinances are normative unless or until they are explicitly modified by later biblical revelation.

REPUGNANT BEAUTY

JUNE 1999

———

A RECENT PHENOMENON WITHIN EVANGELICAL circles is the departure of members from our ranks to enter into communion with the Eastern Orthodox Church. Since on the surface there appears to be a radical difference between Eastern Orthodoxy and historical evangelicalism, one wonders what is the attraction to Eastern Orthodoxy. I have no scientific poll results that would explain this rising trend; all I have is a small sampling of testimonies from some of the people who have made the move. If anything stands out as a common thread in these testimonies it is a disappointment with the impoverished forms of evangelical worship and a disenchantment with the anti-liturgical emphasis of modern evangelicalism. At the same time, one of the positive attractions of the Eastern Orthodox Church is its love for art and beauty as expressed in the prominent place of icons in worship.

However, the use of icons in Eastern worship is one of the points of division between the Eastern Orthodox and Protestants. The ancient iconoclastic controversy was revived afresh in the Protestant Reformation vis-à-vis both Rome and Eastern Orthodoxy. The issue focused on the application of the second commandment and its explicit prohibition of the use of graven images. At the heart of the matter was the strong biblical prohibition against all forms of idolatry, which prohibition was violated by virtually every generation of Israelites.

The golden calf episode recorded in Exodus is at the root of the historic problem. The calf was fashioned at the behest of the people, before whom Aaron acquiesced and sanctioned the event. It is noteworthy that this all occurred when Moses delayed his return from Mount Sinai. Perhaps the people were distressed by the lack of any visible presence of God; perhaps someone had a vision and said God had told them to build a golden calf—we are not sure. But when Joshua heard the noise of the gala celebration, he mistook it for shouts of war before he realized he was hearing the sounds of singing and dancing. This was probably the most well-attended, culturally relevant worship in the history of Israel. It involved a kind of worship that the people enjoyed but God despised. When God alerted Moses to what was going on, He said to him, " 'Go, get down! For your people whom you brought out of the land of Egypt have corrupted themselves. They have turned aside quickly out of the way which I commanded them. They have made themselves a molded calf, and worshiped it and sacrificed to it, and said, "This is your god, O Israel, that brought you out of the land of Egypt!" ' And the LORD said to Moses, 'I have seen this people, and indeed it is a stiff-necked people! Now, therefore, let Me alone, that My wrath may burn hot against them and I may consume them' " (Ex. 32:7–10a).

The golden calf was a substitute graven image for God. The Israelites' worship of it was a clear exercise in idolatry and a violation of the second commandment.

During the Reformation, John Calvin exclaimed that human beings are by nature idol factories. But despite his concern for the purity of worship and the dangers posed by idolatry, Calvin did not castigate all art forms. He understood that God, when He designed the tabernacle and temple in the Old Testament, endowed craftsmen with His Spirit to create objects for "beauty and for glory." Even the sacred ark was adorned with the figures of the cherubim. What Calvin insisted upon was the pure and lawful use of art. He argued, for example, against the use of icons because seeking to make visible the invisible God did violence to the divine majesty.

Eastern Orthodoxy (as well as Rome) has defended the use of icons and statuary in worship on basically two grounds. The first is the precedent of the use of beautiful art in the Old Testament. The second reason, which is pedagogical, is that images are "books for the unlearned." In other words, what cannot be read by the illiterate can be grasped easily in visual form.

The chief concern in this matter is the use and function of images in worship. Augustine argued that it not only was unlawful to worship images, but to dedicate them. Calvin, citing Augustine, said, "Whosoever, therefore, is desirous of being instructed on the true knowledge of God must apply to some other teacher than images" (*Institutes*, I.XI.6).

The chief abuses of icons are the veneration of them, praying before them, and offering sacrifices to them. Again, it was Augustine who argued that people who pray or worship while looking at an image are inclined to think or hope that they are being heard by the image. So the problem is not simply what is revealed in the icon; it is what is hidden. The glory of God is obscured by unauthorized attempts to duplicate His image.

In defense of the use of images, Catholicism has historically retreated to a distinction between "service" and "worship." Calvin remarks, "The worship which they pay to their images they cloak with the name of *idolodulia*, and deny to be *idolatria*. So they speak, holding that the worship which they call *dulia* may (without insult to God) be paid to statues and pictures. Hence, they think themselves blameless if they are only servants and not the worshipers of idols; as if it were not a lighter matter to worship than to serve" (I.XI.11).

In effect, Calvin calls the subtle distinction between *latria* (worship) and *dulia* (service) a distinction without a difference, which distinction was obscured by such early church leaders as Constantius, bishop of Cyprus, who advocated the embracing of images with reverence and said he would pay them the respect due to the Trinity, or the Eastern legate John who declared that it would be better to allow a city to be filled with brothels than be denied the worship of images.

The honor of *dulia* is also given to the saints whose images are widely used. This honor is especially given to Mary, for whom is reserved the veneration of *hyperdulia*.

Though Calvin technically allowed for art that depicted earthly and historical events, as a matter of prudence he counseled against even their use as adornment in the church. This reflected his zeal to avoid anything that might even incline the heart to idolatry. Perhaps he went too far, but Eastern Orthodoxy has gone too far in the opposite direction, with people lighting candles and saying prayers before images, genuflecting, and giving other outward signs of reverence and worship.

These things may be beautiful, but they can be as deadly as they are aesthetically pleasing.

My biggest concern, however, with the Eastern Orthodox Church is not what is taught to the unlearned via images and icons, but what is taught verbally. Eastern Orthodoxy rejects the clear teaching of *sola fide*, salvation by faith alone, and by that rejection rejects the biblical Gospel. Eastern Orthodox churches may be beautiful, but there is nothing so beautiful as the Gospel. Without the Gospel, the beauty of the church changes to ashes.

LEST WE BE SCATTERED

JULY 1999

O NE OF THE MOST FREQUENTLY MISQUOTED verses in the Bible is Proverbs 16:18: "Pride goes before destruction, and a haughty spirit before a fall." The misquotation telescopes the verse so that it says simply, "Pride goes before a fall." Though this misquotation is not textually accurate, it does capture the truth of the proverb. Indeed, pride is a precursor of a fall and the harbinger of destruction.

We see this illustrated dramatically in the biblical narrative of the Tower of Babel:

> Now the whole earth had one language and one speech. And it came to pass, as they journeyed from the east, that they found a plain in the land of Shinar, and they dwelt there. Then they said to one another, "Come, let us make bricks and bake them thoroughly." They had brick for stone, and they had asphalt for mortar. And they said, "Come, let us build ourselves a city, and a tower whose top is in the heavens; let us make a name for ourselves, lest we be scattered abroad over the face of the whole earth." But the LORD came down to see the city and the tower which the sons of men had built. And the LORD said, "Indeed the people are one and they all have one language, and this is what they begin to do; now nothing that they propose to do will be withheld from them. Come, let Us go down and there confuse their language, that they may not understand one another's speech" (Gen. 11:1–7).

The Tower of Babel was the world's first skyscraper, probably a high ramp or ziggurat that carried with it a religious connotation. As Martin Luther noted in his *Lectures on Genesis*, all sorts of fanciful myths and legends developed in the Middle Ages regarding the structure. Some argued that it was built as a place of refuge that would be high enough for people to escape another flood, ignoring God's promise that He never again would destroy the world by a deluge. Others maintained that the structure reached a height of nine miles, so high that from it one could hear the voices of angels singing in heaven. But these speculative tales miss the point of the story and yield little insight.

Whatever it was, the narrative labors the point that the Tower of Babel certainly was not built to the glory of God. It was a monument to human pride. Luther observed, "I believe their motive is expressed in the words, 'Come, let us build *ourselves* a city and a tower.' These words are evidence of smug hearts, which put their trust in the things of this world without trusting God and despise the church because it lacks all power and pomp." Later he added, "Was this not colossal pride and great contempt for God, that without asking God for advice they dared undertake so massive a project on their own responsibility?"

The motive of pride is seen even more clearly in the arrogant declaration "Let us make a name for ourselves." In the Lord's Prayer, the first petition Christ instructed us to make is that the name of God be hallowed. This petition is clearly linked to the subsequent pleas—"Thy kingdom come, Thy will be done, on earth as it is in heaven." The kingdom of God is clearly present in heaven. His will is always done there and His name is hallowed there. But His kingdom is not present and His will is not done where His name is not hallowed. At Shinar, men sought to hallow and exalt their own names. This was Eden redux, in which the temptation to be as gods was replicated.

The construction of this tower to heaven was an attempt at the apotheosis of mankind, the self-divinization of the sons of men. This displays how old "New Age" thinking really is. It reflected what Paul declares to be the universal sin of humanity; the refusal to honor God as God and to be grateful (Rom. 1:21).

The act of building the Tower of Babel was an act of apostasy. It was under the guise of religion, as apostasy usually is, but such religion is pagan idolatry that always seeks to worship the creature rather than the Creator. It involves the substitution of a false god for the true God. Luther comments, "It was no sin in itself to erect a tower and to build a city, for the saints did the same.... This, however, is their sin: they attach their own name to this structure...." In this act, true worship is replaced by man-centered worship.

Genesis tells us that in response to this human act of hubris, "the LORD came down to see the city and the tower which the sons of men had built." This echoes the situation in Eden, when God came into the garden, provoking Adam and Eve to flee for cover. It was not as if the omniscient and omnipresent God was not cognizant of the situation. Rather, the narrative indicates a visitation of God whereby He came to these people in judgment. The pride that goes before destruction and the haughty spirit that precedes a fall is an attitude of defiance toward God. It is an attitude that assumes that God is unaware of what is going on or, if aware, is powerless to do anything about it. Unpunished sin evokes a fearlessness in the sinner by which he grows ever more brash in his defiance. The sinner mistakes God's patience and long-suffering for impotence, and carelessly heaps up for himself wrath against the day of wrath. The longer the judgment is delayed, the worse it is when it falls.

The punishment God meted out at Babel was the confusion of human language and the break-up of a united world order. This judgment struck at the heart of human enterprise, as it stabbed to the core of human political and economic activity. People are now grouped into political blocs, wherein a common language unites one nation against other nations. This breeds international hostility, as nations rise against nations. The language barrier likewise presents a major obstacle to international trade, further aggravating the hostility and proving the axiom that "when goods and services cross borders, soldiers seldom do."

The break-up of human harmony via the confusion of languages has consequences that are both far-reaching and long-lasting. Luther considered the confusion of human language to be a more severe judgment than the Flood itself. How so? After all, the Flood destroyed the entire population of the world, except Noah and his family. Luther's reasoning was this: The Flood harmed only the humans who were alive at the time, while the confusion of languages harmed all mankind until the end of time. The reason God gave for this particular punishment was that nothing sinful human beings proposed to do might be accomplished easily.

Human history is the record of creatures seeking to build empires for themselves. No empire ever has endured over time. This is true both of political and economic empires. The only possible end for pride is destruction. The proud may stand for a season, but sooner or later they will fall.

Today we move inexorably toward a unified global village. The computer gives us a new, universal language. But what happens if the language of computers fails? What happens if the global economy fails? Where will our pride be then?

"Unpunished sin evokes a fearlessness in the sinner by which he grows ever more brash in his defiance."

TABLE TALK

AUGUST 1999

———

T HE PROPHET ISAIAH WROTE, "How beautiful upon the mountains are the feet of him who brings good news, who proclaims peace, who brings glad tidings of good things, who proclaims salvation, who says to Zion, 'Your God reigns!' " (Isa. 52:7).

In the ancient world, the outcome of critical battles could not be known by television or other forms of high-tech, instantaneous communication. There was no CNN. People anxiously awaited news that was carried from the scene by runners. Lookouts were posted high on the city walls, peering to see the first sign of an approaching messenger. When the first glimpse of a runner in the distance was achieved, an experienced lookout could tell the nature of the news by the movement of the runner's feet. Feet kicking up dust and moving rapidly were a sure sign that the messenger was bringing good news. But feet plodding along in the rigors of the "survivor's shuffle" indicated that the downcast runner was a herald of bad news. The feet of the happy runner were considered beautiful because they signaled the announcement of truth that was beautiful.

The gifts of God to His people are beautiful. There is no ugliness in them. If we ask God for a fish, He does not give us a serpent. (It may not be a fish either, but that's for another article.) Like Him, we shrink at the idea of giving ugly gifts to those we love. So at Christmas and on birthdays, we give beautiful gifts to our loved ones, especially our children.

But what of the rest of the year? Every day affords us the opportunity to give something beautiful to our children: We can give them the beauty of truth.

When a teacher dies, I think not only of the loss of the person but also of the loss of access to the knowledge the teacher had accumulated over a lifetime, a gift that is no longer directly accessible to us. When my father died when I was 17 years old, I lost my most trusted mentor. On countless occasions since that moment, I have ached for his presence, not only to enjoy his love but also to have access to his wisdom. There just was not enough time for him to pass along to me the wealth of his knowledge and wisdom. But one thing I do remember vividly from our discussions when I was a youth—he was far more interested in wisdom than in knowledge. He understood that one needs knowledge in order to gain wisdom, but that one can have knowledge without gaining wisdom.

We did not have "homeschooling" when I was a child. Nevertheless, our home was a school. The chief classroom was the dining room table. It was during the dinner hour that I was most frequently exposed to my father's teaching.

Like me, my children were not homeschooled, yet our house was a place of education. In their youth, our ministry was exercised in a study center in the remote mountains of western Pennsylvania. In a manner similar to that of Francis Schaeffer's L'Abri, our students stayed in our home and ate at our table. Every meal was an occasion for "table talk," which was devoted to conversations and discussions of the things of God.

Now that our children are grown, they point back to those conversations as critical moments in their Christian educations. My regret, as well as theirs, is that we didn't have more time for such meetings. These times were a critical part of their education and an essential dimension of their family tradition.

Webster's defines "tradition" as "the passing down of elements of a culture from generation to generation, especially by oral communication," or "a mode of thought or behavior followed by a people continuously from generation to generation," or "a set of such customs and usages viewed as a coherent body of precedents influencing the present."

The English word *tradition* comes from the Latin verb *tradere*, which means "to hand down." Actually, the Latin word contains both a prefix and a root. The prefix is *trans*, which means "over," and the root is *dare*, which means "to give." So the term literally means "to give over." The same combination of prefix and root is found in the Greek word for "tradition," which is *parodosis*.

I stress this for two reasons. The first is that we clearly see the link between the idea of tradition and the idea of a gift. To pass wisdom from one generation to the next is to transfer a vital and beautiful gift. The second is that the passing on of knowledge and wisdom in the form of tradition is a crucial biblical concept.

Because Jesus uttered sharp rebukes to the scribes and Pharisees for replacing the truth of God with the traditions of men, we sometimes draw the invalid inference that Jesus opposed all tradition. That was not the case. Though He repudiated the supplanting of the Word of God by human tradition, He never attacked or denied the virtue of the divine tradition, the things of God for the people of God for all time. We also speak of the Apostolic tradition, which is passed on to all generations of the church. In fact, it may properly be said that the New Testament contains the Apostolic tradition and that the Bible as a whole contains the divine tradition.

In his first epistle to the Corinthians, Paul said, "For I received from the Lord that which I also delivered to you . . ." (1 Cor. 11:23a). These words comprise the introduction to Paul's statement of the institution of the Lord's Supper. As an Apostle, Paul received his content from Christ and then, in turn, "gave it over" to the church. This is the way tradition functions.

It was the responsibility of the parents in Israel to "give over" the truth of God to their children. For example, God spoke to the Israelites through Moses, "And you shall tell your son in that day, saying, 'This is done because of what the Lord did for me when I came up from Egypt.' It shall be as a sign to you on your hand and as a memorial between your eyes, that the LORD's law may be in your mouth; for with a strong hand the LORD has brought you out of Egypt. You shall therefore keep this ordinance in its season from year to year" (Ex. 13:8–10).

My children went to school and to church, where they received a large measure of their education. Their catechetical instruction was especially important to them. But school and church school can only amplify what children learn at home. The chief responsibility for the education of our children rests with we parents. We delegate it at the greatest peril.

The cultural revolution of the 1960s has had a major impact on education. The revolution brought on a new order of customs, thoughts, and values. It created a new tradition that is on a collision course with the divine tradition. We no longer can assume, in this new order, that other people and institutions will pass the divine tradition to our children. That gift now rests chiefly in our hands.

"To pass wisdom from one generation to the next is to transfer a vital and beautiful gift."

STEWARDS OF WEAL AND WOE

SEPTEMBER 1999

———

T HE APOSTLE PETER SETS FORTH A SOLEMN exhortation about the stewardship of ministry:

> As each one has received a gift, minister it to one another, as good stewards of the manifold grace of God. If anyone speaks, let him speak as the oracles of God. If anyone ministers, let him do it as with the ability which God supplies, that in all things God may be glorified through Jesus Christ, to whom belong the glory and the dominion forever and ever. Amen (1 Peter 4:10–11).

In this passage, the Apostle is concerned with stewardship. The term *stewardship* translates the Greek word *oikonomia*, from which the English word *economy* is derived and which literally means "house law" or "house rule." In the Greek culture, a steward was one assigned to the task of managing the affairs of the house.

In our culture, we usually think of *economy* in terms of the management of money. And this is the general realm in which we usually think of stewardship. Biblically, however, the context for stewardship is far broader than mere financial management. For instance, there is an "economy" of managing what Peter calls the "manifold grace of God." That means we are all stewards of divine grace. Simply put, we are accountable to God for how we manage the grace that we receive from Him. We can squander that grace, neglect it, or, in numerous ways, mistreat it. Or we can use it well.

When Peter moves from the general concern of being a good steward of God's grace to a specific application of the principle, he quickly takes up the matter of speaking with respect to the oracles of God. This mandate has a particularly weighty application to all who are ordained to the Gospel ministry as preachers and teachers. Such are entrusted with the stewardship or economy of the Word of God. A steward of the Word of God must be careful not to waste, neglect, or otherwise abuse the grace present in the oracles of God, for these oracles are intended to be of great benefit to the people of God.

When the Apostle Paul chastened the Jews in Romans 2 by saying, "The name of God is blasphemed among the Gentiles because of you," he labored the point that a true Jew is one who is a Jew *inwardly*, not merely *outwardly*. This chapter might lead the reader to the gratuitous conclusion that there was no particular value to being in the Jewish community of Old Testament Israel.

But at the beginning of Romans 3, Paul hastens to disavow such a conclusion by asking, "What advantage then has the Jew, or what is the profit of circumcision?" He answers his own questions in an emphatic way by saying, "Much in every way! Chiefly because to them were committed the oracles of God." Paul declares that there were many advantages to being included in the commonwealth of Israel, but he stresses that the chief advantage was that it was in this locus that the oracles of God were entrusted.

In the New Testament economy, the chief locus in which the oracles of God are entrusted is the church. Later, in his second letter to Timothy, Paul writes: "All Scripture is given by inspiration of God, and is profitable for doctrine, for reproof, for correction, for instruction in righteousness, that the man of God may be complete, thoroughly equipped for every good work" (2 Tim. 3:16–17).

This text speaks to far more than an abstract doctrine of the nature of inspiration. It is weighted with practical concern. It speaks of a certain value, advantage, or profit, which includes doctrine, reproof, correction, and instruction. This indicates that the Apostle did not share the widespread antipathy toward doctrine found in our churches. Rather, he saw sound doctrine as a profit, not a loss; an asset, not a liability. He also valued reproof and correction, which in our day may be assigned to the realm of the politically incorrect because these processes may injure someone's self-esteem. Paul also placed a high value on instruction in righteousness, as opposed to the bliss of ignorance.

All these "profits" have a purpose, according to Paul: "That the man of God may be complete, thoroughly equipped for every good work."

When ministers are poor stewards of the oracles of God, the practical impact of their neglect is devastating—the people are left without sound doctrine, without reproof and correction, and without instruction in righteousness. The final calamity is that the members of the flock are cheated out of the grace of ministry by which they are to be nurtured and are left incomplete and immature because they have not been "thoroughly equipped."

The irony is that empty preaching is sometimes what the people want. They encourage their ministers not to reprove or correct them, teach them doctrine or instruct them in righteousness. They might prefer a less strict and demanding teacher, just as schoolchildren often do.

Paul warns Timothy about this tendency when he writes: "Preach the word! Be ready in season and out of season. Convince, rebuke, exhort, with all longsuffering and teaching. For the time will come when they will not endure sound doctrine, but according to their own desires, because they have itching ears, they shall heap up for themselves teachers; and they will turn their ears away from the truth, and be turned aside to fables" (2 Tim. 4:2–4).

I once knew a pastor who frequently expressed his philosophy of ministry by saying, "We must scratch people where they itch. We must address their felt needs." Scratching people where they itch and addressing their "felt needs" is a stratagem of the poor steward of the oracles of God. This was the recipe for success for the false prophets of Old Testament Israel. The problem with focusing on felt needs is that people often do not feel the real needs they have. For instance, people really need to know the true character of God. They may not particularly feel like they need to know that God is holy, but there are few things, if any, that human beings need to know more desperately than that.

The whole counsel of God is not always popular. This was the problem for Jeremiah in his day. The false prophets were popular while Jeremiah languished in ignominy. God's response was clear: "Thus says the Lord of hosts, 'Do not listen to the words of the prophets who prophesy to you. They make you worthless; they speak a vision of their own heart, not from the mouth of the Lord. They continually say to those who despise Me, "The Lord has said, 'You shall have peace' "; and to everyone who walks according to the dictates of his own heart, they say, "No evil shall come upon you" ' " (Jer. 23:16–17).

God addressed these false prophets earlier in that chapter, saying, " 'Woe to the shepherds who destroy and scatter the sheep of my pasture!' says the Lord" (Jer. 23:1). Thus, the preachers themselves became objects of a divine oracle—an oracle of woe. And such an oracle applies to any minister who, having been entrusted with the oracles of God, betrays that trust.

On the positive side, good stewardship of the whole counsel of God produces many benefits. We have already seen some of the benefits for the people of God: doctrine, reproof, correction, and instruction. But Peter's exhortation points to the ultimate reason for good stewardship of divine grace: "That in all things God may be glorified." *Soli Deo gloria.*

AN INVALUABLE HERITAGE

OCTOBER 1999

———

O N THE RING FINGER OF MY LEFT HAND I wear a wedding band. On the comparable finger of my right hand I wear another ring, one that my wife gave me as a Christmas present. It is a plain gold ring that bears the imprint of my family crest. The crest is a constant reminder of my biological ancestry. However, my biological ancestry also contains something of my spiritual ancestry.

Several years ago, after I had completed an address in Cincinnati, I was approached by an elderly gentleman whose name was Sproul. He told me he was a retired university professor and that he had spent much of his retirement tracing his (and my) family tree. He was full of questions about my immediate family, all designed to help him in his research. Later, he sent me a voluminous manuscript that contained an account of the history of the Sproul family. He had traced our family tree back to the Battle of Hastings in 1066. From there, he had traced the lineage of a knight named Spruill, who had been hired by the king of Scotland as a mercenary.

What stood out in the record, especially from the sixteenth century onward, was the long list of clergymen in Scotland bearing our family name. What was most fascinating and exciting for me was the discovery that the first man ordained by John Knox in the Reformed Church of Scotland was named Robert Campbell Sproul, of whom I am a direct descendant. It is an encouragement and comfort to me that I have biological ancestors who have gone before me as my spiritual ancestors.

My spiritual ancestry, however, extends far beyond the bloodlines of my family tree. I am connected to those from the past who were, as I am now, a part of the household of God. They were within the extended "family" of which I am a member.

I count the saints of the past as not just members of my spiritual family but as my friends. Ours is not a relationship of consanguinity but a relationship of affinity. And these relationships of affinity are important to me because, even though they are rooted in the past, their impact on my life is very much in the present. For instance, I love to read the works of the great saints of the past. They instruct me, and at times I am dazzled by the acuteness of their insight and the scope of their knowledge. But even beyond their instruction in formal learning, I am heartened and encouraged by their example.

Our spiritual ancestors function as role models for us. They are far more than the epicenters of personality cults. History serves us by sifting through the gallery of former superstars and separating the wheat from the chaff. Certain giants from the past retain their status as models for us for good reasons.

There are distinctive differences among such people as Augustine, Thomas Aquinas, Martin Luther, John Calvin, Jonathan Edwards, Knox, and others. One can detect variances at certain points of theology and obvious differences in personality traits; the "style" of Luther stands in vivid contrast to the style of Aquinas or Calvin. However, some common strands are woven tightly through all of them, and several traits stand out.

These men all were conquered, overwhelmed, and spiritually intoxicated by their vision of the holiness of God. Their minds and imaginations were captured by the majesty of God the Father. Each of them possessed a profound affection for the sweetness and excellence of Christ. There was in each of them a singular and unswerving loyalty to Christ that spoke of a citizenship in heaven that was always more precious to them than the applause of men. And the spirit of boldness and courage is seen clearly through the lenses of these models; no one has accused these saints of being wimps.

These qualities tend to be contagious. Just as the cowardice of a few can induce mass panic and send troops into flight, so the courage of a single person can inspire heroic acts by many. In this respect, these models are vastly different from those produced by the music and sports worlds. These saints modeled virtue for people to imitate.

The Scriptures call attention to the importance of role models. Hebrews 11, the roll call of heroes of the Old Testament, cites the faith of people such as Abraham, Joseph, Moses, Rahab, David, and others, of whom it is said "the world was not worthy."

The chronicle of faith concludes with this exhortation: "Therefore we also, since we are surrounded by so great a cloud of witnesses, let us lay aside every weight, and the sin which so easily ensnares us, and let us run with endurance the race that is set before us, looking unto Jesus, the author and finisher of our faith, who for the joy that was set before Him endured the cross, despising the shame, and has sat down at the right hand of the throne of God" (Heb. 12:1–2).

In this text, we find an instance of the popular New Testament metaphor of the race. This race is not a 100-yard dash; it is an endurance test that requires a reservoir of strength the runner can call upon when exhaustion and pain entice him to quit. As the runner reaches for something extra as the crowd cheers him on, so the Christian must tune in to the urging voices of encouragement that emanate from the cloud of witnesses that surrounds him.

These spiritual ancestors point us beyond themselves and their own examples to our supreme champion, Jesus, who is called "the author and finisher of our faith." He is portrayed in this text as One who endured. He endured the cross and despised the shame of His humiliation. He had to run—long, hard, and painfully—before the Father seated Him at His right hand.

The modern church is endangered by the short-sightedness of severe myopia. Like the philosophers who gathered at Mars Hill in Athens, we tend to be preoccupied with what is new. Our vision tends to extend only to the boundaries of our own times. Sometimes we act as if the church began in the twentieth century. But this is hardly the golden age of theology or the acme of spiritual vitality. We may be shod with Nikes, but few if any of us can run as fast or true as those who have gone before us. We have much to learn from those who ran the race before us.

We enjoy a large measure of freedom from the persecution that was a constant threat to our ancestors. I have never had a price put on my head, as did Luther. I have not been exiled from my native land, as was Calvin, nor banished to the wilderness, as was Edwards. I have never been tormented by savage heretics, as was Augustine, or been chained to oars as a galley slave, as was Knox.

I would hope that we not only would learn about these spiritual ancestors but would get to know them as people. We should make friends of them, if even from a distance. The fellowship we enjoy with our friends has a powerful influence on our own behavior. These saints were friends of Christ and can be friends with us.

We have the opportunity to join this marvelous cloud of witnesses, that our modeling may be a legacy to those who will come after us. If the Lord tarries, then we will be the spiritual ancestors of future generations. Let us leave to them an inheritance of virtue, not vice; of courage, not cowardice; of endurance, not quitting.

BOUND FOR GLORY

NOVEMBER 1999

———

I N THE APOSTLES' CREED, a crucial affirmation is made: "I believe in ... the communion of saints." This is referring to a holy fellowship, a *communio sanctorum*, that exists in the church of Christ. Indeed, it *is* the church of Christ.

We all know that the church is not a building; rather, it is people. Though the people of God are likened in the New Testament to a building, this is simply a metaphor for a group whose foundation is the Apostles and prophets, and whose cornerstone is Christ, through whom the foundation is secure. The individual stones or building blocks of the church are its members.

That the church is a community of people is also seen in the metaphor of the human body. Here the church is the *corpus Christi*, the body of Christ. In this metaphor, Christ is seen as the head and the members make up the other parts of the body, such as hands and feet. Just as a healthy body is not composed of isolated parts that have no relationship to one another, the church is a living organism, with each part fashioned to contribute to the well-being of the whole. Although it is composed of individuals whose individuality is not absorbed or negated by the whole, the church is not an institution created for rugged *individualism*. The metaphor is one of unity (not uniformity) and diversity (not chaos or competition). There are diverse gifts and diverse offices, all designed to serve a common purpose and mission. The church's unity is found in its having one Lord, one faith, and one baptism.

But in our day, the visible church is fragmented into a host of denominations. Though all practice baptism and confess the lordship of Christ, there is great diversity concerning the content of the faith. Doctrinal issues, both real and imagined, divide earnest Christians.

This unhappy state of affairs has caused many to complain (mostly internally, mind you) that Christ's High Priestly Prayer in John 17 has not been answered and that the ancient creed that declared the church to be one, holy, catholic, and apostolic should not be proclaimed.

But wait a minute. Are we to assume that the efficacy of the prayers of our Great High Priest and Intercessor have failed? If "the effectual fervent prayer of a righteous man availeth much" (James 5:16b, KJV), are we to conclude that the prayer of Christ was ineffectual, was not fervent enough, or was offered by one less than perfectly righteous? God forbid.

I can only conclude that the prayer of Jesus was effectual and was answered by the Father in a real and transcendent manner. With Augustine, we must conclude that the explanation lies in the difference between the visible church and the invisible church. Though the visible church is fragmented, the invisible church remains one.

The Invisible Church

The invisible church is not called "invisible" because it is imaginary or unreal. It is completely real, as it is made up of all who are truly in Christ, the whole company of believing saints, the entire membership of the elect of God. By contrast, the visible church is always a "mixed body" (a *corpus per mixtum*). It is made up of both wheat and tares. The tares are those who, while they profess faith in Christ, do not actually possess faith in Him. To us, the true number of believers is unknown. We labor at the disadvantage of being able to perceive outward appearances only; we cannot look at the heart. The heart of one who professes faith is invisible to us, but it is visible to God. Thus, to God's eyes, the invisible church is completely visible.

For Augustine, the invisible church was not an entity found chiefly *outside* the visible church, as some "underground church." Rather, he concluded that the invisible church exists *substantially inside* the visible church. We notice that Augustine did not say that the invisible church is found *exclusively* within the visible church. That is because there are situations wherein members of the invisible church may be found outside the visible church.

How so? There are different reasons why Christians may be found outside the visible church, including:

1. They are providentially hindered from joining a visible church body. These would include people who are converted but die before they can formally unite with the church (to wit, the thief on the cross).

2. They are ignorant or derelict in their duty. Some new Christians are so disenchanted with the visible, institutional church that they suppose it is not needful for them to enter formally into church membership. They seek fellowship in para-church groups (which are a poor substitute for the church at best) or attend local churches without joining. This could be a temporary condition for a true believer, though persistence likely would indicate the person is not a true believer. One cannot love Christ and despise His church.

3. They are isolated from other Christians. This might include people in solitary confinement or hermits who live on the fringes of settled human communities where no visible church is present.

4. They belong to an apostate church or a cult that does not qualify as a valid church. For example, though the Mormon community denies the deity of Christ and is not recognized as a valid Christian church by orthodox Christians, it is possible that a true Christian believer could remain in such a body out of ignorance or even disobedience. Though every true believer should leave a cult or an apostate church, some remain, either being unaware of the condition of the institution or being misguided into thinking they ought to stay within it and work as a missionary to it.

5. They have been excommunicated. It is possible that the church, in its zeal for purity, may inadvertently pull up some wheat with the tares. She may unjustly excommunicate an innocent person. Likewise, she may justly excommunicate an impenitent true be-

liever who, after excommunication, comes to true repentance and returns to the church to seek forgiveness and restoration. Still, for a season, that person is deemed an unbeliever and is cast off from the fellowship of the church.

Ultimately, the basis for Christian community is found in our unity with Christ. The New Testament Greek uses two different prepositions that both can be translated by the English word *in*. These two words are *en* and *eis*. Technically, the word *eis* means "into." For me to be inside a room, I must first enter it. To enter it means to go *into* it from the outside. Once this transition has been made, I am *in* or *inside* the room.

When the Bible calls us to "believe in Christ," the preposition that usually is used is *eis* Thus, the call is to believe *into* Christ. When such faith is exercised, an amazing and transcendent transition occurs. When I believe into Christ, from all time thereafter I am "in Christ." But not only am I in Christ, Christ is now in me. Herein is the basis for the communion of saints. The term *communion* means "union with." Every Christian enjoys a mystical union with Christ. We are in Him and He is in us. Christ announced this relationship in the Upper Room as He said, "You are in me, and I am in you" (John 14:20, NIV).

But this communion does not stop with our individual union with Christ. The moment I enter union with Christ, I simultaneously enter a union with every person, living or dead, who also is in union with Christ. This unity of Christ's people exists and manifests the degree to which His High Priestly Prayer has been answered. This unity is no insignificant thing. Indeed, nothing can possibly separate us, for this unity and community are fixed by and in Christ Himself.

This community is a heavenly community, but it also is a community in which we participate right here and right now—a unity that counts forever.

INTO THE NIGHT

DECEMBER 1999

———

T HE SPAN OF FOUR HUNDRED YEARS BETWEEN the close of the Old Testament and the birth of John the Baptist was a time marked by divine silence. The prophetic word had ceased; for four centuries there was no special revelation from God.

To get a feeling for the length of this drought of the prophetic word, consider the span of time from 1599 to 1999. In 1599, the Protestant Reformation was in full swing. However, the Pilgrims had not yet set sail for the New World, and there had been no Descartes, no Newton, no Napoleon, no George Washington. The world has changed enormously in the past 400 years.

The last book that appears in the Old Testament is that of the canonical prophet Malachi. The date of the writing of this book is uncertain, but it clearly is from the fifth century B.C., perhaps from between 450 and 430 B.C. Malachi was a contemporary of Ezra and Nehemiah, who also lived near the end of the Old Testament era, and certain concerns about the spiritual condition of Israel are echoed in the work of all three men. It was a time of spiritual degeneracy and decadence, and a kind of secularism had taken a grip on the nation, including its religious leaders. Moved by the Lord, Malachi addressed a number of key issues that have a great deal of relevance for the church today.

Marriage to Foreign Wives

Malachi complains, "Why do we deal treacherously with one another by profaning the covenant of the fathers? Judah has dealt treacherously, and an abomination has been committed in Israel and in Jerusalem, for Judah has profaned the LORD's holy institution which He loves: he has married the daughter of a foreign god. May the LORD cut off from the tents of Jacob the man who does this, being awake and aware, yet who brings an offering to the Lord of hosts!" (Mal. 2:10b–12).

The profanation of the sacred institution of marriage is called treachery and an abomination to God. The concept of "abomination" was usually associated with the practice of idolatry. Here it is extended as a pejorative term of judgment for those who took marriage partners who were pagans and worshipers of idols. Marrying outside of the covenant community was prohibited by Old Testament law. God had commanded the destruction of pagan altars in the Promised Land, "lest you make a covenant with the inhabitants of the land, and they play the harlot with their gods and make sacrifice to their gods, and one of them invites you and you eat of his sacrifice, and you take of his daughters for your sons, and his daughters play the harlot with their gods and make your sons play the harlot with their gods" (Ex. 34:15–16). The same prohibition is found in Deuteronomy 7:2b–4: "Nor shall you make marriages with them. You shall not give your daughter to their son, nor take their daughter for your son. For they will turn your sons away from following Me, to serve other gods; so the anger of the Lord will be aroused against you and destroy you suddenly."

This Old Testament prohibition against marriages to pagans is continued in the New Testament (see 1 Cor. 7:39 and 2 Cor. 6:14).

Malachi not only protested against profane marriages, but also against the cavalier divorce practices that further desecrated the holy institution of marriage:

> The Lord has been witness between you and the wife of your youth, with whom you have dealt treacherously; yet she is your companion and your wife by covenant. But did He not make them one, having a remnant of the Spirit? And why one? He seeks godly offspring. Therefore take heed to your spirit, and let none deal treacherously with the wife of his youth. "For the Lord God of Israel says that He hates divorce, for it covers one's garment with violence," says the Lord of hosts (Mal. 2:14b–16a).

The entire covenant relationship between God and Israel was likened to a marriage, with Israel as God's bride, just as the church is the bride of Christ. This divine marriage was to be reflected and mirrored in the earthly marriages of God's people. But the word that keeps occurring in Malachi's prophetic judgment against Israel is the word *treacherous*. Treachery is a synonym for betrayal. Thus, when we betray our marriage partners, we betray God Himself.

The spiritual condition at this juncture in the history of Israel is remarkably similar to that of our own day, wherein the institution of marriage has been desecrated in contemporary American customs in an unprecedented manner.

The Neglect of the Tithe

Ezra, Nehemiah, and Malachi all were concerned deeply about the failure of God's people to present their tithes to Him. This is nowhere more clear than in the indictment rendered by Malachi:

> "Will a man rob God? Yet you have robbed Me! But you say, 'In what way have we robbed You?' In tithes and offerings. You are cursed with a curse, for you have robbed Me, even this whole nation. Bring all the tithes into the storehouse, that there may be food in My house, and try Me now in this . . . if I will not open for you the windows of heaven and pour out for you such blessing that there will not be room enough to receive it" (Mal. 3:8–10).

A few years ago, a poll among professed evangelical Christians in America indicated that only 4 percent were tithers. If the poll was accurate, it would mean that 96 percent of so-called evangelical Christians are systematically robbing God and exposing themselves to His curse rather than His blessing. (See also how Nehemiah confronted this problem, in Neh. 13:10–12.)

A Degenerate Clergy

Through the lips of Malachi, God reproaches Israel for dishonoring Him:

> "Where is My reverence? says the Lord of hosts to you priests who despise My name. Yet you say, 'In what way have we despised Your name?' " (Mal. 1:6b).

The priests of Israel had despised God by corrupting worship. They defiled and profaned the table of the Lord. They broke their vows, practiced deceit, and did not give glory to God.

The priests were the clergy of Israel. They were set apart for ministry and were responsible to maintain the covenant with reverence, justice, and truth. When the clergy became corrupt, the covenant was violated, reverence in worship was lost, injustice prevailed in the land, and truth lay slain in the streets.

If America propagates moral decay in our time, judgment for it must begin in the house of God. When pastors fail in their duty, the whole land mourns. It is a corrupt church, not a corrupt government, that brings decadence to the culture. The government merely reflects the social conventions of the culture. It is the church that is to be the conscience of a nation. When that conscience is seared, vice is enshrined as custom.

Social Sins

Via Malachi, God says to Israel: " 'I will be a swift witness against sorcerers, against adulterers, against perjurers, against those who exploit wage earners and widows and orphans, and against those who turn away an alien—because they do not fear Me,' says the LORD of hosts" (Mal. 3:5).

Malachi portrays this host of social sins as a direct result of Israel's infidelity to its covenant with God.

Thus, as the prophetic word falls silent and the Intertestamental Period begins, the Old Testament ends in bleakness—but not without a promise of a future Christmas: "But to you who fear My name the Sun of Righteousness shall arise with healing in His wings ..." (Mal. 4:2a). And from the darkness of the Intertestamental Period, the Son of God arose.

BATTLE OF THE WILLS

JANUARY 2000

———

W HATEVER ELSE WE KNOW ABOUT the nature and character of God, we know that He is a volitional being. This is simply to say that God has a will, and He exercises that will. How sovereignly He exercises His will is a matter of great disagreement, but that He has a will to exercise is not in dispute, at least not in orthodox Christian theology, though it is questioned in popular concepts of God in our culture. These concepts often define God as a mindless, impersonal, will-less "force" or "higher power." Such just as easily could be defined as "cosmic dust" as it could be identified with the God of Abraham, Isaac, and Jacob.

We also know, at least from the Christian perspective, that whatever else humans are, they are volitional beings also. To be sure, they are creaturely beings with creaturely wills, but they are volitional nonetheless.

Though many secular determinists have denied both the reality of mind and the reality of will to human beings, that is not the case with historic Christianity. The issue in the church has been not so much whether we have wills, but the extent to which our wills are free. The issue in theology (as distinguished from philosophy, wherein the question of free will encounters other obstacles) has two foci.

The first has to do with the relationship between man's will and God's will with respect to predestination and divine providence. Here, most agree (at least certainly Calvinists) that in the mystery of concurrence, or the point at which the human will intersects the divine will, man's freedom is neither violated nor destroyed. That is, the human will does not fall victim to coercion; God works out His divine will in and through the choices made by the human will. At no time does He reduce humans to the level of impersonal or non-volitional puppets who can move and act only as their strings are pulled externally. To be sure, all of our acting could not be achieved without the power of God, for it is in Him that we live, and move, and have our being. Yet, in Him we really do *live*, we really do *move* (act and choose), and we really do *have being*. We are free but not autonomous.

Sometimes we hear that the sovereignty of God and the free will of man are antinomies, wherein both sides are true. This reflects a serious misunderstanding of antinomy, not to mention freedom. An antinomy, strictly speaking, is a contradiction, wherein the two poles are mutually exclusive and cannot both be true. But the two statements—God is sovereign and man is free—do not constitute an antinomy.

If, however, we said that God is sovereign and man is autonomous, that would be a bona fide antinomy, or contradiction. It is self-evident that if God is sovereign over His creatures, none of them can be autonomous, or "a law unto themselves." Such a notion not only is repugnant to reason, it is repugnant in the extreme to the teaching of Scripture.

Likewise, if man is autonomous, then God cannot be sovereign. He could have "limited sovereignty," perhaps over trees and rocks, except where men were dealing with the trees and rocks.

The false dilemma or false antinomy is avoided if we understand that God's sovereignty is unlimited and man's freedom, though real, is limited. The popular idea that God's sovereignty is limited by human freedom is pure blasphemy and represents both a pagan view of God and a pagan view of man. If God's sovereignty is limited by human freedom, then it is man and not God who is sovereign. This would make human freedom absolute, and God's sovereignty relative and subject to man. Some seek to advance the notion that God is self-limited by His righteous character, in that it would be immoral for Him to exercise sovereignty over man's will. This reflects a confusion between God's violating human will via coercion and overruling human decisions by His government.

God is free and man is free. However, God is more free than I am. That is what sovereignty is all about. If my will bumps up against God's will, something has to give. I can only exercise my will insofar as God chooses to let me do so. At any point in my life, God has both the power and the right to take my life or otherwise stop me in my tracks. For Him to override my will is perfectly consistent with His righteous character.

The second focus of theological concern regarding free will has to do with the degree to which our liberty has been impaired by the Fall. This is the issue I chronicled historically in my book *Willing to Believe*. This is the issue that was at the heart of the Pelagian controversy that pitted the British monk Pelagius against St. Augustine of Hippo in the fifth century. In that debate, Pelagius argued that man not only was created free but that his nature was created immutable. He denied the reality of the Fall, arguing that Adam's sin affected Adam and only Adam. There was no fall into a state of moral corruption called original sin, which was transmitted to the entire human race.

Against Pelagius, Augustine argued that the Fall produced dire consequences for humanity that involved the loss of original liberty. He distinguished between "freewill" (*liberium arbitrium*) and "liberty" (*libertas*). He argued that since the Fall man still has a free will—that is, he retains the faculty of choosing. He still can act intentionally, according to his desires. What he lost was any desire for the things of God. Thus, he never will choose God precisely because he doesn't want to choose God. This is freedom without liberty. This state of affairs is rooted in man's bondage to sin. The sinner is both free and enslaved at the same time, but not in the same relationship. He is free to do what he wants, but what he wants to do is sin. Therein is his bondage.

Pagan and humanistic views of man, while admitting that we sin, do not agree that we sin because of a fallen nature that is enslaved to sin. Sin is seen as peripheral to human experience, not at its core. The humanist argues that a free will is always an indifferent will that has no pre-inclination to sin but is always able, in any circumstance, to choose sin or righteousness. It is this "indifference" that is on a collision course with the biblical view of man.

Pelagianism was condemned by the church and rarely occurs in history in its unvarnished form, save in the writings of people such as Charles Finney and, perhaps in our own time, Clark Pinnock. The usual struggle is between Augustinianism and Semi-Pelagianism. Semi-Pelagianism, early articulated by John Cassianus, taught that there truly was a Fall and that the Fall left man in such a state of corruption that his will or liberty was seriously impaired. Whereas Pelagius argued that man could make godly choices without the assistance of grace, Semi-Pelagianism insists that grace is a necessary prerequisite for godly choices. The chief difference between Augustinian theology and Semi-Pelagianism is with respect to the degree of moral bondage we are in. The Semi-Pelagian believes that, to some extent, the will is still able to cooperate with or refuse the offer of grace. The grace of regeneration (or its equivalent) is deemed resistible. By contrast, Augustine believed that the grace that liberates the soul from bondage is not cooperative but monergistic. In other words, for the sinner to respond to God, God first must do a work of monergistic grace, by which He unilaterally changes the disposition of the soul of man to make him willing to respond positively to God, and this gracious change is absolutely effectual.

This was the debate between Luther and Erasmus, Calvin and Arminius, and Edwards and the Arminianism of his day. Luther's *The Bondage of the Will*, Calvin's *Institutes*, and Edwards' *The Freedom of the Will* all follow in the footsteps of Augustine regarding this controversial matter.

In simple terms, the issue usually comes down to this: does faith precede regeneration, or does regeneration effectually precede faith? Do we choose Christ, or does He choose us? Orthodox Christianity has argued from Scripture that Christ must choose, for man is not free to do so. And so we have another indication that God's freedom far surpasses our own.

THE IMITATION OF CHRIST

FEBRUARY 2000

———

S EVERAL YEARS AGO, AT THE ANNUAL Christian Booksellers Association convention, I saw the WWJD bracelets for the first time.* I must confess that my initial reaction to them was a bit negative. I thought they were just another Christian "trinket" that would trivialize the depths and riches of the Christian faith, one more piece of hokey merchandise to go with such things on display as mint candies called "Testamints" and Christian toilet paper adorned with Bible verses. In that vast array of spiritual junk food and junk jewelry, my spirit sank at how cheap and tawdry we were making the things of God.

But as I reflected on these bracelets and gave them the benefit of a second glance, I began to gain some appreciation for them. I thought of other acronyms that have served the church well as mnemonic devices. One good example was J.S. Bach's custom of penning "SDG" at the bottom of his compositions. The letters stand for *soli Deo gloria*, one of the prominent mottoes of the Reformation—"To God alone the glory." Such a motto is useful because the siren call for personal glory is so seductive that we need constant reminders to seek the glory of God alone, and not our own.

Of course, virtually all such mottoes are subject to the charge of being hokey and simplistic. That charge could be made against the theological shorthand phrase *sola fide*, which seeks to express, in two simple words, "faith alone," the monumental doctrine of justification by faith alone, which captures the very essence of the Gospel. Such slogans and mottoes embody the principle articulated in another well-worn acrostic, KISS

———

* "What Would Jesus Do?" bracelets were a popular fashion item among Christian youth in the 1990s. They were meant to encourage the wearer to consider Christ's example in daily life.

(keep it simple, stupid). But while the desire for simplicity is a noble one, it is no easy task to simplify the difficult or reduce the complex to basic terms that are understandable. The trick is to simplify without distortion. The simple clarifies; the simplistic distorts. The person who can simplify difficult things without distorting them or making them simplistic first must reach a thorough understanding of the matter he is trying to explain.

Acronyms and acrostics are common and often effective means of communication in our culture. For instance, everyone understands what is meant by the office memo that includes the acrostic ASAP. Such abbreviations may be crude, such as PDQ or CYA, but the message gets through. Then there are acrostics and acronyms that are valuable memory aids. If I want to remember the white keys on the piano that make up an F major 7th chord, I just need to make a "face" (F-A-C-E), and if I have trouble remembering the five Great Lakes, I can think of HOMES (Huron, Ontario, Michigan, Erie, and Superior).

These devices also play a role in Christian learning and experience. Every Reformed person knows the significance of TULIP. In like manner, every Sunday morning when I offer the pastoral prayer in church, I consciously structure my prayer according to the acrostic ACTS, following the pattern of Adoration, Confession, Thanksgiving, and Supplication.

Let us return then to the WWJD bracelets (or bumper stickers, or T-shirts, or whatever). This device reminds us to ask ourselves the question, "What would Jesus do?" It is a call for the Christian to follow the example of Christ in godly living. While the WWJD bracelets are new, this call is not. One of the most famous devotional books ever written was the classic penned by Thomas à Kempis, *On the Imitation of Christ.*

In fact, the call to the *imitatio Christo* is rooted in the New Testament. The Apostle Paul wrote to the Corinthians, "Imitate me, just as I also imitate Christ" (1 Cor. 11:1). Here the Apostle was aware of his own responsibility to be a role model for Christians. He called upon believers not only to receive his teaching as from the Lord, but to follow his example of Christian living. Of course, the Apostolic exhortation was not absolute, as Paul was acutely aware that he was not sinless. The call to imitate Paul ends where Paul fails to imitate his Lord. Hence, he says, "Imitate me, just as I also imitate Christ." This can be understood to mean that we should imitate Paul insofar as he imitates Christ.

Elsewhere, Paul declares to the Ephesians, "Therefore be imitators of God as dear children. And walk in love, as Christ also has loved us and given Himself for us, an offering and a sacrifice to God for a sweet-smelling aroma" (5:1–2). Here, Paul raises the call a notch to the imitation of God Himself. Do not understand this as a cryptic denial of the deity of Christ. To be sure, Christ is fully God, but He is also fully man, and in His humanity He had tasks to perform that we not only cannot emulate, but should not seek to emulate. That obviously also applies to the imitation of God; we are to imitate the righteousness of God without seeking to emulate the being of God.

When Martin Luther called Christians to "Be Christ to your neighbor," he did not mean they should do anything so crass as to assume they could become a substitute for Christ to their neighbors. That is the sentiment of antichrist, who seeks to replace Christ. Luther understood that we cannot atone for our neighbors' sins; only Christ can accomplish that task. Rather, Luther meant that we are to so mirror the love of Christ to our neighbors that they can see something of Him in our witness.

But to answer the question "What would Jesus do?" is no simple matter. If we make a careful study of the life of Jesus, we encounter real surprises. We see Him cursing a fig tree because the tree had the sign of figs, leaves, but no actual fruit. The fig tree was an object lesson in hypocrisy. We see Jesus sending demons into swine and, consequently, the swine to their deaths. We see Him knocking over the tables in the temple as He cleansed the corruption there with a whip. We see Him declaring Himself the Lord of the Sabbath and the one who possesses authority to forgive sins in the earth. What do these actions of Jesus say to us?

When I seek to imitate Christ, I must always be mindful of the wide chasm that exists between His authority and my authority. Though He indeed delegated much authority to His disciples and to His church, no one has the right to supplant the authority the Father vested in Him.

How did Jesus deal with people in terms of human relationships? Again, the pattern is not always easy to discern. Jesus was consistently fair with all whom He encountered, but He was not monolithically gentle. He would never break a bruised reed, but He smashed arrogant reeds. When Jesus dealt with the weak and lowly, He was always tender and gentle. When He dealt with the powerful, He asked no quarter and gave none. We observe Him being tender and gentle with the oppressed but tough and unyielding with the oppressors. His meekness, like that of Moses, who was said to be meek, was not to be confused with weakness. Jesus was not a whimpering doormat. He subjected Himself to the judgment of the world on His own terms in order to accomplish His divine mission. He reminded Pilate that he could have no power at all against Him unless it had been given to him from above. He also declared that none could take His life from Him unless He was willing to lay it down for His sheep.

Paul expounds the call to imitation in Philippians, where he writes, "Let this mind be in you which was also in Christ Jesus" (2:5). Here we are called to imitate the humility of Jesus, who was willing to lose His reputation and take upon Himself the role of a servant for the sake of others. This is the supreme call for the Christian seeking to imitate Jesus—that in all things we seek first the approval of God over the approval of men. What would Jesus do? He would do everything possible to please His Father.

GROUNDED IN GRACE

MARCH 2000

——

T HE HISTORIC DEBATE BETWEEN Protestantism and Roman Catholicism frequently is framed in terms of an argument over works vs. faith and/or merit vs. grace. The magisterial Reformers articulated their view of justification through a theological shorthand device of Latin slogans, and the phrases they used—*sola fide* and *sola gratia*—have become deeply entrenched in Protestant history. *Sola fide*, or "faith alone," denies that our works contribute to the ground of our justification, while *sola gratia*, or "grace alone," denies that any merit of our own contributes to our justification.

The problem with slogans is that in their function as theological shorthand they are capable of being misunderstood easily or of being used as licenses for oversimplifying complex matters. Thus, when faith is sharply differentiated from works, various distortions easily creep into our understanding.

When the Reformers insisted that justification is by faith alone, they did not mean that faith is itself a work of any kind. In seeking to exclude works from the ground of our justification, they did not mean to suggest that faith contributes anything to justification.

The Heart of the Matter

It may be said that the heart of the sixteenth century debate over justification was the issue of the ground of justification. The ground of justification is the basis on which God declares a person just. The Reformers insisted that the biblical view is that the only possible ground for our justification is the righteousness of Christ. This is an explicit reference to the righteousness achieved by Jesus in the living of His own life; it is not the righteousness of Christ *in* us but the righteousness of Christ *for* us.

When we keep the issue of the ground of justification squarely before us, we see that *sola fide* is a shorthand slogan not only for the doctrine of justification by faith alone but also for the notion that justification is by Christ alone. It is in, through, and by the righteousness of Christ alone that God declares us just in His sight.

To say that justification is *by* faith means simply that it is by or through faith that we receive the imputation of Christ's righteousness to our account. Thus, faith is the instrumental cause, or the means, by which we lay hold of Christ.

Rome teaches that the instrumental cause of justification is the sacrament of baptism (in the first instance) and the sacrament of penance (in the second instance). Via the sacrament, the grace of justification, or the righteousness of Christ, is infused (or poured) into the soul of the recipient. Thereupon, the person must assent to and cooperate with this infused grace to such an extent that true righteousness actually *inheres* in the believer, at which point God declares that person just. For God to justify a person, the person must first *become* just.

Thus, Rome believes that for a person to become just he needs three things: grace, faith, and Christ. Rome does not teach that man can save himself by his own merit without grace, by his own works without faith, or by himself without Christ. So what was all the fuss about?

Neither the debates of the sixteenth century nor the recent discussions and joint declarations between Catholics and Protestants have been able to resolve the key issue of the debate, the issue of the ground of justification. Is it the *imputed* righteousness of Christ or the *infused* righteousness of Christ?

In our day, many who confront this centuries-old conflict merely shrug their shoulders and say, "So what?" or "What's the big deal?" Since both sides affirm that the righteousness of Christ is necessary for our justification, and that grace and faith are likewise necessary, to probe more deeply into other technical issues seems like a waste of time or an exercise in theological pedantic arrogance. The whole debate looks to more and more people like a tempest in a teapot.

Two Perspectives

Well, *what is the big deal?* Let me try to answer that from two perspectives, one theological, the other personal and existential.

The big deal theologically is the essence of the Gospel. Deals don't get much bigger than that. The Good News is that the righteousness God demands from His creatures was achieved *for* them by Christ. The work of Christ *counts* for the believer. The believer is justified on the basis of what Jesus did for him, outside of and apart from him, not by what Jesus does in him. For Rome, a person is not justified until or unless righteousness inheres in him. He gets the help of Christ, but God does not reckon, transfer, or impute Christ's righteousness to his account.

What does this mean personally and existentially? Rome's view strikes despair into my soul. If I have to wait until I am inherently righteous before God will declare me righteous, I have a long wait in store for me. In Rome's view, if I commit a mortal sin, I will lose whatever justifying grace I presently possess. Even if I regain it via the sacrament of penance, I still face purgatory. If I die with any impurity in my life, I must go to purgatory to have all impurities "purged." That may require multiple thousands of years to accomplish.

What a radical difference from the biblical Gospel, which assures me that justification in the sight of God is mine the moment I put my trust is Jesus. Because His righteousness is perfect, it can neither be increased nor diminished. And if His righteousness is imputed to me, I now possess the full and total *ground* of justification.

The issue of imputed vs. infused righteousness never can be resolved without repudiating one or the other. They are mutually exclusive views of justification. If one is true, the other must be false. One of these views declares the true biblical Gospel; the other is a false Gospel. They both simply cannot be true.

Again, this issue cannot be resolved by some middle ground. The two incompatible views may be ignored or minimized (as the modern dialogues do through historical revision), but they cannot be reconciled. Neither can they be reduced to a mere misunderstanding—both sides are too intelligent for that to have happened for the past 400 years.

The issue of merit and grace in justification is clouded by confusion. Rome speaks of believers having two kinds of merit: congruous and condign. Congruous merit is gained by doing works of satisfaction in connection with the sacrament of penance. These works are not so meritorious that they impose an obligation upon a just judge to reward them, but they are good enough to make it "fitting" or "congruous" for God to reward them.

Condign merit is a higher order of merit achieved by saints. But even this merit is defined by Rome as being rooted and grounded in grace. It is merit that could not be achieved without the assistance of grace.

The Reformers rejected both congruous and condign merit, arguing that our situation not only is *rooted* in grace, it is gracious at every point. The only merit that counts toward our justification is the merit of Christ. Indeed, we are saved by meritorious works—Christ's. That we are saved by someone else's merit imputed to us is the very essence of the grace of salvation.

It is this grace that must never be compromised or negotiated by the church. Without it, we are truly hopeless and helpless to stand righteous before a holy God.

THE LAST ENEMY

APRIL 2000

———

"**H**ALT! WHO GOES THERE?"
Such might be the words of a sentry who confronts a mysterious stranger in the darkness. The sentry must discern the identity of the trespasser to determine whether he is a friend or foe. Armed to protect his territory, the vigilant guard wants to avoid two evils: (1) the entrance into the compound of an enemy bent on destruction and (2) the mistaken shooting of an ally stumbling about in the dark.

There is an intruder in our garden—the one called death. Our task is to determine whether his grin is the fiendish mask of a mortal enemy or the benign smile of a friend come to rescue us from this vale of tears. Should we greet him with strident protests or with open arms?

The Bible describes death as an enemy. It is not the only enemy of the Christian, but it is described as the "last enemy." In 1 Corinthians, Paul affirms that Christ will reign until He has put all enemies under His feet, and the last of those enemies will be death (15:25–26). It should be a great comfort to the believer to know that the one in whom he places his trust is *Christus Victor*. We see this clearly in Hebrews, where the author describes Jesus as our *archēgos*, or the "supreme champion" of His people.

The champion motif is central not only to Hebrews but to the entire Bible. We think of the famous episode of the match between David and Goliath. The Israelites and Philistines had agreed that the outcome of their war would be determined not by a full confrontation of the armies but by a contest between champions who would represent each side. Goliath, the gigantic champion of the Philistines, struck terror into the hearts of the Jewish soldiers because he appeared invincible. No one volunteered to go up against him until the shepherd boy, David, stepped forward to assume the task. His conquest of Goliath was astonishing, but it pales into insignificance when placed alongside the victory of David's greater Son, who was also David's Lord and David's champion. As David went up against the power of Goliath, Jesus went up against the power of Satan himself.

Notice the link between Paul's teaching in 1 Corinthians 15 and that found in Hebrews 2. First Corinthians 15:26–28 says, "The last enemy that will be destroyed is death. For 'He has put all things under His feet.' But when He says 'all things are put under Him,' it is evident that He who put all things under Him is excepted. Now when all things are made subject to Him, then the Son Himself will also be subject to Him who put all things under Him, that God may be all in all."

Now note Hebrews 2:8ff: "For in that He put all in subjection under Him, He left nothing that is not put under Him. But now we do not yet see all things put under Him. But we see Jesus, who was made a little lower than the angels, for the suffering of death crowned with glory and honor, that He, by the grace of God, might taste death for everyone. For it was fitting for Him, for whom are all things and by whom are all things, in bringing many sons to glory, to make the captain of their salvation perfect through sufferings."

Both 1 Corinthians and Hebrews harken back to Psalm 8, in which the "son of man" fulfills the destiny of the Second Adam and receives from the Father dominion over creation. This placing of all things in or under subjection to Christ has both a present and a future dimension. In His ascension, Christ was invested as the King of kings and Lord of lords. He is already at the right hand of the Father and reigns over all creation. But the whole of creation is not yet in willing submission or subjection to Him. In short, Christ has rebellious subjects. Satan himself is still in rebellion.

The connection between Satan and death is important: "Inasmuch then as the children have partaken of flesh and blood, He Himself likewise shared in the same that through death He might destroy him who had the power of death, that is, the devil, and release those who through fear of death were all their lifetime subject to bondage" (Heb. 2:14–15).

Here it is declared that the devil had the power of death until that power was wrenched away from him by Christ. We must remember that any power or authority Satan ever has is a *delegated* authority, as the ultimate authority over death and everything else is God. But Satan's delegated authority over death is taken from him by Christ. The irony is that Christ's victory over the devil and the power of death is accomplished by means of death. In His death, Jesus is victorious over death. Death cannot hold Him.

Yet there is still a future dimension to this victory, for Paul says that the last enemy that will be destroyed is death. He writes this years after the Cross. Thus, even though Christ dealt a mortal blow to Satan and death in His own death, there still remained a victory to be won.

Something glorious and decisive did take place on the cross with respect to death. The sting of death was removed by the captain of our salvation. Paul writes: "So when this corruptible has put on incorruption, and this mortal has put on immortality, then shall be brought to pass the saying that is written: 'Death is swallowed up in victory.' 'O Death, where is your sting? O Hades, where is your victory?' The sting of death is sin, and the strength of sin is the law. But thanks be to God who gives us the victory through our Lord Jesus Christ" (1 Cor. 15:54–57).

Here is our "Champion Christology." God gives to us a victory that we have not achieved for ourselves. It is won for us by another. Victory over Goliath is not worthy to be compared to victory over death.

So is death now our friend? Or is it still our foe? For believers, death is a friend insofar as it ushers us into the immediate presence of Christ. But insofar as it is still coupled with much suffering, it remains the last enemy that must be totally vanquished. However, our problem with death is not with death itself but with the process that leads up to it. It is *dying* that is still feared by Christians. What Christian would be afraid of death if we could just shut our eyes and wake up in heaven? We know that the other side of death is glory and that death is but the portal or threshold to that glory.

Paul knew the glory of death, as evidenced by his anguish and ambivalence regarding his possible departure from this life. He wrote: "For to me, to live is Christ, and to die is gain. But if I live on in the flesh, this will mean fruit from my labor; yet what I shall choose I cannot tell. For I am hard-pressed between the two, having a desire to depart and be with Christ, which is far better. Nevertheless to remain in the flesh is more needful for you" (Phil. 1:21–24).

Paul here makes a comparison between life and death. It is not a contrast between the good and the bad. Neither is it a comparison between the good and the better. It is a comparison between the good and the *far better*.

Because of Christ's conquest of death, we are called "hyper-conquerors" by Paul: "Yet in all these things we are more than conquerors through Him who loved us" (Rom. 8:37). "All these things" include life and death, and everything in between. Dominion over the curse of death is sealed for those who are beloved of Christ.

In this same passage, Paul answers his own question about what shall separate us from the love of Christ: nothing can do that, not even death. Those of us who are approaching that deadly day have nothing to fear but God Himself.

THEOLOGY IN HARMONY

MAY 2000

———

" **A** RIGHT STRAWY EPISTLE . . ." Such was Martin Luther's early bombastic judgment of the value of the book of James. The words were uttered during a period in which Luther questioned the canonical status of this New Testament book.

Because Luther once questioned the canonical status of James, some scholars have argued that he did not believe in the inerrancy or binding authority of Scripture. Yet Luther repeatedly asserted that the Scriptures never err and the principle of *sola Scriptura* affirms the binding authority of all the Bible. Luther's question was not about the *nature* of Scripture, but about the *scope* or *extent* of Scripture. He was not asking whether Scripture is inerrant or authoritative, but whether James was properly included in the canon of Scripture. Luther never changed his mind about the nature of Scripture, but he did change his mind about its extent by questioning James' inclusion in the canon. At a later point, however, that question was removed from his mind.

Why did Luther ever question the canonical status of James? The answer is clear. Luther's struggle with James grew out of the deepest theological controversy in the history of the church, the struggle over the nature of the Gospel as it was focused in the doctrine of justification by faith alone (*sola fide*). Luther's opponents constantly cited the book of James to repudiate the evangelical understanding of the Gospel. The Roman Catholic community in particular relied heavily on the epistle, especially at the Sixth Session of the Council of Trent, which cited James 2:17 and 2:20 in chapter seven and James 2:24 in chapter 10.

James 2:24 reads, "You see then that a man is justified by works, and not by faith only." On the surface, this text clearly seems to repudiate *sola fide* in that it states explicitly that justification is *by* works and not by faith alone. The problem is intensified by James' earlier statement: "Was not

Abraham our father justified by works when he offered Isaac his son on the altar?" (James 2:21). Thus, James seems to declare that men in general and Abraham in particular are justified by works.

The problem is exacerbated by the fact that James apparently is in conflict not just with Luther, but, more seriously, with the Apostle Paul. In chapter 3 of his epistle to the Romans, Paul declares that justification is by faith apart from the works of the law. But if justification is by works, as James says, then it cannot be by faith apart from works. Conversely, if it is by faith alone, it cannot be by works.

Some critical scholars have argued that Paul and James were simply locked in an irreconcilable contradiction between mutually exclusive doctrines of justification. The irony of this is that most critics see the conflict between Paul and James as irreconcilable, yet at the same time they insist that the differences between the Reformation and Roman Catholic views of justification *are* reconcilable. In fact, recent declarations of accord between Lutherans and Roman Catholics and between some professed evangelicals and Roman Catholics have affirmed that such reconciliation has been achieved.

However, Rome has insisted historically that the ground of justification must be *inherent* righteousness (though resting on grace), while the Reformers insisted that the *only* ground of justification is the imputation of the righteousness of Christ that is not inherent in us. *This* is irreconcilability—the ground of justification cannot possibly be both in us and outside of us at the same time and in the same relationship. The only way reconciliation can be achieved is for at least one party to abandon its historic position. So far, every accord to resolve the conflict that I've seen has witnessed a Protestant retreat from the Reformation position.

By contrast, Paul and James are not irreconcilable. Luther finally accepted James, not because he saw a way to reconcile himself with Roman doctrine, but because he saw that Paul and James were not in ultimate conflict. He realized, as Calvin did, that though Paul and James both discussed the word *justify* and both appealed to the same Old Testament figure—Abraham—they were discussing distinctly different issues. They were not answering the same question.

Paul addresses this question: "How can an unjust person ever be acceptable to a just and holy God?" His answer to this profound human predicament is his exposition of the Gospel, which Good News declares that we are justified freely by what was accomplished for us by Christ in His life and death. By faith we receive the benefit of having our sin/guilt imputed to Christ and His perfect righteousness imputed to us. Paul teaches that the moment Abraham believed (in Gen. 15) God counted or reckoned him just, before he did any works. Paul also labors the point that it is by faith, prior to any works, that we are reconciled to God, because Christ is our righteousness.

James is answering a different question. His concern has to do with what kind of faith justifies. He frames the issue in 2:14: "What does it profit, my brethren, if someone says he has faith but does not have works? Can faith save him?"

The issue here is this: Are we saved by an empty profession of faith? Neither Paul nor Luther ever taught that justification is by profession alone. Both insisted that what was professed must actually be possessed for justification to exist. Both Paul and Luther taught that if true faith is present, it necessarily produces the fruit of works. If works do not follow from "faith," that is proof positive that the "faith" is not genuine but is a mere claim to it. However, even if all good works do come from faith, these works still have no part in the ground of justification. They add no merit to us. The only work that contributes to our justification is the work of Jesus; not the work of Jesus *in* us, but the work of Jesus *for* us. His merit is the only merit that counts for us.

When James says that Abraham was justified when he offered Isaac on the altar, he uses the term *justify* with a different nuance than Paul. He is saying that in this work Abraham demonstrated that his faith was genuine; he "justified" his claim to true faith. Jesus used the term in a similar sense when He said, "Wisdom is justified by her children" (Matt. 11:19b). In other words, true wisdom is shown to be wise by its fruit, so a person who claims to have faith is vindicated on his claim when he shows forth his faith by his works. This is the sum and substance of James' concern in chapter 2, and in this regard he has no conflict with Paul or with Luther.

The Reformers, such as Luther, were reconciled with James. The Roman Catholics have yet to be reconciled with Paul.

THE MATTER OF ART

JUNE 2000

———

EVERY FORM IS AN ART FORM, and every art form communicates something. No art is content-neutral because all art is expressive. Manifestly, that which is expressed, in order to be expressive, must express something.

Art forms are many and varied. Music, painting, sculpture, film, drama, and literature are some of the art forms that both shape and express our culture. The question of the chicken and the egg with respect to art imitating life or life imitating art is a false dilemma. Art surely does imitate life, yet it is also true that art has a powerful impact on shaping society. This is true because art is a creative enterprise.

When the artist creates, he makes a world and invites us to step into it and live in it for a time. This is nowhere more obvious than in the cinema. When audiences scream for Rocky to win or shout warnings to the heroine who is about to be attacked by a hidden killer, we see the empathy that can be produced in the creation of a make-believe world. A movie is a fantasy, a created world in which we are invited to live for about two hours. We become more than observers; we are participants. We taste life in the world of images that we behold.

As an adolescent living in the "Happy Days" of the 1950s, my rite of passage into romance was initiated by kissing parties where the games of choice were "Post Office" and "Spin the Bottle." There was a progression in competency in the art of kissing, as we graduated from a casual kiss to a sustained smooch that we described as kissing "movie-style" (a style that has long perished from the silver screen, being replaced by a more overtly erotic form of kissing). At our adolescent parties, we were translating what we saw in the movies into our own patterns of behavior. This was life imitating art.

Today, when our TV heroes, movie stars, and novel protagonists enter into sexual relations outside of marriage, the message expressed is that such behavior is normal, and therefore good and acceptable. The world portrayed or expressed in these art forms is one in which its creator places his or her imprimatur on such behavior. This message bombards the senses of the participant, teaching an ethic that collides violently with the ethic commanded by the real Creator of the real world.

One of the most powerful of all the art forms is literature. The written word is a medium that is verbal. We understand that non-verbal communication is real and powerful, but it is the verbal that communicates in a particularly cognitive manner.

Literature has been a powerful tool used to chisel the forms of Western civilization. The impact of the great writers has been vast. Literary greats include poets, dramatists, essayists, philosophers, scientists, and novelists.

If we trace the development of the novel in American history, we get a bird's-eye view of the formative changes in American culture. Read the literature of the Colonial period and compare it with the current top 10 on *The New York Times*' best-seller list. Compare the content, the style of expression, and especially the worldviews communicated. The contrast is not merely striking, it is overwhelming.

When my children were young, we took them on a trip to Washington, D.C. Among our sight-seeing experiences was a visit to the National Archives. In the rotunda that houses the U.S. Constitution and the Declaration of Independence, there was also a large assortment of writings composed by eighteenth century leaders, particularly written correspondence. While waiting in line to view the Declaration, I read these more casual writings penned by the framers. I was amazed by the literary grace of their simple letters, their clear articulation of their ideas, and the fluent style of their writing. Again, this experience was a strong exercise in contrast to contemporary forms of written communication.

I had a friend who was an English major in college. He had aspirations of becoming a writer, but in his creative writing class he kept receiving C grades with critical comments from his professor (a woman) indicating that his writing was dull and unimaginative. I mention that his professor was a woman for a reason. This was still in the decade of the 1950s, albeit the late '50s, before the cultural revolution of the 1960s. It was a quaint time when men would rather perish than speak crude vulgarities in the presence of women.

Nevertheless, my friend decided to try a new tack. Riding the crest of the new realism that was just beginning to come into vogue, he wrote a "creative" descriptive paper in which he employed every crudity and filthy word he knew to describe explicit sexual acts between his characters. On this paper he received an A⁺ coupled with effusive praise that concluded with this remark: "Mr. ——, this is excellent work. I didn't know you had it in you." Here the lofty standard of realism was achieved by using the most crude forms of verbal expression my friend could muster.

If this is the way to literary greatness, we wonder what heights Shakespeare, Milton, Melville, Hawthorne, and Edgar Allan Poe might have achieved had they been encouraged to call upon their most graphic crudities to express themselves.

The language of verbal expression is rich and employs a plethora of forms. Even the Bible uses crudities at times. But there is a difference between the crude and the filthy. I think we all know the difference—we may not be able to describe it, but we know it when we see it. We understand the difference between cursing and obscenity, between vulgarism and filth.

Men such as Poe have displayed a mastery of language that marries the craftsmanship of words with exalted plateaus of beauty. Poe understood the power of language and of written words to stimulate the soul to soar to lofty heights.

I wonder whether any literature has ever been penned in English that surpasses "The Whiteness of the Whale," chapter 42 of Herman Melville's *Moby Dick*. In this novel, we find not only a high use of language but a lofty theme, that of a whaling captain's monomaniacal pursuit of a rogue whale that previously left him crippled in body and soul. Here we see a carefully crafted symbolism of an ungodly method of pursuing God Himself.

Great literature expresses great themes in a great way. It pierces to the core of the human predicament and shines a verbal light on truth. In great literature, even that which chronicles misery, evil, oppression, and darkness, there is a loveliness to the bare truth that is expressed. From the power of Poe to the joy of Bunyan, we are moved by an art form that is obscured and in eclipse by the popular and tawdry literature that reflects our current culture.

REJOICING WITH THE GROOM

JULY 2000

———

A WEDDING IS A TIME OF CELEBRATION. It is a time to break out the food and the wine. Similarly, Jesus' presence on earth was a time of celebration for the people of God.

It is axiomatic that there are some people you can never please. They seek prudence, but some fall short of the mark—about three letters shy—and simply become prudes.

Such were the folks who were critical of Jesus. Imagine someone clicking his or her tongue and saying "Tsk, tsk" at Jesus. But that's what they did. However, the same prudes who disapproved of the behavior of Jesus previously shook their fingers at John the Baptist for opposite reasons.

The attitude of these prudes provoked Jesus to ask, "To what then shall I liken the men of this generation, and what are they like? They are like children sitting in the marketplace and calling to one another, saying:

" 'We played the flute for you,
and you did not dance;
we mourned to you,
and you did not weep' " (Luke 7:31–32).

Jesus was charging the Pharisees with being childish. Oh, this criticism from the Lord of Glory had to sting. The Pharisees prided themselves on being so mature, but Jesus exposed them as being jejune. They were like little children who couldn't agree on what game to play. "Let's play checkers." "Naw! I hate checkers, let's play guns." "No way, let's play a video game." "Boring!" And so it goes through suggested game after suggested game. Play the flute, they don't want to dance. OK, let's mourn, but no one will weep.

Jesus applied this childishness to the response of the prudes to John and to Himself: "For John the Baptist came neither eating bread nor drinking wine, and you say, 'He has a demon.' The Son of Man has come eating and drinking, and you say, 'Look, a glutton and a winebibber, a friend of tax collectors and sinners!' But wisdom is justified by all her children" (Luke 7:33–35).

The style of Jesus differed sharply from that of John the Baptist. John was an ascetic. He lived in the desert and followed a rigorous regimen of self-denial, subsisting on locusts and wild honey. By contrast, Jesus went to parties. It is interesting to note the number of gospel narratives in which we find Jesus attending a banquet or feast. Because He went to events of that sort, Jesus acquired the reputation (at least among His enemies) of being a glutton and a wine drinker.

The question for us is, why did Jesus and John the Baptist behave so differently? More specifically, why did Jesus eschew the lifestyle of the ascetic? But we need not resort to idle speculation in order to answer this question. Jesus answered it for us.

> The disciples of John and of the Pharisees were fasting. Then they came and said to Him, "Why do the disciples of John and of the Pharisees fast, but Your disciples do not fast?" And Jesus said to them, "Can the friends of the bridegroom fast while the bridegroom is with them? As long as they have the bridegroom with them they cannot fast. But the days will come when the bridegroom will be taken away from them, and then they will fast in those days" (Mark 2:18–20).

Under the terms of the law of Moses, fasting was required only once a year, on the Day of Atonement. However, people could and would fast voluntarily on other occasions, such as in times of mourning or of deep repentance. The Pharisees, however, had a habit of fasting often, even as frequently as twice a week. And John's disciples apparently fasted as a sign of the repentance John called for in light of his announcement of the time of crisis for Israel, the moment of the arrival of the Messiah who would usher in the kingdom of God.

Once Jesus appeared, however, everything changed. The King of Glory had arrived on the scene. Jesus announced that if people saw Him casting out Satan by the Spirit of God, then they would know the kingdom had come upon them (Matt. 12:28). And so it was.

Jesus described His coming by using the metaphor of the bridegroom. People do not fast at a wedding, nor do they play funeral dirges there. A wedding is a time of celebration. It is designed to be a happy occasion. It is a time to break out the food and the wine. Similarly, Jesus' presence on earth was a time of celebration for the people of God. His presence was a call to rejoicing.

Yet Jesus' explanation contained an ominous word of foreboding. He spoke of the time when He would be taken away from His friends, which would be a time for fasting. To what was Jesus referring?

The answer may be twofold. On the one hand, Jesus was taken from His friends by His suffering and death. Perhaps He was alluding here merely to His absence between His death and His resurrection. On the other hand, He may also have been referring to His departure in His ascension. He spoke repeatedly to His disciples about the coming time when He would leave them to return to His Father.

Yet even as Jesus spoke to His followers about His departure, He comforted them with the promise that He would be with them until the end of the age. Therefore, the church confesses her faith that, as to His human nature, Jesus is no longer present with us, but, in His divine nature, He is never absent from us. Jesus is both present with and absent from His people at the same time, though not in the same way.

With our future hope, we look forward to a full reunion with Christ in heaven. We anticipate with great joy the marriage feast of the Lamb. We are His bride and we await the celebration of the arrival of the Bridegroom.

There is still a significant place for fasting. We have much for which to mourn and much for which to repent. But we also can celebrate the presence of Christ, especially in the sacrament of the Lord's Supper. Among other things, the Lord's Supper is a foretaste of our future marriage feast. We not only look back to the cross but ahead to the banquet, and in the present we celebrate the real presence of Christ with us. This is no religion for prudes.

"With the advent of liberalism came a massive attack on the trustworthiness of the Bible. This attack came not from outside the church but from within it."

—

A FACADE OF FAITH

AUGUST 2000

———

S TUDENTS OF THE LATE SWISS THEOLOGIAN Karl Barth tell the story of his lecture series that focused on the theology of Friedrich Schleiermacher, a German theologian of the late eighteenth and early nineteenth centuries. During the lectures, Barth had a bust of Schleiermacher sitting on his desk, and he would address comments to the mute statue from time to time. At the end of his final lecture, Barth walked up to his desk and, with great aplomb, swept the bust of Schleiermacher off the desktop with his arm. When the statue hit the floor and shattered into pieces, Barth announced, "So much for the theology of Schleiermacher."

Barth's critique of Schleiermacher was but a small portion of his critique of the whole movement of nineteenth century theology that appeared under the rubric of "liberalism." When we speak of a "liberal" in theology, the label usually is not describing someone who is a free-thinker, progressive, or open-minded, or even one inclined to the left politically. In theology, liberalism refers to the specific movement that arose in nineteenth century Europe and came to dominate the academic realm of religion. As a movement, it sought to de-supernaturalize the Christian faith, especially miracles. Thus, it represented a wholesale attack against orthodox Christianity.

Miracles were suspect precisely because they required a supernatural cause, and supernaturalism was anathema to these people. The nineteenth century liberals did not deny the existence of God, but they were so intoxicated by Hegelian philosophy that they embraced a radical immanentism by which God was virtually identified with the cosmic process that was evolving in space and time. The transcendence of God was all but obliterated in this scheme. The focus was not on heaven but on earth. Redemption was not the personal soul coming to terms of reconciliation with God via the atoning work of Christ, but the reconciliation of social groups with each other in terms of humanitarian goals. The Gospel was said to be "this-sided" rather than "that-sided," a matter of earth rather than heaven.

With the advent of liberalism came a massive attack on the trustworthiness of the Bible. This attack came not from outside the church but from within it, causing Dutch theologian Abraham Kuyper to remark that biblical criticism had degenerated into biblical vandalism.

The biggest problem with the Bible, as liberals saw it, was that it declared that God wrought miracles in history. The New Testament record of Jesus was ablaze with miracles. They had to go; they had to be naturalized. So Strauss, Wrede, and others gave fresh explanations to the miracle stories of the Gospels.

For instance, the feeding of the five thousand was recast either as a fraud perpetrated by Jesus and His disciples or as a "moral" miracle. The fraud version had Jesus storing a cache of food inside a large cave, the entrance to which was carefully concealed. With His disciples covertly passing foodstuffs to Him, *a la* a bucket brigade, Jesus kept pulling food out of His sleeves like a magician pulls scarves, presenting the illusion of a miracle. The moral explanation was that Jesus persuaded those who had brought lunches to share with those who had brought nothing. This was a "miracle" that overcame human selfishness, a miracle of ethical value.

Following that line of thinking, Albrecht Ritschl sought to reduce the essence of Christianity to ethical values. The ongoing relevance of Christianity is seen more in the ethics of the Sermon on the Mount than in atonements and resurrections, he said.

Barth's colleague Emil Brunner, in his book *The Mediator*, gave his critique of liberalism with a single word. The word he chose to crystallize the essence of liberalism was *unbelief.* Both Barth and Brunner, though never coming all the way to orthodoxy, were clear in their rejection of the liberalism of the nineteenth century and the neo-liberalism (exemplified by Rudolf Bultmann) of the twentieth century.

Liberalism is not a subset of historic Christianity. J. Gresham Machen rightly said, "An examination of the teachings of liberalism in comparison with those of Christianity will show that at every point the two movements are in direct opposition." Indeed, if the word *liberal* is used in the nineteenth century religious sense, the term *liberal Christian* is an oxymoron. In fact, if the core of liberalism is unbelief, then its presence in the church represents the nadir of apostasy.

The tragedy is that liberalism has captured the mainline churches of Europe and America. It first infiltrated the universities and seminaries, then swept through most of the so-called mainline churches. In Europe, the "triumph" of liberalism ushered in the post-Christian era, as most churches were emptied of their members.

Liberalism sought to maintain an aura of religion, but in the final analysis it was at best a pious fraud. Ministers who did not believe biblical Christianity still needed jobs. They were not prepared to simply abandon their churches and the billions of dollars invested in church real estate and property. It was simpler to redefine Christianity. But the new version of Christianity was hypocritical in that, on the one hand, it rejected any biblical grounds for attaching ultimate significance to Jesus, while at the same time identifying itself with His name. Given the option of changing themselves or changing Jesus, liberals devoted themselves to creating a revised portrait of Jesus, whose real historical identity was deemed unknowable. This is the historical root of the contemporary "Jesus Seminar," which represents the worst of this hypocrisy and double-talk.*

Unfortunately, the historical tragedy of the capitulation of mainline churches to the vacuous theology of liberalism has not been instructive. The new frontier for liberalism is the evangelical church, which every day flirts with more and more of the tenets of liberalism. We must be vigilant, as the leaven of unbelief is more pervasive within the church than at any time previously in church history.

---

* The Jesus Seminar was a group founded in 1985 that sought to identify the historical teachings of Jesus of Nazareth. The group rejected almost all of the sayings attributed to Jesus in the Gospels, and its methodology and results have come under intense criticism.

SEMPER FIDELIS

SEPTEMBER 2000

I N THE NEW GENEVA STUDY BIBLE, there are subheads that divide and introduce various sections of the text of Scripture. In Paul's second letter to Timothy, between 4:8 (the conclusion of the Apostle's declaration of having fought the good fight and having kept the faith) and 4:9, the subhead reads:

The Abandoned Apostle

Paul has just announced to his beloved son in the faith, Timothy, that "I am already being poured out as a drink offering, and the time of my departure is at hand" (4:6). Now, as he faces death, he pleads for Timothy to come to see him. He yearns to see Timothy one last time. He writes:

> Be diligent to come to me quickly; for Demas has forsaken me, having loved this present world, and has departed for Thessalonica—Crescens for Galatia, Titus for Dalmatia. Only Luke is with me. . . . At my first defense no one stood with me, but all forsook me. May it not be charged against them (2 Tim. 4:9–16).

Who was this Demas who forsook Paul? He was a co-worker who labored alongside the Apostle and was with Paul during his first Roman imprisonment. Paul sent greetings from Demas to the Colossians (Col. 4:14) and to Philemon (Philem. 24).

I wonder how many Christians in the early church longed to be next to Paul in his ministry, to be invited into the privileged inner circle of his close friends. Demas had that privilege. Obviously, he was not merely an acquaintance of Paul, someone the Apostle knew from a distance. Rather, he was a close and trusted friend. Therefore, his betrayal recapitulated the treachery inflicted on Christ Himself by the betrayal of Judas Iscariot and the denial of Peter.

Judas and Peter, however, were not the only ones who ran for cover during Jesus' darkest hour. In the Garden of Gethsemane, Jesus declared to His inner circle of friends, Peter, James, and John, that He was deeply distressed and that His soul was exceedingly sorrowful even unto death. He implored His friends to stay with Him and watch (Mark 14:32–34). At this moment, no soldiers were present; none of the enemies of Jesus were there. The disciples were alone with Christ. He didn't ask them to fight; He asked them to watch while He prayed. Three times Jesus came to them. Three times He found them sleeping. They were not able to watch with Him for a single hour. Jesus warned them, saying, "Watch and pray, lest you enter into temptation. The spirit indeed is willing, but the flesh is weak" (Mark 14:38).

It is one thing to be attacked or insulted by one's enemies; it is quite another to be betrayed by a close friend or family member. To be betrayed by someone we love and trust is one of the most painful experiences a human being can endure. You know that what I have just written is true. At this very moment, in all probability, a person's name is in your thoughts and an image of a face has just flashed through your mind. I say this with some confidence, as I have never met a person who has not experienced betrayal at the hands of someone close. This is the pain that makes us guard our hearts against trusting too many people or inviting people into close relationships.

If it is true that we all have been burned by betrayal, is it because there are a few noxious souls out there who go around breaking as many hearts as they can? No. If there are many who have been betrayed, it is because there are many who betray. Not only have we all been abandoned by someone about whom we cared, we probably have played the role of the abandoner and the betrayer.

Mark tells what happened after Jesus warned His disciples and after the soldiers arrived to arrest Him: "Then they all forsook Him and fled" (Mark 14:50). Paul, at least, was not totally abandoned. After he told Timothy of being abandoned by Demas and others, he mentioned two who stayed with him, two who remained faithful. First Paul said, "Only

Luke is with me" (2 Tim. 4:11). Then he added: "But the Lord stood with me and strengthened me, so that the message might be preached fully through me, and that all the Gentiles might hear. Also I was delivered out of the mouth of the lion" (4:17). Here we see the supreme difference between the Lord and His people. All of His disciples deserted Him in His hour of need. Yet He never deserts any of His people in their hours of need.

The reason we betray others and the Lord Himself is that "the spirit indeed is willing, but the flesh is weak." The contrast here is not between the soul and the body. It is between our fallen, sinful natures (the flesh) and the inner man that has been renewed by God. Even as redeemed and regenerate people, we still face the battle Paul described in terms of warfare between the flesh and the spirit. The Lord, however, does not have such an inner conflict. His love and commitment to His people is pure.

For God to love us at all surely is an act of mercy. But the love He gives to us is described in both the Old Testament and the New as analogous to the love that is consummated in the sacred institution of marriage. In the Old Testament, Israel is the bride of Yahweh. In the New Testament, the church is the bride of Christ. When Israel went into idolatry, it was described by the prophets as an act of spiritual adultery.

Adultery on the physical level and in terms of human relationships is rooted in our propensity toward spiritual adultery. When we are unfaithful to each other, we also are being unfaithful to God and revealing our deep depravity.

One of the most important Hebrew words found frequently in the Old Testament is *hesed*. This word is translated in different ways in the English text of the Bible. Sometimes it is translated as "mercy." More often it is translated as "steadfast love." I also have seen it translated as "loyal love."

The mercy of *hesed* is linked to a love that is defined as "steadfast." Steadfast love is never fickle. Neither is it driven by political opportunism. It doesn't use or exploit people. It is not whimsical or capricious. Rather, it is firmly fixed in place and not subject to change. It is steady.

Most important, *hesed* is a love that is loyal. It is a love that is *semper fidelis*, "always faithful." It is a love that is constant. It does not betray or abandon.

Hesed is the love of God that we are called to mirror and reflect in our marriages, families, and friendships. Without it, the flesh will triumph over the spirit, and treachery will vanquish loyalty.

PULLING IN TANDEM

OCTOBER 2000

———

I N OUR DAY, WE FACE A CRISIS WITH RESPECT TO the relationship between faith and reason. The ax of existential and dialectical thought not only has been laid at the root, it has demolished the tree, reducing it to sawdust. I doubt there has ever been a time in Christian history when faith and reason have been as clearly divorced as in our own day. And the divorce has not been amicable. Modern theology not only wants to keep faith at a distance from reason, it doesn't even want to grant reason visiting rights.

Under this prevailing attitude, the great enemy of faith is logic. Logic has always been a martial foe of sloppy thinkers. But now hostility toward it has been dipped in piety, so that it is regarded as an act of spiritual devotion to attack logic, a kind of jihad against the infidel, Aristotle.

Under the influence of Søren Kierkegaard and out of antipathy to the rationalism of Georg W.F. Hegel and nineteenth century liberalism, Karl Barth sought to drive a wedge between faith and reason. He argued in his *Romerbrief* that a Christian does not reach spiritual maturity until or unless he is willing to affirm both poles of a contradiction. Thus, with a stroke of his pen, Barth converted spiritual insanity into spiritual maturity. His co-laborer, Emil Brunner, went a step further by declaring that the contradiction was the hallmark of truth, an idea that, if correct, makes the serpent in Eden an ambassador of truth and the fall a great leap forward for mankind.

Sadly, the children of dialectical thinking today are not so much liberals as conservatives who declare that God Himself is somehow "above" the law of non-contradiction in the sense that He is free and able to affirm real contradictions in His own mind. To show that God is exalted over reason (as He certainly is), theologians project their own muddleheadedness onto Him, giving us a God whose Word can never be trusted because ultimately, in God's own mind, the opposite of what He says may in fact be true.

This method of doing theology is a million miles away from classical orthodoxy. Giants such as Saint Augustine and Saint Anselm understood that there is a difference between faith and reason, but though they carefully distinguished the two, they never resorted to separating or divorcing them. They saw a symbiotic relationship between the two.

In some ways, Anselm stood on the shoulders of Augustine. Augustine's motto was *credo ut intelligam*, "I believe in order that I may understand." For Augustine, faith precedes reason in one respect. Before he could reach a deep understanding of the truths of God, he had to put his trust in God. That opens the door to a whole new understanding of reality. But Augustine's motto was not a license for a leap of faith into the irrational or absurd. In another sense, reason precedes faith, for one cannot believe or trust what is manifestly irrational. To do so, for Augustine, would not be faith but credulity. He insisted that there is an eternal standard for truth that is possessed by all people and that cannot be disposed of. "Do what we will, we cannot help knowing that the world is either one or not one; that three times three are nine; and the like; that is to say, the principles that underlie, for example, logic and mathematics ... and we know them not only to be true, but to be eternally and immutably true, quite independent of our thinking minds."

Against the backdrop of Augustine we see Anselm's motto: *fides quaerens intellectum*, "Faith seeking understanding." Like Augustine, Anselm believed that faith and reason, though distinct, are compatible. They meet at the top, as it were. That is, if used properly, both faith and reason will reach the same conclusions.

Anselm did not seek to arrive at a knowledge of God via reason alone. He did not attempt to prove the existence of God until after he firmly believed in Him. What he sought from reason was *understanding*. Christianity contains mysteries that we do not at present understand. Such mysteries may become clear to us in heaven, but some may never be grasped, as we still will be finite in heaven. Yet there are many things that are mysterious *for a time* but for which more information or explanation provides understanding. That can never happen with contradictions, since real contradictions are inherently unintelligible, even for God.

Anselm understood that the Word of God is addressed not only to the heart, but also, and indeed primarily, to the mind. God's revelation is designed to be understood. Such understanding requires a diligent use of reason.

Anselm was a philosopher, theologian, and apologist. As an apologist, he made ample use of reason. Like the apologists of the early church, he saw the task of apologetics as being two-fold: to *clarify* and to *defend* the truth claims of Christianity. In the early church, when Christians were accused of cannibalism because of rumors that they met in secret to devour somebody's body and blood, the apologists explained the Lord's Supper to put to rest the distortions spread by the enemies of Christianity. But clarification was but the first step of apologetics; the second step was to obey the biblical mandate for giving a reason for the hope that is within us. That is, the second step was to provide a rational defense for the faith, if for no other reason than (as Calvin would say later) to stop the mouths of the obstreperous.

Anselm was a master of both clarification and defense. Though he is famous for his formulation of the ontological argument for the existence of God, he used other arguments as well.

We find the apologetic arguments for God and for the need for the atoning work of Christ in Anselm's three most famous books, the *Proslogion*, the *Monologion*, and *Cur Deus Homo*. His famous ontological argument appears in the *Proslogion*. In the *Monologion*, we find his other arguments for God. In *Cur Deus Homo*, we find his answer to the question, "Why the God-man?"

Anselm is a clear example of a classical apologist, eschewing claims to naked leaps of faith as found in fideism and theologies that wallow in dialectical confusion and irrationality. He was a champion for the rational character of Christianity, that the faith we are to have is to be an intelligible faith and not a flight into irrationality.

THE SECRET GARDEN

NOVEMBER 2000

T HE LORE OF THE AUGUSTINIAN TRADITION includes an incident that allegedly took place after the great saint wrote concerning God's work of creation. Augustine had written that God made all things by divine imperative, speaking the world into being and bringing light out of darkness by the sheer power of His divine fiat. In reaction, skeptics taunted Augustine by asking him this question: "What was God doing before He created the world?" Augustine replied, "Creating hell for curious souls."

Augustine's terse response was not merely an exercise in clever repartee. He was articulating the need for a reverent attitude before God, a holy sense of fear and respect for His incomprehensibility. John Calvin later echoed Augustine's sentiments when he said, "Where God closes His holy mouth, I will desist from inquiry." And Martin Luther was fond of distinguishing between the "revealed God" (*Deus revelatus*) and the "hidden God" (*Deus absconditus*). The hidden God is that aspect of God that remains veiled from our eyes.

What we know about God and His plans is exactly what He has been pleased to reveal. And His revelation is our most precious treasure. However, what He has kept to Himself is none of our business. He has established a fence that guards His unrevealed thoughts and plans from prying eyes and snooping noses. The ground on the other side of the fence that borders the scope of divine revelation is holy ground. No fallen creature can walk there, and every step we take toward this forbidden knowledge is a step away from God's will.

The Bible describes this limiting fence in Deuteronomy 29:24–29:

"All nations would say, 'Why has the LORD done so to this land? What does the heat of this great anger mean?' Then people would say: 'Because they have forsaken the covenant of the Lord God of their fathers, which He made with them when He brought them out of the land of Egypt; for they went and served other gods and worshiped them, gods that they did not know and that He had not given to them. Then the anger of the Lord was aroused against this land, to bring on it every curse that is written in this book. And the Lord uprooted them from their land in anger, in wrath, and in great indignation, and cast them into another land, as it is this day.' The secret things belong to the Lord our God, but those things which are revealed belong to us and to our children forever, that we may do all the words of this law."

Moses was speaking of the wrath of God that would be poured out on the land should the people fall into sin. In response to such an act of providence, he said, future generations of Israelites and foreigners would ask, "Why?" They would supply their own speculations as to the reasons for God's actions. But as Moses went on to say, the secret things belong to the Lord. By contrast, he said, God's people possess what He has revealed to them; it belongs to them and to their children. They are to delight in this knowledge as in a prized possession. It is their richest heritage to pass on to their children. And it is their sacred duty to pass it on, for these revealed things are given to them that they might give to God their obedience.

What are the secret things that remain hidden from us? There are several things that may be included in the list.

In the first place, there are aspects of God's own nature that remain shrouded in mystery. How He governs His creation by a sovereign will that works through human agents without destroying their volition or responsibility is one such mystery. This mystery may be unraveled for us in heaven, but only if God is pleased to move the fence for us at that time. Even in heaven, some mysteries will remain. We are creatures now and we will remain creatures forever. And as long as God is God and we are creatures, there will be limits on our understanding of Him.

In our present state, we are forbidden to look upon the face of God.

Though we live before His face, His face remains invisible to us. We recall Moses' attempt to glimpse His visage in Exodus 33:17–23:

> So the LORD said to Moses, "I will also do this thing that you have spoken; for you have found grace in My sight, and I know you by name." And he said, "Please, show me Your glory." Then He said, "I will make all My goodness pass before you, and I will proclaim the name of the LORD before you. I will be gracious to whom I will be gracious, and I will have compassion on whom I will have compassion." But He said, "You cannot see My face; for no man shall see Me, and live." And the LORD said, "Here is a place by Me, and you shall stand on the rock. So it shall be, while My glory passes by, that I will put you in the cleft of the rock, and will cover you with My hand while I pass by. Then I will take away My hand, and you shall see My back; but My face shall not be seen."

After Adam and Eve were expelled from Paradise and consigned to live out their days east of Eden, sentinels were placed at the entrance to the garden, angels and a flaming sword, stationed there by God to ensure that no fallen creature would trespass in that place. Part of the boundary to Eden is the hiddenness of God's face from our eyes. It is a forbidden sight as long as we remain impure. The problem is not the weakness of our vision. It is a moral problem. The future promise of seeing God is given to the "pure in heart." The beatific vision is restricted to those who have been glorified in heaven.

A second "secret thing" is the future. Though God has been pleased to reveal much about His plans for our redemption, there remains much about our personal futures that He has not revealed. Furthermore, He prohibits us from gazing into future things about which He is silent. Our desire to know the future fuels the horoscope industry, and keeps palm readers and Tarot card sharks in business. These things were emphatically forbidden in the Old Testament, and consultations with sorcerers, witches, necromancers, and so forth were considered heinous crimes. The ouija board is the modern version of these ancient attempts to pry into secret things.

Finally, there is that forbidden territory of knowledge that has to do with our own entertainment. We might call this "carnal knowledge." In this morning's newspaper, I read an article headlined "Addiction to Cybersex Soars." The author documented that in April of 1998, more than 9.6 million people—or 15 percent of all Web users—logged on to the 10 most popular cybersex sites. And seven of 10 did it in secret, ironically recognizing that there are some things that should be hidden. Images of nude people are used to entertain, to advertise consumer goods, and to titillate prurient interests. We are called to avoid this kind of knowledge (Prov. 5:1–2; 8:12). The sage advice of the past still applies: You do not need to live in a garbage can to know that it stinks.

The alternative to such carnal knowledge is found in Paul's exhortation to the Philippians: "Finally, brethren, whatever things are true, whatever things are noble, whatever things are just, whatever things are pure, whatever things are lovely, whatever things are of good report, if there is any virtue and if there is anything praiseworthy—meditate on these things. The things which you learned and received and heard and saw in me, these do, and the God of peace will be with you" (Phil. 4:8–9).

" ... IN LIKE MANNER"

DECEMBER 2000

I N MY BOOK *THE LAST DAYS ACCORDING TO JESUS,* I focused on
the problem believers face with the time-frame references in the New
Testament prophecies concerning the return of Jesus. I pointed out
that much of the ammunition used by higher critics who reject the inspiration of the Bible and who question the deity of Christ is drawn from the
arsenal of New Testament prophecy. Most significantly, the words of Jesus
in the Olivet Discourse, "This generation will by no means pass away till
all these things take place" (Matt. 24:34), have been used to prove that the
Bible is errant and that Jesus Himself was wrong about His predictions.

The irony is that, of all the prophecies in the New Testament, none
demonstrate a more dramatic literal fulfillment than those of Jesus in the
Olivet Discourse. Jesus said that the temple would be destroyed and that
Jerusalem would be conquered and fall into the hands of the Gentiles.
Such ideas were not just radical to Jesus' hearers; they were unthinkable.
Yet in A.D. 70, less than a generation later, Jerusalem was taken and the
temple destroyed by the Romans.

Since these predictions came to pass with uncanny accuracy, we might
expect they would serve as proof positive of the Bible's inspiration and of
the veracity of Jesus' claims to messiahship. However, within the context
of Jesus' predictions concerning Jerusalem and the temple, He included
a prediction of His own coming. If He failed to come in the time frame
He indicated He would, then His prediction was false and He was a false
prophet according to biblical tests. Two out of three is not good enough
to qualify as a true prophet.

In dealing with the problems raised by the critics regarding the Olivet
Discourse, we are left with few alternatives. We can argue that the meaning of the term *generation* as used by Jesus did not refer to the normal sense
of the word as a time frame of roughly 40 years. Or we can argue that the

coming Jesus referred to was His judgment coming on Israel, which did take place in A.D. 70. There are other ways to approach this problem, but I will not detail them here.

The modern eschatological viewpoint known as "preterism" is of two types. Full preterism teaches that all of the New Testament prophecies concerning the coming of Christ and attending events (such as the resurrection from the dead, the Rapture, etc.) took place in A.D. 70. Partial preterism claims that only some of the New Testament prophecies concerning the future coming of Christ have been fulfilled. Partial preterism still looks forward to the final coming of Christ, the Rapture, the resurrection of the dead, and the Last Judgment.

After my book was published, I received a few "nasty-grams" from people who complained that I gave too much credence to full preterism and opened the door to eschatological heresy. However, the vast majority of the mail I received was from full preterists. Those in this group went out of their way to thank me for dealing with the problem of the time-frame references of the New Testament, but expressed disappointment that I did not arrive at a full preterist position.

I remain convinced that the New Testament descriptions of the last resurrection, the Rapture, and the Last Judgment indicate a still-future return of Jesus to consummate His kingdom. Though I think some of His predictions came to pass in A.D. 70, I do not think all of them did.

One of the texts that I do not think full preterists have explained adequately is the account of Christ's ascension in Acts 1:9–11: "Now when He had spoken these things, while they watched, He was taken up, and a cloud received Him out of their sight. And while they looked steadfastly toward heaven as He went up, behold, two men stood by them in white apparel, who also said, 'Men of Galilee, why do you stand gazing up into heaven? This same Jesus, who was taken up from you into heaven, will so come in like manner as you saw Him go into heaven.' "

There is a strong accent here on the visual character of Jesus' ascension. Notice that the words *watched, sight, looked, gazing,* and *saw* are all employed by Luke in his narrative. It is clear that the departure of Christ from this earth was visible to His disciples. This was not an invisible event that took place in the spiritual realm. It was a space-time event that occurred in the empirical realm.

It is also important to note that the literary form of this passage is that of historical narrative, not poetry. And this passage is conspicuously lacking in the graphic imagery of eschatological judgment events, imagery that frequently does not carry literal meaning in Scripture. In other words, the plain sense of this text is that Luke was giving a report of the disciples' eyewitness experience of the departure of Christ.

Though the text does not explicitly say it, it is probable that the cloud that received Jesus out of their sight was the glory cloud, or Shechinah. As this took place, angels appeared who questioned the disciples as to why they stood gazing into heaven. Obviously they were gazing because their eyes had just beheld an amazing sight. Then the angels told them that this same Jesus would come "in like manner" to the way they saw Him ascend.

I think the words of the angels indicate that the return of Christ will be as visible as His departure. This text seems to preclude any possibility of an invisible return of Christ. Of course, when I say this I know that both full preterists and anti-preterists will be quick to point out that when Jesus spoke of His coming in the Olivet Discourse He also described that event in intensely visual imagery and mentioned the glory cloud. It would seem that if I allow prophetic graphic imagery in the Olivet Discourse not to be taken literally, then I must allow for the same usage in Acts. I feel the weight of this problem. It is at difficult points like this that the concept of "Scripture interprets Scripture" is key. While there are topical and genre connections between Acts 1 and Matthew 24, there are key differences (Matt. 24 does not mention a "taken-up ... coming" exchange, which is key to Acts 1). Thus, it is unclear how extensive the parallelism is between the texts.

I am trying in all of this to balance three things: (1) the integrity of the Bible with respect to the time-frame references; (2) the integrity of Jesus with respect to His prediction of His return within a single generation;

and (3) the blessed hope of a yet-future consummation of Christ's ministry in His final return to earth. These three issues define the arena of my concern.

"Of all the prophecies in the New Testament, none demonstrate a more dramatic literal fulfillment than those of Jesus in the Olivet Discourse."

———

THE ROOTS OF DIVISION

JANUARY 2001

———

T HE WORD EPIPHANY REFERS TO A SUDDEN and usually strik-
ing awareness or understanding of reality. It is the type of thing
Archimedes experienced when he stepped into his bathtub and
realized that the water he displaced was equal to the volume of his body.
This discovery prompted him to run naked through the streets of ancient
Syracuse crying, "Eureka! I have found it!"

I recently experienced an epiphany, not in my bathtub but in my study.
Here's what happened:

I was in a booth signing books at the Christian Booksellers Convention
in July in New Orleans. A representative of the Banner of Truth Trust,
a British publisher, came through the line and asked me to stop by his
booth when I was finished. When I visited his booth, he handed me a
book titled *Evangelicals Divided* by Iain H. Murray. He said, "I think you
will find this interesting" (an observation that proved to be a remarkable
understatement).

I read a lot of books. I am an incurable bibliophile. I cannot *not* read. If
I'm left with nothing to read at breakfast, I will read whatever is on the
cereal box. Because I read so much, it is a rare event when I find a book
that yields a true epiphany. But this one did.

As soon as I finished Murray's book, I decided to order 20 copies so I
could give one to every board member of Ligonier Ministries, every member of our executive staff, and every elder of my local church. I placed the
order in July, only to discover that the book would not be released until
September. I didn't realize that my gift copy was a pre-release publication,
one of three copies Banner of Truth had at the time.

The book is a keen critical analysis of the history of evangelicalism in
Great Britain and the United States, focusing chiefly on events within
evangelicalism during the second half of the twentieth century.

Murray begins with a treatment of the thought and influence of Friedrich Schleiermacher, the German theologian who was one of the chief architects of nineteenth century liberalism. He drove a wedge between Christian thinking and Christian feeling, between doctrine and experience, that left a religious heritage in which experience and feeling were everything while doctrine was a matter of indifference.

Liberalism captured the mainline institutions, both ecclesiastical and academic, of Western Europe and the United States, giving rise to the so-called Modernist-Fundamentalist Controversy at the beginning of the twentieth century. The fundamentalists were evangelicals who refused to negotiate the foundational doctrines of historic Christianity. They tended toward separatism and a desire to remain unspotted by the world. Westminster Seminary in Philadelphia, the result of a split by the faculty of Princeton Seminary, was content to remain small in size but enormously large in terms of long-term theological influence.

By the middle of the twentieth century, some leading evangelicals in England and the United States had become concerned about trends in fundamentalism and sought a more vibrant evangelicalism that could enter and remain within the mainstream of religious life. The creation of "neo-evangelicalism" by Harold Ockenga, Billy Graham, and key players at Fuller Seminary, plus the founding of *Christianity Today*, launched this new breed of evangelicals. The vision was good and the motives were righteous. However, according to Murray's analysis, the results were disastrous, both in England and the United States.

The voices of caution from Martin Lloyd-Jones in England and Francis Schaeffer in the United States went largely unheeded. As a result, as evangelicals rose in number, they began to look and think more and more like Schleiermacher. During the 1990s, neo-evangelicalism moved so rapidly that it became a movement that would have been better spelled without the "e" in "neo."

Murray's critique is as kind and gracious as it is revealing and devastating. The icons of modern evangelicalism are shown as falling into egregious strategic errors that have weakened the evangelical faith at its very core. The bridges built to reach the mainstream became a two-way street by which those who sought to influence the liberals were themselves influenced.

The story of how and why this happened could serve as a wake-up call for all of us to fight with all our might against our tendency to value cultural acceptance and the power of numbers above fidelity to the truth of God. We need to read Murray's book and read it again, because what we do today counts forever.

THE BARBER
OF WITTENBERG

FEBRUARY 2001

—

T HANK YOU, PETER BESKENDORF. You have reached across the centuries to influence me and many of my friends. For at least two decades, Peter Beskendorf served as Martin Luther's barber in Wittenberg, Germany. Even more, he was Luther's friend. "Master Peter," as Beskendorf was known in Wittenberg, wielded a razor that was more than sharp enough to cut the throat of the man who sat in his chair with a price on his head. But Luther trusted his valued head to Peter and his ministrations.

Beskendorf once told Luther that he was planning to write a book that would serve as a warning against the power and cunning of Satan. Luther responded by writing 40 lines of humorous verse, beginning with:

No one will become that sharp
That he can know the devil well;
No, tarred he'll be with his own brush,
And will not in peace be left
Unless Christ is there behind him.

I am grateful to Beskendorf because of a question he once asked his illustrious customer. Master Peter recognized the link between Luther's prodigious prayer life and his obvious greatness, so he asked the Reformer to teach him how to pray. Luther responded by penning a small book titled *A Simple Way to Pray*, which he dedicated to his friend. He published it in 1535, and the book went through four editions the first year it was in print.

Luther's response to Beskendorf's request has touched me, and I believe it is valuable to all who struggle with prayer. The guilt Christians carry around because of undisciplined and feeble prayer lives is a burden that screams for relief. It seems that believers in every generation must face the moment when they cry out for help with prayer, just as the disciples did when they said to Jesus: "Teach us to pray."

As pastors, it is not enough for us to exhort our people to pray and admonish them when they neglect prayer. If the flock does not pray, it is likely that they simply do not know how to pray. And if they do not know how to pray, chances are that no one, including their pastor, has taught them how.

Recently, our little church went through a prayer seminar led by Archie Parrish of Serve International, based in Atlanta, Ga. The weekend experience was designed to train us in what Archie calls "kingdom-focused prayer." It involved refocusing our prayers from purely personal concerns and mundane matters to the work of the church and the ministry of Christ. The program involves the creation of "fire teams" consisting of four members who covenant to pray daily for 15 minutes for three months. After the first three months, the time is elevated to 30 minutes a day for another three months, and so on until the prayer time reaches one hour per day. Imagine what happens in a church when scores of people are praying for the ministry for an hour a day.

One of the keys to achieving this focus is following the practical suggestions set forth by Luther in his *A Simple Way to Pray*. We memorize the Lord's Prayer, the Apostles' Creed, and the Ten Commandments. Then we pray through these elements. This does not mean that we simply pray the Lord's Prayer or recite the Creed. Rather, we follow their content to guide and direct our prayers.

I cannot pray through the Lord's Prayer in 15 minutes. It is easy to fill 15 minutes simply on the petition "Hallowed be Thy name."

It is helpful to pray aloud and even to walk around while praying through these matters. Luther routinely prayed for four hours a day.

The Psalms can be added to the list to help us pray. Our group has memorized Psalms 1, 8, and 51 to help us in articulating adoration and confession in our prayers.

Needless to say, I am excited about flooding the church and the world with Christian prayer warriors. God uses prayer as a means to revival and reformation. I hope more and more churches will make use of the resource we have in Archie Parrish's prayer seminars. We need to learn how to pray.

WHAT DIFFERENCE DOES IT MAKE?

MARCH 2001

F EW DOCTRINES, IF ANY, SPARK AS MUCH debate and stir up as much rancor among Christians as the doctrine of election. It is one of those doctrines that divide people so sharply that some would call a perpetual moratorium on discussion about it.

Election is also a doctrine about which few are indifferent. The passions are inflamed on both sides of the divide. Those who oppose it see it as demeaning the significance of human freedom and casting a dark shadow on the goodness of God. Those who embrace it love the assurance and comfort it provides and the triumph of divine grace it reveals.

Well, if it is so divisive, why should we bother about it? As one who has a passion for the doctrine, I am frequently asked, "What difference does it make?" I'm sure Martin Luther was asked the same question repeatedly. Perhaps that's why he declared that the doctrine of election was the "heart of the church." It is interesting that Luther's body was hardly cold in the grave before his followers radically altered and softened his view for future generations of Lutherans, thereby putting a stake in the heart of their church.

Election matters first of all because it concerns the issue of God's truth. If the Augustinian view of election is the Biblical view and if the Bible is true, then that doctrine of election is the truth of God and all who are "of the truth" have the duty to embrace it and proclaim it. On the other hand, if the Augustinian/Reformed view of election is not Biblical and/or not true, then it distorts the truth of God and should be repudiated and abandoned.

Second, the doctrine of election is linked to our assurance of salvation and by it to our sanctification. When Peter set forth the virtues that mark our progress in sanctification, a list strikingly similar to Paul's fruit of the Spirit, he added:

Therefore, brethren, be even more diligent to make your call and election sure, for if you do these things you will never stumble; for so an entrance will be supplied to you abundantly into the everlasting kingdom of our Lord and Savior Jesus Christ. For this reason I will not be negligent to remind you always of these things, though you know and are established in the present truth (2 Peter 1:10–12).

This is a strong and sober Apostolic call to due diligence. It is diligence with respect to election. When a Christian understands election, embraces election, and gains assurance of being numbered among the elect, he becomes firmly grounded in the truth of God—so established in this truth as to be freed from the propensity for stumbling. Assurance and spiritual growth in godliness go hand in hand.

Peter strengthens this call later when he declares that God is not willing that any should perish (2 Peter 3:9). "Any" refers back to the word "us" as its antecedent, and the "us," in turn, to those addressed in the Petrine Epistles, namely the elect. This verse, so far from disrupting or refuting election as the enemies of election claim, actually confirms it.

Third, the doctrine of election affirms the full sovereignty of God and puts to rest any pagan or humanistic notion that God's sovereignty is limited by human freedom. Such a blasphemous view turns the Bible upside down and makes man sovereign instead of God. The Biblical view is that human freedom is real as far as it goes but is always limited by God's sovereignty.

Fourth, the doctrine of election dashes to pieces any foundation for human pride and merit. In this doctrine, the graciousness of grace is fully manifested as the creature realizes that he has nothing of which to boast, because his salvation is a gift of grace alone, with no admixture of human merit or determinative action.

Finally, because of the above reasons and others not here explored, the majesty and excellency of God are so exalted that the creature, by the Holy Spirit, is awakened to true worship. Now we honor God as God and declare our utmost gratitude to Him.

RESURRECTION AND JUSTIFICATION

APRIL 2001

H OW IS THE RESURRECTION OF CHRIST linked to the idea of justification in the New Testament?

To answer this question, we must first explore the use and meaning of the term *justification* in the New Testament. Confusion about this has provoked some of the fiercest controversies in the history of the church. The Protestant Reformation itself was fought over the issue of justification. In all its complications, the unreconciled and unreconcilable difference in the debate came down to the question of whether our justification before God is grounded in the infusion of Christ's righteousness into us, by which we become inherently righteous, or in the imputation, or reckoning, of Christ's righteousness to us while we are still sinners. The difference between these views makes all the difference in our understanding of the Gospel and of how we are saved.

One of the problems that led to confusion was the meaning of the word *justification.* Our English word *justification* is derived from the Latin *justificare.* The literal meaning of the Latin is "to make righteous." The Latin fathers of church history worked with the Latin text instead of the Greek text and were clearly influenced by it. By contrast, the Greek word for justification, *dikaiosynē,* carries the meaning of "to count, reckon, or declare righteous."

But this variance between the Latin and the Greek is not enough to explain the debates over justification. Within the Greek text itself, there seem to be some problems. For example, Paul declares in Romans 3:28, "Therefore we conclude that a man is justified by faith apart from the deeds of the law." Then James, in his epistle, writes, "Was not Abraham our father justified by works when he offered Isaac his son on the altar"

(2:21) and "You see then that a man is justified by works, and not by faith only" (2:24).

On the surface, it appears that we have a clear contradiction between Paul and James. The problem is exacerbated when we realize that both use the same Greek word for justification and both use Abraham to prove their arguments.

This problem can be resolved when we see that the verb "to justify" and its noun form, "justification," have shades of meaning in Greek. One of the meanings of the verb is "to vindicate" or "to demonstrate."

Jesus once said, "Wisdom is justified by all her children" (Luke 7:35). He did not mean that wisdom has its sins remitted or is counted righteous by God by having children, but that a wise decision may be vindicated by its consequences.

James and Paul were addressing different questions. James was answering the question: "What does it profit, my brethren, if someone says he has faith but does not have works? Can faith save him?" (2:14). He understood that anyone can profess to have faith, but true faith is demonstrated as authentic by its consequent works. The claim of faith is vindicated (justified) by works. Paul has Abraham justified in the theological sense in Genesis 15 before he does any works. James points to the vindication or demonstration of Abraham's faith in obedience in Genesis 22.

The Resurrection involves justification in both senses of the Greek term. First, the Resurrection justifies Christ Himself. Of course, He is not justified in the sense of having His sins remitted, because He had no sins, or in the sense of being declared righteous while still a sinner, or in the Latin sense of being "made righteous." Rather, the Resurrection serves as the vindication or demonstration of the truth of His claims about Himself.

In his encounter with the philosophers at Athens, Paul declared: "Truly, these times of ignorance God overlooked, but now commands all men everywhere to repent, because He has appointed a day on which He will judge the world in righteousness by the Man whom He has ordained. He has given assurance of this to all by raising Him from the dead" (Acts 17:30–31).

Here Paul points to the Resurrection as an act by which the Father universally vindicates the authenticity of His Son. In this sense, Christ is justified before the whole world by His resurrection.

However, the New Testament also links Christ's resurrection to *our* justification. Paul writes, "It shall be imputed to us who believe in Him who raised up Jesus our Lord from the dead, who was delivered up because of our offenses, and was raised because of our justification" (Rom. 4:24–25).

It is clear that in His atoning death Christ suffered on our behalf, or for us. Likewise, His resurrection is seen not only as a vindication of or surety of Himself, but as a surety of our justification. Here justification does not refer to our vindication, but to the evidence that the atonement He made was accepted by the Father. By vindicating Christ in His resurrection, the Father declared His acceptance of Jesus' work on our behalf. Our justification in this theological sense rests on the imputed righteousness of Christ, so the reality of that transaction is linked to Christ's resurrection. Had Christ not been raised, we would have a mediator whose redeeming work in our behalf was not acceptable to God.

However, Christ is risen indeed.

ONE NATION, UNDER GOD—DIVIDED

MAY 2001

———

S INCE *TABLETALK* IS NEITHER A DAILY nor a weekly publication, and because articles must be submitted weeks and even months in advance, I am writing for this edition at a bizarre moment in American history. It is Wednesday, Nov. 8, 2000, and the nation is being squeezed in the grip of political paralysis as it waits to learn the outcome of the presidential election.*

Chances are that by the time you read this, the matter will have been settled and the election wrangling will be but a dim memory. Nevertheless, whatever the outcome, it is certain that the razor-thin margin of this election demonstrates a serious rupture of American unity. We are engaged in a real cultural war, with two societies locked in a severe struggle for dominance.

We are living out the consequences of a revolution that took place in the decade of the 1960s. Cultural historians see that revolution as far more impactful upon national life than the American Revolution of the 1770s. The Revolutionary War was fought to *preserve* the American way of life, which was threatened by British imperialism. In the 1960s, the revolution was to *change* the American way of life. It was a values revolution fueled by the sexual revolution and a moral rejection of classical behavioral standards.

More than 30 years later, the nation remains sharply divided. But the

———

* The 2000 U.S. presidential election saw a close and disputed contest between Texas Governor George W. Bush and Vice President Al Gore. The result was in doubt on election night and for more than a month afterward thanks to an extremely close vote and recounts in Florida. The Supreme Court halted the recounts in its *Bush v. Gore* decision on December 12, leading Bush to be declared the winner of Florida by 537 votes, which gave him victory in the Electoral College.

division is not simply about political party preference. The issues have to do with customs, traditions, mores—in short, with competing *ways of life*.

Abortion is still the most contentious issue. This is not a debate about complex ethical issues related to rape or incest. It is a debate about abortion for convenience wrapped in the sacred garb of personal liberty and cunningly tied to the feminist insistence on the "right of a woman over her own body" and her inalienable "right to choose." These slogans display a kind of moral insanity that masks wanton murder with the patina of respectability.

It is now a matter of incontrovertible biological evidence that a fetus, although in a woman's body, is not biologically of her body, for it has its own genetic identity. Thus, the argument from choice is vapid. We have not (yet) embraced the idea that everyone has the right to do whatever he or she wants to do. The very existence of human beings contradicts that premise.

This wanton destruction of human life reveals a cultural change to barbarianism. It reveals a way of life utterly incompatible with Christianity. American Christians must come to grips with the reality that they are living in a pagan land. Even the church has been part of the revolution. In yesterday's election, more than 40 percent of church members voted for candidates who were pro-abortion. (I say pro-abortion rather than "pro-choice" because they are, legally at least, identical terms. A vote for "choice" is a vote for abortion, as every abortionist knows.)

Another aspect of the cultural war is a breakdown of marriage and the family. The very institution of marriage has witnessed wholesale rejection by millions of couples, who choose cohabitation instead. In addition, the speech of Americans, from teen-agers to TV and movie actors, has degenerated into vulgarisms. The customs of courtesy have eroded almost to the vanishing point.

The agitation of politicians has created a class war, with economics being politicized. American politics has become an exercise in socialism, with the transfer of wealth enshrined as the new American way. Estates are double taxed and the system, with its "progressive" or "graduated" income tax, allows people to vote their taxes onto others while exempting themselves. In earlier times, such a practice would have been viewed as exactly what it is—a legal way to steal from others. If I can vote myself your private property, I use the government's gun rather than my own to steal from you. The only way to rectify this injustice is a true flat tax under which every taxpayer pays the same percentage but not the same amount. Then politicians cannot dangle the pork barrel to sway votes with money.

This election of 2000 screams for election reform. I wonder whether the shout will merely be a whimper by the time this article reaches print.

A WARNING
TO PROFESSORS

JUNE 2001

———

W HEN I BEGAN MY TEACHING CAREER at the college level,
I came across a sermon that Jonathan Edwards had written.
It was titled "A Warning to Professors." Since I was a new
college professor, I was certain the sermon was directed at me. Indeed it
was, but not for the reason that I supposed.

The "professors" Edwards had in mind in this sermon were not college
professors or indeed any members of the teaching caste in the academic
world. Rather, he was speaking of those who were professors of Christ,
those who had made outward professions of faith.

All Christians are called to profess Christ before men. Most, if not all,
churches require some kind of public profession from a person seeking to
become a member of the congregation. Such public profession is a duty
of every Christian. But this duty is not what makes a person a Christian.

The church is a *corpus per mixtum*, a "mixed body," where tares grow
among the wheat and goats frolic among the sheep. The tares and the
goats are those who honor Christ with lip service while their hearts are
far from Him. But they will not be able to disguise their true state forever. Jesus' most dreadful warning may well be that given as part of the
conclusion of the Sermon on the Mount. He said:

> "Not everyone who says to Me, 'Lord, Lord,' shall enter the kingdom
> of heaven, but he who does the will of My Father in heaven. Many
> will say to Me in that day, 'Lord, Lord, have we not prophesied in Your
> name, cast out demons in Your name, and done many wonders in Your
> name?' And then I will declare to them, 'I never knew you; depart from
> Me, you who practice lawlessness!' " (Matt. 7:21–23).

In light of this frightening declaration, perhaps we should re-title this sermon, changing it from "The Sermon on the Mount" to "A Warning to Professors." After all, Edwards' warning was but a footnote to this warning from our Lord Himself.

Edwards focused on people who made a profession of faith, joined the church, and participated in worship, but continued to live godless lives. They were the "carnal Christians" of his day, professing faith in Jesus as Savior but not submitting to Him as Lord. But as Jesus warned in His sermon, no one can be His and simultaneously be a lawless person.

To be sure, we are justified by faith alone while we are still sinners, but it is also true that faith without works is dead and that a faith that yields no fruit of obedience will justify no one. True saving faith always and everywhere manifests itself in fruit. The absence of fruit is proof positive of the absence of faith.

We can have a *profession* of faith without fruit but never the *possession* of faith without fruit.

There is a great danger inherent in modern techniques of evangelism. We can become so zealous to win souls for Christ that we can try to "prime the pump," as it were. We can encourage people to make some demonstrable outward response to the preaching of the Gospel. We might ask people to walk forward, to raise a hand, to sign a card, or to recite the "sinner's prayer."

These techniques are not inherently wrong. But they are dangerous and should be used only with prudence. It is all too easy to put so much emphasis upon the external techniques that we "count" every profession of faith as a genuine conversion. This can puff up our statistics and our confidence in the efficacy of our ministries. That is bad, but not nearly so bad as giving assurance to someone who has made a false profession of faith. It's bad that *we* count such a profession as a conversion. It is far worse if *the person* counts it as a conversion and is given a false sense of security while still outside the kingdom of God.

We must look beyond our methods and our techniques to where the real efficacy of evangelism may be found. It is in the power of the Gospel as it is attended by the ministry of the Holy Spirit. That power is not found in the eloquence of the preacher, the force of his rhetoric, or even in the cogency of his argument. The power is in the Gospel. I can preach it. But I cannot effect its increase. That work belongs to God, who alone has the power to revive a single soul.

"We can have a *profession* of faith without fruit but never the *possession* of faith without fruit."

GALILEO REDUX

JULY 2001

———

THE PROSECUTION AND PERSECUTION OF Galileo Galilei stands out as one of the biggest black eyes the church has ever received. Because of that episode, the church to this day is caricatured by her enemies as being an obscurantist institution that prefers fantasy to fact and myth to science. The incident continues to be "Exhibit A" in the scientific community's cynical and skeptical stance toward religion and the church. Religion is painted as the single greatest obstacle to the free inquiry of science and as the chief purveyor of intellectual ignorance.

But there was also the church's initial response to Copernicus' revolutionary paradigm shift from the ancient Ptolemaic view of geocentricity. It had been assumed that the earth was at the center of the solar system, the point around which the sun and all the planets revolved. But Copernicus propounded heliocentricity, the view that the sun was the center point around which the planets ("the wandering stars") revolved.

The Roman Catholic Church greeted Copernicus' thesis as gross heresy. But Rome was not alone in this assessment. The magisterial titans of the Reformation, Martin Luther and John Calvin, joined in the Roman Catholic protest by vehemently opposing Copernicus' views and calling them damnable.

The radical shift to heliocentricity advocated by Copernicus was confirmed by the empirical evidence garnered via Galileo's telescope and later by Johannes Kepler's discovery of the elliptical orbits of the planets. It was further confirmed in a roundabout way by Magellan's circumnavigation of the globe, wherein the international date line was crossed and verified.

Both Rome and the Reformers rejected these findings because they assumed that they were in direct conflict with the Bible. They believed that the Bible taught geocentricity, not heliocentricity. The scene of bishops refusing to look through Galileo's telescope is seen as the nadir of the church's shameful closed-mindedness to any evidence that would undermine her dogma. What the critics often overlook is that many of these bishops were professional scientists as well as clerics, and they were defending the traditional astronomical and cosmological Ptolemaic paradigm with as much of a hidebound closed scientific traditionalism as a religious one. Scientists can be and often are as "dogmatic" about their theories as theologians.

What the church learned from the Galileo episode was that science corrects not the Bible but the church's *misunderstandings* of the Bible. The church's error was "baptizing" the old Ptolemaic view as if it were Holy Writ itself.

The Bible, in claiming to be divine revelation, teaches that God also provides revelation in nature. Whatever God reveals is true and carries the weight of infallibility, regardless of where He reveals it. His "general" revelation in nature is as infallible as His "special" revelation in Scripture. I agree with Augustine and Aquinas that all truth is God's truth and that what God reveals in one locus will never contradict what He reveals somewhere else.

Those who study the Bible are fallible students of Scripture. That is, theologians are not infallible. They can and often do err in their understanding of Scripture. Likewise, scientists who study nature are not infallible. They also can and often do err. If you are uncomfortable about current scientific paradigms, just wait—they will surely change. It is unlikely that the current generation of scientists has the final word on cosmology.

When Biblical theology and scientific theory reach contradictory conclusions, there is one thing I know for sure: They cannot both be right. At least one party must be wrong. It is arrogant for the theologian to assume automatically in such cases that the scientist is wrong. It is also arrogant, as well as foolish, for the scientist to assume that the theologian is wrong. Theology is also a science that is profoundly concerned for truth.

When the two spheres collide, it is time for the philosophy of the second glance. Scientific theories that conflict with theology very well may be wrong and in need of serious revision. History is replete with examples of people who, being hostile toward the things of God, would twist every doctrine of nature to attack Him and His rule. However, we must also remember Copernicus and Galileo lest we miss a correction of our understanding of Scripture that is provided by scientific research.

We see this tension in the fierce debate and crisis with respect to the questions of the age of the earth and the actual meaning of *day* in the Creation narrative. I for one am thoroughly convinced that if the Bible indeed teaches that the universe was formed in seven 24-hour periods, then that is the truth of the matter. But I also recognize that there are legitimate literary questions about that narrative that force us to ask whether that is what the text actually teaches. Douglas Kelly's book on the issue (*Creation and Change: Genesis 1:1–2:4 in the Light of Changing Scientific Paradigms*, published by Christian Focus Publications) persuades me that it is. But I remain convinced that a person can authentically believe in the inerrancy of the Bible and at the same time be persuaded of alternative interpretations of the text, such as the "framework" hypothesis.* Remember Galileo.

---

* The framework theory or interpretation emphasizes the literary structure of the biblical creation account, seeing in the account a set of two triads wherein three kingdoms or realms are created on the first three days and are filled on the next three days.

SCRIPTURE AND TRADITION

AUGUST 2001

———

T HE **BIBLE PUTS A PREMIUM** on the "tradition" that is passed from generation to generation—not the traditions of men, but the divine tradition transmitted by prophets and Apostles. The word *tradition* itself, which means "to give along," hints at the idea that the divine tradition is in large measure a divine gift. For unlike Tevye's cherished tradition, which helped keep the fiddler on the roof from falling off his precarious perch, this tradition is grounded in the authority of God Himself.

Yet in addition to the prophetic and Apostolic tradition inscripturated in the Bible, there exists also a wealth of Christian tradition that extends from the closing of the canon of Scripture to the present. What role does this tradition have in the lives of Christians? What authority does it exercise on and in the church?

The issue of Scripture and tradition was seen as the "formal cause" of the Protestant Reformation. In debating his views on justification at Leipzig and Marburg, Martin Luther was maneuvered by his able antagonists, Johann Eck and Cardinal Thomas Cajetan, to acknowledge that his views clashed with teachings set forth in church councils and by the church fathers. Perhaps even more serious was Luther's contention that popes could and had erred in their teaching. (Although papal infallibility was not officially declared until 1870, it enjoyed a wide acceptance for centuries before that.) Luther argued that popes and councils could err and thus fall short of the supreme authority of Scripture, which, Luther declared, "does never err."

This principle of the sole inerrant authority of the Bible was set in concrete at the Diet of Worms, where Luther is said to have declared:

"Unless I am convinced by sacred Scripture, or by evident reason, I will not recant. My conscience is held captive by the Word of God, and to act against conscience is neither right nor safe.... Here I stand."

In the Roman Church's response to the Reformation, it set forth its view of Scripture and tradition at the Fourth Session of the Council of Trent, declaring:

> These truths and rules are contained in the written books and in the unwritten traditions which, received by the apostles from the mouth of Christ Himself, or from the apostles themselves, the Holy Ghost dictating, have come down to us.... Following, then, the examples of the orthodox Fathers, [the church] receives and venerates ... all the books both of the Old and New Testaments, since one God is author of both; also the traditions, whether they relate to faith or to morals, as having been dictated either orally by Christ or by the Holy Ghost, and preserved in the Catholic Church.

There is a certain ambiguity in this passage. It speaks simply of Scripture *and* tradition. Does this mean simply that what God reveals in Scripture also can be found in the later traditions of the church? Or does it mean that, *in addition to* the revealed truth in Scripture, the Holy Spirit adds more revelation in the tradition?

As a Protestant, I believe that much of the truth of Scripture can also be found in the creeds and confessions of the church and in the teachings of the great theologians of church history. I have enormous respect for that tradition. But I stop short of saying that it is inspired by the Holy Spirit. These traditions lack the authority that is found uniquely in Scripture.

The issue of Trent's intent was clarified somewhat in the twentieth century when an Anglican scholar discovered a remote source that uncovered the first draft of the Fourth Session. In that draft, the council declared that the truth of God was found "partly" (*partim*) in Scripture and "partly" in tradition. This would have removed any ambiguity and made it clear that Rome officially taught a "dual source" of special revelation, the Bible and church tradition. But when that draft was presented to the council, two delegates protested that the wording would undermine the uniqueness and sufficiency of Scripture. Unfortunately, the record ends there. In the final draft, the words "partly" (*partim... partim*) were removed and replaced by the simple word "and" (*et*).

Why the change? Did the council heed the warning of the delegates? Was the change merely stylistic? Was it left intentionally ambiguous? We don't know. But what is ambiguous at Trent is cleared up by later papal encyclicals (such as *Humani Generis*), in which the dual-source theory was declared.

This is why *sola Scriptura* remains a terminal point of division between Roman Catholicism and Protestantism. This is why we must continue, in spite of pressure otherwise, to trust in God's Word as our only rule of faith and practice.

ADDITION AND SUBTRACTION

SEPTEMBER 2001

T HE CHRISTIAN FAITH IS CALLED a "faith" in part because at its core it is confessional. By confessional I do not mean that it acknowledges sins (which, of course, it does) but that it declares affirmations of belief before the world. Christianity is a religion with a content, a body of truths that are embraced and professed. We are distinguished by what we believe.

It sometimes seems that people think the Christian church was born in the twentieth century. The driving force of much church activity today is to be "contemporary" in style, in worship, and in theology. We have witnessed not a mere alteration in style, but a revolution. The church's architecture has changed from the Gothic or Georgian styles, which sought to communicate the transcendence of God, to that of a civic meeting house and now to a secular odium. Gone is the organ, the chancel, the choir, and the pulpit. These anachronisms are replaced by the synthesizer, the stage, the worship team, and the translucent plastic lectern, which often is removed to make room for the drama team. Stained glass has given way to colored lights that change the ambiance of the stage from chancel to cabaret.

The new worship style is designed for and directed to the unbeliever in an effort to be relevant and to meet postmodern people where they are. The thought seems to be that if the world will not welcome the church into its midst, perhaps the church can welcome the world into its midst. However, it appears to me that this revolution, despite its well-intentioned motives of outreach, is nothing less than the secularization of the church. We are, as the late James M. Boice said, "Doing the Lord's work in the world's way."

I am aware that there is nothing sacrosanct about pipe organs, stained glass, pulpits, pews, and chancels. The early church thrived in the catacombs without the benefit of these accoutrements. And we know that traditional church architecture and worship haven't been "working" everywhere. Magnificent cathedrals in Europe have become museums of the past that antedate the "post-Christian era"—or mausoleums for the death of God.

Since the world has rejected the church in its more traditional forms, it is not surprising that zeal for evangelism has turned to experimental forms and styles, that the Gospel message might get through. The church expresses its faith in different forms and styles in different ages and cultures. As cultures change, so does the style of the church.

However, changes in the church's style sometimes are driven by a degrading culture. In our day, it has begun with an addition, leading to a subtraction.

The secular culture has embraced the philosophers of pluralism and relativism, the twin pillars of the larger topic of secularism. Since the world is accepting secularism, pluralism and relativism have been added to the church in an attempt to make it more "relevant."

This leads to the current antipathy to theology. Doctrine is said to divide, while pluralism and relativism unite. Thus, it is assumed that if we are to enjoy the true communion of the saints, we must have done with creeds, since they only spark theological contention and division. Every creed affirms something and, by that affirmation, necessarily denies its opposite. All who are united by creeds are also divided from those who reject the content of those creeds.

I am reminded of the dispute that arose in the sixteenth century between Desiderius Erasmus and Martin Luther. In his *Diatribe* against Luther, Erasmus declared that he preferred to remain "open" on theological issues and make no assertions. This point almost gave Luther apoplexy. He replied that the making of assertions was the very mark of the Christian, and that if you take away assertions you take away Christianity. He reminded Erasmus that the Holy Spirit is not a skeptic and that the assertions He makes are more certain than life itself.

The communion we share with all who are in Christ is a communion not only in spirit but also in doctrine and in worship. We have one Lord, one faith, and one baptism. We have Christ, the Gospel, the Word, and the sacraments.

Throughout church history, Christians have insisted that the Word and the sacraments belong together. Sacraments without the Word become naked symbols. The Word without the sacraments becomes impoverished. Likewise, doctrine and worship can be distinguished but never separated.

I cannot help but wonder whether the revolution in worship today is driven more by the collapse of doctrine through the addition of secularism than by the fresh wind of the Holy Spirit blowing in our midst. The secular culture is hardly one that manifests the fruit of the Spirit. When the church starts to look identical to a dying culture, we must wonder who is influencing whom.

The great myth of our day is the myth of influence, which declares that if we are to influence the culture we must build bridges to it by adopting its methods and styles. But the lesson of history is that, in this game, the world always wins and the church always loses. The church only wins when it keeps the faith—maintains its creed and becomes transformed rather than conformed to the world.

POWER IN THE PULPIT

OCTOBER 2001

R ECENTLY, A LIGONIER MINISTRIES STAFF MEMBER who also is a member of Saint Andrew's Chapel, the church where I preach, remarked, "R.C., when you are in the pulpit, you have a gleam in your eye like I see nowhere else." This person went on to say, "I can tell you really like it."

I hadn't realized that my love for the pulpit was that transparent, although I have confessed to many people who have asked that being the minister of preaching and teaching at Saint Andrew's is one of my favorite things. It is a singular delight for me, and one I never believed I would be privileged to enjoy.

When I was ordained, my "call" was to a teaching position in a college. The teaching ministry to which I was ordained was, and continues to be, my chief vocation. I was not ordained specifically to the pastoral ministry. However, with my ordination to the teaching ministry came all the privileges and responsibilities of the clergy. That meant that I could officiate at weddings and funerals, administer the sacraments, and occupy the pulpit in churches.

Over the years, I have had the privilege of preaching in churches across the nation and overseas. But it is one thing to preach as a guest speaker; it is quite another thing to have your "own" pulpit and congregation. I understand full well that the pulpit does not belong to me and neither does the congregation. These are Christ's lambs whom He purchased with His blood, but it my task is to feed them with His Word. Here the joy of the privilege of preaching meets the burden of responsibility that goes with it.

As the Old Testament priests were called of God to weep between the porch and the altar, so the modern preacher should trail his tears between the study and the pulpit. The pulpit is holy ground. It is that sacred place where the ministry of the Word issues forth.

Notice that we speak not so much of the ministry of the minister but of the ministry of the Word (to which must be added the ministry of the sacraments). We make this distinction because it is imperative that we locate the power in preaching where it belongs. It is not the preacher who is the power of God unto salvation. It is not my preaching that God promises will not return to Him void. The power is in the Word as God attends it with the power of the Holy Spirit. As Paul noted to the Corinthians, we may plant, another may water, but it is God who gives the increase.

What made Charles H. Spurgeon such a powerful preacher was not his eloquence or his personality: It was that God visited his preaching with the power of the Holy Spirit. I am convinced there was a link between Spurgeon's loyalty to the Word and his accuracy in expounding it, and God's blessing upon his preaching.

We preachers always hope God will use our sermons to pierce the hearts of our hearers. Yet we tend to try to make it happen in our own power. Every Sunday after the worship service, I greet our people at the door. Many of them say kind words about the sermon. I appreciate that, but when I get into the car to go home, I still turn to Vesta and ask, "How was my sermon?" She always says nice things about the sermon (she knows how easy it is for her to crush me). Yet no matter what words she uses, I can always tell from her response exactly what she thought. Sometimes she says, "This morning I didn't think of you as my husband, but only as my pastor." When she says that, I know something special happened with the sermon.

I want to preach well. I try hard to do so. But I have to keep asking myself about what it means to preach well. I have come to believe that to preach well is to preach *faithfully*, to expound the text accurately and boldly.

Just yesterday, after church, I listened to *The Bible Study Hour* on the radio. It was a replay of a sermon by the late James M. Boice on justification by faith alone. I realized that it was the first time I had listened to his voice on tape since he died in June 2000. As his voice came over the airways, I was gripped by a host of emotions as memories of our times together in ministry raced through my mind. But in minutes, those memories receded and my grief over his death passed, and I found myself in rapt attention to his words.

Near the end of Dr. Boice's sermon, I turned to Vesta and said, "Who preaches like that today?" The question was rhetorical, as we both knew the answer—not too many. Jim's sermons minister to me; though his life in this world is over, his ministry of the Word continues to bear fruit.

So it is with Spurgeon and other great preachers. God will use a man's labor over and over again if that labor is to the honor and glory of God.

The first year I was a Christian, I heard a minister remark about the vocation of preaching. He said, "God only had one Son, and He made Him a preacher." Even then I had a high view of preaching and the pastoral vocation. Yet my career has been in teaching rather than preaching. Why? The answer is simple. I was afraid of the pastoral ministry. I felt neither worthy of it nor up to its demands. I still feel that way.

It breaks my heart to know how many pastors are wounded by their congregations, how many are discouraged, how many leave their vocations every year. It is a holy vocation, and we need to honor it as such.

THE FLIP SIDE OF GRATITUDE

NOVEMBER 2001

———

W E OFTEN DISTINGUISH BETWEEN LAW and Gospel but rarely distinguish between law and gratitude. Perhaps that is because, at first blush, the two seem unrelated. Law seems to describe some rule of behavior, while gratitude seems to describe a human feeling or emotion. Sometimes we hear it stated that law is about rules, but gratitude is about relationships. And we're told that relationships, not doctrine, are what count in the Christian life. We even have seen the emergence of what is called "relational theology," which usually walks hand-in-glove with its partner, "situational ethics." The tie that binds the two together is relativism. Relational theology is based on a relativistic view of theological truth.

We tend to forget that theology is not an abstract science that has no bearing on human living. On the contrary, it defines the very essence of how the Christian life is to be understood and lived out. I once was discussing theology with a Christian businessman who, being bored with theology, said to me, "Give me some news I can use." He didn't grasp that I was giving him the most useful information I had at my disposal.

It is important that we remember that gratitude is not just an emotional feeling that is optional to the virtuous life. Gratitude is a command. It is part of God's law for our lives.

This issue of *Tabletalk* has explored the sinfulness of ingratitude according to Romans 1. There, ingratitude is viewed as one of the most basic of all human transgressions, as a sin that provokes the wrath of God. Manifestly, ingratitude could not be judged a sin unless it violates the law of God.

We remember the answer to the catechism question "What is sin?"— "Sin is any want of conformity to or transgression of the law of God."

Ingratitude reveals a heart empty of thankfulness, which thereby fails to conform to God's command to be grateful.

Where does God's law require gratitude? There are manifold references to the divine requirement, but here we shall focus on perhaps the most foundational one—the tenth commandment, which in its short form reads simply, "You shall not covet" (Ex. 20:17a). Covetousness represents the flip side of gratitude.

It is important to note here that the literary structure of the Decalogue is elliptical. That is, there is information or content implied in the commandments that is not spelled out explicitly. That means that whatever the Decalogue forbids, by implication it commands the opposite. We know this definitively by virtue of Jesus' teaching on the Law. For instance, when the Decalogue forbids killing, it elliptically is enjoining us to be concerned for the life of our neighbor. When it forbids stealing, it is telling us we must respect our neighbors' private property.

In like manner, what the Law enjoins elliptically prohibits the opposite. For instance, when the Law says we must remember the Sabbath day to keep it holy, it is clear that we are not to forget the Sabbath day. When it calls us to honor our parents, it clearly means that we are not to dishonor them.

Similarly, when God's Law forbids coveting, it implies that we are not to so desire what belongs to our neighbor that we actually steal it, vandalize it, or begrudge it to him by envy or jealousy.

The Law against coveting blankets a multitude of sins. This commandment defines how we are to relate to others. If we are concerned about relationships, then we need to understand that covetousness, envy, and jealousy are deadly sins because they drip with the venom that destroys relationships.

I know a man whom I have honored publicly time and again. For some reason, he finds it difficult to pass up the opportunity to trash me publicly. I once asked another man who has suffered similar attacks upon his person, "Why does that fellow attack you so much?" He replied, "The only reason I can think of is jealousy." Jealousy is the soil that yields the fruit of broken relationships.

But coveting is not merely a barrier to good human relationships. At root, it is a serious sin against God. It is the sin of ingratitude. If I am truly grateful to God for the things I have, there can be absolutely no room in my heart for coveting anyone else's property, status, or anything. But the minute I covet what belongs to someone else, I show discontent with the gifts I have received from the hand of Providence. Gratitude to God precludes coveting anything of my neighbor.

A grateful heart is a heart so full of joy toward God, the giver of every good and perfect gift, the fountain of all blessing, that it has no room in its chambers for jealousy, envy, or covetousness.

In Mario Puzo's best-selling novel on the Sicilian code of silence, *Omertà*, one of the Mafia dons plans his retirement, "knowing that gratitude is the least lasting of virtues, and that gifts must always be replenished." Our gratitude toward God tends to be like this. Our gratitude is only as strong as the memory of our latest blessing. Yet if God were to cease His benefits to us today, replenishing none of His gifts, we would have no just reason to do anything but shout for joy for the rest of our days for the benefits we have already received at His hand.

THE FULLNESS OF TIME

DECEMBER 2001

———

" I N THE BEGINNING GOD CREATED. . . ." These five words, the first ones in the Bible, are like a blaring trumpet blasting the ears of secular naturalists, for they assert three foundational truths on which the children of postmodernism always choke. This triad of truths sets the stage for the entire Biblical history of redemption. These truths are: There is a God, the universe was created by God, and history had a beginning in time.

The issues of God's existence and His creation of the universe are paramount points of conflict with all forms of naturalism. These issues, though worthy of close attention, are beyond the scope of this article. I want to focus on the third point, the truth that the universe had a beginning in time. This reduces my concern from the first five words of the Bible to the first three: "In the beginning . . ."

In the conflict between Christianity and naturalism, the popularity of "big bang" cosmology would seem to force agreement on the point of the universe's having a beginning in time. It is usually argued that the big bang, by which all the energy and matter of the universe exploded from a compressed, infinitesimal "point of singularity," occurred sometime 12 billion to 17 billion years ago (give or take a billion). However, lurking beneath the surface of the theory is the idea that something antedated the beginning, that matter and energy pre-existed the explosion, as far back as eternity. Thus, for some naturalists the big bang does not really describe the beginning as such, merely a radical change in the form and structure of reality for which there is no beginning.

In the ancient world, the Hebrew assertion of a beginning was somewhat radical. The favorite theory of history, embraced particularly (but not exclusively) by Greek philosophers, was the cyclical view. In this view, history is neither linear nor progressive. Rather, it goes around and around in a never-ending circle. It has no point of origin or any specific point of destination. This often is seen as a schema wherein there is no purpose to history. This pessimistic view is explored and countered in the book of Ecclesiastes. The refrain, "Vanity of vanities, all is vanity," describes a view of history wherein the sun sets and rises, but nothing new appears "under the sun."

Against cyclical theories of history stands the Judeo-Christian view of a linear-progressive history that has a specific starting point and a future consummation. This assertion is crucial not only to the conflict between Christianity and naturalism, but to critical theories of Biblical interpretation.

Rudolf Bultmann's neo-gnostic approach to theology was the most influential view of the second half of the twentieth century. He distinguished between the presence of history and myth in the Bible. Working from a naturalistic framework, he denied all things miraculous in the Biblical narrative. In his view, miracles were the mythical husk that needed to be peeled away to reach the kernel of historical truth. It did not bother Bultmann's understanding of faith to say that the Bible was filled with mythology in its quasi-historical narratives. He sought to construct a theology of timelessness. For him, salvation is not wrought within the boundaries of history. Rather, it is "supra-temporal" or "trans-temporal." The supra or trans realm is that which is above the realm of history and is not contained within it. Bultmann argued for a salvation that takes place in the "here and now," on a vertical existential plane, not the horizontal plane of history. In this scheme, the historical content of the Bible doesn't need to be true in the factual sense. In the final analysis, it doesn't even matter if there was a historical Jesus.

Swiss Biblical scholar and historian Oscar Cullmann wrote against this radical violation of Biblical Christianity. By examining the time-frame references of the Bible, Cullmann concluded that Biblical Christianity is unintelligible apart from its historical context. The Hebrew-Christian view of history is tied to Judeo-Christian faith. Christianity is about a God who creates history, governs it, and works out His plan of salvation in it.

To rip the content of the Bible from its historical context is not to rescue it from naturalistic philosophical criticism but to surrender it to philosophical naturalism. A Christian naturalism is an oxymoron.

Cullmann noted the difference between two Greek words for "time," *chronos* and *kairos*. *Chronos* refers to the normal moment-by-moment passage of time, to normal history that is "chronicled." *Kairos* refers to a specific moment in time that is especially significant. A kairotic moment defines the significance of the past and the future. We approximate this distinction by the English words *historical* and *historic*. Everything that happens is historical but not everything is historic. However, everything that is historic is also historical in that it takes place within history. Thus, the kairotic moments of which the Bible speaks are not moments out of time; they take place within the context of *chronos*.

In God's eternal purpose, Jesus' birth took place in the "fullness of time." God had governed history in preparation for that kairotic moment, which happened in real history. Christianity stands or falls with that real history.

"We see a stark difference between the true Good News and the 'good news' of some modern evangelists."

—

ASHAMED OF THE GOSPEL

JANUARY 2002

⸻

ONE OF THE MOST POPULAR New Testament paraphrases ever published in English was called *Good News for Modern Man.* The title was taken from the meaning of the word *Gospel,* which translates the Greek term *euangelion,* which, of course, means "good news."

In Christian jargon, it is now commonplace to hear the term *Good News* used as a synonym for the term *Gospel.* But in reality, the "modern man" who hears modern forms of the Good News hears very little of the Gospel.

The Gospel is indeed good news. But we cannot reverse the subject and the predicate so that we identify good news with the Gospel. We know that not all news is good news. We also know that not all good news is the Gospel. When the boss tells an employee that he is going to get a raise, that's good news—but it is not the Gospel. When the biopsy report comes back negative, that's good news—but it is not the Gospel.

Here we must ask an impolite and perhaps disturbing question: When does an evangelist fail to do the work of evangelism? The answer: when he fails to proclaim the "evangel," that is, the Gospel. Like anyone else, the modern evangelist faces the temptation to sugarcoat the Gospel—with the result that the good news he proclaims is not the Gospel at all. When an evangelist tells a person that "God loves you and has a wonderful plan for your life," he is telling him good news—but it is not the Good News of the Gospel. Likewise, when he proclaims to people that God loves them "unconditionally," he is speaking good news, but not the Gospel.

The Old Testament is filled with examples of false prophets who told people "good news." For instance, Jeremiah was surrounded by such purveyors of false teaching: "From the prophet even to the priest everyone deals falsely. For they have healed the hurt of the daughter of My people slightly, saying, 'Peace, peace!' when there is no peace. Were they ashamed when they had committed abomination? No! They were not at all ashamed, nor did they know how to blush" (Jer. 8:10b–12a).

The message of "peace" from the lips of the false prophets sounded like good news for the people. As a result, the false prophets had far more converts than Jeremiah. But theirs was a false gospel. When the people heard "Peace," they were not troubled. They saw no need for repentance. Indeed, there was no need for anyone to repent if he already had peace with God. In the same way, why should any modern person flee to Christ if he hears that God already loves him unconditionally? If that message is true, does it not mean that we can continue in sin without fear of judgment? If God loves me and has a wonderful plan for my life, how can my impenitence possibly disrupt that plan?

When we look beyond the modern distortions of the Gospel and return to its original proclamation, we see a stark difference between the true Good News and the "good news" of some modern evangelists.

Paul announces the Gospel in his thematic statement of the book of Romans: "For I am not ashamed of the gospel of Christ, for it is the power of God to salvation for everyone who believes, for the Jew first and also for the Greek. For in it the righteousness of God is revealed from faith to faith; as it is written, 'The just shall live by faith'" (1:16–17).

Here Paul speaks of the Gospel of Christ, which he first mentioned in verse 1 ("the gospel of God"). *The true Gospel is one that has its origin in God's revelation.* It is God's Good News about the work of Christ for us. It is God's power unto salvation.

The Gospel is *about* salvation. In Biblical terms, salvation concerns rescue from some calamity. To be cured of a serious disease is to be "saved." To escape defeat in battle is to experience salvation. But these are examples of salvation in a generic sense. We must be careful to distinguish rescue from earthly calamities and rescue from the ultimate calamity that will befall mankind.

The Biblical Gospel is the Good News that God has provided us with salvation *from the wrath that is to come.* By His life and death, Jesus rescues penitent believers from God's judgment. Ultimately, therefore, the salvation of which the Gospel speaks is salvation *from God.*

Since salvation is from God and His wrath, we see why the indiscriminate proclamation of the unconditional love of God is not only *not* the Gospel, but in reality undermines and fundamentally denies the Gospel itself. The modern "gospel" is a gospel without wrath. A gospel without wrath is not the Biblical Gospel.

It is noteworthy that immediately after setting forth the central theme of the epistle to the Romans—the revelation of the Gospel—Paul plunges into a serious discussion of the wrath of God. He says, "For the wrath of God is revealed from heaven against all ungodliness and unrighteousness of men, who suppress the truth in unrighteousness, because what may be known of God is manifest in them, for God has shown it to them" (1:18–19).

Paul explains that all men have suppressed the truth of God that is plainly revealed to them. All have refused to retain God in their knowledge. All have turned to idolatry. As a result, all are exposed to the just wrath of God. Paul brings the whole human race, both Jew and Gentile, to the tribunal of God and shows that all are "under sin."

Judged by the standard of righteousness, men face a judgment they have no hope of escaping, except by trusting in the work of Christ on their behalf. The Gospel is about real salvation by a real Savior from the real wrath of God. When God's wrath is obscured or denied, the Gospel is eclipsed with it. There is no true Good News apart from a correct understanding of the bad news that makes it necessary.

VESSELS FIT FOR DESTRUCTION

FEBRUARY 2002

———

I RECENTLY READ *The Wrath of Almighty God*, a book of essays by Jonathan Edwards (reviewed in this issue of *Tabletalk*, p. 59). I had read these essays before and was more than vaguely familiar with their contents. However, as I read them this time I had an epiphany of sorts. It was not a pleasant one. I suddenly realized I have been guilty of skirting the matter of the wrath of God in my teaching and preaching. I have taken pride in proclaiming the whole counsel of God. But this epiphany revealed that my pride was the sort that precedes destruction and, like a haughty spirit, precipitates a fall.

In subtle ways, it is easy to flee from dealing with the wrath of God, and many preachers and teachers do so. It is not a popular subject, for it violates all the canons of political correctness.

Though an emphasis upon divine wrath was in vogue during the Great Awakening of the eighteenth century, it quickly passed from the scene, and the "scare theology" of the likes of Edwards, John Wesley, and George Whitefield gave way to the more sanguine approach of nineteenth-century liberalism. We can summarize the message of the eighteenth-century preachers as "Man is very bad and God is very mad." The nineteenth-century litany ran, "Man is not so bad and God is not so mad." Today, wrath has been so extricated from the divine character that God is portrayed as loving everyone "unconditionally."

In the early twentieth century, some Continental theologians reacted against the reductionism of liberal theology, which not only reduced God's wrath to a minimum but denied it altogether. These newer theologians insisted that if one is going to have a Biblical view of God, it must contain an element of the reality of God's wrath. Sadly, this attempt to restore a Biblical perspective on divine wrath carried with it perhaps an even more diabolical distortion of the nature of God.

Influenced by the passion motif and the drug of irrationalism that inoculated existential philosophy, these men argued that though God's wrath is real, it is based on an impure and chaotic element within the personality of God Himself. They spoke of the "shadow side" of God that barely concealed the demonic element within His character. Good and evil were said to exist in a dualistic tension within Him. The evil was manifested in the paroxysms of fury that erupted in God, particularly in the Old Testament. The outbursts recorded there included God's rage against Uzzah for touching the ark of the covenant (2 Sam. 6:6–7), His instant execution of Nadab and Abihu for offering "strange fire" on the altar (Lev. 10:1–7), and the swift destruction of Korah and his cohorts in their rebellion against Moses (Num. 16:1–35). His raging fury also was seen in the deluge that wiped out almost the entire human race, the slaughter of the Egyptian children in the Passover, and the merciless annihilation of the Canaanites. These episodes were cited as evidence of irrational and evil anger in God, of God simply venting His wrath for no good reason and to no good end.

This view stands in stark contrast to the Biblical view that God's wrath does not reveal a defect in His character but His perfection. His wrath is a manifestation of His holiness. A holy being who is indifferent to or tolerant of evil is simply not holy.

James M. Boice, whose commentary is guiding our study through Romans this year, once said: "The wrath of God is not ignoble. Rather, it is too noble, too just, too perfect—it is this that bothers us."

In Romans, Paul writes, "For the wrath of God is revealed from heaven against all ungodliness and unrighteousness of men, who suppress the truth in unrighteousness" (1:18). Notice that God's wrath is provoked not by goodness or righteousness. It is not the benign behavior of the creature that incites His wrath. Thus, His wrath is not irrational, that is, it is not for no good reason. The twin terms Paul uses here, *ungodliness* and *unrighteousness*, probably do not refer to two distinct actions but to one act that is both ungodly and unrighteous. In this case, Paul would be using a literary device called *hendiadys*, in which two terms are used to describe a single notion. The act in view is the suppression of God's revelation of Himself through creation, which basal behavior forms the foundation for idolatry. Thus, God's anger has a rational and reasonable object—human wickedness. It is the evil of men that prompts His fury.

The Greek word Paul uses for wrath is *orgē*. It is the same word from which the English word *orgy* is derived. In antiquity, orgies usually were connected with pagan religious rites that involved unrestrained and excessive frenzies of a sexual nature. Obviously God's wrath is not an act of sexual frenzy. The verbal link is with respect to intensity of passion. God's wrath is not mere displeasure. It cannot be dismissed as simple annoyance or mild irritation. Rather, it is a raging fury directed against evildoers. It is a matter of heat that rivals the melting fire of the sun. God is revealed as an all-consuming fire.

These metaphors are designed to awaken all of us to the reality of God's righteous judgment, to jerk us from our ease in Zion by which we rest, complacently assuming that God is incapable of anger.

THIS MAN WAS ALSO WITH HIM

MARCH 2002

———

T HE ROCK. THE BIG FISHERMAN. The Betrayer. Each of these sobriquets has been applied to Simon Peter. Will the real Simon Peter please stand up?

The names given to Peter all fit him in one way or another. Like all of us, Peter was a complex person; no one is truly one-dimensional. At different times and under different circumstances Peter behaved in different manners. At times he was timid and weak, cowering before accusers. At other times he was bold and heroic, standing up against those in positions of power.

Peter earned a reputation for being somewhat impetuous. John names the disciple (who is unnamed in the Synoptic Gospels) who cut off the right ear of the high priest's servant, Malchus, during Jesus' arrest in Gethsemane. It was Peter who took that precipitous and reckless action.

That same impetuosity appeared again when Jesus warned Peter that Satan would sift him as wheat. Peter answered proudly, "Lord, I am ready to go with You, both to prison and to death" (Luke 22:33). In reality, Peter was not ready to join Jesus either in prison or in death. Instead, he fulfilled Jesus' prediction that he would betray Him:

> Having arrested [Jesus], they led Him and brought Him into the high priest's house. But Peter followed at a distance. Now when they had kindled a fire in the midst of the courtyard and sat down together, Peter sat among them. And a certain servant girl, seeing him as he sat by the fire, looked intently at him and said, "This man was also with Him." But he denied Him, saying, "Woman, I do not know Him." And after a little while another saw him and said, "You also are of them." But Peter

said, "Man, I am not!" Then after about an hour had passed, another confidently affirmed, saying, "Surely this fellow also was with Him, for he is a Galilean." But Peter said, "Man, I do not know what you are saying!" (Luke 22:54–60a).

At this point, Matthew notes that Peter prefaced his third denial with curses and swearing. Luke then adds a poignant detail:

Immediately, while he was still speaking, the rooster crowed. And the Lord turned and looked at Peter. Then Peter remembered the word of the Lord . . . [and] went out and wept bitterly (Luke 22:60b–62).

There is irony here. In the space of a little more than an hour, Peter fell under the careful scrutiny of two people. The first was a servant girl, who fixed her gaze intently upon him before accusing him of being one connected to Jesus. This provoked Peter's first denial. Then, immediately following his third denial, Peter was the object of the gaze of Christ. It was a knowing stare. No words were exchanged; none needed to be. I doubt that any human being in all history was subjected to a more devastating look than the one Peter received from the soon-to-be-executed Jesus. It is no wonder that Peter went out and wept bitterly.

The inconsistency of Peter's behavior may be seen not only in the contrast between this shameful denial and his subsequent fearless behavior before the authorities of this world, but also in his capacity for change in short intervals of time.

It was at Caesarea Philippi that Simon was given the name "Peter." The change was made in direct response to his confession regarding the identity of Jesus. When Jesus asked His disciples, "Who do you say that I am?" Simon replied, "You are the Christ, the Son of the living God." Jesus then declared: "Blessed are you, Simon Bar-Jonah, for flesh and blood has not revealed this to you, but My Father who is in heaven. And I also say to you that you are Peter, and on this rock I will build My church" (Matt. 16:15–18a).

Simon was now called "Petros," or "Rock." Yet, presumably only moments later, Jesus gave him still another name. Jesus had just explained to Peter and the others that He had to go to Jerusalem to suffer and die. To this announcement Peter said, "Far be it from You, Lord; this shall not happen to You!" (v. 22).

Then came the new name: "Get behind Me, Satan! You are an offense to Me, for you are not mindful of the things of God, but the things of men" (v. 23).

From "Rock" to "Satan." From benediction to rebuke. From praise to offense. All in a short space of time.

Peter's volatility gradually gave way to rock-hard steadfast faith. After the Resurrection, after Pentecost, and with the memory of the transfigured Jesus still vivid in his mind, Peter became the pillar of the Apostolic church in Jerusalem. His dramatic sermon on the Day of Pentecost was followed by the healing of the lame man by the gate Beautiful. When the lame man begged for alms, Peter said, "Silver and gold I do not have, but what I do have I give you: In the name of Jesus Christ of Nazareth, rise up and walk" (Acts 3:6). The man departed walking, leaping, and praising God.

But not everyone was pleased about this episode. The authorities, troubled by Apostles' preaching of the Resurrection, had Peter and John cast into prison. Then, before the authorities (not a mere servant girl), Peter preached a courageous sermon, provoking even more hostility from them. They therefore commanded Peter and John to speak no more of Jesus. But the Apostles replied: "Whether it is right in the sight of God to listen to you more than to God, you judge. For we cannot but speak the things which we have seen and heard" (Acts 4:19–20).

The authorities saw a different Peter . . . a transformed Peter. With characteristic understatement, Luke records: "Now when they saw the boldness of Peter and John, and perceived that they were uneducated and untrained men, they marveled. And they realized that they had been with Jesus" (v. 13).

Here is the crux of the matter, the key that unlocks the personality of Peter—he was a man who had been with Jesus.

ZEAL WITHOUT KNOWLEDGE

APRIL 2002

——

MANY PEOPLE ARE SURPRISED, and some are shocked, when they hear of my involvement in the charismatic movement years ago. It began in 1965, shortly after I returned from graduate study in Holland to teach philosophy and theology at my alma mater. Some of my senior students who were preparing for ministry kept talking to me excitedly about their experiences with the Holy Spirit and about receiving the gift of tongues. My first response was profound skepticism, because my only previous experience had been with hardcore Pentecostals whose views of sanctification I deemed aberrant. Soon, however, the sheer number of my students involved in this phenomenon, coupled with their high level of competence as students, provoked me to give them the "philosophy of the second glance." I also saw reports that tongues-speaking was breaking out in mainline denominations such as the Presbyterian, Methodist, Episcopalian, and Lutheran churches. Reports of outbreaks at Notre Dame and at Duquesne University also piqued my curiosity.

I began meeting with my students to discuss the matter at my home. These meetings became regular times of prayer that lasted several hours or, on at least one occasion, all night. Because of the marvelous ardor for prayer these students displayed, I began to wonder whether I was missing something in my own spiritual life.

My attention then turned to the New Testament, particularly to Paul's teaching on tongues in 1 Corinthians. In chapters 12–14, Paul deals with abuses of tongues in the Corinthian church and rebukes those who had elevated their gifts over those of others. It was clear that Paul did not put tongues, or *glossolalia*, at the apex of gifts and did not teach tongues as an indispensable sign of the baptism of the Holy Spirit.

In 1 Corinthians 14, Paul gives detailed instructions about the use of tongues. Though he warns sharply against many abuses of tongues, he does not outlaw their use. Indeed, he explicitly says, "Do not forbid to speak with tongues" (v. 39b). Paul also writes: "He who speaks in a tongue edifies himself, but he who prophesies edifies the church. I wish you all spoke with tongues, but even more that you prophesied" (vv. 4–5a). Paul clearly is teaching the comparative superiority of prophecy over tongues. But he is comparing the good and the better, not the good and the bad.

Two things struck me in this passage. The first is that Paul says tongues are edifying for the individual. As a Christian, I certainly wanted everything the Holy Spirit had available to me. Second, the Apostle says he wishes all the Corinthian Christians speak with tongues. Even though he also expresses his preference for prophecy, he still asserts his desire that all speak in tongues. Finally, in verse 18, Paul says, "I thank my God I speak with tongues more than you all."

Since Paul was a tongues-speaker and expressed his desire for all to speak in tongues, I took this to mean that I should pursue this spiritual gift.

The major obstacle I still faced was the question of whether what was happening in the contemporary charismatic movement was indeed a revival of the New Testament gifts. That is, was the modern outbreak of *glossolalia* the same thing that was practiced in the Apostolic church? I found this to be an extremely difficult question to answer given the paucity of references to the phenomenon throughout church history, save for its dawn among deeply heretical groups such as the Montanists.

In any case, I sought the gift and soon was able to join my friends in praying in tongues. But I found no great edification from it and still preferred to pray with understanding.

In the meantime, I continued to investigate the question of whether this was the New Testament phenomenon. As the movement expanded, reports began to come in of people in non-Christian religions practicing "tongues." There were also reports that tongues had been identified as known foreign languages, but none of these reports was verified.

As time passed, several things became clear. First, a neo-Pentecostal theology was becoming popular. Though not monolithic among charismatics, it stressed tongues-speaking as a necessary and indispensable sign of the Biblical concept of the baptism of the Holy Spirit. It also was marked by fantastic claims of miracles and supernatural prophecies with new revelation. The more interpretations of tongues-speaking and prophecies I heard, the more false doctrine and false prophecy I heard. Several people spoke "prophecies" to me about specific things that would occur within a specific time period. Every single prophecy of that sort failed to materialize. I heard manifestly false doctrine, doctrine in clear antithesis to Scripture, being urged upon people via tongues interpretations. Extravagant claims of miracles that I was able to investigate proved to be unfounded. Something obviously was deeply wrong with the picture. In short, the charismatic movement was not delivering the goods.

More and more people were seeking to live the Christian life on the basis of subjective feelings rather than on the Word. I saw a strong revival of "Deeper Life" type views of sanctification that promised Christians a special second work of grace by which they could live the "victorious" Christian life through being "filled with the Spirit."

The church now had two classes of Christians—those who were baptized in the Spirit and those who were not; those who were "Spirit-filled" and those who were not. This dichotomy, I became convinced, not only was not taught in the New Testament but was contrary to what is taught there. I came to realize that the charismatic view of the Day of Pentecost represented a distortion of its Biblical significance. The charismatic view of Pentecost was a low one, not a high one.

I began to see that anyone who is uninhibited enough can utter unintelligible sounds while in a posture of prayer. I don't doubt anyone's experience of praying in such a fashion, but I am concerned it is not a supernatural event and is not the same as what was experienced in the early church.

My final departure from the movement came when I realized that I must live by the Word, as the Spirit never works against the Word but always with it and through it.

I still enjoy fellowship with my charismatic friends and delight in their love for prayer. I am grateful for the real revival in interest in the person and work of the Holy Spirit in the life of the church that this movement has spawned. However, I am very concerned about the false doctrine it has brought in its wake.

"The New Testament concept of hope is bathed with assurance and cloaked with certainty. This hope is faith looking into the future."

—

GLORIOUS VISION

MAY 2002

———

A FTER CHURCH ONE SUNDAY MORNING, one of my parishioners, who comes from my hometown of Pittsburgh, asked me whether I thought our favorite sports team would win its upcoming game. I replied, "I sure hope so."

My answer was not a prediction of the outcome; it was simply an expression of my desire as to the outcome. It described my wish for the future, not my foreknowledge of the event. Indeed, it revealed both my lack of foreknowledge and my lack of assurance.

The combination of a wish (or desire) and the absence of assurance that it will come about is the equation for the common meaning of the word *hope* in our vocabulary. Because of this customary usage of the term, we often stumble when we meet the word *hope* in Scripture. In New Testament terms, hope transcends the flimsy element of wish projection. It is something far greater and far stronger than mere desire. In fact, the Bible elevates it to a place among the great triad of virtues that defines the Christian life—faith, hope, and love. These are the three that abide after all the clutter is cleared away.

In short, the New Testament concept of hope is bathed with assurance and cloaked with certainty. This hope is faith looking into the future.

Though hope and faith are distinguished, they are not disconnected or divorced from each other. There is a certain symbiotic relationship between them. We see this in the way the author of Hebrews defines faith as "the substance of things hoped for, the evidence of things not seen" (11:1).

Here the word *faith* is defined in a manner that collides with the frivolous way it is used in our day. Notice that Hebrews speaks of faith in terms of substance and evidence. Faith without substance is superstition. Faith without evidence is credulity. Scriptural faith is not some blind, irrational leap into the dark. Rather, it both has substance and gives substance.

This is solid faith, faith based upon the surety of the reliability of God. In faith we trust God not only for what He already has done for us, but for what He promises to do in the future.

I frequently say that it is one thing to believe in God, but it is quite another to believe God. When our faith moves beyond a mere intellectual assent to the existence of God to actually trusting His Word, then we experience faith.

Faith in things past carries over to trust in things future. Because God has proven Himself in the past, His promise for the future gives substance to our hope. The Las Vegas oddsmakers are wrong every week in their predictions about the outcomes of sports contests. Howie, Terry, et al., never have a perfect record for the season with their "expert picks." But God doesn't guess about future events. Neither does He offer expert prognostications. His promises carry the substance of who He is. In this sense, we experience hope as faith looking forward.

When Hebrews speaks of faith as the evidence of things unseen, it is making a similar point. The disciples' faith in the resurrection of Christ was not a blind faith resting on the unseen. Christ appeared to them in visible form so they could declare to us what they saw with their eyes and heard with their ears. Faith is the evidence of things unseen in this way: New Testament faith is based on what is seen. The seen then bears witness to and gives credibility to what is unseen. The best evidence for trusting God in the future is His track record in the past. In this sense, faith gives evidence to hope so that the hope we have is not feeble but one that rests powerfully on the assurance of God Himself. It is described as the "anchor of the soul."

> Thus God, determining to show more abundantly to the heirs of promise the immutability of His counsel, confirmed it by an oath, that by two immutable things, in which it is impossible for God to lie, we might have strong consolation, who have fled for refuge to lay hold of the hope set before us. This hope we have as an anchor of the soul, both sure and steadfast, and which enters the Presence behind the veil, where the forerunner has entered for us, even Jesus (Heb. 6:17–20a).

With such hope, our ship is not left anchorless to be tossed to and fro by fickle winds that buffet it. This hope is sure and steadfast. Furthermore, it gets us "behind the veil" and into the "Presence."

In Paul's letter to Titus, he speaks of the "blessed hope" of the church, the glorious appearing of our God and Savior Jesus Christ (2:13). The ultimate dimension of this blessed hope is the promised future experience of what is called the beatific vision, or the vision of God (*visio Dei*). We find this in 1 John:

> Beloved, now we are children of God; and it has not yet been revealed what we shall be, but we know that when He is revealed, we shall be like Him, for we shall see Him as He is. And everyone who has this hope in Him purifies himself, just as He is pure (3:2–3).

The vision of God is called the beatific vision because what is seen carries with it the greatest blessedness a human being can experience. We shall see Him as He is. At present, we have the secondary portrait of the Creator provided by His handiwork in creation. We "see" Him through His works. The people of God in the Old Testament had theophanies, visible manifestations of the invisible God, such as the pillar of cloud, the burning bush, etc. But even then, the face of God remained hidden from view; no one was permitted to see God. That we cannot see Him is not because of a deficiency in our optic powers. The deficiency is in our hearts. Sin is the shield that conceals His face from our eyes.

In the Beatitudes, Jesus promised that the pure in heart are the ones who will see God. Not until our hearts are purified from all sin will we gaze into the unveiled face of God. Then we will see Him as He is.

One glance at the unveiled glory of God will be enough to move the redeemed soul to spiritual ecstasy that will last forever. But the blessed hope promises more than a momentary glance. It promises an eternity of dwelling in the immediate presence of the unveiled glory of God. This is our hope, and it is a hope that cannot possibly leave us disappointed.

DEAD MEN WALKING

JUNE 2002

———

T HERE IS AN ELEMENTARY SCHOOL TEACHER who is surely ubiquitous. Her name is Miss Prim and Proper. I'm sure that she taught cursive writing in your school as well as mine. She nagged us about always dotting our i's and crossing our t's. Attention to detail is far more important in our theology than in our penmanship. For instance, we need to be sure to dot the I in *TULIP*, the well-known acrostic whose letters represent the classic five points of Calvinism. The *T* stands for total depravity, the *U* for unconditional election, the *L* for limited atonement, the *I* for irresistible grace, and the *P* for perseverance of the saints. In the age-old debate between Augustinian and Semi-Pelagian theologies, the crucial point at issue is irresistible grace (although this issue turns back on both total depravity and unconditional election).

Before we consider the qualifier "irresistible," we must define the use of "grace" in this term. The grace that is in view is not some quantifiable substance that is added to or poured into the soul. The grace in this formula has to do with an action or operation. This operation is wrought on us by God the Holy Spirit. It is a divine work or operation that cannot be earned or merited. This fits with the most basic definition for grace in general—"unmerited favor." We can never earn or deserve grace. If grace were earned, it no longer would be grace. Rather, it would be justice.

The specific operation of God that is in view in the doctrine of irresistible grace is the divine work of regeneration. Regeneration literally means "to generate again." It is the concept that rests upon Scripture's teaching concerning rebirth or being born anew. This is the idea expressed in Paul's concept of "quickening," by which the sinful person is raised from spiritual death to spiritual life.

Jesus emphatically and unambiguously taught that regeneration is a necessary condition for seeing and entering the kingdom. It is essential for salvation. To be saved, a person must be born again.

Most Christians agree that regeneration is necessary for salvation. The debate rages over the question of how this necessary condition is met. Historic Semi-Pelagianism teaches that in order to be regenerated one first must have faith. In this schema, it is clear that faith precedes regeneration and that regeneration rests upon a prior response of faith. Thus, God is seen as offering salvation to whosoever will cooperate with His grace.

The problem is that this view sees human beings as having the ability to resist God's grace. Those who reject the offer of grace remain unregenerated and perish in their sins. They have successfully resisted God's offer of salvation.

Another way of describing this view is by using the term *synergism*. The root of this word is *erg*, which in English is defined as a unit of work. It is also found in the word *energy*. The prefix *syn* indicates the idea of "with." Synergism, therefore, refers to an action, work, or operation in which two or more persons are laboring together. It is a joint venture.

In contrast to all forms of Semi-Pelagianism, Augustianian and Reformed theology teaches that the grace of regeneration is a monergistic work that is done by God alone because it is a work only God *can* do. It is a work accomplished on us and in us by which our very natures are changed. It is at once a divine act of re-creation and of liberation. By re-creation we are quickened to spiritual life, or raised from the state of spiritual death. By this re-creation we are born anew. In this divine act, by which the Holy Spirit supernaturally and immediately changes our constituent nature, we are utterly passive. God monergistically ("working alone") brings this to pass. We are as passive as Lazarus was in his resurrection or as passive as Adam was in his original creation.

Regeneration is not a joint venture. We do not cooperate in it because we will not cooperate in spiritual matters while we are still dead in our sins. Our hearts are totally disinclined and indisposed to the things of God. We love darkness and will not have God in our thinking. The desires of our hearts are enslaved to sin. We will never choose Christ until or unless we are liberated from that slavery. In short, we are morally unable to exercise faith until and unless we are first regenerated.

This is why the axiom of Reformed theology is that regeneration precedes faith. Rebirth is a necessary pre-condition for faith. Faith is not possible for spiritually dead creatures. Therefore, we contend that apart from spiritual rebirth there can be no faith.

At the same time, the doctrine of irresistible grace teaches that all who are regenerated indeed come to faith. The "irresistible" may be better described as "effectual." All of God's grace is resistible in the sense that sinners resist it. But the saving grace of regeneration is called irresistible because our resistance to it cannot and does not overpower it.

The grace of regeneration is effectual in that the effect God the Holy Spirit intends to produce actually does come to pass. When the Holy Spirit supernaturally and immediately works to create a person anew, that person is created anew one hundred times out of one hundred. All who receive this grace are changed. All are liberated from the bondage to sin. All are brought to saving faith. The outcome of this work never depends upon the work of unregenerate flesh. The grace is operative, not co-operative.

Of course, once the divine initiative of regeneration has been wrought by the sovereign monergistic work of God, the rest of the Christian life is synergistic. But the transformation of the person from death to life, darkness to light, bondage to liberty is done by God alone, effectually and irresistibly. This is the Biblical basis for the church's confession *soli Deo gloria*.

GETTING TO KNOW ME

JULY 2002

———

"**W**HAT DO YOU WANT TO BE WHEN you grow up?" This question is faced by virtually every person at some point in childhood.

When I was a child, the most common answers among boys included "a cowboy," "a fireman," or "a baseball player." Yet few of us ended up as cowboys, firemen, or baseball players. At some point, as a person leaves childhood, passes through adolescence, and enters adulthood, the question "Who am I?" becomes liberated (at least in part) from childhood fantasy and is answered in more sober terms, terms often dictated by the harsh blows of reality.

What is true for little boys and girls is usually true also for institutions. Just as individuals seek an identity, so do organizations. The church is no exception. During the second century of Christian history, the church was busy answering the question "Who are we?" It was a time of amalgamation, codification, and definition. In that century, the church reflected upon its authority base (Scripture), its theology, and its organization.

It is often the case that organizations, even nations, are forced to define themselves with greater clarity and precision by their competitors and/or enemies. Such was true for the church. Early Christian apologists such as Justin Martyr worked to clarify the nature of the church and Christianity in order to offset misconceptions spread about by outsiders such as pagans and Jews. In like manner, "orthodox" doctrine was hammered out on the anvil of heresy. Then, as now, most heretics claimed to be advocates of true Christianity. Their errors and distortions forced the church to define her beliefs more sharply.

In 2001, Hans Küng, the controversial Roman Catholic theologian, published yet another book about the church. This one was titled simply *The Catholic Church: A Short History*. Küng saw a decisive shift from the activity and self-awareness of the pristine church of the first century to the "institutionalization" of the church in the second century. He notes that, in order to answer the Gnostics, as well as heretics such as Marcion and Montanus, the church set forth clear canons, or standards, about what is truly Christian. They were:

1. A summary creed that was customarily used at baptism. The earliest baptismal creed was the simple statement "Jesus is Lord." Later, the formula was broadened to include affirmations of faith in almighty God and in Jesus Christ, the Son of God born of the Holy Spirit. The rudiments of what became known as "the Symbol," or the Apostles' Creed, were added at this time. Later, more affirmations were added to form the final version of the creed.

2. The New Testament canon. The formulation of the list of authoritative books was provoked in large measure by the work of the heretic Marcion, who produced his own expurgated New Testament. Though the New Testament canon was not finalized until near the end of the fourth century, almost all of it was formally in place by the end of the second century.

3. The episcopal teaching office. This evolved as the church moved in the direction of the monarchical episcopate. It became common to appeal to bishops' teachings to settle theological controversies. Küng argues that this third standard represented a shift from the church of the Apostolic age, which was comprised of free communities without a mono-episcopate or a presbyterate. He views the Apostolic communities as complete and well-equipped churches, which lacked nothing. Later congregationalist churches (and many Puritans) would appeal to these communities as representing the original structure of the church.

Though in some respects saddened by these historical changes, Küng nevertheless says, "The fact cannot be overlooked that with the three standards mentioned above, the Catholic Church created a structure for theology and organization and with it a very resistant inner order."

Küng's assessment does not differ greatly from Protestant analysis. In *A History of the Christian Church*, Williston Walker notes: "Thus out of the struggle with Gnosticism and Montanism came the Catholic Church, with its strong episcopal organization, creedal standard, and authoritative canon. It differed much from the Apostolic Church; but it had preserved historic Christianity and carried it through a tremendous crisis."

Incidentally, Küng notes that all three of the standards established by the church in the second century were attacked in subsequent ages. In the sixteenth century, the Reformation raised questions about the episcopal structure of Rome. The Enlightenment then questioned both the canon of Scripture and the creedal rule of faith.

The second-century church also made significant progress toward defining church life and Christian practice. Early in Christian history, the church made a distinction between proclamation (*kerygma*) and instruction (*didachē*). The apostolic church was a missionary church, reaching beyond the borders of Judaism. The Gentiles were reached by the proclamation of the Gospel in its basic outline. Stress was placed on the person and work of Christ—on His death and resurrection. When converts embraced Christ by faith, they were baptized and entered into the church community. Then they were given more thorough instruction in the faith. To this end, a manual of church order known as the *Didache*, or "The Teaching of the Twelve Apostles," was composed in the second century.

This manual (discovered as recently as 1873) provides simple rules for local congregations, and deals with baptism, abortion (which was regarded as murder), almsgiving, fasting, the Lord's Supper, and other matters. It sets two ways in stark contrast—a way of life and a way of death. Many of the admonitions found within it are explicit quotes from the New Testament Scriptures.

The *Didache* came to be used both as a catechetical tool and as a guide for Christian living. As such, it represents the first post-apostolic written code of Christian morality. Though it is not a part of the canon of Scripture, it offers valuable insights into the early church's self-understanding.

The second-century church developed a strong sense of identity. This process continued well into the third century, when new heresies and new struggles with the state brought even more development and new structures in the church.

MILKING THE RAM

AUGUST 2002

———

O F THE MANY FORMS OF LEGALISM, none is more deadly than that which replaces faith with works or grace with merit as the ground of justification.

The sixteenth-century Reformation was a fight to the death over this issue. It was a struggle for the true Gospel, which had been eclipsed in the medieval church. However, the erosion of the doctrine of justification by faith alone did not begin in the Middle Ages. It had its roots in the New Testament era with the appearance of the "Galatian heresy."

The Galatian agitators, who sought to undermine the authority of the Apostle Paul, argued for a gospel that required works of the law not merely as evidence of justification but as prerequisites for it. This neo-nomianism, or "new lawism," was in direct contradiction to Paul's teaching in Romans: "Now we know that whatever the law says, it says to those who are under the law, that every mouth may be stopped, and all the world may become guilty before God. Therefore by the deeds of the law no flesh will be justified in His sight, for by the law is the knowledge of sin" (3:19–20).

The so-called Judaizers of Galatia sought to add works to faith as a necessary ground for justification. In doing so, they corrupted the Gospel of free grace by which we are justified by faith alone. This distortion provoked Paul to his most vehement repudiation of any heresy he ever combated. After he had affirmed that there was no other gospel than the one he proclaimed and had declared those accursed who sought to preach "any other gospel" (Gal. 1), he then chastened the Galatians:

> O foolish Galatians! Who has bewitched you that you should not obey the truth, before whose eyes Jesus Christ was clearly portrayed among you as crucified? This only I want to learn from you: Did you receive the Spirit by the works of the law, or by the hearing of faith? . . . But

that no one is justified by the law in the sight of God is evident, for "the just shall live by faith" (Gal. 3:1–2, 11).

In the beginning of his epistle, Paul expressed his amazement at how quickly the Galatians had departed from the true Gospel and embraced a "different" gospel that was no gospel at all. However, the seductive voice of legalism has been powerful from the beginning. Works-righteousness schemes have supplanted the Gospel in every age of church history. We think of Pelagianism in the fourth century, Socinianism in the sixteenth century, and Liberalism and Finneyism in the nineteenth century, to name just a few.

But none of these movements has been so complex and systematic in its embrace of a legalistic view of justification as has the Roman Catholic Church. Rome, by adding works to faith and merit to grace as prerequisites for justification, has rekindled the flames of the Galatian heresy.

Though Rome, against pure Pelagianism, insists that grace is necessary for justification, it denies that grace alone justifies. Though it teaches that faith is necessary as the initiation, the foundation, and the root of justification, it denies that we are justified by faith alone. It adds works to faith as a requirement for justification. For God to declare us just, we must be inherently just, according to Rome.

Rome adds merit to grace in two distinct ways. First, there is "congruous merit" (*meritum de congruo*), merit a person acquires by performing works of satisfaction within the context of the sacrament of penance. These works, done with the aid of grace, make it "congruous" or "fitting" for God to justify the person.

Second, there are works of supererogation. These works are above and beyond the call of duty, thus, they yield excess merit. Rome says that when saints achieve more merit than they need to gain entrance into heaven, the excess is deposited into the "Treasury of Merit." Rome calls this the "spiritual goods of the communion of saints."

Out of this treasury the church may dispense merit to those who lack it in sufficient quantity. This is done through "indulgences." The Catechism of the Catholic Church defines an indulgence as follows: "A remission before God of the temporal punishment due to sins whose guilt has already been forgiven, which the faithful Christian who is duly disposed gains under certain prescribed conditions through the action of the church—which, as the minister of redemption, dispenses and applies with authority the treasury of the satisfactions of Christ and the saints."

During the Reformation, a huge controversy grew up around indulgences. The Reformers insisted that the only person whose works had true merit before God was Christ. It is by His works and His merit alone that we can be justified. The value of Christ's merit cannot be augmented or diminished by the works of others. However, in the Roman system, our works not only avail for our own justification, but if they are good enough, they can aid those in purgatory who lack sufficient merit to gain entrance to heaven.

Martin Luther declared that the Roman view of merit was nothing but vain figments and dreamy speculations about worthless stuff. He argued that any view that included our works in our justification was not only blasphemous but ridiculous. He said: "To seek to be justified by the Law is as if a man, already weak and ill, were to go in search of some other greater evil whereby he hoped to cure his ailment, whereas it would, of course, bring him utter ruin, as if a man affected with epilepsy were to add the pestilence to it. ... Here as the proverb puts it, one milks the ram while the other holds the sieve under him."

Luther's proverb declares a double folly. To try to get milk from a ram is foolish enough. But to bring a sieve to catch it merely compounds the folly. Likewise, trying to be justified by any form of legalism is as foolish as trying to get milk from a ram—but with far more dire consequences.

The great tragedy in our day is not just that Roman Catholicism and other religions, such as Islam, codify works as a necessary ground for justification. In practical terms, I fear that the great majority of Protestants also rest their hopes upon their own works. Until we despair of seeking our justification by works, we have not grasped the Gospel.

"TO THE GALLOWS WITH MOSES!"

SEPTEMBER 2002

———

I T WAS JOHANNES AGRICOLA, one of Martin Luther's early zealous comrades and a former student of the Reformer, who uttered the vehement words that serve as the title of this article. Agricola's understanding of the Gospel, as expressed in the formula *sola fide* (justification by faith alone), left no room for the preaching of the moral law of the Old Testament. His full statement was this: "Art thou steeped in sin, an adulterer or a thief? If thou believest, thou art in salvation. All who follow Moses must go to the Devil. To the gallows . . ."

Luther responded negatively to Agricola's statement, coining the term *antinomianism* to describe the sentiment his young comrade was expressing. He also charged Agricola with declaring that "Law belongs in the courthouse, not in the chancel." The idea was that the law was superseded by the Gospel and was abolished in all its parts. The antinomians who followed Agricola argued that the saints are no longer subject to the law.

Ironically, in Luther's own insistence on *sola fide*, many in the Roman Catholic community "heard" the idea that the Gospel totally abrogates the Old Testament law and has no application to the New Testament Christian. In a sense, they saw Agricola's view as the logical conclusion of Luther's doctrine. If works contribute nothing to our justification, they should be of no concern to us. If faith trumps works and the Gospel banishes the law, we can sing the theme song of antinomianism:

Free from the law,
O blessed condition;
We can sin all we want
And still have remission.

It was because of charges to this effect, as well as repeated appeals to James 2, that Luther found it necessary to clarify the nature of saving faith, the relationship of faith to works, and the relationship of the Gospel to the law.

The Reformation qualifier was this: "Justification is by faith alone, but not by a faith that is alone." Luther, in keeping with the epistle of James, argued that saving faith is a *fides viva*, a living faith that always yields the fruit of good works. The Reformation did not see justification as being wrought by a profession of faith, for a profession is easy to come by and may not indicate the possession of true faith itself.

Jesus warned against empty professions when He said: "Not everyone who says to Me, 'Lord, Lord,' shall enter the kingdom of heaven, but he who does the will of My Father in heaven. Many will say to Me in that day, 'Lord, Lord, have we not prophesied in Your name, cast out demons in Your name, and done many wonders in Your name?' And then I will declare to them, 'I never knew you; depart from Me, you who practice lawlessness!' " (Matt. 7:21–23).

There can be no stronger denunciation of antinomianism than that from the lips of Jesus. If good works do not flow from faith, it is proof that the "faith" is no true faith but merely an empty or dead claim to faith. Faith without works is not saving faith. But Luther was careful to note that the works that are the necessary fruit of true faith add no merit or anything to the ground of justification. The only works that justify us are the works of Christ.

Luther repudiated antinomianism in his 1536 treatise titled *Against the Antinomians*, although the debate continued until 1540. Finally, even Agricola recanted his views, though he was never personally reconciled with Luther.

At first, Luther saw the role of law as simply preparing sinners for grace by revealing their sin, but he later broadened his understanding of its use. In 1577, the Lutheran Formula of Concord recognized a threefold use of the law: to reveal sin, to establish decency in society, and to provide a rule of life for Christians.

Though the term *antinomian* (antilaw) was introduced in the sixteenth century by Luther, the power of this heretical idea was known much earlier. In the early centuries of Christianity, the Gnostic heresy fostered a kind of antinomianism that has not yet disappeared from the church. The Gnostics saw salvation as purely a spiritual matter that did not affect the carnal nature of man. They also affirmed that the carnal does not affect the soul, saying that if gold were dipped in filth, it would not lose its beauty but would retain its own nature. Nothing that a "spiritual man" could do would harm his spiritual nature.

Even before the Gnostic antinomianism, the disease was present in the Apostolic community. The scandalous episode of the incestuous man in the Corinthian church was reported to Paul. This man's behavior was not merely an isolated event; it revealed a broader spirit of antinomianism that was corrupting the church.

In his rebuke, Paul wrote: "And you are puffed up, and have not rather mourned, that he who has done this deed might be taken away from among you" (1 Cor. 5:2). Obviously, the Corinthians were taking pride in their "freedom" in the Gospel that tolerated such heinous sin. Paul rebuked them by saying, "Your glorying is not good" (v. 6), then required them to excommunicate the man and to "deliver such a one to Satan for the destruction of the flesh, that his spirit may be saved in the day of the Lord Jesus" (v. 5).

Later, the Apostle warned the Corinthians to guard against deceptive doctrine: "Do not be deceived. Neither fornicators, nor idolaters, nor adulterers, nor homosexuals, nor sodomites, nor thieves, nor covetous, nor drunkards, nor revilers, nor extortioners will inherit the kingdom of God" (6:9b–10).

Paul was not suggesting that anyone who commits these sins has no hope of heaven. But impenitent persistence in such wickedness would be a sign of a dead faith with no fruit of sanctification. Paul clearly understood the Christian's ongoing struggle with sin, but he had no room for a theology of lawlessness by which the sinner cries, "Let us continue in sin that grace may abound."

A FREE AND LASTING LEGACY

OCTOBER 2002

I N THE EARLY 1970s, I was browsing through dusty volumes in a used-book store in downtown (pronounced *dahn-tahn*) Pittsburgh. To my astonishment and delight, I found a copy of a book of sermons written by Abraham Kuyper. Because the volume was in Dutch, few customers had showed any interest in it. Therefore, by the immutable law of supply and demand, the asking price was 25 cents. For one quarter I was able to secure a book that in other parts of the world would be regarded as a treasure. One man's garbage . . .

I first heard of Kuyper while I was a philosophy student in college. My main professor had been deeply influenced by Kuyper and by Kuyper's students. At that time, I had no idea how great an influence this man would have on my own life.

In 1964, I graduated from seminary. I had been married for four years, and we had a 3-year-old daughter. I was tired of going to school and more than ready to get a full-time job. But my theology professor had other plans. Only a few weeks before graduation, my mentor sat me down and insisted that I go on to graduate school. I said, "If I go, where should I go?" Without hesitation he replied, "To the Free University of Amsterdam." He wanted me to study under G.C. Berkouwer, and since Berkouwer held the chair of theology at the Free University, that's where I had to go.

At the time, I was not aware that "The Fu" (the students' affectionate term for the school) had been founded by Kuyper. Kuyper, a theologian, philosopher, and politician in the Dutch Calvinist tradition, founded the university in 1880. He served there as a professor and administrator. He also served his country as a member of Parliament for more than 30 years and was the prime minister of the Netherlands from 1901 to 1905.

At his 70th birthday party in 1907, it was said of him that "the history of the Netherlands in church, in state, in society, in press, in school, and in the sciences of the last forty years, cannot be written without the mention of his name on almost every page."

At first glance, it may seem that Kuyper the educator structured the Free University according to the classical pattern of the medieval university, where theology was regarded as the queen of the sciences and philosophy as her handmaiden. At the Fu, theology and philosophy held center stage. The second glance, however, reveals that Kuyper did not seek to replicate the medieval model because he saw it as too dependent on the role of human reason and natural theology.

The Free University was so called not because there were no tuition costs. The "free" had to do with its status with respect to both church and state. The university was free in the sense that it was independent, bound only by the Word of God. Kuyper had a profound influence on the thought of Herman Dooyeweerd, who was both a student and later a professor of philosophy at the Free University. Dooyeweerd, like his mentor, was deeply concerned about "worldview" thinking and with the "cultural mandate," the task given to Adam and Eve to subdue the earth. For Kuyper and his students, all thought must be brought into subjection to the sovereignty of God. All culture, all science, and all knowledge must be understood in light of God. Fields of inquiry may be distinguished from theology, but never separated from it. Kuyper had no place for a truncated worldview in which theology was relegated to a tiny compartment of spirituality. All of culture was to be under God's sovereignty.

Dooyeweerd, in his massive (and somewhat arcane) four-volume work *A New Critique of Theoretical Thought*, and in other works, leveled a sharp criticism against the secular foundations of Western thought. He argued that secular worldviews are blind to their own "religious" commitments. Secular thinkers are caught in a pretense of their own sense of autonomy. Every thinker has his own "cosmonomic" idea. This idea of cosmic law describes the general structure, grid, or framework into which the scholar or scientist fits and interprets the particular "facts" of his knowledge.

There is a line that runs from Kuyper to Dooyeweerd to Cornelius Van Til and to Francis Schaeffer. Though each of these thinkers had his own unique contributions, there is a common connection among them in the call to bring all knowledge into subjection to God.

For Kuyper and his followers, there was no such thing as "neutral" knowledge or education. One's knowledge is related to God or it ignores Him. For Dooyeweerd, the "heart" refers to the functional center or core of a person's being. Reflecting the Biblical axiom that "As a man thinks in his heart, so is he," Dooyeweerd said the heart of man is either inclined toward God and submissive to Him or is set against Him.

The Free University was Kuyper's legacy to worldview thinking. When I enrolled in the Theological School in 1964, it was located in the inner city of Amsterdam, just around the corner from the Anne Frank house. Today the university has expanded and moved to the suburbs, not far from the international airport of Schiphol. It now comprises 15 faculties; two thousand lecturers and researchers, including three hundred professors; sixteen hundred non-academic staff members; and facilities for fourteen thousand students. It includes a major teaching hospital as part of its program. This great university lives on as one of Kuyper's many legacies.

EVANGELICAL LAP DOGS

NOVEMBER 2002

———

I N THE BOOK OF LEVITICUS, we read God's mandate to His people: "For I am the LORD your God. You shall therefore consecrate yourselves, and you shall be holy; for I am holy. Neither shall you defile yourselves with any creeping thing that creeps on the earth. For I am the LORD who brings you up out of the land of Egypt, to be your God. You shall therefore be holy, for I am holy" (Lev. 11:44–45).

In Creation, man was made in the image of God. Part of the significance of this truth is that, being stamped with the divine image, human beings are called to reflect the character of God.

When God formed Israel as a nation unto Himself, He called the people to holiness, a kind of moral "otherness" or "apartheid." God's people were to be different, to be consecrated or "set apart." They were to be unlike other nations and peoples. And the difference was to be seen in their loyalty and obedience to God.

In one sense, the Old Testament record is the history of Israel's failure to obey this mandate. The people's covenant infidelity was marked by a desire to be like other nations, to abandon the uniqueness to which they were called. Instead of being a light to the Gentiles, they were enticed to embrace the darkness of the world around them. This was seen in the people's clamoring to Samuel for a king. Despite both the warning of Samuel and of God Himself, the people persisted:

Nevertheless the people refused to obey the voice of Samuel; and they said, "No, but we will have a king over us, that we also may be like all the nations, and that our king may judge us and go out before us and fight our battles" (1 Sam. 8:19–20).

Several years ago, I read an analysis of the development of children written from a psychological perspective. The author argued that from birth to
age 5, the most important influence in the life of a child is the mother. From
6 to 12, the most powerful influence is the father. Then, from 13 to 20, the
most significant influence is the person's peer group. Adolescence is seen
as the period of highest pressure to conform to one's immediate culture.

I don't know how accurate this analysis is, but it certainly seems to be
borne out in the behavioral patterns of adolescents. For the teenager, it is
often a fate worse than death to be considered "out of it." To be "with it" is a
powerful seductive force that, sadly, does not end at age 20. The desire to be
accepted by the mainstream of the culture has been a fierce and destructive
force to the people of God in every generation. The tendency to accommodate the faith to the culture did not end with the Old Testament.

We have seen countless examples of universities, colleges, and seminaries chartered with a strong commitment to orthodox Christianity,
only to erode first into liberalism and ultimately into secularism. Why
does this happen? There are multiple, complex reasons for the apostasy
of such institutions, but one key factor is the desire of professors to be
intellectually recognized in the academic world. A slavish genuflection
to the latest trends in academia seduces our leaders into conformity. One
apologist once described this pattern as the "treason of the intellectuals."
If the secular establishment ridicules such tenets as the inspiration of
the Bible, then insecure Christian professors, desperate to be accepted
by their peers, quickly flee from orthodoxy, dragging the colleges, seminaries, and ultimately the churches with them. It is a weighty price to
pay for academic recognition.

In the second half of the twentieth century, the church witnessed the
steady decline of historic evangelicalism to such a degree that the term is
now hardly recognizable. The church lost what Francis A. Schaeffer called
the "antithesis" between a Christian worldview and secularism. The result
is that it is sometimes difficult to distinguish between left-wing evangelicalism and liberalism with respect to methodology, theology, and ethics.

The justification for this erosion among evangelicals is the goal of influencing the world. Martin Luther called for a "profane" Christianity in the literal sense, meaning that the church is called "out of the temple" and into the world. Indeed the world is our mission field, our theater of operations. The difficulty, as always, is to influence the world without surrendering to it. The line is crossed when, in our zeal to reach the world, we accommodate the truth of God to that world.

For a current example of such accommodation, we need look no further than the controversy that is raging with respect to Bible translating. In 1997, it was discovered that a British edition of the New International Version was being produced that included a translators' explanation that one of the goals of the version was to "correct the patriarchalism" of the Bible. Masculine words such as *man, brother,* and *son,* as well as pronouns such as *he* and *him,* would be eliminated in favor of "gender-neutral" terms such as *people* and *children.* This disclosure evoked a hue and cry resulting in a public pledge by the presidents of the International Bible Society and Zondervan Publishing Co. not to proceed with such a translation. In a cordial atmosphere, these men signed guidelines for translation at a meeting in Colorado Springs, Colo., that year.

But in early 2002, the International Bible Society and Zondervan announced the preparation of Today's New International Version (TNIV). The day before the announcement was made in the national media, representatives of Zondervan and the International Bible Society notified the signatories of the Colorado Springs accord that they were withdrawing their names from the agreement.

The defenders of the TNIV translation argue that it is driven not by a feminist agenda or by a desire to be "politically correct." The repeated claims of its authors and publishers is that it is an endeavor to improve the "accuracy" of the English Bible. But if the TNIV is more accurate than the NIV, why does Zondervan intend to continue to publish the NIV? If Zondervan is really committed to accuracy, it would seem that it would have the TNIV replace the NIV altogether.

Actually, the TNIV appears to be a move not toward greater accuracy but away from it. One example: In the Sermon on the Mount, Jesus says,

"Blessed are the peacemakers, for they shall be called sons of God" (Matt. 5:9). The TNIV changes *sons* to *children*. But the Greek word *huios* in its plural form means "sons," not "children." My Latin Bible translates it "sons" (*filii*). My German Bible, my Dutch Bible, and my French Bible translate it "sons." Likewise, every English Bible I own translates it "sons." Indeed, from the first century until today, the whole world has understood what the Greek says.

It was not until the advent of gender-inclusive language (the legacy of radical feminism and political correctness) that any translation dared to change the original text. This is accommodation to the culture. It cannot be explained by pointing to the fluidity and dynamism of human language. Even today, we still distinguish between male and female offspring by referring to them as sons or daughters. In the scope of Scripture, there is a theological import to the word *son* that is lost when it is rendered by the term *child*. The translators may not embrace feminism or political correctness, yet they fall into the trap of accommodating such cultural perspectives.

When a translation moves from the specific to the general (as *sons* to *children*), it is not taking a step toward accuracy but away from it. There is a patriarchal framework to Biblical revelation that is clearly present in the original text. To "change" or "correct" that framework is to take liberties with Scripture that cannot be justified by "dynamic equivalency" or any other methodology.

The task of translation is not to provide a commentary on the original text. The work of interpreting and applying the text to the present culture belongs to pastors, teachers, and students of the Word. When translators undertake this in the name of improved accuracy, they step over a boundary the church has been jealous to guard carefully for two thousand years. Not since Marcion in the second century have we seen attempts to actually change the language of the original text.

YOUR WORD IS NOW FULFILLED

DECEMBER 2002

———

T HE PROPHET HABAKKUK WAS BURDENED DEEPLY. He lived in a land filled with violence and devoid of justice, a land under oppression by a foreign enemy. It perplexed him that the God of Israel could allow His own people to be destroyed by pagans. So he protested that while God was too holy to look at wickedness, He was tolerating it in abundance.

Having voiced his vexing questions, the prophet ascended a rampart, his "watch tower," to await God's reply. When God answered, He instructed Habakkuk to write His words down: "Write the vision and make it plain on tablets, that he may run who reads it. For the vision is yet for an appointed time; but at the end it will speak, and it will not lie. Though it tarries, wait for it; because it will surely come, it will not tarry. Behold the proud, his soul is not upright in him; but the just shall live by his faith" (Hab. 2:2–4).

These words, "the just shall live by faith," are quoted three times in the New Testament. God was telling Habakkuk that the righteous person will live by trusting Him. This call to faith was a summons to trust God's promise of redemption. The promise had been set for an appointed time by the determinate counsel of God. He called it an appointment that would not lie, for it was an appointment grounded in the truth of God Himself. It would not be broken because it could not be broken.

The divine instructions were simple: "Though it tarries, wait for it." This command could be attached to all of the promises of God. Throughout the Old Testament, God promised the coming of the Messiah. He had set an appointment for the Incarnation to occur in the fullness of time—the exact moment in world history that He had decreed from the foundation of the world. This decree made that of Caesar Augustus (Luke 2:1) pale into insignificance, except that it provided the context for the fulfillment of the ultimate plan of God.

When the moment came for Christ's entrance into the world, Israel once again was under foreign domination. It is clear from the New Testament that at the time of His Advent, the Old Testament church was not ready for Him. Four hundred years had passed since Israel had received its last prophetic word from God. The people had grown tired of waiting. In their eyes, the promised Messiah had tarried too long. The quaint promises of their ancient religion now appeared to be simply myths and legends, or even worse, lies.

For the most part Israel had been secularized. The people still maintained the trappings of religion—they still observed their annual festivals, and they still had a professional priesthood and the ministries of the scribes and Pharisees. But this external religion was empty. It was a hypocritical sham that Jesus quickly exposed.

Perhaps the saddest commentary on that day is found in the prologue to John's gospel: "He was in the world, and the world was made through Him, and the world did not know Him. He came to His own, and His own did not receive Him" (John 1:10–11).

God invited Israel to a reception in honor of His Son. But they did not come. Instead, they fled from the receiving line. It was not the pagans who refused to receive Him. It was Israel, God's own people, the people of the covenant, the people who possessed the promise of God, who would not receive Him.

Yet John indicates that despite this national apostasy, God preserved for Himself a remnant. This remnant was a small group of Jews who lived by faith. They were not secularized. They waited for the promise, even though it had tarried for centuries. Of these people John writes: "But as many as received Him, to them He gave the right to become children of God, to those who believe in His name: who were born, not of blood, nor of the will of the flesh, nor of the will of man, but of God" (John 1:12–13).

John speaks of those who were the adopted children of God. These were the people who received Christ. The term translated "right" is better rendered "authority" or "power" to become God's children. These people were born of God and not of human effort.

Luke gives us cameo portraits of some of these members of the remnant that received Jesus. In his infancy narratives, he speaks of Zacharias and Elizabeth, Mary and Joseph, and Anna and Simeon.

Simeon is one of my favorite characters in the Bible. He was a man of persevering faith. He is described by Luke as being just and devout. To be devout is to be a person of devotion. His allegiance to God was not a casual matter. Rather, his commitment revealed a singular passion, a constant and steadfast love, despite the unbelief of those around him.

Luke tells us that Simeon was "waiting for the Consolation of Israel." The phrase *Consolation of Israel* was a Messianic title, an appellation that described one of the functions of the coming Redeemer, who would bring comfort to His people. Where others had forgotten the promises of God or abandoned hope in their fulfillment, Simeon was doing exactly what Habakkuk was instructed to do: he was waiting. He was anointed by the Holy Spirit, and God had revealed to him that he would not die before seeing the coming Messiah.

We don't know when God revealed to him that he would see the Messiah. It probably had been many years earlier, as he is described as a man who had been "waiting."

We are told that Simeon was led to the temple by the Spirit. We don't know whether he came daily to inquire about the Messiah. But one day, when he came to the temple, he saw the parents of Jesus with their child. To their astonishment, Simeon took the babe in his arms and said (or sang) the *Nunc Dimittis:*

> "Lord, now You are letting Your servant depart in peace, according to Your word; for my eyes have seen Your salvation . . ." (Luke 2:29–30).

When he finished these words, he made a grim prophecy to Mary:

> "Behold, this Child is destined for the fall and rising of many in Israel, and for a sign which will be spoken against (yes, a sword will pierce

through your own soul also), that the thoughts of many hearts may be revealed" (vv. 34–35).

Simeon was ready to die. He didn't need to see the public ministry of Jesus, His miracles, death, and resurrection. He had seen enough. He had witnessed the arrival of the Consolation of Israel. It was worth the wait— as are all of God's promises.

LIKE A SHIP
WITHOUT A RUDDER

JANUARY 2003

L IKE A SCRATCHED RECORD ON WHICH the stylus becomes stuck in a single groove, playing the same music over and over again, one refrain sounds repeatedly in the book of Judges: "And the children of Israel again did evil in the sight of the LORD."

Judges covers a crucial period of Old Testament history. It is sandwiched between the books of Joshua and 1 Samuel (with the little book of Ruth squeezed in as well). Joshua records the history of the conquest of Canaan, the move of the Israelites from the wilderness into the Promised Land. Once the conquest was accomplished, Israel settled into the era of the judges, or what Biblical scholars call the period of the amphictyony.

Historians date this period as being roughly between 1200 and 1050 B.C. The Egyptian Empire was waning and Assyria had been weakened. The newest threat to the Israelites was the Philistines, who controlled the seacoast of Canaan and had a monopoly on the manufacture of iron.

During this time, Israel was structured politically into a loose federation of tribes. The judges arose during times of crisis, being especially endowed by the Holy Spirit for their leadership tasks. They were charismatic figures who led the people of Israel by divine empowerment. We read of the exploits of Othniel, Ehud, Shamgar, Deborah, Gideon, Samson, and others. All engaged in defensive war—in battles to save their people from foreign oppression.

The cyclical history of the amphictyony went like this:

1. The Israelites sinned against God.
2. God's anger was kindled against the people.
3. God delivered them into the hands of their enemies.

4. The Israelites groaned under oppression.
5. God raised up judges to deliver the people.

This scenario is repeated over and over again until we come to the end of Judges. The book ends with an ominous note of foreboding: "In those days there was no king in Israel; everyone did what was right in his own eyes."

This was a time of moral decadence. The law of God was ignored and the covenant religion of the nation was supplanted by pagan idolatry. In this state of shambles, it is a wonder that the amphictyony survived at all, let alone lasting almost two hundred years.

The end of the judges period coincides with a transition into the period of the monarchy in Israel. The last judge of Israel, Samuel, is introduced as the protégé of Eli, the venerable priest. Eli's great sin was his failure to discipline his corrupt sons, Hophni and Phinehas.

The amphictyony basically ended on the field of battle. The Israelites had met the Philistines near Ebenezer. In this battle, Israel was soundly defeated and four thousand of its soldiers were killed. When news of this humiliating slaughter reached the elders of Israel, they decided to send Israel's most powerful weapon into battle against the Philistines—the sacred ark of the covenant that symbolized the very presence of God. The Philistines were aware of the incredible victories Israel's armies had won when they had carried the ark into battle. Thus, when the ark arrived and the shout came from the Israelite camp, the Philistines were stricken with terror at the prospect of doing battle with Yahweh.

The sons of Eli were assigned the task of accompanying the ark into battle. But when the battle ensued this time, it was much worse. Israel was defeated again, this time with the loss of thirty thousand of its soldiers. Among the casualties were Hophni and Phinehas. But the supreme humiliation was that the ark of the covenant was captured by the Philistines and carted off to be placed as a trophy in the temple of Dagon.

When news of this disaster reached the central sanctuary at Shiloh, Eli, who was 98 years old and blind, fell over backward, broke his neck, and died. And when Eli's daughter-in-law, the wife of Phinehas, heard the news, she went into labor and gave birth on the spot to a son. She died in childbirth, but not before naming her son "Ichabod."

The name of this forlorn infant encapsulated the situation of Israel at this point in its history. Eli and his sons were dead. The ark of the covenant was captured, Shiloh was taken, and the sanctuary of the amphictyony was destroyed. The line of judges that had served Israel for so long was in ruins. The sole surviving judge was Samuel. For a time, he acted as an itinerant judge in an effort to keep the amphictyony alive. But the people had lost hope in the system. They had no unified government, no national army, and now no real central sanctuary. The "old ways" were deemed to be no longer effective. It was a time when the glory (*kabod*) of God had departed from Israel.

When Samuel grew old, he made his sons to be judges over Israel, but they, like the sons of Eli, did not walk in the ways of their father. The people began to clamor for a king, saying, "Make us a king to judge us like all the nations." God saw this desire to be like the pagan nations to be not a rejection of Samuel but a rejection of God Himself. He viewed it as a desire of the people to not have Him to reign over them.

God granted the wish of the people, giving them over to their own evil impulses. But He did not make this grant without a solemn warning:

"This will be the behavior of the king who will reign over you: He will take your sons and appoint them for his own chariots.... He ... will set some to plow his ground and reap his harvest, and some to make his weapons.... He will take your daughters to be perfumers, cooks, and bakers. And he will take the best of your fields, your vineyards, and your olive groves.... He will take a tenth of your grain.... He will take your male servants, your female servants, your finest young men, and your donkeys.... And you will be his servants. And you will cry out in that day because of your king whom you have chosen for yourselves, and the LORD will not hear you in that day" (1 Sam. 8:11–18).

The rest is history.

"The mindset of relativism and pluralism has so penetrated the church that truth itself is sacrificed on the altar of relational expediency."

—

TOLERATING
THE INTOLERABLE

FEBRUARY 2003

O NE OF THE BANES OF MY EXISTENCE IS trying to recall exactly where I read something. My memory for quotes is good, but my memory for sources is poor. Maybe I read too much, so that I quickly forget where I read things. So it is with a particular John Calvin quote. I once read that no theologian is ever more than 80 percent correct in his theology. Now, I'm more than 80 percent sure that Calvin wrote that, but I am zero percent sure of where he wrote it.

In making this statement, Calvin was saying that even the best and most careful of Christian thinkers is prone to error. And errors tend to multiply if they are systemic. Not only do different theological views abound on particular issues, but widely divergent systems of thought clash with one another. The more incorrect the system is, the higher the likelihood that it will contain a multitude of errors. If my system is correct, then my errors will fall among the particulars or details within the system. If my system is wrong, then the places where I am accurate will tend to fall among the particulars or details.

We also must acknowledge that multiple systems may function in our thinking, systems that exist within systems. For example, there is a large system of thought that we call orthodox or "catholic" Christianity. This system includes those macro-truths that are shared historically by virtually all groups claiming the name of Jesus. These truths include such affirmations as the Trinity, the resurrection of Christ, the fall of man, and others. Historic Protestant groups, such as the Lutheran, Baptist, Methodist, Presbyterian, and Episcopalian churches, affirm the core doctrines I mentioned above, as does Roman Catholicism. They may disagree on questions such as the extent of the Fall, but all agree on the reality of the Fall.

There are three major systems of theology that have claimed to be Christian—Pelagianism, Augustinianism, and Semi-Pelagianism. Pelagianism was declared heretical by the ancient church and is outside the bounds of Christian orthodoxy. It reappeared substantially in sixteenth-century Socinianism, in nineteenth-century liberalism (which extends to our day), and in the quasi-evangelicalism of Charles Finney.

For the most part, historic Christianity can be seen in systems that are either Augustinian or Semi-Pelagian. These systems hold to the essentials of historic Christianity while differing in other, often important matters. The Roman Church falls into the Semi-Pelagian group but differs from Protestant Semi-Pelagianism in that it denies the crucial doctrine of justification by faith alone, which historic Protestantism sees as an essential doctrine of orthodox Christianity.

Within the systems of Augustinianism and Semi-Pelagianism, there are a host of specialized systems, such as Calvinism, Arminianism, dispensationalism, and so forth. Where these systems clash, there must be error. For example, Calvinism and Arminianism cannot both be systemically true. At least one of the systems, if not both, is in error. But where these differences and errors appear, they usually have not been deemed to be heretical. Though all heresies are errors, not all errors rise to the level of heresy. Usually a heresy is an error so severe that it denies or threatens an essential tenet of Christianity.

Throughout history, the church has faced not just errors of greater or lesser severity, but heresy. But heresy has had a "left-handed," or indirect, benefit for the church—it has forced the church to define orthodoxy. The history of the church councils is largely the history of the church in conflict with heresy. For instance, when the heretic Marcion produced his fake canon of Scripture, the church countered by defining the books of the Bible as we now have them. The heresy of Arius led to the Council of Nicaea, which produced the Nicene Creed and the church's confession of the Trinity. Likewise, in response to the heresies of Nestorius and Eutyches, the Council of Chalcedon in 451 defined the dual nature of Christ in terms of His true deity and true humanity.

In every era, heresy pushes the church to greater precision of her confession of faith. This salutary "benefit" of heresy, however, does not make the heresies themselves less odious. Heresies are damnable precisely because they lead people into damnation. They expose people to the anathema of God Himself.

We live in an era that rejects the very idea of heresy. It seems that the only heresy is to accuse someone else of heresy. Heresy trials are as rare as politicians who ignore lobby groups. The mindset of relativism and pluralism has so penetrated the church that truth itself is sacrificed on the altar of relational expediency. We are willing to affirm what we believe but unwilling to deny its antithesis. When Francis A. Schaeffer spoke of "true truth," he meant truth that can be distinguished from its antithesis, or falsehood. But in a pluralistic environment, truth itself is "plural." There are as many "truths" as there are advocates of views. Pluralism is the twin of relativism. Truth is subjective, so there can be no antithesis between what a person professes and its opposite.

Thus, when from within the confines of "evangelicalism" a view of God is propounded that self-consciously departs from orthodox theism, it is treated as a minor dispute among true evangelicals. But open theism is not simply a point of dispute between Arminians and Calvinists.* Though it comes out of the Arminian camp, open theism is as antithetical to historic Arminianism as it is to Calvinism. Neither must it be viewed as one more error on the contemporary theological landscape. Open theism so attacks the Biblical and orthodox doctrine of God that it passes the border between error and heresy. As politically incorrect as the idea of heresy may be, the church must be willing to use this term in this debate. Open theism must be rejected not only as sub-Christian, but as anti-Christian.

Our understanding of God determines our entire theology. When the orthodox doctrine of God goes, nothing can be more systemic. If our doctrine of God is heretical, then our entire belief system will be ground into dust by this heresy

---

* Open theism is a theological view that posits that because humans have free will, God's knowledge of the future is tentative and His providence is not all-encompassing.

WHATEVER HAPPENED TO PREACHING

MARCH 2003

M ORE THAN 30 YEARS AGO, I heard a man declare: "The age of great preachers is over; the age of great congregations has begun." When I heard this assertion, my response was ambivalence.

On the one hand, I was stirred to think of the power that would be unleashed if ministers would really equip the saints for ministry. I didn't think (and I still don't) that the visible church would have any significant impact upon the world unless the laity was mobilized.

In Acts 8:1–4, we read the following: "Now Saul was consenting to [Stephen's] death. At that time a great persecution arose against the church which was at Jerusalem; and they were all scattered throughout the regions of Judea and Samaria, except the apostles. . . . Therefore those who were scattered went everywhere preaching the word."

We notice in this record that the supreme preachers of the early church were the Apostles. During the persecution in Jerusalem, all except the Apostles were scattered. Yet the ones who were scattered went everywhere preaching the Word. This is exhibit A of a mobilized church that had been equipped for ministry. So the idea of an age of great congregations was a thrilling concept to me.

On the other hand, the above announcement included the ominous note that "the age of great preachers is over." That prospect saddened me. I think the church desperately needs great preachers in every age.

Two thoughts have stuck with me since I first heard this comment. First, saying that we can have great preachers or great congregations is an example of the either/or fallacy or the fallacy of the false dilemma. There is no reason we can't have both. Indeed, there is a compelling reason to assume that the two are not only compatible, but virtually necessarily connected. Theoretically, it may be possible to have truly great preachers without great congregations, but such is hard for me to imagine. Great preaching is Gospel preaching, not mere oratorical talent. Great preaching declares the whole counsel of God with power and accuracy. Such preaching simply does not return unto God void. To be sure, there are those who sit under great preaching who never are moved by it, but such preaching is the "foolish" means by which God has chosen to save the world.

My second thought is that it may be possible to have a great congregation without great preaching, but it is hard.

When I was in college, I joined a club called Karux. The word *karux* is derived from the Greek word for "preaching." The club was organized for students who were preparing for the ministry. I suppose that when the club was first established, its founders chose the name Karux because they saw preaching as the primary task of the minister.

The book of Acts contains several examples of what scholars call the *kerygma*. The term *kerygma* may be distinguished from the word *didachē*. *Kerygma* refers to the "proclamation" of the early church, to the content of the message that was preached. *Didachē* refers to the "teaching" of the early church.

We still may distinguish between preaching and teaching, but they should not necessarily be separated. Most of my work focuses upon teaching, but many times when I am teaching I also include preaching; I move from giving information to exhortation. Likewise, when I am preaching, I normally include a large dose of teaching.

As a teacher, I prefer to be a peripatetic. That is, I love to walk around the classroom engaging students in dialogue as I teach. I don't like to be restricted to a single spot behind a desk or a podium. During Ligonier conferences, I roam back and forth upon the platform as I teach.

However, last year our church completed its initial building program. During the planning stages, our building committee asked me whether I wanted to have a pulpit. The committee members were aware that I like to roam while I talk, so they assumed I would not want a pulpit. I told them I not only wanted a pulpit, I wanted an elevated pulpit. Why? To exalt the preacher? God forbid. I wanted an elevated pulpit to elevate the Word of God, as well as to say "no" to the current trend in church architecture of dispensing with pulpits.

The year I was born, the classic movie *Gone with the Wind* was released. I fear that the history of this church era may be summarized by the headline "Gone with the Pulpit." I fear that when the pulpit is removed, so is a high view of preaching. The modern church has exchanged the fixed pulpit for a plexiglass lectern that can be removed easily to make way for the drama team or to remove any sense of preaching as a threatening voice from on high that might be seeker unfriendly. Pulpits are too "churchy," and churchiness is now déclassé. What is in is pop psychology or entertaining anecdotes. (I once heard a well-known preacher give a riveting story. At its conclusion, he said: "What am I illustrating? Nothing. I just think it's a great story." That in itself was an illustration.)

Of course, there are preachers who are preaching the whole counsel of God, sound expositors of the Word, who use portable lecterns and the like. There are also preachers who spew forth secular platitudes from raised and fixed pulpits. I'm speaking of trends and what they signify. Every form is an art form and every art form communicates something. My question and my fear is: What does the disappearance of the pulpit communicate with respect to preaching? The preaching is not in the pulpit; it's in the preacher. But when the pulpit goes, can the preacher be far behind?

OUR FATHER...

APRIL 2003

———

MY FIRST CLASS AT THE Free University of Amsterdam shattered my academic complacency. It was cultural shock, an exercise in contrasts. It started the moment the professor, Dr. G.C. Berkouwer, entered the room. At his appearance, every student stood at attention until he mounted the podium steps, opened his notebook, and silently nodded for the students to be seated. He then began his lecture, and the students, in a holy hush, dutifully listened and wrote notes for the hour. No one ever dared to interrupt or distract the master by presuming to raise his hand. The session was dominated by a single voice—the voice we were all paying to hear.

When the lecture ended, the professor closed his notebook, stepped down from the podium, and hastily left the room, but not before the students once more rose in his honor. There was no dialogue, no student appointments, no gabfest. No student ever spoke to the professor—except during privately scheduled oral exams.

My first such exam was an exercise in terror. I went to the professor's house expecting an ordeal. But as rigorous as the exam was, it was not an ordeal. Dr. Berkouwer was warm and kind. In avuncular fashion, he asked about my family. He showed great concern for my well-being and invited me to ask him questions.

In a sense, this experience was a taste of heaven. Professor Berkouwer was, of course, mortal. But he was a man of titanic intellect and encyclopedic knowledge. I was not in his home to instruct him or to debate him—I was the student and he was the master. There was hardly anything in the realm of theology he could learn from me. And yet, he listened to me as if he really thought he *could* learn something from me. He took my answers to his probing questions seriously. It was as if I were a son being questioned by a caring father.

This event is the best human analogy I can come up with to answer the age-old query, "If God is sovereign, why pray?" However, I must confess that this analogy is frail. Though Berkouwer towered above me in knowledge, his knowledge was finite and limited. He was by no means omniscient.

By contrast, when I converse with God, I am not merely talking to a Great Professor in the Sky. I'm talking to One who has all knowledge, One who cannot possibly learn anything from me that He doesn't already know. He knows everything there is to know, including what's on my mind. He knows what I'm going to say to Him before I say it. He knows what He's going to do before He does it. His knowledge is sovereign, as He is sovereign. His knowledge is perfect, immutably so.

Though the Bible at times limps with human language expressing the idea that God changes His mind, relents, or repents of His plans, it elsewhere reminds us that these human-form expressions are just that, and that God is not a man that He should repent. In Him there is no shadow of turning. His counsel is from everlasting. He has no plan B. Plan B's are "contingency plans," but though God knows all contingencies, He Himself knows nothing contingently.

People ask, "Does prayer change God's mind?" To ask such a question is to answer it. What kind of God could be influenced by my prayers? What could my prayers do to induce Him to change His plans? Could I possibly give God any information about anything that He doesn't already have? Or could I persuade Him toward a more excellent way by my superior wisdom? Of course not. I am completely unqualified to be God's mentor or His guidance counselor. So the simple answer is that prayer does not change God's mind.

But suppose we ask the question of the relationship between God's sovereignty and our prayers in a slightly different way: "Does prayer change *things*?" Now the answer is an emphatic "Yes!" The Scriptures tell us that "the effective, fervent prayer of a righteous man avails much" (James 5:16). This text declares that prayer is effectual. It is not a pious exercise in futility. That which is futile avails nothing. Prayer, however, avails much. That which avails much is never futile.

What does prayer avail? What does it change? In the first place, my prayers change me. The purpose of prayer is not to change God. He doesn't change because He doesn't need changing. But I do. Just as Dr. Berkouwer's questions to me were not for his benefit but for mine, so my time with God is for my edification, not His. Prayer is one of the great privileges given to us along with our justification. A consequence of our justification is that we have access to God. We have been adopted into His family and given the right to address Him as Father. We are encouraged to come boldly into His presence. (Of course, there is a difference between boldness and arrogance.)

But prayer also changes things. In practical terms, we say that prayer works. That which is effectual is that which causes or produces effects. In theology, we distinguish between primary and secondary causality. Primary causality is the power source of all causes. When the Bible says that "in Him we live and move and have our being" (Acts 17:28), it indicates that apart from God's sustaining providence we would be powerless to live, move, or exist. All power that we have is secondary. It always depends upon God for its ultimate efficacy. Yet, it is real. Prayer is one of the means God uses to bring about the ends He ordains. That is, God not only ordains ends; He ordains the means He uses to bring about those ends.

God doesn't need our preaching to save His people. Yet He has chosen to work through our preaching. He empowers our human preaching with His own power. In like manner, He has chosen to work through our prayers. He empowers our prayers so that after we pray we can step back and watch Him unleash His power in and through our prayers.

We pray expectantly and confidently, not in spite of the sovereignty of God, but because of it. What would be a waste of time and breath would be praying to a god who is not sovereign.

"To make God totally identified with creation is to obscure His transcendence and slip into pantheism. But if we make Him totally transcendent, we slip into deism or sheer skepticism."

—

HOLY OTHERS

MAY 2003

———

T HEY WERE HERALDED AS THE ARCHITECTS of a "new orthodoxy." Their distinguished group included such scholars as Karl
Barth, Emil Brunner, Paul Althaus, and, in the early years, Rudolf
Bultmann. Barth was the acclaimed leader of this movement, called variously "dialectical theology" or "neo-orthodoxy."

Like Barth, most of them were educated in the canons of nineteenth-
century liberalism, being molded by the thinking of G.W.F. Hegel, Albrecht
Ritschl, Friedrich Schleiermacher, and others. They also were influenced
by the existential philosophy of Søren Kierkegaard.

And yet, in many ways, the rise of neo-orthodoxy was a sharp reaction
against liberalism. Barth once spent a semester lecturing on the theology
of Schleiermacher. During his lectures, he had on his desk a bust of Schleiermacher, to which he would address questions and criticisms. On the
last day of the class, he finished his lecture, then walked over to the bust
and knocked it to the floor, where it shattered into pieces. Barth wiped
his hands, grinned, and said, "So much for Schleiermacher."

Barth and his allies were concerned about the strong tendency toward
pantheism found in Hegelian and idealistic philosophy. They saw that the
emphasis on the immanence of God so identified Him with the universe
that His transcendence was obscured. If history is seen as the unfolding
of the Absolute Spirit, then God Himself is trapped within and shaped
by the world.

Barth believed this thinking was a result of the invasion of speculative
philosophy into the realm of Biblical revelation, an intrusion of an alien
rationalism that turned God into Reason with a capital R. He wanted a
return to a Biblical theology that was not controlled by logic or other
Aristotelian concepts.

However, Barth's rejection of liberalism did not mean that he simply reaffirmed classic Christian orthodoxy. Indeed, he was sharply critical of orthodoxy, denying the inerrancy of Scripture and with it both general revelation and natural theology. The thought of Thomas Aquinas came in for special criticism. For instance, Barth attacked the Thomist notion of the analogy of being (*analogia entis*), seeing in it the illegitimate use of an abstract concept of being that could apply both to God and to man.

To overcome the emphasis on the immanence of God in liberalism and to reassert the transcendence of God, the neo-orthodox theologians employed a phrase that has since crept into the vocabulary even of otherwise orthodox scholars. It is the term *wholly other*. They said God is not analogous to us but is quite different from us. He is other—not in part but in whole. He is totally different from us.

Thus, in their zeal to rescue God from immanentism, the neo-orthodox theologians fell into the error of the opposite extreme. The term *wholly other* is not only erroneous; it is exceedingly dangerous. Indeed, it does erase the analogy of being, but it also wipes out any possibility of the knowledge of God.

Why is that? To answer this question, I will illustrate by recalling a dialogue I had with a group of theological scholars who were critical of my approach to apologetics because it relied on logic, reason, and natural theology. They argued that God cannot be known from nature because God is wholly other from nature.

I replied by asking them how God can be known. Without hesitation they answered, "By revelation." I pushed the issue by asking, "But how can God reveal Himself?" They responded, "Through His Word [the Bible], through Christ, and through redemptive history."

By now it was clear to me that they were missing the force of my questions. So I put it plainly and directly. I said: "If God is 'wholly other' in the sense in which you are using the concept, if He is utterly and totally dissimilar to us, how could He possibly communicate anything meaningful about Himself to us? There would be no possible point of contact with our understanding between Him and us."

Suddenly the lights went on as they realized that if God were really wholly other, the only way we could speak of Him would be via the way of negation, by saying what He is not. This leaves us with Greek thought (Neoplatonism) with a vengeance. They responded in a manner like to that of a man who smacks himself in the forehead. "Perhaps we shouldn't say God is wholly other," they said.

Precisely. This concept should never be used by orthodox Christianity. It leaves us groping in darkness with only flimsy and unsound appeals to revelation, which revelation is not even possible.

It is because there is some analogy or similarity between us and God that revelation takes place. We really are created in God's image. That fact makes communication between God and us possible.

As a young college student, I attended a series of lectures at Westminster Theological Seminary in Philadelphia. It was in the halcyon days of that institution, when its faculty boasted such luminaries as Ned Stonehouse, E.J. Young, John Murray, and especially Cornelius Van Til. Van Til was a sharp critic of Barth, so sharp that Barth referred to him as a "man-eater."

During the conference, I was seated at the lunch table across from the professor of philosophy. I had just tasted some soup when the professor looked at me and said, "Young man, is God transcendent or immanent?" With an involuntary spasm, I spat the soup out of my mouth and nearly choked to death. I had no idea what the terms *transcendent* and *immanent* meant.

Seeing my embarrassment, the professor rushed to my aid. He explained that God is both transcendent and immanent. He is higher than the cosmos. He rises above and beyond it. His greatness surpasses anything that is creaturely. Yet at the same time, He is "connected to" His creation. He is immanent in His infinite being; He is immanent in history with His redemptive works, especially in the person of the incarnate Christ; He is immanent in His providential government; and He is immanent in our lives in the presence and power of the Holy Spirit. God is both above us and with us. To make Him totally identified with creation is to obscure His transcendence and slip into pantheism. But if we make Him totally transcendent, we slip into deism or sheer skepticism.

God reveals Himself in creation, but He is not the creation. The heavens declare His glory, but He is not the heavens. We are created in His image, but we are not gods. He is not to be identified with anything creaturely, but neither is He so remote as to be "wholly other." Rather, He is holy other. He is transcendent in His majesty, power, and being.

IMAGO DEI

JUNE 2003

——

T HERE ARE FEW THEOLOGICAL CONTROVERSIES more crucial than that which rages over the question of the nature of humanity. In our age, we face a real threat of the "abolition of man."

Modern thinkers have an overwhelming desire to wrench our understanding of ourselves out of any connection with the God of the Bible. But anthropology is married to theology. Take God out of the equation, and the question of the nature of man (*anthrōpos*) is left to stand or fall on its own. When God is driven into exile or vanquished altogether, people follow suit, for we are made in God's image. The image-bearer loses his significance the moment the One whose image he bears is eclipsed.

Thus, the message every young person gets today in the name of science and advanced education is that he or she is a cosmic accident, a grown-up germ that has emerged fortuitously from the slime, garbed temporarily in the guise of intelligence and intentionality (which are really myths that obscure the truth of sheer physical causes). This intelligent animal (*Homo sapiens*) is said to share the destiny of the snail and the octopus, the abyss of nothingness.

Thus, man is reduced to a brute of insignificant origin. And modern culture has embraced this animalistic view of human beings in the arenas of science, law, public education, the arts, and business.

The humanist declares that people still have dignity, but it is a declaration without substance. Cosmic accidents don't have a lot of dignity in the grand scheme of things. For a creature who lives between the poles of an origin of insignificance and a destiny of insignificance, it seems ludicrous to imagine any dignity. If Christianity embraces faith, humanism embraces credulity, as it has a view of humanity that at best is Pollyanna-like. Better the existentialism of Sartre, who at least had the courage to take humanism to its logical conclusion and say man is a "useless passion."

While there is great rancor today over such issues as gender equity and sexual orientation, the deeper question is voiced by the cynic, who asks simply, "Who cares?" What difference does it make whether males exploit females or whether the beast is heterosexual or homosexual in its orientation? We don't get excited about the sexual proclivities of worms, so why care about those of people? If, indeed, people are sophisticated animals, bestial in their fundamental constitution, then ultimately it doesn't really matter much whether towers collapse on them or snipers pick them off one at a time.

At this point, Biblical Christianity is on a collision course with the secular culture, for it offers a radically different view of humans. First, we are not God or gods. We are creatures, indeed creatures of the dust. Second, we are not mere brutes. Though not divine, there is some sense in which we are like God. An image cannot reflect something utterly dissimilar to it. Rather, an image is a likeness of something beyond itself. It is not the original, but it mirrors the original.

Historically, theology has wrestled over the content of the image, over the issue of how we are like God. Traditionally, the point of likeness has been seen in those areas in which we share in the communicable attributes of God.

For example, God is a rational being—He has a mind and intelligence. Though our minds are limited by our creatureliness, we still have the capacity of thinking. (For centuries many assumed that animals cannot think but act only on "instinct," a category that may be a distinction without a difference.)

Also, we understand that God is a volitional being in that He acts according to His divine will. His will is sovereign, but that does not preclude or exclude the existence of lesser volitional creatures. We also enjoy the faculty of volition as we exercise our wills in the making of choices.

Others have sought to establish the image of God (*imago Dei*) in our status. Just as God exercises full dominion over the created order, He has delegated to human beings a lesser dominion over the animal world and the earth. In this role, we function as vicegerents of God, or as His appointed deputies.

Still other attempts have been made to locate the image in our human capacity for "I-Thou" relationships. Karl Barth spoke of man's uniqueness in his being made *Homo relationis*. Just as the persons of the Trinity enjoy an eternal relationship among themselves, so we find our significance in our male/female relationships.

Finally, the question of dignity is tied to the *imago Dei*. From a Biblical perspective, human beings do not have inherent or intrinsic dignity. In other words, our dignity (which is real) is not eternal or self-existent. Rather, we have dignity that is extrinsic—it comes to us from without. We have dignity because God assigns dignity to us. He has taken the initiative to stamp His image upon us.

That we bear the image of the God of glory is an unspeakable blessing. But with this elevated status comes a weighty responsibility. We were made to glorify God—to reflect the character of God. That duty comes in the divine mandate: "You shall be holy, for I the LORD your God am holy" (Lev. 19:2).

It is our ability to reflect the holiness of God that has been shattered by the Fall. Sin distorts the image of God. When the deputy sins, the Regent Himself is slandered.

But even with the Fall, by which the image is marred and the reflection of the Creator is clouded and besmirched, the image itself is not destroyed. Even in our fallenness, the communicable attributes of God are made manifest.

LIKE FATHER, LIKE SON

———

WHEN WE MEET SOMEONE FOR the first time, we usually ask him or her three questions: What is your name? Where do you live? What do you do?

The last question inquires about vocation. We are asking what the person "does for a living." In a word, we are asking about his or her work.

For most of our adult lives, we are engaged in some type of labor. What we do often defines for ourselves and/or for others who we are. Our personhood is tied up with our work. And this is not an improper thing. For instance, in the study of Christology, we distinguish between the person of Christ and the work of Christ. Yet the more we understand the person of Christ, the deeper we can understand the significance of His work. Likewise, the more we probe the meaning of the work, the greater understanding we gain of His person. So person and work go together. To some degree, we are what we do.

It was Karl Marx who challenged man's intellectual capacity as the defining characteristic of human existence. He argued that instead of describing humanity as *Homo sapiens,* we should use the term *Homo faber*—"man the maker." It is the making of tools and goods that defines world history, he said. Marx further theorized that the dialectical pattern of the development of history is determined by the conflict of economic forces. At root, these forces are inseparably related to our labor.

Marx saw the industrial revolution and the triumph of capitalism as bringing on a crisis that touched the very core of human existence. The crisis was one of alienation—chiefly alienation of a person from his labor. In agrarian societies, people were more or less self-sufficient. They produced the goods they consumed. They owned their tools, the means of production, and, most important, the fruit of their own labor. But with the advent of the factory and the forces of mass production, the dilemma

286

became, "How are we going to keep them down on the farm (after they've been to Paris)?" The constancy of regular weekly income that was not dependent on the vicissitudes of the weather or other vagaries of nature enticed many to seek the "security" of being wage earners.

Marx saw this shift as a seduction of free people into slavery. The wage-earner, though he can go home at night, is a virtual slave to the factory owner. He no longer owns the fruit of his labor; instead, he works for someone else who owns the fruit. Marx further understood that whoever owns the tools (the means of production) controls the game.

I learned this lesson as a child while playing baseball in the sandlot. Without the benefit of umpires, we had to monitor our own games. Sometimes disputes were negotiated—"You're out!" "I'm safe!" "You're out!" "I'm safe!"—until one player would say: "It's my ball and my bat. I'm safe!" There could be no more game without the necessary tools of bat and ball, so the argument was settled via political expediency.

Marx's complaint was that when a person was alienated from his labor he became alienated from others, from nature, and from himself. Thus, he called for the overthrow of capitalist society, the end of private ownership (which leads to the enslavement of the proletariat), and the creation of a classless society wherein everybody owns everything.

What he failed so miserably to understand was that when everybody owns everything, then nobody owns anything. The classless society was a fantasy that never materialized because bureaucrats became the new ruling class and production fell so steeply that the human standard of living dropped with it. A real slavery emerged with iron curtains and brick walls.

Marx's dream became a monstrous evil, a monumental failure. Yet he had genuine insights about the makeup of human beings. He also understood that ownership is liberating. This truth is the genius of capitalism—every person, no matter how poor, can become an owner via investment.

Our work is a vital part of our identity. It is not the curse of humanity but the sacred vocation of the human race. It is not work that makes us free, but it is work that makes us obedient.

As creatures made in the image of God, we are to imitate God in certain ways. One such way involves work. God is a working God—a Creator. In His work of Creation, He formed the cosmos, then assigned tasks to His creatures:

> Then God blessed them, and God said to them, "Be fruitful and multiply; fill the earth and subdue it; have dominion over the fish of the sea, over the birds of the air, and over every living thing that moves on the earth" (Gen. 1:28).

We were created to dress, till, and keep the earth. We were made to be fruitful—to be productive as God is productive. And God assigned us these tasks before the Fall. Thus, labor is not a curse; it is a blessing that goes with Creation. The sanctity of human labor is rooted in the work of God Himself and in His call to us to imitate Him.

God's labor did not cease on the seventh day. Though He "rested" from the labor of Creation, He continued to sustain and govern what He had made. Jesus called attention to this truth in one of His disputes with the Pharisees:

> For this reason the Jews persecuted Jesus, and sought to kill Him, because He had done these things on the Sabbath. But Jesus answered them, "My Father has been working until now, and I have been working" (John 5:16–17).

In an agrarian society, as "self-sufficient" as people seemed to be, no one was completely self-sufficient. From creation itself we see a division of labor that makes community not only possible but necessary. When we are hired as part of a work force, we can be productive and fulfilled—if our skills and performance match the corporate needs. When our skills and desires collide with the purposes of the group, then we experience alienation.

For the individual's benefit and the good of the corporation, the alienated person, whether the chief executive or an entry-level clerk, should seek employment elsewhere. A person's labor is sacred. It cannot prosper if mismatched with corporate goals or missions. Blessed is the person whose personal mission is in harmony with the mission of the group. In this situation, both the individual and the group can work together for the glory of God, and escape alienation from labor.

"As creatures made in the image of God, we are to imitate God in certain ways. One such way involves work."

VESSELS OF CLAY

AUGUST 2003

———

I F ANY CHURCH FATHER HAS BEEN subjected to the rigorous twist-ing and distorting of his views to accommodate modern agendas and historical revisionism, it is the third-century apologist Tertullian.

Tertullian, whose full name was Quintus Septimius Florens Tertullian, earned the title of "Father of Latin Theology." He lived mainly in Carthage, in North Africa, between A.D. 160 and 220. Converted in midlife, he applied his skills as a trained lawyer to the intellectual defense of the Christian faith.

Two quotes frequently are attributed to Tertullian. The first is surely genuine; the second highly suspect.

The first quote is this: "What has Athens to do with Jerusalem? What agreement is there between the academy and the church?"

These questions are rhetorical, and the answer to each is assumed to be an emphatic negative. Tertullian fiercely upheld the superiority of Apostolic revelation to speculative philosophy. He was sharply critical of the philosophers of Athens—Plato, Aristotle, and others—but not so critical that he would never appeal to them when they could be enlisted in the cause of the defense of Christianity. Tertullian was engaged in intellectual combat with the heretics of his day, especially with the Gnos-tics, who sought at times to supplant Biblical revelation with their own mystical and speculative theories, and at other times to claim Apostolic endorsement of their views.

Tertullian defended both the authority of Scripture and the authority of the church, standing on the shoulders of Irenaeus.

The second quote is probably spurious, but it is regularly attributed to Tertullian. It is the phrase "*Credo ad absurdum,*" which literally means "I believe because it is absurd." The idea that there is some sort of virtue in believing something because it is absurd is a welcome creed to a post-modern culture heavily influenced by existential irrationalism. A whole tradition of twentieth-century "dialectical" theologians gloried in the irrational, with Karl Barth declaring that one does not become a mature Christian until he is willing to affirm both poles of a contradiction. His compatriot Emil Brunner insisted that the contradiction is the hallmark of truth. These theologians had such an aversion to rationalism that they ended by sacrificing rationality.

This approach to theology breeds fideism, by which faith is not only distinguished from but separated from reason as the sole basis for Christian truth. Fideists tend to be skeptical about the use of reason or evidence to defend Christian truth claims. In their view, to be "rational" is to sink into a sub-Christian or anti-Christian form of pagan Greek thinking.

Even in modern Reformed theology, we see a tendency toward irrationalism, even to the point where some "Reformed" scholars actually argue that the law of non-contradiction does not apply to the mind of God. This view would destroy all confidence in Scripture because whatever the Bible teaches might mean its antithesis in the mind of God. In His thinking, Jesus could be both Christ and Antichrist at the same time and in the same relationship.

For such thinkers, who abhor logic, Tertullian rises as a hero. But when we examine the writings of Tertullian, especially his *Prescriptions against Heretics* (*De Praescriptionibus Haereticorum*), we see that Tertullian was not opposed to reason. The quote attributed to him was actually an allusion to the Biblical idea that what is true may be regarded as foolish by those whose minds are darkened by sin. Tertullian also appealed to natural revelation as the basis for certain truths that were grasped and defended by pagan philosophers. His critique of Gnostic thought provides rich insights sorely needed in our time as we witness the resurgence of Neo-Gnosticism, not only in the culture, but in the church as well.

Like Tertullian, Origen (A.D. 186 to 255) was a third-century apologist. His ministry was exercised, for the most part, in Alexandria, which had been a center of Hellenistic Judaism. The major intellectual center in Egypt yielded such leaders as Clement, who also labored as an apologist.

Origen was not unlike the fabled little girl who had a little curl right in the middle of her forehead. Like this damsel, Origen, when he was good, was very, very good, but when he was bad, he was horrid. In Origen we see the conjoined strengths and weaknesses that tended to characterize the early church fathers. In the sub-apostolic age, the church lacked the titanic power of the original Apostles. Neither did it enjoy the cumulative insight that took centuries to develop and geniuses like Augustine to express.

Among Origen's accomplishments were his apologetic reply to the philosopher Celsus (*Contra Celsus*) and his defense of the divine inspiration of the Bible. Unfortunately, in his defense of the Bible he was weak in his understanding of the historical reliability of Scripture. To defend the Bible, he hastened to employ an allegorical method of interpreting it, a method that harmed the church's understanding of Scripture for centuries to come.

The irony of Origen's allegorical approach to Scripture is seen in his rash act of self-castration. Because both men and women were attending his classes, he sought to guard against sexual temptation. He took Jesus' words, "There are eunuchs who have made themselves eunuchs for the kingdom of heaven's sake" (Matt. 19:12b), in a radically literal way, taking no solace in the allegorizing of this text. This action created a credibility problem for him, and Origen soon came under attack from Bishop Demetrius, who made life miserable for Origen for years to come.

In his teaching, Origen adopted a Greek view of the pre-existence of the soul, taught universalism, raised questions about the physical nature of Christ's resurrection body, and held a defective view of the Trinity. (We must remember that the church was still reflecting deeply on the matter of the Trinity and had not yet come to a fixed understanding of it.) However, his work on prayer has come down as a treasured treatise, as well as his teaching on martyrdom. He expressed hope that his life would end in the highest manner of virtue, by being martyred for Christ's sake. That was not to happen, as he died of natural causes in 255. However, the church historian Eusebius testifies that Origen suffered profound agony during the Decian persecution—being tortured, stretched, and confined to a dungeon in chains.

Origen's personal love for and devotion to Christ gives us a glimpse of Christian piety in the third century.

THE SILENCE OF THE LAMBS

SEPTEMBER 2003

I WOULD LIKE TO MUSE ABOUT and opine regarding the question of why American Christians suffer so little persecution while people in other nations today pay with their lives for their Christian confession. But before I speculate on this matter, I would like to retreat into the past and glance briefly at an episode in the life and ministry of the Apostle Paul:

> And about that time there arose a great commotion about the Way. For a certain man named Demetrius, a silversmith, who made silver shrines of Diana, brought no small profit to the craftsmen. He called them together with the workers of similar occupation, and said: "Men, you know that we have our prosperity by this trade. Moreover you see and hear that not only at Ephesus, but throughout almost all Asia, this Paul has persuaded and turned away many people, saying that they are not gods which are made with hands. So not only is this trade of ours in danger of falling into disrepute, but also the temple of the great goddess Diana may be despised and her magnificence destroyed, whom all Asia and the world worship." Now when they heard this, they were full of wrath and cried out, saying, "Great is Diana of the Ephesians!" So the whole city was filled with confusion, and rushed into the theater with one accord, having seized Gaius and Aristarchus, Macedonians, Paul's travel companions (Acts 19:23–29).

In first-century Ephesus, it was a dangerous business to be a travel companion of Paul. And it seems that being closely linked to Paul and to his Master has been a dangerous enterprise ever since.

If we look at the issues that sparked the riot in Ephesus, we see two major points of conflict. The first was economic; the second, theological. Demetrius and his cohorts were threatened economically because their livelihood depended upon revenues gleaned from the sin of idolatry. If the mission of Paul succeeded, they would be put out of business. The theological issue was the status of pagan religion in the face of the bold claims of the Apostles. Paul preached that there was only one true God and one true Messiah. All other religions were exposed as false, pagan, and idolatrous. This claim to exclusive truth provoked sharp conflict with the pagan world, which resulted in the martyrdom of multitudes of Christians.

Why do such things not happen to Americans? One factor is obvious. The United States was founded by refugees from religious persecution. They desired to create a nation that would be a haven for religious liberty. It was not by accident that the very first amendment to the Constitution guaranteed the free exercise of religion. Since its inception, this nation has taken such a strong stand on behalf of religious liberty that we still enjoy the benefits of that legacy. It may be, however, that we are living on borrowed capital, inasmuch as this country's commitment to the free exercise of religion wanes almost daily. The erosion of this freedom is subtle at times, but it is nevertheless real.

In New England, the same community structure is evident in almost every town. At the very center of the town we see a church (or churches). In our day, more and more communities are developed with no room permitted for the erection of churches. By the fiat of zoning regulations, churches are moved "outside" the boundaries of community life. We may still attend church, but the church is no longer permitted to be in the center of our communities.

In the United States, we are still "free" to exercise our faith, but the arena of that exercise is more and more limited to a "reservation." The unspoken rule is that we must not exercise our faith in the public square. For instance, Franklin Graham was asked to pray in a public meeting, but was excoriated when he dared to pray in the name of Christ. (He broke one of the unspoken rules.)

Still, there remains some constitutional restraint on those who would persecute Christians for their faith. The restraint is there, but it grows more tenuous by the hour.

In addition to our legal protection, we must also face the decline in passion for the cause of Christ by the modern church. Perhaps we have too much to lose by declaring the uniqueness of Christ. When a Christian wanders off the reservation and emulates the message of the Apostles, he meets fierce opposition. Sadly, much of the opposition comes from the Christian community itself. Defense Secretary Donald Rumsfeld said of Washington, D.C., "Your friends are those who stab you in the chest." But when a Christian leaves the reservation, he is usually shot in the back by his own people, who don't want to be hurt if opposition is stirred up.

Avoidance of conflict is a frequent goal of the contemporary church. I discovered this when I published a book on abortion and produced a video series on it for churches. Of some 60 books I have published, the one that had the shortest tenure before going out of print was *Abortion: A Rational Look at an Emotional Issue.* The video series continues to collect dust. When we inquired of churches why they weren't interested in the series, we received the same response time and again: "This might divide the congregation." Who dares to declare in this age that the "pro-choice" position is not only incorrect, but manifestly evil?

America is the place of baseball, Chevrolet, and apple pie. At least it was. Now it seems it is baseball, Chevrolet, and pornography. According to a recent report from the National Coalition for the Protection of Children and Families, Hughes Electronics, which owns DirecTV, is the largest distributor of pornography via satellite in America, with 10.9 million households. (General Motors, the parent company of Hughes Electronics, recently announced plans to sell the business after much pleading by the coalition.) Likewise, Comcast is the largest distributor of pornography via cable, with more than 21 million households.

Such companies are the "silversmiths" of our day. If the church united in its resistance against these corporate giants, I wonder how long we would be asking why we weren't being persecuted.

As long as we compromise the Gospel and seek the safety of the reservation, we have little to fear from the pagan culture that surrounds us. If we become clear with the Gospel, then things will change and we will take our place as companions of the Apostle Paul.

"In the United States, we are still 'free' to exercise our faith, but the arena of that exercise is more and more limited to a 'reservation.'"

THE MEANING OF ENDS

OCTOBER 2003

THE MAJOR RAP AGAINST CALVINISM is contained in the ceaseless mantra that it undermines the church's mission of evangelism. After all, if John Calvin's understanding of predestination is true, then there is no urgency to the evangelistic task. Why bother with vigorous outreach if the number of the elect was settled in eternity and nothing we do or don't do can change the immutable decrees of God?

The response to this criticism is threefold. In the first instance, the reply is Biblical exegesis. The second is the response of historic theology. The third is the testimony of history.

With respect to the first reply, we note that the doctrine of election is not the invention of Calvin—or of Martin Luther, or even of Augustine. It is the teaching of Scripture, to which the aforementioned greats of the church were simply being faithful.

Election is taught throughout Scripture, but most clearly in the teaching of the church's premier theologian, the Apostle Paul. Nowhere is Paul clearer in his proclamation of election than in the ninth chapter of Romans. But Paul also penned the 10th chapter of Romans. There he writes:

> For there is no distinction between Jew and Greek, for the same Lord over all is rich to all who call upon Him. For "whoever calls on the name of the Lord shall be saved." How then shall they call on Him in whom they have not believed? And how shall they believe in Him of whom they have not heard? And how shall they hear without a preacher? And how shall they preach unless they are sent? As it is written: "How beautiful are the feet of those who preach the gospel of peace, who bring glad tidings of good things!" (Rom. 10:12–15).

Here Paul gives a list of sequential rhetorical questions, questions that can be answered only in the negative. The tacit answer to each question is obvious: "They can't." So it goes: How can they call upon Him in whom they have not believed? They can't. How can they believe in Him of whom they have not heard? They can't. How can they hear without a preacher? They can't. How can they preach if they are not sent? They can't.

These questions, with their clearly implied answers, consistently express the Apostle's understanding of the way of salvation, the way in which the eternal purposes of God are carried out in time and space. Paul elsewhere makes it clear that God not only chooses whom He will save but also by what means they shall come to salvation. God not only chooses people, He chooses a method to reach those people. He has chosen the foolishness of preaching as that means. He has purposed that it should be by the power of the Gospel, which is the power of God unto salvation (Rom. 1:16).

Election is not an abstract notion that is not worked out in the reality of history. The elect are saved by faith, by believing in the Gospel preached unto them and heard by them. They respond not in the flesh but in the power of the Holy Spirit working on them and within them.

In theological terms, we make a distinction between ends and means to those ends. With respect to God's sovereignty in election, we understand that He sovereignly decrees not only the ends but also the means to those ends. It is God's sovereign command of evangelism that is His appointed means to the ends He has decreed.

At the heart of the doctrines of grace stands the doctrine of God's sovereignty. What gross folly it would be for a Calvinist to declare that he believes that God is sovereign in His decree of election (the end) but not sovereign in His decree of evangelism (the means). If we had no other reason to evangelize than that a sovereign God commands that we be engaged in evangelism, that reason would be sufficient to bind our consciences absolutely and to impose a holy obligation upon the entire church. Any person who claimed to be a Calvinist while eschewing evangelism would reveal that he is not only not a Calvinist but is guilty of slandering the very Calvinism he claims to embrace.

Thus, in the first instance, we evangelize because we are commanded to do so. But obedience to the divine command is not our only motive for evangelism. Far beyond being a duty and responsibility, evangelism is also an unspeakable privilege and opportunity.

In Romans 10:15, Paul cites this statement of the prophet Isaiah: "How beautiful are the feet of those who preach the gospel of peace, who bring glad tidings of good things!" Here, the feet of those who carry the treasure of the Gospel are called "beautiful." The human agents to whom God entrusts the power of the Gospel are honored by their participation in God's saving plan of redemption.

No preacher, no evangelist, no human being has the power to bring forth the fruit of the Gospel. The power is not in the preacher but in God, who empowers the Gospel for fruit. I can plant or I can water, but only God can bring the increase. Yet planting and watering are great privileges delegated to us by God. He could carry out these activities without us. But He has chosen to include us in the holy drama of redemption.

Finally, the testimony of history to Calvinism does not reveal evangelistic inertia but rather evangelistic boldness and aggression. We recall the Reformation as the greatest awakening in the history of Christendom. This awakening was driven by the human agency of men sold out to the doctrine of election, including Luther, Calvin, and John Knox.

Likewise, the greatest revival in American history, the Great Awakening, was led chiefly by three preachers. The three men God used most powerfully in this evangelistic endeavor were John Wesley, Jonathan Edwards, and George Whitefield. Two of these men were fully committed to Calvinistic theology (Edwards and Whitefield), while the third (Wesley), while not embracing the doctrines of grace, came out of a church communion whose confession of faith was Calvinistic. Whitefield's passion for souls was matched by his passion for the doctrines of grace.

In our own time, we see an ongoing accent on evangelism among Reformed churches and ministries. For instance, the only ministry that I know of that is currently operating in every single nation on planet earth is Evangelism Explosion, a ministry founded by a convinced Calvinist. In the seminary where I teach (Knox Theological Seminary), every member of the faculty is required to be engaged in evangelism on a regular basis. In this respect, we are not only heirs of Knox and the Reformation, but of George Whitefield, as well.

"Far beyond being a duty and responsibility, evangelism is also an unspeakable privilege and opportunity."

FOOL'S GOD

NOVEMBER 2003

———

A S A BOY, I WAS A DEVOTED FOLLOWER of the "Hot Stove League." This league took place between the end of the Major League Baseball season in October and the beginning of the next season in April. It received its name from the image of men ensconced in a hunting cabin and warming themselves around a wood-burning stove while swapping fantasies about possible trades. The dream was that your favorite team could trade some nonproductive player and get a superstar in return, a player who would lead the team to the pennant.

In Pittsburgh, the dream was a fixation. Our joke was that the Pirates were in first place in the National League—if you turned the newspaper upside down. Each year I rooted for the "cellar" team. The only good thing about our team was Ralph Kiner, the Hall of Fame–bound home-run hitter. A ball autographed by No. 4 adorns my desk in the office.

Then came the fateful day—"Doomsday" in the eyes of Pirate fans—when word came over the wires that Kiner was involved in a "blockbuster" trade with the Chicago Cubs. Kiner had been swapped for a couple of mediocre players, plus "a player to be named later." It turned out that this mystery player was the key to the deal. He was a highly promising minor leaguer who, when he came up to the Pirates, was about as hot as his last name. (I'll keep you guessing on that, but it rhymes with "Sneeze.")

With every trade, hopes soar. We part with someone or something we are willing to let go in order that we can gain something we want but presently lack. Sometimes trades benefit both parties, but this ideal is rarely realized.

Though the Kiner trade was a bad deal, it pales into insignificance when compared with the worst of all possible trades. Far and away, the worst trade is a theological one. It is a trade that we might deem foolish—nay, incredibly stupid. But its utter stupidity is exceeded by its wickedness. This trade is one in which God Himself is exchanged for an idol.

In Romans 1 Paul describes this exchange: "...although they knew God, they did not glorify Him as God, nor were thankful, but became futile in their thoughts, and their foolish hearts were darkened. Professing to be wise, they became fools, and changed the glory of the incorruptible God into an image made like corruptible man—and birds and four-footed animals and creeping things. Therefore God also gave them up to uncleanness, in the lusts of their hearts, to dishonor their bodies among themselves, who exchanged the truth of God for the lie, and worshiped and served the creature rather than the Creator, who is blessed forever. Amen" (Rom. 1:21–25).

How dumb is this deal? Swapping the immortal, invisible, only-wise God for a creepy crawler? Or trading the eternal God of majestic glory for a totem pole or a carp?

Imagine a craftsman taking an inert block of wood or stone, then sculpting it into the image of a fish. When his work is finished, he cleans up the chips from the floor, puts away his chisel and hammer, then falls on his knees to pray to the deaf and dumb object he just made for himself. The Old Testament prophets scoffed at those who fashioned idols by their own hands.

And yet, this sort of trade is approved by every human being. There is no sin more basic, no sin more common to humanity than the sin of idolatry. It is the oldest sin known to man.

Why such stupidity? Why such evil? Why do we all have the propensity to swap the truth for the lie? Obviously it is because we desire the lie more than the truth.

The truth about ourselves in light of the glory of God is too painful to behold. It reduces us to radical corruption. It reveals our sin. This revelation is so threatening to us that we stop at nothing to drive God from our thoughts. By nature, we will not have Him in our thinking: He must be banished from our consciousness, exiled from our lives. The vacuum left by His departure may then be filled by more friendly "deities," those we create for ourselves who make no absolute claims upon us.

Simply put, none of us wants to be judged in light of the absolute standard of the holiness of God. We would rather be judged against a lesser standard—say the standard of the snake or the crocodile. The morality of snakes does not embarrass me. The ethics of the crocodile do not intimidate me. I can compete with creatures, but not with God. And so, we exchange the Creator for the creature.

Unfortunately, conversion does not suddenly erase our proclivity for idolatry. This sin lurks at the door of every Christian. It simply manifests itself in more subtle and sophisticated ways than by the fashioning of the image of a snake or a cow.

Idolatry grabs us by the throat when we "remodel" the Biblical God into one of our own liking. We approach God as if His attributes were special dishes offered at a smorgasbord. We carry our tray through the line and select a little love, a portion of grace, and a double helping of mercy. But we plead a special diet when we pass by His holiness, justice, wrath, and sovereignty. By stripping God of His sovereignty, His omniscience, or His omnipotence, we cut Him down to a size we can live with.

It is no wonder that the Law of God puts so much weight on the prohibition against idolatry. The first four of the Ten Commandments all deal with this sin in one way or another.

God and God alone is worthy of our worship. His attributes are not subject to change or negotiation. We must constantly examine our thoughts to insure the God we affirm is the Biblical God in the fullness of His glory. Anything less is an idol of our own making—a lie that has been substituted for the truth.

There is no trading season for God. The only Hot Stove League that seeks to swap Him for something better is the league of hell itself.

THE WORK OF CHRIST

DECEMBER 2003

——

O NE OF THE MOST FRIVOLOUS theological controversies of all time, a dispute that made the question of how many angels can dance on the head of a pin seem respectable by contrast, was the "omphalos debate." This controversy focused on the anatomy of Adam: Did God fashion the first man with or without a belly button (omphalos)? Since the omphalos, or navel, is a result of tying the umbilical cord after birth, it would seem that Adam, having been created in the adult stage of life, had no place to display a navel ring. But perhaps God adorned Adam with a navel to display his solidarity with his progeny.

Who knows? But more important, who cares? This question gives substance to the definition of idle curiosity.

But a related question is not at all a matter of frivolity. This question asks, "Why did the second person of the Trinity, the eternal Logos, become incarnate as a baby?" In other words, why didn't the Word made flesh come fully grown (like Adam) into this world? Why did the Son of Man not descend from heaven on a cloud of glory; go straight to Jerusalem to suffer, die, and rise again; then return via ascension to glory?

Or, to approach the question from a different angle, why didn't Mary and Joseph take their babe to Jerusalem (a journey of only a few miles) and sacrifice Him there on the altar? Could not the baby Jesus have served as a perfect sacrifice for our sin? Would the atonement of the Christ child have been any less efficacious than that of the adult Jesus? After all, wasn't the baby also both divine and human? Was He not also *vere homo, vere Deus* (truly man and truly God)? The church long ago rejected any form of adoptionist Christology that envisioned a human Jesus gradually becoming divine. At no point in Jesus' life was He ever anything less than truly man and truly God.

The New Testament makes much of Jesus' role as the "last Adam" (sometimes called the "New Adam" or the "Second Adam"). As Paul declares: "And so it is written, 'The first man Adam became a living being.' The last Adam became a life-giving spirit. However, the spiritual is not first, but the natural, and afterward the spiritual. The first man was of the earth, made of dust; the second Man is the Lord from heaven. As was the man of dust, so also are those who are made of dust; and as is the heavenly Man, so also are those who are heavenly. And as we have borne the image of the man of dust, we shall also bear the image of the heavenly Man" (1 Cor. 15:45–49).

Although there is a great contrast between the two Adams, we see some crucial similarities. Both Adams were put in a testing place of probation. Both were exposed to the unbridled assault of Satan. But whereas Adam succumbed to the tempter and disobeyed the Creator, Jesus trampled over the evil one by His obedience to God.

At this point, we see why it was critical for Jesus, our Mediator, to spend time on earth before His atoning death. We remember that our salvation rests not only upon the death of Christ, but also upon His life. In the Atonement, He took the curse of God on sin for us. He paid the penalty we deserve. That took care of our guilt before God. However, it did nothing to solve our lack of righteousness or merit before God. For this reason, there is a two-fold imputation in our salvation, according to Scripture. God not only imputes our guilt to Christ; He imputes Christ's righteousness to us. That righteousness or merit of Christ is an achievement. Jesus gained righteousness by obeying the law of God at every point during His life.

At Jesus' baptism, John hesitated, thinking it wrong to baptize the One who was without sin. Why "cleanse" a Lamb without blemish? John protested, saying to Jesus, "I need to be baptized by You, and are You coming to me?" (Matt. 3:14). The words of Jesus' reply are important to our understanding of His role as the last Adam: "Permit it to be so now, for thus it is fitting for us to fulfill all righteousness" (3:15).

"To fulfill all righteousness." You see, Jesus' task included more than the Cross. We distinguish in theology between the passive obedience of

Christ (suffering God's wrath on the cross) and His perfect, active obedience (His perfect fulfillment of the law). Both were necessary for our salvation. Thus, Jesus' mission not only required that He die on the cross, but that He obey every law that God imposed upon His people. (And since God now required baptism of His people, it was required also of Jesus, even though He Himself was sinless.)

This could explain why Jesus didn't descend immediately to Jerusalem and submit to crucifixion. Jesus was baptized in the Jordan and sent to the wilderness to be tempted by Satan at the beginning of His three years of public ministry. That period of active obedience could have been enough to satisfy the Law if Jesus, like Adam, had come on the scene as an adult.

Yet we still have the question of the period from His birth to His baptism. Why was He born to grow into adulthood?

Because of His corporate solidarity with His people, Jesus bore their sins and fulfilled all the demands of the Law. In this role, we see a strong identity between Christ and Old Testament Israel. In His person, Jesus fulfilled the elements of the Old Testament. He was the Tabernacle. He was the Bread from heaven. He was the Light. He was the Mercy Seat.

In the gospel according to Matthew, we are told that Jesus' parents were warned to flee into Egypt to escape Herod's "slaughter of the innocents" (Matt. 2:13–16). They remained in Egypt until the death of Herod. Then we are told that the family's return fulfilled Old Testament prophecy (Matt. 2:15). Here Jesus, as a child, recapitulated the Exodus. He, like Israel, was the "Son" who was called.

The link to Israel is noted often in the gospel of John. Not the least of these references is found in John 15:1. "I am the true vine, and my Father is the vinedresser." It is hard to read these words and not think of Psalm 80: "You have brought a vine out of Egypt; You have cast out the nations, and planted. . . . Return, we beseech You, O God of hosts; look down from heaven and see, and visit this vine and the vineyard which Your right had has planted, and the branch that You made strong for Yourself. . . . Let Your hand be upon the man of Your right hand, upon the son of man whom You made strong for Yourself" (Ps. 80:8, 14–15, 17).

Israel was God's vine, and Jesus, as the true vine, has fulfilled that role. In the metaphor, the vine is planted by God. Israel was a "babe" as a nation at the Exodus. So Jesus, as the true Israel, began as a babe, but He grew to manhood and fulfilled the destiny of Israel for His Father and for His people.

"What the New Covenant has that the Old Covenant lacked is the fulfillment of the promised Messiah. In a word, we have Jesus—the Word made flesh."

—

THE SUPREMACY OF CHRIST

JANUARY 2004

——

I WONDER IF IT IS PROPER to have a "favorite" book of the Bible. The idea scratches like fingernails on a chalk-board. What would induce us to prefer one portion of the Word of God to another? It would seem that to hear God say anything would be such a delight to the soul that every word that proceeds from His mouth would excite the soul to the same degree. Perhaps when we reach glory, our delight in Him and in His Word will be such that it will know no comparative degrees.

In the meantime we are left with our varied inclinations. When I think of "favorite" books of the Bible, I always place Hebrews near the very top. Why? In the first instance, this book masterfully connects the Old Testament and the New Testament. What Augustine said is true: "The New is in the Old concealed, and the Old is in the New revealed." The bridge between the two is Hebrews.

Hebrews is a book of comparisons and contrasts. The New Covenant is seen against the backdrop of the Old. The New is seen as being better. "Better" is the operative word. The New Covenant is better because it is more inclusive (it includes Gentiles); it has a better Mediator; a better High Priest; a better King; and a better revelation of God.

What the New Covenant has that the Old Covenant lacked is the fulfillment of the promised Messiah. In a word, we have Jesus—the Word made flesh.

Indeed, as the author of Hebrews (whom I believe was Paul, possibly through an amanuensis) describes the person and work of Jesus, the comparative quickly changes to the superlative. It is not enough to see Jesus as simply being "better" than what came before. He is more than better; He is the best.

In this regard, Hebrews focuses on the supremacy of Christ. To speak of "supremacy" is to speak of that which is "above" or "over" others. It reaches the level of the "super." In our language it refers to that which (or who) is greatest in power, authority, or rank. It is also used to describe that which (or who) is greatest in importance, significance, character, or achievement—the "ultimate."

In all these areas of consideration, Jesus ranks as the ultimate or supreme—supreme in power, rank, glory, authority, importance, etc.

The high Christology of Hebrews is set against the background of the Old Testament. Hebrews begins with the attestation of Christ as the supreme revelation of God: "God, who at various times and in various ways spoke in time past to the fathers by the prophets, has in these last days spoken to us by His Son, whom He has appointed heir of all things, through whom also He made the worlds; who being the brightness of His glory and the express image of His person, and upholding all things by the word of His power . . ." (Heb. 1:1–3a, NKJV).

Here the supremacy of Christ is His preeminence over the Old Testament prophets. Those prophets spoke the Word of God—but Christ is *the* Word of God. He is not merely a prophet in a long line of prophets. He is the Prophet par excellence. This supreme revelation comes from Him, the One who is more than a prophet—the very Son of God. In this opening passage of Hebrews there is enough weighty Christology to occupy the most astute theologians for their entire lives without exhausting its richness. Here Christ is seen as the Creator of the world and the One who upholds it by His power. He is the Creator of all things and the Heir of all things. He is the very brightness of the glory of God. Again, it is not enough to say that He is the supreme reflection of divine glory. Nay, He is the brightness of that glory. He is the express image of God's person, the One who bears the *imago Dei* supremely.

Next, Hebrews sets forth the contrast between the person and function of angels to Jesus. No angel rises to the level of the only begotten Son of God. Angels are not to be worshiped—yet the angels are commanded to worship Christ. The Kingdom is not given to angels; it is given to Christ who alone is seated at the right hand of God the Father in the position of cosmic authority. In every way Christ has supremacy over the angels and is not to be confused as being one of them.

Then the author of Hebrews details the supremacy of Christ over Moses. Surely Moses is the most exalted person of the Old Testament in his role of Mediator of the Law. We read, "Therefore, holy brethren, partakers of the heavenly calling, consider the Apostle and High Priest of our confession, Christ Jesus, who was faithful to Him who appointed Him, as Moses also was faithful in all His house. For this One has been counted worthy of more glory than Moses, inasmuch as He who built the house has more honor than the house. For every house is built by someone, but He who built all things is God. And Moses indeed was faithful in all His house as a servant, . . . but Christ as a son over His own house, whose house we are. . . ." (Heb. 3:1–6a, NKJV).

The contrasts here are among the servant of the house, the builder of the house, and the owner of the house. The builder and owner are supreme over the servant of the house. Moses could lead the people to the earthly promised land but could not lead them into their eternal rest.

Next, Christ is seen as the supreme High Priest. The high priests of old offered shadows of the reality to come. The sacrifices of old were offered regularly—Christ offers the true sacrifice, once for all. The old priests offered objects different from themselves. The Supreme High Priest offers Himself—a perfect sacrifice. He is both the subject and object of the supreme atoning sacrifice.

Finally, Christ's priesthood differs from the old in that Christ serves both as High Priest and as King. In the Old Covenant, the king was ultimately to come from the tribe of Judah. The priests were to be consecrated from the tribe of Levi (following Aaron). But Jesus was not a Levite. His was a different priesthood from a different order—the order of Melchizedek. Melchizedek makes a strange appearance to Abraham as both king and priest to whom Abraham gives obeisance. Hebrews argues that as Abraham is greater than Levi, and Melchizedek is greater than Abraham, then manifestly Melchizedek is greater than Levi. The eternal high priesthood and kingship is given to Christ in fulfillment of Psalm 110.

These references are but a few of the riches set forth in Hebrews that declare the supremacy of Christ.

THE BLUEPRINT
OF REDEMPTION

———

A PERSISTENT TRADITION CLAIMS THAT UPON being mocked by a skeptic with regard to his doctrine of creation, Saint Augustine was cynically asked, "What was God doing before He created the world?" Augustine's alleged reply was: "Creating hell for curious souls."

The reply was, of course, tongue-in-cheek. The Bible doesn't speak of such a special work of divine creation before creation itself. But Augustine's *bon mot* had a serious point that warned against idle speculation of God's activity in eternity.

However, quite apart from speculation, the Bible has much to say about God's activity "before" the world was made. The Bible speaks often of God's eternal counsel, of His plan of salvation, and the like. It is a matter of theological urgency that Christians not think of God as a ruler who *ad libs* His dominion of the universe. God does not "make it up as He goes along." Nor must He be viewed as a bumbling administrator who is so inept in His planning that His blueprint for redemption must be endlessly subject to revision according to the actions of men. The God of Scripture has no "plan B" or "plan C." His "plan A" is from everlasting to everlasting. It is both perfect and unchangeable as it rests on God's eternal character, which is among other things, holy, omniscient, and immutable. God's eternal plan is not revised because of moral imperfections within it that must be purified. His plan was not corrected or amended because He gained new knowledge that He lacked at the beginning. God's plan never changes because He never changes and because perfection admits to no degrees and cannot be improved upon.

The covenant of redemption is intimately concerned with God's eternal plan. It is called a "covenant" inasmuch as the plan involves two or more parties. This is not a covenant between God and humans. It is a covenant among the persons of the Godhead, specifically between the Father and the Son. God did not become triune at creation or at the Incarnation. His triunity is as eternal as His being. He is one in essence and three in person from all eternity.

The covenant of redemption is a corollary to the doctrine of the Trinity. Like the word *trinity*, the Bible nowhere explicitly mentions it. The word *trinity* does not appear in the Bible, but the concept of the Trinity is affirmed throughout Scripture. Likewise, the phrase "covenant of redemption" does not occur explicitly in Scripture but the concept is heralded throughout.

Central to the message of Jesus is the declaration that He was sent into the world by the Father. His mission was not given to Him at His baptism or in the manger. He had it before His incarnation.

In the great "Kenotic Hymn" of Philippians 2, we get a glimpse of this: "Let this mind be in you which was also in Christ Jesus, who, being in the form of God, did not consider it robbery to be equal with God, but made Himself of no reputation, taking the form of a bondservant, and coming in the likeness of men. And being found in appearance as a man, He humbled Himself and became obedient to the point of death, even the death of the cross. Therefore God also has highly exalted Him and given Him the name which is above every name, that at the name of Jesus every knee should bow, of those in heaven, and of those on earth, and of those under the earth, and that every tongue should confess that Jesus Christ is Lord, to the glory of God the Father" (vv. 5–11, NKJV).

This passage reveals many things. It speaks of the willingness of the Son to undertake a mission of redemption at the behest of the Father. That Jesus was about doing the will of the Father is testified throughout His life. As a young boy in the temple He reminded His earthly parents that He must be about His Father's business. His meat and drink was to do the will of His Father. It was zeal for His Father's house that consumed Him. Repeatedly He declared that He spoke not on His own authority but on the authority of the One who sent Him.

Jesus is the primary missionary. As the word suggests, a missionary is one who is "sent." The eternal Word did not decide on His own to come to this planet for its redemption. He was sent here. In the plan of salvation the Son comes to do the Father's bidding.

The point of the covenant of redemption is that the Son comes willingly. He is not coerced by the Father to relinquish His glory and be subjected to humiliation. Rather, He willingly "made Himself of no reputation." The Father did not strip the Son of His eternal glory but the Son agreed to lay it aside temporarily for the sake of our salvation.

Listen to Jesus as He prays to the Father at the end of His ministry: "Father, the hour has come. Glorify Your Son, that Your Son also may glorify You. . . . And now, O Father, glorify Me together with Yourself, with the glory which I had with You before the world was" (John 17:1–5, NKJV). The covenant of redemption was a transaction that involved both obligation and reward. The Son entered into a sacred agreement with the Father. He submitted Himself to the obligations of that covenantal agreement. An obligation was likewise assumed by the Father—to give His Son a reward for doing the work of redemption.

In his systematic theology, Charles Hodge lists eight promises the Father gave to the Son in this pact made in eternity. Briefly they are: that God would form a purified Church for His Son; that the Son would receive the Spirit without measure; that He would be ever-present to support Him; that He would deliver Him from death and exalt Him to His right hand; that He would have the Holy Spirit to send to whom He willed; that all the Father gave to Him would come to Him and none of these be lost; that multitudes would partake of His redemption and His messianic kingdom; that He would see the travail of His soul and be satisfied.

Because God honored the eternal covenant of redemption, Christ became the heir of His Father's promises. Because this covenant was never violated, we reap its benefits as heirs of God and joint heirs with Christ.

"I BELIEVE IN THE LIFE EVERLASTING"

MARCH 2004

HIS NAME IS "BEECHIE." RECENTLY he surprised us with a serendipitous visit. He called to say he was in Orlando with part of his family and asked if he could make an impromptu visit to our home. We responded with unreserved delight at the prospect of seeing a friend from the past. As I relate this yarn, I am looking at an elementary school class picture from 1946–47 (grade 3). There, sitting Indian style in the center front is Bob Beech, wearing knickers and adorned with his ubiquitous smile. Next to him is Johnny, from my novel *Johnny Come Home*. Almost directly behind Beechie is Vesta, who was Beechie's girlfriend before she was mine.

During our visit, Beechie opened a package that contained pictures and other relics from our past, many stretching over a half century into yesteryear. The visit stimulated a flood of memories—memories of people and of events. We spoke of the kids we grew up with—of Jarl "Gus" Gustafson, Don Whirlow, Bobby Ewalt, Bill Heidish, Rodney Wise (Rodney—where are you? I think of you often), and a host of others.

Beechie and I shared so many memories, especially of sports. We played football, basketball, and baseball together. I remember him going over the middle to catch my passes—of playing the backcourt together on the hardwood and hundreds and hundreds of practice moves for the double play, as he was 4 (second base) to my 6 (shortstop).

Memories were dredged up from the past that had lain fallow over decades, consigned, as it were, to the sea of forgetfulness (to mix my metaphors). Memories were forgotten . . . but only temporarily. Like Plato's sparking the recollection of the slaveboy in the *Meno* dialogue, so Beechie awakened a storehouse of images and names from my past.

I doubt if many people call Robert Beech "Beechie" today—probably about as many as still call me "Sonny." Few make the connection. But there is an indissoluble link between the "Beechie" of 1947 and the Robert Beech of today and the "Sonny" of the same era and the "R.C." of the present.

Every one of us has a past. We are not only the people we are today, but we remain the people we were yesterday and the days before that. My memory contains a record of my personal history—which is an integral dimension of my identity. Memory links my consciousness of my past existence with my consciousness of the present.

We have seen dramas on television and in the movies where the protagonist suffers a virulent attack of amnesia, leaving him in a state of desperation, afflicted by a dreadful loss of personal identity.

Is death a final and permanent form of amnesia? Does it spell the abrupt halt of personal consciousness? The materialist answers with an emphatic "yes"—assuming that once the matter of the brain dissolves, consciousness, or mental function, dissolves with it. That is, without the physical brain, non-physical thought is impossible.

This raises the perennial philosophical question about the nature of the mind (or soul) and its relationship to matter. John Gerstner once mused: "What is mind?"—He replied, "No matter."—"What is matter?" ... "Never mind."

The Christian affirmation of life after death asserts the notion of the continued conscious existence of the soul after the dissolution of the body (as articulated by Charles Hodge). This continuity of personal, conscious existence is the very essence of life after death. If we "continue" in an impersonal manner (lost in the oneness of the "all" of the universe), or in an unconscious state (soul-sleep), then our "continuation" is not what the Scriptures teach about life after death.

The folly of reincarnation is that it assumes on-going life without continuity of consciousness. It is the eternal recurrence of the amnesiac. Oh, one can claim "memories" of former lives à la Bridey Murphy and Shirley MacLaine stimulated by deep hypnosis or other esoteric methods, but for the average person there is zero recall of former existences.* For practical purposes—if there is no conscious memory linking discrete "lives," then there is no essential difference between re-incarnation and death as the absolute end of a life.

The key to on-going life is the essential element of the continuity of personal consciousness. It is really arrogant to assume that a physical brain or body is necessary for consciousness. In our present state, mind may be linked to brain—but that does not indicate a necessary permanent dependence. We see the analogy in nature of inestimable diversity of both body and consciousness. Biblically we encounter angelic spirits who can think and reason without the benefit of physical, human brains. The ultimate proof is seen in the nature of God Himself, who, while lacking a body, exhibits the highest possible level of consciousness.

Lesser arguments may be seen in the rising tide of testimonies of uncanny experiences of those who have been revived from a flat line state only to recall observations of things that occurred after they were declared dead—in many cases observing things that took place outside the rooms where they "died." To be sure the jury is still out on these phenomena, but the reports pose interesting grist for the life-after-death mill.

If I may indulge in a bit of cynicism, I can't resist noting that we've all experienced people who have brains but can't think, and people who think who seem to lack brains. But that would involve an exercise not only of cynicism but of equivocation.

The Bible affirms that life is good, even with the afflictions we must endure. This side of heaven, we resemble Hamlet in his judgment that we would rather "bear those ills we have, than fly to others we know not of. . . ." This fear is that what comes after our eyelids close in death may be worse than what we now endure. But this is not the biblical hope for the Christian. Paul writes: "For to me, to live is Christ, and to die is gain. But if I live on in the flesh, this will mean fruit from my labor; yet what I

---

* An American woman named Virginia Tighe (1923–95) claimed to have been an Irishwoman named Bridey Murphy in a past life. Shirley MacLaine (1934–) is an American actress well known for her claims of past lives.

shall choose I cannot tell. For I am hard pressed between the two, having a desire to depart and be with Christ, which is far better. Nevertheless to remain in the flesh is more needful for you" (Phil. 1:21–24, NKJV).

Here Paul expresses Apostolic ambivalence. He sees the good of his present life, yet yearns for his departure because of his assurance that it will mean gain. He uses the comparative form of the good by choosing the term "better" to describe what follows this life. Indeed the comparative is further modified by the word "far." Thus Paul avers that the state that follows death is "far better" than that which we presently enjoy.

This comparative state is called "the intermediate state." It is intermediate because it stands between our present state and our final state. It is the state of bodiless souls that precedes our final state of resurrection when our souls will be reunited with our glorified bodies to live in the superlative state of human life (the best) forever.

My memories of "Beechie" and my childhood friends will not cease at death. Indeed they will be enhanced as the muddled memories of this present body will give way to unconfused recollections of the past that I will be able to cherish forever. Beechie—that means that we will never forget our friendship together.

NONE RIGHTEOUS

APRIL 2004

———

T HE PSALMIST ASKED THE QUESTION: "If the Lord marks iniquity, who should stand?" This query is obviously rhetorical. The
only answer, indeed the obvious answer is no one.

The question is stated in a conditional form. It merely considers the
dire consequences that follow if the Lord marks iniquity. We breathe a
sigh of relief saying, "Thank heavens the Lord does not mark iniquity."

Such is a false hope. We have been led to believe by an endless series of
lies that we have nothing to fear from God's scorecard. We can be confident that if He is capable of judgment at all, His judgment will be gentle.
If we all fail His test—no fear—He will grade on a curve. After all, it is
axiomatic that to err is human and to forgive is divine. This axiom is so
set in concrete that we assume that forgiveness is not merely a divine
option, but a veritable prerequisite for divinity itself. We think that not
only may God be forgiving, but He must be forgiving or He wouldn't be
a good God. How quick we are to forget the divine prerogative: "I will
have mercy on whomever I will have mercy, and I will have compassion
on whomever I will have compassion" (Rom. 9:15, NKJV).

In our day we have witnessed the eclipse of the Gospel. That dark shadow
that obscures the light of the Gospel is not limited to Rome or liberal
Protestantism; it looms heavily within the Evangelical community. The
very phrase "preaching the Gospel" has come to describe every form of
preaching but the preaching of the Gospel. The "New" Gospel is one that
worries not about sin. It feels no great need for justification. It readily
dismisses the imputation of Christ's righteousness as an essential need
for salvation. We have substituted the "unconditional love" of God for
the imputation of the righteousness of Christ. If God loves us all unconditionally, who needs the righteousness of Christ?

The reality is that God does mark iniquity, and He manifests His wrath against it. Before the Apostle Paul unfolds the riches of the Gospel in his epistle to the Romans, he sets the stage for the need of that Gospel: "For the wrath of God is revealed from heaven against all ungodliness and unrighteousness of men . . ." (Rom. 1:18).

This text affirms a real revelation of real wrath from a real God against real ungodliness and unrighteousness of real men. No appeal to some invented idea of the unconditional love of God can soften these realities.

The human dilemma is this: God is holy, and we are not. God is righteous, and we are not. To be sure, it is openly admitted in our culture that "No one is perfect." Even the most sanguine humanist grants that humanity is marred. But, on balance . . . ah, there's the rub. Like Muslims we assume that God will judge us "on balance." If our good deeds outweigh our bad deeds, we will arrive safely in heaven. But, alas, if our evil deeds outweigh our good ones, we will suffer the wrath of God in hell. We may be "marred" by sin but in no wise devastated by it. We still have the ability to balance our sins with our own righteousness. This is the most monstrous lie of all. We not only claim such righteousness; we rely on such righteousness, which righteousness in fact does not exist. Our righteousness is a myth, but by no means a harmless one. Nothing is more perilous than for an unrighteous person to rest his future hope in an illusion.

It was against such an illusion that Paul stressed by citing the Psalmist: "For we have previously charged both Jews and Greeks that they are all under sin. As it is written: 'There is none righteous, no, not one; there is none who understands; there is none who seeks after God. They have all turned aside; they have together become unprofitable; there is none who does good, no, not one'" (Rom. 3:9–12, NKJV).

What comprises just under four verses of the New Testament is so radical that if the modern church would come to believe it, we would experience a revival that would make the Reformation pale into insignificance. But the church today does not believe the content of these verses: There is none righteous—not one.

Who believes that apart from Jesus not a single human being, without exception, is righteous? Not a single unregenerate person can be found who understands God.

Seeking God? We have totally revised corporate worship to be sensitive to "seekers." If worship were to be tailored for seekers, it would be directed exclusively to believers, for no one except believers ever seeks God.

Every person turns aside from God. All become unprofitable in spiritual matters. At rock bottom no one even does good—no, not one.

Good is a relative term. It is defined against some standard. If we establish what that standard is, we can congratulate ourselves and take comfort in our attainment of it. But if God establishes the standard, and His standard includes outward behavior (that our actions conform perfectly to His law) and internal motivation (that all our acts proceed from a heart that loves Him perfectly), then we quickly see that our pretended "goodness" is no goodness at all. We then understand what Augustine was getting at when he said that man's best works are nothing more than "splendid vices."

So what? The equation is simple. If God requires perfect righteousness and perfect holiness to survive His perfect judgment, then we are left with a serious problem. Either we rest our hope in our own righteousness, which is altogether inadequate, or we flee to another's righteousness, an alien righteousness, a righteousness not our own inherently. The only place such perfect righteousness can be found is in Christ—that is the good news of the Gospel. Subtract this element of alien righteousness that God "counts" or "imputes" for us, and we have no biblical Gospel at all. Without imputation, the Gospel becomes "another gospel," and such a "gospel" brings nothing but the anathema of God.

With the righteousness of Christ promised to us by faith, we have the hope of our salvation. We become numbered among those blessed to whom the Lord does not impute sin (Rom. 4:8).

ABUNDANT LOVE

MAY 2004

———

I N HIS MONUMENTAL BIOGRAPHY OF Jonathan Edwards, George Marsden cites a passage from Edwards' *Personal Narrative*: "Since I came to this town [Northampton], I have often had sweet complacency in God in views of his glorious perfections, and the excellency of Jesus Christ. God has appeared to me, a glorious and lovely being chiefly on account of his holiness. The holiness of God has always appeared to me the most lovely'of all his attributes" (p. 112).

If we take note of Edwards' language, his choice of words to describe his enraptured delight in the glory of God, we observe his accent on the sweetness, loveliness, and excellence of God. He reports of enjoying a "sweet complacency" in God. What does he mean? Is not the term *complacency* a word we use to describe a certain smugness, a resting on one's laurels, a sort of lazy inertia that attends a superficial sort of satisfaction? Perhaps. But here we see a vivid example of how words sometimes change their import over time.

What Edwards meant by a "sweet complacency" had nothing to do with a contemporary dose of smugness. Rather, it had to do with a sense of pleasure. This "pleasure" is not to be understood in a crass hedonistic, or sensual, sense but rather a delight in that which is supremely pleasing to the soul.

The roots of this meaning of "complacency" are traced by the Oxford English Dictionary (vol. 3), where the primary meaning given is "the fact or state of being pleased with a thing or person; tranquil pleasure or satisfaction in something or some one." References are cited for this usage from John Milton, Richard Baxter, and J. Mason. Mason is quoted, "God can take no real complacency in any but those that are like him."

I labor the earlier English usage of the word *complacency* because it is used in a crucial manner in the language of historic, orthodox theology. When speaking of God's love, we distinguish among three types of that love—the love of benevolence, the love of beneficence, and the love of complacency. The reason for the distinctions is to note the different ways in which God loves all people, in one sense, and the special way He loves His people, the redeemed.

Love of Benevolence

Benevolence is derived from the Latin prefix *bene*, which means "well," or "good," and it is the root for the word *will*. Creatures who exercise the faculty of the will by making choices are called volitional creatures. Though God is not a creature, He is a volitional being insofar as He also has the faculty of willing.

We are all familiar with Luke's account of the nativity of Jesus in which the heavenly host praises God declaring: "Glory to God in the highest. And on earth peace, goodwill toward men" (Luke 2:8–14, NKJV). Though some argue that the blessing is given to men of goodwill, the root meaning is the same. The love of benevolence is the quality of good will toward others. The New Testament is replete with references of God's good will to all humanity even in our fallenness. Though Satan is a malevolent being (one who harbors bad will both toward us and God), it can never properly be said of God that He is malevolent. He has no malice in His purity, no maliciousness in His actions. God does not "delight" in the death of the wicked—even though He decrees it. His judgments upon evil are rooted in His righteousness, not in some distorted malice in His character. Like an earthly judge weeps when he sends the guilty for punishment, God rejoices in the justness of it but gets no glee from the pain of those justly punished.

This love of benevolence, or good will, extends to all people without distinction. God is loving, in this sense, even to the damned.

Love of Beneficence

This type of love, the love of beneficence, is closely linked to the love of benevolence. The difference between benevolence and beneficence is the difference between disposition and action. I may feel well-disposed toward someone, but my goodwill remains unknown until or unless I manifest it by some action. We often associate beneficence with acts of kindness or charity. We note here that the very word "charity" is often used as a synonym for love. In the sense of beneficence, acts of kindness are acts of the love of beneficence.

Jesus emphasized this aspect of God's love in teaching regarding those who benefit from God's providence: "You have heard that it was said, 'You shall love your neighbor and hate your enemy.' But I say to you, love your enemies, bless those who curse you, do good to those who hate you, and pray for those who spitefully use you and persecute you that you may be sons of your Father in heaven; for He makes His sun rise on the evil and on the good, and sends rain on the just and the unjust. For if you love those who love you, what reward have you?" (Matt. 5:43 ff., NKJV).

In this passage, Jesus enjoins the practice of love toward one's enemies. Notice that this love is not defined in terms of warm, fuzzy, or sanguine feelings but in terms of behavior. In this context, love is more of a verb than a noun. To love our enemies is to be loving toward them. It involves doing good to them.

In this regard, the love we are to display is a reflection of God's love toward His enemies. To those who hate and curse Him, He shows the love of beneficence. God's benevolence (good will) is demonstrated by His beneficence (kind actions). His sun and rain are given equally to the just and the unjust.

We see then that God's benevolent love and His beneficent love are universal. They extend to the whole of humanity.

But here is the chief difference between these types of love and God's love of complacency. His love of complacency is not universal, nor is it unconditional. Sadly, in our day, the glorious character of this type of divine love is routinely denied or obscured by a blanket universalization of the love of God. To announce to people indiscriminately that God loves them "unconditionally" (without carefully distinguishing among the distinctive types of divine love) is to promote a perilous false sense of security in the hearers.

God's love of complacency is the special delight and pleasure He takes first of all in His only-begotten Son. It is Christ who is the beloved of the Father, supremely; He is the Son in whom the Father is "well pleased."

By adoption in Christ, every believer shares in this divine love of complacency. It is the love enjoyed by Jacob, but not by Esau. This love is reserved for the redeemed in whom God delights—not because there is anything inherently lovely or delightful in us—but we are so united to Christ, the Father's Beloved, that the love the Father has for the Son spills over onto us. God's love for us is pleasing and sweet to Himself—and to us—as Jonathan Edwards understood so well.

ONE HOLY CATHOLIC AND APOSTOLIC CHURCH

JUNE 2004

———

"ONE NATION, UNDER GOD, INDIVISIBLE, with liberty..." We say it. We argue about it (especially the "under God" part). But is it true? In reality, how united is the United States? The "more perfect union" sought by Lincoln is hardly perfect in terms of harmony. We are a nation—morally, philosophically, and religiously—deeply divided. Yet there remains the outward shell of formal and organizational unity. We have union without unity.

As it is with the "United" States, so it is with the unity of the Christian church. The "oneness" of the church is one of the classic four descriptive terms to define the church. According to the Council at Nicaea (AD 325), the Church is one, holy, catholic, and Apostolic.

Few church bodies today give much regard to being Apostolic. Fewer still seem concerned with the dimension of the holy. When these two qualities become irrelevant to the minds of church people, it is a mere chimera to speak of catholicity and unity.

The church, organizationally, is hopelessly fragmented. Since the birth of the "Ecumenical Movement," the church has seen more splits than mergers. The crisis of disunity is on the front pages following the Episcopal Church's decision to consecrate a practicing, impenitent homosexual to the role of bishop.*

Is unity a false hope? Is it, in its historic expressions, merely an illusion? To answer these questions we must consider the nature of the unity of the church.

In the first instance, the deepest and most significant unity of the Church

———

* Gene Robinson (1947–) is a retired Episcopalian priest and bishop who in 2003 became the first openly gay bishop in a major Christian denomination.

is its spiritual unity. Though we can never separate the formal from the material with respect to the Church's unity, we can and must distinguish them.

It was Augustine who taught most deeply about the distinction between the visible church and the invisible Church. With this classic distinction Augustine did not envision two separate ecclesiastical bodies, one apparent to the naked eye and another beyond the scope of visual perception. Now, did he envision one church that is "underground" and another one above ground, in full view?

No, he was describing a church within a church. Augustine took his cue from our Lord's teaching that until He purifies His Church in glory, it will continue in this world as a body that will include "tares" along with the "wheat." The tares are weeds that grow along with the flowers in Christ's garden.

Because of the presence of wheat and tares simultaneously in the church, we know that believers co-exist with unbelievers, the regenerate alongside the unregenerate. It was this situation that prompted Augustine to describe the church as a "mixed body" (*corpus per mixtum*). The invisible Church is the Church made up of true believers. It is the Church comprised of the regenerate, or as Augustine observed, the "elect."

Jesus made it clear that there are some, indeed many who profess faith but do not possess it. His piercing warning is the climax of the Sermon on the Mount: "Not everyone who says to Me, 'Lord, Lord,' shall enter the kingdom of heaven, but he who does the will of My Father in heaven. Many will say to Me in that day, 'Lord, Lord, have we not prophesied in Your name, cast out demons in Your name, and done many wonders in Your name?' And then I will declare to them, 'I never knew you; depart from Me, you who practice lawlessness!' " (Matt. 7:21–23, NKJV).

Elsewhere Jesus noted that people honored Him with their lips while their hearts were far from Him. The claim on the lips of the tares is that they labored for Christ. Yet Jesus will dismiss them. He will ask them (nay, command them) to leave. He will declare that they were never at any time part of His true Church. "I never knew you." These are not one-time sheep who became goats. They are the sons and daughters of Judas who were unbelievers from the beginning.

We notice also that Jesus said that the number of such self-proclaiming believers, who are not really regenerate, is declared to be "many." This should elicit caution in our assumptions of the success of our methods and techniques of evangelism. We tend to be quite sanguine with our "evangelistic statistics" when we assume the conversion of all who answer an altar call, make a "decision for Christ," or recite the "sinner's prayer." These tools can help measure outward professions, but they do not give us a glimpse into the heart. All we can ever see of a person's profession is his fruit. And even the fruit can be deceptive. God, and God alone, can read the human heart. Our gaze cannot penetrate beyond the outward appearance.

Augustine also maintained that the invisible Church exists substantially within the visible church. There may be rare instances when a true believer never connects with a visible church if providentially hindered. The thief on the cross never had the opportunity to attend new member classes in a local church.

However, for the most part, the true members of Christ's invisible Church are found within the visible church. Though the visible church a truly regenerate person may belong to differs from the church another regenerate person belongs to, the two believers are, in reality, already united in the one true, invisible Church.

The union of believers is grounded in the mystical union of Christ and His Church. The Bible speaks of a two-way transaction that occurs when a person is regenerated. Every converted person becomes "in Christ" at the same time Christ enters into the believer. If I am in Christ and you are in Christ, and if He is in us, then we experience a profound unity in Christ.

The High Priestly Prayer of Jesus in John 17 in behalf of the unity of His followers was not a failure or unfulfilled plea. God has been pleased to ensure a unity among believers that, though invisible, is nevertheless real. It is a common bond grounded in one Lord, one faith, and one baptism.

"The subjective appropriation of the work of the Son is accomplished by the application of that redemption by the Holy Spirit. It is the Spirit who regenerates us."

—

"CAN THESE BONES LIVE?" THE EFFECTUAL CALLING OF THE HOLY SPIRIT

JULY 2004

I T WAS THE EARLY SPRING OF 1958. I had spent the entire morning hours, till noon, on my knees beside my bed. It was the most passionate prayer experience of my young Christian life. I had been converted in September of 1957 and was now facing the deepest crisis of my nascent spiritual pilgrimage.

At issue was this: my girlfriend was coming to campus. She was the girl I loved and desired to marry. My resolve toward matrimony with her was kindled when I was in the eighth grade, five years earlier.

The previous months were difficult for her. She received a letter I wrote to her the night I became a Christian. She read it with zero comprehension of what I was talking about. At first she was puzzled by my new religious fervor. Her bewilderment turned to grave concern as our mutual friends warned her that I had gone off the deep-end and morphed into a religious fanatic. Then concern gave way to hostility knowing she could not spend her life with a religious nutcase.

Each day she fielded my letters that were laced with quotations from the Bible and testimonies of each new experience I had with Christ. Soon we both understood that our relationship was headed for a train wreck, one not unlike the one she and I experienced in Alabama in 1983*—hence my prayer vigil. This was not mere intercession. It was importunity, spiritual begging with a vengeance. I knew that unless she became a Christian, there was no way we could ever marry.

------

* Dr. and Mrs. Sproul were aboard the *Sunset Limited* when it derailed on the Big Bayou Canot Bridge near Mobile, Ala., in 1993. Forty-seven passengers were killed.

I picked her up at the bus station, and she checked in at the girls' dorm on campus. After dinner I took her to our weekly Bible study in the parlor of the church across the street from "Old Main." There in the course of the opening of the Word, her heart was opened as well, and she made the transition from the kingdom of darkness to the kingdom of light. She met the Master, and He redeemed her.

That night her sleep came in fits and starts. She kept pinching herself asking silently, "Do I still have it?" Satisfied that indeed she still had it, she drifted off to sleep.

First thing the next morning I picked her up at the dorm to begin our journey home for the weekend. On the way down Route 19 toward Pittsburgh, she looked at me with a radiant smile and said, "Now I know who the Holy Spirit is."

She had grown up in church. She sang in the choir. She heard the words of Scripture, but they bounced off her recalcitrant heart. She had no ears to hear, no eyes to behold the excellency of Jesus. Until that night in New Wilmington, Pennsylvania, the Holy Spirit was a mere abstraction, a third of the ritual of the weekly benediction. But now she knew Him as the third person of the Trinity.

Less than twenty-four hours as a Christian, and she had no training in theology. She was illiterate with respect to the content of the Bible. But she was, by intuition, already a Calvinist. She understood that her conversion was not caused by my prayers or by my oratory. She knew the cause did not reside in the inclinations of her own flesh. She knew her faith was not self-created. No, she clearly knew that what was wrought in her soul was wrought by the immediate, supernatural, and efficacious work of God the Holy Spirit.

The accomplishment of all that was needed objectively for her redemption had been achieved by Christ centuries earlier. But the personal application to her soul, the subjective appropriation of the objective work of Christ, was done by the Holy Spirit.

It was John Calvin who was known as the "theologian of the Holy Spirit." He was dubbed this not because he manifested the gifts of tongues or became so preoccupied with the Spirit as to lean toward a unitarianism of the third person of the Trinity. He was called the theologian of the Holy Spirit because of his biblical emphasis upon the work and ministry of the Holy Spirit in our redemption. He understood that just as the Bible sets forth the divine work of Creation as a triune activity involving the Father, the Son, and the Holy Spirit, so, in a similar fashion, Scripture reveals the work of redemption as the threefold activity of the Godhead. In our redemption, it is the Father who designs and plans our redemption. It is the Father who sends the Son into the world and, together with the Son, sends the Holy Spirit.

In the administration of redemption, though all three persons of the Godhead are co-equal in being, glory, and eternality, there is nevertheless an economic subordination that takes place. The Son comes to do the will of the Father. His task is to satisfy the demands of God's justice and righteousness. His meat and His drink is to do the will of the Father. He speaks with authority, but it is an authority not His own. Rather, it is an authority delegated to Him by the Father.

His perfect obedience is both active and passive. Actively, He kept every jot and tittle of the Law. In that endeavor, He was perfectly successful. He is more than sinless. To be sinless is to be free from all fault, taint, or blemish. It is to be innocent of guilt. But the Son is more than innocent. He is righteous. He achieves perfect merit. He fulfills the details of the covenant by which God promised the reward of blessing to those who achieved obedience. It is the fruit of Christ's active obedience that is the ground of our justification and the righteousness that is imputed to us by faith.

In His passive obedience, like the silent lamb at the slaughter, the Son acquiesces to the dreadful punishment of the curse of God. He drinks the cup of the bitterness of God's wrath to its dregs.

In His active and passive obedience, the Son accomplishes our redemption objectively. Yet, for that redemption to avail for us, it must be appropriated subjectively. Faith is required as the necessary instrument for us to receive the benefits of Christ's accomplished work of redemption.

The subjective appropriation of the work of the Son is accomplished by the application of that redemption by the Holy Spirit. It is the Spirit who regenerates us. In that regeneration, He generates the faith in us that is necessary for our appropriation of the work of Christ.

That application via regeneration and faith is not a joint venture between the sinner and the Spirit. The Spirit does not regenerate those who believe. No, He regenerates the unbelieving sinner unto faith. He quickens to spiritual life those who are dead in sin. He changes the recalcitrant heart of the sinner, making the unwilling willing to come to Christ. He makes the indisposed disposed to Him, the disinclined fully inclined. Our salvation is entirely of God—God the Father, God the Son, and God the Holy Spirit. *Soli Deo Gloria.*

WHO DO YOU SAY THAT I AM?

AUGUST 2004

———

"I N THE BEGINNING WAS THE WORD. And the Word was with God, and the Word was God."

The introductory segment of the prologue of the gospel of John was the most carefully examined text of the New Testament for the first three centuries of Christian history. Of all the theological issues and questions facing the early church, none was more acute than the church's understanding of the person of Jesus Christ.

The New Testament devotes plentiful attention to the person and work of Jesus—what He said, what He did, where He came from, and where He went. But nothing captivated the minds of the intellectual leaders of the early church as much as the question, "Who was He?"

The question "Who was Jesus?" forced attention on the Johannine concept of the *Logos*. This Greek term, simply translated "word," was the deepest idea about Jesus introduced in the New Testament.

We note the distinction John makes when he writes: "The Word was with God and the Word was God." At worst, John falls into a ghastly contradiction between two assertions made about the Logos with barely a breath taken between them. When we say someone or something is with another that normally indicates a distinction between them. We note an obvious difference between distinction and identity. When we assert that two things are identical we usually mean there is no difference or distinction between them. Yet, here John does two things: On the one hand he distinguishes between the Logos and God, while on the other hand he identifies the Logos with God.

Contradiction? Not necessarily, though we live in an era in which theologians, both liberal and conservative, are not only content with, but take delight in contradictions. However, if we are to retain theological sanity, we must reject the idea that these assertions are in fact contradictory. Nor do we wish to succumb to the popular but deadly notion now popular in formerly Reformed circles, that real contradictions can be resolved in the mind of God. This new irrationalism gives us an irrational God with an irrational Bible and an irrational theology; all defended by an irrational apologetics. This movement rests on the false premise that the only alternative to irrationalism is rationalism. But one need not be a rationalist in order to be rational. Flights into the absurd may delight existential philosophers, but they slander the Holy Spirit of truth.

Nor can we solve the tension in John by appealing to the absence of the definite article (as do the Mormons and Jehovah's Witnesses) and render the text: "And the Word was a God." This feeble attempt at resolution yields only polytheism.

It was this type of question that impelled the church to examine and test Christological formulations for three centuries. The watershed confession of the fourth-century Nicene Creed did not leap suddenly on the scene like Athena out of the head of Zeus. The formulation of the doctrine of the Trinity was codified in the fourth century but was by no means born at that time. Tri-unity in the Godhead had its roots in the fertile soil of the first-century biblical text.

At issue from the beginning was the question of monotheism. It was discussed in terms of the idea of Monarchianism. We are familiar with the words monarch or monarchy in normal conversation, as we use them with respect to butterflies and rulers. In Greek, the term has a prefix and a root.

Ironically, the root of monarch—"arch"—appears in John 1. The Apostle writes, "In the beginning . . . ," and the word translated "beginning" is *archē*. This word also means "chief" or "ruler." In English we speak of archangels, arch-enemies, architects (chief builders), arch-bishops, etc. In all of these words, *archē* means "chief" or "ruler." Thus, when we add the prefix "mono" to the root *archē*, we get the idea of "one ruler." A monarch, then, is a single ruler over any given realm (usually a king or a queen).

In the early centuries, the church had to maintain the clearly taught notion of monotheism, with the equally clear affirmation of the deity of Christ. How monotheism could be maintained while affirming the deity of Christ reached crisis proportions in the third century and on into the fourth.

The third century witnessed the strong assault against Christianity by various forms of Gnosticism, which bred a kind of Monarchianism called "Modalistic Monarchianism." To understand this we must grasp something of the meaning of the term "mode." A mode was a particular "level" or "manifestation" of a given reality. The popular idea among Gnostics was that God is the ultimate reality. His Being radiates, or emanates, from the core of His Being. Each radiation or emanation represents a tier or level of His being. The further that emanation, or tier, is from the core of the divine Being, the less "pure" is its divine Being.

The heretic Sabellius taught such a concept. He compared the relationship of the Logos to God as being analogous, as a sunbeam is to the sun. The sunbeam is of the same essence or being of the sun, yet can be distinguished from the sun. In modern terms we say that the sun is ninety-three million miles away from us, yet we are warmed by its rays that are near at hand. Sabellius argued that Jesus was of the "same essence" (Greek *homo-ousios*) as God but was less than God. Sabellius and his Modalistic Monarchianism was condemned as heresy in Antioch in 267, and the church used the expression "like essence" (*homoi-ousios*) to refer to the Logos. Here the idea was that the Logos, though distinguished from the Father, shared fully "in like manner" with the Father in His divine Being.

Soon after the defeat of Sabellius and Modalistic Monarchianism, a new and more virulent form of Monarchianism arose. Ironically its cradle was Antioch, the very place where Sabellius was condemned. The new heresy has been called "Dynamic Monarchianism," and sometimes, "Adoptionism." The Antioch school of Lucien, Paul of Samosata, and others produced their most formidable representative—Arius. It was the teaching of Arius and his followers that provoked the critical Council of Nicaea and the Nicene Creed in 325. Since this will be discussed further in this issue of *Tabletalk*, I will restrict my comments here to indicate that Arius clearly denied the eternal deity of the Logos. He defended himself, ironically, by appealing to the orthodox phrase "like essence" (*homoi-ousios*). The Logos is only "like" God; He is not God Himself. Most heretics like Arius tried to mask their heresy by using orthodox language to convey it. The Arian threat was so great that the church reversed her choice of terms for defining the relationship of the Logos to the Father. The term the church had previously rejected in the third-century dispute with Sabellius, *homoousios* ("same essence"), was elevated to orthodoxy. Now the term, of course, was not used to revert to Sabellius' modalism; rather, it was used to assert that the Logos is of the same divine essence as God—co-eternal, co-essential, not created.

The importance of this word choice underlines in red how seriously the church took the threat of Arianism and how resolute the church was to maintain her confession of the full deity of Christ. This was the defining moment of fourth-century Christianity.

THE FRUIT OF PATIENCE

SEPTEMBER 2004

THE PROPHET HABAKKUK WAS SORELY DISTRESSED. His misery was provoked by the spectacle of the threat of the pagan nation of Babylon against Judah. To this prophet it was unthinkable that God would use an evil nation against His own people; after all, Habakkuk mused, "God is too holy even to look upon evil." So the prophet protested by mounting his watchtower and demanding an answer from God: "And the LORD answered me: 'Write the vision; make it plain on tablets, so he may run who reads it. For still the vision awaits its appointed time; it hastens to the end—it will not lie. If it seems slow, wait for it; it will surely come; it will not delay. Behold, his soul is puffed up; it is not upright within him, but the righteous shall live by his faith'" (Hab. 2:2–4).

The final words of this utterance, "the righteous shall live by faith," are cited three times in the New Testament by the familiar words, "the just shall live by faith." In this phrase, "faith" refers to "trust in God." It involves trusting in the future promises of God and waiting for their fulfillment. The promise to Habakkuk is one of just thousands given by God in Scripture to His people. Such promises characteristically come with the admonition that though they tarry, we must wait for them.

Waiting for God is at the heart of living by faith. The Christian does not share the cynical skepticism dramatized by the theatrical production *Waiting for Godot*. The end of Christian hope is never shame or embarrassment, because we have a hope that is a sure anchor for our souls. It is this hope in the trustworthy promises of God that is the ground of the Christian's virtue of patience.

We are told that we live in a culture that is consumed by consumerism. Madison Avenue daily feeds our instant gratification, which is not merely a weakness; it is an addiction in our time. The epidemic of credit-card indebtedness bears witness to this malady. We want our luxuries, our pleasures, and our niceties, and we want them now. The antiquated virtue by which stewardship capitalism had its impetus was the principle of "delayed gratification." One postponed immediate consumption in favor of investing for future growth. By that principle, many prospered—but not without the necessary exercise of patience.

When the Bible speaks of patience, particularly as one of the fruits of the Spirit, and as one of the characteristics of love, it speaks of it as a virtue that goes far beyond the mere ability to await some future gain. It involves more than the rest or peace of the soul that trusts in God's perfect timing. The patience that is in view here focuses more on interpersonal relationships with other people. It is the patience of longsuffering and of forbearing in the midst of personal injury. This is the most difficult patience of all. When we are injured by others, we long for vindication, a vindication that is speedy. We fear that the axiom "justice delayed is justice denied" will work its havoc in our souls. The parable of the unjust judge speaks eloquently to this human struggle, when our Lord asks rhetorically: "Will not God give justice to His elect, who cry to Him day and night?" The parable that calls us not to faint in times of trial ends with the haunting question: "When the Son of Man comes, will He find faith on earth?" The parable ties together patience and faith. If we look at the triad of virtues underscored in the New Testament—faith, hope, and love—we see that each one of these virtues contains within it the necessary ingredient of patience. Paul tells us in 1 Corinthians 13 that love suffers long. This longsuffering, forbearing patience is to be the Christian's reflection of the character of God. It is part of God's character to be slow to anger and quick to be merciful. Part of the incomprehensibility of God in terms of my own relationship with Him is this: I cannot fathom how a holy God has been able to put up with me marring His creation to the degree I have for three score and five years. For me to live another day requires a continuation of God's gracious patience with my sin. The bare and simple question is this, "How can He put up with me?" The mystery is compounded when we add to the patience of God not only His patience with me but His patience with you, and you, and you, and you—multiplied exponentially throughout the whole world. It becomes even more difficult to fathom when we see a sinless Being being more patient with sinful beings than sinful beings are with each other.

God's patience is long but not infinite. He warns that there is a border to His longsuffering, which He will not extend. Indeed, He has appointed a day in which He will judge the world, and that day will mark the endpoint of God's striving with us. It will also mark the day of vindication for His longsuffering saints.

To be sure, a longsuffering patience is one of the most difficult exercises we can achieve. It is subjected to trial everyday. Such trials can eat away at our love, our hope, and our faith. This erosion can leave us broken and embittered. In this regard, we must tie ourselves to the mast and look to the manifold witnesses that Scripture provides of the people of God who endured such trials and tribulations. We look to Job, the classic paragon of patience who cried from the dung-heap: "Though he slay me, I will trust in him." The patience of Job was merely an outward display of the faith of Job, the hope of Job, and the love of Job.

BIBLICAL SCHOLASTICISM

OCTOBER 2004

———

I N AN AGE WHEREIN THE GROUND OF theology has been saturated by the torrential downpour of existential thinking, it seems almost suicidal, like facing the open floodgates riding a raft made of balsa wood, to appeal to a seventeenth-century theologian to address a pressing theological issue. Nothing evokes more snorts from the snouts of anti-rational zealots than appeals to sages from the era of Protestant Scholasticism.

"Scholasticism" is the pejorative term applied by so-called "Neo-Orthodox" (better spelled without the "e" in Neo), or "progressive" Reformed thinkers who embrace the "Spirit" of the Reformation while eschewing its "letter" to the seventeenth-century Reformed thinkers who codified the insights of their sixteenth-century magisterial forebears. To the scoffers of this present age, Protestant Scholasticism is seen as a reification or calcification of the dynamic and liquid forms of earlier Reformed insight. It is viewed as a deformation from the lively, sanguine rediscovery of biblical thought to a deadly capitulation to the "Age of Reason," whereby the vibrant truths of redemption were reduced to logical propositions and encrusted in dry theological tomes and arid creedal formulations such as the Westminster Confession of Faith.

The besetting sin of men like Francis Turretin and John Owen was their penchant for precision and clarity in doctrinal statements. As J.I. Packer observed in his introduction of John Owen's classic work *The Death of Death in the Death of Christ*: "Those who see no need for doctrinal exactness and have no time for theological debates which show up divisions between so-called Evangelicals may well regret its reappearance....Owen's work is a constructive broad-based biblical analysis of the heart of the gospel, and must be taken seriously as such.... Nobody has the right to dismiss the doctrine of the limitedness of the atonement as a monstrosity of Calvinistic logic until he has refuted Owen's proof that it is part of the uniform biblical presentation of redemption, clearly taught in plain text after plain text."

The "monster" created by Calvinistic logic to which Packer refers is the doctrine of limited atonement. The so-called "five points of Calvinism" (growing out of a dispute with Remonstrants [Arminians] in Holland in the early seventeenth century) have been popularized by the acrostic T-U-L-I-P, spelling out the finest flower in God's garden: T—Total Depravity; U—Unconditional Election; L—Limited Atonement; I—Irresistible Grace; P—Perseverance of the Saints.

Many who embrace a view of God's sovereign grace in election are willing to embrace the TULIP if one of its five petals is lopped off. Those calling themselves "four-point Calvinists" desire to knock the "L" out of TULIP.

On the surface, it seems that of the "five points" of TULIP, the doctrine of limited atonement presents the most difficulties. Does not the Bible teach over and over that Jesus died for the whole world? Is not the scope of the atonement worldwide? The most basic affirmation the Evangelical recites is John 3:16: "For God so loved the world . . ."

On the other hand, it seems to me that the easiest of the five points to defend is limited atonement. But this facility must get under the surface to be manifested. The deepest penetration under that surface is the one provided by Owen in *The Death of Death in the Death of Christ.*

First, we ask if the atonement of Christ was a real atonement. Did Jesus really, or only potentially, satisfy the demands of God's justice? If indeed Christ provided a propitiation and expiation for all human beings and for all their sins, then, clearly, all persons would be saved. Universal atonement, if it is actual, and not merely potential, means universal salvation.

However, the overwhelming majority of Christians who reject limited atonement also reject universal salvation. They are particularists, not universalists. They insist on the doctrine of justification by faith alone. That is, only believers are saved by the atonement of Christ.

If that is so, then the atonement, in some sense, must be limited, or restricted, to a definite group, namely believers. If Christ died for all of the sins of all people, that must include the sin of unbelief. If God's justice is totally satisfied by Christ's work on the cross, then it would follow that God would be unjust in punishing the unrepentant sinner for his unbelief and impenitence because those sins were already paid for by Christ.

People usually get around this by citing the axiom, "Christ's atonement was sufficient for all, but efficient only for some." What does this mean? The Calvinist would interpret this axiom to mean that the value of Christ's sacrifice is so high, His merit so extensive, that its worth is equal to cover all the sins of the human race. But the atonement's benefits are only efficient for believers, the elect.

The non-Calvinist interprets this axiom in slightly different terms: Christ's atonement was good enough to save everyone—and was intended to make salvation possible for everyone. But that intent is realized only by believers. The atonement is efficient (or "works") only for those who receive its benefits by faith.

As I said, this is still a form of "limited atonement." Its efficacy is limited by human response. Sadly, this kind of limit puts a limit on the saving work of Christ far greater than any limit of the atonement viewed by Reformed theology.

The real issue was the design, or purpose, of God's plan in laying upon His Son the burden of the Cross. Was it God's purpose simply to make salvation possible for all but certain for none? Did God have to wait to see if any would respond to Christ to make His atonement efficient? Was it theoretically possible that Jesus would die "for all" yet never see the fruit of His travail and be satisfied?

Or was it God's eternal purpose and design of the Cross to make salvation certain for His elect? Was there a special sense in which Christ died for His own, for the sheep the Father had given Him?

Here our understanding of the nature of God impacts strongly and decisively our understanding of the design and scope of the Atonement. To deal with every biblical text that bears on those questions, the best source I know of is John Owen's *The Death of Death in the Death of Christ.*

A LOVING PROVISION

NOVEMBER 2004

I N RECENT YEARS, WE HAVE BEEN treated to the invention of a word previously unknown, or at least not used. That word that has entered into the general vocabulary of our time is the word *oxymoron.* A typical example of an oxymoron might be the phrase "jumbo shrimp." The words that are used to describe a particular thing seem to be self-contradictory, or at least standing in an antithetical relationship. From this perspective, one might say that in theology the phrase "common grace" is such an oxymoron. I say this for this reason: God's grace can never be reduced to the level of experience that may be deemed "common." Though God's grace in one sense is commonplace, it is always and everywhere an expression of something that He gives that is undeserved by the creature. That God bestows any grace at all upon fallen creatures is indeed an uncommon manifestation of His sovereign generosity. We neither merit nor deserve such benefits.

Having said this, however, we need to look at the specific intent of the use of the term *common* with respect to grace. Common grace is distinguished not so much from what we might call uncommon grace, but rather from what we call "special grace." Common grace refers to several concepts or experiences that we observe as Christians. On the one hand, we realize that in God's divine providence He pours out benefits that are enjoyed not simply by believers, but by believers and non-believers alike. With respect to such benefits and such activities, the common grace of God is linked closely to two distinct aspects of the love of God. As I explained in my article from the May 2004 issue of *Tabletalk,* we distinguish among three distinct types of the love of God, two of which involve common grace.

The first of these aspects is God's love of benevolence. The term *benevolence* means simply "good will." And God's love for the human race may be defined in terms of His having a generally kind disposition to all of His creatures, fallen as they may be. This, of course, does not negate God's stance of wrath and anger towards those who continue in disobedience and in resisting the proper worship and gratitude the creature owes to God. But God's love of benevolence reflects His good will towards all creatures.

This disposition, or kindness, that God displays towards all creatures indiscriminately is linked to the second type of love that we use to define God's character. That is His love of beneficence. Where *benevolence* has to do with God's will, *beneficence* has to do with God's actions as they pertain to His activity on behalf of the whole created realm. We see that He not only has a divine kindness towards His creatures, He *acts* with a loving provision for the whole human race.

Jesus said that rain falls upon the just as well as the unjust. If we have two farmers living side by side, laboring each day to bring forth produce from the soil, we know that both farmers require the light of the sun, as well as a sufficient amount of rain to bring forth a healthy crop. If the two farmers are distinguished in terms of faith, one being a regenerate believer and the other an unregenerate non-believer, we don't expect the sun simply to shine on the believer's fields and the rain simply to moisten his crop, while at the same time God withholds the gifts of rain and sunshine from the unregenerate. On the contrary, both farmers reap the benefits of the grace of God. He owes neither farmer the gifts of rain and sunshine, as both of those come from His sovereign bounty. Nevertheless, He pours out these gifts to both believer and unbeliever, commonly. So, in this respect, when we speak of the love of God in His beneficence, His beneficence is common; that is, the whole world benefits from God's grace to a certain degree.

We look also to the gifts that God gives and provides for people. We can go to unbelieving medical doctors who practice their trade perhaps with a superior skill than believers. It is not simply the believer who is a gifted physician, a gifted musician, or a gifted accountant. God blesses all sorts of people with gifts and talents, and these gifts all flow from His grace. They are not restricted simply to believers.

In like manner, God's law is given to benefit the whole of mankind. God established government initially with an angel guarding the entrance to Paradise. Such government involves a restraint of evil. When God gives such restraints to evil, that restraining power gives benefit to the whole world. As fallen as the world is, and as many atrocities that are committed by wicked individuals or corrupt governments, the world would manifest much greater depravity and decadence if not for the restraint of evil by God's common grace. We see that God, in His common grace, restrains evil from going unchecked, even among the most wicked people and nations.

Finally, those endeavors to which we as Christians give our attention that have salutary benefits for the whole are acts of common grace. For example, we march with the atheist and those of other religions to combat common evils such as abortion and human rights violations. These issues are not issues reserved for Christians but for the welfare of the entire human community. Common grace matters call the Christian often to work in arenas where there is a mixture of wheat and tares growing together.

In the final analysis, the grace that is most significant for our concern is that special grace of regeneration, or that special love of God called His love of complacency, the benefits of which are directed solely to His elect. Only the elect receive that grace, and that's what distinguishes the elect from the non-elect. We must not think of common grace as a saving grace given indiscriminately or provided indiscriminately by God's intent to the whole human race. That would be to step into a semi-Pelagian or Arminian understanding of common grace. Common grace does not include within it the divine and sovereign selective grace that is reserved for His elect.

MORE THAN CONQUERORS

DECEMBER 2004

———

"I F YOU HAVE IT, YOU NEVER LOSE IT; if you lose it, you never had it." This pithy adage gives expression to the doctrine in the church that some call the doctrine of eternal security, while others refer to it as the "perseverance of the saints." Among the latter group, the perseverance of the saints makes up the fifth point of the so-called "Five Points of Calvinism" that are encapsulated in the acronym TULIP—the "P," the final point, standing for "perseverance of the saints." Another way of expressing the doctrine in pithy categories is by the phrase "once in grace, always in grace."

The idea of the perseverance of the saints is distinguished from the doctrine of the assurance of salvation, though it can never by separated from it. There are those Christians in church history who have affirmed that a Christian can have assurance of his salvation, but that his assurance is only for the moment. One can know that he is in a state of grace today, but with that knowledge, or assurance, there is no further guarantee that he will remain in that state of grace tomorrow or the day after tomorrow, or unto death. On the other hand, those who believe in the perseverance of the saints believe also that one can have the assurance of salvation, not only for today, but forever. So again, we see that perseverance is distinguished from assurance but can never be divorced from it.

Now we face the question, why is it that Reformed people, classically and historically, have hung so tenaciously to the doctrine of the perseverance of the saints? What are the reasons given for holding this particular doctrine?

The first reason that is given is based on reason itself. That is, the doctrine of the perseverance of the saints may be seen as the logical conclusion to, or as a rational inference from, the doctrine of predestination.

At this point, many theologians demur, saying that we should not construct our theology on the basis of logical inferences drawn from other doctrinal premises. However, if such inferences are not only possible inferences but necessary inferences, then I think it's legitimate to draw such inferences. However, such inferences ought to be drawn from the truth of the Bible, as our doctrine consists not only of what is explicitly set forth in Scripture but what, by good and necessary consequence, is deduced from the premises of Scripture. Perhaps the danger of drawing the doctrine of perseverance simply as a logical inference from predestination is that the vital, visceral significance of the doctrine could get lost in theological abstraction. But despite that danger, we must see that if we have a full understanding of the biblical doctrines of predestination and election, we would understand that the whole purpose of God's divine decree of election is not to make salvation a temporary possession of the elect but to make that salvation a permanent reality for those whom He predestines unto salvation. Again, predestination is not unto part-time, or temporary, faith but unto full-time and permanent faith.

The second basis for our holding the doctrine of perseverance is the actual and explicit promises of Scripture. The Scriptures teach us that what God begins in us, He will complete. Peter tells us that we are to praise God who, according to His great mercy, regenerated us for a living hope through the resurrection of Jesus Christ from the dead, to an incorruptible, unspotted, and unfading inheritance that has been kept in the heavens for you, who are guarded by God's power, through faith for salvation that is ready to be revealed in the last time (1 Peter 1:3–5). The promises of God, as Peter indicates here, are unspotted, and they are incapable of fading away. The inheritance that we have is secure.

When we look at the work of Christ on our behalf, we not only see His atonement, which has secured the payment for our sins, we see the ascension of Christ and His ministry at the right hand of the Father as our Great High Priest. Here we see in the ministry of Jesus an intercession for those whom the Father has given Him, and a taste of that type of intercession is given to us in the High Priestly Prayer recorded in John 17, where Jesus prays that none whom the Father has given to Him would ever be lost.

Despite the promises of the New Testament, the intercession of Christ on our behalf, and the doctrine of election that point to the certainty of perseverance, we still must take seriously the warnings of apostasy that frequently occur in the New Testament. Paul himself talks about how he has to pummel his body to subdue it, lest he, in the final analysis, becomes a castaway. He speaks of those who have departed from the faith.

At the end of Paul's ministry, in his final letter to Timothy, he decried the departure of Demas, who had forsaken Paul, because Demas, a previous co-worker alongside the Apostle, loved this present world. And so the assumption is that Demas, as well as others who started out with a vital profession of faith, ended in the destruction and the abyss of apostasy. How else do we understand the urgent warnings given in the sixth chapter of Hebrews? Here we have to say, without straining the text, that the New Testament, despite these warnings of apostasy, makes it clear that those who commit such acts of full and final apostasy were never really believers in the first place. John writes in his epistle: "Those who went out from us were never really among us" (1 John 2:19).

We read in chapter 6 of Hebrews, at the end of the most chilling warning against apostasy: "But we are persuaded of better things from you, things that accompany salvation" (v. 9b). People within the visible church, as was the case in Old Testament Israel, certainly do fall away from the profession of faith that they have made and end in destruction. The same is true in the New Testament community. People can join themselves to the visible church, profess faith in Christ but under duress fall away—in some cases fully and finally. We must conclude from the teaching of Scripture that such cases of apostasy are wrought by people who made a profession of faith, and whose profession was not authentic.

Finally, our basis for confidence in perseverance is really not so much in our ability to persevere as it is in God's power and grace to preserve us. If we were left to ourselves, in our human weakness, not only could we fall away, we most certainly would fall away. However, the reason we do not fall away, the reason we do endure to the end is because of the grace of our heavenly Father, who by grace called us in the first place. He sustains us by preserving us, even unto our glorification.

"The promises of God are unspotted, and they are incapable of fading away. The inheritance that we have is secure."

HOW SHOULD WE THEN WORSHIP?

JANUARY 2005

T HREE-QUARTERS OF THE WAY THROUGH the twentieth century, Francis A. Schaeffer asked the question, "How should we then live?" His book of the same name answered the questions raised by the radical shift in our culture from modernity to post-modernity. The question that we face in our generation is closely related to it: "How should we then worship?" The "how?" of worship is a hotly disputed matter in our day. The issue has been described as the war of worship. If there has been a worship war in the church in America in the last thirty years, then surely by now its outcome has been decided. Far and away, the victorious mode of worship in our day is that form roughly described as contemporary worship. "Contemporary" in this context is contrasted with "traditional," which is seen as being outmoded, passé, and irrelevant to contemporary individuals. Those who deem the contemporary shift in worship as a deterioration are in the minority, so it behooves us to explore the "how" question that Schaeffer first raised.

The "how" question is related to the other questions usually pursued by the journalists who seek to unwrap the details of a particular story. They ask the questions: "Who, what, where, when, and how?" In like manner, the best place for us to answer the "how" question of worship is to begin with the "who" question. Manifestly the most important question we ask is, "Who is it that we are called upon to worship with our hearts, our minds, and our souls?" The answer to that question at first glance is exceedingly easy. From a Christian perspective, the obvious reply is that we are called upon to worship the triune God. As easy as this answer is on the surface, when we see the concern given to this question throughout the Old and New Testaments, we realize that as fallen creatures it is one of our most basic and fundamental inclinations to worship something, or someone, other than the true God. It's not by accident that the first four commandments of the Ten Commandments focus attention on the true God whom we are to worship according to His Being. The New Testament likewise calls us to honor God with true worship. Paul reminds us that at the heart of our fallenness is a refusal to honor God as God or to show proper gratitude to Him with praise and thanksgiving. So it is imperative that the Christian, at the beginning of his pursuit to understand what true worship is, gets it clear that the object of our worship is to be God and God alone.

When we move to the "where" question, it doesn't appear to matter that much. We recall Jesus' discussion with the woman at the well when He said that the New Testament church has no appointed central sanctuary where all true worship must take place. It's not necessary for Christians to migrate to Jerusalem in order to offer authentic worship to God. Yet at the same time we notice throughout biblical history that people met together in a variety of locations, including house churches in the early years after Christ's ascension. The house church phenomenon of the first century was not something intended to avoid institutional churches or to seek an underground church as such, but it was basically built on the foundation of convenience because the church was so small that the number of believers could easily meet in a home. As the church grew in number, it became necessary to find a place where a larger group could assemble for the solemn worship of God, as an act of corporate praise and celebration. So today it would seem that the obvious answer to the "where" question is that we should be worshiping together with other Christians as we gather in local churches.

The "when?" is also a question that is given attention biblically. Obviously, it is the obligation of the believer to worship God everyday, at all times. But God appoints special times and seasons for the gathering of His people in corporate worship. In the Old Testament, that special time was established early to be on the Sabbath. The term *sabbath* means seventh, or a cycle of one in seven. In the Old Testament economy, it was on the seventh day of the week. After the resurrection and the split of the Christian community from Judaism, it was changed from the seventh day of the week to the first day of the week, though the seven-day cycle remained intact. We understand that when the Christian community meets in solemn assembly, the communion of saints means that not only are Christians joined together locally in their own particular congregations, but that the worship of God goes beyond the walls of each individual church and incorporates churches around the nation and around the world, who, for the most part, are meeting at the same time. But the "where" and the "when" questions pale into insignificance when we return our attention to the "how" question. And the "how" question is ultimately determined by the "who" question.

We are to worship God how God wants us to worship Him. This is the apparent crisis in the revolution of worship in our day. The driving force behind the radical shift in how we worship God today is not because of a new discovery of the character of God but rather through pragmatic studies on what works to attract people to corporate worship. Thus, we devise new ways of worship that will accommodate the worship of the people of God to those who are outside the covenant community. We are told that churches ought to be seeker-sensitive, that is, they ought to design worship to be appealing to people who are unbelievers. That may be a wonderful strategy for evangelism, but we must remember that the purpose of Sabbath worship is not primarily evangelism. Worship and evangelism are not the same thing. The solemn assembly is to be the assembling together of believers, of the body of Christ, to ascribe worship and honor and praise to their God and to their Redeemer. And the worship must not be designed to please the unbeliever or the believer. Worship should be designed to please God.

We remember the tragic circumstances of the sons of Aaron in the Old Testament, who offered strange fire before the Lord, which God had not commanded. As a result of their "experiment" in worship, God devoured them instantly. In protest, Aaron went to Moses inquiring about God's furious reaction. Moses reminded Aaron that God had said that He must be regarded as holy by all who approach Him.

I believe that the one attribute of God that should inform our thinking about worship more than any other is His holiness. This is what defines His character and should be manifested in how we respond to Him. To be sure, God is both transcendent and immanent. He is not merely remote and aloof and apart from us. He also comes to join us. He abides with us. He enters into fellowship. He brings us into His family. We invoke His presence. But when we are encouraged to draw near to Him in New Testament worship, we are encouraged to draw near to a God who, even in His immanence, is altogether holy.

The modern movement of worship is designed to break down barriers between man and God, to remove the veil, as it were, from the fearsome holiness of God, which might cause us to tremble. It is designed to make us feel comfortable. The music we import into the church is music that we draw from the world of entertainment in the secular arena. I heard one theologian say recently that he was not only pleased with this innovative style of worship and music but thought that what the church needs today is music that is even more "funky." When we hear clergy and theologians encourage the church to be more funky in worship, I fear that the church has lost its identity. Rather, let us return to Augustine who agreed that we can use a variety of music in our worship, but all that is done should be done with a certain gravitas, a certain solemnity, always containing the attributes of reverence and awe before the living God. The "what?" of worship, the "where?" of worship, the "when?" of worship, and especially the "how?" of worship must always be determined by the character of the One who is the living God.

ANCIENT PROMISES

FEBRUARY 2005

———

"**T**HE NEW IS IN THE OLD CONCEALED**; the old is in the new revealed." This famous statement by Saint Augustine expresses the remarkable way in which the two testaments of the Bible are so closely interrelated with each other. The key to understanding the New Testament in its fullest is to see in it the fulfillment of those things that were revealed in the background of the Old Testament. The Old Testament points forward in time, preparing God's people for the work of Christ in the New Testament.

The history of redemption began with creation itself. The book of Genesis, the first book of the Pentateuch, starts with the beginning, or the "genesis," of the universe as expressed in the revelation of God's mighty work of creation. The creation of the universe culminated in the narrative of the creation of humanity. This was followed very shortly by humanity's cataclysmic plunge into ruin as a result of the sin of Adam and Eve. From the third chapter of Genesis through the end of the Bible, the rest of the narrative history is the history of God's work of redeeming a fallen humanity. Genesis shows that the same God who is the God of creation is also the God of our redemption.

The book of Genesis gives us an overview of the patriarchal period and the covenants that God made with them. They form the foundation for everything that follows in redemptive history. Beginning with Noah and moving toward Abraham, Isaac, Jacob, and the sons of Jacob, the story unfolds God's consistent pattern of redemption, which looks ahead for centuries, as God's people awaited the ultimate fulfillment of the patriarchal promises. These promises were fulfilled in the person and work of Jesus.

The book of Genesis ends with the children of Israel migrating into Egypt to be rescued by the intervention of Joseph, who ruled as the nation's prime minister. Exodus opens with the scene having changed from one of benevolent circumstances under Joseph to one of dire circumstances, as the immigrant nation of Israel had been enslaved by Pharaoh. The stirring account in Exodus is the Old Testament watershed work of divine redemption. It sets forth for us the narrative of the divine rescue of the slaves held captive in Egypt. The captives were redeemed by the triumph of God and His mercy over the strongest military force of this world embodied in Pharaoh and his army. It points forward to an even greater liberation by a greater Mediator from slavery to sin.

From this Old Testament group of slaves, God molded a nation and called them His people. Through the mediatorial work of their earthly leader, Moses, God gave to this people His law. The ultimate expression of the Law is found in the Decalogue, or the Ten Commandments. The Decalogue sets forth the moral law, by which God's people are to live. Ultimately the Law was designed to drive people to an awareness of their need for a redeemer. Exodus also added to the Ten Commandments a multitude of laws called the Holiness Code, which demonstrated, by way of case law, the practical applications of the moral law found in the Decalogue.

In the latter part of Exodus, and moving into the book of Leviticus, we see the laws governing worship, ritual, and the establishment of the priesthood, all of which are engaged as anticipating types, or shadows, of the work of the Christ who was to come. Of particular import is the institution of sacred festivals such as the Feast of Weeks, the Feast of the Ingathering, and, most importantly, the Day of Atonement. The drama of these events again prefigures the fulfillment of them in their ultimate form in the perfect sacrifice that was offered on the cross by Jesus.

The books of Numbers and Deuteronomy, which round out the first five books of the Bible called the "Pentateuch," or the "Torah," continue to develop the historical patterns of the experiences of Israel from the days of the Exodus up until the departure of Moses at Moab. In these books, we also see the roles God assigns to the various tribes of Israel, as well as the giving of the second law (*deuteronomos*, the book of Deuteronomy), which again set forth the terms of the covenant God made with Israel.

It spelled out the obligations, responsibilities, sanctions, and the blessings that were integral to that covenant. The establishment of curses and blessings set the foundation for the perfect ministry of Jesus, who, as our Mediator in the New Testament, satisfied the demands of the curse of our sin upon us and won for us, through His perfect obedience, the blessings promised in that covenant.

From Genesis through Deuteronomy, we have the most important theological foundation to provide the framework for our comprehensive understanding of the Christian faith. In earlier centuries, for someone to be recognized as a serious theologian, it would have been expected of that person to have written at least a commentary on the book of Genesis, because so many of the themes found in Genesis and the rest of the Pentateuch are central to understanding the work of Christ. Indeed, in the Pentateuch, the entire New Testament is concealed, yet the revelation therein opens a gateway for us to understand all of the rest of the revelation that God provides from Joshua through Revelation.

In our day the covenantal structure of redemption is often obscured. What should be plain by even a cursory reading of the Pentateuch is passed off into darkness and replaced by some other structure or framework invented by human speculation.

The covenant structure of redemption does not end in the fifth book of the Pentateuch. It continues throughout the Old Testament.

At the advent of Christ, Mary sang the *Magnificat*, in which she rejoiced in the mercy of God that is "from generation to generation." She sang of the remembrance of God's ancient promises to the Patriarchs:

He has helped His servant Israel,
In remembrance of His mercy.
As He spoke to our fathers.
To Abraham and to his seed forever (Luke 1:54–55, NKJV).

HUMILIATION TO EXALTATION

MARCH 2005

I T JUST HANGS THERE. It dangles as if it were simply an afterthought attached to the second chapter of Genesis. But we know there are no afterthoughts in the mind and inspiration of the Holy Ghost. Thus, we look at this passage to give us a clue about our condition prior to the misery of sin. Chapter 2, verse 25, reads, "They were both naked, the man and his wife, and were not ashamed." This tells us that before sin came into the world, there was no shame. There was no embarrassment. The experience of humiliation was completely unknown and foreign to the human race. However, along with the first experience of sin came the awful burden of the weight of personal shame and embarrassment. Shame and embarrassment are feelings and experiences that occur to us in various degrees. The worst kind of shame, the most dreadful form of embarrassment, is that which results in utter and complete humiliation. Humiliation brings with it not merely the reddened face of embarrassment but also the sense of despair as we lose our dignity and our reputations are cast into ruin.

Yet it was precisely into this domain of shame and humiliation that our Savior came voluntarily in the incarnation. The popular hymn "Ivory Palaces" depicts this descent from glory—the Son of Man's voluntary departure from the ivory palace that is His eternal dwelling place. He chose willingly to make Himself of no reputation, to become a man and a servant, obedient even unto death. It is this humiliation that Christ willingly accepted for Himself, which stands at the beginning of the entire progress that He travels on His road to glory and to His final exaltation. The progress, as the New Testament traces it, is one that moves from humiliation in the birth of Jesus to His exaltation in His resurrection, ascension, and return.

The quality of exaltation is the exact opposite, a strong antithesis, to the quality of humiliation. In exaltation, dignity is not only restored, but it is crowned with the glory that only God can bestow. And so when we look at the biblical theme of the exaltation of Jesus, we look at the way in which the Father rewards His Son and declares His glory to the whole creation.

We are told that no one ascends into heaven except the One who descends from heaven, and we are also told that in baptism, we are given the mark and the sign of our participation with Jesus in both His humiliation and His exaltation. The promise of participating in the exaltation of Christ is given to every believer—but there is a catch. There is a warning, and that warning is clear: unless we are willing to participate in the humiliation of Jesus, we would have no reason to expect ever to participate in His exaltation. But that is the crown that is set before us, that we, who have no right to everlasting glory and honor, will nevertheless receive it because of what has been achieved in our stead by our perfect Redeemer.

In 1990, I wrote a book titled *The Glory of Christ.* The writing of that book was one of the most thrilling experiences I've ever had in writing. My task on that occasion was to demonstrate that while there is a general progression from humiliation to exaltation in the life and ministry of Jesus, this progression does not run in an unbroken line that moves uninterrupted from humiliation to exaltation. Rather, the book explains that even in Jesus' general progress from humiliation to exaltation, in His worst moments of humiliation, there are interjections by the grace of God, wherein the Son's glory is also manifest.

For example, when we consider the nativity of Jesus, it is easy to focus our attention on the sheer impoverishment that went with His being born in a stable and in a place where He was unwelcome in the resident hotel or inn. There was an overwhelming sense of debasement in the lowliness of His birth. Yet, at the very moment that our Lord entered humanity in these debasing circumstances, just a short distance away the heavens broke out with the glory of God shining before the eyes of the shepherds with the announcement of His birth as the King.

Even when He goes to the cross, in the worst moments of His humiliation, there still remains a hint of His triumph over evil, where His body is not thrown into the garbage dump outside of Jerusalem; rather, following the prophetic prediction of Isaiah, chapter 53, Jesus' body was tenderly laid to rest in the tomb of a wealthy man. His death was ignominious, but His burial was one that was a great honor in ancient terms. His body was adorned with the sweetest spices and most costly perfumes, and He was given the burial plot of honor. Therefore, God, in the midst of the suffering of His obedient servant, would not allow His holy One to see corruption.

And throughout the pages of Scripture, we see these glimpses here and there, breaking through the veil and the cloak of Jesus' humanity, piercing the armor of the humiliation and debasement that was His lot during His earthly sojourn. These moments, or glimpses, of glory should be for the Christian a foretaste of what lies ahead, not only for the ultimate exaltation of Jesus in the consummation of His kingdom, but also a taste for us of heaven itself, as we become the heirs and joint-heirs of Jesus. Jesus' final lot, His destiny, His legacy, promised and guaranteed by the Father, is glory, and that glory He shares with all who put their trust in Him.

In common language, the terms *exaltation* and *humiliation* stand as polar opposites. One of the most magnificent glories of God's revealed truth and most poignant ironies is that in the cross of Christ these two polar opposites merge and are reconciled. In His humiliation, we find our exaltation. Our shame is replaced by His glory. The songwriter had it right when he wrote, "My sinful self, my only shame, my glory, all the cross."

B.B. WARFIELD, DEFENDER OF THE FAITH

APRIL 2005

T WENTY-FIVE YEARS AGO I GAVE an address at a college in western Pennsylvania. After the service was completed, an elderly gentleman and his wife approached me and introduced themselves as Mr. and Mrs. Johannes Vos. I was surprised to learn that Dr. Vos was the son of the celebrated biblical theologian Geerhardus Vos who had written a classical work on redemptive history titled *Biblical Theology*, which is still widely read in seminaries. During the course of my conversation with them, Dr. Vos related to me an experience he had as a young boy living in Princeton, New Jersey, where his father was teaching on the faculty of Princeton Theological Seminary. This was in the decade of the 1920s, a time in which Princeton Theological Seminary was still in its heyday; it was the time we now refer to as "old Princeton." Dr. Vos told me of an experience he had in the cold winter of 1921. He saw a man walking down the sidewalk, bundled in a heavy overcoat, wearing a fedora on his head, and around his neck was a heavy scarf. Suddenly, to this young boy's horror and amazement, as the man walked past his home, he stopped, grasped his chest, slumped, and fell to the sidewalk. Young Johannes Vos stared at this man for a moment, then ran to call to his mother. He watched as the ambulance came and carried the man away. The man who had fallen had suffered a major heart attack, which indeed proved to be fatal. His name was Benjamin Breckinridge Warfield.

I was thunderstruck by this narrative that was told to me by the now elderly Johannes Vos. I felt like I was somehow linked to history by being able to hear a firsthand account through somebody telling me of the last moments of the legendary B.B. Warfield's life. At the time of his death,

Warfield had been on the faculty of Princeton and had distinguished himself as its most brilliant theologian during his tenure.

My first exposure to the writings of B.B. Warfield was somewhat seren-dipitous. As a young college student, I had the daily dilemma of trying to parlay my meager funds into enough money to sustain myself. I was trying to live on a five-dollar-a-week allowance, out of which had to come the payment of my meals and the nightly ritual of a long distance tele-phone call to my fiancée. Obviously, even in the 1950s, five dollars did not stretch far enough to provide all of these needs. Therefore, I had to find ways to become semi-entrepreneurial and scrounge up a few extra dollars, so that I could eat and enjoy the conversation with my bride to be. I took up barbering without a license, giving my fellow students haircuts for a dollar to help defray my expenses. But my great break came when one of my professors told me of a new publishing company that was doing business out of a man's garage in Nutley, New Jersey. It was called the Presbyterian and Reformed Publishing Company. The publishing house was looking for student representatives on various campuses to help distribute its products, and my professor asked if I would be inter-ested in such an enterprise. I leapt at the chance, not motivated by any desire to propagate Reformed theology, but merely out of a pure eco-nomic motive. Within a few days there arrived at my dormitory a large cardboard box that was so heavy I could hardly lift it. It included all of the then published works of the Presbyterian and Reformed Publishing Company. There was a note inside indicating to me that these books were samples that I would have at my disposal, that I might familiarize myself with the works that were published by the company. Included were several of the works of Cornelius Van Til, a couple of volumes that had been published into English by G.C. Berkouwer, along with the com-plete works of B.B. Warfield.

While I initially had no idea of the wealth of scholarship that was con-tained in this single box of books, I quickly grasped their significance as I started to read through them to familiarize myself with the content of the products I would be selling on campus for the next couple of years. I had no idea at that time that G.C. Berkouwer, to whom I was first introduced through these books, would be my mentor in graduate school in Holland. Nor did I think that I would ever have the opportunity to meet Cornelius Van Til and exchange ideas and concepts with him while eating cookies on his front porch in eastern Philadelphia near the campus of Westminster Theological Seminary. Though the providence of God was kind to me in allowing me to meet two out of the three of these titans of theology, I knew that the only way I would ever have the opportunity to meet B.B. Warfield was to wait until glory, since he had departed this world before I was born.

When we think of Presbyterian and Reformed theology in the nineteenth century, there are four names that stand out among the rest. In the northern church there was the extremely capable theologian Charles Hodge, who actually had taught Warfield in his undergraduate studies. The southern church was blessed with the work of James Henley Thornwell and Robert Lewis Dabney. Each of these four men had been strongly influenced by the classical Reformed thought of seventeenth-century Geneva, especially through the work of Francis Turretin.

Of the four, I am convinced that Warfield was the most able and the most brilliant. He combined a keen grasp of biblical knowledge along with all of the nuances of systematic theology. Indeed, early in his seminary teaching, he taught at Western Theological Seminary in Pittsburgh, which became perhaps the most liberal seminary among Presbyterian seminaries before it merged in the late 1950s with Pittsburgh-Xenia Seminary to become Pittsburgh Theological Seminary. His distinguished work at Western Seminary led Warfield to be given an invitation to teach at his alma mater Princeton Theological Seminary, where he distinguished himself as a mighty champion of the Reformed faith. He was a contemporary of Abraham Kuyper and Herman Bavinck who were both from the Netherlands. Though he was closely related to those Dutch theologians' understanding of historic Calvinism, Warfield was more in line with the Scottish Reformed tradition than that of the Dutch. He had what seemed at the time to be a minor disagreement with Abraham Kuyper over the best way to defend Christian truth in the science of apologetics. That difference escalated among some of the students of Warfield and Kuyper. In 1929, Princeton Theological Seminary split, and its greatest thinkers moved to Philadelphia to become Westminster Theological Seminary. Cornelius Van Til, a brilliant young theologian who followed in the footsteps of Kuyper and Bavinck, affirmed a position on apologetics different from B.B. Warfield. One of Van Til's most able students was John Gerstner. The irony is that though Gerstner was a student directly of Van Til, he came to the conclusion that Warfield was correct in this intramural debate with Kuyper. As a result, Gerstner continued the Warfield tradition, and Van Til continued the tradition of Kuyper. The students of Van Til include men such as John Frame and the late Greg Bahnsen.

As a student of John Gerstner, I was introduced early to Warfield and was convinced of the view of Warfield over Kuyper. To this day, we see these two strands of apologetics competing for acceptance within the Reformed community. It's only to our detriment that we don't have in our own day men of the stature of Warfield or Kuyper to carry these issues on. In the meantime, I am profoundly grateful for the legacy that has enriched the whole church as a result of the theological contributions of B.B. Warfield. I believe that Warfield is second only to Jonathan Edwards as America's greatest theologian.

SHEPHERDING THE FLOCK

MAY 2005

―――

WHEN WE EXAMINE LIFE IN THE early Christian church, we see a remarkable phenomenon recorded for us in the book of Acts. In Acts 8:1–2 we read, "At that time a great persecution arose against the church which was at Jerusalem; and they were all scattered throughout the regions of Judea and Samaria, except the Apostles. And devout men carried Stephen to his burial, and made great lamentation over him." A little bit later in the text we read these words: "Therefore those who were scattered went everywhere preaching the word" (Acts 8:4). We notice here that the people described as going everywhere preaching the Word were not the Apostles. They were the laity of the first-century church. The Apostles remained in Jerusalem and were not numbered among those who fled during the great persecution. It is obvious from this text in Acts that one of the functions of the leaders of the early church was to equip the laity so that the ministry of the Gospel could be effected through their labors. This was a precursor of what Luther had in mind in the sixteenth century when he advocated the doctrine of the "priesthood of all believers." In that doctrine, Luther did not intend to obscure the distinction between laity and clergy but simply intended to point out that all Christians are to be involved in fulfilling the mission of the church.

At the same time, the New Testament makes it clear that there are those appointed to be leaders in the local church, and they are called by various names, but in the main we think of the pastor as the leader of the local church. The supreme paradigm, or model, for pastoral ministry is seen in the work of Jesus Himself. One of the titles that the New Testament bestows upon Him is that of the Good Shepherd. The metaphor of the shepherd who cares for his flock becomes then the metaphor that defines the work of the local pastor. But what does it mean to be a shepherd over the flock?

In the first place, to be a shepherd over the flock of sheep means that it is the shepherd's responsibility to lead the sheep. If anyone has observed the behavior of sheep who are left unguided, without the care and constant supervision of a shepherd, he is aware that sheep tend to move willy-nilly in all directions without any order to their movement. They are prone to getting lost, getting injured, and being left in a state of vulnerability unless they are cared for by a shepherd. So it is with the flock of Christ. It is the chief responsibility of the pastor, who is the shepherd, to lead the sheep.

One of the great tragedies in the church of the twenty-first century, particularly in Protestantism, is that while pastors are given the responsibility for leading their congregations, rarely do they receive a level of authority that matches that responsibility. For the most part, they are considered hirelings by the governing boards of the local church, whether it be a board of elders, deacons, or a consistory. So that the pastor, in being subordinate to the elder board, always has to keep one eye on his supervisors before he takes the reins to lead the flock of Christ. This is one of the reasons why so many pastors have compromised the preaching of the Gospel. They have been so fearful that they would lose their jobs by being bold in their preaching and passionate in their concern for the sheep that they keep one eye on the sheep and the other eye on those who hire and fire them. This is not the biblical model. From Old Testament times beginning with Moses into the New Testament, those who were called to be elders and deacons were to be placed in a position to give aid and assistance to the shepherd, who was given the authority and responsibility to lead the flock. Some pastors are very effective in leading without that authority simply by the sheer force of their personality or the skills they have in leading.

Secondly, the shepherd is responsible to feed the sheep. This was set forth with great emphasis in Jesus' discourse with Peter after the resurrection, when He inquired of Peter's love for his Master. Jesus three times gave the mandate to Peter to feed His sheep—to tend the flock. Sheep without food soon grow thin, weak, emaciated, and sickly—ultimately perishing. It is the first responsibility of the pastor to make sure that the sheep under his care are fed, nourished, and nurtured by the whole counsel of the Word of God. The New Testament rebukes the believer who is satisfied with milk and flees from serious learning of the things of God by avoiding the difficult digestion of the meat of the Word of God. But a good shepherd weans his sheep from the elemental principles of milk that is given to babes, and he gives them a diet that will cause them to become strong and fully equipped to do the ministry of the Gospel. That feeding is given at the responsibility of the pastor.

Thirdly, the pastor is called to tend the flock. Following again John's imagery from nature, when a sheep is wounded or becomes ill, it is to be noticed by the good shepherd, who takes that sheep from the flock and gives the special attention needed by the sheep to be restored to fullness of health. So it is that the good pastor is one who knows the aches, the pains, the joys, and the sorrows of each member of his congregation, so that he can tend to their needs and so that they aren't overcome by physical maladies or by spiritual and psychological distress. He is there to encourage the sheep and to see to it that they grow to the fullness of maturity in the life of Christ, conforming to Christ's very image.

It is the responsibility of the pastor to equip the sheep by teaching them and training them. There is a difference between teaching and training. Teaching involves the imparting of information from one person to another. Training requires more hands-on participation, showing someone how to master a particular skill. It is not enough for a pastor simply to communicate information through expositional preaching or to explain the doctrines of the faith to his flock. He is also called to see to it that they are trained in certain skills necessary for growth in the faith. It is the pastor's responsibility to teach his sheep how to pray, how to worship, how to evangelize, how to be engaged profitably in the mercy ministries of the church. In all of these enterprises, the pastor is to mirror and reflect the ministry of Jesus Himself, who gave of Himself completely to those given to Him by the Father. So the pastor must see his congregation as a flock of sheep that is entrusted to him by the Father and by the Lord Jesus Christ, that he may help the saints become all that they can become in the ministry of the Gospel.

> "It is the responsibility of the pastor to equip the sheep by teaching them and training them."

CULTURAL REVOLUTION

JUNE 2005

——

I N THE EARLY YEARS OF THE 1950s the phenomenon of broad-cast television was beginning to sweep America. In these early days, however, it was still a small minority of American households that proudly owned a television set. At this time, a ban was executed by the networks prohibiting the use of the word "virgin" in television broad-casts. The censorship of this word was explained in light of the term's close connection to matters of sexuality. So sensitive were the original producers of television towards offending the ethics and mores of the American public that words as seemingly harmless as the word "virgin" were banished from the airwaves in order to keep at arm's length all possible sexual innuendos.

Obviously, we have come a long way from the days of Ozzie and Harriet and the dawn of television broadcasting. However, since that time, the American culture has gone through its most radical cultural revolution in its history. The cultural revolution of the decade of the sixties contained within it a major cultural upheaval with respect to sexual mores. The old taboos against premarital and extramarital sexual relationships were destroyed by the new sex ethic. The new sex ethic was heralded by social scientists such as Alfred Kinsey and later by *The Chapman Report* and other chroniclers. What society now accepted in practice and in the arts showed a dramatic shift from an earlier time when chastity was regarded as a virtue. Every aspect of the media, in terms of cultural expression, made massive use of the new morality. Today one can hardly read a novel, watch a television program, see a movie in the theater, or even look at the advertisements in magazines and in stores without being acutely aware of this radical shift. Sex is the number-one seller for every conceivable sort of consumer product from razor blades to automobiles. If it's sexy, it sells.

The cultural revolution brought in its wake a completely different climate with respect to casual sex, extramarital sex, and, in more recent times, homosexual practices. This new climate has produced a level of erotic stimulation that no generation in human history has had to deal with in the past.

Because of this shift in cultural acceptability, young people particularly are bombarded every single day of their lives with every conceivable sort of erotic stimulation. Of course, as long as there have been men and women, there have been biological urges and sexual appetites to deal with in terms of seeking to live chaste and virtuous lives. There is a sense in which fallen humanity has always had to struggle with the erotic impulses of the human heart, but at the same time there has been a massive escalation of temptation brought in the wake of the explosion of erotic stimulation in our day.

The advent of the computer and the use of the Internet has rapidly increased this escalation. Though I am technologically challenged—I do not know how to go online, have never written an email message, much less have an email address—I am still aware that pornography on the Internet is a multibillion dollar industry in our country. My limited use of the Internet boils down to this, each day one of my associates graciously and professionally downloads for me the latest information coming out of Pittsburgh, Pennsylvania, on the developments of the Pittsburgh Steelers football team—one of my passions. What strikes me in reading the print on these articles is that frequently in the margins of these major articles there are seductive pictures of scantily clad young beauties that beckon for further investigation. It's clear that pornography, even in a sports article, is but a click or two away.

Given the bombardment of the external stimulation that the young person today receives, it is well advised for the church, even though we are called to maintain the call to holiness and virtue that is ours from Scripture, to have at the same time compassion for people who are overwhelmed by temptation. It would be good for us to remember the encounter of Jesus with the woman caught in adultery, who while treating her with

His loving kindness and tender mercy and forgiving her for her sin, nevertheless commanded her to cease from that behavior henceforth, saying, "Go and sin no more."

If we examine the biblical ethic with respect to sexual behavior, we see that from the Old Testament through the New Testament, the ethic is virtually monolithic. Take, for example, the technical study of the word *porneia* as it is used in the Scriptures. In Kittel's *Theological Dictionary of the New Testament*, we read, "The New Testament is characterized by an unconditional repudiation of all extramarital and unnatural intercourse" (p. 590). He recognizes that if anything is part of the original message of the New Testament it is this unequivocal judgment with respect to sexual purity and immorality.

In Paul's letter to the Romans, Paul expresses the corruption of our humanity that flows out of our base idolatry, and the subsequent judgment of God upon that. We read in Romans 1:24–32: "Therefore God gave them up in the lusts of their hearts to impurity, to the dishonoring of their bodies among themselves, because they exchanged the truth about God for a lie and worshiped and served the creature rather than the Creator, who is blessed forever. Amen. For this reason God gave them up to dishonorable passions. For their women exchanged natural relations for those that are contrary to nature; and the men likewise gave up natural relations with women and were consumed with passion for one another, men committing shameless acts with men and receiving in themselves the due penalty for their error. And since they did not see fit to acknowledge God, He gave them up to a debased mind to do what ought not to be done. They were filled with all manner of unrighteousness, evil, covetousness, malice. They are full of envy, murder, strife, deceit, maliciousness. They are gossips, slanderers, haters of God, insolent, haughty, boastful, inventors of evil, disobedient to parents, foolish, faithless, heartless, ruthless. Though they know God's decree that those who practice such things deserve to die, they not only do them but give approval to those who practice them." In this the Apostle Paul sees that sexual immorality, particularly with respect to its expression in homosexual activity, represents the extreme degree to which human moral corruption sinks. He sees these practices as being the result of a debased mind, a mind that is filled with unrighteousness, and that the people who do these things in defiance to God, at the same time encourage others to do it as well.

When society gives its approval to forms of illicit sexual behavior, that becomes the strongest temptation of all to people who are susceptible to doing what everybody else is doing. That's why it is the task of the Christian in the twenty-first century to underscore the unique call that God gives to us to be people who are non-conformists to a fallen and pagan culture. We are to seek to live transformed lives and to have our minds informed not by what other people are doing in the secular culture, not by what is deemed acceptable in television episodes or movie scenes of extramarital sex or by homosexual relationships, but we are to have our minds informed by the Word of God. I know of no other antidote for us to heal our sick souls in the midst of this crisis.

RADICAL CORRUPTION

JULY 2005

I N God's work of creation, the crowning act, the pinnacle of that divine work, was the creation of human beings. It was to humans that God assigned and stamped His divine image. That we are created in the image of God gives to us the highest place among earthly beings. That image provides human beings with a unique ability to mirror and reflect the very character of God.

However, since the tragic fall of Adam and Eve in the garden of Eden, that image has been subject to serious change and corruption. As a result, we speak of the "shattering of the image." The term *shatter* may go too far, however, because it could suggest the idea that the image is now destroyed and that no vestige of it is left in our humanity. Such is not the case. Though the image has been radically blurred and corrupted, there remains some aspect of that image left in our humanity, which remaining vestige is the basis for human dignity. Human dignity is not inherent; it is derived. It is not intrinsic; it is extrinsic. Human beings have dignity because God, who has dignity inherently and intrinsically, has assigned such dignity to us.

When we speak of the fall and of original sin, we are not speaking of the first sin committed by Adam and Eve; we are speaking of the radical consequences of that sin, which followed to all future generations of mankind. In Reformed circles, the doctrine of original sin has often been described by the phrase "total depravity." That it's called "total depravity" is explained in one sense because the letter "T" fits so neatly into the historic acrostic TULIP, which defines the so-called "five points of Calvinism."

Nevertheless, the word *total* with respect to our depravity may seriously mislead. It could suggest that our fallen natures are as corrupt and depraved as possible. But that would be a state of *utter* depravity. I prefer to use the phrase "radical corruption," perhaps because the first initial of each word suits my own name and nature, R.C., but more so because it avoids the misunderstanding that results from the phrase "total depravity." Radical corruption means that the fall from our original state has affected us not simply at the periphery of our existence. It is not something that merely taints an otherwise good personality; rather, it is that the corruption goes to the *radix*, to the root or core of our humanity, and it affects every part of our character and being. The effect of this corruption reaches our minds, our hearts, our souls, our bodies—indeed, the whole person. This is what lies behind the word *total* in "total depravity."

What is most significant about the consequences of the fall is what it has done to our ability to obey God. The issue of our moral capability after the fall is one of the most persistently debated issues within the Christian community. Virtually every branch of Christendom has articulated some doctrine of original sin because the Bible is absolutely clear that we are fallen from our created condition.

However, the degree of that fall and corruption remains hotly disputed among Christians. Historically, that dispute was given fuel by the debate between the British monk Pelagius and the greatest theologian of the first millennium, Saint Augustine of Hippo. In defining the state of corruption into which mankind has fallen, Augustine set up some parallels and contrasts between man's estate before the fall and his condition after the fall. Before the fall, Augustine said that man was *posse peccare* and *posse non peccare*, that is, man had the ability to sin and the ability not to sin. Not sinning was a possibility that Adam had in the Garden.

In addition to this, Augustine distinguished between our original estate, which involved both the *posse mori* and the *posse non mori*. This distinction refers to our mortality. Adam was made in such a way that it was possible for him to die. At the same time, he had the possibility before him of living forever had he not fallen into sin. So both the possibility of sinning and not sinning and the possibility of dying or not dying existed as options for Adam before the fall, according to Augustine.

He further argued that the consequence of the fall upon the human race can be defined this way: since the fall, man no longer has the *posse non peccare* or the *posse non mori*. All human beings now have lost the natural ability to keep from sinning and thus to keep from dying. We are all born in the state of sin and as mortal creatures, destined to death. After the fall, Augustine defines our condition as having the *posse peccare*. We retain the ability to sin, but now we have the dreadful condition of the *non posse non peccare*. This double negative means that we no longer have the ability to not sin. Likewise, we have now the *non posse non mori*. It is not possible for us not to die. It is appointed to all of us once to die and then the judgment. The only exceptions to this would be those who remain alive at the coming of Christ.

When we get to heaven, things will change again. There we will no longer have the *posse peccare* and the *non posse non peccare*. There we will only have *non posse peccare*. We will no longer be able to sin or to die. It all comes down to this, to the issue of moral ability. Augustine was saying that apart from the regenerating work of the Holy Spirit that God performs in the souls of the elect, no person in his own power is able to choose godliness, to choose Christ, or to choose the things of God. That ability to come to Christ, as our Lord Himself declared in John chapter 6, is an ability that can only be the result of the regenerating power of God the Holy Spirit. That position spelled out by Augustine remains the orthodox position of historic Reformed theology.

THE PELAGIAN CONTROVERSY

AUGUST 2005

———

" **G**RANT WHAT THOU COMMANDEST, and command what Thou dost desire." This passage from the pen of Saint Augustine of Hippo was the teaching of the great theologian that provoked one of the most important controversies in the history of the church, and one that was roused to fury in the early years of the fifth century.

The provocation of this prayer stimulated a British monk by the name of Pelagius to react strenuously against its contents. When Pelagius came to Rome sometime in the first decade of the fifth century, he was appalled by the moral laxity he observed among professing Christians and even among the clergy. He attributed much of this malaise to the implications of the teaching of Saint Augustine, namely that righteousness could only be achieved by Christians with the special help of divine grace.

With respect to Augustine's prayer, "Oh God, grant what Thou commandest, and command what Thou dost desire," Pelagius had no problems with the second part. He believed that God's highest attribute was indeed His righteousness, and from that righteousness He had the perfect right Himself to obligate His creatures to obey Him according to His law. It was the first part of the prayer that exercised Pelagius, in which Augustine asked God to grant what He commands. Pelagius reacted by saying that whatever God commands implies the ability of the one who receives the command to obey it. Man should not have to ask for grace in order to be obedient.

Now, this discussion broadened into further debates concerning the nature of Adam's fall, the extent of corruption in our humanity that we describe under the rubric "original sin," and the doctrine of baptism.

It was the position of Pelagius that Adam's sin affected Adam and only

Adam. That is to say, as a result of Adam's transgression there was no change wrought in the constituent nature of the human race. Man was born in a state of righteousness, and as one created in the image of God, he was created immutably so. Even though it was possible for him to sin, it was not possible for him to lose his basic human nature, which was capable always and everywhere to be obedient. Pelagius went on to say that it is, even after the sin of Adam, possible for every human being to live a life of perfect righteousness and that, indeed, some have achieved such status.

Pelagius was not opposed to grace, only to the idea that grace was necessary for obedience. He maintained that grace *facilitates* obedience but is not a necessary prerequisite for obedience. There is no transfer of guilt from Adam to his progeny nor any change in human nature as a subsequence of the fall. The only negative impact Adam had on his progeny was that of setting a bad example, and if those who follow in the pathway of Adam imitate his disobedience, they will share in his guilt, Pelagius asserted, but only by being actually guilty themselves. There can be no transfer or imputation of guilt from one man to another according to the teaching of Pelagius. On the other side, Augustine argued that the fall seriously impaired the moral ability of the human race. Indeed, the fall of Adam plunged all of humanity into the ruinous state of original sin. Original sin does not refer to the first sin of Adam and Eve, but refers to the consequences for the human race of that first sin. It refers to God's judgment upon the whole human race by which He visits upon us the effects of Adam's sin by the thoroughgoing corruption of all of his descendants. Paul develops this theme in the fifth chapter of his epistle to the Romans.

The key issue for Augustine in this controversy was the issue of fallen man's moral ability—or lack thereof. Augustine argued that prior to the fall, Adam and Eve enjoyed a free will as well as moral liberty. The will is the faculty by which choices are made. Liberty refers to the ability to use that faculty to embrace the things of God. After the fall, Augustine said the will, or the faculty, of choosing remained intact; that is, human beings are still free in the sense that they can choose what they want to choose. However, their choices are deeply influenced by the bondage of sin that holds them in a corrupt state. And as a result of that bondage to sin, the original liberty that Adam and Eve enjoyed before the fall was lost.

The only way that moral liberty could be restored would be through God's supernatural work of grace in the soul. This renewal of liberty is what the Bible calls a "royal" liberty (James 2:8). Therefore, the crux of the matter had to do with the issue of moral inability as the heart of original sin. The controversy yielded several church verdicts including the judgment of the church in a synod in the year 418, where the Council of Carthage condemned the teachings of Pelagius. The heretic was exiled to Constantinople in 429. And once again, Pelagianism was condemned by the church at the Council of Ephesus in 431. Throughout church history, again and again, unvarnished Pelagianism has been repudiated by Christian orthodoxy. Even the Council of Trent, which teaches a form of semi-Pelagianism, in its first three canons—especially in the sixth chapter on justification—repeats the church's ancient condemnation of the teaching of Pelagius that men can be righteous apart from grace. Even as recently as the modern Roman Catholic catechism, that condemnation is continued.

In our own day, the debate between Pelagianism and Augustinianism may be seen as the debate between humanism and Christianity. Humanism is a warmed-over variety of Pelagianism. However, the struggle within the church now is between the Augustinian view and various forms of semi-Pelagianism, which seeks a middle ground between the views of Pelagius and Augustine. Semi-Pelagianism teaches that grace is necessary to achieve righteousness, but that this grace is not imparted to the sinner unilaterally or sovereignly as is maintained by Reformed theology. Rather, the semi-Pelagian argues that the individual makes the initial step of faith before that saving grace is given. Thus, God imparts the grace of faith in conjunction with the sinner's work in seeking God. It seems a little mixing of grace and works doesn't worry the semi-Pelagian. It is our task, however, if we are to be faithful first to Scripture and then to the church's ancient councils, to discern Augustine's truth and defend it aright.

CUR DEUS HOMO

SEPTEMBER 2005

——

I N THE ELEVENTH CENTURY, one of the church's most brilliant thinkers, Anselm, archbishop of Canterbury, wrote three important works
that have influenced the church ever since. In the field of Christian
philosophy, he gave us his *Monologium* and his *Proslogium*; in the field of
systematic theology, he penned the great Christian classic *Cur Deus Homo*,
which being translated means "Why the God-Man?"

In this work, Anselm set forth the philosophical and theological foundations for an important aspect of the church's understanding of the
atonement of Christ, specifically the satisfaction view of the atonement.
In it, Anselm argued that it was *necessary* for the atonement to take place
in order to satisfy the justice of God. That viewpoint became the cen-
terpiece of classical Christian orthodoxy in the Middle Ages, in terms
of the church's understanding of the work of Christ in His atonement.
Since then, however, the satisfaction view of the atonement has not been
without its critics.

In the Middle Ages, questions were raised about the propriety of thinking that the atonement of Jesus was made necessary by some abstract
law of the universe that required God's justice to be satisfied. This gave
rise to the so-called *Ex Lex* debate. In the *Ex Lex* debate, the question was
raised as to whether God's will functioned *apart* from any law or *outside*
of any law (*ex lex*), or whether the will of God was itself subjected to some
norm of righteousness or cosmic law that God was required to follow
and, therefore, His will was exercised under law (*sub lego*). The question
was: Is God apart from law or is He under law?

The church's response to this dilemma was to say basically "a pox on
both houses," and to declare that God is neither apart from law nor under
law in these respective senses. Rather, the church responded by affirming
that God is both apart from law and under law, in so far as He is free from

any restraints imposed upon Him by some law that exists outside of Himself. In that sense, He is apart from law and not under law. Yet at the same time, God is not arbitrary or capricious and works according to the law of His own nature. The church declared that God is a law unto Himself. This reflects not a spirit of lawlessness within God, but that the norm for God's behavior and God's will is based on what the seventeenth-century orthodox theologians called "the natural law of God."

The natural law of God, as a theological expression, can be easily misunderstood or confused with the broader concept that we encounter in political theory and in theology of the so-called "law of nature" (*lex naturalis*). In that sense of the phrase, the law of nature refers to those things that God reveals in the world of nature about certain principles of ethics. In distinction from this common use of the term *natural law*, what the seventeenth-century Westminster divines had in view when they spoke of the natural law of God was this: that God operates according to the law of His own nature. That is to say, God never acts in such a way that would contradict His own holiness, His own righteousness, His own justice, His own omnipotence, and so on. God never compromises the perfection of His own being or character in what He does.

When the church confesses the necessity of the satisfaction of God's righteousness, this necessity is not something that is imposed upon God from the outside, but it is a necessity imposed upon God by His own character and nature. It is necessary for God to be God, never to compromise His own holiness, righteousness, or justice. It is in this sense that an atonement that satisfied His righteousness is deemed necessary.

In more recent times, modern thinkers have objected to the satisfaction view of the atonement on the grounds that it casts a shadow over the free grace and love of God. If God is a God of love, why can He not just forgive people gratuitously from the pure motivation of His own love and grace, without being concerned about satisfying some kind of justice, whether it's a law of His own nature or a law imposed from without? Again, this view of the atonement fails to understand that God will never negotiate His own righteousness, even out of His desire to save sinners.

In the atonement, we see that God both manifests His gracious love towards us and yet at the same time, manifests a commitment to His own righteousness and justice. Justice is served by the work of Christ who satisfies the demands of God's righteousness, thereby maintaining God's commitment to righteousness and justice. God satisfied the demands of His righteousness by giving to us a Substitute who stands in our place, offering that satisfaction for us. This displays marvelously the graciousness of God in the midst of that satisfaction. God's grace is illustrated by the satisfaction of His justice in that it is done for us by the One whom He has appointed. It is God's nature as the Judge of all the world to do what is right. And the Judge who does what is right never, ever violates the canons of His own righteousness.

The Bible explains the cross in terms of both propitiation and expiation, the twin accomplishments of Christ in our behalf. Propitiation refers specifically to Christ's work of satisfaction of God's righteousness. He pays the penalty for us that is due our sins. We are debtors who cannot possibly pay the moral debt that we have incurred by our offense against the righteousness of God, and God's wrath is satisfied and propitiated by the perfect sacrifice that Christ makes on our behalf. But that's only one aspect of the work. The second is expiation. In expiation, our sins are removed from us, remitted by having our sins transferred or imputed to Christ, who vicariously suffers in our stead. God is satisfied, and our sin is removed for us in the perfect atonement of Jesus. This fulfills the dual sense in which sin was atoned for on the old-covenant Day of Atonement, both by the sacrifice of one animal and the symbolic transfer of the sins of the people to the back of the scapegoat, who was then sent into the wilderness, removing the sins from the people.

A SNARE IN YOUR MIDST

OCTOBER 2005

———

WHEN IS A CHURCH NOT A CHURCH? This question has received various answers throughout history, depending on one's perspective and evaluation of certain groups. There exists no monolithic interpretation of what constitutes a true church. However, in classic Christian orthodoxy certain standards have emerged that define what we call "catholic," or universal, Christianity. This universal Christianity points to the essential truths that have been set forth historically in the ecumenical creeds of the first millennium and are part of the confession of virtually every Christian denomination historically. However, there are at least two ways in which a religious group fails to meet the standards of being a church.

The first is when they lapse into a state of apostasy. Apostasy occurs when a church leaves its historic moorings, abandons its historic confessional position, and degenerates into a state where either essential Christian truths are blatantly denied or the denial of such truths is widely tolerated.

Another test of apostasy is at the moral level. A church becomes apostate *de facto* when it sanctions and encourages gross and heinous sins. Such practices may be found today in the controversial systems of denominations, such as mainline Episcopalianism and mainline Presbyterianism, both of which have moved away from their historic confessional moorings as well their confessional stands on basic ethical issues.

The decline of a church into apostasy must be differentiated from those communions that never actually achieved the status of a viable church in the first place. It is with respect to this phenomenon that the consideration of cults and heretical sects is usually delineated. Here again we find no universal monolithic definition for what it is that constitutes a cult or a sect. Both terms are capable of more than one meaning or denotation. For example, all churches that practice rites and rituals have at their core a concern for their "cultus." The cultus is the organized body of worship that is found in any church. However, this cultic dimension of legitimate churches can be distorted to such a degree that the use of the term *cult* is applied in its pejorative sense. For example, the dictionary may define the term *cult* as a religion that is considered to be false, unorthodox, or extremist. When we talk about cults in this regard, what comes to mind are the radical distortions in fringe groups, such as the Jonestown phenomenon. There, a group of devotees attached themselves to their megalomaniacal leader, Jim Jones, and illustrated their devotion to such a degree that they willingly submitted to Jones' direction to take their Kool-Aid laced with cyanide. This is cultic behavior with a vengeance. The same kind of thing could be seen among the Branch Davidians, the followers of Father Divine in Philadelphia, and other lesser groups that have come and gone over the course of church history.*

It is noteworthy that almost any compendium that treats the history of cults will include within its studies large bodies of religion such as Mormons and Jehovah's Witnesses. Nevertheless, the sheer size and endurance of such groups tend to give them more credibility as time passes and as more people associate with their beliefs. When we look at groups such as the Mormons and the Jehovah's Witnesses, we find elements of truth within their confessions. Yet at the same time, they express clear denials of what historically may be considered essential truths of the Christian faith. This certainly includes their unabashed denial of the deity of Christ. Jehovah's Witnesses and Mormons have this denial in common. Though both place Jesus in some type of exalted position within their respective creeds, He does not attain the level of deity. Both groups consider Christ an exalted creature. Following the thinking of the ancient heretic Arius, Mormons and Jehovah's Witnesses argue that the New Testament does not teach the deity of Christ; rather, they argue it teaches He is the exalted

---

* The Branch Davidians were the followers of cult leader David Koresh (1959–93); they are well known for a standoff with federal agents near Waco, Tex., that ended on April 19, 1993, with a fire that killed seventy-six members. Father Divine (1876–1965) was an African American spiritual leader and founder of the International Peace Mission movement; he claimed to be the second coming of Christ.

firstborn of all creation. They say He is the first creature made by God, who then is given superior power and authority over the rest of creation. Though Jesus is lifted up in such Christology, it still falls far short of Christian orthodoxy, which confesses the deity of Christ. Passages in the New Testament such as Jesus being "begotten" and His being the "firstborn of creation" are incorrectly used to justify this creaturely definition of Christ.

In the first three centuries of Christian history, the biblical passage that dominated reflection on the church's understanding of Christ was the prologue of the gospel of John. This prologue contains the affirmation of Christ's being the *Logos*, or the eternal Word of God. John declares in his gospel that the *Logos* was "with God in the beginning, and was God." This "with God" suggests a distinction between the *Logos* and God, but the identification by the linking verb "was" indicates an identity between the *Logos* and God. The way in which this identity is denied by Mormons and Jehovah's Witnesses and other cultists is by substituting the indefinite article in the text, rendering it that the *Logos* was "a god." In order to wrest this interpretation from the text, one must have a prior affirmation of some form of polytheism. Such polytheism is utterly foreign to Judeo-Christian theology, where deity is understood in monotheistic terms.

The threat of cultic distortions is something the church must struggle with in every generation and in every age. It is also important to understand that even legitimate churches may contain within it practices that reflect the behavior of the cults. Cults can emerge within the structures of certain churches. In the Roman communion, for example, we see in Haiti a mixture of Roman Catholic theology with the cultic practices of voodoo. Also in that same communion there is no question that large groups of people venerate Mary to a degree that is beyond the limits espoused by that church itself, degenerating their worship into a cult mentality. But such can be the case among Lutherans, Presbyterians, or any group, when orthodoxy is sacrificed for the devotion to idols.

"True systematic theology seeks to understand the system of theology that is contained within the whole scope of sacred Scripture."

—

THE FIVE POINTS OF CALVINISM

NOVEMBER 2005

———

T HE LATE THEOLOGIAN CORNELIUS VAN TIL once made the observation that Calvinism is not to be identified with the so-called five
points of Calvinism. Rather, Van Til concluded that the five points
function as a pathway, or a bridge, to the entire structure of Reformed
theology. Likewise, Charles Spurgeon argued that Calvinism is merely a
nickname for biblical theology. These titans of the past understood that
the essence of Reformed theology cannot be reduced to five particular
points that arose as points of controversy centuries ago in Holland with
the Remonstrants, who objected to five specific points of the system of
doctrine found in historic Calvinism. Those five points have become
associated with the acrostic TULIP: Total depravity, Unconditional election, Limited atonement, Irresistible grace, and Perseverance of the saints.

It is the task of this article to approach the question of Reformed theology from the perspective of what is called in philosophy the *via negativa*.
This method of approaching truth defines things in terms of what they
are not; hence, it is called the "way of negation." For example, when we
speak of the nature of God, we say that He is infinite, which simply means
that He is "not finite." This is an example of the use of the way of negation.
When we have a clear understanding of how to employ this method, the
way of affirmation, its opposite, becomes manifest. As we look at what
Reformed theology is not, it helps us to understand what it is.

We begin by saying that Reformed theology is not a chaotic set of disconnected ideas. Rather, Reformed theology is systematic. We live in a
time when systems of thought are decried in a postmodern world, not
only in the secular arena of ideas, but even within Christian seminaries.
Historically, the principle of systematic theology has been this: The Bible,

being the Word of God, reflects the coherence and unity of the God whose Word it is. To be sure, it would be a distortion to take a foreign system of thought and force it upon Scripture, making Scripture conform to it as if it were some kind of procrustean bed. That is not the goal of sound, systematic theology. Rather, true systematic theology seeks to understand the system of theology that is contained within the whole scope of sacred Scripture. It does not impose ideas upon the Bible; it listens to the ideas that are proclaimed by the Bible and understands them in a coherent way.

The next point we make by way of negation is that Reformed theology is not anthropocentric. That is to say, Reformed theology is not centered on human beings. The central focal point of Reformed theology is God, and it's the doctrine of God that permeates the whole of the substance of Reformed thought. Thus Reformed theology, by way of affirmation, can be called theocentric.

Though it is not often helpful to speak about paradoxes in our understanding of truth, there is nevertheless one paradox I like to maintain. On the one hand, the doctrine of God proper, that is, the doctrine of the nature, attributes, and character of God, affirmed by various creeds of Reformation thought, has little that is different from other theologies and other expressions of faith found among Lutherans, Roman Catholics, Methodists, and the like. At the same time, and herein lies the paradox, the most distinctive dimension of Reformed theology is its doctrine of God. Though it sounds like I'm writing out of both sides of my pen, let me hasten to clarify this paradoxical assertion. After Reformed theology articulates its doctrine of the nature and character of God in the first principles of its system of doctrine, it does not thereafter forget its affirmations when it addresses other doctrines. Rather, our understanding of the character of God is primary and determinant with respect to our understanding of all other doctrines. That is to say, our understanding of salvation has as its control factor, right at the heart of it, our understanding of the character of God.

Reformed theology is not anti-catholic. This may seem strange since Reformed theology grows directly out of the Protestant movement of the sixteenth century, which movement was called "Protestant" because it involved a "protest" against the teaching and activity of Roman Catholicism. But the term *catholic* refers to catholic Christianity, the essence of which may be found in the ecumenical creeds of the first thousand years of church history, particularly the early creeds and church councils, such as the Council of Nicaea in the fourth century and the Council of Chalcedon in the fifth century. That is to say, those creeds contain common articles of faith shared by all denominations that embrace orthodox Christianity, doctrines such as the Trinity and the atonement of Christ. The doctrines affirmed by all Christians are at the heart and core of Calvinism. Calvinism does not depart on a search for a new theology and reject the common base of theology that the whole church shares.

Reformed theology is not Roman Catholic in its understanding of justification. This is simply to say that Reformed theology is evangelical in the historical sense of the word. In this regard, Reformed theology stands strongly and firmly with Martin Luther and the magisterial Reformers in their articulation of the doctrine of justification by faith alone. It affirms the *solas* of the Reformation, which are the formal and material causes of the sixteenth-century Reformation. Those two principles are the doctrines of *sola Scriptura* and *sola fide*. Neither of these doctrines are explicitly declared in the five points of Calvinism; yet, in a sense, they become the foundation for the other characteristics of Reformed theology. These introductory statements about what Reformed theology is not are given a much broader and deeper expression in my book *What Is Reformed Theology?*, which was written to help laypersons and Christian leaders understand the essence of Reformed theology. In this article I am giving the bare-bones approach to the doctrine, reminding *Tabletalk* readers that Reformed theology so far transcends the mere five points of Calvinism that it is an entire life and world view. It is covenantal. It is sacramental. It is committed to transforming culture. It is subordinate to the operation of God the Holy Spirit, and it has a rich framework for understanding the entirety of the council of God revealed in the Bible.

BORN OF THE VIRGIN MARY

DECEMBER 2005

———

LONG WITH THE GREAT THEOLOGIAN and philosopher Anselm of Canterbury we ask the question, *Cur Deus homo?* Why the God-man? When we look at the biblical answer to that question, we see that the purpose behind the incarnation of Christ is to fulfill His work as God's appointed Mediator. It is said in 1 Timothy 2:5–6: "For there is one God and one Mediator between God and men, the Man Christ Jesus, who gave Himself. . . ." Now, the Bible speaks of many mediators with a small or lower case *m*. A mediator is an agent who stands between two parties who are estranged and in need of reconciliation. But when Paul writes to Timothy of a solitary Mediator, a single Mediator, with a capital *M*, he's referring to that Mediator who is the supreme Intercessor between God and fallen humanity. This Mediator, Jesus Christ, is indeed the God-man.

In the early centuries of the church, with the office of mediator and the ministry of reconciliation in view, the church had to deal with heretical movements that would disturb the balance of this mediating character of Christ. Our one Mediator, who stands as an agent to reconcile God and man, is the One who participates both in deity and in humanity. In the gospel of John, we read that it was the eternal *Logos*, the Word, who became flesh and dwelt among us. It was the second person of the Trinity who took upon Himself a human nature to work out our redemption. In the fifth century at the Council of Chalcedon in 451, the church had to fight against a sinister teaching called the Monophysite heresy. The term *monophysite* is derived from the prefix *mono*, which means "one," and from the root *physis*, which means "nature" or "essence." The heretic Eutyches taught that Christ, in the incarnation, had a single nature, which he called a "theanthropic nature." This theanthropic nature (which combines the word *theos*, meaning "God," and *anthrōpos*, meaning "man") gives us a Savior who is a hybrid, but under close scrutiny would be seen to be one who was neither God nor man. The Monophysite heresy obscured the distinction between God and man, giving us either a deified human or a humanized deity. It was against the backdrop of this heresy that the Chalcedonian Creed insisted Christ possesses two distinct natures, divine and human. He is *vere homo* (truly human) and *vere Deus* (truly divine, or truly God). These two natures are united in the mystery of the incarnation, but it is important according to Christian orthodoxy that we understand the divine nature of Christ is fully God and the human nature is fully human. So this one person who had two natures, divine and human, was perfectly suited to be our Mediator between God and men. An earlier church council, the Council of Nicaea in 325, had declared that Christ came "for us men, and for our salvation." That is, His mission was to reconcile the estrangement that existed between God and humanity.

It is important to note that for Christ to be our perfect Mediator, the incarnation was not a union between God and an angel, or between God and a brutish creature such as an elephant or a chimpanzee. The reconciliation that was needed was between God and human beings. In His role as Mediator and the God-man, Jesus assumed the office of the second Adam, or what the Bible calls the last Adam. He entered into a corporate solidarity with our humanity, being a representative like unto Adam in his representation. Paul, for example, in his letter to the Romans gives the contrast between the original Adam and Jesus as the second Adam. In Romans 5, verse 15, he says, "For if by the one man's offense many died, much more the grace of God and the gift by the grace of the one Man, Jesus Christ, abounded to many." Here we observe the contrast between the calamity that came upon the human race because of the disobedience of the original Adam and the glory that comes to believers because of Christ's obedience. Paul goes on to say in verse 19: "For as by one man's disobedience many were made sinners, so also by one Man's obedience many will be made righteous." Adam functioned in the role of a mediator, and he failed miserably in his task. That failure was rectified by the perfect success of Christ, the God-man. We read later in Paul's letter to the Corinthians these words: "And so it is written, 'The first man Adam became a living being.' The last Adam became a life-giving spirit. However, the spiritual is not first, but the natural, and afterward the spiritual. The first man was of the earth, made of dust; the second Man is the Lord from heaven. As was the man of dust, so also are those who are made of dust; and as is the heavenly Man, so also are those who are heavenly. And as we have borne the image of the man of dust, we shall also bear the image of the heavenly Man" (1 Cor. 15:45–49).

We see then the purpose of the first advent of Christ. The Logos took upon Himself a human nature, the Word became flesh to effect our redemption by fulfilling the role of the perfect Mediator between God and man. The new Adam is our champion, our representative, who satisfies the demands of God's law for us and wins for us the blessing that God promised to His creatures if we would obey His law. Like Adam, we failed to obey the Law, but the new Adam, our Mediator, has fulfilled the Law perfectly for us and won for us the crown of redemption. That is the foundation for the joy of Christmas.

CHRISTIAN LOSES HIS BURDEN

JANUARY 2006

———

A S A SEMINARY STUDENT, I remember my favorite professor often setting forth arguments for particular theological positions. On many occasions, as these debates proceeded, the professor stopped in mid-sentence, paused, looked at his students and said, "I sense that you do not feel the weight of this argument." His regular reference to the "weight" of arguments was an interesting metaphor for me. Arguments that we do not take seriously are those that we take lightly. The whole idea of weight or weightiness is one that is found throughout the Bible. In the first instance, the glory of God is described in terms of His inherent and eternal weightiness. Those who take God lightly are those who have no regard for His glory.

One of the most important areas in which the whole idea of weight comes to bear in the New Testament has to do with the Law. In Paul's letter to the Romans, in chapter 3, verse 9, after he has set forth the unrighteousness of both Jew and Gentile, he makes the comment, "What then? Are we better than they? Not at all. For we have previously charged both Jews and Greeks that they are all under sin" (NKJV). Again in verses 19–20 of the same chapter, the Apostle writes, "Now we know that whatever the law says, it says to those who are under the law, that every mouth may be stopped, and all the world may become guilty before God. Therefore by the deeds of the law no flesh will be justified in His sight, for by the law is the knowledge of sin" (NKJV).

In our day, the weightiness of the Gospel itself has been eclipsed. I doubt if there's a period in the history of the church in which professing evangelicals have been as ignorant of the elements of the biblical Gospel as they are today.

There is a stark contrast between the second best-seller in the history of the English language, second only to the Bible, namely, John Bunyan's *Pilgrim's Progress*, and the runaway best-seller of the last two years, *The Purpose Driven Life*. In Bunyan's *Pilgrim's Progress*, we see set forth in masterful literary style the depths and the riches of the biblical Gospel. When we compare it to *The Purpose Driven Life*, we see a book in which it is difficult to find a full explanation of the biblical Gospel. Justification, the relief from the burden of sin that weighs down the soul, is all but absent in the setting forth of a new and different gospel of achieving or discovering purpose in one's life. One of the leaders of the recent emerging church movement boasts that he has not mentioned the word "sin" in the last ten years of his preaching.* He wants to make sure that his people will not feel crushed by guilt or by a loss of their self-esteem. When the acute awareness of guilt is removed from the conscience, there is no sense of the burden of sin. There is no sense of being under the crushing weight of the law of God that bears down upon our souls relentlessly.

However, if we turn our attention to the insights of Bunyan set forth in the Christian classic *Pilgrim's Progress*, we see a story that focuses on the groaning pressure of a man who is weighed down to the depths of his soul with a burden of which he is unable to rid himself. It is like the Apostle Paul's description in Romans 7 of the body of death that crushes the spirit. In the very first paragraph on the first page of *Pilgrim's Progress*, Bunyan pens these lines:

> As I walked through the wilderness of this world, I lighted on a certain place, where was a den; and I laid me down in that place to sleep: and as I slept I dreamed a dream. I dreamed, and behold I saw a man clothed with rags, standing in a certain place, with his face from his own house, a book in his hand, and a great burden upon his back. I looked, and saw him open the book, and read therein; and as he read,

---

* The emerging church is a movement of the late twentieth and early twenty-first centuries that seeks to reconcile traditional Christianity with a postmodern world. It emphasizes "conversation" rather than propositional truth and is generally skeptical of institutional Christianity.

he wept and trembled: and not being able longer to contain, he brake out with a lamentable cry; saying, "What shall I do?"

When preachers announce from their pulpits that God loves people unconditionally, there is hardly any reason for the hearer to feel any burden or cry out with any lament, saying, "What shall I do?" If indeed God loves us unconditionally and requires nothing of us, then obviously there is no need for us to do anything. But if God has judged us according to the righteousness of His perfect Law and has called the whole world before His tribunal to announce that we are all guilty, that none of us is righteous, that none of us seeks after God, that there is no fear of God before our eyes, that we are in the meantime, before the appointed day of judgment, treasuring up wrath against the day of wrath, then anybody in his right mind (and even those in their wrong mind) would have enough sense to cry out the same lamentation, "What shall I do?" The story of Christian is the story of a man who is burdened by the weight of sin. His conscience was smitten by the Law, but where the Law is eliminated in the church, no one needs to fear divine judgment. Without the Law there is no knowledge of sin, and without a knowledge of sin, there is no sense of burden. The pilgrim knew the Law, he knew his sin, and he realized he had a burden on his back that he could not, with all of his effort and his greatest strivings, ever remove. His redemption must come from outside of himself. He needed a righteousness not his own. He needed to exchange that weighty sack of sin on his back for an alien righteousness acceptable in the sight of God. For the pilgrim there was only one place to find that righteousness, at the foot of the cross. The crucial moment in Christian's life is when he comes to the cross. We read the description: "He ran thus till he came to a place somewhat ascending; and upon that place stood a cross, and little below in the bottom, a sepulchre. So I saw in my dream, that just as Christian came up with the cross, his burden loosed from off his shoulders, and fell from off his back; and began to tumble, and so continued to do so until it came to the mouth of the sepulchre, where it fell in, and I saw it no more."

Shortly thereafter, Christian sang his song of deliverance: "Thus far did I come laden with my sin, nor could aught ease the grief that I was in, till I came hither. What a place is this! Must here be the beginning of my bliss? Must here the burden fall from off my back? Must here the strings that bound it to me, crack? Blessed cross! Blessed sepulchre! Blessed rather be the Man that there was put to shame for me."

This is the description of how salvation comes. It comes as a result of the atoning work of Christ and the exchange of our sin from our backs to His, as well as the cloak of His righteousness being transferred from His account to ours. Anything that eliminates this double exchange, this double imputation of sin and righteousness, falls short of the biblical Gospel. It's time once more for the Christian community to follow the *Pilgrim's Progress.*

AN HISTORICAL FAITH

FEBRUARY 2006

———

"ONCE UPON A TIME . . ." These words signal the beginning of a fairy tale, a story of make believe, not an account of sober history. Unlike beginning with the words "once upon a time," the Bible begins with the words, "In the beginning God . . ." This statement, at the front end of the entire Bible, introduces the Pentateuch or the first five books of the Old Testament, and it sets the stage for God's activity in linear history. From the opening chapters of Genesis to the end of the book of Revelation, the entire dynamic of redemption takes place within the broader setting of real space and time, of concrete history.

The historical character of Judeo-Christianity is what markedly distinguishes it from all forms of mythology. A myth finds its value in its moral or spiritual application, while its historical reality remains insignificant. Fairy tales can help our mood swings, but they do little to give us confidence in ultimate reality. The twentieth century witnessed a crisis in the historical dimension of biblical Christianity. German theologians made a crucial distinction between ordinary history and what they called "salvation history," or sometimes "redemptive history." This distinction was based in the first instance on the obvious character of sacred Scripture, namely, that it is not only a record of the ordinary events of men and nations. It is not a mere chronicle of human activity but includes within it the revelation of God's activity in the midst of history. Because the Bible differs from ordinary history and was called "salvation history," it was a short step from there to ripping the biblical revelation out of its historical context altogether. No one was more important in the snatching of the Gospels out of history than the German theologian Rudolf Bultmann. Bultmann devised a new theology that he called "a theology of timelessness." This theology of timelessness is not interested in the past or in the future as categories of reality. What counts according to Bultmann is the *hic et nunc*, the "here and now," or the present moment. Salvation doesn't take place on the horizontal plane of history, but it takes place vertically in the present moment or what others called "the existential moment."

We might ask the question: How long does a moment last? There is a parallel between Descartes' concept of the "point" and the existentialist's concept of the "moment." When Descartes searched for a middle position between the physical and the mental, the extended and the non-extended, he described a mathematical point as the transition between the two realms. The point serves as a hybrid between the physical and the non-physical in the sense that a point takes up space, but has no definite dimensions. In similar fashion, the function of the existential moment in salvation for people like Bultmann is this, that the moment is in time but has no definite duration. On the one hand, it participates in time; on the other hand, it transcends time and is what some have called "supratemporal," that is, beyond time. When salvation is understood in these terms, the whole notion of linear history becomes basically insignificant and unimportant. The old quest for the historical Jesus can then be abandoned as being a fool's errand. Again, for Bultmann's existential Gospel, salvation comes directly and immediately from above. It comes from the vertical plane, in a moment of existential crisis.

Bultmann went on to make a distinction between history and mythology, arguing that the Bible is a mixture of both. In order for the Bible to be relevant to modern people, it must first be stripped of its mythological husk in order to penetrate the salvific core. That is, it must be submitted to the task of "demythologizing."

Not everybody in twentieth-century biblical scholarship embraced the thought of Bultmann with respect to redemption and history. Some of his critics accused him of being a neo-gnostic for lifting salvation out of the plane of the knowable.

Herman Ridderbos, the Dutch New Testament scholar, agreed that biblical history is *redemptive* history, but it is at the same time redemptive *history*. Though the content of Scripture is deeply concerned with redemption, that redemption is inseparably tied to the reality of the historical context in which it takes place. One need not be a philosopher or a theological scholar to understand the difference between the words, "once upon a time," and the words, "in the year that king Uzziah died," or, "a decree went out from Caesar Augustus." The biblical concept of redemption in history sees God moving in space and time, preparing His people for the consummation of His plan of salvation. Christ comes to the earth not at an accidental point in history but "in the fullness of time" (Gal. 4:4).

Oscar Cullmann, the Swiss scholar, wrote strenuously combating the vertical, existential theology of Bultmann by doing a fascinating study of the concept of time itself in Scripture. He emphasized, for example, the distinction between two Greek words, both of which can be translated by the English word *time*. The two Greek words are *kairos* and *chronos*. *Chronos* refers to the moment-by-moment passage of time. It is the word from which English words like *chronicle, chronology,* or *chronometer* are derived. It refers to the ordinary passage of time in history. *Kairos* refers to a particularly pregnant moment in history that is of enduring significance. A kairotic moment is a moment that shapes the history of everything that comes after it. In the Old Testament, for example, the exodus was a kairotic moment. In the New Testament, the birth of Jesus, the cross, and the resurrection are all kairotic moments. The closest word we have to this in English is the word *historic*. Every event that takes place in history is historical, but not every event that takes place in history is deemed historic. To be historic it has to have special significance and special impact on life. So the Bible is the record of God's historic works of redemption within the context of space and time. Take the Gospel and its message out of the context of history, and Christianity is destroyed altogether.

THE LIBERAL AGENDA

MARCH 2006

——

W HEN ANY DISCUSSION DEVELOPS CONCERNING Christianity and liberalism, it is crucial that one gives a proper definition of liberalism. The term *liberal* can mean anything from being free in one's thinking to being a proponent of the latest fad in the realm of theology or any other ideology. The term *liberal* shifts with the sands of time in as much as yesterday's liberal may be considered today's conservative without changing views.

However, when we speak of liberalism in the field of theology, we are not thinking of a frame of mind or a philosophical bent but a distinct historical movement that captured the minds of many churchmen in the nineteenth century. Nineteenth-century liberalism followed closely on the heels of enlightenment thought and was married philosophically to many of the ideas that defined modernism. The root idea that defined liberalism was the influence of the philosophy of naturalism. Naturalism asserts that all reality can be explained in purely natural categories without any appeal to the supernatural. As a result, nineteenth-century liberalism saw a wholesale attack on all things supernatural contained within historic orthodox Christianity.

The principal targets of nineteenth-century liberalism included the miracles attributed to Jesus in the New Testament (not to mention all of the miracles recorded in the Old Testament). Those events that are defined or described in Scripture as being miraculous, indeed, caused by the supernatural agency of God, were rejected as naïve, pre-scientific myths that found their way into the original documents of Scripture. The miraculous acts of Jesus were explained away. For example, the feeding of the five thousand was sometimes described as an act of fraud by which Jesus had hidden a cache of fish and loaves in a cave with a secret opening concealed by His long flowing robe. And like the magician who pulls sausages or scarves endlessly out of his sleeves, so Jesus, standing in front of the concealed entrance of the cave, was assisted in His magical work by the disciples, who, working as a bucket brigade, were feeding the fish and loaves through the secret entrance into Jesus' cloak, out His sleeves, to the masses. Another tack taken by the liberals was to give a moral explanation to the miracles of Jesus. In the case of the feeding of the five thousand, what Jesus did was to persuade those who brought lunches with them to share their food with those who had brought none. This was an "ethical miracle," by which Jesus promoted the ethic of sharing with one's fellow human beings.

Next on the target list were the supernatural aspects of the life of Jesus. Of particular concern for nineteenth-century liberals was their assault against the virgin birth. Not only was the virgin birth rejected, but every supernatural aspect of Jesus' life, including the transfiguration, His atonement as a transcendent supernatural event, His resurrection, His ascension, and His return at the end of the age. All of these things were cast aside as so many accretions of early church mythology. Obviously, since the Bible reports the person and work of Christ in supernatural terms involving angels, miracles, and the fulfillment of predictive prophecy, all of those aspects found in sacred Scripture were also rejected. The Bible was the favorite target of this assault, by which critical scholars rejected all predictive prophecy and anything that smacked of the supernatural, reducing the Bible to just another human book of the ancient world.

This new wave of thinking swept through Europe, with its roots principally in Germany, and then it crossed the ocean to theological seminaries in the United States and produced a crisis within many churches. What does one do with billions of dollars' worth of church property and the thousands of people who are ordained to be clergy who no longer believe the historic content of orthodox Christianity? Some took the position that the only honest response to this skepticism was to resign from the ministry and find employment in another line of work. However, the overwhelming majority of those who espoused this view decided simply to restructure the mission of the church. The mission of the church became no longer an enterprise of bringing personal redemption supernaturally between the soul and God; rather, it sought social redemption by alleviating, as far as possible, human suffering. This gave way to the birth of the so-called "social gospel," which saw the good news found in the church's mission to meet the humanitarian needs of society. The Gospel itself was given a new definition in terms of social action. Along with the denials of particular aspects of historic Christianity, a denial of the importance of Christian doctrine also came in its wake. Doctrine was something that was derived from the teaching of the Bible, and since the Bible was now suspect, there was no need for any significant maintenance of orthodox Christian doctrine.

In every age, the church is threatened by heresy, and heresy is bound up in false doctrine. It is the desire of all heretics to minimize the importance of doctrine. When doctrine is minimized, heresy can exercise itself without restraint. In the twentieth century, the Swiss theologian Emil Brunner wrote his treatise on the person of Christ titled *The Mediator*. In that book, Brunner used one word to describe the essence of nineteenth-century liberalism: "unbelief." He saw in liberalism not a simple change of nuance in the content of the Christian faith but a wholesale rejection of the very heart and soul of biblical Christianity. The twentieth century saw the continuation of the impact of liberalism, particularly in the mainline denominations in America, with the advent of so-called neo-liberalism following the radical criticism of men like Rudolf Bultmann and his successors.

This liberal agenda has by no means disappeared from the life of the church. It has gained almost total control of the mainline denominations and has made its influence felt strongly within evangelical circles. Within evangelicalism itself, we have seen a serious erosion of biblical authority, a willingness to negotiate the biblical Gospel itself, and a widespread rejection of doctrine as being unimportant and in no way foundational to the Christian faith. Liberalism stands in every generation as a flat rejection of the faith. It must not be viewed as a simple subset or denominational impulse of Christianity; it must be seen for what it is—the antithesis of Christianity based on a complete rejection of the biblical Christ and His Gospel.

TRIUNE MONARCHY

APRIL 2006

———

T HE MOST BASIC AFFIRMATION THE SCRIPTURES make regarding the nature of God is that He is one. The Shema of Deuteronomy 6 reads as follows: "Hear, O Israel: the LORD our God, the LORD is one" (v. 4). These words that preface the great commandment are axiomatic to the biblical understanding of the nature of God. Old and New Testaments together bear witness to the eternal truth that there exists one God—monotheism. Another term for *monotheism* is the word *Monarchianism*, meaning that the God of the Bible is a monarch. *Monarch* comes from a Greek word that has a prefix and a root. The prefix *mono* means "one" or "single." The root word *archē* means "beginning, chief, or ruler." We hear of archbishops, archenemies, archangels, all of which employ the root term *archē*.

A monarchy is a form of government in which the rule is restricted to one person, a king or a queen, as distinguished from the rule of the few (oligarchy) or the rule of many (plutarchy). The doctrine of the Trinity, central to Christian confession, is not the result of abstract speculation. Rather, it is the result of the church's reflection on the teaching of the Bible. With respect to the doctrine of the Trinity, or what I call "triune monarchy," the church was faced with two distinct issues. The first was the responsibility to exercise fidelity to the Bible. The second was to be clear in its rejection of heretical doctrine.

Two virulent Monarchian heresies emerged in the first three hundred years of the Christian church. The first was called Modalistic Monarchianism, as expressed in the heretical views of Sabellius. This form of Monarchianism will be treated in another article in this issue of *Tabletalk*. Suffice to say, it was condemned at Antioch in 267 AD. Perhaps even more serious was the "Dynamic Monarchianism" of Arius, which threatened Christian orthodoxy in the beginning of the fourth century. It resulted in the Council of Nicaea and the Nicene Creed. The theological struggles of the first three centuries were based upon the church's desire to be faithful to biblical monotheism (Monarchianism) and at the same time to be faithful to the attribute of deity for each of the three persons in the Godhead.

The church looked at the role of Jesus in creation and in redemption as the only begotten Son of the Father who wrought for us our redemption. There are multiple manifestations of biblical claims for Jesus as God, as seen, for example, in the kenotic hymn of Philippians 2:6–11, in the high Christology of the book of Hebrews, in the "I am" sayings found in the gospel of John, in the worship that is given to Jesus without rebuke (Matt. 14:33), such as in the case of Thomas at Christ's resurrection appearance (John 20:24–29). But there is no passage of Scripture that more occupied the attention of the theologians of the early church than that found in the prologue to the gospel of John (1:1–18). In this prologue, Jesus is identified as the incarnate Logos, the Word who became flesh. This concept is so profound in the opening verses of John's gospel that it preoccupied the finest minds of the church for the first three hundred years of the church's existence.

What is so striking about John's prologue is found in its opening words: "In the beginning was the Word, and the Word was with God, and the Word was God. He was in the beginning with God. All things were made through Him, and without Him was not any thing made that was made. In Him was life, and the life was the light of men" (1:1–4). These few verses are staggering in their affirmation. On the one hand, the Logos is distinguished from God, inasmuch as John writes that in the beginning the Word was with God. By using the term *with*, the Logos is distinguished from God, even though He was with Him from the beginning. But then the profundity intensifies in the very next clause where the affirmation is made that the Word was God. On the one hand, the Word is distinguished from God. On the other hand, the Word is identified with God. A Christology that honors these two affirmations of the prologue of John must include an identification of the second person of the Trinity with God, while at the same time having some distinction in it that would distinguish the Father from the Son and, subsequently, from the Holy Spirit.

So in the formula of the Trinity, the church bows to sacred Scripture, honoring both the unity of God and the distinctions among the persons of the Godhead. The formula made use of terms such as *person, subsistence, hypostasis,* in an attempt to get at the unity and the distinction within God Himself. In addition to affirming the deity of Jesus, without which deity it would be blasphemous for Him to be an object of worship in the church, the Holy Spirit is also described in the Scriptures in terms of divine attributes. He is omnipotent. He is omniscient. He is infinite. He is eternal. He is actively involved in the divine work of creation, and in conjunction with His being the author of life and human intelligence, He is active in empowering the work of Christ in redemption. We see in the Bible that the work of creation involves the Father, the Son, and the Holy Spirit, just as the work of redemption includes the Father, the Son, and the Holy Spirit. All three are testified to uniformly by the Scriptures as being divine. They are not three gods, because the unity of God remains axiomatic in the Monarchianism of sacred Scripture. The church still declares that the Lord our God is one. He is one being, though we must distinguish within that one being the subsistences of Father, Son, and Holy Spirit.

Therefore, the church distinguishes among the three persons but sees these distinctions as not essential in character. They are essential in the sense of being absolutely vital and important for a true understanding of God, but they are not essential insofar as the distinctions among the three persons of the Godhead are not distinctions of essence, substance, or being, for God is one.

"Once relativism is embraced, there are no brakes on the roller coaster of sensational epistemology."

—

THE DA VINCI CONSPIRACY

MAY 2006

Y ES, VIRGINIA, THERE REALLY IS A lunatic fringe on the ideological spectrum. We commonly hear perspectives described as
left-wing or right-wing. Beyond that, the descriptions become
more precise in terms of radical right and radical left. If we cross the
border beyond the radical of right or left, we enter into the domain of
the lunatic fringe. There is a lunatic fringe on the right, which would
include neo-Nazis, skinheads, and the like. On the radical left there is
also a lunatic fringe that would include within it radical conspiratorial-
ists and even academicians who are educated beyond their intelligence.
For example, the Jesus Seminar represents the lunatic fringe of the theological world. The proper response to their views is not patient, critical
analysis but scorn and ridicule. Their theories and hypotheses are not
worthy of serious rebuttal.

In the realm of ideological discussion, there is always a curious phase
called the "journalistic phase." The journalistic phase is the phase that feeds
upon sensationalism. It grabs the headlines and the interest of reporters
because it is so far out that it is news. The Jesus Seminar has fascinated
news makers by virtue of its being so radically new. The same sort of
thing catches headlines with the cultural success of a book like *The Da
Vinci Code*. *The Da Vinci Code* sensationalizes historical evaluations of
the New Testament documents and their portrait of Jesus of Nazareth.

We are a people absorbed by finding flaws in the famous. We are incurably iconoclastic, relishing the fall of the mighty. We love to sing "O How
the Mighty Have Fallen" when we see famous people caught in criminal
acts or moral improprieties. Notice the attention given to the criminal
trials of high-profile people such as O.J. Simpson. Whenever the mighty
or the hero of the culture falls into corruption, it provokes juicy discussion with delicious elements for a public hungry for controversy. No

one in the historical stage of history is represented with less flaws than Jesus of Nazareth. Indeed, even beyond the church and her confession, Jesus is often perceived as being flawless. Yet there is no more delicious target for sensational fiction writing than Jesus. To sully His character by salacious innuendos is the ultimate form of iconoclasm. Add to the mix the appetite for conspiracy and cover-up, and it's easy to see how *The Da Vinci Code* can be catapulted to the top of the best-selling list. It adds to the critical exposure of Jesus' hidden love life, the additional cover-up involving clues from one of the most high-profile artists in history, Leonardo da Vinci. The famous painting of the Last Supper itself supposedly reveals one of these enormous clues.

Why are we so gullible as to take this kind of thing seriously? The author, who is writing a fictional work, nevertheless claims to be basing his story on real historical data. That claim adds to the fictional dimension of the book. We have here fictional fiction with a fictional claim to historical sobriety. The claims of historical knowledge in this book rely on completely non-credible sources. The actual historical source for the salacious speculations of the behavior of Jesus is found in the pseudo-gospels of the second and third centuries. Very early in church history these pseudo-documents were exposed as frauds that were advanced by the early Gnostic community.

Who were the Gnostics that produced such fraudulent literature? The Gnostics were so named because they claimed to have a special type of knowledge that was unavailable to other people. They borrowed their name from the Greek word for knowledge, which is *gnōsis*. The Gnostics eschewed normal categories of knowledge, such as found universally in human epistemology, namely that we learn what we learn by a combined use of sense perception (empiricism) and rational deduction from the data (rationalism). The Gnostics rejected both and claimed a superior way of knowing through immediate apprehension of truth by mystical intuition. These people who claimed to be "in the know" advanced their intellectual theories as being superior to the insights given by the first-century Apostles. They claimed to have a knowledge that superseded the knowledge of the first-century eyewitnesses of Jesus. There was no end to their fanciful speculations that they claimed were rooted in their own special mystical revelation. In a word, the Gnostics were anti-science and anti-sober history.

It's important for us to understand the rudiments of Gnosticism in as much as we live in what has been called a neo-gnostic culture. Our culture has been defined by an intoxication with New Age theories that share many things in common with Gnosticism. The most obvious point of commonality is the substitute of mystical insight for rational and empirical investigation. We also live in an age that is characterized by the embracing of philosophical and moral relativism. Relativism and Gnosticism are not one and the same thing, but they have so many common elements that they are compatible with each other. Once relativism is embraced, there are no brakes on the roller coaster of sensational epistemology. It opens the door for the kind of literature that makes *The Da Vinci Code* well read and its author, Dan Brown, famous. The flaws of this book reveal far more about the flaws in the character of its author than it does about alleged flaws of the most impeccable character in history.

THE PROBLEM OF PAIN

JUNE 2006

——

T HE PROBLEM OF EVIL HAS BEEN defined as the Achilles' heel of the Christian faith. For centuries people have wrestled with the conundrum, how a good and loving God could allow evil and pain to be so prevalent in His creation. The philosophical problems have generated an abundance of reflection and discussion, some of which will be reiterated in this issue, but in the final analysis, the problem is one that quickly moves from the abstract level into the realm of human experience. The philosophical bumps into the existential.

Historically, evil has been defined in terms of privation (*privatio*) and negation (*negatio*), especially in the works of Augustine of Hippo and Thomas Aquinas. The point of such definitions is to define evil in terms of a lack of, or negation of, the good. We define sin, for example, as any want of conformity to, or transgression of, the law of God. Sin is characteristically defined in negative terms. We speak of sin as *dis*obedience, law*less*ness, *im*morality, *un*ethical behavior, and the like. So that, above and beyond the problem of evil always stands the standard of good by which evil is determined to be evil. In this regard, evil is parasitic. It depends upon a host outside of itself for its very definition. Nothing can be said to be evil without the prior standard of the good. Nevertheless, as much as we speak of evil as a privation or negation of the good, we can't escape the power of its reality.

At the time of the Reformation, the magisterial Reformers embraced the definition of evil they inherited from the earlier church fathers in terms of *privatio*, of privation and negation. They modified it with one critical word. *Privatio* began to be described as *privatio actuosa* (an actual, or real, privation). The point of this distinction was to call attention to the reality of evil. If we think of evil and pain simply in terms of negation and privation, and seek to avoid the actuality of it, we can easily slip into the absurd error of considering evil an illusion.

Whatever else evil is, it is not illusory. We experience the pangs of its impact, not only in an individual sense, but in a cosmic sense. The whole creation groans, we are told by Scripture, waiting for the manifestation of the sons of God. The judgment of God upon the human race was a judgment that extended to all things over which Adam and Eve had dominion, including the whole earth. The curse is spread far beyond the house of Adam into every crevice of God's creation. The reality of this curse puts a weighty burden and uncomfortable cloak upon all of life. It is indeed a cloak of pain.

Many years ago I had a dear Christian friend who was in the hospital going through a rigorous series of chemotherapy treatments. The chemotherapy at that time provoked a violent nausea in her. When I spoke to her about her experience, I asked her how her faith was standing up in the midst of this trial. She replied, "R.C., it is hard to be a Christian with your head in the toilet." This graphic response to my question made a lasting impression on me. Faith is difficult when our physical bodies are writhing in pain. And yet, it is at this point perhaps more than any other that the Christian flees to the Word of God for comfort. It is for this reason that foundational to the Christian faith is the affirmation that God is sovereign over evil and over all pain. It will not do to dismiss the problem of pain to the realm of Satan. Satan can do nothing except under the sovereign authority of God. He cannot throw a single fiery dart our way without the sovereign will of our heavenly Father.

There is no portion of Scripture that more dramatically communicates this point than the entire Old Testament book of Job. The book of Job tells of a man who is pushed to the absolute limit of endurance with the problem of pain. God allows Job to be an unprotected target for the malice of Satan. Everything dear to Job is stripped from him, including his family, his worldly goods, and his own physical health. Yet, at the end of the day, in the midst of his misery, while his home is atop a dunghill, Job cries out: "The LORD gave, and the LORD has taken away; blessed be the name of the LORD" (1:21). It is easy to quote this utterance from Job in a glib and smug manner. But we must go beyond the glib and penetrate to the very heart of this man in the midst of his misery. He was not putting on a spiritual act or trying to sound pious in the midst of his pain. Rather, he exhibited an astonishing level of abiding trust in his Creator. The ultimate expression of that trust came in his words, "Though He slay me, yet will I trust Him" (13:15). Job prefigures the Christian life, a life that is lived not on Fifth Avenue, the venue of the Easter parade, but on the *Via Dolorosa*, the way of sorrows that ends at the foot of the cross. The Christian life is a life that embraces the sacrament of baptism, which signifies, among other things, that we are baptized into the death, humiliation, and the afflictions of Jesus Christ. We are warned in Scripture that if we are not willing to embrace those afflictions, then we will not participate in Jesus' exaltation. The Christian faith baptizes a person not only into pain, but also into the resurrection of Christ. Whatever pain we experience in this world may be acute, but it is always temporary. In every moment that we experience the anguish of suffering, there beats in our hearts the hope of heaven—that evil and pain are temporary and are under the judgment of God, the same God who gave a promise to His people that there will be a time when pain will be no more. The *privatio* and the *negatio* will be trumped by the presence of Christ.

PAUL: A SERVANT OF JESUS CHRIST

JULY 2006

——

W HEN I LOOK BACK OVER FORTY YEARS of teaching, I sometimes think I must be the most inarticulate writer and speaker
in the history of the world. I wonder about that when I
read interpretations of my teaching from the pens of other people, particularly from those who are hostile to what I declare. Frequently the
distortions are so great that I cannot recognize my own position in the
criticism. It may be helpful in trying to interpret mine or any other
teacher's declarations by looking at their geographical backgrounds. I
grew up in the city of Pittsburgh, in a blue-collar environment, yet in
a white-collar home, and so one can see that the perspective I have on
life will differ from those people who grew up in southern California or
Alabama. Nevertheless, to interpret my teachings simply on the basis
of my Pittsburgh background would be utter nonsense. My perspective
is not identical to every person who ever grew up in Pittsburgh. In like
manner, one could examine my educational background and look at
the viewpoints of my main mentors. As a student of G.C. Berkouwer in
the Netherlands, one can certainly see dimensions of influence on my
thought from that theologian. But to identify my general approach in
theology to Berkouwer's would be to distort my own views. It would
even be incorrect to identify my theology totally with that of my main
mentor, the late John H. Gerstner. The reason for this is that I have
had many mentors in addition to those I've already mentioned, and
also, through my own studies of the Bible and of church history, I have
developed some positions that one cannot find in these other people.
Still, it may be valuable from time to time to examine the background

and education of theologians to get a deeper understanding of their teachings. Such investigation indeed may be beneficial while at the same time perilous.

I mentioned my own experience simply to call attention to a much greater issue, one that far transcends how people interpret or misinterpret me, namely, how we go about seeking a correct understanding of the biblical writers in general and for the benefit of this issue of *Tabletalk*, the teaching of the Apostle Paul in particular. In the New Testament, Paul himself indicates in one of his defenses that he was from Tarsus, which he describes as no mean city. Tarsus was a city that was cosmopolitan in antiquity, and, as a melting pot, it became a place where the exchange of many diverse ideas commonly took place. That Paul was exposed to views that arose beyond the borders of his own home town is something we can take virtually for granted. Paul goes on to cite his background as a student at the feet of the renowned rabbi Gamaliel. It is without doubt that Paul's thinking was shaped to some degree by his great mentor Gamaliel. We know that Paul was immersed academically in the content of the Old Testament as well as in the writings of the rabbinic scholars of his day. But to interpret Paul solely on the grounds of the teachings of the rabbinic scholars of antiquity would be to negate critical factors of influence in the development of Paul's thought.

In our day, two very significant movements have occurred in biblical scholarship that have brought with it deleterious effects on biblical doctrine. The first such development is what is called "atomistic" exegesis or interpretation. This approach to the Scriptures sees the individual books and individual passages of those books, the "atom bits of teaching," as ideas that must be interpreted only in their immediate contexts and not in the context of the whole scope of Scripture, or even of the whole scope of a particular writer's expressions. For example, one scholar may say he will interpret Paul's teaching of justification as set forth in Ephesians without any consideration of what Paul said of the doctrine in Galatians or in Romans. Each passage is treated as an atom of insight, and whether that atom coheres with bits of teaching found elsewhere in the author's writing or in the whole of Scripture is irrelevant. The Reformation rule of interpreting the Bible—that the Bible is its own interpreter and that we are not to set one portion of Scripture against another—is thrown to the winds in this approach. Indeed, even among professing evangelicals, to insist on coherency in the Word of God is to offend them. They have bought into the notion of relativism, that even the Bible, as the inspired Word of God, can at times be contradictory and incoherent, because coherency and consistency are virtues that theologians impose upon our doctrine of God and are not to be found in the Scriptures themselves. This approach to biblical interpretation and to the doctrine of God is utterly fatal.

But beyond the epidemic influence of atomistic exegesis is the current vogue of interpreting New Testament writers in terms of rabbinic Judaism, particularly with respect to Paul. Since Paul himself was an expert in rabbinic thought, the conclusion is reached (by a gratuitous leap) that all Paul's teaching can be made clear by looking at the background of rabbinic teaching that formed Paul's perspective. Indeed, even the so-called "new perspective" on Paul involves an attempt to reconstruct the old perspective that Paul himself brought to the doctrines of the New Testament, which perspective was basically shaped by rabbinic views.

This approach to Pauline interpretation involves two crucial errors. The first is that it assumes no room for the supreme influence on Paul of his right theological expressions, namely, the superintendence of the Holy Ghost, while the Apostle, acting as an agent of revelation, set forth his doctrine. Equally important is the ignoring of the radical transformation that occurred to Paul by his encounter with Jesus on the road to Damascus. Paul himself claims Jesus as the supreme influence in shaping his thought, not Gamaliel or the rabbinic scholars of antiquity. We notice that when Paul writes his letters, he does not identify himself by saying, "Paul, a bond servant or slave of Gamaliel." No, he says, "Paul, a bond slave of Jesus Christ." It is the teaching of Christ, who revealed His perspective and His own mind to Paul, that stands as the supreme foundation for Pauline theology. To ignore that is to assume no real conversion, no real changing of Paul's mind, no real transformation of Paul's thinking. To gain insight into Paul, it may help to study his background, but when we look at that background as a control for Paul's expression, we fall into the trap of the worst kind of deconstruction.

THE BATTLE
FOR GRACE ALONE

AUGUST 2006

———

T HE EARLY PART OF THE FIFTH CENTURY witnessed a serious controversy in the church that is known as the Pelagian controversy. This debate took place principally between the British monk Pelagius and the great theologian of the first millennium, Augustine of Hippo. In the controversy, Pelagius objected strenuously to Augustine's understanding of the fall, of grace, and of predestination. Pelagius maintained that the fall affected Adam alone and that there was no imputation of guilt or "original sin" to Adam's progeny. Pelagius insisted that people born after the fall of Adam and Eve retained the capacity to live lives of perfect righteousness unaided by the grace of God. He argued that grace "facilitates" righteousness but is not necessary for it. He categorically rejected Augustine's understanding that the fall was so severe that it left the descendants of Adam in such a state of moral corruption that they were morally unable to incline themselves to God. The doctrines of Pelagius were condemned by the church in 418 at a synod in Carthage.

Though Pelagianism was rejected by the church, efforts soon emerged to soften the doctrines of Augustine. In the fifth century the leading exponent of such a softening was John Cassian. Cassian, who was the abbot of a monastery in Gaul, together with his fellow monks, completely agreed with the condemnation of Pelagius by the synod in 418, but they objected equally to the strong view of predestination set forth by Augustine. Cassian believed that Augustine had gone too far in his reaction against the heresy of Pelagius and had departed from the teachings of some of the church fathers, especially Tertullian, Ambrose, and Jerome. Cassian said that Augustine's teaching on predestination "cripples the force of preaching, reproof, and moral energy . . . plunges men into despair and introduces a certain fatal necessity." This reaction against the implied fatalism of predestination led Cassian to articulate a position that has since become known popularly as "semi-Pelagianism." Semi-Pelagianism, as the name implies, suggests a middle ground between Pelagius and Augustine. Though grace facilitates a life of righteousness, Pelagius thought it was not necessary. Cassian argues that grace not only facilitates righteousness, but it is an essential necessity for one to achieve righteousness. The grace that God makes available to people, however, can and is often rejected by them. The fall of man is real and serious, but not so serious as Augustine supposed, because a certain level of moral ability remains in the fallen creature to the extent that the fallen person has the moral power to cooperate with God's grace or to reject it. Augustine argued that the very cooperation with grace was the effect of God's empowering the sinner to that cooperation. Augustine again insisted that all of those who were numbered among the elect were given the gift of the grace of regeneration that brought them faith. Again, for Cassian, though God's grace is necessary for salvation and helps the human will to do good, in the final analysis it is man, not God, who must will the good. God does not give the power to will to the believer because that power to will is already present despite the fallen condition of the believer. Further Cassian taught that God desires to save all people, and the work of Christ's atonement is effectual for everyone.

Cassian understood that predestination was a biblical concept, but he made divine prescience primary over God's choice. That is to say, he taught that though predestination is an act of God, God's decision to predestine is based upon His foreknowledge of how human beings will respond to the offer of grace. For Cassian, there is no definite number of persons that are elected or rejected from eternity, since God wishes all men to be saved, and yet not all men are saved. Man retains moral responsibility and with that responsibility the power to choose to cooperate with grace or not. In the final analysis, what Cassian was denying in the teaching of Augustine was the idea of irresistible grace. For Augustine, the grace of regeneration is always effectual and will not be denied by the elect. It is a monergistic work of God that accomplishes what God intends it to accomplish. Divine grace changes the human heart, resurrecting the sinner from spiritual death to spiritual life. In this act of God, the sinner is made willing to believe and to choose Christ. The previous state of moral inability is overcome by the power of regenerating grace. The operative word in Augustine's view is that regenerating grace is monergistic. It is the work of God alone.

Pelagius rejects the doctrine of monergistic grace and replaces it with a view of synergism, which involves a work of cooperation between God and man.

The views of Cassian were condemned at the Council of Orange in 529, which further established the views of Augustine as expressions of Christian and biblical orthodoxy. However, with the conclusion of the Council of Orange in the sixth century (529), the doctrines of semi-Pelagianism did not disappear. They were fully operative through the Middle Ages and were set in concrete at the Council of Trent in the sixteenth century. They continue to be a majority view in the Roman Catholic Church, even to the twenty-first century.

The majority view of predestination, even in the evangelical world, is that predestination is not based on God's eternal decree to bring people to faith but on His foreknowledge of which people will exercise their will to come to faith. At the heart of the controversy in the fifth and sixth centuries, the sixteenth century, and today, remains the question of the degree of corruption visited upon fallen human beings in original sin. The controversy continues. The difference between the Pelagian controversy and the issues with semi-Pelagianism is that Pelagianism was seen by the church then and now as a sub-Christian and indeed anti-Christian approach to fallen humanity. The semi-Pelagian controversy, though a serious one, is not deemed to be a dispute between believers and unbelievers, but an intramural debate between believers.

EXCEPTIONAL MEDIOCRITY

SEPTEMBER 2006

⸻

I N MY BOOK *The Hunger for Significance* I explored the desire commonly found among us to find some basis for dignity, for value, for worth in our lives. I wrote at that time: "Modern man has an aching void. The emptiness we feel cannot be relieved by a new car, a better job, a bigger house. It can only be filled by understanding that each human life is significant. Our lives cannot be reduced to meaninglessness."

The modern quest for significance and human dignity is often prompted by the overwhelming aura of despair that penetrates the cultural worldview in which we live. We are repeatedly told that we are cosmic accidents who have oozed fortuitously from the slime. Our origins are meaningless and our destiny is annihilation. Yet in the midst of those two poles of despair, the search for significance and dignity is one that is often attended by a sense of urgency.

In this issue of *Tabletalk*, we're exploring the quest for excellence, which in many cases is inseparably related to our fundamental aspiration for significance. There can be different and at times conflicting motives for the search for excellence. That search can be based simply upon a desire to excel at something in which we are engaged. On the one hand, the motive for this kind of excelling can be one of competitive dominance. Historically, we've defined our humanness via the term *Homo sapiens*. Friedrich Nietzsche, the nihilistic philosopher of the nineteenth century, argued that what most defines human existence is not our wisdom (*sapiens*) but our will to power, our will to conquer. The lust for power that drives tyrants and dictators is something that we characteristically see as evil, but Nietzsche regarded it as virtue. For him, the super-man (*Übermensch*) is one who above all else is a conqueror. He is the one who allows his inherent will to power to go not only unchecked but to be fed lustfully by every means available. In the world in which we live, the will to power is often seen as a desire to climb the corporate ladder, to reach the peak of authority and power, so that we can dominate other people. In this regard, the competitive desire for domination by which we can exercise sovereignty over weaker people is a manifestation, not of inherent humanness, but of inherent human fallenness. It is a manifestation of the depths of corruption that lurks in the heart of each one of us.

On the other hand, a strong desire to excel may be motivated by an attempt to reach goals of achievement. The aspiration to significance that is inherent in every human being is, in and of itself, not a sinful appetite. The aspiration to significance is given to us, I believe, by our Creator. As His creatures, made in His image, we know that the dignity we possess is not intrinsic but extrinsic. That is, it is a dignity assigned to us by God. We have value and worth, because God declares us valuable. It is God who calls us to labor to the highest level of excellence and achievement of which we are capable. It is by His hand that we receive gifts to use in this world. The faithful exercise of those gifts is what should drive our desire to excel. In and of itself, aspiration to significance is not a bad thing, but, indeed, such worthy desires that beat in the human heart can run amuck. The aspiration to significance, if not checked by godly ethics, can easily transform itself into the Nietzschian will to power.

The legitimate motive for excellence is to seek achievement for the end to glorify God. That is the chief purpose for which we are created, to bear witness to His glory. One thing that does not bear witness to the glory of God is a human addiction to mediocrity, a smug satisfaction with the status quo. Rather, the Scriptures call us to seek a high calling—the high calling that is ours in Christ Jesus. Such a high calling cannot be achieved when we wallow in sloth. Slothfulness and laziness are twin vices that are roundly and soundly condemned by sacred Scripture. The biggest reason we fail to achieve excellence is that we are unwilling to work to such an extent that excellence can be achieved. No one achieves excellence in any worthy enterprise without diligent and disciplined labor. The enemy of achievement in this sense is sloth. On the other hand, even with the most sanctified human heart, the quest for excellence will always be tainted with a corrupt sense of pride. If we were to achieve the highest goals possible in this world, to scale the heights of human achievement in unprecedented manners, we would still be at best unprofitable servants who have no right to boast in anything but in the glory of God and the precious redemption that is ours in Christ Jesus.

Let us therefore seek to excel, let us push ourselves to the highest limits of endurance to achieve the highest possible level of excellence in all that we do, while at the same time watching ever vigilantly for the evil impulse of pride to vitiate any value to our labor. Let us work hard; let us excel to God's glory. *Soli Deo gloria.*

THE COVENANT OF WORKS

OCTOBER 2006

———

C OVENANT THEOLOGY IS IMPORTANT FOR many reasons. Though covenant theology has been around for millennia, it finds its more refined and systematic formulation in the Protestant Reformation. Its importance, however, has been heightened in our day because of its relationship to a theology that is relatively new. In the late nineteenth century, the theology called "dispensationalism" emerged as a new approach to understanding the Bible. The old *Scofield Reference Bible* defined dispensationalism in terms of seven distinct dispensations or time periods within sacred Scripture. Each dispensation was defined as "a period of time during which man is tested in respect of obedience to some specific revelation of the will of God" (p. 5, *Scofield Reference Bible*). Scofield distinguished seven dispensations including that of innocence, conscience, civil government, promise, law, grace, and the kingdom period. Over against this diversified view of redemptive history, covenant theology seeks to present a clear picture of the unity of redemption, which unity is seen in the continuity of the covenants that God has given throughout history and how they are fulfilled in the person and work of Christ.

Beyond the ongoing discussion between traditional dispensationalists and Reformed theology with respect to the basic structure of biblical revelation, there has arisen in our day an even greater crisis with respect to our understanding of redemption. This crisis focuses on the place of imputation in our understanding of the doctrine of justification. Just as the doctrine of imputation was the pivotal issue in the sixteenth-century debate between the Reformers and the Roman Catholic understanding of justification, so now the issue of imputation has raised its head again even among professing evangelicals who repudiate the Reformation understanding of imputation. At the heart of this question of justification and imputation is the rejection of what is called the covenant of works. Historic covenantal theology makes an important distinction between the covenant of works and the covenant of grace. The covenant of works refers to the covenant that God made with Adam and Eve in their pristine purity before the fall, in which God promised them blessedness contingent upon their obedience to His command. After the fall, the fact that God continued to promise redemption to creatures who had violated the covenant of works, that ongoing promise of redemption is defined as the covenant of grace.

Technically, from one perspective, all covenants that God makes with creatures are gracious in the sense that He is not obligated to make any promises to His creatures. But the distinction between the covenant of works and grace is getting at something that is of vital importance, as it has to do with the Gospel. The covenant of grace indicates God's promise to save us even when we fail to keep the obligations imposed in creation. This is seen most importantly in the work of Jesus as the new Adam. Again and again the New Testament makes the distinction and contrast between the failure and calamities wrought upon humanity through the disobedience of the original Adam and the benefits that flow through the work of the obedience of Jesus, who is the new Adam. Though there is a clear distinction between the new Adam and the old Adam, the point of continuity between them is that both were called to submit to perfect obedience to God.

When we understand Christ's work of redemption in the New Testament, we focus our attention largely on two aspects of it. On the one hand, we look at the atonement. It's clear from the New Testament teachings that in the atonement Jesus bears the sins of His people and is punished for them in our place. That is, the atonement is vicarious and substitutionary. In this sense, on the cross, Christ took upon Himself the negative sanctions of the old covenant. That is, He bore in His body the punishment due to those who violated not only the law of Moses, but also the law that was imposed in paradise. He took upon Himself the curse that is deserved by all who disobey the law of God. This, Reformed theology describes in terms of "the passive obedience of Jesus." It points to His willingness to submit to His reception of the curse of God in our stead.

Beyond the negative fulfillment of the covenant of works, in taking the punishment due those who disobey it, Jesus offers the positive dimension that is vital to our redemption. He wins the blessing of the covenant of works on all of the progeny of Adam who put their trust in Jesus. Where Adam was the covenant breaker, Jesus is the covenant keeper. Where Adam failed to gain the blessedness of the tree of life, Christ wins that blessedness by His obedience, which blessedness He provides for those who put their trust in Him. In this work of fulfilling the covenant for us in our stead, theology speaks of the "active obedience" of Christ. That is, Christ's redeeming work includes not only His death, but His life. His life of perfect obedience becomes the sole ground of our justification. It is His perfect righteousness, gained via His perfect obedience, that is imputed to all who put their trust in Him. Therefore, Christ's work of active obedience is absolutely essential to the justification of anyone. Without Christ's active obedience to the covenant of works, there is no reason for imputation, there is no ground for justification. If we take away the covenant of works, we take away the active obedience of Jesus. If we take away the active obedience of Jesus, we take away the imputation of His righteousness to us. If we take away the imputation of Christ's righteousness to us, we take away justification by faith alone. If we take away justification by faith alone, we take away the Gospel, and we are left in our sins. We are left as the miserable sons of Adam, who can only look forward to feeling the full measure of God's curse upon us for our own disobedience. It is the obedience of Christ that is the ground of our salvation, both in His passive obedience on the cross and His active obedience in His life. All of this is inseparably related to the biblical understanding of Jesus as the new Adam (Rom. 5:12–20), who succeeded where the original Adam failed, who prevailed where the original Adam lost. There is nothing less than our salvation at stake in this issue.

THE BATTLE
FOR THE TABLE

NOVEMBER 2006

———

THERE HAVE BEEN CENTURIES OF DEBATE over the church's understanding of the doctrine of the Lord's Supper. Before we survey the critical issues involved, we need to understand that the main reason why the argument continues, and at times becomes fierce, is because the church understands the vital importance of this sacrament in its life and worship.

The fundamental disagreement over the Lord's Supper focuses on four distinct views. These views include: first, the view of transubstantiation articulated by the Roman Catholic communion; second, the doctrine of consubstantiation articulated by the Lutheran community (we must note, however, that the word *consubstantiation*, though it is used widely in theological circles to describe the Lutheran view, is not a term that the Lutherans tend to embrace, and so we should honor their attempt to disavow this particular word); third, the Reformed and Anglican affirmation of the real presence of Christ in the Lord's Supper; and fourth, the memorial-sign view of the sacrament espoused by Ulrich Zwingli and by the majority of those in the Baptist communities.

It is important to note at this point that there is major agreement among Roman Catholics, Lutherans, Anglicans, and the Reformed that Christ is truly present in the Lord's Supper. They all go beyond the view of the Supper as a bare sign or memorial, as espoused by many evangelicals.

The debate among Catholics, Lutherans, and Reformed people is one that focuses on the mode of Christ's presence in the Lord's Supper. At the bottom, this debate is not so much sacramental as it is Christological.

Historically, the Roman Catholic Church has articulated her view of the Lord's Supper in terms of the doctrine of transubstantiation. This doctrine was clearly affirmed by the Ecumenical Council of Trent in the sixteenth century and was reaffirmed as recently as the papal encyclical issued by Paul VI in 1965, entitled *Mysterium Fide*. Transubstantiation uses language that was borrowed from the philosopher Aristotle. In defining the nature of objects in the world, Aristotle distinguished between the "essence," or "substance," of an object and its external, perceivable qualities that he called the "accidens." Therefore, Aristotle distinguished between substance and accidens of all beings in the created world. By use of this terminology, the Roman Catholic Church teaches the miracle of the Mass, in which the substance of the bread and wine that is used in the Lord's Supper is miraculously changed into the substance of the body and blood of Christ.

This miracle, however, contains two aspects. While the substance of the bread and wine are changed to the body and blood of Christ, nevertheless, the accidens of bread and wine remain the same. That is, before the miracle occurs, the bread and wine look like bread and wine, taste like bread and wine, and feel like bread and wine. After the miracle of their transformation occurs, they still look like bread and wine, feel like bread and wine, and taste like bread and wine. That is because after the miracle occurs, the substance of bread and wine has changed into the substance of the body and blood of Christ, while the accidens of bread and wine remain. Therefore the miracle is twofold. For Rome there is the substance of one thing with the accidens of another, and the accidens of another thing with the substance of something else.

Interestingly, last century a debate erupted over a similar point, particularly in Holland among the Dutch Catholics. They attempted to get beyond the language of Aristotle and keep the idea of the miracle intact without being tied to the philosophical formulation of Aristotelian terms. Edward Schillebeeckx, as well as the writers of the Dutch Catechism, adopted a view called "transignification," which they said maintained the reality of the real presence of Christ without the formulation of Trent. Paul VI responded to this in *Mysterium Fide* (1965) by insisting that not only is the church committed to the substance of the doctrine of transubstantiation, but it is committed to the formulation of it as well.

Martin Luther saw a frivolous use of the word *miracle* in Rome's understanding of transubstantiation and said that it is not necessary to talk about the substance of one and the accidens of another when we can just affirm the true corporeal presence of Christ "in, under, and with" the elements of bread and wine. Luther didn't use the word *consubstantiation*. It was the Reformed church's attempt to faithfully articulate Luther's view by using the term *consubstantiation*, which means that Christ is substantively present with the substantive presence of bread and wine. In both the Roman and Lutheran view of the matter, for Christ to be present in His human nature in more than one place at the same time requires that some kind of communication of divine attributes takes place between God and the human Jesus. This was the chief objection that Calvin and the other Reformers launched against both Luther and Rome, because they saw in it a violation of the Council of Chalcedon, which taught that the two natures of Christ are united without confusion or without mixture. For Jesus in His human nature, to which His body certainly belongs, to be present at more than one place at the same time would require the deification of His body, which the Reformers saw as a thinly veiled Monophysite heresy.

John Calvin insisted, as did the Anglicans, on the true presence of Christ, but he also insisted that the presence of Christ is through His divine nature. His human nature is no longer present with us. It is in heaven at the right hand of God. We still are able to commune with the human nature of Christ by means of our communion with the divine nature, which does indeed remain united to the human nature. But that human nature remains localized in heaven. In the debate, Calvin fought a war on two fronts. On the one hand, in dealing with the Lutherans and the Roman Catholics, he refused to use the term *substance* with respect to the presence of Jesus in the sacrament. But over against those disciples of Zwingli, who wanted to reduce the sacrament to a mere symbol and memorial, Calvin insisted upon the term *substance*. Here the term *substance* had two different nuances. With respect to Luther and Rome, the term *substance* meant "corporeal" or "physical." With respect to the debate with Zwingli, Calvin used the term *substance* as a synonym for "real" or "true."

In addition to this aspect of the controversy, the Reformation theologians also rejected Rome's notion that in the Lord's Supper a true sacrifice of Christ is offered to God. Catholicism says that though this sacrifice is not bloody, it nevertheless is a real sacrifice (the Council of Trent used the word *sacrificium*). In this understanding, the Reformers saw a violation of the once-for-all offering of Christ on the cross.

The debate goes on, as the church tries to plumb the depths and the riches of this sacrament that was instituted by Jesus and practiced on a regular basis in the primitive Christian church, and this debate has survived even to our day.

WHY FORGIVE?

DECEMBER 2006

———

W HEN SOMEONE ORDERS US TO DO SOMETHING, or imposes an obligation, it is natural for us to ask two questions. The first question is, "Why should I?" and the second is, "Who says so?" The why and the authority behind the mandate are very important to the question of forgiveness.

To answer the question of why we should be forgiving people, let us look briefly at the teaching of Jesus in the New Testament. In Matthew's gospel, chapter 18, verse 21 and following, we read this account:

> Then Peter came up and said to him, "Lord, how often will my brother sin against me, and I forgive him? As many as seven times?"
>
> Jesus said to him, "I do not say to you seven times, but seventy times seven. Therefore the kingdom of heaven may be compared to a king who wished to settle accounts with his servants. When he began to settle, one was brought to him who owed him ten thousand talents. And since he could not pay, his master ordered him to be sold, with his wife and children and all that he had, and payment to be made. So the servant fell on his knees, imploring him, 'Have patience with me, and I will pay you everything.' And out of pity for him, the master of that servant released him and forgave him the debt.
>
> "But when that same servant went out, he found one of his fellow servants who owed him a hundred denarii, and seizing him, he began to choke him, saying, 'Pay what you owe.' So his fellow servant fell down and pleaded with him, 'Have patience with me, and I will pay you.' He refused and went and put him in prison until he should pay the debt. When his fellow servants saw what had taken place, they were greatly distressed, and they went and reported to their master all that had taken place. Then his master summoned him and said to him, 'You wicked servant! I forgave you all that debt because you pleaded

with me. And should not you have had mercy on your fellow servant, as I had mercy on you?' And in anger his master delivered him to the jailers, until he should pay all his debt.

"So also my heavenly Father will do to every one of you, if you do not forgive your brother from your heart."

In this parable, the point of Jesus' teaching is clear, that the *why* for forgiving others is rooted in the fact that we have been the recipients of extraordinary mercy and compassion. We are all debtors who cannot pay their debts to God. Yet God has been gracious enough to grant us forgiveness in Jesus Christ. It is no wonder that in the Lord's Prayer, Jesus instructs His disciples to say, "Forgive us our debts as we forgive our debtors." There is a parallel, a joint movement of compassion, that is first received from God and then we in turn exercise the same compassion to others. God makes it clear that if we lack that compassion and harbor vengeance in our heart, rather than being ready to forgive again and again, we will forfeit any forgiveness that has been given to us.

Thus, the foundation for a forgiving spirit is the experience of divine grace. It is by grace that we are saved. It is by grace that we live. It is by grace that we have been forgiven. Therefore, the why of forgiving is to manifest our own gratitude for the grace that we have received. Again, the parable of Jesus points to one who took the grace that he received for granted and refused to act in a way that mirrored and reflected the kindness of God. Why should we forgive? Simply, because God forgives us. It is not an insignificant thing to add on to the why the point that we are commanded by that God of grace to exercise grace in turn.

When we look at the question of forgiveness, however, we also have to ask the second query, "Who says so, and under what conditions are we to keep this requirement?" If we turn our attention to another gospel, we see in Luke 17 the following (vv. 1–4):

And he said to his disciples, "Temptations to sin are sure to come, but woe to the one through whom they come! It would be better for him if a millstone were hung around his neck and he were cast into the sea than that he should cause one of these little ones to sin. Pay attention to yourselves! If your brother sins, rebuke him, and if he repents, forgive him, and if he sins against you seven times in the day, and turns to you seven times, saying, 'I repent,' you must forgive him."

It's important that we look closely at this directive from Jesus regarding forgiveness. It is often taught in the Christian community that Christians are called to forgive those who sin against them unilaterally and universally. We see the example of Jesus on the cross, asking God to forgive those who were executing Him, even though they offered no visible indication of repentance. From that example of Jesus, it has been inferred that Christians must always forgive all offenses against them, even when repentance is not offered. However, the most that we can legitimately infer from Jesus' actions on that occasion is that we have the right to forgive people unilaterally. Though that may be indeed a wonderful thing, it is not commanded. If we look at the commandment that Jesus gives in Luke 17:3, He says, "If your brother sins, rebuke him." Notice that the first response to the offense is not forgiveness but rather rebuke. The Christian has the right to rebuke those who commit wrong doing against him. That's the basis for the whole procedure of church discipline in the New Testament. If we were commanded to give unilateral forgiveness to all, under all circumstances, then the whole action of church discipline to redress wrongs, would itself be wrong. But Jesus says, "If your brother sins, rebuke him, and if he repents . . . ,"—here is where the command becomes obligatory—if the offender repents, then it is mandatory for the Christian to forgive the one who has offended him. If we refuse to give forgiveness when repentance has been manifest, then we expose ourselves to the same fate as the unforgiving servant. We open ourselves to the wrath of God. If, indeed, I offend someone and then repent and express my apology to them, but he refuses to forgive me, then the coals of fire are on his head. Likewise, if we fail to give forgiveness, when one who has offended us repents of the offense, we expose ourselves to the coals of fire, and we are in worse shape than the one who has given the offense. In other words, it is transgression against God when we refuse to forgive those who have repented for their offenses to us. This is the teaching of Jesus. It is the mandate of Jesus. As we are united in Christ, we are to show that union by extending the same grace to others that He extends to us.

"The foundation for a forgiving spirit is the experience of divine grace. It is by grace that we are saved."

"R.C. Sproul was a rare theologian who explained the deepest of subjects in the simplest of terms, and he did so in a way that grabbed people's attention and interest. His gifts shine in the column he regularly wrote, Right Now Counts Forever. On subjects from sports to politics to sexuality, and of course, the life of the church, Sproul's wisdom and wit show us how the truth of God's Word illuminates and transforms all of life."

—Dr. Joel R. Beeke
President and professor of systematic theology and homiletics
Puritan Reformed Theological Seminary
Grand Rapids, Mich.

"R.C. Sproul's legacy is vast, including visual, audio, and print resources stimulating countless believers worldwide. Now, Ligonier has added to it with this thrilling thesaurus, gathered from more than forty years of his monthly contributions to *Tabletalk*. In the early years, he shared his spiritual perception of current affairs, including politics, economics, inflation, the newest A-list books and 'the American dream'; it was as if he had all of these in one hand and his Bible in the other. In the later years, he was more immediately concerned with theological and doctrinal truths. His exposition and application of biblical revelation on subjects such as the doctrine of God, Christology, Jesus' substitutionary death, atonement, the true nature of sin and the new birth, theodicy, the measure and manner of God's forgiveness, conscience, Christian liberty, and scores of other subjects are brilliantly handled.

"I do have a quibble. At one point he wrote, 'There is nothing in my thought that hasn't been said before far more eloquently than I can ever hope to articulate'—commendably modest, but thankfully untrue."

—Dr. John Blanchard
Preacher, teacher, apologist, and author
Banstead, England

"You hold in your hand a veritable gold mine of Christian truth. Flowing from the pen of Dr. R.C. Sproul, here is his work of more than forty

years writing his monthly column Right Now Counts Forever in *Tabletalk* magazine. Dr. Sproul was arguably the greatest teacher of theology in our generation. He was also a lucid and cogent writer, able to take profound truth and make it accessible to everyday readers. This book will take you to the heights of heaven as Dr. Sproul addresses a wide breadth of issues and topics. Though now seated in a cloud of witnesses above, Dr. Sproul continues to instruct us in the vital essentials of Christian living. This book should be required reading for every believer."

—Dr. Steven J. Lawson
President, OnePassion Ministries
Dallas

"This collection of columns from four decades offers a treasure trove of timeless reflection on the timely. Dr. Sproul tackles football, commercials, ethical issues, best-selling books, politics, and philosophy—and that's merely the first year of columns alone. You will find wit and humor, always accompanied by deep and faithful theological and biblical reflection. Here you will find wisdom that never goes out of style."

—Dr. Stephen J. Nichols
President, Reformation Bible College
Chief academic officer, Ligonier Ministries

"Spanning more than forty years, Dr. Sproul's prophetic insights on a wide range of ethical and theological issues provide a fascinating historical narrative of cultural change, both in society at large and, sadly, the evangelical church, as well as a breathtakingly clear Christian (biblical) response. Cultural attitudes may have changed as the effects of postmodernity took hold in the late twentieth century, but it is clear from these pages that the Bible is sufficient to address each one. I will be consulting this volume often as issues arise for which I need a clear biblical response."

—Dr. Derek W.H. Thomas
Senior minister, First Presbyterian Church
Columbia, S.C.

Right Now Counts Forever

R.C. SPROUL

RIGHT
NOW
COUNTS
FOREVER

Volume IV: 2007–2018

 LIGONIER MINISTRIES

Right Now Counts Forever, Volume IV: 2007–2018
© 2021 by the R.C. Sproul Trust

Published by Ligonier Ministries
421 Ligonier Court, Sanford, FL 32771
Ligonier.org

Printed in China
RR Donnelley
0000321
First printing

ISBN 978-1-64289-314-4 (Hardcover)
ISBN 978-1-64289-315-1 (ePub)
ISBN 978-1-64289-316-8 (Kindle)

Cover design: Metaleap Creative
Interior typeset: Katherine Lloyd, The DESK

Ligonier Ministries edited and adapted Dr. R.C. Sproul's original text to create this volume. We are thankful to Mrs. Vesta Sproul for her invaluable help on this project.

Bible quotations are the author's translation or are taken from one of the following versions:

The ESV® Bible (The Holy Bible, English Standard Version®), copyright © 2001 by Crossway, a publishing ministry of Good News Publishers. Used by permission. All rights reserved.

The New American Standard Bible® (NASB), Copyright © 1960, 1962, 1963, 1968, 1971, 1972, 1973, 1975, 1977, 1995 by The Lockman Foundation. Used by permission. www.Lockman.org

The New King James Version®. Copyright © 1982 by Thomas Nelson. Used by permission. All rights reserved.

The Holy Bible, New International Version®, NIV®. Copyright © 1973, 1978, 1984, 2011 by Biblica, Inc.™ Used by permission of Zondervan. All rights reserved worldwide. www.zondervan.com The "NIV" and "New International Version" are trademarks registered in the United States Patent and Trademark Office by Biblica, Inc.™

The King James Version. Public domain.

Cataloging-in-Publication Data is available from the Library of Congress
LCCN 2020038106 (print) | LCCN 2020038107 (ebook)
LC record available at https://lccn.loc.gov/2020038106
LC ebook record available at https://lccn.loc.gov/2020038107

CONTENTS

"In order to grasp the meaning of sin, we cannot define it apart from its relationship to law. It is God's law that determines what sin is."

—

COSMIC TREASON

JANUARY 2007

———

T HE QUESTION, "WHAT IS SIN?" is raised in the Westminster
Shorter Catechism. The answer provided to this catechetical question
is simply this: "Sin is any want of conformity to or transgression
of the law of God."

Let us examine some of the elements of this catechetical response. In
the first instance, sin is identified as some kind of want or lack. In the
Middle Ages, Christian theologians tried to define evil or sin in terms of
privation (*privatio*) or negation (*negatio*). In these terms, evil or sin was
defined by its lack of conformity to goodness. The negative terminology
associated with sin may be seen in biblical words such as dis*obedience*,
*god*less*ness*, or im*morality*. In all of these terms, we see the negative being
stressed. Further illustrations would include words such as *dishonor, anti-
christ*, and others.

However, to gain a complete view of sin, we have to see that it involves
more than a negation of the good, or more than a simple lack of virtue.
We may be inclined to think that sin, if defined exclusively in negative
terms, is merely an illusion. But the ravages of sin point dramatically to
the reality of its power, which reality can never be explained away by
appeals to illusion. The Reformers added to the idea of *privatio* the notion
of actuality or activity, so that evil is therefore seen in the phrase *privatio
actuosa*. This stresses the active character of sin. In the catechism, sin is
defined not only as a want of conformity but an act of transgression, an
action that involves an overstepping or violation of a standard.

In order to grasp the meaning of sin, we cannot define it apart from its
relationship to law. It is God's law that determines what sin is. In the New
Testament, the Apostle Paul, particularly in Romans, labors the point that
there is an inseparable relationship between sin and death and between
sin and law. The simple formula is this: No sin equals no death. No law

1

equals no sin. The Apostle argues that where there is no law, there is no sin, and where there is no sin, there is no death. This rests upon the premise that death invades the human experience as an act of divine judgment for sin. It is the soul who sins that dies. However, without law there can be no sin. Death cannot enter into the human experience until first God's law is revealed. It is for this reason that the Apostle argues that the moral law was in effect before God gave Israel the Mosaic code. The argument rests upon the premise that death was in the world before Sinai, that death reigned from Adam to Moses. This can only mean that God's moral law was given to His creatures long before the tablets of stone were delivered to the nation of Israel.

This gives some credence to Immanuel Kant's assertion of a universal moral imperative that he called the *categorical imperative*, which is found in the conscience of every sentient person. Since it is God's law that defines the nature of sin, we are left to face the dreadful consequences of our disobedience to that law. What the sinner requires in order to be rescued from the punitive aspects of this law is what Solomon Stoddard called a righteousness of the Law. Just as sin is defined by a lack of conformity to the Law, or transgression of the Law, the only antidote for that transgression is obedience to the Law. If we possess such obedience to the Law of God, we are in no danger of the judgment of God.

Solomon Stoddard, the grandfather of Jonathan Edwards, wrote in his book *The Righteousness of Christ* the following summation of the value of the righteousness of the Law: "It is sufficient for us if we have the righteousness of the law. There is no danger of our miscarrying if we have that righteousness. The security of the angels in Heaven is that they have the righteousness of the law, and it is a sufficient security for us if we have the righteousness of the law. If we have the righteousness of the law, then we are not liable to the curse of the law. We are not threatened by the law; justice is not provoked with us; the condemnation of the law can take no hold upon us; the law has nothing to object against our salvation. The soul that has the righteousness of the law is out of the reach of the threatenings of the law. Where the demand of the law is answered, the law finds no fault. The law curses only for lack of perfect obedience. Yea, moreover, where there is the righteousness of the law, God has bound himself to give eternal life. Such persons are heirs of life, according to the promise of the law. The law declared them heirs of life, Galatians 3:12, 'The man that doth them, shall live in them'" (*The Righteousness of Christ*, p. 25).

The only righteousness that meets the requirements of the Law is the righteousness of Christ. It is only by imputation of that righteousness that the sinner can ever possess the righteousness of the Law. This is critical for our understanding in this day where the imputation of the righteousness of Christ is so widely under attack. If we abandon the notion of the righteousness of Christ, we have no hope, because the Law is never negotiated by God. As long as the Law exists, we are exposed to its judgment unless our sin is covered by the righteousness of the Law. The only covering that we can possess of that righteousness is that which comes to us from the active obedience of Christ, who Himself fulfilled every jot and tittle of the Law. His fulfilling of the Law in Himself is a vicarious activity by which He achieves the reward that comes with such obedience. He does this not for Himself but for His people. It is the background of this imputed righteousness, this rescue from the condemnation of the Law, this salvation from the ravages of sin that is the backdrop for the Christian's sanctification, in which we are to mortify that sin that remains in us, since Christ has died for our sin.

THE BOOK OF JOB: WHY DO THE RIGHTEOUS SUFFER?

FEBRUARY 2007

———

I N THE ARENA OF BIBLICAL studies, there are five books that are generally included under the heading of "wisdom literature" or "the poetic books of the Old Testament." They are the books of Proverbs, Psalms, Ecclesiastes, Song of Solomon, and Job. Of these five books, one stands out in bold relief, manifesting significant differences from the other four. That is the book of Job. The wisdom that is found in the book of Job is not communicated in the form of proverb. Rather, the book of Job deals with questions of wisdom in the context of a narrative dealing with Job's profound anguish and excruciating pain. The setting for this narrative is in patriarchal times. Questions have arisen as to the authorial intent of this book, whether it was meant to be historical narrative of a real individual or whether its basic structure is that of a drama with a prologue, including an opening scene in heaven, involving discourse between God and Satan, and moving climactically to the epilogue, in which the profound losses of Job during his trials are replenished.

In any case, at the heart of the message of the book of Job is the wisdom with respect to answering the question as to how God is involved in the problem of human suffering. In every generation protests arise saying that if God is good, then there should be no pain, no suffering or death in this world. Along with this protest against bad things happening to good people have also been attempts to create a calculus of pain, by which it is assumed that an individual's threshold of suffering is in direct proportion to the degree of their guilt or the sin they have committed. A quick response to this is found in the ninth chapter of John, where Jesus responds to the disciples' question regarding the source of the suffering of the man born blind.

In the book of Job, the character is described as a righteous man, indeed the most righteous man to be found on the earth, but one whom Satan claims is righteous only to receive blessings from the hand of God. God has put a hedge around him and has blessed him beyond all mortals, and as a result the Devil accuses Job of serving God only because of the generous payoff he receives from his Maker. The challenge comes from the evil one for God to remove the hedge of protection and see whether Job will then begin to curse God. As the story unfolds, Job's suffering goes in rapid progression from bad to worse. His suffering is so intense that he finds himself sitting on a dung heap, cursing the day he was born, and crying out in relentless pain. His suffering is so great that even his wife counsels him to curse God, that he might die and be relieved of his agony. What unfolds further in the story is the counsel given to Job from Job's friends, Eliphaz, Bildad, and Zophar. Their testimony shows how hollow and shallow is their loyalty to Job, and how presumptive they are in assuming that Job's untold misery must be grounded in a radical degeneracy in Job's character.

Job's counsel reaches a higher level with some deep insights by Elihu. Elihu gives several speeches that carry with them many elements of biblical wisdom, but the final wisdom to be found in this great book comes not from Job's friends or from Elihu, but from God Himself. When Job demands an answer from God, God responds with this rebuke, "Who is this that darkens counsel by words without knowledge? Dress for action like a man; I will question you, and you make it known to me" (Job 38:1–3). What ensues from this rebuke is the most intense interrogation of a human ever brought to bear by the Creator. It almost seems at first glance as if God is bullying Job, in as much as He says, "Where were you when I laid the foundations of the earth?" (v. 4). God raises question after question in this manner. "Can you bind the chains of the Pleiades? Or loose the belt of Orion? Can you lead forth the Mazzaroth in their season, or can you guide the Bear with its children?" (vv. 31–32). Obviously, the answers to these rhetorical questions that come in machine gun rapidity is always, "No, no, no." God hammers away at the inferiority and subordination of Job in His interrogation. God continues with question after question about Job's ability to do things that Job cannot do but that God clearly can do.

In chapter 40, God says to Job finally, "Shall a faultfinder contend with the Almighty? He who argues with God, let him answer it" (v. 2). Now, Job's response is not one of defiant demand for answers to his misery. Rather he says, "Behold, I am of small account; what shall I answer you? I lay my hand on my mouth. I have spoken once, and I will not answer; twice, but I will proceed no further" (vv. 4–5). And again God picks up the interrogation and goes even more deeply in the rapid fire interrogation that shows the overwhelming contrast between the power of God, who is known in Job as El Shaddai, and the contrasting impotence of Job. Finally, Job confesses that such things were too wonderful. He says, "I had heard of you by the hearing of the ear, but now my eye sees you; therefore I despise myself, and repent in dust and ashes" (42:5–6).

What is noteworthy in this drama, is that God never directly answers Job's questions. He doesn't say, "Job, the reason you have suffered is for this or for that." Rather, what God does in the mystery of the iniquity of such profound suffering, is that He answers Job with Himself. This is the wisdom that answers the question of suffering—not the answer to why I have to suffer in a particular way, in a particular time, and in a particular circumstance, but wherein does my hope rest in the midst of suffering.

The answer to that comes clearly from the wisdom of the book of Job that agrees with the other premises of the wisdom literature: the fear of the Lord, awe and reverence before God, is the beginning of wisdom. And when we are befuddled and confused by things that we cannot understand in this world, we look not for specific answers always to specific questions, but we look to know God in His holiness, in His righteousness, in His justice, and in His mercy. Therein is the wisdom that is found in the book of Job.

THE NEW BIRTH

MARCH 2007

———

R EGENERATION PRECEDES FAITH. THIS ASSERTION that captures
the heart of the distinctive theology of historic Augustinian and
Reformed thought is the watershed assertion that distinguishes
that theology from all forms of semi-Pelagianism. That is, it distinguishes
it from *almost* all forms of semi-Pelagianism.

There is one historic position of semi-Pelagianism that advocates the
view of a universal benefit that embraces all mankind as a result of the
atonement of Jesus. This universal benefit is the universal regeneration of
all men—at least to the degree that rescues them from the moral inability
of their original sin and now empowers them with the ability to exercise
faith in Christ. This new ability to believe makes faith possible but by
no means effectual. This type of regeneration does not bring in its wake
the certainty that those who are born again will in fact place their trust
in Christ.

For the most part, however, the statement "Regeneration precedes faith"
is the watershed position that creates apoplexy in the minds of semi-
Pelagians. The semi-Pelagian would argue that despite the ravages of the
fall, man still has an island of righteousness left in his soul, by which he
still can accept or reject God's offer of grace. This view, so widely held
in evangelical circles, argues that one must believe in Christ in order to
be born again, and so the order of salvation is reversed in this view by
maintaining that faith precedes regeneration.

However, when we consider the teaching on this issue as found in John's
record of Jesus' discussion with Nicodemus, we see the emphasis that
Jesus places on regeneration as a necessary condition, a *sine qua non*, for
believing in Him. He says to Nicodemus in John 3:3: "Truly, truly, I say to
you, unless one is born again, he cannot see the kingdom of God." Then
again in verses 5–7, Jesus says, "Truly, truly, I say to you, unless one is

born of water and the Spirit, he cannot enter the kingdom of God. That which is born of the flesh is flesh, and that which is born of the Spirit is spirit. Do not marvel that I said to you, 'You must be born again.' " The must-ness of regeneration of which Jesus speaks is necessary for a person to see even the kingdom of God, let alone to enter it. We cannot exercise faith in a kingdom that we cannot enter apart from rebirth.

The weakness of all semi-Pelagianism is that it invests in the fallen, corrupt flesh of man the power to exercise faith. Here, fallen man is able to come to Christ without regeneration, that is, before regeneration. On the other hand, the axiom that regeneration precedes faith gets to the very heart of the historic issue between Augustinianism and semi-Pelagianism.

In the Augustinian and Reformation view, regeneration is seen first of all as a supernatural work of God. Regeneration is the divine work of God the Holy Spirit upon the minds and souls of fallen people, by which the Spirit quickens those who are spiritually dead and makes them spiritually alive. This supernatural work rescues that person from his bondage to sin and his moral inability to incline himself towards the things of God. Regeneration, by being a supernatural work, is obviously a work that cannot be accomplished by natural man on his own. If it were a natural work, it would not require the intervention of God the Holy Spirit.

Secondly, regeneration is a monergistic work. "Monergistic" means that it is the work of one person who exercises his power. In the case of regeneration, it is God alone who is able, and it is God alone who performs the work of regenerating the human soul. The work of regeneration is not a joint venture between the fallen person and the divine Spirit; it is solely the work of God.

Thirdly, the monergistic work of regeneration by the Holy Spirit is an immediate work. It is immediate with respect to time, and it is immediate with respect to the principle of operating without intervening means. The Holy Spirit does not use something apart from His own power to bring a person from spiritual death to spiritual life, and when that work is accomplished, it is accomplished instantaneously. No one is partly regenerate, or almost regenerate. Here we have a classic either/or situation. A person is either born again, or he is not born again. There is no nine-month gestation period with respect to this birth. When the Spirit changes the disposition of the human soul, He does it instantly. A person may not be aware of this internal work accomplished by God for some time after it has actually occurred. But though our awareness of it may be gradual, the action of it is instantaneous.

Fourthly, the work of regeneration is effectual. That is, when the Holy Spirit regenerates a human soul, the purpose of that regeneration is to bring that person to saving faith in Jesus Christ. That purpose is effected and accomplished as God purposes in the intervention. Regeneration is more than giving a person the possibility of having faith, it gives him the certainty of possessing that saving faith.

The result of our regeneration is first of all faith, which then results in justification and adoption into the family of God. Nobody is born into this world a child of the family of God. We are born as children of wrath. The only way we enter into the family of God is by adoption, and that adoption occurs when we are united to God's only begotten Son by faith. When by faith we are united with Christ, we are then adopted into that family of whom Christ is the firstborn. Regeneration therefore involves a new genesis, a new beginning, a new birth. It is that birth by which we enter into the family of God by adoption.

Finally, it's important to see that regeneration is a gift that God disposes sovereignly to all of those whom He determines to bring into His family.

A GRIEF OBSERVED

APRIL 2007

———

WHAT'S WRONG WITH THIS PICTURE? I'm speaking of my assignment for this month's issue of *Tabletalk*. Over the years, my articles have been generally written out of a concern to communicate content of a biblical or theological nature that I approach from the perspective of a student. This time I've been given the sobering assignment of writing about a topic, not merely from a biblical or theological perspective, but from a personal, anecdotal perspective. The editors of *Tabletalk* have asked me to write about grief, reflecting on how I have experienced grief in my own life and then commenting on how to deal with grief biblically as Christians should.

Before I discuss personal grief, I want to comment on the nature of grief. When we speak of the reality of grief, we are talking about pain. The pain that we describe by the use of this word, however, is not the pain of a minor irritation. It is not the pain of a broken bone, a fractured leg, a pierced shoulder. It is a pain that penetrates the skin of a person and plunges to the deepest recesses of the person's being. It is a pain that grips the soul with a vise-like pincer that brings with the pain an excruciating sense of mourning. We use the term *grief* to describe pain that assaults the deepest level of our being. We often use the metaphor of the broken heart, yet we know that hearts don't break like a glass that falls on the floor or like bones that are shattered in an accident. The broken heart really describes a weeping soul, a soul that is cloaked in the darkest night.

When we speak of grief, we speak about an emotion of which the Scriptures are profoundly aware. We speak of an emotion that was most poignantly manifested in the life and the experience of our Lord Himself. Jesus was described as a man of sorrows, acquainted with grief. His acquaintanceship with grief was not merely a sympathetic or empathetic awareness of other people's pain. Rather, His experience of grief was a pain that He felt within Himself. To be sure, His pain was the result of His perception, not of His own shortcomings, but of the great evils that plague this world. We think of Jesus coming to the holy city, the city that He visited as a boy, the city that incorporated all of the promises that God had made to His people Israel, the city that was Zion's holy hill. He came to that city, the city of promise, at a time when its corruption had reached its highest point. The nadir of unbelief was encrusted around the city of Jerusalem. When Jesus observed this city, He cried out in a lament, saying, "O Jerusalem, Jerusalem, the city that kills the prophets. . . . How often would I have gathered your children together as a hen gathers her brood under her wings, and you would not!" It's the grief that Jesus experienced when He noticed those women weeping for Him as He was moved, pushed, and shoved towards the cross at Golgotha. He said to these bystanders, "Daughters of Jerusalem, do not weep for me, but weep for yourselves and for your children" (Luke 23:28). Our Lord's grief was rooted and grounded in His compassion for a fallen world.

On the other hand, when we experience grief, our grief is usually wrapped up with some kind of personal loss. We remember C.S. Lewis' profound insights to this human predicament in his book *A Grief Observed*.

In my own experience, when I think of grief, there are only a few personal recollections that force their way into my mind. The first and most painful was the grief associated with the death of my father when I was seventeen years old. This was the man who, humanly speaking, was the anchor of my soul, the rock of stability in our home and in my life. When he was reduced to frailty and became incapacitated by multiple strokes, and wasted away finally to death itself, I was driven to despair. The loss of this man, who was my greatest earthly hero, left a scar on my soul that remains even to this day. I also think personally of my sense of loss when my dear friend Jim Boice was taken home to glory in 2000. It was not simply the loss of a friend, but a loss of a comrade in an ongoing battle that left me with such sorrow. The pangs of that sorrow were multiplied by my sense of loss, not only to me, but to the church of our time. When this champion was removed from our midst, I wanted to cry with David, "O how the mighty have fallen." I wanted to say, "Tell it not in Gath, publish it not in Ashkelon." Let no one take opportunity at the passing of this man to rejoice in any apparent defeat to the power of the cross.

Beyond those personal losses, the loss of friends, the loss of comrades, always bring to me a certain measure of grief. In my own heart, however, I know that nothing grieves me more than to see the Gospel compromised in the church. It's not the wickedness of the pagan that breaks my heart. It's the compromise of the Christian that grieves my soul. Finally, when I look at grief, as I experience it in my life and read of it in Scriptures, I know that with it always comes the clear and present danger of an emotion that can turn sour. Yet the emotion itself is perfectly legitimate. If we fail to deal with our grief, if our mourning goes beyond sorrow into bitterness, then we have allowed pain to abscess and become poison. We must examine the griefs we experience and take care that they never become the occasion for sin. They never did that to Jesus. We pray they won't do it to us.

OUR FATHER

JUNE 2007

———

T HE NEXT TIME YOU ATTEND A PRAYER MEETING, pay close attention to the manner in which individuals address God. Invariably,
the form of address will be something like this, "Our dear heavenly
Father," "Father," "Father God," or some other form of reference to God
as Father. Not everyone customarily addresses God in the first instance
in prayer by using the title "Father." However, the use of the term *Father*
in addressing God in prayer is overwhelmingly found as the preference
among people who pray. What is the significance of this? It would seem
that the instructions of our Lord in giving the model prayer, "The Lord's
Prayer," is emulated by our propensity for addressing God as Father. Since
Jesus said, "When you pray, say, 'Our Father,' " that form of address has
become the virtual standard form of Christian prayer. Because this form
of prayer is used so frequently, we often take for granted its astonishing
significance.

The German scholar Joachim Jeremias has argued that in almost every
prayer that Jesus utters in the New Testament, He addresses God as Father.
Jeremias notes that this represents a radical departure from Jewish custom and tradition. Though Jewish people were given a lengthy number
of appropriate titles for God in personal prayer, significantly absent from
the approved list was the title "Father." To be sure, the Jews would use the
term "Father" indirectly by addressing God as the Father of people, but
never by way of a direct address, in which the person praying addressed
God in personal terms as "Father." Jeremias also notes that the serious
reaction against Jesus by His contemporaries indicated that they heard
in His addressing God as Father a blasphemous utterance by which Jesus
was presuming, by this term of address, a certain equality that He enjoyed
with the Father. Jeremias goes on to argue that there is no record of any
Jew addressing God directly as Father until the tenth century A.D. in Italy,

with the notable exception of Jesus. Though Jeremias' findings have been challenged in some quarters, it remains a matter of record that Jesus' use of the term "Father" in personal prayer is an extraordinary use.

Since the science of comparative religion reached its zenith in the nineteenth century and liberal theologians sought to reduce the core essence of all religion to the universal fatherhood of God and the universal brotherhood of man, it has followed from such liberal assumptions that to consider God as Father would be a most basic assumption in any religion. However, when we look again at the way in which the term functions in the New Testament and in the teaching of the Apostles, we see that there is no doctrine of universal fatherhood of God in the Bible, except for His role as the creator of all men. Rather, the fatherhood of God has as its primary reference a filial (father/son) relationship that is restricted.

In the first and most important case, God has only one child, His only-begotten Son, the *monogenēs*, which restricts this filial relationship to Christ. We do not have the natural right to call God "Father." That right is bestowed upon us only through God's gracious work of adoption. This is an extraordinary privilege, that those who are in Christ now have the right to address God in such a personal, intimate, filial term as "Father." Therefore, we ought never to take for granted this unspeakable privilege bestowed upon us by God's grace. We note in the Lord's Prayer that Jesus instructs us that now when we pray, we are to refer to God as "Our Father." Again the "ourness" of this relationship is grounded in the unique ministry of Jesus by which, through adoption, He is our elder brother and He gives to us those privileges that by nature belong only to Him. Now, by adopting us, He says that we may regard God, not only as His Father, but as our Father.

The first petition of the Lord's Prayer is found in the words, "Hallowed be Thy Name." The opening address, "Our Father, who art in Heaven," is simply that, an address. From that address, Jesus instructs His disciples to offer certain petitions in prayer. The first and chief of those petitions is that we pray that the name of God will be hallowed. This is also extraordinary in that as the prayer continues, we ask that the will of God be done on earth as it is in heaven and that His kingdom would come on earth as it is in heaven. Both of these desires can only be met when and if the God of the kingdom of heaven and of earth is treated with supreme reverence, honor, and adoration. When we fail to observe the third commandment, when we fail to honor God as God, and use His name as a curse word, or in a flippant, careless manner, we fail to fulfill this first petition. Perhaps nothing is more commonplace in our culture than the expression that comes from people's lips on many occasions, when they say simply, "Oh, my God." This careless reference to God indicates how far removed our culture is from fulfilling the petition of the Lord's Prayer. It should be a priority for the church and for every individual Christian to make sure that the way in which we speak of God is a way that communicates respect, awe, adoration, and reverence. How we use the name of God reveals more clearly than any creed we ever confess our deepest attitudes towards the God of the sacred name.

"The Christianity of the Bible is a religion that is uncompromisingly supernatural. If we take away the supernatural, we take away Christianity."

—

A SUPERNATURAL FAITH

JULY 2007

———

"THE GOD HYPOTHESIS IS NO LONGER NECESSARY to explain the origin of the universe or the development of human life." This assertion was at the very heart of the movement that took place in the eighteenth century that we call the Enlightenment or the *Aufklärung*. This movement spread from Germany to France and then to England. The French Encyclopedists (writers of an encyclopedia during the eighteenth century that promoted secular humanism) were militant in their denial of the need for the existence of God. His existence was seen as no longer necessary because He had been supplanted by the "science" of that period that explained the universe in terms of spontaneous generation. Here we see an example of pseudoscience supplanting sound philosophy and theology.

Added to this, we have the agnosticism of the titanic philosopher Immanuel Kant, who argued that it is impossible for science or philosophy to acquire knowledge of the metaphysical realm of God. It was declared that all knowledge must be restricted to the realm of the natural. With the combination of Kant's agnosticism and the hypothesis of the Enlightenment, the door was open wide to a thoroughgoing philosophy of naturalism. This philosophy captured in its wake the academic theologians of Europe in the nineteenth century.

Out of this came nineteenth-century liberalism with its militant anti-supernatural perspective. The liberalism of that era denied all of the supernatural elements of the Christian faith, including the virgin birth of Jesus, His miracles, His atoning death, and His resurrection. The supernatural was stripped altogether from Christianity. Commenting on this in the twentieth century, the Swiss theologian Emil Brunner described nineteenth century liberalism as mere "unbelief in disguise."

The twentieth century saw a continuation of the impact of naturalism with the so-called neo-liberalism of German theology, particularly as it was manifested in the writings of Rudolf Bultmann. Bultmann saw the Bible as a mixture of history and mythology. He believed that which was mythological had to be removed from the text of the Bible in order to speak relevantly to modern people. Of course, from Bultmann's perspective, the supernatural trappings of the New Testament were all a part of the mythological husk that had to be stripped away from the ethical core of the Bible. The impact of liberalism and neo-liberalism on the church left it basically as a worldly, nature-bound religion that sought refuge in a humanitarian social agenda. This is the approach to Christianity that has all but completely captured many of today's mainline churches throughout the world.

However, in the last few decades, we have witnessed a comeback of sorts of the supernatural. Yet this increasing interest in the supernatural has been driven in large measure by a fascination with the occult. People are now interested in demons, witches, spiritualists, and other occultic phenomena.

The Christianity of the Bible is a religion that is uncompromisingly supernatural. If we take away the supernatural, we take away Christianity. At the heart of the worldview of both Testaments is the idea that the realm of nature is created by One who transcends that nature. That God Himself is "supra" or above and beyond the created universe. The first principle of the Bible is that God must never be identified with the realm of nature but always and everywhere be seen as the Lord over nature. The difference between the natural and the supernatural is the difference between that which is restricted to this world and that which participates in the realm of the divine, the realm that is above and beyond the reach of what is found in simple nature.

In no way does this affirmation of supernature in the Bible denigrate the importance of the natural. The natural realm is where God's work of redemption is played out in space and time. But that work of redemption is not a natural process of human evolution or development; rather, it involves an intrusion from above, from the transcendent realm of God, which addresses the spiritual nature of our humanity.

With the renewed interest in the supernatural that comes with the occult, we must be ever vigilant to make sure that whatever understanding we have of the supernatural is an understanding that is informed by the Bible and not by paganism. Sheer naturalism is paganism with a vengeance, but so is the occult. What we need is an understanding of the supernatural that comes to us from the supernatural, from the Author of the supernatural, who reveals to us in His Word the content of the supernatural realm—so that our understanding of angels, or demons, or of spiritual beings comes from God's self-revelation and not from human speculation, neo-gnostic magic, or other forms of pagan intrusions. Again, we must insist that without the supernatural, Christianity loses its very heart, and this writer cannot understand why anybody would attach any great significance to Christianity at all once it's been stripped of its supernatural elements.

THE ATHANASIAN CREED

AUGUST 2007

———

Q UICUMQUE VULT—THIS PHRASE IS THE title attributed to what is popularly known as the Athanasian Creed. It was often called the Athanasian Creed because for centuries people attributed its authorship to Athanasius, the great champion of Trinitarian orthodoxy during the crisis of the heresy of Arianism that erupted in the fourth century. That theological crisis focused on the nature of Christ and culminated in the Nicene Creed in 325. At the Council of Nicaea of that year the term *homoousios* was the controversial word that finally was linked to the church's confession of the person of Christ. With this word the church declared that the second person of the Trinity has the same substance or essence as the Father, thereby affirming that the Father, the Son, and the Holy Spirit are equal in being and eternality. Though Athanasius did not write the Nicene Creed, he was its chief champion against the heretics who followed after Arius, who argued that Christ was an exalted creature but that He was less than God.

Athanasius died in 373 A.D., and the epithet that appeared on his tombstone is now famous, as it captures the essence of his life and ministry. It read simply, "*Athanasius contra mundum*," that is, "Athanasius against the world." This great Christian leader suffered several exiles during the embittered Arian controversy because of the steadfast profession of faith he maintained in Trinitarian orthodoxy.

Though the name "Athanasius" was given to the creed over the centuries, modern scholars are convinced that the Athanasian Creed was written after the death of Athanasius. Certainly, Athanasius' theological influence is embedded in the creed, but in all likelihood he was not its author. The present title, *Quicumque Vult*, follows the custom in the Roman Catholic Church that is used for encyclicals and creedal statements. These ecclesiastical affirmations get their name from the first word or words of the Latin text. The Athanasian Creed begins with the words *quicumque vult*, which mean "whoever wishes" or "whosoever wishes," inasmuch as this phrase introduces the first assertion of the Athanasian Creed. That assertion is this: "Whosoever wishes to be saved must, above all, keep the catholic faith." The Athanasian Creed seeks to set forth in summary version those essential doctrines for salvation affirmed by the church with specific reference to the Trinity.

With respect to the history of the origins of the Athanasian Creed, it is generally thought now that the creed was first written in the fifth century—though the seventh century is also given its due, since the creed does not show up in the annals of history until 633 at the fourth Council of Toledo. It was written in Latin and not in Greek. If written in the fifth century, several possible authors have been mentioned because of the influence of their thought including Ambrose of Milan and Augustine of Hippo, but it likely was the French saint Vincent of Lérins.

The content of the Athanasian Creed stresses the affirmation of the Trinity in which all members of the Godhead are considered uncreated and co-eternal and of the same substance. In the affirmation of the Trinity the dual nature of Christ is given central importance. As the Athanasian Creed in one sense reaffirms the doctrines of the Trinity set forth in the fourth century at Nicaea, in like manner the strong affirmations of the fifth-century council at Chalcedon in 451 are also recapitulated therein. As the church fought with the Arian heresy in the fourth century, the fifth century brought forth the heresies of Monophysitism, which reduced the person of Christ to one nature, *mono physis*, a single theanthropic (God-man) nature that was neither purely divine or purely human. In the Monophysite heresy of Eutyches, the person of Christ was seen as being one person with one nature, which nature was neither truly divine nor truly human. In this view, the two natures of Christ were confused or co-mingled together. At the same time the church battled with the Monophysite heresy, she also fought against the opposite view of Nestorianism, which sought not so much to blur and mix the two natures but to separate them, coming to the conclusion that Jesus had two natures and was therefore two persons, one human and one divine. Both the Monophysite heresy and the Nestorian heresy were clearly condemned at the Council of Chalcedon in 451, where the church, reaffirming its Trinitarian orthodoxy, stated their belief that Christ, or the second person of the Trinity, was *vere homo* and *vere Deus*, truly human and truly God. It further declared that the two natures in their perfect unity coexisted in such a manner as to be without mixture, confusion, separation, or division, wherein each nature retained its own attributes. So with one creedal affirmation, both the heresy of Nestorianism and the heresy of Monophysitism were condemned.

The Athanasian Creed reaffirms the distinctions found at Chalcedon, where in the Athanasian statement Christ is called "perfect God and perfect man." All three members of the Trinity are deemed to be uncreated and therefore co-eternal. Also following earlier affirmations, the Holy Spirit is declared to have proceeded both from the Father "and the Son," affirming the so-called *filioque* concept that was so controversial with Eastern Orthodoxy. Eastern Orthodoxy to this day has not embraced the *filioque* idea.

Finally, the Athanasian standards examined the incarnation of Jesus and affirmed that in the mystery of the incarnation the divine nature did not mutate or change into a human nature, but rather the immutable divine nature took upon itself a human nature. That is, in the incarnation there was an assumption by the divine nature of a human nature and not the mutation of the divine nature into a human nature.

The Athanasian Creed is considered one of the four authoritative creeds of the Roman Catholic Church, and again, it states in terse terms what is necessary to believe in order to be saved. Though the Athanasian Creed does not get as much publicity in Protestant churches, the orthodox doctrines of the Trinity and the incarnation are affirmed by virtually every historic Protestant church.

DUTY AND HONOR

SEPTEMBER 2007

———

S EVERAL YEARS AGO I WAS participating in a discussion with some business men in Jackson, Mississippi. In the course of the conversation, one of the men made reference to a man who was not present at the meeting. He said, "He is an honorable man." When I heard this comment, my ears perked up as I thought for a moment I was hearing a foreign language being spoken. I realized that I was in the middle of the Deep South where customs of old had not entirely been eradicated, yet I still could not get over that somebody in this day and age was using the word *honor* as a descriptive term for a human being. The term *honor* has become somewhat archaic. We may think of the famous speech that General Douglas MacArthur gave at West Point titled "Duty, Honor, Country," but that was more than a half a century ago. Today, the word *honor* has all but disappeared from the English language. Virtually, the only time I see the word in print is on bumper stickers that declare that the owner of the automobile has a child who is on the "Honor Roll," but "Honor Roll" is perhaps the last vestigial remnant of a forgotten concept.

I speak about honor because the dictionary lists the term *honor* as the chief synonym for the word *integrity*. My concern in this article is to ask: "What is the meaning of integrity?" If we use the pedestrian definitions given to us by lexicographers, such as we find in Webster's dictionary, we read several entries. In the first instance, integrity is defined as "uncompromising adherence to moral and ethical principles." Second, integrity means "soundness of character." Third, integrity means "honesty." Fourth, integrity refers to being "whole or entire." Fifth and finally, integrity means to be "unimpaired in one's character."

Now, these definitions describe persons who are almost as rare as the use of the term *honor*. In the first instance, integrity would describe someone whom we might call "a person of principle." The person who is a person of principle is one, as the dictionary defines, who is uncompromising. The person is not uncompromising in every negotiation or discussion of important issues, but is uncompromising with respect to moral and ethical principles. This is a person who puts principle ahead of personal gain. The art of compromise is a virtue in a politically correct culture, which political correctness itself is modified by the adjectival qualifier *political*. To be political is often to be a person who compromises everything, including principle.

We also see that integrity refers to soundness of character and honesty. When we look to the New Testament, for example, in the epistle of James, James gives a list of virtues that are to be manifested in the Christian life. In the fifth chapter of that letter at verse 12, he writes, "But above all, my brothers, do not swear, either by heaven or by earth or with any other oath, but let your 'yes' be yes, and your 'no,' be no, so that you may not fall under condemnation." Here James elevates the trustworthiness of a person's word, the simple statement of yes or no, as a virtue that is "above all." What James is getting at is that integrity requires a kind of honesty that indicates that when we say we will do something, our word is our bond. We should not require sacred oaths and vows in order to be trusted. People of integrity can be trusted on the basis of what they say.

In our culture, we see again and again the distinction between a politician and a statesman. One person I know made that distinction in these terms: A politician is a person who looks to the next election, while a statesman is a person who looks to the next generation.

There is, admittedly, a kind of cynicism inherent in such a distinction, the idea being that politicians are people who will compromise virtue or compromise principle in order to be elected or to stay in office. Such lack of virtue is found not only in politicians, but it is found in the churches every day, which appears at times to be filled with ministers who are quite prepared to compromise the truth of the Gospel for the sake of their current popularity. This is the same lack of integrity that destroyed the nation of Israel in the Old Testament, where the false prophets proclaimed what they knew the people wanted to hear, rather than what God had commanded them to say. That is the quintessence of the lack of integrity.

When we come to the New Testament, we look at the supreme exam-ple of a lack of integrity in the judgment accorded Jesus by the Roman procurator Pontius Pilate. After examining and interrogating Jesus, Pilate made the announcement to the clamoring crowd: "I find no fault in Him." Yet after this declaration, Pilate was willing to deliver the faultless One into the hands of the raging mob. This was a clear act of political com-promise where principle and ethics were thrown to the wind in order to appease a hungry crowd.

We look back again to the Old Testament to the experience of the prophet Isaiah in his vision recorded in chapter 6 of that book. We remember that Isaiah saw the Lord high and lifted up as well as the seraphim singing the Trisagion: "Holy, Holy, Holy." In response to this epiphany, Isaiah cried out, "Woe is me," announcing a curse upon himself. He said the reason for his curse was because "I am undone" or "ruined." What Isaiah expe-rienced in that moment was human disintegration. Prior to that vision, Isaiah was perhaps viewed as the most righteous man in the nation. He stood secure and confident in his own integrity. Everything was being held together by his virtue. He considered himself a whole, integrated person, but as soon as he saw the ultimate model and standard for integrity and virtue in the character of God, he experienced disintegration. He fell apart at the seams, realizing that his sense of integrity was at best a pretense.

Calvin indicated that this is the common lot of human beings, who as long as they keep their gaze fixed on the horizontal or terrestrial level of experience are able to congratulate themselves and consider themselves with all flattery of being slightly less than demigods. But once they raise their gaze to heaven and consider even for a moment what kind of being God is, they stand shaking and quaking, becoming completely disavowed of any further illusion of their integrity.

The Christian is to reflect the character of God. The Christian is to be uncompromising with respect to ethical principles. The Christian is called to be a person of honor whose word can be trusted.

GOOD INTENTIONS GONE BAD

OCTOBER 2007

———

THE ADAGE TELLS US THAT there is a destination, the road to which is paved with good intentions. It is the destination that we would prefer not to reach. Good intentions can have disastrous results and consequences. When we look at the revolution of worship in America today, I see a dangerous road that is built with such intentions. The good purposes that have transformed worship in America have as their goal to reach a lost world—a world that is marked by baby boomers and Generation Xers who have in many ways rejected traditional forms and styles of worship. Many have found the life of the church to be irrelevant and boring, and so an effort to meet the needs of these people has driven some radical changes in how we worship God.

Perhaps the most evident model developed over the last half century is that model defined as the "seeker-sensitive model." Seekers are defined as those people who are unbelievers and are outside of the church but who are searching for meaning and significance to their lives. The good intention of reaching such people with evangelistic techniques that include the reshaping of Sunday morning worship fails to understand some significant truths set forth in Scripture.

In Romans 3, Paul makes abundantly clear that unconverted people do not seek after God. Thomas Aquinas understood this and maintained that to the naked eye it may seem that unbelievers are searching for God or seeking for the kingdom of God, while they are in fact fleeing from God with all of their might. What Aquinas observed was that people who are unconverted seek the "benefits" that only God can give them, such as ultimate meaning and purpose in their lives, relief from guilt, the presence of joy and happiness, and things of this nature. These are benefits the Christian recognizes can only come through a vital, saving relationship with Christ. The gratuitous leap of logic comes when church leaders think that because people are searching for benefits only God can give them, they must therefore be searching after God. No, they want the benefits without the Giver of the benefits. And so structuring worship to accommodate unbelievers is misguided because these unbelievers are not seeking after God. Seeking after God begins at conversion, and if we are to structure our worship with a view to seekers, then we must structure it for believers, since only believers are seekers.

When we look at the early church, we see that the Christians of the first century gathered on the Lord's Day, devoting themselves to the study of the Apostles' doctrine, to fellowship, to prayer, and to the breaking of bread (Acts 2:42). This was not an assembly of unbelievers. It was an assembling together of believers. Of course, as our Lord warned, there are always present among believers people who have made false professions of faith. There are always the tares that grow alongside of the wheat (Matt. 13:36–43). But one does not structure the church to meet the felt needs and desires of the tares. The purpose of corporate assembly, which has its roots in the Old Testament, is for the people of God to come together corporately to offer their sacrifices of praise and worship to God. So the first rule of worship is that it be designed for believers to worship God in a way that pleases God.

The Old Testament has manifold examples of His severe displeasure that was provoked when the people decided to structure worship according to what they wanted rather than to that which God commanded. Perhaps the most vivid illustration of that is found in Leviticus 10, in the narrative account of the sudden execution of the sons of Aaron, Nadab and Abihu, for their attempts at offering strange fire upon the altar. These young priests "experimented" in a manner that was displeasing to God, and God's response that He spoke to Aaron through Moses was this: "Among those who are near me I will be sanctified, and before all the people I will be glorified" (Lev. 10:3). Corporate worship is not the place to celebrate the profane or the secular. It may be more attractive to Generation Xers to turn Sunday morning worship into an imitation of Starbucks, but it hardly can be thought to be pleasing to God.

Another erroneous assumption made in the attempt to restructure the nature of worship is that the modern generation has been so changed by cultural and contextual influences—such as the impact of the electronic age upon their lives—that they are no longer susceptible to traditional attempts of being reached by expository preaching. Early in the twentieth century, the liberal preacher Harry Emerson Fosdick pointed out that people were no longer interested in coming to church to hear what some Apostle or prophet wrote a couple thousand years ago. Such words and messages were completely irrelevant according to Fosdick, and so the focus of preaching has moved in many cases away from an exposition of the Word of God. We assume this alteration is necessary if we're to reach the people who have been trapped within the changes of our current culture. The erroneous assumption is that in the last fifty years, the constituent nature of humanity has changed, as if the heart can no longer be reached via the mind. It also assumes that the power of the Word of God has lost its potency, so that we must look elsewhere if we are to find powerful and moving experiences of worship in our church. Though the intentions may be marvelous, the results, I believe, are and will continue to be catastrophic.

CROSSING THE CHANNEL

NOVEMBER 2007

———

T HE RAPID SPREAD OF THE Protestant Reformation from Wittenberg, Germany, throughout Europe and across the Channel to England was not spawned by the efforts of a globe-trotting theological entrepreneur. On the contrary, for the most part Martin Luther's entire career was spent teaching in the village of Wittenberg at the university there. Despite his fixed position, Luther's influence spread from Wittenberg around the world in concentric circles—like when a stone is dropped into a pond. The rapid expanse of the Reformation was hinted at from the very beginning when the Ninety-five Theses were posted on the church door (intended for theological discussion among the faculty). Without Luther's knowledge and permission, his theses were translated from Latin into German and duplicated on the printing press and spread to every village in Germany within two weeks. This was a harbinger of things to come. Many means were used to spread Luther's message to the Continent and to England.

One of the most important factors was the influence of virtually thousands of students who studied at the University of Wittenberg and were indoctrinated into Lutheran theology and ecclesiology. Like Calvin's Academy in Geneva, Switzerland, the university became pivotal for the dissemination of Reformation ideas. Wittenberg and Geneva stood as epicenters for a worldwide movement.

The printing press made it possible for Luther to spread his ideas through the many books that he published, not to mention his tracts, confessions, catechisms, pamphlets, and cartoons (one of the most dramatic means of communication to the common people of the day was through messages encrypted in cartoons).

In addition to these methods of print, music was used in the Reformation to carry the doctrines and sentiments of Protestantism through the writing of hymns and chorales. Religious drama was used not in the churches but in the marketplace to communicate the central ideas of the movement—the recovery of the biblical Gospel.

Another overlooked aspect of the expansion of the Reformation is the impact of the fine arts on the church. Woodcuts and portraitures were produced by the great artists of the time—Albrecht Dürer, Hans Holbein, Lucas Cranach the Elder, and Peter Vischer. The portraits of the Reformers made their message more recognizable, as it was associated with their visage in the art world.

Students from England who studied at Wittenberg also had a major impact in bringing the Reformation across the Channel to Great Britain. Probably the most important person in the English Reformation was William Tyndale, whose translation of the Bible into English was of cataclysmic importance. In 1524, he left England for the Continent and studied for a period of time at Wittenberg. His first edition of the New Testament was published in Flanders in 1526, five years after the fated Diet of Worms during which Luther gave his famous "Here I Stand" speech. Thousands of these Bibles were smuggled into England. Many were burned as the work of a heretic, but still others escaped the fire and produced a theological fire of their own.

Another important person was Robert Barnes, an Augustinian monk from Cambridge who was burned at the stake in 1540. Seven years before his martyrdom, he had matriculated at the University of Wittenberg. There also was Martin Bucer, an important Reformer who was invited by the English Protestants to come to Britain and become a professor at the University of Cambridge in 1551.

In addition to those who influenced the English Reformation directly from Luther's Germany, were those whose influence came by a more circuitous route, that is, via Geneva, Switzerland. John Calvin himself had to flee from Paris because of the views he learned from his friends who had been influenced by the teachings of Martin Luther. This Frenchman found his refuge in Geneva, where his pulpit and teaching ministry became known around the world. Geneva became a city of refuge for exiles who fled there for safety from all over Europe. Of the countries that sent exiles to Calvin's Geneva, none was more important than England and the British Isles. John Knox, who led the Reformation in Scotland, spent some time in Switzerland at the feet of Calvin, learning his Reformation theology there. Though Calvin was twenty-six years younger than Luther, Luther's views made a dramatic impact on the young Calvin's life while he was still in his twenties. Though Calvin is usually associated with the doctrine of predestination, it is often overlooked that there was nothing in Calvin's view of predestination and election that was not first articulated by Luther, especially in Luther's famous work *The Bondage of the Will*.

When Calvin was teaching in Geneva, Bloody Mary came to the throne of England. Under her reign, many Protestants were burned at the stake. Those who survived the stake fled in large numbers to Geneva. Some of the exiles from England under Calvin's tutelage set upon the task of translating the Bible into English. This Bible, called the Geneva Bible, was the first Bible to have theological notes printed in the margin, which notes were heavily influenced by Calvin's preaching. This Bible was the predominant Bible among the English for the next hundred years before it was supplanted by the popular King James Version. It was the original, official version of the Scottish Presbyterian church. It was the Bible of Shakespeare, the Bible the Pilgrims brought with them on the *Mayflower* to America, and it was the Bible of choice among America's early colonists.

From Wittenberg directly to England, or from Wittenberg to Geneva to England, in this roundabout route, the seeds of the Reformation that were planted in Germany sprouted into full bloom as they made their way into the English empire. To trace the pathway from Wittenberg to London, one must follow a series of circuitous routes, but the origin of that movement in Wittenberg is unmistakable, and its influence continues even to this day.

THE KING OF KINGS

DECEMBER 2007

T HE GOSPEL OF LUKE ENDS WITH a supremely jarring statement: "Then he led them out as far as Bethany, and lifting up his hands he blessed them. While he blessed them, he parted from them and was carried up into heaven. And they worshiped him, and returned to Jerusalem with great joy, and were continually in the temple blessing God" (24:50–53).

What is jarring about this passage is, as Luke reports the departure of Jesus from this world, the response of His disciples was to return to Jerusalem with "great joy." What about Jesus' departure would instill in His disciples an emotion of sheer elation? This question is made all the more puzzling when we consider the emotions the disciples displayed when Jesus earlier had told them that His departure would come soon. At that time, the idea that their Lord would leave their presence provoked in them a spirit of profound remorse. It would seem that nothing could be more depressing than to anticipate separation from the presence of Jesus. Yet, in a very short period of time, that depression changed to unspeakable joy.

We have to ask what it is that provoked such a radical change of emotion within the hearts of Jesus' disciples. The answer to that question is plain in the New Testament. Between the time of Jesus' announcement to them that He would soon be going away and the time of His actual departure, the disciples came to realize two things. First, they realized why it was that Jesus was leaving. Secondly, they understood the place to which He was going. Jesus was leaving not in order that they might be left alone and comfortless, but that He might ascend into heaven. The New Testament idea of ascension means something far more weighty than merely going up into the sky or even to the abode of the heavenlies. In His ascension, Jesus was going to a specific place for a specific reason. He was ascending into heaven for the purpose of His investiture and coronation as the King of kings and Lord of lords. The New Testament title used to describe Jesus in His kingly role is the "King of kings" and likewise the title "Lord of lords." This particular literary structure means more than Jesus' establishment in a position of authority by which He will rule over lesser kings. Rather, it is a structure that indicates the supremacy of Jesus in His monarchical majesty. He is King in the highest possible sense of kingship.

In biblical terms, it is unthinkable to have a king without a kingdom. Since Jesus ascends to His coronation as king, with that coronation comes the designation by the Father of a realm over which He rules. That realm is all creation.

There are two gross errors in modern theology regarding the biblical concept of the kingdom of God. The first is that the kingdom has already been consummated and that nothing is left for the reign of Christ to be made manifest. Such a view can be described as over-realized eschatology (last things). With the realization of the fullness of the kingdom, there would be no more to look forward to in terms of the triumph of Christ. The other error is that which a vast number of Christians believe, that the kingdom of God is something totally futuristic—that is, in no sense does the kingdom of God exist already. This view takes such a strong attitude toward the future dimension of the kingdom of God that even such New Testament passages as the Beatitudes of Matthew 5–7, have no application to the church today because they belong to the future age of the kingdom, which has not yet begun.

Both of the above views do violence to the clear teaching of the New Testament that the kingdom of God has indeed begun. The King is already in place. He has already received all authority on heaven and on earth. That means that at this very moment the supreme authority over the kingdoms of this world and over the entire cosmos is in the hands of King Jesus. There is no inch of real estate, no symbol of power in this world that is not under His ownership and His rule at this very moment. In Paul's letter to the Philippians, in chapter 2, in the so-called kenotic hymn, it is said that Jesus is given the name that is above all names. The name that He is given that rises above all other titles that anyone can receive, is a name that is reserved for God. It is God's title *Adonai*, which means the "One who is absolutely sovereign." Again, this title is one of supreme governorship for the One who is the King of all of the earth.

The New Testament translation of the Old Testament title *adonai* is the name *lord*. When Paul says that at the name of Jesus every knee must bow and every tongue confess, the reason for the bowing in obeisance and for confessing is that they are to declare with their lips that Jesus is Lord—that is, He is the sovereign ruler. That was the first confession of faith of the early church.

Then Rome, in her misguided, pagan tyranny tried to enforce a loyalty oath to the emperor cult of religion, in which all people were required to recite the phrase *kaisar kyrios*—"Caesar is lord." The Christians responded by showing every possible form of civil obedience, by paying their taxes, by honoring the king, by being model citizens; but they could not in good conscience obey the mandate of Caesar to proclaim him lord. Their response to the loyalty oath, *kaisar kyrios*, was as profound in its ramifications as it was simple in its expression, *Iēsous ho kyrios*, Jesus is Lord. The lordship of Jesus is not simply a hope of Christians that someday might be realized; it is a truth that has already taken place. It is the task of the church to bear witness to that invisible kingdom, or as Calvin put it, it is the task of the church to make the invisible kingdom of Christ visible. Though invisible, it is nevertheless real.

THE SIGNIFICANCE
OF C.S. LEWIS

JANUARY 2008

———

C.S. LEWIS EMERGED AS A TWENTIETH-CENTURY ICON in the world of Christian literature. His prodigious work combining acute intellectual reasoning with unparalleled creative imagination made him a popular figure not only in the Christian world but in the secular world as well. The Chronicles of Narnia and the Space Trilogy, though rife with dramatic Christian symbolism, were devoured by those who had no interest in Christianity at all, but were enjoyed for the sheer force of the drama of the stories themselves. An expert in English literature, C.S. Lewis functioned also as a Christian intellectual. He had a passion to reach out to the intellectual world of his day in behalf of Christianity. Through his own personal struggles with doubt and pain, he was able to hammer out a solid intellectual foundation for his own faith. C.S. Lewis had no interest in a mystical leap of faith devoid of rational scrutiny. He abhorred those who would leave their minds in the parking lot when they went into church. He was convinced that Christianity was at heart rational and defensible with sound argumentation. His work showed a marriage of art and science, a marriage of reason and creative imagination that was unparalleled. His gift of creative writing was matched by few of his twentieth-century contemporaries. His was indeed a literary genius in which he was able to express profound Christian truth through art, in a manner similar to that conveyed by Bach in his music and Rembrandt in his painting. Even today his introductory book on the Christian faith—*Mere Christianity*—remains a perennial best seller.

We have to note that although a literary expert, C.S. Lewis remained a layman theologically speaking. Indeed, he was a well-read and studied layman, but he did not benefit from the skills of technical training in theology. Some of his theological musings will indicate a certain lack of technical understanding, for which he may certainly be excused. His book *Mere Christianity* has been the single most important volume of popular apologetics that the Christian world witnessed in the twentieth century. Again, in his incomparable style, Lewis was able to get to the nitty-gritty of the core essentials of the Christian faith without distorting them into simplistic categories.

His reasoning, though strong, was not always technically sound. For example, in his defense of the resurrection, he used an argument that has impressed many despite its invalidity. He follows an age-old argument that the truth claims of the writers of the New Testament concerning the resurrection of Jesus are verified by their willingness to die for the truths that they espoused. And the question is asked: Which is easier to believe—that these men created a false myth and then died for that falsehood or that Jesus really returned from the grave? On the surface, the answer to that question is easy. It is far easier to believe that men would be deluded into a falsehood, in which they really believed, and be willing to give their lives for it, than to believe that somebody actually came back from the dead. There has to be other reasons to support the truth claim of the resurrection other than that people were willing to die for it. One might look at the violence in the Middle East and see 50,000 people so persuaded of the truths of Islam that they are willing to sacrifice themselves as human suicide bombs. History is replete with the examples of deluded people who have died for their delusions. History is not filled with examples of resurrections. However, despite the weakness of that particular argument, Lewis nevertheless made a great impact on people who were involved in their initial explorations of the truth claims of Christianity.

To this day, people who won't read a Bible or won't read other Christian literature will pick up *Mere Christianity* and find themselves engaged by the acute mental processes of C.S. Lewis. The church owes an enormous debt to this man for his unwillingness to capitulate to the irrationalism that marked so much of Christian thought in the twentieth century—an irrationalism that produced what many describe as a "mindless Christianity."

The Christianity of C.S. Lewis is a mindful Christianity where there is a marvelous union between head and heart. Lewis was a man of profound sensitivity to the pain of human beings. He himself experienced the crucible of sanctification through personal pain and anguish. It was from such experiences that his sensitivity developed and his ability to communicate it sharply honed. To be creative is the mark of profundity. To be creative without distortion is rare indeed, and yet in the stories that C.S. Lewis spun, the powers of creativity reached levels that were rarely reached before or since. Aslan, the lion in the Chronicles of Narnia, so captures the character and personality of Jesus; it is nothing short of amazing. Every generation, I believe, will continue to benefit from the insights put on paper by this amazing personality.

"When Israel violated the terms of her covenant, God sent his prosecuting attorneys to file suit against them, to declare his controversy with the people."

—

COVENANT PROSECUTORS

FEBRUARY 2008

——

I DON'T REMEMBER THE EXACT WORDS. They went something like this: "He was a thundering paradox of a man." These words served as the opening lines of William Manchester's classic biography of General Douglas MacArthur. In this work, MacArthur was shown as a multi-faceted man whose essence could not be crystallized by a single attribute. In like manner, the prophets of the Old Testament were men of multi-faceted and multi-dimensioned responsibilities and behavior. Some of the roles carried out by these prophets include the following: First, the prophets of Israel were agents of revelation. They did not say, "In my opinion." Instead, they introduced their statements or oracles with "Thus saith the Lord." Though the Old Testament prophets as agents of revelation are popularly conceived as being principally men involved in foretelling, that is, predicting future events, in reality the emphasis of their activity was involved in forthtelling. Forthtelling meant that they were declaring the Word of God to their own time and to their own generations.

The second dimension of the role of the Old Testament prophet was that of being reformers. We must distinguish here between the work of reformation and the work of revolution. The Old Testament prophets had no desire to root up and cast down or to destroy the cultic structure of the nation. Rather, they called the people to return to orthodoxy, not to abandon their history. They called for a return to the terms of the original covenants that God had made with them, to obedience to the law that God had revealed through Moses, and, most importantly, to the practice of true worship as distinguished from all forms of idolatry and hypocrisy. They spoke boldly against formalism, externalism, and ritualism. But in their critique, they did not repudiate the formal, the external, or the ritual. Rather, it was the *ism* attached to these concepts that expressed the hypocrisy of Jewish worship during the prophetic era. The rituals, the externals, and the forms had been distorted by false forms of worship.

Third, the prophet carried out the role of the covenant prosecutor. There were legal ramifications in terms of the relationship between God and His people. The structure of that relationship was the covenant, and all covenants had stipulations associated with them as well as sanctions. There was a penalty for disobedience, as well as a reward for obedience. When Israel violated the terms of her covenant, God sent His prosecuting attorneys to file suit against them, to declare His controversy with the people. We see this in Hosea's announcement when he called the people of Israel to solemn assembly, saying that the Lord has a controversy with His people. The announcement and pursuit of this controversy by reason of law had the prophets speaking not as priestly defenders of the people, but rather as divine prosecuting attorneys pronouncing God's judgment and wrath upon them.

Fourth, the role of the prophet in Israel, individually and corporately, was to serve in a concrete way as the conscience of the nation. Israel was structured as a divine theocracy. There was no hard-pressed separation of church and state. When the state and the people in it wandered from the ethical structure of the nation, it was the prophet who would prick the consciences of the people and of the kings. Part of the reason the prophets lived such perilous lives was because they were called to speak boldly to the rulers of the nation, which rulers did not appreciate the intervention of the prophet. Rare was the king such as David who gave heed to the intervention of Nathan and who responded with profound repentance (2 Sam. 12:1–15). Normally, the course of the rulers was to follow the way of Ahab, to seek the very life of that prophet who dared to call him to repentance (1 Kings 19:1–3). In our own culture, where we have a so-called separation of church and state, it is not the role or responsibility of the church to rule the nation. But it is the responsibility of the church to be the conscience of the nation and to call the state to repentance when the state becomes demonized and fails to serve in the cause of righteousness.

Finally, the prophets were known as rugged individualists. There were indeed schools of professional prophets who worked together executing their trade for their own livelihood. Traditionally, these were the ones who became the false prophets of Israel. The true prophets were those who usually met with God alone in the wilderness and were given a divine summons to stand against the crowd and against the false prophets. Jeremiah, for example, felt the ignominy and the anguish of always being outnumbered by the false prophets who united in their cause against the truth boldly proclaimed by him. It was Elijah who thought that he was the only one left who had not bowed his knee to Baal. God rebuked him and reminded him that he had preserved 7,000 for Himself, who had not bowed the knee to Baal. These incidents reflect the commonplace experience of the Old Testament prophet who, time after time, was called to stand alone against a secularized nation and an immoral culture. They stood their ground for the truth of God and in many cases paid the ultimate price for it. It's on the shoulders of the prophets of the Old Testament that the New Testament church establishes the agents of revelation—which are the Apostles in the language of the new covenant. And so the foundation of the church of Christ is the foundation of the prophets and the Apostles.

THE DARK NIGHT OF THE SOUL

MARCH 2008

———

T HE DARK NIGHT OF THE SOUL. This phenomenon describes a malady that the greatest of Christians have suffered from time to time. It was the malady that provoked David to soak his pillow with tears. It was the malady that earned for Jeremiah the sobriquet "The Weeping Prophet." It was the malady that so afflicted Martin Luther that his melancholy threatened to destroy him. This is no ordinary fit of depression, but it is a depression that is linked to a crisis of faith, a crisis that comes when one senses the absence of God or gives rise to a feeling of abandonment by Him.

Spiritual depression is real and can be acute. We ask how a person of faith could experience such spiritual lows, but whatever provokes it does not take away from its reality. Our faith is not a constant action. It is mobile. It vacillates. We move from faith to faith, and in between we may have periods of doubt when we cry, "Lord, I believe; help Thou my unbelief."

We may also think that the dark night of the soul is something completely incompatible with the fruit of the Spirit, not only that of faith but also that of joy. Once the Holy Spirit has flooded our hearts with a joy unspeakable, how can there be room in that chamber for such darkness? It is important for us to make a distinction between the spiritual fruit of joy and the cultural concept of happiness. A Christian can have joy in his heart while there is still spiritual depression in his head. The joy that we have sustains us through these dark nights and is not quenched by spiritual depression. The joy of the Christian is one that survives all downturns in life.

In writing to the Corinthians in his second letter, Paul commends to his readers the importance of preaching and of communicating the Gospel to people. But in the midst of that, he reminds the church that the treasure we have from God is a treasure that is contained not in vessels of gold and silver but in what the Apostle calls "jars of clay." For this reason he says, "that the surpassing power belongs to God and not to us." Immediately after this reminder, the Apostle adds, "We are afflicted in every way, but not crushed; perplexed, but not driven to despair; persecuted, but not forsaken; struck down, but not destroyed; always carrying in the body the death of Jesus, so that the life of Jesus may also be manifested in our bodies" (2 Cor. 4:7–10).

This passage indicates the limits of depression that we experience. The depression may be profound, but it is not permanent, nor is it fatal. Notice that the Apostle Paul describes our condition in a variety of ways. He says that we are "afflicted, perplexed, persecuted, and struck down." These are powerful images that describe the conflict that Christians must endure, but in every place that he describes this phenomenon, he describes at the same time its limits. Afflicted, but not crushed. Perplexed, but not in despair. Persecuted, but not forsaken. Struck down, but not destroyed.

So we have this pressure to bear, but the pressure, though it is severe, does not crush us. We may be confused and perplexed, but that low point to which perplexity brings us does not result in complete and total despair. Even in persecution, as serious as it may be, we are still not forsaken, and we may be overwhelmed and struck down as Jeremiah spoke of, yet we have room for joy. We think of the prophet Habakkuk, who in his misery remained confident that despite the setbacks he endured, God would give him feet like hind's feet, feet that would enable him to walk in high places.

Elsewhere, the Apostle Paul in writing to the Philippians gives them the admonition to be "anxious for nothing," telling them that the cure for anxiety is found on one's knees, that it is the peace of God that calms our spirit and dissipates anxiety. Again, we can be anxious and nervous and worried without finally submitting to ultimate despair.

This coexistence of faith and spiritual depression is paralleled in other biblical statements of emotive conditions. We are told that it is perfectly legitimate for believers to suffer grief. Our Lord Himself was a man of sorrows and acquainted with grief. Though grief may reach to the roots of our souls, it must not result in bitterness. Grief is a legitimate emotion, at times even a virtue, but there must be no place in the soul for bitterness. In like manner, we see that it is a good thing to go to the house of mourning, but even in mourning, that low feeling must not give way to hatred. The presence of faith gives no guarantee of the absence of spiritual depression; however, the dark night of the soul always gives way to the brightness of the noonday light of the presence of God.

NORMA NORMATA:
THE RULE THAT IS RULED

APRIL 2008

———

T HE LATIN WORD *CREDO* MEANS simply "I believe." It represents the first word of the Apostles' Creed. Throughout church history it has been necessary for the church to adopt and embrace creedal statements to clarify the Christian faith and to distinguish true content from error and false representations of the faith. Such creeds are distinguished from Scripture in that Scripture is *norma normans* ("the rule that rules"), while the creeds are *norma normata* ("a rule that is ruled").

Historically, Christian creeds have included everything from brief affirmations to comprehensive statements. The earliest Christian creed is found in the New Testament, which declares, "Jesus is Lord." The New Testament makes a somewhat cryptic statement about this affirmation, namely, that no one can make the statement except by the Holy Spirit. What are we to understand by this? On the one hand, the New Testament tells us that people can honor God with their lips while their hearts are far from Him. That is to say, people can recite creeds and make definitive affirmations of faith without truly believing those affirmations. So, then, why would the New Testament say that no one can make this confession save by the Holy Spirit? Perhaps it was because of the cost associated with making that creedal statement in the context of ancient Rome.

The loyalty oath required by Roman citizens to demonstrate their allegiance to the empire in general and to the emperor in particular was to say publicly, "*Kaisar Kyrios,*" that is, "Caesar is lord." In the first-century church, Christians bent over backward to be obedient to civil magistrates, including the oppressive measures of Caesar, and yet, when it came to making the public affirmation that Caesar is lord, Christians could not do so in good conscience. As a substitute for the phrase, "Caesar is lord," the early Christians made their affirmation by saying, "Jesus is Lord." To do that was to provoke the wrath of the Roman government, and in many cases, it cost the Christian his life. Therefore, people tended not to make that public affirmation unless they were moved by the Holy Spirit to do so. The simple creed "Jesus is Lord" or more full statements such as the Apostles' Creed give an outline of basic, essential teachings. The creeds summarize New Testament content.

The creeds also used that summary content to exclude the heretics of the fourth century. In the affirmation of the Nicene Creed, the church affirmed categorically its belief in the deity of Christ and in the doctrine of the Trinity. These affirmations were seen as essential truths of the Christian faith. They were essential because without inclusion of these truths, any claim to Christianity would be considered a false claim.

At the time of the Reformation, there was a proliferation of creeds as the Protestant community found it necessary, in the light and heat of the controversy of that time, to give definitive statements as to what they believed and how their faith differed from the Roman Catholic Church's theology. Rome itself added her creedal statements at the Council of Trent in the middle of the sixteenth century as a response to the Protestant movement. But each Protestant group, such as the Lutherans, the Swiss Reformed, and Scottish Reformed, found it necessary to clarify the truths that they were affirming. This was made necessary, not only because of disagreements within Reformed parties, but also to clarify the Protestant position against frequent misrepresentations set forth by their Roman Catholic antagonists. The seventeenth-century confessional statement known as the Westminster Confession is one of the most precise and comprehensive creedal statements growing out of the Reformation. It is a model of precision and biblical orthodoxy. However, because of its length and comprehensive dimension, it is difficult to find two advocates of the Westminster Confession who agree on every single precise point. Because of that, churches that use the Westminster Confession or other such confessions, usually limit requirements of adherence by an acknowledgment of "the system of doctrine contained within." These later Protestant creeds not only intended to affirm what they regarded as essentials to Christianity, but specifically to clarify the details of the particular religious communion that would use such comprehensive confessions of faith.

In our day, there has been a strong antipathy emerging against confessions of any stripe or any degree. On the one hand, the relativism that has become pervasive in modern culture eschews any confession of absolute truth. Not only that, we have also seen a strong negative reaction against the rational and propositional nature of truth. Creedal statements are an attempt to show a coherent and unified understanding of the whole scope of Scripture. In that sense, they are brief statements of what we historically have called "systematic theology." The idea of systematic theology assumes that everything that God says is coherent and not contradictory. So, though these creeds are not created out of pure rational speculation, nevertheless, they are written in such a way as to be intelligible and understood by the mind. Without such confessions, theological anarchy reigns in the church and in the world.

COSMIC TREASON

MAY 2008

———

"THE SINFULNESS OF SIN" SOUNDS like a vacuous redundancy that adds no information to the subject under discussion. However, the necessity of speaking of the sinfulness of sin has been thrust upon us by a culture and even a church that has diminished the significance of sin itself. Sin is communicated in our day in terms of making mistakes or of making poor choices. When I take an examination or a spelling test, if I make a mistake, I miss a particular word. It is one thing to make a mistake. It is another to look at my neighbor's paper and copy his answers in order to make a good grade. In this case, my mistake has risen to the level of a moral transgression. Though sin may be involved in making mistakes as a result of slothfulness in preparation, nevertheless, the act of cheating takes the exercise to a more serious level. Calling sin "making poor choices" is true, but it is also a euphemism that can discount the severity of the action. The decision to sin is indeed a poor one, but once again, it is more than a mistake. It is an act of moral transgression.

In my book *The Truth of the Cross* I spend an entire chapter discussing this notion of the sinfulness of sin. I begin that chapter by using the anecdote of my utter incredulity when I received a recent edition of *Bartlett's Familiar Quotations*. Though I was happy to receive this free issue, I was puzzled as to why anyone would send it to me. As I leafed through the pages of quotations that included statements from Immanuel Kant, Aristotle, Thomas Aquinas, and others, to my complete astonishment I came upon a quotation from me. That I was quoted in such a learned collection definitely surprised me. I was puzzled by what I could have said that merited inclusion in such an anthology, and the answer was found in a simple statement attributed to me: "Sin is cosmic treason." What I meant by that statement was that even the slightest sin that a creature commits against his Creator does violence to the Creator's holiness, His glory, and His righteousness. Every sin, no matter how seemingly insignificant, is an act of rebellion against the sovereign God who reigns and rules over us and as such is an act of treason against the cosmic King.

Cosmic treason is one way to characterize the notion of sin, but when we look at the ways in which the Scriptures describe sin, we see three that stand out in importance. First, sin is a debt; second, it is an expression of enmity; third, it is depicted as a crime. In the first instance, we who are sinners are described by Scripture as debtors who cannot pay their debts. In this sense, we are talking not about financial indebtedness but a moral indebtedness. God has the sovereign right to impose obligations upon His creatures. When we fail to keep these obligations, we are debtors to our Lord. This debt represents a failure to keep a moral obligation.

The second way in which sin is described biblically is as an expression of enmity. In this regard, sin is not restricted merely to an external action that transgresses a divine law. Rather, it represents an internal motive, a motive that is driven by an inherent hostility toward the God of the universe. It is rarely discussed in the church or in the world that the biblical description of human fallenness includes an indictment that we are by nature enemies of God. In our enmity toward Him, we do not want to have Him even in our thinking, and this attitude is one of hostility toward the very fact that God commands us to obey His will. It is because of this concept of enmity that the New Testament so often describes our redemption in terms of reconciliation. One of the necessary conditions for reconciliation is that there must be some previous enmity between at least two parties. This enmity is what is presupposed by the redeeming work of our Mediator, Jesus Christ, who overcomes this dimension of enmity.

The third way in which the Bible speaks of sin is in terms of transgression of law. The Westminster Shorter Catechism answers the fourteenth question, "What is sin?" by the response, "Sin is any want of conformity to, or transgression of, the law of God." Here we see sin described both in terms of passive and active disobedience. We speak of sins of commission and sins of omission. When we fail to do what God requires, we see this lack of conformity to His will. But not only are we guilty of failing to do what God requires, we also actively do what God prohibits. Thus, sin is a transgression against the law of God.

When people violate the laws of men in a serious way, we speak of their actions not merely as misdemeanors but, in the final analysis, as crimes. In the same regard, our actions of rebellion and transgression of the law of God are not seen by Him as mere misdemeanors; rather, they are felonious. They are criminal in their impact. If we take the reality of sin seriously in our lives, we see that we commit crimes against a holy God and against His kingdom. Our crimes are not virtues; they are vices, and any transgression of a holy God is vicious by definition. It is not until we understand who God is that we gain any real understanding of the seriousness of our sin. Because we live in the midst of sinful people where the standards of human behavior are set by the patterns of the culture around us, we are not moved by the seriousness of our transgressions. We are indeed at ease in Zion. But when God's character is made clear to us and we are able to measure our actions not in relative terms with respect to other humans but in absolute terms with respect to God, His character, and His law, then we begin to be awakened to the egregious character of our rebellion.

Not until we take God seriously will we ever take sin seriously. But if we acknowledge the righteous character of God, then we, like the saints of old, will cover our mouths with our hands and repent in dust and ashes before Him.

TWILIGHT OF THE IDOLS

JUNE 2008

———

T HE NINETEENTH-CENTURY PHILOSOPHER Friedrich Nietzsche is famous for his declaration that "God is dead." That brief dictum does not give the whole story. According to Nietzsche, the cause of the Deity's demise was compassion. He said, "God is dead; He died of pity." But before the God who was the God of Judeo-Christianity perished, Nietzsche said that there were a multitude of deities who existed, such as those who resided on Mount Olympus. That is, at one time there was a plurality of gods. All of the rest of the gods perished when one day the Jewish God, Yahweh, stood up in their assembly and said, "Thou shalt have no other gods before me." Hearing this, according to Nietzsche's satirical summary, all of the rest of the gods and goddesses died. They died of laughter.

In our day, where pluralism reigns in the culture, there is as much satirical hostility to the idea of one God as there was in Nietzsche's satire. But today, that repugnance to monotheism is not a laughing matter. In the culture of pluralism, the chief virtue is toleration, which is the notion that all religious views are to be tolerated, all political views are to be tolerated. The only thing that cannot be tolerated is a claim to exclusivity. There is a built-in, inherent antipathy towards all claims of exclusivity. To say that there is one God is repulsive to the pluralists. To say that one God has not revealed Himself by a plurality of avatars in history is also repugnant. A single God with an only begotten Son is a deity who adds insult to injury by claiming an exclusive Son. There cannot be only one Mediator between man and God. There must be many according to pluralists today. It is equally a truism among pluralists that if there is one way to God, there must be many ways to God, and certainly it cannot be accepted that there is only one way. The exclusive claims of Christianity in terms of God, in terms of Christ, in terms of salvation, cannot live in peaceful coexistence with pluralists.

Beyond the question of the existence of God and of His Son, and of a singular way of salvation, there is also a rejection of any claim to having or possessing an exclusive source of divine revelation. At the time of the Reformation, the so-called *solas* of the Reformation were asserted. It was said that justification is by faith alone (*sola fide*), that it is through Christ alone (*solus Christus*), that it is through grace alone (*sola gratia*), and that it is for God's glory alone (*soli Deo gloria*). But perhaps most repugnant to the modern pluralist is the exclusive claim of *sola Scriptura*. The idea of *sola Scriptura* is that there is only one written source of divine revelation, which can never be placed on a parallel status with confessional statements, creeds, or the traditions of the church. Scripture alone has the authority to bind the conscience precisely because only Scripture is the written revelation of almighty God. The implications of *sola Scriptura* for pluralism are many. Not the least of them is this: It carries a fundamental denial of the revelatory character of all other religious books. An advocate of *sola Scriptura* does not believe that God's revealed Word is found in the Bible and in the Book of Mormon, the Bible and in the Koran, the Bible and in the Upanishads, the Bible and in the Bhagavad Gita; rather, the Christian faith stands on the singular and exclusive claim that the Bible and the Bible alone is God's written word.

The motto of the United States is *e pluribus unum.* However, since the rise of the ideology of pluralism, the real *Unum* of that motto has been ripped from its foundation. What drives pluralism is the philosophical antecedent of relativism. All truth is relative; therefore, no one idea or source can be seen as having any kind of supremacy. Built into our law system is the idea of the equal toleration under the law of all religions. It is a short step in people's thinking from equal toleration under the law to equal validity. The principle that all religions should be treated equally under the law and have equal rights does not carry with it the necessary inference that therefore all religions are valid. Even a cursory, comparative examination of the world's religions reveals points of radical contradiction among them, and unless one is prepared to affirm the equal truth of contradictories, one must not be able to embrace this fallacious assumption.

Sadly, with a philosophy of relativism and a philosophy of pluralism, the science of logic doesn't matter. Logic is escorted to the door and is firmly booted out of the house onto the street. There is no room for logic in any system of pluralism and relativism. Indeed, it's a misnomer to call either a system, because it is the idea of a consistent, coherent view of truth that is unacceptable to the pluralist. The fact that people reject exclusive claims to truth does not invalidate those claims. It is the Christian's duty to hold firm to the uniqueness of God and of His Christ and not compromise with the advocates of pluralism.

"Since all truth is God's truth, all aspects of scientific inquiry are to be within the province of biblical and Christian learning."

—

ALL TRUTH
IS GOD'S TRUTH

JULY 2008

———

DURING THE NINETEENTH-CENTURY potato famine in Ireland, my great-grandfather Charles Sproul fled his native land to seek refuge in America. He left his thatched roof and mud floor cottage in a northern Ireland village and made his way barefoot to Dublin—to the wharf from which he sailed to New York. After registering as an immigrant at Ellis Island, he made his way west to Pittsburgh, where a large colony of Scots-Irish people had settled. They were drawn to that site by the industrial steel mills led by the Scot Andrew Carnegie.

My great-grandfather died in Pittsburgh in 1910, but not until he instilled a profound love for the tradition and yore of Ireland with his sons and grandsons. Thirty years ago, one of my cousins made a pilgrimage to north Ireland to seek his roots in the town from which our great-grandfather came. As he inquired about the whereabouts of any Sprouls, he was told by an elderly gentleman that the last surviving member of our family had perished when he stumbled on his way home from the local pub in a profound state of inebriation. He fell into a canal and drowned.

This leaves us with the stereotype of the Irish as hard-drinking, two-fisted men, who consider bricks to be "Irish confetti." This caricature of the Irish, however, obscures some very important dimensions of Irish history. In the eighth century, missionary settlers to Ireland were very important to the Christianization of the British Isles that had been inhabited largely by pagans and barbarians. The monasteries in Ireland were noted for their devotion to scholarship, for copying biblical texts, and especially for adorning the biblical texts with magnificent illuminations. Their passion for scholarship and art quickly spread to Great Britain where the codification of ancient law was established, which has made an impact even on our land to this day.

One of the most important scholars of this period was a man called Bede, known as the "Venerable." He resided in England and is considered to be the first great European historian. The Irish also produced a master-piece that combined scholarship and beauty in the famous Book of Kells.

But it was in the second part of the eighth century that the great impetus for a revival of scholarship took place. It was under the reign of Charles the Great (Charlemagne), crowned as the first holy Roman emperor, that a new revival of arts and sciences took place. This revival, called the "Carolingian Renaissance," foreshadowed the great Renaissance that would sweep through Europe in the late Middle Ages, beginning chiefly with the work of the Medici patrons in Italy, which found its zenith in the labors of Lorenzo the Magnificent.

In the Holy Roman Empire of the eighth century, Charlemagne was determined to recover the best of classical and biblical learning. He became a patron of scholarship and appointed as his chief intellectual assistant Alcuin, who was from Great Britain. Charlemagne was one of the most illustrious members of the Carolingian dynasty that began with his father, Pepin the Short, and lasted until the tenth century. The Renaissance was a recovery of classical language and biblical truth. The later Renaissance at the time of the sixteenth century with its most famous personage, Erasmus of Rotterdam, found its motto in the words *ad fontes*, that is, "to the sources." The motto declared the intent of the scholars of that day to return to the wellspring—"to the sources" of ancient philosophy, culture, and especially the biblical languages. So a renewed study of the Greek philosophers, Plato and Aristotle, coupled with a zeal for the recovery of the biblical languages, spearheaded both the later Renaissance as well as the Carolingian Renaissance that came about under the leadership of Charlemagne.

Before the Carolingian Period, Augustine, in his passion for scholarship, was convinced that it was the duty of the Christian to learn as much as possible about as many things as possible. Since all truth is God's truth, all aspects of scientific inquiry are to be within the province of biblical and Christian learning. It was not by accident that the great discoveries of Western science were spearheaded by Christians who took seriously their responsibilities to exercise dominion over the earth in service to God. Rather than seeing learning, scholarship, and the pursuit of beauty as being ideas foreign to the Christian enterprise, the eighth-century revival, following the earlier lead of Augustine, saw a pursuit of God Himself in the pursuit of knowledge and of beauty. They saw that God is the source of all truth and of all beauty.

Throughout the centuries, Christian influences dominated the world of art as well as the world of scholarship. The legacy of this period has enriched the whole scope of Western history even to this day. It is imperative that we in the twenty-first century learn from the pioneers of the past who did not despise classical scholarship, but saw it as something to be harnessed in the service of the kingdom of God.

FAITH & REASON

AUGUST 2008

———

I N THIS POSTMODERN CULTURE WE HAVE WITNESSED a fascinating revival of ancient Gnosticism. The Gnostics of antiquity were called by that name because they asserted that they had a superior type of knowledge that surpassed the insights found even in the Apostles of the New Testament. They maintained that the insights of the Apostles were limited by the natural limitations suffered by human beings tied to rationality. True knowledge, according to these heretics, was found not through reason or sense perception, but through a highly developed mystical intuition. In like manner, in this postmodern world we've seen a wide spread rejection of rationality. This rejection of rationality has infiltrated the church with a vengeance. We see frequent attempts to remove the Christian faith from all considerations of rationality. It is being argued today that biblical revelation is only intelligible by intuition or by a particularly sensitive poetic imagination. This carries with it the idea that biblical revelation is unintelligible through reason.

For good cause, the church in recent centuries has had to reject rationalism in its many faceted forms. There is no monolithic philosophy of rationalism; rather, rationalism wears various faces. On the one hand, we think of rationalism as distinct from empiricism with respect to how we come to know what we know. Second, Enlightenment rationalism contrasts reason not with sense perception but with revelation, arguing that revelation is unreasonable and the only truth that can be known is that which can be known by natural reason. The third and most complex form of rationalism is Hegelian rationalism, which defines reason with a capital R, and reality is the unfolding in space and time of ultimate reason. None of these philosophies represents historic Christianity. Christianity is not based on rationalism. However, the rejection of rationalism in the modern church often carries with it the rejection of rationality. This rejection is itself irrational. When we reject humanism, we don't reject being human. If we reject existentialism, we don't reject existence. So, if we reject an "ism" attached to reason, it does not mean that we are to reject reason itself.

Any discussion of faith and reason has to ask the question, "What is faith?" The biblical answer, according to the author of Hebrews, is that faith is the substance of things hoped for, the evidence of things not seen (11:1). The author goes on to say that by faith we understand that the world was formed by the Word of God. The first thing we notice in this assertion is that faith is something that is substantial, not ephemeral. Secondly, faith represents a type of evidence. It is the evidence of the unseen. At the heart of the concept of New Testament faith is the idea of trust, namely, that faith involves placing one's trust in something. In this regard all human creatures are subject to depending at one point or another on faith. I am not an expert in medicine, so I must give a certain trust to the diagnoses offered to me by experts in the field. That trust may be provisional until I find that it is not based in substance or evidence. But in the meantime, to trust what we do not see is not necessarily a matter of being irrational. Without reason, the content of biblical faith would be unintelligible and meaningless. So we say that biblical faith is not the same as reason, but that faith is rational and reasonable. The first assertion that faith is rational means that faith is intelligible. It is not absurd or illogical. If biblical revelation were absurd and irrational, it would be utterly unintelligible and meaningless. The content of the Bible cannot pierce the soul of a sentient creature without first going through the mind. It was Augustine who declared that faith without evidence is credulity. At this point we understand that though faith is rational, it is also reasonable. Biblical faith does not call people to crucify their intellect or take irrational leaps of faith into the darkness with the hope that Christ will catch us. Rather we are called to leap out of the darkness and into the light.

When the Scriptures say that faith is the evidence of things not seen, what are we to understand that to mean? The example given is that by faith we understand the world was formed by the Word of God. None of us was an eyewitness of the action of God in creation. Yet we trust that the universe has come into being by the act of God's divine work of creation because we have come on reasonable grounds to believe that God's Word is trustworthy. Because we are convinced that God's Word is trustworthy and that that conviction is a reasonable conviction, we can trust God's Word even for those things that we cannot see. John Calvin also argued the point that true faith is not believing against evidence. Rather, true faith involves trusting in the evidence that God has amply provided in and through His Word. That faith is not without what Calvin called evidences; rather, it is a faith that surrenders to or acquiesces to the evidences.

We must be on our guard and vigilant at every moment against the intrusion of irrationality coming from existential philosophy, neo-orthodox theology, and the resurgence of mysticism set forth in neo-Gnosticism. What is at stake is the coherence and intelligibility of God's divine work.

STATISM

SEPTEMBER 2008

———

"**A** DECREE WENT OUT FROM CAESAR AUGUSTUS that all the world should be registered...." In Luke 2, the well-known passage introducing the nativity story, the title accorded to the Roman emperor is Caesar Augustus. Had this census been mandated earlier under the monarchy of Julius Caesar, the Scripture would read: "A decree went out from Julius Caesar..." Had Octavian followed the model of Julius, he would have called himself Octavianus Caesar, and then the text would read: "A decree went out from Octavianus Caesar..." But we note Octavius' explicit change of his personal name to the title *Caesar Augustus*. This indicates the emerging dimension of the emperor cult in Rome, by which those who were elevated to the role of emperor were worshiped as deities. To be called "august" would mean to be clothed with supreme dignity, to which is owed the reverence given to the sacred. The elevation of the emperor in Rome to this kind of status was the ancient zenith of statism.

About thirty years ago, I shared a taxi cab in St. Louis with Francis Schaeffer. I had known Dr. Schaeffer for many years, and he had been instrumental in helping us begin our ministry in Ligonier, Pennsylvania, in 1971. Since our time together in St. Louis was during the twilight of Schaeffer's career, I posed this question to him: "Dr. Schaeffer, what is your biggest concern for the future of the church in America?" Without hesitation, Dr. Schaeffer turned to me and spoke one word: "Statism." Schaeffer's biggest concern at that point in his life was that the citizens of the United States were beginning to invest their country with supreme authority, such that the free nation of America would become one that would be dominated by a philosophy of the supremacy of the state.

In statism, we see the suffix "ism," which indicates a philosophy or worldview. A decline from statehood to statism happens when the government is perceived as or claims to be the ultimate reality. This reality then replaces God as the supreme entity upon which human existence depends.

In the nineteenth century, Hegel argued in his extensive and complex study of Western history that progress represents the unfolding in time and space of the absolute Idea (Hegel's vague understanding of God), which would reach its apex in the creation of the Prussian state. The assumption that Hegel made in the nineteenth century was made before the advent of Hitler's Third Reich, Stalin's Russia, and Chairman Mao's communist China. These nations reached an elevation of statism never dreamed of by Hegel in his concept of the Prussian state.

In America, we have a long history of valuing the concept of the separation of church and state. This idea historically referred to a division of labors between the church and the civil magistrate. However, initially both the church and the state were seen as entities ordained by God and subject to His governance. In that sense, the state was considered to be an entity that was "under God." What has happened in the past few decades is the obfuscation of this original distinction between church and state, so that today the language we hear of separation of church and state, when carefully exegeted, communicates the idea of the separation of the state from God. In this sense, it's not merely that the state declares independence from the church, it also declares independence from God and presumes itself to rule with autonomy.

The whole idea of a nation under God has been challenged again and again, and we have seen the exponential growth of government in our land, particularly the federal government, so that the government now virtually engulfs all of life. Where education once was under the direction of local authorities, it now is controlled and directed by federal legislation. The economy that once was driven by the natural forces of the market has now come under the strict control of the federal government, which not only regulates the economy, but considers itself responsible for controlling it. Where we have seen the largest measure of the loss of liberty is with respect to the function of the church. Though the church is still somewhat tolerated in America (in a way it was not tolerated in Mao's

Red China and under Stalin), it is tolerated only when it remains outside of the public square. In other words, the church has been relegated to a status not unlike that given to the native Americans, where the tribes were allowed to continue to exist as long as they functioned safely on a reservation, outside of any significant influence on the government. So although the church has not been banished completely by the statism that has emerged in America, it has been effectively banished from the public square.

Throughout the history of the Christian church, Christianity has always stood over against all forms of statism. Statism is the natural and ultimate enemy to Christianity because it involves a usurpation of the reign of God. If Francis Schaeffer was right—and each year that passes makes his prognosis seem all the more accurate—it means that the church and the nation face a serious crisis in our day. In the final analysis, if statism prevails in America, it will mean not only the death of our religious freedom, but also the death of the state itself. We face perilous times where Christians and all people need to be vigilant about the rapidly encroaching elevation of the state to supremacy.

TOTA SCRIPTURA

OCTOBER 2008

———

I N CENTURIES PAST, THE CHURCH was faced with the important task of recognizing which books belong in the Bible. The Bible itself is not a single book but a collection of many individual books. What the church sought to establish was what we call the canon of sacred Scripture. The word *canon* comes from a Greek word that means "standard or measuring rod." So the canon of sacred Scripture delineates the standard that the church used in receiving the Word of God. As is often the case, it is the work of heretics that forces the church to define her doctrines with greater and greater precision.

We saw the Nicene Creed as a response to the heresy of Arius in the fourth century, and we saw the Council of Chalcedon as a response to the fifth-century heresies of Eutyches and Nestorius, with respect to the church's understanding of the person of Christ. In like manner, the first list of canonical books of the New Testament that we have was produced by a heretic named Marcion.

Marcion's New Testament was an expurgated version of the original biblical documents. Marcion was convinced that the God of the Old Testament was at best a demiurge (a creator god who is the originator of evil) who in many respects is defective in being and character. Thus, any reference to that god in the New Testament in a positive relationship to Jesus had to be edited out. And so we receive from Marcion a bare-bones profile of Jesus and His teaching, divorced from the Old Testament. Over against this heresy, the church had to define the full measure of the Apostolic writings, which they did in establishing the New Testament and Old Testament canon.

Another crisis emerged much later in the sixteenth century, in the midst of the Protestant Reformation. Though the central debate, what historians call the material cause of the Reformation, focused on the doctrine of justification, the underlying dispute was the secondary issue of authority. In Luther's defense of *sola fide* or faith alone, he was reminded by the Roman Catholic Church that she had already made judgments in her papal encyclicals and in her historical documents in ways that ran counter to Luther's theses. And in the middle of that controversy, Luther affirmed the Protestant principle of *sola Scriptura*, namely that the conscience is bound by sacred Scripture alone, that is, the Bible is the only source of divine, special revelation that we have. In response, the Roman Catholic Church at the fourth session of the Council of Trent declared that God's special revelation is contained both in sacred Scripture and in the tradition of the church. This position, called a dual-source view of revelation, was reaffirmed by subsequent papal encyclicals. And so we see the dispute between Scripture alone versus Scripture plus tradition. In that controversy, the issue had to do with something that was an addition to the Bible, namely, the church's tradition.

Since that time, the opposite problem has emerged, and that is not so much the question of what is added to Scripture, but rather what has been subtracted from it. We face now an issue not of Scripture addition but of Scripture reduction. The issue that we face in our day is not merely the question of *sola Scriptura* but also the question of *tota Scriptura*, which has to do with embracing the whole counsel of God as it is revealed in the entirety of sacred Scripture. There have been many attempts in the last century to seek a canon within the canon. That is to say, restricted portions of Scripture are deemed as God's revelation, not the whole of Scripture. In this case, we have seen movements that have been described by historians as neo-Marcionite. That is, the activity of canon reduction sought by the heretic Marcion in the early church has now been replicated in our day.

Perhaps most famous for this in the twentieth century was the German theologian Rudolf Bultmann, who made a significant distinction between what he called kerygma and myth. He taught that the Scriptures contained truths of historical value and of theological value that were salvific in their content, but that those truths were hidden and contained within a husk of mythology. For the Bible to be relevant to modern man, it must be demythologized. The husks must be broken in order that the kernel of truth buried under the mythological husk can be brought to the surface.

Beyond the radical reductionism of Bultmann, we have seen more recently attempts among professing evangelicals, and even within the Reformed community, to seek a different type of reduction of Scripture. We have seen views of so-called "limited inspiration" or "limited inerrancy." That is to say, the Spirit's inspiration of the Bible is not holistic, but rather is limited to matters of faith and doctrine. In this scenario, proponents suggest we can distinguish between doctrinal matters that are of divine origin and what the Bible teaches in matters of science and history, and, in some cases, ethics. Therefore, there are portions within the Bible that are not equally inspired by God. In this case, we see the reappearance of a canon within a canon. The problem that arises is a serious one. Perhaps most severe is the question, who is it who decides what part of the Bible really belongs to the canon? Once we remove ourselves from a view of *tota Scriptura*, we are free then to pick and choose what portions of Scripture are normative for Christian faith and life, just like picking cherries from a tree.

To do this we would have to revisit the teaching of Jesus, wherein He said that man does not live by bread alone but by every word that proceeds from the mouth of God. We would have to change it, to have our Lord say that we do not live by bread alone but by only some of the words that come to us from God. In this case, the Bible is reduced to the status where the whole is less than the sum of its parts. This is an issue that the church has to face in every generation, and it has reappeared today in some of the most surprising places. We're finding, in seminaries that call themselves Reformed, professors advocating this type of canon within the canon. The church must say an emphatic "no" to these departures from orthodox Christianity, and she must reaffirm her faith not only in *sola Scriptura*, but in *tota Scriptura* as well.

ECCLESIASTICAL MYOPIA

NOVEMBER 2008

———

ec·cle·si·as·ti·cal

\i-klē-zē-as-ti-kəl\ adj (15c) 1: of or relating to a church esp. as an established institution ...

my·o·pia

\mī-ō-pē-ə\ n (ca. 1752) ... 2: a lack of foresight or discernment: a narrow view of something

PERHAPS THE MOST REMARKABLE STATEMENT I ever heard a man utter from the pulpit was: "He has a penurious epistemology, which tends to be myopic." I was seated in the balcony of the church when that statement was made, and I could not restrain myself from laughing aloud. I nudged my wife Vesta and said, "I just might be the only person in the church who understood what that man said." What is a penurious epistemology? A penurious epistemology is a theory of knowledge that is poverty-stricken or on the verge of bankruptcy. Such a view of knowledge, if it tends towards myopia, is simply suffering a bad case of near-sightedness. I'm afraid that the American church suffers from a similar sort of myopia.

Our vision tends to extend only to the borders of our own nation or at best across the Atlantic to western Europe. We tend to think that Christianity is fundamentally a Western religion. Such a view is penurious, indeed. The Bible, through the lips of Jesus, calls the church to extend the reach of the gospel to the corners of the earth—to every tribe, to every tongue, and to every nation. The whole world is the mission of the

Christian faith. The strength of Christianity does not stand or fall with the strengths of the church in America or western Europe.

If in our ecclesiastical myopia we restricted our vision to the United States and Europe, it would be easy for us to become profoundly discouraged, particularly regarding Europe. The historians are saying that western Europe has now entered a post-Christian era where only a tiny fraction of the populace attends church regularly. The beautiful churches that dot the scene on the continent have become museums in many cases.

Though there still exists a vibrant Christianity in the United States, we have also seen serious decline in the substance of our faith and commitment. The discouragement that ensues from an evaluation of what's happening in America and in Europe is unwarranted, however, when we evaluate the church from a global perspective.

Though the Christian faith may be on the wane in certain sections of the West, there is a burgeoning vitality found in Korea, in Africa, in Latin America, and even now in China. The excitement of the discovery of the Reformed tradition in the Ukraine, for example, is contagious throughout the eastern part of Europe and into Russia. Sociologists and historians have predicted that by the year 2050 the strongest center for Christianity will be in Africa and Latin America.

The good news is that the inroads of the faith in these areas of the globe have been profound. The bad news is that there has been a lack of substantive doctrine feeding the people of these lands—as is often the case with fresh revivals and awakenings to Christianity. So often a syncretism exists in which superstitious elements of animistic religion are mingled and blended with the Christian faith. However, as these churches mature, we can anticipate an increase of sound theology with a diminution of elements of pagan syncretism.

One of the strongest churches in the world is the church in Korea, which has enjoyed explosive growth over the last forty years. The contagion of that Asian form of Christianity is penetrating all parts of the world. It is not an unusual thing to now see missionaries being sent from the Third World countries into Europe and even into the United States, as the ebb and flow of Christian fervor moves from one geographical spot to another. Many times I have heard people lament the spiritual aridity of America's New England. The irony is that no part of our nation has ever had a more powerful visitation of the Holy Spirit than New England enjoyed in the Great Awakening during the middle of the eighteenth century. That Great Awakening, however, gave way to unitarianism and secularism. One wonders that if God pours out a profound blessing on a particular geographical region and that blessing is neglected or repudiated, does a kind of *ichabod* ensue in which God removes His lampstand from their midst, along with His glory (1 Sam. 4:20–22; Rev. 2:5)? We should take heed in this country that the profound spiritual benefits and blessings that we have enjoyed in our brief history may be removed and passed to other nations that are more receptive to the truths of God.

Here in the West, we have become immunized or inoculated against the deep things of God, living our Christian lives on a superficial plain of churchiness and religiosity. This type of Christianity will not do. It would be no surprise to me if we, in a very short time, will be looking to Africa, to eastern Europe, to Asia, and to Latin America to discover the real power of the Christian gospel.

THE MYSTERY OF INIQUITY

DECEMBER 2008

———

IT HAS BEEN CALLED THE Achilles' heel of the Christian faith. Of course, I'm referring to the classical problem of the existence of evil. Philosophers such as John Stuart Mill have argued that the existence of evil demonstrates that God is either not omnipotent or not good and loving—the reasoning being that if evil exists apart from the sovereign power of God, then by resistless logic, God cannot be deemed omnipotent. On the other hand, if God does have the power to prevent evil but fails to do it, then this would reflect upon His character, indicating that He is neither good nor loving. Because of the persistence of this problem, the church has seen countless attempts at what is called theodicy. The term *theodicy* involves the combining of two Greek words: the word for God, *theos*, and the word for justification, *dikaios*. Hence, a theodicy is an attempt to justify God for the existence of evil (as seen, for instance, in John Milton's *Paradise Lost*). Such theodicies have covered the gauntlet between a simple explanation that evil comes as a direct result of human free will or to more complex philosophical attempts such as that offered by the philosopher Leibniz. In his theodicy, which was satirized by Voltaire's *Candide*, Leibniz distinguished among three types of evil: natural evil, metaphysical evil, and moral evil. In this three-fold schema, Leibniz argued that moral evil is an inevitable and necessary consequence of finitude, which is a metaphysical lack of complete being. Because every creature falls short of infinite being, that shortfall must necessarily yield defects such as we see in moral evil. The problem with this theodicy is that it fails to take into account the biblical ideal of evil. If evil is a metaphysical necessity for creatures, then obviously Adam and Eve had to have been evil before the fall and would have to continue to be evil even after glorification in heaven.

To this date, I have yet to find a satisfying explanation for what theologians call the mystery of iniquity. Please don't send me letters giving your explanations, usually focusing on some dimension of human free will. I'm afraid that many people fail to feel the serious weight of this burden of explanation. The simple presence of free will is not enough to explain the origin of evil, in as much as we still must ask how a good being would be inclined freely to choose evil. The inclination for the will to act in an immoral manner is already a signal of sin.

One of the most important approaches to the problem of evil is that set forth originally by Augustine and then later by Thomas Aquinas, in which they argued that evil has no independent being. Evil cannot be defined as a thing or as a substance or as some kind of being. Rather evil is always defined as an action, an action that fails to meet a standard of goodness. In this regard, evil has been defined in terms of its being either a negation (*negatio*) of the good, or a privation (*privatio*) of the good. In both cases, the very definition of evil depends upon a prior understanding of the good. In this regard, as Augustine argued, evil is parasitic—that is, it depends upon the good for its very definition. We think of sin as something that is being unrighteous, involving disobedience, immorality, and the like. All of these definitions depend upon the positive substance of the good for their very definition. Augustine argues that though Christians face the difficulty of explaining the presence of evil in the universe, the pagan has a problem that is twice as difficult. Before one can even have a problem of evil, one must first have an antecedent existence of the good. Those who complain about the problem of evil, must now also have the problem of defining the existence of the good. Without God there is no ultimate standard for the good.

In contemporary days, this problem has been resolved by simply denying both evil and good. Such a problem, however, faces enormous difficulties, particularly when one suffers at the hands of someone who inflicts evil upon them. It is easy for us to deny the existence of evil, until we ourselves are victims of someone's wicked action.

However, though we end our quest to answer the origin of evil, one thing is certain, since God is both omnipotent and good, we must conclude that in His omnipotence and in His goodness, there must be a place for the existence of evil. We know that God Himself never does that which is evil. Nevertheless, He also ordains whatsoever comes to pass. Though He does not do evil, and does not create evil, He does ordain that evil exists. If it does exist, and if God is sovereign, then obviously He must have been able to prevent its existence. If He allowed evil to enter into this universe, it could only be by His sovereign decision. Since His sovereign decisions always follow the perfection of His being, we must conclude that His decision to allow evil to exist is a good decision.

Again, we must be careful here. We must never say that evil is good, or that good is evil. But that is not the same thing as saying, "It is good that there is evil." Again, I repeat, it is good that there is evil, else evil could not exist. Even this theodicy does not explain the "how" of the entrance of evil into the world. It only reflects upon the "why" of the reality of evil. One thing we know for sure, that evil does exist. It exists if nowhere else in us and in our behavior. We know that the force of evil is extraordinary and brings great pain and suffering into the world. We also know that God is sovereign over it and in His sovereignty will not allow evil to have the last word. Evil always and ever serves the ultimate best interest of God Himself. It is God in His goodness and in His sovereignty that has ordained the final conquest over evil and its riddance from His universe. In this redemption we find our rest and our joy—and until that time, we live in a fallen world.

PRINCIPLE VS. PRAGMATISM

JANUARY 2009

———

S OME YEARS AGO, I DROVE along the Pennsylvania Turnpike about two o'clock in the morning with a friend after having spent all day at a steel corporation in eastern Pennsylvania dealing with labor management issues. My companion was a man who had lost his job as a highly paid executive in the industry for being too concerned about the welfare and dignity of the laborers in his plant. As we were making this drive in the wee hours of the morning, I noticed my friend was at the point of exhaustion, and so I asked him the question: "Why are you doing this?" He looked over at me as if to indicate that my question was a foolish one, and he replied simply: "Because it's the right thing to do."

In stark contrast to that, in this past year I have witnessed the worst type of corruption within the church that I have seen in my lifetime. I was chairing the board of a Christian institution of learning as we dealt with a question of the propriety of the teaching of one of the professors. The task of the board was to guard the purity of the doctrine of the institution. The motion was made to suspend the professor for a brief period of time in order to give him an opportunity to amend his views. As chairman, I did not vote, but the motion carried by a vote of eight to two.

During the discussion, one of the men who voted against the resolution asked this question: "Can't we deal with this question in a more pragmatic way?" Another board member responded by saying, "No, it is our responsibility to act not according to pragmatism but according to principle." The motion to suspend was passed by a margin of eight-to-two. The pragmatist who was outvoted, instead of submitting to the vote or bringing in a minority report, went around the board and did everything in his power to have the board's decision overthrown. Accomplishing this, his next move was to see to it that board members with whom he disagreed were ousted from the board. Through Machiavellian machinations of corruption, this pragmatist was able to succeed. In his wake, he left the demolition of a strategically important institution of Christian learning.

What is pragmatism? Pragmatism is the only philosophy native to America. Pragmatism eschews any hope of discovering ultimate truth. It is skeptical with respect to objective principles of righteousness and defines truth as "that which works." In this philosophy, the end always justifies the means. The driving force behind decisions within the scope of pragmatism is the force of expediency.

We remember in the days of the trial of Jesus of Nazareth, two of the important players were Caiaphas and Pontius Pilate. Both men made their decisions to have Jesus executed on the basis of expediency (Mark 15:15; John 11:45–53). Caiaphas and Pontius Pilate were pragmatists with a vengeance.

Several years ago, I had the opportunity to have lunch with a ranking senator of the United States Congress. During our discussion, I raised an ethical issue that the Senate faced at that time and asked him why the Senate didn't act on that particular issue. He replied that he agreed with me that the Senate certainly should act on it, but he added that they could not do it that year because it was an election year. I moved to my second question and asked about another issue that needed the Senate's attention. Again he agreed that it should be addressed, but not that particular year because it was an election year.

After we got to the sixth or seventh question where the mantra was repeated again ("not this year because it's an election year"), I looked at the senator and asked, "Is there anybody up here on Capitol Hill who thinks about the next generation instead of the next election?" I guess it was too idealistic of me to think that our nation's leaders would be a bit more concerned for the welfare of the nation than for their own political war chest. No nation (or Christian institution, for that matter) can survive when its leaders are driven by a spirit of pragmatism or make their decisions according to political expediency.

Expediency is an obscene word. It is the word that is ever and always at war with principle. A person who is a Christian is called of God to live by biblical principles. The principles that the Bible reveals to guide our steps are the necessary elements for authentic righteousness. Take away principle, and righteousness is slain in the streets. We need an awakening in the culture and in the church to principle—to working according to truth and to living according to biblical revelation. Without principle, the church as well as the culture will decay, and the church will become a mere echo of the unprincipled pragmatism of secularism.

THE WITNESS OF MATTHEW

FEBRUARY 2009

———

I
N THE HISTORY OF BIBLICAL STUDIES, we have seen in the last two centuries the rise of so-called "higher criticism." So much of higher criticism is fueled by skepticism with respect to the reliability of the biblical texts. Since orthodox Christians stand opposed to many of the arguments of higher critics, they sometimes overlook valuable insights that can be gained through critical analysis of the text. Some of these analyses can be very helpful to our endeavor of seeking an accurate understanding of the Bible.

One element of critical scholarship that can do this is that dimension known as source criticism. As the title suggests, this type of criticism attempts to reconstruct the way in which the Synoptic Gospels (Matthew, Mark, and Luke) came to be written.

The general assumption among source critics is that Mark was the first written gospel. This is seen by an analysis of Matthew and Luke—both Matthew and Luke have material in their gospels that is common to the gospel of Mark. At the same time, there is common material found in Luke and in Matthew that is not found in Mark. The scholars then try to account for this common information found in these two gospels that is absent from Mark's gospel. The working hypothesis is that Matthew and Luke, in addition to having Mark as a source for their information, had a second independent source that Mark did not use. This second independent source is called simply the "Q-source."

That letter *Q* is used since it is the first letter of the German word *Quelle*, which is simply the word for source. That is to say, the Q-source is a source that is unknown to us but known to the gospel writers Matthew and Luke. Much of this analysis is speculative and hypothetical. Scholars differ as to whether the alleged Q-source was a written source shared by Matthew and Luke, or simply an oral tradition they both had access to. Wherever we land in our conclusions about the method by which the gospel writers compiled their texts, the very analysis that we have seen gives us one clear benefit. By isolating material that is found in Matthew and only in Matthew, or isolating material that is found in Luke and only in Luke, or isolating material found in Mark and only in Mark, we get clues as to the audience to which the author was directing his information and also his major themes in the particular gospel.

For example, in looking at the gospel of Matthew, we find more citations and allusions to Old Testament Scriptures than in any of the other gospels. This fact alone lends credence to the idea that Matthew was directing his gospel primarily to a Jewish audience to show how Jesus, the long-awaited Messiah, fulfilled Old Testament prophecy.

We also see in Matthew's gospel a strong condemnation of the Jewish clergy of that period of history who were responsible for seeing to the destruction of Jesus. The scribes and the Pharisees are particularly singled out, as Matthew records for us the judgment of woes spoken against the scribes and the Pharisees for their hypocrisy. On a somewhat related matter, we also find in Matthew more information concerning Jesus' teaching on hell than we find anywhere else in the four gospels.

If we were to look, however, for one single theme that seems to be the most central and most important theme of the entire gospel of Matthew, it would be the theme of the coming of the kingdom. We see in the first instance that the term *gospel* refers to the gospel of the kingdom—the good news of the announcement of the breakthrough of the kingdom of God. In Matthew's case, he uses the phrase "kingdom of heaven" rather than the terminology "kingdom of God." He does this not because he has a different view of the meaning or content of the kingdom of God; rather, out of sensitivity to his Jewish readers, he makes common use of what is called *periphrasis*, a certain type of circumlocution to avoid mentioning the sacred name of God. So for Matthew, the doctrine of the kingdom of heaven is the same kingdom that the other writers speak of as the kingdom of God.

Matthew talks about the break-through of the kingdom and the arrival of Jesus in His incarnation. He announces the coming of the kingdom at the beginning of Jesus' public ministry, and at the end of the book Matthew speaks about the final consummation of the coming of that kingdom in the Olivet Discourse. So from the first page of Matthew to the last page, we see the unifying theme of the coming of the kingdom of God in the appearance of the king Himself, who is the Messiah of Israel and the fulfillment of the kingdom given to Judah.

The gospel of Matthew is rich in detailed information about the teaching of Jesus and particularly in His parables, which are not always included in the other gospels. Again, the central focus of the parables of Jesus is the kingdom, where He introduces parables by saying, "The kingdom of heaven is like unto this . . ." or "the kingdom of heaven is like unto that . . ." If we are to understand the significance of the appearance of Jesus in the fullness of time to inaugurate the kingdom and the whole meaning of redemptive history, we see that focus come into clear view in the Gospel according to Saint Matthew.

THE DIVINE FOUNDATION OF AUTHORITY

MARCH 2009

———

"You're out!" "I'm safe!" "Out!" "Safe!" "Out!" "It's my ball, and it's my bat, and I say that I'm safe." This is how we settled disputes over plays in our pickup baseball games played without the benefit of a referee or umpire. When a disputed play could not be resolved through reason or through yelling, the one who possessed the equipment usually determined the outcome. It was a child's game in which might made right. It was the nascent expression of the cynical statement: "He who owns the gold, rules."

These illustrations indicate that at some level ownership is involved in authority. The very word *authority* has within it the word *author*. An author is someone who creates and possesses a particular work. Insofar as God is the foundation of all authority, He exercises that foundation because He is the author and the owner of His creation. He is the foundation upon which all other authority stands or falls.

We use the term *foundation* with respect to the imagery of a building. Houses and commercial buildings are erected upon a foundation. As Jesus indicated in His parables, if the foundation is not solid, the structure will not stand. The house that is built upon the sand will crumble at the first sign of a windstorm. Instead, Jesus commended the building of the house upon a rock. The foundation has to be firm in order for the house to stand.

In the sixteenth century, the critical dispute that arose in the Protestant Reformation focused on two central issues. Historians speak of one as being the material cause, that is, the matter around which the dispute centered. That material cause was the doctrine of justification. The battle was fought over the issue of what is required for a person to be justified in the sight of God. The other issue, the formal one, lurked only slightly under the surface of the external debate about justification: the question of authority. When Luther defended his doctrine in his disputes with Cardinal Cajetan and with the theologian Johann Eck, the Roman Catholic experts called attention to the decrees of earlier church councils and of papal encyclicals to refute Luther's arguments. Luther in response argued that the edicts of church councils and even the encyclicals of popes can err and often do err. The only final authority Luther would recognize, upon which the controversy could be resolved, was the authority of Scripture, because that authority carried the weight of God's authority itself.

As a result, the Diet of Worms culminated with Luther's expression: "Unless I am convinced by sacred Scripture or by evident reason, I cannot recant because my conscience is held captive by the Word of God, and to act against conscience is neither right nor safe. Here I stand. God help me. I can do no other." In that statement, Luther was affirming publicly his commitment to the principle of *sola Scriptura*, that the Bible alone is the only authority that can bind the conscience of a person absolutely because it is the only authority that carries with it the intrinsic authority of God Himself.

In the Scriptures we see that God creates the universe and owns the universe. It is His possession, and He governs it by His own authority. The authority by which God governs all things is His autonomous authority. To say that God's authority is autonomous is to say that God is a law unto Himself. He is not bound by some abstract system of law that exists outside of Himself or independent from Him (*ex lex*). Nor is God under some external law (*sub lego*); rather, He is a law unto Himself. This does not mean that He acts or behaves in an arbitrary manner. Rather, God's activity is directed by God's own character. And His character is completely righteous. All that He does flows out of His own internal righteousness. His external authority comes from His internal righteousness. In this sense God's authority is intrinsic. It is found within Himself. It is not borrowed, delegated, or assigned from any other source.

In the same manner, all lesser authorities on heaven and on earth are only as valid as they are delegated by God's authority. Whatever authority we possess is extrinsic rather than intrinsic. It exists only by delegation. This was the issue in the garden of Eden. The primal sin of Adam and Eve could be described as the grasping for autonomy. They sought to take for themselves the authority that belonged only to God. To act on one's own authority against the authority of God is the essence of disobedience and of sin. When we grasp authority ourselves and do what is right in our own minds, we are attacking the very foundation of life and of the welfare of human beings.

"You're out!" "I'm safe!" This question has to be determined by some foundation other than the possession of bats and balls. Justice must reign if we are to escape a life and a world without foundations. Any authority that rules without divine foundation is tyranny.

THE WORD OF GOD IN THE HANDS OF MAN

APRIL 2009

———

IT WAS MANY YEARS AGO when my grandmother related to me games that she played as a little girl in the 1880s. One game she mentioned was one that she and her Methodist girlfriends played with their Roman Catholic friends. In a playful jest of the words of the Mass, my grandmother would say, "Tommy and Johnny went down to the river to play dominoes." Here the word *dominoes* was a play on the use of the term *Domine* that occurred so frequently in the Catholic rite of the Mass. The children, of course, were revealing their lack of knowledge of the words of the Mass because they were spoken in Latin.

In a similar vein, those who are interested in the arts of prestidigitation know that all magicians, as they ply their trade, use certain sayings to make their magic come to pass. They will recite certain incantations, such as "abracadabra," "presto chango," and perhaps most famous of all, "hocus pocus." Even today we use "hocus pocus" to describe a type of magical art. It is an incantation used for the magician to perform his magic. But from where does the phrase "hocus pocus" come?

The origin of it is once again borrowed from people's misunderstanding of the language used in the Roman Catholic Mass. In the words of institution uttered in Latin in the ancient formula, the statement was recited as follows: "*hoc est corpus meum.*" This phrase is the Latin translation of Jesus' words at the Last Supper: "This is my body." But in the Mass to the unskilled ear, the supposed miracle of the transformation of the elements of bread and wine into the body and blood of Christ were heard under the rubric of language that sounded like "hocus pocus." These kinds of derivations are a direct result of people's being involved in some kind of drama where the words that are spoken remain unknown to them.

In the Middle Ages, the church was committed to performing the Mass in the ancient tongue of Latin. That tongue was understood by educated people, and particularly by the clergy, but it was not intelligible to the laity. As early as the ninth century, questions were raised about the propriety of keeping the words of God obscured from the layperson by being restricted to Latin. The Bible itself was literally chained to the lecterns of the churches, so that it could not fall into the hands of people who were unskilled in the languages. It was not given to the common person to interpret the Bible for himself or to have it read in the common language of the people. It took centuries for the church to get over this struggle, and it provoked issues of heresy and of persecution. Prior to the sixteenth-century Reformation, among English-speaking people, the work of Tyndale and Wycliffe was brought under the censure of the church because these men dared to translate the Bible into a language other than Latin.

In 1521, the Imperial Diet of Worms ended dramatically when Luther, in the presence of the Holy Roman Emperor, refused to recant of his writing and stated to the assembly gathered: "Unless I'm convinced by sacred Scripture or by evident reason, I will not recant. For my conscience is held captive by the Word of God. Here I stand, I can do no other. God help me." With those dramatic words, the Diet exploded in shouts of protest, while Luther's friends faked a kidnapping, whisked him away from Worms and secreted him to the Wartburg Castle in Eisenach. There for a full year, Luther, disguised as a monk, worked on his project of translating the New Testament into the German language from the original Greek text. Some regard this work of setting forth the Bible in the vernacular as one of the most important contributions that Luther made to the life of the church.

But it was not received with equanimity everywhere. The great renaissance scholar, Erasmus of Rotterdam, whose motto was *ad fontes* ("to the sources"), who was known for his mastery of ancient languages, protested against Luther's presumption to interpret the Bible into the vernacular. Erasmus did have enough respect for Luther to see that Luther was a world-class philologist in his own right. But he chastened Luther for daring to go against the church in translating the Bible into German. He counseled Luther by saying that if the Bible were to be translated into the common tongue and given to the people for their own reading, it would "unloose a floodgate of iniquity."

Erasmus was convinced that giving the Bible into the hands of the people in their own language would give them a license to turn the Bible into a wax nose to be twisted and shaped and distorted into any inclination or private opinion that the individual could stretch from the Scriptures. Luther affirmed this, that if unskilled people are given the right to read the Scriptures for themselves in their own language, much mischief will occur from it, and people will use the Bible to try to justify the wildest of all possible heresies. On the other hand, Luther was convinced of the perspicuity of Scripture, namely, that its central message of salvation is so clear that even a child can understand it. Luther believed that the salvific words communicated in Scripture are so vitally important that it is worth setting the opportunity for salvation before the people even though some dire consequences might flow from such reading. He responded to Erasmus by saying, "If a floodgate of iniquity be opened, so be it."

In the wake of the translation of the Bible into the common language came the basic principle of private interpretation. That principle of private interpretation was soundly condemned by the Roman Catholic Church in the fourth session of the Council of Trent in the middle of the sixteenth century. But the die was cast, and since that time, the Bible has been translated into thousands of languages, and attempts are afoot to get the Bible translated into every language that can be found anywhere on the face of the earth. The prophetic concerns of Erasmus in many ways have come true with the vast proliferation of denominations, each calling themselves biblical. Yet at the same time, the gospel of salvation in Christ has been made known abroad throughout the world because the Bible has been given in the vernacular and made available to all people. To be sure, private interpretation does not give a license for private distortion. Anyone who presumes to interpret the Bible for himself must assume with that right the awesome responsibility of interpreting it correctly.

THE PERILS FACING THE EVANGELICAL CHURCH

MAY 2009

———

W HEN WE CONSIDER THE PREDICAMENT that the evangelical church of the twenty-first century faces in America, the first thing we need to understand is the very designation "evangelical church" is itself a redundancy. If a church is not evangelical, it is not an authentic church. The redundancy is similar to the language that we hear by which people are described as "born-again Christians." If a person is born again of the Spirit of God, that person is, to be sure, a Christian. If a person is not regenerated by the Holy Spirit, he may profess to be a Christian, but he is not an authentic Christian. There are many groups that claim to be churches that long ago repudiated the *evangel*, that is, the gospel. Without the gospel, a gathering of people, though they claim otherwise, cannot be an authentic church.

In the sixteenth century, the term *evangelical* came into prominence as a description of the Protestant church. In many cases, the terms *evangelical* and *Protestant* were used interchangeably. Today, that synonymous use of the adjectives no longer functions with any accuracy. Historic Protestants have forgotten what they were protesting in the sixteenth century. The central protest of the Reformation church was the protest against the eclipse of the gospel that had taken place in the medieval church.

When we turn our attention to the first century, to the churches about which we learn from the biblical record, we know that all of the churches addressed in the New Testament, including the churches in Ephesus, Corinth, Thessalonica, and the seven churches of Revelation, were evangelical churches. They all embraced the biblical gospel. Yet at the same time, these churches were different in their strengths, in their weaknesses, and in their compositions. An evangelical church is not necessarily a monolithic community. There may be unity among evangelical churches but not necessarily uniformity. The distinctions of the seven churches of Revelation are set forth clearly in that book. They manifest different greatnesses and frailties, but they all faced perils. Each confronted the dangers that assaulted the church in the first century. They faced hazards of varying proportions, but there was a common threat to the health of the New Testament church from many sides. Those dangers manifested in the first century are repeated in every age of the church. They certainly loom large at our time in the early years of the twenty-first century.

Among what I see as the three most critical perils the church faces today are, first of all, the loss of biblical truth. When the truth of the gospel is compromised or negotiated, the church ceases to be evangelical. We live in a time of crisis with respect to truth, where many churches see doctrine merely as something that divides. Therefore, they stress relationships over truth. That is a false distinction, as a commitment to truth is a commitment that should manifest itself in vital, living relationships. Relationships can never be a substitute for embracing the truth of God. So the either/or fallacy of doctrine or relationship cannot be maintained under careful biblical scrutiny.

A second widespread peril to the church today is the loss of any sense of discipline. When the church fails to discipline its members for gross and heinous sins, particularly sins of a public nature, that community becomes infected with the immorality of the secular culture. This occurs when the church so desperately wants to be accepted by the pagan culture that it adopts the very morality of the pagan community and imitates it, baptizing it with religious language.

The third crucial peril facing the church today is the loss of faithful worship. There are different styles of worship that can be pleasing to God. However, all worship that is pleasing to God is worship grounded in Spirit and in truth. We can have lively worship, manifesting great interest and excitement, with doctrine and truth eliminated. On the other hand, we can have what some call a dead orthodoxy, where the creedal truths of the historic Christian faith remain central to the worship of the church, but the worship itself does not flow from the heart and lacks spiritual vitality.

Another element that threatens the evangelical church is the ongoing erosion of evangelical faith by the impact of liberal theology. Liberal theology saw its heyday in the nineteenth century and raised its head again with the neo-liberalism that captured the mainline churches of the twentieth century. Yet it is by no means dead. Perhaps the place where liberalism is manifesting itself most dangerously is within the walls of churches that have historically been strongly evangelical. David F. Wells describes the crisis of the twenty-first century church as "vacuous worship." A vacuous worship is one that is empty of content. It is satisfied with platitudes, pop psychology, and entertainment. Such worship is devoid of the Word of God and of the authentic sacrifice of praise.

Dr. James Montgomery Boice, before his death, lamented his concern that the church was being enticed "to do the Lord's work in the world's way." We try to transfer principles of success drawn from Madison Avenue and from other secular institutions and imitate them in the life of the church. Such a process is deadly.

In every generation, including our own, the same perils to the spiritual strength that Jesus rebuked in the seven churches of Revelation threaten us anew. These include such things as a lack of love, a lack of truth, a compromising spirit with the world, a lukewarm devotion, and a double-minded conviction, to name but a few. There were rebukes and encouragements given to these churches by our Lord that every church in every age must take seriously, examining ourselves to make sure that we are not manifesting the same departures from biblical truths that these churches were. We must be vigilant and diligent if we are to maintain a godly witness in our day.

GRACE ALONE

JUNE 2009

———

S OLI *DEO GLORIA* IS THE MOTTO THAT grew out of the Protestant Reformation and was used on every composition by Johann Sebastian Bach. He affixed the initials *SDG* at the bottom of each manuscript to communicate the idea that it is God and God alone who is to receive the glory for the wonders of His work of creation and of redemption. At the heart of the sixteenth-century controversy over salvation was the issue of grace.

It was not a question of man's need for grace. It was a question as to the extent of that need. The church had already condemned Pelagius, who had taught that grace facilitates salvation but is not absolutely necessary for it. Semi-Pelagianism since that time has always taught that without grace there is no salvation. But the grace that is considered in all semi-Pelagian and Arminian theories of salvation is not an efficacious grace. It is a grace that makes salvation possible, but not a grace that makes salvation certain.

In the parable of the sower we see that regarding salvation, God is the one who takes the initiative to bring salvation to pass. He is the sower. The seed that is sown is His seed, corresponding to His Word, and the harvest that results is His harvest. He harvests what He purposed to harvest when He initiated the whole process. God doesn't leave the harvest up to the vagaries of thorns and stones in the pathway. It is God and God alone who makes certain that a portion of His Word falls upon good ground. A critical error in interpreting this parable would be to assume that the good ground is the good disposition of fallen sinners, those sinners who make the right choice, responding positively to God's prevenient grace. The classical Reformed understanding of the good ground is that if the ground is receptive to the seed that is sown by God, it is God alone who prepares the ground for the germination of the seed.

The biggest question any semi-Pelagian or Arminian has to face at the practical level is this: Why did I choose to believe the gospel and commit my life to Christ when my neighbor, who heard the same gospel, chose to reject it? That question has been answered in many ways. We might speculate that the reason why one person chooses to respond positively to the gospel and to Christ, while another one doesn't, is because the person who responded positively was more intelligent than the other one. If that were the case, then God would still be the ultimate provider of salvation because the intelligence is His gift, and it could be explained that God did not give the same intelligence to the neighbor who rejected the gospel. But that explanation is obviously absurd.

The other possibility that one must consider is this: that the reason one person responds positively to the gospel and his neighbor does not is because the one who responded was a better person. That is, that person who made the right choice and the good choice did it because he was more righteous than his neighbor. In this case, the flesh not only availed something, it availed everything. This is the view that is held by the majority of evangelical Christians, namely, the reason why they are saved and others are not is that they made the right response to God's grace while the others made the wrong response.

We can talk here about not only the correct response as opposed to an erroneous response, but we can speak in terms of a good response rather than a bad response. If I am in the kingdom of God because I made the good response rather than the bad response, I have something of which to boast, namely the goodness by which I responded to the grace of God. I have never met an Arminian who would answer the question that I've just posed by saying, "Oh, the reason I'm a believer is because I'm better than my neighbor." They would be loath to say that. However, though they reject this implication, the logic of semi-Pelagianism requires this conclusion. If indeed in the final analysis the reason I'm a Christian and someone else is not is that I made the proper response to God's offer of salvation while somebody else rejected it, then by resistless logic I have indeed made the good response, and my neighbor has made the bad response.

What Reformed theology teaches is that it is true the believer makes the right response and the non-believer makes the wrong response. But the reason the believer makes the good response is because God in His sovereign election changes the disposition of the heart of the elect to effect a good response. I can take no credit for the response that I made for Christ. God not only initiated my salvation, He not only sowed the seed, but He made sure that that seed germinated in my heart by regenerating me by the power of the Holy Ghost. That regeneration is a necessary condition for the seed to take root and to flourish. That's why at the heart of Reformed theology the axiom resounds, namely, that regeneration precedes faith. It's that formula, that order of salvation that all semi-Pelagians reject. They hold to the idea that in their fallen condition of spiritual death, they exercise faith, and then are born again. In their view, they respond to the gospel before the Spirit has changed the disposition of their soul to bring them to faith. When that happens, the glory of God is shared. No semi-Pelagian can ever say with authenticity: "To God alone be the glory." For the semi-Pelagian, God may be gracious, but in addition to God's grace, my work of response is absolutely essential. Here grace is not effectual, and such grace, in the final analysis, is not really saving grace. In fact, salvation is of the Lord from beginning to end. Yes, I must believe. Yes, I must respond. Yes, I must receive Christ. But for me to say "yes" to any of those things, my heart must first be changed by the sovereign, effectual power of God the Holy Spirit. *Soli Deo gloria.*

THE THEOLOGIAN

JULY 2009

———

T HINKERS IN THE ANCIENT WORLD sought to plumb the depths
of ultimate reality. With that quest for ultimate reality came the
birth of the discipline of philosophy. Some philosophers focused
on one particular aspect of philosophy called metaphysics (ultimate
being). Others focused their attention on epistemology (the science of
knowing). Still others stressed in their investigation the basic principles
and elements of ethics (the study of the good and the right). And others focused on the ultimate foundations for aesthetics (the study of the
beautiful). One philosopher stood out as being deeply involved in the
study of all of these matters as well as others. His name was Aristotle.
Because Aristotle's philosophical investigation was so comprehensive
that it encompassed all of the above concerns of philosophy, he earned
for himself the supreme epithet, namely, "the Philosopher." Among
students of philosophy, if passing mention is made of the title "the Philosopher," everybody understands that that title can be a reference to
only one person—Aristotle.

In a similar manner, the study of theology historically has brought
to the surface outstanding thinkers and scholars. Some are known for
their specific ability to create a synthesis between theology and secular
philosophy. Augustine, for example, was known for his ability to take
precepts from the philosophy of Plato and blend them with biblical theology. Much of Augustine's theology was therefore of a philosophical
kind. The same could be said to a certain degree of Thomas Aquinas,
who gave us a similar synthesis between Aristotelian philosophy and
Christian thought. Among the sixteenth-century magisterial Reformers,
we notice that Luther, being a brilliant student of language, brought to
the theological table an uncanny ability to provide vignettes of insight
into particular questions of truth. But Luther was not a systematician by

nature, and so he could not be the theologian of theologians. He never developed a full-orbed systematic theology for the instruction of the church. That task in the sixteenth century was left to the genius of the Genevan theologian John Calvin.

Calvin brought to the study of theology a passion for biblical truth and a coherent understanding of the Word of God. Of all of the thinkers of the sixteenth century, Calvin was most noted for his ability to provide a systematic theological understanding of Christian truth. His magnum opus, *Institutes of the Christian Religion*, remains to this day a titanic work in the field of systematic theology. Luther did not live long enough to recognize the full impact of Calvin's work, though he did see that Calvin would become a towering figure. It was left to one who knew Calvin and his work more extensively, namely, Philip Melanchthon, Luther's assistant and an impressive scholar in his own right, to give Calvin the sobriquet "the Theologian." Thus, if one mentions "the Philosopher," we understand that to mean a reference to Aristotle. On the other hand, if one mentions "the Theologian," the heirs of the Reformation think exclusively of John Calvin.

In our day there seems to be an ongoing battle between advocates of systematic theology and advocates of biblical theology. We are living in a time of unprecedented antipathy toward rationality and logic. Where systematic theology used to reign supreme in theological seminaries, it has all but vanished, exiled to the perimeter of academic studies. This antipathy toward rationality and logic finds its nadir in the modern allergy against systematic theology, with nothing to fill its place except the expansion of biblical theology. A possible tendency exists in biblical theology to interpret the Bible atomistically without a concern for coherency and unity. This dichotomy between biblical theology and systematic theology is a classic example of the fallacy of the false dilemma, sometimes called the either/or fallacy. If we look to John Calvin, we see a scholar whose mastery of the content of Scripture was unparalleled. Calvin had a passion for the Bible, as well as a monumental knowledge of the Bible, and yet he is known as a systematic theologian. He was not a systematic theologian in the sense that he took some extra-biblical philosophical system and forced it upon the Bible. For him, a system was not a preconceived Procrustean bed to which the Bible was forced to conform. On the contrary, Calvin's system of doctrine was the result of his attempt to find the coherent substance of the Bible itself. That is, Calvin worked out the system that is within Scripture, not a system that is imposed upon Scripture. Calvin was convinced that the Word of God is coherent and that God does not speak in contradictions or in illogical statements. It has been said a multitude of times that consistency is the hobgoblin of small minds. If that is in fact true, then one would have to come to the conclusion that the smallest mind in the universe is the mind of God, because God in His thinking is altogether consistent and altogether coherent. It is in that appreciation of the nature of God that Calvin sought passionately to set forth the unity of the Word of God. In that regard, he has done a masterful service to the history of Christian thought. Some people see Calvinism, bearing the name of John Calvin, as an odious distortion of the Word of God. Those who appreciate Calvin's commitment to biblical truth see Calvinism as "a nickname for biblical Christianity," as Spurgeon said.

Calvin in debate could draw on his encyclopedic knowledge of biblical passages, as well as the ability to quote at length from ancient thinkers such as Augustine and Cicero. But above all things, Calvin sought to be true to the Word of God. He was the biblical theologian par excellence who was at the same time a singularly gifted systematic theologian.

We owe a great debt to this man. He is God's gift to the church, not only for the sixteenth century but for all time. We therefore join the multitudes who are celebrating the 500th birthday of John Calvin in the year 2009.

WILL MAN ROB GOD?

AUGUST 2009

———

I N THE LAST BOOK OF the Old Testament, God spoke through the prophet Malachi. He raised a provocative question: "Will man rob God?" This is somewhat startling because it suggests something that on the surface would appear to be impossible. How could anybody rob God of anything? Does it mean that we storm the ramparts of heaven and break into the inner sanctum of the divine treasury and help ourselves to things that God alone possesses? Such a thing is manifestly impossible. The strongest robber in the world could never scale the heights of heaven and defile the possessions of an omnipotent God, and so the very idea of robbing God seems absurd. Yet God gives answer to this question immediately dispelling any absurdity connected with it. He explains pointedly how indeed it is possible for human creatures to be guilty of theft against God. He answers his question, "Will a man rob God?" by saying, "Yet you have robbed me." The Israelite response is: "How have we robbed you?" To which God replies, "In your tithes and contributions" (3:8). God announces that to withhold the full measure of the tithe that He requires from His people is to be guilty of robbing God Himself. Because of this, He pronounces a curse upon the whole nation and commands them afresh to bring to Him all of the tithes.

When we think of tithing in Old Testament categories, we understand that the requirement involves returning to God the first fruits of one's prosperity. We are required to give ten percent of our gross annual income or gain. If a shepherd's flock produced ten new lambs, the requirement was that one of those lambs be offered to God. This offering is from the top. It is not an offering that is given after other expenses are met or after other taxes have been paid.

Recently, I read an article that gave an astonishing statistic that I find difficult to believe is accurate. It declared that of all of those people in America who identify themselves as evangelical Christians, only four percent of them return a tithe to God. If that statistic is accurate, it means that ninety-six percent of professing evangelical Christians regularly, systematically, habitually, and impenitently rob God of what belongs to Him. It also means that ninety-six percent of us are for this reason exposing ourselves to a divine curse upon our lives. Whether this percentage is accurate, one thing is certain—it is clear that the overwhelming majority of professing evangelical Christians do not tithe.

This immediately raises the question: "Why?" How is it possible that somebody who has given his life to Christ can withhold their financial gifts from Him? I have heard many excuses or explanations for this. The most common is the assertion that the tithe is part of the Old Testament law that has passed away with the coming of the New Testament. This statement is made routinely in spite of the complete lack of New Testament evidence for it. Nowhere in the New Testament does it teach us that the principle of the tithe has been abrogated. The New Testament does teach us, however, that the new covenant is superior to the old covenant. It is a covenant that gives more blessings to us than the old covenant did. It is a covenant that with its manifold blessings imposes greater responsibilities than the Old Testament did. If anything, the structure of the new covenant requires a greater commitment to financial stewardship before God than that which was required in the old covenant. That is to say, the starting point of Christian giving is the tithe. The tithe is not an ideal that only a few people reach but rather should be the base minimum from which we progress.

Church history also bears witness that many in the early church did not consider the tithe as having been abrogated in the new covenant. One of the earliest (turn of the second century) extrabiblical documents that survives to this day is the book of the *Didache*. The *Didache* gives practical instruction for Christian living. In the *Didache*, the principle of the giving of the first fruits or the tithe is mentioned as a basic responsibility for every Christian.

A second argument that people give to avoid the tithe is that they cannot tithe because they "cannot afford it." What that statement really means is that they cannot pay their tithe and pay all the other expenses that they have incurred. Again, in their minds the tithe is a last resort in the budget. Their giving to God is something that is at the bottom of the list of priorities. It's a weak argument before God to say, "Lord, I didn't tithe because I couldn't afford it"—especially when we consider that the poorest among us has a higher standard of living than ninety-nine percent of the people who have ever walked on the face of the earth.

There are many more excuses that people give to avoid this responsibility, yet the New Testament tells us. "Let the thief no longer steal" (Eph. 2:28a). If we have been guilty of stealing from God in the past by withholding our tithe from Him, that behavior must cease immediately and give way to a resolution to begin tithing at once, no matter what it costs. It's an interesting phenomenon in the life of the church, that people who in 1960 gave a dollar to the offering plate every week, still give that same dollar today. Everything else in their living costs has been adjusted to inflation except their giving. We also have to remind ourselves that if we give gifts to God, we cannot call them tithes if these gifts fall beneath the level of ten percent.

One of the sad realities of failure to tithe is that in so doing we not only are guilty of robbing God, but we also rob ourselves of the joy of giving and of the blessings that follow from it. I have yet to meet a person who tithes who has expressed to me regret for being a tither. On the contrary, I hear from tithers not a sense of judgment towards those who don't but rather a sense of compassion towards them. Frequently, I hear tithers saying, "People who don't tithe just don't know what they're missing." It is a cliché and a truism that you can't out-give God. That statement has become a cliché because it is so true. In the text in Malachi, we find something exceedingly rare coming from the lips of God. Here God challenges His people to put Him to a test: "Put me to the test, says the Lord of hosts, if I will not open the windows of heaven for you and pour down for you a blessing until there is no more need" (3:10). Have you put God to that test? Have you tried Him to see if He will not open heaven itself and empty His own treasuries upon you? We need to stop robbing Him and thus receive from Him the blessing that He promises.

"How is it possible that somebody who has given his life to Christ can withhold their financial gifts from Him?"

IS THE REFORMATION OVER?

SEPTEMBER 2009

———

Is THE REFORMATION OVER? There have been several observations rendered on this subject by those I would call "erstwhile evangelicals." One of them wrote, "Luther was right in the sixteenth century, but the question of justification is not an issue now." A second self-confessed evangelical made a comment in a press conference I attended that "the sixteenth-century Reformation debate over justification by faith alone was a tempest in a teapot." Still another noted European theologian has argued in print that the doctrine of justification by faith alone is no longer a significant issue in the church. We are faced with a host of people who are defined as Protestants but who have evidently forgotten altogether what it is they are protesting.

Contrary to some of these contemporary assessments of the importance of the doctrine of justification by faith alone, we recall a different perspective by the sixteenth-century magisterial Reformers. Luther made his famous comment that the doctrine of justification by faith alone is the article upon which the church stands or falls. John Calvin added a different metaphor, saying that justification is the hinge upon which everything turns. In the twentieth century, J.I. Packer used a metaphor indicating that justification by faith alone is the "Atlas upon whose shoulder every other doctrine stands." Later Packer moved away from that strong metaphor and retreated to a much weaker one, saying that justification by faith alone is, "the fine print of the gospel."

The question we have to face in light of these discussions is, what has changed since the sixteenth century? Well, there is good news and there is bad news. The good news is that people have become much more civil and tolerant with theological disputes. We don't see people being burned at the stake or tortured on the rack over doctrinal differences. We've also seen in the past years that the Roman communion has remained solidly steadfast on other key issues of Christian orthodoxy, such as the deity of Christ, His substitutionary atonement, and the inspiration of the Bible, while many Protestant liberals have abandoned these particular doctrines wholesale. We also see that Rome has remained steadfast on critical moral issues such as abortion and ethical relativism. In the nineteenth century at Vatican Council I, Rome referred to Protestants as "heretics and schismatics." In the twentieth century at Vatican II, Protestants were referred to as "separated brethren." We see a marked contrast in the tone of the different councils. The bad news, however, is that many doctrines that divided orthodox Protestants from Roman Catholics centuries ago have been declared dogma since the sixteenth century. Virtually all of the significant Mariology decrees have been declared in the last 150 years. The doctrine of papal infallibility, though it de facto functioned long before its formal definition, was nevertheless formally defined and declared *de fide* (necessary to believe for salvation) in 1870 at Vatican Council I. We also see that in recent years the Roman communion has published a new Catholic catechism, which unequivocally reaffirms the doctrines of the Council of Trent, including Trent's definition of the doctrine of justification (and thus affirms that council's anathemas against the Reformation doctrine of justification by faith alone.) Along with the reaffirmations of Trent have come a clear reaffirmation of the Roman doctrine of purgatory, indulgences, and the treasury of merits.

At a discussion among leading theologians over the issue of the continued relevance of the doctrine of justification by faith alone, Michael Horton asked the question: "What is it in the last decades that has made the first-century gospel unimportant?" The dispute over justification was not over a technical point of theology that could be consigned to the fringes of the depository of biblical truth. Nor could it be seen simply as a tempest in a teapot. This tempest extended far beyond the tiny volume of a single teacup. The question, "what must I do to be saved?" is still a critical question for any person who is exposed to the wrath of God.

Even more critical than the question is the answer because, the answer touches the very heart of gospel truth. In the final analysis, the Roman Catholic Church affirmed at Trent and continues to affirm now that the basis by which God will declare a person just or unjust is found in one's "inherent righteousness." If righteousness does not inhere in the person, that person at worst goes to hell and at best (if any impurities remain in his life) goes to purgatory for a time that may extend to millions of years. In bold contrast to that, the biblical and Protestant view of justification is that the sole grounds of our justification is the righteousness of Christ, which righteousness is imputed to the believer, so that the moment a person has authentic faith in Christ, all that is necessary for salvation becomes theirs by virtue of the imputation of Christ's righteousness. The fundamental issue is this: is the basis by which I am justified to be saved a righteousness that is my own? Or is it a righteousness that is, as Luther said, "an alien righteousness," a righteousness that is *extra nos*, apart from us—the righteousness of another, namely, the righteousness of Christ? From the sixteenth century to the present, Rome has always taught that justification is based upon faith, on Christ, and on grace. The difference, however, is that Rome continues to deny that justification is based on Christ alone, received by faith alone, and given by grace alone. The difference between these two positions is the difference between salvation and its opposite. There is no greater issue facing a person who is alienated from a righteous God.

At the moment the Roman Catholic Church condemned the biblical doctrine of justification by faith alone, she denied the gospel and ceased to be a legitimate church, regardless of all the rest of her affirmations of Christian orthodoxy. To embrace her as an authentic church while she continues to repudiate the biblical doctrine of salvation is a fatal attribution. We're living in a time where theological conflict is considered politically incorrect, but to declare peace when there is no peace is to betray the heart and soul of the gospel.

IS THE CHURCH FULL
OF HYPOCRITES?

OCTOBER 2009

BOUT THIRTY YEARS AGO, my close friend and colleague, Archie Parrish, who at that time led the Evangelism Explosion (EE) program in Fort Lauderdale, came to me with a request. He indicated that on the thousands of evangelistic visits the EE teams made, they kept a record of responses people made to discussions of the gospel. They collated the most frequent questions and objections people raised about the Christian faith and grouped these inquiries or objections into the ten most frequently encountered. Dr. Parrish asked if I would write a book answering those objections for evangelists to use in their outreach. That effort resulted in my book *Objections Answered*, now called *Reason to Believe*. Among the top ten objections raised was the objection that the church is filled with hypocrites. At that point in time, Dr. D. James Kennedy responded to this objection by replying, "Well, there's always room for one more." He cautioned people that if they found a perfect church, they ought not to join it, since that would ruin it.

The term *hypocrite* came from the world of Greek drama. It was used to describe the masks that the players used to dramatize certain roles. Even today, the theatre is symbolized by the twin masks of comedy and tragedy. In antiquity, certain players played more than one role, and they indicated their role by holding a mask in front of their face. That's the origin of the concept of hypocrisy.

But the charge that the church is full of hypocrites is manifestly false. Though no Christian achieves the full measure of sanctification in this life, that we all struggle with ongoing sin does not justly yield the verdict of hypocrisy. A hypocrite is someone who does things he claims he does not do. Outside observers of the Christian church see people who profess to be Christians and observe that they sin. Since they see sin in the lives of Christians, they rush to the judgment that therefore these people are hypocrites. If a person claims to be without sin and then demonstrates sin, surely that person is a hypocrite. But for a Christian simply to demonstrate that he is a sinner does not convict him of hypocrisy.

The inverted logic goes something like this: All hypocrites are sinners. John is a sinner; therefore, John is a hypocrite. Anyone who knows the laws of logic knows that this syllogism is not valid. If we would simply change the charge from "the church is full of hypocrites" to "the church is full of sinners," we would be quick to plead guilty. The church is the only institution I know of that requires an admission of being a sinner in order to be a member. The church is filled with sinners because the church is the place where sinners who confess their sins come to find redemption from their sins. So in this sense, simply because the church is filled with sinners does not justify the conclusion that the church is filled with hypocrites. Again, all hypocrisy is sin, but not all sin is the sin of hypocrisy.

When we look at the problem of hypocrisy in the New Testament era, we see it most clearly displayed in the lives of those who claimed to be the most righteous. The Pharisees were a group of people who by definition saw themselves as separated from the normal sinfulness of the masses. They began well, seeking a life of devoted godliness and submission to the law of God. However, when their behavior failed to reach their ideals, they began to engage in pretense. They pretended they were more righteous than they were. They gave an outward facade of righteousness, which merely served to conceal a radical corruption in their lives.

Though the church is not filled with hypocrites, there is no denying that hypocrisy is a sin that is not limited or restricted to New Testament Pharisees. It is a sin with which Christians must grapple. A high standard of spiritual and righteous behavior has been set for the church. We often are embarrassed by our failures to reach these high goals and are inclined to pretend that we have reached a higher plateau of righteousness than we've actually attained. When we do that, we put on the mask of the hypocrite and come under the judgment of God for that particular sin. When we find ourselves enmeshed in this type of pretense, an alarm bell should go off in our brains that we need to rush back to the cross and to Christ and to understand where our true righteousness resides. We have to find in Christ, not a mask that conceals our face, but an entire wardrobe of clothing, which is His righteousness. Indeed, it is only under the guise of the righteousness of Christ, received by faith, that any of us can ever have a hope of standing before a holy God. To wear the garments of Christ in faith is not an act of hypocrisy. It is an act of redemption.

ALL TRUTH
IS GOD'S TRUTH

NOVEMBER 2009

———

F EW BOOKS I HAVE READ HAVE MADE a lasting impression on my mind and thought. One of them I read over fifty years ago. The title of the book was *The Metaphysical Foundations of Modern Science*, and it made a lasting impression upon me because it clearly set forth the importance of understanding that all scientific theories presuppose certain philosophical premises. The philosophical premises that are the underpinning of scientific inquiry are often taken for granted and never given even a cursory exploration. But in a time when fierce debate rages between science and theology, it is important that we step back and ask questions about the pre-scientific theoretical foundations for the whole enterprise of knowledge.

The word *science* means "knowledge." We tend to have a restricted view of the word as if knowledge only applies to the realm of empirical investigation. Besides material knowledge, we also have to take into account formal truth. In this regard we must consider mathematics as a genuine science, because math in its formal dimension yields real knowledge. In fact, if we look at the history of scientific progress, we see that the engine that has driven new break-throughs and brought to bear new paradigms has more often than not been the engine of formal mathematics. But it is astonishing to see how frequently people engaged in material scientific research glibly pass over the philosophical presuppositions of their own work.

In Carl Sagan's famous book entitled *Cosmos*, based on his television series of the same title, he makes the following statement: "*Cosmos* is a Greek word for the order of the universe. It is, in a way, the opposite of chaos. It implies the deep interconnectedness of all things." In this seemingly harmless definition of the entire structure of Sagan's work, he assumes that the universe under investigation by science is a cosmos rather than a chaos. He speaks of cosmos "implying a deep interconnectedness of all things." This is the grand presupposition of scientific inquiry, namely, that the universe we are seeking to know is coherent. There is an implied deep and profound interconnectedness of all things. The alternative to cosmos, as Sagan has indicated, is chaos. If the universe is at root chaotic, then the whole scientific enterprise collapses. If the universe is chaotic and disconnected, then no knowledge is possible at all. Even discreet bits of atomic data cannot be understood within the framework of utter chaos, so the presupposition of a coherent, rational order of all things is the screaming presupposition of scientists.

This idea of an assumed coherency has its roots in ancient philosophical inquiry. Ancient Greeks, for example, sought ultimate reality. They sought a foundational principle for unity that would make sense out of diversity. This ultimate unity is what the science of theology provides. The science of theology provides the necessary presupposition for modern science. This is precisely the point that led prominent philosopher Antony Flew to his conversion from atheism to deism—namely, the essential necessity of a coherent foundation to reality to make any knowledge possible. This ultimate coherency cannot be provided by the contingency of this world. It requires a transcendent order.

In the Middle Ages, a crisis ensued in the realm of philosophy with the revival of what Muslim thinkers called "integral Aristotelianism." In their attempt to achieve a synthesis between Aristotelian philosophy and Muslim theology, these thinkers produced a concept called the "double-truth theory." The double-truth theory argued that what was true in religion could be false in science, and what was true in science could at the same time be false in religion. To translate that into contemporary categories, it would go something like this: As a Christian, one could believe that the universe came into being through the purposive act of a divine Creator while at the same time believing that the universe emerged gratuitously as a cosmic accident. These two truths examined by logic would appear to be contradictory. Nevertheless, the double-truth theory would say that truth is contradictory, and one could hold these contradictory ideas at the same time. This kind of intellectual schizophrenia rules the day in our own time where people think that God had nothing to do with the formation of the cosmos from Monday to Saturday only to become creationists on Sunday, failing to see that the two concepts are utterly irreconcilable.

At this point, the question is raised, "Well, does logic really count in our attempt to understand reality?" Again, if we're going to assume coherency and cosmos, logic has to count not just for something but for everything. Thomas Aquinas responded to the Aristotelianism of the medieval Muslim philosophers by replacing double truths with the concept of mixed articles, distinguishing nature and grace (not dividing them, as many of his critics allege). Aquinas said that there are certain truths that can be known through special revelation that are not discerned from investigation of the natural world, while at the same time there are certain truths learned from the study of nature that are not found, for example, in the Bible. One does not find the circulatory system of the human body clearly set forth in Scripture. What Aquinas was saying was that there are certain truths that are mixed articles, truths that can be known either from the Bible or by a study of nature. Among those mixed articles, he included the knowledge of the existence of a Creator.

The fundamental point, of course, that Aquinas was arguing, in agreement with his famous predecessor, Augustine, was that all truth is God's truth, and that all truth meets at the top. If science contradicts religion, or if religion contradicts science, at least one of them must be wrong. There have been times in history where the scientific community has corrected not the Bible but poor interpretations of the Bible, as we saw in the Galileo scandal. On the other hand, biblical revelation can act as intellectual brakes upon scientific theories that are groundless. In any case, if knowledge is possible, what Sagan assumed must continue to be assumed—namely, that for truth to be known, for science to be possible, there must be a coherent reality that we are seeking to know.

MOVING TOWARD
THE GOAL OF HISTORY

DECEMBER 2009

———

"**W**HAT GOES AROUND, COMES AROUND.**"** This American idiom suggests a view of history that has more in common with ancient Greek philosophy than with the Judeo-Christian understanding of history. The grand difference between the ancient view of history and that found in Scripture is the difference between what is called "cyclical" and "linear-progressive." A cyclical view indicates that there was no beginning to the universe and no goal for it; rather, history creates itself and eventually repeats itself—forever. It was this ancient perspective that generated the skepticism that inspired Friedrich Nietzsche's view of "the myth of eternal recurrence."

Over against this view stands the biblical view of linear-progressive history. This understanding does not say that history moves in a steady incline, moving toward some evolutionary climax; rather, it indicates a movement of history that looks more like a corporate chart displaying troughs and peaks while in the long term moving in an upward direction. The most important part of this linear-progressive view of history is that, as the Bible says, the world had a beginning, and that at the beginning an action began, a movement guided by divine providence to an ultimate *telos*—a culmination of purpose, aim, or goal. This purpose or *telos* of history is both personal and cosmic. Every individual moves from birth to death, from a beginning to an end that continues beyond the grave into the ages. In like manner, the world itself looks forward to a future that has been ordained by its Creator.

The term *eschatology* in our theological vocabulary refers to the study of the *eschaton*, or the end times. It is a mistake to think of the end times as being something that remains exclusively in the future. The New

Testament makes it clear that the end times have already begun. The coming of Christ in His first advent, in which He inaugurated His kingdom, displays that the goal of creation is not totally future but has a present reality initiated by the coming of Jesus and emphasized by His resurrection from the dead and by His ascension to the right hand of God where He reigns now as King of kings and Lord of lords.

It is also important for us to understand that in terms of biblical eschatology, the end of the world does not indicate an annihilation of the world but a renovation and redemption of it. The New Testament makes it evident that the final renovation of creation is cosmic in scope, that the whole universe groans together in travail waiting for the redemption of the sons of men (Rom. 8:18–23). Questions of our future, personal and cosmic, are all subject to the inquiries associated with eschatology. The question of life after death—the issues of heaven, hell, and resurrection—are all integral to our study of eschatology. An understanding of the last judgment also falls under the scope of this consideration.

As people who live in the present, who have a past that we are aware of and a future that is not altogether clearly known, we nevertheless have the future promises set forth by God in His Word as an anchor for our souls. The Bible speaks of our confidence in the future in terms of the idea of "hope." In biblical categories, hope does not indicate an unfulfilled wish that we have a desire to see come to pass. Instead, our hope is that which rests upon a certain conclusion in the future that God has promised for His people. Here hope is described by the metaphor of the anchor—the anchor of the soul (Heb. 6:13–20). An anchor is not something that is tenuous or ephemeral. It has weight, it has solidity, and it is that which gives security to a ship that is moored in open water. In like manner, we live our lives in the midst of the waves that crash against us, but we are not tossed to and fro with no anchor. Our anchor is the promise of God for the future that He has laid up for His people.

It is easy to become so preoccupied with the future that we forget the past and almost ignore the marvelous reality that God has already accomplished for His people in history. History is the domain of Christ's incarnation, atonement, resurrection, and ascension, and we can't understand our hope for the future without understanding those things that God has already brought to pass in His plan of redemption. At the same time, we must not be so occupied with the past and with the present that we forget the hope that God has set before us in the future. So, how we live today is in large measure determined by how we understand the past as well as how we understand the future. It is because God is a God of history, a God of purpose, a God of *telos* that the present has eternal significance. It's because God is the Lord of history that right now counts forever.

FOR MY GOOD?

JANUARY 2010

———

I N 1993, MY WIFE AND I WERE INVOLVED IN an historic train wreck. The crash of the *Sunset Limited* into an inlet from Mobile Bay killed more passengers than any Amtrak accident in history. We survived that eerie accident but not without ongoing trauma. The wreck left my wife with an ongoing anxiety about being able to sleep on a train at night. The wreck left me with a back injury that took fifteen years of treatment and therapy to overcome. Nevertheless, with these scars from the trauma we both learned a profound lesson about the providence of God. Clearly, God's providence in this case for us was one of benign benevolence. It also illustrated to us an unforgettable sense of the tender mercies of God. In as much as we are convinced that God's providence is an expression of His absolute sovereignty over all things, I would think that a logical conclusion from such a conviction would be the end of all anxiety.

However, that is not always the case. Of course, our Lord Himself gave the instruction to be anxious for nothing to His disciples and, by extension, to the church. His awareness of human frailties expressed in our fears was manifested by His most common greeting to His friends: "Fear not." Still, we are creatures who, in spite of our faith, are given to anxiety and at times even to melancholy.

As a young student and young Christian, I struggled with melancholy and sought the counsel of one of my mentors. As I related my struggles, he said, "You are experiencing the heavy hand of the Lord on your shoulder right now." I had never considered God's hand being one that gave downward pressure on my shoulder or that would cause me to struggle in this way. I was driven to prayer that the Lord would remove His heavy hand from my shoulder. In time, He did that and delivered me from melancholy and a large degree of anxiety.

On another occasion I was in a discussion with a friend, and I related to him some of the fears that were plaguing me. He said, "I thought you believed in the sovereignty of God." "I do," I said, "and that's my problem." He was puzzled by the answer, and I explained that I know enough about what the Bible teaches of God's providence and of His sovereignty to know that sometimes God's sovereign providence involves suffering and affliction for His people. That we are in the care of a sovereign God whose providence is benevolent does not exclude the possibility that He may send us into periods of trials and tribulations that can be excruciatingly painful. Though I trust God's Word that in the midst of such experiences He will give to me the comfort of His presence and the certainty of my final deliverance into glory, in the meantime I know that the way of affliction and pain may be difficult to bear.

The comfort that I enjoy from knowing God's providence is mixed at times with the knowledge that His providence may bring me pain. I don't look forward to the experience of pain with a giddy anticipation; rather, there are times when it's necessary for me and for others to grit our teeth and to bear the burdens of the day. Again, I have no question about the outcome of such affliction, and yet at the same time, I know that there are afflictions that will test me to the limits of my faith and endurance. That kind of experience and knowledge makes it easy to understand the tension between confidence in God's sovereign providence and our own struggles with anxiety.

Romans 8:28, which is a favorite for many of us, states that "all things work together for good to those who love God, to those who are the called according to His purpose" (NKJV). There's no other text that demonstrates so clearly and magnificently the beauty of God's sovereign providence than that one. The text does not say that everything that happens to us, considered in and of itself, is good; rather, it says that all things that happen are working together for our good. That is the master plan of God's redemptive providence. He brings good out of evil. He brings glory out of suffering. He brings joy out of affliction. This is one of the most difficult truths of sacred Scripture for us to believe. I've said countless times that it is easy to believe in God but far more difficult to believe God. Faith involves living a life of trust in the Word of God.

As I live out the travail that follows life on this side of glory, hardly a day goes by that I am not forced to look at Romans 8:28 and remind myself that what I'm experiencing right now feels bad, tastes bad, is bad; nevertheless, the Lord is using this for my good. If God were not sovereign, I could never come to that comforting conclusion—I would be constantly subjected to fear and anxiety without any significant relief. The promise of God that all things work together for good to those who love God is something that has to get not only into our minds, but it has to get into our bloodstreams, so that it is a rock-solid principle by which life can be lived.

I believe this is the foundation upon which the fruit of the Spirit of joy is established. This is the foundation that makes it possible for the Christian to rejoice even while in the midst of pain and anxiety. We are not stoics who are called to keep a stiff upper lip out of some nebulous concept of fate; rather, we are those who are to rejoice because Christ has overcome the world. It is that truth and that certainty that gives relief to all of our anxieties.

TILTING AT SCARECROWS

FEBRUARY 2010

———

> "We are not justified by faith by believing in justification by faith. We are justified by faith by believing in the gospel itself—in other words, that Jesus is Lord and that God raised him from the dead."
>
> —N.T. Wright, "New Perspectives on Paul,"
> in *Justification in Perspective*, p. 261

I N THE PAST FEW YEARS, the British bishop and New Testament scholar N.T. Wright has emerged as an icon of biblical theology around the world. His excellent work on the resurrection of Christ has influenced many people including his own country's most famous philosopher and former atheist Antony Flew, who has converted to deism. Wright is also known, however, for being one of the chief architects of the so-called new perspective on Paul, in which he recasts the doctrine of justification in such a way as to transcend the historic dispute between Roman Catholicism and Reformation Protestantism. In a sense, Wright says, "A pox on both your houses," claiming that both Rome and the Reformation misunderstood and distorted the biblical view of justification. In his response to John Piper's critique of his work, Wright drips patronizing disdain for Piper and for those who embrace the traditional Protestant view of justification. He is critical of theological traditions that he thinks miss the biblical point.

In the course of debate, one of the most effective and fallacious arguments often used is called the "straw man" fallacy. The value of a scarecrow is that it is a counterfeit human being designed to scare away a few crows. It is an effective device, but not nearly as effective as a real farmer patrolling his fields with a shotgun. The farmer made of straw is not nearly as formidable as the real one. This is usually the case in the difference between the authentic and the counterfeit. The straw man fallacy occurs when

one creates a false view of his opponent's position in a distorted caricature by which he then easily dismantles that position in total refutation.

One of the statements that N.T. Wright employs, using this same stratagem, is the statement that "we are not justified by faith by believing in
justification by faith." To intimate that Protestant orthodoxy believes
that we are justified by believing in the doctrine of justification by faith
is the king of all straw men. It is the Goliath of scarecrows, the King Kong
of straw man fallacies. In other words, it is a whopper. I am aware of no
theologian in the history of the Reformed tradition who believes or argues
that a person can be justified by believing in the doctrine of justification
by faith. This is a pure and simple distortion of the Reformed tradition.

In Wright's statement we see a straw man argument that falls by its
own weight. It contains more straw than the stick figure can support. The
doctrine of justification by faith alone not only does not teach that justification is by believing in the doctrine of justification by faith alone, but
in fact, teaches that which is totally antithetical to the idea. The phrase
"justification by faith alone" is theological shorthand for saying justification is by Christ alone. Anyone who understands and advocates the
doctrine of justification by faith alone knows that the focal point is that
which justifies—trust in Christ and not trust in a doctrine.

One of the key terms in the phrase "justification by faith" is the word
by, which signals that faith is the means or tool that links us to Christ and
His benefits. The concept indicates that faith is the "instrumental" cause
of our justification. What is in view in the Protestant formulation is a distinction from the Roman Catholic view of the instrumental cause. Rome
declares the sacrament of baptism in the first instance and penance in
the second instance to be the instrumental causes of justification. So the
dispute of what instrument is the basis by which we are justified was and
remains critical to the classical dispute between Rome and Protestantism.
The Protestant view, following Paul's teaching in the New Testament, is
that faith is the sole instrument by which we are linked to Christ.

Closely related to this is the hotly disputed issue of the grounds of our
justification before God. Here is where the biblical concept of imputation

is so important. Those who deny imputation as the grounds of our justification declare it to be a legal fiction, a miscarriage of justice, or even a manifestation of cosmic child abuse. Yet at the same time, it is the biblical explanation for the ground of our redemption. No biblical text more clearly teaches this concept of transfer or imputation than that of Isaiah 53, which the New Testament church singled out as a crucial prophetic explanation of the drama of redemption. The New Testament declares Christ to be our righteousness, and it is precisely our confidence in the righteousness of Christ as the grounds for our justification that is the focus of the doctrine of justification by faith. We understand that believing the doctrine of *sola fide* will save no one. Faith in a doctrine is not enough to save. However, though we cannot be saved by believing in the doctrine of justification, the denial of that same doctrine can indeed be fatal because to deny the doctrine of justification by faith alone as the Apostle Paul indicated in Galatians is to reject the gospel and substitute something else for it, which would result in what Paul declares to be anathema. The gospel is too important to be dismissed by tilting at scarecrows.

THE ASCENSION

MARCH 2010

———

T HESE MEN HAD SPENT THREE YEARS in a state of unspeakable joy. They had witnessed what no human beings before them had ever seen in the entire course of history. Their eyes peered openly at things angels themselves longed to look into but were unable. Their ears heard what ancient saints had a fierce desire to hear with their own ears. These men were the disciples of Jesus of Nazareth. They were His students. They were His companions. Where He went, they went. What He said, they heard. What He did, they saw with their own eyes. These were the original eyewitnesses of the earthly ministry of the Son of God.

But one day, these men heard from the lips of their teacher the worst of all possible news. Jesus told them that He was leaving them. He told them that the days of their intimate companionship in this world were coming to a hasty end. Imagine the shock and profound panic that filled the hearts of these disciples when Jesus said that it was just about over.

In John 16 we read what Jesus said: " 'A little while, and you will see me no longer; and again a little while, and you will see me.' So some of his disciples said to one another, 'What is this that he says to us, "A little while, and you will not see me, and again a little while, and you will see me"; and, "because I am going to the Father"?' So they were saying, 'What does he mean by "a little while"? We do not know what he is talking about.'

"Jesus knew that they wanted to ask him, so he said to them, 'Is this what you are asking yourselves, what I meant by saying, "A little while and you will not see me, and again a little while and you will see me"? Truly, truly, I say to you, you will weep and lament, but the world will rejoice. You will be sorrowful, but your sorrow will turn into joy. When a woman is giving birth, she has sorrow because her hour has come, but when she has delivered the baby, she no longer remembers the anguish, for joy that a human being has been born into the world. So also you have sorrow now, but I will see you again, and your hearts will rejoice, and no one will take your joy from you'" (John 16:16–22).

Just shortly before this enigmatic statement, Jesus had said to His disciples: "But now I am going to him who sent me, and none of you asks me, 'Where are you going?' But because I have said these things to you, sorrow has filled your heart. Nevertheless, I tell you the truth: it is to your advantage that I go away, for if I do not go away, the Helper will not come to you. But if I go, I will send him to you" (vv. 5–7).

In the first instance, Jesus says that their hearts will not simply be touched by sorrow or grief or disappointment, but there will be a fullness of sorrow that saturates the chambers of their hearts. They will be overcome with grief. Their mourning will reach the limits of its human capacity. But Jesus says the condition that they will experience will be temporary, that the sense of abandonment they may feel for a moment will give way to unspeakable joy.

Jesus also explains why He must leave them. He says that it is expedient or necessary for Him to go away so that the disciples may be filled with the Holy Spirit. What sounds like an absolute disadvantage, Jesus promises will turn into an advantage. In Acts 1:9–11 we read, "And when he had said these things, as they were looking on, he was lifted up, and a cloud took him out of their sight. And while they were gazing into heaven as he went, behold, two men stood by them in white robes, and said, 'Men of Galilee, why do you stand looking into heaven? This Jesus, who was taken up from you into heaven, will come in the same way as you saw him go into heaven.'" The disciples watched Jesus leave them. They gazed, staring intently into the heavens as long as their eyes had any sight of Him, at which point two angels came and asked them why they were staring into heaven. The angels then told them that the same Jesus who visibly and bodily ascended would come in like manner at a later time.

Luke tells us in his gospel account of the ascension (24:50–53): "Then he led them out as far as Bethany, and lifting up his hands he blessed them. While he blessed them, he parted from them and was carried up into heaven. And they worshiped him and returned to Jerusalem with great joy, and were continually in the temple blessing God." We notice here the complete fulfillment of what Jesus had predicted—the fullness of their sorrow that had completely engulfed them at the hearing of the news of His departure, had given way not only to contentment, not only to acceptance, not only to joy, but to a great and fulfilling joy. They returned from their last sight of Jesus with their hearts filled with elation. How can that be? The obvious answer is found in that the disciples came to understand the significance of the ascension. As hard as it was to fathom, they came to believe that Jesus' absence from them was of more benefit than His bodily presence with them, the reason being where He was going and what He was about to undertake.

In John 3:13 Jesus declared, "No one has ascended into heaven except he who descended from heaven, the Son of Man." That verse sounds difficult at first glance when we realize that in the Old Testament, Enoch ascended into heaven in the sense that he was carried there, as was Elijah when the chariots of fire lifted him up into the heavens. When Jesus speaks of ascension, He's not speaking of merely "going up." He is speaking of something in technical terms. He is thinking in terms of the Psalms of Ascent that celebrated the anointing of a king (Pss. 120–34). When Jesus says no one ascends into heaven, it is true that no one ascends or goes to heaven in the same manner or for the same purpose that He went there. He was lifted up on clouds of glory in order to go to His Father for the purpose of His coronation as our King—as the King of kings and the Lord of lords. He ascended into heaven to fulfill His role as our Great High Priest, interceding for His people daily. So as He sits at the right hand of the Father, exercising His lordship over the whole world and His intercession before the Father on behalf of His people, He improves our condition dramatically. Not only this, but before Pentecost could come and the Holy Spirit could be poured out upon the church, empowering the church for its missionary enterprise to the whole world, it was necessary for Christ to ascend so that together with the Father He might dispatch from heaven the Holy Spirit in all of His power.

As hard as it is to imagine, the condition that we enjoy right now on this side of the atonement, on this side of the resurrection, this side of the ascension, and this side of Pentecost is, redemptively speaking, a greater situation than that which the disciples enjoyed during their three-year tenure in the presence of the Lord Jesus. We celebrate the ascension because we celebrate our King.

THE TIMES, THEY ARE A-CHANGING

APRIL 2010

———

O NE OF THE OLDEST MYSTERIES OF theoretical thought is the question: What is time?

Immanuel Kant defined time and space as "pure intuitions." We see time as inextricably related to matter and motion. Without matter and space [matter and motion], we have no way to measure the passing of time. Time, it seems, is always in motion. It can never be stopped.

Historically, we have measured the passing of time with various material objects: the sundial, which displays the movement of shadows across its face; the sand pouring through the hourglass; the hands moved by gears within a watch and the minute and hour hands moving around a circle of numbers. I think of staring at a large wall clock and watching the sweeping motion of the second hand. I look at twelve on the dial and wait for the second hand to pass it. My eyes glance below to the number six, and I know that the second hand has not reached it yet, but as the hand sweeps towards the bottom of the face, I get the sensation of time moving so swiftly toward the future at number six. Then, instantly, the second hand is past it, and what a moment ago was future now lies in the past. Sometimes when I experiment with such exercises, I want to call for the clock to stop. But it will not stop—it cannot stop. As the axiom declares, "Time marches on."

Everything in creation is subject to time. Everything in creation is mutable. Everything in creation goes through the process of generation and decay. God and God alone is eternal and immutable. God and God alone escapes the relentless onslaught of time.

We not only measure moments in time, but we measure periods that take place in terms of ages, eras, and epochs. In our own generation, we have seen various transitions of the human cultures in which we find ourselves situated, hurled against the backdrop of time (as Martin Heidegger indicated in his epic book *Being and Time*). We say that times are changing. That doesn't mean that time itself changes. There are still sixty seconds in a minute, sixty minutes in an hour, twenty-four hours in a day. But cultures are constantly shifting in their patterns, in their values, and in their commitments. In my life I have witnessed dramatic changes to the culture in which I find myself. I can think of where I was and what I was doing when I heard of the announcement of the death of Franklin Delano Roosevelt. I remember where I was and what I was doing when I heard the news on the radio of the United States testing its first atomic bomb (before Hiroshima and Nagasaki). I remember where I was and what I was doing at the end of World War II, the assassination of John F. Kennedy, the Russian launch of Sputnik into space, and the news of man's first walk on the moon. But what I remember perhaps more than anything is an entire decade—the decade of the 1960s—in which the United States of America went through an unbloody revolution that changed the culture so dramatically that people who lived before that decade feel like aliens in a culture dominated by a post-1960s worldview. The revolution of the '60s spelled the end of idealism and ushered in several radical changes in the culture, including the sexual revolution. The sanctity of marriage was more explicitly undermined. Clean, wholesome speech in the public sphere became increasingly rare. The sanctity of life with respect to the unborn underwent attack legislatively, and moral relativism became the norm in our culture.

With this moral relativism came technological advances that also altered our daily lives. The knowledge explosion rocked by the advent and proliferation of the use of the computer has brought a new culture of people who live more or less "online." This relativistic culture brought with it a culture of *eros* and heightened addiction to pornography, as well as a culture of drugs with the subsequent invasion of addiction and suicide.

The times in which we live are times that are exceedingly challenging to the church of Jesus Christ. The great tragedy of the church in the post-1960s revolution is that the face of the church has changed along with the face of the secular culture. In a fatal pursuit of relevance, the church has often become merely an echo of the secular culture in which it lives, having a desperate desire to be "with it" and acceptable to the contemporary world. The church itself has adopted the very relativism it seeks to overcome. What is demanded by times such as ours is a church that addresses the temporal while at the same time remaining tethered to the eternal—a church that speaks, comforts, and heals all things mortal and secular without itself abandoning the eternal and the holy. The church must always face the question of whether its commitment is to sanctity or profanity. We need churches filled with Christians who are not enslaved by the culture, churches that seek more than anything to please God and His only begotten Son, rather than to attract the applause of dying men and women. Where is that church? That is the church Christ established. That is the church whose mission is to minister redemption to a dying world, and that is the church we are called to be. God help us and our culture if our ears become deaf to that call.

MAKING MOLEHILLS OUT OF MOUNTAINS: THE CRISIS OVER JUSTIFICATION

MAY 2010

———

T HE CRISIS REGARDING THE DOCTRINE of justification that provoked the Protestant Reformation in the sixteenth century has not yet been resolved. Thus, the Reformation is by no means over. The dispute over justification that split the church back then threatens to fracture contemporary, evangelical Christianity. At issue during the Reformation was the relationship of justification to sanctification. It was a question of the order of salvation. The difference is not a tempest in a teapot; it's one by which salvation itself is defined.

The Roman Catholic Church depended upon the Latin fathers who understood the doctrine of justification against the background of the Latin word *iustificare*. It is this word from which we get our English word *justify*, literally, "to make righteous." However, the actual Greek term that is used in the New Testament means "to declare righteous." What, then, is the difference? In the Protestant understanding of the New Testament, justification occurs when God declares that a person is just. That declaration takes place the moment a person puts his or her faith in Christ. Sanctification is the process that follows justification by which those who have been declared just by God are actually conformed to the image of Christ. But the glorious good news of the gospel is that we don't have to wait until we become just in order to be counted just by God.

Catholics argued in the sixteenth century and have continued to argue, as recently as the *Catechism of the Catholic Church* in 1994, that God will declare a person just only when that person has achieved inherent righteousness. True, that righteousness cannot be gained apart from grace, apart from faith, or apart from Christ. But with the help of these means of grace, the Catholic argues, that righteousness may and must be attained before God will make His declaration that a person is just. That is why, according to Rome, if a person dies with imperfections or impurities still present in his soul, before he can go to heaven, he must first go to purgatory, where his abiding imperfections are purged away. That time in purgatory could last millions of years in order for the cleansing necessary to bring about total purity. What was anathema to Rome about Martin Luther's teaching, among other things, was his famous formula defining justification as bringing sinners into a state whereby we are *simul iustus et peccator*—at the same time just and sinner. We are just by virtue of God declaring us just in Christ, but we still struggle with abiding sin.

Another way of looking at the difference between the Roman Catholic doctrine of justification and the classic Protestant doctrine is the difference between what may be called "analytical" justification and "synthetic" justification.

An analytical statement is true by definition. For example, we may say that "a bachelor is an unmarried man." In that statement, there is nothing in the predicate that isn't contained in the subject. However, if we say, "the bachelor is a poor man," poorness is not automatically contained within the notion of bachelorhood, and so we have added something to the concept of bachelorhood by mentioning poverty. This something that is added makes this a synthetic statement. For Rome, justification occurs only when under analysis God sees that a person is inherently just. In the Protestant view, our justification is synthetic because God judges us not on the basis of our own righteousness, but on the basis of a righteousness that has been added to us by faith, namely, the righteousness of Christ.

When we argue that justification is by faith alone, we mean that all that is necessary in order for a person to receive all of the benefits of Christ's redeeming work is the presence of actual saving faith. Rome agrees that faith is necessary for justification, as well as grace and Christ, but Catholics struggle with the term *alone*. They do not believe that justification is by faith alone but by faith plus works (the works of satisfaction that are a necessary ingredient of the sacrament of penance). Rome believes that justification is by grace plus merit—the merit that is gained by doing works of satisfaction—by Christ plus a person's own righteousness. Again, we can't have that righteousness without the presence of faith, grace, and Christ. Nevertheless, in the final analysis, that righteousness is truly the person's own righteousness.

The ultimate issue between Rome and the Reformation is the issue of the ground of justification. Luther rightly argued that the basis of our justification is our connection to "an alien righteousness"—a righteousness that, properly speaking, is not our own but belongs to someone else. It is a righteousness that Luther spoke of as *extra nos*—apart from us. That righteousness, of course, is the righteousness of Christ that is imputed to all who believe in Him.

In our own day, a full-scale assault has been launched within evangelicalism against the classical doctrine of justification by faith alone. Arguments are raised attacking the concept of imputation and the concept of Christ's achieving of His own righteousness through His active obedience to the Mosaic law and serving as our representative as the second and final Adam. These issues are being debated strenuously even now within the bounds of evangelical seminaries, particularly in light of the influence of the British New Testament scholar N.T. Wright, who, while rejecting both the Roman Catholic and the Reformation views of justification, has particularly raised issues about imputation.

This crisis again confronts the church with what Luther once called "the issue upon which the church stands or falls." Without the doctrine of justification by faith alone, the gospel is not merely compromised, it is lost altogether. And in the place of the good news comes the bad news: that before we can ever enter our heavenly rest, we must, with whatever means of grace are available, reach the point, either in this world or in purgatory, where we attain a pure righteousness that is inherent in us. If I have to wait for that in order to enter into my rest, I cannot imagine anything other than an eternity of restlessness.

FUELING REFORMATION

JUNE 2010

———

I'M ALWAYS PUZZLED WHEN I SEE church billboards announcing a coming revival. They give the times and the dates when the church will be engaged in revival. But I wonder, how can anybody possibly schedule a revival? True revivals are provoked by the sovereign work of God through the stirring of His Holy Spirit in the hearts of people. They happen when the Holy Spirit comes into the valley of dry bones (Ezek. 37) and exerts His power to bring new life, a revivification of the spiritual life of the people of God.

This kind of thing cannot be manipulated by any human program. Historically, no one scheduled the Protestant Reformation. The Welsh revival was not on anyone's agenda, nor was the American Great Awakening penciled into someone's date book. These epic events in church history resulted from the sovereign work of God, who brought His power to bear on churches that had become virtually moribund.

But we have to understand the difference between revival and reformation. Revival, as the word suggests, means a renewing of life. When evangelism is a priority in the church, such outreach will often bring about revival. However, these revivals of spiritual life do not always result in reformation. Reformation indicates changing forms of church and society. Revivals grow into reformations when the impact of the gospel begins to change the structures of the culture. Revival can produce a multitude of new Christians, but these new Christians have to grow into maturity before they begin to make a significant impact on the surrounding culture.

Reformation can involve a change for the better. We must not be so naïve as to think that all change is necessarily good. Sometimes when we feel that we are in the doldrums or that progress has been stultified, we cry out for change, forgetting for the moment that change may be regressive rather than progressive. If I drink a vial of poison, it will change me, but not for the better. Nevertheless, change is often good.

In our day, we have seen the rise of what has been called the "New Calvinism," which tends to focus primarily on the so-called five points of Calvinism. This movement within the church has attracted a great deal of attention, even in the secular media.

Yet it would be wise to not identify Calvinism exhaustively with those five points. Rather, the five points function as a pathway or a bridge to the entire structure of Reformed theology. Charles Spurgeon himself argued that Calvinism is merely a nickname for biblical theology. He and many other titans of the past understood that the essence of Reformed theology cannot be reduced to five particular points that arose centuries ago in Holland in response to controversy with the Arminians, who objected to five specific points of the system of doctrine found in historic Calvinism. For the purposes of this article, it might be helpful to look at both what Reformed theology is and is not.

Reformed theology is not a chaotic set of disconnected ideas. Rather, Reformed theology is systematic. The Bible, being the Word of God, reflects the coherence and unity of the God whose Word it is. To be sure, it would be a distortion to force a foreign system of thought upon Scripture, making Scripture conform to it as if it were some kind of procrustean bed. That is not the goal of sound systematic theology. Rather, true systematic theology seeks to understand the system of theology that is contained within the whole scope of sacred Scripture. It does not impose ideas upon the Bible; it listens to the ideas that are proclaimed by the Bible and understands them in a coherent way.

Reformed theology is not anthropocentric. That is to say, Reformed theology is not centered on human beings. The central focal point of Reformed theology is God, and the doctrine of God permeates the whole of Reformed thought. Thus, Reformed theology, by way of affirmation, can be called theocentric. Indeed, its understanding of the character of God is primary and determinant with respect to its understanding of all other doctrines. That is to say, its understanding of salvation has as its

RIGHT NOW COUNTS FOREVER

control factor—its heart—a particular understanding of God's sovereign character.

Reformed theology is not anti-catholic. This may seem strange since Reformed theology grew directly out of the Protestant movement against the teaching and activity of Roman Catholicism. But the term *catholic* refers to catholic Christianity, the essence of which may be found in the ecumenical creeds of the first thousand years of church history, particularly those of the early church councils, such as the Council of Nicaea in the fourth century and the Council of Chalcedon in the fifth century. That is to say, those creeds contain common articles of faith shared by all denominations that embrace orthodox Christianity, doctrines such as the Trinity and the atonement of Christ. The doctrines affirmed by all Christians are at the heart and core of Calvinism. Calvinism does not depart on a search for a new theology and reject the common base of theology that the whole church shares.

Reformed theology is not Roman Catholic in its understanding of justification. This is simply to say that Reformed theology is evangelical in the historical sense of the word. In this regard, Reformed theology stands strongly and firmly with Martin Luther and the magisterial Reformers in their articulation of the doctrine of justification by faith alone, as well as the doctrine of *sola Scriptura*. Neither of these doctrines is explicitly declared in the five points of Calvinism; yet, in a sense, they become part of the foundation for the other characteristics of Reformed theology.

All this is to say that Reformed theology so far transcends the mere five points of Calvinism that it is an entire worldview. It is covenantal. It is sacramental. It is committed to transforming culture. It is subordinate to the operation of God the Holy Spirit, and it has a rich framework for understanding the entirety of the counsel of God revealed in the Bible.

So it should go without saying that the most important development that will bring about reformation is not simply the revival of Calvinism. What has to happen is the renewal of the understanding of the gospel itself. It is when the gospel is clearly proclaimed in all of its fullness that God exercises His redeeming power to bring about renewal in the church and in the world. It is in the gospel and nowhere else that God has given His power unto salvation.

If we want reformation, we have to start with ourselves. We have to start bringing the gospel itself out of darkness, so that the motto of every reformation becomes *post tenebras lux*—"after darkness, light." Luther declared that every generation must declare freshly the gospel of the New Testament. He also said that anytime the gospel is clearly and boldly proclaimed, it will bring about conflict, and those of us who are inherently adverse to conflict will find it tempting to submerge the gospel, dilute the gospel, or obscure the gospel in order to avoid conflict. We, of course, are able to add offense to the gospel by our own ill-mannered attempts to proclaim it. But there is no way to remove the offense that is inherent to the gospel message, because it is a stumbling block, a scandal to a fallen world. It will inevitably bring conflict. If we want reformation, we must be prepared to endure such conflict to the glory of God.

WHEN TO STOP, WHEN TO GO, WHEN TO SLOW DOWN

JULY 2010

———

T HE COLLEGE I ATTENDED WAS situated in a small western Pennsylvania town in an area heavily populated by one of the largest gatherings of Amish people found in the United States. The Amish are a delightful group totally committed to separation from this world. They go out of their way to avoid any social mixing with the non-Amish, or the "Gentiles," who are present among them. They are easy to discern, as the clothing they wear is a clearly defined uniform, commonly consisting of blue denim. The men wear beards. Their clothes are never adorned with buttons but are gathered together with hooks and eyes.

The Amish make their way about the area in horse-drawn buggies. They studiously avoid the use of any modern devices and conveniences, such as cars, tractors, electricity, or running water. An Amish house can easily be identified by the presence of sheets hanging over the windows rather than the more ornate curtains that would indicate the home of somebody more worldly.

In any case, the entire system of Amish religion is dedicated to a kind of separatism that sees the use of modern conveniences such as electricity and gasoline-operated engines as a descent into worldliness. The lifestyle of the Amish is driven in large measure by an ethical commitment that regards such separation as necessary for spiritual development.

The rest of the Christian community regards the use of buttons, electricity, and gasoline as a matter of moral or ethical indifference. That is, there is no inherent or intrinsic ethical content with respect to the use of the gasoline engine. To be sure, the use of the gasoline engine may be the occasion of sin if we use our cars in an ungodly manner, risking people's lives and limbs by reckless speeding, for example. Yet the very existence of an automobile and its function in society has no intrinsic, ethical content. We regard automobiles, electricity, or telephones as matters that are *adiaphora*—things that are morally or ethically indifferent.

The concept of adiaphora was developed in the New Testament when the Apostle Paul had to address emerging ethical concerns in the nascent Christian community. Christians coming out of a background of idolatry were particularly sensitive to issues such as whether it was appropriate to eat meat that had been offered to idols. After using such meat in their godless religious ceremonies, the pagans sold it in the marketplace. Some early Christians were convinced that such meat was tainted by its very use in pagan religion, so they went to great lengths to avoid it, thinking, according to their scruples for godliness, it was necessary to have no connection with such meat. Paul pointed out that the meat itself was not inherently good or evil, so the eating of meat offered to idols was a matter of ethical indifference. Yet at the same time, the Apostle gave significant instructions as to how the Christian community is to relate to those people who develop scruples about certain behaviors that are not by nature ethically charged.

This problem that faced the early church persists in every Christian generation. Though we don't struggle with the question of eating meat offered to idols today, we have other issues that touch upon the question of adiaphora. American fundamentalism, for example, has elevated adiaphora to a matter of major concern. In some areas of the church and of the Christian community, questions of watching television, going to movies, wearing makeup, dancing, and the like are considered matters of spiritual discernment. That is to say, people are instructed that true spirituality necessitates the avoidance of dancing and going to the movies, as well as other matters of this sort.

The problem with this particular approach to ethics is that these elements, on which the Bible is silent, become ethical matters of the highest consideration for some Christians. In a word, the adiaphora become elevated to the status of law, and people's consciences become bound where God has left them free. Here a form of legalism emerges that is on a collision course with the biblical principal of Christian liberty. Even more important is that a substitute morality replaces the true ethical criteria that the Bible prescribes for godly people.

Although on the surface it seems rigid and severe to define spirituality as involving the avoidance of dancing, wearing makeup, and going to movies, in reality it vastly oversimplifies the call to godliness that the Bible gives to Christian people. It is much easier for someone to avoid going to movies, for example, than it is to manifest the fruit of the Spirit. True godliness concerns much weightier matters than superficial ways of distinguishing ourselves from our unbelieving neighbors.

At the same time, when these adiaphorous matters are elevated into the status of law, and people become convinced that God requires them to follow a certain path, the Bible gives instructions on how we are to be sensitive to them. It is not a matter of Christian liberty to bash or to ridicule those who have these scruples. We are called to be sensitive to them. We are not to offend unnecessarily those referred to in the Bible as weaker brothers. On the other hand, sensitivity to the weaker brother stops at the point where he elevates his sensitivity to become the law or defining rule of Christian behavior.

In every age and in every culture, discerning the difference between that which God requires and prohibits for His people, and that which is indifferent, requires a significant knowledge of sacred Scripture, as well as an earnest desire to be obedient to the Lord. There is enough in principle to keep us busily engaged in the pursuit of godliness and obedience without adding to it matters that are ethically indifferent.

How this issue applies to the big question of Christian worship is no small matter. But wrestle through it we must if we are to remain obedient to the living God and receive what He offers as the church worships Him—a taste of heaven.

SETTING THE STAGE: THE FIRST MILLENNIUM

AUGUST 2010

VOLUMES HAVE BEEN WRITTEN GIVING detailed analyses of the extraordinary things that occurred in the first thousand years of church history, events that influenced everything that came after them. In this brief overview, I'm going to look at five dimensions of activity that had monumental impact for the future history of Christianity.

Five extraordinary developments arose during the first thousand years AD, which deeply influenced the faith and practice of the next millennium.

The first such matter was the rise of the so-called "mono-episcopacy." By the end of the first century, it was seen that the bishop of Rome had grown exceedingly more influential than other bishops of that period. Within the next century or so, the authority and power of the bishop of Rome was consolidated for all future history of the Roman Catholic Church. The singular authority that became located in the bishop of Rome gave the church a unifying base. The influence of the pope in the first thousand years of the church is almost impossible to measure.

In that light, we see the second major impact come to the fore—the innovations brought to Christianity by perhaps the most important pope of the first millennium: Gregory the Great. In his activities he consolidated the power vested in the sacraments of the church and spawned the vast sacerdotal system (priests through ordination receiving the ability to act as mediators of God's grace to man through the sacraments) with which all future Catholicism would be associated.

A third element that had great influence on the future of Christianity was the rise of the monastic movement. Beginning with the extreme asceticism of people such as Anthony of the Desert (ca. 251–356), this radical brand of self-denial became institutionalized with the rise of various monastic orders, most of which exist to this day. These orders include the Benedictines, the Augustinians, the Franciscans, and others that date back several centuries.

Perhaps most important in the first thousand years were the ecumenical councils. Of the several ecumenical councils, clearly the two most important were those that were convened in the fourth and in the fifth centuries. The fourth century saw the convening of the Council of Nicaea and the production of the historic Nicene Creed. Here the church gave its definition of the deity of Christ over against the heretic Arius, who argued that though Jesus was the first creature created by God and in that sense the firstborn of God, He nevertheless remained a creature and so was not to be worshiped as the second person of the Trinity.

The tension that was provoked by the Arian controversy and the years of deliberation and discussion that ensued finally culminated in the Council of Nicaea in 325. In that council the full deity of Christ was affirmed, and Christ, the divine Logos, the second person of the Trinity, was declared to be co-essential and co-eternal with the Father. This formula gave the church a way to distinguish among the persons of the Godhead, while at the same time attributing a singular divine essence to the three. The anti-trinitarian Christology of Arius saw the beginning of its defeat with this ecumenical council.

The fifth century saw the convening of perhaps the most important Christological council in all of church history at Chalcedon in 451. Here orthodox Christianity had to fight a battle on two fronts. On the one hand was the opposition to the orthodox view of the nature of Christ in His incarnation by Eutyches. Eutyches was a monophysite—he declared that Jesus had only one nature. This nature was called a single "theanthropic nature," meaning a divinely human nature or a humanly divine nature. This position, saying that Christ had one nature (Greek: *monophysis*), obscured both the real deity and the real humanity that were united in the incarnation of Christ.

On the other side of the debate, the Nestorians argued that if Jesus had two natures, He had to have had two persons as well, so they separated the two natures of Christ into two persons. Over against both heresies, Chalcedon gave its famous formula by which it declared that Christ is truly God and truly man, with the natures perfectly united in such a way that they are not confused—the natures are without mixture, confusion, division, or separation; each nature retains its own attributes. This was a watershed council because it set the boundaries or parameters of Christo-logical speculation. The two natures were not to be merged or confused; the human nature, for example, would not be absorbed or swallowed up in the divine nature and vice versa. At the same time, the two natures were not to be separated so as to lose their unity in the one person.

Throughout history since Chalcedon, the church in virtually every generation has had to face the tendencies of either confusing the two natures or dividing or separating the two natures. Orthodoxy in the fifth century declared that the natures must be distinguished yet never separated. They must be distinguished and never be co-mingled.

The other noteworthy event of the first millennium was the extraordinary impact of Augustine of Hippo, perhaps the greatest theologian of that millennium. Augustine was called to defend the church against the heresies of the Donatists in their disputes about baptism and, more importantly, against the heretical views of Pelagius, who denied original sin, arguing that even apart from grace the descendants of Adam could achieve lives of perfection. Augustine's theology of salvation shaped the future history of Christianity, particularly as it helped quicken Luther and Calvin for the Protestant Reformation. At the same time, Augustine's view of the church solidified the power of the monoepiscopacy and the Roman magisterium for all future generations.

These five aspects of the first millennium are only illustrative of a vast number of things that in the providence of God developed over this period of time. Sadly, at the end of this millennium, the church was already groping in the darkness and biblical soteriology had declined to such a degree that the gospel was rapidly becoming obscured, even becoming almost totally eclipsed until it was recovered in the sixteenth century Reformation.

"There's nothing in redemptive history that would make beauty, goodness, or truth suddenly passé or insignificant."

—

BUILDING WITH CONVICTION

SEPTEMBER 2010

———

WHEREVER PEOPLE COME TOGETHER TO worship God, whether it be on a desert island or in a burgeoning metropolis, whether it be on the plains of Africa or in the cold winter of Siberia, people are concerned to worship Him in terms of the good, the true, and the beautiful. In the book of Exodus, we see the origin of the tabernacle, which was the house of God. This was the house where people came to meet with the living God. In order to prepare that house, the Lord gave meticulous instructions, down to the finest details, as to how the place of meeting was to be constructed. We know that homes or houses come in all shapes and sizes. Some are ornate, others are simple, merely providing the basics that are needed for shelter. There are grass huts, tepees, igloos, castles, and Victorian mansions. The tabernacle had a particular design. It was the dwelling place where God would meet with His people. More chapters are devoted in the Old Testament to the building of the tabernacle than there are chapters in the entire book of Romans. This demonstrates the concern our Lord has for how He is worshiped.

Since the very beginning, from Cain and Abel to the New Testament model, God has required that true worship be done in Spirit and in truth (John 4:24). God is the source, the fountainhead, and the norm of all that is true. His judgment comes crashing down through the ages on all forms of false worship and idolatry. Idolatry is so pernicious because it distorts and smothers the truth of God. In like manner, God is the source, the fountainhead, and the norm of all that is good. Evil in all of its forms represents a transgression or departure from the good. In the context of worship, goodness is to be part of the focus of attention. Finally, God is the source, the fountainhead, and the norm of all that is beautiful. Just as everything that is true points to God, and everything that is good points to God, so everything that is authentically beautiful also points to the source and fountainhead of that beauty.

The Old Testament tabernacle was but a shadow of things that were to come. What it foreshadowed was fulfilled in the perfect sacrifice of the incarnate Christ, who was, during His first advent, God "tabernacling" among us. Since the essence of the foreshadowing of the tabernacle was fulfilled in Christ, many have come to the conclusion that we have nothing further to learn from its construction. They say we are not to look at it as a model for New Testament churches, as it has no further significance since Jesus altogether fulfilled its function. Upon taking a second glance however, the question is raised: Are there transferable principles found in the construction of the tabernacle that may be useful for the construction of houses of worship in the New Testament? I believe there are.

When we look at the instructions for the building of the Old Testament tabernacle, down to the particular threads and linens that were used in the garments of Aaron and the priests, we learn they were designed "for glory and for beauty" (Ex. 28:2, 40). But for whose glory were they designed? Not for the human beings who ministered in the tabernacle. Arguably, the glory that is in view is the glory of the Lord. The beauty is to manifest that same glory. It is the beauty of God that is on display in the tabernacle. Since Christ fulfilled all of the aspects of the sacrificial system undertaken in the Old Testament tabernacle, does that mean that God's concern for His glory and for His beauty has passed away? I think not. God has lost nothing of His glory or of His beauty. The principle of seeking to show forth His glory and His beauty in the places where we meet Him is not something that can be lightly discarded.

We know this to be the case because the finest materials available to human beings were used to adorn the sanctuary by God's own command. The most skilled artisans were employed to construct the sacred vessels. The first people mentioned in the Bible as being filled with the Holy Spirit were the artisans whom God selected for this undertaking. Again,

His dwelling, His place of meeting with His people, was to manifest His glory and His beauty, indeed the beauty of holiness.

In our day, we have seen a widespread movement to abandon all the "churchiness" of churches. Instead of using architectural styles designed to call attention to the transcendent majesty of God—the beauty of His holiness and glory—we have moved in the direction of pure functionality. Churches are designed now for creature comfort and for utilitarian purposes. We have even seen the pulpits of churches being removed or the use of portable pulpits so as to not get in the way of productions. Contrarily, in the churches of Christian history, particularly in Reformation churches, the pulpit rose as the dominant feature of the interior of the building, indicating the central importance of the Word of God, the absolute significance of God's truth. At the same time, the preaching of the Word of God calls the people out of sin and to righteousness, emphasizing the central importance of goodness to the Christian life. Something, then, has been lost in the move to pure functionality.

In the final analysis, we ask, what happened to beauty? Modern churches tend to look like prefabricated warehouses, or they're designed to be functional music halls so that the production of music may have center stage. In the Old Testament, the whole person was engaged in worship. The mind was engaged with the Word of God. The music of the choirs and the instruments mentioned in many of the psalms were part of the design of worship. There was an auditory beauty. There was a visual beauty. There was even an olfactory beauty with the sweet aroma of incense that was part of the experience of worship. All five senses, as well as the mind, were engaged in biblical worship. If we are to worship God fully in truth and in Spirit, we need to incorporate beauty among the gathering of His people wherever possible. This is the model that God followed when He designed the tabernacle, His dwelling place in Israel.

There's nothing in redemptive history that would make beauty, goodness, or truth suddenly passé or insignificant. These elements, which point to God, are always and everywhere, in every time and in every nation, significant elements of godly worship.

JUSTIFICATION BY DEATH?

OCTOBER 2010

———

I N THE SIXTEENTH CENTURY, Christendom underwent one of the most extensive and serious schisms in its history. The chief article that caused the controversy to end in division was the doctrine of justification by faith alone. The Protestant Reformation was not a tempest in a teapot. The issue that divided the Roman Catholics from the Protestant Reformers was not a secondary or tertiary doctrine. The dispute focused on the essence of the gospel. Some have argued that *sola fide* (faith alone) is central to the Christian faith but not essential. I contend, however, that it is essential to the gospel in that, without *sola fide*, we do not have the gospel. And without the gospel, we have no salvation.

One would think after so many centuries of dissemination of the doctrine of justification by faith alone, particularly in Protestant countries, that the doctrine would be firmly entrenched in the minds of Christian people. But such is not the case. Those who hold to justification by faith alone are clearly in a minority. More popular views are the doctrines of justification by works and justification by a combination of faith and works. These really reflect not so much Christian views of the matter as a Muslim one. In the Muslim view, a person's eternal destiny is determined by the scales of justice. If one's good works outweigh the bad deeds, then the person goes to heaven. If the bad deeds outweigh the good deeds, the person goes to hell. This view is held by many professing Christians, who still entertain the idea that they can gain entrance into heaven and into the kingdom of God by living a good life. As long as they refrain from egregious sins such as murder, grand theft, or adultery, they think they have kept their moral slates clean enough to get them past the gates of judgment.

As fallacious as that view is, there is a view even more insidious in its subtlety and thus more pervasive—the cultural view of justification that is widely held in the West. That doctrine is the doctrine of justification by death. It is an implicit universalism that assumes everyone goes to heaven when he or she dies. Perhaps the most rank evildoers, such as Adolf Hitler or Joseph Stalin, may not make it, but the average person certainly has nothing to worry about.

I was informed of how pervasive this doctrine is when I asked my son, when he was a child, the second diagnostic question made popular by Evangelism Explosion. I asked him: "If you were to die tonight and God were to say to you, why should I let you into My heaven, what would you say?" His eyes lit up and he looked at me with a shocked expression as if the question I had just proffered was the most stupid he had ever heard. With a simple shrug, he said, "Well, I would say He should let me in because I'm dead." In other words, "Doesn't everyone who dies enter into God's redeeming presence?" Here was a son of a father who was by profession a theologian—a Reformed theologian—who not only had failed to grasp the doctrine of justification by faith alone but wasn't even sidelined by a doctrine of justification by works. He was content to rest on his assumption of justification by death.

Of course, my young son's confession of faith, or the lack thereof, is by no means an isolated instance in our culture. Nothing transforms sinners into valorous saints more miraculously or more frequently than death. Go to the funeral of the most wicked sinner you know and you will hear a eulogy that guarantees that person's entrance into the kingdom of God.

What drives this pervasive belief in justification by death? I think there are several factors. One is a misinformed idea of the character of God. We are told ad nauseum that God loves everyone unconditionally. The necessary inference that people draw from that is simple: If God loves me unconditionally, then there are no conditions that I must meet in order to enter into heavenly bliss. In a sense, God, if He is loving, is obligated to give me eternal life.

The second driving factor is a widespread denial of hell. The whole concept of hell is so ghastly and difficult even to comprehend that we have a visceral response of denial to it. We cannot imagine any of our loved ones ever being assigned to such a dreadful place. We also find in our culture a rejection of the whole idea of a final judgment. Never mind that our Lord taught again and again that each one of us will stand before God and will be held accountable for his or her sins—to the extent that even every idle word we speak will be brought into judgment. No one escapes the judgment of God. We all must stand before that final tribunal and be judged not on a curve, not according to how we stack up against other people in this world, but how we stand according to God's standard of righteousness, a standard that none of us will ever reach.

The Bible speaks of two ways in which people die. There are those who die in faith and, because of that faith, are linked to the atoning work of Christ and receive the benefits of His atoning work, including entrance into His kingdom. The other way that the Bible speaks of dying is dying in sin. Those who die in sin are those who die in a state of impenitence. Such people have never bowed the knee to the living God and cried out from their helplessness for His grace. Instead of clinging to the cross and coming with nothing in our hands, it is our nature as fallen creatures to try to bring something in our hands that will pay the price that needs to be paid for our redemption. This is the height or, perhaps, the nadir of folly. The only thing we can be sure of is that death will give us judgment. The question is, do we have that faith by which we are linked to the righteousness of Christ and all the benefits of His ministry on our behalf, or will we stand alone at that judgment bar of Christ?

BE PREPARED

NOVEMBER 2010

———

N EVER ARGUE WITH THE MAN WITH the microphone. On several occasions, I've been invited to appear on radio or television programs for interviews by controversial hosts. For the most part, I have declined these interviews because of the format in which they are structured. Though they promise the opportunity for open debate, such debate is rarely forthcoming. There are certain hosts who are ruthless in their treatment of their guests and get away with it because of the power of the microphone. Whoever controls the microphone controls the game. If the host makes a particular statement, the guest must rely on the mercy of the person with the microphone in order to offer a rebuttal to the host. At any time in the course of such discussions, the comments of the guest can be silenced.

I use this illustration frequently in talking with students who encounter hostile professors in college or in seminary. In their efforts to defend the truth claims of Christianity, students often valiantly charge in where angels fear to tread and are attacked viciously by the professor. I try to communicate to them that, as valiant as their attempts may be, they are in most cases exercises in futility because the professor controls the discussion. The classroom is not a place where open debate is usually encouraged. To the contrary, on the campuses of many universities and even seminaries, open season has been declared on Christian students. For some reason, it seems that professors in such settings take delight in trying to undermine the faith of their students. This is one reason why the New Testament warns us that not many should become teachers, for with teaching comes a greater judgment.

At the same time, our Lord Himself warned against those who bring harm to one of His little ones. In most cases, it is easy for a man or woman with a doctorate and years of experience in higher education to humiliate a student, no matter how strong the student's faith is or how articulate the student may be. It's a mismatch, and it's a mismatch that unscrupulous teachers greedily seize upon.

These teachers explain their tactics by saying they're simply trying to open the closed minds of the students or to bring them to deliverance from their slavery to outmoded ideas. The excuses are as endless as they are mindless. In the first week of my first year attending seminary, a professor was sharply critical of a student for coming to the seminary with too many preconceived ideas. The idea the seminary student brought with him that the professor described as an unwarranted preconception was his belief in the deity of Christ. I was shocked when I saw a student being humiliated for having the audacity to come to seminary with the idea already formed in his mind that Christ is the incarnate Son of God. The real question, however, was this one: Why was the professor, who was supposedly committed to the creedal statements of the seminary, denying the deity of Christ in such a situation? But this type of thing happens far more regularly than many people realize.

When I was on the faculty of a Christian college many years ago, I had a constant stream of students come to me with questions about the relationship between the truths affirmed in the New Testament about Christ and similar mythological affirmations found in the famous work *Metamorphoses* by the poet Ovid. It became clear that it was the delight of the English professor in his humanities class, which included a study of Ovid, to draw parallels between the New Testament teachings about Jesus and the myths presented in *Metamorphoses*.

I had the opportunity to meet in a friendly atmosphere with this professor over coffee in the student union, and I began asking him questions about his knowledge of the biblical worldview compared to the worldview of Ovid. I pointed out the remarkable number of differences between Ovid's worldview and that of the New Testament, which the professor acknowledged existed, and I said: "It's just simply not good teaching to point out similarities between different positions without at the same time acknowledging the significant differences between them. In your critique of Christianity, you have failed to mention these differences, which is not a sound approach to the matter." He was contrite and committed not to do that anymore. But again, that was one incident out of literally tens of thousands that take place every year on campuses, not only at secular universities, but at church-related colleges and even in theological seminaries, as I've already mentioned.

One of the problems we have here is the criteria we use when choosing colleges or universities to attend in the first place. So often parents are impressed by the beauty of the campus of the particular institution or by their own remembrance of the commitment of the institution a generation ago, overlooking the reality that the approach to Christianity changes in various institutions as the faculty changes. The most significant barometer for choosing any kind of institution of higher learning is not the beauty of its campus but its faculty.

If you're looking to send your children to an institution that has a Christian history or a Christian relationship, do not assume that the current faculty is fully persuaded of the truth claims of Christianity. You may indeed be throwing your children into the fire of a crucible they are not expecting and are not really prepared to withstand. I am not for educating people in a sheltered environment where there is no interaction with the secular mindset and with pagan worldviews, but we need to be fully prepared to understand when and where those worldviews come into collision with Christianity and how to avoid collisions that may be disastrous.

DO WE BELIEVE
THE WHOLE GOSPEL?

DECEMBER 2010

———

*U*NBELIEF. THIS ONE WORD EXPRESSES the judgment Emil Brunner, the Swiss "crisis theologian," used to describe nineteenth-century liberal theology. The rise of such liberalism was a conscious synthesis between naturalism in the world of philosophy and historic Christianity. Liberalism sought to de-supernaturalize the Christian faith and to restrict the modern significance of Jesus and the New Testament to ethical considerations, particularly with respect to the needs of human beings, and especially with respect to their material needs.

This provoked a significant dilemma for the organized church, first in Europe and then in America. If an institution repudiates the very foundation upon which it is built and for which it exists, what happens to the billions of dollars' worth of church property and its numerous ordained professionals? The clergy were left with nothing to preach except social concerns. In order to maintain a reason for the continued existence of Christianity as an organized religion, nineteenth-century liberalism turned to a new gospel, dubbed the "social gospel." This was a gospel that focused on considerations of humanitarianism and had at the core of its agenda a commitment to "social justice."

The use of the term "social justice" involved an ironic twisting of words. What was in view in this philosophy was basically the redistribution of wealth, following the template of socialism. The false assumption of this so-called social justice was that material wealth can be gained only by means of the exploitation of the poor. Ergo, for a society to be just, the wealth must be redistributed by government authority. In reality, this so-called social justice degenerated into social injustice, where penalties were levied on those who were legitimately productive and non-productivity was rewarded—a bizarre concept of justice indeed.

The rise in importance of the social gospel provoked a controversy known in church history as the "modernist-fundamentalist controversy," which raged in the early years of the twentieth century. This controversy witnessed an unholy dichotomy between two poles of Christian concern. On the one hand, there was the classic concern of personal redemption accomplished by Christ through His atoning death on the cross, which brought reconciliation for those who put their trust in Jesus. On the other hand there was the consideration of the material well-being of human beings in this world right now. It included the consideration of clothing the naked, feeding the hungry, giving shelter to the homeless, and caring for the poor.

Many evangelicals at this period in history, in order to preserve the central significance of the proclamation of the gospel of Jesus Christ, gave renewed emphasis to evangelism. In many cases, this emphasis upon evangelism was done to the exclusion of the other pole of biblical concern, namely, mercy ministry to those who were poor, afflicted, and suffering. So glaring was the dichotomy between liberal and evangelical concerns that, sadly, many evangelicals began to distance themselves from any involvement in mercy ministries, lest their activities be construed as a surrender to liberalism.

The fallacy of the false dilemma takes two important truths and forces one to choose between them. The assumption of the either/or fallacy is that of two particular matters, only one is true while the other is false; therefore, one is required to choose between the true and the false. The either/or fallacy that stood before the church in this period was either the gospel of personal redemption or the gospel of social concern for the material welfare of human beings.

Even a cursory reading of the New Testament, however, makes it clear that the concerns of Jesus and of the New Testament writers cannot be reduced to an either/or dilemma. The problem with this fallacy, as with all fallacies, is that truth becomes severely distorted. The New Testament does not allow for this false dilemma. The choice that the church has is never between personal salvation and mercy ministry. It is rather a both/and proposition. Neither pole can be properly swallowed by the other. To reduce Christianity either to a program of social welfare or to a program of personal redemption results in a truncated gospel that is a profound distortion.

Historically, before the outbreak of nineteenth-century liberalism, the church did not seem to struggle with this false dichotomy. For centuries, the church understood her task as both to proclaim the saving gospel of the atoning work of Christ and, at the same time, to follow Jesus' example of ministry to the blind, to the deaf, to the imprisoned, to the hungry, to the homeless, and to the poor. The ministry of the church, if it is to be healthy, must always be firmly committed to both dimensions of the biblical mandate, that we may be faithful to Christ Himself. If we reject either the ministry of personal redemption or of mercy to the afflicted, we express "unbelief."

KNOWING SCRIPTURE

JANUARY 2011

———

I T HAS OFTEN BEEN CHARGED THAT THE Bible can't be trusted because people can make it say anything they want it to say. This charge would be true if the Bible were not the objective Word of God, if it were simply a wax nose, able to be shaped, twisted, and distorted to teach one's own precepts. The charge would be true if it were not an offense to God the Holy Spirit to read into sacred Scripture what is not there. However, the idea that the Bible can teach anything we want it to is not true if we approach the Scriptures humbly, trying to hear what the Bible says for itself.

Sometimes systematic theology is rejected because it is seen as an unwarranted imposition of a philosophical system on the Scriptures. It is seen as a preconceived system, a Procrustean bed into which the Scriptures must be forced by hacking off limbs and appendages to make it fit. However, the appropriate approach to systematic theology recognizes that the Bible itself contains a system of truth, and it is the task of the theologian not to impose a system upon the Bible, but to build a theology by understanding the system that the Bible teaches.

At the time of the Reformation, to stop unbridled, speculative, and fanciful interpretations of Scripture, the Reformers set forth the fundamental axiom that should govern all biblical interpretation. It is called the analogy of faith, which basically means that Holy Scripture is its own interpreter. In other words, we are to interpret Scripture according to Scripture. That is, the supreme arbiter in interpreting the meaning of a particular verse in Scripture is the overall teaching of the Bible.

Behind the principle of the analogy of faith is the prior confidence that the Bible is the inspired Word of God. If it is the Word of God, it must therefore be consistent and coherent. Cynics, however, say that consistency is the hobgoblin of little minds. If that were true, then we would have to say that the smallest mind of all is the mind of God. But there is nothing inherently small or weak to be found in consistency. If it is the Word of God, one may justly expect the entire Bible to be coherent, intelligible, and unified. Our assumption is that God, because of His omniscience, would never be guilty of contradicting Himself. It is therefore slanderous to the Holy Spirit to choose an interpretation of a particular passage that unnecessarily brings that passage into conflict with that which He has revealed elsewhere. So the governing principle of Reformed hermeneutics or interpretation is the analogy of faith.

A second principle that governs an objective interpretation of Scripture is called the *sensus literalis*. Many times people have said to me, incredulously, "You don't interpret the Bible literally, do you?" I never answer the question by saying, "Yes," nor do I ever answer the question by saying, "No." I always answer the question by saying, "Of course, what other way is there to interpret the Bible?" What is meant by *sensus literalis* is not that every text in the Scriptures is given a "woodenly literal" interpretation, but rather that we must interpret the Bible in the sense in which it is written. Parables are interpreted as parables, symbols as symbols, poetry as poetry, didactic literature as didactic literature, historical narrative as historical narrative, occasional letters as occasional letters. That principle of literal interpretation is the same principle we use to interpret any written source responsibly.

The principle of literal interpretation gives us another rule, namely that the Bible in one sense is to be read like any other book. Though the Bible is not like any other book in that it carries with it the authority of divine inspiration, nevertheless, the inspiration of the Holy Spirit over a written text does not turn verbs into nouns or nouns into verbs. No special, secret, arcane, esoteric meaning is poured into a text simply because it's divinely inspired. Nor is there any such mystical ability we call "Holy Ghost Greek." No, the Bible is to be interpreted according to the ordinary rules of language.

Closely related to this point is the principle that the implicit must be interpreted by the explicit, rather than the explicit interpreted by the implicit. This particular rule of interpretation is violated constantly. For example, we read in John 3:16 that "whoever believes in him should not perish but have eternal life," and many of us conclude that since the Bible teaches that anyone who believes shall be saved, it therefore implies that anyone can, without the prior regenerative work of the Holy Spirit, exercise belief. That is, since the call to believe is given to everyone, it implies that everyone has the natural ability to fulfill the call. Yet the same gospel writer has Jesus explaining to us three chapters later that no one can come to Jesus unless it is given to him of the Father (6:65). That is, our moral ability to come to Christ is explicitly and specifically taught to be lacking apart from the sovereign grace of God. Therefore, all of the implications that suggest otherwise must be subsumed under the explicit teaching, rather than forcing the explicit teaching into conformity to implications that we draw from the text.

Finally, it is always important to interpret obscure passages by those that are clear. Though we affirm the basic clarity of sacred Scripture, we do not at the same time say that all passages are equally clear. Numerous heresies have developed when people have forced conformity to the obscure passages rather than to the clear passages, distorting the whole message of Scripture. If something is unclear in one part of Scripture, it probably is made clear elsewhere in Scripture. When we have two passages in Scripture that we can interpret in various ways, we want always to interpret the Bible in such a way as to not violate the basic principle of Scripture's unity and integrity.

These are simply a few of the basic, practical principles of biblical interpretation that I set forth years ago in my book *Knowing Scripture.* I mention that book here because so many people have expressed to me how helpful it has been to guide them into a responsible practice of biblical interpretation. Learning the principles of interpretation is exceedingly helpful to guide us in our own study.

THE GOODNESS OF THE LAW

MARCH 2011

———

"**O**H HOW I LOVE YOUR LAW!**" (Ps. 119:97). What a strange statement of affection. Why would anyone direct his love toward the
law of God? The law limits our choices, restricts our freedom,
torments our consciences, and pushes us down with a mighty weight
that cannot be overcome, and yet the psalmist declares his affection for
the law in passionate terms. He calls the law sweeter than honey to his
mouth (Ps. 119:3).

What is it about the law of God that can provoke such affection? In
the first place, the law is not an abstract set of rules and regulations. The
law reflects the will of the Lawgiver, and in that regard it is intensely
personal. The law reflects to the creature the perfect will of the Creator
and at the same time reveals the character of that being whose law it is.
The law of God proceeds from God's being and reflects His character.
When the psalmist speaks of his affection for the law, he makes no division between the law of God and the Word of God. Just as the Christian
loves the Word of God, so we ought to love the law of God, for the Word
of God is indeed the law of God.

The second reason why the psalmist has such a positive view of the law
is that the law, by revealing God's character, exposes our fallenness. It is
the mirror that reflects our own images—warts and all—and becomes
the pedagogue, the schoolmaster that drives us to Christ. The law does
not drive us out of the kingdom but it ushers us into the kingdom by
directing us to the One who alone is able to fulfill its demands.

God's law also is a guide for us. The psalmist calls it "a lamp to my feet
and a light to my path" (119:105). The imagery here suggests a person
walking on a narrow path on a moonless night, groping in the dark to

find the correct way. A wrong turn could result in a fall from a precipice or tripping into painful brambles. But the law serves as a lamp to show us where we should place our feet as we walk. It shows us how not to stray into the way of destruction. In that respect, the law with its light grants wisdom to one who meditates upon it. By this wisdom, we discern what righteousness is and what is the right thing to do in the complex situations of our lives. The light that shines from the law reveals the snares that have been set in our pathway by the enemy and gives us the wisdom to avoid them. It becomes a hiding place, a shield, and the source of our hope.

The law also acts as a restraint upon us. Our nature in the fall is one of lawlessness. The power of conversion rescues us from bondage to sin, but it does not deliver us from all temptations. We need the restraint of law to keep our sinful impulses and fallen inclinations in check. In this regard, we may use the metaphor of the bridle. The bridle and the bit are put on the horse so that the horse can be kept from running wildly into destruction. Speed limits on the highway do not stop speeding, but they do produce a certain restraint to keep impulses under control.

The most wonderful function of the law, however, is that it shows us what is pleasing to God. The godly man is the one who meditates on the law day and night (Ps. 1:2), and he does so because he finds his delight therein. By delighting in the precepts of God, he becomes like a tree planted by rivers of living water, bringing forth its fruit in its season (Ps. 1:3). Our Lord said, "If you love Me keep My commandments" (John 14:15), but we cannot show that love for Him unless we know what the commandments are. A knowledge of the law of God gives to us the pattern of loving obedience. If we love the Lord, we must also love His law. To love God and despise His law is a contradiction that must never be the profile of the Christian. The psalmist says that God hates the double-minded man, and the double-minded man says that he loves God while at the same time he eschews the law of the Lord (Ps. 119:113). The psalmist says that the precepts, judgments, and testimonies of God are wonderful because they keep the soul and they preserve us from sins dragging us back into slavery and dominion (v. 129). The law in this regard is redemptive—not that we find our redemption by keeping the law, but that the Redeemer is shown to us through the law.

Finally, the psalmist says, "Your word is very pure; Therefore your servant loves it" (v. 140, NKJV). Those things that are pure, that are perfect, are worthy objects of our affection. All of these functions of the law are seen in the sweetness and the loveliness of the law that God reveals. He gives us His law not to take away our joy but rather that our joy may be full. His law is never given in a context of meanness but in the context of His love. We love the law of God because God loves His law and because that law is altogether lovely.

PREACHING CHRIST

APRIL 2011

————

T HE CHURCH OF THE TWENTY-FIRST CENTURY faces many crises. One of the most serious is the crisis of preaching. Widely diverse philosophies of preaching vie for acceptance among contemporary clergy. Some see the sermon as a fireside chat; others, as a stimulus for psychological health; still others, as a commentary on contemporary politics. But some still view the exposition of sacred Scripture as a necessary ingredient to the office of preaching. In light of these views, it is always helpful to go to the New Testament to seek or glean the method and message found in the biblical record of apostolic preaching.

In the first instance, we must distinguish between two types of preaching. The first has been called *kerygma*; the second, *didachē*. This distinction refers to the difference between proclamation (*kerygma*) and teaching or instruction (*didachē*). It seems that the strategy of the Apostolic church was to win converts by means of the proclamation of the gospel. Once people responded to that gospel, they were baptized and received into the visible church. They then underwent a regular, systematic exposure to the teaching of the Apostles, through regular preaching (homilies) and in particular groups of catechetical instruction. In the initial outreach to the Gentile community, the Apostles did not go into great detail about Old Testament redemptive history. That knowledge was assumed among Jewish audiences, but it was not held among the Gentiles. Nevertheless, even to the Jewish audiences, the central emphasis of the evangelistic preaching was on the announcement that the Messiah had come and ushered in God's kingdom.

If we take time to examine the sermons of the Apostles that are recorded in the book of Acts, we see a somewhat common and familiar structure to them. In this analysis, we can discern the Apostolic *kerygma*, the basic proclamation of the gospel. Here the focus in the preaching was on the person and work of Jesus. The gospel itself was called the gospel of Jesus Christ. The gospel is about Him; it involves the proclamation and declaration of what He accomplished in His life, in His death, and in His resurrection. After the details of His death, resurrection, and ascension to the right hand of God were preached, the apostles called the people to be converted to Christ—to repent of their sins and receive Christ by faith.

When we seek to extrapolate from these examples how the Apostolic church did evangelism, we must ask: What is appropriate for the transfer of Apostolic principles of preaching to the contemporary church? Some churches believe that a person is required to preach the gospel or to communicate the *kerygma* in every sermon preached. This view sees the emphasis in Sunday morning preaching as one of evangelism, of proclaiming the gospel. Many preachers today, however, say they are preaching the gospel on a regular basis when in some cases they have never preached the gospel at all, because what they call the gospel is not the message of the person and work of Christ and how His accomplished work and its benefits can be appropriated to the individual by faith. Rather, the gospel of Christ is exchanged for therapeutic promises of a purposeful life or having personal fulfillment by coming to Jesus. In messages such as these, the focus is on us rather than on Him.

On the other hand, in looking at the pattern of worship in the early church, we see that the weekly assembly of the saints involved a coming together for worship, fellowship, prayer, the celebration of the Lord's Supper, and devotion to the teaching of the Apostles. If we were there, we would see that the Apostolic preaching covered the whole of redemptive history and the sum of divine revelation, not being restricted simply to the evangelistic *kerygma*.

So, again, the *kerygma* is the essential proclamation of the life, death, resurrection, ascension, and rule of Jesus Christ, as well as a call to conversion and repentance. It is this *kerygma* that the New Testament indicates is the power of God unto salvation (Rom. 1:16). There can be no acceptable substitute for it. When the church loses her *kerygma*, she loses her identity.

ANSELM

MAY 2011

———

A NSELM HELD THE POSITION OF archbishop of Canterbury from 1093 to 1109. A Benedictine monk, philosopher, and theologian, he stands as one of the most significant thinkers in the history of the western church.

His influence is not due to the sheer volume of his writings but to his ability to expound profound subjects biblically and thoughtfully in just a few words. In general, the assumption exists that to make a significant contribution to the body of literature that shapes scholarly thought requires the production of massive tomes. Anselm's impact completely overthrows this notion.

His thought has had far-reaching consequences, even to this day. Anselm, more than any of the other thinkers of antiquity, plumbed the depths of the substitutionary, satisfaction view of the atonement. In his book *Cur Deus Homo* (Why the God-man?), he saw the work of Christ on the cross as an act of propitiation by which Jesus satisfied the demands of God's justice. Neither the Devil nor human desires were satisfied, but God Himself. Neither was the wrath of God satisfied so much as His justice, which Anselm defined as His righteousness or rectitude.

Paul writes that in the drama of justification, through the work of Christ, God is both "just and the justifier" (Rom. 3:26). He labors the point that in the atoning work of Jesus God does not simply overlook the sin of fallen humanity and give us a pass. Rather, He ensures His own character is not compromised and thereby establishes His justice. God requires the payment by Christ, as our substitute, to maintain His justice. The cross is simultaneously God's foremost manifestation of justice and grace. His justice is displayed in that Jesus pays for sin, and His grace is seen in that redemption is offered to us through Jesus' work. It is the perfect Mediator who satisfies God's justice and saves God's people.

This truth impacted not only the church's thinking about the atonement but also, unfortunately, the Roman Catholic Church's understanding of the Mass as a repetition of the atoning work of Christ. Rome twisted Anselm's thought to make it fit its sacerdotal system of salvation, using his words in ways Anselm never intended. Thus, the Mass is considered an unbloody sacrifice involving satisfaction.

After *Cur Deus Homo*, the second work for which Anselm is famous is a little book called *Monologion*. In this book, he seeks to answer the question of the relationship between faith and reason. He argues that since revelation is at the foundation of all truth, the Christian begins by believing and trusting in God's revelation. In approaching revelation, the Christian does not abandon the intellect. Instead, he grasps the rational coherence of revelation. This is the ongoing task of the Christian thinker, the starting point of faith. We do not come to a rational understanding of God's revelation before we are able to believe; rather, we must first put our trust in that revelation in order to see its coherence. Anselm's famous slogan was *Credo ut intelligam* ("I believe in order that I may understand").

In this little book, following the process of faith seeking understanding, Anselm works out a cosmological argument for the existence of God. The essence of this argument is that only God, in His creative power, gives us sufficient reason for the existence of the universe. But the cosmological argument has been formulated in many ways and times by many different people.

What makes Anselm stand out in the history of philosophy and apologetics is his extraordinary argument set forth in his third book, *Proslogion.* Anselm desired to give a simple and quick proof for the existence of God based on the nature of God's being. Hence, this proof has been called the ontological argument for the existence of God. It flows from and rests upon an understanding of God's being.

Again basing his assumptions on the revelation by which God has made Himself known to all people, Anselm argues that every person has some idea of God. The idea that we have of God is not that of a mere mythical structure, but of a God who truly exists. There is a sense in which the very idea of God carries with it the idea of His existence. In an interesting twist of words, Anselm stated the argument this way: God is that than which nothing greater can be conceived. Since we conceive of God, we must conceive of Him as existing in reality and not just in the mind. Anselm understood that the mind is able to consider things that do not exist, but the idea of God being that than which no greater can be conceived, cannot be conceived as nonexistent. If we are conceiving of God simply as a formal concept but not attributing to Him existence, we have not reached the idea of Anselm's God. This is because there would still be a being greater than a being that exists only in the mind and not in reality. That being, than which no greater can be conceived, must exist in reality as well as the mind or it is not that being than which no greater can be conceived.

This is the kind of argument that has given philosophers Excedrin headaches for centuries, but the impact of it remains powerful, as does the impact of the body of work of the ancient archbishop of Canterbury.

DEFINING THE DEBATE

JUNE 2011

———

T HE QUESTION OF SABBATH OBSERVATION, historically, has provoked many debates and controversies involving separate issues. The first great debate about the Sabbath is whether, as an Old Testament ordinance particularly emphasized in the Mosaic covenant, it is still obligatory in the context of new covenant Christianity. Augustine, for example, believed that nine of the Ten Commandments (the so-called "moral law" of the Old Testament) were still intact and imposed obligations upon the Christian church. His lone exception was the commandment with respect to the Sabbath day. Since Paul spoke about keeping Sabbaths or not keeping Sabbaths as a matter adiaphorous (indifferent), Augustine was persuaded that the Old Testament Sabbath law had been abrogated. Others have argued that because the Sabbath was instituted originally not in the Mosaic economy but in creation, it maintains its status of moral law as long as the creation is intact.

The second major controversy is the question about the day of the week on which the Sabbath is to be observed. Some insist that since the Sabbath was instituted on the seventh day of creation, when God rested from His labors, and since the Old Testament Israelites celebrated the Sabbath on the seventh day of the week, which would be Saturday, we should follow that pattern. Others have insisted that the New Testament changed the Sabbath to the first day of the week because of the significance of the resurrection of Jesus on that day. They also point to the New Testament practice of Christians coming together on Sunday as the Lord's Day for worship. The argument focuses on whether the Sabbath is a cyclical command that requires worship and rest on every seventh day or whether it is specified to a particular day of the week. John Calvin argued that it would be legitimate to have the Sabbath day on any day if all of the churches would agree, because the principle in view was the regular assembling of the saints for corporate worship and for the observation of rest.

Within the Reformed tradition, the most significant controversy that has appeared through the ages is the question of how the Sabbath is to be observed. There are two major positions within the Reformed tradition on this question. To make matters simple, we will refer to them as the Continental view of the Sabbath and the Puritan view of the Sabbath. Both views acknowledge that the Sabbath is still in effect. Both views agree that the Sabbath is a time for corporate worship. Both agree that the Sabbath is a day of rest when believers are to abstain from unnecessary commerce. But two areas are in dispute between the two schools and the most important of these is the question of recreation. Is recreation a legitimate form of rest-taking, or is recreation something that mars a sacred observation of the Sabbath day?

The Puritan view argues against the acceptability of recreation on the Sabbath day. The text most often cited to support this view is Isaiah 58:13–14 and following: "If you turn back your foot from the Sabbath, from doing your pleasure on my holy day, and call the Sabbath a delight and the holy day of the Lord honorable; if you honor it, not going your own ways, or seeking your own pleasure, or talking idly; then you shall take delight in the Lord, and I will make you ride on the heights of the earth; I will feed you with the heritage of Jacob your father, for the mouth of the Lord has spoken."

The crux of the matter in this passage is the prophetic critique of people doing their own pleasure on the Sabbath day. The assumption that many make with respect to this text is that doing one's own pleasure must refer to recreation. If this is the case, the prophet Isaiah was adding new dimensions to the Old Testament law with respect to Sabbath-keeping. Whereas the rest of the Old Testament law is virtually silent with respect to recreation, this text in Isaiah is cited to indicate a further revelation from God about Sabbath observance—a prohibition of recreation.

There is another way to understand Isaiah 58, however, following the thinking of those who hold the Continental view of the Sabbath. The distinction in Isaiah 58 is between doing what is pleasing to God and doing what is pleasing to ourselves in opposition to what is pleasing to God. Presumably, what is in view in the prophetic critique is God's judgment against the Israelites for violating the Mosaic law with respect to the Sabbath day, particularly regarding involvement in commerce. There were Israelites who wanted to be able to buy and sell seven days a week, not simply six days a week. Therefore, they violated the Sabbath commandment by seeking their own pleasure, which was to do business on the Sabbath rather than to do that which was pleasing to God. According to this view, the text has nothing to say directly or indirectly about recreation on the Sabbath day.

There is an old story, which may be apocryphal, that when John Knox came to Geneva to visit John Calvin at his home on the Sabbath, he was shocked to find Calvin engaged in lawn bowling. If the story is true, it may indicate that the theologian most devoted to Sabbath-keeping in history, Calvin, did not see recreation as a violation of the Lord's Day, but as a part of the rest-taking or recreation that is to be part of this day. Recreation would never have been acceptable to Calvin if it had interrupted or supplanted the time devoted to worship on the Sabbath.

One other point of debate remains between the two sides on this issue. It has to do with works of mercy performed on the Sabbath. The example of Jesus is cited, that on the Sabbath He engaged not only in worship and rest but also in works of mercy. Such works brought Him into conflict with the Pharisees over the question of Sabbath-keeping. Some have drawn the conclusion that since Jesus performed works of mercy on the Sabbath, the Christian is obligated to do the same. However, the fact that Jesus did works of mercy on the Sabbath, though it clearly reveals that it is lawful to do so on the Sabbath, does not obligate us to do such works on the Sabbath. That is to say, Jesus' example teaches us that we *may* do works of mercy on the Sabbath but not that we *must* do such works on the Sabbath.

All of these issues continue to be examined and debated as the church seeks to understand how God is best honored on this day.

THE BONDS OF BROTHERHOOD

JULY 2011

---

*F*RATERNITY ... WHAT DOES THIS word mean? It can refer to several distinct types of associations or relationships, and the church can learn valuable lessons by exploring these in more depth. The term *fraternity* may prompt us to recall the motto of the French Revolution: "Liberty, Fraternity, Equality." Fraternity, along with equality and liberty, ranked right at the top of the concerns of that revolution. The term may cause us to think of college campus groups such as those depicted in the radical fraternity film *Animal House*. Beyond the college level, there is a wide variety of organizations of men in this world that are "fraternal orders," such as the Elks, police groups, and various service clubs.

The idea of fraternity is also manifested in the field of competitive sports, particularly with respect to team sports. The saying "There is no 'I' in team" is a cliché because it is so true. For teams to function efficiently and effectively, there must be fraternity and teamwork. Again and again we witness superstar players in the realm of professional sports being traded by their clubs because they create such a destructive atmosphere in the locker room.

No team can function well strictly on the strength of a single individual. In basketball, for example, players who are ballhogs destroy the spirit of teamwork. If the ball is passed to a ballhog, he is very unlikely to pass it to a teammate, but more likely to take an ill-advised shot. In football, a play run by the offense involves blocking, running, passing, tackling, and other dimensions of the sport. The whole affair is an orchestration of the various elements. Even baseball operates on the basis of a team working in harmony. Babe Ruth never won a game by himself.

Ironically, when we look at the arena of athletics, we see that the idea of fraternity exists not only in team sports but also in the context of individual sports. Perhaps the supreme example of an individual sport is boxing. It is *mano a mano*, one man against another. There is no tag team in the boxing ring. The boxer stands toe-to-toe against his opponent with his support systems in his corner. In the ring—the battlefield—he must fight alone. How many times have we seen the drama of a tense bout between two equally-matched opponents, each doing his best to knock the other one out or to do enough bodily harm to win the fight on points? And yet, when the final bell rings, we often see these two gladiators come to the center of the ring and hug with an obvious sense of affection. Why do they do this? It is because a fighter is trained in his individual sport not only to compete with his opponent but to respect him. When he is engaged in a match that tests him to the ultimate degree, he comes away exhausted, battered, maybe even beaten, but nevertheless still possessing enormous respect for his opponent. There is a kind of fellowship, a kind of fraternity, that only individual gladiators such as these men understand.

The same thing may be seen in golf, even though most matches test individual ability. From time to time, golfers join together as teammates, and there is the sense among them that they are part of a fraternity that is higher than each one in his individual accomplishments.

But there is no fraternity as important or as significant as the church and the communion of saints. Obviously, the church is not an organization exclusive to men, so perhaps we can speak of the church as both a fraternity and a sorority. But in any case, the idea of team participation is clearly present. There is no such thing as a one-person church.

Certainly we are not saved or justified by the faith of our families, friends, or associates. In one sense, redemption is an intensely individual matter. But once we are justified, once we are in a state of salvation, we are immediately put into a group. We are immediately put into the church.

The church exists as a corporate body. There is a corporate solidarity that defines the identity of the New Testament church. There is no room for rugged individualism. No one has been given all the gifts of the Holy Spirit; no one has an opportunity to "hog" the ministry.

What is needed in the church is a kind of familial relationship that is a brotherhood and a sisterhood. It can be learned in part outside of the church in other endeavors, such as the world of sports or even the battlefield. But the deepest knitting together of human beings for a common cause, a common faith, and a common Lord exists in the church of Jesus Christ.

THE UNHOLY PURSUIT OF GOD IN *MOBY DICK*

AUGUST 2011

I
T SEEMS THAT EVERY TIME a writer picks up a pen or turns on his word processor to compose a literary work of fiction, deep in his bosom resides the hope that somehow he will create the Great American Novel. Too late. That feat has already been accomplished and is as far out of reach for new novelists as is Joe DiMaggio's fifty-six-game hitting streak or Pete Rose's record of cumulative career hits for a rookie baseball player. The Great American Novel was written more than a hundred and fifty years ago by Herman Melville. This novel, the one that has been unsurpassed by any other, is *Moby Dick*.

My personal copy of *Moby Dick* is a leather-bound collector's edition produced by Easton Press under the rubric "The Hundred Greatest Books Ever Written."

Note that the claim here is not that Moby Dick is one of the hundred greatest books written in English, but rather that it is one of the hundred greatest books written in any language.

Its greatness may be seen not in its sometimes cumbersome literary structure or its excursions into technicalia about the nature and function of whales (cetology). No, its greatness is found in its unparalleled theological symbolism. This symbolism is sprinkled abundantly throughout the novel, particularly in the identities of certain individuals who are assigned biblical names. Among the characters are Ahab, Ishmael, and Elijah, and the names *Jeroboam* and *Rachel* ("who was seeking her lost children") are given to two of the ships in the story.

In a personal letter to Nathaniel Hawthorne upon completing this novel, Melville said, "I have written an evil book." What is it about the book that Melville considered evil? I think the answer to that question lies in the meaning of the central symbolic character of the novel, Moby Dick, the great white whale.

Melville experts and scholars come to different conclusions about the meaning of the great white whale. Many see this brutish animal as evil because it had inflicted great personal damage on Ahab in an earlier encounter. Ahab lost his leg, which was replaced by the bone of a lesser whale. Some argue that Moby Dick is Melville's symbol of the incarnation of evil itself. Certainly this is the view of the whale held by Captain Ahab himself. Ahab is driven by a monomaniacal hatred for this creature, this brute that left him permanently damaged both in body and soul. He cries out, "He heaps me," indicating the depth of the hatred and fury he feels toward this beast. Some have accepted Ahab's view that the whale is a monstrous evil as that of Melville himself.

Other scholars have been convinced that the whale is not a symbol of evil but the symbol of God Himself. In this interpretation, Ahab's pursuit of the whale is not a righteous pursuit of God but natural man's futile attempt in his hatred of God to destroy the omnipotent deity. I favor this second view. It was the view held by one of my college professors—one of the five leading Melville scholars in the world at the time I studied under him. My senior philosophy research paper in college was titled "The Existential Implications of Melville's *Moby Dick*." In that paper, which I cannot reproduce in this brief article, I tried to set forth the theological structure of the narrative.

I believe that the greatest chapter ever written in the English language is the chapter of *Moby Dick* titled "The Whiteness of the Whale." Here we gain an insight into the profound symbolism that Melville employs in his novel. He explores how whiteness is used in history, in religion, and in nature. The terms he uses to describe the appearance of whiteness in these areas include *elusive, ghastly,* and *transcendent horror,* as well as *sweet, honorable,* and *pure.* All of these are descriptive terms that are symbolized in one way or another by the presence of whiteness. In this chapter Melville writes,

But not yet have we solved the incantation of this whiteness, and learned why it appeals with such power to the soul; and more strange and far more portentous—why, as we have seen, it is at once the most meaning symbol of spiritual things, nay, the very veil of the Christian's Deity; and yet should be as it is, the intensifying agent in things the most appalling to mankind. Is it that by its indefiniteness it shadows forth the heartless voids and immensities of the universe, and thus stabs us from behind with the thought of annihilation, when beholding the white depths of the milky way? Or is it, that as in essence whiteness is not so much a colour as the visible absence of colour; and at the same time the concrete of all colours; is it for these reasons that there is such a dumb blankness, full of meaning, in a wide landscape of snows—a colourless, all-colour of atheism from which we shrink?

He then concludes the chapter with these words: "And of all these things, the albino whale was the symbol. Wonder ye then at the fiery hunt?"

If the whale embodies everything that is symbolized by whiteness—that which is terrifying; that which is pure; that which is excellent; that which is horrible and ghastly; that which is mysterious and incomprehensible—does he not embody those traits that are found in the fullness of the perfections in the being of God Himself?

Who can survive the pursuit of such a being if the pursuit is driven by hostility? Only those who have experienced the sweetness of reconciling grace can look at the overwhelming power, sovereignty, and immutability of a transcendent God and find there peace rather than a drive for vengeance. Read *Moby Dick*, and then read it again.

9/11 TEN YEARS LATER

SEPTEMBER 2011

———

A FULL DECADE HAS PASSED SINCE AMERICA suffered the tragedy of 9/11. Ten years ago, I repeatedly heard the question raised:
"Where was God in all of this? Where was God on 9/11 when the
planes crashed into the twin towers in New York, the Pentagon in Washington, D.C., and a field near Shanksville, Pennsylvania?" My answer then
was the same as it is now: God was in the precise place on 9/11 that He
was on the day before and the day after. He was on His throne then and
continues to be on His throne now because He is the Lord God omnipotent
who reigns. He reigns day in and day out in consistent manifestation of
His immutable sovereignty. God is immutable, unchanging, even though
people and cultures continually change.

When we look at the casualties on 9/11, we see that they were light
compared with the casualties suffered in bloody battles during previous
times of war. They were light compared to the casualties of Antietam and
Gettysburg. They were light compared to the casualties of Hiroshima
and the Battle of the Bulge. The victims were few compared to those
who were slaughtered in the Holocaust and in the purges under Joseph
Stalin in Russia.

But the emotional scars have been enormous in our culture. The most
vivid symbol of the changes caused by that cultural crisis may be the
lines at airports as people undergo security scanning, an intrusion into
their privacy and schedules, before they can board planes for travel. We
also see it in the security that surrounds other modes of transportation
and public events.

In the days, weeks, and months immediately following 9/11, appealing
to God to intervene for the welfare of our country became very common. Suddenly, calls for the separation of church and state, particularly
the separation of the state from God, were set aside as we looked to the

Creator to help bail us out from the consequences of the terrorist attack on our homeland. Bumper stickers with the request "God bless America" seemed to be ubiquitous.

When two evangelical leaders, Pat Robertson and the late Jerry Falwell, suggested that 9/11 may have been a divine judgment upon our sinful culture, they were hissed, booed, and shouted down to the point that they issued public recantations. The American psyche has no place for a God who judges people or nations. God can bless us, but God forbid He ever judges us.

We are like Habakkuk, who, in his consternation over the fact that God used a foreign power to chasten His own people, stationed himself in a watchtower, demanding an answer from God as to how He could allow such wickedness to prevail. Unlike Habakkuk's reaction when God answered that question in His Holy Word, our lips do not quiver, our legs do not shake, our bellies do not tremble, nor does rottenness enter our bones (Hab. 3:16). Rather than repent in dust and ashes before a holy God, we continue to shake our fists in His face, demanding a more benevolent providence from His hand.

But God does not say to us as Americans: "My country right or wrong." God requires nations as well as individuals to repent of their attempts to be autonomous, sovereign rulers, trying to displace Him. Any nation that seeks to supplant God's sovereignty with its own is doomed. It is doomed to failure, it is doomed to destruction, and it is doomed to insignificance.

Many things have changed in the last ten years, but some have not. Saddam Hussein is gone, but terrorism is still here. Osama bin Laden is dead, but there still is no peace in the Middle East. Islam has grown exponentially in the West, but it has demonstrated again and again that it is, in fact, not a religion of peace. Its symbol today is the symbol it has had from its beginning—the scimitar or sword. This symbol stands in vivid contrast to the cross, the symbol of the Christian faith. Islam has a theology that glorifies conquest; Christianity has a theology of the cross. In Islam, it is still a virtue to slay an infidel, and this virtue is sought by suicide bombers around the world. But in God's sight, it is still a virtue to love our enemies and to pray for those who deceitfully use us.

My fear is that we haven't learned very much from 9/11. On 9/11, ten years ago, more babies were destroyed in the wombs of their mothers than people were killed in the terrorist attack in New York. That destruction continues to this day. The greatest attacks on the sanctity of life come not from al-Qaeda but from those who destroy their young. God will not continue to tolerate any nation that practices that culture of death and barbarism.

What is most tragic is that when we were given a wake-up call ten years ago on 9/11, we pushed the snooze button and went back to sleep.

"The American psyche has no place for a God who judges people or nations. God can bless us, but God forbid He ever judges us."

DEATH DOES NOT

OCTOBER 2011

———

T**HE GUNS OF SECULAR NATURALISM,** when aimed at the Christian faith, resemble not so much shotguns as carefully aimed rifles. The chief target of the naturalist is the biblical doctrine of creation. If the doctrine of creation falls, all of Judeo-Christianity falls with it. Every skeptic understands that. Thus the constant shooting at Genesis 1.

But along with the assault against divine creation comes an assault against the biblical teaching of a historical Adam who is involved in a historical fall, the result of which is the entrance of death into the world. If Adam can be confined to the genre of mythology and the fall set aside with him, then we see death as a purely natural phenomenon with no relationship to sin.

Much is at stake with the biblical teaching of the fall because this doctrine is linked to the doctrine of redemption. The historical function of the first Adam is matched and conquered by the historical life of the last Adam, Jesus Christ.

In the eighteenth century, when Jonathan Edwards wrote his lengthy treatise on original sin, he argued not simply from biblical teaching. He also maintained that if the Bible itself were completely silent about a historical fall, natural reason would have to suggest that idea based on the reality of the universal presence of sin. If sin is simply a result of bad decisions that some people make, we would assume that at least 50 percent of the people born in this world would choose the right path rather than the sinful one that is so damaging to our humanity. The fact that 100 percent of the human race falls into sin indicates that there must be an inherent moral defect in the race. Of course, Edwards points to the fall, a historical event, to account for this universal fatal flaw.

In the Genesis account, we are told that the soul that sins will die. In His warning to our original parents with respect to disobedience, God declared that "the day that you eat of it you shall surely die" (Gen. 2:17). But the record goes on to say that the day Adam and Eve disobeyed their Maker, they did not experience the fullness of what the Greek translation of the Old Testament calls *thanatos*—physical death. Because of this, some have argued that the death that God promised was not physical death but rather spiritual death.

To be sure, spiritual death set in the very day that Adam and Eve sinned. But the fact that they did not experience physical death that day was not a result of God being lax regarding His warnings and judgments. Rather, it was a result of God's tempering His justice with mercy and allowing for the redemption of His fallen creatures, even though Adam and Eve were still ultimately destined to succumb to physical death.

Since the fall, every human being born into this world as a natural son of Adam arrives "DOA." He is "dead on arrival" in a spiritual sense when he is born. But this spiritual death is not the same as biological death, though biological death is also the inevitable destiny of every sinning person. So, though we arrive "DOA" in a spiritual sense, we nevertheless arrive biologically alive. We live out our days on this planet on death row, living under the burden of the death sentence that is imposed on us for sin.

In Romans 5, Paul links the entrance of death into the world to sin. In verses 12–14 he writes,

> Therefore, just as sin came into the world through one man, and death through sin, and so death spread to all men because all sinned—for sin indeed was in the world before the law was given, but sin is not counted where there is no law. Yet death reigned from Adam to Moses, even over those whose sinning was not like the transgression of Adam, who was a type of the one who was to come.

Later, in verse 17, Paul continues, "For if, because of one man's trespass, death reigned through that one man, much more will those who receive the abundance of grace and the free gift of righteousness reign in life through the one man Jesus Christ." Here Paul is arguing that even though the Mosaic law had not yet appeared on tablets of stone at Mount Sinai, nevertheless God had written His law so indelibly on each human heart that this law was present even before the Ten Commandments. The reason that Paul argues for that reality is because death reigned from Adam until Moses. Since death is the penalty for sin, and sin is defined in terms of transgression of law, the conclusion the Apostle stresses is that death came into the world because of the violation of the law of God.

When the contrast between the first Adam and the last Adam, Jesus Christ, is worked out in the New Testament, we see in the work of Christ the conquest over the last enemy—death. The Puritan Divine John Owen wrote a classic book titled *The Death of Death in the Death of Christ.* Owen was saying that, in Christ's death, He took upon Himself the curse that is inseparably linked to the punitive measure of death itself. Yet for those who put their trust in Christ, that curse is removed, so that now, for all who are in Christ, death is no longer a curse. Its sting has been removed. The mockery of the grave has been silenced and now death is merely a transition from this life to the next. The contrast that is given in the New Testament is not that this life is bad and the next life is good. On the contrary, the apostle Paul says that this life is good, but to die and to be with Christ is better. So death represents for the believer a gain, indeed, an extraordinary gain.

When we close our eyes in death, we do not cease to be alive; rather, we experience a continuation of personal consciousness. No person is more conscious, more aware, and more alert than when he passes through the veil from this world into the next. Far from falling asleep, we are awakened to glory in all of its significance. For the believer, death does not have the last word. Death has surrendered to the conquering power of the One who was resurrected as the firstborn of many brethren.

AMEN

NOVEMBER 2011

———

A ND ALL THE PEOPLE SAID ... "Amen!" The "amen corner" has had an important place in the life of the church throughout the ages. However, it is rare to find such a spot among Presbyterians. We are known as God's frozen chosen for a reason. It has been said that the Methodists like to shout "Fire," the Baptists like to shout "Water," and the Presbyterians like to softly say, "Order, order." Nevertheless, in spite of the idiosyncrasies of various ecclesiastical persuasions, the function of the word *amen* far transcends denominational usages in the modern era.

The term *amen* was used in the corporate worship of ancient Israel in two distinct ways. It served first as a response to praise given to God and second as a response to prayer. Those same usages of the term are still in vogue among Christians. The term itself is rooted in a Semitic word that means "truth," and the utterance of "amen" is an acknowledgment that the word that has been heard, whether a word of praise, a word of prayer, or a sermonic exhortation, is valid, that is, sure and binding. Even in antiquity, the word *amen* was used in order to express a pledge to fulfill the terms of a vow. So, this little word is one that is centered on the idea of the truth of God.

The truth of God is such a remarkable element of Christian faith that it cannot be overlooked. There are those who think that truth is negotiable or, even worse, divisive, and it therefore should not be a matter of passionate concern among believers. But if we are not concerned about truth, then we have no reason to have Bibles in our homes. The Bible is God's Word, and God's Word is true. It is not just true but is truth itself. This is the assessment made of it by the Lord Jesus Christ Himself (John 17:17).

Therefore, when we sing a hymn that reflects biblical truth and end it with the sung word *amen*, we are giving our approbation of the content of the praise in the hymn. When we have a choral "amen" at the end of the pastoral prayer, again we are emphasizing our agreement with the validity and surety of the content of the prayer itself.

Worship in biblical terms is a corporate matter. The corporate body is made up of individuals, and when an individual sounds the "amen," the individual is connecting to the corporate expression of worship and praise. However, we are told in the Scriptures that the truths of God are "yea" and "amen" (2 Cor. 1:20), which simply means that the Word of God is valid, it is certain, and it is binding. Therefore, the expression "amen" is not simply an acknowledgment of personal agreement with what has been stated; it is an expression of willingness to submit to the implications of that word, to indeed be bound by it, as if the Word of God would put ropes around us not to strangle or retard us but to hold us firmly in place.

There is, perhaps, no more remarkable use of the term *amen* in the New Testament than on the lips of Jesus. Older translations render statements of our Lord with the preparatory words, "Verily, verily, I say unto you." Later translations update that to "Truly, truly, I say unto you." In such passages, the Greek word that is translated as "verily" or "truly" is the word *amen*. Jesus does not wait for the disciples to nod their agreement or submission to His teaching at the end of His saying; rather, He begins by saying, "Amen, amen, I say unto you." What is the significance of this? Namely, that Jesus never uttered a desultory word; every word that came from His lips was true and important. Each word was, as "amen" suggests, valid, sure, and binding.

Furthermore, even in His own pedagogy, Jesus took the opportunity on occasion to call strict attention to something He was about to say by giving it tremendous emphasis. His practice was somewhat akin to the sounding of a whistle and an announcement over a loudspeaker on a ship: "Now hear this, this is the captain speaking." When that announcement is made on a ship, everyone listens, realizing that when the captain speaks to the entire crew, what he is saying is of the utmost importance and urgency. However, the authority of Jesus far transcends that of a captain of a seagoing vessel. Jesus has been given all authority in heaven and on earth by the Father. So when He gives a preface to a teaching and says,

"Amen, amen, I say unto you," our listening ears should be fine-tuned to take note instantly of what our Lord is going to say following the preface, for it is of the utmost importance.

We also notice that Jesus uses the Hebrew technique of repetition by saying not merely, "Amen, I say unto you," but "Amen, amen." This form of repetition underlines the importance of the words that are to follow. Whenever we read in the text of Scripture our Lord giving a statement that is prefaced by the double "amen," it is a time to pay close attention and be ready to give our response with a double amen to it. He says "amen" to indicate truth; we say it to receive that truth and to submit to it.

DIVORCE

DECEMBER 2011

———

I N 1948, THE FAMOUS HARVARD social historian Pitirim Sorokin wrote an essay in which he sounded an alarm about the rapid disintegration of the stability of the American culture. In this essay, Sorokin pointed out that in 1910 the divorce rate in America was ten percent. Yet from 1910 to 1948, the rate of divorce in America escalated from ten to twenty-five percent. Sorokin indicated that if a quarter of the homes in any given nation are broken by divorce, the stability of the nation cannot endure. Its culture is torn to shreds. Arguing that the family unit is the most basic and foundational unit of every society, he said that when that unit breaks, the society itself suffers a shattered continuity.

One wonders what Sorokin would think if he observed the situation that exists in America today. Since 1948, the divorce rate has gone from twenty-five percent up to and beyond fifty percent: that is, at least half of those marriages that are contracted in America end in divorce. This also means that at least half of the families that are united by marriage suffer a fracture; in a word, they are broken.

The fallout from this startling statistic includes the growing disenchantment with the institution of marriage itself in unprecedented numbers. From the beginning of time and the institution of marriage by God in the garden of Eden, matrimony has been pursued by nearly everyone. However, many people are now eschewing marriage and are choosing cohabitation without the covenant bond of marriage. This situation is not only dangerous but, from a biblical perspective, involves gross and heinous sin. Cohabitation without marriage is seen by God as sexual immorality.

Obviously, the majority in America is not concerned about departure from a biblical ethic. But what is even more disconcerting is that many young people who are members in good standing of evangelical Christian churches opt for cohabitations without fear of rebuke or discipline from church authorities. This says as much about the church as it does the people who are living in wanton sin. In addition to those cohabitating outside of marriage, we also see a multitude of young women who choose to be single parents without entering into marriage or even without cohabitating with the fathers of their children. The single mother is becoming almost an institution in American culture. This spells a serious situation of brokenness that affects the very fabric of American society.

The issue of divorce can be measured objectively by simply examining the statistics of marriages and dissolutions of marriages that are accomplished legally. But in addition to this objective statistic, we find other forms of brokenness within the context of marriage. It is not only divorce that breaks a home; when parents are addicted to illicit drugs or abuse other substances, the family structure is equally broken. The threat to the family unit is ultimately a manifestation of the fallenness of our human nature. Sin violates family unity. Sin is the force by which families are broken. And sinners have no power within themselves to repair that which is broken. The broken home seems to suffer a fate similar to Humpty Dumpty. All the king's horses and all the king's men were not able to repair the fracture that this poor mythical egg experienced.

The number of people seeking to survive within the context of brokenness has now reached multiple millions. The comforting factor is that if we are involved in such brokenness, our experience is not unique, anomalous, or something that takes place in solitary confinement. Rather, those of us who are involved in broken homes are surrounded by multitudes experiencing the same pain due to the dissolution of family stability. This is an area, of course, that not only asks for but screams for the church's ministry.

The New Testament puts a priority on the church's concern for widows and orphans. Widows and orphans are human beings who have suffered broken families not through divorce but through death. Obviously, the church's concern must extend beyond those whose brokenness has been caused by death. Anyone who is involved in a broken family relationship needs the ministry and care of the church. One good thing that has come out of this destruction of the American family is the church's awakening to the need to minister to single mothers and fathers, to recovering substance abusers, and to all who are trying to repair their lives after going through difficult divorces. Divorce can no longer be seen simply as an extreme case of marital failure. Since it has reached not only epidemic but pandemic proportions, it cries out for the application of the means of grace to those who suffer as a result of it.

A church that closes its doors and its hearts to those who are in broken situations cannot be considered a church at all. The church exists, principally, to minister to those who are broken. It was said of our Lord Himself that He would not break the bruised reed (Isa. 42:3). Victims of broken homes are bruised people; the bruises will not go away without help. This is a wound that time does not have the capacity to heal. It requires the healing of God Himself, which He often ministers through His church. This is our concern as Christians, and one we dare not neglect. How we handle these situations will have an eternal impact, not only for the individuals involved, but for cultures and nations whose structure is marred by brokenness.

THE THINGS OF GOD

JANUARY 2012

———

I T IS ONE THING FOR A STUDENT TO DISAGREE with his teacher. But it is another thing entirely for a student to rebuke his teacher for his teaching. Yet, that is precisely what the Apostle Peter did.

He had the gall to confront the incarnate Word of God, the One who embodies all truth, and rebuke Him for what He was teaching (Mark 8:32).

To make matters worse, the Greek word translated as "rebuke" is used biblically in connection with the condemnation of demons. When Jesus silenced demons, He did it by rebuking them, judging them worthy of condemnation (Matt. 17:18; Mark 1:25; 9:25; Luke 4:35; 9:42). It is clear that Peter's protest was not mild; he stood up to Jesus with the full measure of hostility. The Apostle who had said, "You are the Christ, the Son of the living God," and who had heard Jesus say, "Blessed are you, Simon Bar-Jonah" (Matt. 16:16–17a), presumed to correct and admonish his Master.

What was the nature of Peter's rebuke? He said, "Far be it from you, Lord! This shall never happen to you" (v. 22b). Peter was saying that all the things Jesus had predicted (His betrayal and execution) most certainly would not happen to Him. Why? Because Peter was prepared to prevent them from happening—or so he thought.

Jesus' response was equally sharp. Mark tells us: "But turning and seeing his disciples, he rebuked Peter and said, 'Get behind me, Satan! For you are not setting your mind on the things of God, but on the things of man' " (8:33). Here again is the Greek word that the gospel writers use to describe how Jesus spoke to demons. Now Mark uses it to describe what Jesus said to Peter, and Jesus' words drive home the severity of this correction, for the Lord called His disciple "Satan."

Why did Jesus equate Peter with the devil? I believe it was because Peter presented the same temptation the devil brought to Jesus in the wilderness at the beginning of His ministry. In his record of Jesus' final temptation, Matthew writes,

> Again, the devil took him to a very high mountain and showed him all the kingdoms of the world and their glory. And he said to him, "All these I will give you, if you will fall down and worship me." Then Jesus said to him, "Be gone, Satan! For it is written, 'You shall worship the Lord your God and him only you shall serve.' " (4:8–10)

Satan asked Jesus to bow down to him. "Nobody will see it," he suggested. "If you'll do it, I will give you all of the kingdoms of this world. You won't have to go through the Via Dolorosa ("the way of grief"). There will be no cross; there will be no cup of wrath; there will be no suffering." The promise of this temptation was the acquisition of a throne without the experience of pain and suffering.

Our Lord withstood that temptation just as He withstood all of Satan's offers. But Luke tells us that Satan "departed from him until an opportune time" (4:13b). There is foreboding there, the hint that Satan wasn't finished with his temptation.

Who could have foreseen that the "opportune time" would follow on the heels of the highest confession of faith among the disciples? Who could have foreseen that Satan would speak through the spokesman of the disciples, the man who had said, "You are the Christ"? But Jesus recognized the work of Satan right away.

Jesus told Peter: "You are not setting your mind on the things of God, but on the things of man" (Mark 8:33). Peter was not looking at the Messiah from God's point of view but was thinking of the Messiah as a political leader who would deliver the Jews from Roman subjugation. For Peter, it was inconceivable that the Messiah should suffer—even though the Old Testament said He would.

Jesus showed Peter that there are two ways of looking at things—God's way and man's way. This is the divide between godliness and godlessness. The godly person is deeply concerned about the things of God, but the godless person has no concern for the things of God. Instead, he is preoccupied with this world.

We need to evaluate ourselves on these criteria from time to time. We need to ask ourselves: "Where is my heart? What is my chief concern? Am I preoccupied with the things of this world, or does my heart beat for the things of God? Am I seeking first the kingdom of God and His righteousness? Or is there some other priority, some ambition, some goal to which all of my energy is devoted?"

We especially need to ask ourselves these questions if we find that Jesus' teaching offends us and prompts us to question or even rebuke Him. May we never be so foolhardy.

FOR GLORY AND BEAUTY

FEBRUARY 2012

———

T HE WEEK BEFORE CHRISTMAS, when I was in third grade, my grandmother took me to downtown Pittsburgh so that I could buy gifts for my family and, for the first time in my life, my girlfriend. I wanted to buy something romantic for her, so I selected a small decorative pin. It looked to me as if it was made of gold, but it really wasn't. However, I was able to have her initials engraved on the pin, and the lady behind the counter gift-wrapped it for me. It made a nice gift, and when I gave it to my girlfriend, she giggled and swooned over it. That must have been a formative experience for me because, all these years later, I still love to give my then-girlfriend-but-now-my-wife jewelry.

It is interesting to me that people of all ages and from all civilizations and cultures are fascinated with jewels and precious metals for no reason other than their beauty. These things are precious to us not because we can eat them or use them as tools, but because they serve as adornments. By their inherent beauty, they enhance human beauty and the work of man's hands.

When God brought the people of Israel out of Egypt and led them to Sinai to receive His law, He dictated the building of the tabernacle, the first sanctuary. The instructions for this large, ornate tent are astonishing in their detail. God gave the Israelites precise measurements for each part of the tabernacle and extensive instructions about the materials that were to be used. But even before He gave these instructions, God commanded the Israelites to take up an offering for the sanctuary. Did God instruct the Israelites to give money to buy building materials? Did He tell them to donate canvas and wooden poles for the tent? No, He commanded them to bring very different materials. God said:

> "Speak to the people of Israel, that they take for me a contribution. From every man whose heart moves him you shall receive the contribution

for me. And this is the contribution that you shall receive from them: gold, silver, and bronze, blue and purple and scarlet yarns and fine twined linen, goats' hair, tanned rams' skins, goatskins, acacia wood, oil for the lamps, spices for the anointing oil and for the fragrant incense, onyx stones, and stones for setting, for the ephod and for the breast-piece. And let them make me a sanctuary, that I may dwell in their midst." (Ex. 25:2–8)

It is clear that most, if not all, of these items were not essential for the construction of a functional tent. Obviously, God did not want a tent that was merely functional. He commanded the Israelites to give items that would adorn and beautify the tabernacle.

Later, God gave similarly detailed instructions for the garments that Aaron would wear as the high priest. In these instructions, God said something very interesting. He commanded Moses: "You shall make holy garments for Aaron your brother, for glory and for beauty" (Ex. 28:2). A utilitarian robe for Aaron would not do; God wanted him to minister in garments that were skillfully woven and beautifully adorned. Simply put, the God of heaven and earth is deeply concerned about and appreciative of beauty.

The Christian faith is like a stool with three legs, but we have a tendency to make our stools with only one or two legs. The three legs that properly belong to the Christian faith, the three elements of the faith, are the good, the true, and the beautiful. It is obvious that God is concerned about good-ness, for He is the fountainhead of everything that is good (Gen. 1:31; James 1:17). As His people, we are called to mirror and reflect who He is, which means we are called to reflect the good. Likewise, God is deeply concerned about truth, for He is Himself the essence of truth (Isa. 65:16; John 14:6). Therefore, we are to be people who love and practice truth. Finally, as we have seen, God is highly concerned about that which is beautiful. As we read and study the Scriptures, we have to come to the conclusion that there is an ultimate source of beauty—the character of God. Just as the normative standard for goodness and truth is God, so the ultimate stan-dard of beauty is God, and He is very interested in beauty in His creation.

However, we often fail to reflect this concern of His. We settle for the utilitarian and the functional in so many aspects of church life when we should be reaching for what is truly beautiful.

When God built a church, He wanted it to be beautiful. That tells us that whatever we do in the church, we should do it tastefully. The life of the church should be adorned with beauty as a visible expression of our desire to honor God.

"God is deeply concerned about truth, for He is Himself the essence of truth."

———

THE COMING OF THE KINGDOM

MARCH 2012

T HE GOSPEL OF MARK IS NOTABLE FOR its lack of extended accounts of Jesus' teaching. Furthermore, Mark gives us noticeably fewer parables than do Matthew and Luke. However, in chapter 4 of his gospel, Mark records four parables. He begins with the lengthy parable of the sower, then follows with three short, pithy parables, each clearly communicating one central idea, as do most parables. All three of these parables teach us something about the kingdom of God.

In 4:26–29, Mark writes:

> And he said, "The kingdom of God is as if a man should scatter seed on the ground. He sleeps and rises night and day, and the seed sprouts and grows; he knows not how. The earth produces by itself, first the blade, then the ear, then the full grain in the ear. But when the grain is ripe, at once he puts in the sickle, because the harvest has come."

In this parable, as in the parable of the sower, Jesus taps the metaphor of sowing and seed. Here, however, Jesus does not talk about the different soils into which seed is sown, but about one of the most remarkable dimensions of nature. We plant seeds and go to bed. Overnight, rain falls on the seeds. The next day, sunlight warms them. Germination occurs and tiny green shoots emerge from the ground. Soon, the crop is ready for harvesting. Jesus said the spread of the kingdom of God is much like this process. It begins small, but while our attention is elsewhere, so to speak, the kingdom grows. Like the growth of a seed, it is a mysterious process.

I find it comforting to know that this is how God's kingdom works. This parable teaches me that the things I say and do, though they seem infinitely insignificant to me, may have eternal significance as God uses me in the building of His kingdom. Of His own good pleasure, He works through what we do and say not to exalt us but to glorify Himself.

Once, when I was standing at the church door after a service, a young man came up to me and began to tell me that he had heard me speak fifteen years before at a small church in Pennsylvania. He told me that following that service, he had asked me a question, and he was able to repeat my answer to him verbatim all those years later. He said, "When I went home, I could not get your words out of my head, and God used the comment you made that day to convict me to go into the ministry." As I reflected on his story, I wondered how many other words I had spoken to people that had helped them or, perhaps, wounded them, leaving scars on their souls that they carry to this day. We have no idea how powerful a simple word can be, for good or ill.

Every year in the United States, thousands of pastors leave the ministry. Some leave for moral reasons, but most leave because they feel unappreciated by their congregations. They feel like they're spinning their wheels, that they're preaching their hearts out but nothing is happening. They need to hear this parable. Or they need to listen to Paul when he says, "So neither he who plants nor he who waters is anything, but only God who gives the growth" (1 Cor. 3:7). God can and does use their faithful preaching of His Word, though the preachers themselves may never see their words' effect.

Yet sometimes God does give us a glimpse into how He has used us and our words to glorify Himself. Over the years, I've been a part of countless pastors conferences and seminars. It always amazes me how ministers in vastly different settings have similar stories about their preaching experiences. So often, I have heard preachers talk about those occasions when they stood in the pulpit and gave a sermon that they did not consider particularly compelling, even though they put their heart and soul into preparing for it. These same pastors have told me that those sermons are what their people remembered and benefited from years later. God used what these preachers considered weak and unremarkable for great good. I can also testify that this has often been my own experience.

That's the way the kingdom is. We often do not know what God does with our service. We plant the seed, go to bed, and, while we sleep, God germinates the seed so that life grows and eventually produces a full harvest. Then God Himself reaps for His own glory. We simply need to forget about trying to see the fruit of our service immediately. It does not matter if we ever see it. We are called to take the light and let it shine, then let God do with it whatever He pleases.

JESUS: THE ONLY SAVIOR

APRIL 2012

I CANNOT IMAGINE AN AFFIRMATION THAT would meet with more resistance from contemporary Westerners than the one Paul makes in 1 Timothy 2:5: "For there is one God, and there is one mediator between God and men, the man Christ Jesus."

This declaration is narrow and downright un-American. We have been inundated with the viewpoint that there are many roads that lead to heaven, and that God is not so narrow that He requires a strict allegiance to one way of salvation. If anything strikes at the root of the tree of pluralism and relativism, it is a claim of exclusivity to any one religion. A statement such as Paul makes in his first letter to Timothy is seen as bigoted and hateful.

Paul, of course, is not expressing bigotry or hatefulness at all. He is simply expressing the truth of God, the same truth Jesus taught when He said: "I am the way, and the truth, and the life. No one comes to the Father except through me" (John 14:6). Paul is affirming the uniqueness of Christ, specifically in His role as Mediator. A mediator is a go-between, someone who stands between two parties that are estranged or involved in some kind of dispute. Paul declares that Christ is the only Mediator between two parties at odds with one another—God and men.

We encounter mediators throughout the Bible. Moses, for example, was the mediator of the old covenant. He represented the people of Israel in his discussions with God, and he was God's spokesman to the people. The prophets in the Old Testament had a mediatorial function, serving as the spokesmen for God to the people. Also, the high priest of Israel functioned as a mediator; he spoke to God on behalf of the people. Even the king of Israel was a kind of mediator; he was seen as God's representative to the people, so God held him accountable to rule in righteousness according to the law of the Old Testament.

Why, then, does Paul say there is only one mediator between God and man? I believe we have to understand the uniqueness of Christ's mediation in terms of the uniqueness of His person. He is the God-man, that is, God incarnate. In order to bring about reconciliation between God and humanity, the second person of the Trinity united to Himself a human nature. Thus, Jesus has the qualifications to bring about reconciliation—He represents both sides perfectly.

People ask me, "Why is God so narrow that He provided only one Savior?" I do not think that is the question we ought to ask. Instead, we should ask, "Why did God give us any way at all to be saved?" In other words, why did He not just condemn us all? Why did God, in His grace, give to us a Mediator to stand in our place, to receive the judgment we deserve, and to give to us the righteousness we desperately need? The astonishing thing is not that He did not do it in multiple ways, but that He did it in even one way.

Notice that Paul, in declaring the uniqueness of Christ, also affirms the uniqueness of God: "There is one God." This divine uniqueness was declared throughout the Old Testament; the very first commandment was a commandment of exclusivity: "You shall have no other gods before me" (Ex. 20:3).

So Paul brings all these strands together. There is only one God, and God has only one Son, and the Son is the sole Mediator between God and mankind. As I said above, that is very difficult for people who have been immersed in pluralism to accept, but they have to quarrel with Christ and His Apostles on this point. The Bible offers no hope that sincere worshipers of other religions will be saved without personal faith in Jesus Christ. As Paul said in Athens, "The times of ignorance God has overlooked, but now he commands all people everywhere to repent" (Acts 17:30). There is a universal requirement for people to profess faith in Christ.

Perhaps you are concerned to hear me talk in such narrow terms of the exclusivity of Christ and of the Christian faith. If so, let me ask you to think through the ramifications of putting leaders of other religions on the same level as Christ. In one sense, there is no greater insult to Christ than to mention Him in the same breath as Muhammad, for example. If Christ is who He claims to be, no one else can be a way to God. Furthermore, if it is true that there are many ways to God, Christ is not one of them, because there is no reason one of many ways to God would declare to the world that He is the only way to God.

As we celebrate the death and resurrection of Christ this month, it is good for us to remember the uniqueness of Christ. May we never suggest that God has not done enough for us, considering what He has done for us in Christ Jesus.

WISDOM AND KNOWLEDGE

MAY 2012

———

I N COLLEGE, I MAJORED IN PHILOSOPHY. On the very first day of the very first course that I took in philosophy, the professor wrote the word *philosophy* on the chalkboard, then broke it down to show its etymological origin. The word comes from two Greek words, which is appropriate, for the Greeks are usually seen as the founding fathers of Western philosophy. The prefix *philo* comes from the Greek word *phileō*, which means "to love." The root comes from the Greek word *sophia*, which means "wisdom." So, the simple meaning of the term *philosophy* is "love of wisdom."

When I came to understand this meaning, I assumed that by studying philosophy I would learn about wisdom in a practical sense. However, I soon discovered that Greek philosophy stressed abstract questions of metaphysics (the study of ultimate being or of ultimate reality) and epistemology (the study of the process by which human beings learn). It's true that one of the subdivisions of philosophy is ethics, particularly the science of normative ethics—the principles of how we ought to live. That was certainly a concern of the ancient Greeks, particularly Socrates. But even Socrates was convinced that proper conduct, or right living, is intimately connected with right knowledge.

There is a section of the Old Testament known as the Wisdom Literature—the books of Job, Psalms, Proverbs, Ecclesiastes, and the Song of Solomon. Here, we see a completely different philosophical emphasis, one that is based on the initial assumption of the Bible. Many people regard the assertion that there is one god over all creation as a late development in Greek philosophy. In a sense, it was the conclusion of their thought. But for the Jews, the assertion of God's sovereignty was primary. The first line of the Old Testament says, "In the beginning, God created the heavens and the earth" (Gen. 1:1). Monotheism is not at the end of the trail; it is at the very beginning.

Genesis offers no argument or proof for the existence of God. One of the reasons for this is that the Jews were convinced that God had already done the job Himself: the heavens declared the glory of God (Ps. 19:1). The Jews were not concerned about whether there is a God but about what He is like: What is His name? What are His attributes? What is His character? The whole Old Testament focuses on God's self-disclosure to His covenant people.

The Wisdom Literature makes a startling affirmation: "The fear of the LORD is the beginning of wisdom" (Ps. 111:10; Prov. 9:10). For the Jews, wisdom meant a practical understanding of how to live a life that is pleasing to God. The pursuit of godliness was a central concern of the writers of the Wisdom Literature. They affirmed that the necessary condition for anyone to have true wisdom is a fear of the Lord.

Such fear is not terror or horror. As Martin Luther said, it is a filial fear, the fear of a child who is in awe of his father and doesn't want to do anything that would violate his father and disrupt their loving relationship. In a word, this concept has to do with reverence, awe, and respect. When the writers of the Wisdom Literature say that the fear of the Lord is the beginning of wisdom, they are saying that the absolute, essential starting point if you want to acquire true wisdom is reverence and adoration for God.

Showing a contrast, the psalmist tells us, "The fool says in his heart, 'There is no God' " (Ps. 14:1a). Wisdom is contrasted with foolishness. However, in the Hebrew literature, the term *fool* does not describe a person who lacks intelligence. To be foolish to the Jew is to be irreligious and godless. The fool is the person who has no reverence for God, and when you have no reverence for God, inevitably your life will show it.

The Wisdom Literature also makes a sharp distinction between wisdom and knowledge. A person can have unbounded knowledge and not have wisdom. But the reverse is not the case; no one can have wisdom if he does not have knowledge. The anti-intellectual spirit of our times declares: "I don't need to study. I don't need to know the Bible. All I need is to have a personal relationship with Jesus." That viewpoint is on a collision course with what the Wisdom Literature teaches. The purpose for learning the things of God is the acquisition of wisdom, and we cannot have wisdom without knowledge. Ignorance breeds foolishness, but true knowledge—the knowledge of God—leads to the wisdom that is more precious than rubies and pearls.

We want to be rich, successful, and comfortable, but we do not long for wisdom. Thus, we do not read the Scriptures, the supreme textbook of wisdom. This is foolishness. Let us pursue the knowledge of God through the Word of God, for in that way we will find wisdom to live lives that please Him.

THE CHURCH IS ONE

JUNE 2012

———

I N THE SEVENTEENTH CHAPTER OF his gospel, the Apostle John recounts the most extensive prayer that is recorded in the New Testament. It is a prayer of intercession by Jesus for His disciples and for all who would believe through their testimony. Consequently, this prayer is called Jesus' High Priestly Prayer. Christ implored the Father in this prayer that His people might be one. He went so far as to ask the Father that "they may be one even as we are one" (v. 22b). He desired that the unity of the people of God—the unity of the church—would reflect and mirror the unity that exists between the Father and the Son.

Early in church history, as the church fathers were hammering out the cardinal doctrines of the faith, they wrestled with the nature of the church. In the fourth century, in the Nicene Creed, the church was defined with four adjectival qualifiers: one, holy, catholic, and Apostolic. These early saints believed, as Scripture teaches, that the church is one, a unity.

We know that the prayers of Christ, our High Priest, are efficacious and powerful. We know that the early church experienced remarkable unity (Acts 2:42–47; 4:32). Yet the church today, in its visible manifestation, is probably more fragmented and fractured than at any time in church history. There are thousands of denominations in the United States and even more around the world. How, then, are we to understand Christ's prayer for the unity of the church? How are we to understand the ancient church's declaration that the church is one?

There have been different approaches to this. In the twentieth century, we witnessed the rise of relativistic pluralism, a philosophy that allows for a wide diversity of theological viewpoints and doctrines within a single body. In the face of numerous doctrinal disputes, some churches have tried to maintain unity by accommodating many differing views.

Such pluralism has frequently succeeded in maintaining unity—at least organizational and structural unity.

However, there's always a price tag for pluralism, and historically, the price tag has been the confessional purity of the church. In the sixteenth and seventeenth centuries, when the Protestant movement began, various ecclesiastical groups created confessions, creedal statements that set forth the doctrines these groups embraced. In the main, these documents reiterated that body of doctrine that had been passed down through the centuries, having been defined in the so-called ecumenical councils of the first several centuries. These confessions also spelled out the particular beliefs of these various groups. For centuries, Protestantism was defined confessionally. But in our day, the older confessions have been largely relativized as churches try to broaden their confessional stances in order to achieve a visible unity.

There has always been a certain level of pluralism within historic Christianity. The church has always made a distinction between heresy and error. It is a distinction not of kind but of degree. The church is always plagued with errors, or at least members who are in error in their thinking and beliefs. But when an error becomes so serious that it threatens the very life of the church, when it begins to approach a doctrinal mistake that affects the essentials of the Christian faith, the church has had to stand up and say: "This is not what we believe. This false belief is heresy and cannot be tolerated within this church." Simply put, the church has recognized that it can live with differences that are not of the essence of the church, matters that are not essentials of the faith. But other matters are far more serious, striking at the very basics of the faith. So, we make a distinction between those errors that impact the *being* of the church— major heresies—and lesser errors that impact the *well-being* of the church.

Today, however, the church, in order to achieve unity, increasingly negotiates central truths, such as the deity of Christ and the substitutionary atonement. This must not be allowed to happen, for the Bible calls us to "the unity of the faith" (Eph. 4:13), a unity based on the truth of God's Word. Believers who are trying to be faithful to the Scriptures know that the New Testament writers stress the need for us to guard the truth of the faith once delivered (Jude 3; 1 Tim. 6:20a) as well as the need for us to beware those who would undermine the truth of the Apostolic faith by means of false doctrine (Matt. 7:15).

The Christian faith is lived on the razor's edge. The Apostle Paul says, "If possible, so far as it depends on you, live peaceably with all" (Rom. 12:18). We need to bend over backward to keep peace and maintain unity. Yet, at the same time, we are called to be faithful to the truth of the gospel and to maintain the purity of the church. That purity must never be sacrificed to safeguard unity, for such unity is no unity at all.

THE BISHOP
OF OUR SOULS

JULY 2012

———

THE TITLES THAT THE NEW TESTAMENT WRITERS use for Jesus make for a fascinating and enlightening study. One of the most obscure and perplexing of these titles is found in 1 Peter 2:25, where the Apostle writes, "For you were straying like sheep, but have now returned to the Shepherd and Overseer of your souls." In the classical language of the King James Version, this title is rendered as "Shepherd and Bishop of your souls." Many evangelicals react negatively to the idea of Jesus as our Bishop. What did Peter have in mind when he spoke of Jesus in this way?

Although Peter's letter is the only place in the New Testament where Christ is called our Bishop, the concept is deeply rooted in Scripture. We even find a hint of it in the song of Zechariah, father of John the Baptist. Zechariah said, "Blessed be the Lord God of Israel, for he has visited and redeemed his people" (Luke 1:68). In the Old Testament, the promises of redemption that God made to His people included a promise of a day of divine visitation. The Jews were taught to expect a visit from God. Zechariah, however, said God had visited and redeemed His people. He spoke this way because he understood that the appearance of the Messiah was at hand, and He would be heralded by Zechariah's own son.

What does this have to do with the title of "bishop"? The Greek word translated as "visited" in Luke 1:68 is *episkeptomai*, which is a verb form of the noun *episkopos*, the Greek word that is translated as "bishop" or "overseer" in 1 Peter 2:25. That word, *episkopos*, is reflected in the name of the Episcopalian Church, which is governed by bishops.

The word *episkopos* is composed of a prefix and a root. The prefix is *epi-*, which serves to intensify the word with which it is combined. The root is *skopos*, which gives us the English word "scope." We find this root in such words as telescope, periscope, and microscope, all of which are instruments that help us to see things. If we were to add the prefix *epi-* to the word *scope*, we would have an instrument for intensive observation. That is precisely what an *episkopos* was in ancient Greece, except that it was a person, not an instrument. The *episkopos* was a high-ranking military officer who inspected the troops to be sure they were ready for battle. With that background, we can see that a bishop is one who is given oversight in the church, with the responsibility to look closely into all matters under his supervision.

Jesus, then, is our Bishop, our *Episkopos*, who has oversight of us as our Lord. He is vested with the power to look into our lives, to gauge our readiness for combat with the forces of darkness.

The sad fact, however, is that we do not usually like to undergo His inspection. Do you remember how Adam and Eve reacted when God visited the garden of Eden after they had eaten from the forbidden tree? They hid themselves. They understood themselves to be naked in His presence, unable to conceal their sin from His close scrutiny (Gen. 3:8–10). Adam and Eve wanted nothing to do with an *episkopos*. It was much the same when Jesus came in His incarnation. The Scriptures tell us that "He came to his own, and his own people did not receive him" (John 1:11). Like Adam and Eve, the Jews wanted nothing to do with this heavenly Visitor. Indeed, all fallen human beings are terrified of exposure to God's scrutiny.

The Jews in Old Testament times looked forward to the coming of the Messiah. But the prophets warned them that the day of His appearing might not be the wonderful experience they expected. They hoped to see God judge their enemies, but the prophets said that the *Episkopos* would judge His own people if they were not ready to receive Him, if they were faithless and disobedient.

But Zechariah sang his song from the perspective of a child of God, one who was glad to see the coming of the heavenly Visitor and who welcomed His scrutiny. For all who are ready, a visit from the *Episkopos* is a welcome thing, for they understand that His scrutiny is directed toward the care of the souls under His supervision.

The Bishop of our souls knows us better than we know ourselves. Although ministers and bishops are called to follow our Lord's example, we will never have a pastor or elder who cares for our souls anywhere near the degree to which Christ, our Bishop, does.

Do you want God to know you? Do you pray as David did: "Search me, O God, and know my heart!" (Ps. 139:23a)? Those are the words of a person who knows the forgiving grace of God. Once we experience God's grace and tender mercy, we want more. The Christian delights in being known by the Bishop of his soul.

WHEN TOWERS FALL

AUGUST 2012

———

W
HEN A CATASTROPHE HAPPENS IN our world, it is virtually certain that a question will come up: "Where was God?"
People always seem to question how a good God could allow
a terrible thing to happen.

The same question came up in Jesus' time, as we see from an incident
recorded in Luke's Gospel:

> There were some present at that very time who told him about the Galile-
> ans whose blood Pilate had mingled with their sacrifices. And he answered
> them, "Do you think that these Galileans were worse sinners than all
> the other Galileans, because they suffered in this way? No, I tell you;
> but unless you repent, you will all likewise perish. Or those eighteen on
> whom the tower in Siloam fell and killed them: do you think that they
> were worse offenders than all the others who lived in Jerusalem? No, I
> tell you; but unless you repent, you will all likewise perish." (13:1–5)

Some people asked Jesus a question about an atrocity that had occurred
at the hands of Pontius Pilate, the Roman governor of Judea. It seems that
some people who were in the midst of worship were massacred by Pilate's
soldiers. The people who came to Jesus were troubled about this and asked
Him how God could have allowed it to happen to His chosen people.

Jesus answered their question with a question: "Do you think that these
Galileans were worse sinners than all the other Galileans, because they
suffered in this way?" This response shows us that those who brought
the original question to Jesus were assuming that all the suffering that
people endure in this world is proportionately related to their degree of
sinfulness, an idea that remains pervasive today.

Of course, suffering and death came into this world in the first place
because of sin. So, Jesus' questioners were correct in assuming that there

is a connection between moral evil and physical suffering. But Jesus took that opportunity to remind them that we cannot leap to the conclusion that all people suffer in direct proportion to their degree of sin.

The Bible makes this point very clearly. It shows that the wicked sometimes prosper and the righteous sometimes suffer deeply. The book of Job especially belies the idea of a proportionate relationship between sin and suffering by showing that even though Job was the most upright man in the world, he was visited with untold misery, and then had to endure the questioning of his "friends," who assumed he must have fallen into terrible sin.

Thus, when Jesus asked His disciples: "Do you think that these Galileans were worse sinners than all the other Galileans, because they suffered in this way?" the answer was obvious. No, they were not worse sinners than anyone else. Jesus wanted to get the idea of a proportionate connection between sin and suffering out of the disciples' minds lest they think that they were better people in God's sight because they had not suffered and died. So, He warned them: "Unless you repent, you will all likewise perish."

To drive His point home, Jesus mentioned a similar incident: "Or those eighteen on whom the tower in Siloam fell and killed them: do you think that they were worse offenders than all the others who lived in Jerusalem?" Again, the answer was clearly no. These victims were no worse and no better than any other Jews. So, once more He warned them: "Unless you repent, you will all likewise perish."

Those who were killed by the Roman troops and those who died when the tower fell may have been upstanding citizens. But in the vertical dimension, in their relationship to God, none of them was innocent, and the same is true for us. Jesus was saying, "Instead of asking Me why a good God allowed this catastrophe, you should be asking why your own blood wasn't spilled." Jesus was reminding His hearers that there is ultimately no such thing as an innocent person (except Him). Thus, we should not be amazed by the justice of God but by the grace of God. We should be asking why towers do not fall on us each and every day.

When anything painful, sorrowful, or grievous befalls us, it is never an act of injustice on God's part, because God does not owe us freedom from tragedies. He does not owe us protection from falling towers. We are debtors to God and cannot repay. Our only hope to avoid perishing at the hands of God is repentance.

Jesus was not being insensitive or harsh with His disciples. He simply had to jolt them out of a false way of thinking. We would do well to receive His jolt with gladness, for it helps us see things from the eternal perspective. We can deal with catastrophes in this world only by understanding that behind them stands the eternal purpose of God and by realizing that He has delivered us from the ultimate catastrophe—the collapse of the tower of His final judgment on our heads.

"We should not be amazed by the justice of God but by the grace of God."

LOVE THAT IS PATIENT AND KIND

SEPTEMBER 2012

FIRST CORINTHIANS 13 IS ONE OF THE most famous passages in all of Scripture, for in it the Apostle Paul gives us a marvelous exposition of the character of godly love. He starts by showing the importance of love, writing that if we have all kinds of gifts, abilities, and achievements but lack love, we are nothing (vv. 1–3). Then, in verse 4, he begins to describe what godly love looks like, saying, "Love is patient and kind," or, in the wording of a more traditional translation, "Love suffers long and is kind" (NKJV). I find myself intrigued by this pairing—patience and kindness. Why did Paul place these traits first in his description of love, and why did he pair them?

Paul tells us that love is patient, that it "suffers long." I like this more traditional translation because it conveys the idea that loving others can be difficult. Loving people means we do not write them off the first time they offend us. In our relationships, we tend to be far more patient with some people than with others. If a longtime friend does something to irritate or annoy me, I usually say, "Oh, that's just his way, that's his personality, we're all human, none of us is perfect." I make allowances for him. But if I meet another person and find that he behaves in exactly the same way my friend behaved, I might want nothing more to do with him. We tolerate things in our friends that we will not tolerate in strangers.

Longsuffering love does not keep a scorecard. The first time you offend me, I could say, "Strike one," and then give you two more strikes before you're out. But if my love suffers long, you can get to the seventy-seventh strike, and I'll still be hanging in there with you.

Why does Christian love suffer long? It is because Christians imitate Christ, who imitates God the Father, and longsuffering is a chief characteristic of

God. The Bible often makes the point that God is slow to anger, that He is longsuffering with His stiffnecked people. For instance, God describes Himself this way: "The LORD, the LORD, a God merciful and gracious, slow to anger, and abounding in steadfast love and faithfulness" (Ex. 34:6). Likewise, Paul speaks of "the riches of his kindness and forbearance and patience" (Rom. 2:4).

If you are a Christian, how long did God endure your unbelief before you were redeemed? How long has He endured your abiding sin? If not for the longsuffering of God, we would perish. If God treated us with as much impatience as we treat other people, we would be suffering in hell right now. He has endured our disobedience, our blasphemy, our indifference, our unbelief, and our sin, and He still loves us. That is who God is. That is how He manifests His love. He shows His love by His patience, which is a long-lasting patience.

We are called not only to be patient but to suffer long. We are not to be patient with people's sins, foibles, and shortcomings only as long as they cause us no pain. Suffering long means loving when we are experiencing hurt and pain. It means that we "keep loving one another earnestly, since love covers a multitude of sins" (1 Peter 4:8). In this way, we reflect the love of God, who suffers long.

Why, then, does Paul couple patience/longsuffering with kindness? It is possible for us to suffer injury or hostility for a long time while being hostile and plotting revenge in return. But that is not what the Bible means by longsuffering. Longsuffering includes kindness, for we are to be kind in response to the cause of our suffering. Kind people are not rude, not severe, not mean. They have generous hearts. They are sensitive and tender to other people.

My father, I believe, was a model of this trait. He was truly kind. He demonstrated to me the kindness of God. I hated it when I came home from school and found I was in trouble for something I had done. My mother would say, "Your father wants to have a session with you." I had to go into my dad's office and close the door, and he would say, "Well, son, we have to have a talk." He would take me apart without ever raising his voice, without ever manifesting anger to me, and somehow, after he took me apart, he was able, very gently, to put me back together again. Afterward, I would leave his office walking on air. I felt happy, but I also knew I needed to do better the next time. He inspired me because his manner was so kind.

A truly kind person is a rarity, I'm afraid. But kindness ought to be linked with longsuffering as a manifestation of love. Simply put, love is neither impatient nor unkind. This is a picture of the love of God, the same love that the Holy Spirit cultivates in God's people.

THINKING LIKE JESUS

OCTOBER 2012

———

SEVERAL YEARS AGO, I WAS ASKED to give a convocation address at a major theological seminary in America. In that address, I spoke about the critical role of logic in biblical interpretation, and I pleaded for seminaries to include courses on logic in their required curricula. In almost any seminary's course of study, students are required to learn something of the original biblical languages, Hebrew and Greek. They are taught to look at the historical background of the text, and they learn basic principles of interpretation. These are all important and valuable skills for being good stewards of the Word of God. However, the main reason why errors in biblical interpretation occur is not because the reader lacks a knowledge of Hebrew or of the situation in which the biblical book was written. The number one cause for misunderstanding the Scriptures is making illegitimate inferences from the text. It is my firm belief that these faulty inferences would be less likely if biblical interpreters were more skilled in basic principles of logic.

Let me give an example of the kind of faulty inferences I have in mind. I doubt I have ever had a discussion on the question of God's sovereign election without someone quoting John 3:16 and saying, "But doesn't the Bible say that 'God so loved the world that He gave His only begotten Son that whosoever believes in Him should not perish but have everlasting life'?" I immediately agree that the Bible says that. If we were to translate that truth into logical propositions, we would say that all who believe will have eternal life, and no one who has eternal life will perish, because perishing and eternal life are polar opposites in terms of the consequences of belief. However, this text says absolutely nothing about human ability to believe in Jesus Christ. It tells us nothing about who will believe. Jesus said, "No one can come to me unless the Father who sent me draws him" (John 6:44). Here we have a universal negative that describes ability. No person has the ability to come to Jesus unless a particular condition is met by God. Yet this is forgotten in light of John 3:16, which says nothing about a prerequisite for faith. So, John 3:16, one of the most famous texts in all of the Bible, is routinely, regularly, and systematically butchered with faulty inferences and implications.

Why do such illegitimate inferences happen? Classical Christian theology, particularly Reformed theology, talks about the *noetic* effects of sin. The English word *noetic* derives from the Greek word *nous*, which is often translated as "mind." So, the noetic effects of sin are those consequences of the fall of man on the human intellect. The entire human person, including all of our faculties, was ravaged by the corruption of human nature. Our bodies die because of sin. The human will is in a state of moral bondage, in captivity to the evil desires and impulses of the heart. Our minds, likewise, are fallen, and our very ability to think has been severely weakened by the fall. I would guess that Adam's IQ before the fall was off the charts. I doubt that he was given to making illegitimate inferences in his time of tending the garden. Rather, his mind was sharp and acute. But he lost that when he fell, and we lost it with him.

However, the fact that we are fallen does not mean that we no longer have the ability to think. We are all prone to error, but we also can learn to reason in an orderly, logical, and cogent fashion. It is my desire to see Christians think with the utmost cogency and clarity. So, as a matter of discipline, it is much to our benefit to study and master the elementary principles of reasoning so that we can, by the help of God the Holy Spirit, overcome to a certain degree the ravages of sin upon our thinking.

I do not think for a moment that any of us, as long as sin is in us, will ever become perfect in our reasoning. Sin prejudices us against the law of God for as long as we live, and we have to fight to overcome these basic distortions of the truth of God. But if we love God, not only with all of our hearts, our souls, and our strength, but also with our minds (Mark 12:30), we will be rigorous in our attempts to train our minds.

Yes, Adam had a keen mind before the fall. But I believe the world has never experienced such sound thinking as was manifested in the mind of Christ. I think that part of the perfect humanity of our Lord was that He never made an illegitimate inference. He never jumped to a conclusion that was unwarranted by the premises. His thinking was crystal clear and coherent.

We are called to imitate our Lord in all things, including His thinking. Therefore, make it a matter of chief and earnest business in your life to love Him with all of your mind.

WISELY HANDLING THE BIBLE'S WISE SAYINGS

NOVEMBER 2012

———

E VERY CULTURE SEEMS TO HAVE ITS OWN UNIQUE, collected
wisdom, pithy insights of the wise. Oftentimes, these tidbits of wisdom are preserved in the form of the proverb. We have proverbial
sayings in American culture. I am thinking of sayings such as "A stitch
in time saves nine" or "A penny saved is a penny earned."

The Bible, of course, has an entire book of such pithy sayings—the book
of Proverbs. However, this compilation of proverbial wisdom is different
from all other such collections in that these sayings reflect not just human
wisdom but divine wisdom, for these proverbs are inspired by God.

Still, we must be very careful in how we approach and implement these
wise sayings. Simply because they are inspired does not mean that the
biblical proverbs are like laws, imposing a universal obligation. Yet, some
people treat them as if they were divine commandments. If we regard
them in that way, we run into all kinds of trouble. Even divinely inspired
proverbs do not necessarily apply to all life situations. Rather, they reflect
insights that are generally true.

To illustrate this point, let me remind you of two of our own culture's
proverbs. First, we often say, "Look before you leap." That is a valuable
insight. But we have another proverb that seems to contradict it: "He who
hesitates is lost." If we tried to apply both of these proverbs at the same
time and in the same way in every situation, we would be thoroughly
confused. In many situations, wisdom dictates that we examine carefully
where we should place our steps next so that we are not moving blindly.
At the same time, we cannot be so paralyzed in our evaluation of the
pros and cons of our next move that we hesitate too long before making
a decision and lose opportunities when they present themselves to us.

Naturally, it does not really bother us to find seemingly contradictory proverbs in our own cultural wisdom. But when we discover them in the Bible, we find ourselves wrestling with questions about the trustworthiness of Scripture. Let me cite one well-known example. The book of Proverbs says, "Answer not a fool according to his folly" (26:4a). Then, in the very next verse, we read, "Answer a fool according to his folly" (26:5a). How can we follow these opposite instructions? How can both be statements of wisdom?

Again, just as in the example I gave above, the answer depends on the situation. There are certain circumstances when it is not wise to answer a fool according to his folly, but there are other circumstances when it is wise to answer a fool according to his folly. Proverbs 26:4 says, "Answer not a fool according to his folly, *lest you be like him yourself*" (emphasis added). If someone is speaking foolishness, it is generally not wise to try to talk to him. Such a discussion will go nowhere, and the one who tries to carry on the discussion with the fool is in danger of falling into the same foolishness. In other words, there are circumstances when we are better off saying nothing.

At other times, however, it can be helpful to answer a fool according to his folly. Proverbs 26:5 says, "Answer a fool according to his folly, *lest he be wise in his own eyes*" (emphasis added). Although it was made an art form by the ancient Greek philosophers, the Hebrews understood and in biblical teaching sometimes used one of the most effective ways of arguing with another person. I am referring to the *reductio ad absurdum*, which reduces the other person's argument to absurdity. By means of this technique, it is possible to show a person the necessary, logical conclusion that flows out of his argument, and so demonstrate that his premises lead ultimately to an absurd conclusion. So, when a person has a foolish premise and gives a foolish argument, it can at times be very effective to answer the fool according to his folly. You step over onto his territory and say, "Okay, I'll take your position for argument's sake, and I'm going to take it to its logical conclusion and show you the foolishness of it."

So, the book of Proverbs is concerned to give us practical guidelines for daily experience. It is a neglected treasure of the Old Testament, with untold riches lying in wait in its pages to guide our lives. It holds real, concrete advice that comes from the mind of God Himself. If we want wisdom, this is the fountain from which to drink. He who is foolish will neglect this fountain. He who is hungry for God's wisdom will drink deeply from it. We need to listen to the wisdom of God so that we can cut through the many distractions and confusions of modern life. But, as with the entirety of the Word of God, we need to be zealous to learn how to handle the book of Proverbs properly.

SIGHT, PLACE, AND THE PRESENCE OF GOD

DECEMBER 2012

———

A GREAT DEBATE AND CONTROVERSY OVER what is proper worship before God is going on in our time. As I have wrestled with this question, I keep going back to the Old Testament. I know this is a dangerous practice because we now live in the New Testament era, but the Old Testament gives detailed, explicit instructions for worship, whereas the New Testament is almost silent on the conduct of worship. In the Old Testament, I find a refuge from speculation, from human opinion, and from the vagaries of human taste and preference because there I find God Himself explicitly demanding that certain things take place in worship. I believe it is both possible and right to mine principles for worship from the Old Testament, for the Old Testament books remain part of the canon of Scripture, and while there is a certain discontinuity between the Old and New Testaments, there is also a continuity that we must not discount.

One of the principles I learn from the Old Testament is this: the whole person is to be engaged in the experience of worship. Certainly, the minds, hearts, and souls of the worshipers are to be engaged, but when we come to worship on Sunday morning, we do not come as disembodied minds, hearts, or souls. None of our experiences are purely intellectual, emotional, or spiritual. The experience of human life also involves physical aspects. This means that all five senses are involved in the experience of living. We are creatures who live life not merely with our minds, hearts, and souls, but with our senses of sight, hearing, smell, taste, and touch.

I do not have enough space in this brief article to touch on how all five senses are engaged in worship, or even to explore the full dimensions of even one of the senses. So, I want to consider just one way in which the visual sense can be impacted so that our hearts are moved to worship.

Surveys routinely tell us that the two leading reasons why people stay away from church are that they find worship boring and they find the church irrelevant. These reasons, especially the first one, astound me. I have often said that if God Himself were to announce that He would appear at my church one Sunday morning at 11 a.m., there would be standing room only at the appointed hour. I am sure that no one would come to that service, witness God's arrival, and go away saying, "I was bored." When we read the biblical accounts of people's encounters with God, we see the whole gamut of human emotions. Some people weep, some cry out in fear, some tremble, some pass out. However, we never read of anyone who was bored in God's presence.

So, given the fact that worship is, in its most basic sense, a meeting with God, how can we account for the surveys that tell us people come away from church feeling bored? I must conclude that they are experiencing no sense of the presence of God. That is tragic, because if people have no sense of the presence of God, they cannot be moved to worship and glorify God.

One of the elements that helps people gain a sense of the real presence of God is the form of the worship environment. I used to enjoy asking my seminary students, who were Protestants, whether they had ever been in one of the great Roman Catholic Gothic cathedrals. Many had, so I would ask them to share their visceral response upon walking into a cathedral. Most would say, "I felt a sense of awe" or "I felt a sense of the transcendence of God." That gave me the opportunity to point out how the architecture of the cathedrals, the form of the worship environment in those buildings, put my students in the "mood" for worship, as it were. That, of course, was the very reaction the cathedrals were designed to spark. Great care and thought went into the design of the cathedrals. The designers wanted a form that would quicken in people a sense of the loftiness of God, of the otherness of God. It saddens me that Protestants do not usually take the same care in church design. Our worship environments are often utilitarian. Sanctuaries are designed along the lines of cinemas or television studios. Such environments are not wrong, but many people would testify that such settings do not inspire worship in the way traditional church interiors do.

It behooves us, I think, to note the great care with which God gave His people plans for the tabernacle, their first worship environment. Like the temple that followed, the tabernacle was a place of beauty, glory, and transcendence. It was like no other place in the lives of God's people. We need to understand that our church architecture communicates something to our visual senses, and, therefore, that architecture can promote or hinder our sense of the presence of God.

"The whole person is to be engaged in the experience of worship."

A CHARITABLE REACTION

JANUARY 2013

———

H AS ANYONE EVER SAID SOMETHING UNKIND to you or about you? I think we all have had that experience. Becoming victims of slander or malicious gossip can be difficult to bear. However, God calls us to exhibit a very specific kind of response in such circumstances.

Years ago, I received a letter from a friend who is a pastor at a church in California. In it, the pastor included a copy of an article that had appeared in the *Los Angeles Times*. Although the article included a photo of him standing in his church and holding his Bible, it was basically a vicious personal attack against him.

When I saw that picture and read that article, I felt a great deal of empathy for my friend because I had recently had a similar experience. A person I believed was my friend made some very unkind statements about me publicly, and word had gotten back to me. My feelings basically vacillated between despondency and anger, even though I knew I needed to respond with joy (Matt. 5:11–12).

I believe the greatest book ever written about the virtue of love in the Christian life is Jonathan Edwards' classic *Charity and Its Fruits*. In this book, Edwards included a chapter on how we are to respond to false charges. There, he makes the biblical point that such attacks should not surprise us; rather, we should expect them:

> Men that have their spirits heated and enraged and rising in bitter resentment when they are injured act as if they thought some strange thing had happened to them. Whereas they are very foolish in so thinking for it is no strange thing at all but only what was to be expected in a world like this. They therefore do not act wisely that allow their spirits to be ruffled by the injuries they suffer.

Edwards' point is that if the Christian expects to be slandered and keeps his eyes focused on God when it happens, he will not be depressed over it.

Edwards reinforces the concept that other human beings can harm only my worldly pleasure. A person can injure my body, steal my money, or even destroy my reputation. However, all of these things have to do only with the cares and pleasures of this world. But we have an inheritance that is laid up in heaven, a treasure no one can steal or defile (1 Peter 1:4). It is protected by the Lord Himself.

We might be tempted to think that Edwards was a spiritual giant who could handle personal attacks with ease, while we are "ordinary" believers. How, then, can we not be distressed when we are hurt by people we thought were our friends? Yet while it is true that it is part of our human nature to respond to personal attacks with sadness, anger, or bitterness, these feelings are part of our fallen humanity. They are not fruits of the Holy Spirit. This means that Edwards, as great a saint as he was, was not calling "ordinary" Christians to do anything extraordinary. We are all called to bear our injuries with joy, patience, love, and gentleness.

This kind of response is required of all of us because the Christian life is about the imitation of Christ (1 Cor. 11:1). We are being molded into His image, so we are to strive to live as He lived. Our Lord was slandered and falsely accused of all kinds of offenses, but He opened not His mouth in protest (Isa. 53:7). Like a lamb, He accepted these vitriolic attacks, and, in the very moment of His passion, He prayed for the forgiveness of those who were attacking Him (Luke 23:34). This is how we are called to react to our enemies (1 Peter 4:13). Therefore, every false accusation, every slander, every ill word spoken about me is an opportunity for me to grow in my sanctification.

Edwards helped me see that I had allowed my soul to become distressed, and that was sin. Instead of seeing the attack on me as an occasion to imitate Christ and to grow in my sanctification, I had resisted God's Spirit, who had brought this painful event into my life for my edification, that I might remember where my treasure is.

R . C .   S P R O U L

The key to responding to attacks and insults as Christ would is to nurture love for God. Edwards writes:

> As love to God prevails, it tends to set persons above human injuries, in this sense, that the more they love God the more they will place all their happiness in him. They will look to God as their all and seek their happiness in portion in his favor, and thus not in the allotments of his providence alone. The more they love God, the less they set their hearts on their worldly interests, which are all that their enemies can touch.

We need to keep Edwards' insight in mind as we deal with the inevitable attacks and insults that come our way in this life.

SUFFERING AND THE GLORY OF GOD

FEBRUARY 2013

———

I ONCE VISITED WITH A WOMAN WHO WAS dying from uterine cancer. She was greatly distressed, but not only from her physical ailment. She explained to me that she had had an abortion when she was a young woman, and she was convinced that her disease was a direct consequence of that. In short, she believed cancer was the judgment of God on her.

The usual pastoral response to such an agonizing question from someone in the throes of death is to say the affliction is not a judgment of God for sin. But I had to be honest, so I told her that I did not know. Perhaps it was God's judgment, but perhaps it was not. I cannot fathom the secret counsel of God or read the invisible hand of His providence, so I did not know why she was suffering. I did know, however, that whatever the reason for it, there was an answer for her guilt. We talked about the mercy of Christ and of the cross, and she died in faith.

The question that woman raised is asked every day by people who are suffering affliction. It is addressed in one of the more difficult passages in the New Testament. In John 9, we read: "As he passed by, he saw a man blind from birth. And his disciples asked him, 'Rabbi, who sinned, this man or his parents, that he was born blind?' Jesus answered, 'It was not that this man sinned, or his parents, but that the works of God might be displayed in him' " (vv. 1–3).

Why did Jesus' disciples suppose that the root cause of this man's blindness was his sin or his parents' sin? They certainly had some basis for this assumption, for the Scriptures, from the account of the fall onward, make it clear that the reason suffering, disease, and death exist in this world is sin. The disciples were correct that somehow sin was involved in this man's affliction. Also, there are examples in the Bible of God causing affliction because of specific sins. In ancient Israel, God afflicted Moses' sister, Miriam, with leprosy because she questioned Moses' role as God's spokesman (Num. 12:1–10). Likewise, God took the life of the child born to Bathsheba as a result of David's sin (2 Sam. 12:14–18). The child was punished, not because of anything the child did, but as a direct result of God's judgment on David.

However, the disciples made the mistake of particularizing the general relationship between sin and suffering. They assumed there was a direct correspondence between the blind man's sin and his affliction. Had they not read the book of Job, which deals with a man who was innocent and yet was severely afflicted by God? The disciples erred in reducing the options to two when there was another alternative. They posed their question to Jesus in an either/or fashion, committing the logical fallacy of the false dilemma, assuming that the sin of the man or the sin of the man's parents was the cause of his blindness.

The disciples also seem to have assumed that anyone who has an affliction suffers in direct proportion to the sin that has been committed. Again, the book of Job dashes that conclusion, for the degree of suffering Job was called to bear was astronomical compared with the suffering and afflictions of others far more guilty than he was.

We must never jump to the conclusion that a particular incidence of suffering is a direct response or in direct correspondence to a person's particular sin. The story of the man born blind makes this point.

Our Lord answered the disciples' question by correcting their false assumption that the man's blindness was a direct consequence of his or his parents' sin. He assured them that the man was born blind not because God was punishing the man or the man's parents. There was another reason. And because there was another reason in this case, there might always be another reason for the afflictions God calls us to endure.

Jesus answered His disciples by saying, "It was not that this man sinned, or his parents, but that the works of God might be displayed in him" (v. 3). What did He mean? Simply put, Jesus said that the man was born blind so that Jesus might heal him at the appointed time, as a testimony to Jesus' power and divinity. Our Lord displayed His identity as the Savior and the Son of God in this healing.

When we suffer, we must trust that God knows what He is doing, and that He works in and through the pain and afflictions of His people for His glory and for their sanctification. It is hard to endure lengthy suffering, but the difficulty is greatly alleviated when we hear our Lord explaining the mystery in the case of the man born blind, whom God called to many years of pain for Jesus' glory.

JESUS CHRIST, ANOINTED ONE

MARCH 2013

T HROUGHOUT THE NEW TESTAMENT, we encounter many titles for Jesus of Nazareth—"Son of God," "Son of Man," "Lord," and others. However, the title that is given to Jesus most often in the New Testament is one that is familiar to us, but one that we do not understand well. It is the title "Christ."

Why do I say that we do not understand this title well? I say it because "Christ" is used so often in conjunction with "Jesus" that we tend to think of it as His last name. However, "Christ" is not a secondary name for Jesus; He would have been known as "Jesus Bar Joseph," meaning "Jesus, son of Joseph." Rather, "Christ" is Jesus' supreme title. But what does it mean?

The meaning of *Christ* is drawn from the Old Testament. God promised the ancient Israelites that a Messiah would come to deliver them from sin. The idea of the Messiah is carried over into the New Testament with the title *Christ*. The Greek word *Christos*, from which we get the English word *Christ*, is the translation of the Hebrew term *Mashiach*, which is the source for the English word *Messiah*. *Mashiach*, in turn, is related to the Hebrew verb *masach*, which means "to anoint." Therefore, when the New Testament speaks of Jesus Christ, it is saying "Jesus the Messiah," which literally means, "Jesus the Anointed One."

In Old Testament times, people were subject to anointing when they were called to the offices of prophet, priest, and king. For example, when Saul became the first king of Israel, Samuel the prophet anointed his head with oil in a ceremonial fashion (1 Sam. 10:1). This religious rite was performed to show that the king of Israel was chosen and endowed by God for the kingship. Likewise, the priests (Ex. 28:41) and prophets (1 Kings 19:16) were anointed at God's command. In a sense, anyone in the Old Testament who was set apart and consecrated for a servant task was a messiah, for he was one who received an anointing.

But the people of Israel looked forward to that promised individual who was to be not merely a messiah but *the* Messiah, the One who would be supremely set apart and consecrated by God to be their Prophet, Priest, and King. So, at the time Jesus was born, there was a strong sense of anticipation among the Jews, who had been waiting for their Messiah for centuries.

Amazingly, when Jesus began His public ministry, few recognized Him for who He was, despite overwhelming evidence that He possessed an anointing from God that far surpassed that which had rested on any other man. We know that there was great confusion about Him even after He had been ministering for some time. At one point, Jesus asked His disciples, "Who do people say that the Son of Man is?" (Matt. 16:13b). He was taking the pulse of His culture, getting feedback regarding the rumors about Himself. In response to Jesus' question, the disciples ticked off various views that were being put forward: "Some say John the Baptist, others say Elijah, and others Jeremiah or one of the prophets" (v. 14). Jesus was being identified with all kinds of people, but none of these speculations was correct.

Then Jesus asked the disciples, "But who do you say that I am?" (v. 15b). Peter answered with what is known as the great confession, a statement of his belief as to the identity of Jesus: "You are the Christ, the Son of the Living God" (v. 16). With these words, Peter declared that Jesus was the *Christos*, the *Mashiach*, the Anointed One.

Then Jesus said an interesting thing. He told Peter that he was blessed to have this understanding of Jesus' identity. Why did He say this? Jesus explained: "For flesh and blood has not revealed this to you, but my Father who is in heaven" (v. 17). Peter had received a divine insight that Jesus was the Messiah; it was not something that he had discerned by his own ability. Again, this amazes me because one would think that nearly everyone who encountered Jesus would have recognized Him immediately as the Messiah. After all, there is no shortage of information in the Old Testament about the coming Messiah—where He would be born, how

He would behave, and what power He would manifest—and everyone could see what Jesus had done—raising people from the dead, healing all sorts of maladies, and teaching with great authority. But, of course, they did not. Jesus' anointing was not immediately apparent.

Many people today have positive things to say about Jesus as a model of virtue, a great teacher, and so on, but they stop short of saying He is Messiah. This is the great divide between Christians and unbelievers. Only one who has been born again can confess that Jesus is the Christ. Can you?

"Only one who has been born again can confess that Jesus is the Christ. Can you?"

THE SONS OF GOD

APRIL 2013

―――

I N THE TWENTIETH CENTURY, the German biblical scholar Rudolf
Bultmann gave a massive critique of the Scriptures, arguing that the
Bible is filled with mythological references that must be removed
if it is to have any significant application to our day. Bultmann's major
concern was with the New Testament narratives, particularly those that
included records of miracles, which he deemed impossible. Other scholars, however, have claimed that there are mythological elements in the
Old Testament as well. Exhibit A for this argument is usually a narrative
that some believe parallels the ancient Greek and Roman myths about
gods and goddesses occasionally mating with human beings.

In Genesis 6, we read this account: "When man began to multiply on
the face of the land and daughters were born to them, the sons of God
saw that the daughters of man were attractive. And they took as their
wives any they chose.... The Nephilim were on the earth in those days,
and also afterward, when the sons of God came in to the daughters of
man and they bore children to them. These were the mighty men who
were of old, the men of renown" (vv. 1–4).

This narrative is basically a preface to the account of the flood God sent
to eradicate all people from the earth, except for the family of Noah. Of
course, the flood narrative itself is often regarded as mythological, but
this preparatory section, where we read of the intermarriage of "the sons
of God" and "the daughters of man," is seen as blatant myth.

The assumption in this interpretation of Genesis 6 is that "the sons of
God" refers to angelic beings. Why do some biblical interpreters make
this assumption? The simple answer is that the Scriptures sometimes
refer to angels as sons of God, and it is assumed that the reference in Genesis 6 means the same. This is certainly a possible inference that could
be drawn, but is it a necessary inference? I would answer no; I do not

believe this text necessarily teaches the idea of sexual relations between angels and human beings.

To understand this difficult passage, we have to look at the broader application of the phrase "sons of God." Pre-eminently, it is used for Jesus Himself; He is the Son of God. As noted, it is sometimes used to refer to angels (Job 1:6; 21:1; Ps. 29:1). Also, it is sometimes used to speak of followers of Christ (Matt. 5:9; Rom. 8:14; Gal. 3:26). So, the concept of divine sonship in the Scriptures is not always linked to a biological or ontological relationship (relationship of being). Rather, it is chiefly used to set forth a relationship of obedience. This means Genesis 6 could simply be speaking about the intermarriage of those who manifested a pattern of obedience to God in their lives and those who were pagans in their orientation. In other words, this text likely describes marriages between believers and unbelievers.

The immediate context of Genesis 6 supports this conclusion. Following the narrative of the fall in Genesis 3, the Bible traces the lines of two families, the descendants of Cain and of Seth. Cain's line is recounted in Genesis 4, and this line displays proliferating wickedness, capped by Lamech, who was the first polygamist (v. 19) and who rejoiced in murderous, vengeful use of the sword (vv. 23–24). By contrast, the line of Seth, which is traced in Genesis 5, displays righteousness. This line includes Enoch, who "walked with God, and . . . was not, for God took him" (v. 24). In the line of Seth was born Noah, who was "a righteous man, blameless in his generation" (6:9). Thus, we see two lines, one obeying God and the other willfully disobeying Him.

Therefore, many Hebrew scholars believe that Genesis 6 is describing not the intermarriage of angels and human women but the intermarriage of the descendants of Cain and Seth. The two lines, one godly and one wicked, come together, and suddenly everyone is caught up in the pursuit of evil, such that "every intention of the thoughts of [man's] heart was only evil continually" (v. 5). We do not need to surmise an invasion of the earth by angels in order to make sense of this chapter.

Resolving the interpretive difficulties of Genesis 6 reminds us to be

RIGHT NOW COUNTS FOREVER

very careful about drawing inferences from Scripture that are not necessarily warranted. The descriptive terms "sons of God" and "daughters
of man" do not give us license to make the assumption of interaction
between heavenly beings and earthly beings. We have to be very careful
when we look at a difficult text like this to see how the language is used
in the broader context of Scripture. It is a very important principle that
Scripture is to be interpreted by Scripture.

STRANGE FIRE

MAY 2013

———

T HERE IS AN INCIDENT IN THE BIBLICAL RECORD that causes abiding consternation for many of God's people. It is the story of how two of the sons of Aaron, Nadab and Abihu, were slain suddenly by God.

> Now Nadab and Abihu, the sons of Aaron, each took his censer and put fire in it and laid incense on it and offered unauthorized fire before the Lord, which he had not commanded them. And fire came out from before the LORD and consumed them, and they died before the LORD. Then Moses said to Aaron, "This is what the LORD has said: 'Among those who are near me I will be sanctified, and before all the people I will be glorified.'" And Aaron held his peace. (Lev. 10:1–3)

Aaron, of course, was the older brother of Moses and the first high priest of Israel. God had consecrated Aaron and his sons to the holy vocation of the priesthood. It was in the context of their priestly service that two of Aaron's four sons, Nadab and Abihu, each got a censer—a kind of vessel that was used in antiquity to contain the incense that was burned as an offering before God—put fire in them, put incense on them, and offered what the book of Leviticus calls "unauthorized fire."

What is "unauthorized fire," or, as it is rendered in other translations, "profane fire" or "strange fire"? We use the word *profane* to refer to that which is less than holy, but the word *profane* comes from the Latin *profanus*, which literally means "outside the temple." So, in a literal sense, Moses, as the author of Leviticus, is saying that the fire that Nadab and Abihu introduced to the altar had not been purified or consecrated. For that, God took their lives. On the surface, it seems that this was cruel and unusual punishment. These young priests clearly violated some prescription that God had set forth for the offering of incense in the holy place, but it may have been no more than a prank or a mischievous innovation. Was it really necessary for God to rebuke their action so decisively?

To understand this incident more fully, we have to go back to the book of Exodus. Just before God gave His Ten Commandments, He told Moses that He soon would come to him in a thick cloud so that the people might hear Him speaking and believe (19:9). To prepare for that stupendous vision, God commanded the people to consecrate themselves (v. 10). He also set strict borders around Mount Sinai, saying that whoever touched the mountain would die (v. 12). When God came, "there were thunders and lightnings and a thick cloud on the mountain and a very loud trumpet blast, so that all the people in the camp trembled" (v. 16). God called Moses to ascend the mountain, but before revealing His law, God sent Moses back down the mountain to repeat and expand the warning. He said:

> Go down and warn the people, lest they break through to the Lord to look and many of them perish. Also let the priests who come near to the Lord consecrate themselves, lest the Lord break out against them. (vv. 21–22)

So, at the very formation of the nation of Israel, God laid down the fundamental laws of consecration for the priests. He warned them that if they were not consecrated or if they violated their consecration, He would "break out" against them. Nadab and Abihu violated the holy law of the priesthood. When they did so, God killed them, reminding Israel of the sanctity of His presence. That is why Moses reminded Aaron, "This is what the LORD has said: 'Among those who are near me I will be sanctified, and before all the people I will be glorified.'" When he heard this, Aaron "held his peace." Even amid his grief, he knew his sons had committed a grave offense against Israel's holy God.

One aspect of the modern church that most saddens and concerns me is that believers are no longer encouraged to have a healthy fear of God. We seem to assume that the fear of the Lord is something that belonged to the Old Testament period and is not to be a part of the life of the Christian.

But fear of God involves not simply a trembling before His wrath, but a sense of reverence and awe because of His glorious holiness.

Even though we are living on the finished side of the cross, the fear of the Lord is still the beginning of wisdom (Ps. 111:10a). God is still a consuming fire, a jealous God (Deut. 4:24). When we come into His presence, we are to come as children, as those who have been reconciled, but there is to be a godly fear inspired by respect for the One with whom we are dealing.

THE BASIS OF A CHRISTIAN MARRIAGE

JUNE 2013

———

S OME YEARS AGO, I ATTENDED an interesting wedding. I was especially struck by the creativity of the ceremony. The bride and the groom had brainstormed with the pastor in order to insert new and exciting elements into the service, and I enjoyed those elements. However, in the middle of the ceremony, they included portions of the traditional, classic wedding ceremony. When I began to hear the words from the traditional ceremony, my attention perked up and I was moved. I remember thinking, "There is no way to improve on this because the words are so beautiful and meaningful." A great deal of thought and care had been put into those old, familiar words.

Today, of course, many young people not only are saying no to the traditional wedding ceremony, they are rejecting the concept of marriage itself. More and more young people are coming from broken homes, and as a result, they have a fear and suspicion about the value of marriage. So we see couples living together rather than marrying for fear that the cost of that commitment may be too much. They fear it may make them too vulnerable. This means that one of the most stable and, as we once thought, permanent traditions of our culture is being challenged.

One of the things I like most about the traditional wedding ceremony is that it includes an explanation as to why there is such a thing as marriage. We are told in that ceremony that marriage is ordained and instituted by God—that is to say, marriage did not just spring up arbitrarily out of social conventions or human taboos. Marriage was not invented by men but by God.

We see this in the earliest chapters of the Old Testament, where we find the creation account. We find that God creates in stages, beginning with the light (Gen. 1:3) and capping the process with the creation of man (v. 27). At every stage, He utters a benediction, a "good word." God repeatedly looks at what He has made and says, "That's good" (vv. 4, 10, 12, 18, 21, 25, 31).

But then God notices something that provokes not a benediction but what we call a malediction, that is, a "bad word." What was this thing that God saw in His creation that He judged to be "not good"? We find it in Genesis 2:18, where God declares, "It is not good that the man should be alone." That prompts Him to create Eve and bring her to Adam. God instituted marriage, and He did it, in the first instance, as an answer to human loneliness. For this reason, God inspired Moses to write, "Therefore a man shall leave his father and his mother and hold fast to his wife, and they shall become one flesh" (v. 24).

But while I like and appreciate the words of the traditional wedding ceremony, I believe the form of the ceremony is even more important. This is because the traditional ceremony involves the making of a covenant. The whole idea of covenant is deeply rooted in biblical Christianity. The Bible teaches that our very redemption is based on a covenant. Much could be said here about the character of the biblical covenants, but one vital facet is that none of them is a private matter. Every covenant is undertaken in the presence of witnesses. This is why we invite guests to our weddings. It is so they will witness our vows—and hold us accountable to keep them. It is one thing for a man to whisper expressions of love to a woman when no one will hear, but it is quite another thing for him to stand up in a church, in front of parents, friends, ecclesiastical or civil authorities, and God Himself, and there make promises to love and cherish her. Wedding vows are sacred promises made in the presence of witnesses who will remember them.

I believe marriage is the most precious of all human institutions. It's also the most dangerous. Into our marriages we pour our greatest and deepest expectations. We put our emotions on the line. There we can achieve the greatest happiness, but we also can experience the greatest disappointment, the most frustration, and the most pain. With that much at stake, we need something more solemn than a casual promise.

Even with formal wedding ceremonies, even with the involvement of authority structures, roughly fifty percent of marriages fail. Sadly, among the men and women who stay together as husband and wife, many would not marry the same spouse again, but they stay together for various reasons. Something has been lost regarding the sacred and holy character of the marriage covenant. In order to strengthen the institution of marriage, we might want to consider strengthening the wedding ceremony, with a clear, biblical reminder that marriage is instituted by God and forged in His sight.

THE JUDGMENT OF CHARITY

JULY 2013

———

E VERY TIME I READ THE GOSPELS, I am struck by how Jesus seems to have found Himself in the middle of controversy wherever He went. I am also struck by how Jesus handled each controversy differently. He did not follow the example of Leo "The Lip" Deroucher, the former manager of the New York Giants, and treat every person He encountered in the same manner. Although He expected everyone to play by the same rules, He shepherded people according to their specific needs.

The Old Testament depicts the Good Shepherd as One who carries both a staff and a rod, for His responsibility is both to guide His sheep and to protect them from ravenous wolves (Ps. 23:4). In the Gospels, we see Jesus exercise His protective rod most often against the scribes and Pharisees. When Jesus dealt with these men, He asked no quarter and gave none. When He pronounced the judgment of God on them publicly, He used the oracle of woe that was used by the Old Testament prophets: "Woe unto you Scribes and Pharisees, hypocrites! For you travel across sea and land to make a single proselyte [convert], and when he becomes a proselyte, you make him twice as much a child of hell as yourselves" (Matt. 23:15).

Jesus dealt with many of the religious leaders of His day so forcefully because of their hard-hearted hypocrisy. Other people who were cognizant of their sin and ashamed of it—these He addressed with love and encouragement. Consider the woman at the well (John 4). Jesus sat and talked with a Samaritan woman, which was unheard of for a Jewish rabbi in those days because of common biases against women and Samaritans. He patiently drew a confession of sin out of her and revealed His Messianic office to her. Jesus treated her as a bruised reed and smoldering wick, tenderly confronting but not crushing her (Matt. 12:15–21).

Among many other things, I think Christ's example teaches us how we are to deal with those with whom we disagree. Sometimes we must be forceful and sometimes we must be gentle—forceful with the wolves and gentle with Jesus' lambs.

There are disagreements we have with our brothers, but also disagreements we have with those who claim to be our brothers but who may, in fact, be wolves in sheep's clothing. Such wolves always represent a clear danger to the safety, health, and well-being of Christ's sheep. No quarter can be given to wolves, but we are called to exercise gentleness toward those whose disagreements with us do not touch the heart of Christian orthodoxy.

To know the difference between when to be gentle and when to be forceful is one of the most difficult matters for mature Christians to discern. I don't have a formula that is easily applied, but I do know that we are always called to deal with the disputes and disagreements we have on the basis of charity, that is, love.

Charity and Its Fruits by Jonathan Edwards is the deepest exposition of I Corinthians 13 that I know of. I've read it at least half-a-dozen times, probably more. In this work, Edwards writes:

> A truly humble man, is inflexible in nothing but in the cause of his Lord and master, which is the cause of truth and virtue. In this he is inflexible because God and conscience require it; but in things of lesser moment, and which do not involve his principles as a follower of Christ, and in things that only concern his own private interests, he is apt to yield to others.

The humility of which Edwards is speaking here is a humility that must be brought to every disagreement that erupts among believers. It is a humility that brings to the fore what in church history many have called the judgment of charity. The judgment of charity works something like this: When we disagree with one another, I believe that we are called as Christians to assume the motives of the person with whom we disagree are pure motives. This is the approach we are to have with those with whom we have an honest difference in biblical interpretation but who love the Bible and aren't trying to change what it teaches. Such people are unwilling to compromise the essential truths of the Christian faith.

Now, the judgment of charity assumes in a Christian dispute that the brother or sister with whom we are disagreeing is disagreeing honestly and with personal integrity. Here I think of my friend John MacArthur. If I disagree about something with John—I don't care what it is—and we go to the mat and talk about it, John will change his position—no matter the cost—if I can persuade him that the Bible teaches my view and not his. That's because what he wants more than anything else is to be faithful to the Word of God.

That's what I mean by the judgment of charity. We don't impugn people's motives and don't assume the worst of them when we disagree with them. We make a distinction between best-case and worst-case analysis. The problem we all have as sinners on this side of glory is that we tend to reserve best-case analysis to our own motives and give worst-case analysis to our brother's and sister's motives. That's just the opposite of the spirit we're called to have in terms of biblical humility.

A PILGRIM PEOPLE

AUGUST 2013

———

THERE IS JUST SOMETHING ABOUT being at home, isn't there? I am reminded of this every time I travel. As I write this column, it has been only a few weeks since we returned from a Ligonier study cruise in the Caribbean. We had a wonderful time of study and fellowship with Ligonier's friends and supporters, many of whom are likely reading this column right now. Despite my enjoyment of the trip, however, I was happy to return home. I feel the same way every time I travel. I love my homeland and am happy to come back to the United States even after a blessed journey.

Even though I am glad to come back to America, I must admit that when I come home to my country, I long to be elsewhere. At the end of the day, the United States is but an inn, a place to rest on the way to my true home—the city of heaven. As a Christian, I realize that I will never be truly home until I am with my Savior in heaven. The old spiritual puts it well: "This world is not my home . . . I'm just a passin' through."

God's people have always been what we would call a "pilgrim people." The constitution of the old covenant church in the exodus gave the ancient Israelites the names pilgrims and sojourners. Living a semi-nomadic existence in the desert, they had no permanent place to call their own. Even their place of worship was a tent—the tabernacle—that had to be taken down when the Lord called Israel to move and put back up when they established a new camp. Later, John's description of the incarnation picks up this theme. The Word of God who "became flesh and dwelt among us" (John 1:14) translates with the English term *dwelt* a Greek term with the same root that means "tent" or "tabernacle." Christ literally "pitched His tent" or "tabernacled" among us.

Because of this, Christ is the ultimate Pilgrim revealed to us in Scripture. He became the supreme Sojourner in the incarnation, leaving His home in heaven in our behalf. He came to this world to journey along with the children of Abraham, Isaac, and Jacob on their way to their heavenly home.

Hebrews 11:13 puts it this way: The old covenant saints, having seen the promises from afar, "acknowledged that they were strangers and exiles on the earth." Moses, Abraham, and the others went forth from their earthly homes in faith, seeking for that heavenly home that the Lord promised them. They desired "a better country, a heavenly one," and so "God is not ashamed to be called their God, for he has prepared for them a city" (v. 16).

Though the hall of faith in Hebrews 11 focuses on old covenant believers, the pilgrimage of God's people did not end once they settled in Canaan, first conquered Jerusalem, or even when they returned to the Promised Land after the exile. The Christian church is a pilgrim people. The Apostle Peter is clear: "Dearly beloved, I beseech you as strangers and pilgrims, abstain from fleshly lusts, which war against the soul" (1 Peter 2:11; KJV). We still await the holy city and heavenly Jerusalem. That is the home we were made for. "Behold the tabernacle of God is with men, and he will dwell with them, and they shall be his people, and God himself shall be with them, and be their God" (Rev. 21:3).

On this side of heaven, the Lord gives us a glimpse of our heavenly home in many ways, especially when we gather for corporate worship. I've experienced this in my home church, Saint Andrew's Chapel, where every Lord's Day we gather and cross the threshold from the secular to the sacred. But I've also seen it when I have worshipped in foreign lands.

About twenty years ago, I traveled through Eastern Europe to preach and teach in several lands that had been closed to Christian missionaries during Communist rule, which had ceased just a few years earlier. At one church in Transylvania, I had the opportunity to preach one Sunday morning, and when I looked out over the congregation, I saw many elderly women, whose faces were etched with wrinkles born from years of toiling the land with primitive tools. Though they were dressed head to toe in black—black skirts, black blouses, and black babushkas—there was nonetheless a serenity about them. They looked almost angelic. These women were listening intently to my sermon, and sometimes I even saw a tear roll down one of their cheeks.

Standing there, I heard my preaching translated into their native Romanian language, and I marveled at what was happening. I felt a real kinship with them, a bond forged from nothing of this world. We had nothing in common. We spoke different languages, came from different cultures, followed different customs, and otherwise had nothing to tie us together. But we did have the blessed tie that binds—a shared love for God's Word. We were all citizens of heaven, passing through this world in different geographies but with a profound union that resulted from our common union with Christ. I and those peasant women were pilgrims on our way to the heavenly country.

God gives us many blessings in this world and in our earthly homes. Nevertheless, "this world is not [our] home . . . [we're] just a passin' through."

A SURE HOPE
FOR THE FUTURE

SEPTEMBER 2013

———

I 'VE SPOKEN AT MORE CONFERENCES than I can remember, and one of the highlights of these events is the book signing wherein attendees visit with the conference speakers and the speakers sign their books. These signings are a privilege because they give the speaker a glimpse at the impact his words have had on people. I've talked to seminarians, grandmothers, businessmen, and just about anyone else you can think of during these signings. On occasion, children have even given me pictures that they drew for me.

As enjoyable as these signings can be, there's one phenomenon I haven't been able to get used to fully, and that's the request to sign one book that I didn't write—the Bible. I'm happy to do it, however, and often the people who want me to sign their Bible ask me for my life's verse. The first time someone asked me for such a verse, I was perplexed. "What's a life verse?" I asked, never having heard of this tradition whereby people pick one verse from the Bible to base their lives upon. In any case, I chose Romans 12:12 the first time I was asked to provide a life verse during a book signing. This verse features one of Paul's great summaries of the Christian life: "Rejoice in hope, be patient in tribulation, be constant in prayer."

When I think of what it means to be patient in tribulation, to be constant in prayer, and to find joy in our hope that lies ahead, I think of one person who embodies that triad of virtues more than almost anyone else in history. I'm talking about the most famous patient man of all time— Job. If ever a man was called upon to hang on to his faith and his devotion to God in the midst of travail, it was Job.

I'm sure we all know Job's story well. It opens with a little glimpse into heaven. Satan challenged God and asserted with a perverse kind of glee that humanity had rebelled against its Creator and no longer stood on His side. The Lord responded by putting forth Job as an example of one man who still loved and served Him. But Satan countered that Job served God only because of what he could get from such service, so the Lord put Job to the test to show the Accuser that he was wrong. What happened was that Satan attacked Job more violently than he did anyone else in the history of the world except for Jesus.

To make matters worse, Job then had to deal with three "friends" who told him that he suffered because of his own sin. But Job patiently and repeatedly asserted his innocence, demanding to know the reasons for his suffering since he was a righteous man who hadn't done anything to deserve such pain.

Job wasn't patient in the sense that he had a plastic smile on his face and whistled through all of his misery and affliction. Instead, Job was patient in the sense that he did two things: he hung on and he refused to curse God. Job definitely complained—loudly—and he challenged God, asking Him many questions. But unlike his "friends," Job always spoke rightly about God (Job 42:8). Moreover, in the midst of all his suffering, Job made what I believe is one of the most heroic statements a human being ever uttered. In the midst of abject misery he cried out, "Though he slay me, I will hope in him" (Job 13:15).

Scripture says the just shall live by faith, which doesn't mean believing something when you're not sure if it's true. It means that the just shall live by trusting God. Paul distills the essence of the Christian life when he says, "Rejoice in your hope," since our joy is vested in the future that God promises for His people. Our joy as strangers and sojourners in this valley of tears is that God has prepared a place for us—a better world that will be consummated at Christ's return.

Paul's use of the word *hope* isn't the way we use the term today to refer to things that are uncertain. He and the other biblical authors talk about hope that is certain, hope that cannot fail, and hope that will never disappoint or embarrass you (Rom. 5:5). The New Testament calls hope the anchor of the soul (Heb. 6:13–20). Why? What is it that makes it certain? The answer is God's sure promises and the demonstration of His faithfulness in the history of Israel, in the lives of the Apostles, and, most clearly, in the person and work of Jesus Christ.

Job had very little joy, but there was still a part of his spirit that rejoiced in the midst of his tribulation. Elsewhere he says, "I know that my Redeemer lives, and I will see Him standing on that day." He knew that there is One who would vindicate his prayers, who would restore him some day. The exact details of the vindication he had in mind is up for speculation, for he lived long before the fullness of God's revelation in Christ. But we do know that Job was certain of one thing, namely, that God would not allow his pain, suffering, and affliction to be the last chapter. Job groaned in the present, but he never lost his confidence in the future.

ANSWERING EVIL

OCTOBER 2013

D R. JOHN GERSTNER, MY ESTEEMED mentor, certainly had a way of getting my attention and helping me to think more clearly. I still remember when I told him that I thought the problem of evil is irresolvable. Having noted that the best apologists and theologians in church history haven't answered all the questions raised by the existence of evil in this world, I told him that no one would ever solve the problem on this side of eternity. He turned and rebuked me. "How do you know the problem of evil will never be solved?" he asked. "Perhaps you or another thinker are the one God has appointed to solve this issue."

With all due respect to Dr. Gerstner, I think he overestimated his students. I haven't changed my opinion on the problem of evil since that conversation. In the many years I've taught philosophy, apologetics, and theology, and in the many conversations I've had with hurting people, a full answer to the problem of evil remains elusive. If anything, recent events make the problem seem more acute. In the past year alone, we've dealt with terrorists bombing the Boston Marathon as well as the Sandy Hook Elementary School shooting in Connecticut. Hurricane Sandy killed nearly 300 people in the Northeastern United States. We could also mention the hundreds of thousands who died in tsunamis in 2004 and 2011. The list is almost endless.

Putting a human face on evil can make it more understandable—it's no surprise that evil people do evil things. Nature's violence can be more troubling. How do we deal with natural disasters that do not respect persons but rather indiscriminately claim the lives of the elderly, infants, and the handicapped along with able-bodied children and adults? "How," many people—even many Christians—ask, "could a good God allow such things to happen?"

There's been no shortage of speculation in the attempt to answer these questions. Well-meaning individuals have suggested countless theodicies—attempts at justifying and vindicating God for the presence of evil in the world. In his eighteenth-century book *Theodicy*, philosopher Gottfried Leibniz tried to explain evil by suggesting that we live in the "best of all possible worlds." Other thinkers have said evil is necessary to make us virtuous people or to preserve the reality of free will. Such answers fail to satisfy, and they usually sacrifice the sovereignty of God in the process.

I don't think God has revealed to us a full and final answer to the problem of evil and suffering. However, that doesn't mean that He's been silent on the issue. Scripture does give us some helpful guidelines:

First, evil is not an illusion—it's all too real. Some religions teach that evil is unreal, but the Bible never minimizes the truth of misery and pain. Moreover, the biblical characters show us that a stoic detachment from evil is not the right response. They tear their clothing, offer up lamentations to God, and cry real tears. Our Savior Himself walked the *Via Dolorosa* as the Man of Sorrows who knew our grief.

Second, God is not capricious or arbitrary. He does not act irrationally, nor does He show or permit violence purposelessly. That doesn't mean we always know why a particular evil occurs at a given place or time. Because we don't know all the reasons behind each particular evil, we can't make facile connections between guilt and disaster, between a person's sin and the evil that befalls him. Texts including the book of Job and John 9 keep us from universally declaring that pain is a specific punishment for specific sin. That means that when inexplicable disasters occur, we must say with Martin Luther, "Let God be God." Job's cry that "the Lord gave, and the Lord has taken away; blessed be the name of the Lord" (Job 1:21) was not a superficial display of piety or a denial of pain. Instead, Job bit his lip and clenched his stomach as he remained faithful in the middle of tragedy and unmitigated suffering. Job knew who God was, and he refused to curse Him.

Third, this isn't the best of all possible worlds. This world is fallen. Suffering is here only because sin has marred an otherwise good creation. Of course, that doesn't mean all suffering is tied to a particular sin or that we can draw a one-to-one correlation between the degree of a person's sin and the degree of his suffering. However, suffering belongs to the full complex of sin that people visit upon this world. As long as creation suffers from the violence of men, it returns this violence. The Bible tells us that creation gets angry with its human masters and exploiters. Instead of stewarding the earth wisely and replenishing it, we exploit and pollute it. Until Christ returns with the new heavens and earth, we'll deal with tempests, earthquakes, and floods. Until then, we'll yearn for a renewed creation.

Finally, evil is not ultimate. Christianity never denies the horror of evil, but neither does it regard evil as having any power above or equal to God. Scripture's final word on evil is triumph. Creation groans as it awaits its final redemption, but this groaning is not futile. Over all creation stands the resurrected Christ—*Christus Victor*—who has triumphed over the powers of evil and will make all things new.

FAITH HAS ITS REASONS

NOVEMBER 2013

C HRISTIANS FROM EVERY THEOLOGICAL TRADITION have for centuries confessed their faith by reciting the Apostles' Creed. Elsewhere I have taught on the actual content of this creed, but if there is one aspect of this confession that we often fail to reflect on, it is the creed's opening words: *I believe.*

Here I want to consider faith in relation to what are often seen as its opposites—reason and sense perception. Epistemology is the division of philosophy that seeks to answer one question: How do we know what we know, or how do we know what is true? Reason, sense perception, or some combination of the two have been among the most common answers to this basic question.

Our minds function according to certain categories of rationality. We try to think in a logically coherent manner. Our judgments and deductions are not always correct and legitimate, but our minds always look for logical, intelligible patterns. Some people say that we find true knowledge exclusively within the mind. These "rationalists" stress the mind and reason as the sources of true knowledge.

The mind processes information that we acquire with our five senses. Our minds act on what we see, hear, feel, smell, and taste. Perception is the experience of being in touch with the external world, and "empiricists" emphasize sense perception as the true basis for knowledge.

The scientific method combines sense perception and reason. In scientific experiments we gather facts with our senses. Our minds then draw conclusions, reasoning through what our five senses discover. Some want to oppose this way of learning to faith, but I don't find in Scripture the idea that faith is irrational or anti-sense perception. According to God's Word, reason and sense perception form the foundation of knowledge. Faith rests on this foundation but takes us beyond it.

We live in the most anti-intellectual age of history, and even many Christians believe we can compartmentalize faith as a way of knowing completely separate from sense perception and reason. Yet as Augustine told us centuries ago, how could we receive knowledge from God if it were not accessible to the human mind? Could we say that "Jesus is Lord" without some understanding of what the term Lord means, what the verb is indicates, and who the name Jesus refers to? We can't believe the gospel without our minds understanding it to a degree.

Christianity also features a book—the Bible—that is designed for our understanding. Why would God give us a written document if faith bypasses reason entirely? Moreover, sense perception is key to the biblical story. Luke wrote down those things to which he had eyewitness testimony (Luke 1:1–4). Peter said the Apostles didn't proclaim clever myths but what they saw with their eyes and heard with their ears (2 Peter 1:16). The biblical writers tell us about actual events in history that they experienced. Christianity isn't ahistorical. God reveals Himself with reference to history: He is "the God of Abraham, of Isaac, and of Jacob" (Ex. 3:16).

Faith never requires us to crucify our minds or deny our senses. It's not virtuous to take a "leap of faith" if that means we plunge into irrationality. The Bible never calls us to leap into the darkness but to leap out of the darkness into the light.

The New Testament defines faith as the substance of things hoped for and the evidence of things unseen (Heb. 11:1). This doesn't mean faith is against what we see. We are called to trust Him whom we haven't seen—God—but He hasn't remained wholly invisible. We have seen the Lord's handiwork in this world, which Calvin called "a magnificent theater of natural revelation." One day we'll see Him directly in the beatific vision of His glory, but until then, He has not left Himself without a witness in creation.

Revelation is the third category of knowledge. Christianity is a revealed religion. The Christian God is not mute. When we talk about faith as the evidence of things not seen, we're talking about believing the Lord who has spoken. Not just believing *in* God but *believing* God. Believing God for things we cannot see now is the essence of faith, but it's not an irrational or unscientific faith. God makes it very rational for me to believe He's there. He's shown Himself in the created order. He's broken into time and space. Jesus came in the flesh, was seen, and rose from the dead in history. The Apostles testify to these events in Scripture, recording those things they witnessed with their senses.

It's not irrational to believe in the One who vindicated Himself as the incarnation of truth. This is not blind faith but faith that embraces testimony. The real opposites of faith are not reason and sense perception but credulity and superstition. Credulity, or naive believism, believes something that has no basis in reality. Superstition believes in magical things that have nothing to do with Scripture.

We find superstition and credulity throughout the church. That's why we continually measure our faith by the Word of God and make sure we are assenting to the reasonable, historical testimony of the prophets and the Apostles to the triumph of Christ. Faith is not mere intellectual assent. We aren't saved simply because we affirm the truth of certain facts but because we trust the Person whom those facts reveal. So, faith is definitely more than knowledge. But it is not less.

ESCAPING THE CAGE STAGE

DECEMBER 2013

———

MY FRIEND MICHAEL HORTON OFTEN comments on the phenomenon of "cage-stage Calvinism," that strange malady that seems to afflict so many people who have just seen the truth of the Reformed doctrines of grace. We've all known one of these "cage-stage Calvinists." Many of us were even one of them when we were first convinced of God's sovereignty in salvation.

Cage-stage Calvinists are identifiable by their insistence on turning every discussion into an argument for limited atonement or for making it their personal mission to ensure everyone they know hears—often quite loudly—the truths of divine election. Now, having a zeal for the truth is always commendable. But a zeal for the truth that manifests itself in obnoxiousness won't convince anyone of the biblical truth of Reformed theology. As many of us can attest from personal experience, it will actually push them away.

Roger Nicole, the late Swiss Reformed theologian and colleague of mine for several decades, once remarked that all human beings are by nature semi-Pelagian, believing that they are not born as slaves to sin. In this country, particularly, we have been indoctrinated into a humanistic understanding of anthropology, especially with respect to our understanding of human freedom. This is the land of the free, after all. We don't want to believe that we are burdened by negative inclinations and outright enmity toward God, as the Bible teaches us (Rom. 3:9–20). We think that true freedom means having the ability to come to faith without the vanquishing power of saving grace. When we realize that this is not true, that Scripture paints a bleak picture of the human condition apart from grace, that it says it is impossible for us to choose rightly, we want to make sure that everybody else knows it as well. Sometimes we are even angry that no one told us about the true extent of our depravity and the majesty of God's sovereign grace before.

This gives birth to cage-stage Calvinists, those newly minted Reformed believers who are so aggressive and impatient that they should be locked in a cage for a little while so that they can cool down and mature a little in the faith. At times, someone who becomes convinced of the biblical doctrines of grace finds himself in conflict with friends and family because of his discovery of Reformed theology. More than once I've been asked how one should handle hostility from loved ones regarding Reformed theology. If Reformed convictions are causing problems, should one just drop the subject altogether? Are we responsible for convincing others of the truth of the doctrines of grace?

The answer is both yes and no. First let's consider the "no." Scripture says that "neither he who plants nor he who waters is anything, but only God who gives the growth" (1 Cor. 3:7). Paul is speaking primarily of evangelism in that verse, but I think we can apply it to growth in Christ even after conversion. The Holy Spirit convinces us of truth, and one's coming to embrace Reformed theology shows this quite clearly. Given our semi-Pelagian inclinations, it takes a tremendous amount of exposure to the Word of God to overcome that natural bias against the doctrines of grace. People hold tenaciously to a particular view of free will that is not taught in Scripture. Calvin once remarked that if you mean by free will a will that is unencumbered by the weight of sin, you've used a term that's far too exalted to apply to us. It takes a lot to overcome the exalted view that most sinners have of themselves. Only the Spirit can finally convince people of His truth.

Recognizing the Spirit's work, however, does not mean we are silent or stop believing the truth of Scripture. We don't give up the doctrines of grace to keep peace in the family or with friends. John Piper puts it well when he says that we not only have to believe the truth, that it's not enough even to defend the truth, but we must also contend for the truth. That does not mean, however, that we are to be contentious people by nature. So yes, we are to share what we have learned about God's sovereign grace with those around us.

However, if we really believe the doctrines of grace, we learn how to be gracious about it. When we remember how long it took us to get past the difficulties we once had with the full biblical picture of divine sovereignty and our enslavement to sin, we can view our non-Reformed friends and family more sympathetically and share the truth with them more graciously. One of the first things a person who is excited about his discovery of the doctrines of grace must learn quickly is to be patient with friends and family. God took time with us to convince us of His sovereignty in salvation. We can trust Him to do the same with those we love.

INTO THE WORLD

JANUARY 2014

———

I'VE LONG BEEN FASCINATED WITH THOSE MOMENTS in Jesus' life when the veil of His human flesh gave way to a vision of His refulgent glory as the Son of God. What must it have been like to be one of His disciples and to know Him as a man but then to see with clarity His deity in an encounter of dazzling light? The most spectacular of these encounters was His transfiguration, that moment when His transcendent radiance paralyzed Peter, James, and John with awe (Matt. 17:1–13). All they wanted at that moment was to bask in Jesus' glory forever—and so that is what they asked for.

It has always struck me that Jesus said no to that request. Instead, Jesus came down from the Mount of Transfiguration with His disciples and went back into the world. Jesus' going back into the world has served as a model for the church's ministry until the present day. When Christ calls people into His kingdom, He doesn't pull them out of the world forever. He sends them back out with the gospel.

Jesus did that with the Apostles just after His resurrection. He came to the upper room, where they were hiding in fear, and told them that they were to wait for the Spirit to be poured out. But at that point, there was to be no more waiting. Once the Spirit came, they were to go out into the world (Luke 24:36–49). And that is what they did. The Apostles entered the marketplace with the authority of Christ behind them, and they upset the world.

Paul is a model for engagement with the world. We are familiar with his confrontation with the philosophers at the Areopagus in Athens, but these philosophers knew where to find him because he was "in the marketplace every day," reasoning with the people who were there (Acts 17:16–34). The marketplace in Athens was more than a mere shopping mall. It was the center of community life. It was the place where people gathered to play, shop, hear lawsuits, and attend events. It was a decidedly public location, the place where one could engage with the world. No one went to the marketplace to hide. Paul went there to find unbelievers and minister to them.

During the Protestant Reformation, Martin Luther preached that the church had to move out of the heavenly temple into the world. By this he meant that Christ has relevance not just for the community of believers but for the whole world as well. Jesus is not bound to the inner courts of the Christian community, and if we think that He is, then we are being disobedient or, perhaps, have no faith at all. His gospel is for all nations, and all of us are responsible to help fulfill the Great Commission to make disciples of all peoples (Matt. 28:18–20).

Throughout church history, many have taught the idea of what we might call "salvation by separation," believing that we achieve holiness by avoiding contact with sinners. This doctrine predates Christianity, however, having been invented by the Pharisees, who were scandalized by Jesus' ministry to tax collectors, prostitutes, and lepers. But if Christ's holiness did not require withdrawing from the world, then neither does ours. He came to seek and to save the lost, and the lost are gathered in the world—in our Father's world. To stay out of the public sphere, away from sinners, is never a permanent option for the Christian.

I say "permanent option" because generations of believers have seen wisdom in having new Christians withdraw from the world for a season—not into monastic isolation but for a time of concentrated growth with fellow believers. Upon reaching spiritual maturity, however, they must see the world as God's theater of redemption, that place where He meets with sinners through the gospel witness of believers and calls His elect to faith. Martin Luther noted that it is the coward who flees from the real world permanently and hides his fear with piety.

The church is not a ghetto or a reservation. True, the world wants to put us there, to force us out of the world into the four walls of the church building, outside of which we are never to speak of sin or the salvation that comes only in Christ. However, we don't have to let the world do that. I fear that all too often we blame the world for our failure to engage it when, in reality, we are more comfortable hiding from the world's hostility. Our fallen culture will do whatever it can to hide our light under a bushel. We dare not invent our own bushels to help them in their goal. Christ has commissioned us to be light and salt in this world (Matt. 5:13–16). We have no option but to obey.

"To stay out of the public sphere, away from sinners, is never a permanent option for the Christian."

THE SPIRIT'S INTERNAL WITNESS

FEBRUARY 2014

——

N EARLY FORTY YEARS AGO, I was a part of a group known as the International Council on Biblical Inerrancy. Concerned about the impact of liberal higher criticism, we gathered to define what it means that the Bible does not teach any error and to articulate a defensible position on the trustworthiness of God's Word that Christians could use to combat misunderstandings and misrepresentations of the church's historic position on the Bible. The council developed the Chicago Statement on Biblical Inerrancy, which deals with many issues related to the inspiration and truthfulness of Scripture. Article XVII of this statement asserts, in part, that "the Holy Spirit bears witness to the Scriptures, assuring believers of the truthfulness of God's written Word."

By this article we wanted to make it clear that the Bible is the Holy Spirit's book. He is involved not only in the inspiration of Scripture, but is also a witness to Scripture's truthfulness. This is what we call the "internal testimony" of the Holy Spirit. In other words, the Holy Spirit provides a testimony that takes place inside of us—He bears witness to our spirits that the Bible is the Word of God. Just as the Spirit bears witness with our spirits that we are children of God (Rom. 8:16), He assures us of the sacred truth of His Word.

Despite its importance, the internal testimony of the Spirit is subject to misunderstanding. One of these misunderstandings relates to how we defend the truthfulness of the Bible. Do we need to provide an apologetic—a defense—for sacred Scripture that relies on evidence from archaeology and history, on demonstrating the Bible's internal consistency, and on logical argumentation? Some misconstrue the doctrine of the internal testimony to mean that the presentation of evidence to the veracity of the Bible is unnecessary and even counterproductive. All we need to do is rest on the fact that the Holy Spirit tells us that the Bible is God's Word both in direct biblical statements and in His internal work of confirming Scripture's truthfulness.

Those who hold this position usually want to stress that the authority of God's Word depends on God Himself and believe that subjecting His Word to empirical testing is to make the Bible's truthfulness dependent on our own authority to evaluate its truth claims. At one level, this concern is laudable. Scripture's authority depends on its being the revelation of God, above whom there is no higher authority. But when we are talking about proof for the veracity of Scripture, we are not talking about the authority of God's Word but about how we know which of the books that claim to be the Word of God are actually from Him. Here, subjective experience cannot be our only court of appeal. We need some sort of objective testimony to determine whether the Bible, Qur'an, or Bhagavad Gita is the Word of God because they all claim to be the Word of God.

This is where what John Calvin called the *indicia* come into play. The *indicia*—indicators—are testable, analyzable, falsifiable, or verifiable aspects of proof. They include such things as archaeological evidence, Scripture's conformity to what we know about history from other sources, its internal consistency, its majesty and beauty, and so forth. These things give us objective confidence that the Bible is indeed the Word of God. Both Calvin and the Westminster Confession of Faith tell us that these indicators are enough in themselves to convince people that Scripture alone is the Word of God.

However, these authorities both recognize the difference between proof and persuasion, and it is really the work of persuasion that we are discussing when we look at the internal testimony of the Spirit. Human beings are adept at rejecting objective evidence when it does not confirm their prejudice, no matter how clear or compelling the evidence may be. Some people will not be persuaded by all the proof in the world because they are not truly open to the evidence.

My experience as an apologist and minister has shown me that the real reason most people reject Christianity is not for lack of evidence. The proof from external sources regarding the truth of the biblical account is too overwhelming. No, the real issue is a moral one. The person not reconciled to God in Christ and living in disobedience does not want Scripture's claim that God has a full and final claim on his life to be true. He wants to get rid of the book as fast as he can.

This is where the internal witness of the Spirit comes in. Only those whom God the Holy Spirit has regenerated will submit to Scripture as His inerrant and infallible Word. The Holy Spirit does not give us a new argument for the truth of the Bible, but He confirms in our hearts the truth of Scripture as it is displayed in both the internal marks of Scripture (harmony and majesty of its contents) and the external marks of Scripture (historical accuracy). Objective proofs for the Bible are many and compelling, but they cannot force people to believe against their wills. Sinners are only persuaded to receive the Bible as God's Word as the Holy Spirit changes their hearts and assures them that they can trust and rely on what Scripture says.

FOR THE GLORY OF GOD

MARCH 2014

———

A T THE CHURCH I CO-PASTOR, Saint Andrew's Chapel in Sanford, Florida, we are deliberate about making sure that both our church members and visitors understand the doctrinal basis of our fellowship. As a small way of helping to further that end, we note in our church bulletin every Sunday morning that "we affirm the *solas* of the Protestant Reformation."

By way of reminder, the five *solas* are five points that summarize the biblical theology recovered and proclaimed during the Protestant Reformation. As we note in our bulletin, these five *solas* are:

- *Sola Scriptura*: The Bible is the sole written divine revelation and alone can bind the conscience of the believer absolutely.
- *Sola Fide*: Justification is by faith alone. The merit of Christ, imputed to us by faith, is the sole ground of our acceptance by God, by which our sins are remitted, and imputed to Christ.
- *Solus Christus*: Christ is the only mediator through whose work we are redeemed.
- *Sola Gratia*: Our salvation rests solely on the work of God's grace for us.
- *Soli Deo Gloria*: To God alone belongs the glory.

Each *sola* is important, but the first four really exist to preserve the last one, namely, the glory of God. By *sola Scriptura*, we declare the glory of God's authority by noting that only His inspired Word can command us absolutely. *Sola fide*, *solus Christus*, and *sola gratia* all exalt God's glory in salvation. God and God alone—through His Son, Jesus Christ—saves His people from sin and death. We need the glory of God to be reinforced because it is the hardest truth of all for people to accept. The refusal to glorify God in an appropriate and proper way is basic to our corrupt state. As Paul says in his penetrating description of human fallenness in Romans 1: "They did not honor him as God" (v. 21).

So often when we talk about God, we describe Him in such a way that He isn't recognizable as the God of the Bible. I've said more than once that if our god is not sovereign, our god is not God. But I must go further. If we don't acknowledge the sovereignty of God, if we don't acknowledge the justice of God, if we don't acknowledge the omniscience of God, the immutability of God, then whatever god it is we are acknowledging, it is not God. We're not glorifying God as God, we're glorifying something less than God as if it were God, and to glorify something other than God or something less than God as if it were God is the very essence of idolatry.

Idolatry is our most basic sin, and in it an exchange is made: God reveals His truth about Himself, and we trade in that truth and walk out with the lie. We exchange the glory of God for the glory of the creature. This can be done in a crass way of worshiping something that we craft with our own hands such as a statue or an icon. But there is also a more sophisticated, intellectual sort of idolatry—the reconstruction of our doctrine of God in such a way as to strip Him of those attributes with which we are uncomfortable. All of us have a propensity to reconstruct a god who is not holy, who is not wrathful, who is not just, who is not sovereign. We find it easy to take the attributes of God we like and reject the ones we don't. When we do that, we are as guilty of idolatry as a person who is worshiping a graven image.

Every day in America, we hear one of the great pernicious lies about God, namely, that we all worship the same god. We are told that whatever we call him or it—Allah or Yahweh or Tao or Buddha—it doesn't matter. We all worship the same thing. To that I reply, "No, we don't." The scary part about religion in general is that it underscores man's guilt before God, but then goes on to create ineffective solutions to this guilt. The impetus for creating alternatives to the religion that God reveals in nature and in Scripture is idolatry. But even if we boldly confess this truth, we must be on guard against idolatry even within the Christian community. Because we are fallen creatures, we can be religious and be idolaters at the same time. All of us can remake God in our own image, downplaying or ignoring those aspects of His character we do not like. If we do that, we are withholding the glory that belongs to God alone.

The whole goal of our salvation is to bring us to a place where we worship God and we honor Him as God. The great danger is that we make ourselves the center of concern, and we steal the glory of God. In all that we do, the driving passion of the Christian must always be *Soli Deo Gloria*, to God alone be the glory. And the only way for this passion to be realized is to honor God as God, to understand Him as He has revealed Himself in His Word and not according to the mere opinions of fallen creatures.

THE FALL
OF A BELIEVER

———

W E MAY LIVE IN A CULTURE THAT believes everyone will be saved, that we are "justified by death" and all you need to do to go to heaven is die, but God's Word certainly doesn't give us the luxury of believing that. Any quick and honest reading of the New Testament shows that the Apostles were convinced that nobody can go to heaven unless they believe in Christ alone for their salvation (John 14:6; Rom. 10:9–10).

Historically, evangelical Christians have largely agreed on this point. Where they have differed has been on the matter of the security of salvation. People who would otherwise agree that only those who trust in Jesus will be saved have disagreed on whether anyone who truly believes in Christ can lose his salvation.

Theologically speaking, what we are talking about here is the concept of *apostasy*. This term comes from a Greek word that means "to stand away from." When we talk about those who have become apostate or have committed apostasy, we're talking about those who have fallen from the faith or at least from the profession of faith in Christ that they once made.

Many believers have held that yes, true Christians can lose their salvation because there are several New Testament texts that seem to indicate that this can happen. I'm thinking, for example, of Paul's words in 1 Timothy 1:18–20:

> This charge I entrust to you, Timothy, my child, in accordance with the prophecies previously made about you, that by them you may wage the good warfare, holding faith and a good conscience. By rejecting this, some have made shipwreck of their faith, among whom are

Hymenaeus and Alexander, whom I have handed over to Satan that they may learn not to blaspheme.

Here, in the midst of instructions and admonitions related to Timothy's life and ministry, Paul warns Timothy to keep the faith and to keep a good conscience, and to be reminded of those who didn't. The Apostle refers to those who made "shipwreck of their faith," men whom he "handed over to Satan that they may learn not to blaspheme." This second point is a reference to Paul's excommunication of these men, and the whole passage combines a sober warning with concrete examples of those who fell away grievously from their Christian profession.

There is no question that professing believers can fall and fall radically. We think of men like Peter, for example, who denied Christ. But the fact that he was restored shows that not every professing believer who falls has fallen past the point of no return. At this point, we should distinguish a serious and radical fall from a total and final fall. Reformed theologians have noted that the Bible is full of examples of true believers who fall into gross sin and even protracted periods of impenitence. So, Christians do fall and they fall radically. What could be more serious than Peter's public denial of Jesus Christ?

But the question is, are these people who are guilty of a real fall irretrievably fallen and eternally lost, or is this fall a temporary condition that will, in the final analysis, be remedied by their restoration? In the case of a person such as Peter, we see that his fall was remedied by his repentance. However, what about those who fall away finally? Were they ever truly believers in the first place?

Our answer to this question has to be no. First John 2:19 speaks of the false teachers who went out from the church as never having truly been part of the church. John describes the apostasy of people who had made a profession of faith but who never really were converted. Moreover, we know that God glorifies all whom He justifies (Rom. 8:29–30). If a person has true saving faith and is justified, God will preserve that person.

In the meantime, however, if the person who has fallen is still alive, how do we know if he is a full apostate? One thing none of us can do is read the heart of other people. When I see a person who has made a profession of faith and later repudiates it, I don't know whether he is a truly regenerate person who's in the midst of a serious, radical fall but who will at some point in the future certainly be restored; or whether he is a person who was never really converted, whose profession of faith was false from the start.

This question of whether a person can lose his salvation is not an abstract question. It touches us at the very core of our Christian lives, not only with regard to our concerns for our own perseverance, but also with regard to our concern for our family and friends, particularly those who seemed, for all outward appearances, to have made a genuine profession of faith. We thought their profession was credible, we embraced them as brothers or sisters, only to find out that they repudiated that faith.

What do you do, practically, in a situation like that? First, you pray, and then, you wait. We don't know the final outcome of the situation, and I'm sure there are going to be surprises when we get to heaven. We're going to be surprised to see people there who we didn't think would be, and we're going to be surprised that we don't see people there who we were sure would be there, because we simply don't know the internal status of a human heart or of a human soul. Only God can see that soul, change that soul, and preserve that soul.

THE COMFORT OF JESUS' PRAYERS

MAY 2014

———

A S AN ORDAINED MINISTER, I've had experience going to the Scriptures with a number of people in order to help them see what God has to say about many different subjects. Over the years, one of the most common questions that I've been asked has to do with the meaning of Christ's work for the security of the believer's salvation. The New Testament gives us many categories for understanding that those who are truly saved will persevere. There is the category of justification, which tells us that we have received the imputation of Christ's righteousness through faith in Him alone and that we are at peace with God—not a cease-fire that can be broken at the slightest provocation, but an everlasting peace wherein the Lord never takes up arms against us again (Rom. 5:1). There is also the category of sanctification, which says God always finishes the work of salvation that He starts: "He who began a good work in you will bring it to completion at the day of Jesus Christ" (Phil. 1:6).

In the Philippians passage, we typically understand that it is God, by the Holy Spirit, who is working out our salvation in us, bringing us into conformity to Christ. That, of course, is true, but we should not miss that Jesus is at work as well. Our greatest consolation regarding our perseverance comes from what the New Testament reveals about the present work of Christ. We often speak of the "finished work of Christ," which is simply shorthand to indicate the completion of Christ's atonement—the finalization of His purchase of redemption for us, His taking upon Himself the curse of God. However, Christ's work of salvation did not end there. He had more to do after the cross. He was raised for our justification, and then He ascended into heaven, where He is seated at God's right hand, where He reigns as King of kings and Lord of lords, governing creation and ruling His church (Acts 2:33; Rom. 4:23–25; 1 Cor. 15:25).

That is not all. One of the chief emphases of the New Testament in terms of His present work for His people is His intercession. Christ's priestly work did not end on the cross. Every day, in the presence of the Father, Christ intercedes for His people. If, as James says, the fervent prayer of a righteous person "has great power as it is working" (James 5:16), how much more do Jesus' prayers avail for His people?

One of the most important sources of comfort with respect to the intercession of Christ in behalf of the believer is found in Jesus' great High Priestly Prayer, which itself was a profound prayer of intercession. Remarkably, even we are mentioned in this great prayer of intercession. We read in John 17:1–9:

> Father, glorify me in your own presence with the glory that I had with you before the world existed. I have manifested your name to the people whom you gave me out of the world. Yours they were, and you gave them to me, and they have kept your word. . . . For I have given them the words that you gave me, and they have received them and have come to know in truth that I came from you; and they have believed that you sent me. I am praying for them. I am not praying for the world but for those whom you have given me, for they are yours.

Look again at verse 9: "I am praying for them. I am not praying for the world but for those whom you have given me, for they are yours." That's the crux of the matter. Jesus is praying for all those who belong to God, not for everyone on the planet. The Father has chosen a people for Himself—and the same people belong to Christ as well. None of them is lost except the son of destruction—Judas—who being a son of destruction, was never God's child to begin with. Those for whom Jesus prays are the people whom God has chosen, and none of them is lost (vv. 10–19). This includes not only the disciples in the Upper Room who witnessed Jesus' prayer but also those of us who believe in Him today. I said that we are mentioned in Jesus' prayer, and here we are: "I do not ask for these only, but also for those who will believe in me through their word" (v. 20). We came to believe through the words of the Apostles, and so Jesus prays for us. This is Christ's prayer. We persevere because we are preserved by our High Priest's intercession.

If we take great comfort in the intercessory prayer of a friend or of a pastor, how much more comfort can we experience from the full assurance that Jesus is praying for us? We know that Jesus' prayers never fail. He knows the mind of God perfectly. He knows what to pray for so that we persevere to the end. Moreover, Jesus says the Father will give us whatever we ask for in His name (15:16). If this is so, certainly the Father will not fail to give His own beloved Son what He asks for, and He asks for us to persevere.

The greatest illustration of the efficacy of Jesus' prayer is Peter. Like Judas, Peter had a great fall. Unlike Judas, Peter was restored and persevered in faith. Both of them denied Jesus, but only Peter repented. Why? Luke 22:31–32 gives the answer. Satan asked to capture Peter permanently, but Jesus prayed for Peter, and that ensured that he would repent. Jesus did not pray for Judas, but He prayed for Peter, and so Peter persevered in faith and repentance. That is great assurance for us all. Those for whom Jesus prays remain in faith over the long haul. If we believe in Christ, He is praying for us every day.

THE PURPOSES OF GOD

JUNE 2014

———

"**W**HY?**" THIS SIMPLE QUESTION IS** loaded with assumptions about what philosophers call "teleology." Teleology, which comes from the Greek word for "goal" or "end" (*telos*), is the study of purpose. The "why" questions are purpose questions. We seek the reasons things happen as they do. Why does the rain fall? Why does the earth turn on its axis? Why did you say that?

When we raise the question of purpose, we are concerned with ends, aims, and goals. All these terms suggest intent. They assume meaning rather than meaninglessness. Despite the best attempts of nihilist philosophers to deny that anything has ultimate meaning and significance, the perennial question "Why?" shows that they haven't been successful. In fact, even the cynic's glib retort of "Why not?" is a thinly veiled commitment to purpose. To explain why we're not doing something is to give a reason or purpose for not doing it. Purpose remains in the background. Human beings are creatures committed to purpose. We do things for a reason—with some kind of goal in mind.

Still, there is complexity in this quest for purpose. We distinguish between proximate and remote purposes, the proximate being what is close at hand and the remote referring to the distant and ultimate purpose. To use a sports analogy, the proximate goal for the Pittsburgh Steelers offensive line is to make a first down. Making a touchdown is the more remote goal. A goal that is even further on for the team is to win the game. Finally, the ultimate goal is to win the Super Bowl.

The most famous Old Testament illustration of the relation between remote and proximate purposes is found in the story of Joseph. At the story's end, Joseph's brothers express their fear that he will take revenge on them for all that they had done to him. Joseph's response shows us a remarkable concurrence at work between proximate and remote purposes.

He said, "You meant evil against me, but God meant it for good" (Gen. 50:20). Here, the proximate and the remote seemed to be mutually exclusive. The divine intention was the exact opposite of the human intention. Joseph's brothers had one goal; God had a different one. The astounding reality here is that the proximate purpose served the remote purpose. This did not absolve the brothers of culpability. Their intent and actions were evil. Yet God deemed it good to let the brothers have their way with Joseph—to a limited extent—that He might achieve His ultimate purpose.

We all experience what seem to be tragic accidents. Some years ago, one of the pastors of Saint Andrew's Chapel cut his hand severely while working in a cabinet shop. He did not mean to slice his hand; he intended to cut the wood for the cabinet he was working on. Proximately speaking, he had an accident. He asked, "Why did God permit my hand to get cut up?"

The question looks for a final purpose to the accident. It assumes what we know to be true, namely, that God could have prevented the accident. If we deny this, we deny the God who is. If He could not have prevented it, He would not be omnipotent—He would not be God. Moreover, our question "Why?" assumes another truth: that the question has an answer. We know God had a purpose for the accident.

For questions like these, we may not get a full answer in this life. We may never know on this side of glory all of the reasons why a tragedy occurs. Nevertheless, there is an answer to this most important question: "Is God's purpose in allowing this accident to happen a good one?"

If we know anything about God, we already know the answer to the question. The Lord's purposes and intentions are always altogether good. There is no hint of arbitrariness or wicked intent in the will of God. The pleasure of His will is always the good pleasure of His will. His pleasure is always good; His will is always good; His intentions are always good.

Paul's incredible promise that "for those who love God all things work together for good, for those who are called according to his purpose" (Rom. 8:28) is a statement of teleology. Here, Paul addresses the remote rather than the proximate. Note that he doesn't say all things *are* good but that they *work together* for good—for a final and ultimate goal. The Apostle insists that the proximate must always be seen in light of the remote. The difficulty we face is that we do not yet possess the full light of the remote. On this side of heaven, we see through a glass darkly. Yet, we are not utterly devoid of light. We know enough about God to know He has a good purpose for all things even when that good purpose eludes us.

God's good purpose shows us that the appearance of vanity and futility in this world is just that—mere appearance. To trust in God's good purpose is the essence of godly faith. Thus, no Christian can be an ultimate pessimist. The wickedness and tragedy we daily endure can lead to a proximate pessimism, but not an ultimate one. I am pessimistic about human government and the innate good will of men. I am fully optimistic about divine government and the intrinsic good will of God.

We do not live in a world of chance or chaos. It began with a purpose, it is sustained with a purpose, and it has an ultimate purpose. This is my Father's world, and His rule is purposeful, not capricious and arbitrary. Purposelessness is a manifest impossibility.

THE HOLY LOVE OF GOD

JULY 2014

———

L ONG AGO, AUGUSTINE OF HIPPO pointed out that the desire of every human heart is to experience a love that is transcendent. Regrettably for us today, however, I don't think there's any word in the English language that's been more stripped of the depth of its meaning than the word *love*. Due to the shallow romanticism of secular culture, we tend to view the love of God in the same way popular music, art, and literature view love. Yet the Bible says God's love is far different—and greater.

First John 4:7–11 gives us this classic statement with respect to the love of God:

> Beloved, let us love one another, for love is from God, and whoever loves has been born of God and knows God. Anyone who does not love does not know God, because God is love.... In this is love, not that we have loved God, but that he loved us and sent his only Son to be the propitiation for our sins. Beloved, if God so loved us, we also ought to love one another.

Here the Apostle grounds his admonition for Christians to love one another in the very character of God. "Love is from God," he tells us. What he means is that Christian love comes from God Himself. This love is not natural to fallen humanity. It originates in God and is a divine gift to His people. When we are transformed by the power of the Holy Spirit, we are given a capacity for this supernatural love that has God as its source and foundation. When John says that "whoever loves has been born of God and knows God," he is not teaching that every human being who loves another is therefore born of God. The kind of love of which he speaks comes only from regeneration. Without the Holy Spirit's transformation of the human heart, no one has this capacity for love. No unregenerate person has this kind of love, and no regenerate person lacks such love. Therefore, a person who does not have the ability to love in the way John describes has not been born again. "Anyone who does not love [in this manner] does not know God."

John does not stop there. Not only is love *from* God but God *is* love. Note that John does not use the word *is* as an equals sign. We cannot reverse the subject and the predicate in *God is love* and say *love is God.* John is not making a crass identification between love and God so that anyone who has a romantic feeling in his heart or any affection for another person has thereby encountered God. When he says God is love, he's using a bit of hyperbole. In other words, love is such an intimate aspect or attribute of the character of God, that you can, in a manner of speaking, say that He is love. Any view of Him that neglects to include within it this profound sense of divine love is a distortion of who God is.

Of course, the normal problem we face is not that people ignore God's love; rather, people separate His love from His other attributes. I don't know how many times I've taught on God's sovereignty, holiness, or justice, only to hear the objection, "But my God is love"—as if God's love is incompatible with justice, sovereignty, or holiness.

Our most fundamental inclination as fallen human creatures is to exchange the truth that God reveals about Himself for a lie, and to serve and worship the creature rather than the Creator (Rom. 1:18–32). We commit idolatry every time we substitute a lesser concept for His glory, whether that substitution takes the crass form of stone gods or the more sophisticated form of redefining God's character to suit our tastes. A god stripped of justice, of holiness, of sovereignty, and the rest is as much an idol as a statue of wood or stone. We must be careful not to substitute for the biblical God a god who is exhausted in his character by the one attribute of love, especially as popular culture defines it.

As Christians we believe in a God who is simple and not made up of parts. God is not one part sovereign, one part just, one part immutable, one part omniscient, one part eternal, and one part loving. Rather, He is all of His attributes at all times. To understand any single attribute, we must understand it in relation to all His other attributes. The love of God is eternal and sovereign. The love of God is immutable and holy. We treat all of His other attributes in the same way. God's justice is loving and eternal. His holiness is loving and omniscient. Our concept of the love of God will stay on track only as we understand His love in relationship to His other attributes.

Whatever else God's love is, it is holy. His love is therefore characterized by the qualities that define holiness—transcendence and purity. First, God's love is transcendent. It is set apart and different from everything we experience in creation. Second, God's love is pure. His love is absolutely flawless, having no selfishness, wickedness, or sin mixed in with it. God's love is not ordinary or profane. It is a majestic, sacred love that goes far beyond anything creatures can manifest. No shadow of evil covers the brightness of the pure glory of the love of God.

The love of God is in a class by itself. It transcends our experience. Nevertheless, it is a love that He shares in part with us and expects us to manifest to each other. He grants to His people—insofar as is possible given the Creator-creature distinction—His holy love (Rom. 5:5).

DIVINE INCOMPREHENSIBILITY

AUGUST 2014

———

W HAT CAN WE KNOW ABOUT GOD? That's the most basic question of theology, for what we can know about God and whether we can know anything about Him at all determine the scope and content of our study. Here we must consider the teaching of the greatest theologians in history, all of whom have affirmed the "incomprehensibility of God." By using the term *incomprehensible*, they are not referring to something we are unable to comprehend or know at all. Theologically speaking, to say God is incomprehensible is not to say that God is utterly unknowable. It is to say that none of us can comprehend God exhaustively.

Incomprehensibility is related to a key tenet of the Protestant Reformation—the finite cannot contain (or grasp) the infinite. Human beings are finite creatures, so our minds always work from a finite perspective. We live, move, and have our being on a finite plane, but God lives, moves, and has His being in infinity. Our finite understanding cannot contain an infinite subject; thus, God is incomprehensible. This concept represents a check and balance to warn us lest we think we have captured altogether and mastered in every detail the things of God. Our finitude always limits our understanding of God.

If we misunderstand the doctrine of God's incomprehensibility, we can easily slide into two serious errors. The first error says that since God is incomprehensible, He must be utterly unknowable, and anything we say about God is gibberish. But Christianity affirms the rationality of God alongside the incomprehensibility of God. Our minds can go only so far in understanding God, and to know God we need His revelation.

But that revelation is intelligible, not irrational. It is not gibberish. It is not nonsense. The incomprehensible God has revealed Himself truly.

Here we allude to the Reformational principle that God is both hidden and revealed. There is a mysterious dimension of God that we do not know. However, we aren't left in darkness, groping around for a hidden God. God has also revealed Himself, and that is basic to the Christian faith. Christianity is a revealed religion. God the Creator has revealed Himself manifestly in the glorious theater of nature. This is what we call "natural revelation." God has also revealed Himself verbally. He has spoken, and we have His Word inscripturated in the Bible. Here we're talking about special revelation—information God gives us that we could never figure out on our own.

God remains incomprehensible because He reveals Himself without revealing everything there is to know about Him. "The secret things belong to the Lord our God, but the things that are revealed belong to us and to our children forever" (Deut. 29:29). It's not as if we have no knowledge of God or as if we have consummate knowledge of God; rather, we have a working knowledge of God that is useful and crucial for our lives.

This raises the question as to how we can meaningfully speak about the incomprehensible God. Theologians have an unfortunate tendency to swing between two poles. The pole of skepticism, which we considered above, assumes that our language about God is utterly meaningless and has no reference point with regard to Him. The other pole is a form of pantheism that falsely assumes we have captured or contained God. We steer clear of these errors when we understand that our language about God is built upon analogy. We can say what God is like, but as soon as we equate whatever it is that we use to describe God with His essence, we have committed the error of thinking that the finite has contained the infinite.

Historically, we see the vacillating between the two aforementioned errors in Protestant liberalism and Neoorthodoxy. Nineteenth-century liberal theology identified God with the flow of history and with nature. It promoted a pantheism in which everything was God and God was everything. Against that backdrop, Neoorthodoxy objected to identifying God with creation, and it sought to restore God's transcendence. In their zeal, Neoorthodox theologians spoke of God as "wholly other." That idea is problematic. If God is wholly other, how do you know anything about Him? If God is utterly dissimilar from us, how could He reveal Himself? What means could He use? Could He reveal Himself through a sunset? Could He reveal Himself through Jesus of Nazareth? If He were wholly other from human beings, what common basis for communication between God and mankind could there ever be? If God is utterly dissimilar from us, there is no way for Him to speak to us.

Understanding that we relate to the Lord by way of analogy solves the problem. There is a point of contact between man and God. The Bible tells us that we are created in the image of God (Gen. 1:26–28). In some sense, human beings are like God. That makes it possible for communication to occur. God has built this capacity for communication into creation. We are not God, but we are like Him because we bear His image and are made in His likeness. Therefore, God can reveal Himself to us, not in His language, but in our language. He can talk to us. He can communicate to us in a manner that we can understand—not exhaustively, but truly and meaningfully. If you get rid of analogy, you end in skepticism.

THE BLESSING
OF GREAT TEACHERS

SEPTEMBER 2014

———

S INCE I'VE SPENT THE MAJORITY OF MY professional career as a teacher of Scripture, philosophy, and theology, I've often had the opportunity to think about matters of pedagogy and other issues related to instruction. One thing that's always struck me as I have considered what it means to be an effective teacher is that most of the great teachers in history were themselves students of other great instructors. Socrates taught Plato; Plato taught Aristotle; and Aristotle taught Alexander the Great. The entire history of Western ideas has been affected by these four men. In theology, we see that Ambrose of Milan taught Augustine, and Augustine, through his writings, taught both Martin Luther and John Calvin. We owe a great debt to Ambrose, who by discipling Augustine got the ball rolling for the Reformation, in a manner of speaking.

That great teachers produce other great teachers tells us that we can't take the search for a teacher lightly. In fact, our choices of the instructors under whom we sit are among the most crucial and life-altering decisions we will ever make. We should take great care in selecting our instructors, particularly when we're considering those who will train us for our vocations. I've seen too many young people choose a school because it had a beautiful campus or national championship football team, or because of its location. I've seen too many young men and women not consider the faculty when they are evaluating different options for higher education. Yet it is the faculty that matters most. These are the people who have a definitive impact on our future. We have to think carefully about who will be teaching us and what they will teach us at every stage of life, but particularly during our college years.

Several teachers during my undergraduate and graduate years of study had an impact on me that resonates to this day. As an undergraduate student, I chose philosophy as my major because I had a great philosophy professor as my faculty advisor. I was drawn to this man, Dr. Thomas Gregory, for his erudition and kindness. I ultimately ended up majoring in philosophy more out of my respect for the man than out of an innate affection for philosophy. I took every course that Dr. Gregory taught and, under his personal influence, developed a love for the history of ideas and the importance of logical thought.

When I was in seminary, I was privileged to have yet another incredible instructor—Dr. John Gerstner—who became my mentor in theology. He was instrumental in my decision to pursue doctoral studies. He insisted that I pursue a doctorate, and though I was initially reluctant, I told him that I would go on to further studies only if I could sit under the best teachers available. Imagine my surprise when Dr. Gerstner identified those individuals as G.C. Berkouwer and the faculty at the Free University of Amsterdam. After talking with Dr. Gerstner at length about it that day, I booked my family's journey to the Netherlands the next. That decision was one of the most important decisions I have ever made, and I don't regret it.

Three years ago, Ligonier Ministries opened Reformation Bible College to provide formal training in the things of God for young men and women. When we were planning the college, I was insistent that we hire the best faculty possible because I knew the quality of our education and its faithfulness to Scripture would be determined finally by our instructors and the material they would present to our students.

It's ultimately no surprise that great teachers produce other great teachers. That seems to be the way God has designed us. In Scripture, we are called again and again to be disciples, or more precisely, learners. We need teachers if we are to learn, and great teachers raise up great learners who can then go on to produce other great learners. Christ is our preeminent example of this. Because He was a great teacher, He knew what to do in order to take a ragtag bunch of fishermen, Zealots, and tax collectors, and make them into the most influential bunch of learners the world has ever known. From their ranks we have been blessed with great teachers—Matthew, John, Peter, and others whose work continues to impact the world to this day. Of course, these men were inspired by the Holy Spirit in a manner that other teachers aren't. However, Christ's use of them to make disciples of all nations remains a model of how great teachers produce other great teachers.

No matter how great our earthly teachers may be, they will err. We will have to weigh their words against the Spirit-inspired teachings of the Apostles and prophets. But we dare not think we can ever reach a point where we cannot benefit from the teaching of others. Great teachers who are faithful to God's Word are a blessing to God's church. He will use them to build us up so that we can build up others.

"Great teachers who are faithful to God's Word are a blessing to God's church."

THE SECRET TO A HAPPY LIFE

OCTOBER 2014

——

J AMES IS SOMETIMES CALLED THE "New Testament book of Proverbs." That's because of passages such as James 4 that give us a series
of loosely linked aphorisms of practical, godly wisdom. This chapter
begins with our universal concern about conflict:

> What causes quarrels and what causes fights among you? Is it not this,
> that your passions are at war within you? You desire and do not have,
> so you murder. You covet and cannot obtain, so you fight and quarrel.
> You do not have, because you do not ask. You ask and do not receive,
> because you ask wrongly, to spend on your passions. (James 4:1–3)

The world is marked by warfare. There's global war and national conflict; there's warfare in the church; there's warfare in the community;
there's warfare in the home—there's conflict all around us. James says
that these quarrels, fights, disputes, and contentions come from within,
from the fallenness of our hearts. The motivation for these conflicts is
envy, or covetousness, which is a transgression we rarely hear about in
our own day.

Conflict is the fruit of covetous hearts that want what others have.
Now, it's not inherently wrong to want something we don't have. James'
statement that we do not have because we do not ask implicitly calls us to
ask God to give us our desires. We should feel no shame when we desire
good things as long as our desire does not make those good things into
idols. The warning against covetousness comes into play when James
acknowledges that sometimes we ask *wrongly* for what we don't have.
Sometimes we ask for good things in the wrong spirit.

What does this mean? Consider that we ask for things because we believe they will make us happy. This turns into covetousness when we believe that we have an inalienable right to pursue pleasure as the source of happiness. Maximizing pleasure is our culture's chief goal, but happiness and pleasure are profoundly different.

I'm not opposed to pleasure. I enjoy pleasure. But remember, sin is tempting because it can be pleasurable—in the short term. We sin because we think it will feel good. Every time we sin, we believe the original lie of Satan, who tempts us that we will be happy if we get the pleasure we want. Hedonism, which defines the good in terms of the pleasurable, is the oldest philosophy to oppose God.

However, sin never brings happiness—the state of inner delight, blessedness, and contentment wherein there is no room for greed or covetousness. Christians know moments of happiness, when we are alone in the presence of God, in fellowship with Him, and it is enough to know our sins have been forgiven. But soon we forget and we're worrying about the bills. Suddenly, we say, "If I just had a little bit more money, if I just had a better car, if I just had a nicer house, I'd finally be happy."

After explaining conflict's source, James reveals what ends it and brings true happiness:

> But he gives more grace. Therefore it says, "God opposes the proud, but gives grace to the humble." Submit yourselves therefore to God.... Humble yourselves before the Lord, and he will exalt you. (James 4:6–7, 10)

Humility is the secret to a happy life. What is humility? Scripture does not say the humble person is Mr. Milquetoast, the wishy-washy person, the spineless man who is a doormat for the world; rather, the humble person is one who fears God. The fear of the Lord is the beginning of wisdom, and such fear flows from a heart that is in awe of God and bows to His authority.

The opposite of humility is arrogance. To think God owes us every pleasure we want manifests an unspeakable arrogance that presumes to critique God's provision for us. Every time we start fighting over what we don't have, our struggle is ultimately with the Lord. Is anything more foolish than warring with God? Opposition from God is opposition with a capital *O*. He's the last being I want to have opposing me. God opposes the proud, so we need to get this maxim from James into our souls: "God opposes the proud, but gives grace to the humble."

If there's anything that we ought to be in a passionate quest to achieve, it's the grace of God. By definition, grace is not something you can earn. You can receive grace only if God in His mercy gives it to you. It's a gift. You can't buy, earn, or merit it. God gives grace to the humble because they understand the graciousness of grace. Humility willingly submits one's life to God's sovereign mercy. Humble people recognize that the Lord doesn't owe them anything.

Do we want more grace? Let's try a little more humility. Do we seek less opposition from God? Let's do away with our pride. We must remember that we are unworthy servants throwing ourselves on the mercy of the court. When we enter God's presence and demand that He give us something or try to persuade Him to give us something as if we were His counselors who advise Him of a better way of doing things, we've entered into His presence not boldly as the Bible calls us to do, but arrogantly. We must come to Him in thanksgiving and praise for the grace we've already received. The more humble we are, the more grace we get. The prouder we are, the more God opposes us.

THE CHURCH'S ONE FOUNDATION

NOVEMBER 2014

———

MORE THAN FORTY YEARS AGO, Los Angeles experienced a terrible earthquake, one of the worst in the city's history. I remember the event because just before the earthquake, I had driven a friend of mine to the airport so that he could catch a flight to Los Angeles, where he was a pastor. The earthquake affected his church, and he later told me that at first everything seemed to be fine with the sanctuary building. Although there was no visible damage of any significance, a later inspection revealed that the foundation of the church had shifted to such a degree that they had to close the church and rebuild the sanctuary because it was no longer safe. To any casual observer, it seemed like the sanctuary was stable. However, in reality it was unfit for use, and it had to be demolished and rebuilt upon a sure foundation.

In Psalm 11:3, David asks the question, "If the foundations are destroyed, what can the righteous do?" David draws on an analogy in the physical realm to depict a particular spiritual concern that he had. If the failure of a building's physical foundation spells the end for the entire building, the failure of God's people to maintain the foundation of truth means disaster for their spiritual health and well-being.

We can apply this idea to the church. If the foundation of the church is shaken, can the church survive? No. But what is the foundation of the church? Answering that question correctly will help us guard the foundation and preserve His truth.

I've often taught on this subject—the foundation of the church—in my years of ministry. I've often pointed out that while the author of the line, "The church's one foundation is Jesus Christ our Lord," had his heart in the right place when he was writing his hymn, the line itself is a conduit of misinformation. With respect to the foundation of the church, Scripture does speak of Jesus as the foundation: "For no one can lay a foundation other than that which is laid, which is Jesus Christ" (1 Cor. 3:11). However, that is not all that the New Testament says about the church's foundation. Paul says in Ephesians 2:20 that Jesus is actually "the cornerstone." Jesus is called the foundation because He is the linchpin, as it were, for the entire foundation. But there are other stones in this foundation.

What, then, is the rest of the foundation? The foundation, Paul tells us, consists of the prophets and the Apostles (Eph. 2:18–21). In Revelation 21, we read of the magnificent vision of the New Jerusalem, the heavenly city that comes down from above. Verse 14 tells us that "the wall of the city had twelve foundations, and on them were the twelve names of the twelve apostles of the Lamb." Even the heavenly Jerusalem is based upon the foundation of the apostles.

Historically, the Christian church is, in its very essence, Apostolic. The term *Apostle* comes from the Greek word *apostolos*, which means "one who is sent." In the ancient Greek culture, an *apostolos* was first of all a messenger, an ambassador, or an emissary. But he wasn't just a page. He was an emissary who was authorized by the king to represent the king in his absence, and he bore the king's authority.

The first Apostle in the New Testament was actually Jesus, for He was sent by His Father into the world. We get the fullest picture of what it is to be an Apostle by looking at what He says in the New Testament about this role of His. Jesus said, "I do nothing on my own authority, but speak just as the Father taught me" (John 8:28). Christ told His disciples, "For I have not spoken on my own authority, but the Father who sent me has himself given me a commandment—what to say and what to speak" (12:49). He said, "All authority in heaven and on earth has been given to me" (Matt. 28:18). Jesus was granted authority by God the Father to speak on behalf of the Father and to deliver His Father's Word, so Jesus' teaching had God's authority.

The Apostles spoke with a transferred authority from Christ to deliver His teachings. The Apostles taught with the authority of Jesus, who taught with the authority of God. Therefore, as the church father Irenaeus argued long ago, to reject Apostolic authority is to reject the authority of Jesus. And in the final analysis, to reject the authority of Jesus is to reject the authority of God.

What we have here in the concept of Apostolic authority is of vital importance to the Christian faith. But how do we recognize Apostolic authority? By submitting to the Apostolic tradition. In 1 Corinthians 15:3 Paul tells us, "I delivered to you, first of all, that which I also received," and he uses the term *paradosis*, which is the Greek term we translate as "tradition." *Paradosis* literally means "a giving over, a transfer," and that's what the New Testament is. It is the Apostolic tradition that the church has received. The church received it from the Apostles, who received it from Christ, who received it from God. That's why when we reject the teaching of the Apostles—the Apostolic tradition of the New Testament— we're rejecting the very authority of God.

OUR BEAUTIFUL GOD

DECEMBER 2014

———

I've always found it interesting that the Bible often makes reference to the beautiful. In fact, if you took the time to look up every reference to "beauty" or every reference to "the beautiful" in a concordance, you would see that the word *beauty* in one form or another occurs frequently in the pages of sacred Scripture, particularly in the Old Testament. First Chronicles 16:29 is one of the places where we read of beauty: "Give to the Lord the glory due His name; Bring an offering, and come before Him. Oh, worship the Lord in the beauty of holiness!" (NKJV). This passage conjoins the holiness and glory of God with respect to the idea of beauty. We are called to come into the presence of God and to worship what is beautiful about Him—His glory and holiness.

Other texts also talk about God's beauty. "One thing have I asked of the Lord, that will I seek after: that I may dwell in the house of the Lord all the days of my life, to gaze upon the beauty of the Lord and to inquire in his temple" (Ps. 27:4). In Psalm 29, David calls upon us to worship the Lord in the beauty of holiness. In both places, the Lord (or significant aspects of His character) are called "beautiful."

I'm afraid that the idea of the beauty of God has been all but eclipsed in our contemporary culture, both in the secular community and in the church as well. I've said many times that there are three dimensions of the Christian life that the Scriptures are concerned about—the good, the true, and the beautiful. Yet we tend to cut off the third from the other two. Some Christians reduce their concern for the things of God purely to the ethical realm, to a discussion of righteousness or of goodness with respect to our behavior. Others are so concerned about purity of doctrine that they're preoccupied with truth at the expense of behavior or at the expense of the holy. Rarely, at least in many Protestant circles, do we find a focus on the beautiful.

This reflects a striking imbalance given that the Bible is concerned with goodness, truth, and beauty. God, Scripture tells us, is the ground or fountain of all goodness. All goodness finds its definition in His character. In the final analysis, God's character is the measure of goodness. At the same time, the Scriptures speak about God as the author, source, and foundation of all truth. In the same way and in the same dimension, the Scriptures speak about the beauty of God. His Word tells us that all things beautiful find their source and foundation in the character of God Himself. So, God is ultimately the norm of the good, the norm of the true, and the norm of the beautiful.

We live in a time of crisis in the secular culture and in the church with regard to the beautiful. I hear all the time from Christian artists—musicians, sculptors, painters, architects, writers, dramatists, and others—that they feel cut off from the Christian community. They tell me that they are treated as pariahs because their vocation is considered worldly and unworthy of Christian devotion. That's a sad commentary on our state of affairs, particularly when we look at the history of the church and we see that the Christian church has produced some of the greatest giants in music, in art, and in literature. Where else but in Christian history do you find a Milton, a Handel, a Bach, or a Shakespeare—men who have been pioneers of greatness in the arts?

If you were to go to the Louvre in Paris or to the Rijksmuseum in Amsterdam and peruse the history of art, you would see that it's dominated by a religious orientation, and specifically, a Christian orientation. Ever since the people of God have existed in community, art has been a significant concern. When we go to the Old Testament, for example, we see there that the first people filled with the Holy Ghost were the artisans and craftsmen that God selected to prepare the objects for the tabernacle. That's divine inspiration—these artists were inspired by God the Holy Spirit. He inspired them for their craftsmanship of the tabernacle and its furniture, for the metalworking in the tent, and for the making of the gowns and robes for Aaron—which were to be made for glory and for beauty. God was concerned not only to use artists in the building of

His sanctuary in the Old Testament, but also to endow those very artists with the power of His Holy Spirit to ensure that what they were doing met with the standards of beauty He set.

At the same time, we also see in the Old Testament strong prohibitions against the misuse of art. One of the Ten Commandments even prohibits the making of graven images that become part of the practice of idolatry, and so there is a hedge put around the use of art in the Old Testament. Though there were some forms of art that received the blessing of God, there were other forms of art that did not receive the blessing of God.

One cannot come away from the pages of Scripture with a simplistic conclusion that all art is good art or that all art is bad art, that art is always lawful or that art is always unlawful. What we can come away with is the understanding that God saw art and what it communicates as being important enough to include in His tabernacle—to include the beautiful where people would meet to worship Him. Beauty is important to God because He is beautiful, and so what is beautiful must be of importance to His people as well. Christian artists should be encouraged to create beautiful art, and Christian people should be encouraged to appreciate the beautiful alongside the true and the good, for the Lord Himself is beautiful.

PREACHING
AND TEACHING

JANUARY 2015

———

O VER THE YEARS, I'VE MADE NO SECRET of my admiration for men such as Martin Luther and John Calvin, who were so instrumental in the recovery of the gospel during the Protestant Reformation of the sixteenth century. I'm amazed by their towering intellects and their ability to stand firm amid much danger. Their love for biblical truth is an example to follow, and as I approach twenty years of weekly preaching at Saint Andrew's Chapel, I'm particularly grateful for their pastoral model. Both of these men were "celebrities" in their day, but neither of them spent his years traveling Europe in order to consolidate a movement of followers. Instead, both of them devoted themselves to their primary vocation of preaching and teaching the Word of God. Both men were tireless preachers—Luther in Wittenberg, Germany, and Calvin in Geneva, Switzerland. They took the ministry of the Word of God seriously, so when they talk about the task of the preacher, I pay close attention.

More than a decade ago, I was invited to give a lecture on Martin Luther's view of preaching, and I found that preparing for that exercise was invaluable for my own work as a preacher. I also discovered that what Luther had to say about preaching was not only for the pastor but also for the entire church, and it's amazing how timely his words remain in our day.

One of the emphases that we find again and again in Luther's writings is that a preacher must be "apt to teach." In many ways, this is no great insight, for he's just restating the qualifications that are set forth in the New Testament for church elders (1 Tim. 3:2). Yet given what we expect from our preachers today, Luther's words—echoing biblical revelation— need to be heard anew. The concept that the primary task of the minister is to teach is all but lost in the church today. When we call ministers to our churches we often look for these men to be adept administrators, skilled fundraisers, and good organizers. Sure, we want them to know some theology and the Bible, but we don't make it a priority that these people be equipped to teach the congregation the things of God. Administrative tasks are seen as more important.

This is not the model that Jesus Himself commended. You remember the encounter that Jesus had with Peter after His resurrection. Peter had denied Jesus publicly three times, and Jesus went about restoring the Apostle, telling him three times to "feed my sheep" (John 21:15–19). By extension, this calling is given to the elders and ministers of the church because the people of God who are assembled in the congregations of churches all over the world belong to Jesus. They are His sheep. And every minister who is ordained is consecrated and entrusted by God with the care of those sheep. We call it the "pastorate" because ministers are called to care for the sheep of Christ. Pastors are Christ's undershepherds, and what shepherd would so neglect his sheep that he never took the time or trouble to feed them? The feeding of our Lord's sheep comes principally through teaching.

Typically, we distinguish between preaching and teaching. Preaching involves such things as exhortation, exposition, admonition, encouragement, and comfort, while teaching is the transfer of information and instruction in various areas of content. In practice, however, there is much overlap between the two. Preaching must communicate content and include teaching, and teaching people the things of God cannot be done in a neutral manner but must exhort them to heed and obey the Word of Christ. God's people need both preaching and teaching, and they need more than twenty minutes of instruction and exhortation a week. A good shepherd would never feed the sheep only once a week, and that's why Luther was teaching the people of Wittenberg almost on a daily basis, and Calvin was doing the same thing in Geneva. I'm not necessarily calling for the exact practices in our day, but I'm convinced that the church needs to recapture something of the regular teaching ministry evident in the work of our forefathers in the faith. As they are able, churches should be creating many opportunities to hear God's Word preached and taught. Things such as Sunday evening worship, midweek services and Bible classes, Sunday school, home Bible studies, and so on give laypeople the chance to feed on the Word of God several times each week. As they are able, laypeople should take advantage of what is available to them by way of instruction in the deep truths of Scripture.

I say this not to encourage the creation of programs for the sake of programs, and I don't want to put an unmanageable burden on church members or church staffs. But history shows us that the greatest periods of revival and reformation the church has ever seen occur in conjunction with the frequent, consistent, and clear preaching of God's Word. If we would see the Holy Spirit bring renewal to our churches and our lands, it will require preachers who are committed to the exposition of Scripture, and laypeople who will look for shepherds to feed them the Word of God and take full advantage of the opportunities for biblical instruction that are available.

DOUBT AND OBEDIENCE

FEBRUARY 2015

———

O NE COMMENT THAT CHRISTIAN PASTORS sometimes hear from people they are counseling is that it would be easier for them to have a strong faith if they could see God doing the same kinds of miracles today as are recorded in the Bible. The unspoken assumption is that seeing is believing—that the people who lived in Jesus' day found themselves more readily trusting Him because they could see His great works.

Such comments show the need for a closer reading of Scripture, for there are many cases where seeing great miracles didn't move observers to faith. For example, John 11 records Jesus' raising Lazarus from the dead—a convincing sign if there ever was one. Yet the authorities took the miracle as a reason to oppose Jesus, not to believe in Him (vv. 45–53).

Scripture also records occasions when even God's people experienced disbelief after seeing many miracles. Consider Joshua 7, which records what happened at Ai not long after the Israelites conquered Jericho. After the conquest of Jericho, when a shout brought the walls "tumbling down" (chap. 6), you can imagine what the feelings were among the people of Israel. God had delivered them in a dramatic, supernatural way, removing from their path the most formidable obstacle to the conquest of Canaan. He had delivered on His promise that He would give them every place where Joshua set his foot. So, you would think there would be nothing but elation and confidence among the troops and especially in the heart of Joshua. But what transpires is a major comeuppance for Joshua and the Israelites. After a scouting party reports that Ai should be easy to conquer, Joshua sends a force to take the city, but it is quickly routed, and thirty-six people are killed (7:2–5). How does Joshua respond?

Joshua tore his clothes and fell to the earth on his face before the ark of the LORD until the evening. . . . And Joshua said, "Alas, O Lord GOD, why have you brought this people over the Jordan at all, to give us into the hands of the Amorites, to destroy us? Would that we had been content to dwell beyond the Jordan! O Lord, what can I say, when Israel has turned their backs before their enemies! For the Canaanites and all the inhabitants of the land will hear of it and will surround us and cut off our name from the earth. And what will you do for your great name?" (vv. 6–9)

Here we see Joshua, the one who in the past has always been courageous, the man of faith who gave the good report to the nation that Israel could take Canaan. Now he's rending his garments and complaining to the Lord, saying, "Why didn't You just leave well enough alone? We could have lived happily ever after on the other side of the Jordan, but now we're humiliated and the news of this defeat will go all through the Promised Land." Joshua, in a moment of disbelief, is saying to God, "What have You done for me lately?" His faith is so fragile that after one minor setback, he loses his confidence and is in mourning. Joshua thought he understood the full measure of God's commitment to him and to his army, and he is beside himself when this defeat takes place at the hands of an enemy that Israel should have been able to run over without the help of God. Now even with God's promise, they suffer this humiliating defeat. All of a sudden, Joshua's wondering, "Was God's promise of success an illusion? Was I hearing things? God promised that we'd never be defeated, and now we're defeated." What Joshua endures here, as we see in his fasting, mourning, and seeking God's face, is a crisis of faith.

Why were the Israelites defeated? Joshua 7:1 tells us: "The people of Israel broke faith in regard to the devoted things, for Achan . . . of the tribe of Judah, took some of the devoted things. And the anger of the Lord burned against the people of Israel." Yes, God promised Israel victory, but He also commanded the people to exercise scrupulous obedience to the terms of this conflict. God instituted the ban against the Canaanites, meaning that in this conquest of holy war the soldiers could not take any personal loot or booty. And one man in the army disobeyed. Achan succumbed to the temptation to line his own pockets with the spoils from the victory at Jericho. And because of one man's sin, God held the whole nation of Israel accountable. Because of this trespass, God's anger is expressed against Israel, and His providential judgment causes this defeat.

Scripture warns us that on this side of glory, there is not a one-to-one correlation between obedience and blessing. Faithful people are often successful, but sometimes they experience great defeat. The faithless often suffer for their wrongdoing, but sometimes they enjoy many outward successes. Nevertheless, success and strong, confident faith are some of the blessings that the Lord gives to those who keep His commandments (Ps. 1). Though God has not promised to act in the same miraculous manner today as He did in the days of old, we can expect Him to move in our behalf. We don't merit righteousness before our Father by our obedience, and the Lord's grace is so vast that He regularly blesses us in spite of our disobedience. Still, perhaps we would see more blessing and experience less doubt if we were to serve Him more faithfully.

WHAT IS GRACE?

MARCH 2015

A NUMBER OF DECADES AGO AT THE Ligonier Valley Study Center, we sent out a Thanksgiving card with this simple statement: "The essence of theology is grace; the essence of Christian ethics is gratitude." In all the debates about our role versus God's role in sanctification—our growth in holiness—we'd stay on the right track if we'd remember this grace-gratitude dynamic. The more we understand how kind God has been to us and the more we are overcome by His mercy, the more we are inclined to love Him and to serve Him.

Yet we can't get the grace-gratitude dynamic right if we aren't clear on what grace means. What is grace? The catechisms many of us learned as children give us the answer: "Grace is the unmerited favor of God." The first thing that we understand about grace is what it's not—it's not something we merit. In fact, if that is all we ever understand about grace, I'm sure God will rejoice that we know His grace is unmerited. So, here's our working definition of grace—it is *unmerit*.

Paul's epistle to the Romans sheds light on what we mean when we say that grace is *unmerit*. In 1:18–3:20, the Apostle explains that on the final day, for the first time in our lives, we will be judged in total perfection, in total fairness, in absolute righteousness. Thus, every mouth will be stopped when we stand before the tribunal of God. This should provoke fear in the hearts of fallen people, as condemnation is the only possible sentence for sinful men and women: "All have sinned and fall short of the glory of God" (3:23).

But those who trust in Christ Jesus have hope, for if we are in Him by faith, we have been "justified freely by His grace." Note that justification is accomplished not by obligation, but freely through grace on account of the redemption purchased by Jesus alone. There's no room for boasting, for we are justified not by our works but by grace alone through faith alone. Paul goes on to cite Abraham as the preeminent example of one who was justified by faith alone and therefore free from God's sentence of condemnation. If the basis for Abraham's salvation, his justification, was something that Abraham did—some good deed, some meritorious service that he performed, some obligation that he performed—if it were on the basis of works, Paul says, he would have had something about which to boast. But Abraham had no such merit. All he had was faith, and that faith itself was a gift: "Abraham believed God, and it was counted to him as righteousness" (4:3; see Eph. 2:8–10).

Romans 4:4–8 is a key passage here:

> Now to the one who works, his wages are not counted as a gift but as his due. And to the one who does not work but believes in him who justifies the ungodly, his faith is counted as righteousness, just as David also speaks of the blessing of the one to whom God counts righteousness apart from works: "Blessed are those whose lawless deeds are forgiven, and whose sins are covered; blessed is the man against whom the Lord will not count his sin."

That's grace. Paul couldn't say it any other way. To him who works, it's debt; if you merit something, it means that someone is obligated to pay you. If I hire you as an employee and promise to pay you one hundred dollars if you work eight hours, I must pay you for working the eight hours. I'm not doing you a favor or giving you grace. You've earned your pay. You've fulfilled the contract, and I'm morally obliged to give you your wages.

With respect to the Lord, we are debtors who cannot pay. That's why the Bible speaks of redemption in economic language—we were bought with a price (1 Cor. 6:20). Only someone else—Christ—can pay our debt. That's grace. It's not our good works that secure our rescue but only the works of Christ. It's His merit, not ours. We don't merit anything. He grants us His merit by grace, and we receive it only by faith. The essence of grace is its voluntary free bestowal. As soon as it's a requirement, it's no longer grace.

Grace should never cease to amaze us. God has an absolute, pure, holy standard of justice. That's why we cling with all our might to the merit of Jesus Christ. He alone has the merit to satisfy the demands of God's justice, and He gives it freely to us. We haven't merited it. There's nothing in us that elicits the Lord's favor that leads to our justification. It's pure grace.

And the more we understand what God has done for us as sinners, the more willing we are to do whatever He requires. The great teachers of the church say the first point of genuine sanctification is an increasing awareness of our own sinfulness. With that comes, at the same time, an increasing awareness of God's grace. And with that, again, increasing love and increasing willingness to obey Him.

When we truly understand grace—when we see that God only owes us wrath but has provided Christ's merit to cover our demerit—then everything changes. The Christian motivation for ethics is not merely to obey some abstract law or a list of rules; rather, our response is provoked by gratitude. Jesus understood that when He said, "If you love Me, keep My commandments." If I may have the liberty to paraphrase: "Keep My commandments not because you want to be just, but because you love Me." A true understanding of grace—of God's unmerited favor—always provokes a life of gratitude and obedience.

SACRAMENTAL ASSISTANCE

APRIL 2015

——

W E ALL HAVE THOSE MOMENTS IN our lives that we say were formative for the shaping of who we are today. We celebrate birthdays in our homes every year. We remember our wedding anniversaries and the dates on which we first met our spouses or made a life-changing career decision. Often, these events have sights and smells that are associated with them, or particular sights and smells bring to mind particular episodes or feelings. If your mother made you a special batch of chicken soup every time you got sick, smelling hot chicken broth might evoke fond memories of her and her care. Finding a treasured doll or stuffed animal from your childhood will likely take you back to those days and the experiences you enjoyed.

This human tendency to remember important events by means of tangible objects carries right over into the religious sphere. We understand that the life and worship of the church involves what we call "Word and sacrament." In Protestant churches particularly, there has been a tremendous emphasis on the preaching of the Word, but historically, the celebration of the sacraments in Protestantism has also been vital. Sadly, there has been a neglect of the sacraments among modern evangelicals, though there are encouraging signs that this trend is being reversed. Nevertheless, the celebration of God-ordained sacraments has been a constant throughout the history of God's people. From the days of the Old Testament all the way through the New Testament, God has been concerned not only to speak to His people through His Word, but also to communicate in other ways and in other methods, one of the most important of which is through the sacraments.

When we speak of the sacraments, we are usually referring specifically to baptism and the Lord's Supper, those signs and seals instituted by Christ to remember His death and His work in cleansing His people from sin. But theologians also use terms such as *sacrament* or *sacramental* in a broader sense. Such terms can be applied to many ways in which God has communicated to His people through object lessons, through signs or ordinary symbols that take on extraordinary meaning. For example, we have the rainbow, which was the sign given to Noah that the Lord would never destroy the earth again with a flood. He used that common, natural phenomenon of the rainbow as a sign of an uncommon, special, divine promise of His persevering and preserving providence. Now, every time we see a rainbow, we are involved in the sacramental life of the faith, not in the technical sense of sacraments, but rather in the sense of the broader meaning of external objects that are used to enhance and support the communication of the verbal promises of God. Old covenant believers also had circumcision as a visible reminder that they had been cut out of the world to be the Lord's holy people. Moreover, the prophets often dramatized the Word of God through visible signs such as a plumb line, a broken jar, or other such things. Perhaps the preeminent sacramental celebration under the old covenant was the Passover, the meal that was eaten to commemorate God's deliverance of the Israelites from Egyptian slavery. Here we see the sign joined to the Word of God, as is to be the case whenever a God-ordained sacrament is celebrated. As the meal was being eaten, the families in Israel were to retell the story of the exodus, to recount the divinely sent plagues and God's message to Israel through Moses that were part and parcel of the liberation from Egypt.

Under the new covenant, we remember, for example, the Lord's Supper, when Jesus took the Old Testament sacrament of Passover and filled it with new meaning and new content. He took the bread and the wine of the Passover meal and made them signs and seals of His broken body and shed blood, which are the purchase price of our redemption. He said to eat the bread and drink the wine in remembrance of Him. Jesus knew His people; He knew what we were like, that sometimes our faithfulness to Christ is only as intense and as strong as the vivacity of our recollection of our most recent blessing at the hands of God. But we come down from those mountaintop experiences and we tend to forget what God has done for us in the past. The sacraments represent the Lord accommodating Himself to this weakness of ours in order to assist us in remembering what He has done for us.

We are weak, sinful people who need all the assistance we can get in order to remember what the Lord has done for us. If we neglect the sacraments He has given His people and fail to understand the importance of the sacramental aspects of our faith, we are turning down precious helps that provide additional confirmation of His promises. When joined to the Word of God, the sacraments strengthen our faith, further our sanctification, and assure us of the Lord's unwavering faithfulness to us—His forgetful and often unfaithful people.

A CALL FOR ENDURANCE

I'M NOT A PROPHET OR THE SON OF A PROPHET. I've made a lot of predictions and guesses about the future that haven't come true. As I told the congregation of Saint Andrew's Chapel a few weeks ago during a sermon, I'm not infallible, nor have I ever claimed to be infallible.

On occasion, however, my predictions of the future have been accurate. When you've been writing a monthly column for as long as I have, you invariably comment on cultural matters and the direction that the culture is heading. Recently, I was reading a column I wrote twenty-five years ago for the January 1990 issue of *Tabletalk*, and I was amazed at how prescient it turned out to be.

I wish I could say I'm happy about that. In the column I addressed the specter of a new dark age in our culture. I wasn't referring to a new dark age in terms of the stunted growth of knowledge. What was true then remains true today: we have more knowledge than we know what to do with. Knowledge in every field of study is growing so rapidly that no one can absorb it all. Scholars must choose increasingly narrow specializations to have hope of gaining expertise, and then it is only expertise in a relative sense. This reality has only grown worse with the advent of the Internet and the way it makes truth—and falsehood—more easily accessible than our forefathers ever dreamed.

The dark age to which I was referring was an age of moral darkness, a darkness due to the eclipse of God. Twenty-five years ago our culture would not have God in its thinking, and the same is true today. As a society, we have preferred for the Light to be shrouded. We've chosen to close our minds to the truth. And yet, the Light remains. Just as a solar eclipse obscures but does not destroy the light, our moral darkness hides but does not eliminate the Light. We see the truth of the Apostle Paul's teaching that we suppress the truth in unrighteousness—but we cannot destroy the truth (Rom. 1:18–32). Humanity remains incurably religious, and we retain the innate sense that we must live by a moral code. But on account of our suppression of the truth, this moral code is twisted to reflect the darkness of our own hearts, not the immutable moral law of God.

Futile thinking continues to result from this. Our darkened minds attempt to shroud the truth of our Creator, and we as a society fail to honor Him. This has led to the loss of honor itself, to the sacrifice not only of divine dignity but of human dignity as well.

Twenty-five years ago, I predicted that this eclipse would manifest itself in various cultural struggles such as abortion. Though we have seen the rise of crisis pregnancy centers and bans on partial birth abortion, our culture continues to endorse abortion on demand.

I also predicted that the state would zealously protect its supposed autonomy, interpreting the separation of church and state to mean the separation of the state and God. As I write this column, the state and federal courts of the United States have declared that "homosexual marriage" is a right in the majority of U.S. states, and come June the Supreme Court will rule on whether the Constitution guarantees this right to all U.S. citizens. Since the law is being determined by collective preference and not the revelation of God in the natural order, I have little doubt that the highest court in the land will feel no shame in casting aside God's definition of marriage in favor of the current spirit of the age. In all this, some churches have already capitulated. They are either silent on these matters of life and human sexuality, or they have bowed to cultural pressure to abandon what God says on these matters.

Yet I do not mean to paint a picture of gloom and doom. There are faithful believers and churches who are not capitulating. God's kingdom continues to grow around the world. The light of divine truth shines brightly even though at times the darkness seems overwhelming. Our Lord is building His church, and He will not be thwarted (Matt. 16:18). At times it may seem as if the darkness is winning, but God's Word stands firm. People around the world are hungry for His truth, and by the Lord's grace, His people are taking it to the nations.

Twenty-five years ago, I predicted that a tremendous struggle was coming. We are living in the midst of it. Such is the plight of the church militant in every generation. The struggle manifests itself in different forms, but it is essentially the same. We are called in our generation to be faithful to the gospel, for the honor of God is at stake. And when the honor of God is at stake, so is the honor of every human being, for it is God who grants dignity to men and women. Our high calling is to remain faithful to the Lord in this struggle, to fight for the truth of God's Word and not to compromise. If we remain faithful, we are promised a sure and great reward: "The one who conquers will not be hurt by the second death" (Rev. 2:11b).

THE REFORMED DOCTRINE OF GOD

JUNE 2015

———

O VER THE YEARS, I'VE HAD OPPORTUNITIES to teach systematic theology in a variety of settings, from seminary classrooms to university courses to Sunday school classes in the local church. But no matter where I've taught systematics, the first place I typically start is the doctrine of God. Theology, of course, studies God and His character and ways, so it's appropriate to begin with a look at His nature and attributes before examining what the Bible has to say about redemption, the church, the last things, and the other categories of systematic theology.

Whenever I've taught the doctrine of God, I've started out with two statements that have seemed to fill many of my students with no small amount of consternation. It's been my practice to tell them that on the one hand there's nothing particularly unique about the doctrine of God confessed in the Reformed tradition of Christian theology. Presbyterians, Reformed Baptists, the Dutch Reformed, and other Reformed Christians affirm the same attributes of God that Lutherans, Anglicans, Methodists, the Eastern Orthodox, and Roman Catholics all do. There's nothing radically different about our doctrine of God.

Yet, when those same students have asked me what's the most significant distinctive of Reformed theology, I've said it's our doctrine of God. Now, that does sound completely contradictory to my first statement, but I say that the Reformed doctrine of God sets us apart from other traditions for the reason that I know of no other theology that takes seriously the doctrine of God with respect to every other doctrine. In most systematic theologies, you get an affirmation of the sovereignty of God on page one of your theology text, but then once you move on to soteriology (doctrine of salvation), eschatology (doctrine of last things), and anthropology (doctrine of humanity), and so on, the author has seemingly forgotten what he said about God's sovereignty on page one.

Reformed theologians, however, self-consciously see the doctrine of God as informing the whole scope of Christian theology. That's one of the reasons why Calvinists tend to focus so much on the Old Testament. We're concerned about the character of God as defining everything—our understanding of Christ, our understanding of ourselves, our understanding of salvation. We turn to the Old Testament because it's one of the most important sources that you find anywhere in the universe on the nature and character of God. Reformed Christians tend to take the Old Testament very seriously because it's such a vivid revelation of the majesty of God.

Just think of the key revelations of God in the Old Testament. At our recent Ligonier Ministries National Conference, I looked at Isaiah 6, which is probably the single text I've preached on more often than any other in my preaching career. There we find one of the most vivid disclosures of divine holiness in all of Scripture. Then, of course, there's the Lord's revelation of Himself and His covenant name to Moses at the burning bush that we read about in Exodus 3. That's a must read chapter for anyone seeking to understand God's independence and self-existence. When I've sought a reminder of our Creator's commitment to truth and His faithfulness to keep His covenant promises, I've often turned to Genesis 15, where God swears by Himself to fulfill His pledge to Abraham to give him innumerable descendants. And for a vivid portrayal of God's unfailing, effectual love for His people—His bride—you can hardly find a better place to go in Scripture than the book of Hosea.

I could offer many more examples, but what do these episodes all have in common? These revelations of God all take place at various crisis points in the lives of God's people. Both Isaiah and Moses were about to be sent on a great mission to proclaim the greatness of the Lord to hardened people. What did they need most at a time like that? Not a promise of success— indeed, Isaiah was told that his message would harden hearts (Isa. 6:8–13). No, what they needed was an understanding of the Lord's character. When God wanted to give them assurance, He gave them Himself. The same was true of Abraham and Hosea. Humanly speaking, Abraham had little evidence to believe that God would give him many descendants. So, the Lord assured the patriarch of His faithfulness by committing Himself to His own destruction—an impossibility—should He not keep His Word. Hosea lived in a day when it seemed as if God had fully and finally cast off His people for their unfaithfulness. What hope could the Lord provide that He loved Israel with an everlasting love? It was the revelation of Himself as the Husband who is perfect in love and faithfulness.

Reformed theology's doctrine of God and its emphasis on all of His attributes at every point in the unfolding of salvation sets it apart from other Christian understandings of the Lord. And our doctrine of God is drawn from Genesis through Revelation, from the Old Testament as much as from the New Testament. Why, therefore, wouldn't we soak up the whole counsel of God and read both testaments with great devotion?

FAMILY VALUES

JULY 2015

———

ALTHOUGH THE ACTUAL ELECTION IS about a year and a half away, we're already starting to see prospective candidates throw their hats into the ring for the 2016 U.S. presidential race. Caucuses, primaries, debates, get-out-the-vote efforts, fund-raising, and so much more will occupy the attention of the news media as it covers the candidates' attempts to become the so-called leader of the free world. As is true every four years, we'll see party platforms crafted and each person in the race claiming that his or her positions on the issues are the truest embodiment of American values.

Regardless of whether the term *family values* is bandied about during the election cycle, we're likely to see candidates talking about the importance of issues that pertain to families. Here I have to quibble just a bit with the term *family values*, and that's because of our modern propensity to confuse the concept of values with the concept of ethics. They are not synonymous ideas. *Ethics* is an objective science, one that seeks to determine concrete standards of right and wrong. Values, on the other hand, refers to preferences. They are, in large measure, subjective. We speak, for example, of the "subjective theory of value," which says that the value of goods and services in an economy is determined by the worth an individual or group of individuals attributes to them. All things being equal, if an item or service is highly desired, it will go up in price. If desire for an item or service is low, it will cost less.

In the Christian worldview, ethical standards are fixed because they are objective standards of right and wrong that reflect our transcendent Creator. In contrast, values change over time according to personal preference. That does not mean, however, that ethics and values are unrelated. Biblically speaking, the two go hand in hand. We are called to align our values with what God values, and what God values is outlined in His revealed ethical norms in Scripture. This is as true of family values as it is of economic values, political values, and so forth.

Biblical revelation tells us that family values are tied to how we should value people. When it comes to the family, Scripture is quite clear that children are gifts from God, and therefore they are of inestimable value. I'm reminded of the story of Abraham in Genesis 15 when he is concerned about his lack of an heir. That great patriarch was one of the wealthiest men in his day. He was "very rich in livestock, in silver, and in gold" (Gen. 13:2). But Abraham was not concerned for his riches above all else. There was something he wanted more—a son to be his heir. Despite his wealth, he felt impoverished because he had no children. He longed for the children God promised him when he was called out of Ur (12:1–3).

That says much about Abraham's values. But Abraham isn't the only person we read about in Scripture who highly valued children. We feel the anguish of Hannah in her plea for a son, and we rejoice with her in the birth of Samuel (1 Sam. 1). Solomon tells us that "children are a heritage from the Lord, the fruit of the womb a reward," and blessed is the man who fills his house with children just as he fills a quiver with arrows (Ps. 127:3–5). And who can forget Jesus' command that His disciples not keep the "little children" from coming to Him (Matt. 19:13–14)? Our Savior, who Himself never married or had children, placed a high value on children.

The Bible doesn't prescribe a set number of children for each family. We know that in a fallen world, there are sometimes conditions that prevent couples from having children. Nevertheless, it does tell us that to have children is a great blessing. The creational principle that we are to be fruitful and multiply (Gen. 1:28) echoes throughout the Bible, confronting all who would view children as a burden. The family values revealed in Scripture condemn the values of Planned Parenthood, abortion on demand, and every other group or philosophy that denies the dignity of children whether they are presently in the womb or not. Any candidate or individual who espouses "family values" while turning a blind eye to the slaughter of a million children every year via America's abortion clinics has rejected the ethics of God's Word and should fear the judgment of God.

Periodically, we hear of the supposed economic burden children bring. Recent statistics estimate that it costs more than $250,000 to raise a child from birth to age eighteen. Yet Christians do not consider their sons and daughters to be burdens. We know they are gifts from God to be treasured and to be raised in the fear and admonition of our Lord (Eph. 6:4). No matter the financial cost, it is a small price to pay for the joys we receive from the hugs of our children and grandchildren. May the Lord bless His church with children who love and serve Him.

THE PROPER PLACE OF LOVE

AUGUST 2015

———

H
OW MANY PEOPLE DO YOU KNOW that have made it to the hall
of fame in music, art, literature, or sports because of their love?
We elevate people to the status of heroes because of their gifts,
their talents, and their power, but not because of their love. Yet, from
God's perspective, love is the chief of all virtues. But what is love?

Love is said to make the world go round, and romantic love certainly
makes the culture go round in terms of advertising and entertainment.
We never seem to tire of stories that focus on romance. But we're not referring to romantic love when we speak of the Christian virtue of love. We're
talking about a much deeper dimension of love, a virtue so paramount
that it is to distinguish Christians from all other people. Moreover, love
is so important to the Bible's teachings that John tells us, "God is love"
(1 John 4:7–8). Whatever else we say about the Christian virtue of love, we
must be clear that the love God commands is a love that imitates His own.
The love of God is utterly perfect. And we are called to reflect and mirror
that love to perfection, to be perfect as He is perfect (Matt. 5:48). Now, of
course, none of us loves perfectly, which is why we must be covered with
the perfect righteousness of Christ by faith in Him alone. Nevertheless,
it's important for us to return time and again to Scripture to find out what
love is supposed to look like, for we're so easily satisfied with a sentimen-
tal, maudlin, romantic, or superficial understanding of love.

First Corinthians 13 plumbs the depths of what love really means. It's
a measuring rod by which we can examine ourselves carefully to see
whether this love resides in our hearts and is manifested in our lives. Given
that truth, I'm surprised that 1 Corinthians 13 is one of the most popular
passages in all of Scripture instead of being one of the most despised. I

can't think of any chapter in Scripture that more quickly reveals our sins than this chapter. It's popularity may be due to its being one of the most misunderstood and least applied chapters in the Bible. There's a sense in which we're ambivalent toward it. We're drawn to it because of the grandeur of its theme and the eloquence of its language, yet at the same time we're repulsed by this chapter because it reveals our shortcomings. We want to keep some safe distance from it because it so clearly demonstrates to us our lack of real love.

This chapter is part of an Apostolic admonition to Christians who were torn apart by contentions in the church. They were behaving in an immature, fleshly manner, and at the heart of this ungodly behavior was a manifestation of certain talents, abilities, and gifts without the presence of love in their lives. In the opening verses, Paul speaks of love as the sine qua non of Christian virtue (1 Cor. 13:1–3). He's speaking with hyperbole, intentionally exaggerating things to make his point. He starts off comparing love to the gift of tongues. Paul says, in effect, "I don't care if you are fluent in fifty languages or if you have the gift to speak foreign languages miraculously. I don't care if God has endowed you with the ability to speak the language of the heavenly host. If you don't have love, the eloquence of your speech becomes noise. It becomes dissonance, an irritating and annoying racket." He says here that if we speak in the tongues of men and of angels but have not love, we become a sounding brass or a clanging symbol—mere noise. All the beauty of speech is lost when love is absent.

Paul then compares love to the gifts of prophecy and understanding, miraculous endowments that God gave to people during the Apostolic era. These tremendous gifts were nothing compared to love. The Apostle says that you can have a miraculous endowment, you can receive power from God the Holy Spirit, but it is to be used in the context of the grace of love. And without that love, the use of the divine power is a charade. Jesus had to warn even His own disciples about the danger of using a God-given gift without love. Jesus empowered His disciples to participate in His ministry of exorcism, and they went out on their mission and came back clicking their heels. They were so excited at the effectiveness of their ministry that they were rejoicing in the power Christ had given them. But what did Jesus say? Don't rejoice because you have been given power over Satan, but rejoice that your names have been written in heaven (Luke 10:1–20). The disciples were caught up with the power instead of the grace that was underlying that power. They were intoxicated with the gift, and were forgetting the One who gave it.

The bottom line is that the gifts of God can be used without love. When that happens, their value is destroyed. The essence of love, 1 Corinthians 13 tells us, is to seek the welfare of others. A person who reflects God's love is driven to give of himself for others, not to wield his power for his own benefit. But we are people who are more interested in power, in doing rather than being. We're more concerned to seize the supernatural power that God can give rather than the supernatural love that is shed abroad in our hearts by the Holy Spirit (Rom. 5:5). We have misplaced priorities. Thanks be to God that His love for us is greater than our love for Him. May He strengthen us to pursue love above all else, a love that reflects His love for us in Christ (5:8).

WHY A STUDY BIBLE?

SEPTEMBER 2015

———

THE EDITORS OF *TABLETALK* ASKED me to speak about study Bibles and what drove Ligonier Ministries, in particular, to publish a thoroughly revised and updated version of the *Reformation Study Bible*. I'm glad to take up this task, as I continue to believe that a good study Bible is one of the most important tools for helping people grow in the things of God.

Another article this month will deal with the history of study Bibles, so I won't go into detail on that specific subject. However, I do want to point out that our efforts to produce a study Bible are born of the same passion that drove men in years past to get the Word of God into the minds and hearts and souls of every person. This passion compelled William Tyndale to cross the whole continent of Europe, moving from city to city to escape execution, translating the ancient Hebrew into words that a literate plowboy could read and understand. After the Diet of Worms, Martin Luther fled in a faked kidnapping episode to the Wartburg castle. There, he donned a disguise and undertook the task of putting the Bible into the German vernacular. This was anathema to the Roman church—Luther was told that if he were to translate the Bible into the common tongue, he would open a floodgate of iniquity. Hundreds of different denominations would arise, each claiming to base their faith on the Bible. Luther agreed that that could very well happen. But, he said, if getting the gospel that is plain enough for every child to understand into the hands of the normal person carries with it the risk that some will misinterpret Scripture and open a floodgate of iniquity, then so be it. Luther understood the importance of every person's knowing Scripture, and he knew that the church had to get it out to the masses even though misuse of the Bible was possible. As long as the church is faithful to this Word, she cannot be held accountable for its misuse.

At Ligonier, we're confident in the power of the Word of God to convert sinners and equip Christians for every good work. We want the gospel to go forth to every nation, even if some may take that gospel and twist it to their own ends. But we want the people of God to grow deeper in their faith and to explore the depths of the gospel, which is simple enough for all to understand and yet so deep that in our lifetime we can only begin to scratch the surface of its meaning and application. For that, sound teaching is indispensable, and that's why our goal has been to provide a study Bible grounded in the Reformed tradition of Christian theology.

Reformed theology, which C.H. Spurgeon said is merely a nickname for biblical Christianity, is our passion here at Ligonier. We want to spread the knowledge of the gospel to as many people as possible to help churches around the world understand the substance of its message. Everything we do through Ligonier Ministries is directed toward that end, including the *Reformation Study Bible*.

There is distaste in our day, even in the church, for doctrine. People say, "I can live the Christian life without being concerned about doctrine." Well, if you are not concerned about doctrine, then the best thing you can do with your Bible is throw it away, because that is what the Bible is—it is sixty-six divinely revealed books of doctrine. On the night before His execution, Jesus met in the upper room with His disciples and prayed His High Priestly Prayer. He poured out His soul to the Father in behalf of His followers—His disciples and those who would believe through the ministry of the original disciples. And His prayer was for their sanctification. He said to His heavenly Father, "Sanctify them through thy truth; your word is truth" (John 17:17). Now, if you want to be sanctified, if you want to grow in conformity to the image of Christ, you need to know the truth of God. You need to know doctrine. The whole point of a good study Bible, such as the *Reformation Study Bible*, is to help you learn the theology that God reveals in His sacred Word that will shape your life and bring you into conformity with Christ.

The original Geneva Bible, which you will read about in this issue of *Tabletalk*, was developed to help people learn the theology revealed in

God's Word. It is in the spirit of that Geneva Bible that we produced the original *New Geneva Study Bible*, and then the *Reformation Study Bible*. We wanted a resource that, like the Geneva Bible, faithfully taught the Scriptures and presented the key tenets of Reformed theology rediscovered in the Protestant Reformation. And in that same spirit, we have the completely new, reworked edition of the *Reformation Study Bible*—which really excites me.

"The only teacher who has no need of learning is God Himself. A great teacher is teachable. If he is not, he will have precious little to teach."

—

TEACHABLE TEACHERS

OCTOBER 2015

O NE OF THE MOST FRUSTRATING aspects of teaching is encountering students who are not really teachable. Every pastor has had to deal with people who are settled in their opinions and not open to correction. Church elders must at times pursue church discipline all the way to excommunication because the person being disciplined is not teachable and refuses to repent.

It is bad enough when students or parishioners are not teachable, but there is something even worse. I'm talking about teachers who are not teachable. These are teachers who don't think that the words of this biblical proverb apply to them: "Give instruction to a wise man, and he will be still wiser; teach a righteous man, and he will increase in learning" (Prov. 9:9). In fact, this verse might be more pertinent for those who seek to teach vocationally than for those who do not. If teachers are to impart knowledge and wisdom to their students, will not the best teachers seek to grow in their knowledge and wisdom so that they will have more to teach to others? Becoming a teacher does not mean that one has "arrived" in terms of knowledge; the best teachers understand where they are lacking and seek to be taught so that they will increase in wisdom and learning.

Most of us have been blessed to sit under great teachers, whether they were public or private school instructors, pastors, Sunday school teachers, parents, or others. It's also likely that most of us have had at least one poor teacher, one who didn't seek to learn more about his subject or grow in the skill of teaching. I've known teachers who did all their work the first year they had to teach and have been coasting ever since. They made lesson plans right out of college and have used those same plans for years without changing them. Needless to say, these teachers have not been great teachers.

It's critical that teachers be lifelong learners. No great teacher gets everything right the first time. Excellent instructors keep on revising their material and adjusting their skills throughout their teaching careers. Simply put, they keep learning.

Spend any time with a good teacher, and it won't be long before he tells you that one of the best ways to learn is to have to teach others. By way of personal example, I learned that principle in college before I was ordained to the full-time teaching ministry. During my undergraduate years, my college inaugurated a major in philosophy, and I was the first student to sign up. In fact, I was the only person in my graduating class to graduate with a degree in that major. Yet though I was the only senior to take the major, my philosophy courses were full of other students who took them as electives but were not philosophy majors themselves.

Many of these students asked me, the philosophy major, to tutor them in preparation for their exams. Some of them thought they were imposing on me to help them. What they didn't realize was that they were helping me to learn philosophy as much as I was helping them to learn it. The best possible preparation I ever had for my own philosophy exams was to teach the material to someone else before I was tested on it. As I explained the content to others, I quickly became aware of those areas of weakness in my own understanding of the material. This encouraged me to study even further and to become more adept at articulating key philosophical concepts.

The point is that wise teachers learn not only from their preparation and not only from other teachers but also from their students. The insightful questions of my best students have made it possible for me to become a better and more biblical theologian. These questions have forced me to reconsider things from different angles and have opened up new avenues of study that I never considered before. I confess that at times this has been a painful process, forcing me to deal with my own pride. It can be humbling to learn from students, but it's necessary and helpful.

Over the years, I've learned that if I as a teacher am threatened by the questions or knowledge of my students, I will never grow as a teacher.

I've prayed that God would enable me never to become defensive, tentative, and ultimately unteachable. I've prayed that for my students as well, especially those who are called to vocational ministry. Those who are willing to see the questions and knowledge of their students as opportunities to expand their learning will become better, if not great, teachers.

The only teacher who has no need of learning is God Himself. A great teacher is teachable. If he is not, he will have precious little to teach. Flee from the teacher who knows it all, and look for instructors who are teachable.

PROVIDENCE AND CONTENTMENT

B LAISE PASCAL, THE FAMOUS FRENCH philosopher and math-
ematician, noted that human beings are creatures of profound
paradox. We're capable of both deep misery and tremendous grandeur, often at the same time. All we have to do is scan the headlines to
see that this is the case. How often do celebrities who have done great
good through philanthropy get caught up in scandals?

Human grandeur is found in part in our ability to contemplate ourselves,
to reflect upon our origins, our destiny, and our place in the universe. Yet,
such contemplation has a negative side, and that is its potential to bring
us pain. We may find ourselves miserable when we think of a life that is
better than that which we enjoy now and recognize that we are incapable of achieving it. Perhaps we think of a life free of illness and pain, yet
we know that physical agony and death are certain. Rich and poor alike
know that a life of greater wealth is possible but grow frustrated when
that wealth is unobtainable. Sick or healthy, poor or rich, successful or
unsuccessful—we are all capable of growing vexed when a better life
remains outside of our grasp.

Scripture prescribes only one remedy to this frustration: contentment.

Biblical contentment is a spiritual virtue that we find modeled by the
Apostle Paul. He states, for example, "I have learned in whatever situation
I am to be content" (Phil. 4:11). No matter the state of his health, wealth,
or success, Paul found it possible to be content with his life.

In Paul's era, two prominent schools of Greek philosophy agreed that
our goal should be to find contentment, but they had very different ways
of getting there. The first of these, Stoicism, said *imperturbability* was
the way to contentment. Stoics believed that human beings had no real

control over their external circumstances, which were subject to the whims of fate. The only place they could have any control was in their personal attitudes. We cannot control what happens to us, they said, but we can control how we feel about it. Thus, Stoics trained themselves to achieve imperturbability, an inner sense of peace that would leave them unbothered no matter what happened to them.

The Epicureans were more proactive in their search for contentment, looking to find a proper balance between pleasure and pain. Their aim was to minimize pain and maximize pleasure. Yet even achieving a goal in this arena can result in frustration. We might never obtain the aimed-for pleasure, or, having obtained it, we might realize that it does not bring what we thought it would.

Paul was neither a Stoic nor an Epicurean. Epicureanism leads eventually to an ultimate pessimism—we can't get or maintain the pleasure we seek, so what's the point? The Apostle's doctrine of the resurrection and the renewal of creation does not allow for such pessimism. Creation "will be set free from its bondage to corruption and obtain the freedom of the glory of the children of God" (Rom. 8:18–25; see 1 Cor. 15). Paul also rejected the passive resignation of Stoicism, for he was no fatalist. Paul actively pressed toward his goals and called us to work out our salvation with fear and trembling, believing that God works in and through us to bring about His purposes (Phil. 2:12).

For the Apostle, true contentment was not complacency, and it was not a condition, on this side of glory, that could admit no feelings of discontent and dissatisfaction. After all, Paul frequently expresses such feelings in his epistles as he considers the sins of the church and his own shortcomings. He did not rest on his laurels but worked zealously to solve problems both personally and pastorally.

Paul's contentment pertained to his personal circumstances and the state of his human condition. Whether he suffered lack or enjoyed material prosperity, he had "learned" to be content wherever God placed him (Phil. 4:12). Note that this was something he learned. It was not a natural gifting but something he had to be taught.

What was the secret to contentment that he had learned? Paul tells us in Philippians 4:13: "I can do all things through him who strengthens me."

In short, the Apostle's contentment was grounded in his union with Christ and in his theology. He saw theology not as a theoretical or abstract discipline but rather as the key to understanding life itself. His contentment with his condition in life rested on his knowledge of God's character and actions. Paul was content because he knew his condition was ordained by his Creator. He understood that God brought both pleasure and pain into his life for a good purpose (Rom. 8:28). Paul knew that since the Lord wisely ordered his life, he could find strength in the Lord for any and all circumstances. Paul understood that he was fulfilling the purpose of God whether he was experiencing abundance or abasement. Submission to God's sovereign rule over his life was the key to his contentment.

As we continue to wrestle with the desires of the flesh, we can be tempted to believe God owes us a better condition than we presently enjoy. To believe such a thing is sin, and it leads to great misery, which is overcome only by trusting in the Lord's sustaining and providential grace. We will find true contentment only as we receive and walk in that grace.

PERFECTLY HUMAN

DECEMBER 2015

———

O VER THE PAST TWO CENTURIES, much has been written in evangelical circles on the deity of Christ. This has been good and necessary, for many people deny that Jesus is the Son of God incarnate. Sometimes I fear, however, that this emphasis on Christ's deity has led to an imbalance in our doctrine of Christ. It's proper to highlight our Lord's deity, but Scripture also emphasizes His humanity. If Jesus were only God and not truly man, He could not save us. His humanity is inseparable from His being the second Adam, fulfilling all righteousness, and taking upon Himself all the obligations of God's law that must be fulfilled for us to receive life eternal (Lev. 18:5; Rom. 2:13).

The New Testament proclaims Jesus Christ as *vera homo*, truly human, as well as *vera Deus*, truly God. References to Jesus' true humanity abound. John numbers those who deny a real incarnation with the antichrist (2 John 1:7). Paul speaks of Christ as "born of a woman" (1 Cor. 11:12; Gal. 4:4). The Gospels reveal Christ as having the basic characteristics of humanity. He walks, He talks, He becomes tired, He eats, He drinks, He cries, He manifests every human emotion and every dimension of the physical aspect of mankind (see, for example, Matt. 8:24; Luke 7:34; John 11:35). There's a full identification of Jesus with humanity—except with respect to one vital distinction: the moral distinction. Christ perfectly obeys the Father; we don't.

Christ's sinlessness is vital to the biblical understanding of redemption. If Jesus is to be our mediator, if He is to be our redeemer, it's essential that He be sinless. How could His atoning life have any significance if He committed even one sin? He's called the lamb without blemish because His perfection is integral to His redemptive role as the mediator who offers up a perfect sacrifice to the Father to fulfill the old covenant and satisfy the wrath of God. The sinlessness of Jesus is critical to the full biblical understanding of His sacrificial death. Not only does Christ take what should be ours—namely, punishment for sin—but through imputation He gives to those who are in Him by faith alone the inheritance He receives for His perfect obedience (Rom. 3:21–26).

Some have denied the sinlessness of Christ in the name of protecting His humanity. If there's anything that binds us together in common humanity, if there's anything true of all men of all races and creeds, it's that we fall short of our standards. We transgress our own laws, not to mention the laws of God. I don't know anything more common to humanity than sin. If one man in this world today lived ten minutes in perfect obedience to God, that would be nothing less than astonishing. But Christ's entire life was marked by sinlessness (1 Peter 2:22). So, how could a sinless Christ be truly human if sinlessness violates what is so common to human behavior?

What we're really asking is this: Is sinfulness intrinsic to true humanity? We can answer only in the negative. To say that sinfulness is intrinsic to authentic humanity requires two conclusions: first, that Adam before the fall was not a human being; second, and more seriously, that Christians in a state of perfected glory in heaven will no longer be human.

Everything Scripture says about human beings and sin suggests that men and women, as originally created, were without sin but were nevertheless truly human. Moreover, the Bible teaches that when we are glorified, we will be without sin but yet truly human. Sin isn't a necessary attribute of true humanity; it's a foreign intrusion into humanity as created by God. To affirm that sin is intrinsic to our humanity denies the true humanity both of our origins and of our destiny.

Christ's sinlessness is vindicated most powerfully in His resurrection. The penalty of sin, biblically speaking, is death (Gen. 2:15–17; Rom. 6:23). But it was impossible for death to hold Him (Acts 2:24). Why? Since Jesus was guilty of no personal sin, death had no rightful claim over Him. He bore our sin and guilt, and that is why He died; but once our debt of sin was canceled, there was nothing left to keep Him buried (Col. 2:13–15). Jesus, being perfectly righteous, had to be raised, for it would have been unjust for God to allow a sinless man to rot in the grave. Christ was raised for our justification, resurrected to prove that He fully satisfied God's demands on behalf of His people (Rom. 4:25).

When we confess the sinlessness of Jesus, we are not confessing merely that Jesus is a good man, nor a very good man, nor the best man who has ever lived. We are confessing that Jesus is the perfect man. There's a significant difference between the good, the better, the best, and the perfect. It amazes me that many people will say that Jesus is a good man but not that He is the perfect man. But how can Jesus be a good man if He has falsely claimed to be a perfect man? Only a bad man would claim to be perfect if he was not perfect. To be equal with the Father, to be sent from God, to be the Savior of the world—a good man would not claim such things of himself if they were not true. Jesus can't be merely a good man. He is either the perfect man or He's not a good man.

Christ is not only truly human—He is perfectly human. Only He has fulfilled the vocation of human beings to love the Lord above all else. That makes Him the most human person who has ever lived, because only He has done what human beings were made to do.

TERMS FOR THE COVENANT

JANUARY 2016

———

REFORMED THEOLOGY, AS MANY HAVE SAID, is covenant theology, for the concept of covenant has shaped the development of Reformed thinking. We should expect as much because of our doctrine of sola Scriptura, which says that the Bible is the only infallible authority for Christian faith and practice. Therefore, we want to structure all theological understanding according to Scripture. This demands covenant theology, since covenant is an organizing principle in Scripture.

Given the importance of the biblical doctrine of covenant, all Christians should have at least a basic understanding of what the Bible means by the term *covenant*. In the Old Testament, the Hebrew word we translate as "covenant" is *berith*, and it was used for centuries by the ancient Israelites. However, after Alexander the Great conquered the Eastern Mediterranean world and brought with him the Greek language, many Jews became more familiar with Greek than with Hebrew. Consequently, a Greek translation of the Hebrew Old Testament was made during the third century B.C. We know this translation as the Septuagint, and it had a tremendous impact on the writers of the Greek New Testament.

One challenge that the Jews who produced the Septuagint faced was the decision about how best to translate the Hebrew term *berith* or "covenant," since there wasn't any Greek word that precisely matched the Hebrew term. Eventually, the word chosen by the Septuagint translators was the Greek word *diathēkē*, and this was adopted by the New Testament writers, who, for the most part used *diathēkē* for the concept of "covenant."

Some confusion arises here, however, because the Greeks used the word *diathēkē* in the sense of "testament." That's because a testament in Greek culture, at least at that time, included several nuances that made it different from the Hebrew concept of covenant. First, in Greek culture, a *diathēkē*—a testament—could be changed at any time by the testator while the testator was still alive. The testator could make up his last will and testament and then get irritated at his heirs and write them out of his will. And that continues to this day, for we know that people are sometimes disinherited, or written out of the will of a friend or family member. But that's significantly different from a *diathēkē*—a testament or covenant—made by God. When God makes a covenant with His people, He can punish them for covenant breaking, but He never cancels the covenant promises He has made.

Another difference between the Greek understanding of *diathēkē* as a testament and the Hebrew understanding of *berith* as a covenant is that in the Greek world, the benefits of the testament, or *diathēkē*, did not accrue until after the testator died. Obviously, when God makes a covenant, His people don't have to wait for Him to die to inherit the blessings of that covenant, because He's incapable of dying.

Given those two great weaknesses, why did the Septuagint translators and the New Testament authors choose the Greek word *diathēkē* ("testament") to translate the Hebrew *berith* ("covenant")? Because it was a better choice than the alternative Greek term—*synthēkē*. That word features the prefix *syn-*, which we see in such English terms as *synonym, syncretism,* and *synchronization.* It simply means "with." And the idea of a *synthēkē* in Greek culture was an agreement between equal partners, an agreement with the consent of peers. The Jewish translators wanted to maintain that the covenants that God makes with His people are made between a superior and a subordinate, not between two equal parties. So, the word *synthēkē* was rejected.

The Septuagint translators and New Testament authors chose *diathēkē* because in its original use, before the Greeks came to use it to mean "testament," it had reference to what is called "the disposition for one's self." A *diathēkē* had to do with an individual's disposition of his goods or property for himself; that is, it referred to his sovereign determining of his heirs. To this day, that's how we understand the concept of a testament or will. That aspect of disposition is an element that reflects the Hebrew concept because in His covenant, God sovereignly determines to give promises to whom He will give promises. He made a covenant with Abraham, not Hammurabi. He chose the Jews, not the Philistines. He entered into a covenant relationship with them and said, "I will be your God and you will be my people." That's a choice God made, not the Jews. So, even though the Greek word *diathēkē* includes aspects that don't overlap with the Hebrew notion of a covenant, it carries the key notion of sovereign determination.

This might seem pedantic, but there's one important point to take away from this discussion. If God's covenant were a *synthēkē* made between two equal parties, all would be lost. Our role in maintaining the covenant relationship would be fully equal to His. But we are sinners who cannot keep covenant perfectly. A *synthēkē* would mean no salvation. A *diathēkē* is different. Because it is God's sovereign administration with an unequal party, the onus for the fulfillment of the covenant's promises is on the greater party—the Lord Himself. He swore by Himself to uphold the covenant (Gen. 15; Heb. 6:13–20). His honor is on the line, and if He fails, His glory suffers. But we know that God cannot fail, that He will not surrender His glory (Isa. 48:11). In the Lord's *diathēkē*, or covenant, He guarantees the fulfillment of His Word for His name's sake, which means the redemption of His people is secure.

OUR STORY

FEBRUARY 2016

———

WHEN **I** RETURN TO THE FIRST FEW chapters of Genesis, I'm able not only to review the events of early human history but also to see how humanity hasn't outgrown our earliest aspirations. Perhaps most illustrative of my point is the story of the Tower of Babel in Genesis 11. We read in verse 1 that "the whole earth had one language and the same words." Note the unity preserved from the original pre-fall creation. In the garden of Eden there were no translators; everyone spoke the same language. And even though sin intruded to destroy the harmony of the original creation, at least people could understand each other in the initial years of human expansion. They could speak the same language and communicate with some degree of harmony.

Speaking the same language and having the same values, this humanity built a city: "Come, let us build ourselves a city and a tower with its top in the heavens" (v. 4). From the beginning, the dream of human progress, the dream of the human spirit has been to build a city of such magnificence that it reaches to the pinnacle of heaven itself. It's part of our nature as human beings to build monuments to human accomplishment. We can go through the cities of this world and see magnificent human achievements. We can view the Eiffel Tower from almost any point in and around Paris. No tourist in New York City fails to look for the Statue of Liberty or the Empire State Building. We can't go to Asia without wanting to walk on the Great Wall of China. When we go to Egypt, to the pyramids, we see monuments of ancient kings. Brick and mortar, steel and glass—we use whatever we can to somehow say that we are important, that we are significant, that we want to be remembered long after we are dead and gone.

Listen to the sentiment expressed in Genesis 11: "Let us make a name for ourselves" (v. 4). Friedrich Nietzsche, the nineteenth-century atheist philosopher, said the most fundamental drive of the human heart is the "will to power," a lust for dominance. This is what drives fallen humanity. It's the legacy of Eden, the living out of the serpent's seduction when he said, "You shall be as gods." Why should God get all the glory? Why should the monuments of this world only be to the praise and honor of the Creator? Can't we share in that? Can't we claim it for ourselves? Can't we supplant Him as the Sovereign One? Let's gather together and build a city. Let's make monuments that even God cannot bring down, monuments that will endure forever: statues, walls, cathedrals, skyscrapers, and more.

I remember sitting transfixed and watching Walter Cronkite and some former astronauts describe the first landing of human beings on the moon. When I heard the words of Neil Armstrong, "That's one small step for a man; one giant leap for mankind," I was as excited as anybody else by this incredible accomplishment, this conquest of a whole new frontier. But there was also something that bothered me when I heard those words. It sounded like the Tower of Babel all over again, a boasting in human achievement rather than bowing in prayer, saying, "This is for Your glory, O God. This is the fulfillment of the scientific enterprise You gave us in Eden to have dominion over the earth."

We've been called to have dominion over the earth to the glory of God, but we want dominion for the glory of man. That's what was going on at Babel—a distortion, an evil twisting of the legitimate task that God had given mankind. There's nothing wrong with building. There's nothing wrong with sowing and reaping. Those are the tasks God gave to us in creation, but they're to be done under the authority of God. They're to be done *coram Deo*, before the face of God, under the authority of God, and unto the glory of God.

But what happened in the cosmic revolt? Man wanted to build a city for himself, to build his own kingdom, to make a name for himself, not for God. And this is not a story of ancient defects of human beings. This is our story. We're the players in this drama. Babel is representative of the whole human enterprise that we are so busily engaged in. "Let's build a city. Let's make a name for ourselves."

Then we read in chapter 11 of Genesis that "the LORD came down to see the city and the tower, which the children of man had built" (v. 5). God inspected the city of man, and He didn't like what He saw:

> The LORD said, "Behold, they are one people, and they have all one language, and this is only the beginning of what they will do. And nothing that they propose to do will now be impossible for them. Come, let us go down and there confuse their language, so that they may not understand one another's speech." So the LORD dispersed them from there over the face of all the earth, and they left off building the city. Therefore its name was called Babel, because there the LORD confused the language of all the earth. (vv. 6–9a)

The greatest building project mankind ever attempted was resisted by God. And it ended in chaos and confusion.

Every attempt of man to build his own ultimate city and kingdom will end in chaos. Any success we enjoy will be short-lived, for the Lord will bring into judgment every hidden thing, every secret thought (Eccl. 12:14). Nothing built for the glory of man will survive His scrutiny. But what is done for God's glory will endure forever.

DIFFERENCE OR CONTRADICTION?

MARCH 2016

W E LIVE IN A DAY WHEN CONSISTENCY OF thought is demeaned by many people, and individuals maintain that contradiction is the hallmark of truth, particularly in religious matters. Yet, in practice, human beings seek consistency. Consider liberal Protestantism. Decades ago, most of the mainline denominations abandoned the infallibility and inerrancy of Scripture. Originally, these denominations thought they could continue affirming the other core tenets of Christianity. As the years passed, however, it became clear that the rejection of the infallibility and inerrancy of the Scriptures leads to the denial of Christian orthodoxy on other matters. Most churches that abandoned biblical inerrancy and infallibility eventually rejected the atonement, biblical sexual ethics, and other teachings. Those denominations had to do that for consistency's sake. To deny that God's Word is without error is to deny that we have a trustworthy revelation from Him. Thus, it doesn't ultimately matter what the Bible says about anything.

When it comes to studying the actual consistency of Scripture, it's not long before we have to deal with allegations that the Bible is full of contradictions. This can be devastating to the Christian faith, because we know that if the Bible has real contradictions, it's not a consistent account, and if it's not a consistent account, it can't be divinely inspired.

The main thing I want to say about this issue is that most alleged contradictions turn out not to be contradictions at all. When I was a seminary student, my professors frequently taught the theories of "higher" critics who refused to affirm the infallibility of Scripture. One of my fellow seminarians, a brilliant fellow, struggled with these theories. He had come to seminary believing in Scripture's consistency, but by the time he was a senior, he was one of the casualties of the exposure to this relentless skepticism about the Bible. I remember one discussion in the hallway of the seminary where he said: "R.C., how can you still believe in the inerrancy of Scripture after all we've gone through here? Don't you see that the Bible is full of contradictions?"

At the time, he couldn't list even ten examples of contradictions in the Bible. So I suggested he go home and come up with thirty contradictions that we could look at together. When we met the next day, he brought a list of about twenty. He gave me the first "contradiction," and we looked at the apparently contradictory passages together, and we found that there was variation between the two accounts. But variation and contradiction aren't the same thing. We're familiar with how two eyewitnesses might see the same crime but report it differently. They remember different things about the event because of their different perspectives, but the details of the two accounts don't conflict. In fact, the authorities like to have many witnesses to a crime because comparing the stories gives a fuller view of what happened. The same thing happens when historians research an event and read eyewitness accounts of it.

As my friend and I looked at the first alleged biblical problem, we found it was possible for the two accounts to agree. Then, we looked at the rest of the "contradictions." Some examples were more challenging than others, but what happened was this: in every example, we concluded together that there were no real contradictions.

Read the Bible carefully, and you'll find variations of perspective. Consider the Gospels' presentation of the resurrection. For example, Matthew 28:1–10 and Mark 16:1–8 say there was one angel at the empty tomb, while Luke 24:1–12 mentions the presence of two angels at Jesus' grave. That was one of the "contradictions" my friend brought to me. So I said we should assume for the sake of argument that two angels were present. If so, would it not be possible for one eyewitness to be more concerned about who wasn't there—Jesus—than he was about the number of angels present, especially if one of them did not speak? The disciple could have said, "I went there, and I saw an angel, who said x, y, and z," without mentioning the second angel because the presence of two angels wasn't that significant to the disciple who was writing. I asked my friend, "What word is conspicuously absent from this disciple's report that must be there to have a true contradiction?" The answer was clear: the word *only*. If there were two angels, we know there had to be at least one; thus, since Mark and Matthew don't say there was *only* one angel there, there's no contradiction between them and Luke. Instead, there's variation in perspectives because they're relying on different eyewitness reports of the same event. Such variation is exactly what we should expect from independent accounts.

It took many centuries and many different writers to give us the Bible. It didn't drop from heaven on a parachute. The doctrine of inspiration doesn't mean we won't find difficult-to-reconcile texts in Scripture. The Bible is a divine book—but it's also a very human book, not in that it is filled with human errors but in that it reflects how human beings tell stories. No two people write in exactly the same way, and no two human beings report their perspectives on the same event identically. Two people can accurately represent the same event without covering all the same details. That's the kind of thing we find in Scripture. Difference does not mean contradiction.

EXPLAINING ANOMALIES

APRIL 2016

———

U NBELIEVERS OFTEN ALLEGE THAT THE Bible is "full of contradictions." I've noted in many places over the years, however, that
most of the contradictions people suggest really do not qualify
as contradictions but merely reflect the difference in perspective we get
when several eyewitnesses describe the same event but give different
details. In such cases, the accounts do not contradict one another; rather,
each account may emphasize different aspects of the same event, such
that we get a fuller picture when we see how the details can be harmo-
nized. Variations in perspective are exactly what we should expect even
in a divinely inspired text, for the Holy Spirit did not override the personalities and styles of the individual authors when they wrote. Instead,
the Spirit worked through their concerns to give us an inerrant record of
what happened even as each writer focuses on some details and not others.

The vast majority of supposed "contradictions" in Scripture are relatively
easy to reconcile. However, for the sake of honesty, I must acknowledge
that there are a handful of problems in Scripture that are exceedingly difficult. For instance, it's hard at times to square 1 and 2 Chronicles with 1
and 2 Kings, particularly with respect to when certain kings reigned, how
long they ruled, and when they took the throne. Some have done the yeo-
man's work of figuring out how these accounts fit together, which requires
detailed knowledge of how ancient Near Eastern peoples recorded dates,
periods of co-regency when two kings ruled at the same time, and other
such things. No universally accepted solution has yet been found for every
problem, but the work continues, and there's every reason to believe we
will have better answers as we learn more about how ancient Near Eastern
writers, including the authors of Kings and Chronicles, did their work.

I'm confident such problems will eventually be solved because we serve
a God who speaks truthfully and consistently, and because archaeological

discoveries continue to confirm the biblical account. As an example, for many years all we knew about Pontius Pilate came from the Bible and a few other extrabiblical documents, so some people questioned whether Pilate ever existed. But in 1961, an ancient inscription mentioning Pilate was found in what was once the city Caesarea Maritima on the Mediterranean coast, thereby confirming that Pilate was indeed procurator of Judea during Jesus' time. Another formerly "assured result of higher criticism" that "disproved" the Bible relates to the story of Abraham. For a long time, there was no archaeological evidence that camels had been domesticated in the patriarchal period, and many people said that proved the Genesis account to be fictional because the Abraham story includes domesticated camels. But eventually, archaeological discoveries pushed back the domestication of camels hundreds of years—well into the patriarchal period.

Other discrepancies in the biblical account have yet to be resolved, but that doesn't mean we should doubt Scripture's truthfulness. Here, I'm simply following the course of ordinary science. Every so often, we see massive changes in scientific theory, paradigm shifts in which there is a change in the overarching model adopted to make sense of the data. Scientific paradigms are structural theories that explain reality, but every scientific paradigm has had to deal with anomalies, for every paradigm suffers from the presence of details that it cannot neatly explain. But you don't throw out the paradigm the first time you find an anomaly the paradigm cannot explain. You wait, you study, you get more data, and so on.

The paradigm doesn't shift until you get enough of these anomalies challenging the system. Copernican astronomy did not replace Ptolemaic astronomy because there were only a few details Ptolemy's system couldn't explain. The Ptolemaic system worked for many centuries until too many anomalies were discovered. The Copernican model was then adopted because it better explains the data and has fewer anomalies.

Overall, the trend with respect to apparent biblical discrepancies is that the number of them is decreasing. If maybe there were once a hundred such difficulties, that list has been pared down to a handful. At this point, we don't throw the Bible out based on a handful of unresolved difficulties when everything indicates a greater confidence in Scripture's truthfulness than we had before.

We tend to be too quick in accusing normal people, let alone the Bible, of contradictions. Now, we're all capable of inconsistency, incoherency, and contradiction. But common courtesy requires at least that we give others the benefit of a second glance. We should strive to figure out how someone can consistently affirm two seemingly contradictory positions. In giving that second glance, we often find that what others are saying is not as contradictory as it first seemed. If we extend this courtesy to others, how much more do we owe it to the Apostles? Before we accuse Paul of a contradiction, we ought to have enough respect for his importance to see if what he says in Ephesians really contradicts what he says in Galatians.

One of the most satisfying and faith-increasing exercises in my own lifetime has involved giving focused attention to alleged biblical difficulties. That's because the more I study them and see their resolutions, the more I back away from the text in utter amazement that the Bible can be so coherent and so consistent and so unified at the tiniest level of the fine details. Its symmetry, its complexity, and its harmony are astonishing.

CHRIST'S CALL
TO MAKE DISCIPLES

MAY 2016

———

O NE OF THE MOST EXCITING TIMES of my life was when I was converted to Christ. I was filled with a zeal for evangelism. However, much to my consternation, when I told my friends about my conversion to Christ, they thought I was crazy. They were tragically amused, remaining unconvinced despite my sharing the gospel with them. Finally, they asked me, "Why don't you start a class and teach us what you have learned about Jesus?" They were serious. I was elated. We scheduled a time to meet—but they never showed up.

Despite my profound desire for evangelism, I was a failure at it. This realization came to me early in my ministry. Yet, I also discovered that there are many people whom Christ has called and whom He has gifted by His Spirit to be particularly effective in evangelism. To this day, I'm surprised if anyone attributes their conversion in some part to my influence. In one respect, I'm glad that the Great Commission is not a commission principally to evangelism.

The words preceding Jesus' commission were these: "All authority in heaven and on earth has been given to me" (Matt. 28:18). He then went on to say, "Go therefore and make disciples of all nations" (v. 19). When Jesus gave this commission to the church, He was speaking authoritatively. He gave a mandate to the church of all ages not simply to evangelize but to make disciples. That raises a significant question: What is a disciple?

The simplest definition of *disciple* is one who directs his mind toward specific knowledge and conduct. So, we might say that a disciple is a learner or pupil. The Greek philosophers Socrates, Plato, and Aristotle had disciples. Socrates described himself as a disciple of Homer, whom Socrates regarded as the greatest thinker in Greek history.

We tend to think of Homer as a poet rather than as a philosopher. But Socrates saw him as the supreme teacher of ancient Greece. Socrates had his own student—his chief disciple—whose name was Plato. Plato had his disciples, the chief one being Aristotle. Aristotle also had his disciples, the most famous being Alexander the Great. It is astonishing to think about how dramatically the ancient world was shaped by four men: Socrates, Plato, Aristotle, and Alexander the Great. In fact, it is nearly impossible to understand the history of Western civilization without understanding the influence of those four individuals, who in their own way were each disciples of another.

Aristotle was known as a "peripatetic" philosopher. That is, he was a nomadic teacher who walked from place to place, not teaching in a fixed location. The students of Aristotle would follow him as he walked the streets of Athens. In one respect, Aristotle's disciples lived life with him, learning from him in the course of a normal daily routine.

These concepts help illuminate the nature of discipleship. However, they fail to capture the full essence of biblical discipleship. Biblical discipleship involves walking with the Teacher and learning from His words, but it is more than that.

Jesus was a rabbi and, of course, the most important peripatetic teacher and disciple-maker in history. Wherever He walked, His students would follow. At the beginning of Jesus' public ministry, He chose particular individuals to be His disciples. They were required to memorize the teachings that He spoke as He walked. What's more, people didn't file an application to get into the School of Jesus. Jesus selected His disciples. He went to prospective disciples where they were and gave this simple command: "Follow me." The command was literal—He called them to drop their present duties. They had to leave their work, their families, and their friends to follow Jesus.

Yet, Jesus was more than just a peripatetic teacher. His disciples called Him "Master." Their entire way of life changed because they followed Jesus not merely as a great teacher but as the Lord of all. That's the essence of discipleship—submitting fully to the authority of Christ, the One whose lordship goes beyond just the classroom. Jesus' lordship encompasses all of life. The Greek philosophers learned from their teachers but then tried to improve on that teaching. Christ's disciples have no such warrant. We are called to understand and teach only what God has revealed through Christ, including the Old Testament Scriptures, for they point to Christ; and the New Testament Scriptures, for they are the words of those whom Christ appointed to speak in His name.

The Great Commission is the call of Christ for His disciples to extend His authority over the whole world. We are to share the gospel with everyone so that more and more people might call Him "Master." This calling is not simply a call to evangelism. It isn't merely a call to get members for our churches. Rather, Christ calls us to make disciples. Disciples are people who have wholeheartedly committed to follow the thinking and conduct of the Master. Such discipleship is a lifelong experience of learning the mind of Christ and following the will of Christ, submitting ourselves in full obedience to His lordship.

Thus, when Jesus tells us to go to all nations, we are to go into all the world with His agenda, not our own. The Great Commission calls us to work with other believers in the church in order to produce disciples and flood this world with knowledgeable, articulate Christians who worship God and follow Jesus Christ passionately.

PRINCIPLES AND SITUATIONS

JUNE 2016

———

E VERY SO OFTEN, I RUN ACROSS a news story that's emblematic of our times. Recently, I read of a case wherein a woman contracted with a man to be a surrogate mother. The man agreed to pay her to bear the children, who were conceived by in vitro fertilization using the man's sperm and eggs donated from another woman. Triplets were conceived, but the man wants to abort one of them, and the contract he signed gives him the legal right to do so. The woman does not want to abort the child, so she has sued to prevent it and has offered to raise the unwanted child herself. But the man does not want that, and now thinks it would be better to put the child up for adoption himself.

The commodification of children, the nonchalant manner in which the man wants to get rid of one of the babies, and other issues raised by this case send chills down one's spine. Here we see the logical results of what happens when human beings have no fixed, objective standard of right and wrong.

Modern science and technology have introduced questions that the church has never had to deal with before. When it comes to many biomedical issues, we don't have the advantage of two thousand years of careful research, debate, and insight into complex and weighty problems. The availability of life-support systems, cloning, in vitro fertilization, and other technologies have introduced new dilemmas and pose new ethical questions.

It's not that we don't have basic principles to apply to these issues, for Scripture does provide them. The difficulty lies in applying these principles to new situations we've never faced before. And we aren't facing abstract theoretical questions but life-or-death questions that must be answered in concrete instances. Pastors, for example, are often called to help determine when to extend and when to end life support for a patient.

Without clear, normative principles, we're left rudderless in these situations. Our decisions apply principles in specific situations, but the situations cannot dictate the decisions. And we can't decide to make no decision. To make no decision is to make a decision.

We need principles that are absolute and normative; otherwise, the decisions we make will be arbitrary, and we'll have no basis for distinguishing right decisions from wrong decisions. Our human-enacted laws can be helpful, but they can never provide absolute norms. This is particularly clear in societies where the laws are enacted according to popular will. We will find conflict and contradiction between the laws of one society wherein laws are made by an elected body and the laws of another society that makes laws in a similar way. In the United States, abortion is legal. In Chile, abortion is illegal. Does this mean that it is ethically right to abort American babies but wrong to abort Chilean babies? Was it ethically wrong to have an abortion before *Roe v. Wade* but ethically proper after *Roe v. Wade*? The answer is yes if popularly enacted laws and court decisions are the absolute norm.

Only the character of God as revealed in His law provides us with absolute norms for ethical issues. It gives us fixed principles to apply in specific situations. God's law is both situational and non-situational. It's situational because it must always be applied in specific situations, but it's non-situational because the situation itself never dictates the good. The unchanging principle from the law determines the good.

In popular culture, we see a definition of right and wrong that says we must do what love requires in any situation. Why not let two men or two women get married? we are asked. After all, they love each other. How is it loving to bring a child into a situation of poverty? we are often asked in the abortion debate.

On the one hand, it's correct that we must always do what love requires. Love is the linchpin of God's law, the very fulfillment of the commandments (Rom. 13:10). But love isn't a vacuous feeling; it's something objective.

Love is defined by God Himself, for Scripture tells us that "God is love" (1 John 4:8). And the God who is love has given us a law that defines and applies what love looks like in concrete situations. For instance, Paul lays out the principle that we must "walk in love," but then he immediately tells us that "sexual immorality and all impurity or covetousness must not even be named among you, as is proper among saints" (Eph. 5:2–3). God defines love as being the rejection of sexual immorality, impurity, and covetousness. Anything that includes such things cannot be love even if the designation of love is claimed.

In most ethical decisions, we must apply more than one principle. This requires wisdom, but we won't be prepared to balance these principles unless we know them. That's why we must continue to study the law and the principles revealed therein, principles that are not subject to the shifting sands of relativism. At the final judgment, we will have to answer for what we have done with this law, for we are the creatures and God is the Creator. He has the absolute right to demand from His creatures what He defines as right. The will of the creature must submit itself to the will of the Creator, and if we don't bow to His lordship, we will be judged accordingly.

God's law is the absolute, objective norm that is to govern the behavior of all people. It's not a norm hidden from us, but it has been revealed. So, we have the responsibility to know and do what righteousness requires.

WHAT IS THE CHURCH?

JULY 2016

———

P**AUL GIVES GREAT ATTENTION TO** ecclesiology, the doctrine of the church, in his letter to the Ephesians. In fact, we could say Ephesians answers this question: What is the church? In Ephesians 2:19–22, the chief metaphor Paul uses is that of a building—the household of God. Christians are part of the household in the sense that they have been adopted into the family of God, which is another image that Scripture uses to describe the church. But here the accent is not so much on the family of the household as it is on the house of the household: "[We] are fellow citizens with the saints and members of the household of God, built on the foundation of the apostles and prophets" (vv. 19–20a).

Paul says the foundation of this building called the church is made up of the prophets and the Apostles, that is, the Old Testament prophets and New Testament Apostles. Why? It's because the prophets and Apostles are the agents of revelation by whom God speaks to His people. They delivered the Word of God. Another way of saying this is that the foundation of the church is the Word of God.

That's why we must pay close attention to our doctrine of Scripture. The attacks launched against the integrity, authority, sufficiency, and trustworthiness of Scripture are attacks not upon a side alcove of this building. They don't put a dent in the roof of the church. They're attacks on the church's very foundation. To have a church without Apostolic authority, without the Word of God as its foundation, is to build a church on sand rather than on rock. The foundation of the prophets and the Apostles is necessary for the entire edifice of the church to stand securely.

Paul continues the building metaphor in 2:20b: "Christ Jesus Himself being the cornerstone." Christ is the cornerstone, the point that holds the foundation together. Take out the cornerstone, and everything falls apart. "In [Christ] the whole structure, being joined together, grows into a holy temple in the Lord. In him you also are being built together into a dwelling place for God by the Spirit" (vv. 21–22). The church is a new temple built in Christ, by Christ, and for Christ. Obviously, Paul isn't saying the church is a building made out of mortar and brick, but that we are the stones, the living stones, as 1 Peter 2:5 tells us. Each believer is part of this church just as each stone is part of a building. The church, the new temple, is still under construction. Every day, new stones are added. This new temple will not be finished until Jesus returns to consummate His kingdom. Christ is still building His church, not by adding cement but by adding people who are the stones that hold together in Him.

Paul continues in Ephesians 3:14–19,

> For this reason I bow my knees before the Father, from whom every family in heaven and on earth is named, that according to the riches of his glory he may grant you to be strengthened with power through his Spirit in your inner being, so that Christ may dwell in your hearts through faith—that you, being rooted and grounded in love, may have strength to comprehend with all the saints what is the breadth and length and height and depth, and to know the love of Christ that surpasses knowledge, that you may be filled with all the fullness of God.

The Apostle Paul explains the doctrine of the church so that we might understand what God has done and so that we may understand who we are. And in calling us to understand who we are and what we're called to do, Paul says that we're the church. We're the church that God ordained from the foundation of the world. We're His people; we're His household, so let the church be the church.

We're living in a time of crisis. Many Christians are decrying the decadence of American culture and complaining about the government and its value system. I understand that, but if we want to be concerned for our nation and culture, our priority must be the renewal of the church. We are the light of the world.

Government merely reflects and echoes the customs embraced by the people in a given generation. In a real sense, our government is exactly what we want it to be, or it wouldn't be there. Change in culture doesn't always come from the top down. It often comes from the bottom up. The change we need to work for, chiefly, is renewal within the church. As the church becomes the fellowship of citizens of heaven who manifest what it means to be the household of Christ, and when the church walks according to the power of the Holy Spirit—then the people of God will shine as the light of the world. When people see that light, they will give glory to God (Matt. 5:16). This will change the world. But Paul says, first of all, let the church be the church. We must remember who we are, who the foundation is, who the cornerstone is, who the head of our building is, who the Lord of the church is.

Do we love the church? I doubt if there have been many times in our history when there has been as much anger, hostility, disappointment, and disillusionment with the institutional church as there is today. It's hard not to be critical of the church because in many ways the church has failed us. But if the church has failed, that means we have failed. We are called to serve the church in the power of God the Holy Spirit.

We, the church, have been made for this task by the indwelling presence and power of God's Spirit. Yet, we are called not so much to rise up but to bow down. And if we bow down to our Lord, as Paul says in Ephesians 3:14, the church will be the church, and our light will pierce the darkness.

BEARING AND ENDURING

AUGUST 2016

———

"LOVE BEARS ALL THINGS, believes all things, hopes all things, endures all things" (1 Cor. 13:7). I want to focus on the bearing and enduring aspects of love. Those aren't the same thing, but there is a close link between bearing and enduring because being able to bear pain is important to being able to endure. And if love is going to endure in the Christian life, love must be able to bear a certain amount of pain and disappointment.

I think Paul is talking about the grace of God in the gift of love that makes it possible for us to deal with suffering. So much of the New Testament speaks to the reality of human pain and suffering, and suffering is something that we are called to bear and exhorted to endure. Now when we talk about endurance, we're talking about being able to stay at or with something which is usually over a protracted, but certainly finite, period of time. We distinguish between sprint type races and endurance races. Different abilities and strengths are required to run the hundred-yard dash than are required to run a twenty-six-mile marathon. But both races have a definite, finite period of time—one may last ten or so seconds, and the other may last two to three hours. When Scripture talks to us about the reality of suffering, it always reminds us that suffering is for a season. And the promise of God for the Christian is that there will not be an eternal, relentless experience of pain for the redeemed; rather, the promise is a complete end to all suffering. That promise for the future is repeated again and again in Scripture to give us hope, to strengthen our resolve and our ability to bear and to endure pain when it strikes in this world. God's Word tells us the suffering we're called upon to endure in this world is not worthy to be compared with the glory that awaits the saints at their life's end. But in the meantime, the whole of life may seem to be an endurance race.

Years ago, I had the privilege of visiting the home of a former Miami Dolphins quarterback and meeting his wife, who was dying of cancer. It was a privilege because she was a deeply committed Christian woman. I sat next to her, she looked at me, a single tear flowing from her eyes, and she said, "R.C., I just don't know how much more I can take. It's gotten to the place where it seems unbearable."

She wasn't complaining or bitter. She was simply tired. We prayed together. I left, and several days later I got the report that she had died. She had fought the good fight for the faith, she had finished the race, and she had kept the faith. And her pain was over—forever. I look at her life, and I ask myself whether I could endure that kind of prolonged, protracted suffering without becoming absolutely impossible to be around, without becoming bitter and angry. But this is where the rubber meets the road. Will we love God when we're hurting, when the pain of our experience is so intense?

Pain and suffering tend to eat away not only at our love but also at our faith, because we begin to wonder if God is loving and if He is even real. We ask how in the world He can let this relentless pain grip our lives. That's why it's so important for us to keep our attention on the Word of God. We are told not to be surprised when suffering comes our way. The New Testament doesn't say that suffering might occur—it says it's a certainty. Remember what Paul says in 2 Corinthians 11 when he talks about what he bore for the sake of the gospel: beatings, stonings, being left for dead, shipwrecks, days and nights at sea, fighting with wild beasts, and constantly being the target of human hostility. Why was he willing to bear those things? Because he understood the divine purpose for suffering and the divine promise not only of relief from suffering, but of the redemption of the suffering itself. In this interim between Christ's resurrection and return, Christians are called to participate in the afflictions of Christ (Col. 1:24). By bearing and enduring pain, we walk in the footsteps of Jesus and mirror and reflect Him to onlookers. Pain and suffering are opportunities to show the love that God has shed abroad in our hearts.

Coming back to the quarterback's wife, we could look at her pain and say, "Here is a woman that God did not love." Or we could look at her and say, "Here is a woman whom God loved so deeply that He would entrust such pain and suffering to her, knowing that she would endure." That's real greatness. That's real achievement.

One problem we have in our day is the popular belief that God never wills pain or suffering. Many teach that if you trust in Jesus, all your problems will be over, and you'll never have to live with deprivation, persecution, or pain. Have the people who say such things ever read the New Testament? Just a cursory reading tells you that if you are in Christ, you will suffer, you will be afflicted, you will be persecuted. The Christian life is a pilgrimage filled with pain, affliction, and persecution. And the more we love God, and the more consistent we are with the love of which the Apostle speaks in 1 Corinthians 13, the more we will be hated and persecuted, and we will find it necessary to bear and endure all things. But what makes this possible is love.

Between "bearing" and "enduring," we are told that love "believes all things, hopes all things." It's only as we believe the Word of God and have confidence in our future that we're able to bear and to endure.

THE MOST SOLEMN MANDATE

SEPTEMBER 2016

———

I DON'T KNOW HOW MANY TIMES I've heard parents who are members of churches say to me:

I intentionally never discuss theology or religion with my children, because I want them to believe whatever they come to believe honestly and not because they've been indoctrinated by us in the home. I don't want them to be slaves to a parental tradition. I want them to experience reality on its own terms and come to whatever conclusion they are drawn from the evidence.

Such sentiments mystify me because they are at such odds with the teaching of Scripture. Just consider Deuteronomy 6:4–9:

Hear, O Israel: The Lord our God, the Lord is one. You shall love the Lord your God with all your heart and with all your soul and with all your might. And these words that I command you today shall be on your heart. You shall teach them diligently to your children, and shall talk of them when you sit in your house, and when you walk by the way, and when you lie down, and when you rise. You shall bind them as a sign on your hand, and they shall be as frontlets between your eyes. You shall write them on the doorposts of your house and on your gates.

What I find remarkable about this text is how closely it places the mandate to teach our children to what Jesus calls the greatest commandment, namely, "You shall love the Lord your God with all your heart and with all your soul and with all your might" (v. 5; see Matt. 22:36–40). There is no commandment more important than to love our Creator, but what's the very next command in Deuteronomy 6? That the law of God is to be on our hearts and taught to our children. The divine mandate is that parents should teach the Lord's commandments to their children. Not that the parents should send their children somewhere else to learn these things, but the responsibility is given to the parents.

Moreover, Deuteronomy 6 doesn't say that "you shall teach them casually, occasionally, once in a while to your children." No, it says,

> You shall teach them diligently to your children, and shall talk of them when you sit in your house, and when you walk by the way, and when you lie down, and when you rise. You shall bind them as a sign on your hand, and they shall be as frontlets between your eyes. You shall write them on the doorposts of your house and on your gates. (vv. 7–9)

That is, these things are to be taught so diligently that they are going to be taught every single day, in every place, even in every room of our homes.

I don't think there's a mandate to be found in sacred Scripture that is more solemn than this one. That we are to teach our children the truth of God's Word is a sacred, holy responsibility that God gives to His people. And it's not something that is to be done only one day a week in Sunday school. We can't abdicate the responsibility to the church. The primary responsibility for the education of children according to Scripture is the family, the parents. And what is commanded is the passing on of tradition.

In our forward-looking age, many look upon tradition with scorn. It is seen as the province of reactionaries and conservatives who refuse to get with the times. But when we look at Scripture, we find it has much to say about tradition, some of it negative, some of it positive. One of the judgments of God upon the nation of Israel and upon the teachers of Israel was that they began to substitute human traditions for the Word of God, with the human traditions taking the place of Scripture. Because of that error, we may jump to the conclusion that we should, therefore, never communicate traditions.

Yet when we come to the New Testament, we find a distinction made between the traditions of men and the tradition of God. The Apostle

Paul, for example, claims that he did not invent out of his own mind the message that he proclaimed to the churches and was passing on to the churches—the *paradosis*, the tradition, of God. *Paradosis* is the Greek word for "tradition," and it comes from the same root as the Greek term for "gift" as well as the prefix *para-*, which means "alongside of" or "passing on." Literally, the meaning of "tradition" in the Scriptures is the passing on of a gift. The gift that is to be passed on is the gift of the knowledge of God, of what He has revealed about Himself in His Word, of what He inspired the prophets and Apostles to tell us in sacred Scripture.

It's my responsibility as a parent and it's your responsibility as a parent to pass on that gift. If you aren't a parent, it's your responsibility to support the work of the church and those who are parents in passing on that gift. It is a great and glorious calling to lead our children into the truth of God's Word. Indeed, there is no more solemn mandate given to parents and adults in the church than to raise up covenant children in the fear and admonition of the Lord.

THE MOST VALUABLE
AIM OF APOLOGETICS

OCTOBER 2016

E
XODUS 3 NARRATES THE WELL-KNOWN account of God's reveal-
ing Himself to Moses in the burning bush and commissioning
him to tell Pharaoh to release the Israelites from slavery in Egypt.
But that was only part of Moses' mission. The other task to which the
Lord called Moses was to address the Israelites. He was to command the
Israelites in the name of God to engage in the largest strike in history.
In absolute defiance of the power and authority of Pharaoh, they were
to leave Egypt and go out to the desert to worship God at His mountain.
And, of course, these events ended in the exodus.

Just think of Moses' task. Moses, an old man who had been tending
sheep in the wilderness for years, was to somehow get an appointment
with Pharaoh, the most powerful ruler on earth in that day. But in many
respects it was even more difficult to go to the people of Israel and say,
"Never mind the chariots of Egypt and the armies of Pharaoh. Follow me
and I will lead you to the Promised Land." What slave in his right mind
would take Moses at his word? And that is the problem that is addressed
particularly in Exodus 4, where Moses says to God, "They will not believe
me or listen to my voice, for they will say, 'The LORD did not appear to
you.'" And the Lord gave Moses many proofs to show the Israelites that
his claims were credible.

In this encounter, Moses raised the question of apologetics, the question of how the believer is to defend the faith as reasonable. He had to
convince the Israelites of the truth of the mandate and that it came from
God. He was dealing with the in-house problem of apologetics, namely,
that he had to persuade the church—the people of God—of the veracity
of the Word of God and its claim on their lives.

The task of apologetics, of defending the truth of Christianity, has at least three main aims. I think most Christians are familiar with two of these. First, apologetics is to provide an answer to the critics of the Christian faith, to those who seek to undermine the rational basis for Christianity or who critique it from the standpoint of another philosophy or religion. Paul did that in Acts 17 when he confronted the Epicureans and the Stoics, followers of two popular philosophical schools in his day. Early Christian apologists such as Justin Martyr wrote to the Roman emperor to defend Christians against false accusations of atheism (because Christians did not worship the Roman gods) and cannibalism (because pagans misunderstood the Lord's Supper).

The second major aim of apologetics is to tear down the intellectual idols of our culture. Here, apologetics operates on the offensive, pointing out the inconsistencies and errors of other faiths and worldviews.

The third, and what I believe is the most valuable, aim of apologetics is to encourage the saints, to shore up the church—just as the first concern that Moses had was to be able to demonstrate that God had called him to go to the Israelites and lead them out of Egypt. Moses was an apologist to his own people.

The toughest three years of my life were my seminary years, because I was a zealous Christian studying in a citadel of unbelief. Every day, the precious doctrines of our faith were attacked viciously by my professors. One professor lashed out at a student in my class for coming to seminary with too many preconceived ideas, such as the deity of Christ. Another professor attacked a student when he preached on the cross. "How dare you preach the substitutionary atonement in this day and age!" the professor said. There was a hostility that was palpable in the air, and it was discouraging. All kinds of questions were raised, and even though I understood the philosophical assumptions behind the critics' attacks, there were still many questions I was not equipped to answer. Intuitively I knew these men were wrong, but I couldn't answer them.

At that time, there was basically one major seminary in the United States that was faithful to historic Reformed theology—Westminster

Theological Seminary in Philadelphia. After classes were over at my seminary for the day, I used to read Westminster professors such as J. Gresham Machen, John Murray, Ed Stonehouse, Ed Young, and others. And they would give me answers to the questions I had. After a while, when I heard a question I wasn't able to answer, I had confidence that God had raised up great men of learning who knew far more than I did and were able to answer these skeptical questions.

I said to the Ligonier staff many years ago: "The work that we do in apologetics may not be understood in all of the details by all the Christians who hear it. But if we can answer these questions and show the credibility of Christianity, the folks in the church will not be devastated by the voices of skepticism that surround them." We've known students in our churches who've gone to college—even professedly "Christian" institutions—and had a crisis of faith. In many cases, they've hung on by their fingernails because they were being beaten down every day, ridiculed and scorned for their faith in Christ. What such kids need is the task of apologetics inside the church, to calm their fears. And it is not just college students, it is all of us who live in this fallen world. Because if Satan can't take away our faith, he might be able to intimidate us to such a degree that we are paralyzed, that we are not quite as bold as we were before. And so, not everybody is called to be a professional apologist, but we are all called to study apologetic issues and to see that there are reasons for the hope that is within us.

LEARNING FROM THE JUDGES

NOVEMBER 2016

———

CERTAIN PERIODS OF HISTORY STAND out to me as particularly instructive for the course of all of history. That is, sometimes we can zero in on one period of time in the past, observe how the entire span of human history recapitulates that particular period, and then learn from that period what we should do today. One of these instructive periods is the period of the judges of Israel.

This period, narrated for us in the books of Judges and Ruth and the opening chapters of 1 Samuel, spans a period of roughly 350 years. If you want a sense of how wide an expanse of time this represents, think back to the middle of the seventeenth century in America. Think of all the history that has transpired in America from a period of 125 years before the Revolutionary War up to the present day. That's the same time span that the period of the judges covers. For this period of about three and a half centuries, there was no king in Israel, no single leader of the nation. Israel was living in the land of Canaan as a tribal federation, led by a succession of individuals whom God raised up in times of crisis and empowered to perform particular tasks. Under the power of the Holy Spirit, Samson exercised great physical strength against the Philistines. Deborah and Barak were anointed to defeat the evil King Jabin. And so on.

Now, the reason I believe the period of the judges is instructive for the flow of all history is the pattern we see during those three-hundred-and-fifty years. Repeatedly during this era, the book of Judges tells us, the Israelites would find themselves in a cycle that began this way: "The people of Israel did what was evil in the sight of the LORD." And each time we read that phrase in the book of Judges, we see that God would raise up enemies of Israel—the Midianites, the Philistines, the Moabites, and others—as tools of chastisement against His people. Those pagan nations would oppress the Israelites, who would then cry out for relief and repent of their sins. Then, God would raise up one of the judges who, under the power of the Holy Spirit, would defeat the enemies of Israel and bring deliverance. One scholar calls this a cycle of relapse, retribution, repentance, and rescue. Following each relapse into gross sin recorded in the book of Judges is the retributive justice of God whereby He pours out His judgment and wrath against His own people. Under the weight of that retributive justice of God, the people are then brought to repentance, and they bewail their situation and await their rescue by God, who redeems them.

The grim history of Israel's sin in the period of the judges goes against what the people pledged. When Joshua brought the people together to renew their covenant with the Lord just before his death, the Israelites promised two things, one positive and one negative. Positively, they promised to obey God. Negatively, they promised not to forsake Him for idols.

And this is significant in light of the promise God made again and again to the patriarchs. When He committed Himself to Jacob, for example, He said, "I will not leave you" (Gen. 28:15). This covenant pledge of God to those who are in a relationship with Him is a key theme of Scripture. The book of Judges attests to that, that even though God chastened His people, He was chastening His children whom He loved. And though they felt forsaken for a season, God did not utterly abandon them.

However, the record is that the people forsook Him. That's the big difference between the God of Israel—the God of the covenant—and His people. God does not forsake us, but we are prone to forsake Him. What provoked the forsaking of God during the period of the judges was the Israelites' great desire to be like their neighbors. God had called them to nonconformity. God had called them to be a holy nation. God had called them to be godly and to flee from idolatry, but that was unpopular in those days. It's often been unpopular in church history. And without a doubt, it's unpopular today as well.

The people of God relived the cycle of relapse, retribution, repentance, and rescue over and over again throughout biblical history. And, dare I say, the church has seen a similar cycle over the past two thousand years as well. But we have a tendency to think such things cannot happen in the life of the church today. We refuse to take note of this recurring pattern of the actions of God, believing that God will not bring calamity upon a people who forsake Him. But the God of Israel is a God who promises both blessing and curse, both prosperity and calamity. We should not be surprised to see trouble for the church when it has been worldly, when it has been unfaithful to the Lord. Sometimes, of course, the church suffers because of its faithfulness, because the forces of darkness respond with hostility against the advance of gospel transformation. At other times, however, the church suffers because of widespread, persistent unfaithfulness. That happened during the era of the judges, and it can happen today as well.

Nevertheless, we read in the book of Judges that when the Israelites repented, God delivered them. No matter how badly God's covenant people fail, our Lord is quick to rescue His church when she repents. His people forsake Him, but He never forsakes them. Judgment begins at the house of God (1 Peter 4:17), but it is a judgment that is disciplinary, not destructive. It's designed to move us to repentance and faithfulness. And the era of the judges shows us that the Lord will not fail to rescue and preserve His church when His church repents and cries out to Him.

NO SHORTCUTS TO GROWTH

DECEMBER 2016

———

I'M STILL AMAZED WHENEVER I SEE THE bumper sticker that reads, "Visualize world peace." The idea is that if I, and enough other people, create the right mental picture of peace, it will soon come to pass. It's astounding that some people actually believe that silly technique will bring about such a desirable goal.

Then, there's the popular "Coexist" bumper sticker. You may have seen it, the one spelled out with the symbols of different religions—the Islamic crescent forming the C, the Christian cross forming the T, and so on. The idea seems to be that if we religious people would just stop focusing on our differences, we could achieve world harmony. If we understood that our beliefs are all ultimately the same, all of the problems of war and strife would go away.

The funny thing is, we'll reject such sentiments when they appear on a bumper sticker, but we'll accept them elsewhere. How many business seminars promise increased profit if we only focus on the positive or visualize a goal? Eastern mysticism, where much of the bumper-sticker theology we're talking about finds its ultimate origin, dresses it up with more acceptable religious practices. Meditate regularly, repeating a mantra as you visualize the oneness of all things, and the human race will move toward unity. But there's also a version sold to us as the Christian key for victorious living. Speak your desire, claim it's yours in Jesus' name, visualize it will happen, and then it will be yours. Your healing, wealth, relationship success, happy family, improved marriage will come as soon as you name it and claim it or practice the power of positive thinking.

We're looking for the right technique, the secret that will turn our wishes into reality. We laugh at the world's spiritual magic, only to baptize it and practice it ourselves. We'll read Scripture hoping to find the shortcut to spiritual growth while missing the true but non-shortcut answer—the key is not in the Bible; it is the Bible.

One reason we look for spiritual shortcuts is related to our modern age where shortcuts and rapid results abound. We can quickly relieve pain with medicine, find our way to restaurants with our smartphones, and get immediate answers to our questions online. These aren't inherently bad things, but they tend to foster false expectations. If technology can relieve our illnesses and make our jobs easier, it surely can give rest to our souls, right?

We assume the answer is yes, and there are all too many "experts" out there who'll encourage that assumption. Just look at the self-help section at your local bookstore, even at your local Christian bookstore. Book after book promises to hold the key to our happiness in twelve steps or less. The fact that none of the promises pan out doesn't deter people from buying those books or new authors from repackaging old, ineffective answers in fancier dress.

But we can't ultimately blame our search for shortcuts on modern technology. Our innate desire since the fall for autonomy, to be masters of our own fates, drives us to search out soul-building techniques that will improve us. We see our faith not as an end in itself but as a means to greater fulfillment. Evangelists routinely implore people to come to Christ, saying that He will make them happier, more confident in themselves, and more spiritual. Jesus becomes a means to improve our marriages and finances while releasing us from all manner of compulsions and negative character traits.

Can Christ do all those things? Of course He can. But Jesus is not a means to other ends—He is the end, the goal of our lives. He doesn't come into our lives to give us special techniques to make our lives better; He works in and through us, changing us for the sake of His glory. He provides believers no mystic secrets to take them to a higher plane of spirituality. There's no hidden truth available to only a few, no method that guarantees quick maturity in Him as long as we master it.

We're saved by grace alone and justified by faith alone, but having been saved, we don't just wait around to die. Christianity is about spiritual growth as well, and spiritual growth involves effort—the hard work of sanctification. We manifestly don't work for our regeneration or our justification. Both acts are monergistic, accomplished by God alone. Only the Holy Spirit can change our hearts. Only the righteousness of Christ, the righteousness of the Son of God secured by His perfect obedience to the Father, can secure our right standing before God. Sanctification, however, includes our efforts. We say it is synergistic because both God and we are doing something. Yet, we aren't equal partners. God wills and works in us according to His good pleasure so that we progress in holiness (Phil. 2:12–13). But as God works in us, we work as well, pursuing Him in prayer, relying on the means of grace—the preached Word and the sacraments—seeking to be reconciled to those we have offended. There's no shortcut for sanctification. It's a process, and one that all too often seems overly plodding, with progress taking years to discern.

God's work is easy for Him. He doesn't look for shortcuts because He never grows weary. We get tired and frustrated, however. We're tempted to look for the simple path, the quick answer, the effortless way forward. But there is none. Sanctification requires diligently attending to the means God has given us. The growth may be slow, almost imperceptible at times, but it is sure.

No technique of the devil's can stop the process of Christ making us into His image. Those whom He calls He sanctifies.

Casually attending to the things of the Lord will not result in our nurture. Visualizing or seeking a secret formula won't help. We must work out our salvation with fear and trembling, knowing that Christ, by His Spirit, is working in us.

THE REVOLUTION THAT ENSLAVES

JANUARY 2017

———

W HAT'S THE MOST SIGNIFICANT REVOLUTION we've ever experienced in the United States? I imagine most Americans would say it was the American Revolution, which marked the beginning of our existence as a country. Some might make the case that it was the Industrial Revolution, which transformed our nation into a world power. Yet both answers, I think, are wrong.

The most far-reaching, epochal revolution in American history began about fifty years ago and is now reaching its zenith. No war has been fought in terms of military conflict, but this revolution has killed millions of unborn people. Approximately three thousand lives, in fact, will be lost to this revolution before midnight tonight. And this number does not include the revolution's other casualties. Bodies will be mutilated in the name of "changing" one's gender. Sexually transmitted diseases will sterilize, leave lasting physical and emotional scars, and even pronounce death sentences on men and women. Young women will get pregnant and be abandoned, leaving them to raise children in fatherless homes. Pornography will warp people's views of sex and relationships.

I'm talking about the sexual revolution, which has wrought far more changes to the cultural behavior of America than the War of Independence fought against England in the eighteenth century. This sexual revolution is a war that's been fought not against any earthly king but against the King of the cosmos, the Lord Himself. It's a war with roots that stretch much further back than the sixties—to Eden, when Adam and Eve joined Satan's cosmic revolt. As we inaugurate a new president this month, the revolution continues, draped in the flag of free speech, free sex, and freedom from oppression. However, the freedom being sought isn't freedom from unjust civil laws but from natural law and the eternal moral law of God. The freedom embraced is the ungodly "freedom" of moral autonomy, of our trying to be a law unto ourselves, of our raising our fists to heaven and declaring that God will not be Lord over us.

The sexual revolution has the same philosophical roots that fueled Friedrich Nietzsche's goal of casting off what he saw as the weakness of Judeo-Christian morality. In Nietzsche's eyes, the morality rooted in the Scriptures kept the authentic individual in chains. In the name of authenticity, of embracing the most basic human drive of the "will to power," Nietzsche looked for humanity to set itself free from outside moral constraints. Nietzsche was eventually driven to insanity, but the moral insanity he argued for has gained ascendancy in our day. In one sense, the West has accomplished what Nietzsche desired—a "liberation" from God, and evidence for this is the sexual anarchy of our culture. However, such liberation cannot ultimately be accomplished. We're still accountable to the Lord and will face judgment. Moreover, the freedom found is proving to be no freedom at all, but rather enslavement to the unforgiving demands of the false gods of unrestrained eros and libido.

The sexual revolution is a war that is fought on many fronts. It includes the abuse of "free speech" to legalize the vilest and most explicit forms of pornography. It includes attacking all notions of traditional gender norms and labeling as "hateful bigots" those who want bathrooms segregated by biological sex differences. It involves abortion on demand and the elimination of every restriction on the procedure. It includes making promiscuity the norm and chastity the aberration. It includes elevating homosexuality as a positive good. The human sex drive is now liberated from all forms of oppression that would deny us our inalienable right to pleasure, and sexual pleasure—however we define it for ourselves—is seen as necessary to human happiness and fulfillment.

The fruit and fuel of the sexual revolution is widespread moral relativism. Our society has rejected wholesale the very notion of vice—with one exception. The only vice our culture now recognizes is the refusal to join the revolutionaries in their quest for sexual "liberation." Stay on

God's side, and the revolution will demand that you pay a high price economically and socially.

Saddest of all, many churches fall over themselves to accommodate the changes wrought by the sexual revolution. Entire denominations are rushing to catch up to the culture. If there's any sin of which we must repent, it's the sin of affirming what God has always said about sexual morality. But if we go along with this trend, we'll have no good news to preach, for we'll have no sin from which we need the gospel to rescue us. We know that God will still mark the sin, but if the church won't call sin sin, it cannot call anyone to repent of it and escape divine condemnation by turning to Christ. Sexual immorality and the kingdom of God are incompatible. No person who impenitently violates God's sexual ethic has any part in His kingdom. If we don't proclaim this to lost people, they will remain lost.

The New Testament gospel is about forgiveness—forgiveness for all types of sin. Forgiveness is not needed if sin does not exist (1 John 1:8–10). But Jesus—as well as Paul, Moses, and the other prophets and Apostles—recognized adultery, homosexuality, and other forms of sexual immorality as sin (Lev. 18:5; Matt. 5:27–30; John 7:53–8:11; 1 Cor. 6:9–11). The good news of the gospel is that every sexual sin is forgivable; all that's required is repentance and faith in Christ alone. But it is one thing to forgive sin; it is quite another to sanction it. To give license to sin is not to free people, but to enslave them.

CARING FOR WIDOWS

FEBRUARY 2017

———

I N BIBLICAL TERMS, TO BE RELIGIOUS DOES NOT necessarily mean you are godly. To be religious can mean simply that you're involved in the trappings of religion, that you may be a member of a false religion. Yet, the Scriptures sometimes speak of religion in a positive sense, in the sense of practice that is the fruit of true faith in Christ and commitment to His Word.

The Apostle James focuses on religion as the practice of those who have true faith in Jesus, and he says that true religion demonstrates the presence of saving trust in the Lord (James 2:14–26). What true godliness looks like, he tells us, is not a matter of merely holding to right doctrine with our minds, though that is essential. No, true godliness means that doctrine shapes our lives to such a degree that we manifest the kind of life God wants us to live. And James gives us a succinct definition of true religion, of true godliness: "Pure and undefiled religion before God and the Father is this: To visit orphans and widows in their trouble, and to keep oneself unspotted from the world." James elevates the activity of caring for widows and orphans as the very essence of pure and undefiled religion. That strikes me as being very significant, and it's an idea that is neglected in the church today.

In this article, I want to focus particularly on widows. Widows and their care figure prominently in the agenda that God has set for His church. One of the earliest problems that arose in the Apostolic church was that the widows were being neglected. And if that was a problem in the first-century church, how much more likely is it that we, twenty centuries later, would be guilty of neglecting the widows in our midst?

After my grandfather died, my grandmother moved into our home and lived with us for many years as I was growing up. On several occasions, she would talk to me late at night and weep, telling me of the burden of pain she had in feeling like she had not only lost her husband but that she had also lost her place in the community. Once her husband passed, she suddenly felt excluded from the things she was intimately involved with alongside him while he was alive. When a person loses her lifelong mate, it's like losing an integral, intimate part of one's self because husband and wife, we are told, in the mystery of marriage are one flesh. So, the pain of widowhood brings a unique dimension of loneliness. It's jarring to suddenly be alone when one has been accustomed to the constant companionship with one's spouse over a long period of time. Since God is the great Comforter of His people, it makes sense that He would have such concern for widows given the pain they experience.

Now, why does James not mention the widowers? After all, the widower also experiences that same pang of suffering that goes with losing a lifelong mate. Well, every man that I've ever talked to always says they want to go first because they can't imagine living life without their wives. I can't prove it, but I think that's one of the reasons why the normal life expectancy of the man is shorter than the life expectancy of the woman, because God is gracious to us men, and He knows that we're not as strong as women. But what I do know for sure is that widows have always experienced particular difficulties in every age and culture. They faced particular problems in the ancient world. There weren't insurance programs, annuities, or other sorts of things, and without a husband, the widow was usually the most vulnerable and helpless person in the community. Widows had little or no means of support in ancient societies. Thus, the care of the widows was given to the church both in the Old Testament and in the New.

Jesus frequently pays attention to widows in His teaching. Just consider the story of the widow's mite in Mark 12:41–45. Who is it that normally gets the attention in the church? The people who are the big donors, the ones whose donations are so important to the ongoing funding of the church's budget. Few pay attention to the poverty-stricken person who makes a tiny donation that's insignificant to the budget's bottom line. But Jesus noticed what everyone else overlooked. He told His hearers to look at the poor widow. Even though the woman gave only the equivalent of two pennies to the temple, she put in more than all the rest of the people who donated heavily to the treasury because in giving out of her own poverty, she gave out of her devotion to God.

One of the most tender moments recorded in the New Testament is found in John 19:16b–27. While Christ was on the cross, He looked in the direction of His mother, who was an eyewitness to His passion, and He said to her, "Woman, behold your son!" He was not asking His mother to look at Him. Obviously, she already was looking at Him. Then, Jesus said to John, "Behold your mother!" In His dying moments, Jesus was commending the care of His widowed mother to His beloved disciple, John. On the cross, Jesus said to John, "John, you take care of My mother. She's a widow, so let her be to you as your own mother." To Mary, He said, "Mother, let John be to you as your own son."

What are sons for? To look after their mothers. What are mothers for but to look after their children? When you think of all of the years and the opportunities where mothers have looked after their children when they enter into their loneliness, the first line of care is to be the surviving family. But it by no means stops there, because the larger family is the church. James, the brother of Jesus, sees this mandate to care for widows as so important that he uses it to describe the crystallized essence of true religion. Do you think you're religious, but you don't care about the widows? Your religion is an exercise in futility, because James says pure and undefiled religion is the care of widows and of orphans in times of trouble.

LIVING UNDER AUTHORITY

MARCH 2017

——

A S I READ THE SCRIPTURES, particularly the New Testament, there is a theme that recurs again and again regarding the Christian's willingness to be in submission to various types of authority. Given the rebellious spirit of our age, that frightens me. It's all too easy for us to get caught up in an attitude that will bring us into open defiance of the authority of God.

Let's turn our attention to 1 Peter 2:11–16:

> Beloved, I urge you as sojourners and exiles to abstain from the passions of the flesh, which wage war against your soul. Keep your conduct among the Gentiles honorable, so that when they speak against you as evildoers, they may see your good deeds and glorify God on the day of visitation. Be subject for the Lord's sake to every human institution, whether it be to the emperor as supreme, or to governors as sent by him to punish those who do evil and to praise those who do good. For this is the will of God, that by doing good you should put to silence the ignorance of foolish people. Live as people who are free, not using your freedom as a cover-up for evil, but living as servants of God. Honor everyone. Love the brotherhood. Fear God. Honor the emperor.

Peter is speaking to people who were subjected to brutal, fierce, and violent persecution—the kind of activity that can incite within us the worst possible responses, including anger, resentment, and hatred. But Peter pleads with those people who were the victims of the hatred of their culture to behave in an honorable manner before the watching world. Paul gives a similar plea time and time again that we're to try to live at peace with all men as much as possible.

The "therefore" of verse 13 introduces a key manifestation of living honorably before the watching world. We're to submit ourselves to the ordinances of man. Why? I find the answer startling and fascinating. The Apostle's admonition is that we're to submit for the Lord's sake. But how is obedience to human ordinances done for the Lord's sake? How does my obedience to my professors, my boss, or the government in any way benefit Christ?

To understand this, we have to understand the deeper problem that all of Scripture is dealing with—the problem of sin. At the most fundamental level, sin is an act of rebellion and disobedience to a higher law and Lawgiver. The biggest problem with the world is lawlessness. The reason people are violated, killed, and maimed in battle, the reason there are murders, robberies, and so forth is that we're lawless. We disobey, first of all, the law of God. The root problem in all of creation is disobedience to law, defiance of authority. And the ultimate authority of the universe is God Himself.

But God delegates authority as He reigns and rules over His creation. God raises up human governments. It is God who instituted government in the first place (Rom. 13). That's why Christians are called to honor and pray for the king, pay their taxes, and submit as much as possible to the authorities in all things—because the authorities are instituted by God. Moreover, He shares supreme authority with Christ, who said, "All authority in heaven and on earth has been given [by the Father] to me" (Matt. 28:18). So, no ruler in this world has any authority except that which has been delegated to him by God and by His Christ, who is the King of kings and Lord of lords. Thus, disobedience to the lawful commands of earthly authorities is ultimately disobedience to God and to Christ because they ordained the governing authorities.

The world has gone crazy in lawlessness, but we're to be different. Wherever we find ourselves under authority—and we all find ourselves submitting to various authorities—we're to submit to that authority. Nobody in this world is autonomous. Every one of us has not just one boss, but several bosses. Everyone I know, including me, is accountable not to just one person but to all kinds of authority structures. Throw a brick through a store window, and you'll find out quickly that you're accountable, that you're under authority, that there are laws to be obeyed and law enforcement officers to make sure the laws are obeyed.

Christians are free in Christ, but we aren't to use our liberty as a license for sin, because even though on the one hand we're free, on the other hand we remain indentured servants. We're bondservants to God. We're slaves of Jesus Christ. So, even if the rest of the world is running on the track of anti-authority and anti-submissiveness, we aren't allowed to join in. We're called to be scrupulous to maintain order. There is such a thing as law and order that God Himself has ordained in the universe. And we're called to bear witness to that, even by suffering through uncomfortable, inconvenient, and sometimes painful submission to the lawful rules of even those authorities who do not recognize God, for even the godless authorities have been established by God.

I think we all have experiences where we bristle and chafe under authority and under mandates with which we vehemently disagree. Let me just suggest as a matter of practical consideration that if we look to these human institutions or these human persons who are tyrannical, unfair, unjust, and all that, and we seek to submit to them individually or even institutionally, considered in and of themselves, we will find it extremely difficult to submit with any kind of good attitude. But if somehow we can look through them, look past them, look over them, and see the One whom the Father has invested with ultimate cosmic authority, namely, Christ Himself, we'll have an easier time submitting. We'll find help with our struggle to submit when we recognize we're submitting ultimately to Christ, because we know He'll never tyrannize or abuse us.

AGAINST THE SOPHISTS

APRIL 2017

———

I F ANYONE IS A SHOO-IN FOR THE hall of fame of educators historically, it is Socrates. Socrates stands as a giant in the history of educational philosophy, and the importance of Socrates and of his ideas is not only for ancient history but also for today. Socrates was a man with a passion and a profound concern for salvation. Socrates was trying to save Greek civilization. The reason he was concerned about saving Greek civilization is because in his day a dreadful crisis had emerged that was a clear and present danger to the ongoing stability of Greece. It was an educational crisis that arose as a result of Sophism.

To understand that crisis, we have to back up a little bit. We have to go back to the sixth century BC to the beginning years of the science of Western philosophy in the pre-Socratic era. The earliest Greek philosophers were not simply abstract dreamers or speculative thinkers, but they were at the same time the leading scientists of the period. They were concerned about questions of biology, chemistry, astronomy, and questions of physics. Unlike us, they didn't make an absolute distinction between the study of physics and the study of metaphysics, which is the study of things above and beyond the realm of the physical. The pre-Socratic philosophers were looking for ultimate reality, the reality behind the physical world.

However, an impasse came when the best thinkers, people such as Parmenides and Heraclitus, failed to agree on what is ultimate truth. As a result of that impasse in philosophical and scientific inquiry, a new school of thought emerged in Athens. This school of thought embraced skepticism, believing that if the greatest minds of the culture couldn't agree on what ultimate truth is, then it must mean that ultimate truth is beyond the scope of human learning. The conclusion that this new school came to was not only that we cannot know ultimate truth, but that even to search for ultimate truth is a fool's errand. The only knowledge we can possess is the knowledge of what we can see, taste, smell, touch, and hear. All we can attain is knowledge of this realm, knowledge of the immediate context in which we live. We don't know if there are absolute truths. What really matters is the day-to-day experience of living, and so we have to direct our attention away from this quest for ultimate truth and toward an understanding of practical living. So, Greek education shifted away from a pursuit of truth for truth's sake to a pursuit of technique, methodology, and ways in which the person's practical concerns could be considered. The name of this school of thought was Sophism, and its adherents were known as Sophists.

In the context of a modern debate, you may have heard one side say to the other, "You're just engaging in sophistry." By this, the accusing side means that their opponents are using superficial, uninformed, and simplistic reasoning, a reasoning that doesn't ascend to the higher principles. The word *sophistry* comes from what we know about the Sophists, who emphasized instruction in rhetoric, which has to do with public speaking. Now, it is perfectly legitimate for people to master the craft of vocabulary and the use of words properly in public speech. But remember, the Sophists believed that truth itself is unknowable, so they created a disjunction between proof and persuasion. Proof involves the presentation of solid evidence by cogent reasoning whereby the premises are demonstrated by their logical conclusions. Persuasion, on the other hand, has to do with emotional response. A person can be persuaded without ever really thinking things through. In other words, instead of responding to carefully conceived and constructed arguments, people can respond to slick forms of persuasion. For the Sophists, it didn't matter whether their speech was true. What mattered is whether it worked. Would the speech persuade? If it persuaded people, it did not matter whether it was true. The argument did not have to be sound as long as it was convincing. Sadly, this philosophy lives on in so much of modern advertising and political discourse.

Socrates came into this environment and said that if Sophism triumphs in our culture, it will be the end of civilization because this kind of skepticism and superficial persuasion rips life out of the context of truth. If nothing can be discerned as true, then what will be destroyed are the norms by which people determine what is good and what is evil. And if we cannot know the good, Socrates said, ethics will disintegrate and civilization will return to barbarianism.

When our educational system is ruled by skepticism, we are on the fast track to civilizational suicide. We're seeing it all around us as so many people in our culture are committed to a philosophy of relativism, which foundationally is no different from the assumptions brought to the realm of education by the ancient Sophists. This relativism is reinforced in much of our educational system, which has been shaped by the philosophy of pragmatism. Pragmatism says that we cannot know anything of ultimate truth, and so our task is to learn what works. That's Sophism all over again.

The crisis we face today is the revival of the skepticism that fueled Sophism. This skepticism drives education, ethics, business, and even the political decisions that emanate out of Washington. And we need a Socrates who is willing to go into the streets to engage people in serious discussion to probe their thinking, to show them that this approach makes knowledge itself impossible and can only end in ignorance.

WHICH LAWS APPLY?

MAY 2017

———

T O THIS DAY, THE QUESTION of the role of the law of God in the Christian life provokes much debate and discussion. This is one of those points where we can learn much from our forebears, and John Calvin's classic treatment of the law in his *Institutes of the Christian Religion* is particularly helpful. Calvin's instruction comes down to us in what he calls the threefold use of the law with respect to its relevance to the new covenant.

The law, in its first use, reveals the character of God, and that's valuable to any believer at any time. But as the law reveals the character of God, it provides a mirror to reflect to us our unholiness against the ultimate standard of righteousness. In that regard, the law serves as a schoolmaster to drive us to Christ. And one of the reasons that the Reformers and the Westminster divines thought that the law remained valuable to the Christian was because the law constantly drives us to the gospel. This also was one of the uses of the law that Martin Luther most strongly emphasized.

Second, the law functions as a restraint against sin. Now, on the one hand, the Reformers understood what Paul says in Romans 7 that in a sense the law prompts people to sin—the more of the law unregenerate people see, the more inclined they are to want to break it. Yet despite that tendency of the law, there still is a general salutary benefit for the world to have the restraints upon us that the law gives. Its warnings and threats restrain people from being as bad as they could be, and so civil order is preserved.

Third, and most important from Calvin's perspective, is that the law reveals to us what is pleasing to God. Technically speaking, Christians are not under the old covenant and its stipulations. Yet, at the same time, we are called to imitate Christ and to live as people who seek to please the living God (Eph. 5:10; Col. 1:9–12). So, although in one sense I'm not covenantally obligated to the law or under the curse of the law, I put that out the front door and I go around the back door and I say, "Oh Lord, I want to live a life that is pleasing to You, and like the Old Testament psalmist, I can say, 'Oh how I love Thy law.' " I can meditate on the law day and night because it reveals to me what is pleasing to God.

Let me give you a personal example. Several years ago, I was speaking in Rye, N.Y., at a conference on the holiness of God. After one of the sessions, the sponsors of the conference invited me to someone's house afterward for prayer and refreshments. When I arrived at the house, there were about twenty-five people in the parlor praying to their dead relatives. To say I was shocked would be an understatement. I said, "Wait a minute. What is this? We're not allowed to do this. Don't you know that God prohibits this, and that it's an abomination in His sight and it pollutes the whole land and provokes His judgment?" And what was their immediate response? "That's the Old Testament." I said, "Yes, but what has changed to make a practice that God regarded as a capital offense during one economy of redemptive history now something He delights in?" And they didn't have a whole lot to say because from the New Testament it is evident that God is as against idolatry now as He was then.

Of course, as we read Scripture, we see that there are some parts of the law that no longer apply to new covenant believers, at least not in the same way that they did to old covenant believers. We make a distinction between moral laws, civil laws, and ceremonial laws such as the dietary laws and physical circumcision. That's helpful because there's a certain sense in which practicing some of the laws from the Old Testament as Christians would actually be blasphemy. Paul stresses in Galatians, for example, that if we were to require circumcision, we would be sinning. Now, the distinction between moral, civil, and ceremonial laws is helpful, but for the old covenant Jew, it was somewhat artificial. That's because it was a matter of the utmost moral consequences whether they kept the ceremonial laws. It was a moral issue for Daniel and his friends not to eat as the Babylonians did (Dan. 1). But the distinction between the moral, civil, and ceremonial laws means that there's a bedrock body of

RIGHT NOW COUNTS FOREVER

righteous laws that God gives to His covenant people that have abiding significance and relevance before and after the coming of Christ.

During the period of Reformed scholasticism in the seventeenth and eighteenth centuries, Reformed theologians said that God legislates to Israel and to the new covenant church on two distinct bases: on the basis of divine natural law and on the basis of divine purpose. In this case, the theologians did not mean the *lex naturalis,* the law that is revealed in nature and in the conscience. By "natural law," they meant those laws that are rooted and grounded in God's own character. For God to abrogate these laws would be to do violence to His own person. For example, if God in the old covenant said, "You shall have no other gods before Me," but now He says, "It's OK for you to have other gods and to be involved in idolatry," God would be doing violence to His own holy character. Statutes legislated on the basis of this natural law will be enforced at all times.

On the other hand, there is legislation made on the basis of the divine purpose in redemption, such as the dietary laws, that when their purpose is fulfilled, God can abrogate without doing violence to His own character. I think that's a helpful distinction. It doesn't answer every question, but it helps us discern which laws continue so that we can know what is pleasing to God.

LOVING GOD WITH OUR MINDS

JUNE 2017

———

T HE HUMAN MIND IS ONE OF THE MOST incredible aspects of creation. It is more powerful than the largest supercomputer and can solve great problems and make great discoveries. That makes the noetic effects of sin especially tragic.

The noetic effects of sin describe the impact of sin upon the *nous*— the mind—of fallen humanity. The faculty of thinking, with which we reason, has been seriously disturbed and corrupted by the fall. In our natural, unregenerate state, there is something dramatically wrong with our minds. As a consequence of our suppressing the knowledge of God in our sin, we have been given over to a debased mind (Rom. 1:28).

It's terrible to have a reprobate mind, a mind that now in its fallen condition doesn't have a scintilla of desire to love God. But that is the kind of mind we chose for ourselves in Adam, so in our natural fallen condition, there is nothing more repugnant to our minds than the love of God. While we remain unregenerate, we have such an antipathy to loving God by nature that we choke at the very thought of Christ's command to love God with our minds (Matt. 22:37).

Our minds have been corrupted by sin, but that does not mean our ability to think has been annihilated. The best pagan thinkers can still spot errors of logic without being born again. You don't have to be regenerate in order to get a Ph.D. in mathematics. The fallen mind retains the ability to follow formal argumentation to a degree, but that ends when discussion about the character of God begins because that is where bias is so severe and hostility so great that many of the most brilliant people stumble. In fact, if a person begins their thinking by refusing to acknowledge what they know to be true—that there is a God—then the more brilliant they are, the further away from God their reasoning will lead them.

Any consideration of the human mind, therefore, must begin with the understanding that by nature the mind does not love God at all, and it will not love God at all unless and until God the Holy Spirit changes its disposition immediately and sovereignly to set the affections on Him. Regeneration is the necessary condition for loving God with our minds. Without it, there is no love of God. So, we must get rid of this idea that's pervasive in the evangelical world that unbelieving people are seekers of God. The natural man does not seek after God. Unregenerate people who look like they are seeking after God, as Thomas Aquinas said, are seeking the benefits only God can give, not God Himself.

Note, however, that all of the mind's antipathy toward God is not eliminated the minute we're born again. After regeneration, for the first time in our lives, we are disposed to the things of God rather than against them. We are given a desire to have God in our thinking rather than despising the idea of having God in our thinking. But the residual effects and the power of our fallen human condition remain and are not eliminated entirely until we're glorified in heaven. The whole pilgrimage of the Christian life in our sanctification, then, is one in which we are seeking to love God more and more with our minds.

Jonathan Edwards once said that seeking after God is the main business of the Christian. And how do we seek after God? By pursuing the renewal of our minds. We don't get the love of God from a hip replacement, a knee replacement, or even a heart transplant. The only way we can be transformed is with a renewed mind (Rom. 12:1–2). A renewed mind results from diligently pursuing the knowledge of God. If we despise doctrine, if we despise knowledge, that probably indicates that we're still in that fallen condition where we don't want God in our thinking. True Christians want God to dominate their thinking and to fill their minds with ideas of Himself.

Isn't it strange that our Lord says that we are called to love God with our minds? We don't usually speak of love in terms of an intellectual activity. In fact, most of our understanding of love in our secular culture is described in passive categories. We speak not of jumping in love but falling in love, like it was an accident.

But real love is not an involuntary thing. It is something we do purposefully based on our knowledge of the person we love. Nothing can be in the heart that is not first in the mind. And if we want to have an experience of God directly where we bypass the mind, we're on a fool's errand. It can't happen. We might increase emotion, entertainment, or excitement, but we're not going to increase the love of God because we can't love what we don't know. A mindless Christianity is no Christianity at all.

If we want to love God more, we have to know Him more deeply. And the more we search the Scriptures, and the more we focus our minds' attention on who God is and what He does, the more we understand just a tiny little bit more about Him and the more our souls break out in flame. We have a greater ardor to honor Him. The more we understand God with our minds, the more we love Him with our minds.

To love God with our minds is to hold Him in high esteem, to think about Him with reverence and with adoration. The more we love God with our minds, the more we'll be driven to do that other thing that is alien to us in our fallen condition, namely, to worship Him. To pursue God with our minds simply for intellectual enjoyment and without the ultimate purpose of loving and worshiping Him is to miss what it means to love Him with our minds. True knowledge of God always bears fruit in greater love for God and a greater desire to praise Him. The more we know Him, the more glorious He will appear to us. And the more glorious He appears to us, the more inclined we will be to praise Him, to honor Him, to worship Him, and to obey Him.

WHEN ALL THINGS ARE MADE NEW

JULY 2017

———

A S A PASTOR AND THEOLOGIAN, I've had to think about a lot of hard questions over the years. Truth be told, however, the most difficult problem I've faced is the problem of suffering. We all face suffering in some way, and we all know people who've lived such painful lives that we wonder how they can go on.

We don't ever want to downplay or deny the pain that suffering brings. Christianity isn't a system of Stoic denial wherein we pretend that everything is OK even when we are enduring the worst things. At the same time, we dare not forget the Christian hope that one day suffering will be gone forever. When we deal with suffering, we tend to have our gaze completely locked on the present, but the Christian answer to suffering, while making it incumbent upon us to alleviate present suffering as much as we are able, looks beyond the present to the future.

The very essence of secularism is the thesis that the *hic et nunc*, the here and now, is all there is. There is no realm of the eternal. But as Christians, we are called to consider the present in light of the eternal. This is what Jesus preached again and again. What does it profit a man if in this time and in this place he gains the whole world, but he loses his own soul (Luke 9:25)?

Scripture says that the end defines the significance of the beginning (Eccl. 7:8). God alone knows the end from the beginning comprehensively, but in His Word, He gives us a glimpse of the end toward which we are moving. And if we can focus our attention on the end and not merely on the now and the pain we experience here, we can begin to understand our pain in the right perspective.

In unfolding the new heaven and the new earth, Revelation 21–22 gives us one of the clearest glimpses of the future. Let me touch on a few of the highlights.

"Behold, the dwelling place of God is with man. He will dwell with them, and they will be his people, and God himself will be with them as their God. He will wipe away every tear from their eyes" (21:3–4). When I was a little boy, life was tough. There was a boy in our community who was much bigger than I was, and he was a bully. Sometimes he would beat me up, and I would run home crying. And my mother would be in the kitchen, and she'd have her apron on, and she'd say, "Come here." I'd come in, and then she'd lean over and wipe away my tears—one of the most tender forms of communication—with the edge of her apron. When my mother wiped away my tears, I was truly comforted, and I was encouraged to go back into the battle. But I'd go back out, and sooner or later I'd get hurt again, and I would cry again, and my mother would have to wipe my tears away again. But when God wipes away our tears, they will never flow again for all eternity. (Unless, of course, they are tears of joy.)

That's the eternal perspective. That's the end from the beginning. Right now we live in the valley of tears, but that situation is not permanent because God will wipe away our tears.

John also says, "Death shall be no more, neither shall there be mourning, nor crying" (v. 4). Death, sorrow, crying, pain—these all belong to the former things that will pass away. I can imagine having conversations with you in the new Jerusalem, and you'll say, "Remember back then when we used to worry about the problem of suffering?" And I'll say, "I hardly remember what that was."

Then, in verse 22, we read about something else that will be missing. Not only will there be no sorrow or death, but there will be no temple in the new Jerusalem of the new heaven and earth. But how can the new Jerusalem be the holy city without a temple? Well, John means that there will be no temple building. There will be another kind of temple, John says—"the Lord God the Almighty and the Lamb." The most beautiful earthly sanctuary in this world will be passé in the new Jerusalem because we'll be in the presence of God and of the Lamb.

"No longer will there be anything accursed" (22:3). You know that song "Joy to the World"? I love the line in the song that ends with "far as the curse is found." How far is that? In this present darkness, the curse extends to the end of the earth—to our lives, to our labors, to our businesses, to our relationships. All suffer under the pangs of the curse of a fallen world. That's why there's a cosmic yearning, where all of creation groans together waiting for the manifestation of the sons of God, waiting for that moment when the curse is removed (Rom. 8:19). There won't be any weeds or any tares in the new Jerusalem. The earth won't resist our plows because the curse won't be found. "But the throne of God and of the Lamb will be in it, and his servants will worship him" (Rev. 22:3).

And then we get the highest hope, the most incredible promise in the New Testament—we will see God's face (v. 4). All of our lives we can come close to the Lord, we can sense His presence, and we can talk with Him, but we cannot see His face. But if we persevere through the pain and the suffering of this present world, the vision of God waits for us on the other side. Can you imagine it? Can you imagine looking into the unveiled glory of God for one second? It will make every pain I've ever experienced in this world worth it to see that.

"These words are trustworthy and true" (v. 6)—not salve or opium to dull our present pain but the truth of Almighty God, who made us, who knows us, who by the suffering of His Son has redeemed His people. He has now guaranteed that if we are in Christ by faith alone, we are bound for glory, and nothing can derail that train. So these former things that cause us so much grief will pass away, and He will make all things new.

THE ROLE OF EXPERIENCE

AUGUST 2017

———

W E'RE LIVING IN A DAY WHEN personal experience has been elevated above everything else as the final criterion of right and wrong. Just think of all of the people who try to justify themselves on the basis of what they feel. Divorce is routinely excused on the basis of a married couple's no longer feeling like they are in love. We are told that homosexuality should be embraced as a moral good because some homosexuals report having felt an attraction to the same sex from a young age. Even many professing Christians make their decisions about right and wrong based on what they feel.

It's hard to have a discussion with someone who makes their experience the final arbiter of reality. Many people embrace the old adage that "a person with an experience is never at the mercy of a person with an argument." Ultimately, we have to disagree with this assertion, but not because experience is not a valuable tutor. It can help us connect theory to practice and abstract concepts to concrete situations. It assists us in sifting through the nuances of living in this complex world. There are even some experiences that seem to prove that experience trumps argumentation. I think of the example of Roger Bannister. Before 1954, many people argued that no human being could run a mile in under four minutes. Bannister broke that record, proving by experience that the argument was invalid.

The problem is not that experience can never outweigh an argument; we know from the history of science that the experience of empirical investigation has often overturned prevailing arguments. The problem is the idea that the person with an experience is never at the mercy of a person with an argument. In many cases, sound argument trumps experience. This is particularly true when the debate concerns personal experience versus a sound understanding of the Word of God.

I remember one occasion on which a lady approached me and said, "Dr. Sproul, for thirty years I have been married to a kind man and a good provider who is not a Christian. Finally, I could no longer stand not having in common with him the most important thing in my life—my faith. So, I left him. But he's been calling me daily and begging me to come back. What do you think God wants me to do?"

"That's easy," I said. "Your husband's lack of Christian faith is no grounds for a divorce according to 1 Corinthians 7. So, God's will is that you return to him."

The woman did not like my answer and said it wasn't a good one because I didn't know what it was like to live with her husband. I responded, "Ma'am, you did not ask me what I would do if I were in your shoes. Perhaps I would have backed out long before you did, but that's irrelevant to the matter. You asked me about the will of God, and that is clear in this situation. Your experience is not a license to disobey God." I'm thankful to report that when the woman saw that she was asking God to make an exception just for her, she repented and returned to her husband.

That woman's argument is duplicated every day among many Christians who subject the Word of God to their experience. Too often, when our experience conflicts with the Word of God, we set aside the Scriptures. We might take refuge in public opinion or the most recent psychological studies. We allow the common experience of people around us to become normative, denying the wisdom and authority of God in favor of the collective experience of fallen human beings.

Truthfully, we all know that experience is often a good teacher. But experience is never the best teacher. God, of course, is the best teacher. Why? Because He instructs us from the perspective of eternity and from the riches of His omniscience.

Sometimes we try to cover up our reliance on experience with more orthodox-sounding language. I can't tell you the number of times I've heard Christians tell me that the Holy Spirit led them to do things Scripture clearly forbids or that God gave them peace about their decision to act in a way that is clearly contrary to the law of God. But that's blasphemous slander against the Spirit, as if He would ever countenance sin. It's bad enough to blame the devil for our own decisions, but we put ourselves in grave danger when we appeal to the Spirit to justify our transgressions.

One of the most powerful devices of manipulation we've ever designed is to claim that we have experienced the Spirit's approval of our actions. How can anyone dare contradict us if we claim divine authority for what we want to do? The result is that we end up silencing any questions about our behavior. But Scripture tells us that the Holy Spirit leads us to holiness, not to sin, and if the Spirit inspired the Scriptures, any experience we have that suggests we can go against biblical teaching cannot be from Him.

As long as we live on this side of heaven, we must deal with the fallenness of our bodies and souls. Seeking to make our experience determinative of right and wrong means repeating Adam and Eve's sin. Why did they disobey the Lord? Because they trusted their experience that told them "the tree was good for food, and that it was a delight to the eyes, and that the tree was to be desired to make one wise" (Gen. 3:6). They ignored the promises and warnings God revealed to them regarding the fruit of the forbidden tree. Experience can and should teach us, but it can never be the final arbiter of right and wrong. That role belongs to our Creator alone, and His Word gives us the standards by which we must live.

"We aren't satisfied with the old, proven answers God has revealed."

—

WISDOM NEW AND OLD

SEPTEMBER 2017

———

R ECENTLY, I THOUGHT OF A CONVERSATION I had with a friend some years ago. He told me about a discussion he had with some others. In our discussion, my friend mentioned that he had asked the question, "What do you think life will be like on this planet a thousand years from now?"

My friend and I began to speculate about the same question. We thought that maybe in fifty years there will be no more automobiles or highways. Instead, we will be able to move around with battery packs on our backs and fly through lanes in the air. We won't worry about collisions, because we will have sophisticated collision avoidance systems.

Today, I don't know if that prediction will come true, but I think that in future centuries people will certainly look back at the twenty-first century and feel sorrow for the tough life we have now. For example, when we get sick, we go to the hospital and have people cut us open with knives and do surgery, but in the years to come we will be treated in ways that are far less invasive. Just consider how things have rapidly changed in our own lifetimes. I've read that if you go to your local hardware store, 50 percent of the products that you find there were not in existence ten years ago. The changes are so quick and so startling and dramatic that it's very difficult for us to keep pace.

When I think about the rapidity of change, I'm often disturbed by the arrogance we have with respect to our knowledge. Because of all of the tremendous discoveries and advancements, we think we are so much smarter than people who lived long ago. For some, in fact, natural science has become a god and the scientists are the new high priests. Thus, modern people so often look down upon those in the ancient world who believed in God. We think of them as primitive, naive, prescientific, and so on. Consider the man who, two thousand years ago, came to the edge of a forest. And walking through, he said, "Here is a forest made up of trees, some tall trees and some short, some green trees and some brown." People in our day often will think this man unintelligent because he couldn't identify the different species of trees, he didn't understand how photosynthesis operates, he didn't understand how water is drawn up through the root system and pumped up to the tallest extremities of the trees. We think he is unlearned because our knowledge has advanced so magnificently since that time two thousand years ago.

But are we really any smarter? All we have done is look more closely at what is. If you would have asked that traveler two thousand years ago, "Sir, why is there a forest here, rather than no forest?" he could have given an answer to that question as intelligent as the world's greatest botanist could give today because the ultimate questions of life transcend superficial analysis. But we think that because we can look more deeply at the visible world that we have somehow gotten closer to the fundamental nature of reality. Yet, we haven't gotten closer at all. If we measure Western culture by Scripture, society as a whole is further away from the fundamental nature of reality today than it was two thousand years ago. And that's because even though the basic issues of life are the same today as they were then, we aren't satisfied with the old, proven answers God has revealed.

We don't look to past wisdom to get the answers to the deep questions: Why are we here? What is the purpose of life? How do we define what is true, what is good, and what is beautiful? We are people who are always looking for what is new. The new is where we are absorbed; it is what grabs our attention. We don't want to learn what is old. We're hoping that around the corner something new is going to give our lives meaning that it lacks today, when in reality, the deepest truths of life are already available to us. We can learn so much from the history of the world, from church history, from economic history, and so on to help us in the present, but we don't want to learn. We violate time and again proven principles in such areas as economics and ethics, and we think these violations are going to work even though they've never worked before. The reason we keep doing it is because we have ignored the past and we haven't learned from those who have gone before us. We think they have nothing to say because they aren't what is new, and yet when we as believers work to apply the old wisdom revealed by God, we find it is more current, more satisfying, and more effective than anything "new" being touted today.

There are new products and there are new people, new faces, new homes, and new this and new that. But the things that really grab us—relationships, behavioral patterns, the deepest yearnings in our heart—are the things that we find people killing over, fighting over, weeping over, and pleading over in antiquity. The real issues of life don't change; only the context and the environment and the accoutrements change. Fundamentally, in terms of the depth dimension of human existence, there is nothing new. That's what the Preacher in Ecclesiastes tells us, and it is a theme that is repeated throughout sacred Scripture.

Our calling as believers is to be thankful for the many technological and scientific advances that have come to us today, but at the same time we are not to be arrogant and think we have everything figured out whereas past generations were hopelessly lost. For God revealed Himself first to the ancients, and He has been working in history among His people to illumine their understanding of His truth. We ignore this wisdom at our peril when we run after what is "new" and ignore what is "old."

THE TRAUMA OF HOLINESS

OCTOBER 2017

———

A S WE READ THE WORKS OF nineteenth-century atheists, we find that they were not particularly concerned to prove that God does not exist. These atheists tacitly assumed God's nonexistence. Instead, they said that after the Enlightenment, now that we know there is no God, how can we account for the almost universal presence of religion? If God doesn't exist and human religion is not a response to the existence of God, why is it that man seems to be incurably *Homo religiosus*—that man in all of his cultures seems to be incurably religious? If there's no God, why is there religion?

One of the most popular and famous answers was the argument offered by Sigmund Freud. As a psychiatrist, Freud knew that people are afraid of lots of different things. Such fears are understandable, as there are all kinds of things in our world that represent a clear and present danger to our well-being. Other people can rise up individually in anger and try to murder us, or they may unite and attack us on a grand scale in warfare. But in addition to the human sphere of fear and danger, there's also the impersonal realm of nature, particularly in previous ages when people did not have the protection against the natural world that we enjoy in this world of modern technology. Though natural terrors still strike us with fear at times, in the past people were exposed in a greater way to storms, famines, and floods. When diseases such as cholera or the plague could wipe out entire populations, life seemed more fragile and nature seemed more threatening.

Today we perceive that science has the responsibility of somehow taming the unruly forces of nature such as hurricanes, tornadoes, floods, and fires. And in many ways, science has been successful in helping us prevent natural disasters from doing their worst and in helping us recover quickly after nature assaults us. But, Freud said, the ancient man's dilemma was how to deal with these things when their destructive impacts were much worse and harder to recover from. You can talk to a human attacker, sign a peace treaty with a foreign power, or otherwise negotiate your safety with people who might threaten you, but how do you bargain with disease, storms, or earthquakes? These forces of nature are impersonal. They don't have ears to hear. They don't have hearts to which we can appeal. They have no emotions.

So, Freud argued, religion emerged as humans personalized nature and made it something they could negotiate with. Human beings invented the idea that natural disasters were inhabited by personal spirits: a storm god, an earthquake god, a fire god, and gods related to various sicknesses. These gods wielded natural forces to cause disaster. Having personalized these dangers, human beings could apply the techniques that we use to negotiate with personal hostile forces to the impersonal forces of nature. We could, for example, plead with the storm god, pray to the storm god, make sacrifices to the storm god, repent before the storm god in order to remove the threat. Eventually, human beings consolidated all the gods into one single deity who was in control over all these forces of nature and then pleaded with him.

I'm fascinated by Freud's argument because it's a reasonable explanation for how people could become religious. It is possible, theoretically, that there could still be religion even if there were no God. We know that we are capable of imagining things that don't really exist. In fact, the Bible is replete with criticism of false religion that invents idols.

Yet there's a difference between possibility and actuality. That what Freud said is possible doesn't mean that it actually happened that way. The major hole in his theory is this: If Freud's theory is true, why, then, was the God of the Bible "invented"? This holy God, we see in Scripture, inspires far greater trauma in those whom He encounters than any natural disaster. We see, for example, how even righteous Isaiah was completely undone by meeting the God of Israel face-to-face (Isa. 6:1–7). Well-meaning Uzzah was struck dead when trying to steady the ark of this holy God (2 Sam. 6:5–10). Peter, James, and John at first saw the revelation of Christ's deity and their hearing of the Father's voice not as a blessing but as a terror (Matt. 17:1–8).

Why, to redeem us from the threat of trauma, would we invent a God whose character is infinitely more threatening than anything else we fear? I can see humanity inventing a benevolent god or even a bad god who is easily appeased. But would we invent a holy God ? Where does that come from? For there is nothing in the universe more terrifying, more threatening to a person's sense of security and well-being than the holiness of God. What we see throughout the Scriptures is that God rules over all of the threatening forces that we fear. But this same God, in and of Himself, frightens us more than any of these other things. We understand that nothing poses a greater threat to our well-being than the holiness of God. Left to ourselves, none of us would invent the God of the Bible, the being who is a threat to our sense of security more primal and more fundamental than any act of nature.

Martin Luther and the other Reformers understood the holy character of this God. For them, the recovery of the gospel was such good news because they knew the trauma of holiness and that the only way to endure the presence of this holy God's judgment is to be covered in the holiness and righteousness of Christ. Five hundred years after the Protestant Reformation, the church desperately needs men and women who understand the trauma of God's holiness, for in understanding that holiness we see that the gospel is the only thing that can give us confidence that when we meet this God face-to-face, His holiness will embrace us and not cast us into eternal judgment. May God in His grace grant to all of us a renewed vision of His majestic holiness.

THE ETERNAL LOVE OF GOD

NOVEMBER 2017

——

I**T'S ESSENTIAL THAT WE UNDERSTAND** the love of God in conjunction with the other attributes of God. God's love, for instance, is holy love. But all of the attributes of God come into play as well, even His eternity. God's love, like God Himself, is eternal. When we talk about God's eternity, we're talking about something greater than duration. When we say God is eternal, we are saying that God is self-existent, that He has no beginning. He derives His existence or His being from no other source; rather, He has the power to be in and of Himself. He's not dependent upon anything outside Himself for His own life or being.

There is no point at which God began. Before God ever made a world, He already existed. And the Scriptures make clear that as He existed from all eternity, there was already in His nature from all eternity the attribute of love. God didn't become loving at the time of creation, for He has always been a God of love. Since that's the case, and since there was nothing else besides God from all eternity, we have to ask, what was the object of the divine love from all eternity? The question has something of a complex answer.

When we think of creation, we make a distinction between creation and redemption. God created His world in a state of goodness, the world was plunged into ruin through the fall of the human race, and then the rest of history is the story of God's work of redemption by which He is salvaging His people from this enormous collapse of the fall.

But before creation or redemption, God was. And God, before creation, knew about the fall, and from all eternity, He had a plan of redemption. And that plan of redemption was born of His triune character such that the work of redemption would be carried out by all three members of the

Godhead. So, in theology we talk about the covenant of redemption, the covenant that the Father, Son, and Holy Spirit made with one another, from all eternity, to save a people from sin.

The Father sent the Son into the world, but the Son did not reluctantly enter creation to effect our redemption. The Father covenanted to send the Son and the Son covenanted to willingly descend from heaven and take upon Himself a human nature, subject Himself to humiliation, and become obedient even unto death in order to redeem His people. And then, from all eternity, the Holy Spirit covenanted with the Father and the Son to apply the work of Christ to God's people, so that the work of redemption is the work of the Father, the Son, and the Holy Ghost. Like creation, redemption is a Trinitarian work. The Father created the heavens and the earth through the eternal Son in the power of the Spirit (Gen. 1:1–2; John 1:1, 10). Creation and redemption are both accomplished by the Holy Trinity.

The Bible also tells us that one thing that motivated God from all eternity to implement redemption is His love for His creation. God gave His only begotten Son because He loves the world (John 3:16). But we would be mistaken if we thought that the primary object of the love of God was the world or even the people whom He redeems. It's certainly true that God loves us, and on account of that love He sent Christ to be a propitiation for our sin. But the Father first loves the Son. It's absolutely true that God loves us, but we must remember that He loves us in the Son. We are included in the work of redemption because the Father sees us as belonging to the Son, whom He loves. "The Father loves the Son" (John 3:35), and in love He chose us in the Son for adoption as sons of the Father (Eph. 1:3–6). The Scriptures speak of God's love for us, an eternal love for us that is rooted and grounded in the Father's love for the Son.

"See what kind of love the Father has given to us, that we should be called children of God; and so we are" (1 John 3:1). Notice the amazement John expresses here. What kind of love is this that we should be called the children of God? He can't get over it. He doesn't take this love for granted. He doesn't hold that anyone who's a creature is automatically a child of the Creator. John knows that to be counted a member of the family of

God is a privilege granted by grace alone, and that it's the greatest privilege any mortal could ever experience. And our being called the children of God as an expression of the incredible love of God is grounded in our adoption. We are not by nature children of God. Only by adoption are we regarded as the children of God.

Romans 8 articulates this well. Paul spends much of Romans 1–7 saying that by nature we are in the flesh, that is, hostile to God and under His wrath. We have none of the Spirit of God in us by our biological birth. But Paul says this of those whom God regenerates and justifies: "You, however, are not in the flesh but in the Spirit, if in fact the Spirit of God dwells in you. Anyone who does not have the Spirit of Christ does not belong to him. But if Christ is in you, although the body is dead because of sin, the Spirit is life because of righteousness" (8:9–14). To be a child of God is not natural but supernatural. No unregenerate person, no one who lacks the presence of the Holy Ghost, has the privilege of being a child of God. But all who are indwelt by the Spirit of God are numbered in God's family. "You did not receive the spirit of slavery to fall back into fear, but you have received the Spirit of adoption as sons, by whom we cry, 'Abba! Father!' The Spirit himself bears witness with our spirit that we are children of God" (vv. 15–16).

Because of the Father's love for Christ, the Father has adopted us into the royal family, making us joint heirs with Christ. We are beloved of the Father because He is beloved of the Father, and we ought never to forget that. He is the eternal object of the Father's affection, and we are the Father's gifts of love to His Son. We are adopted by the Father in Christ, and the Father loves us because we are in the Son.

WHAT IS THE MIND?

DECEMBER 2017

———

W HAT IS THE MIND? I remember one theologian who played a word game in seeking to answer that question. He said, "What is the mind?" And he said, "No matter." And then when someone said, "Well, what is matter?" he said, "Never mind."

He was trying to communicate that what we call the mind, though we recognize it is inseparably related to the physical organ of the brain, cannot be absolutely equated with the brain. The brain may be the seat of the mind, it may be the organ that the body uses to think, but there is a difference between the physical organ that does the thinking and the thinking itself. So, we ask the question, "What is thought?" Is thought merely a biochemical, electrical impulse that can be measured in exclusively physical categories? Or is there something nonphysical or spiritual about thought that is basic to our existence as human beings?

We know that as people we think, we have ideas and concepts in our minds, and we have a tendency to locate the source of that thinking in our heads, not in our fingers or toes. We also know that physical injuries to the brain and chemical imbalances can alter patterns of thought. We recognize the existence of mental illness where people lose the capacity to think rationally, and yet people who are perfectly healthy mentally also at times think irrationally. So, we often wonder where the line is between mental illness and mental soundness—between sanity and insanity. It's often been said that there's a thin line between genius and insanity, between those who think at extraordinary depths and those who somehow cross the border into madness. That thin line between genius and insanity is one that some people skate back and forth over frequently.

Is there ever a time when we're not thinking? At times, we may not be thinking in some deep, logical order or analysis. We may be daydreaming. But even while we're daydreaming, we're having thoughts. We're having ideas that we're aware of. But there is also the phenomenon wherein we're asleep and sometimes our train of thought takes bizarre turns. We've all been awakened in the middle of the night by a nightmare, when the thinking in our sleep frightened us or alarmed us.

These issues further multiply the difficulty of sorting out exactly what it means to have a mind and to think. As Christians, we understand that the Scriptures teach plainly that being moral creatures is inherent to our humanity. Being a moral creature entails the ability to think and behave in a way that corresponds to or opposes some moral standard. The standard, of course, is the law of God, and God holds us accountable for our obedience to His law.

To be able to think is part of what it means for us to be moral creatures, but other things are also involved. Historic Christianity has recognized that another part of being a moral being is the possession of a will. Moral creatures must be volitional creatures. They must have the ability to make choices, to make decisions. As moral creatures, we possess a will.

But then we have to ask another question: What is the will? Jonathan Edwards, a key thinker on the nature and function of the human will, said, "The will is the mind choosing." He meant that for a person to exercise their will, for a person to make a moral choice, that person has to be in a state of awareness. What we do when we're unconscious is not normally considered to be of a moral nature. We also distinguish in our bodily functions between those that are voluntary and those that are involuntary. We don't choose every second to have our hearts beat and push blood throughout the circulatory system. The heart beats as an involuntary organ. We don't consciously decide to make it do what it does.

But to make a moral decision requires some kind of understanding of the moral issues or options involved, so that the mind is intimately engaged in our choices. So as human beings, we can't assume that our ethical decisions are mindless acts; rather, our actions result from the choices that we make, which are informed by our thinking. That's why Scripture exhorts us to renew our minds, so that we will begin to think in categories that please God, so that our thinking will influence our choices in conformity to the law of God. The mind, then, is vital to the Christian life.

Over against this biblical view is physical determinism. The famous twentieth-century psychologist B.F. Skinner concluded that all of our responses are determined by our environment and by our physical makeup. This idea that our physical makeup determines our behavior has spread to many disciplines. Of course, it can be valuable to consider how physical influences may affect our thinking, but there are significant problems with the notion that every decision is determined by our environment and physical makeup. First, we would be unable to hold anyone accountable for their behavior. If people's environment and physical makeup absolutely determine their decisions, how can they be guilty or innocent of anything? They make no choices; they only respond to their "programming."

Second, the great argument against the notion of physical and environmental determinism is that it falls under its own weight. We'd have to say that anything Skinner said about the nature of the mind and of volition would itself be conditioned by his biochemical composition and his background, and that would give his ideas no more credence than anyone else's ideas. I could just as well listen to the responses and the instincts of a gorilla or a hippopotamus as to anyone's thinking, because physical and environmental determinism of the mind and will eliminate cogency from the very act of thinking.

GOD'S GOOD PLEASURE IN ELECTION

JANUARY 2018*

I F WE ARE GOING TO TAKE THE BIBLE SERIOUSLY, we have to have some doctrine of predestination. The idea of predestination wasn't invented by Calvin or Luther or Augustine. Paul says in Ephesians 1:4–6 that in love, God "predestined us for adoption to himself as sons through Jesus Christ, according to the purpose of his will, to the praise of his glorious grace, with which he has blessed us in the Beloved." So, predestination is a biblical word, and it's a biblical concept.

But the very concept of predestination raises the question, why does God elect certain people and not others? We know that it's not based on anything that we do. It's not based on our running, our willing, or our doing anything. It's based solely on the purpose of God, as Paul says in Ephesians. But that raises another question: If the reason for the Lord's selecting some to receive the tremendous benefit of salvation but not others is not rooted in those whom He chooses (Rom. 9:1–18), doesn't that mean that somehow God is arbitrary?

Let's take a moment to define what we mean by the term *arbitrary*. People who are arbitrary do what they do without any reason. They just do it, and when you ask them why they did it, they might respond, "No reason. Just on a whim." We don't have a lot of respect for capricious people who do things for no reason. Now, are we going to attribute to God that kind of impetuous or motiveless behavior—that He is arbitrary and capricious? Scripture certainly won't allow us to do that.

Here we must make a distinction between God's doing something for

---

* Dr. Sproul went to be with the Lord on December 14, 2017. Because *Tabletalk* is edited and printed several months ahead of time, his January and February 2018 columns were written before his passing.

no reason and His doing something for no reason found in us. We say clearly that His grace is given not for any reason in us. But the fact that there is no reason in me for my salvation does not mean there is no reason behind God's action. Scripture actually tells us over and over again that God has a reason behind His choice of some for salvation and His not choosing others for redemption.

Ephesians 1:11 fleshes out the purpose behind predestination by telling us that predestination is "according to the purpose of him who works all things according to the counsel of his will." The counsel of God's will has to do with the wisdom, the plan, the thought processes of God. The very word "counsel" suggests intelligence and an intelligent reason for acting, and God never wills apart from His own counsel. A person who is completely arbitrary has no counsel, takes no counsel, listens to no counsel. He just does it. And so the very word "counsel" should alert us that the biblical idea here of God's sovereign grace is rooted in the wisdom of God, in His own thought, which is perfect. It's not irrational—it's eminently rational and far from arbitrary.

Another key word that is used again and again with respect to predestination and election in the Bible is the word *purpose.* We saw in Ephesians 1:4–6 that predestination is according to God's purpose. Someone who does something arbitrarily does it for no purpose. But, the New Testament makes it clear that there is a divine purpose in God's electing grace, and part of that is to make manifest the riches of His grace, to display His mercy (Rom. 9:22–24)—that is, to reveal something about His marvelous character, which His grace certainly does. It makes manifest His awesome, marvelous, beautiful mercy. There's also another purpose, and that's the purpose of honoring Christ. Remember the promise to Christ that He would see the travail of His soul and be satisfied (Isa. 53:11)? According to His own counsel, God determined from the foundation of the world that the cross of Jesus Christ would yield its appointed fruit and that Christ would be satisfied by the results of His pain, suffering, and death.

Notice that when the New Testament speaks of election and predestination, it always speaks of our being elect, or chosen, in the Beloved, in

Christ. Ultimately, the New Testament tells us that people are chosen for salvation so that God the Father can bestow His glory, love, and affection on God the Son (Eph. 1:3–6). Ultimately, we're redeemed not because of our worthiness but because of the worthiness of Christ. God is gracious to me in order to reward One who does deserve a reward—His only begotten Son. Do you see the intersection here of grace and justice? It is right or just that Christ should receive an inheritance, and we are that inheritance. That we are that inheritance is grace for us and justice for Christ.

The final thing I want to note is found in Ephesians 1:5. We are chosen "according to"—on the basis of—"the good pleasure" of God's will (NKJV). God chooses and elects us according to what kind of pleasure? "According to the good pleasure of His will." That word, "good," makes all the difference in the world, because there's no such thing as the bad pleasure of God's will. God does not take pleasure in evil, even if we take pleasure in evil. In fact, we sin because it's so pleasurable to us. If it weren't pleasurable, we wouldn't be enticed to it or tempted by it. But there is no evil will in God. The only thing that has ever pleased God is goodness, the only pleasure that He's ever had is a good pleasure, and the only purpose that He's ever had is a good purpose.

Clearly, then, in the mystery of the grace of God, He is never whimsical, capricious, or arbitrary. Though the reason for our salvation does not rest in us, that does not mean that God is without a purpose in choosing His elect. He does have a purpose, and it is a good one.

"Forgiveness is objective but the feeling of forgiveness is subjective."

—

THE PROBLEM OF FORGIVENESS

FEBRUARY 2018

———

FORGIVENESS IS A PROBLEM FOR MANY PEOPLE due to their misunderstanding of what forgiveness involves and confusion about what forgiveness really is. Part of the issue is that sometimes we are unable to distinguish between forgiveness and feeling forgiven. Sometimes our feelings can get out of sync with the reality of forgiveness.

Once a man came to talk to me about feeling greatly distressed because of his guilt. He said that he had committed a particular sin and had prayed and prayed about it but hadn't received any relief. He wanted to know what he had to do to experience God's forgiveness. But since he had confessed his sin and begged God to forgive him, I told him that he needed to ask God to forgive him for a different sin—the sin of arrogance. God says, "If we confess our sins, he is faithful and righteous to forgive us our sins and to cleanse us from all unrighteousness" (1 John 1:9). When we don't believe that God has in fact forgiven us when we have confessed our sin, we are calling into question His faithfulness. We are saying that God's promise cannot be trusted. That is supreme arrogance, so we need to ask God's forgiveness for our refusing to believe His promise.

There is more to this problem of forgiveness. When we sin, one of the most difficult things for us is accepting free, gracious, merciful forgiveness. We are creatures of pride. We think that God's forgiveness is fine for other people, but when we do something wrong, we want to make up for it. However, this is absolutely impossible for anyone to do. God requires perfect holiness. Once perfection is lost, we cannot regain it. We are debtors with a debt we cannot pay. This is difficult for us to accept because we want to be able to pay our own way. It's because of our pride and arrogance, both fruits of our sinfulness, that we refuse to accept the forgiveness of God.

Back to the distinction between forgiveness and feeling forgiven: forgiveness is objective but the feeling of forgiveness is subjective. I can feel forgiven but not be forgiven because I haven't repented. I can excuse myself when God has not excused me, and that false feeling of forgiveness can lead me astray. But I can also not feel forgiven even when I actually have been forgiven. If God declares that a person is forgiven, that person is in fact forgiven. Our lack of feeling forgiven does not negate the reality of what God has done.

What is the authority in our lives? Our feelings, which are subjective, or the Word of God, which is objective truth? The Christian must live practically each day by the Word of God rather than by his feelings. The issue of forgiveness is not whether we feel forgiven, but whether we have repented. If we confess our sin and ask God for forgiveness through Christ, we can be assured that He forgives us. Sometimes we don't forgive ourselves even though God has forgiven us. But who are we to refuse to forgive one whom God has forgiven? What makes us so wicked that God's forgiveness is not enough to cover our sin? In effect, we're saying that we're so evil that even the grace of God can't help us. No, we're so proud that we refuse God's grace.

Now let's look at what forgiveness is. The Bible teaches that when God forgives us, He forgets our sins. This doesn't mean He erases them from His memory. It means that He doesn't hold them against us anymore.

How many times has someone told you that he has forgiven a sin you committed against him, and then, the next time you have a fight, he brings up what you did the last time? That person has, in a sense, rescinded his forgiveness. God doesn't do that. If I am pardoned by God, it is settled and is never to be brought up again. God puts those sins aside and will never speak of them. However, we oft reopen old wounds. We allow them to disturb the relationship. If I have forgiven someone, I should never again mention that sin. Forgiveness means not bringing it up.

There is another issue to look at, and that is our obligation to forgive others who sin against us. If such people confess their sin and repent, it is our moral obligation to forgive. However, if they don't repent, we are not required to forgive. We may forgive, as Jesus did for those who killed Him (Luke 23:34). But in doing that, Jesus didn't command that we must always forgive those who don't repent. You can go to those who have wronged you and tell them they have offended you (see Matt. 18:15). If they repent, you have won them. But you are not called to forgive if they don't repent. You are not allowed to be bitter or vindictive. You have to be loving, caring, concerned, and compassionate, but you don't have to forgive. You can still talk about it and seek public vindication.

Here is one last problem related to forgiveness that we deal with oft as elders in Christ's church. A husband or wife commits adultery, repents deeply, and then asks his or her spouse for forgiveness. In such a situation, the offended spouse must forgive the guilty partner. However, that spouse is not obligated to stay married to that partner. The Bible makes a provision for the dissolution of a marriage in the event of adultery. The person is required to treat the repentant person as a brother or sister in Christ but not as a spouse.

Another example is a man stealing from us fifty times in our office and repenting each time. We must forgive him, but we can ask for restitution. We don't have to keep him in our employ, but we must still treat him as a brother in Christ. This situation is an important practical application of the concept of forgiveness. We can have forgiveness and restored relationships, but that does not necessarily mean there are no lasting consequences for our sin.

COMBINED INDEX

Anderson, Bowden, **2:**66;

angel, **1:**138; **2:**28, 37, 58, 187–88, 237, 334; **3:**69, 310, 347, 391; **4:**333–34

anger, **1:**16, 22, 82, 89, 91, 118, 131; **2:**76, 121, 138, 269–71, 297; **3:**9, 15, 140, 181–82, 229–30, 265, 340, 346, 431; **4:**206–7, 217–18, 293–94, 346, 368, 390

Anglican, **2:**262, 285; **3:**210, 426

animism, **2:**186

Anna, **3:**96, 263

Anne (saint), **2:**293

Anointed One, **4:**223–24

Anselm, **3:**179–80, 380, 390; **4:**157–59

Anthony of the Desert, **4:**133

anthropology, **2:**143; **3:**283

antichrist, **1:**125; **4:**250, 304

Antietam, **4:**169

antinomianism, **1:**42–43; **2:**115, 236, 266; **3:**251–53

Antioch, **3:**337, 403

anxiety, **2:**177, 313; **4:**43, 110–12

Apollo, **2:**9; **3:**11

Apollos, **3:**2–4

apologetics, **1:**155; **2:**108–9, 127, 142, 223; **3:**75, 77–78, 180, 258, 280, 290–91, 336, 365; **4:**36, 244, 257, 353–55

apostasy, **1:**123; **2:**30, 140, 246; **3:**120, 173, 258, 262, 350, 383; **4:**262–63

apostate, **2:**325–26; **3:**137, 383; **4:**262, 264

Apostles, **1:**25, 150, 171; **2:**108, 183, 197, 203–4, 259, 335; **3:**44–45, 55, 65, 98, 100–101, 103, 135, 193, 209, 233, 246–47, 272, 292, 294–95, 366, 408; **4:**14, 27, 41, 45–46, 58, 155–56, 191, 243, 247–49, 253, 262, 267, 279, 284–85, 337, 344, 352, 364

Apostles' Creed, **3:**45, 55, 135, 193, 246; **4:**45–46, 247

Apostolic, **2:**6, 81, 108, 116, 179, 259, 323–24; **3:**3, 44, 84, 125, 148, 196, 209, 233, 235, 246–47, 253, 290, 319, 327; **4:**155–56, 196, 198, 284–85, 311, 344, 365

Aquinas, Thomas. *See* Thomas Aquinas

archaeology, **2:**37–39; **4:**256

Archimedes, **1:**95; **3:**189

architecture, **1:**96, 130; **2:**34, 165; **3:**212–13; **4:**215–16

Areopagus, **2:**162, 201; **3:**58, 84, 133; **4:**253

Arianism, **2:**60–61, 222; **3:**48, 270, 337–338, 384, 403; **4:**20–21, 134

Aristotelianism, **2:**170, 225; **4:**105–6

Aristotelian philosophy, **2:**223–24; **4:**91, 105

Aristotle, **2:**1, 133, 171, 223–25, 258, 316, 319; **3:**88, 178, 290, 427; **4:**48, 56, 91–92, 277, 338–39

Armageddon, **1:**74, 93

Arminianism, **2:**263, 285, 309–10; **3:**2–3, 20–21, 146, 270–71, 347; **4:**88–89

Armstrong, Neil, **4:**330

Arnold, Eddy, **1:**143

arrogance, **1:**142; **2:**129, 150, 253; **3:**108, 152, 277; **4:**281, 387, 403

art, **1:**29, 97, 146, 148, 158–59; **2:**51–53, 66, 113, 123, 133, 208, 218, 291; **3:**87–90, 107, 115–17, 163–64, 166, 251, 274; **4:**14, 24, 30, 35, 55, 57, 82, 212, 271, 287–88, 310

ascension, **2:**26; **3:**67–69, 76

asceticism, **2:**31; **4:**133

Aslan, **2:**167; **4:**37

Assyria, **3:**265

Athanasian Creed, **4:**20–22

Athanasius, **2:**162

atheism, **1:**59, 120–21, 146; **2:**192; **3:**78, 347; **4:**105, 113, 168, 329, 354

Athena, **3:**336

Athens, **1:**171; **2:**83, 132, 217–18; **3:**58, 84, 133, 198, 290; **4:**191, 253, 339, 371

atonement, **1:**59, 120–21; **2:**5–6, 89, 138, 203, 251, 274, 309, 324–25; **3:**21, 65, 70, 199, 242, 304, 343–44, 349, 380–82, 387, 389, 418, 424; **4:**7, 99, 109, 119, 128, 157, 197, 250, 265, 332, 354

Augustine, **1:**158, 175, 191; **2:**22, 28, 32–33, 47, 140, 162, 170–71, 190, 194, 224, 232, 252, 254, 271, 283–85, 299, 307–8, 310, 316; **3:**1, 4–5, 36, 116–17, 132, 134, 136, 145–46, 179, 181, 207, 292, 297, 309, 313, 322, 328–29, 355–56, 375–79, 410, 417–19; **4:**21, 56–57, 59, 71, 91, 93, 106, 135, 160, 271, 277, 399

Augustinianism, **2:**224, 308–9; **3:**146, 270, 379; **4:**8

Augustinians, **2:**308; **4:**134

authority of God, **1:**39; **2:**12, 175, 280; **3:**209, 411; **4:**81, 257, 285, 330, 368, 384

authority of Scripture, **1:**48, 79, 86; **2:**93, 320; **3:**159, 209, 290; **4:**80

autonomy, **1:**8, 36, 43; **2:**65, 70, 154, 237, 239, 242, 266, 318; **3:**11, 255; **4:**62, 81, 302, 360

Don Quixote, **1**:108; **2**:186
"Don't Worry, Be Happy" (McFerrin), **2**:272
Dooyeweerd, Herman, **3**:255
Dostoevsky, Fyodor, **1**:120, 180; **2**:196
double truth theory, **2**:225
doubt, **1**:141, 159, 170; **2**:2, 125–28, 131, 143, 161, 223, 277; **3**:40, 45, 102, 114, 178, 200, 232, 236, 317, 393, 414; **4**:35, 42, 208–9, 294, 302, 336, 346, 357
Dracula, Count, **2**:331
drama, **1**:1, 45, 90; **2**:6, 9, 36, 58, 97, 123, 132, 192; **3**:163, 212, 274, 299, 357; **4**:4, 6, 30, 35, 82, 101, 115, 157, 164, 330
D'Souza, Dinesh, **2**:134
dualism, **1**:13, 146–47; **2**:144, 187
dual nature of Christ, **3**:270; **4**:21
Duke University, **2**:134
dulia, **2**:292; **3**:117
Dürer, Albrecht, **4**:30
Dutch Reformed, **4**:304

early church, **2**:108, 116, 259; **3**:1, 77, 117, 174, 180, 213, 236, 247, 272–73, 292, 335, 366, 401, 404; **4**:27, 34, 65, 95, 128, 131, 156, 196
Easter, **3**:67, 412
Eastern Orthodoxy, **3**:115–18; **4**:22, 304
East Germany, **2**:92, 331–32
Eastwood, Clint, **1**:66
Ebenezer, **3**:266
Ecclesiastes, **2**:9–11, 167, 210, 212; **3**:85, 222; **4**:4, 193, 389
ecclesiology, **4**:29, 344
Eck, Johann, **3**:209; **4**:80
economics, **1**:49, 51, 99, 123, 127–29; **2**:134, 238, 286; **3**:60, 201; **4**:388
Ecumenical Movement, **3**:327
Eddy, Nelson, **1**:143
"Edelweiss," **2**:165–66
Eden, garden of, **1**:89; **2**:28, 237, 239, 335; **3**:23, 120–21, 178, 183, 374; **4**:81, 178, 200, 329–30, 362
Ed Sullivan show, **1**:18
education, **1**:9, 23, 25–26, 38, 61, 71–72, 84–87, 122–23, 150–51; **2**:18, 20, 94–96, 134–35, 137, 155, 157, 204–5, 238, 260, 320–21; **3**:46–47, 61–62, 91, 124–25, 256, 283, 414; **4**:62, 143, 277–78, 351, 372–73

Edwards, Jonathan, **1**:25, 175; **2**:75–76, 98, 101–2, 122, 128, 140, 147–48, 158–59, 162, 205, 283–85, 309; **3**:1–3, 5, 20–21, 40, 50–51, 88, 132, 134, 146, 203–4, 228, 299, 323, 326, 365; **4**:2, 172, 217–19, 236, 378, 397
Egypt, **1**:130; **3**:61, 116, 125, 182, 257, 291, 306, 356–57; **4**:184, 299, 329, 353–54
eighteenth century, **1**:96; **2**:307–8; **3**:20–21, 164, 228; **4**:17, 69, 172, 362
Einstein, Albert, **2**:7, 39, 72–73
elders, **2**:137–38; **3**:266, 367; **4**:289–90, 317, 405
election (doctrine of), **1**:192; **2**:118, 129, 148, 251, 285, 309; **3**:195–96, 242, 297–99, 343, 349–50, 387; **4**:31, 90, 208, 250, 400
election (political), **1**:93, 112–13, 127; **2**:317; **3**:200–202; **4**:24, 74, 307
Electoral College, **3**:200
Eli, **2**:329; **3**:266–67
Elijah, **1**:16; **4**:41, 118, 166, 224
Elisabeth. *See* Elizabeth (Bible character)
Elizabeth (Bible character), **1**:138; **2**:291; **3**:96, 263
Elizabeth I (queen), **2**:91, 262; **3**:20
Ellington, Duke, **2**:167
Elliot, Elisabeth, **1**:184
Elliot, Jim, **1**:184
Ellis Island, **2**:255; **4**:55
El Shaddai, **2**:300; **4**:6
Emmanuel, **2**:209
emotions, **1**:19; **2**:282; **3**:216; **4**:32, 215, 233, 391
empiricism, **2**:75; **3**:93, 408; **4**:58
end times, **4**:107–8
endurance, **1**:2–3, 59, 123; **2**:252; **3**:133–34, 384, 411, 422; **4**:111, 347
enemies, **1**:141; **2**:20, 101–3, 119–20, 177–78, 180, 210; **3**:11, 16, 18, 56, 77–78, 155, 168, 175, 180, 196, 206, 245, 265, 325, 336; **4**:49, 170, 200, 218–19, 293, 357
England, **1**:50; **2**:91–93, 217–18, 261–62, 285; **3**:11, 20–21, 72, 190, 294; **4**:17, 29–31, 56, 69, 362
Enlightenment, **1**:36, 96; **2**:52, 238, 246–47, 307, 316; **3**:93, 247; **4**:17, 58, 390
Enoch, **2**:252; **4**:118, 227
entitlement, **2**:155
envy, **1**:98–100; **2**:120; **3**:8–9, 219–20, 372; **4**:280

Sadducees, **3:**96
Sade, Marquis de, **2:**75
Sagan, Carl, **3:**8; **4:**104
Saint Andrew's Chapel, **3:**215; **4:**239, 259, 269, 289, 301
St. Giles Cathedral, **2:**92
St. Jacques, Raymond, **1:**45–46
St. Vitus Cathedral, **2:**165
Salem witches, **1:**108
salvation, **1:**59, 170, 172, 192; **2:**6, 22, 33, 36–38, 82, 86, 101, 105, 107, 114–15, 129–31, 146–48, 154, 179–80, 196–97, 219, 221, 244, 250–51, 268, 275, 293, 308, 310, 328, 334; **3:**68, 72–76, 80, 85, 95, 118, 154, 156–57, 195–96, 216, 222, 226–27, 243, 251, 253, 263, 298, 305–6, 313, 315, 320, 322, 343–44, 348–50, 388, 391, 396–99, 418, 425; **4:**2–3, 7, 21, 51–52, 84, 88–90, 99–100, 123, 127, 129, 135, 140, 148, 156, 158, 164, 190, 250, 252, 254, 259, 261–62, 264–65, 296, 304–6, 321, 328, 361, 371, 399–401
Salvation Army, **1:**109
Samaria, **2:**81, 203, 257; **3:**272, 366
Samaritans, **1:**172; **4:**235
Samson, **4:**356
Samuel, **2:**177, 329; **3:**265; **4:**223, 308, 356
Sanballat, **3:**16–17
sanctification, **1:**162, 169–70, 177; **2:**22–23, 35–36, 131, 191, 228–29, 243, 245, 274–75; **3:**24, 72, 195, 234, 236, 253; **4:**3, 37, 101, 123, 218, 222, 265, 297, 361, 378
sanctity of life, **1:**82, 98; **2:**48; **4:**121, 171
Sandy Hook shooting, **4:**244
Sanguillén, Manny, **2:**161
Sanhedrin, **2:**5
Santa Claus, **2:**207–8, 249
Sartre, Jean-Paul, **1:**125; **2:**211; **3:**283
Satan, **1:**162; **2:**131, 185–89, 192–93; **3:**23, 25, 27, 156–57, 169, 192, 231, 233, 253, 305–6, 324, 411; **4:**4–5, 181–82, 242, 263, 267, 281, 312, 355, 362
Saul, **1:**29; **2:**13, 52, 177, 242; **3:**272; **4:**223
Savior, 2;49, 81, 107, 114–16, 180, 254, 289, 293, 321, 335; **3:**100, 196, 204, 227, 241, 359, 391
Sayers, Dorothy, **2:**96
scapegoat, **3:**382
scare theology, **2:**75; **3:**228

Schaeffer, Francis, **1:**82; **2:**21, 153, 156, 171, 286; **3:**91, 124, 190, 256, 258, 271, 352; **4:**61, 63
Schleiermacher, Friedrich, **3:**279
Schlessinger, Laura, **3:**42
scholasticism, **3:**342
Schopenhauer, Arthur, **2:**9
Schweitzer, Albert, **3:**101
science, **1:**59, 101, 125, 137, 140, 146, 149, 157, 187; **2:**20, 37–38, 52, 66–67, 83–88, 94, 96, 108, 133, 142, 165, 171, 213, 218, 225, 238, 258, 281; **3:**50, 89, 93, 103, 108, 206–7, 218, 255, 283, 365; **4:**14, 17, 35, 53, 57, 66, 91, 104–6, 193, 307, 336, 341, 371, 383, 390
scientific method, **1:**101; **2:**52, 94; **4:**247
Scofield Reference Bible, **2:**263; **3:**423
Scotland, **2:**91–93, 261–62; **3:**19, 131; **4:**31
Scots Confession, **2:**285
Scrooge, Ebenezer, **2:**207
second Adam, **3:**156, 305
second century, **1:**4; **3:**245–47, 260; **4:**95
second coming, **3:**101, 384
Second Vatican Council, **2:**293
secularism, **1:**38–39, 86, 123; **2:**223, 247; **3:**19, 213, 258; **4:**69, 75, 380
Seed of the woman, **2:**336
self-denial, **2:**31; **3:**168; **4:**133
selfishness, **1:**117; **3:**82, 172; **4:**273
semi-Pelagianism, **2:**308–10; **3:**379, 418–19; **4:**7–8, 89, 250–51
Senate, **2:**28, 132; **4:**74
senses, **1:**95, 132, 150, 158–59, 163, 165; **2:**1–2, 83, 94, 125, 142–43, 169–70, 277; **3:**93–94, 164, 198, 380; **4:**42, 139, 214, 216, 247–49
sensus literalis, **3:**104; **4:**150
separation of church and state, **1:**16; **4:**40, 62, 169, 302
separatism, **3:**190; **4:**130
Septuagint, **4:**326–27
seraphim, **4:**25
Sermon on the Mount, **1:**139; **2:**48; **3:**172, 203–4, 259, 328
serpent, **1:**146; **2:**185, 237, 239, 307, 336; **3:**23, 123, 178; **4:**330
Serve International, **3:**193
Servetus, Michael, **2:**283
servile fear, **2:**258, 327
Seth, **4:**227

ABOUT THE AUTHOR

DR. R.C. SPROUL was founder of Ligonier Ministries, founding pastor of Saint Andrew's Chapel in Sanford, Fla., first president of Reformation Bible College, and executive editor of *Tabletalk* magazine. His radio program, *Renewing Your Mind*, is still broadcast daily on hundreds of radio stations around the world and can also be heard online. He was author of more than one hundred books, including *The Holiness of God*, *Chosen by God*, and *Everyone's a Theologian*. He was recognized throughout the world for his articulate defense of the inerrancy of Scripture and the need for God's people to stand with conviction upon His Word.